# Dictionary of Literary Biography

1. *The American Renaissance in New England*, edited by Joel Myerson (1978)
2. *American Novelists Since World War II*, edited by Jeffrey Helterman and Richard Layman (1978)
3. *Antebellum Writers in New York and the South*, edited by Joel Myerson (1979)
4. *American Writers in Paris, 1920-1939*, edited by Karen Lane Rood (1980)
5. *American Poets Since World War II*, 2 parts, edited by Donald J. Greiner (1980)
6. *American Novelists Since World War II, Second Series*, edited by James E. Kibler Jr. (1980)
7. *Twentieth-Century American Dramatists*, 2 parts, edited by John MacNicholas (1981)
8. *Twentieth-Century American Science-Fiction Writers*, 2 parts, edited by David Cowart and Thomas L. Wymer (1981)
9. *American Novelists, 1910-1945*, 3 parts, edited by James J. Martine (1981)
10. *Modern British Dramatists, 1900-1945*, 2 parts, edited by Stanley Weintraub (1982)
11. *American Humorists, 1800-1950*, 2 parts, edited by Stanley Trachtenberg (1982)
12. *American Realists and Naturalists*, edited by Donald Pizer and Earl N. Harbert (1982)
13. *British Dramatists Since World War II*, 2 parts, edited by Stanley Weintraub (1982)
14. *British Novelists Since 1960*, 2 parts, edited by Jay L. Halio (1983)
15. *British Novelists, 1930-1959*, 2 parts, edited by Bernard Oldsey (1983)
16. *The Beats: Literary Bohemians in Postwar America*, 2 parts, edited by Ann Charters (1983)
17. *Twentieth-Century American Historians*, edited by Clyde N. Wilson (1983)
18. *Victorian Novelists After 1885*, edited by Ira B. Nadel and William E. Fredeman (1983)
19. *British Poets, 1880-1914*, edited by Donald E. Stanford (1983)
20. *British Poets, 1914-1945*, edited by Donald E. Stanford (1983)
21. *Victorian Novelists Before 1885*, edited by Ira B. Nadel and William E. Fredeman (1983)
22. *American Writers for Children, 1900-1960*, edited by John Cech (1983)
23. *American Newspaper Journalists, 1873-1900*, edited by Perry J. Ashley (1983)
24. *American Colonial Writers, 1606-1734*, edited by Emory Elliott (1984)
25. *American Newspaper Journalists, 1901-1925*, edited by Perry J. Ashley (1984)
26. *American Screenwriters*, edited by Robert E. Morsberger, Stephen O. Lesser, and Randall Clark (1984)
27. *Poets of Great Britain and Ireland, 1945-1960*, edited by Vincent B. Sherry Jr. (1984)
28. *Twentieth-Century American-Jewish Fiction Writers*, edited by Daniel Walden (1984)
29. *American Newspaper Journalists, 1926-1950*, edited by Perry J. Ashley (1984)
30. *American Historians, 1607-1865*, edited by Clyde N. Wilson (1984)
31. *American Colonial Writers, 1735-1781*, edited by Emory Elliott (1984)
32. *Victorian Poets Before 1850*, edited by William E. Fredeman and Ira B. Nadel (1984)
33. *Afro-American Fiction Writers After 1955*, edited by Thadious M. Davis and Trudier Harris (1984)
34. *British Novelists, 1890-1929: Traditionalists*, edited by Thomas F. Staley (1985)
35. *Victorian Poets After 1850*, edited by William E. Fredeman and Ira B. Nadel (1985)
36. *British Novelists, 1890-1929: Modernists*, edited by Thomas F. Staley (1985)
37. *American Writers of the Early Republic*, edited by Emory Elliott (1985)
38. *Afro-American Writers After 1955: Dramatists and Prose Writers*, edited by Thadious M. Davis and Trudier Harris (1985)
39. *British Novelists, 1660-1800*, 2 parts, edited by Martin C. Battestin (1985)
40. *Poets of Great Britain and Ireland Since 1960*, 2 parts, edited by Vincent B. Sherry Jr. (1985)
41. *Afro-American Poets Since 1955*, edited by Trudier Harris and Thadious M. Davis (1985)
42. *American Writers for Children Before 1900*, edited by Glenn E. Estes (1985)
43. *American Newspaper Journalists, 1690-1872*, edited by Perry J. Ashley (1986)
44. *American Screenwriters, Second Series*, edited by Randall Clark, Robert E. Morsberger, and Stephen O. Lesser (1986)
45. *American Poets, 1880-1945, First Series*, edited by Peter Quartermain (1986)
46. *American Literary Publishing Houses, 1900-1980: Trade and Paperback*, edited by Peter Dzwonkoski (1986)
47. *American Historians, 1866-1912*, edited by Clyde N. Wilson (1986)
48. *American Poets, 1880-1945, Second Series*, edited by Peter Quartermain (1986)
49. *American Literary Publishing Houses, 1638-1899*, 2 parts, edited by Peter Dzwonkoski (1986)
50. *Afro-American Writers Before the Harlem Renaissance*, edited by Trudier Harris (1986)
51. *Afro-American Writers from the Harlem Renaissance to 1940*, edited by Trudier Harris (1987)
52. *American Writers for Children Since 1960: Fiction*, edited by Glenn E. Estes (1986)
53. *Canadian Writers Since 1960, First Series*, edited by W. H. New (1986)
54. *American Poets, 1880-1945, Third Series*, 2 parts, edited by Peter Quartermain (1987)
55. *Victorian Prose Writers Before 1867*, edited by William B. Thesing (1987)
56. *German Fiction Writers, 1914-1945*, edited by James Hardin (1987)
57. *Victorian Prose Writers After 1867*, edited by William B. Thesing (1987)
58. *Jacobean and Caroline Dramatists*, edited by Fredson Bowers (1987)
59. *American Literary Critics and Scholars, 1800-1850*, edited by John W. Rathbun and Monica M. Grecu (1987)
60. *Canadian Writers Since 1960, Second Series*, edited by W. H. New (1987)
61. *American Writers for Children Since 1960: Poets, Illustrators, and Nonfiction Authors*, edited by Glenn E. Estes (1987)
62. *Elizabethan Dramatists*, edited by Fredson Bowers (1987)
63. *Modern American Critics, 1920-1955*, edited by Gregory S. Jay (1988)
64. *American Literary Critics and Scholars, 1850-1880*, edited by John W. Rathbun and Monica M. Grecu (1988)
65. *French Novelists, 1900-1930*, edited by Catharine Savage Brosman (1988)
66. *German Fiction Writers, 1885-1913*, 2 parts, edited by James Hardin (1988)
67. *Modern American Critics Since 1955*, edited by Gregory S. Jay (1988)
68. *Canadian Writers, 1920-1959, First Series*, edited by W. H. New (1988)
69. *Contemporary German Fiction Writers, First Series*, edited by Wolfgang D. Elfe and James Hardin (1988)
70. *British Mystery Writers, 1860-1919*, edited by Bernard Benstock and Thomas F. Staley (1988)
71. *American Literary Critics and Scholars, 1880-1900*, edited by John W. Rathbun and Monica M. Grecu (1988)
72. *French Novelists, 1930-1960*, edited by Catharine Savage Brosman (1988)
73. *American Magazine Journalists, 1741-1850*, edited by Sam G. Riley (1988)
74. *American Short-Story Writers Before 1880*, edited by Bobby Ellen Kimbel, with the assistance of William E. Grant (1988)
75. *Contemporary German Fiction Writers, Second Series*, edited by Wolfgang D. Elfe and James Hardin (1988)
76. *Afro-American Writers, 1940-1955*, edited by Trudier Harris (1988)
77. *British Mystery Writers, 1920-1939*, edited by Bernard Benstock and Thomas F. Staley (1988)

78 *American Short-Story Writers, 1880–1910,* edited by Bobby Ellen Kimbel, with the assistance of William E. Grant (1988)

79 *American Magazine Journalists, 1850–1900,* edited by Sam G. Riley (1988)

80 *Restoration and Eighteenth-Century Dramatists, First Series,* edited by Paula R. Backscheider (1989)

81 *Austrian Fiction Writers, 1875–1913,* edited by James Hardin and Donald G. Daviau (1989)

82 *Chicano Writers, First Series,* edited by Francisco A. Lomelí and Carl R. Shirley (1989)

83 *French Novelists Since 1960,* edited by Catharine Savage Brosman (1989)

84 *Restoration and Eighteenth-Century Dramatists, Second Series,* edited by Paula R. Backscheider (1989)

85 *Austrian Fiction Writers After 1914,* edited by James Hardin and Donald G. Daviau (1989)

86 *American Short-Story Writers, 1910–1945, First Series,* edited by Bobby Ellen Kimbel (1989)

87 *British Mystery and Thriller Writers Since 1940, First Series,* edited by Bernard Benstock and Thomas F. Staley (1989)

88 *Canadian Writers, 1920–1959, Second Series,* edited by W. H. New (1989)

89 *Restoration and Eighteenth-Century Dramatists, Third Series,* edited by Paula R. Backscheider (1989)

90 *German Writers in the Age of Goethe, 1789–1832,* edited by James Hardin and Christoph E. Schweitzer (1989)

91 *American Magazine Journalists, 1900–1960, First Series,* edited by Sam G. Riley (1990)

92 *Canadian Writers, 1890–1920,* edited by W. H. New (1990)

93 *British Romantic Poets, 1789–1832, First Series,* edited by John R. Greenfield (1990)

94 *German Writers in the Age of Goethe: Sturm und Drang to Classicism,* edited by James Hardin and Christoph E. Schweitzer (1990)

95 *Eighteenth-Century British Poets, First Series,* edited by John Sitter (1990)

96 *British Romantic Poets, 1789–1832, Second Series,* edited by John R. Greenfield (1990)

97 *German Writers from the Enlightenment to Sturm und Drang, 1720–1764,* edited by James Hardin and Christoph E. Schweitzer (1990)

98 *Modern British Essayists, First Series,* edited by Robert Beum (1990)

99 *Canadian Writers Before 1890,* edited by W. H. New (1990)

100 *Modern British Essayists, Second Series,* edited by Robert Beum (1990)

101 *British Prose Writers, 1660–1800, First Series,* edited by Donald T. Siebert (1991)

102 *American Short-Story Writers, 1910–1945, Second Series,* edited by Bobby Ellen Kimbel (1991)

103 *American Literary Biographers, First Series,* edited by Steven Serafin (1991)

104 *British Prose Writers, 1660–1800, Second Series,* edited by Donald T. Siebert (1991)

105 *American Poets Since World War II, Second Series,* edited by R. S. Gwynn (1991)

106 *British Literary Publishing Houses, 1820–1880,* edited by Patricia J. Anderson and Jonathan Rose (1991)

107 *British Romantic Prose Writers, 1789–1832, First Series,* edited by John R. Greenfield (1991)

108 *Twentieth-Century Spanish Poets, First Series,* edited by Michael L. Perna (1991)

109 *Eighteenth-Century British Poets, Second Series,* edited by John Sitter (1991)

110 *British Romantic Prose Writers, 1789–1832, Second Series,* edited by John R. Greenfield (1991)

111 *American Literary Biographers, Second Series,* edited by Steven Serafin (1991)

112 *British Literary Publishing Houses, 1881–1965,* edited by Jonathan Rose and Patricia J. Anderson (1991)

113 *Modern Latin-American Fiction Writers, First Series,* edited by William Luis (1992)

114 *Twentieth-Century Italian Poets, First Series,* edited by Giovanna Wedel De Stasio, Glauco Cambon, and Antonio Illiano (1992)

115 *Medieval Philosophers,* edited by Jeremiah Hackett (1992)

116 *British Romantic Novelists, 1789–1832,* edited by Bradford K. Mudge (1992)

117 *Twentieth-Century Caribbean and Black African Writers, First Series,* edited by Bernth Lindfors and Reinhard Sander (1992)

118 *Twentieth-Century German Dramatists, 1889–1918,* edited by Wolfgang D. Elfe and James Hardin (1992)

119 *Nineteenth-Century French Fiction Writers: Romanticism and Realism, 1800–1860,* edited by Catharine Savage Brosman (1992)

120 *American Poets Since World War II, Third Series,* edited by R. S. Gwynn (1992)

121 *Seventeenth-Century British Nondramatic Poets, First Series,* edited by M. Thomas Hester (1992)

122 *Chicano Writers, Second Series,* edited by Francisco A. Lomelí and Carl R. Shirley (1992)

123 *Nineteenth-Century French Fiction Writers: Naturalism and Beyond, 1860–1900,* edited by Catharine Savage Brosman (1992)

124 *Twentieth-Century German Dramatists, 1919–1992,* edited by Wolfgang D. Elfe and James Hardin (1992)

125 *Twentieth-Century Caribbean and Black African Writers, Second Series,* edited by Bernth Lindfors and Reinhard Sander (1993)

126 *Seventeenth-Century British Nondramatic Poets, Second Series,* edited by M. Thomas Hester (1993)

127 *American Newspaper Publishers, 1950–1990,* edited by Perry J. Ashley (1993)

128 *Twentieth-Century Italian Poets, Second Series,* edited by Giovanna Wedel De Stasio, Glauco Cambon, and Antonio Illiano (1993)

129 *Nineteenth-Century German Writers, 1841–1900,* edited by James Hardin and Siegfried Mews (1993)

130 *American Short-Story Writers Since World War II,* edited by Patrick Meanor (1993)

131 *Seventeenth-Century British Nondramatic Poets, Third Series,* edited by M. Thomas Hester (1993)

132 *Sixteenth-Century British Nondramatic Writers, First Series,* edited by David A. Richardson (1993)

133 *Nineteenth-Century German Writers to 1840,* edited by James Hardin and Siegfried Mews (1993)

134 *Twentieth-Century Spanish Poets, Second Series,* edited by Jerry Phillips Winfield (1994)

135 *British Short-Fiction Writers, 1880–1914: The Realist Tradition,* edited by William B. Thesing (1994)

136 *Sixteenth-Century British Nondramatic Writers, Second Series,* edited by David A. Richardson (1994)

137 *American Magazine Journalists, 1900–1960, Second Series,* edited by Sam G. Riley (1994)

138 *German Writers and Works of the High Middle Ages: 1170–1280,* edited by James Hardin and Will Hasty (1994)

139 *British Short-Fiction Writers, 1945–1980,* edited by Dean Baldwin (1994)

140 *American Book-Collectors and Bibliographers, First Series,* edited by Joseph Rosenblum (1994)

141 *British Children's Writers, 1880–1914,* edited by Laura M. Zaidman (1994)

142 *Eighteenth-Century British Literary Biographers,* edited by Steven Serafin (1994)

143 *American Novelists Since World War II, Third Series,* edited by James R. Giles and Wanda H. Giles (1994)

144 *Nineteenth-Century British Literary Biographers,* edited by Steven Serafin (1994)

145 *Modern Latin-American Fiction Writers, Second Series,* edited by William Luis and Ann González (1994)

146 *Old and Middle English Literature,* edited by Jeffrey Helterman and Jerome Mitchell (1994)

147 *South Slavic Writers Before World War II,* edited by Vasa D. Mihailovich (1994)

148 *German Writers and Works of the Early Middle Ages: 800–1170,* edited by Will Hasty and James Hardin (1994)

149 *Late Nineteenth- and Early Twentieth-Century British Literary Biographers,* edited by Steven Serafin (1995)

150 *Early Modern Russian Writers, Late Seventeenth and Eighteenth Centuries,* edited by Marcus C. Levitt (1995)

151 *British Prose Writers of the Early Seventeenth Century,* edited by Clayton D. Lein (1995)

152 *American Novelists Since World War II, Fourth Series,* edited by James R. Giles and Wanda H. Giles (1995)

153 *Late-Victorian and Edwardian British Novelists, First Series,* edited by George M. Johnson (1995)

154 *The British Literary Book Trade, 1700–1820,* edited by James K. Bracken and Joel Silver (1995)

155 *Twentieth-Century British Literary Biographers*, edited by Steven Serafin (1995)

156 *British Short-Fiction Writers, 1880–1914: The Romantic Tradition*, edited by William F. Naufftus (1995)

157 *Twentieth-Century Caribbean and Black African Writers, Third Series*, edited by Bernth Lindfors and Reinhard Sander (1995)

158 *British Reform Writers, 1789–1832*, edited by Gary Kelly and Edd Applegate (1995)

159 *British Short-Fiction Writers, 1800–1880*, edited by John R. Greenfield (1996)

160 *British Children's Writers, 1914–1960*, edited by Donald R. Hettinga and Gary D. Schmidt (1996)

161 *British Children's Writers Since 1960, First Series*, edited by Caroline Hunt (1996)

162 *British Short-Fiction Writers, 1915–1945*, edited by John H. Rogers (1996)

163 *British Children's Writers, 1800–1880*, edited by Meena Khorana (1996)

164 *German Baroque Writers, 1580–1660*, edited by James Hardin (1996)

165 *American Poets Since World War II, Fourth Series*, edited by Joseph Conte (1996)

166 *British Travel Writers, 1837–1875*, edited by Barbara Brothers and Julia Gergits (1996)

167 *Sixteenth-Century British Nondramatic Writers, Third Series*, edited by David A. Richardson (1996)

168 *German Baroque Writers, 1661–1730*, edited by James Hardin (1996)

169 *American Poets Since World War II, Fifth Series*, edited by Joseph Conte (1996)

170 *The British Literary Book Trade, 1475–1700*, edited by James K. Bracken and Joel Silver (1996)

171 *Twentieth-Century American Sportswriters*, edited by Richard Orodenker (1996)

172 *Sixteenth-Century British Nondramatic Writers, Fourth Series*, edited by David A. Richardson (1996)

173 *American Novelists Since World War II, Fifth Series*, edited by James R. Giles and Wanda H. Giles (1996)

174 *British Travel Writers, 1876–1909*, edited by Barbara Brothers and Julia Gergits (1997)

175 *Native American Writers of the United States*, edited by Kenneth M. Roemer (1997)

176 *Ancient Greek Authors*, edited by Ward W. Briggs (1997)

177 *Italian Novelists Since World War II, 1945–1965*, edited by Augustus Pallotta (1997)

178 *British Fantasy and Science-Fiction Writers Before World War I*, edited by Darren Harris-Fain (1997)

179 *German Writers of the Renaissance and Reformation, 1280–1580*, edited by James Hardin and Max Reinhart (1997)

180 *Japanese Fiction Writers, 1868–1945*, edited by Van C. Gessel (1997)

181 *South Slavic Writers Since World War II*, edited by Vasa D. Mihailovich (1997)

182 *Japanese Fiction Writers Since World War II*, edited by Van C. Gessel (1997)

183 *American Travel Writers, 1776–1864*, edited by James J. Schramer and Donald Ross (1997)

184 *Nineteenth-Century British Book-Collectors and Bibliographers*, edited by William Baker and Kenneth Womack (1997)

185 *American Literary Journalists, 1945–1995, First Series*, edited by Arthur J. Kaul (1998)

186 *Nineteenth-Century American Western Writers*, edited by Robert L. Gale (1998)

187 *American Book Collectors and Bibliographers, Second Series*, edited by Joseph Rosenblum (1998)

188 *American Book and Magazine Illustrators to 1920*, edited by Steven E. Smith, Catherine A. Hastedt, and Donald H. Dyal (1998)

189 *American Travel Writers, 1850–1915*, edited by Donald Ross and James J. Schramer (1998)

190 *British Reform Writers, 1832–1914*, edited by Gary Kelly and Edd Applegate (1998)

191 *British Novelists Between the Wars*, edited by George M. Johnson (1998)

192 *French Dramatists, 1789–1914*, edited by Barbara T. Cooper (1998)

193 *American Poets Since World War II, Sixth Series*, edited by Joseph Conte (1998)

194 *British Novelists Since 1960, Second Series*, edited by Merritt Moseley (1998)

195 *British Travel Writers, 1910–1939*, edited by Barbara Brothers and Julia Gergits (1998)

196 *Italian Novelists Since World War II, 1965–1995*, edited by Augustus Pallotta (1999)

197 *Late-Victorian and Edwardian British Novelists, Second Series*, edited by George M. Johnson (1999)

198 *Russian Literature in the Age of Pushkin and Gogol: Prose*, edited by Christine A. Rydel (1999)

199 *Victorian Women Poets*, edited by William B. Thesing (1999)

200 *American Women Prose Writers to 1820*, edited by Carla J. Mulford, with Angela Vietto and Amy E. Winans (1999)

201 *Twentieth-Century British Book Collectors and Bibliographers*, edited by William Baker and Kenneth Womack (1999)

202 *Nineteenth-Century American Fiction Writers*, edited by Kent P. Ljungquist (1999)

203 *Medieval Japanese Writers*, edited by Steven D. Carter (1999)

204 *British Travel Writers, 1940–1997*, edited by Barbara Brothers and Julia M. Gergits (1999)

205 *Russian Literature in the Age of Pushkin and Gogol: Poetry and Drama*, edited by Christine A. Rydel (1999)

206 *Twentieth-Century American Western Writers, First Series*, edited by Richard H. Cracroft (1999)

207 *British Novelists Since 1960, Third Series*, edited by Merritt Moseley (1999)

208 *Literature of the French and Occitan Middle Ages: Eleventh to Fifteenth Centuries*, edited by Deborah Sinnreich-Levi and Ian S. Laurie (1999)

209 *Chicano Writers, Third Series*, edited by Francisco A. Lomelí and Carl R. Shirley (1999)

210 *Ernest Hemingway: A Documentary Volume*, edited by Robert W. Trogdon (1999)

211 *Ancient Roman Writers*, edited by Ward W. Briggs (1999)

212 *Twentieth-Century American Western Writers, Second Series*, edited by Richard H. Cracroft (1999)

213 *Pre-Nineteenth-Century British Book Collectors and Bibliographers*, edited by William Baker and Kenneth Womack (1999)

214 *Twentieth-Century Danish Writers*, edited by Marianne Stecher-Hansen (1999)

215 *Twentieth-Century Eastern European Writers, First Series*, edited by Steven Serafin (1999)

216 *British Poets of the Great War: Brooke, Rosenberg, Thomas. A Documentary Volume*, edited by Patrick Quinn (2000)

217 *Nineteenth-Century French Poets*, edited by Robert Beum (2000)

218 *American Short-Story Writers Since World War II, Second Series*, edited by Patrick Meanor and Gwen Crane (2000)

219 *F. Scott Fitzgerald's* The Great Gatsby: *A Documentary Volume*, edited by Matthew J. Bruccoli (2000)

220 *Twentieth-Century Eastern European Writers, Second Series*, edited by Steven Serafin (2000)

221 *American Women Prose Writers, 1870–1920*, edited by Sharon M. Harris, with the assistance of Heidi L. M. Jacobs and Jennifer Putzi (2000)

222 *H. L. Mencken: A Documentary Volume*, edited by Richard J. Schrader (2000)

223 *The American Renaissance in New England, Second Series*, edited by Wesley T. Mott (2000)

224 *Walt Whitman: A Documentary Volume*, edited by Joel Myerson (2000)

225 *South African Writers*, edited by Paul A. Scanlon (2000)

226 *American Hard-Boiled Crime Writers*, edited by George Parker Anderson and Julie B. Anderson (2000)

227 *American Novelists Since World War II, Sixth Series*, edited by James R. Giles and Wanda H. Giles (2000)

228 *Twentieth-Century American Dramatists, Second Series*, edited by Christopher J. Wheatley (2000)

229 *Thomas Wolfe: A Documentary Volume*, edited by Ted Mitchell (2001)

230 *Australian Literature, 1788–1914*, edited by Selina Samuels (2001)

231 *British Novelists Since 1960, Fourth Series*, edited by Merritt Moseley (2001)

232 *Twentieth-Century Eastern European Writers, Third Series*, edited by Steven Serafin (2001)

233 *British and Irish Dramatists Since World War II, Second Series*, edited by John Bull (2001)

234 *American Short-Story Writers Since World War II, Third Series*, edited by Patrick Meanor and Richard E. Lee (2001)

235 *The American Renaissance in New England, Third Series*, edited by Wesley T. Mott (2001)

236 *British Rhetoricians and Logicians, 1500–1660*, edited by Edward A. Malone (2001)

237 *The Beats: A Documentary Volume*, edited by Matt Theado (2001)

238 *Russian Novelists in the Age of Tolstoy and Dostoevsky*, edited by J. Alexander Ogden and Judith E. Kalb (2001)

239 *American Women Prose Writers: 1820–1870*, edited by Amy E. Hudock and Katharine Rodier (2001)

240 *Late Nineteenth- and Early Twentieth-Century British Women Poets*, edited by William B. Thesing (2001)

241 *American Sportswriters and Writers on Sport*, edited by Richard Orodenker (2001)

242 *Twentieth-Century European Cultural Theorists, First Series*, edited by Paul Hansom (2001)

243 *The American Renaissance in New England, Fourth Series*, edited by Wesley T. Mott (2001)

244 *American Short-Story Writers Since World War II, Fourth Series*, edited by Patrick Meanor and Joseph McNicholas (2001)

245 *British and Irish Dramatists Since World War II, Third Series*, edited by John Bull (2001)

246 *Twentieth-Century American Cultural Theorists*, edited by Paul Hansom (2001)

247 *James Joyce: A Documentary Volume*, edited by A. Nicholas Fargnoli (2001)

248 *Antebellum Writers in the South, Second Series*, edited by Kent Ljungquist (2001)

249 *Twentieth-Century American Dramatists, Third Series*, edited by Christopher Wheatley (2002)

250 *Antebellum Writers in New York, Second Series*, edited by Kent Ljungquist (2002)

251 *Canadian Fantasy and Science-Fiction Writers*, edited by Douglas Ivison (2002)

252 *British Philosophers, 1500–1799*, edited by Philip B. Dematteis and Peter S. Fosl (2002)

253 *Raymond Chandler: A Documentary Volume*, edited by Robert Moss (2002)

254 *The House of Putnam, 1837–1872: A Documentary Volume*, edited by Ezra Greenspan (2002)

255 *British Fantasy and Science-Fiction Writers, 1918–1960*, edited by Darren Harris-Fain (2002)

256 *Twentieth-Century American Western Writers, Third Series*, edited by Richard H. Cracroft (2002)

257 *Twentieth-Century Swedish Writers After World War II*, edited by Ann-Charlotte Gavel Adams (2002)

258 *Modern French Poets*, edited by Jean-François Leroux (2002)

259 *Twentieth-Century Swedish Writers Before World War II*, edited by Ann-Charlotte Gavel Adams (2002)

260 *Australian Writers, 1915–1950*, edited by Selina Samuels (2002)

261 *British Fantasy and Science-Fiction Writers Since 1960*, edited by Darren Harris-Fain (2002)

262 *British Philosophers, 1800–2000*, edited by Peter S. Fosl and Leemon B. McHenry (2002)

263 *William Shakespeare: A Documentary Volume*, edited by Catherine Loomis (2002)

264 *Italian Prose Writers, 1900–1945*, edited by Luca Somigli and Rocco Capozzi (2002)

265 *American Song Lyricists, 1920–1960*, edited by Philip Furia (2002)

266 *Twentieth-Century American Dramatists, Fourth Series*, edited by Christopher J. Wheatley (2002)

267 *Twenty-First-Century British and Irish Novelists*, edited by Michael R. Molino (2002)

268 *Seventeenth-Century French Writers*, edited by Françoise Jaouën (2002)

269 *Nathaniel Hawthorne: A Documentary Volume*, edited by Benjamin Franklin V (2002)

270 *American Philosophers Before 1950*, edited by Philip B. Dematteis and Leemon B. McHenry (2002)

271 *British and Irish Novelists Since 1960*, edited by Merritt Moseley (2002)

272 *Russian Prose Writers Between the World Wars*, edited by Christine Rydel (2003)

273 *F. Scott Fitzgerald's* Tender Is the Night: *A Documentary Volume*, edited by Matthew J. Bruccoli and George Parker Anderson (2003)

274 *John Dos Passos's* U.S.A.: *A Documentary Volume*, edited by Donald Pizer (2003)

275 *Twentieth-Century American Nature Writers: Prose*, edited by Roger Thompson and J. Scott Bryson (2003)

276 *British Mystery and Thriller Writers Since 1960*, edited by Gina Macdonald (2003)

277 *Russian Literature in the Age of Realism*, edited by Alyssa Dinega Gillespie (2003)

278 *American Novelists Since World War II, Seventh Series*, edited by James R. Giles and Wanda H. Giles (2003)

279 *American Philosophers, 1950–2000*, edited by Philip B. Dematteis and Leemon B. McHenry (2003)

280 *Dashiell Hammett's* The Maltese Falcon: *A Documentary Volume*, edited by Richard Layman (2003)

281 *British Rhetoricians and Logicians, 1500–1660, Second Series*, edited by Edward A. Malone (2003)

282 *New Formalist Poets*, edited by Jonathan N. Barron and Bruce Meyer (2003)

283 *Modern Spanish American Poets, First Series*, edited by María A. Salgado (2003)

284 *The House of Holt, 1866–1946: A Documentary Volume*, edited by Ellen D. Gilbert (2003)

285 *Russian Writers Since 1980*, edited by Marina Balina and Mark Lipovetsky (2004)

286 *Castilian Writers, 1400–1500*, edited by Frank A. Domínguez and George D. Greenia (2004)

287 *Portuguese Writers*, edited by Monica Rector and Fred M. Clark (2004)

288 *The House of Boni & Liveright, 1917–1933: A Documentary Volume*, edited by Charles Egleston (2004)

289 *Australian Writers, 1950–1975*, edited by Selina Samuels (2004)

290 *Modern Spanish American Poets, Second Series*, edited by María A. Salgado (2004)

291 *The Hoosier House: Bobbs-Merrill and Its Predecessors, 1850–1985: A Documentary Volume*, edited by Richard J. Schrader (2004)

292 *Twenty-First-Century American Novelists*, edited by Lisa Abney and Suzanne Disheroon-Green (2004)

293 *Icelandic Writers*, edited by Patrick J. Stevens (2004)

294 *James Gould Cozzens: A Documentary Volume*, edited by Matthew J. Bruccoli (2004)

295 *Russian Writers of the Silver Age, 1890–1925*, edited by Judith E. Kalb and J. Alexander Ogden with the collaboration of I. G. Vishnevetsky (2004)

296 *Twentieth-Century European Cultural Theorists, Second Series*, edited by Paul Hansom (2004)

297 *Twentieth-Century Norwegian Writers*, edited by Tanya Thresher (2004)

298 *Henry David Thoreau: A Documentary Volume*, edited by Richard J. Schneider (2004)

299 *Holocaust Novelists*, edited by Efraim Sicher (2004)

300 *Danish Writers from the Reformation to Decadence, 1550–1900*, edited by Marianne Stecher-Hansen (2004)

301 *Gustave Flaubert: A Documentary Volume*, edited by Éric Le Calvez (2004)

302 *Russian Prose Writers After World War II*, edited by Christine Rydel (2005)

## *Dictionary of Literary Biography Documentary Series*

1. *Sherwood Anderson, Willa Cather, John Dos Passos, Theodore Dreiser, F. Scott Fitzgerald, Ernest Hemingway, Sinclair Lewis,* edited by Margaret A. Van Antwerp (1982)

2. *James Gould Cozzens, James T. Farrell, William Faulkner, John O'Hara, John Steinbeck, Thomas Wolfe, Richard Wright,* edited by Margaret A. Van Antwerp (1982)

3. *Saul Bellow, Jack Kerouac, Norman Mailer, Vladimir Nabokov, John Updike, Kurt Vonnegut,* edited by Mary Bruccoli (1983)

4. *Tennessee Williams,* edited by Margaret A. Van Antwerp and Sally Johns (1984)

5. *American Transcendentalists,* edited by Joel Myerson (1988)

6. *Hardboiled Mystery Writers: Raymond Chandler, Dashiell Hammett, Ross Macdonald,* edited by Matthew J. Bruccoli and Richard Layman (1989)

7. *Modern American Poets: James Dickey, Robert Frost, Marianne Moore,* edited by Karen L. Rood (1989)

8. *The Black Aesthetic Movement,* edited by Jeffrey Louis Decker (1991)

9. *American Writers of the Vietnam War: W. D. Ehrhart, Larry Heinemann, Tim O'Brien, Walter McDonald, John M. Del Vecchio,* edited by Ronald Baughman (1991)

10. *The Bloomsbury Group,* edited by Edward L. Bishop (1992)

11. *American Proletarian Culture: The Twenties and The Thirties,* edited by Jon Christian Suggs (1993)

12. *Southern Women Writers: Flannery O'Connor, Katherine Anne Porter, Eudora Welty,* edited by Mary Ann Wimsatt and Karen L. Rood (1994)

13. *The House of Scribner, 1846–1904,* edited by John Delaney (1996)

14. *Four Women Writers for Children, 1868–1918,* edited by Caroline C. Hunt (1996)

15. *American Expatriate Writers: Paris in the Twenties,* edited by Matthew J. Bruccoli and Robert W. Trogdon (1997)

16. *The House of Scribner, 1905–1930,* edited by John Delaney (1997)

17. *The House of Scribner, 1931–1984,* edited by John Delaney (1998)

18. *British Poets of The Great War: Sassoon, Graves, Owen,* edited by Patrick Quinn (1999)

19. *James Dickey,* edited by Judith S. Baughman (1999)

See also DLB 210, 216, 219, 222, 224, 229, 237, 247, 253, 254, 263, 269, 273, 274, 280, 284, 288, 291, 294, 298, 301

## *Dictionary of Literary Biography Yearbooks*

1980 edited by Karen L. Rood, Jean W. Ross, and Richard Ziegfeld (1981)

1981 edited by Karen L. Rood, Jean W. Ross, and Richard Ziegfeld (1982)

1982 edited by Richard Ziegfeld; associate editors: Jean W. Ross and Lynne C. Zeigler (1983)

1983 edited by Mary Bruccoli and Jean W. Ross; associate editor Richard Ziegfeld (1984)

1984 edited by Jean W. Ross (1985)

1985 edited by Jean W. Ross (1986)

1986 edited by J. M. Brook (1987)

1987 edited by J. M. Brook (1988)

1988 edited by J. M. Brook (1989)

1989 edited by J. M. Brook (1990)

1990 edited by James W. Hipp (1991)

1991 edited by James W. Hipp (1992)

1992 edited by James W. Hipp (1993)

1993 edited by James W. Hipp, contributing editor George Garrett (1994)

1994 edited by James W. Hipp, contributing editor George Garrett (1995)

1995 edited by James W. Hipp, contributing editor George Garrett (1996)

1996 edited by Samuel W. Bruce and L. Kay Webster, contributing editor George Garrett (1997)

1997 edited by Matthew J. Bruccoli and George Garrett, with the assistance of L. Kay Webster (1998)

1998 edited by Matthew J. Bruccoli, contributing editor George Garrett, with the assistance of D. W. Thomas (1999)

1999 edited by Matthew J. Bruccoli, contributing editor George Garrett, with the assistance of D. W. Thomas (2000)

2000 edited by Matthew J. Bruccoli, contributing editor George Garrett, with the assistance of George Parker Anderson (2001)

2001 edited by Matthew J. Bruccoli, contributing editor George Garrett, with the assistance of George Parker Anderson (2002)

2002 edited by Matthew J. Bruccoli and George Garrett; George Parker Anderson, Assistant Editor (2003)

## *Concise Series*

**Concise Dictionary of American Literary Biography,** 7 volumes (1988-1999): *The New Consciousness, 1941-1968; Colonization to the American Renaissance, 1640-1865; Realism, Naturalism, and Local Color, 1865-1917; The Twenties, 1917-1929; The Age of Maturity, 1929-1941; Broadening Views, 1968-1988; Supplement: Modern Writers, 1900-1998.*

**Concise Dictionary of British Literary Biography,** 8 volumes (1991-1992): *Writers of the Middle Ages and Renaissance Before 1660; Writers of the Restoration and Eighteenth Century, 1660-1789; Writers of the Romantic Period, 1789-1832; Victorian Writers, 1832-1890; Late-Victorian and Edwardian Writers, 1890-1914; Modern Writers, 1914-1945; Writers After World War II, 1945-1960; Contemporary Writers, 1960 to Present.*

**Concise Dictionary of World Literary Biography,** 4 volumes (1999-2000): *Ancient Greek and Roman Writers; German Writers; African, Caribbean, and Latin American Writers; South Slavic and Eastern European Writers.*

Dictionary of Literary Biography® • Volume Three Hundred Two

# Russian Prose Writers After World War II

Dictionary of Literary Biography® • Volume Three Hundred Two

# Russian Prose Writers After World War II

Edited by
Christine Rydel
*Grand Valley State University*

A Bruccoli Clark Layman Book

THOMSON
★
GALE

Detroit • New York • San Francisco • San Diego • New Haven, Conn. • Waterville, Maine • London • Munich

ST. PHILIP'S COLLEGE LIBRARY

**THOMSON GALE**

Dictionary of Literary Biography
Volume 302: Russian Prose Writers
After World War II
Christine Rydel

**Advisory Board**
John Baker
William Cagle
Patrick O'Connor
George Garrett
Trudier Harris
Alvin Kernan

**Editorial Directors**
Matthew J. Bruccoli and Richard Layman

© 2005 Thomson Gale, a part of The Thomson Corporation.

Thomson and Star Logo are trademarks and Gale is a registered trademark used herein under license.

*For more information, contact*
Thomson Gale
27500 Drake Rd.
Farmington Hills, MI 48331-3535
Or you can visit our Internet site at
http://www.gale.com

**ALL RIGHTS RESERVED**
No part of this work covered by the copyright hereon may be reproduced or used in any form or by any means—graphic, electronic, or mechanical, including photocopying, recording, taping, Web distribution, or information storage retrieval systems—without the written permission of the publisher.

For permission to use material from this product, submit your request via Web at http://www.gale-edit.com/permissions, or you may download our Permissions Request form and submit your request by fax or mail to:

*Permissions Department*
Thomson Gale
27500 Drake Rd.
Farmington Hills, MI 48331-3535
Permissions Hotline:
248-699-8006 or 800-877-4253, ext. 8006
Fax: 248-699-8074 or 800-762-4058

While every effort has been made to ensure the reliability of the information presented in this publication, Thomson Gale does not guarantee the accuracy of the data contained herein. Thomson Gale accepts no payment for listing; and inclusion in the publication of any organization, agency, institution, publication, service, or individual does not imply endorsement of the editors or publisher. Errors brought to the attention of the publisher and verified to the satisfaction of the publisher will be corrected in future editions.

---

**LIBRARY OF CONGRESS CATALOGING-IN-PUBLICATION DATA**

Russian prose writers after World War II / edited by Christine Rydel.
　　p. cm. — (Dictionary of literary biography ; v. 302)
"A Bruccoli Clark Layman Book"
Includes bibliographical references and index.
　　　　ISBN 0-7876-6839-7 (cloth : alk. paper)
　　　　1. Russian prose literature—20th century—Bio-bibliography—Dictionaries. 2. Authors, Russian—20th century—Biography—Dictionaries. I. Rydel, Christine. II. Series.

PG3094.R866 2004
891.78′440809′03—dc22
　　　　　　　　　　　　　　　　　　　　　　　　　　　　　2004014753

---

Printed in the United States of America
10 9 8 7 6 5 4 3 2 1

*For Sergius*

# Contents

Plan of the Series . . . . . . . . . . . . . . . . . . . . . . . . . . xv
Introduction . . . . . . . . . . . . . . . . . . . . . . . . . . . . . .xvii

Fedor Aleksandrovich Abramov
   (1920–1983) . . . . . . . . . . . . . . . . . . . . . . . . . . .3
   *David Gillespie*

Chingiz Aitmatov (1928– ) . . . . . . . . . . . . . . . . . . .9
   *Erika Haber*

Vassily Aksyonov (Vasilii Pavlovich Aksenov)
   (1932– ) . . . . . . . . . . . . . . . . . . . . . . . . . . . . . . .15
   *Konstantin V. Kustanovich*

Andrei Amalrik (1938–1980) . . . . . . . . . . . . . . . . .35
   *Jonathan Z. Ludwig*

Natal'ia Vladimirovna Baranskaia
   (1908– ) . . . . . . . . . . . . . . . . . . . . . . . . . . . . . . .40
   *Benjamin M. Sutcliffe*

Vasilii Ivanovich Belov (1932– ) . . . . . . . . . . . . . .46
   *David Gillespie*

Andrei Georgievich Bitov (1937– ) . . . . . . . . . . . .52
   *Cynthia Simmons*

Iurii Vasil'evich Bondarev (1924– ) . . . . . . . . . . .64
   *Alexandra Smith*

Lidiia Chukovskaia (1907–1996) . . . . . . . . . . . . . .72
   *Sibelan Forrester*

Iulii Daniel' (Nikolai Arzhak)
   (1925–1988) . . . . . . . . . . . . . . . . . . . . . . . . . . .77
   *Jefferson Gatrall*

Vladimir Dmitrievich Dudintsev
   (1918–1998) . . . . . . . . . . . . . . . . . . . . . . . . . . .83
   *Peter Rollberg*

Evgeniia Ginzburg (1904–1977) . . . . . . . . . . . . . .89
   *Jane Gary Harris*

Lidiia Iakovlevna Ginzburg
   (1902–1990) . . . . . . . . . . . . . . . . . . . . . . . . . . .95
   *Jane Gary Harris*

Anatolii Tikhonovich Gladilin
   (1935– ) . . . . . . . . . . . . . . . . . . . . . . . . . . . . . 103
   *Boris Lanin*

Daniil Granin (1918– ) . . . . . . . . . . . . . . . . . . . . 108
   *Alexandra Smith*

Irina Grekova (Elena Sergeevna Venttsel')
   (1907–2002) . . . . . . . . . . . . . . . . . . . . . . . . . . 115
   *Nadya L. Peterson*

Fazil' Abdulevich Iskander (1929– ) . . . . . . . . . 120
   *Marina Kanevskaya*

Iurii Pavlovich Kazakov (1927–1982) . . . . . . . . . 138
   *Naum Leiderman*

Anatolii Kuznetsov
   (A. Anatoly) (1929–1979) . . . . . . . . . . . . . . . 150
   *Jennifer Ryan Tishler*

Vladimir Emel'ianovich Maksimov
   (1930–1995) . . . . . . . . . . . . . . . . . . . . . . . . . . 155
   *Peter Rollberg*

Nadezhda Iakovlevna Mandel'shtam
   (1899–1980) . . . . . . . . . . . . . . . . . . . . . . . . . . 164
   *Beth Holmgren*

Vladimir Rafailovich Maramzin
   (1934– ) . . . . . . . . . . . . . . . . . . . . . . . . . . . . . 172
   *Lev Loseff*

Iurii Markovich Nagibin (1920–1994) . . . . . . . . 177
   *Alexandra Smith*

Viktor Platonovich Nekrasov
   (1911–1987) . . . . . . . . . . . . . . . . . . . . . . . . . . 187
   *Michael Falchikov*

Vera Fedorovna Panova (1905–1973) . . . . . . . . . 194
   *Nadya L. Peterson*

Boris Pasternak
   (1890–1960) . . . . . . . . . . . . . . . . . . . . . . . . . . 202
   *Karen Evans-Romaine*

## Contents

Valentin Grigor'evich Rasputin
(1937– ) .................................. 230
*David Gillespie*

Anatolii Naumovich Rybakov
(1911–1994) ............................. 242
*Boris Lanin*

Varlam Tikhonovich Shalamov
(1907–1982) ............................. 250
*Janet Tucker*

Vasilii Makarovich Shukshin
(1929–1974) ............................. 266
*John Givens*

Konstantin Mikhailovich Simonov
(1915–1979) ............................. 280
*Marina Balina*

Andrei Siniavsky
(Abram Tertz) (1925–1997) ........... 296
*Catharine Theimer Nepomnyashchy*

Vladimir Alekseevich Soloukhin
(1924–1997) ............................. 317
*Alexandra Smith*

Aleksandr Solzhenitsyn (1918– ) ........... 324
*Edward E. Ericson Jr. and Alexis Klimoff*

Arkadii Natanovich Strugatsky (1925–1991)
and Boris Natanovich Strugatsky
(1933– ) ................................. 356
*Alexandra Smith*

Vladimir Fedorovich Tendriakov
(1923–1984) ............................. 366
*Alexandra Smith*

Iurii Valentinovich Trifonov
(1925–1981) ............................. 373
*David Gillespie*

Aleksandr Valentinovich Vampilov
(A. Sanin) (1937–1972) ................ 387
*J. Alexander Ogden*

Georgii Vladimov (1931–2003) ............. 397
*Svetlana McMillin*

Vladimir Nikolaevich Voinovich (1932– ) ... 406
*Helen Segall*

Sergei Pavlovich Zalygin (1913–2000) ...... 422
*Jennifer Ryan Tishler*

Aleksandr Aleksandrovich Zinov'ev (1922– ) ... 429
*Boris Lanin*

Checklist of Further Readings .............. 437
Contributors ................................ 443
Cumulative Index .......................... 447

# Plan of the Series

*. . . Almost the most prodigious asset of a country, and perhaps its most precious possession, is its native literary product—when that product is fine and noble and enduring.*

Mark Twain*

The advisory board, the editors, and the publisher of the *Dictionary of Literary Biography* are joined in endorsing Mark Twain's declaration. The literature of a nation provides an inexhaustible resource of permanent worth. Our purpose is to make literature and its creators better understood and more accessible to students and the reading public, while satisfying the needs of teachers and researchers.

To meet these requirements, *literary biography* has been construed in terms of the author's achievement. The most important thing about a writer is his writing. Accordingly, the entries in *DLB* are career biographies, tracing the development of the author's canon and the evolution of his reputation.

The purpose of *DLB* is not only to provide reliable information in a usable format but also to place the figures in the larger perspective of literary history and to offer appraisals of their accomplishments by qualified scholars.

The publication plan for *DLB* resulted from two years of preparation. The project was proposed to Bruccoli Clark by Frederick G. Ruffner, president of the Gale Research Company, in November 1975. After specimen entries were prepared and typeset, an advisory board was formed to refine the entry format and develop the series rationale. In meetings held during 1976, the publisher, series editors, and advisory board approved the scheme for a comprehensive biographical dictionary of persons who contributed to literature. Editorial work on the first volume began in January 1977, and it was published in 1978. In order to make *DLB* more than a dictionary and to compile volumes that individually have claim to status as literary history, it was decided to organize volumes by topic, period, or genre. Each of these freestanding volumes provides a biographical-bibliographical guide and overview for a particular area of literature. We are convinced that this organization—as opposed to a single alphabet method—constitutes a valuable innovation in the presentation of reference material. The volume plan necessarily requires many decisions for the placement and treatment of authors. Certain figures will be included in separate volumes, but with different entries emphasizing the aspect of his career appropriate to each volume. Ernest Hemingway, for example, is represented in *American Writers in Paris, 1920–1939* by an entry focusing on his expatriate apprenticeship; he is also in *American Novelists, 1910–1945* with an entry surveying his entire career, as well as in *American Short-Story Writers, 1910–1945, Second Series* with an entry concentrating on his short fiction. Each volume includes a cumulative index of the subject authors and articles.

Between 1981 and 2002 the series was augmented and updated by the *DLB Yearbooks*. There have also been nineteen *DLB Documentary Series* volumes, which provide illustrations, facsimiles, and biographical and critical source materials for figures, works, or groups judged to have particular interest for students. In 1999 the *Documentary Series* was incorporated into the *DLB* volume numbering system beginning with *DLB 210: Ernest Hemingway*.

We define literature as the *intellectual commerce of a nation:* not merely as belles lettres but as that ample and complex process by which ideas are generated, shaped, and transmitted. *DLB* entries are not limited to "creative writers" but extend to other figures who in their time and in their way influenced the mind of a people. Thus the series encompasses historians, journalists, publishers, book collectors, and screenwriters. By this means readers of *DLB* may be aided to perceive literature not as cult scripture in the keeping of intellectual high priests but firmly positioned at the center of a nation's life.

*DLB* includes the major writers appropriate to each volume and those standing in the ranks behind them. Scholarly and critical counsel has been sought in deciding which minor figures to include and how full their entries should be. Wherever possible, useful refer-

*\*From an unpublished section of Mark Twain's autobiography, copyright by the Mark Twain Company*

ences are made to figures who do not warrant separate entries.

Each *DLB* volume has an expert volume editor responsible for planning the volume, selecting the figures for inclusion, and assigning the entries. Volume editors are also responsible for preparing, where appropriate, appendices surveying the major periodicals and literary and intellectual movements for their volumes, as well as lists of further readings. Work on the series as a whole is coordinated at the Bruccoli Clark Layman editorial center in Columbia, South Carolina, where the editorial staff is responsible for accuracy and utility of the published volumes.

One feature that distinguishes *DLB* is the illustration policy—its concern with the iconography of literature. Just as an author is influenced by his surroundings, so is the reader's understanding of the author enhanced by a knowledge of his environment. Therefore *DLB* volumes include not only drawings, paintings, and photographs of authors, often depicting them at various stages in their careers, but also illustrations of their families and places where they lived. Title pages are regularly reproduced in facsimile along with dust jackets for modern authors. The dust jackets are a special feature of *DLB* because they often document better than anything else the way in which an author's work was perceived in its own time. Specimens of the writers' manuscripts and letters are included when feasible.

Samuel Johnson rightly decreed that "The chief glory of every people arises from its authors." The purpose of the *Dictionary of Literary Biography* is to compile literary history in the surest way available to us—by accurate and comprehensive treatment of the lives and work of those who contributed to it.

The DLB Advisory Board

# Introduction

In the twentieth century Russian writers struggled mightily to gain control of their destinies—perhaps never more so than in the forty-year span that began at the end of World War II and ended with Mikhail Gorbachev's rise to power in 1985. This period brought challenges to the monolithic authority of the state over the arts in the form of boycotts, protests, underground literature (samizdat), publishing abroad *(tamizdat)*, and emigration. The government countered with arrests, imprisonment, exile, confinement in mental institutions, physical and psychological harassment, and, in extreme cases, disenfranchisement, along with forced expulsion from the Union of Soviet Socialist Republics (U.S.S.R.; commonly shortened to Soviet Union). Of course, not all writers were dissidents; many managed, quite willingly, to publish through official channels in state-run publishing houses *(gosizdat)*. Consequently, these forty years also brought the emergence of two factions of writers: the conservatives, who remained true to the principles of socialist realism (discussed in the introduction to *DLB 272: Russian Writers Between the World Wars*), and the liberals, who demanded artistic freedom. Nevertheless, in spite of their differences, both camps fell prey to the vicissitudes of history, internal politics, and foreign policy that grew out of the Soviet Union's involvement in World War II.

At the conclusion of that war the homeland of Russian literature was a vast and ruined battlefield littered with unburied corpses, burned-out machinery, and enormous heaps of rubble that had once been towns and cities. Some twenty-one million people had died in the epic struggle to throw the Germans out of the land and to pursue them, by various routes, all the way to Berlin. Because they had successfully rid the country of the Nazi enemy, Joseph Stalin and the Communist Party of the Soviet Union (CPSU) enjoyed their first true popularity. But when Stalin announced that the task at hand was to rebuild Soviet society, a challenge fully as daunting as that of "building socialism" in the 1930s, his clarion call was not greeted with universal joy.

The Russians realized that "rebuilding" also meant reversion to the repressive policies that had been in force until 1943. In that momentous year of the Stalingrad victory and the Teheran Conference, at which Stalin, U.S. president Franklin D. Roosevelt, and British prime minister Winston S. Churchill decided how to defeat Adolf Hitler, popular support for the war was rewarded by remarkable concessions to the Soviet people: in 1943 Stalin did away with the policy of militant atheism, had some of his underlings meet Russian Orthodox Church leaders in public, and allowed the election of a new patriarch. Soviet officials looked the other way as a market economy solved the food shortages. Peasants and industrial workers responded by starting or expanding private garden plots. Most important for literature, cultural controls were relaxed with the understanding that writers would support the patriotic struggle; for intellectuals, at least, war became more relaxed and creative than peace. As the troops marched back from Germany two years later, many citizens—not just intellectuals—hoped for something more than "rebuilding socialism."

The regime moved quickly to cut off these incipient dreams that threatened its system. The leniency in trade and agriculture ended, and rigid planning returned to the economy. In 1946, at about the same time that the U.S.S.R.'s Western allies discovered the "Iron Curtain," Stalin ordered that a cultural purge should begin in Leningrad; the task was given to Andrei Aleksandrovich Zhdanov, one of his most obedient lieutenants. In 1949, on Stalin's orders, Lavrentii Pavlovich Beria, head of the MVD (Ministerstvo vnutrennih del [Ministry of Internal Affairs]), carried out a minor purge of the Communist Party: in the so-called Leningrad Affair many leading party figures were either shot or died in custody. Throughout the late 1940s, despite an abnormally high death rate, the enormous population of the dreaded labor-camp system remained constant: a steady stream of political prisoners, forcibly repatriated war refugees, and former German prisoners of war more than made up for those who died.

Seen from outside, the U.S.S.R. seemed to grow in power and prestige. Having spurned the offer of Marshall Plan aid, the Soviet Union walled itself off from the world economy and rebuilt its heavily damaged infrastructure. Soviet science produced nuclear weapons. Shortly after consolidating its control over all of Eastern Europe, Moscow welcomed China into the growing family of Marxist dictatorships. In 1949 the concerned Western powers established the North Atlantic Treaty Organization (NATO) with the express mission of defending Europe from the perceived Soviet threat. The following year war broke out in the Korean Peninsula pitting the Communist North, backed by China and encouraged by the U.S.S.R., against the United Nations, led by the United States. Few in the West had any real idea of the crisis building up within Stalin's empire.

One of the many ironies of the Soviet experiment was that the thoroughgoing attempt to realize the promises of a doctrine of extreme equality had produced exactly the opposite result. More than any other event, the great Purge of 1934 to 1938 had transformed the upper echelons of the Communist Party into one of the most privileged ruling elites in history. As might be expected, the preservation and enhancement of special advantages became the primary interest of this elite group. The party chiefs did not have to worry about the long-suffering, war-blasted people, but they knew well how they themselves had risen to high estate. They greatly feared the institutions of terror; the sham courts of law; the security organs, renamed the MGB (Ministerstvo Gosudarstvennoi Bezopasnosti [Ministry of State Security]); the prison and camp empire known as the gulag; and the execution cellars of the Lubianka, a notorious Moscow prison and the headquarters of state security forces. (Though *GULag* actually stands for Gosudarstvennoe upravlenie lagerov [State Supervision of Camps], popular usage has adopted the word to mean the camp system itself. By convention, *GULag* refers to the supervisory apparatus, while *gulag* designates the camps themselves.)

Stalin's postwar moves not surprisingly greatly alarmed the Communist Party: his actions clearly pointed at the dawn of yet another Great Purge. The dictator kept shifting his personal favor from one group of party leaders to another in a most disturbing way. The Leningrad Affair was particularly upsetting. In 1952, at the Nineteenth Party Congress (the first held since 1938), Stalin proposed to pack the highest party committee, the Presidium (formerly the Politburo), with new men of his own choosing. Then, in January 1953, in an incident known as the "Doctors' Plot," several elite physicians with Jewish names were arrested for treason and murder. This plot all too eerily recalled the "Kirov Affair" that had touched off the Great Purge in 1934 (discussed in the introduction to *DLB 272*).

Thus, it was a great relief for the party leadership when Stalin suffered a massive stroke and died on 5 March 1953. The news stunned the population at large and set off a variety of events as different as violent camp uprisings and mass demonstrations of sincere lamentation. Behind the scenes, however, the upper echelons moved swiftly to dismantle the purge mechanism and to arrest and execute Beria, the one man in a position to institute a new terror. The direction of the new policy was unmistakable. Soon, millions of camp inmates began the process of a phased return to their former homes. Bulldozers arrived at the campsites and scraped them from the face of the earth. Significantly, a collective leadership downgraded the MGB (*Ministry* of State Security) to the KGB (Komitet gosudarstvennoy bezopasnosti [*Committee* of State Security]). Negotiations began that ultimately ended the Korean War with an armistice that was signed on 27 July 1953. An era of reform seemed to be at hand.

After the death of Stalin, the U.S.S.R. enjoyed considerable respect in the world at large because it was a nuclear power that had served as the pattern state for China and because it continued to exercise hegemony over Eastern Europe. But international power and prestige obscured inherent contradictions. Soviet socialism promised a radiant future and the transformation of human nature, but it had actually produced only an oppressive military-industrial complex and a privileged Communist Party elite known as the *nomenklatura*. Many problems emerged, not the least of which was that the entire postwar industrial infrastructure had been rebuilt according to an already obsolete prewar technology. The component of the Soviet system that touched literature the most, however, was enforced denial of reality. Even after obliterating most of the camps, in an arrangement that lasted until the late 1980s, the party leadership retained some KGB establishments, such as camps and psychiatric wards, that were reserved for evangelical Christians, intellectual dissidents, writers, poets, and others who could not refrain from telling the truth.

From 1953 to 1956, in an effort to mollify the populace, the party made a concerted effort to humanize the existing system and to satisfy the needs and wishes of the people. For four tense years, as former camp inmates returned with stories of their treatment, the upper echelons sought a leader equal to the task. By 1956 Nikita Khrushchev emerged as first secretary of the party. At the Twentieth Party Congress in 1956 he surprised the world with his "secret speech" denouncing Stalin for crimes against the party. The speech launched a campaign of "de-Stalinization" that expelled many of the old guard from their leadership positions; nevertheless, Khrushchev's motives were sincere: he wished to realize the promise of socialism.

Anxious to avoid problems in Eastern Europe, the party in the four years of collective leadership unwittingly created an impression that its hegemony was about to collapse. For example, by organizing the satellite states into an alliance called the Warsaw Pact in 1955, the U.S.S.R. seemed to give a tacit nod to the idea of satellite sovereignty. The neutralization and troop withdrawals of the Austrian State Treaty (1955) looked like the beginning of a retreat. Khrushchev's secret speech appeared to confirm this impression. In Poland, where military force had squashed popular labor protest in the summer of 1956, a Communist reformer, Władysław Gomułka, took control as a measure of reconciliation. Khrushchev and a delegation of hard-liners made a surprise visit to Warsaw to protest this action, but they met a Gomułka ready to make war rather than back down. The two sides negotiated a deal whereby Poland was permitted not only to move away from Stalinist policies but also to exercise home rule and to tolerate the Catholic Church in return for allegiance to the Warsaw Pact.

In Hungary, where similar protests erupted, Soviet authorities waited too long to placate protesters by introducing a reformer. Their man, Imre Nagy, was virtually captured by a revolution and ended up by withdrawing Hungary from the Warsaw Pact and ordering Soviet forces out of the country. At first, under the impression that Nagy would receive American support, the Soviets withdrew their tanks. But when they realized that the United States would do nothing, they returned and brutally crushed the Hungarian Uprising and Nagy. To maintain control, however, Moscow had to install another reformer, Janos Kadar, who in time negotiated the same deal that Poland enjoyed. Another important consequence of the secret speech was the Soviet Union's break with China. Although it took almost a decade to mature, the split between the two Communist great powers had its origin in Chinese outrage that the U.S.S.R. had had the effrontery to cast down their idol, Stalin. In a matter of years, the Chinese were insulting the Soviet Communist Party with the label "revisionist."

In general, Soviet domestic politics followed the same pattern as foreign affairs, with Khrushchev in the role of a Communist reformer. In 1957, with the aid of the armed forces, the first secretary faced down a putsch by disgruntled Stalinists, punishing them only with early retirement and demotions to positions far removed from the center of affairs. The way was then clear for reforms to proceed, with 1980 declared the year in which the Soviet populace would enjoy benefits similar to those of modern Sweden. The highly publicized Twenty-second Party Congress of 1962 even voted to remove Stalin's name from all monuments and his embalmed body from display in the Lenin Mausoleum.

Russian literature did not immediately benefit from the reforms. In 1957, for example, Boris Pasternak could not get his manuscript for *Doktor Zhivago* (translated as *Doctor Zhivago,* 1958) past the censorship, because it transgressed the limits of socialist realism. Pasternak had the novel published in Milan, Italy. The next year it was awarded the Nobel Prize in literature, but Khrushchev's regime refused to let the author go to Stockholm to accept the honor. Real change came in the wake of the Twenty-second Party Congress, however, when, in a daring move, Khrushchev turned to the dissident writers for support.

In November 1962 the first secretary personally authorized an event that had an impact equal to that of the secret speech: *Novyi mir* (New World), a leading literary journal, published Aleksandr Solzhenitsyn's *Odin den' Ivana Denisovicha* (translated as *One Day in the Life of Ivan Denisovich,* 1963), which realistically portrays life in Stalin's gulag. What followed was a flood of literary works that broke with the policy of denying reality. To be sure, these works had the effect of promoting de-Stalinization, but before long writers indicted the entire system. Not all of this literature was published, however, because alarmed officials blocked as much of it as they could; consequently, many works circulated only privately in the U.S.S.R. (samizdat) or abroad (*tamizdat*).

Along with the reform program, the U.S.S.R. embarked on an adventurous course of foreign affairs and astounding accomplishments that enhanced an external image of power and success. The outstanding examples include Sputnik 1, the first Earth-orbiting satellite, launched on 4 October 1957; so-called summit conferences between the Soviet premier and the president of the United States; the first unmanned Moon landing, accomplished by the Luna 2 spacecraft on 14 September 1959; the U-2 incident, in which Gary Powers, the pilot of an American spy plane, was shot down on 1 May 1960; Khrushchev's visit to the United Nations on 29 September 1960; Iurii Gagarin's first human Earth orbit on 12 April 1961; the construction of the Berlin Wall on the night of 12–13 August 1961; and the Cuban Missile Crisis of 18 to 29 October 1962. Once again, however, foreign affairs concealed growing problems within. On 16 October 1964 the world was stunned to learn that Khrushchev's colleagues had had him deposed and sent into forced retirement, supposedly for "adventurism" but actually because his policies were correctly perceived as threatening the privileged position of the *nomenklatura*.

The *nomenklatura* had reason to worry when they brought Khrushchev's reign to an end. Just as in 1953, there was no obvious successor, and the country was run by a tenuous collective leadership. It took the *nomenklatura* seven more years to realize that the

U.S.S.R. had failed to modernize its industrial sector, but in 1963 its agriculture was already a recognized disaster. In that year the U.S.S.R. had to initiate annual massive grain imports from the United States. Communist China succeeded in stealing the mantle of international Marxism, and the reformed regimes of Poland and Hungary mocked Soviet hegemony in Eastern Europe. At home, a growing body of dissident literature promoted reforms of the Soviet system by exposing its crimes, follies, and misfortunes.

Dissidence emerged at once as the most deadly of the government's problems—and the easiest with which to deal. De-Stalinization clearly ended with the 1964 arrest of the poet Iosif Aleksandrovich Brodsky for "parasitism" and escalated with the 1965 arrest of Andrei Siniavsky and Iulii Daniel', samizdat and *tamizdat* authors who were sentenced to the camps after their trial in February 1966. In response, a "dissident movement" developed and went underground. The party itself, however, did not want to revert completely to Stalinism out of fear of terror and out of recognition that something had to be done to make the system work. Neo-Stalinism thus turned into a facade behind which the party sought ways to preserve the tenure and privileges of its own elite.

The new regime was officially established at the Twenty-third Party Congress in 1966, with Leonid Brezhnev elected as party first secretary and Aleksei Kosygin as Soviet prime minister. Both had been protégés of Khrushchev, and both occupied illusory positions; behind the scenes, Khrushchev's chief opponent, the sinister head of party ideology, Mikhail Andreevich Suslov, directed a collective of aging party chiefs known as the "gerontocracy." Over time Kosygin withered away, leaving Brezhnev as the sole figurehead. The collective made every effort to present him as a "new Stalin," even to the point of awarding him the Lenin Prize for Literature for his ghostwritten memoirs. The party also made him the most highly-decorated soldier in Russian and Soviet history, despite the fact that he had performed no real military service. This charade was no more absurd than almost anything else that was happening in these increasingly surrealistic times.

So little meaningful reform emerged from the years under Brezhnev that the entire period was given the label "the age of *zastoi* (stagnation)." Massive annual importations of grain continued as the agricultural sector sank into lethargy. Industry declined to the point of zero growth. Little could be done as long as the CPSU and the command economy were considered sacred cows. Two other problems characterized this period: the planned economy had no way to measure costs or production other than to adapt and adopt the price structure of the "capitalist world"; and to supply ordinary consumer goods to the people and imported luxury items to the *nomenklatura*, the system had to tolerate an illegal black market. Not surprisingly, criminal elements generically described as "mafia" and private traders publicly branded *spekulanty* (speculators) dominated most of the illegal commerce. Yet another problem plagued the system: to pay for gigantic military expansion, the U.S.S.R. relied on enormous exports of oil to Europe. Paradoxically, a "first world" power rested on a "third world" economy.

Following the Siniavsky-Daniel' trial, Russian writers and poets entered a quarter century of life on the verge of catastrophe. Under its new director, Iurii Andropov, appointed on 18 May 1967, the KGB became increasingly more sophisticated. During Brezhnev's long tenure it had faced many challenges, including ethnic restlessness, Jewish demands to allow immigration to Israel, and, above all, dissent. The security organs dealt in various creative ways with these problems. Citizens suspected of ties with dissidents or of having dissident tendencies were subjected to all manner of surveillance, harassed, and stripped of their jobs and apartments, and their children were denied educational opportunities. Victims such as General Piotr Grigorenko and the political writer Vladimir Konstantinovich Bukovsky survived to tell of the tortures they had endured in KGB psychiatric wards. Others languished in prisons such as the notorious Kresty in Leningrad or in labor camps such as Perm 43.

Prominent dissidents whose public persecution might cause further problems were sent into internal exile. The physicist Andrei Sakharov, father of the Soviet nuclear program, was exiled to Gorky (now renamed Nizhniy Novgorod) from January 1980 until December 1986, late in the Gorbachev regime. Perhaps the most innovative tactic of all was expulsion from the U.S.S.R. The most notorious case, and the one that became the pattern for many others, was that of Solzhenitsyn, who wrote an extensive and brilliant exposé of the Stalinist camp system, *Arkhipelag GULag, 1918–1956: Opyt khudozhestvennego issledovaniia* (1973–1975; translated as *Gulag Archipelago, 1918–1956: An Experiment in Literary Investigation,* 1974–1978). After the KGB learned of this manuscript in 1974, Solzhenitsyn sent the first volume for publication abroad; two novels he had written after 1963, *V kruge pervom* (1968; translated as *The First Circle,* 1968) and *Rakovyi korpus* (1968; translated as *The Cancer Ward,* 1968) had earlier been published in the West without Solzhenitsyn's authorization. But this time he was stripped of his Soviet citizenship and forced on board an airliner bound for Europe. The new technique worked well in the short run because it removed writers' influence within the country and simultaneously deprived them of the dissident environment.

The international event that corresponded to the Siniavsky-Daniel' trial as a herald of neo-Stalinism was the 1968 "Prague Spring." The centerpiece of this episode was a limited set of reforms that the Czechoslovak Communist Party chief, Alexander Dubček, introduced under the slogan "socialism with a human face." Dubček, however, lost control of the reform process as younger comrades organized nonparty political associations and demanded an end to censorship. Alarmed older Communists appealed to Moscow for help, and the Kremlin asked the Warsaw Pact to discipline its wayward member. Tank columns rolled into Prague on 21 August. The U.S.S.R. justified intervention with the "Brezhnev Doctrine" that declared the right of all socialist countries to act whenever the socialism of any of them was threatened. Some Soviet dissidents made a public protest; they were all arrested, but news of the disturbance leaked out and revealed the existence of an opposition movement.

Most of the years of *zastoi* correspond to the "era of détente," which began with the 1970 SALT (Strategic Arms Limitation Talks) I negotiations for mutual limitation of nuclear weapons and proceeded until the United States, damaged by its fiasco in Vietnam, seemed ready to concede international equality. The U.S.S.R. took advantage of this "window of opportunity" to build up a blue-water navy complete with atomic submarines, to assemble a huge army of tanks confronting NATO forces in Europe, and to extend aid and encouragement to Marxist movements in Africa and southeast Asia. The high point of the process came with the signing of the 1975 Helsinki Accords, whereby the United States recognized the existing boundaries in Europe and the Soviet Union promised to respect human rights. The Soviet promises were unenforceable, but at least dissidents got international attention by forming Helsinki Watch Groups to document the hypocrisy. In December 1979, acting according to the Brezhnev Doctrine, Soviet forces invaded Afghanistan. Shocked out of complacency, the American government refused to seek ratification of the new SALT II agreements and withdrew its financially important participation in the 1980 Moscow Olympics. Détente was over. In reply, Brezhnev introduced SS-20 medium-range nuclear missiles into Eastern Europe.

The end times of *zastoi* actually began in Poland. In 1978 the Roman Catholic Church elected Karol Wojtyla Pope John Paul II–the first Polish Pope in history. In the following year the Polish regime wisely allowed the Pope to visit his homeland. Unwisely, it decided to let the Church preside over the triumph, the experience of which taught the Poles how to mobilize their energies outside of party control. In 1980, the same year in which the American elections produced the overtly anti-Communist administration of Ronald Reagan, a strike in the shipyards of Gdańsk resulted in the formation of an openly revolutionary movement called Solidarność (Solidarity). As Polish popular loyalty clearly shifted to Solidarność, the Polish Communist Party turned to naked military force by elevating General Wojciech Jaruzelski to the office of first secretary. Jaruzelski, acting on the advice of the Brezhnev regime, imposed martial law on 13 December 1981. When Brezhnev died on 10 November 1982, Poland resembled a powder keg about to explode at any minute, taking all of Eastern Europe with it.

In the vote for Brezhnev's successor, Andropov (who had just stepped down as head of the KGB), cut out Konstantin Chernenko, Brezhnev's chosen heir. Lacking real support and, for that matter, a real program, Andropov had little choice but to maintain the status quo; his one innovation was to have people arrested for not showing up for work. On his watch international standing plummeted when Soviet air force MIGs stalked and shot down a civilian airliner, Korean Air Lines Flight 007, on 31 August 1983 and when the United States countered the SS-20s with medium-range Pershing missiles in Western Europe. Andropov died on 9 February 1984 and was briefly succeeded by Chernenko, who died on 10 March 1985. Waiting in the wings was his protégé, Gorbachev, who took over a Communist empire on the verge of collapse.

Throughout the four decades from 1945 to 1985, when five Communist Party leaders sought to subordinate everything to their own political agendas, Russian literature put up a surprising resistance. The postwar struggle began on 9 February 1946 when Stalin dashed their hopes for the immediate future in a speech in which he told his country that the hard times were not yet over. On 14 August the Central Committee issued an edict condemning the journals *Zvezda* (Star) and *Leningrad* as too liberal and denounced the writers Mikhail Mikhailovich Zoshchenko (treated in *DLB 272*) and Anna Andreevna Akhmatova (treated in *DLB 295: Russian Writers of the Silver Age, 1890–1925*). The edict further directed writers to adopt a more anti-Western stance in their works, a situation that continued until the end of 1949. Aware of growing unrest among the intelligentsia, however, Stalin accused Soviet linguists of being too reactionary in 1950; by 1951 the official press took his lead and asked for new life and greater reality in literature. This apparent waning of control over writers went on until Stalin's death in 1953, after which the reins loosened with each passing month.

As early as 16 April 1953 the poet Ol'ga Fedorovna Berggolts published "Razgovor o lirike" (Conversation about Lyrics) in the newspaper *Literaturnaia gazeta* (Literary Gazette), in which she called for true expressions of love in lyric poetry. She bemoaned the fact that recent Russian poetry remained devoid of feeling and pointed out that even dedicated Soviet workers needed love. More pronounced appeals for greater freedom in literature appeared in articles by Il'ia Grigor'evich Erenburg and Vladimir Mikhailovich Pomerantsev. In "O rabote pisatelia" (About the Writer's Work), published in the journal *Znamia* (Banner) in October 1953, Erenburg said that writers needed to explore the inner world of human beings, not only their socio-economic milieu. Pomerantsev's article "Ob iskrennoste v literature" (About Sincerity in Literature) in *Novyi mir* (December 1953), however, caused the most controversy and discussion; it deplored the woodenness of Soviet literature and demanded "unvarnished" truth. The establishment reacted almost immediately with sharp criticism of Pomerantsev in *Literaturnaia gazeta* (30 January 1954).

Along with critical articles, works of belles lettres began to appear that put theory into practice. Vera Fedorovna Panova's novel *Vremena goda; iz letopisei goroda Enska* (1954, The Seasons: From the Chronicles of the Town of Ensk; translated as *Span of the Year*, 1957) investigates the private lives of people as it exposes a corrupt bureaucracy. Leonid Genrikhovich Zorin's play *Gosti* (1954, Guests) further attacks the bureaucratic state. Erenburg's novel *Ottepel'* (1954; translated as *The Thaw*, 1955), the title of which gave a name to the ensuing period, dares to discuss Russia's recent past and even alludes to the aborted Doctors' Plot of 1953. Once again, an author chooses to describe the inner lives of his characters, who try to keep their integrity under official pressure to conform. The second volume of *Ottepel'*, which came out in 1956, lacks the reforming fervor of the first. In June 1954 the Communist Party organization of the Moscow writers met to discuss the fast-growing liberal trends they perceived in literature. As a result, in August *Novyi mir* received official censure, and Konstantin Mikhailovich Simonov replaced the more liberal Aleksandr Trifonovich Tvardovsky as its editor. In December the Second Congress of Soviet Writers convened, and the neo-Zhdanovite Aleksei Aleksandrovich Surkov reasserted the conservative party line regarding the role of literature. Nevertheless, his speech did not entirely quash strong support for liberalization.

Khrushchev's secret speech at the Twentieth Party Congress in February 1956 gave carte blanche to the liberals. At that meeting, for the first time since 1930, delegates discussed two opposing views of literature: the socialist realist model versus more innovative forms. In the August through November 1956 issues of *Novyi mir* Vladimir Dmitrievich Dudintsev published his novel *Ne khlebom edinym* (translated as *Not by Bread Alone*, 1957), which investigates further the themes of the first "Thaw" literature: how to retain individual integrity against the will of a corrupt bureaucratic elite. Though not a particularly well-written novel, it strengthened the momentum of the liberals. In fact, in 1956, the so-called Year of Protest, Soviet writers were "freer than they had been since the 20s," according to Edward J. Brown in his *Russian Literature since the Revolution* (1982). For example, Daniil Granin could see in print his story "Sobstvennoe mnenie" (A Personal Opinion; *Novyi mir*, 1956), which offers a pessimistic look at the fate of someone who has forsaken his conscience for gain. A two-volume set, *Literaturnaia Moskva* (Literary Moscow), and the almanac *Den' poezii, 1956* (Poetry Day, 1956) further attest to the growing freedoms of Soviet writers. The Hungarian revolt of October 1956, however, brought about a reversal of fortune for the writers.

In early 1957 Khrushchev repeatedly warned Soviet authors to heed the lessons of the suppression of the revolt and not follow the lead of the Hungarian intellectuals. Nevertheless, the new implementation of conservative policies never reached the terror levels of the Stalinist period: authors who had been asked to recant their liberal views refused, and all remained unharmed. The successful launch of Sputnik in October 1957 returned more authority to party views on literature; the liberals' struggle to write as they chose continued, however. This tense state of literary affairs continued well into 1958. Although Khrushchev still criticized intellectuals and aesthetes, he also rehabilitated several writers. Yet, when Pasternak won the Nobel Prize in 1958, he was not allowed to attend the ceremonies in Stockholm; but in the same year Tvardovsky regained his post as editor of *Novyi mir*. He even won the Lenin Prize for literature in 1961.

Speeches at the Twenty-first Party Congress in 1961 by Tvardovsky and by the conformist writer and editor of the conservative journal *Oktiabr'* (October) Vsevolod Anisimovich Kochetov effectively "drew the line in the sand." According to Brown, "Tvardovsky's speech . . . called for a literature sincerely engaged with the life of real people and free of political tutelage; Kochetov's rejoinder reminded the delegates of the past achievements of socialist realism and demanded a literature permeated with Communist ideas and presenting heroic perspectives." Brown further demonstrates how the debate clearly formed the parties: conservative neo-Stalinists versus the liberals. Even journals became identifiable by their biases. To the conservative camp belonged *Neva, Moskva* (Moscow), and *Oktiabr'*; the liberals controlled *Novyi mir, Iunost'* (Youth), and *Inostrannaia literatura* (Foreign literature). Brown explains that

"The existence of factions explains the apparently vacillating literary policies of the Party since 1954." Khrushchev listened to both sides and changed his mind over the course of several years. Although Khrushchev allowed the publication of Solzhenitsyn's *Odin den' Ivana Denis'evicha* in 1962, by 1963 he was sanctioning his "hatchet man" Vladimir Vladimirovich Ermilov's vigorous conservative campaign against modern art and the incipient "underground" literature. With Khrushchev no longer in office in 1964, the conservatives quickly gained more power.

At the 1966 Party Congress, Mikhail Aleksandrovich Sholokhov (treated in *DLB 272*), who had received the Nobel Prize in 1965 for his epic novel *Tikhii Don* (1928, 1929, The Quiet Don; translated in two volumes as *And Quiet Flows the Don,* 1930, and *The Don Flows Home to the Sea,* 1941), labeled Siniavsky and Daniel' traitors. During this period many writers had to recant their seditious positions. Sholokhov had his say again at the Fourth Congress of Writers that met in Moscow in the last week of May 1967. At first the congress maintained a festive mood in honor of the fiftieth anniversary of the October (November, in New Style) Revolution. The keynote speech by Konstantin Fedin (treated in *DLB 272*) calmly acknowledged two trends in current Soviet literature. On the other hand, Sholokhov's speech hinted at sedition among the ranks of authors—especially the 10 percent who chose to "boycott" the meeting. He deplored the fact that only approximately 13 percent of the members of the Union of Soviet Writers were under forty and that the median age of the assembly was sixty. He attributed this wide discrepancy to the defiance of young writers, especially their public protests. Sholokhov then attacked everyone who demanded "freedom of the press." Brown provides an excerpt from the speech:

> Recently quite a few voices have been raised in the West in favor of "freedom" of creation for us Soviet writers. These are uninvited cheerleaders, who include the CIA . . . some United States senators, rabid White Guards [anti-Soviets in the 1918–1920 Civil War], the defector [Svetlana] Alliluyeva [Stalin's daughter], and the notorious [Aleksandr Fedorovich] Kerensky [former political leader and later émigré], who had long been a political corpse. It is in this bizarre company that our zealots of freedom of the press find themselves.

In actuality, Sholokhov was directing this attack at Solzhenitsyn, who had written and distributed a letter in defense of freedom of the press and against the norms of repression and injustice that, in his opinion, truly characterized official policy toward writers.

At this time there was, indeed, a great deal of public protest over the Siniavsky and Daniel' trial. A letter signed by sixty-two members of the Union of Soviet Writers—old and young alike—was sent to the Presidium of the Twenty-third Party Congress; it said that the limits placed on writers were too restrictive and that the Siniavsky-Daniel' trial caused great damage to the prestige of the Soviet Union. Such protests drew a harsh reaction from the Union of Writers and the KGB, both of which began to exert even greater control over the writers; several were imprisoned or expelled from the country. The invasion of Czechoslovakia and liquidation of the liberal Prague Spring also led to more severe control. Protest over the invasion led to the confinement in a mental institution of one of the organizers, the poet Natalia Evgen'evna Gorbanevskaia. But at the same time, there appeared in the official press works of "forgotten" writers, such as *Master i Margarita* (1966, 1967; translated as *The Master and Margarita,* 1967), by Mikhail Afanas'evich Bulgakov, and short works of Andrei Platonovich Platonov (both treated in *DLB 272*). Harsh repression was the norm in the late 1960s and the 1970s, however, and sent many writers to samizdat and tamizdat. Pasternak, Siniavsky, Daniel', and Solzhenitsyn were compelled to send their work abroad; in all, almost half of the authors treated in this volume originally published some or all of their works in the West. Novels, stories, and memoirs about the gulag and the Great Terror that found a tamizdat audience include Lidiia Korneevna Chukovskaia's *Opustely dom* (1965; translated as *The Deserted House,* 1967) and *Spusk pod vodu* (1972; translated as *Going Under,* 1972), Evgeniia Ginzburg's two-volume *Krutoi marshrut* (1967, 1979, Steep Journey; translated as *Journey into the Whirlwind,* 1967, and *Within the Whirlwind,* 1981), Nadezhda Iakovlevna Mandel'shtam's chilling memoirs *Vospominaniia* (1970, Memoirs; translated as *Hope against Hope,* 1970) and *Vtoraia kniga* (1972, Second Book; translated as *Hope Abandoned,* 1974), Vladimir Emel'ianovich Maksimov's *Karantin* (1973, The Quarantine), Georgii Nikolaevich Vladimov's *Vernyi Ruslan: Istoriia karaul'noi sobaki* (1975; translated as *Faithful Ruslan: The Story of a Guard Dog,* 1979), Varlam Tikhonovich Shalamov's *Kolymskie rasskaz* (1978; translated as *Kolyma Tales,* 1980), and Andrei Amalrik's *Zapiski dissidenta* (1982, Notes of a Dissident; translated as *Notes of a Revolutionary,* 1982). Even the Strugatsky brothers, Arkadii Natanovich and Boris Natanovich, popular authors of science fiction published regularly in the Soviet Union, sent their novels *Gadkie lebedi* (1972; translated as *The Ugly Swans,* 1979) and *Khromaia sud'ba* (1987, A Lame Fate) to the West in order to have an open forum for their ideas. The talented Vladimir Rafailovich Maramzin expresses a sense of disillusionment and despair in his experimental writing that appeared in both samizdat and tamizdat.

Yet, the other half of the authors treated in this volume managed to publish in the official press while mostly remaining true to their principles. The decade and a half after World War II became the period of the long novel, with a major theme being the war itself. Among the works of the many practitioners of the craft, certain war novels stand out: Konstantin Simonov's *Dni i nnochi* (1944; translated as *Days and Nights,* 1945), *Zhivye i mertvye* (1960; translated as *The Living and the Dead,* 1962), and *Soldatami ne rozhdaiutsia* (1964, One Is Not Born a Soldier); Panova's *Sputniki* (1946, Fellow Travelers; translated as *The Train,* 1949); Viktor Platonovich Nekrasov's *V okopakh Stalingrada* (1947, In the Trenches of Stalingrad; translated as *Front-Line Stalingrad,* 1962); and Iurii Vasil'evich Bondarev's *Batal'ony prosiat ognia* (1958, The Battalions Request Fire) and *Poslednye zalpy* (1959; translated as *The Last Shots,* 1959).

In the middle of the 1950s short forms of fiction increased in popularity. In tune with the temporary loosening of restrictions after Stalin's death, short-story writers took up Pomerantsev's call for more sincerity in literature and began to look at the personal lives of individuals in everyday situations: their characters go hunting and fishing, fall in and out of love, become estranged from or reconciled with their parents or children, and fall into reveries evinced by sensory perceptions such as the smell of bread. The best representatives of this tendency are Iurii Pavlovich Kazakov, Iurii Markovich Nagibin, and Vladimir Fedorovich Tendriakov.

They, in turn, paved the way for the next group of fresh, new writers, known collectively as the *shestidesiatniki* (men of the 1960s) or the "youth movement." Fed up with "the system" and distrustful of their fathers, whom they saw as hypocrites and compromisers, these young people felt cheated. Deming Brown describes them in his *Soviet Russian Literature since Stalin* (1978): "The new generation felt it had been betrayed and misled by loving but compromised parents, who had given them a false and morally unstable upbringing by lying to them in an effort to protect them. The realization caused not scorn and resentment but puzzlement, compassion, and respect for their parents' sufferings, and redoubled hatred of an ossified authoritarianism that they had ceased to respect." Nevertheless, by the end of the 1960s most of these writers had resolved their differences with the previous generation and had begun concentrating on the vagaries and trials of being young. Many of them wrote of those moments in a youth's life when he realizes what it means to be an adult. The new generation of writers concentrated heavily on the psychology of their characters, who are usually at loose ends; some are aimless wanderers seeking meaning in human existence. The writers explored the possibility that a question can have more than one correct answer—or no answer. They also searched for moral guides, and their characters often experience moral crises. The young writers also wanted their readers to feel close to their characters and to that end often use first-person narration. They tried to find an intimate voice in which to convey their innermost thoughts and feelings to the reader. But most of all, these writers wanted to break with the smug complacency that they saw in the previous generation. Especially after the preponderant drabness of the official literature, the works of the new generation of writers were exciting to read. Experimentation with form, language play, crisp dialogue, quirky characters, and multiple narrators brought a fresh approach to Soviet literature. Not insignificantly, all of these writers at one time or another needed to publish in the West; in the heady immediate post-Stalinist period, however, their works appeared in the mainstream Soviet press. Among the most important writers of the youth movement are Maksimov, Vasily Pavlovich Aksyonov, Andrei Georgievich Bitov, Anatolii Tikhonovich Gladilin, Vladimir Nikolaevich Voinovich, and Fazil' Abdulevich Iskander.

Some of the best writing in the post-Stalin years investigates the life of the peasants and became known as "village prose"; and though often critical of the plight of the peasant, none of its practitioners had to resort to publication either in samizdat or *tamizdat.* The life of the Russian peasant has attracted writers as far back as the eighteenth century and continues to attract them today. In his *Russian Writing since 1953: A Critical Survey* (1987), David Allen Lowe offers a reason for the popularity of the theme: "The rural setting appeals to Russian readers because it reproduces either their roots or the milieu in which they still live." The writers of village prose satisfied both criteria and also brought a new and varied dimension to the topic. They also wanted to deflate the crudely optimistic depiction of happy life on the collective farm that socialist realist novels offered.

A tendency to write exposés of the grim life on the collective occupied early examples of village prose, but as the genre matured it combined narratives with sociological, ethnographic, historical, ecological, and philosophical overtones. Therefore, the sketches, stories, and novels describe conflicts when urbanization and industrialization began to spoil the pristine beauty of the land, as well as encroach on traditional peasant values and customs. Some writers of village prose revel in such customs and in the quaintness of peasant speech, but generally do so without resorting to sentimentalism; others try to set history straight and reveal the negative effects of forced collectivization. Some writers with a more philosophical bent look for and, according to Lowe, "find beauty and solace in the very

Russianness of the village." Some of the latter have used that very Russianness to endorse a supernationalistic platform.

Fedor Aleksandrovich Abramov, Vasilii Ivanovich Belov, and Valentin Grigor'evich Rasputin are the most typical of the village-prose writers, while Vasilii Makarovich Shukshin, Vladimir Alekseevich Soloukhin, and Sergei Pavlovich Zalygin add a different texture to the genre. Abramov's tetralogy, *Brat'ia i sestry* (Brothers and Sisters), made up of the novels *Brat'ia i sestry* (1959), *Dve zimy i tri leta* (1969; translated as *Two Winters and Three Summers*, 1984), *Puti-pereputia* (1973, Roads and Crossroads), and *Dom* (1979, The House), begins in the war years and traces the hard life on the collective farm for the Priaslin family—especially the women. He bemoans the collapse of peasant traditions and the wearing away of moral values as life becomes easier. Belov's story "Privychnoe delo" (1966, That's How It Is) evokes great sympathy for the peasant, reveres nature, and suggests that in the rural setting one has a greater chance of finding spiritual fulfillment. His *Plotnitskie rasskazy* (1968, Carpenter's Tale) reveals the mindless cruelty of forced collectivization. Rasputin, the most prominent of the village-prose writers, grieves for a lost way of life, both spiritual and ecological, in Siberia. His novella "Proshchanie s Matiory" (1977; translated as *Farewell to Matera*, 1979) shows the destruction of a small island for the sake of a hydroelectric plant. Soloukhin searches the back roads and lost villages of the country in a lyrical search for beauty, which he finds especially in lost icons in works such as *Vladimirskie proselki* (1958, Back Roads of the Vladimir District; translated as *A Walk in Rural Russia*, 1966) and "Chernye doski" (1969, Black Boards; translated as *Searching for Icons in Russia*, 1971). Zalygin, like Belov, writes of forced collective farming in his well-received novel *Na Irtyshe* (1965, On the Irtysh). One of the most popular authors, Shukshin, does not strictly belong to the village-prose school, but his characters generally come from the country and make up a motley crew of alienated wanderers. His novel *Kalina krasnaia* (1971, Red Kalina Berry; translated as "Snowball Berry Red," 1979) details the unhappy fate of a newly released prisoner who tries to make a new life for himself. According to Lowe, Shukshin loosely fits into village-prose writing because his "oeuvre as a whole has a distinctly anti-urban orientation."

In contrast to the village-prose writers, many authors of the 1960s and 1970s prefer urban themes and include some of the youth-movement writers such as Aksyonov, Bitov, and Gladilin. The best representative of urban writing, however, is Iurii Valentinovich Trifonov, who is the most successful in reproducing the sights and sounds of the city and catching the tones and nuances of urban speech. Trifonov captures especially well the life of the intelligentsia and the moral choices they constantly face. One of his most notable stories, "Obmen" (1969, The Exchange), places a man between his idealistic, dying mother and his avaricious, materialistic wife, who schemes to exchange their apartment for the mother's after her death. Shortly before she dies, the mother tells her son that he has already made a more profound exchange: he has lost his soul in a quest for a comfortable life. Trifonov also offers a striking description of the 1940s in his acclaimed *Dom na naberezhnoi* (1983; translated as "The House on the Embankment," 1983).

Natal'ia Vladimirovna Baranskaia and I. (Irina Nikolaevna) Grekova (pseudonym of Elena Sergeevna Venttsel) bring a woman's point of view to the urban scene. Baranskaia's first novella, "Nedelia kak nedelia" (1969, A Week Like Any Other; translated as "The Alarm Clock in the Cupboard," 1989) simply observes one week in the life of a working woman in her various roles as wife, mother, and scientist as she races from home to work to shopping to work to home and manages to get almost everything done. Baranskaia exposes in diary form the extreme hardships and unfair treatment life in Soviet Russia imposed on women, in spite of the official claims that women enjoyed equal rights with men. Grekova also presents the life of Soviet citizens from a feminine point of view. Her characters are usually older career women who once may have had to jump the same hurdles as Baranskaia's young heroine but have learned through hard experience to achieve some measure of balance and harmony in their lives. They have also learned how to treat human triumphs and failings with equanimity. Her best story, "Damskii master" (1963; translated as "The Ladies' Hairdresser," 1975), describes the relationship between an older woman and her young, ambitious hairdresser. Though the latter is talented, he faces frustration and disappointment at every turn. Lowe believes that the story "cagily suggests that Soviet society crushes creativity in any form at any level."

Grekova thus may have subtly expressed the dominant subtext of the period dealt with in this volume. The forty years or so that followed the end of World War II provided at best a topsy-turvy environment that kept writers a bit off-kilter. The sometimes capricious, sometimes arbitrary, and sometimes calculated vacillation of the Soviet leadership in their policies concerning literature and the arts may have tried to crush the creativity of Russia's artists, but in the end the artists prevailed. The cliché that artists must suffer for their art became a tragic reality in the Soviet Union; yet, the writers of this period were willing to face the consequences—no matter how dire. Whether they wrote in Aesopian language to publish in *gosizdat*, went underground and circulated their manuscripts in samizdat, sent their manuscripts abroad to be published in *tamizdat*, or even divorced themselves from their homeland and native tongue by emigrating, the postwar Russian writers fought to keep the traditions of Russian literature alive. As for the writers who toed the official line: they may have enjoyed the favor of the state and reaped its rewards, but they also may have suffered like Trifonov's hero when they made their own moral "exchange."

Whether the writers in this period described the war, the Great Terror, the gulag experience, exile, repression, or simply everyday life in the city or in the country, they generally turned to a problem that Edward J. Brown describes as a "major theme of Russian literature since the Revolution: the fate of the individual human being in a mass state." In the literature sometimes the state won, chiefly because of its power; at other times individuals triumphed, mainly because of their moral convictions. One can confidently say that the same is true of the Russian prose writers after World War II whose literary biographies appear in this volume.

*—Christine Rydel*

## Acknowledgments

This book was produced by Bruccoli Clark Layman, Inc. Charles Brower, Philip B. Dematteis, and Patricia Hswe were the in-house editors.

Production manager is Philip B. Dematteis.

Administrative support was provided by Carol A. Cheschi.

Accountant is Ann-Marie Holland.

Copyediting supervisor is Sally R. Evans. The copyediting staff includes Phyllis A. Avant, Caryl Brown, Melissa D. Hinton, Philip I. Jones, Rebecca Mayo, Nadirah Rahimah Shabazz, Joshua Shaw, and Nancy E. Smith.

Pipeline manager is James F. Tidd Jr.

Editorial associates are Jessica R. Goudeau and Joshua M. Robinson.

In-house prevetter is Catherine M. Polit.

Permissions editor is Amber L. Coker.

Layout and graphics supervisor is Janet E. Hill. The graphics staff includes Zoe R. Cook and Sydney E. Hammock.

Office manager is Kathy Lawler Merlette.

Photography editors are Mark J. McEwan and Walter W. Ross.

Digital photographic copy work was performed by Joseph M. Bruccoli.

Systems manager is Donald Kevin Starling.

Typesetting supervisor is Kathleen M. Flanagan. The typesetting staff includes Patricia Marie Flanagan and Pamela D. Norton.

Walter W. Ross is library researcher. He was assisted by the following librarians at the Thomas Cooper Library of the University of South Carolina: Jo Cottingham, interlibrary loan department; circulation department head Tucker Taylor; reference department head Virginia W. Weathers; reference department staff Laurel Baker, Marilee Birchfield, Kate Boyd, Paul Cammarata, Joshua Garris, Gary Geer, Tom Marcil, Rose Marshall, and Sharon Verba; interlibrary loan department head Marna Hostetler; and interlibrary loan staff Bill Fetty, Nelson Rivera, and Cedric Rose.

The editor thanks Professors Neil Cornwell and Marcus Levitt for invaluable help with this volume. Yet again, the editor could not have completed the volume without Lydia C. Thiersen. Thanks are also due Nicole A. LaRoque for her diligent work on the manuscripts in their earliest form. The editor furthermore expresses her sincere thanks to Penelope Hope and Tracy Simmons Bitonti, in-house editors of previous volumes she edited in this series; they taught her a great deal. In-house editors Patricia Hswe, Charles Brower, and Philip B. Dematteis helped to make the current volume a better one. The editor owes her deepest appreciation, however, to Edward Alan Cole, sine qua non.

Dictionary of Literary Biography® • Volume Three Hundred Two

# Russian Prose Writers After World War II

# Dictionary of Literary Biography

# Fedor Aleksandrovich Abramov
(29 February 1920 – 14 May 1983)

David Gillespie
*University of Bath*

BOOKS: *M. A. Sholokhov: Seminarii,* by Abramov and Viktor Vasil'evich Gura (Leningrad: Uchpedgiz, Leningradskoe otdelenie, 1958; enlarged, 1962);

*Brat'ia i sestry* (Leningrad: Lenizdat, 1959);

*Bezotsovshchina: Povest' i rasskazy* (Moscow & Leningrad: Sovetskii pisatel', 1962);

*Dve zimy i tri leta,* book 2 of *Brat'ia i sestry* (Leningrad: Sovetskii pisatel', 1969); translated by D. B. Powers and Doris C. Powers as *Two Winters and Three Summers* (Ann Arbor, Mich.: Ardis, 1984);

*Puti-pereput'ia,* book 3 of *Brat'ia i sestry* (Moscow: Sovremennik, 1973);

*Priasliny: Trilogiia* (Moscow: Sovremennik, 1974);

*Proletali lebedi* (Moscow: Detskaia literatura, 1979); translated by Raissa Bobrova, Eve Manning, Dudley Hagen, Cynthia Rosenberger, and Amanda Calvert as *The Swans Flew By and Other Stories* (Moscow: Raduga, 1986);

*Dom,* book 4 of *Brat'ia i sestry* (Leningrad: Sovetskii pisatel', 1979);

*Trava-murava* (Moscow: Molodaia gvardiia, 1983; Moscow: Khudozhestvennaia literatura, 1984);

*Chem zhivem-kormimsia* (Leningrad: Sovetskii pisatel', Leningradskoe otdelenie, 1986);

*Trava-murava: Byli-nebyli* (St. Petersburg: Kul't-inform-press, 1993);

*Chistaia kniga* (St. Petersburg: Neva, 2000);

*Neuzheli po etomu puti idti vsemu chelovechestvu? Putevye zametki Frantsiia, Germaniia, Finliandiia, Amerika* (St. Petersburg: SpbGU, 2000).

**Editions and Collections:** *Brat'ia i sestry. Bezotsovshchina. Zhila-byla semuzhka* (Leningrad: Lenizdat, 1962);

*Rasskazy* (Moscow & Leningrad: Khudozhestvennaia literatura, 1966);

*Fedor Aleksandrovich Abramov (from Aleksei Turkov,* Fedor Abramov: Ocherk, *1987; Jean and Alexander Heard Library, Vanderbilt University)*

*Brat'ia i sestry, Bezotsovshchina, Sosnovye deti* (Moscow: Sovetskaia Rossiia, 1970);

*Brat'ia i sestry: Dve zimy i tri leta* (Leningrad: Sovetskii pisatel', 1971);

*Dereviannye koni* (Leningrad: Sovetskii pisatel', 1972);

*Posledniaia okhota* (Moscow: Sovetskaia Rossiia, 1973);

*Pelageia i Al'ka* (Arkhangel'sk: Severo-Zapadnoe knizhnoe izdatel'stvo, 1974);

*Izbrannoe*, 2 volumes (Leningrad: Khudozhestvennaia literatura, 1975);

*Izbrannoe*, 2 volumes (Moscow: Izvestiia, 1976);

*Oleshina izba* (Arkhangel'sk: Severo-Zapadnoe knizhnoe izdatel'stvo, 1976);

*Dereviannye koni* (Moscow: Sovremennik, 1978);

*Dereviannye koni. Pelageia, Al'ka, Bezotsovshchina, Vokrug da okolo, Zhila-byla semuzhka* (Leningrad: Lenizdat, 1979; Leningrad: Sovetskii pisatel', 1989);

*Brat'ia i sestry*, books 1-2 (Moscow: Sovremennik, 1980);

*Pelageia, Al'ka* (Moscow: Sovremennik, 1980);

*Zhila-byla semuzhka* (Leningrad: Detskaia literatura, 1980);

*Sobranie sochinenii*, 3 volumes (Leningrad: Khudozhestvennaia literatura, 1980-1982);

*Babilei* (Leningrad: Sovetskii pisatel', 1981);

*Dve zimy i tri leta* (Izhevsk: Udmurtiia, 1982);

*Trava-murava* (Moscow: Sovremennik, 1982);

*Povesti* (Moscow: Sovetskaia Rossiia, 1983);

*Brat'ia i sestry*, books 3-4 (Leningrad: Khudozhestvennaia literatura, Leningradskoe otdelenie, 1984);

*Zharkim letom* (Leningrad: Sovetskii pisatel', 1984);

*Povesti i rasskazy* (Leningrad: Lenizdat, 1985);

*Dela rossiisskie* (Moscow: Molodaia gvardiia, 1987);

*Pashnia zhivaia i mertvaia. Ocherki, rasskazy, stikhi (with A. Chistiakov)* (Leningrad: Sovetskii pisatel', 1987);

*Slovo v iadernyi vek: Stat'i, ocherki, vystupleniia, interv'iu, literaturnye portrety, vospominaniia, zametki* (Moscow: Sovremennik, 1987);

*Dom* (Moscow: Vysshaia shkola, 1988);

*Povesti* (Moscow: Detskaia literatura, 1988);

*O khlebe nasushchnom i khlebe dukhovnom* (Moscow: Molodaia gvardiia, 1988);

*Iz kolena Avvakumova* (Moscow: Sovremennik, 1989);

*Sobranie sochinenii*, 6 volumes (Leningrad: Khudozhestvennaia literatura, 1990-1995);

*Brat'ia i sestry*, 2 volumes (Minsk: Iunatstva, 1994);

*Tak chto zhe nam delat'? Iz dnevnikov, zapisnykh knizhek, pisem. Razmyshleniia, somneniia, predosterezheniia, itogi* (St. Petersburg: Neva, 1995).

**Editions in English:** *The New Life: A Day on a Collective Farm*, translated, with an introduction, by George Reavey (New York: Grove, 1963);

*The Dodgers*, translated by D. Floyd (London: Flegon, 1963);

"Olesha's Cabin," translated by Paul Gorgen, in *The Barsukov Triangle, The Two-Toned Blond and Other Stories*, edited by Carl Proffer and Ellendea Proffer (Ann Arbor, Mich.: Ardis, 1984), pp. 129-148;

"The House," translated by Robert Porter, in *Understanding Soviet Politics through Literature: A Book of Readings*, edited by Porter and Martin Crouch (London: Allen & Unwin, 1984), pp. 119-125;

"A Journey into the Past" and "Diary," translated by David Gillespie, in *The Life and Work of Fedor Abramov*, edited by Gillespie (Evanston, Ill.: Northwestern University Press, 1997), pp. 67-89, 91-111.

OTHER: *Sovetskaia literatura*, edited by Abramov and others (Leningrad: Izdatel'stvo Leningradskogo universiteta, 1958);

*Rasskazy leningradskhikh pisatelei*, edited by Abramov and others (Leningrad: Lenizdat, 1981).

Fedor Abramov was one of the foremost of the *derevenshchiki*, or village prose writers, who were prominent in Soviet Russian literature in the 1960s and 1970s. His works are almost always set in villages in the north of European Russia, and his prose is distinguished by its consistent adherence to realism. Unlike other *derevenshchiki*, he does not idealize the Russian national character, nor does he mythologize the supposed moral and spiritual values of the Russian peasant. Rather, Abramov chooses to show the inner strength required to survive the onslaught of collectivization, war, and neglect that have characterized the twentieth-century history of the Soviet Russian rural community.

Abramov was born on 29 February 1920 in the village of Verkola, in Arkhangel'sk province, into the family of a peasant, Aleksandr Stepanovich Abramov. Aleksandr Stepanovich died when Abramov was still a child, and the absence of a strong father figure is a feature of Abramov's writings. Abramov was the youngest of five children; his siblings were Mikhail, Nikolai, Vasilii, and Mariia. As the oldest, Mikhail assumed many duties of the head of the house after the death of Aleksandr Stepanovich. Abramov's mother, Stepanida Pavlovna (Zavarzina) Abramova, came from an Old Believer family who guided the boy's spiritual development—according to Abramov's widow, Liudmila Vladimirovna Krutikova-Abramova, herself a noted literary scholar. She adds that his Aunt Irina greatly influenced the formation of Abramov's moral character. At school he experienced difficulties because of his family's social origin (that of a "middle peasant"). In 1938, nonetheless, he entered the arts faculty of Leningrad State University, and at the outbreak of war in 1941 he joined the army. He was twice wounded and, after recuperating, worked in Arkhangel'sk as a political instructor and then in 1943–1945 as a counterespionage agent in the feared SMERSH (short for the expression "Smert' shpionam!" ["Death to spies!"]). After the war he returned to the university, graduated, and wrote his dissertation (for the *kandidat* degree, equivalent to graduate study between the M.A. and Ph.D.) on the work of Mikhail Aleksandrovich Sholokhov. From 1951 to 1958 he taught at the Department of Soviet Literature at Leningrad State University. He left the university in 1958 to pursue a literary career, joining the Soviet Writers' Union in 1960.

Although Abramov's first publication, a poem, appeared in a local newspaper in 1937, his earliest serious writings were journalistic articles. In 1949 he put his name to an article that attacked leading literary scholars of the day, including Boris Mikhailovich Eikhenbaum, Mark Konstantinovich Azadovsky, and Viktor Maksimovich Zhirmunsky. Not until April 1954, however, did his name become famous. That year he published the article "Liudi kolkhoznoi derevni v poslevoennoi proze" (People of the Collectivized Village in Post-War Prose) in the journal *Novyi mir* (New World), then under the editorship of Aleksandr Trifonovich Tvardovsky. In his article Abramov criticized recent literary works that were about the countryside, in particular for their dishonesty and "varnishing of reality." He called on writers to show the "truth" of village life, including the problems of agriculture, and thereby implicitly indicated that works of Socialist Realism had falsified reality. Some of these works had been awarded the Stalin Prize, and Abramov's article was seen as an early salvo of the Thaw that followed the death of the dictator, which had occurred a little more than a year before.

"Liudi kolkhoznoi derevni v poslevoennoi proze" is significant in another respect. It serves as Abramov's own literary credo, for in his subsequent fiction and nonfiction writings he strives to depict the real state of affairs in villages, usually based on his own observations and experience. Although Abramov had lived in Leningrad since before the war, he returned to his home village during the summer months, usually staying with relatives, and in 1974 bought a small house. He maintained contact with his fellow villagers throughout his remaining years, writing about their problems and even addressing open letters to them in the periodical press.

In 1958 his novel *Brat'ia i sestry* (Brothers and Sisters) appeared in *Novyi mir;* published in book form in 1959, it was the first part of a tetralogy that Abramov completed only in 1978. Set from the 1940s (during World War II), to the 1970s, the novel tells about the life of a fictional village, Pekashino (modeled after Verkola), and, in particular, about the Priaslin family.

Rooted in Abramov's own life, *Brat'ia i sestry* is based on his observations as a wounded soldier sent to the rear to recuperate. It offers a fictional confirmation of the ideas that he related in his 1954 article, and he does not flinch from showing the difficulties of village life during the war. The inner strength of the villagers, especially the women, who make up most of the population, is especially noteworthy. The title refers to Joseph Stalin's patriotic call to arms in his address to the Soviet people on 3 July 1941 in the aftermath of Adolf Hitler's invasion. The unity of the nation in its fight against a common enemy is explicitly asserted by one of the characters:

> So, they say, the war arouses different instincts in a man. You've probably read about it. But I see that with us this is not the case. People try their utmost to help one another. The people's conscience is roused so that you can see the soul of every individual. And you'll notice that there are hardly any disagreements or squabbles. Well, how can I put it? Brothers and sisters, you see.... You understand what I'm getting at?

Abramov's determination to depict rural reality–both its flaws and its strengths–brought him difficulties when he published the semidocumentary sketch "Vokrug da okolo" (Round and About) in 1963. The editor of the journal *Neva,* in which the work appeared, lost his job, and Abramov himself could not publish any new books for several years. "Vokrug da okolo" is set on a collective farm called Novaia zhizn (The New Life). The name is ironic, since life obviously is far from easy and in some ways no better than under the old tsarist system. The sketch caused outrage among conservative critics as a "crude distortion of life" and continues to be Abramov's most unabashed and stark account of village life published in his lifetime (subsequent book editions, however, considerably toned down the content).

He returned to print with some short stories in 1965, but his reputation for honesty and truthfulness was reaffirmed with a series of works published between 1968 and 1973. In 1968 in *Novyi mir,* Tvardovsky published the sequel to *Brat'ia i sestry. Dve zimy i tri leta* (Two Winters and Three Summers, published 1969 in book form) is set in the immediate postwar years. An uncompromising work, like "Vokrug da okolo," it received hostile reviews from conservative critics. *Dve zimy i tri leta* does not shrink from showing the excessive demands that are put upon the peasants by the state–through taxation and grain yields, for example. Life for them is grim and almost desperate. Not for nothing at the end of the novel does the main character, Mikhail Priaslin, ask himself: "How could he survive? Where

*Abramov outside his home in Dalekaia Pinega (from Aleksei Turkov,* Fedor Abramov: Ocherk, *1987; Jean and Alexander Heard Library, Vanderbilt University)*

could he go?" Passages censored from this novel were published in 1989.

*Dve zimy i tri leta* soon was followed by some of Abramov's best short fiction. *Pelageia* (published 1969 in *Novyi mir*) is the story of a hard-working old peasant woman who embodies all the strengths and virtues of the Russian village, although, in line with Abramov's determination to be truthful, she is not without her faults. The same is true of Milent'evna, a character in *Dereviannye koni* (Wooden Horses, published 1970 in *Novyi mir*) who represents a dying rural world and culture. In *Al'ka* (published 1972 in *Nash sovremennik* [Our Contemporary]) the title character is Pelageia's daughter; now urbanized and therefore morally corrupted, she returns to her roots but finds that she has nothing in common with village life. These short pieces reflect certain social processes of the time, the increasing urbanization of the country, and the perceived loss of spiritual values and even national identity.

The last two installments of Abramov's tetralogy were *Puti-pereput'ia* (Roads and Crossroads, published 1973 both in *Novyi mir* and as a book) and *Dom* (The House, published 1978 in *Novyi mir*, published 1979 in book form). *Puti-pereput'ia,* which suffered censorship problems before it was published, is set in the late 1940s and early 1950s, when the peasantry continued to be at the mercy of the authorities. Yet, although the narrative again focuses on the Priaslin family, the party functionaries Podrezov and Ganichev are also brought to the fore, as representatives of a ruthless and oppressive political authority. *Dom* shows Pekashino in the 1970s; it is relatively more affluent, though beset by problems recognizably modern—such as environmental mismanagement, increasing alcoholism, and social alienation.

A distinctive feature of Abramov's writings published in his lifetime is the absence of any real confrontation with the recent past—especially with collectivization, a major theme for other *derevenshchiki*. *Dom* does include some references to the past, with embedded narratives about characters who took part in the revolution and civil war. It even features biblical references that hint at the religious dimension of Russia's suffering. All four novels are linked in their use of imagery and symbolism, whereby human actions are seen in harmony with the natural world, especially the passing of the seasons, and the peasant's work on the land is described in painstaking and convincing detail. The natural elements, the earth, and the forest provide the true context for the working out of human lives and the passing of history, and much of the language is based on that of the northern dialect, thus maintaining narrative authenticity.

Examination of the historical past, though, is the dominant motif of Abramov's writings that were not published until after his death, most of them through the untiring efforts of his widow Krutikova-Abramova. Short stories such as "Frantik" (The Dog Frantik, published 1987 in *Nash sovremennik*) and "SOE" (Socially Dangerous Element, published 1988 in *Ogonek* [The Flame]) point to the author's disgust and outrage at the arbitrariness and cruelty of collectivization and the violence inflicted on a peaceful peasant population and way of life. Yet, the most powerful of these works—and perhaps Abramov's greatest single work of fiction—is the short story "Poezdka v proshloe" (A Journey into the Past), begun in the early 1960s, completed in 1974, and published only in 1989 in *Novyi mir*.

The text of the story as published in *Novyi mir* is supplemented by eighteen pages of drafts from various years, as well as by Abramov's personal notes and recollections of collectivization and "dekulakization" and even by some letters he wrote in his school days. The central character is Nikifor Kobylin, who has a comic-sounding nickname, Miksha. He is now a middle-aged peasant and poacher (he spent some time in prison for crashing a truck when he was drunk). Miksha is fond of recalling his uncles Aleksandr and Mefodii Kobylin, his mother's brothers, both of whom had been active during collectivization and ferociously upheld party policy. In fact, when his own father was arrested in 1937, Miksha renounced his surname (Varzumov) and his patronymic and took the surname of his uncles.

Into his life comes the mysterious official Kudasov, who asks to be shown around part of a river upstream that is to be made into a fish farm. They both head off into the northern taiga *(suzem)* and make their way to a now deserted village that used to house those kulaks who were exiled from the south during collectivization. Miksha discovers that Kudasov is, in fact, the same young boy he had fought thirty years before—the son of one of the kulaks who, as a fifteen-year-old boy, had killed his uncle Aleksandr Kobylin. His uncle had been buried with all the solemnity afforded a Red partisan and fearless fighter for the cause, and his memory is revered in the local museum.

However, the reality is different, as Abramov demythologizes those regarded as "heroes" and strips away the lies and distortions about collectivization that the party and the country had lived behind for more than thirty years. Miksha's uncle had in reality been a drunken thug with a keen interest in young girls and had raped Kudasov's fifteen-year-old sister. Kudasov then took revenge, knifing the uncle in the back one night. These facts emerge through Miksha's awakened consciousness, as he is made to face up to a devastating truth that had lingered for decades in his subconscious.

When Kudasov leaves, Miksha visits several people in the village old enough to remember his father, Ivan Varzumov, in an effort to rediscover his own past and his own identity. The reader learns that Ivan was an incredibly brave man who would protect others from the drunken excesses of the Kobylin brothers, and he was respected by all in the village. Yet, Miksha himself is not forgiven for having turned his back on his father and refusing his name. As a retired schoolteacher who spent seventeen years in the GULag (abbreviation for Soviet prison camp system) says to him: "No, Kobylin, not everything that is in the past can be forgotten." Miksha gets drunk and makes his way to the cemetery where his father is buried. Next to his father's grave, which he had never before visited, Miksha freezes to death. The story is concluded in ironic fashion as Miksha's death is announced in the local newspaper as a warning against the dangers of alcoholism: "We must fight drunkenness!"

In the space of a few pages in "Poezdka v proshloe," Abramov manages to summarize the main themes of "village prose" and reach a catharsis. He achieves these ends by relating most of the narrative through the eyes of Miksha himself; the eventual realization of an awful truth is conveyed through quasi-direct discourse and interior monologue. The devastating psychological effects of class warfare in the countryside are still palpable decades later. The official lies and platitudes about the recent past hide monstrous truths, and the party is responsible for terror and mass murder (in one of the notes accompanying the text Abramov remarks that "the number of victims of Stalin's regime is roughly equal to our losses in the war with Germany"). Most importantly, the memory of Stalin's terror is still alive, and historical truth will out.

Abramov died following an operation on 14 May 1983. He was buried 19 May in Verkola. At the time of his death he was working on *Chistaia kniga* (2000, The Pure Book), designed as a panorama of northern Russian life. It encompasses events from 1905 to 1937 and displays all strata of society, from peasants to revolutionaries to churchmen to the intelligentsia. The incomplete version, nevertheless, is filled with a rejection of revolutionary extremism but also includes descriptions of rural crafts, peasant culture, and language. Much of it is written in the dialect of the north, and the dialogue is particularly hard to follow. Abramov viewed *Chistaia kniga* as his main work in life. He was reclaiming history for the people, so that Russians could understand their country, and themselves, better.

Other writings that appeared in the 1990s confirm Abramov's anxieties about Soviet history and his faith in Russia. "Kto on?" (1993, Who Is He?) and "Belaia loshad'" (1995, The White Horse) both offer autobiographical reflections on World War II and its cost. In the former piece Abramov attempts to atone for his own involvement in injustices perpetrated by SMERSH, and in the latter he laments the loss of a generation sent out to fight with one rifle per three men—and against tanks. His diaries, too, reveal the real thoughts and torments of a man unable to speak the truth about his time, although he is fully aware of its iniquities.

The works by Fedor Aleksandrovich Abramov published in the 1990s demonstrate to what extent he suffered at the hands of the censorship and literary bureaucracy from the 1960s until the time of his death. They also ensure that he is remembered not only as a "village writer" who eschewed the lyrical and the sentimental (unlike some of his fellows) and depicted the hard and sometimes cruel realities of rural life. Rather, these posthumous publications have shown that, as with the injustices and miseries of twentieth-century Russian history, the truth will emerge.

**References:**
Iurii Andreevich Andreev, "Bol'shoi mir: O proze F. Abramova," *Neva,* 3 (1973): 172–182;

Nadezhda I. Azhgikhina, "Protivostoianie," *Oktiabr',* 9 (1989): 181–187;

Gilda Baikovitch, "Rabelais, Bakhtin and Village Prose: The Case of Fedor Abramov," *Slovo,* 1–2 (1998): 1–20;

Deming Brown, *The Last Years of Soviet Literature: Prose Fiction, 1975–1991* (Cambridge: Cambridge University Press, 1993);

Brown, *Soviet Russian Literature since Stalin* (Cambridge: Cambridge University Press, 1978);

Shamil' Zagirovich Galimov, *Fedor Abramov. Tvorchestvo, lichnost'* (Arkhangel'sk: Severo-Zapadnoe knizhnoe izdatel'stvo, 1989);

Galimov, *Uroki chelovechnosti: Literatura i sever* (Arkhangel'sk: Severo-Zapadnoe knizhnoe izdatel'stvo, 1984);

Elena Sh. Galimova, comp., *Fedor Abramov i Sever* (Arkhangel'sk: GO SSSR, 1992);

Leonid Vasil'evich Khanbekov, *Velen'em sovesti i dolga: Ocherk tvorchestva Fedora Abramova* (Moscow: Sovremennik, 1989);

Liudmila Vladimirovna Krutikova-Abramova, *Dom v Verkole: Dokumental'naia povest'* (Leningrad: Sovetskii pisatel', 1988);

Krutikova-Abramova, "Fedor Abramov i tsenzura," *Moskva,* 10 (1990): 176–196;

Krutikova-Abramova, "Fedor Abramov ob Aleksandre Tvardovskom," in *Tvorchestvo Aleksandra Tvardovskogo: Issledovaniia i materialy,* edited by Petr Sozontovich Vykhodtsev and Natal'ia Aleksandrovna Groznova (Leningrad: Nauka, 1989), pp. 204–281;

Krutikova-Abramova, comp., *Zemlia Fedora Abramova* (Moscow: Sovremennik, 1986);

Dina Germanovna Kul'bas, *Esteticheskie printsipy F. Abramova* (Kurgan: Zaural'e, 1998);

Feliks Feodos'evich Kuznetsov, "Obostrennost' grazhdanskoi sovesti: Razmyshleniia nad publitsistikoi Fedora Abramova," *Novyi mir,* 6 (1985): 229–248;

Kuznetsov, *Samaia krovnaia sviaz': Sud'by derevni v sovremennoi proze* (Moscow: Prosveshchenie, 1977);

Ia. Lipkevich, "Operedivshii vremia," *Neva,* 2 (1990): 182–190;

Georgii Iosifovich Lomidze, "Sila realizma," *Voprosy literatury,* 5 (1963): 47–68;

Vladimir Emel'ianovich Maksimov, "Skorb' ne po adresu," *Kontinent,* 37 (1983): 383–386;

Iurii Mikhailovich Okliansky, *Dom na ugore: O F. Abramove i ego knigakh* (Moscow: Khudozhestvennaia literatura, 1990);

Okliansky, "Mirskoi nabat Fedora Abramova," *Voprosy literatury,* 8 (1989): 77–114;

Kathleen Parthé, *Russian Village Prose: The Radiant Past* (Princeton: Princeton University Press, 1992);

N. N. Shneidman, *Soviet Literature in the 1980s: Decade of Transition* (Toronto: Toronto University Press, 1989);

Petr Strokov, "Zemlia i liudi," *Ogonek,* no. 22 (1968): 25–29;

Igor' N. Sukhikh, "Drama mysli," *Literaturnoe obozrenie,* 7 (1989): 9–15;

Vsevolod Alekseevich Surganov, *Chelovek na zemle: Istoriko-literaturnyi ocherk* (Moscow: Sovetskii pisatel', 1975);

Aleksei Turkov, *Fedor Abramov: Ocherk* (Moscow: Sovetskii pisatel', 1987);

Igor' Petrovich Zolotusskt, *Fedor Abramov: Lichnost', knigi, sud'ba* (Moscow: Sovetskaia Rossiia, 1986).

**Papers:**

Fedor Aleksandrovich Abramov's papers are held by his widow, Liudmila Vladimirovna Krutikova-Abramova.

# Chingiz Aitmatov
*(12 December 1928 –    )*

Erika Haber
*Syracuse University*

BOOKS: *Litsom k litsu: Sbornik rasskazy* (Frunze: Kyrgyzstan, 1958);

*Dzhamilia: Povest'* (Moscow: Pravda, 1959); translated by Fainna Solasko as *Jamila,* edited by Olga Shartse (Moscow: Foreign Languages Publishing House, 1964);

*Verbliuzhii glaz: Povesti i rasskazy* (Moscow: Sovetskii pisatel', 1962);

*Povesti gor i stepei* (Moscow: Sovetskii pisatel', 1963; enlarged edition, Moscow: Molodaia-gvardiia, 1965); translated by Fainna Glagoleva and Shartse as *Tales of the Mountains and Steppes* (Moscow: Progress Publishers, 1969);

*Materinskoe pole: Povesti i rasskazy* (Frunze: Khudozhestvennaia literatura, 1964); translated by James Riordan as *Mother Earth and Other Stories* (London: Faber & Faber, 1989);

*Povesti i rasskazy* (Moscow: Molodaia gvardiia, 1970)—includes "Belyi parokhod (posle skazki)," translated by Mirra Ginsburg as *The White Ship* (New York: Crown, 1972);

*The Ascent of Mount Fuji: A Play,* by Aitmatov and Kaltai Mukhamedzhanov, translated by Nicholas Bethell (New York: Farrar, Straus & Giroux, 1975);

*Rannie zhuravli: Povesti* (Moscow: Molodaia gvardiia, 1976)—includes "Rannie zhuravli," translated by Eve Manning as *The Cranes Fly Early: A Short Novel* (Moscow: Raduga, 1983);

*Pegii pes, begushchii kraem moria; Rannie zhuravli: Povesti* (Moscow: Sovetskii pisatel', 1977); translated as *Piebald Dog Running along the Shore and Other Stories* (Moscow: Raduga, 1989);

*V soavtorstve s zemleiu i vodoiu: Ocherki, stat'i, besedy, interv'iu* (Frunze: Kyrgyzstan, 1978);

*I dol'she veka dlitsia den'* (Frunze: Kyrgyzstan, 1981); republished as *Burannyi polustanok (I dol'she veka dlitsia den'): Roman* (Moscow: Molodaia gvardiia, 1981); translated by John French as *The Day Lasts More than a Hundred Years,* foreword by Katerina Clark (Bloomington: Indiana University Press, 1983; London: Macdonald, 1983);

*Sobranie sochinenii v trekh tomakh,* 3 volumes (Moscow: Molodaia gvardiia, 1982–1984);

*Ekho mira: Povesti, rasskazy, publitsistika* (Moscow: Pravda, 1985);

*Plakha; I dol'she veka dlitsia den'* (Riga: Liesma, 1986); "Plakha" translated by Natasha Ward as *The Place of the Skull* (London: Faber & Faber, 1989; New York: Grove Press, 1989);

*Stat'i, vystupleniia, dialogi, interv'iu* (Moscow: Novosti, 1988);

*The Time to Speak Out,* edited by Galina Dzyubenko, translated by Paula Garb (Moscow: Progress Publishers, 1988);

*Time to Speak* (New York: International Publishers, 1989);

*Chingiz Aitmatov (photograph © by Inge Morath/Magnum Photos, Inc.)*

*Beloe oblako Chingiskhana: Povest' k romanu* (Bishkek: "Balasagyn" / Moscow: Planeta, 1991);

*Tavro Kassandry: Izbrannye proizvedeniia* (Moscow: EKSMO Press, 1995)—comprises "Tavro Kassandry," "Pegii pes, begushchii kraem moria," "Plach pereletnoi ptitsy," "Beloe oblako Chingiskhana," and "Bakhiana";

*Plach okhotnika nad propast'iu: Ispoved' na iskhode veka,* by Aitmatov and Mukhtar Shakhanov (Almaty: Rauan, 1996).

**Edition and Collection:** *I dol'she veka dlitsia den' (Beloe oblako Chingiskhana): Roman; Litsom k litsu: povest'* (Bishkek: Glavnaia redaktsiia Kyrgyzskoi sovetskoi entsiklopedii, 1991);

*Sobranie sochinenii v semi tomakh,* 7 volumes, edited by Rustan Rakhmanaliev (Moscow: "Turkestan," 1998).

**Editions in English:** *Short Novels,* translated by Olga Shartse and Fainna Glagoleva (Moscow: Progress Publishers, 1963)—comprises "To Have and to Lose," "Duishen," and "Mother-Earth";

*Farewell, Gulsary,* translated by John French (London: Hodder & Stoughton, 1970);

*The White Steamship,* translated by Tatyana Feifer and George Feifer (London: Hodder & Stoughton, 1972).

PLAY PRODUCTION: *Voskhozhdenie na Fudzhiamu,* by Aitmatov and Kaltai Mukhamedzhanov, Moscow, Sovremennik Theater, 1973; translated by Nicholas Bethell as *The Ascent of Mount Fuji,* Washington, D.C., Arena Theater, 1975.

PRODUCED SCRIPTS: *Pervyj uchitel,* motion picture, Kirghizfilm/Mosfilm, 1965;

*Proshschaj, Gjulsary!* motion picture, Mosfilm, 1968;

*Dzhamilya,* motion picture, Mosfilm, 1969;

*Belyj parokhod,* motion picture, Kirghizfilm, 1976;

*Rannie zhuravli,* motion picture, 1979;

*Voskhozhdenie na Fudzhiamu,* motion picture, Kirghizfilm, 1988;

*Smerch,* motion picture, Tajikfilm, 1988.

OTHER: Sagymbai Orozbak uulu, *Manas,* 4 volumes, edited by Aitmatov and others (Frunze: Kyrgyzstan, 1978–1982);

*Do the Russians Want War?* edited by Aitmatov (Moscow: Progress Publishers, 1985);

"On Craftsmanship," in V. Novikov, *Chinghiz Aitmatov,* (Moscow: Raduga, 1987), pp. 101–181;

"Globale Industrialisierung," in *Alptraum und Hoffnung: Zwei Reden vor dem Club of Rome,* by Aitmatov and Günter Grass (Göttingen: Steidl, 1989).

The best-known non-Russian prose writer in the former Soviet Union and the present-day Russian Federation, Chingiz Aitmatov has helped to bring the history and traditions of the Kirghiz and Kazakhs to the attention of the world. Many of his short stories, novellas, and novels depict the struggles of traditional cultures caught up in rapid change and modernization. The style of his writing—a blend of legend, myth, and realistic details of contemporary life—significantly contributes to the popularity and enduring quality of his prose. His stylistic innovations helped to modify and expand the requirements of socialist realism. Widely promoted and officially decorated by the Soviet government, Aitmatov held editorial positions on prestigious journals, served as president of the Kirghiz Film Union, and sat on the board of the Soviet Writers' Union. In the 1980s he held several important posts in the government of Mikhail Gorbachev.

Chingiz Torekulovich Aitmatov was born on 12 December 1928 in the mountain village of Sheker in the Kirghiz Republic (now Kyrgyzstan) to Torekul Aitmatovich and Nagima Khamzaevna. Like most Kirghiz, he grew up in an extended family in which he learned the oral legends, folklore, and traditions of his native culture. His parents were highly educated and bilingual; in addition to teaching the children about their Kirghiz heritage, the parents also exposed them to Russian language, literature, and culture. Consequently, Aitmatov grew up fully bilingual and with a strong knowledge of the Russian classics.

During the Stalinist purge of non-Russians from the Communist Party in 1937 Aitmatov's father—who was second party secretary for the region—and two uncles were arrested and shot on charges of "bourgeois nationalism." Aitmatov's early stories often feature fatherless boys and describe the special bond that exists between father and son.

In 1941 Aitmatov left school to contribute to the war effort in World War II. At fourteen he became secretary of the village soviet and a tax collector. After the war, he studied at a veterinary college in Kazakhstan and then at the Kirghiz Institute of Agriculture in Frunze (now Bishkek); while at the institute he began writing short stories in Kirghiz. He graduated with a degree in animal husbandry in 1953. To reach a larger audience, he translated his stories into Russian and then began writing in that language. These early stories helped him gain entrance into the prestigious Gorky Literary Institute in Moscow. After graduation in 1958, he returned home to work as a correspondent for the newspaper *Pravda* (Truth) but continued to write fiction.

The 1959 publication of his novella *Dzhamilia* (translated as *Jamila,* 1964) in the liberal journal *Novyi mir* (The New World) brought Aitmatov literary success and international recognition. Unlike his earlier stories, it shows some distance from socialist realist models, especially in character development and themes. Dzhamilia is a young woman who abandons her husband from an arranged marriage to be with her true love, a war deserter and thief. Aitmatov presents her actions in a positive light; while Kirghiz critics denounced the work as demeaning and unrepresentative of their culture, it was widely translated and published abroad.

Aitmatov joined the Communist Party in 1959. He soon became an influential public figure, serving on the editorial boards of important literary journals and newspapers such as *Novyi mir, Innostrannaia literatura* (Foreign Literature), and *Literaturnaia gazeta* (Literary Gazette). Exhibiting distinct departures from the tenets of socialist realism, his mature stories and novels deal with topics such as government corruption, the loss of traditional customs and native languages, agricultural failures, Joseph Stalin's concentration camps, drug and alcohol abuse, and environmental destruction. He developed a devoted reading public, and in 1963 he received the Lenin Prize in literature—the highest honor the Soviet Union could bestow on an author. This official recognition afforded him a measure of security that enabled him to take more risks.

In 1966 Aitmatov published "Proshchai Gul'sary!" (translated as *Farewell, Gul'sary*, 1970), a bold and powerful work that draws parallels between the lives of an elderly man and the beloved old horse he formerly owned and describes how the indifference and corruption of local Communist Party bosses cause both man and animal considerable suffering. Aitmatov was awarded the State Prize for the novella in 1968. In the 1980s the work was adapted for the stage and played to sold-out audiences at the Sfera Theater in Moscow.

In 1973 Aitmatov collaborated with the Kazakh dramatist Kaltai Mukhamedzhanov on the play *Voskhozhdenie na Fudzhiamu* (translated as *The Ascent of Mount Fuji*, 1975). Because of its sensitive content, the work was not published in the Soviet Union. A group of old school friends reunite for an overnight camping trip in Kyrgyzstan. They discuss memories, grievances, and another friend who is not present: because one of them had denounced him to the government at the end of World War II, he had been sent to the concentration camps and had returned home a broken man. No one in the group admits guilt; yet, all are complicit because of their silence. The work ends on an ambiguous note: as authorities begin asking about the death of a camper who was killed by a rock thrown from the top of the mountain, the group sneaks away to elude questioning. The play was staged at the Sovremennik Theater in Moscow in 1973 and at the Arena Theater in Washington, D.C., in 1975; in 1988 Aitmatov wrote the screenplay for a movie version.

*Title page for Aitmatov's novel* Plakha, *translated in 1989 as* The Place of the Skull, *which blames the social ills of contemporary Russia on the people's estrangement from traditional spirituality (Ralph Brown Draughon Library, Auburn University)*

Three of Aitmatov's most popular stories appeared in the 1970s. Attempts at blending native traditional myth and Soviet reality, these stories are largely presented from a child's perspective and feature a strong affinity for nature; Aitmatov often depicts children and nature as innocent victims of a ruthless and uncaring modern society. Interpolated into each story are legends or myths that contrast the wisdom and moral strength of a traditional native culture to the corruption and shallowness of contemporary society. In the poignant "Belyi parokhod (posle skazki)" (1970; translated as *The White Ship*, 1972) an orphan raised on the traditional values of his grandfather is unable to accept the evil realities of contemporary Soviet life and kills himself. In the semi-autobiographical "Rannie zhuravli" (1975; translated as *The Cranes Fly Early: A Short Novel*, 1983) a group of boys are taken from school to help with the war effort during World War II; according to folklore, the early return of cranes signifies good luck, but the boys meet an unfortunate end. "Pegii pes, begushchii kraem moria" (1977; translated as "Piebald Dog Running along the Shore," 1989) takes place in the Soviet Far East among the minority Nivkh peoples; the exotic locale, details of the traditional culture, and the compelling plot of a boy's initiation into manhood that goes terribly wrong were enormously appealing to the Soviet public. Critics attacked the tragic tone and unhappy endings of these stories, but they sealed Aitmatov's popularity with readers.

Aitmatov's first novel began to appear serially in *Novyi mir* in November 1980. Aitmatov had originally titled the work "Obruch" (Iron Hoop) to emphasize the theme of oppression that runs through it; to diffuse this focus, the *Novyi mir* editors chose the title *Burannyi polustanok* (The Snowstorm Station). It was published in book form in 1981 as *I dol'she veka dlitsia den'* (The Day Lasts Longer than a Hundred Years), a title taken from Boris Pasternak's poem "Edinstvennye dni" (Unique Days). Pasternak had angered the Soviet authorities by sending his Nobel Prize–winning novel *Doktor Zhivago* (1958; translated as *Doctor Zhivago*, 1958) abroad for publication (it had first appeared in Italian translation in 1957 as *Il Dottor Zivago*). The novel was translated into English in 1983 as *The Day Lasts More than a Hundred Years*.

Much wider in scope and more complex than anything Aitmatov had published previously, *I dol'she veka dlitsia den'* consists largely of the reminiscences of an elderly Kazakh as he travels to a sacred cemetery to bury his friend according to traditional Muslim rituals. During his solitary journey, at a railway station in the middle of the Kazakh steppe, Edigei recalls the joys and sorrows of his long, hard life. He also recounts Kazakh legends connected with the sacred cemetery and the life of his friend. One legend tells how earlier inhabitants of the steppe were subjugated by invaders who captured the young men, shaved their heads, placed the udders of newly slaughtered camels on their scalps, and left them in the sun to allow the "cap" to dry and tighten on their heads. Many died from the torture, but those who survived became obedient slaves: they had no reason to rebel since they had lost all memory of their previous lives and identities. One slave killed his own mother when she came to rescue him, because he no longer recognized her. The legends reinforce the themes of the importance of memory and identity that run through the realistic plotline of the book.

The novel also includes an ambiguous science-fiction subplot that extends these themes to a more expansive setting. A joint American-Soviet space mission makes contact with intelligent life on a planet in another galaxy without consulting the ground station for permission; when the ground controllers learn of this transgression, they cut off the communication with the aliens and abandon the team in space. Two protective rings of rockets are stationed around the earth to protect it from penetration from the aliens. Edigei's effort to bring his friend's body to its final resting place is ultimately in vain because access to the cemetery has been cut off by the construction of the Soviet ground station.

The story of the joint American-Soviet space team caused Soviet critics considerable discomfort, and they played down this plot element in their reviews. Despite the controversial content, however, the novel was praised by Georgii Mokeevich Markov, head of the Writers' Union, as a model of mature socialist realism. A national-minority version of the highly popular Russian Village Prose genre, it was what Soviet critics had been demanding from authors throughout the 1970s. The ambiguous themes and intricate structure of the novel allowed for multiple interpretations, making it much more interesting than canonical socialist realism, and it enjoyed huge success with readers. In the foreword to the 1983 English translation Katerina Clark notes that issues of *Novyi mir* that included installments of the novel were so hard to obtain that an American correspondent in Moscow had to have copies made in the United States for his Soviet friends.

Aitmatov's second novel, *Plakha* (translated as *The Place of the Skull*, 1989), appeared in 1986. Like many works published in the early days of Gorbachev's policy of glasnost (openness), it focuses on the ills of contemporary society: alcoholism, drug abuse, family breakdown, and plundering of the environment. Using a Russian, the Christ-like Avdii, rather than a Kirghiz or Kazakh as his main character, Aitmatov argues that the Russians, too, have suffered from being cut off from their spirituality and traditional culture. Avdii professes a Christian ideology with which he tries to redeem representatives of corrupt contemporary society. The work includes a subplot, reminiscent of Mikhail Bulgakov's novel *Master i Margarita* (1966, 1967; translated as *The Master and Margarita*, 1967), about the confrontation between Christ and Pontius Pilate. The most poignant subplot is reminiscent of one of Aitmatov's lyrical Kirghiz or Kazakh legends: the cubs of a pair of wolves are stolen and sold; grieving and angry, the anthropomorphized wolves terrorize the town and carry off a two-year-old boy to replace their lost cubs. The boy's father goes in pursuit and accidentally shoots his son along with one of the fleeing wolves.

Although Aitmatov was praised for raising important sociopolitical issues, critical reception of the work was lukewarm; readers who had eagerly awaited the publication of a new novel by Aitmatov were disappointed as well. The various subplots do not hold together, and the ambiguity that worked so well in *I dol'she veka dlitsia den'* is lacking; here, Aitmatov's moralizing is unmitigated and overpowering. The story of the wolf pair, however, redeems the book as a work of art rather than a mere glasnost novel.

In 1989 Aitmatov became a member of the Congress of People's Deputies of the Soviet Union. Also that year he was appointed chairman of the Supreme Soviet's Commission on Issues Pertaining to the Development of Culture and Language, which was charged with modernizing the linguistic policies of the Soviet Union. The commission established the right of the country's minority cultures to use and develop their national languages. Aitmatov also served on the presidential council that oversaw Gorbachev's reform efforts during the period of perestroika (restructuring).

As Aitmatov became more involved with politics, his literary output declined both in quantity and quality. *Novyi mir* announced that it would publish a new novel by Aitmatov titled "Bogomater' v snegakh" (Madonna of the Snows) in 1989; although excerpts have appeared, the complete work has never come out. The novel was to deal with Stalin's image; but according to Noah N. Shneidman in his *Russian Literature 1988–1994: The End of an Era* (1995), Aitmatov has come to believe that Stalin's image "is a worn-out subject, lately much abused."

In 1990 the journal *Znamia* (Banner) published an additional chapter of *I dol'she veka dlitsia den'* that it called a "povest' k romanu" (novella to the novel); titled "Beloe oblako Chingiskhana" (White Cloud of Genghis Khan), the addition was published in book form in 1991 and included in later editions of the novel. In a prefatory note Aitmatov explains that the censor had cut the chapter from the original publication of the novel because it depicts the arrest, interrogation, torture, and death of a minor character, the schoolteacher Abutalip, during Stalin's purges. The chapter also includes a myth, "Sarozekskaia kazn'" (Serozek Execution), in which God punishes Genghis Khan for his excessive pride; Khan's sins are an allegory for the crimes of Stalin and his henchmen in taking the lives of innocents during the purges. The publication of this chapter, nine years after the appearance of the novel, gives a more adequate idea of Aitmatov's intent in writing the work.

In late 1990 Aitmatov was appointed ambassador to Luxembourg. After the dissolution of the Soviet Union in 1991, he stayed on as Russian ambassador and also became a member of the newly elected Russian parliament. Early in 1994 he announced that he was leaving the ambassadorship to devote himself more fully to his writing, and in 1995 he published the story

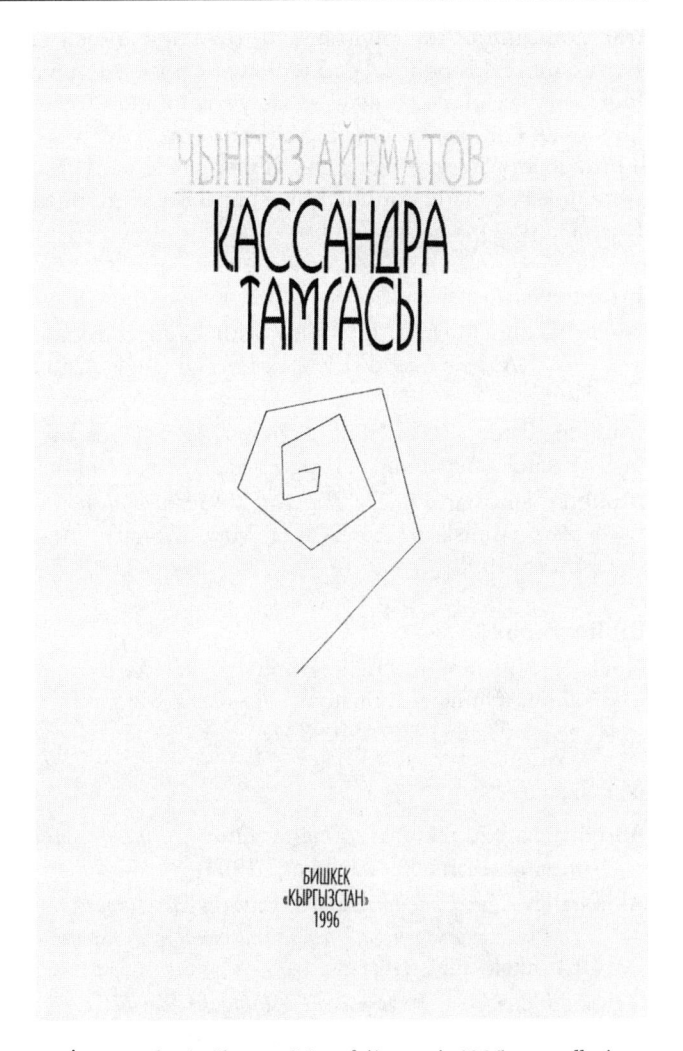

*Title page for the Kyrgyz edition of Aitmatov's 1995 story collection* Tavro Kassandry: Izbrannye proizvedeniia *(The Brand of Cassandra; Suzzallo and Allen Libraries, University of Washington)*

collection *Tavro Kassandry: Izbrannye proizvedeniia* (The Brand of Kassandra). The title piece follows the prevailing literary trends in Russia in being a work of pure science fiction: a famous geneticist working in a secret center creates a humanoid with artificial intelligence; the experiment ends in tragedy when the creature becomes violent toward the human race. The pessimistic story is an allegory of the corruption of individuals who are greedy for power and fame at the cost of civilization. It was widely criticized in the Russian media for lacking the mythic and folkloric elements that had characterized Aitmatov's best writing.

Though a non-Russian, Chingiz Aitmatov publishes primarily in Russian. His innovative literary style helped break down the rigidities of socialist realism and opened the way for more stylistic experimentation and creativity in Soviet prose. His writings have communicated his concerns for the preservation of native traditions and of the environment to a wide audience. Furthermore, his political and diplomatic positions gave him a powerful voice in the last years of the Soviet Union and in its successor, the Russian Federation. Through his literary work and his practical activities, Aitmatov has made considerable contributions both to Russia and to his native Central Asia.

**Interviews:**

Noah N. Shneidman, "Interview with Chingiz Aitmatov," *Russian Literature Triquarterly,* 16 (1979): 265–268;

Daisaku Ikeda, *Odavelichiiu dukha: Dialogi* (Moscow: Izdatel'skaia gruppa "Progress": "Litera," 1994);

Mukhtar Shakhanov, *The Plaint of the Hunter above the Abyss,* translated by Walter May (Almaty: Atamura, 1998).

**Bibliography:**

Noah N. Shneidman, "Bibliography of Works by and about Chingiz Aitmatov," *Russian Literature Triquarterly,* 16 (1979): 340–341.

**References:**

Abdyldazhan Akmataliev, *Chingiz Aitmatov i vzaimosviazi literatur* (Bishkek: "Adabiiat," 1991);

Akmataliev, *Znachenie tvorcheskoi aktivnosti Ch. Aitmatova v ptrotsesse vzaimoobogashcheniia natsional'nykh literatur* (Bishkek: Ilim, 1994);

Gennadii Bazarov, *Prikosnovenie k lichnosti: Shtrikhi k portretu Chingiz Aitmatova* (Frunze: Kyrgyzstan, 1983);

Boris Chlebnikov and Norbert Franz, *Chingiz Ajtmatov* (Munich: Edition text + kritik, 1993);

Tat'iana Timofeevna Davydova, *Sovremennaia kirgizskaia povest': Uroki Chingiza Aitmatova* (Frunze: "Adabiiat," 1989);

Georgii Dmitrievich Gachev, *Chingiz Aitmatov: V svete mirovoi kul'tury,* afterword by Evgenii Kuz'mich Ozmitel' (Frunze: "Adabiiat," 1989);

Gachev, *Chingiz Aitmatov i mirovaia literatura* (Frunze: Kyrgyzstan, 1982);

Pavel E. Glinkin, *Chingiz Aitmatov* (Leningrad: "Prosveshchenie," Leningradskoe otdelenie, 1968);

Irmtraud Gutschke, *Menschheitsfragen, Märchen, Mythen: Zum Schaffen Tschingis Aitmatows* (Halle: Mitteldeutscher Verlag, 1986);

Kalyk Ibraimov, *Mif i miroponimanie v gumanisticheskoi filosofii Chingiza Aitmatova: Monograficheskoe issledovanie* (Bishkek: Kyrgyzstan, 1998);

Arkadii Isenov, *Psikhologizm sovremennoi prozy: Na materialakh tvorchestva Chingiza Aitmatova* (Alma-Ata: "Zhazushy," 1985);

Nina Kolesnikoff, *Myth in the Works of Chingiz Aitmatov* (Lanham, Md.: University Press of America, 1999);

Larisa Iosifovna Lebedeva, *Krutoe voskhozhdenie: Zametki o kirgizskoi literature* (Frunze: Kyrgyzstan, 1981);

Lebedeva, *Povesti Chingiza Aitmatova* (Moscow: Khudozhestvennaia literatura, 1972);

Viktor Levchenko, *Chingiz Aitmatov: Problemy poetiki, zhanra, stilia* (Moscow: Sovetskii pisatel', 1983);

Pariza Mansurovna Mirza-Akhmedova, *Natsional'naia epicheskaia traditsiia v tvorchestve Chingiza Aitmatova* (Tashkent: Fan, 1980);

Joseph P. Mozur, *Doffing "Mankurt's Cap": Chingiz Aitmatov's "The Day Lasts More than a Hundred Years" and the Turkic National Heritage,* Carl Beck Papers in Russian and East European Studies, 0889-275X, no. 605 (Pittsburgh: University of Pittsburgh Center for Russian and East European Studies, 1987);

Mozur, *Parables from the Past: The Prose Fiction of Chingiz Aitmatov* (Pittsburgh: University of Pittsburgh Press, 1995);

V. Novikov, *Chingiz Aitmatov* (Moscow: Raduga, 1987);

Galina Fedorovna Poliakova, *Predanie o Rogatoi materi-olenikhe v "Belom parokhode" Chingiza Aitmatova: Istoriko-literaturnyi analiz* (Moscow: Indrik, 1999);

Robert Porter, "Chingiz Aitmatov: The Provincial Internationalist," in his *Four Contemporary Russian Writers* (Oxford, New York & Munich: Berg, 1989), pp. 52–86;

Rustan Rakhmanaliev, ed., *Chingiz Aitmatov v sovremennom mire: Avtor–kniga–chitatel'. Opyt sotsiokul'turnogo i knigovedcheskogo issledovaniia* (Frunze: Kyrgyzstan, 1989);

Zharkyn Mamatovna Ryskulova, *Vospriiatie tvorchestva Chingiza Aitmatova v angloiazychnykh stranakh* (Frunze: Ilim, 1987);

Abdykadyr Sadykov, ed., *Sovremennyi literaturnyi protsess i tvorchestvo Chingiza Aitmatova: tezisy dokladov I soobshchenii respublikanskoi nauchno-teoreticheskoi konferentsii* (Frunze: Ilim, 1985);

Noah N. Shneidman, *Russian Literature 1988–1994: The End of an Era* (Toronto, Buffalo & London: University of Toronto Press, 1995);

Shneidman, "Soviet Literature at the Crossroads: The Controversial Prose of Chingiz Aitmatov," *Russian Literature Triquarterly,* 16 (1979): 244–264;

Leonid Fedorovich Stroilov, *Tvorchestvo Chingiza Aitmatova v zapadnoevropeiskoi kritike* (Frunze: Kyrgyzstan, 1988);

Vladimir Il'ich Voronov, *Chingiz Aitmatov* (Moscow: Sovetskii pisatel', 1976).

# Vassily Aksyonov
## (Vasilii Pavlovich Aksenov)
*(20 August 1932 - )*

Konstantin V. Kustanovich
*Vanderbilt University*

BOOKS: *Kollegi: Povest'* (Moscow: Sovetskii pisatel', 1961); translated by Alec Brown as *Colleagues* (London: Putnam, 1962);

*Kollegi: P'esa* (Moscow: VUOAP, 1961);

*Katapul'ta* (Moscow: Sovetskii pisatel', 1964)—includes *Apel'siny iz Marokko,* translated by Susan Brownsberger as "Oranges from Morocco," in *The Steel Bird and Other Stories* (Ann Arbor, Mich.: Ardis, 1979);

*Pora, moi drug, pora* (Moscow: Molodaia gvardiia, 1965); translated by Olive Stevens as *It's Time, My Friend, It's Time* (London: Macmillan, 1969);

*Na polputi k lune* (Moscow: Sovetskaia Rossiia, 1966);

*Zhal', chto vas ne bylo s nami* (Moscow: Sovetskii pisatel', 1969);

*Liubov' k elektrichestvu* (Moscow: Politizdat, 1971);

*Moi dedushka – pamiatnik; povest' ob udivitel'nykh prikliucheniiakh leningradskogo pionera Gennadiia Stratofontova, kotoryi khorosho uchilsia v shkole i ne rasterialsia v trudnykh obstoiatel'stvakh* (Moscow: Detskaia literatura, 1972);

*Geografiia liubvi* (Moscow: VAAP, 1975);

*Liubov' k elektrichestvu: Drama iz vremen pervoi russkoi revoliutsii* (Moscow: VAAP, 1975);

*Sunduchok, v kotorom chto-to stuchit: Sovremennaia povest'-skazka bez volshebstva, no s prikliucheniiami* (Moscow: Detskaia literatura, 1976);

*Zatovarennaia bochkotara. Randevu* (New York: Serebriannyi vek, 1980); *Zatovarennaia bochkotara* translated as "Surplussed Barrelware," and *Randevu* as "Rendezvous," by Joel Wilkinson and Slava Yastremsky in *Surplussed Barrelware* (Ann Arbor, Mich.: Ardis, 1985);

*Zolotaia nasha zhelezka* (Ann Arbor, Mich.: Ardis, 1980); translated by Ronald E. Peterson as *Our Golden Ironburg: A Novel with Formulas* (Ann Arbor, Mich.: Ardis, 1989);

*Vassily Aksyonov (courtesy of Konstantin V. Kustanovich)*

*Ozhog* (Ann Arbor, Mich.: Ardis, 1980); translated by Michael Glenny as *The Burn* (New York: Random House, 1984);

*Aristofaniana s liagushkami* (Ann Arbor, Mich.: Ermitazh, 1981)—comprises *Vsegda v prodazhe,* translated by Paul Cubberly as *Always on Sale* (Clayton, Australia: Monash University Drama Series, 1988);

*Potselui, orkestr, ryba, kolbasa . . .* , translated by Daniel Charles Gerould and Jadwiga Kosicka as *Your Murderer* (Amsterdam: Harwood Academic, 2000); *Chetyre temperamenta,* translated by Boris Jakim as *The Four Temperaments,* in *Metropol: Literary Almanac,* edited by Aksyonov and others (Ann Arbor, Mich.: Ardis, 1982); *Aristofaniana s liagushkami;* and *Tsaplia,* translated as *The Heron* by Edythe Haber in *Quest for an Island* (New York: PAJ, 1987);

*Ostrov Krym* (Ann Arbor, Mich.: Ardis, 1981); translated by Michael Henry Heim as *The Island of Crimea* (New York: Random House, 1983);

*The Paperscape: A View from the Flag Tower of the Smithsonian Institution Building: An Attempt at Introspection: Or How Some Stack of Paper Turns into a Russian Novel,* Occasional Paper, no. 161 (Washington, D.C.: Kennan Institute for Advanced Studies, 1982);

*Pravo na ostrov* (Ann Arbor, Mich.: Ermitazh, 1983);

*Bumazhnyi peizazh* (Ann Arbor, Mich.: Ardis, 1983);

*Skazhi izium* (Ann Arbor, Mich.: Ardis, 1985); translated by Antonina W. Bouis as *Say Cheese!* (New York: Random House, 1989);

*Poiski zhanra* (Frankfurt am Main: Posev, 1986);

*V poiskakh grustnogo bebi* (New York: Liberty, 1987); translated by Heim and Bouis as *In Search of Melancholy Baby* (New York: Random House, 1987);

*Moskovskaia saga* (Moscow: Tekst, 1993, 1994); the first part translated by Morris and John Glad as *Generations of Winter* (New York: Random House, 1994); the second part translated by Glad as *The Winter's Hero* (New York: Random House, 1996);

*Negativ polozhitel'nogo geroia* (Moscow: Vagrius/Izograf, 1996);

*Novyi sladostnyi stil'* (Moscow: Izograf, 1997); translated by Christopher Morris as *The New Sweet Style* (New York: Random House, 1999);

*Kesarevo svechenie* (Moscow: Izografus/EKSMO, 2001).

**Editions and Collections:** *Sobranie sochinenii,* volume 1 (Ann Arbor, Mich.: Ardis, 1987);

*Pravo na ostrov* (Moscow: Moskovskii rabochii, 1991);

*Randevu* (Moscow: Tekst & RIF, 1991);

*Sobranie sochinenii,* 5 volumes (Moscow: Iunost', 1994);

*Rasskazy. Povesti. Roman* (Ekaterinburg: U-Faktoriia, 1999);

*Rasskazy. Povesti. Roman. Esse* (Ekaterinburg: U-Faktoriia, 1999);

*Zheltok iaitsa* (Moscow: Izografus/EKSMO, 2003).

**Editions in English:** *A Starry Ticket,* translated by Alec Brown (London: Putnam, 1962); Russian version published as *Zvezdnyi bilet* (Copenhagen: Akademisk Boghandel, 1970);

*The Steel Bird and Other Stories,* translated by Susan Brownsberger, Rae Slonek, and others (Ann Arbor, Mich.: Ardis, 1979)—includes "Little Whale, Varnisher of Reality" and "The Steel Bird";

*Surplussed Barrelware,* translated by Joel Wilkinson and Slava Yastremsky (Ann Arbor, Mich.: Ardis, 1985);

*Quest for an Island* (New York: PAJ, 1987)—includes "The Hollow Herring";

*The Destruction of Pompeii and Other Stories* (Ann Arbor, Mich.: Ardis, 1991).

PLAY PRODUCTIONS: *Kollegi,* Moscow, Malyi teatr, 28 February 1962; Leningrad, Oblastnoi teatr dramy i komedii, 18 April 1962;

*Vsegda v prodazhe,* Moscow, Sovremennik, 2 June 1965;

*Geografiia liubvi,* Tsaritsyno, Moscow Region, Oblastnoi TiuZ, Spring 1974;

*Liubov' k elektrichestvu, Gor'ky Tiuz,* Spring 1976;

*Tsaplia,* Paris, Théâtre National de Chaillot, 17 February 1984; Moscow, Sfera, 11 July 1991.

PRODUCED SCRIPTS: *Kollegi,* television, Leningrad Television Studio, 16 February 1961;

*Kollegi,* Mosfil'm, 1962;

*Moi mladshii brat,* Mosfil'm, 1962;

*Kogda razvodiat mosty,* Lenfil'm, 1962;

*Puteshestvie,* Mosfil'm, 1966;

*Mramornyi dom,* Gor'ky Studio, 1972;

*My Dream Is Wild,* Mosfil'm, 1980.

RECORDING: *Vasily Aksyonov, Arnost Lustig, and Elisavietta Ritchie Reading from Their Work,* Archive of Recorded Poetry and Literature, Gertrude Clarke Whittal Poetry and Literature Fund, Library of Congress, Washington, D.C., 17 April 1989.

OTHER: *Dzhin Grin – neprikasaemyi (Kar'era agenta TsRU No. 14),* by Aksyonov, Ovidii Gorchakov, and Grigorii Pozhenian, as Grivadii Gorpozhaks (Moscow: Molodaia gvardiia, 1972);

*Metropol',* compiled by Aksyonov and others (Moscow & Ann Arbor, Mich.: Ardis, 1979); translated as *Metropol,* edited by Aksyonov and others (Toronto: George J. McLeod, 1982; New York: Norton, 1982);

E. L. Doctorow, *Regtaim,* translated by Aksyonov (Moscow: Inostrannaia literatura, 2000).

Vassily Aksyonov occupies a distinctive place in the history of Russian literature after the rule of Joseph Stalin. Critics traditionally categorize Aksyonov among the *shestidesiatniki*—people in 1960s Russia who were in the avant-garde of the new liberal movement and became protesters and dissidents toward the end of the decade. Yet, this definition bothers him. He claims that the period produced different, sometimes opposite, trends in the arts and in culture; the term *shestidesiatniki* therefore lacks any specific meaning. Another reason why Aksyonov dislikes inclusion in this group is that most of the surviving *shestidesiatniki* represent a bygone movement completely superfluous in the context of contemporary Russian culture, but such irrelevance is not the case with Aksyonov and his work.

In the more than forty years of his writing career Aksyonov has not ceased looking for new ways to expand his artistic horizons. He started as a troubadour of new hopes, born in the aftermath of Stalin's death and in the waning years of Socialist realism. In 1959 he abruptly changed his course and immersed himself in producing carnivalesque satire rooted in Russian symbolism, commedia dell'arte, and ancient Greek comedy. Later, he incorporated the philosophical depth of Leo Tolstoy and the grotesque elements of Nikolai Vasil'evich Gogol in his writing. His life and career have led him from the bitter cold of Magadan, in the Russian Far East, to the warmth and beaches of southern California. Once a pariah, a son of "enemies of the people," Aksyonov is now a world-renowned writer and the Clarence J. Robinson Professor of Russian Literature and Writing at George Mason University in Fairfax, Virginia. Most important, his books, including the latest novels, continue to be in demand in Russia—not only among his own generation but also among young readers. Few writers have such an enduring creative life, one combined with success and the admiration of diverse readers.

Aksyonov was born Vasilii Pavlovich Aksenov on 20 August 1932 in Kazan', the capital of the Tatar Republic, located on the Volga River. Both his parents were dedicated Communists who occupied prestigious positions in the party. His father, Pavel Vasil'evich Aksenov, was the chairman of the Kazan' City Council, and his mother, Evgeniia Solomonovna Ginzburg, was a professor of history at Kazan' University—where Tolstoy and Vladimir Ilyich Lenin had studied and Nikolai Ivanovich Lobachevsky, the father of non-Euclidean geometry, had taught. In 1935–1937 Ginzburg also headed the Culture Department at the Kazan' newspaper *Krasnaia Tatariia* (Red Tatarstan). Aksyonov's parents had children from previous marriages—Pavel Vasil'evich's daughter, Maia, and Ginzburg's son, Aleksei. A nanny, an illiterate but wise peasant woman, cared for the children while the parents worked.

Aksyonov's family led a harmonious and happy life. But it came to an abrupt end in 1937, one of the darkest years in the history of the Soviet Union, at the peak of Stalin's purges. On 8 February, Ginzburg was expelled from the party; exactly a week later she was arrested by the Narodnyi komissariat vnutrennykh del (NKVD, People's Commissariat for Internal Affairs), the Soviet secret police. She was accused of belonging to a Trotskyite organization and conspiring against the Communist Party. The charges against her, like those against other victims of the purges, were fabricated by the investigators and substantiated by false evidence obtained from terrorized witnesses. Ginzburg was sentenced to ten years in prison, followed by five years of deprivation of civil rights. A year later her sentence was changed to ten years of hard labor in the camps. In July 1937 Pavel Vasil'evich followed his wife through the circles of Stalinist hell with a sentence more severe. At first he was condemned to die, but one of his appeals from death row resulted in a miraculous decision: his death sentence was commuted to fifteen years in the camps, followed by five years of deprivation of civil rights.

Within a six-month period, the five-year-old Aksyonov had lost both his parents to the prison camps. The Soviet government took charge of such children of enemies of the people, usually by sending them to special orphanages, where they were destined to experience a life of abuse and a forced change of identity. In order to erase all ties with their families, the government would issue new names to the children. Yet, Aksyonov was lucky. After a long search an uncle found the boy in an orphanage in Kostroma and was able to bring him back to Kazan' for a meager but safe existence with the family of Pavel Vasil'evich's sister. In a country soon devastated by war and the loss of at least forty million people on the battlefields and to Stalin's atrocities and in the camps, many children had no fathers; many lived in families that had just enough money to afford only the barest of necessities. Despite such privations Aksyonov's childhood and adolescence passed under relatively normal circumstances. He went to school, read avidly, and played with his peers, who either did not know about his parents' lot or did not care.

In 1947 Aksyonov's mother completed her ten-year term and was released, albeit without the rights to vote or be elected. She chose to stay, however, in Magadan, a city in the remote northeastern region of Kolyma, the center of the gulag archipelago. Since so many prisoners who returned to major cities, such as Moscow and Leningrad, were quickly rearrested and sent back to the camps, Ginzburg felt that staying away from these places was safer for her. Her older son, Aleksei, had died in 1942 during the siege of Leningrad. Now free, she made plans to reunite with her only surviving son and in 1948 began the difficult task of bringing Aksyonov to Magadan.

After eleven years of separation, the teenage Aksyonov genuinely wanted to see his mother again, and his love for her was his main motivation. At the same time, in keeping with the vogue that American culture was enjoying then in the Soviet Union, he also harbored a deep infatuation with the United States. Although literature and the arts were under strict government control, there were opportunities for Soviets—the youth in particular—to enjoy remnants of Western culture. American movies often played at the cinema, where the average Soviet could see such classics from 1939 as *Mr. Smith Goes to Washington,* which was titled in Russian *Pod vlast'iu dollara* (In the Power of the Dollar); *Stagecoach,* or *Puteshestvie budet opasnym* (The Trip Will Be Dangerous); and *The Roaring Twenties,* or *Sud'ba soldata v Amerike* (A Soldier's Fate in America). The government did not see anything harmful in showing such movies, and the titles in Russian suggested anticapitalist content. At the same time, however, these movies exposed the youth of the nation to American jazz, dance, clothes, and behavior—attributes of American culture that became more significant than the plot of the motion pictures themselves. Some Soviet youth developed such a great fascination with things American that they wore narrow pants, shoes on platform soles of white India rubber, and coats that had big shoulder pads and called themselves "shtatniki" (derived from the Russian word for "states," *shtaty*). In this "America-obsessed" atmosphere the teenage Aksyonov asked in letters to his mother whether Alaska was just a short distance from Kolyma and if there were tribes in Kolyma closely related to the Iroquois.

Soon, Aksyonov was living in Magadan with his mother and her common-law second husband, Anton Valter, a Russian German doctor who was serving a term of exile. (Pavel Vasil'evich was still in the prison camps.) In 1949 Ginzburg was arrested a second time, but she was given a sentence less harsh than before: permanent exile in the Krasnoiarsk region. Although she obtained permission to stay in Magadan, life became even harder. First, she lost her job as a music teacher at a kindergarten, and Valter remained a prisoner subject to certain restrictions. Aksyonov attended high school in Magadan and after graduation returned to Kazan', where, at Valter's encouragement, he enrolled in medical school. The labor camps created by Stalin were self-sufficient, and all the positions—from construction and timber workers to physicians and administrators—were filled by prisoners. Employment as a physician meant the possibility of working in a warm hospital with a better food ration than the pound of bread and the watered-down gruel received by other prisoners. The now seventeen-year-old Aksyonov was not counting on a normal life in the future; he prepared himself to share in his parents' destiny.

This pragmatic view was the result of Aksyonov's reality at the time. In 1953, in his fourth year of medical school, he was expelled for hiding the fact that his parents were enemies of the people. Many years later he learned that the Ministerstvo vnutrennykh del (MVD, Ministry of Interior Affairs), the secret police that was organized after the NKVD but before the Komitet gosudarstvennoi bezopasnosti (KGB, State Security Committee), already had a dossier on him, which might have meant an imminent arrest. He made a trip to Moscow in search of justice, and by some stroke of luck, or perhaps because by that time Stalin was dead, he won a reinstatement. The administration of Kazan' State University received an order to readmit him. Rather than return to his medical studies there, however, Aksyonov decided to transfer to Leningrad Pavlov Medical Institute. One of his reasons was that his mother's sister, Nataliia, lived in Leningrad.

In Leningrad, Aksyonov made new friends who, like himself, looked to the West—to the United States, in particular—for cultural values. The Soviet government gradually eased its ideological controls. This period, known as "The Thaw," began immediately after Stalin's death. It especially gained momentum after the Twentieth Congress of the Communist Party in February 1956; on the last day of the Congress, Nikita Sergeevich Khrushchev gave the so-called secret speech, in which he exposed and denounced the crimes of the Stalin era. These actions were feeble attempts to bring normalcy to the country and alleviate the all-encompassing fear that reigned among its citizens. Stalin's name was no longer sacred, and hundreds of thousands of prisoners started returning from the camps. As they returned, the process of their official exoneration began. Aksyonov's parents were among the returnees; they had survived eighteen years of privations in the camps and in exile. The family was no longer intact, however: Ginzburg, together with Valter and their adopted daughter, Tonia, settled down in L'vov, the largest city in western Ukraine—much of its population practiced Catholicism, which Valter observed; Pavel Vasil'evich went back to Kazan'.

In 1956 Aksyonov graduated from medical school and began working as a quarantine doctor at the Leningrad port. He had applied for a visa, which would permit him to sail abroad as a doctor. International travel was impossible for most Soviets, and Aksyonov's dream to venture abroad did not come to pass. After one and a half years, his application was denied; in the eyes of the KGB, as a son of enemies of the people, he had a tainted record. In 1958–1959 he worked in the Leningrad region, in the town of Voznesenskoe, near Lake Onega. He married Kira Liudvigovna Mendeleva in 1958, and soon they had a son, Aleksei. Later the family moved to the Moscow region, where Aksyonov worked at a tuberculosis sanitarium.

For Aksyonov's generation the late 1950s were formative years. The de-Stalinization initiated by Khrushchev allowed for relative ideological freedom, although literature and other forms of cultural production still remained under strict government control. The Thaw engendered a colossal boom in the cultural life of the Soviet Union. Both Russian and foreign authors, who had been forbidden and mostly forgotten, reappeared in new Soviet editions. The American writer Ernest Hemingway and the German writer Erich Maria Remarque, whose works had not been published in the Soviet Union since the 1930s, again became idols of the Russian intelligentsia. Two volumes of a miscellany, *Literaturnaia Moskva* (Literary Moscow, 1956), published poetry by Marina Ivanovna Tsvetaeva and Anna Andreevna Akhamatova, as well as an article by Boris Leonidovich Pasternak. Equally important were the publications of new, younger writers. In a short story titled "Rychagi" (Levers), Aleksandr Iashin (Aleksandr Iakovlevich Popov) castigates the bureaucracy of the Communist Party, insinuating that Soviet people are no more than levers cynically used by the party to fulfill its ends. The prose writer Iurii Markovich Nagibin and the poets Evgenii Aleksandrovich Evtushenko and Robert Ivanovich Rozhdestvensky wrote about human emotions rather than about victories on the industrial and agricultural fronts. Movies such as *Letiat zhuravli* (Cranes Are Flying, 1957) and *Ballada o soldate* (Ballad about a Soldier, 1960) depicted the tragedies resulting from the war rather than the triumphs of the Soviet army, which had dominated Soviet cinema in previous years.

To cater to the aspirations of the young generation of writers and poets, a new literary monthly, *Iunost'* (Youth), was founded in 1955. Aksyonov published his first two short stories, "Asfal'tovye dorogi" (Asphalt Roads) and "Nasha Vera Ivanovna" (Our Vera Ivanovna), in the July 1959 issue. The stories portray a young country doctor and almost certainly are based on Aksyonov's own experiences as a physician. In 1961 the same journal published his first novel, *Kollegi* (translated as *Colleagues*, 1962), which immediately brought him high acclaim and popularity among the liberal reading audience. Official critics also responded favorably to this publication. In 1962 a motion picture adaptation of the novel was sanctioned

*Cover for the 1983 English-language edition of Aksyonov's novel* Ostrov Krym *(1981), a satirical fantasy in which Crimea is a paradisiacal island nation separate from the Soviet Union (Richland County Public Library, Columbia, South Carolina)*

and produced. After publishing *Kollegi,* Aksyonov quit his job and became a professional writer.

The novel, like the two short stories published earlier, is based on Aksyonov's life as a young doctor. The protagonists are three friends, Aleksei Maksimov, Aleksandr Zelenin, and Vladislav Karpov, all of whom have just graduated from Leningrad Medical Institute. One can already see in this early work the main features that characterize Aksyonov's writings in his later years. He is a sensitive chronicler of the zeitgeist. Rather than create rich psychological portraits of his characters, he depicts symbolic figures who embody the most topical and pressing issues of his era. In this respect he follows the poetics of the Russian symbolists at the turn of the century–above all, those of Aleksandr Aleksandrovich Blok and Andrei Bely (Boris Nikolaevich Bugaev). In *Kollegi*, as well as in other early works, Aksyonov successfully performs a difficult balancing act. On the one hand, respecting the orthodox tenets of Socialist realism, he writes fiction that is easily categorized as typical, conflict-free Soviet literature: the main opposition is not between good and evil but between good and better; Communism and the revolution are still the sacred ideals by which to measure things; and by definition the working class is progressive and good, while the intelligentsia—especially the class of young urbanites—has yet to find the right path in life. On the other hand, Aksyonov's early fiction reflects the doubts that arose in the young generation, after Khrushchev exposed the crimes of the Stalin era, and presents the new values of this generation. He realized that a frank, straightforward depiction of new trends among the young intelligentsia would destroy right away any hope for publication. Hence, in his early prose one finds a significant share of political correctness, Soviet-style.

For example, Maksimov, one of the protagonists, is presented as a cynic who does not believe in the slogans and pronouncements of the official ideology. As if arguing with the trite notions of Socialist realism, he declares that life is not only work but offers many enticements—music, poetry, wine, sports, clothes, cars, mountains, sea, sunsets, and women. Maksimov is a passionate, romantic, and kind young man and a devoted friend; yet, a positive hero in Soviet fiction cannot manifest outrageously bourgeois tastes. Therefore, Aksyonov must demonstrate Maksimov's loyalty and make him announce that he loves his country and his government and is prepared to give his arm, his leg, or even his life for them. The three doctors also look toward the West for new values in life. Their work at a seaport and later, they hope, on merchant ships will provide them with opportunities to meet Western seamen and visit Western ports. The friends have a taste for jazz, Western fashions, and modernist art, but Aksyonov was aware that these very attributes of modern life would be subject to attacks from the Communist Party. As a result, in the novel he employs the usual derisive phrasing when referring to jazz: while symphony sounds are described as "powerful, alarming, and thunderous," jazz produces merely "cacophonic clucking." *Kollegi* was well received by both official critics and liberal readers but for opposite reasons. The critics found all the necessary elements of Socialist realism, while the liberal audience understood Aksyonov's technique of "giving Caesars to Caesar" and enjoyed the daring deviations from the party line, as articulated by the three lovable protagonists.

Within three years Aksyonov wrote three more novels, balancing liberal concepts with orthodox Soviet ideology. His second, *Zvezdnyi bilet* (published 1961 in *Iunost'*; translated as *A Starry Ticket*, 1962), was more daring in its portrait of Soviet youth and clearly leaned toward Western cultural paradigms. In the book three high-school graduates choose a westward direction in their search for the meaning of life: they go to Estonia, a kind of surrogate Western Europe for the Soviets, who could not travel to the real Europe. The young men frequent little cafés and bars in Tallinn, sip cognac, play poker, and smoke cigarettes on the beach. Seventeen-year-old Dima, the central figure of the novel, has an affair with the beautiful Galia, who resembles the French actress Brigitte Bardot. Although the novel ends on the mandatory optimistic note—the protagonists outgrow their immature attachment to this dissolute way of life to become conscientious, hardworking fishermen—Soviet critics could not tolerate the "decadent" behavior of the protagonists; they did not approve of the slang that the characters used liberally or the sexual episodes (between Galia and an older man and then Galia and Dima). Most of the reviews had expressive headlines such as "A Starry Ticket—But Where To?" "The False Ticket," "False Romanticism," "Does *Youth* Need This?" and, finally, "Off the Main Line."

In his next two novels, *Apel'siny iz Marokko* (published 1964 in *Iunost'*; translated as "Oranges from Morocco," 1979) and *Pora, moi drug, pora* (published 1964 in *Molodaia gvardiia*; translated as *It's Time, My Friend, It's Time,* 1969), Aksyonov curbs his pro-Western orientation somewhat, especially in the first one, in which the action takes place in the Russian Far East and most of the protagonists are simple workers. Yet, his protagonists remain the same romantic heroes, be they workers or members of the intelligentsia. Young men, honest and noble, they are always prepared to get into a fight for a good cause and always entangled in relationships that are far from platonic though never debauched. These male heroes never lie to their women and are incapable of taking advantage of them for purely sexual purposes. Through hard work they find the answers to weighty, existential questions. The depiction of the working class in the process of building socialism was one of the main tasks of Socialist realist literature, and—as these novels show—Aksyonov remembered this directive well.

Despite a certain amount of criticism from conservatives, Aksyonov's life appeared the epitome of the successful literary career. In fewer than three years he had become a leading figure in Soviet literature; he represented the views and dreams of the most energetic, educated, and liberal portion of the population. He belonged to the Moscow circle of young, extremely popular new-wave authors, a talented group that included the poets Evtushenko, Bella Akhatovna Akhmadulina, Bulat Shalvovich Okudzhava, and Andrei

Andreevich Voznesensky. His books were readily published and immediately sold out. Besides *Kollegi, Zvezdnyi bilet* was also adapted as a motion picture. In 1961 Aksyonov adapted *Kollegi* into a play, and in 1962 alone it was performed more than 1,600 times in forty-nine theaters. He was allowed to travel abroad—a privilege few Soviets could enjoy. Of course, these trips abroad were not private travels but official functions, such as conferences and congresses, at which he served as a representative of Soviet literature. In 1962 he went to Poland and, at the end of the same year, to Japan; his visit to the capitalist country was an even higher honor and showed the trust of the Communist government in Aksyonov. Another trip to Argentina was scheduled for March 1963: he was to attend a movie festival, where the motion-picture version of *Kollegi* would be screened.

At the same time, the carnival mood of the late 1950s and early 1960s was beginning to subside. The Communist Party was not only unwilling to loosen the reins that firmly controlled the arts but even tightened them. A significant event occurred in December 1962 at a showing of artworks at a Moscow exhibition hall known as the Manezh. The reactionaries who organized the exhibit invited Khrushchev and other members of the government to attend; they fully expected the response that ensued. Seeing the paintings and sculptures that challenged the Socialist realist canon in a daring manner, Khrushchev became outraged. Scarcely educated in the arts, he could not comprehend these works and associated them with pernicious bourgeois ideology. He threatened, scolded, and insulted the artists as if they were his personal slaves. Though in Japan at the time, Aksyonov discerned from afar this clear sign of imminent "frost."

Aksyonov's dissatisfaction with the politics of the cultural sphere explains the pessimistic undertones that appeared in some of his works at this time. In his short stories "Papa, slozhi!" (in *Novyi mir,* 1962; translated as "Papa, What Does it Spell?") and "Malen'kii Kit, lakirovshchik deistvitel'nosti" (in *Na polputi k lune,* 1966; translated as "Little Whale, Varnisher of Reality," 1979), the protagonists undergo both personal and professional crises. The stories mirror the real situation in Aksyonov's life during this period. His relationship with his wife, Kira, was not good. In 1970 he met Maia Afanas'evna Zmeul, with whom he has lived since and experienced wide-ranging travels and trials; they married in 1980. Professionally, Aksyonov also became tired of playing "cat-and-mouse" games with the establishment. Publication in the leading journals and by important publishing houses was no longer enough for him. A desire to express his frustrations led him to formulate a new function for his writings. In 1963 he turned to social satire. He also experimented with new forms, introducing fantastic elements into his writings and writing dramatic works.

The radical turn to satire took place after 7 and 8 March 1963. Aksyonov was invited to the Kremlin for a "Meeting of the Leaders of the Party and the Government with the Workers of Literature and Arts," a gathering of about eight hundred prominent writers and artists from around the U.S.S.R. The party and the government were represented by the highest figures of the Kremlin, including Leonid Ilyich Brezhnev, Mikhail Andreevich Suslov, Aleksei Nikolaevich Kosygin, and Leonid Fedorovich Il'ichev, Khrushchev's advisor on culture and ideology. Khrushchev himself chaired the two-day event. What promised to be an amicable function, the main purpose of which was to raise the ideological consciousness of the "engineers of human souls" (Stalin's designation for Soviet writers), turned into an opportunity for nightmarish personal attacks, filled with insults and threats, upon the writers and artists.

The first victim was Il'ia Grigor'evich Erenburg, a veteran author whose novel *Ottepel'* (The Thaw, 1954) had given the name to the liberalization process that occurred in the late 1950s in the Soviet Union. In the early 1960s Erenburg's memoir came out in the liberal journal *Novyi mir* (The New World), and in it he had attempted to rehabilitate Russian avant-garde art, which had been eradicated by Socialist realism. Still in hysterics over the Manezh incident of December 1962, Khrushchev attacked Erenburg at the March meeting for promoting formalism in art. On the second day he turned his attention to the younger writers, and Voznesensky and Aksyonov were singled out. At this point the composure of the attendees broke down. In his own memoir Aksyonov recalled that the distorted faces of the audience, the majority of whom were literary functionaries and the old Stalinist guard, reflected the horrifying visages found in the paintings of Francisco Goya. The charges against the two writers were ridiculous and insignificant: Voznesensky had said in interviews, paraphrasing Fyodor Dostoevsky, that "beauty governs the world"; Aksyonov once expressed his apprehension that the cult of personality had not been completely vanquished. But the party needed to teach the liberals a lesson about who was master. Khrushchev simply declared that those who tried to deviate from the course of the Communist Party in literature and the arts would be crushed.

The March meeting had no immediate visible effect on the status of the young writers; rather it served as a strong warning. Aksyonov even managed to go to Argentina, although this trip was probably approved because of some mix-up in the official machine rather than the goodwill of party bureaucrats. In 1964 the journal *Molodaia gvardiia* (Young Guard) published his novel *Pora, moi drug, pora;* it appeared in book form in 1965. Also in 1964 his first collection of short stories, *Katapul'ta* (The Catapult), came out, and in 1966 another, *Na polputi k lune* (Halfway to the Moon), was published.

Both Aksyonov and Voznesensky remember the March meeting as one of the most harrowing and humiliating experiences of their lives, and it prompted the former to change the course of his work completely. The humiliation that Aksyonov endured in the Kremlin—intended to put him on the right track—did the opposite. He stopped flirting with Socialist realism, abandoned the romantic search for an ideal hero, and embarked on a new genre—fantastic satire. Aksyonov himself refers to these works as "Total'naia satira" (total satire) and emphasizes their social function. A predominant theme in these new works is the conflict between totalitarianism, impersonated by grotesque figures bestowed with evil power, on the one hand, and the artist and his Muse, on the other. Often the principle of creativity opposing the oppressive totalitarian force is embodied by a small group of talented people—poets, musicians, or visual artists—while the figure of the muse is a combination of Christ (in his hypostasis as the Savior) and the "Prekrasnaia Dama" (Beautiful Lady) of the Russian symbolists. In their clash with totalitarian forces the artists usually perish, but then they rise and find themselves in a sort of paradise, free from any oppression. This Edenic place is an ideal space where all the characters, including the former oppressors, merge in harmonious unity, and the artists are, at last, able to engage in creative activity without interference.

Aksyonov's first work in the genre of total satire was the play *Vsegda v prodazhe* (written 1963; staged in 1965; published 1981; translated as *Always on Sale,* 1988). For the first time in his writing career, he abandoned the Socialist realist principle of "bezkonfliktnost" (conflictlessness) and built the plot around an opposition between good and evil. *Vsegda v prodazhe* centers on tenant relationships in a contemporary Moscow apartment house. Treugol'nikov and Kistochkin are the two protagonists, who are also rivals; they embody, respectively, romantic idealism and cynical, inhumane totalitarianism. The former resembles Aksyonov's heroes of the earlier novels—valiant and moral young men—while the latter is a pragmatic cynic who is trying to corrupt other tenants and eventually gain absolute control over them. Yet, Aksyonov's goal here is not simply to depict the antagonism between two individuals but to create a metaphor for his position vis-à-vis the current political situation in the Soviet Union. The protagonists in *Vsegda v prodazhe* are metaphoric figures rather than realistic characters. In this and many later works Aksyonov does not develop psychological portraits as much as he creates masks that represent specific social and political tendencies. The technique, in principle, is similar to the masks of commedia dell'arte. By deliberately making the main participants of the conflict—Treugol'nikov, Kistochkin, and Kistochkin's helper, the Waitress—schematic, Aksyonov emphasizes the symbolic character of the play, which becomes still more pronounced by the introduction of elements of surrealism in this essentially realistic text.

In 1964, as a direct response to the notorious March meeting, Aksyonov wrote his second play, *Potselui, orkestr, ryba, kolbasa . . .* (1981; translated as *Your Murderer,* 2000). The villain's name, Pork Kabanos, who usurps power in a nonexistent Latin American country, mocks Khrushchev: *kabanos* (wild boar) alludes both to Khrushchev's "piggish" appearance and to the vicious and irrational character of his attack in March. The protagonist is a writer named Alekhandro. He, his lover, Mariia, and his friends—the composer Gregoro and painter Mikaelo—seek refuge on a small island in order to work freely on their creations. Eventually, they face the dilemma of starving or selling out to a whiskey company. They start working for the company but then rebel and are subsequently executed by the Department of Public Harmony, headed by Pork Kabanos. In the end, they rise from the dead and find themselves on the same island but free of Pork Kabanos; in addition, they have been given a coconut tree which supplied them with ham, champagne, and chocolate. The play addresses concerns that Aksyonov and his fellow artists had to face after the March meeting—such as the artist's conformity (to an oppressive regime), which is induced by the "carrot" of privileges and by the "stick" of persecution.

In the late 1960s Aksyonov continued to develop as a theme the conflict between art and totalitarianism. In 1965 he completed the novel *Stal'naia ptitsa* (published 1977 in the journal *Glagol* [The Word]; translated as "The Steel Bird," 1979); in 1967 he finished writing the play *Chetyre temperamenta* (1981; translated as *The Four Temperaments,* 1982); and in 1968 he wrote the novella *Randevu* (published 1971 in *Avrora* [Aurora]; translated as *Rendezvous,* 1985), as well as the play *Aristofaniana s liagushkami* (Aristophaniana with Frogs, 1981). Like *Vsegda v prodazhe* and *Potselui, orkestr, ryba, kolbasa . . . ,* these new works have protagonists who embody creativity, freedom, and a carnivalesque spirit of opposition to the official dogmatic and oppressive culture. They are writers, poets, artists, or composers, or they are multitalented artists such as Leva Malakhitov in *Randevu*. Sometimes the reader is able to identify among them actual representatives of the contemporary Soviet cultural scene. In *Stal'naia ptista,* for example, the names of two tenants, Vas'ka Aksiomov and Tolik Proglotilin, are easily identifiable as Aksyonov and Anatolii Tikhonovich Gladilin, both prose writers of the young generation. At the end of *Randevu,* Aksyonov lists the idols of Soviet pop culture in the 1960s, thus connecting the action in the novel to a specific period. Among these idols are the poets Voznesensky, Evtushenko, and Rozhdestvensky; the actor, poet, and folksinger Vladimir Semenovich Vysotsky; the chess champions Tigran Petrosian and Boris Vasil'evich Spassky; the composer Dmitrii Dmitrievich Shostakovich; and famous Americans such as Louis Armstrong, Ella Fitzgerald, John Updike, and Arthur Miller. Although the settings in these works vary—from Moscow in *Stal'naia ptitsa* and *Randevu,* to a fantastic tower in *Chetyre temperamenta,* to ancient Greece and Hades, the kingdom of the dead, in *Aristofaniana s liagushkami*—allusions to the Soviet Union abound. The graphomaniacs in *Aristofaniana s liagushkami* speak with a Ukrainian accent, as did many Soviet leaders, including Khrushchev and Brezhnev. The protagonists in *Chetyre temperamenta* read poetry by Pasternak, Blok, and Vladimir Vladimirovich Maiakovsky.

Most of Aksyonov's fantastic pieces did not find a publisher. None of his plays, nor the novel *Stal'naia ptitsa,* was published in the Soviet Union. In 1965, however, the play *Vsegda v prodazhe* was staged by the prominent Moscow theater Sovremennik, where it was performed for five seasons. Two other novels written during the 1960s, *Zatovarennaia bochkotara* (published 1968 in *Iunost';* translated as *Surplussed Barrelware,* 1985) and *Randevu,* were published in censored versions in journals. The allegorical meaning of Aksyonov's works was easy to discern; most of the works did not even reach the official censor, as editors at literary journals and publishing houses knew what could pass and what could not.

During this period the political situation in the Soviet Union grew worse. In 1964 Khrushchev was ousted and the Brezhnev era of Stagnation began. Aleksandr Isaevich Solzhenitsyn, who was nominated that year for the Lenin Prize in literature—the highest prize in the Soviet Union—could not publish any works after 1963 and in 1969 was expelled from the Union of Soviet Writers. In 1966 two other writers, Andrei Donatovich Siniavsky and Iulii Markovich Daniel', were sentenced to seven and five years of hard labor, respectively, for publishing their fiction in the West. The final blow to the process of liberalization was delivered in August 1968, when Soviet tanks rolled onto the squares in Prague and put an end to the Prague

*Cover for the 1985 English-language collection of Aksyonov's writings; the title work, a translation of the novel* Zatovarennaia bochkotara *(1968), is about the travels of a band of hitchhikers on a magical barrel truck (Richland County Public Library, Columbia, South Carolina).*

Spring. The despair that the liberal intelligentsia experienced was twofold: people cringed with shame for the crimes committed by their country and felt utter hopelessness for their own political future. But even during this time of Stagnation and political oppression there were short periods when change for the better seemed possible. As a result, between the Siniavsky and Daniel' trial and the invasion of Czechoslovakia, Aksyonov wrote and published *Zatovarennaia bochkotara,* arguably his best work of the 1960s.

By 1967, when the novel was written, Aksyonov's talent had developed and matured in the tradition of Bely and Mikhail Afanas'evich Bulgakov—a tradition rooted in the writings of Gogol. Russian readers, however, did not know this Aksyonov. They knew the Aksyonov of *Kollegi* and *Zvezdnyi bilet,* in which he moved cautiously between new ideas and beliefs and the Socialist realist canon. They also knew Aksyonov from his short stories, which many believed were of higher literary quality than his novels. *Zatovarennaia bochkotara* was therefore a revelation for Soviet readers, and it met with an immediate and resounding success. Although the novel was inspired by Aksyonov's trip with his father to the Riazan' region, where Pavel Vasil'evich was born, the reader will not find in it a realistic portrayal of life in the Russian countryside. The novel is a phantasmagoric account of a truckload of empty barrels (barrelware) being transported to a warehouse in the town of Koriazhsk. On his way there the truck driver, Volodia Teleskopov, picks up hitchhikers who also need to get to Koriazhsk. The hitchhikers come from all walks of life: there is Gleb, a young handsome sailor; Irina, a comely geography teacher; Vadim Afanas'evich Drozhzhinin, a refined intellectual; a small, old but playful grandmother who collects insects for a biological lab; and Mochenkin, an old man who, as an informer and spy, is a legacy of the Stalinist era. None of the hitchhikers, however, is the protagonist of the novel. The central "character" is the Barrelware, a feminine entity similar to the Muse figures in Aksyonov's other works, who is also a sacred locus—a space that harmonizes reality, rehabilitates villains, and unites people in a loving community. In this novel Aksyonov creates a fairy-tale-like narrative that describes travel with adventures, misadventures, and dreams. The Barrelware works magic: the trip to Koriazhsk, which should last no more than a few hours, takes days, and the truck continues to be driven without gas. Eventually, the travelers arrive in Koriazhsk, but by the time they do, they have developed so much love for each other and the Barrelware that they do not want to part, and the trip goes on.

In *Zatovarennaia bochkotara* the reader no longer finds a sharp conflict between art and the oppressive regime. Only a few coded references to Lenin and the revolution remain. For example, the train that passes through Koriazhsk is scheduled to depart at 19:17, the year of the October Revolution, and the villain who arrives on this train wears a visor cap and vest, Lenin's customary getup in the portraits and statues of him. While Aksyonov wrote this novel in 1967, the government was organizing jubilant celebrations of the fiftieth anniversary of the October Revolution and already preparing for the hundredth anniversary of Lenin's birth in 1970. By this time the sacredness of Lenin and the revolution largely had dissipated in the minds of the liberal intelligentsia, and scores of jokes about Lenin and the Russian Civil War hero Vasilii Ivanovich Chapaev were circulating the country. In the context of these jokes and the general cynicism toward official propaganda, the ironic allusions to Lenin and the revolution in the novel should be perceived not as an exposure or satire of the Soviet regime but as a postmodernist deconstruction of Soviet myths.

But Aksyonov himself did not proceed down this postmodernist path. Perhaps the most noteworthy facet of this novel is its poetics. Aksenov playfully fills his text with allusions to characters from Russian literature and popular jokes and songs. He creates a pastiche—to us Frederik Jameson's term—of literary styles and personages. The novel's function, therefore, is not the representation of reality but construction of a postmodernist text that constantly refers to other literary and cultural texts, pursuing the purpose of ironic demythologization of culture. *Zatovarennaia bochkotara* can thus be considered the first Russian postmodernist work of fiction. A year later, Venedikt Erofeev wrote his *poema Moskva–Petushki* (Moscow–Petushki, 1970; translated as *Moscow to the End of the Line*, 1980), a dark version of *Zatovarennaia bochkotara*, which also deconstructs cultural and literary myths. And only in the early seventies, approximately four years after the publication of *Zatovarennaia bochkotara*, did Russian postmodernism enter the phase of intensive, albeit clandestine, development within many different poetic and artistic movements, such as Sots Art, Moscow Conceptualism, and Metarealism. Instead, after the Soviet invasion of Czechoslovakia in August 1968, he reverted to the mode of total satire. He believed that the artist had to choose between pure art and art with a clear ideological goal. In his play *Aristofaniana s liagushkami* Euripides and Aeschylus compete before Dionysus for the honor of bringing poetry back to Athens. The former is an advocate of pure art, while the latter affirms the ideological function of art. According to Aeschylus, the artist must be a teacher and prophet and must show the people the right path. Dionysus chooses him, together with the satirist Aristophanes, to go back to Athens and lead people to freedom.

The development of the theme "art versus the Soviet regime" reaches its climax in Aksyonov's magnum opus, the novel *Ozhog* (1980; translated as *The Burn*, 1984), on which he had begun working in 1969, following the events in Czechoslovakia. That year, too, his third book of short stories, approved for publication in January 1968, finally came out. It was his last work of fiction in book form before he left the Soviet Union eleven years later. He managed to place three more works in literary journals and published a biography of the revolutionary Leonid Borisovich Krasin in 1971, as well as two children's books in 1972 and 1976. Krasin's biography provided him with sufficient income to complete *Ozhog* in 1975.

*Ozhog* is a complex work with two parallel plots developing on two chronological planes. The main action takes place in Moscow and at times in other parts of the Soviet Union during the late 1960s and early 1970s. It describes the life of the Moscow artistic elite as Aksyonov himself experienced it. Many places, events, and characters are easily recognizable, giving the story the verisimilitude of a realistic text. At the same time, as in his previous works of total satire, Aksyonov adds a symbolic constituent to his text. The five protagonists, all bearing the patronymic Apollinarievich—an obvious allusion to the Greek god of music and poetry—represent five kinds of creativity. One Apollinarievich is a writer; another is a musician; the third is a sculptor; the fourth is a physician; and the fifth is a scientist. In the beginning Aksyonov shows them in a state of depression and creative stagnation. Rejecting the path of political conformism within the Soviet system, they have stopped working on their respective projects; instead, they drink and indulge themselves in sexual escapades. At a certain point they surrender to the illusion of a possible compromise with the system and begin working again. The illusion, however, is short-lived; their treacherous friends and the rigidity of a system incapable of any compromises undermine their hopes. Thus, the lives of the Apollinarieviches merge in a symbolic stream of events that represents the waxing and waning of hopes for a creative life within the Soviet system. The Moscow part of *Ozhog* is a carnivalesque narrative often bordering on the grotesque. This carnival does not liberate or remove the tension of social pressures by turning the world upside down. A carnival of drunken carousing, it serves the purpose of obscuring for a while the meaninglessness of life, when reality resembles nightmare and nightmares become reality.

The parallel plot is a realistic narrative through which Aksyonov's writing reaches psychological depths that became characteristic of his later works. It tells the touching story of the teenager Tolia von Steinbok, the adolescent hypostasis of all five Apollinarieviches, who has to face a horrifying world of injustice, oppression, and violence. *Ozhog* has strong autobiographical traces; for example, Tolia lives in Magadan with his mother and her common-law husband, a German doctor—as did Aksyonov in his late-adolescent years. Like the Apollinarieviches, Tolia tries to negotiate a reasonable give-and-take between his sense of what is right and just and the ideological pressures at school. He has a passionate desire "not to be different from others, to live in this Stalinist world and deceive himself . . . to accept slogans, lies, and the Leader as God-given values, not to be afraid of questionnaires and not to pay attention to the columns of slaves." But when the NKVD arrests his mother for the second time, he has to make a choice. There is a limit to the degree of conformism—and its accompanying humiliation—that his conscience allows him to tolerate. After the arresting officers lead his mother away, he sits in the kitchen alone, smokes his first cigarette, drinks his first glass of wine, and says his first prayer. These acts are not ones of typical teenage rebellion against adult morality; rather, they signify rebellion against the hypocrisy and cruelty of a system that orphans him for the second time. From then on Tolia is on the side of "the enemies of the people," because his innocent mother and her noble and courageous friends belong to this category, while "the people" are represented by the sadistic NKVD officers and anti-Semitic schoolteachers. In this novel the outcome of the conflict between art and totalitarianism is much more pessimistic than in his earlier works of "total satire." In *Ozhog*, Aksenov revisits the trip he made with his father to the Riazan' region that inspired him to write *Zatovarennaia bochkotara*. But the general mood and the portrayal of "the simple Russian folk" are much darker in *Ozhog* than in the novella. The peasants in his father's village are thieves and alcoholics, and the analogue to the pathetic but touching and benevolent old man Mochenkin from *Zatovarennaia bochkotara* is a mad, unrepentant torturer, executioner, and rapist. While in his previous works the main conflict is resolved in an abstract utopia, in *Ozhog* the salvation—though only hinted at in the last pages—comes directly from God. This is the first work by Aksenov in which religion, or Christianity to be precise, occupies an important place.

While working on *Ozhog* in the early 1970s, Aksyonov wrote another short novel, *Zolotaia nasha zhelezka* (1980; translated as *Our Golden Ironburg*, 1989). *Ozhog* was written "for the drawer"; because of the obscenities, graphic descriptions of drunken orgies, and anti-Soviet satire in the novel, Aksyonov could not even hope to publish it in the Soviet Union. *Zolotaia nasha zhelezka*, on the other hand, is a short, mild, and less bitter version of *Ozhog* and features many characters and motifs that also appear in the latter novel. Yet, not simply a by-product of a larger work altered to suit a Soviet publisher, *Zolotaia nasha zhelezka* also has characters from other works by Aksyonov, such as Serafima and Volodia Teleskopov, who appeared in *Zatovarennaia bochkotara*. According to Aksyonov himself, *Zolotaia nasha zhelezka* was a nostalgic piece—a farewell to youth, to the hopes of the 1960s, and to the wonderful spirit of love and creativity that united young writers and poets of his generation. He felt that this chapter of Soviet political and literary history had to be closed, and he submitted the work to *Iunost'*, the same journal that published his early novels. But times had changed, and the novel, submitted in 1973, was rejected.

In the late 1960s and early 1970s the political situation continued to worsen. In 1972 the poet Joseph Brodsky was forced to emigrate. In 1974 Solzhenitsyn was arrested, put on a plane, and flown to Germany. The literary scene grew increasingly desolate; the government seemed to favor only the nationalist values of village writers *(derevenshchiki)*, whose works expressed nostalgia for the old Russia. (An exception was Iurii Valentinovich Trifonov—one of the most talented Russian writers who, in the early 1970s, published several short novels on moral topics.) Liberal authors, such as Aksyonov, Gladilin, Georgii Nikolaevich Vladimov, and Vladimir Nikolaevich Voinovich, could not get their works published.

By 1975, at the peak of the détente between the United States and the Soviet Union, the situation changed slightly for the better and a "mini" thaw took place. The authorities allowed Aksyonov to travel to the United States and accept a visiting professor position at the University of California, Los Angeles, where he lectured on Russian literature. He also visited France, Germany, and Italy. Moreover, his mother, Evgeniia Ginzburg, was not persecuted for the unauthorized Western publication of her memoir about Stalin's camps, *Krutoi marshrut* (The Steep Route, 1967; translated as *Journey Into the Whirlwind*, 1967), but was even allowed to travel to France and Germany. During this short thaw, which ended abruptly in 1979 with the Soviet invasion of Afghanistan, Aksyonov published two works in *Novyi mir:* a fictionalized account of his trip to the United States, *Kruglye sutki non-stop* (Non-Stop Round the Clock, 1976) and *Poiski zhanra* (Search for a Genre, 1978). In the former he writes about his visit to the country of his youthful dreams. A cheerful, bright description of California and her "beautiful people," it includes his reflections on American literature and jazz and on the youth movements of the 1960s and 1970s. Unlike many other Russian travelers who have written about America, Aksyonov avoids generalizations. His account is amicable yet objective, told with kind humor and filled with thoughtful observations. In his fictional digressions, the two opposites of his artistic world reappear: the romantic Muse in the guise of Blok's Beautiful Lady and Unknown Lady (here a tall suntanned woman who leads the author on his literary discovery of the United States) and the villain, the author's postmodernist alter ego Memozov, who continuously embarrasses him with his cynical rejection of civilized behavior and traditional values. As in *Zolotaia nasha zhelezka,* in which he is also a villain, Memozov cuts a grotesque figure. He personifies Aksyonov's ambivalence toward the function of art—an ambivalence that becomes a central theme in *Poiski zhanra.*

*Poiski zhanra* was the last novel Aksyonov published in the Soviet Union before his forced emigration. The protagonist, Pavel Apollinarievich Durov, bears the same patronymic as the five Apollinarieviches in *Ozhog* and the four "brothers," the Apollinarieviches, in *Zolotaia nasha zhelezka*. This similarity places Durov, a magician whose surname refers to the well-known Russian circus dynasty, among people engaged in creative work. A magician of a different, higher kind than that of a circus conjurer, Durov works miracles of art. Driving around the country, he picks up hitchhikers, who turn to him with their problems, and he helps them by working miracles with his never-specified art. (From a digression in the text one can deduce that he is a writer.) The interactions between Durov and his fellow travelers allow Aksyonov to create a metaphor of art that actively affects people's lives.

Aksyonov lays this metaphor bare in six "scenes," or digressions, which address questions that have often occupied Russian writers and that became especially important for Soviet artists working under tight government control. Should art be concerned with topical questions of everyday life, or should it withdraw into the aloofness of pure art? What is the artist's duty to the people? What forms should artistic works take—should they be simple and accessible to everybody, or intricate and esoteric? The main text of the novel, describing Durov's encounters on the road, provides the material that elucidates Aksyonov's answers to these questions. As in *Aristofaniana s liagushkami* and other works, he leans toward the social function of art—"working miracles" in order to deliver truth to the people. But to be able to achieve such an end, the artist has to win the people's trust by never compromising his art. A conformist artist who sells his talent to the establishment is similar to a counterfeiter. Aksyonov alludes here not only to scores of Soviet writers who earned their privileged positions by submissively creating ideological trash but also to his own fall—when he wrote the docu-novel "Love to Electricity" about the revolutionary Krasin to provide some income during the early 1970s.

In the late 1970s the political climate worsened again. Aksyonov found himself in an ever-deepening feud with the authorities and the KGB. The secret police knew that the manuscript for *Ozhog* had been smuggled to the West, and they were afraid of still another scandal caused by an anti-Soviet publication. The feud reached its climax in connection with the "*Metropol'* affair." In early 1978 Aksyonov and the young critic and prose writer Viktor Vladimirovich

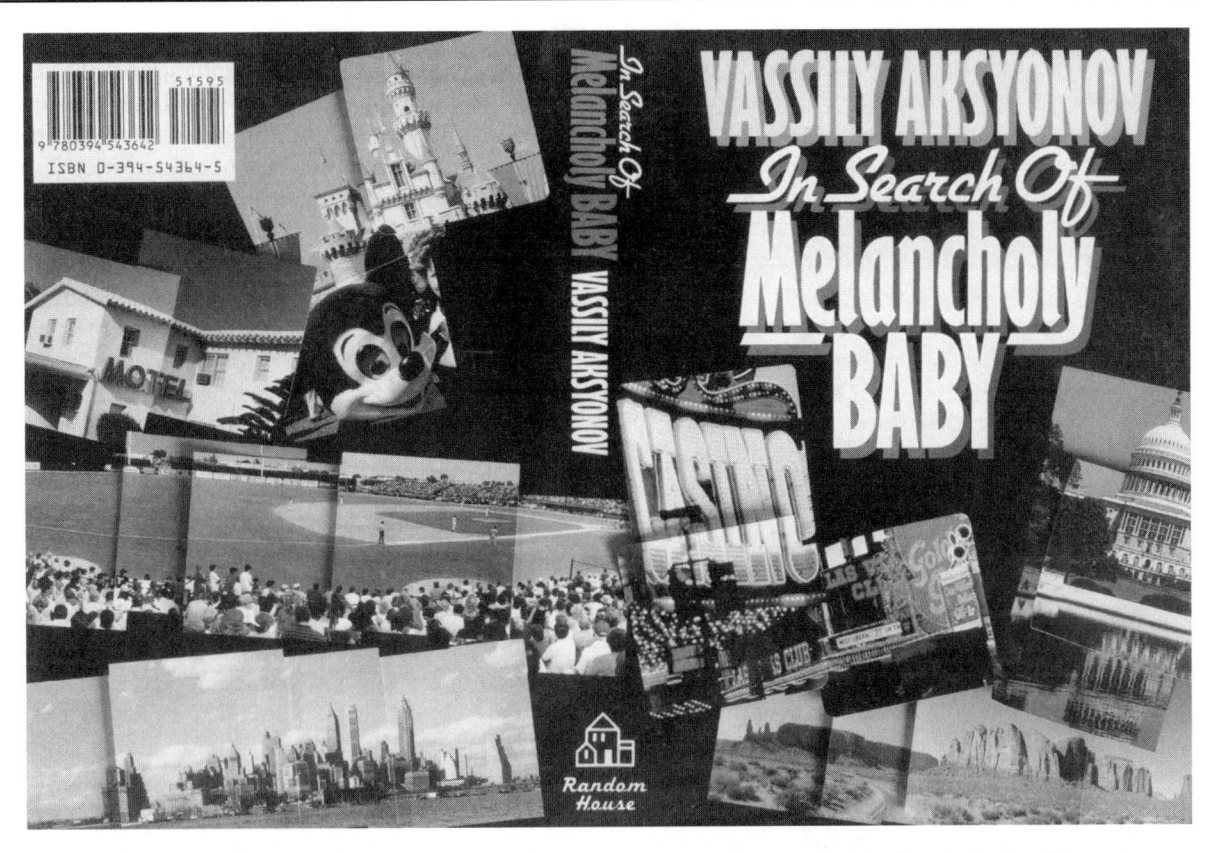

*Dust jacket for the 1987 English-language edition of Aksyonov's* V poiskakh grustnogo bebi *(1987), based on his experiences in the United States after settling there permanently in 1980 (Richland County Public Library, Columbia, South Carolina)*

Erofeev came up with the idea of publishing a volume of uncensored works by contemporary authors. It was not intended as a collection of dissident texts; the main goal was to assert the artist's independence in an environment in which nothing was published without the approval of Glavlit, the censorship administration. About two dozen other writers and artists joined the project. The list included established prose authors such as Andrei Georgievich Bitov and Fazil' Abdulovich Iskander, the poets Akhmadulina and Voznesensky, and the popular bard Vysotsky. Among the lesser-known contributors was Evgenii Anatol'evich Popov, a talented writer from Siberia. Permission to publish the volume was requested by the participants, but they received no response from the authorities. When the collection, titled *Metropol'* (1979; translated, 1982), was officially submitted to the State Committee on Printing for uncensored publication in 1979, a vicious campaign against the writers began. Erofeev and Popov were expelled from the Union of Soviet Writers; work and publication opportunities for the rest were significantly curtailed or eliminated entirely. In protest of Erofeev's and Popov's expulsion, Aksyonov and two poets, Inna L'vovna Lisnianskaia and Semen Izrailevich Lipkin, resigned from the union. Eventually, the volume appeared in the West, brought out by Ardis. Ardis was owned and operated by the Slavic specialists Carl and Ellendea Proffer and during this era published some of the best works of Russian literature—works that would not have passed censorship in the Soviet Union.

In 1980 Aksyonov received permission to go on another lecture tour in the United States, but he knew the trip would be his permanent departure from the Soviet Union. After his membership in the Writers' Union was rescinded, life and work in his country, as he knew it, became impossible, and the thought of emigration haunted him. That the KGB forced Aksyonov to go abroad by using dirty tricks, blackmail, and threats was a thinly masked maneuver to get rid of him without a scandal; this tactic had already been tried on many other dissidents. Troublemakers would be allowed, or even encouraged, to accept an invitation from a Western country; soon after their arrival abroad, they would be stripped of their Soviet citizenship for "actions damaging the prestige of the U.S.S.R. and incompatible with Soviet citizenship," and immediately the host country would offer political asylum to the victim. In 1975 the tactic was used on the writer Vladimir Emilianovich Maksimov; in 1978 the dissident general Petr Grigor'evich Grigorenko, the renowned cello player Mstislav Leopol'dovich Rostropovich, and his wife, the opera singer Galina Pavlovna Vishnevskaia, fell victim to it; and in 1981 the writers Raisa Davydovna Orlova, Lev Zinov'evich Kopelev, and Voinovich were forced to emigrate. On 20 November 1980 a decree of the Supreme Soviet stripped Aksyonov of his Soviet citizenship. He now had to start life anew in the United States.

Shortly before his departure from the Soviet Union, he completed the play *Tsaplia* (1984; translated as *The Heron*, 1987) and the novel *Ostrov Krym* (1981; translated as *The Island of Crimea*, 1983). The theme of confrontation between totalitarianism and creativity that is present in *Tsaplia* had occupied him for a long time—the plot, specific characters, and motifs of the play appear in both *Zolotaia nasha zhelezka* and *Ozhog*—and the routing of *Metropol'* by the literary establishment gave Aksyonov a new impetus to revisit this idea. He employs the same symbolic method as in his earlier works of total satire. The characters are Soviet citizens of various occupations and degrees of loyalty or opposition to the regime, but in fact their affections and feuds are manifestations of a cosmic battle between good and evil. Evil is associated with Stalinism, Nazism, and the Brezhnev era of Stagnation and corruption, while good is embodied in a shy Lithuanian seamstress who also appears as a heron—a homely but touching modification of Anton Pavlovich Chekhov's *Chaika* (1896, Seagull). She lives in Lithuania but every night crosses the border by flying to Poland. The heron is another example of the Muse figure in Aksyonov's works. She imbues the space around her with love and creative energy and miraculously expunges totalitarianism from it. Her flights to Poland betray the author's unchanging longing for the West and his dream of freedom and dignity. At the end the heron perishes but leaves an egg—an embryo of hope for a future birth.

The novel *Ostrov Krym* depicts Crimea not as a Soviet peninsula on the Black Sea but as a free island with a booming capitalist economy, well-developed democratic institutions, and a powerful army. This make-believe island owes its independent status and prosperity to the White Army, which in the novel, at the end of the Russian Civil War, managed to stop the Reds at the strait separating the island from the mainland. Aksyonov models this island on both Taiwan (and its relationship to mainland China) and California, with its plenitude, laid-back beach life, and laissez-faire spirit. The novel opens a new chapter in his "search for a genre." He moves from the symbolic method of total satire to straightforward realist narration. Apart from the fantastic premise of the plot, the text has no figurative meaning and thus departs from the norm of his previous works.

*Ostrov Krym* is a political pamphlet that mocks the naiveté of people's attempts to find logic in the actions and policies of the Soviet government and to look for a meaningful coexistence with the regime. The protagonist, Andrei Arsen'evich Luchnikov, a publisher of the influential Crimean newspaper *Kur'er* (Courier), is obsessed with the idea of a reunion between Crimea and the Soviet Union. The plot switches back and forth between the island and the Soviet Union of 1979, the year Aksyonov took stock of his life before departing for the United States. In this narrative that resembles a thriller Luchnikov leads the advocates of reunification, or "Common Fate," to victory—only to witness the unruly and disorganized Soviet military machine crushing the blissful life of the residents on the beautiful island. In this novel Aksyonov reflects bitterly not only on his own futile search for relative independence within the Soviet ideological system but also on the naive belief of the American Left in the possibility of a meaningful dialogue with the Soviet Union.

The apocalyptic portrayal of the invasion and the incompetence of the Soviet military machine produces an uncanny sense of prescience regarding another, real invasion. The novel was finished in 1979, one month before the Soviet invasion of Afghanistan, which completely halted détente. In *Ostrov Krym*, in a demonstration of his prophetic talent, Aksyonov predicts perestroika five years before it actually commences. He writes about the coming changes: "Stalinism is dying, there is no doubt about it. Our entire country is on the threshold of a new historical period, maybe even more mysterious than the Revolution."

*Ostrov Krym* was the last work Aksyonov wrote in the Soviet Union. In the United States he not only remained a prolific writer but also devoted much time to his new profession as a teacher of creative writing and Russian literature. After his arrival in the West, he taught at the University of Southern California. He then received a Kennan Institute Fellowship for 1981–1982 and spent that time writing the novel *Bumazhnyi peizazh* (1983, Paperscape). In 1982–1983 he taught at George Washington University and then at Goucher College and Johns Hopkins University for five years. Since 1988 Aksyonov has been teaching at George Mason University. His fiction of the 1980s and 1990s shows unsurpassed mastery in many styles and genres. The long story "Sviiazhsk" (1981; translated as "The Hollow Herring," 1986) continues the realistic trend in Aksyonov's prose that was manifest already in *Ostrov*

*Krym;* the somber, pensive mood of the story, however, distinguishes it from the playful, ironic style of the novel. "Sviiazhsk" lacks the modernist devices and permeating irony of which Aksyonov was so fond in his earlier works. Instead, it is a touching account of a Soviet basketball coach, Oleg Shatkovsky, and the mystical ties that connect people and times through God. The secret baptism Oleg received in his childhood and his visit to a convent during his adolescent years work a miracle many years later, turning a depressed functionary into an enthusiastic team leader. The sign of the cross that Oleg makes in front of television cameras inspires the players, who also cross themselves, and brings victory over the invincible rival team, the Tanks. This triumph costs Oleg not only his job but also, apparently, his life. Salvation finally comes from a remote relative, a Christ-like figure who stirs childhood memories in Oleg that bring him to faith. In both style and subject matter "Sviiazhsk" is a Tolstoyan story of a man who has become a jaded automaton in his private and professional life but who in the end undergoes a spiritual crisis and finds God. Like much that Aksyonov has written, the story has strong autobiographical overtones and bespeaks his growing faith in Christianity.

*Bumazhnyi peizazh* is the complete opposite of "Sviiazhsk." Here, Aksyonov enjoys some postmodernist play with Soviet discourses during the Brezhnev era and creates ironic masks for his characters. Like *Ozhog,* however, *Bumazhnyi peizazh* also has references to concrete events and figures important to 1970s Soviet cultural life. The attentive reader will recognize confrontations on the literary front between conformist and nonconformist writers; the persecution of dissidents by the KGB; and the collective letters written to support or castigate Solzhenitsyn and the physicist Andrei Dmitrievich Sakharov, to condemn the invasion of Czechoslovakia, or to demand that Crimean Tatars be allowed to return to their homeland. Behind the names of the characters hide Aksyonov's contemporaries—friends as well as foes: those who withstood the political pressure of the times and those who surrendered to it. With varying degrees of proximity to the prototypes, the characters resemble writers and poets such as Brodsky, Evtushenko, Chingiz Torekulovich Aitmatov, Iurii Vasil'evich Bondarev, Vasil' Vladimirovich Bykov, and Aleksandr Borisovich Chakovsky. There are also characters resembling the ballet dancer Mikhail Baryshnikov and the motion-picture director Andrei Arsen'evich Tarkovsky. One of the main antagonists in the novel, Al'fred Feliaev, the Party secretary for ideology in the Frunzensky District of Moscow, is inspired by Al'bert Beliaev, the chief nemesis of *Metropol'*. Thus, this Gogolesque tale of a little man, Igor' Ivanovich Velosipedov, who often gets into trouble for his naiveté, if not for his stupidity, is also a retrospective and somewhat nostalgic look at the Soviet—or Muscovite—cultural scene of the 1970s.

Though after emigration Aksyonov continued writing short stories and novellas, such as *Bumazhnyi peizazh,* he leaned increasingly toward the writing of novels. In the early and mid 1980s he wrote two books of the genre that can be defined as documentary fiction. *Skazhi izium* (1985; translated as *Say Cheese!* 1989) is a phantasmagoric tale based on the trials and tribulations of the *Metropol'* creators. The novel presents them as a group of photographers compiling an album of uncensored photographs. Admitting that the book tells the story of *Metropol',* Aksyonov himself warns his reader at the beginning not to look for a direct correspondence between the characters and the actual participants of the miscellany. Nevertheless, here—as in *Ozhog* and *Bumazhnyi peizazh*—the specific features and actions of real literary figures are possible to identify. *Skazhi izium* resembles *Ozhog* and *Bumazhnyi peizazh* in another respect as well; like the other two works, it has strong religious undertones. The novel has a typical Aksyonovian ending: a carnivalesque scene on Red Square, where the entire population of the Soviet Union—including the Politburo, the KGB, and their victims, the photographers—gathers in front of the Chief Photographer Vadim Raskladushkin in one harmonious and loving whole. Vadim is an angel who heals all wounds, reconciles all enemies, and transforms the evil party functionaries and members of the KGB. Salvation lies in Christian love and comes from God through a Christ-like figure.

*V poiskakh grustnogo bebi* (1987; translated as *In Search of Melancholy Baby,* 1987) is a kind of sequel to *Kruglye sutki non-stop,* Aksyonov's account of his first trip to the United States. In the earlier piece he attempted to match the real United States with the romantic image of a country of westerns, jazz, and the Beat generation, which he and other "Americophiles" had formed in their youth during the late 1940s and early 1950s. His visit to California in the mid 1970s helped seal this match, or correspondence. When Aksyonov wrote *V poiskakh grustnogo bebi,* he already had been living in the United States for more than five years and was no longer a carefree guest but a resident. The book is a sober systematic account of the United States and displays a more profound and objective analysis. Aksyonov tries to understand and justify those manifestations of American life that he cannot immediately embrace. In this approach his work differs considerably from dozens of other descriptions of the United States, written by Russian travelers who develop an immediately hostile reaction to any phenomenon of American life that does not fit their own cultural stereotypes. There is little fiction in *V poiskakh grustnogo bebi;* the digressions, or as he calls them "Sketches for the Novel Melancholy Baby," serve as links between his youthful infatuation with the United States in the remote past, his present experience of the country, and the portrait of it in a future novel. Names and motifs from some digressions surface later in the novel *Novyi sladostnyi stil'* (1997; translated as *The New Sweet Style,* 1999).

In April 1985 Mikhail Sergeevich Gorbachev became the secretary general of the Communist Party. A new period in Russian history—perestroika—began. One of the main achievements of the new political system was the abolition of censorship. In a short time virtually all restrictions were removed from the publishing industry, and the country enjoyed unprecedented freedom. The works of Brodsky, Solzhenitsyn, Nikolai Sergeevich Gumilev, Evgenii Ivanovich Zamiatin, Vladimir Vladimirovich Nabokov, and other previously forbidden authors were sold at bookstores, book markets, and on the tables of street vendors. Aksyonov's first publication in the Soviet Union after his emigration, *Zolotaia nasha zhelezka,* appeared in 1989 in the journal *Iunost',* which had rejected it earlier, during the Soviet period. Soviet publishers also discovered the underground literature of the 1970s and 1980s—literature usually referred to as Russian postmodernism, or Moscow conceptualism. The works of Timur Iur'evich Kibirov, Dmitrii Aleksandrovich Prigov, Lev Semenovich Rubinshtein, Evgenii Anatol'evich Popov, and Vladimir Georgievich Sorokin became a permanent feature in literary journals and weeklies. But the ironic deconstruction of Soviet mythology, which is the main artistic purpose in these writers' works, can be traced to Aksyonov's *Zatovarennaia bochkotara, Randevu, Poiski zhanra,* and *Ozhog.* Aksenov's influence is especially evident in the works of Popov, Sorokin, and another highly popular writer of the younger generation, Viktor Olegovich Pelevin.

Yet, by the mid 1990s, when the Soviet Union and its myths were gone—at least for the more educated readers who once enjoyed postmodernist irony—the relevance of these writings was lost, too. The "avant-garde" of everyday life was so overwhelming that readers needed more traditional literature to escape the onslaught of social and political changes. Aksyonov has always been sensitive to the dynamics of new literary developments in his country. In his early writings he dared to looked for liberal values beyond the Iron Curtain, when it still hung intact. His *Zatovarennaia bochkotara* was a precursor of 1970s postmodernism. In the late 1980s and early 1990s, during the peak of interest in postmodernism, he already felt the need for reorientation and began working on an epopee, *Moskovskaia saga* (Moscow Saga, 1993, 1994; translated as *Generations of Winter,* 1994), modeled after Tolstoy's *Voina i mir* (1868, 1869, *War and Peace*). The book consists of three parts and portrays life in the Soviet Union under Stalin—from the fall of 1925 to the spring of 1953, the year of Stalin's death. *Moskovskaia saga* describes the fate of a big family, consisting of the patriarch, a renowned surgeon, Boris Nikitich Gradov; his wife, Mary; their children, Nikita, Kirill, and Nina; and several grandchildren, relatives, and friends. Aksyonov leads his characters through the last years of the Novaia ekonomicheskaia politika (NEP, New Economic Policy) period; the early years of Stalin's totalitarian rule; the horrors of the purges and camps in the late 1930s; World War II; and the postwar collapse of hope for a better future.

As always, Aksyonov uses his characters to comment on important political and cultural issues of the time, placing them in the center of major historical events. Thus, Boris III, acting the part of a coward, agrees to participate in Stalin's alleged conspiracy that leads to the death of the military commander Mikhail Vasil'evich Frunze on the operating table. Almost thirty years later, in 1953, Boris III finds courage and pays off his old debt, defending his Jewish colleagues in the infamous Doctor's Plot. Only Stalin's death saves him from perishing in a camp. His son Nikita is also tortured by a bad conscience: Nikita was among the Red troops that brutally suppressed the Kronshtadt Rebellion in 1921. But at the end of World War II he is redeemed by refusing to shoot at Polish soldiers to whom he earlier guaranteed safe passage. Helplessly, his son, Boris IV, witnesses how the Nazis quell the Warsaw uprising, while the Soviet army denies the Polish rebels assistance. Events and coincidences connect the Gradov family to the main villains of the epoch, Lavrenty Pavlovich Beria and Stalin. Aksyonov intricately weaves the lives of his characters into the fabric of several historical figures and events.

The resemblance of *Moskovskaia saga* to *Voina i mir* is intentional. Even the headings of the second and third parts—"Voina i tiur'ma" (War and Jail) and "Tiur'ma i mir" (Jail and Peace)—recall the title of Tolstoy's novel. The characters and their relationships also resemble those in Pasternak's *Doktor Zhivago* (1958). Aksyonov uses these parallels to demonstrate how drastically the nation changed in the course and aftermath of the revolution. The Gradovs and their friends are honest and moral people, but the ideals of the revolution and Communism that they so readily embrace make them surrender their moral values step by step. At first, they genuinely believe that the horrors of the revolution and Stalinism are unfortunate by-products of the revolutionary process. As the Russian saying goes, "When trees are felled chips are flying around." Later, this belief turns into an immunizing self-deception that helps them stomach their own conformism in an atmosphere of total fear. In the end, however, they heroically reject totalitarian ideology and either rebel openly, as Boris III, his son Nikita, and daughter Nina do, or withdraw into religion, as Boris's other son, Kirill, does.

Drinking, feasting, and sexual acts are important preoccupations in the novel. While acts such as drinking or sex can be signs of friendship or love, in Aksyonov's novel these acts have no such meaning. Women sleep with executioners, voluntarily and with gusto, and noble men knowingly share their beds with NKVD informers. Natasha Rostova's infatuation with Anatol' Kuragin in *Voina i mir* or Lara's affair with Komarovsky in *Doktor Zhivago* are tragic occurrences in their lives; in *Moskovskaia saga* not only promiscuity but promiscuity with villains is a nonevent. These feasts and affairs become symbols of "feasting during the plague" when nothing matters any longer. In this light *Voina i mir* and even *Doktor Zhivago* serve as reference points for *Moskovskaia saga* and show the horrifying depth of the fall of a nation mesmerized by lofty ideals.

By the time *Moskovskaia saga* was published in Moscow in 1993, Aksyonov had visited Russia as an émigré on many occasions, and he had been more than welcome. All the liberal newspapers in Moscow carried interviews with, and articles about, him; informers and conformists—the same people who had denounced him at the meetings and in the press and spread ill rumors about him—sought his friendship. In 1990 his Soviet citizenship was restored, and in 1991 the new government granted him an apartment. In the early 1990s Aksyonov spent long stretches of time in Moscow witnessing and participating in the exciting events that were shaking the country. Together with millions of other advocates of perestroika, he shared the triumph and euphoria of victory over the attempt to reel back the reforms in August 1991.

Aksyonov's experiences in the United States and Russia became the subject matter of his next novel, *Novyi sladostnyi stil'*, a work rich in cultural commentary on life in the two countries from the 1980s to the mid 1990s. The central character is Aleksandr Iakovlevich Korbakh, a poet, bard, and director of the stage and screen who is forced by the KGB to emigrate and who now lives in the United States. In the course of the story Korbakh rises from parking-garage attendant and drug pusher in Los Angeles to professor at a leading American university in Washington, D.C. Later, he becomes a Hollywood movie director and the president of a financial foundation that sponsors various worthy

*Dust jacket for the 1996 English-language edition of the second part of Aksyonov's* Moskovskaia saga *(1993–1994, Moscow Saga), his epic novel about the fortunes of a large family in Stalinist Russia (Collection of Patricia Hswe)*

projects during the Gorbachev and post-Gorbachev eras.

Aksyonov molds Korbakh from his own biography but also endows the protagonist with talents and biographical facts of great artists, including Vysotsky, Tarkovsky, and the theater director Iurii Petrovich Liubimov. Combining so many talents in his protagonist, Aksyonov revives a device he had previously used in *Randevu*: the novel is not about one person but about the tribulations of creativity caught between Soviet totalitarianism and the lack of understanding in American academia and the American art establishment. In copious digressions and reflections scattered throughout the text he expresses his abhorrence for both the KGB and the cowardly world of the Soviet artistic elite, as well as his frustration with the Procrustean bed of political correctness and leftist idealism in

American liberal circles. At the same time, the author affectionately describes devoted actors both in Russia and the United States who are completely absorbed by their work in the theater and sacrifice their entire lives to it.

In terms of narrative style a Gogolian tendency prevails in *Novyi sladostnyi stil'*. Irony again becomes the predominant narrative feature–as it was in Aksyonov's works of "total satire" during the Soviet period. The narration is relaxed and free-flowing, and the narrator frequently interjects the text with his comments and ruminations. As in *Moskovskaia saga*, drinking, eating, and sex are abundant; here, however, they are not acts of despair but features of the carnivalesque, Rabelaisian reality that informs the entire text. Aksyonov also has shed much of the bitterness and anger characteristic of his earlier satirical works. In its general mood the novel is closer to *Zatovarennaia bochkotara* and *Poiski zhanra* than to *Ozhog*, *Randevu*, and the plays. Finally, the portraits of the main characters acquire greater psychological depth, which is especially apparent in the depiction of the protagonist and his relationship with Nora.

In the 1990s Aksyonov's works also reflect changes in his ongoing spiritual search. Christianity, which appears as the only path to salvation in *Ozhog*, *Bumazhnyi peizazh*, and *Skazhi izium*, gives way, in the digressions of *Moskovskaia saga*, to eclectic mysticism based on oriental spiritual thought. At the end of *Novyi sladostnyi stil'* Korbakh discovers that he is a reincarnation of his Jewish ancestor who lived in the territory of Israel many centuries ago. The questions of Jewishness and assimilation bother Korbakh, who experiences an identity crisis both in Russia and in the United States. This time the protagonist finds his ultimate salvation and reunites with his love and son in the land of Israel, where he always "feels some kind of rise of spirit, solemn and at the same time softly pacifying." Aksyonov seems to disagree with Pasternak, who in *Doktor Zhivago* calls for assimilation and denounces Judaism in favor of Christianity.

Aksyonov's first book published in the new millennium demonstrates his indefatigable search for new literary paths. The word "novel" on the title sheet of *Kesarevo svechenie* (2001, Caesarian Radiance) assumes new meaning in this book, the structure of which bears little resemblance to the traditional format of this genre. This "big" novel (more than six hundred pages long) includes three plays, a "small" novel, essays, memoirs about dead friends, and verses–not only in the form of poetic digressions, a common feature of Aksyonov's prose, but as a separate part, similar to the "Poems of Iurii Zhivago" in *Doktor Zhivago*. The styles in this work vary, ranging from Aksyonov's favorite relaxed flow of ironic text and traditional narrative prose to somber philosophical writing. The autobiographical figure of the author, Stas Vaksino, an American professor and former Soviet writer with a dissident past, freely interacts with his characters and discusses the nuances of his trade with the readers. At the same time, the characters are aware that they are literary figures and occasionally ask the author to redirect the plot. While in his previous works Aksyonov proved to be a shrewd commentator on topical political and cultural issues, in this book he moves them to the background. His emphasis shifts to a contemplation of the secrets of the literary profession and to experimentation with styles, forms, and genres.

Although Stas, Aksyonov's alter ego, is the central figure of the novel, he is not its protagonist. The protagonists are Slava Gorelik and Natasha (Kakasha) Svetliakova. Both were born by cesarean section and possess–perhaps as some sort of consequence–enthralling and luminescent personalities. In fact, the names Gorelik and Svetliakova are derived from the Russian words that mean, respectively, "to burn" and "light." The two characters separate after their first night together–Slava is sent to jail for three years–and they are then exposed to all imaginable and unimaginable adventures, finally reuniting in a utopia. Gorelik and Svetliakova become ecological heroes; from greedy oil companies they extract inventions of generators of clean energy, which had been buried in the companies' vaults.

At the end, the novel achieves tragic dimensions. In the third play, which concludes the book, Slava and Natasha are shown in the future, in the middle of the twenty-first century. He is a hundred years old and she is ninety-three. Wealthy as they are, they can afford to live in a fully automatic house and to be sustained by organ transplants and various high-tech therapies. They are pathetic old people, subject to attacks of senile rage and hatred, which subside after the appropriate therapy. The couple still has daily sex and carries on public appearances, but they have lost their vitality and luminescence. A fear of dying drives them to have their clones made, but they are disappointed in the results. They cannot recognize themselves in their genetic copies: the clones lack their radiance, energy, and tremendous appetite for life. The clones play sports and exercise, but do not have sex with each other–a crucial and signifying activity in Aksyonov's world. Finally, the time comes when no therapy can save the old couple. They die together, but at the moment of their death, the clones change, and the reader sees the same Slava and Natasha, only seventy-five years younger. The circle closes: the religious dream of eternal life and youth is granted by contemporary science.

The themes of aging, love, and death occupy ever greater positions in Vassily Aksyonov's latest works. They have replaced political polemics and satire. While the delightful wittiness and richness of his language has been preserved, the prose style of his later works is more profound and philosophical. Now in his seventies, he is soon to retire from academia, but he has no intention of giving up his creative work. On the contrary, he enjoys writing as never before and will continue to indulge his readers with many more exciting and unexpected literary discoveries.

**Interviews:**

B. Ezerskaia, *Mastera (interv'iu s russkimi deiateliami iskusstva, zhivushchimi za rubezhom),* volume 2 (Ann Arbor, Mich.: Ermitazh, 1982), pp. 9–62;

Edward Možejko, Boris Briker, and Per Dalgård, eds., *Vasili Pavlovich Aksënov: A Writer in Quest of Himself* (Columbus, Ohio: Slavica, 1986), pp. 14–25, 26–31;

A. Mirchev, *15 interv'iu* (New York: Izdatel'stvo imeni A. Platonova, 1989);

V. Sinel'nikov, "Ia v osnovnom pishu dlia russkikh chitatelei . . . ," *Iskusstvo kino,* 3 (1990): 51–60;

N. Riurikova and M. Sergienko, "Vse vperedi!" *Kinostsenarii,* 2 (1996): 59–67.

**Bibliographies:**

"A Bibliography of Works by and about V. P. Aksenov," in *Vasili Pavlovich Aksënov: A Writer in Quest of Himself,* edited by Edward Možejko, Boris Briker, and Per Dalgård (Columbus, Ohio: Slavica, 1986), pp. 253–268;

"Bibliographicheskii ukazatel'," in *Vasilii Aksenov: Literaturnaia sud'ba,* edited and compiled by V. P. Skobelev and L. A. Fink (Samara: Izdatel'stvo Samarskogo gosudarstvennogo universiteta, 1994), pp. 152–202.

**References:**

Lauren Elaine Bennett, "Blokian Images of the Feminine in Vasilii Aksenov's Post-Thaw Prose," M.A. thesis, University of Virginia, 1993;

Laura Berhara, "Roll Out the Barrels: Emptiness, Fullness, and the Picaresque-Idyllic Dynamic in Vasilii Aksenov's 'Zatovarennaia bochkotara,'" *Slavic Review,* 56 (Summer 1997): 212–232;

Boris Bolshun, "On Certain Lexical Peculiarities of V. Aksenov's Novel *Ozhog*," dissertation, University of Michigan, 1985;

Per Dalgård, *The Function of the Grotesque in Vasilij Aksenov,* translated by Robert Porter (Århus, Denmark: Arkona, 1982);

Nina Aleksandrovna Efimova, *Intertekst v religioznykh i demonicheskikh motivakh V. P. Aksenova* (Moscow: Izdatel'stvo Moskovskogo universiteta, 1993);

Alan Jay French, "Youth and Conflict in the Works of Vasilij Aksenov," M.A. thesis, George Washington University, 1971;

Zina Gimpelevich, "The Intelligentsia: What It Used to Be and What It Is in Aksenov's *Skazhi izium,*" *Canadian Slavonic Papers,* 37 (March–June 1995): 201–217;

Rufus K Griscom, "A Study of an Author in Transition–Vasili Aksenov," M.A. thesis, Brown University, 1969;

Rolf Hellebust, "Metal in the Works of Vasilii Aksenov," *Canadian Slavonic Papers,* 40 (March–June 1998): 91–105;

D. Barton Johnson, "Vasilij Aksionov's Aviary: The Heron and The Steel Bird," *Scando-Slavica,* 33 (1987): 45–61;

John Vincent Kitterman, "The Submerged Son: A Psychoanalysis of Totalitarianism and Authoritarianism in the East European and Latin American Novel," dissertation, University of Virginia, 1992;

Konstantin V. Kustanovich, *The Artist and the Tyrant: Vassily Aksenov's Works in the Brezhnev Era* (Columbus, Ohio: Slavica, 1992);

Kustanovich, "The Narrative World of Vasilij Aksenov's Prose," dissertation, Columbia University, 1986;

David Lowe, "E. Ginzburg's *Krutoj marshrut* and V. Aksenov's *Ozhog*: The Magadan Connection," *Slavic and East European Journal,* 2 (1983): 200–210;

Olga Matich, "Vasilii Aksenov and the Literature of Convergence: *Ostrov Krym* as Self-Criticism," *Slavic Review,* 47 (Winter 1988): 642–651;

Arnold B. McMillin, "Bilingualism and Word Play in the Work of Russian Writers of the Third Wave of Emigration: The Heritage of Nabokov," *Modern Language Review,* 89 (April 1994): 417–426;

McMillin, "Vasilii Aksenov's Writing in the USSR and the USA," *Irish Slavonic Studies,* 10 (1989): 1–16;

McMillin, "Western Life As Reflected in Aksenov's Work before and after Exile," in *Under Eastern Eyes: The West As Reflected in Recent Russian Émigré Writing,* edited by McMillin (New York: St. Martin's Press, 1992), pp. 50–61;

Priscilla Meyer, "Aksenov and Soviet Prose of the 1950s and 1960s," dissertation, Princeton University, 1971;

Meyer, "Aksenov and Stalinism: Political, Moral and Literary Power," *Slavic & East European Journal,* 30 (Winter 1986): 509–525;

Edward Možejko, Boris Briker, and Per Dalgård, eds., *Vasili Pavlovich Aksënov: A Writer in Quest of Himself* (Columbus, Ohio: Slavica, 1986);

Marina Raskin, "The Emergence of Fantasmagoric Realism in Contemporary Russian, Hebrew, and British Literatures: Vasily Aksenov, Amos Oz, and Kingsley Amis," dissertation, Purdue University, 1988;

Christopher Franz Rühe, "Jazz with a Russian Accent: Jazz Narrative in the Prose of Vassily Aksyonov," M.A. thesis, University of Virginia, 1997;

Cynthia Simmons, "The Poetic Autobiographies of Vasilij Aksenov," *Slavic & East European Journal,* 40 (Summer 1996): 309–323;

Simmons, *Their Fathers' Voice: Vassily Aksyonov, Venedikt Erofeev, Eduard Limonov, and Sasha Sokolov* (New York: Peter Lang, 1993);

V. P. Skobelev and L. A. Fink, eds., *Vasilii Aksenov: Literaturnaia sud'ba* (Samara: Izdatel'stvo Samarskogo universiteta, 1994);

Greta N. Slobin, "Aksenov beyond 'Youth Prose': Subversion through Popular Culture," *Slavic & East European Journal,* 31 (Spring 1987): 50–64;

Alexander Suslov, "The 'New Art' Tradition in Modern Russian Prose," dissertation, Georgetown University, 1984;

Lisa Ryoko Wakamiya, "Russian Emigré Literature of the Third Wave and the Creation of Exilic Identity: Vasilii Aksenov, Eduard Limonov, and Zinovii Zinik," dissertation, University of California, Los Angeles, 2000;

Adam Weiner, "The Prosaics of Catharsis in Aksenov's Moscow Saga," *Russian Review,* 57 (January 1998): 87–103.

**Papers:**

Vassily Aksyonov's papers are at the Fenwick Library, George Mason University.

# Andrei Amalrik

*(12 May 1938 – 11 November 1980)*

Jonathan Z. Ludwig
*Rice University*

BOOKS: *Prosushchestvuet li Sovetskii Soiuz do 1984 goda?* (Amsterdam: Fond imeni Gertsena, 1969); translated by Amalrik as *Will the Soviet Union Survive until 1984?* preface by Henry Kamm, commentary by Sidney Monas (New York: Harper & Row, 1970; London: Allen Lane, 1970; revised edition, introduction by Leopold Labedz, New York: Harper & Row, 1971; revised and enlarged edition, Harmondsworth, U.K.: Penguin, 1980; New York: Harper & Row, 1981);

*Nezhelannoe puteshestvie v Sibir'* (New York: Harcourt Brace Jovanovich, 1970); translated by Manya Harari and Max Hayward as *Involuntary Journey to Siberia,* introduction by Hayward (New York: Harcourt Brace Jovanovich, 1970; London: Collins & Harvill, 1970);

*P'esy* (Amsterdam: Fond imeni Gertsena, 1970); translated, with an introduction, by Daniel Weissbort as *Nose! Nose? No-se! and Other Plays* (New York: Harcourt Brace Jovanovich, 1973);

*Stat'i i Pis'ma 1967–1970* (Amsterdam: Fond imeni Gertsena, 1971);

*SSSR i Zapad v odnoi lodke* (London: Overseas Publications Interchange, 1978);

*Raspoutine,* translated and annotated by Basile Karlinsky, preface by Léonide Pliouchtch (Paris: Seuil, 1982); Russian version published as *Rasputin: Dokumental'naia povest'* (Moscow: Slovo, 1992);

*Zapiski dissidenta* (Ann Arbor: Ardis, 1982); translated by Guy Daniels as *Notes of a Revolutionary,* introduction by Susan Jacoby (New York: Knopf, 1982; London: Weidenfeld & Nicolson, 1982);

*Pogruzhenie v triasinu: Anatomiia zastoia,* by Amalrik and others, edited by A. N. Zav'ialova and N. K. Sazanovich (Moscow: Progress, 1991).

**Edition:** *Zapiski dissidenta* (Moscow: Slovo, 1991).

**Edition in English:** *East-West; and Is Uncle Jack a Conformist? Two plays,* translated by Daniel Weissbort, Methuen New Theatrescript, no. 4 (London: Eyre Methuen, 1976).

OTHER: "Russia and the Perplexing Prospects of Liberty," in *Eurocommunism: Its Roots and Future in Italy and Elsewhere,* edited by G. R. Urban (New York: Universe Books, 1978), pp. 236–254.

The dissident writer, playwright, poet, and historian Andrei Amalrik is best known for his 1969 essay *Prosushchestvuet li Sovetskii Soiuz do 1984 goda?* (translated as *Will the Soviet Union Survive until 1984?* 1970), the first work to predict openly the dissolution of the Soviet empire. His other books include the memoir *Nezhelannoe puteshestvie v Sibir'* (1970; translated as *Involuntary Journey to Siberia,* 1970), which recounts his first term of exile from Moscow; *P'esy* (*Plays,* 1970; translated as *Nose! Nose? No-se! and Other Plays,* 1973), a volume of absurdist plays; a biography of Grigorii Rasputin (translated, 1982; Russian version, 1992); a memoir of his later life, *Zapiski dissidenta* (1982; translated as *Notes of a Revolutionary,* 1982); and a collection of traditional poetry. Most of his works were published only abroad.

Andrei Alekseevich Amalrik was born in Moscow on 12 May 1938 into a family of dissidents: one of his paternal uncles was executed in a Stalinist purge, and another was sent to a prison camp. His father, Aleksei Amalrik, a student of history at Moscow University, was drafted into the army shortly after the Soviet Union invaded Poland in 1939. After the German army reached Moscow in 1941, the father was arrested for expressing the opinion that Joseph Stalin, who had decimated both the military officer corps and the populace as a whole, was himself to blame for the defeats. He was sent to the concentration camp on the island of Iagry in the White Sea. Amalrik and his mother were evacuated to Orenburg, on the frontier where Europe meets Asia, after the German bombardment of Moscow in 1941. Because of a shortage of competent officers, the father was

35

*Title page for the 1970 English-language edition of Amalrik's* Prosushchestvuet li Sovetskii Soiuz do 1984 goda? *(1969), in which he openly predicts the fall of the Soviet state (Thomas Cooper Library, University of South Carolina)*

released in 1942 to serve at the battle of Stalingrad. Amalrik and his mother returned to Moscow in 1943. Amalrik himself showed signs of rebellion as a boy: he did not want to join the Young Pioneers, the youth organization dedicated to instilling Communist ideology in its members. He often skipped school and was expelled for various periods of time, including all of the ninth grade. As a result, he had to take his high-school examinations externally.

Amalrik enrolled at Moscow University in 1959; like his father, he majored in history. His dissertation, "Normanny i Kievskaia Rus'" (The Norsemen and Kievan Russia), which argued that early Russian civilization was heavily influenced by Norse traders, contradicted the official Soviet doctrine that Russian culture and civilization were produced solely by the Slavs themselves. While his professors agreed that the work was brilliant, they told him that he would have to change his conclusions or else withdraw them and submit only his research to receive his degree. He refused to do either and was expelled in 1963. The action foreclosed any possibility of an academic career.

By this time Amalrik's father, who had been wounded by a mine in 1944 and had later suffered a series of strokes, had been officially declared an invalid. So that he would have time to care for his father, Amalrik took a variety of temporary jobs in 1963–1964; among these positions were cartographer, construction worker, postal worker, newspaper proofreader, laboratory assistant, translator, automobile-race timekeeper, movie projectionist, and artist's model.

Amalrik's love of stagecraft had begun in his childhood, when he spent time with an aunt who worked in a theater; at thirteen he constructed his own puppet theater and wrote and performed plays with two friends, and at fourteen he interviewed producers and actors to understand their professions better. In 1962 he read Velimir Vladimirovich Khlebnikov's *Mister Lenin* and felt an urge to write his own play. He made little progress, but in 1963 he read Eugène Ionesco's *La cantatrice chauve* (produced, 1950; published, 1953; translated as *The Bald Soprano,* 1958) and was so inspired that he wrote his first play in three days. Shortly thereafter, influenced by the works of Samuel Beckett, whom he considered a master of artistic organization, he completed five of the six plays that were later collected in *P'esy: Moia tetia zhivet v Volokolamske* (translated as *My Aunt is Living in Volokolamsk*), *Vostok-Zapad* (translated as *East-West: A Dialogue in Suzdal*), *Chetyrnadtsat' liubovnikov nekrasivoi Meri-Ènn* (translated as *The Fourteen Lovers of Ugly Mary-Ann*), *Konformist li diadia Dzhek?* (translated as *Is Uncle Jack a Conformist?*), and *Skazka prop belogo bychka* (translated as *The Story of the Little White Bull*). He also began to take an interest in avant-garde painters such as Anatolii Zverev and Dmitrii Plavinsky. He met other writers, artists, and—most dangerous for the time—foreigners, including an American diplomat and several journalists who shared his interest in avant-garde culture.

While writing his dissertation, Amalrik had corresponded with a Danish professor of Slavic languages who was sympathetic to his conclusions. In 1963 he took the dissertation to the Danish embassy and asked the officials to forward it to the professor. Fearing that Amalrik might be a Soviet agent sent to entrap them, the officials contacted the Ministry of Foreign Affairs, which turned the dissertation over to the KGB (Komissariat gosudarstvennoi bezopasnosti [State Security Committee]). This incident and Amalrik's collecting of avant-garde art aroused the government's suspicion, and he was put under surveillance by the Moscow Criminal Investigation Department.

In May 1965 Amalrik was arrested as a "parasite," because he did not have regular employment. The 1961 statute under which he was charged was ostensibly intended to deport alcoholics, workers with substantial absenteeism records, and other vagrants from cities such as Moscow and Leningrad to areas with inadequate workforces. Because he was living with and caring for his invalid father, Amalrik should have been exempt from prosecution; but as the statute was actually designed to be used against intellectuals who avoided full-time jobs to pursue artistic or scholarly endeavors that were not officially sanctioned, he was a prime target. While he was under preliminary detention, the police searched his apartment and confiscated the manuscripts for the five plays. The officer in charge told Amalrik that if he had explained that he was a writer, he could have avoided prosecution under the parasite statute: writing, the officer asserted, was true work; it just took time to be recognized. Also seized were the paintings by Zverev that were hanging on the walls of Amalrik's apartment and Zverev's illustrations for Amalrik's plays.

Under interrogation Amalrik asserted that the only person he had allowed to read the plays was Zverev, so that the latter could provide illustrations. The interrogator then leveled the accusation that the drawings and, therefore, the plays themselves were pornographic. Amalrik maintained that this characterization applied only to the illustrations; nevertheless, he was charged under Article 228 of the Russian Criminal Code with the production, harboring, and dissemination of pornography. Several days later he was questioned again about his plays by an interrogator who obviously had not read them. The next day all charges were suddenly dropped: the Union of Artists had declared that Zverev's paintings and illustrations were not pornography but the work of a madman; they declined to give an opinion of Amalrik's plays, stating that they were unable to define pornography. The charge of parasitism was then summarily reinstated. In the trial, however, the judge continued to discuss the plays, ignoring the issue of whether Amalrik had actually held legitimate employment. He was found guilty of parasitism and sentenced to two and a half years of internal exile with hard labor.

Amalrik was sent to a collective farm in the Tomsk region of Siberia. There he received news that his father was seriously ill. He was granted permission to visit his father for eighteen days, but bureaucratic delays prevented him from leaving Siberia until after his father had died. While in Moscow, Amalrik married Giuzel Makudinova, one of the avant-garde painters whose works he collected. She returned to Siberia with him.

In 1966 a court ruled that the parasite law did not apply to sole family members of officially declared invalids. The Amalriks were allowed to return to Moscow, and Andrei was given permission to seek employment as a journalist.

In 1969 Amalrik's essay *Prosushchestvuet li Sovetskii Soiuz do 1984 goda?* was published in Amsterdam. In the introduction added to the English version Amalrik says that in the fall of 1966 he had begun expressing to small groups of friends his belief that a crisis was approaching in the Soviet Union. In November 1967 he sent letters summarizing his ideas to *Literaturnaia gazeta* (Literary Gazette) and *Izvestiia* (News), both of which refused to publish them. In 1969 Amalrik wrote an article titled "Prosushchestvuet li Sovetskii Soiuz do 1980 goda?" (Will the Soviet Union Survive until 1980?). A friend well versed in English literature suggested that he change the date to 1984–the title of George Orwell's antitotalitarian 1949 novel. Amalrik agreed to the change, as 1984 was exactly fifteen years in the future.

In his essay Amalrik considers the significance of the changes that began after the death of Stalin and, in particular, after Communist Party First Secretary Nikita Khrushchev's "secret speech" denouncing Stalin at the Twentieth Congress of the party in February 1956. Were these changes, he asks, a sign of a potential restructuring of the Soviet system or a signal of its final decay and disintegration? While many others at the time held the former view, Amalrik argues for the latter. The Soviet Union is a top-heavy bureaucratic regime that has lost its revolutionary energy, is devolving toward entropy, and is teetering on the brink of stagnation and death. It must fundamentally change to survive, but its bureaucratic nature renders it incapable of doing so.

Many leftist Western intellectuals, as well as many Russian ones, placed a great deal of faith in a burgeoning Soviet middle class that had slowly been developing since the days of Stalin and would, in their minds, reenergize the Soviet government and make it more open, democratic, and reform minded. Amalrik, however, argues that the hoped-for constructive movement of the relatively small middle class will be doomed when faced with the violent and destructive power of the lower class. A typical trait of the Russian psyche, Amalrik says, when seeing how well one's neighbors are doing, is to desire not to bring oneself up to their level but to bring them down

*Title page for Amalrik's* Nezhelannoe puteshestvie v Sibir' *(1970; translated that year as* Involuntary Journey*), an account of his 1965 arrest, trial, and exile to Siberia (Joint University Libraries, Nashville, Tennessee)*

to one's own. This spiteful tendency will negate any opportunity for stability or improvement.

Another issue affecting the longevity of the Soviet Union, according to Amalrik, is its foreign policy—in particular, its relationship with China. Amalrik sees China as going through the same three revolutionary stages as the Soviet Union: it has already passed through the international stage and is currently in the national stage, exemplified by Mao Tse-tung's Cultural Revolution. Next will come the military-expansionist stage, and this final stage is what will threaten the U.S.S.R. China can expand in only one direction: north into Siberia. This expansion will lead to a war in which the U.S.S.R.'s supply and communication lines will be stretched dangerously thin. Furthermore, the guerrilla tactics Russia has successfully used against invading armies will not work as an offensive technique: the territory in which this war will be waged, Central Eurasia, is either sparsely populated or populated by non-Russians, which will make it easier for Chinese troops to maintain a foothold and run infiltration missions. Finally, Amalrik argues, citing an unnamed Soviet military expert, the Soviet infantry soldier is inferior to his Chinese counterpart. All these factors will lead to certain, if not quick, defeat. The Soviet Union will have to pull troops from Europe to support the Asian war effort, leaving a power vacuum that will allow the Eastern Bloc to break away from the Soviet Union. East and West Germany will reunify, and Romania and Czechoslovakia will immediately declare either neutrality or an intent to link themselves with the West. No Soviet response will be possible. Ethnic nationalism in republics such as Ukraine will threaten the stability and continuance of the Soviet Union itself.

Amalrik wrote *Nezhelannoe puteshestvie v Sibir'* in the late 1960s and smuggled the manuscript out to the West; it was published in New York in 1970. The first half is dedicated to his arrest, the search of his apartment, his interrogations, and his trial; Amalrik says that these experiences seemed as surreal and absurd as his plays. The second half is a detailed description of his life in Siberia. This part of the Soviet Union, which seemed as distant to educated citizens of Moscow or Leningrad as it did to the rest of the world, contains the most underprivileged populace in the nation. The Russian intelligentsia have traditionally had an idealized view of the peasantry, with whom they have had little contact; works such as *Nezhelannoe puteshestvie v Sibir'* and Aleksandr Solzhenitsyn's *V kruge pervom* (1968; translated as *The First Circle*, 1968) describe the disenchantment of intellectuals who were forced to work on collective farms. Amalrik says that forced collectivization has destroyed the peasants' traditional instincts and attachment to the Russian soil, destroying their mystique.

When these works were published in the West, and Amalrik was not immediately arrested, rumors arose that he was a KGB collaborator. They were dispelled when he was arrested in May 1970 and convicted the following November of slandering the Soviet state in his writings. He was again sentenced to imprisonment in a labor camp and spent nearly five years in Siberia. After his forced exile from the Soviet Union in 1976, Amalrik and his wife lived in the Netherlands, the United States, and France; he describes his experiences in Siberia and in exile in *Zapiski dissidenta,* posthumously published in 1982. On 11 November 1980, in Spain to attend an international conference on Soviet compliance with the 1975 Helsinki Accords on security and cooperation in Europe, he was killed in an automobile accident that was regarded with suspicion throughout the dissident community. The disintegration of the Soviet Communist regime that he had predicted occurred eleven years later; though it was not caused by a war with China, it was preceded by the breakup of the Eastern Bloc that he had also foreseen.

**References:**

Svetlana A. Borisova, "Soviet Dissidents, the Emergence of Their Dissent and the Importance of the Issues They Raised: A Case Study of Andrei Amalrik and Vladimir Bukovsky," M.A. thesis, Ohio State University, 1994;

John Glad, "Andrei Alekseevich Amalrik," in *Handbook of Russian Literature,* edited by Victor Terras (New Haven: Yale University Press, 1985), p. 20;

Andrea Gotzes, *Das dramatische Personal in den Stücken A. A. Amal'riks* (Mainz: Liber, 1985);

Jerilyn Ann Heinicke, "Eastern European Theater: Vaclav Havel and Andrei Amalrik," dissertation, Pennsylvania State University, 1993;

John Keep, "Andrei Amalrik and 1984," *Russian Review,* 30 (1971): 335–345;

Nancy Kindelan, "Dark Images of Dissidence: Modernism and Andrei Amalrik's *Nose! Nose? No-se!*" *Journal of Dramatic Theory and Criticism,* 7 (Fall 1992): 89–103;

Felicia Hardison Londre, "Andrei Amalrik's Dramatic Chronicles of Alienation," *Theater Three,* 10–11 (1992): 117–127;

Herta Schmid, "Postmodernism in Russian Drama: Vampilov, Amalrik, Aksenov," in *Approaching Postmodernism,* edited by Douwe W. Fokkema and Hans Bertens (Amsterdam: Benjamins, 1986);

John Brockway Schmor, "The Drama of Andrei Amal'rik–an Analysis," M.A. thesis, University of Oregon, 1989;

Jenny Stelleman, "Sense in a Fairy Tale about Non-Sense: 'Skazka pro belogo bychka' A. A. Amal'rik," *Russian, Croatian and Serbian, Czech and Slovak, Polish Literature,* 37, no. 4 (1995): 603–616.

# Natal'ia Vladimirovna Baranskaia

(18 December 1908- )

Benjamin M. Sutcliffe
*University of Pittsburgh*

BOOKS: *Otritsatel'naia Zhizel'* (Moscow: Molodaia gvardiia, 1977);

*Zhenshchina s zontikom* (Moscow: Sovremennik, 1981);

*Portret, podarennyi drugu* (Leningrad: Lenizdat, 1982);

*Den' pominoveniia* (Moscow: Sovetskii pisatel', 1989)–includes enlarged version of "Nedelia kak nedelia," which first appeared in *Zhenshchina s zontikom*;

*Stranstvie bezdomnykh: Zhizneopisanie: Semeinyi arkhiv. Starye al'bomy. Pis'ma raznykh let. Dokumenty. Vospominaniia moikh roditelei, ikh druzei. Moi sobstvennye vospominaniia*, with afterword by Il'ia Khanukaevich Urilov (Moscow, 1999).

**Edition in English:** *A Week Like Any Other: Novella and Short Stories,* as Natalya Baranskaya, translated by Pieta Monks (London: Virago, 1989)–includes "A Week Like Any Other," "The Petunin Affair," and "Lubka."

OTHER: *Russkaia periodicheskaia pechat'. (1702–1894). Spravochnik,* compiled, with contributions, by Baranskaia, N. S. Bulgakova, T. G. Denisman, and others (Moscow: Gospolitizdat, 1959);

*Zhizn' i lira. O zhizne velikogo russkogo poeta Aleksandra Pushkina, o ego chudesnoi lire, o tekh mestakh Rossii, gde on zhil, rabotal, radovalsia i liubil i tak mnogo stradal,* with contributions by Baranskaia, compiled by Evdoksiia Fedorovna Nikitina (Moscow: Kniga, 1970).

SELECTED PERIODICAL PUBLICATIONS–UNCOLLECTED: "The Alarm Clock in the Cupboard" (first English translation of "Nedelia kak nedelia"), translated by Beatrice Stillman, *Redbook* (March 1971): 179–201;

"Muzhchiny, beregite zhenshchin," *Literaturnaia gazeta,* 46 (1971): 13;

"The Retirement Party" (translation of "Provody"), translated by Anatole Forostenko, *Russian Literature Triquarterly,* 9 (1974): 136–144;

"Chemu raven iks?" *Iunost',* 5 (1974): 43–51;

"The Spell" (translation of "Koldovstvo"), translated by Sigrid McLaughlin, in *The Image of Women in Contemporary Soviet Fiction* (New York: St. Martin's Press, 1989), pp. 113–124;

"The Kiss" (translation of "Potselui"), translated by Wanda Sorgente, in *Balancing Acts* (Bloomington: Indiana University, 1989), pp. 1–5;

"Avtobiografiia bez umolchanii," *Grani,* 156 (1990): 122–148;

*Natal'ia Vladimirovna Baranskaia (Stranstvie bezdomnykh, 1990; Perkins Library, Duke University)*

"Laine's House" (translation by "Dom Laine"), translated by Gerald Mikkelson and Margaret Winchell, in *Soviet Women Writing* (New York: Abbeville Press, 1990), pp. 203-214;

"Avtobus s chernoi polosoi," *Grani,* 166 (1992): 5-51;

"Ptitsa," *Grani,* 166 (1992): 52-64;

"Vstrecha," *Grani,* 168 (1993): 38-41;

"Lesnaia poliana," *Grani,* 168 (1993): 42-62;

"Udivitel'nye shariki," *Grani,* 168 (1993): 62-86;

"Fotografiia Zoiki na fone dvora," *Grani,* 168 (1993): 86-113.

Natal'ia Baranskaia's life prepared her for the role she played in the history of twentieth-century Russian literature: documenting both the quotidian and national tragedy from a woman's viewpoint. A well-educated working mother who raised two children on her own, she knows firsthand the burdens faced by female members of the Russian intelligentsia. Personal experiences and those of her generation reinforced Baranskaia's belief that compassion and responsibility are moral imperatives.

Baranskaia was born Natal'ia Vladimirovna Radchenko on 18 December 1908 in St. Petersburg to Liubov' Nikolaevna Radchenko and Vladimir Nikolaevich Rozanov. Both parents, who never married, were involved in revolutionary activity. In 1906 they were elected to the Central Committee of the Russian Social-Democratic Workers' Party (Mensheviks) at the Fourth Congress of the party. In 1910 they were arrested and, upon their release, immigrated first to Switzerland and then to Germany. In 1915 the seven-year-old Rozanova returned to Russia with Liubov' Nikolaevna, while Vladimir Nikolaevich remained in the West. In 1921, living again in Russia, he was sentenced to death by a revolutionary tribunal because of his Menshevik activities. This verdict was changed to imprisonment, and he was later freed under amnesty. In 1922 Roznova entered Moscow's Model School No. 1 in Moscow and participated in the Blue Blouse propaganda group. In 1926 she began studying in Higher State Literature Courses despite her mother's second arrest and subsequent exile to Voronezh.

Rozanova graduated in 1930 from the Department of History and Ethnology at Moscow State University and in the same year received a degree in literature from the Advanced State Literature Course. At nineteen she married a fellow student, whom she identifies only by the initials "V. M. L." She later discovered that he was an *agent provocateur* who testified against former friends and inspired Baranskaia to write the dark fantastic story "Avtobus s chernoi polosoi" in 1975. They divorced in 1932. She subsequently met Nikolai Nikolaevich Baransky while living near Moscow. Baransky became her second husband in 1936. After the June 1941 German invasion of the U.S.S.R., by which time they had a son and daughter, Nikolai was mobilized and died on 12 August 1943. Baranskaia received notice of his death in October 1943 while living in Altai, where she and the children had been evacuated after first being sent to Saratov. In November of the same year Baranskaia and her son and daughter returned to Moscow. From 1943 until the death of Joseph Stalin in March 1953, Baranskaia struggled to provide for her children and not discourage them with the bitterness she felt toward the Soviet government for both wartime privation and the arrests of the 1930s. The latter had claimed family members and acquaintances, as Baranskaia describes in *Stranstvie bezdomnykh: Zhizneopisanie: Semeinyi arkhiv. Starye al'bomy. Pis'ma raznykh let. Dokumenty. Vospominaniia moikh roditelei, ikh druzei. Moi sobstvennye vospominaniia* (1999, The Journey of the Homeless: A Biography: Family Archive. Old Albums. Letters from Various Years. Documents. Recollections of My Parents and Their Friends. My Own Recollections). She was also horrified by the anti-Semitic sentiments behind Stalin's postwar campaigns against "rootless cosmopolitans" and the discovery of the fictionalized "Doctors' Plot." In 1952 her first publication appeared. "Puteshestvie iz Peterburga v Moskvu A. N. Radishcheva i ustnoe narodnoe tvorchestvo 18 veka" (A. N. Radishchev's Journey from Petersburg to Moscow and Oral Folk Art in the Eighteenth Century) came out in *Izvestiia AN SSR (Otdelenie iazyka i literatury)* (Bulletin of the USSR Academy of Sciences [Division of Language and Literature]). Baranskaia's pre-1969 publications have been overlooked by critics, who focus instead on her fictional and semi-autobiographical writings.

In 1958 she helped to found and oversee the Pushkin Memorial Museum on Arbat Street in Moscow until 1966, when she left the museum. Her "retirement," as she notes in *Stranstvie bezdomnykh* and "Autobiografiia bez umolchanii," was caused by official anger over her inviting the dissident poet Joseph Brodsky to an exhibition. The exhibition included a photograph of the poet Anna Andreevna Akhmatova, Akhmatova's former husband Nokolai Stepanovich Gumilev, who had been executed in 1921, and their son, who was arrested several times and imprisoned from 1949-1956. The administration was also upset over her earlier refusal to condemn Boris Leonidovich Pasternak for his novel *Doktor Zhivago* (1957).

In *Stranstvie bezdomnykh* Baranskaia notes that after her retirement "The 'gift of words' appeared," and at the age of fifty-eight she began to write fiction. Her narratives are shaped by the themes of maternal love, women's strength, war and loss, and by the connections among mothers, homeland *(rodina)*, and nature. Many of the events and situations that she ascribes to her fictional characters arise from her own life.

In 1969 Baranskaia published her best-known and most influential work, "Nedelia kak nedelia" (translated as "The Alarm Clock in the Cupboard," 1989), in the journal *Novyi mir* (New World), then headed by the liberal critic and author Aleksandr Trifonovich Tvardovsky. This *povest'*, or novella, is about the life of Ol'ga Nikolaevna Voronkova, a twenty-six-year-old married mother of two, who is also the narrator. Told in the present tense, "Nedelia kak nedelia" describes events that occur during the workweek and the weekend; it is divided into seven chapters that correspond to the days of the week, Monday through Sunday. The exception to this temporal framework is a flashback to Ol'ga's university days, when she fell in love with Dima, the man who became her husband. Images of movement dominate the novella, and its narrative style is derived from Ol'ga's half-completed thoughts as she rushes from one task to another.

Ol'ga struggles to balance work at a Moscow scientific institute with an ongoing cycle of chores, sick children, and other domestic crises. Her son, Kot'ka, attends kindergarten, and her daughter, Gul'ka, is in nursery school. Baranskaia presents the central theme of the novella, motherhood, in its most banal manifestation—as an endless and exhausting series of crises, shortages, and disasters narrowly avoided. Since Ol'ga and Dima live in a neighborhood that, while new, is distant from the center of the city, she must travel on buses, trams, and subways to reach her place of work. During the week that is the focus of the novella, she and her coworkers (all women, except for one supervisor) are filling out a questionnaire, the aim of which is to find out why Russian women are reluctant to give birth. (Baranskaia's novella appeared at the beginning of a demographic crisis in the U.S.S.R. tinged with racist overtones; the government was alarmed by falling birthrates in Soviet Russia, while the populations of republics in Central Asia and the Caucasus were increasing.) In discussing the problem of marriage and children with her coworkers, Ol'ga tells both herself and the reader that she is fortunate: Dima is faithful and reliable, does not drink, and takes an interest in Kot'ka and Gul'ka. He does, however, assume that Ol'ga will mend his pants and quiet the children while he does some reading for work (a "luxury" for which Ol'ga has no time).

"Nedelia kak nedelia" drew much publicity and spawned debates in Soviet newspapers about the professional and domestic difficulties women then were facing. It was one of the first works published in the Soviet Union that substantially discussed the tribulation of women's *byt*, or everyday life. Baranskaia received a large amount of mail from women who thanked her for bringing their problems to the attention of the public. Translated into several foreign languages, "Nedelia kak nedelia" was republished in a longer version in 1989 in the volume *Den' pominoveniia* (Day of Remembrance).

"Nedelia kak nedelia" has been interpreted in two different ways. For many Soviet critics, especially during the 1970s, it illustrated the problems faced by women as members of society who raise children and encounter complications in maintaining both a home and a career. Baranskaia herself asserted this opinion in a 1981 interview. Many Western feminists, however, see her novella as evidence of women's exploitation at the hands of a fundamentally indifferent society and state. In this sense Ol'ga's continual sense of frustration and impending failure reflects her inability to fulfill the impossible demands of a male-oriented society. She likewise is unable to see the larger pattern of gendered discrimination that victimizes her.

In 1970–1978 Baranskaia published several short stories and novellas in major literary journals and collections issued by prominent publishers. In 1977 several appeared in the book *Otritsatel'naia Zhizel'* (Negative Giselle). One of these stories, "Proisshestvie s Petuninym" (translated as "The Petunin Affair," 1989), is unusual. The narrator is Petunin, a middle-aged man who works for a newspaper in the fictional provincial city of Lopatinsk and is assigned to help with a television broadcast on the evils of alcoholism. (Depictions of alcoholism can be found in many of Baranskaia's works.) Petunin begins to realize that his new supervisor, the energetic Petriaev, is using the broadcast as a means of self-promotion. The broadcast is a scandalous failure: Petriaev drinks from a pitcher in which water has been replaced with vodka, and the live broadcast is cut short. Petunin is blamed, and Petriaev—supported by the local Communist Party organization—launches a campaign against him. Petriaev's secretary, Nina, defends Petunin, who meanwhile has been given a temporary assignment in a distant town. Nina and Petunin later become lovers. This final development occurs mainly because Nina's son, Petia, has become fond of Petunin; the similarity of their names also evokes the close connection between them.

Setting is also significant. In *A History of Russian Women's Writing, 1820–1992* (1994) Catriona Kelly notes that the office setting in much of the story shows "the fluid and dynamic relationships of the workplace, a locus dominated by women in most Baranskaia narratives." While the office is replaced by Ol'ga's institute in "Nedelia kak nedelia," the emphasis on conversation and camaraderie remains.

*Liubka* (translated as "Lubka," 1989), a *povest'* that also appeared in the collection *Otritsatel'naia Zhizel'*, begins with old women criticizing their eighteen-year-old neighbor Liubka as she walks by proudly. The young woman then is publicly harangued at a housing hearing, where she must defend her behavior against the hostile and hypocritical neighbors from her communal apartment. The neighbors accuse her of hosting loud parties for various young people who, the neighbors imply, stay the night. The third-person narrator retells the sad details of Liubka's life via flashbacks that Baranskaia intersperses throughout the hearing. Praskov'ia, Liubka's mother, is a helpless alcoholic who lost her husband during World War II and then drifted from one man to another. (She does not know the identity of Liubka's father.) Liubka left high school without receiving her diploma after being humiliated by the friends of Sen'ka, an older classmate, with whom she reluctantly had sex. Her mother, who is asleep through most of the hearing, adored Liubka as a child—in Russian the name Liubka means "love." Mikhail, a Komsomol activist at Liubka's factory, defends her by embellishing her involvement at work. The housing authority decides merely to reprimand Liubka instead of forcing her to move to another city. She and Mikhail begin dating, and the *povest'* ends with her half-serious announcement to her friends that there will be no more parties at her apartment, since she may be getting married.

As with "Proisshestvie s Petuninym," the themes of alcoholism and single motherhood play a prominent role in *Liubka*. In discussing her protagonist's precocious and disappointing sexual experiences, Baranskaia also gives a sympathetic picture of Soviet youth, who at that time were facing problems created in large measure by an often uncaring and hypocritical older generation. Yet, the novella also bears a strong allegiance to clichéd commonplaces of Soviet literature: the Komsomol takes an active and sympathetic interest in Liubka, and its personification—Mikhail—ultimately "reforms" her through his proposal of marriage. Likewise, Zalomin, the chairman of the court, is more interested in helping Liubka than in punishing her. By extension the attitude of the state toward young people can be read as a recognition of, and an attempt to correct, the difficulties they encounter.

"Otritsatel'naia Zhizel'," the title story of the 1977 collection, describes what happens when Klavdiia Ivanovna takes Slava, her adolescent daughter, to the Bolshoi Ballet. During the performance the third-person narrator describes the thoughts of mother and teenager. Slava laughs at her mother's old-fashioned and pompous sense of fashion, which Klavdiia has derived from "self-improvement" books with ridiculous titles such as

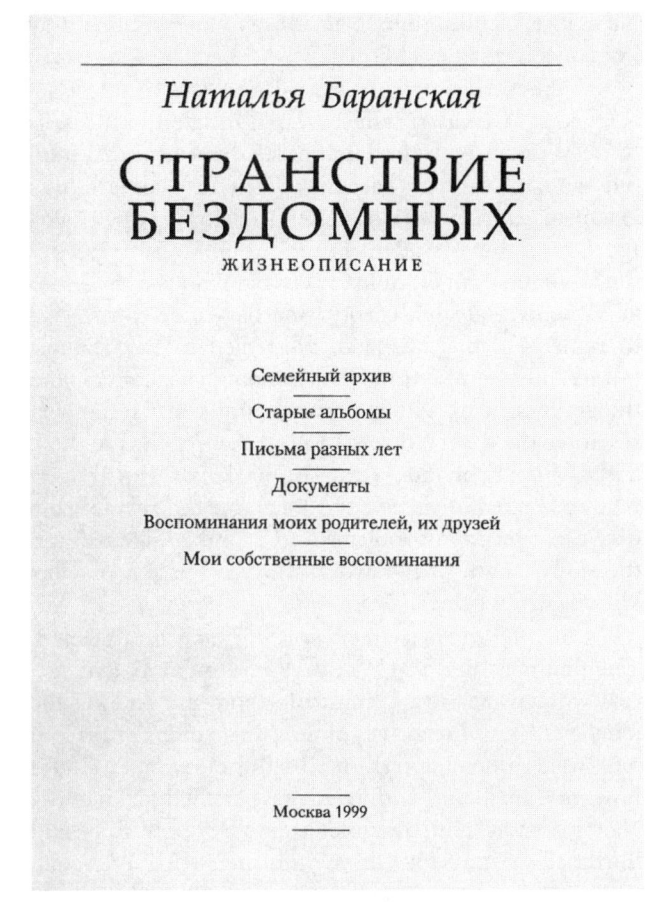

*Title page for Baranskaia's* Stranstvie bezdomnykh: Zhizneopisanie: Semeinyi arkhiv. Starye al'bomy. Pis'ma raznykh let. Dokumenty. Vospominaniia moikh roditelei, ikh druzei. Moi sobstvennye vospominaniia *(The Journey of the Homeless: A Biography: Family Archive. Old Albums. Letters from Various Years. Documents. Recollections of My Parents and Their Friends. My Own Recollections; Perkins Library, Duke University)*

*Khoroshii vkus* (Good Taste) and *Iskusstvo odevat'sia* (The Art of Dressing). Klavdiia worries about how the loose morals of Giselle, the heroine of the opera, will influence Slava. The narrator shows, however, that such moral concerns exist alongside the corrupting love of material objects repeatedly depicted in Soviet literature of the 1960s and 1970s.

Baranskaia's long story "Tsvet temnogo medu" (The Color of Dark Honey) appeared in 1977 in the journal *Sibir'* (Siberia). Blending history and fiction, the story describes Natal'ia Nikolaevna Pushkina in the first few months after the 1837 death of her husband, the famous poet Aleksandr Sergeevich Pushkin. While historians and memoirists traditionally have blamed Natal'ia's flirtatious manner for Pushkin's death (he was killed in a duel with Baron Georges d'Anthès-Heeckeren, who had been pursuing Pushkin's wife for some time), in "Tsvet temnogo medu" Baranskaia sees

Natal'ia as victimized by high-society maneuvers and by her concern for her children.

The title story of Baranskaia's 1981 collection, *Zhenshchina s zontikom,* which was translated in 1989 as "The Woman with the Umbrella," describes a mysterious woman (carrying an umbrella) who wanders by a group of *dachniki,* or vacationers, relaxing near a lake. Igor', a graduate student in the group, converses with the woman stranger, Sofiia L'vovna, who is a professor at Moscow State University. She has come to the lake to remember her husband, who died in the Stalinist purges. The rural setting, the gossiping vacationers, and the grave tone of "Zhenshchina s zontikom" somewhat resemble the short stories of Anton Pavlovich Chekhov. This comparison applies to Baranskaia's works as a whole: her use of irony; the focus on the relationship between everyday problems and moral problems; and the short length of her works are reminiscent of Chekhov's own writings.

In 1989 the novel *Den' pominoveniia* was published. The plot describes the World War II memories of several women on a train, most of whom are making the journey to visit the graves of their husbands. The novel has twenty-one chapters, in which each woman relates how her husband and relatives perished during the Nazi invasion, and Baranskaia employs both first- and third-person narrators throughout the work. Although the women are strangers when they first board the train on 9 May 1970, in many cases their fates already have intersected. For example, while in exile during the war, the Muscovite Mariia Nikolaevna asked the Siberian Feodos'ia Nikitichna for milk; Nonna Romanovna's children were sent to the Altai orphanage where Mariia Nikolaevna worked after fleeing the capital. Those who lived under German occupation relate horrifying acts of brutality and incongruous mercy. Some of the women discuss prewar memories: Mariia Nikolaevna remembers the muted fear she and her husband felt during the mass arrests of 1937. The novel also describes folk songs and rural courtship rituals and alludes to the famines and upheavals of collectivization.

As is typical in Soviet (and post-Soviet) literature, none of the women make reference to the 1939–1941 cooperation between German and Soviet forces. Likewise, there are veiled and overt references to American warmongering but no mention of the disastrous 1979–1989 Soviet involvement in Afghanistan. *Den' pominoveniia* is a testament to national apocalypse, in which memory proves to be selective and exclusionary. It blends autobiography and fiction and ends with Baranskaia's own statement concerning her husband's death in 1943. Mariia Nikolaevna's life reflects that of Baranskaia, in that her patronymic, Nikolaevna, comes from the first name of the author's second husband; in addition, she, too, must flee to Altai and then contend with cold and hunger after returning to wartime Moscow.

This novel is the apotheosis of Baranskaia's principal themes—motherhood as moral force, wartime privation, the importance of personal responsibility, and the connection between mothers, homeland, and nature. Writing in the *Dictionary of Russian Women Writers* (1994), Helena Goscilo sees these themes as "essentialist convictions regarding the primacy of women's maternal conviction; their capacity for stoic patience, love, and acceptance." Women are presented as an often idealized collection of positive attributes reaffirming traditional Slavic and Western ideas of woman as physically and spiritually pure. In *Fruits of Her Plume: Essays on Contemporary Russian Women's Culture* (1993), Thomas Lahusen compares *Den' pominoveniia* to Chingiz Torekulovich Aitmatov's *I dol'she veka dlitsia den'* (1981, The Day Lasts Longer than a Hundred Years), which also focuses on connections among ecology, cultural memory, and loss—although here the maternal motif is not as all-encompassing as in *Den pominoveniia.*

In 1999 Baranskaia published *Stranstvie bezdomnykh,* a work of more than five hundred pages. Its lengthy subtitle summarizes its contents: an account of Baranskaia's family from the late 1800s until 1941. In his afterword to the book Il'ia Khanukaevich Urilov calls *Stranstvie bezdomnykh* a description of the "fate of the Russian intelligentsia," or more precisely, how Baranskaia represents this fate. Urilov suggests that the intellectuals of Russia ultimately are viewed as victims, and particular emphases are placed on the purges of the Stalin years and, by extension, on Baranskaia's changing assessment of the ideologies that created them. In describing the relationship between the individual and collective experience, *Stranstvie bezdomnykh* resembles *Den' pominoveniia.* The latter work begins where the former ends: the horrors of the German invasion and the difficult years following the war.

Despite its unifying themes (motherhood, loss, and responsibility) and style, Baranskaia's work is difficult to classify vis-à-vis Russian literary history. She wrote mainly during the Stagnation and inertia that marked the administration of Leonid Ilych Brezhnev. Yet, her works also have many of the characteristics of literature written during the period of the Thaw, which followed Stalin's death: documentary style (as in "Nedelia kak nedelia," in which daily events are recounted) and an emphasis on literature as conveying personal experience. These themes exist alongside ones common during the Brezhnev years: connections between daily life and moral problems (deliberations over the fate of the wayward protagonist in the novella *Liubka*) and a focus on urban life. In this respect Baranskaia's stories often resemble those of Iurii Valentinovich

Trifonov, who focused on both individual responsibility and collective trauma (the Stalinist purges and, to a lesser extent, World War II). Many of these themes also dominated both perestroika and post-Soviet literature, however: the few references to Stalinism in *Den' pominoveniia* are developed in Anatolii Naumovich Rybakov's *Deti Arbata* (1987; translated as *Children of the Arbat,* 1988) and in the first volume of Vassily Aksyonov's *Moskovskaia saga* (1993, 1994, Moscow Saga), titled *Pokoleniia zimy* (translated as *Generations of Winter,* 1994). Russian literature of the 1980s and 1990s also expanded on references to sexual promiscuity (as seen in Baranskaia's *Liubka*) and rape (as seen in her *Den' pominoveniia*).

Despite her assertions that her works are not feminist, Baranskaia incorporates themes and situations in her narrative fiction that often are conducive to a feminist interpretation by critics. *Den' pominoveniia* equates the violence of war with a world of men estranged from both women (in the form of wives, mothers, and daughters) and nature. In a similar manner, in "Nedelia kak nedelia" Kot'ka thinks that his father, Dima, is physically hurting his mother, Ol'ga, during an argument; the boy is mistaken, but the novella, nonetheless, hints at domestic abuse, which authors such as Liudmila Stefanovna Petrushevskaia have explored extensively. Men are also destructive in less direct ways. For example, Liubka's life has been marred both by her absent father and by the crass Sen'ka. Dima's reluctance to do housework embitters Ol'ga, but she still considers herself luckier than any of her married coworkers.

Baranskaia's work does not connect isolated instances of abuse, mistreatment, or discrimination, however, into a systematic differentiation between the duties and expectations of men and women. She does not believe that society conditions women according to inherently "marginalizing" attitudes. Rather, Baranskaia stresses that women—a category that her works often make synonymous with "mother"—are distinct from their male counterparts. A heightened degree of responsibility and morality comes with this distinction, as shown by the suffering mothers of *Den' pominoveniia.*

Regardless of her relationship with feminism, Natal'ia Vladimirovna Baranskaia created a precedent for the depiction of women's lives in mainstream, official literature. During the 1960s and 1970s her oeuvre influenced Viktoriia Samoilovna Tokareva, and, along with Irina Grekova (pseudonym of Elena Sergeevna Venttsel'), shaped women's prose. These authors and their successors illustrated the difficulties of balancing professional and home life—an elaboration of the "double burden" of work and household described in "Nedelia kak nedelia." During perestroika and the post-Soviet years, the portrayals of women's problems grow more stark, from the psychic and physical abuse that Petrushevskaya pairs with the family to Svetlana Vladimirovna Vasilenko's depictions of rape and abortion. (Of these authors, only Vasilenko labels herself a feminist.) All of these women authors and Russian culture as a whole are indebted to Baranskaia for using the medium of literature to draw attention to women's experiences and problems.

**Interviews:**

Samuel Rachlin, Interview with Natal'ia Baranskaia, in *Russian Women* [documentary], Danish Televison Studios, 1981;

Pieta Monks, "Natalya Baranskaya," in *Writing Lives: Conversations between Women Writers,* edited by Mary Chamberlain (London: Virago, 1988), pp. 25–36;

Sylvia Gressler, "Natalja Baranskaja zu einigen Aspekten ihres werkes. Ein Interview," *Osteuropa,* 7 (1990): 558–592.

**Bibliographies:**

Helena Goscilo, "Baranskaia, Natal'ia Vladimirovna," in *Dictionary of Russian Women Writers,* edited by Marina Ledkovsky, Charlotte Rosenthal, and Mary Zirin (Westport, Conn.: Greenwood Press, 1994), pp. 55–57;

Maureen Riley, "Natal'ia Baranskaia," in *Russian Women Writers,* 2 volumes, edited by Christine B. Tomei (New York: Garland, 1999), II: 1277–1299;

T. A. Shchepakova, "Baranskaia, Natal'ia Vladimirovna," in *Russkie pisateli 20 veka: Biograficheskii slovar',* edited by P. A. Nikolaev (Moscow: Bol'shaia rossiiskaia entsiklopediia, 2000), pp. 72–73.

**References:**

E. Kashkarova, "Zhenskaia tema v proze 60-kh godov: Natal'ia Baranskaia kak zerkalo russkogo feminizma," *Vse liudi sestri,* 5 (1996): 57–69;

Catriona Kelly, *A History of Russian Women's Writing, 1820–1992* (Oxford: Clarendon Press, 1994), pp. 397–409;

Vadim Evgen'evich Kovsky, "Chelovek v mire tvorchestva," *Znamia,* 11 (1970): 224–226;

Thomas Lahusen, "'Leaving Paradise' and *Perestroika: A Week Like Any Other* and *Memorial Day* by Natal'ia Baranskaia," in *Fruits of Her Plume: Essays on Contemporary Russian Women's Culture,* edited by Helena Goscilo (Armonk, N.Y.: M. E. Sharpe, 1993), pp. 205–224;

Iurii Ivanovich Surovtsev, "Vozmozhnosti 'kamernoi' povesti," *Zvezda,* 2 (1971): 191–201;

Nicholas Žekulin, "Changing Perspectives on the Prose of Natalia Baranskaya," *Canadian Slavonic Papers,* 35 (1993): 235–248.

# Vasilii Ivanovich Belov
*(23 October 1932 –   )*

David Gillespie
*University of Bath*

BOOKS: *Dereven'ka moia lesnaia* (Vologda: Vologodskoe knizhnoe izdatel'stvo, 1961);

*Znoinoe leto* (Vologda: Vologodskoe knizhnoe izdatel'stvo, 1963);

*Rechnye izluki* (Moscow: Molodaia gvardiia, 1964);

*Tisha da Grisha* (Moscow: Sovetskaia Rossiia, 1966);

*Za tremia volokami* (Moscow: Sovetskii pisatel', 1968);

*Plotnitskie rasskazy* (Arkhangel'sk: Severo-Zapadnoe knizhnoe izdatel'stvo, 1968);

*Katiushin dozhdik* (Voronezh: Tsentral'no-Chernozemskoe knizhnoe izdatel'stvo, 1969);

*Sel'skie povesti* (Moscow: Molodaia gvardiia, 1971);

*Den' za dnem* (Moscow: Sovetskii pisatel', 1972);

*Kholmy: Povesti, rasskazy, ocherki* (Moscow: Sovremennik, 1973);

*Idu domoi (Rasskazy)* (Arkhangel'sk: Severo-Zapadnoe knizhnoe izdatel'stvo, 1973);

*Nad svetloi vodoi (P'esa v dvukh aktakh)* (Moscow: VAAP, 1975);

*Tseluitsia zori* (Moscow: Molodaia gvardiia, 1975);

*Utrom v subbotu* (Arkhangel'sk: Severo-Zapadnoe knizhnoe izdatel'stvo, 1976);

*Rasskazy o vsiakoi zhivnosti* (Moscow: Detskaia literatura, 1976);

*Kanuny* (Moscow: Sovremennik, 1976; enlarged edition, Moscow: Molodaia gvardiia, 1989);

*Gudiat provoda* (Moscow: Sovetskaia Rossiia, 1978);

*Vospitanie po doktoru Spoku. Sbornik prozy* (Moscow: Sovremennik, 1978);

*Po 206-oi (Tseny iz raionnoi zhizni)* (Moscow: VAAP, 1979);

*Povesti i rasskazy* (Moscow: Izvestiia, 1980);

*Lad: Ocherki o narodnoi estetike* (Moscow: Molodaia gvardiia, 1982);

*Povesti* (Moscow: Khudozhestvennaia literatura, 1982);

*Tri p'esy* (Moscow: Sovetskii pisatel', 1983);

*Razdum'ia na rodine* (Moscow: Sovremennik, 1986; enlarged, 1989);

*Vse vperedi* (Moscow: Sovetskii pisatel', 1987);

*Bukhtiny vologodskie* (Moscow: Sovremennik, 1988);

*Remeslo otchuzhdeniia: Biurokratiia i ekologiia* (Moscow: Sovetskaia Rossiia, 1988);

*From the frontispiece for the 1994 edition of* Kanuny; *Suzzallo and Allen Libraries, University of Washington*

*Bobrishnyi ugor* (Moscow: Detskaia literatura, 1988);

*Za tremia volokami Povesti* (Moscow: Khudozhestvennaia literatura, 1989);

*Takaia voina. Rasskazy* (Moscow: Sovetskaia Rossiia, 1989);

*God velikogo pereloma* (Moscow: Khudozhestvennaia literatura, 1991);
*Vnemli sebe* (Moscow: Skify, 1993);
*God velikogo pereloma* (Moscow: Golos, 1994);
*Vologodskie bukhtiny: Starye i perestroechnye* (Vologda: Russkii Sever-Partner, 1997);
*Chas shestyi* (Moscow: Golos, 1999);
*Zapiski na khodu* (Moscow: Paleia, 1999);
*Povsednevnaia zhizn' russkogo Severa* (Moscow: Molodaia gvardiia, 2000);
*Povest' ob odnoi doroge* (Moscow: Sovetskii pisatel', 2001);
*Tiazhest' kresta: Shukshin v kadre i za kadrom,* by Belov and Anatolii Dmitrievich Zabolotsky (Moscow: Sovetskii pisatel', 2002);
*Medovyi mesiats* (Moscow: Druzhba narodov, 2002).

**Editions and Collections:** *Sobranie sochinenii,* 5 volumes (Moscow: Sovremennik, 1991–1993);
*V krovnom rodstve* (Kurgan: Zaural'e, 1996);
*Propavshie bez vesti* (Vologda: Russkii Sever-Partner, 1997);
*Tikhaia moia rodina . . . Rasskazy, povest'* (Ua: Kitap, 1998).

**Editions in English:** *Morning Rendezvous: Stories* (Moscow: Raduga Publishers, 1983);
*The Best Is Yet To Come* (Moscow: Raduga Publishers, 1989).

OTHER: Anatolii Peredreev, *Lebed' u dorogi: Stikhotvoreniia, perevody, razmyshleniia o poezii,* compiled by Sh. A. Peredreeva, foreword by Belov (Moscow: Sovremennik, 1990).

In the 1960s and 1970s Vasilii Ivanovich Belov was known as one of the most lyrical of the village writers, and some of his works from those years have become classical examples of "village prose." His interest in the fate of the Russian rural community, its culture, and traditions have led him into much darker areas, however, especially since the years of glasnost. In addition, unafraid of courting controversy over the explicit anti-Semitic sentiments of some of his later works, he has associated himself with extreme nationalistic views. Still, there is a clear trajectory in his thinking—one that is of great interest in any consideration of Russian literature at the end of the twentieth century.

Vasilii Ivanovich Belov was born on 23 October 1932 in the village of Timonikha, Vologda district, into the family of a peasant; his parents were Ivan Fedorovich Belov and Anfisa Ivanovna (Kokliushkina) Belova. He attended school in a neighboring town and worked at various jobs (carpenter, electrician, and tractor driver) before doing military service in 1952–1955. He joined the Communist Party in 1956, the same year he began his literary career by working as a journalist at a local newspaper. In 1959–1964 he studied at the Moscow Literary Institute and was accepted into the Union of Soviet Writers in 1963. Since 1964 he has lived mainly in Vologda. Since the 1980s Belov has become increasingly involved in the Writers' Union; he served in 1990 as secretary of the Russian Writers' Union. In 1981 he was awarded the State Prize in literature.

Belov's interest is in the old village and the old ways. When he touches on modern issues his mood is invariably dark and downbeat. His first published work was a book of poetry, *Dereven'ka moia lesnaia* (My Little Village in the Forest, 1961). Though naive and sentimental, the poems of this collection embody the germ of his thought (they lack, however, the political and ideological ramifications of later works). Here he introduces the theme of the "prodigal son," who returns to his rural roots after time spent away, usually in the city. The joy of returning to the countryside and the idyll of childhood are prominent motifs, as is the sadness of lost values and customs, such as the songs that are now forgotten. Yet, the natural world survives, and villagers continue to live and work in harmony with nature and in accordance with the passage of the seasons.

Belov's first major prose work, the novella *Derevnia Berdiaika* (The Village Berdiaika, first published 1961 in *Nash sovremennik* [Our Contemporary]) continues these themes. A man returns to his native village after some time working in the town and, although much of the communal spirit remains, is troubled by the changes taking place. Human activity nonetheless runs according to the rhythms of nature. Life returns after the dead night of winter, and the community remains united in the defense of one of their own against the urban-based authorities. In subsequent works of the early 1960s, delight in the natural world, often lyrically expressed in the author's word pictures and vivid evocations, is accompanied by anxiety over the increasing incursions of the modern world. Thus, in the short story "Na rodine" (Back Home, published in *Vologodskii komsomolets,* 1962) the narrator's memory of a sweet idyllic childhood spent in the bosom of nature is interrupted by the roar of a jet overhead. In "Za tremia volokami" (Beyond Three Portages, first published 1965 in *Sever* [The North]) a soldier returning to his native village remembers the tranquility of his childhood. With little more than a mile to go, he becomes increasingly excited at the prospect of seeing his home and is devastated to discover that his village has now disappeared; instead of houses there are only fields.

With the publication of "Privychnoe delo" (That's How It Is) in *Sever* in 1966, Belov came into the public eye. He not only captured a way of life that many thought had disappeared but also introduced a

*Cover for the 1994 edition of Belov's novel* Kanuny (The Eves), *first published in 1976, expanded and republished in 1989*

character who is of his time and yet as old as the forests themselves. Ivan Afrikanovich Drynov is a peasant with a child-like understanding of the unity of the natural world and an intuitive appreciation of the majesty and beauty of nature. As he walks through frost-covered fields his consciousness merges with the snow, sun, and sky—"with all the smells and sounds of the everlasting Spring"—and time stands still. Even his animals have their own personalities and ways of looking at the world. Ivan Afrikanovich has a store of words and expressions that show his link with the oral heritage of folk culture, and the course of human life correlates with the passage of the seasons.

The organic unity of this world is broken when the outside world intrudes. Ivan Afrikanovich is persuaded by his brother-in-law to look for work and earn more money in the town. As he leaves by train his wife Katerina—traumatized by the prospect of looking after nine children alone and by the work she continues to do in the fields—suffers a heart attack and dies. Social disruption therefore leads to personal tragedy. Afterward, as he reflects on her passing, Ivan Afrikanovich comes to an understanding of death not as the end of all things but, rather, as a natural process. He realizes that life in all its manifestations goes on and that he is a fundamental link in the natural scheme of things.

In creating the character of Ivan Afrikanovich, Belov offered Soviet literature a new type of hero, one that was radically different from the politically enlightened "positive hero" demanded by Socialist Realism. Some critics attacked Ivan Afrikanovich because of his social passivity and called for the depiction of "people capable of changing things," but Belov's hero offered a rejection of ideology and positivism. Here was a character formed from centuries of life and work on the land and in harmony with the natural world, a national type based on recognizably Russian values and traditions.

Belov's most important short story is "Bobrishnyi ugor" (Bobrishnyi Hill, published in *Lituraturnaia Rossiia*, 1967), precisely because it offers the key to his perception of nature. In this story Belov suggests that the village is man's home and the source of his inspiration. The natural world is where man's morality is determined—through his emotional and spiritual interaction with the forces of nature: "When we fish we are no longer ourselves, we have dissolved, become part of eternal nature, we have merged with the river, the bushes and the grass, the sky, the wind and the birds, when you forget who you are." This sense of home and spiritual communion is essential for man's inner peace and his workings in the greater world.

Belov returned to this type in his next major work of fiction, *Plotnitskie rasskazy* (Carpenters' Tale, published in 1968 in *Novyi mir* [New World] and in book form), although the idyll of rural life is disturbed here not by the urban threat but by history. Olesha Smolin has a saint-like passivity and acceptance of the world; he is an honest tiller of the soil and is consistently associated with the color white. He is contrasted, however, with Aviner Kozonkov, a malicious and destructive old peasant who took part in collectivization some thirty years earlier (not out of any ideological conviction but in order to settle scores with those he imagined had wronged him). Olesha and Aviner may be opposites, but they comprise the inseparable and integral, if mutually antagonistic, aspects of village life. As Olesha says, "All our lives we've been arguing, but we can't live without each other. He pops by every day, and at the slightest thing he's threatening me with his stick. That's how it's been since we were kids."

In *Plotnitskie rasskazy* the narrative is filtered through the consciousness of Konstantin Zorin, a modern urban dweller who returns to the village of his childhood. In the 1970s Belov continued to develop Zorin as a character, locating him in the urban milieu and in the midst of destructive relationships that are symptomatic, in Belov's view, of life in the city. The cycle *Vospitanie po doktoru Spoku* (Bringing Up Children According to Dr Spock, first published 1974 in *Sever,* published 1978 in book form) is an unrelenting picture of alcoholism, promiscuity, crime, familial breakdowns, and social alienation; "emancipated" women in particular are the target of Belov's sarcasm. The few moments of peace and happiness arise when Zorin recalls his childhood in the village or ventures out into the countryside.

Another work that looks at the experience of social progress and modernization from the viewpoint of the peasant is "Bukhtiny vologodskie" (Tall Tales from Vologda, first published 1969 in *Novyi mir*). This work is a phantasmagoric excursion into the world of folk culture, and the nonsensical adventures of the stove maker Kuz'ma Barakhvostov are related by Kuz'ma himself (the verb *barakhvostit'* is defined as spreading gossip, slander, or rumor). Kuz'ma has a life both before he was born (he wonders whether he should come out of the womb or wait) and after he dies (he tells the reader of his plans for the future). He has a dog called Kabysdokh (meaning "drop dead" in Russian). While fighting in the war, Kuz'ma is wounded in the left leg, which consequently ends up shorter than the right. He arranges a swap with his friend Andrei, who has been wounded in the right leg, now shorter than his left. Thus, Kuz'ma's legs become longer, while Andrei's legs become shorter. Kuz'ma then gets a job (and his own car) in the capital, forgets about his family in the village, travels to the United Nations in New York, and even makes several journeys into space.

Kuz'ma, who was born in 1917, has a life that embraces key moments of Soviet history, which Belov presents as absurd and unreal. The country, in its headstrong urge for progress, has lost its links with the past, enabling truth and falsehoods to become indistinguishable. When Kuz'ma "dies," he is refused admission to hell because it is full of sinners already; when he is told that he has no conscience, he tries to buy one in the market. But people have sold theirs already, saying "We needed the money very much." He is also forbidden to tell any more "bukhtiny," as they now have become the property of the state. In Kuz'ma's world bears drink vodka and can repair weapons; dogs chase men; and hares chase dogs.

In other stories Belov implies that old peasants serve as a link between the past and the present; they are living reminders of the course of twentieth-century history. Other peasants are at one with the natural world, treating their animals as if they were humans. Children, too—whether they are from the village or the town—delight in the natural world, both in their waking and sleeping hours (they even dream about animals). Yet, when modern ways intrude, the consequence is conflict and disharmony. Sometimes this intrusion results in comic effect, as in "Manikiur" (The Manicure, published in *Literaturnaia Rossia,* 1970), in which a villager visits her brother in town. He tries to introduce her to urban fashions, and, as she sits in the hairdresser's salon while receiving a manicure, all she can think about is how she will be able to milk the cows with painted fingernails. Similarly, the old woman in "Prosvetlenie" (Enlightenment, published in *Nash sovremennik,* 1971) wakes up one night, when the electricity is suddenly switched on, to see her daughter in bed with a boyfriend.

In 1972 Belov published "Kanuny" (The Eves), the first two parts of his novel on collectivization, in the journal *Sever;* the final part, "Kanuny: Chast' 3-ia" (The Eves: Part Three), appeared in *Novyi mir* in 1987. The work (comprising parts 1 and 2) was first published in book form in 1976, and a complete edition of the novel appeared in 1989. *Kanuny* relates the "eves" of collectivization and its calamitous effect on the peasantry from the point of view of the peasants themselves. It features a cross section of the rural population, from ordinary, hardworking peasants to Communist Party activists, from priests to industrial workers, and from secret-police officials to intellectuals. The party activists are associated consistently with demonic imagery, while the religious motifs become stronger in the course of the novel—as does Belov's conviction that the woes of Russia are directly attributable to Jewish and Masonic plots to destroy the country. Belov's novel not only angrily denounces party policy in the countryside in the late 1920s, but it also includes many lyrical moments that remind readers of his stories of the 1960s. Nature is personified; trees bleed when they are cut down; and, when the secret police arrive, real storm clouds gather over the village of Ol'khovitsa. The novel incorporates several debates on the political aspects of collectivization by various party members, as well as philosophical discussions on immortality and the soul by the intellectual Prozorov (a name suggesting "insight") and Father Irinei. Ultimately, the village is doomed, and life is about to change forever.

The spiritual and cultural legacy of a village is the theme of "Lad (Ocherki o narodnoi estetike)" (Harmony [Sketches on Folk Asthetics], first published 1979–1981 in *Nash sovremennik*). This series of essays subsequently came out in book form (as *Lad: Ocherki o narodnoi estetike,* 1982) in a sumptuously illustrated and designed edition. This documentary work covers all aspects of village life and celebrates the rich culture, crafts, and art of the Russian north. Here, too, men and animals share the same

*Cover for the 1989 English-language edition of Belov's pessimistic novel* Vse vperedi *(1987), in which he decries the immoral, self-destructive behavior of contemporary Muscovites (Howard-Tilton Memorial Library, Tulane University)*

reality; human life accords with the passage of the seasons; and there is the same rhythm and unity in human affairs as there is in the natural world. Belov spares no detail in describing the work of carpenters, millers, shepherds, boot makers, joiners, boatmen, stove makers, even beggars—all of them working "not in a struggle with surrounding nature, but in communion with it." Thus, knitting, sewing, handiwork, wickerwork, lacework, silver engraving, and wood carving have a spiritual quality, for they embody the human soul. Recording the life of the villager from childhood to old age, Belov shows how a young village lad learns to fish and make an ax as he grows up and then how he comes to grips with the conventions of courting. The lessons learned during a childhood spent in such idyllic rural surroundings provide a solid moral base for the healthy maturation of the child. Yet, Belov's work is an elegy for a lost way of life (and, at that, an idealized one, in which villagers are seen as moral paragons, and the concept of "sin" was almost unheard of).

The organic unity and inherent goodness of this world is in stark contrast to that described in *Vse vperedi* (The Best Is Yet to Come, first published 1986 in *Nash sovremennik,* published 1987 in book form). This novel is set during the course of ten years amid the empty and crippled lives of Muscovites. Belov's ire is especially aimed at emancipated women who drink and behave shamelessly and encourage each other to have abortions against their husbands' wishes. Social progress has led to a rift between man and nature ("violence toward the natural world has gone out of moral control"), and the benefits of technological civilization are leading mankind to "self-attrition and self-destruction." The world that Belov portrays here has lost its moral base and is alienated from its culture and its past. The novel is antimodern, antiurban, antiwomen, and blatantly anti-Semitic (the original edition of *Kanuny* had several anti-Semitic passages removed before it could be published as a book). On publication the work aroused much controversy.

In the late 1980s and 1990s Belov essentially was writing about the end of a way of life. In "God velikogo pereloma" (The Year of the Great Turning Point, first published 1989 and 1991 in *Novyi mir,* 1994 in *Nash sovremennik;* published 1994 in book form), a sequel to *Kanuny,* the peasants increasingly view the destruction of their community as the end of the world—as an allusion to the arrival of a triumphant Antichrist. The third part of this novel has an explicitly biblical context: the title *Chas shestyi* (The Sixth Hour, first published 1997–1998 in *Nash sovremennik,* published 1999 in book form) is taken from John 19:15, in which the Jews demand that Pilate crucify Christ. In *Chas shestyi* the reader learns that the Jews and the Masons together were responsible for the execution of the French monarch Louis XVI in 1793 and that Joseph Stalin believes his duty is to protect the Soviet state from further Zionist depredations: "The Masons and the Jews headed by Lenin have infested the Revolution like flies."

In other works of the 1990s Belov mercilessly attacks the post-Soviet state. "Semeinye prazdniki" (Family Celebrations, published 1994 in *Moskva* [Moscow]) is set against the background of the October 1993 crisis and Boris Nikolaevich Yeltsin's destruction in Moscow of the Belyi dom (White House), the government building that was home to the Russian parliament. Belov's hatred of Western democracy is unabated, and he calls for Russia to support Serbia as the last bastion of Orthodoxy. The story "Bukhtiny vologodskie zaviral'nye (perestroechnye)" (Tall and Far-Fetched Tales from Vologda [of the Perestroika Period], published 1996 in *Nash sovremennik*) resurrects Kuz'ma Barakhvostov to take swipes at Yeltsin and, particularly, at Mikhail Sergeevich Gorbachev, both of whom have reduced Russia to a "colony" of Western-led market forces. Still, even here there is some humor, especially when Barakhvostov bumps into Gorbachev and Vladimir Volfovich Zhirinovsky in the men's room of the State Duma, and Moscow mayor Iurii Mikhailovich Luzhkov gives him his own Mercedes in which to drive around Moscow.

Vasilii Ivanovich Belov's writings of the 1980s and 1990s do not do justice to his reputation as one of the great prose writers of Leonid Ilyich Brezhnev's Russia—as a writer whose characters Ivan Afrikanovich and Olesha Smolin provided a different set of moral and spiritual values from those advocated by the literature of Socialist Realism. Belov not only laments the loss of an age-old way of life and the alienation of modern man from his natural environment but also tries to preserve the memory of that life in his best writings.

**Bibliography:**

E. N. Aref'eva and Emma Aristakhovna Volkova, comps., *Vasilii Ivanovich Belov: Bibliograficheskii ukazatel' literatury* (Vologda: Vologodskaia oblastnaia biblioteka imeni I. V. Babushkina, 1982).

**References:**

Lev Aleksandrovich Anninsky, "Tochka opory. Eticheskie problemy sovremennoi prozy," *Don*, 6–7 (1968): 168–181, 178–187;

Leonid Fedorovich Ershov, *Pamiat' i vremia* (Moscow: Sovremennik, 1984), pp. 212–246;

Geoffrey A. Hosking, *Beyond Socialist Realism: Soviet Fiction Since "Ivan Denisovich"* (London: Paul Elek & Granada, 1980; New York: Holmes & Meier, 1980), pp. 57–70;

Hosking, "Vasilii Belov–Chronicler of the Soviet Village," *Russian Review*, 34, no. 2 (1975): 163–185;

T. V. Krivoshchapova, "Rol' prozaicheskikh fol'klornykh zhanrov v tvorchestve Vasiliia Belova," *Vestnik Moskovskogo universiteta. Seriia X, Filologiia*, 4 (1976): 33–44;

Arnold McMillin, "Town and Country in the Work of Vasilii Belov," in *Selected Papers from the Second World Congress for Soviet and East European Studies: Russian Literature and Criticism*, edited by Evelyn Bristol (Berkeley, Cal.: Berkeley Slavic Specialties, 1982), pp. 130–143;

Aleksandr Viktorovich Pankov, comp., *"Kanuny" Vasiliia Belova: S raznykh tochek zreniia* (Moscow: Sovetskii pisatel', 1991);

Kathleen F. Parthé, *Russian Village Prose: The Radiant Past* (Princeton: Princeton University Press, 1992);

Iurii Seleznev, *Vasilii Belov: Razdum'ia o tvorcheskoi sud'be pisatelia* (Moscow: Sovetskaia Rossiia, 1983);

Petr Sozontovich Vykhodtsev, "Trud – nravstvennost' – iskusstvo. O knige V. Belova 'Lad,'" *Russkaia literatura*, 1 (1982): 32–46;

Sergei Pavlovich Zalygin, "Rasskaz i rasskazchik," *Nash sovremennik*, 11 (1971): 113–119.

# Andrei Georgievich Bitov
(27 May 1937 -    )

Cynthia Simmons
*Boston College*

BOOKS: *Bol'shoi shar* (Moscow & Leningrad: Sovetskii pisatel', 1963);

*Takoe dolgoe detstvo* (Leningrad: Sovetskii pisatel', 1965);

*Dachnaia mestnost'* (Moscow: Sovetskaia Rossiia, 1967);

*Aptekarskii ostrov* (Leningrad: Sovetskii pisatel', 1968);

*Puteshestvie k drugu detstva* (Leningrad: Detskaia literatura, 1968);

*Obraz zhizni* (Moscow: Molodaia gvardiia, 1972);

*Dni cheloveka* (Moscow: Molodaia gvardiia, 1976);

*Sem' puteshestvii* (Leningrad: Sovetskii pisatel', 1976);

*Uroki Armenii* (Erevan: Sovetakan grokh, 1978);

*Pushkinskii dom* (Ann Arbor, Mich.: Ardis, 1978); translated by Susan Brownsberger as *Pushkin House* (New York: Farrar, Straus & Giroux, 1987);

*Voskresnyi den'* (Moscow: Sovetskaia Rossiia, 1980);

*Gruzinskii al'bom* (Tbilisi: Merani, 1985);

*Stat'i iz romana* (Moscow: Sovetskii pisatel', 1986);

*Chelovek v peizazhe* (Moscow: Sovetskii pisatel', 1988);

*Uletaiushchii Monakhov: Roman-punktir* (Moscow: Molodaia gvardiia, 1990);

*My prosnulis v neznakomoi strane* (Leningrad: Sovetskii pisatel', 1991);

*Sobranie sochinenii,* volume 1 (Moscow: Molodaia gvardiia, 1991-   );

*Trudoliubivyi Pushkin* (Moscow: Aiurveda, 1991);

*Vpervye v Rossii* (Moscow: PPP, 1993);

*Vychitanie zaitsa* (Moscow: Olimp PPP BaGaZh, 1993);

*Nachatki astrologii russkoi literatury* (Moscow: Mir kul'tury/Fortuna-Limited, 1994);

*Oglashennye* (Moscow: BaGaZh, 1995); translated by Susan Brownsberger as *The Monkey Link: A Pilgrimage Novel* (New York: Farrar, Straus & Giroux, 1995);

*Imperiia v chetyrekh izmereniiakh,* 4 volumes (Moscow: TKO ACT / Khar'kov: Folio, 1996);

*Novyi Gulliver: Aine kliaine arifmetika russkoi literatury* (Tenafly, N.J.: Hermitage, 1997);

*V chetverg posle dozhdia* (St. Petersburg: Pushkinskii fond, 1997);

*Zapiski novichka* (Moscow: LOKID, 1997);

*Andrei Bitov (from* Chelovek v peizazhe, *1988; William T. Young Library, University of Kentucky)*

*Derevo: 1971–1997* (St. Petersburg: Pushkinskii fond, 1998);

*Neizbezhnost' nenapisannogo: Godovye kol'tsa, 1956–1998–1937* (Moscow: Vagrius, 1998);

*Obosnovannaia revnost'* (Moscow: Panorama, 1998);

*Kniga puteshestvii po imperii* (Moscow: Ast-Olimp, 2000);

*Piatoe izmerenie: Na granitse vremeni i prostranstva* (Moscow: Nezavisimaia gazeta, 2002);

*Puteshestvie iz Rossii* (Moscow: Vagrius, 2003).

**Editions and Collections:** *Rannii Bitov,* 2 volumes (Leningrad: Podval, 1960);

*Kniga puteshestvii* (Moscow: Izvestiia, 1986);

*Pushkinskii dom* (Moscow: Sovremennik, 1979);

*Sobranie sochinenii* (Moscow: Sovetskaia Rossiia, 1991);

*Dachnaia mestnost': Dubl'* (St. Petersburg: Fond Russkoi poezii, 1999);

*Zhizn' v vetrenuiu pogodu* (Moscow: Vagrius, 1999);

*Pushkin, Aleksandr Sergeevich, 1799–1837. Predpolozhenie zhit': 1836* (Moscow: Nezavisimaia gazeta, 1999).

**Editions in English:** *Life in Windy Weather,* translated by Priscilla Meyer and others, edited by Meyer (Ann Arbor, Mich.: Ardis, 1986)–includes "Autobiography" and "Life in Windy Weather";

*Ten Short Stories* (Moscow: Raduga, 1991);

*A Captive of the Caucasus: Journeys in Armenia and Georgia* (London: Harvill, 1993);

*Life without Us=Zhizn' bez nas* [bilingual edition], translated by Susan Brownsberger (New York: Slovo/Word, 1998).

OTHER: Vladimir Vladimirovich Nabokov, *Krug,* with introduction by Bitov (Leningrad: Khudozhestvennaia literatura, 1990), pp. 3–20;

Genrikh Sapir, *Izbrannye stikhi,* with introduction by Bitov (Moscow, Paris & New York: Tret'ia volna, 1993);

*Predpolozhenie zhit': 1836,* compiled by Bitov (Moscow: Nezavisimaia gazeta, 1999);

Osip Emil'evich Mandel'shtam, *Shum vremeni,* with foreword by Bitov (Moscow: Vagrius, 2002);

*Dve vody: Fotografii,* compiled by D. Klokov and S. Larionov, with an essay by Bitov (St. Petersburg: Sleza, 2003).

SELECTED PERIODICAL PUBLICATIONS– UNCOLLECTED: "Soldat. Iz vospominanii o semeistve Odoevtsevykh," *Zvezda,* 7 (1973): 24–40;

"Pod znakom Al'biny. Iz khroniki semeistva Odoevtsevykh," *Druzhba narodov,* 7 (1975): 88–99;

"Dlia kogo pishet kritik?" *Voprosy literatury,* 3 (1976): 76–82;

"Chuzhaia sobaka i drugie rasskazy," *Chast' rechi. Al'manakh literatury i iskusstva,* 2–3 (1981–1982): 76–94;

*Roman-prizrak 1964–1977. Opyt bibliografii neizdannoi knigi,* as E. Khappenenn, *Wiener Slawistischer Almanach,* 9 (1982): 431–475;

"Dospekh tiazhel, kak pered boem' (Razmyshlenye na granitse poezii i prozy)," *Voprosy literatury,* 7 (1983): 194–203;

"Blizkoe retro, ili kommentarii k obshcheizvestnomu," *Novyi mir,* 4 (1989): 135–164;

"Odnoklassniki," *Novyi mir,* 5 (1990): 224–242;

"Rasskazy. Esse: Zub bolit, ili Porka Spinozy," *Literaturnoe obozrenie,* 10 (1992): 37–48;

"Andrei Platonov Today: A Roundtable Discussion," *Soviet Studies in Literature: A Journal of Translations,* 26 (1996): 91–105.

As both a creative writer and an essayist, Andrei Bitov superbly represents the Russian public intellectual of a special generation. He is old enough to have some recollections of World War II. He experienced postwar reconstruction in Leningrad and the promise of a bright future for Soviet youth. In the spirit of technological progress he chose a career path in the sciences, specifically in geology, but eventually abandoned the field for the life of a writer. Bitov recognized his avocation in the atmosphere of Nikita Sergeevich Khrushchev's "Thaw"; he suffered at the hands of the censors during Leonid Ilyich Brezhnev's "Stagnation"; and he finally achieved full public voice in the years of Mikhail Sergeevich Gorbachev's glasnost. Bitov's published works span more than four decades, and their perspectives encompass an even broader chronology of a "thinking person's" life, as experienced during Joseph Stalin's Soviet Union through post-Communist Russia. Bitov's themes, and at times his artistic method, reflect the burden of changes in Russian and Western culture in the second half of the twentieth century.

Bitov has written a condensed autobiography, which begins with his birth in 1937 and continues up to 1963, when he became a professional writer. He explains his rationale for this endpoint: "In 1963 my biography ends, I became a professional in the sense that my sole occupation is literature and I have no other means of existence–what follows is not biography but books, which feed me not by my writing them but by being published." From 1963 onward he identifies himself with his body of works. He categorizes it for the reader, as well, in a chronology that reflects the writing of the works and not necessarily their date of publication. Yet, the ontology of themes and styles reflect, albeit indirectly, a continuing biography of the writer.

Andrei Georgievich Bitov was born at the height of the Stalinist purges on 27 May 1937 in Leningrad, the native city of his parents, Georgii Leonidovich Bitov and Ol'ga Alekseevna (Kedrova) Bitova. Bitov was the second son; his brother, Oleg, was older by five years. Bitov's first memory, however, was not the "Terror" but the horrendous war and siege of Leningrad that followed on its heels. His family remained in the city during the first, and most horrible, year of the siege. As he recalls in his "Autobiography," which introduces the English collection of short stories *Life in Windy Weather* (1986): "I remember surprisingly peaceful and everyday scenes (after all, I had no earlier recollections) like: corpses, bomb sites, half a meter of ice in the hall, and that catastrophic little piece of bread the size of a postage stamp, our daily ration." In March 1942 Bitov was evacuated, along with his mother and Oleg, over frozen Lake Ladoga to the Urals where his father was working in Revda and then to Tashkent.

When they returned from evacuation in 1944, he started school. Bitov describes his family's long history in the city and commitment to pre-Soviet values of high culture: "My big family didn't have to keep up with the latest to consider itself cultured. Its tastes were independent and distant from the times: the most contemporary writer was Leonid Andreev, the most recent composer–Rakhmaninov." Bitov's choice of postsecondary training in geology reflected both the love of travel or "displacement" (as Bitov terms it), which his mother helped him to develop, and the emphasis in Soviet society on the material and technical. He discovered, however, that he was ill suited to the sciences; he recounts that a viewing of Federico Fellini's motion picture *La Strada* (1954) opened to him the world of contemporary reality and art.

While still at the Leningrad Mining Institute, Bitov became involved with a literary society and group of amateur poets (among which were the poets Aleksandr Semenovich Kushner and Gleb Iakovlevich Gorbovsky). In order to remain in their company, Bitov began to write what he himself terms "bad" poetry; he became so engrossed in his writing, however, that he fell behind in his studies and was expelled from the institute. Other "universities" followed–Bitov worked as a stevedore and a lathe operator and in construction units in the army. The year 1958 was a turning point in his life. He married Inga Petkevich, returned to the institute, gave up writing poetry, and began writing prose. Bitov applied himself in his studies and continued to write, and during field expeditions in the summer he gathered the material for his first books. In 1962, the year of his graduation from the institute, Bitov's daughter, Anya, was born, and he signed an agreement for his first book and first screenplay. The following year he abandoned his career as a geologist. At this point his personal biography, as he sees it, ended, and the life of his books began.

Bitov discusses the publication history of his writing in the commentary to volume one of his *Sobranie sochinenii* (Collected Works, 1991). As was typical in the Soviet Union when Bitov started out as a writer, uncensored publication meant that an author and his work had to conform to prevailing ideological precepts. There were periods of greater and lesser stringency, however, as well as notable exceptions to the rule. As Bitov observes in the commentary, despite the criticism and censorship that his works habitually invoked, he nonetheless was able to publish several collections of short stories in the period 1958–1978: *Bol'shoi shar*; *Takoe dolgoe detstvo* (Such a Long Childhood, 1965); *Dachnaia mestnost'* (A Summer Place, 1967); *Aptekarskii ostrov* (Apothecary Island, 1968); and *Obraz zhizni* (Way of Life, 1972).

With the appearance of his first stories Bitov established himself as part of the "molodaia proza" (young prose) phenomenon and, more specifically, as a writer of "molodaia malaia proza" (young short prose). The works of writers associated with this broad category were published between 1955 and 1967; Vassily Aksyonov (Vasilii Pavlovich Aksenov) and Anatolii Tikhonovich Gladilin were among these authors. Addressing a variety of themes, these young writers shared the concerns of early adulthood. Most significant, contrary to the tenets of Socialist Realism, which was the prevailing policy of Communist authorities toward the arts, young prose addressed coming-of-age themes from a personal and psychological, rather than societal, perspective.

The title story in *Bol'shoi shar* is one of only two that, according to Bitov, reflect his early childhood in war-torn Leningrad; the other is "Noga (Aptekarskii ostrov)" (The Leg [Apothecary Island]). Among the other stories in the collection, the dominant theme is self-realization at the threshold of adolescence and early adulthood. The dilemma of trying to capture reality in the present has intrigued Bitov throughout his life and career, but as shown in several stories in *Bol'shoi shar*, the protagonists become conscious of this enigma in conjunction with their growing self-awareness. For example, in "Odna strana" (One Country) Boris, a geologist who is twenty-three years old (the same age as Bitov when he wrote the story), travels on an expedition through Uzbekistan. He ponders his relationships to his mother and to his beloved as they are constituted in his memory of them and in his imaginings of them. Separated from one another, the three of them exist for each other only intangibly. Bitov suggests that a human relationship depends ultimately on individual perspective or consciousness. Reality is constituted individually in an amalgam of experiences and perceptions. It varies and continually fluctuates. Yet, Bitov does not reject here (in postmodern fashion) overlapping meanings. The title of the story, "Odna strana," alludes to the ability to understand what one's country is–and, by association, who oneself is–by experiencing what the country, or self, is not. In Uzbekistan the protagonist Boris learns what Russia is not, and the experience reveals to him the things that differentiate and characterize his native territory. Similarly, away from the human ties that bind, Boris realizes what, for him, make love and relationships real. In addition, the story emblematizes in a significant way the essential displacement and "borderline" mentality of Bitov's writing as a whole: in "Odna strana," when Boris comes "home" to Leningrad, he longs to return to Central Asia. Bitov suggests that life is more meaningful and real when one lives within the difference.

Boris's desire to travel, to live and think independently, and to search for meaning qualify him as a worthy representative of the concerns of "molodaia proza." Other stories in *Bol'shoi shar* that fit well within this tradition are "Inostrannyi iazyk" (A Foreign Language) and "Zeny net doma" (My Wife Is Not at Home), which focus on young affairs of the heart and the impediments to communication between men and women. "Strashnaia sila" (A Terrible Force) describes the repercussions suffered by the adolescent protagonist Vitia for independent thinking and nonconformity (the latter was an even greater aberration of the prescribed homogeneity of Soviet society).

The collection as a whole introduces several problems and topics that Bitov revisited and developed further in the years after the heyday of "molodaia proza" had passed. Nearly all the stories in *Bol'shoi shar* consider the nature of truth. In "Dver" (The Door), for example, a boy tries to determine whether a woman, with whom he is infatuated, is deceiving him with a nighttime male visitor. The stories also treat psychological connections to the past. In "Iubilei" (The Jubilee) an elderly man prefers to live in his childhood memories; they have become more real for him than the present. In the final, eponymous story of the collection the shifting parameters of time and space, which serve in general to unsettle the reader, prove the possibility of a "miracle." "Bol'shoi shar," is about a little girl, Tonia, who experiences transcendent joy in postwar, postsiege Leningrad, when, during a parade, she spies a red balloon—which is, from her perspective, enormous in size. She sets off on an odyssey to find such a balloon. In the process Tonia breaks rules, such as when she wanders through the unsettled streets of the city, and she overcomes obstacles: when she finds the mysterious place where the balloons are sold, she finds her way back to her apartment; she then asks her caregiver (Tonia's mother likely did not survive the war) for the requisite amount of money, and, amazingly, she receives it. When Tonia returns to her apartment with the red balloon, and her father asks her where she found it, she gives him the name of the street—a street that, to his knowledge, does not exist in Leningrad. "Bol'shoi shar" reveals the serendipitous potential of Bitov's occasionally excruciating analysis of "being." In reading the story one cannot be sure of what has been or what seems now to be, and likewise one cannot limit the possibilities for what may come to pass.

Included in Bitov's third book, *Dachnaia mestnost'*, is a story that, in several ways, came to symbolize his attitude toward art and the creative process. "Zhizn' v vetrenuiu pogodu" (translated as "Life in Windy Weather," 1986) describes the writer Aleksei's move, with his wife and young son, to live in the country. The

*Cover for the 1987 English-language edition of Bitov's* Pushkinskii dom *(1978), a "roman-muzei" (museum novel) that incorporates many allusions to other works of Russian literature (Richland County Public Library, Columbia, South Carolina)*

correspondences between this fictional tale and Bitov's own life were made clear with the publication of *Life in Windy Weather* in English, which includes a companion piece to this story; it is the journal "Zapiski iz-za ugla" (Notes from the Corner), first published in *Novy i Mir* in 1990 though written in 1963 at Bitov's dacha in Toskovo. His intention was to publish both works together as "Dachnaia mestnost'." The notes chronicle the time in which the story takes place, but in them the writer is identified as Bitov, not Aleksei. The ability to compare experiences lived by the author to the fictionalization of such experiences adds another layer to "Zhizn' v vetrenuiu pogodu," a narrative about writing and creativity.

In the story Aleksei, by moving to the country, divests himself of the trappings of the city and his reputation as a writer. Stripped of the formal patterns of his life, he fears that inspiration will never visit him again. By fits and starts Aleksei learns a lesson similar to that learned by the young geologist in "Odna strana"—that one discovers more about a subject when a new perspective is gained. As Aleksei observes in the story, this is what good art always does. It travels to a distant border—to the country, for instance—and reports back from a distance. The recurring motif of wind, which is both liberating and destructive, symbolizes Aleksei's increasingly unfettered perception. He finds much in the country that is new and unspoiled. Now cut off from distractions, he takes the time to observe how his young son experiences life. In the country Aleksei cannot help but notice the forces of nature, but his son, as a new being, draws the father's attention to the life force and the cycle of creation. Eventually, Aleksei comes genuinely to "see"—he acquires insights into his own behavior and into his relationships with his wife and father. At the end of the story he has regained the urge to write. The reader understands that Aleksei has not simply recaptured what was lost. He has reentered the creative process from a new "portal," which promises to enhance and "authenticate" his art.

The story "Puteshestvie k drugu detstva" (Journey to a Childhood Friend), also in *Dachnaia mestnost'*, combines the concerns of "molodaia proza" with the themes and stylistic features that had characterized Bitov's writing for some time. The narrator of the story, a journalist, receives a commission to write about a positive hero—an activity that actually was prescribed within the tenets of Socialist realism. (The quest for an exemplary Russian hero arguably burdened Russian writers and critics to a greater extent than in most other national literatures.) The narrator calls to mind a childhood friend whose character and accomplishments qualify him as a true Soviet hero. He sets out to visit his old friend, named Genrikh, but the "trip" he really takes is one typical for many protagonists in Bitov's works. In the liminal space of the airport, the narrator travels in a psychological sense, ruminating freely on the nature of valorous deeds and what truly makes a man a hero. He recalls Genrikh and the various ways his friend, in the past, qualified as a Soviet hero. Genrikh knew how to fit in and not trouble the status quo. Unlike the narrator, Genrikh engaged in manly activities—he rode a motorcycle and hunted. And in a career chosen for him by his parents, Genrikh distinguished himself in the natural sciences (he was a volcanologist).

Genrikh symbolizes the Socialist Realist positive hero of Bitov's generation—the story is subtitled "Nasha biografiia" (Our Biography); that is, he is someone who necessarily performed valorous deeds. The story pivots not only on the contrast between the narrator and Genrikh but also on the notion of valor as a defining trait of the hero. While waiting at the airport, the journalist-narrator observes an encounter between two ordinary people. A young woman, pregnant and abandoned by her lover, is traveling to find the father of her child. She expects to be rejected. She tells her story to a man, whose appearance is plain in every respect, and he offers to marry her. The narrator has no great hope for their future life together, but he recognizes the value of the man's proposal, a simple act. Through this subplot in "Puteshestvie k drugu detstva," Bitov suggests that the good deed carries greater significance than the prescribed, extraordinary and often unreachable act of valor.

Some of the stories that appear in the 1968 collection, *Aptekarskii ostrov*, were published earlier in *Bol'shoi shar*. Most of the other stories first came out in literary journals, and they reveal some characteristic themes of young prose. On one level the story "Bezdel'nik" (The Idler) presents yet another young Soviet man faced with the numbing reality of a scheduled life of uninteresting work. The idler Alesha has a fantasy life, often fed by alcohol, that leads to censure from his boss. In the end Alesha refuses to defend himself. Allowing his mind to wander, not listening to the offer of a last chance from his boss, the idler ensures his own dismissal.

On another level, however, "Bezdel'nik" demonstrates a method of intertextual dialogue that appears in other of Bitov's early stories. This intertextual approach became his trademark. Though a short text, "Bezdel'nik" echoes myriad Russian classics and their heroes: Alesha's uncreative office work recalls that described in Nikolai Vasil'evich Gogol's tale "Shinel'" (1842, The Overcoat); his sense of alienation and lack of appreciation by others portray him as a late-twentieth-century version of the "superfluous man," a construct of nineteenth-century Russian literature. In addition, he experiences his own version of Raskolnikov's memory of the beaten mare (from Fyodor Dostoevsky's *Prestuplenie i nakazanie* [Crime and Punishment, 1867]) but with a twist: although in "Bezdel'nik" onlookers come to the horse's aid, the symbolic significance of this "literary" happy resolution has no effect on Alesha's personal dilemma—he is still unable to achieve his goal of securing sick leave from work. Like Raskolnikov, Alesha also is drawn to the free and mysterious "Islands" of St. Petersburg. Bitov then mediates these connections to Raskolnikov through the introduction of another frequent visitor of the Islands, Nikolai Apollonovich, which is also the name of the protagonist in Andrei Bely's early-twentieth-century novel *Peterburg* (1913, Petersburg). Furthermore, the tension between fathers, as representatives of the system, and sons, as "revolutionaries"—depicted in *Peterburg* and descending from Ivan Sergeevich Turgenev's *Ottsy i deti* (1862, Fathers and Children)—reverberates in the idler Alesha's arguments with his own father. Stories such as "Bezdel'nik" prefigure the critical debate in Bitov scholarship, particularly with respect to the novel *Pushkinskii dom* (1978; translated as *Pushkin House*, 1987), over whether the copious meanings formed intertextually (with preceding words and works of literature) serve in the end to subvert Bitov's art.

The story "Penelopa" (Penelope), also in *Aptekarskii ostrov*, does not give rise to free-ranging literary associations in the same way as "Bezdel'nik." Bitov has a particular work of literature in mind, however, and saves the reader the effort of recalling it: "Penelopa" is subtitled "Nevskii Prospekt" (Nevsky Prospect), which is also the title of a short story by Gogol. The protagonists of Gogol's "Nevskii prospekt" (1842) fall victim to the "cult of St. Petersburg"; in accordance with this cult, the atmosphere of Peter the Great's "city on a swamp" (or on the souls of the many serfs who died building it) is represented as unreal or supernatural. On Nevsky Prospect, the main thoroughfare of the city, Gogol's characters Piskarev and Pirogov are deceived as to the true nature of the women who capture their attention there. Yet, there is also a realistic explanation for the deception—their potential paramours exist for them only through the prism of their own flawed perceptions. They have projected onto these women their own desires and have in a sense "created" them. Bitov's protagonist vacillates between the image of a woman he could desire—which he creates when he "dresses" a woman he encounters in a movie theater—and the reality of that unattractive and pathetic "creature." The reader meets this autobiographical protagonist in other early stories by Bitov, who identifies him with his full name, Aleksei Monakhov. His surname is based on the Russian word for monk, *monakh*, which conveys the character's sense of urban isolation.

The 1976 collection *Dni cheloveka* (The Days of Man) consists of the fragmentary novel *Rol', Roman-punktir* (Role, Novel with Ellipses) and "Molodoi Odoevstev, geroi romana" (The Young Odoevstev, Hero of a Novel), a fragment of a novel that was to become *Pushkinskii dom;* fragmentation, which Bitov has addressed as a literary critic, is characteristic of his approach to the genre of the novel. The collection also includes the essay "Ptisy, ili Novye svedeniia o cheloveke" (Birds, or New Information about Man). Three of the stories collected in *Dni cheloveka*—"Dver'," "Sad" (The Garden), and "Infant'ev"—had appeared previously in book form. While the stories in *Dni cheloveka* chronicle the development of his autobiographical hero Monakhov, Bitov preferred another combination of tales for the character's life history. In the 1990 collection *Uletaiushchii Monakhov: Roman-punktir* (Vanishing Monakhov: A Novel with Ellipses) and in the English translation of his stories *Life in Windy Weather* (in which the fragmentary novel Uletaiushchii Monakhov is titled *The Lover*), Bitov altered the combination imposed by the publisher in *Dni cheloveka*. The 1990 version conforms to Bitov's original conception, whereby the last of the five stories is "Vkus" (Taste) and not "Infant'ev."

In *Dni cheloveka* and its later incarnations, *Uletaiushchii Monakhov* and *The Lover,* the reader discerns that the boy in "Dver'" and Alesha, the young man in "Sad," are the same person—the character Aleksei Monakhov in "Tretii rasskaz" (The Third Story), originally titled "Obraz" (The Image). In the first story a boy suspects deception in the object of his infatuation, an older woman; in the second Alesha is deceived by his lover, Asia; and in the third Monakhov meets Asia ten years after the end of their relationship. "Tretii rasskaz" is positioned in the middle of *Dni cheloveka*, and it anchors the other stories thematically. Monakhov is now old enough to reflect upon the passions of youth—to recognize their illusions but also to lament their passing. When he meets Asia again, he is a married man awaiting the birth of his first child. He realizes that in his youthful infatuation he had created an image of Asia that did not correspond to the reality of her narcissistic and inconstant nature. Yet, Monakhov regrets the disappearance of that image, or more important, of the emotion it had aroused in him. Now he understands better what puzzled him when he knew Asia earlier. At the end of "Sad" Aleksei ponders the puzzling fragments he has been reading on the nature of love, which indicate that love depends neither on the lover nor the beloved. In "Tretii rasskaz" Monakhov recognizes that the reader thinks of love as a waxing and waning force in nature. At the end of the story he accepts the dissipation of the youthful force. Yet, whether the birth of his son—on which the story ends—will unleash in him a vital, if different, life force is unclear. Bitov answers this question most directly in "Zhizn' v vetrenuiu pogodu," which is not included in *Dni cheloveka, Uletaiushchii Monakhov,* or *The Lover*. As a father Aleksei discovers his most authentic creative energy in the country while observing his young son's discovery of the material world—the child's youthful vitality and naiveté awaken in the writer the spirit of artistic creation.

In "Les" (The Forest), published in *Dni cheloveka* and originally titled "Uletaiushchii Monakhov," Monakhev in a sense comes full circle. Rather than becoming someone deceived in love, he is now an unfaithful husband; rather than being the young man who loses the attentions of his beloved to an older man, he is the older man who conquers the object of a young man's desire. The epithet *uletaiushchii,* or vanishing (literally flying away), which modifies the name Monakhov in the title, can be interpreted in several ways. Monakhov is aging and waning, a reality highlighted by his dying

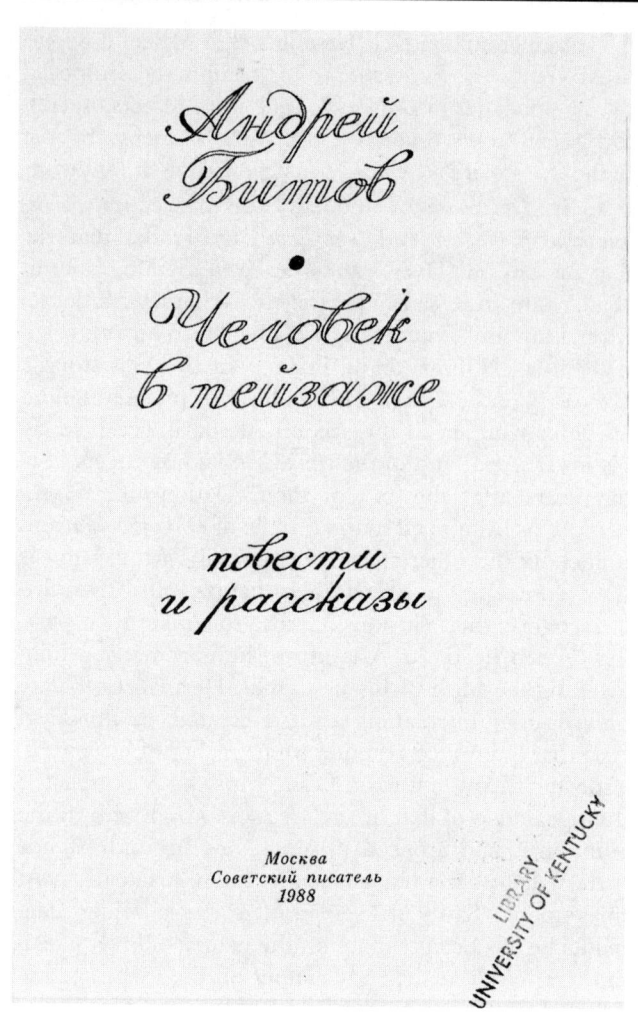

*Title page for Bitov's 1988 story collection* Chelovek v peizazhe *(The Man in the Landscape). In the title story the protagonist falls through the contemporary Russian landscape into the oppressive history of the country (William T. Young Library, University of Kentucky).*

father and the overt theme of the story concerning the "ages of man"; the epigraph to the story, from Ps. 103:15, reads: "The days of man are but as grass: for he flourisheth as a flower of the field." Monakhov is both vanishing and flying away. In "Les" Monakhov sets out for Tashkent; when he does, he is choosing to leave rather than just go on a trip. He is not inspired about the business that takes him to Uzbekistan or about the visit to his aging parents, whom he has not seen in years. He departs for an unintentional odyssey, and his desire to get away constitutes a search.

A series of events gradually leads Monakhov, a flawed hero, to a revelation. In the course of visiting Tashkent, he slowly moves from a position as an abstract observer of his life to a role of engagement, particularly with the people of his past and present, and thus toward a new understanding of their interconnectedness. Only now, in their waning years, as they are disappearing from life, Monakhov recognizes the life force of his parents—their love of him and their preservation, through their being, of his childhood experiences. The infatuation of Lenechka, an eighteen-year-old boy, with Natasha, Monakhov's lover in Tashkent, recalls for Monakhov the passion of his own youth. Moreover, he is reminded of the futility of his (and Lenechka's) youthful passion when he witnesses a young man's death at the Tashkent airport: a passenger, racing to make his flight, is killed by the propeller of the plane; caught up in the blade, the young man, who calls to Monakhov's mind Lenechka, seems to "fly away." Monakhov then also "flies away"; he distances himself, both literally and figuratively, from the time, space, and experiences of his youth. However, although Monakhov's life forces are waning, he finally accepts and appreciates the process of living (and dying) and the revitalizing energy of human connectedness. At the end of the story, back in Moscow and lying in bed next to his wife, with the sound of airplanes flying overhead in the night, Monakhov feels himself receiving the essence of his dying father and understands the relevance of an allegory his father once told him, about what happens after a tree dies in a forest. Upon the death of a tree, the surrounding trees of the forest "reabsorb" the life that is in its remains. As in "Tretii rasskaz," Monakhov at this point realizes the power of family ties and the regenerative effect (on those who are "fading") of new life and of lives yet to be.

In "Vkus," the final story of *Dni cheloveka,* Bitov portrays Monakhov some years later, when the character has lost, yet once more, his tenuous hold on the meaning of life. Monakhov is fleeing again: he leaves his second wife behind in Moscow in order to ruminate and work in the dacha community of Peredel'kino, the writer's colony where Boris Leonidovich Pasternak lived in his later years; Bitov incorporates Pasternak's poetry, and the reader can infer that a scene in the story takes place at Pasternak's grave. The narrator describes Monakhov's predominant sensation of morbid circularity, of life as a dead end or eternal return. On the train, as he begins his foray into the country, Monakhov ponders, in now typical fashion, the insincerity of his moribund relationship with his second wife. Everything is played out and replayed in Monakhov's life, and his actions even during this "retreat" only confirm his assessment. He meets a young woman who is a double of Asia, the great love of his youth. What follows in the story is prescribed—the scripted conversations, the heavy drinking, the affair, and the self-recrimination. The deadliness of this cycle is only reinforced by the news, which Monakhov receives from an old school friend, that Asia has died. The theme of death is predominant in "Vkus" and presages the political novel that was to come, excerpts of which were also published in *Dni cheloveka*.

During the time that Bitov wrote and published his collections of short fiction, from the late 1950s to the mid 1970s, he also was working on *Pushkinskii dom*, the novel that made him a celebrated author. Fragments of the novel appeared in various periodicals before its publication in book form in the United States in 1978. The excerpts from *Pushkinskii dom* and the controversial novel that they promised—which some had already read in samizdat (the underground press)—strained relations, already tense, between Bitov and the Communist authorities. The publication of *Pushkinskii dom* in 1978 and Bitov's co-editorship of the banned literary almanac *Metropol'* (Metropol) in 1979 marked the beginning of a period of official disfavor. Between 1978 and 1985 Bitov was able to publish works that previously had appeared in print and only a few new articles. In retrospect he has noted certain advantages to this period of "silence": "Because I wasn't under pressure, I was able to plumb my work . . . I chose to write different books, I traveled to the interior of the country, since I couldn't go abroad, I had lots of friends, lovers, drank a lot of vodka. And then I had children."

After divorcing Inga in 1973, Bitov had married Ol'ga Shamborant that same year; in 1977 their son, Ivan, was born. He and Ol'ga remained married until 1979. In 1988 Bitov's second son, Georgii, was born, and that year Bitov married Georgii's mother, Natal'ia Gerasimova.

Completed in 1971 but published in its entirety in Russia only in 1987, when it appeared in the journal *Novyi mir* (The New World), *Pushkinskii dom* continues to receive considerable critical attention. The narrator identifies the iconoclastic genre of the work as a "museum novel." It is at once a long narrative and a concatenation of "extratextual" allusions, mostly to works of Russian literature. From the start the title suggests the significance of Russian literature to the book. Pushkin House, the former Customs House in St. Petersburg, is where the Institute of Russian Literature (of the Russian, or Soviet-U.S.S.R., Academy of Sciences) is located. It is also a museum. Yet, Bitov's Pushkin House exists on an abstract level as well—much as Bely's novel *Peterburg* represents both the city of St. Petersburg and the idea of the city. *Pushkinskii dom* concerns the interconnections of Russian literature per se as much as it does the relationship of the protagonists to Russian literature. Critics who emphasize the intertextual "dialogues" in the novel consider the work a prime example of a fatally fragmented postmodern text—in which metatextual associations destabilize and supercede the literary text itself.

The titles of the prologue to the novel and of three sections invoke famous works of Russian literature and their many, already intricate, relationships in the general history of ideas. For instance, Bitov titles the prologue "Chto delat'" (What Is to Be Done), which begs comparison not only to Nikolai Gavrilovich Chernyshevsky's 1863 novel of that name but also to Leo Tolstoy's dialogue with Chernyshevsky in *Tak chto zhe nam delat'?* (1886, What Then Should We Do?) and even with Vladimir Il'ich Lenin's 1902 treatise *Chto delat* (What Is to Be Done). Section 1 bears the name of Turgenev's 1862 novel, *Ottsy i deti*. Section 2, "Geroi nashego vremeni" (A Hero of Our Time), calls forth not only Mikhail Iur'evich Lermontov's 1840 novel of the same name but also the particularly sensitive question in Russian literature of the representation of the "hero." Only in the final section, "Bednyi vsadnik" (The Humble Horseman), does Bitov recall a work of literature with a play on words. The title "Bednyi vsadnik" is based on the title *Mednyi vsadnik* (1837, The Bronze Horseman), Aleksandr Sergeevich Pushkin's narrative poem, in which Pushkin brings together both the thematic and stylistic concerns of his body of works.

The protagonist of *Pushkinskii dom* is Leva Odoevtsev, a young man who first appears in the opening section of the novel, titled "Ottsy i deti." Generations of the aristocratic Odoevtsevs dedicated themselves to philology. Leva's father is living the comfortable life of a scholar while Leva is studying in graduate school. However, mystery and silence surround Leva's grandfather, a renowned linguist, who, the text implies, was denounced in the Stalinist purges, arrested, and subsequently disowned by the family. "Ottsy i deti" primarily concerns Leva's attempt to "find" his father and grandfather and thereby find himself. An air of secrecy in the Odoevtsev household prevents Leva from developing a sense of his relationship to the past and, therefore, his own sense of what is real. His parents' falseness about the past has infected their ability to be emotionally sincere.

Leva attempts to "recognize" his father in two men who return to Leningrad from the camps and from exile during the political "thaw" of the 1960s, when the story takes place. Leva is drawn initially to one of them, an old friend of the family, "Uncle Dickens," an iconoclast with several ties to the pre-Soviet period. But just as his grandfather Modest Platonovich, now "rehabilitated," returns to Leningrad, Leva wakes up to the reality that Uncle Dickens is not beyond human weakness (and cannot be his father; after all, he already has one). Yet, when Leva visits his grandfather in a seemingly foreign space on the outskirts of the city, the latest "reality" that Leva has constructed—of a refined and long-suffering grandfather—crumbles before the actual man, now coarse and bitter. This wreck of a man, however, shocks Leva into awareness. At the end of "Ottsy i deti" Leva is asked by his superiors to stand watch at Pushkin House during the October holidays. He falls asleep and is awakened by a call from an old acquaintance, Mitishat'ev.

The second section, "Geroi nashego vremeni,'" which is subtitled "Versiia i variant pervoi chasti" (Version and Variant of the First Part), retells Leva's childhood with a focus on his loves, infatuations, and peer relationships. The chronicle commences with the death of Stalin in 1953, which has immediate and far-reaching consequences for Leva. Stalin's death leads to the abolition of same-sex education, and the adolescent Leva is introduced to the world of girls. His guide in this process is the same Mitishet'ev whose call he receives at the end of section 1. Leva envies Mitishat'ev's worldliness but seems inherently incapable of wholly admiring, or trusting, this lowly "operator." Ambivalence characterizes all of the adolescent's relationships. The section opens in an atmosphere of insincerity. Insincerity also envelops Leva's troubled relationships with his "loves," Faina, Al'bina, and Liubasha, as well as his relationship with his cohort Mitishat'ev. Leva both deceives and is deceived. Section 2 ends with the convergence of these variant histories of him. Once again he is in Pushkin House and awakened by the phone; the reader learns of Mitishat'ev's intention to visit Leva during his watch.

Section 3, "Bednyi vsadnik," takes place entirely within the Pushkin House museum, and the locale reverberates with characters and words written long before. The October holidays serve as an appropriate background to the maelstrom inside the museum. The city is alive with reveling and drinking, and when characters begin to drop in on Leva, the reader has a sense of experiencing real and imagined carnivals. Literary allusions abound, for example, to devils (Fedor Sologub's *Melkii bes* [The Petty Demon], 1907), and to masquerades (Lermontov's *Maskarad* [The Masquerade], 1835). Mitishat'ev brings along a literary hack and informer, as well as two common Natashas, who represent negative doubles of their probable namesakes (Tolstoy's Natasha Rostova from *Voina i mir* [War and Peace, 1868, 1869] and the actress who played the title character in a motion-picture adaptation of his novel *Anna Karenina* [1875-1877]). Leva's colleague Blank also appears, without explanation. Leva is caught between "masks"—the one he wears before his colleague Blank versus the face he presents to Mitishat'ev. The young men barely feign interest in the unattractive Natashas or respect for the hack informer von Gottich. Yet, these unmaskings of underlying sentiments pale before the ultimate confrontation and revelation that take place once the supporting characters have left Pushkin House, in the final chapter, "Duel'" (Duel).

"Duel'" bears a list of epigraphs that recall seven famous duels in Russian literature, from serious representations in the early nineteenth century to hazy recollections of the custom, to a parody of it. The duel in Bitov's novel takes place between Leva and Mitishat'ev. Returning from a stroll in the festive streets of Leningrad, the two men drink more vodka, and the provocations and revelations commence. Mitishat'ev implies that he has deceived Leva with Faina and then breaks Pushkin's death mask. He suggests a duel with Pushkin's dueling pistols. Leva agrees. They take their places—the narrator, referring to himself as the "author," turns his back to the scene—and a shot is fired; the narrator "discovers" Leva lying unconscious on the floor. Mitishat'ev then flees.

Three epilogues follow "Duel'," and in the second of them the reader learns that Leva has not died. Nor has Uncle Dickens—his resurrection is the author's gift to the reader. Leva's Al'bina arrives at Pushkin House to help with repairs. These epilogues remind the reader of the devices of fiction and the deception that lies at its core. Although Leva has learned a lesson about honesty and integrity, he remains inscribed in the Soviet world of distortions, and, ultimately, Leva himself is a fiction. In the final pages the narrator offers an excerpt from a chapter of Bog est' "God Is," written by Modest Platonovich, Leva's grandfather; Leva "foisted" the manuscript on the narrator-author before they went their separate ways. It states "Unreality is a condition of life. Everything is shifted and exists a step away, with a purpose other than it was named for. On the level of reality, only God is alive. He is reality. All else is divided, multiplied, canceled out, factored—annihilated. To exist on the honesty of authentic reasons is beyond a man's strength now. It voids his life, since his life exists only through error." Modest Platonovich writes that in realizing this lesson he is free. His only choice, however, is to avoid complicity in the distortion of the word—to remain mute. Bitov's final word, however, is *Pushkinskii dom,* the novel itself. Taken as a whole, his fiction, or word trick, serves to reveal the deceptions. Words, rather than silence, set Bitov "free."

For the proposed third volume of his collected works, Bitov gathered various nonfiction pieces that can be classified as travel literature. As is characteristic of the genre, Bitov—in his travels throughout the Caucasus—reveals as much (or more) about the place from which he has departed as he does about the place at which he has arrived. In *Uroki Armenii* (Lessons of Armenia, 1978) he recognizes the appropriateness of the Armenian alphabet. It looks hammered and evokes both the violence of Armenian history and the ruggedness of the people and the terrain. In comparison to this orthography, the contemporary form of the Cyrillic alphabet appears ugly and inadequate to him. At least the original Cyrillic alphabet, before its alteration by language reforms, came closer to "the Russian landscape, Russian architecture, the Russian character." Even in this genre, however, Bitov alludes to the "other places" of literature. With respect to Armenia, he evokes the "ur-texts" of Pushkin's *Puteshestvie v Arzrum* (1836, Journey to Arzrum) and Osip Emil'evich Mandel'shtam's *Puteshestvie v Armeniiu* (1933, Journey to Armenia). In Bitov's dialogue with these texts, he struggles, ultimately, to overcome them. He attempts to discover the Armenia that has not been distorted by the Russian gaze or by Soviet forces of assimilation. Although ultimately impossible (as Leva's grandfather writes, only God is real) Bitov seeks, in *Uroki Armenii*, some truth in the journey.

In the tolerance of the era of Gorbachev and glasnost, some works that Bitov wrote long before were finally published in Russia, such as *Stat'i iz romana* (Articles from a Novel) and *Kniga puteshestvii* (The Book of Journeys); both works appeared in 1986. They confirm Bitov's continuing significance as a literary critic-theorist and travel writer. His impressions of the Caucasus and Central Asia serve to introduce to his generation of Russians many of the non-Slavic regions of the Soviet Empire. Important to Bitov's reemergence in print was the 1987 publication of three fictional works in prestigious literary journals (in addition to the appearance that year of *Pushkinskii dom* in *Novyi mir*): "Fotografiia Pushkina (1799–2099)" (Pushkin's Photograph [1799–2099]) in *Znamia* (Banner); "Chelovek v peisazhe" (A Man in the Landscape) in *Novyi mir;* and "Prepodavatel' simmetrii" (The Teacher of Symmetry) in *Iunost'* (Youth).

Bitov's most significant work of the post-Soviet period came out in Russia in 1995. *Oglashennye* (translated as *The Monkey Link: A Pilgrimage Novel*, 1995) is a trilogy of tales written during the course of more than twenty years: "Ptitsy, ili Novye svedeniia o cheloveke" first appeared in book form in the collection *Dni cheloveka;* Bitov completed "Chelovek v peisazhe" in 1983, and it was published initially in the literary journal *Novyi mir* in 1985; the third tale, "Ozhidanie obez'ian" (Awaiting Monkeys), which is subtitled "Roman-stranstvie" (A Pilgrimage Novel), is the only one that was written after the fall of the Soviet Union. In an approach familiar to readers of Bitov's works, the narrator-author reflects on Russian and human existence from the vantage point of alien territory.

Bitov began this trilogy just as he ended *Pushkinskii dom,* and he carries over into "Ptitsy, ili Novye

*Title page for Bitov's* Uletaiushchii Monakhov: Roman-punktir *(Vanishing Monakhov: A Novel with Ellipses), one of several works that feature his autobiographical hero, Aleksei Monakhov (William T. Young Library, University of Kentucky)*

svedeniia o cheloveke" the motif of freedom found in the words of Modest Platonovich's "God Is." For Leva's grandfather, freedom prevails in God and acts of transcendence: "And yet, under other conditions, I might never have looked up and learned that I was *free*." During a visit to the Kurish Spit, the westernmost tip of the Soviet Union, the journalist-narrator of "Ptitsy, ili Novye svedeniia o cheloveke" recognizes in the archetypically sacred image of the bird a similar ability to transcend. He wonders how humans can overlook the bird's capability to go out of this world and get a clear perspective "looking down." The writer has traveled far to gain a fresh perspective, both geographically and psychologically. His narrator shares the author's ever growing interest in the benefits of ecology—he encourages the reader to take this lesson from the birds.

Rather than a plea to look carefully around (and up) and learn, "Chelovek v peisazhe" presents a blinkered view from the underside of perceived reality. In an allegory of the Brezhnev era of "Stagnation," the protagonist falls through a "landscape" of Russian reality and descends through the oppressive Russian past. Hope resides only in the possibility of passing down and out of the worst of the hellish places; at the nadir all might turn inside out. The writing of this story coincides with one of the bleakest periods in Bitov's writing career (his virtual silencing after the publication of *Pushkinskii dom* and the occurrence of the *Metropol'* affair) and the Soviet invasion of Afghanistan.

In "Ozhidanie obez'ian," the third tale of the trilogy, Bitov openly mocks the failed promise of the Soviet paradise and all those (including himself) who were in any way complicit in the lie. The narrator-pilgrim of the tale travels to Abkhazia, to Moscow, and back. He visits (and ponders) a monkey colony and revisits the era and abuses of Soviet collectivization. "Ozhidanie obez'ian" is the most formally complex tale in the trilogy and thus most in need of the interpretive apparatus that Bitov himself has supplied. The novel alludes heavily to works of Russian and world literature and resonates with citations. This novel, in particular, flaunts its postmodern stylistics—Bitov has published it physically ensconced in other texts, such as commentaries and indices. The final tenor of the novel, though cautionary, suggests that transfiguration is possible.

Since the collapse of the Soviet Union in the early 1990s, Andrei Georgievich Bitov's role as a cultural commentator has grown. Russian intellectuals attend his public lectures and turn to his essays, such as those found in *My prosnulis' v neznakomoi strane* (1991, We Awoke in an Alien Country) and *Piatoe iznerenie: Na granitse vremeni i postranstva* (2002, The Fifth Dimension: On the Border of Time and Space) to reflect on their past and attempt to imagine their future. The significance of his contributions to Russian literature in the second half of the twentieth century is comparable to that of Dostoevsky's work in the second half of the nineteenth century. Unlike Dostoevsky, Bitov did not have access to the world of publishing. Yet, as a writer of both fiction and nonfiction, he represents the Russian intellectual's inquiry into the artistic, political, and social issues of his era.

**Letters:**

Stephen Hagen, "An Unpublished Letter by Andrei Bitov," *Scottish Slavonic Review*, 5 (1985): 108–118.

**Bibliographies:**

Wolf Schmid, "Materialen zu einer Bitov-Bibliographie," *Wiener Slawistischer Almanach*, 4 (1979): 481–495;

Schmid, "Nachtrag zur Bitov-Bibliographie," *Wiener Slawistischer Almanach*, 5 (1980): 327–334.

**References:**

M. Amusin, "Roman A. Bitova Pushkinskii dom i peterburgskii tekst," *Russian, Croatian and Serbian, Czech and Slovak, Polish Literature*, 43 (1998): 413–429;

Harold Baker, "Bitov Reading Proust through the Windows of Pushkin House," *Slavic and East European Journal*, 41 (1997): 604–626;

Baker, "Modest Platonovich in Bitov's *Pushkin House*: A Theory of History and Culture," in *Twentieth-Century Russian Literature: Selected Papers from the Fifth World Congress of Central and East European Studies, Warsaw, 1995*, edited by Karen L. Ryan and Barry P. Scherr (Basingstoke, U.K.: Macmillan / New York: St. Martin's Press, 2000), pp. 206–214;

Olga Hassanoff Bakich, "A New Type of Character in the Soviet Literature of the 1960s: The Early Works of Andrei Bitov," *Canadian Slavonic Papers*, 2 (1981): 125–133;

Peter Barta, "Bitov's Perilous Passage: 'Penelopa,' Odyseus and Plato on Nevskii," *Slavonic and East European Review*, 4 (1998);

Amy L. Cash, "Beyond the Boundary: The Dissolution of Traditional Boundaries in Andrei Bitov's Pushkin House," M.A. thesis, Duke University, 2000;

Ellen Chances, "Andrei Bitov: The Attenuated Boundary Between Art and Life," *Slavic and East European Arts*, 2 (1990): 148–158;

Chances, *Andrei Bitov: The Ecology of Inspiration* (Cambridge: Cambridge University Press, 1993);

Chances, "Andrei Bitov's 'Armenia Lessons': Culture and Values," *Armenian Review*, 41 (1988): 41–52;

Chances, "Andrei Bitov's 'Zhizn' v vetrenuiu pogodu': The Creative Process in Life and Literature," *Slavic Review*, 50 (1991): 400–409;

Chances, "Authenticity as the Tie that Binds: Andrej Bitov's 'Armenia Lessons,'" *Russian Literature*, 28 (1990): 1–9;

Chances, "'In the Middle of the Contrast': Andrei Bitov and the Act of Writing in the Contemporary World," *World Literature Today: A Literary Quarterly of the University of Oklahoma*, 67 (1997): 65–68;

Chances, "'Sunny Side Up': Creativity in Andrei Bitov's 'Sun,'" *Canadian American Slavic Studies*, 22 (1988): 329–336;

E. E. Chudnovskaia, "Za ramkami ocherka (O proze A. Bitova)," *Gosudarstvennyi pedagogicheskii institut. Uchenye zapiski* (Tashkent), 11 (1997): 89–100;

Sergei Aleksandrovich Fomichev, "O literaturovedenii chistom i nechistom. O zavedomykh gipotezakh i Leve Odoevtseve," *Zvezda*, 4 (1978): 202–212;

Dzhon Fridman, "Iskrivlenie real'nosti i vremen v poiske istiny v romanakh *Pushkinskii dom* i *Shkola dlia durakov* (Nenauchnyi ocherk)," *Dvadtsat' dva*, 48 (1986): 201–210;

Revaz Gabriadze, "O rasskaze 'Vkus' i o romane *Uletaiushchii Monakhov*," *Literaturnaia Gruziia*, 1 (1983): 58–61;

M. M. Girshman and S. V. Kuzin, "Osobennosti avtorskoi pozitsii i organizatsiia povestvovaniia v rasskaze: Bitova 'Soldat,'" *Voprosy russkoi literatury: Respublikanskii Mezhvedomstvennyi nauchnyi sbornik*, 1 (1977): 69–76;

Stephen George Sidney Hagen, "The Stories of Andrei Bitov, 1958–1966. A Search for Individual Perception," M.A. thesis, University of Durham, 1980;

Rolf Hellebust, "Fiction and Unreality in Bitov's *Pushkin House*," *Style*, 25 (1991): 265–279;

Marina L. von Hirsch, "Literature as Commentary in Andrei Bitov's Prose: The Nabokov Link," dissertation, Florida State University, 1997;

Iurii Karabichevsky, "Tochka boli. O romane Andreia Bitova, *Pushkinskii dom*," *Grani*, 106 (1977): 141–203;

Anton Kuznetsov, "Izobretenie Kumenngo Topora," *Voprosy literatury*, 1 (1998): 281–297;

Inga Kuznetsova, "Andrei Bitov: Serebrianaia lozhka v ptich'em gnezde," *Znamia*, 2 (1998): 206–212;

Mark Naumovich Lipovetsky, "Razgrom museia. Poetika romana A. Bitova *Pushkinskii dom*," *Novoe literaturnoe obozrenie*, 11 (1995): 230–244;

Ronald Meyer, "Andrei Bitov's 'Bednyj Vsadnik,'" in *James Daniel Armstrong in Memoriam*, edited by Charles E. Gribble and others (Columbus, Ohio: Slavica, 1994), pp. 121–137;

Meyer, "Andrei Bitov's Memoir of Pushkin," *Studies in Comparative Communism*, 21(1988): 379–387;

Meyer, "Andrei Bitov's *Pushkin House*," *Russian Literature Triquarterly*, 22 (1988): 195–204;

Meyer, "Andrei Bitov's *Pushinskii Dom*," dissertation, Indiana University, 1986;

Henrietta Mondry, "*Literaturnost'* as a Key to Andrey Bitov's *Pushkin House*," in *The Waking Sphinx: South African Essays on Russian Culture*, edited by Mondry (Johannesburg: University of the Witwatersrand, 1989), pp. 195–201;

Julie Kay Nachtigal, "Unreality as Condition of Life: A Postmodern View on Andrei Bitov's *Pushkin House*," M.A. thesis, Arizona State University, 1996;

Alice Stone Nakhimovsky, "Looking Back at Paradise Lost: The Russian Nineteenth Century in Andrei Bitov's *Pushkin House*," *Russian Literature Triquarterly*, 22 (1988): 195–204;

Pekka Pesonen, "Bitov's Text as Text: The Petersburg Text as Context in Andrey Bitov's Prose," in *Literary Tradition and Practice in Russian Culture*, edited by Valentina Polukhina, Joe Andrew, and Robert Reid (Amsterdam: Rodopi, 1993), pp. 325–341;

Elizabeth Rich and Adam Perri, "Andrei Bitov," *South Central Review: The Journal of the South Central Modern Language Association*, 12 (1995): 28–35;

I. B. Rodnianskaia, "Obraz i rol'," *Sever*, 12 (1977): 111–119;

Rodnianskaia, "Preodolenie opyta, ili dvadtsat' let stranstvii," in *Literaturnoe semiletie* (Moscow: Knizhnyi sad, 1995), pp. 176–197;

Stephanie Sandler, "Andrei Bitov and the Mystifications of Self and Story," in *Commemorating Pushkin: Russia's Myth of a National Poet* (Stanford: Stanford University Press, 2004), pp. 266–299;

Wolf Schmid, "Andrei Bitov – master 'ostrovideniia,'" *Wiener Slawistischer Almanach*, 27 (1991): 5–11;

Kurt Shaw, "Chasing the Red Balloon: Psychological Separation in the Early Fiction of Andrej Bitov, 1958–1962," dissertation, University of Kansas, 1988;

Shaw, "French Connections: The Three Musketeers Motif in Andrei Bitov's *Pushkinskii dom*," *Canadian Slavonic Papers*, 37 (1995): 187–199;

Olga Slavnikova, "Sushestvovanie v edinstvennon chisle," *Novyi mir*, 7 (1999): 205–210;

Sven Spieker, "Andrei Bitov's Bookish Landscapes: Traveling through the Texts in *Uroki Armenii*," *Wiener Slawistischer Almanach*, 24 (1989): 171–185;

Spieker, *Figures of Memory and Forgetting in Andrej Bitov's Prose: Postmodernism and the Quest for History* (New York: Peter Lang, 1996);

Igor Sukhikh, "Sochinenie na shkol'nvia Temu: 1964–1971, 1978. . . . Pushkinskii dom A. Bitova," *Zvezda*, 2 (2002): 224–234;

Petr Vail and Aleksandr Genis, "Khimera simmetrii. Andrei Bitov," *Sintaksis*, 18 (1987): 80–91;

Evgenii Vertlib, "Andrei Bitov. *Pushkinskii Dom*," *Russian Language Journal*, 34 (1980): 225–228;

Solomon Volkov, "Bitov's ABC," *Slovo-Word*, 19 (1996): 86–98.

# Iurii Vasil'evich Bondarev
## (15 March 1924 -    )

Alexandra Smith
*University of Canterbury, New Zealand*

BOOKS: *Na bol'shoi reke* (Moscow: Sovetskii pisatel', 1953);

*Iunost' komandirov* (Moscow: Sovetskii pisatel', 1956);

*Batal'ony prosiat ognia* (Moscow: Sovetskii pisatel', 1958);

*Poslednie zalpy* (Moscow: Sovetskii pisatel', 1959); translated by L. Lukoshkova as *The Last Shots* (Moscow: Foreign Languages Publishing House, 1959);

*Trudnaia noch'* (Moscow: Voenizdat, 1959);

*Pozdnim vecherom* (Moscow: Molodaia gvardiia, 1962);

*Tishina* (Moscow: Sovetskii pisatel', 1962); translated by Elizaveta Fen as *Silence: A Novel of Post War Russia* (London: Chapman & Hall, 1965); republished as *Silence: A Novel* (Boston: Houghton Mifflin, 1966);

*Stil' i slovo* (Moscow: Sovetskaia Rossiia, 1965);

*Tishina. Dvoe* (Moscow: Sovetskaia Rossiia, 1966);

*Goriachii sneg*, 2 volumes (Moscow: Khudozhestvennaia literatura, 1970); translated by Robert Daglish as *The Hot Snow* (Moscow: Progress, 1976);

*Vzgliad v biografiiu* (Moscow: Sovetskaia Rossiia, 1971);

*Igra* (Moscow: Pravda, 1972);

*Povesti* (Moscow: Sovremennik, 1973);

*Literatura — narodu* (Moscow: Sovetskaia Rossiia, 1974);

*Bereg* (Moscow: Molodaia gvardiia, 1975); translated by Keith Hammond as *The Shore* (Moscow: Raduga, 1984);

*Ozhidanie: Stranitsy iz zapisnoi knizhki* (Moscow: Sovetskaia Rossiia, 1976);

*Poisk istiny* (Moscow: Sovremennik, 1976; enlarged, 1979);

*Maliariia* (Moscow: Pravda, 1977);

*Mgnoveniia* (Moscow: Molodaia gvardiia, 1977; enlarged, 1983; enlarged edition, Moscow: Sovremennik, 1987);

*Chelovek neset v sebe mir* (Moscow: Molodaia gvardiia, 1980);

*Vybor* (Moscow: Molodaia gvardiia, 1981); translated by Monika Whyte as *The Choice* (Moscow: Raduga, 1983);

*Khranitel' tsennostei* (Moscow: Pravda, 1982);

*Iurii Vasil'evich Bondarev (from Ekaterina Nikolaevna Gorbunova, Iurii Bondarev: Ocherk tvorchestva, 1989; Jean and Alexander Heard Library, Vanderbilt University)*

*Mgnoveniia: Miniatiury* (Moscow: Sovetskaia Rossiia, 1988);

*Iskushenie* (Moscow: Molodaia gvardiia, 1992);

*Sluchainost'* (Moscow: RBP, 1995);

*Neprotivlenie* (Moscow: Molodaia gvardiia, 1996);

*Bermudskii treugol'nik* (Moscow: Molodaia gvardiia, 2000).

**Collections:** *Batal'ony prosiat ognia. Poslednie zalpy* (Moscow: Khudozhestvennaia literatura, 1966);

*Sobranie sochinenii,* 4 volumes (Moscow: Molodaia gvardiia, 1973–1974);

*Sobranie sochinenii,* 6 volumes (Moscow: Khudozhestvennaia literatura, 1984–1986);

*Sobranie sochinenii,* 8 volumes, edited by Petr Fedorovich Aleshkin (Moscow: Golos: Russkii arkhiv, 1993–1996).

PRODUCED SCRIPTS: *Poslednie zalpy,* by Bondarev and Leon Saakov, motion picture, Mosfil'm, 1960;

*49 dnei,* by Bondarev, Vladimir Fedorovich Tendriakov, and Grigorii Balkanov, motion picture, Mosfil'm, 1962;

*Tishina,* by Bondarev and Vladimir Basov, motion picture, Mosfil'm, 1964;

*Napravlenie glavnogo udara,* by Bondarev, Oskar Ieremeevich Kurganov, and Iurii Nikolaevich Ozerov, motion picture, DEFA-Studio für Spielfilme/Mosfil'm/Zespol Filmowy, 1969;

*Osvobozhdenie,* by Bondarev, Kurganov, and Ozerov, television, DEFA-Studio für Spielfilme/Mosfil'm, 1970;

*Goriachii sneg,* by Bondarev, Evgenii Grigor'ev, and Gavriil Egiazarov, motion picture, Mosfil'm, 1972;

*Osvobozhdenie: Kinoepopeia,* by Bondarev, Kurgamov, and Ozerov, motion picture, Voenizdat, 1976;

*Vot opiat okno,* by Bondarev, G. Goryshin, and Izrail Metter, television, Lentelefilm, 1982;

*Bereg,* by Bondarev, Aleksandr Alov, and Vladimir Naumov, motion picture, Mosfil'm/Allianz Filmproduktion, 1984;

*Batal'ony prosiat ognia,* by Bondarev and Aleksandr Bogoliubov, television, Gosteleradio/Mosfil'm, 1985;

*Vybor,* by Bondarev and Naumov, motion picture, Adriana International Corporation/Mosfil'm/Sovinfilm, 1987.

OTHER: *Altaiskie milliony,* edited by Bondarev (Moscow: Sovetskaia Rossiia, 1973);

*Nivy Rossii,* edited by Bondarev, compiled by Pavel Alekseevich Kareli (Moscow: Sovetskaia Rossiia, 1981);

*Rasskazy sovetskikh pisatelei,* 3 volumes, edited by Bondarev and others, compiled by Gennadii Gusev (Moscow: Khudozhestvennaia literatura, 1982);

Mikhail Iur'evich Lermontov, *Sobranie sochinenii,* 4 volumes, edited by Bondarev (Moscow, 1985);

Ivan Alekseevich Bunin, *Sobranie sochinenii,* 6 volumes, edited by Bondarev and others (Moscow: Khudozhestvennaia literatura, 1987);

Valentin Savvich Pikul', *Polnoe sobranie sochinenii,* 28 [out of 30] volumes, edited by Bondarev and others (Moscow: Patriot, 1992–1998).

Iurii Bondarev is a prominent war writer whose novels and stories about World War II made a significant contribution to the development of Soviet Russian literature from the 1960s to the 1980s. Although he has always written within the boundaries of official government dictates, he nevertheless tries to look objectively at the morality of his generation. His works generally portray the hazards of war and the complex relationships that develop among people during perilous times.

Iurii Vasil'evich Bondarev was born in Orsk, in the Orenburg region, on 15 March 1924. His father, Vasilii Vasil'evich Bondarev (1896–1988), worked as an investigator. His mother, Klavdiia Iosifovna Bondareva (1900–1978), introduced him to Russian classical literature. In 1931 Bondarev's family moved to Moscow. There, Bondarev graduated from School No. 516 in 1941, where he first started writing fiction. In 1942–1945, after graduating from Berdichev Infantry College, Bondarev served as an artillery officer. He participated in important battles in Stalingrad, Ukraine, Poland, and Czechoslovakia. In 1944 he joined the Communist Party and remained a member until 1991. In 1946–1951 he studied at the Gor'ky Literary Institute, where he took creative-writing courses under the supervision of the prose master Konstantin Georgievich Paustovsky.

Bondarev's first story was published in 1949, the same year he was elected to the Writers' Union, and his first collection of stories, *Na bol'shoi reke* (In the Big River), appeared in 1953. Bondarev's wartime experience frames most of his works. His first novella, *Iunost' komandirov* (The Youth of Commanders, 1956), portrays the students of a military college who are training to become specialists for the artillery forces; among them are the young men Aleksei Dmitriev, Boris Briantsev, and Tolia Drozdov. Most students of this college are veterans of World War II, and their postwar experiences are the focus of Bondarev's discourse on the trauma that haunted several generations of Soviets in the 1940s and 1950s. As Bondarev demonstrates in his novella, the transition to peaceful life for most war veterans was not easy and was marked by various psychological traumas. In the course of the narrative Captain Mel'nichenko learns about the death of his wife; Aleksei finds out about the death of his mother during the Leningrad blockade; and Major Gradusov has cause to reassess his life. All of these characters need time to come to terms with life in peacetime; they must learn to live again.

In an unobtrusive manner Bondarev invites his readers to experience life along with his characters in a distinctive way–that is, to grow to appreciate the simple pleasures of everyday life without war. Thus, for example, Aleksei observes: "I did not have a tram ride for four years. I would like to remind myself how to do it." Aleksei spends two weeks in provincial Berezansk, where he is overwhelmed by the beauty of life. Yet, he longs for the worldview of his war years–an outlook that was based on something ordinary, simple, and clear. He feels that something is missing in postwar life, and the memory of war continually haunts him. Furthermore, Aleksei's wartime friend Boris betrays and slanders him. Shocked by the immoral action of his friend, Aleksei learns to appreciate moral values more than anything else in his life, and as a result he quits his military career. Boris's love for a girl, Maia, enables his transformation into a mature adult. In *Iunost' komandirov* Bondarev brings values to the fore that were forgotten in 1930s and 1940s Soviet society, such as humanist values, bonds with other people, and aesthetic appreciation. Not coincidentally, Bondarev refers to Aleksei as a hero from Leo Tolstoy's *Voina i mir* (1869–1869, *War and Peace*), "Andrei Bolkonsky, who is wearing his Byronic cape." The analogies between Bondarev's novella and Tolstoy's epic novel appear intentionally, because Bondarev is not preoccupied with the depiction of grand battles and universal truths. He is concerned with the psychological and moral issues that are relevant to the life of ordinary Soviet citizens. In a Tolstoyan vein Bondarev depicts important historical events from a human perspective. In an interview for *Literaturnaia gazeta* (The Literary Gazette) he said: "Historical events do not interest me as such; they interest me only in the way they relate to the fate of the individual, or to the fate of the nation."

Bondarev's first major works also include the novella *Batal'ony prosiat ognia* (The Battalions Request Fire, first published 1957 in *Molodaia gvardiia* [The Young Guard], published 1958 in book form) and *Poslednie zalpy* (1959; translated as *The Last Shots*, 1959). They display his interest in the heroic actions of small military units, or of individuals who are opposed to abstract notions of heroism and patriotism as manifested in Soviet propagandist media. Furthermore, Bondarev questions the ethical grounds for military expediency. According to literary editor Mikhail Ivanovich Kuznetsov's account, most of Moscow was discussing the novella *Batal'ony prosiat ognia*–in libraries, canteens, editorial offices, and at writers' gatherings–

shortly after its appearance in the journal *Molodaia gvardiia*. In the novella the few survivors of Colonel Guliaev's battalions discover the truth about their role in an important military operation that had led to heavy losses. The mission of the battalion, as the characters later learn, was to distract the Germans from a larger operation to the north of the Dnepr River region, where there was also fighting. Bondarev's characters encounter a dilemma over their own moral choices and the values of the Soviet state. *Batal'ony prosiat ognia*, which was adapted for television in 1985, reinforces Tolstoy's view that in history ordinary soldiers are the ones who matter, not the commanders and planners who are at a remove from immediate danger.

Bondarev's dramatic and realistic description of the tragic destruction of two battalions opens up a critical evaluation of the Soviet authorities' plans for, and attitudes toward, ordinary people. Thus, at the end of the battle Boris Ermakov sees the Soviet planes that were presumably sent to assist Colonel Guliaev's battalions. As Bondarev writes, Ermakov is "Ready to cry and denounce the sky bringing him some assistance," and the soldier produces a terrifying cry full of frustration and powerlessness: "Too late! Too late!" To come to terms with the betrayal of most of the members of the two battalions is difficult for Ermakov. That their commanders used them and that their lives were wasted in the most senseless manner are incomprehensible. In their reviews of this novella many Soviet critics commented on Bondarev's ability both to depict a shocking truth and to combine lyric and epic aspects in the representation of war. According to Oleg Nikolaevich Mikhailov, Bondarev introduced a new aesthetic to Soviet literature, to the extent that weapons of destruction, such as tanks and planes, come alive in the narrative in order to terrify and, simultaneously, evoke admiration.

The problems of war veterans trying to adapt to civilian life and narrow the gap between "the generation that grew up in war" and "the generation that grew up in the rear" are addressed in Bondarev's novel *Tishina* (1962; translated as *Silence: A Novel of Post War Russia*, 1965). It portrays two war veterans, Sergei and Konstantin, whose expectations of a better life in Russia were shaped during World War II. In their postwar life they are troubled by the new ideological "wars" that Joseph Stalin and his party henchman Andrei Aleksandrovich Zhdanov are leading, as well as by the memory of Stalin's purges of the 1930s. In *Tishina*, which was adapted for motion pictures in 1964, Bondarev reflects on the consequences of the terror instigated by Zhdanov; by Stalin's "Doctors' Plot" (in which the Soviet leader accused nine doctors–many of them Jewish–of trying to kill him and other key government figures); and by Stalin's 1952–1953 anti-Semitic campaign against "rootless cosmopolitans." The novel concludes with Stalin's death. As Frank Ellis points out, "memory, guilt, duty, and loyalty are the main themes" of *Tishina*. The protagonist, Sergei Vokhmintsev, encounters a former soldier, Captain Uvarov, whose oversight of orders during the war resulted in the arrest and punishment of an innocent officer. Sergei is convinced that Uvarov should be held responsible for the death of twenty-eight artillery soldiers killed near Zhukovtsy. Furthermore, the officer who was slandered by Uvarov was sent to one of the battles, among the soldiers expected to be killed first. As a result he did not survive the war. When Sergei meets Uvarov in a restaurant after the war, he punches him in the face.

Uvarov epitomizes cowardice and opportunism, traits that frequently appear in Bondarev's characters. These opportunistic characters often avoid punishment, successfully manipulate the system, and thrive in the postwar Soviet Union. In a paradoxical twist, Uvarov—who burned his Communist Party card during the war—enjoys the trust of the party in the postwar period. Bondarev's sympathy with Sergei's rejection of Uvarov suggests that the author's moral choice is in conflict with contemporary social values. Thus, Bondarev's novel tells the story of one of Sergei's neighbors, an artist, Mukomolov, who is being victimized in a campaign against cosmopolitans. Sergei's father is arrested for alleged involvement in ideological sabotage; a safe containing important party documents, with which his father had been entrusted, went missing during the war. The arrest was instigated by the report of their neighbor Bykov. While attempting to clear his father's name, Sergei was told by a Soviet official that "nobody is arrested by mistake in the Soviet state." Furthermore, Sergei's father, an old Communist of integrity, sends a secret letter from prison to his son. It states: "It is impossible to believe that all the monstrous things I have seen here can survive under cover of love for Stalin."

As a party member, Sergei was expected to notify his party committee of the arrest of his relative. Yet, he fails to do so, and as a result his party card is taken away from him. Sergei's loyalty to the state, which secured victory during the war, is undermined by such an act of humiliation. He quits the university and finds a job in Karaganda in Kazakhstan. Sergei's friend Konstantin Korabel'nikov also quits the university in support of his friend. Soviet reality, as portrayed in *Tishina*, is terrifying in its antihumanist cruelty: people are arrested, psychologically intimidated, and interrogated; families and careers are destroyed; and children are brainwashed. The psychological drama created by

*Bondarev about the time his first collection of stories,* Na bol'shoi reke *(1953, In the Big River), was published (from Iurii Vladimirovich Idashkin,* Postizhenie podviga: Rasskazy o tvorchestve IU. V. Bondareva, *1980; Jean and Alexander Heard Library, Vanderbilt University)*

Bondarev in this novel is reinforced through his use of surreal overtones. For example, at the beginning of the novel, Sergei has a nightmare in which he is chased away in the ruins of a destroyed city by war planes that also appear to him as "frightening gigantic spiders." In a symbolic manner this dream implies that the memory of the past signifies death. At the end of the dream, Sergei sees himself frozen from fear inside one of the buildings: "He felt the icy wind blowing into his back from the open door; and he understood that behind his back is death." The second part of the novel depicts the events of 1953 and has some optimistic overtones associated with the death of Stalin. The title of the novel alludes to the silence of the Soviet people—a silence that ensures their survival and leads to moral degradation. Thus, Vokhmintsev accuses the Communist Morozov of taking part in this process of forgetting the truth: "Such people as Uvarov and Sviridov undermine the cause of the communist party, faith and justice in this cause. And you, and others like you, you keep silent and use the international situation and other arguments to justify this phenomenon. Your clever silence goes to hell, when bones are broken! And you try to use an argument of something like pragmatic egoism." The novel addresses the issue of personal responsibility that is overlooked by other Soviet writers of this period. *Tishina* might be seen as an indictment of Stalin's regime, even after all the sacrifices that the Soviet people had to bear in order to win their victory over Adolf Hitler's Germany.

Another important work of this period is Bondarev's novella *Rodstvenniki* (Relatives, published 1969 in the journal *Oktiabr'* [October]). It tells of a young man, Nikita, who arrives in Moscow from Leningrad to see his uncle Professor Georgii Lavrent'evich Grekov. Nikita has brought a letter from his late mother, Vera Lavrent'evna Grekova, in which she asks her brother to take care of her son. As the story unfolds, the seemingly successful professor has some conflicts with his two sons, Alexei and Valerii—to the extent that Aleksei, a war veteran, lives modestly with his young family and does not wish to accept any help from his father. Furthermore, Nikita learns one day that in the past Professor Grekov misled the police, and his report brought about Nikita's mother's arrest and imprisonment. Nikita is shocked to discover that Professor Grekov, who made Nikita's mother suffer for several years, did not kill himself or become a monk but "continued to live and organize birthday parties." The novella addresses important moral questions relating to Stalinism and to those who should be made accountable for the crimes of this period. Vera Grekova thus writes in her letter: "I hope that history will be an objective judge, and repay everyone accordingly." Valerii—the younger son of Professor Grekov—and Nikita drive from their summer cottage to Moscow to find out the whole truth about Professor Grekov's past. On the way there, however, they are involved in a car accident, which kills Valerii and prevents him from finding out the truth about his father. Nikita is severely injured in the accident. In *Rodstvenniki*, Bondarev presents the theme of an individual's moral responsibility in an uncompromising manner and as an issue of grave importance. Although most critics have overlooked this novella, Vasilii Vladimirovich Bykov, a prominent Soviet writer of war fiction, observed that Bondarev's novella conveys "the absolute and unpleasant truth about the period." Bykov thinks that *Rodstvenniki* is superior to Bondarev's other works because it reveals "the intensity of the moral nerve" that became a matter of great importance to the postwar generation of Soviet youth.

Bondarev's most acclaimed novel to date, *Goriachii sneg* (1970; translated as *The Hot Snow*, 1976), discusses the Battle of Stalingrad in an epic vein. It portrays several Soviet soldiers and officers, as well as the generals working for the headquarters. One of the generals is given the symbolic name Bessonov, meaning "sleepless," for he epitomizes the professional qualities of untiring dedication that Bondarev admires. Bondarev brings to the fore Bessonov's total dedication to his job, fairness in dealing with people, and, above all, his human qualities. In a laconic manner he portrays Bessonov's meeting with Stalin as businesslike, but this seemingly unremarkable conversation becomes more and more meaningful to Bessonov as the story unfolds. In the meeting Stalin is portrayed in a favorable light: as a person who understands the important aspects of planning for a forthcoming battle. Stalin gives Bessonov important advice about how to make soldiers overcome their image of German soldiers as mighty and powerful. In this conversation Stalin also refers to the treachery of General Andrei Andreevich Vlasov (a Nazi collaborator) and to Bessonov's independent mind—suggesting that Stalin would like Bessonov to prove himself superior to Vlasov.

*Goriachii sneg* creates an atmosphere of national unity and overwhelming patriotism not unlike that found in Tolstoy's depiction of Russians in *Voina i mir*. For his novel, as Bondarev explains in "Chelovek neset v sebe mir" (A Person Represents the World), the title essay of a collection published in 1980, he used military memoirs and personal conversations with various high-ranking military commanders, including Marshal Georgii Konstantinovich Zhukov. *Goriachii sneg* provides readers with some significant psychological insights into the mentality of humble Soviets whose sense of duty and loyalty to their country turned them into heroes. It is also permeated with melodramatic overtones. For example, the female protagonist Zoia Elagina gets killed without realizing her dreams of becoming a mother of many children and having a quiet family life as soon as the war finishes. In addition, the novel highlights the mass destruction of advanced technology in modern times. Mikhail Aleksandrovich Sholokhov considered *Goriachii sneg*, which was made into a movie in 1972, Bondarev's most significant achievement. "Bondarev not only demonstrated to us the moral attitude of the Soviet soldier to the events that took place around him," commented Sholokhov, "but he also revealed to us what the great sense of personal responsibility for everything that happened during the war comprised."

Bondarev's novel *Bereg* (1975; translated as *The Shore*, 1984; adapted 1984 as a motion picture), a philosophical work with strong autobiographical overtones, is about Nikitin, a successful Soviet writer and war veteran, who visits West Germany. He discusses the past with Ditsman, a German editor, who points out that if in the past they had been separated from each other by the memory of the 1940s, in the 1970s they are divided by political systems. Reflecting on his expectations at the end of World War II, Nikitin says, "In 1945 I believed that everything would change after the war, that the whole world and life in general would be one endless holiday." In the novel the juxtaposition of war scenes with contemporary events suggests that Nikitin and other war veterans cannot forget the past. He keeps remembering his friend, Lieutenant Andrei Kniazhko, who was killed in one of the battles at the end of the war; Kniazhko wanted to stop firing at the young German soldiers who were screaming for help. Nikitin confesses to his German friends that he had never met anyone like Kniazhko, and he misses him. The story of Kniazhko has an unmistakable touch of humanism that was highly praised by German reviewers of the novel. One German newspaper stated that *Bereg* was "permeated with the tender atmosphere of humanity that makes this book especially appealing." According to Bondarev, his novel represents a bridge from the past to the present, an idea that is manifested in the symbolic title, which signifies the shore to which the main character, because of his spiritual quest, is drawn: "This is a novel about happiness, love, and about the quest for the meaning of life." As Bondarev explains, everyone should find for himself his own shore—his own truth that makes him happy. "Every person," asserts Bondarev, "seeks a shore within himself and outside. The fact of whether a person finds his shore or not determines how happy or unhappy he is." Some Soviet critics compare Nikitin to the character of Pierre Bezukhov in *Voina i mir*. In all the major novels written by Bondarev many war veterans are presented as philosophers who are on a spiritual quest for the truth. In this respect their war experiences are depicted as an awakening of their moral consciousness. Bondarev's novels are concerned with individuals, rather than with Soviet conditions on a level comparable to the novels of the 1920s and 1930s. In this respect Bondarev is a Soviet prose writer who cultivates a short story or novella in preference to epic and historical narratives.

Soviet critics see Bondarev's novel *Vybor* (1981; translated as *The Choice*, 1983; adapted 1987 as a motion picture) as a polyphonic and philosophical work. It tells of a talented Moscow artist, Vasil'ev, and his wife, Mariia, who travel to Venice. This trip to the city that Vasil'ev loves becomes a backdrop for a psychological drama. He learns from his wife that she has received a letter from Il'ia Ramzin, a friend from the past whom they thought had been killed in the war. A successful Soviet artist, Vasil'ev finds meeting with Il'ia awkward; he considers Il'ia, who settled in the West, a traitor. Il'ia needs a visa for travel to the U.S.S.R., and he asks his old friend Vasil'ev to use his influence to help him obtain the visa. At the end of the novel, when Il'ia returns to the Soviet Union and reunites with his mother after a forty-year absence, he realizes that he has become a displaced person. He chooses to die and be buried in his native land.

Apparently, Il'ia's survival during the war was secured by his escape to Germany because of complex

*Title page for the volume collecting two of Bondarev's novellas about valorous military units:* Batal'ony prosiat ognia *(1958, The Batallions Request Fire) and* Poslednie zalpy *(1959; translated as* The Last Shots, *1959; Thomas Cooper Library, University of South Carolina)*

circumstances. Later, after his return to the U.S.S.R., he seems to experience feelings of guilt that drive him to commit suicide. In his suicide note he writes to Vasil'ev: "I do not know what people deserve more: compassion or hatred." In their discussion of the novel some Soviet critics stated that Il'ia epitomizes an ambition that grew to pathological proportions and that subsequently he stands for a worldview of extreme individualism. Bondarev portrays Il'ia's lack of empathy for people in a Nietzschean vein. Il'ia defines himself as a person beyond any political trends and beyond good and evil. "There is no God," explains Il'ia to his friend, "neither here, nor there." He maintains that human beings are tragically lonely everywhere, and everyone is subjected to cruel experiments of Nature. In a provocative way in *Vybor,* Bondarev also ponders the nature of success through the character of the established Soviet artist Vasil'ev. At the end of the novel the narrator realizes that "sooner or later it will be necessary to pay for the fifteen years of quiet life, for the so called successful career, recognition . . . trips abroad to exhibit his works." Here, Bondarev raises concerns about the ethics of representation in the postwar period–hence Vasil'ev's idealization of the prewar period as a lost paradise.

In Russia, Bondarev is also well known as an author of many essays on culture, literature, and philosophy. Most of his nonfiction pieces are collected in *Vzgliad v biografiiu* (1971, A Gaze at Biography) and *Poisk istiny* (1976, The Quest for Truth). His collection of short stories and essays, *Mgnoveniia* (1988, Moments), touches upon aesthetic values, Western culture, observations on war veterans, childhood, and his contemporaries. It conveys Bondarev's scattered thoughts on various subjects that do not create a coherent worldview. In the essay "Neukliuzhest' istiny" (The Awkwardness of Truth), for example, Bondarev states that he loves "Ancient Greek tragedy" but does not appreciate the Hellenistic sculpture that shapes everything in canonical classical forms; in "Madonna Litta" he proclaims Leonardo da Vinci's Madonna to be the mother of life on earth, someone whom he would like to worship forever; in "Omertvenie chuvstva" (The Death of Emotion) he proffers his critical responses to French contemporary culture, which he deems pornographic and pathological, for it lacks the concept of beautiful love; and in "Genial'noe polotno" (Canvas of Genius) he mocks avant-garde modes of representation and suggests that the music of Johannes Brahms and Wolfgang Amadeus Mozart portrays human life in a more expressive manner than the canvases of some Impressionists. In some of his recent comments Bondarev has defined the post-Soviet era as a "timeless period, without great ideas, a natural way of life, or morality." He sees contemporary Russian freedom as a right to "spit into the future at something saintly, pure, and innocent." At present his attitudes represent various conservative tendencies in contemporary Russian society.

Iurii Vasil'evich Bondarev and his wife, Valentina Nikitichna Bondareva, reside in Moscow; they have two daughters: Elena, a specialist in English studies, and Ekaterina, an artist. His major literary achievements are in Soviet war literature and the literature of reconstruction. He is a member of the board of the Writers' Union, serving since 1971 as chairman; he also belongs to the Union of Cinematographers. In 1975–1989 he participated in the Supreme Soviet of the Russian Soviet Federated Socialist Republic of the former Soviet Union (R.S.F.S.R.). In 1995 he became cochairman of the International Union of Writers. In addition, Bondarev has been awarded many prestigious prizes for his achievements in Soviet and Russian literature: the Lenin Prize (1972), the U.S.S.R. State Prize (1974 and 1983), the R.S.F.S.R. State Prize (1975), and the Leo Tolstoy Prize (1993). His later work is marked by conservative and anti-Western tendencies. His novels and stories have been translated into more than seventy languages, including English, German, French, Japanese, and Italian. Finally, his major works have been the bases of various movies devoted to World War II, including the epic motion picture *Osvobozhdenie* (1970, Liberation), for which Bondarev wrote the script in cooperation with the movie director Iurii Nikolaevich Ozerov and with Oskar Ieremeevich Kurganov.

**References:**
Viktoriia Vladimirovna Buznik, "Pamiat' voiny: iz pisem chitatelei k Iuriiu Vasi'evichu Bondarevu," *Russkaia literatura,* 3 (1995): 96–113;

Nikolai Mikhailovich Fed', "Gor'kii vkus istiny: Razmyshleniia o romane Iuriia bondareva 'Igra,'" *Moskva,* 10 (October 1985): 184–195;

Fed', *Khudozhestvennye otkrytiia Bondareva* (Moscow: Sovremennik, 1988);

Fed', "Neobychnaia iniga, ili rozhdenie novogo zhanra," *Nash sovremennik,* 5 (May 1987): 172–185;

Ekaterina Nikolaevna Gorbunova, *Iurii Bondarev: Ocherk tvorchestva* (Moscow: Sovetskaia Rossiia, 1989);

Gorbunova, "Problema vybora i viny: k sporam vokrug romanov Iu. Bondareva," *Oktiabr',* 5 (May 1988): 180–188;

Iurii Vladimirovich Idashkin, *Grani talanta: O tvorchestve Iuriia Bondareva* (Moscow: Khudozhestvennaia literatura, 1983);

Idashkin, *Iurii Bondarev* (Moscow: Khudozhestvennaia literatura, 1987);

Idashkin, "Oglianis; Vo gneve," *Voprosy literatury,* 7 (1986): 144–171;

Idashkin, *On Craftsmanship: Iurii Bondarev,* translated by Christopher English (Moscow: Raduga, 1983);

Vladimir Ivanovich Korobov, *Iurii Bondarev* (Moscow: Sovremennik, 1984);

Korobov, "Utverzhdenie i otritsanie: Bondarevu–60 let," *Oktiabr',* 3 (March 1984): 190–195;

Konstantin Kovalev, "V poiskakh pravdy o sebe: O mirosozertsanii geroia romana Iu. Bondareva 'Igra,'" *Molodaia gvardiia,* 3 (1986): 270–278;

A. Mansurova, "Roman Bondareva 'Goriachii sneg' i ego mesto v sovremennoi sovetskoi literature," *Filologicheskie nauki,* 17, no. 3 (1975): 41–47;

Oleg Nikolaevich Mikhailov, *Iurii Bondarev* (Moscow: Sovetskaia Rossiia, 1976);

Mikhailov, "Sud'ba: o romane Iu. Bindareva 'Bereg,'" *Moskva,* 9 (1975): 196–206;

Aleksandr Ivanovich Ovcharenko, "Ot voiny k miru: o tvorchestve Iuriia Bondareva," *Nash sovremennik,* 5 (1983): 163–178;

Aleksandr Viktorovich Pankov, "Dolgii put' poznaniia; k 60-letiiu Iu. Bondareva," *Znamia,* 3 (March 1984): 225–230;

Viktor Ivanovich Polozhii, *Kontseptsiia geroicheskoi lichnosti v tvorchestve Iuriia Bondareva* (Kiev: Nauk. Dumka, 1983);

N. N. Shneidman, "Iurii Bondarev," in his *Soviet Literature in the 1980s: Decade of Transition* (Toronto: University of Toronto Press, 1989), pp. 124–132;

Shneidman, *Russian Literature 1988–1994: The End of an Era* (Toronto: Toronto University Press, 1995), pp. 67–72;

A. S. Silaev, "Chelovek iskusstva v romane Bondareva 'Vybor,'" *Voprosy russkoi literatury,* 1, no. 51 (1988): 62–68;

Anatolii Vasilenko, "Nuzhno li chitat' novyi roman Iuriia Bondareva?" *Molodaia gvardiia,* 10 (1995): 229–233.

# Lidiia Chukovskaia
*(24 March 1907 – 7 February 1996)*

Sibelan Forrester
*Swarthmore College*

BOOKS: *Istoriia odnogo vosstaniia* (Moscow: Izd-vo detskoi lit-ry, 1940);

*N. N. Miklukho-Maklai* (Moscow: Geografgiz, 1948);

*Dekabrist Nikolai Bestuzhev: Issledovatel' Buriatii* (Moscow: Geografgiz, 1950);

*Dekabristy, issledovateli Sibiri* (Moscow: Geografgiz, 1951);

*Boris Zhitkov: Kritiko-biograficheskii ocherk* (Moscow: Sovetskii pisatel', 1955);

*S. Georgievskaia, Kritiko-biograficheskii ocherk* (Moscow: Izd-vo detskoi lit-ry, 1955);

*V laboratorii redaktora* (Moscow: Iskusstvo, 1960);

*Opustelyi dom: Povest'* (Paris: Piat' kontinentov, 1965); republished as "Sof'ia Petrovna," *Novyi zhurnal* (New York), no. 83 (June 1966): 5–45; no. 84 (September 1966): 5–46; translated by Aline Werth as *The Deserted House* (New York: Dutton, 1967; London: Barrie & Rockliff, 1967); translation revised by Eliza Kellogg Klose as *Sofia Petrovna* (Evanston, Ill.: Northwestern University Press, 1988); translated by David Floyd as *Sofia Petrovna* (London: Collins Harvill, 1989);

*"Byloe i dumy" Gertsena* (Moscow: Khudozhestvennaia literatura, 1966);

*Going Under*, translated from the manuscript by Peter M. Weston (London: Barrie & Jenkins, 1972); Russian version published as *Spusk pod vodu* (New York: Chekhova, 1972);

*Zapiski ob Anne Akhmatovoi: 1938–1941* (Paris: YMCA-Press, 1976); revised and enlarged as *Zapiski ob Anne Akhmatovoi* (Paris: YMCA-Press, 1984; Moscow: Kniga, 1989); revised by Chukovskaia and translated by Milena Michalska, Sylvia Rubasheva, and Peter Norman as *The Akhmatova Journals* (London: Harvill, 1994; New York: Farrar, Straus & Giroux, 1994); revised Russian version published as *Zapiski ob Anne Akhmatovoi* (St. Petersburg: Neva, 1995; Kharkiv: Folio, 1996); revised and enlarged as *Zapiski ob Anne Akhmatovoi v trekh tomakh*, 3 volumes (Moscow: Soglasie, 1997);

*Lidiia Chukovskaia (from Zapiski ob Anne Akhmatovoi: 1938–1941, volume 2, 1976; Thomas Cooper Library, University of South Carolina)*

*Otkrytoe slovo* (New York: Khronika, 1976; edited by Vladimir Glotser, Moscow: IMA Press, 1991);

*Po ètu storonu smerti: Iz dnevnika 1936–1976* (Paris: YMCA-Press, 1978);

*Protsess iskliucheniia: Ocherk literaturnykh nravov* (Paris: YMCA-Press, 1979; Moscow: Novoe vremia, 1990);

*Pamiati detstva* (New York: Chalidze, 1983); translated by Eliza Kellogg Klose as *To the Memory of Child-*

*hood* (Evanston, Ill.: Northwestern University Press, 1988); Russian version republished (Moscow: Moskovskii rabochii, 1989);

*Stikhotvoreniia* (Moscow: Gorizont, 1992).

**Editions and Collections:** *Sof'ia Petrovna; Spusk pod vodu: Povesti* (Moscow: Moskovskii rabochii, 1988);

*Izbrannoe* (Moscow: Gorizont" / Minsk: Aurika, 1997);

*Sochineniia v 2-kh tomakh,* 2 volumes (Moscow: Gud'ial Press, 2000);

*Pamiati detstva: Vospominaniia o Kornee Chukovskom* (St. Petersburg: Limbus Press, 2000).

OTHER: *Slovo predostavliaetsia detiam,* edited by Chukovskaia (Tashkent, 1942).

Lidiia Chukovskaia was an editor and the author of children's books, criticism, fiction, poetry, and a variety of journalistic works. She played Boswell to the banned poet Anna Andreevna Akhmatova during the darkest days of Stalinist repression, and for twenty years, beginning during the "Thaw," she was a leading figure in the Soviet dissident movement. For her many admirers in Russia and abroad her importance lies more in her personality than in her publications, but her writing seems sure to remain crucial to Russian history and literature.

Lidiia Korneevna Chukovskaia was born on 24 March 1907 in St. Petersburg to the literary critic, memoirist, author of children's verse, editor, and translator Kornei Ivanovich Chukovsky (born Nikolai Vasil'evich Korneichukov) and Maria Borisovna Chukovskaia. She had an older brother, Nikolai, and two younger siblings, Boris and Maria; the latter died of tuberculosis as a child. Her early education was mostly at the family's home in the Finnish dacha community of Kuokkala (today Repino); she evokes those early years lovingly in her memoirs, *Pamiati detstva* (1983; translated as *To the Memory of Childhood,* 1988), which are devoted mainly to her father. Unlike most of the local Russians, who only stayed there in the summer, the Chukovskys lived in Kuokkala year-round from 1910 to 1917. Chukovskaia learned early the value of reading, as well as the idea that writers and artists were special beings. Moreover, as her father noted in his diary, she was a "born humanist," oriented toward other people and their particular needs and gifts. After the abdication of Tsar Nikolas II the family moved to Petrograd, which became Leningrad in 1924. There, despite their difficult financial situation during the years of war communism, Chukovskaia attended the fine schools of the former capital: the Tagantsev Gymnasium and the Tenishev School, where Osip Emil'evich Mandel'shtam and Vladimir Nabokov had been pupils before the revolution.

In 1924 Chukovskaia enrolled at the Leningrad Institute for the History of the Arts, where she attended lectures on literature by such leading theoretical lights as Iurii Nikolaevich Tynianov, Boris Mikhailovich Eikhenbaum, and Viktor Maksimovich Zhirmunsky. In 1926 she was arrested, apparently for objecting to arbitrariness in the conduct of her Komsomol (Communist Youth) chapter, and exiled to Saratov. After eleven months, her father arranged for her to return to Leningrad. In 1928 she graduated from the Philological Faculty of Leningrad University and became an editor at Detgiz, the children's literature branch of the Leningrad State Publishing House Gosizdat, where she worked with her father's friend, the poet and critic Samuil Iakovlevich Marshak. Chukovskaia received Marshak's help and advice as she began her career, and she writes extensively about him and her experiences at Detgiz in *V laboratorii redaktora* (In the Editor's Laboratory, 1960). She began to publish her own children's works in magazines in 1928 under the pseudonym Aleksei Uglov. Chukovskaia's first marriage, in 1929 to the up-and-coming critic and editor Tsezar' Samoilovich Vol'pe ended in divorce in 1933; their daughter Elena (Liusha) was born in August 1931.

In 1937 several Detgiz workers were denounced by a colleague as *vrediteli* (wreckers, supposedly working to undermine the Soviet system). Chukovskaia and all of her friends lost their jobs, and several were arrested; the atmosphere of dread and confusion is reflected in her novel *Sof'ia Petrovna* (1966; translated as *The Deserted House,* 1967). Chukovskaia's second husband, the astrophysicist and author Matvei Petrovich Bronshtein, was arrested late that year and sentenced to "ten years of imprisonment without the right to correspond"—meaning that he was probably executed immediately (the family did not receive confirmation of his death until 1957). Warned by her father that the NKVD (Narodnyi komissariat vnutrennykh del [People's Commissariat for Internal Affairs]) had come to search her apartment and, clearly, to arrest her, as well, Chukovskaia spent several months after Bronshtein's arrest moving from city to city, staying with friends and relatives and not seeing her daughter for weeks at a time. She returned to Leningrad only after the wave of arrests and exiles had subsided.

Chukovskaia had encountered Akhmatova in passing, but in 1938 the two began to meet regularly. Chukovskaia decided that she must record every word of their conversations for posterity. Her ability to memorize verse quickly and accurately was an asset in helping to preserve Akhmatova's new poetry, especially the long poem *Rekviem* (1963; translated as *Requiem,* 1976).

*Drawing of Chukovskaia by the poet Vladimir Vladimirovich Maiakovsky, 1915 (from* Pamiati detstva, *second edition, 1989; translated as* To the Memory of Childhood, *1988; Thomas Cooper Library, University of South Carolina)*

Akhmatova would jot a new poem or stanza on a scrap of paper; Chukovskaia would memorize it, and then Akhmatova would burn it. Both the poetry and the notes on their conversations put Chukovskaia in considerable danger, and she wrote some of the notes in code.

Among her many writings, Chukovskaia is probably best known for *Sof'ia Petrovna*. Written between November 1939 and February 1940, the novel is the only known surviving prose work about the Terror that was actually composed at the time. The heroine, Sof'ia Petrovna Lipatova, bears little resemblance to Chukovskaia herself; she is a fairly unreflective, self-satisfied woman with middle-class tastes and limited understanding of history or culture. After the death of her doctor husband, Sof'ia Petrovna goes to work as a typist at a publishing house to provide for her son, Kolia. Kolia not only has the requisite socialist-realist traits of athletic handsomeness, intelligence, and enthusiasm for the new society but is also a decent human being who defends his best friend, Alik, from anti-Semitism at school. Her experiences on the job and the slightly condescending lectures of her son mold Sof'ia Petrovna into a productive citizen, broadened and fulfilled by her work though still quick to judge the other typists according to her middle-class standards.

After Kolia moves to Sverdlovsk to work in a factory, Sof'ia Petrovna becomes even prouder of him for his engineering feats and the cogwheel he invents. Then Alik arrives to tell her that Kolia has been arrested. Along with Alik and Kolia's girlfriend, Natasha, who works with Sof'ia Petrovna at the publishing firm, Sof'ia Petrovna joins the lines outside the prison to try to learn his fate and help him. Sof'ia Petrovna cannot understand what is happening as first Natasha and then she lose their jobs; several people at the publishing company are arrested; and the other residents of the communal apartment turn against her. Finally, Natasha commits suicide, and Sof'ia Petrovna becomes insane. At the end Sof'ia Petrovna receives a letter from Kolia, begging her to help him; but she burns it in fear. With this gesture she renounces her son and the truth, which is too much for her to comprehend.

Chukovskaia showed the manuscript of *Sof'ia Petrovna* to Akhmatova and received her tacit approval. Fearing that it would be found, since she remained under suspicion as the wife of an "enemy of the people," she asked a friend, Isidor Moiseevich Glikin, to keep the only copy; he did so at the risk of his life. Glikin starved to death during the blockade of Leningrad, but his sister Rozaliia kept the notebook.

In July 1941, soon after the German army invaded the Soviet Union, Chukovskaia was evacuated to Chistopol in Central Asia; there she briefly met the poet Marina Ivanovna Tsvetaeva and had further conversations with Akhmatova. Returning to Leningrad after the war, she found strangers living in her apartment. She moved to Moscow, dividing her time between an apartment in the city and her father's dacha in the writer's village Peredelkino, sixteen miles to the southwest.

Chukovskaia's second novel, *Spusk pod vodu* (1972; translated as *Going Under*, 1972), was written between 1949 and 1957. The narrator, Nina Sergeevna, resembles the author far more than does Sof'ia Petrovna: she is an intellectual, a writer, a mother, and the widow of a scientist who died in the gulag. Like Chukovskaia, Nina Sergeevna has a refined ear for poetry: she can distinguish the music in a colleague's verse written in Yiddish, a language she does not know. The text takes the form of diary written during Nina Sergeevna's four-week stay at a writer's retreat/sanatorium in February and March 1949, ostensibly to work on a translation. As the title suggests, Nina Sergeevna uses the time away from her daughter and their room in an unpleasant communal apartment to venture below the surface of everyday life into memory and the mystery of her husband's fate. The sanatorium brings her into contact with interesting people: the Yiddish poet and war hero Veksler; a famous movie director and his glamorous wife; and Nikolai Bilibin, an author who has returned from the prison camps and can tell her what might have happened to her husband. Though Bilibin is married, a romance begins to bud during their conversations. Veksler is arrested and driven away in the middle of the night, reflecting the anti-Semitic campaign of the last years of Joseph Stalin's rule and its toll on the creative intelligentsia. Nina Sergeevna's search for the truth in her own past seems to inspire various workers at the sanatorium to reveal their family tragedies to her. The horrors of the past enter the story in a vivid flashback to the late 1930s and the death of the baby of a woman who stood beside Nina Sergeevna in a Leningrad prison line all day in the cold for news of her husband, who had been arrested simply for being a Finn. Nina Sergeevna is a rigorously honorable person who refuses to approve of the media's attacks on admired cultural figures but is also unwilling, perhaps because of her survivors' guilt, to forgive others who lack her strength and resistance. When Bilibin's new work turns out to be straight socialist realism, telling nothing of the truth of his own experiences, she scolds him mercilessly and ends their friendship—realizing afterward that she has caused still more pain to a man whose health and character were already badly shaken. Nina Sergeevna returns to Moscow, to the dry, choking atmosphere in which truth is the thing most feared, and the people who have spoken the truth to her remind her not to say anything that might get them into trouble.

In 1952 Chukovskaia resumed her meetings with Akhmatova. Their conversations, which continued until the poet's death in 1966, form the later volumes of *Zapiski ob Anne Akhmatovoi* (Notes on Anna Akhmatova, 1997).

In 1953 Chukovskaia recovered the notebook with the manuscript for *Sof'ia Petrovna* from the effects of Glikin's late sister and came close to publishing it; she tells the story in *Protsess iskliucheniia: Ocherk literaturnykh nravov* (The Process of Expulsion: A Sketch of Literary Morals, 1979). The liberal journal *Novyi mir* (New World) turned the manuscript down in 1962, but it was accepted by the prestigious publisher Sovetskii pisatel' (Soviet Writer) for publication as a book. Publication was halted in 1963 because of a change in the political climate. Remarkably, Chukovskaia sued for and won the remaining 40 percent of her royalties. The

*Cover for the first volume of Chukovskaia's* Zapiski ob Anne Akhmatovoi: 1938–1941 *(1976, Notes on Anna Akhmatova), in which she transcribes conversations with her friend and fellow dissident poet (Thomas Cooper Library, University of South Carolina)*

novel was published in 1965 in Paris in a somewhat inaccurate émigré edition as *Opustelyi dom* (The Emptied House); the title, which Chukovskaia did not approve, was taken from a line in Akhmatova's *Rekviem*. The novel appeared in its original form and with the correct title the following year in a New York Russian-language magazine. *Sof'ia Petrovna* is widely read and taught both as a work of literature and as a piece of historical evidence; most readers in Russia have seemed to approach it as evidence, rather than as art.

Chukovskaia had refused to shun Boris Leonidovich Pasternak when he was under attack after winning the 1958 Nobel Prize; that choice was less a public statement of support for the poet than a disagreement with her brother Nikolai, a writer who had gone along with the Soviet writers' establishment. As the liberalization of the Thaw ended, she helped monitor Iosif Aleksandrovich Brodsky's trial in 1964; she wrote a critical open letter on behalf of Andrei Donatovich Siniavsky and Iurii Markovich Daniel' during their 1966 trial to Mikhail Aleksandrovich Sholokhov, who took part in their persecution; she welcomed Aleksandr Solzhenitsyn to stay in Peredelkino after his archive was confiscated; and she defended the dissident physicist Andrei Sakharov. Her father's death in 1969 deprived her of the limited protection that his age and fame had offered her; even before he died she had had trouble publishing her writings, and after his death the journal publication of her childhood memoirs was stopped. Chukovskaia made her father's Peredelkino dacha an unofficial museum and worked with his longtime secretary, Klara Izrailevna Lozovskaia, to keep it in repair and show it to visitors.

On 9 January 1974 Chukovskaia was expelled from the Writers' Union for her protest activities and for publishing abroad without permission. Her expulsion deprived her of any legal way to make a living from her professional work; her writings spread via samizdat and foreign publication. Her autobiographical poems documenting and mourning her own and others' losses of beloved people and places were published in Paris in 1978 as *Po ètu storonu smerti: Iz dnevnika 1936–1976* (On This Side of Death: From a Diary, 1936–1976). The royalties from foreign publications paid for her medications and for treatment for her failing vision: Chukovskaia was almost blind and had to write with a large magnifying glass, using felt-tip pens she was sent from abroad.

Unlike so many others, Chukovskaia lived to see her vindication: *Sof'ia Petrovna* and *Spusk pod vodu* were published in Moscow in 1988 and reviewed in major journals such as *Novyi mir;* the first volume of *Zapiski ob Anne Akhmatovoi* was published in Moscow in 1989. Other writers Chukovskaia had championed were welcomed back to Russia both in publications and in person. Access to better medical care and operations on her cataracts improved her vision. She even enjoyed the satisfaction of being proved right in her warnings: she had argued in letters that by cutting the masses off from the country's intelligentsia, and especially from its greatest writers, the government was creating an ignorant and embittered populace that would eventually reject its own heritage. Chukovskaia died in Moscow on 7 February 1996 and was widely eulogized in the Russian press.

Lidiia Korneevna Chukovskaia's writing combines loyalty, fearless retelling of tragedy, and an outstanding literary background. She was devoted to the highest achievements of Russian culture, loved and supported the individuals who produced that culture, and maintained a faith in a network of supporters who valued the writer's or dissident's work and would come forward to offer assistance at crucial moments. Her judgments could be harsh and categorical, though she was aware how easy it was to compel people to compromise and remain silent when their loved ones were hostages to the regime. Chukovskaia worked to document and explain the monstrousness of Stalinism, while never forgetting the lives that were lost and the grieving survivors. From Stalin's ascension to power until the mid 1980s her striving to preserve and document Russia's cultural, historical, and literary heritage was as radical a challenge as any kind of more purely creative work might have been. In the end, as she strove to serve her country and its art, defining her artistic mission in terms of selflessness, Chukovskaia discovered a powerful, memorable voice as a writer.

**Biography:**

Beth Holmgren, *Women's Works in Stalin's Time: On Lidiia Chukovskaia and Nadezhda Mandelstam* (Bloomington: Indiana University Press, 1993).

**References:**

E. Breibart, "Khranitel'nitsa traditsii: Lidiia Korneevna Chukovskaia," *Grani,* no. 104 (1977): 171–182;

Sibelan Forrester, "Chukovskaya, Lidiya Korneevna," in *Women in World History,* 17 volumes, edited by Anne Commire and Deborah Klezmer (Waterford, Conn.: Yorkin, 1999–2002), III: 741–746;

Bella Hirshon, *Lydia Korneevna Chukovskaya: A Tribute* (Melbourne, Australia: University of Melbourne, 1987);

Beth Holmgren, *Women's Works in Stalin's Time: On Lidiia Chukovskaia and Nadezhda Mandelstam* (Bloomington: Indiana University Press, 1993);

Sarah Pratt, "Angels in the Stalinist House: Nadezhda Mandel'shtam, Lidiia Chukovskaia, Lidiia Ginzburg, and Russian Women's Autobiography," in *Engendering Slavic Literatures,* edited by Pamela Chester and Sibelan Forrester (Bloomington: Indiana University Press, 1996), pp. 158–173;

Stephanie Sandler, "Reading Loyalty in Chukovskaia's *Zapiski ob Anne Akhmatovoi,*" in *The Speech of Unknown Eyes: Akhmatova's Readers on Her Poetry,* volume 2, edited by Wendy Rosslyn (Nottingham, U.K.: Astra Press, 1990), pp. 267–282;

Svetlana Shnitman-McMillin, "Lidiia Korneevna Chukovskaia 1907–1996," in *A Reference Guide to Russian Literature,* edited by Neil Cornwell (London & Chicago: Fitzroy Dearborn, 1998), pp. 228–232.

# Iulii Daniel'
## (Nikolai Arzhak)
*(15 November 1925 – 30 December 1988)*

Jefferson Gatrall
*Columbia University*

BOOKS: *Govorit Moskva: Povest',* as Nikolai Arzhak (Washington, D.C.: Filipoff, 1962); translated by John Richardson as "This Is Moscow Speaking," in *Dissonant Voices in Soviet Literature,* edited by Patricia Blake and Max Hayward (New York: Pantheon, 1962), pp. 262–306;

*Ruki. Chelovek iz MINAPa,* as Arzhak (Washington, D.C.: Filipoff, 1962); translated by M. V. Nesterov as *The Man from M.I.S.P. and Hands* (London: Flegon Press, 1966);

*Iskuplenie: Rasskaz,* as Arzhak (New York: Inter-Language Literary Associates, 1964);

*Stikhi iz nevoli,* Biblioteka samizdata, no. 3 (Amsterdam: Fond imeni Gertsena, 1971); translated by David Burg and Arthur Boyars as *Prison Poems* (London: Calder & Boyars, 1971; Chicago: J. P. O'Hara, 1972).

**Collections:** *Govorit Moskva: Povesti i rasskazy* (N.p.: Mezhdunarodnoe Literaturnoe Sodruzhestvo, 1966);

*Govorit Moskva: Proza, poeziia, perevody* (Moscow: Moskovskii rabochii, 1991).

**Edition in English:** *This is Moscow Speaking and Other Stories,* translated by Stuart Hood, Harold Shukman, and John Richardson, foreword by Max Hayward (London: Harvill Press, 1968; New York: Dutton, 1969).

OTHER: "V raionnom tsentre," in *Chistye prudy* (Moscow: Moskovskii rabochii, 1989), pp. 250–264.

*Iulii Daniel' (from* Govorit Moskva: Povesti i rasskazy, *1969; Thomas Cooper Library, University of South Carolina)*

Iulii Daniel' is best remembered as the codefendant of the more celebrated and outspoken author and critic Andrei Siniavsky in one of the most sensational trials of the 1960s in the Soviet Union. Between September 1965 and February 1966 the two writers were arrested, convicted, and sentenced to forced-labor camps for publishing abroad, under pseudonyms, allegedly "anti-Soviet" literary works. The first political trial for more than a decade in the Soviet Union, "the case of Siniavsky and Daniel'" has been regarded by many critics as a cultural signpost marking the end of the Nikita Khrushchev Ottepel (Thaw) and the beginning of the Leonid Brezhnev Zastoi (Stagnation); more specifically, the trial is widely considered the opening chapter in the "dissident movement" under Brezhnev. While Daniel''s stature as a dissident icon was reaffirmed at the end of the 1980s with the publication of many of his works in the Soviet Union for the first time, less critical attention has been paid to the specifically literary aspects of his poetry and prose. His prose works, especially the four he wrote under the nom de plume Nikolai Arzhak, combine realism, fantasy, and political satire and can be placed alongside the experimental writings of such writers as Siniavsky and Boris Samoilovich Iampol'sky within the context of Russian modernism in the 1960s. Critics have noted Fyodor Dostoevsky, Franz Kakfa, Mikhail Mikhailovich Zoshchenko, Il'ia Ilf, Evgenii Petrov, and the Serapion brothers among those who influenced Daniel''s prose and Boris Leonidovich Pasternak and Nikolai Alekseevich Zabolotsky as major influences on his poetry.

Iulii Markovich Daniel' was born in Moscow on 15 November 1925 to Mark Mendelevich Daniel', a pro-Soviet writer of Yiddish plays and fiction in the 1920s and 1930s, and Mina Pavlona Daniel'. At eighteen Daniel' was drafted into the army; he served on the Ukrainian and Belorussian fronts during World War II and was discharged after receiving serious and ultimately chronic wounds to his hands in August 1944. In 1946 he studied Russian literature for a year in Khar'kiv; there he met Larisa Iosifovna Bogoraz, whom he married in 1950. In 1947 he transferred to the Moscow Regional Pedagogical Institute. After graduating from the institute in 1951, Daniel' moved with his wife and their newborn son, Aleksandr, to Kaluga, where he became a teacher of Russian literature. They returned to Moscow two years later. Daniel' continued to teach until 1957, when he turned to translating to provide more time for his writing. From then until 1965 he translated poems from languages including Ukranian, Armenian, Balkar, and Yiddish as part of a state-sponsored effort to make the poetry of the Soviet Union's many ethnic groups more widely known.

In terms of literary output, the 1957–1965 period was the most productive of Daniel''s career; all of his major prose works were either composed or completed during these years. From 1952 to 1958 he worked on a historical novella, "Begstvo" (1989, Flight), set during the reign of the empress Catherine the Great. The hero, Sveshnikov, is an erudite, antimonarchist peasant who received a classical education from a priest in his home village before gaining the patronage of Shuvalov, an enlightened scholar and aristocrat in St. Petersburg. Shuvalov encourages Sveshnikov to write poetry but deems the one poem he composes too anticlerical to be publishable. Sveshnikov's gift for languages attracts the attention of Catherine's court, and he enters St. Petersburg high society under the protection of Field Marshall Grigory Potemkin. His anticlerical poem is, however, discovered by the head of Catherine's chancellery, who uses it to force him to leave St. Petersburg. Sveshnikov returns to his village, where he is ordered to help build a home for his new master. He decides instead to flee from the bondage of serfdom and travels to the south of Russia. Through Potemkin's influence Sveshnikov is eventually granted his freedom; but he falls ill during the plague of 1771 and dies just after learning of his new status.

Daniel''s first novella fits comfortably within the somewhat widened formal parameters of socialist realism during the Thaw; yet, he manages deftly to interweave official Soviet historiography with the plight of a nonconforming writer who, not unlike Daniel' and many of his colleagues, labors under an oppressive regime. The novella was printed by the Children's State Publishing house, but distribution was interrupted at the time of Daniel''s arrest before any of the copies were sold. After Daniel' was freed from prison in 1970, Boris Mikhailovich Kogut, a high-ranking KGB (Komissariat gosudarstvennoi bezopasnosti [State Security Committee]) official, gave him the only extant copy of the novella; a shortened version was serialized in 1989 in three issues in the journal *Pioner* (Pioneer).

From 1956 to 1958 Daniel' wrote a short story, "Ruki" (translated as "Hands," 1966), which was published abroad in 1962 under a pseudonym, Nikolai Arzhak, borrowed from a popular song about thieves. In the story the factory worker Vasily Malnilin explains to an acquaintance why his hands shake chronically. A revolutionary hero and a Communist Party member during the Civil War, Manilin was recruited to the Cheka, the first of many Soviet secret-police agencies. On one assignment he was ordered to execute three village priests. Although not a believer, Manilin felt increasingly ill at ease while executing the first two victims and took a break. Returning, Malnilin fired several shots at point-blank range at the third priest; but the man was unharmed, tore open his cassock, and shouted religious invective at his would-be executioner. When the priest remarked that Manilin's hands were bloody, the Chekist agent threw down his gun and ran past his laughing colleagues, who had played a joke on him by loading his gun with blanks during his break. Manilin was fired from the Cheka, and his hands have trembled ever since from the "nervous shock" he received. The story is a subtle character sketch of an executioner turned victim; while the central episode affords a display of religious symbolism, the work remains grounded in psychological realism. Perhaps the most distinctive feature of the story is Daniel''s effective use of slang in Manilin's monologue with his silent interlocutor. Apparently based on a true incident, "Ruki" introduces the related themes of guilt and complicity to which Daniel' returned a few years later in his two major novellas.

At about the same time he finished "Ruki," Daniel' completed a short satirical piece titled "V raionnom tsentre" (1989, In the District Office). The district director of Novo-Oproshchensk, Vasilii Gaidukov, believes that he has turned into a cat. After a late Communist Party meeting, he strips naked in his office, exits through the window, and disappears into the night. In a parody of the often xenophobic rhetoric of Soviet officialdom, local party bureaucrats conduct an investigation and develop the hypothesis that Gaidukov must have been kidnapped by foreign secret-service agents for "their own self-interested criminal goals." After spending the night in the house of a fisherman, the director returns to work the next day during a meeting about his disappearance and confirms that he had been kidnapped by foreign agents. He is unable to repress his feline nature for long, however: his audience flees in terror from his uncanny meowing, and the director again disappears, this time for good. Daniel' left a draft of the story in his desk before his trial; remarkably, it was still there, seemingly untouched by Soviet authorities, when he returned from prison five years later. It was published in 1989.

In 1961 Daniel' wrote perhaps the most politically inflammatory of all his works, the satirical novella *Govorit Moskva* (1962; translated as "This Is Moscow Speaking," 1962). The novella opens with the government's announcement of an "Open Day of Murder" on which citizens will be permitted, with certain exceptions and provisos, to kill whomever they wish. As the appointed day approaches, Anatolii Kartsev attempts to communicate to others his anxieties about what the motives behind this announcement might be. His concerns are met with apathy or opportunism. In a parody of Marxist utopianism, one acquaintance argues that the decree represents a logical step in the "democratization of the organs of executive authority." Painters and poets spread the official line on the Open Day of Murder with rote pomp and circumstance, and Kartsev's girlfriend breaks up with him when he refuses to help her kill her husband. On the day itself Kartsev wanders the streets, encounters a blood-stained corpse, and is almost mugged by a man who claims to be acting "for the sake of the Motherland." In an ironic anticlimax, however, the day passes with relatively little carnage nationwide. With a translator's eye for the localized conflicts preoccupying the various non-Russian nationalities within the Soviet Union, Daniel' writes that while not one person was killed in the three Baltic states, Georgians were reported to have slaughtered Armenians, and Armenians in Nagorno-Karabakh to have massacred Azerbaijanis. Kartsev concludes that the Soviet citizenry has already been too terrorized by the state to take its own initiative on a day of terror.

In terms of style, Kartsev's moral seriousness as first-person narrator provides a counterweight to the fantastic premise of the novella and its satirical portrayal of Soviet public life. Thematically, the notion that

*Cover for the 1966 Russian-language edition published in New York of Daniel''s story collection* Govorit Moskva: Povesti i rasskasy *(This Is Moscow Speaking: Stories and Tales). The first Russian-language publication was in Washington, D.C., in 1962 (Thomas Cooper Library, University of South Carolina).*

such a day of public murder could take place allows Daniel' to unearth signs of the lingering potential for Joseph Stalin–era purges such as the arbitrariness of official party pronouncements, the complicity of the intelligentsia in state policy, and the apathy of the populace in the face of mass murder. The first of Daniel''s Arzhak works to appear abroad, *Govorit Moskva* was initially published in Polish translation in the Parisian émigré journal *Kultura* (Culture) in January 1962. It quickly appeared in other languages, including English and the original Russian.

In 1961 Daniel' also wrote "Chelovek iz MINAPa" (1962; translated as "The Man from M.I.S.P.," 1966), the most fantastic and least overtly political of his four Arzhak works. Volodia Zalessky develops the "unusual gift" of being able to select the sex of babies at conception. If he concentrates on imagining the face of Karl Marx while having intercourse, the baby will be a boy; for girls he images Klara Zetkin, the German organizer of the first International

*Title page for* Iskuplenie: Rasskaz *(Atonement: Stories), the last collection of fiction Daniel' published in his lifetime (Olive Kettering Library, Antioch College)*

Woman's Day in 1911. Working on a referral basis, he puts his ability to civic use by helping housewives have children of the desired sex. When the husband of one of his clients returns to find his wife in bed with Zalessky, however, Zalessky is put on trial at the Ministry of Scientific Profanation (MISP), where he studies and the husband works. The trial turns in Zalessky's favor when he provides the telephone numbers of satisfied clients. After scientists verify the validity and uniqueness of his ability, he is given a full-time position and a dacha outside Moscow where he can practice his trade for the state. On strictly literary grounds, "Chelovek iz MINAPa" is the most humorous and wide-ranging of Daniel''s three satires. He parodies various aspects of Soviet society, including Stalin-era pseudo-sciences (most directly Trofim Lysenko's Marxist-based biology), the small-time trials endemic in Soviet academic institutions, Communist Party initiatives to increase the size of the Soviet population, the cult of personality, and, not least, the peccadilloes of Soviet married life. "Chelovek iz MINAPa" was published abroad together with "Ruki" in 1963.

Daniel' adopts a more realistic mode of writing in his last Arzhak work, the novella *Iskuplenie* (translated as "Atonement," 1968), which was published abroad in 1964. After Khrushchev's criticism at the Twentieth Communist Party Congress in 1956 of Stalin's excesses, the cases of hundreds of thousands of political prisoners were reviewed; by the early 1960s the return of falsely convicted prisoners and the exposure of those who had informed on them had become commonplace. The narrator of *Iskuplenie,* the painter Viktor Volsky, is confronted by Feliks Chernov, a rehabilitated prisoner recently released from Stalin's camp system. Chernov accuses Volsky of having denounced him to the Soviet authorities in 1951 and threatens to reveal this fact to all of Volsky's acquaintances if the painter does not leave Moscow immediately. As Chernov contacts more and more of Volsky's friends, the painter becomes increasingly isolated; even his girlfriend leaves him. Moreover, although he is innocent of having informed on Chernov, Volsky begins to feel burdened by his "sins of omission": he shares in the collective guilt of having remained silent while millions were sent to Stalin's camps. In the final chapter Volsky is celebrating his birthday, evidently in an insane asylum.

Daniel' weaves a labyrinth of moral ambiguities in this novella. Some critics have noted the Dostoevskian roots of the "everyone is guilty" theme. Others have suggested that Daniel' is the first Soviet writer to probe seriously the notion of collective guilt in relation to Stalin's mass terror. In terms of style, Daniel' makes extensive use in *Iskuplenie* of the techniques of interior monologue and moral allegory he employed in "Ruki" and *Govorit Moskva*. He also incorporates several original prison songs of the type that had begun to circulate throughout the Soviet Union with the return of prisoners from the camps.

*Iskuplenie* was the last work of fiction Daniel' completed. In September 1965 he and his friend Siniavsky were arrested for violating Article 70 of the Soviet constitution, which prohibited conducting "agitation or propaganda with the purpose of subverting or weakening the Soviet regime," by publishing four "anti-Soviet" works abroad under the respective pseudonyms Nikolai Arzhak and Abram Tertz. While awaiting trial, the writers were imprisoned for five months, first in the Lubianka and later in the Lefortovo prisons, both in Moscow. On 5 December 1965 a small demonstration in support of the two writers took place on Pushkin Square in Moscow. The arrests were officially made public in January 1966 with the publication of two newspaper articles by minor Soviet literary figures

*Daniel' in 1966 (left), before his trial on charges that he published "anti-Soviet" works, and during his sentence of five years of forced labor in prison camps in Mordovia and Siberia (from Max Hayward and Leopold Labedz, eds.,* On Trial: The Case of Sinyavsky [Tertz] and Daniel [Arzhak], *1966; Jean and Alexander Heard Library, Vanderbilt University)*

denouncing their works. The trial–the first ever in the Soviet Union in which writers were tried specifically for what they had written–lasted from 10 to 14 February and became an immediate international sensation. Along with his more famous codefendant, Daniel' became not only a cause célèbre among Western intellectuals and writers but also a household name in the Soviet Union and abroad. Soviet citizens sent signed open letters and petitions in support of Daniel' and Siniavsky to such newspapers as *Izvestiia* (News) and to government bodies as the Presidium of the Supreme Soviet and the Supreme Court of the Union of Soviet Socialist Republics. With the exception of the recent Nobel laureate Mikhail Sholokhov, not one major literary figure in the Soviet Union or in the West publicly supported the prosecution's case. As underground transcripts of the closed trial circulated in the Soviet Union and abroad, Siniavsky's and Daniel''s spirited defense, which broke with the pattern of confession and recantation typical of show trials under Stalin, became the stuff of legend.

The court found both writers guilty and sentenced Daniel' to five years of forced labor and Siniav-sky to seven. Daniel' served most of his sentence in the Mordovian camp system in European Russia, spending the final fourteen months in the Vladimir camp in Siberia. Between his arrest and his release from prison five years later Daniel' wrote a cycle of poems titled *Stikhi iz nevoli* (1971; translated as *Prison Poems,* 1971). The cycle is divided into parts according to the places in which the poems were written; all of them relate in one way or another to Daniel''s trial and imprisonment. Daniel' opens the cycle with a call to his readers, written in October 1965, to remember him after he has gone. He promises to give them "each a verse." In "Dom" (House) Daniel' describes, in mundane detail and prosaic style, a building he sees from his cell window in the Lubianka. In "Prigovor" (The Sentence), written in Mordovia, he announces his acceptance of his sentence in a way that evokes a sense of his own guilt for sins of omission. The longest poem, "A v eto vrem'ia . . ." (But at That Time . . .), is an examination of the prison system as a whole; written in a raw language and an often fragmented manner, it is dedicated to those who were not broken by the camps. Other pieces include stylized prison songs, love poems, addresses to his friends, meditations on the role of the writer, and irreverent reflections on his Jewish heritage. Stylistically, the poems incorporate prison slang, folk songs, irregular rhythms, and a wry wit. Although Daniel' had been writing verse since at least 1952, *Stikhi iz nevoli*, which appeared in print in Amsterdam near the time of his release in September 1971, was his only published book of poetry.

Barred from returning to Moscow, Daniel' divorced Bogoraz soon after his release from prison and settled in Kaluga with his second wife, Irina Pavlovna Uvarova. Unable to publish his own works openly, he was permitted to translate poetry under the pseudonym IU. Petrov. During the 1970s and 1980s he translated Scottish folk ballads and works by Johann Wolfgang von Goethe; William Wordsworth; George Gordon, Lord Byron; Voltaire (François Marie Arouet); Victor Hugo; Charles Baudelaire; Arthur Rimbaud; Sir Walter Scott; the Spanish dramatist Ramón Maria del Valle-Inclan; the Georgian poet Galaktion Tabidze; the Armenian poet Daniel Varuzhan; and the Latvian poet Knut Skujenieks. In July 1988 five of his prison poems were published for the first time in the Soviet Union in the magazine *Ogonek* (The Flame). Daniel' died of a stroke on the following 30 December. During the next two years many of his works were published in magazines and journals in the Soviet Union; most of them had never appeared there previously. They included poems, "Begstvo," "V raionnom tsentre," and several unfinished prose pieces on which he had worked in the years following his release. These newly published works were collected, along with his four Arzhak stories and the *Stikhi iz nevoli* poems cycle, in a 1991 volume produced by the Kniga publishing house.

Iulii Daniel''s oeuvre amounts to only a few hundred pages. Unlike Siniavsky, who went abroad after his release from prison, Daniel' was effectively silenced in the Soviet Union for the remaining two decades of his life. What Daniel' did write, however, shows him to have been an accomplished satirist, a skillful poet, a prodigious translator, and, perhaps most important, a moral authority whose ideas found their expression in literature. While Daniel' had aspired most of all to be a poet, he deserves a place in the canon of Russian modernist literature for his experiments in prose. And while the reclusive Daniel' may have shied away from the title of "dissident," he earned his status as an icon of dissent.

**Letters:**

"*Ia vse sbivaius' na literaturu–*": *Pis'ma iz zakliucheniia, stikhi,* edited by Aleksandr Iul'evich Daniel' (Moscow: Zven'ia, 2000).

**References:**

Galina Andreevna Belaia, "'Yea So Shall It Be Known to All. . . ,'" translated by Catharine T. Nepomnyashchy, *Russian Studies in Literature,* 28, no. 1 (1991–1992): 12–24;

Richard L. Chapple, "The 'Crime and Punishment'-ness of Yuli Daniel's 'Atonement,'" *South Central Bulletin,* 35 (1975): 120–121;

Chapple, "The Theme of Atonement in Yuli Daniel's 'Atonement,'" *South Atlantic Bulletin,* 40, no. 4 (1975): 53–60;

Edith W. Clowes, "Kafka and Russian Experimental Fiction in the Thaw, 1956–1965," *Modern Language Review,* 89 (January 1994): 149–165;

Margaret Dalton, *Andrei Siniavskii and Julii Daniel': Two Soviet "Heretical" Writers* (Würzburg: Jal, 1973);

L. S. Eremina, ed., *Tsena metafory, ili, Prestuplenie i nakazanie Siniavskogo i Danielia* (Moscow: Kniga, 1989);

Boris Andreevich Filippov, "Priroda i tiur'ma (O tvorchestve Abrama Tertsa i Nikolaia Arzhaka)," *Grani,* 60 (1966): 75–93;

Aleksandr Ginzburg, ed., *Belaia kniga po delu A. Siniavskogo i IU. Danielia* (Frankfurt am Main: Posev, 1967);

Michael Glenn, "Sinyavsky and Daniel on Trial," *Survey,* 66 (1968): 145–147;

Max Hayward, "The Moscow Trial," *Partisan Review,* 33 (1966): 228–239;

O. Mozhaiskaia, "Otvet frantsuzskoi intelligentsii na prizyv Larisy Daniel' i Pavla Litvinova," *Grani,* 67 (1968): 199–205;

Lilia Pann, "Iulii," *Oktiabr',* 12 (January 1995): 182–189;

Ritta H. Pitman, "The Case of Yuli Markovich Daniel'," *Chapman,* 11 (Spring 1989): 34–36;

Boris Iosifovich Shragin, "Iskuplenie Iuliia Danielia," *Sintaksis,* 16 (1986): 3–33;

*Siniavskii i Daniel' na skam'e podsudimykh* (New York: Mezhdunarodnoe Literaturnoe Sodruzhestvo, 1966); edited and translated by Hayward as *On Trial: The Soviet State versus "Abram Tertz" and "Nikolai Arzhak"* (New York: Harper & Row, 1966);

Knut Skujenieks, "Pamiati druga," *Daugava,* 6 (June 1989): 40–44;

Iuliia Vishnevskaia, "Arkhivnyi detektiv, ili Kto napisal stsenarii suda nad Siniavskim i Danielem," *Literaturnaia gazeta,* 4 November 1992, p. 3.

**Papers:**

Iulii Daniel''s papers are in the Rossiiskii gosudarstvennyi arkhiv literatury i iskusstva [Russian State Archive of Literature and Art] in Moscow.

# Vladimir Dmitrievich Dudintsev

*(16 July 1918 – 22 July 1998)*

Peter Rollberg
*George Washington University*

BOOKS: *U semi bogatyrei* (Moscow: Sovetskii pisatel', 1952);

*Stansiia "Nina"* (Moscow: Pravda, 1952); translated by E. Ketrova as *Nina and Other Stories* (Moscow: Foreign Languages Publishing House, 1954);

*Na svoem meste* (Moscow: Sovetskii pisatel', 1954);

*Ne khlebom edinym* (Moscow: Sovetskii pisatel', 1957); translated by Edith Bone as *Not by Bread Alone* (New York: Dutton, 1957);

*Povesti i rasskazy* (Moscow: Trudrezervizdat, 1959);

*Rasskazy* (Moscow: Moskovskii rabochii, 1963);

*Novogodniaia skazka* (Moscow: Sovetskii pisatel', 1965); translated by Max Howard as *A New Year's Tale* (London: Hutchison, 1960);

*Belye odezhdy* (Moscow: Sovetskii pisatel', 1988);

*Mezhdu dvumia romanami* (St. Petersburg: Neva, 2000).

**Editions:** *Ne khlebom edinym* (Moscow: Khudozhestvennaia literatura, 1968);

*Ne khlebom edinym* (Moscow: Sovremennik, 1979).

**Edition in English:** *A New Year's Tale,* translated by Gabriella Azrael (New York: Dutton, 1960).

Vladimir Dmitrievich Dudintsev was born on 16 July 1918 (29 July 1918, new style) in the town of Dupiansk, in the Khar'kov region of Ukraine, into a family of gentry stock. His father, Semen Nikolaevich Baikov, a captain of the White Army, was executed by Red Army troops in Khar'kov shortly after his son's birth, as was the boy's grandmother. Dudintsev's mother, an operetta singer, remarried. The stepfather, a land surveyor named Dmitrii Ivanovich Dudintsev, was a cultured man whose trips to the countryside—and detailed reports of these trips—became the first lessons in life and verisimilitude for the precocious boy.

In the late 1920s the family moved to Moscow. At the age of twelve Dudintsev tried his hand at writing fiction. He attended a literary circle for children under the direction of Isia Arkad'evich Rakhtanov. The boy's first poem was published in 1930 in *Pionerskaia pravda* (Pioneer Truth). During the next few years he wrote more poems and some short stories for newspapers and journals such as *Molodoi bol'shevik* (Young Bolshevik) and *Rabochaia Moskva* (Workers' Moscow). These early publications and his membership in the literary circle personally acquainted the adolescent with famed authors such as Isaak Emmanuilovich Babel', Il'ia Grigor'evich Erenburg, and Eduard Georgievich Bagritsky, as well as the greats of Soviet theater such as Vsevolod Emil'evich Meierkhol'd and Solomon Mikhailovich Mikhoels. In 1934 Dudintsev won third prize in a national literary competition dedicated to the Seventeenth Party Congress. Yet, despite his literary achievements, he decided to enroll in the Institute of Law at Moscow University in 1936. He graduated with a law degree in 1940.

Dudintsev was drafted in June 1941, after Nazi Germany attacked the Soviet Union. (This period of

*Vladimir Dmitrievich Dudintsev (from* Belye odezhdy, *1988; William T. Young Library, University of Kentucky)*

World War II was known in the former Soviet Union as the Great Patriotic War.) He attended artillery school and enlisted as an officer; during the first months of the war, he served as commander of an infantry batalion. He was wounded four times, most severely in December 1941 near Leningrad. After his discharge from frontline service on 31 December 1941, he worked in the office of a military attorney in Siberia until the end of the Great Patriotic War in May 1945. Dudintsev's experience of the war in its initial stage proved eye-opening in more than one way: while passionately fighting the Nazi invaders, he noticed the often painful inefficiency of Soviet airplanes against their German counterparts and realized for the first time "how senseless and dangerous it is to mask one's own weaknesses and deny reality by issuing pompous statements."

In 1942 Dudintsev married Natal'ia Fedorovna Gordeeva, with whom he had four children. Specific facts about the births of the children are difficult to attain; what is known is that his third child, a daughter, was born in 1950; his last child, a son named Ivan, was born in 1956. In 1946–1951 Dudintsev worked as a correspondent for the daily *Komsomol'skaia pravda* (Komsomol Truth), a job he was offered after winning a national literary competition. Only in his late twenties at the time, Dudintsev was awarded the prize on equal parts with the celebrated author Konstantin Georgievich Paustovsky. Dudintsev's fiction—mostly short stories—was published in important journals such as *Ogonek* (The Flame) and *Novyi mir* (New World). His first book publication was a collection of short stories, *U semi bogatyrei* (At the Seven Knights), which appeared in 1952. Literary critics widely agree that these early narratives were not distinct from regular Socialist-Realist fare; they typically were explicit in their didacticism and constructed along simple narrative lines. In his later years, as a mature author, Dudintsev himself did not think too highly of them. Rather, he viewed his early attempts as exercises of literary craft written in order to make a living (they were republished in several collections in the 1950s and early 1960s but have not reappeared since then).

Dudintsev found his true vocation as a literary champion for lofty ethical ideals in an often cynical and hypocritical society with his first novel, *Ne khlebom edinym* (translated as *Not by Bread Alone*, 1957), first published in *Novyi mir* in 1956 and then as a book in 1957. The title alone leaves little doubt about its underlying concept: positive moral values are the only acceptable foundation for genuine creativity, and Soviet society, like any other, has to be measured by the realization of these values. The qualitative jump from bland short stories featuring uncomplicated plots to a dramatically charged novel such as *Ne khlebom edinym* is striking. At times one can hardly believe that the stories and the novel come from the same author.

Dudintsev wrote *Ne khlebom edinym* not for eternity but for his contemporaries. He was driven by a literal understanding of the term *sotsial'nyi zakaz* (social order), which implies a practical purpose for literature in a socialist society. According to his own account, *Ne khlebom edinym* was ten years in the making, and this length of time indicates that he had sensed some of the deep changes in Soviet society long before their actual arrival—that is, years before the death of Joseph Stalin and the Twentieth Congress of the Communist Party, an event that apparently inspired the writing of the novel. But whatever factors may have determined the actual history of its writing, the impression that *Ne khlebom edinym* made on Soviet and foreign readers in the 1950s and 1960s was staggering. Its sharp, uncompromising social criticism hardly suffices to explain the overwhelming enthusiastic approval of the public. As critic Boris Nikol'sky testified in his foreword to Dudintsev's *Mezhdu dvumia romanami* (2000, In between Two Novels), *Ne khlebom edinym* became a watchword of sorts for an entire generation—a generation of idealists who refused to accept the unreformability of the Soviet Stalinist system into a truly Communist one. It was translated into more than twenty foreign languages and read by hundreds of thousands of people inside and outside the U.S.S.R.; the German edition alone sold more than a million copies (the novel was published in virtually all Western countries but not in all Eastern bloc members).

In what has become an unfortunate literary cliché, critics and historians typically point to the "artistic shortcomings" of the novel. Monograph after monograph on Soviet literature lists Dudintsev's supposedly "weak characterizations," "clumsy transitions," and "static, wordy scenes." While these remarks accurately characterize his earlier prose work, they cannot be upheld for *Ne khlebom edinym*. This unkind, fatuous, unjustified treatment was repeated by Western critics after official Soviet reviewers had set it as the norm during the Communist Party campaign against the novel that began in late 1957. Regarding Soviet literary hacks—some of whom, like Konstantin Mikhailovich Simonov, had initially endorsed the novel as a "timely contribution"—there could be no doubt that they were carrying out orders from the Central Committee, trying to downplay the social significance of the novel. Some of Dudintsev's secret well-wishers later claimed that they were tearing *Ne khlebom edinym* apart with "aesthetic" arguments in order to protect it as a whole, or by distracting the Party leaders from its dangerous subject matter. Whatever the underlying motives of some of their Western colleagues, a fresh re-reading today, in the aftermath of the dissolution of the Soviet Union, is needed. The book has more subtextual levels than might be indicated by the mere struggle of an idealist against a stone wall of Party and academic critics over a technical innovation. Among those often-neglected levels are unequivocal religious symbolism, allusions to classical literary works, and an astute psychological analysis that grants the novel a human appeal reaching beyond Soviet specifics. Against the background of the mostly gray mainstream of Soviet fiction published in the mid 1950s, *Ne khlebom edinym* stands out as a professionally written, analytical, intelligent, and ethically uncompromising work with its own distinctive charisma.

At the heart of this novel lies the life of a creative mind: the trials, tribulations, victories, and defeats of an unhappy, lonely searcher in a specific sociopolitical situation—namely, the Soviet Union of the late 1940s. The two main settings are "Muzga Station" in Siberia—modeled as a center of the Soviet defense industry—and Moscow the capital, with its ministries, institutes, stores, and a maze of communal apartments that sometimes serve as hiding places for frustrated inventors. The variety of milieus featured in *Ne khlebom edinym* is indicative of Dudintsev's social alertness. His awareness of class disparities filled a gap in post-Stalinist literature, which was disingenuous in its claim of social equality. Dudintsev was the first nondissident Soviet writer to contrast the miserable living conditions of the majority with the luxurious flats inhabited by the higher echelons of the Soviet *nomenklatura*, with their chauffeured cars and special stores. His harsh realism is at its best when depicting the difficulty of everyday survival during the Soviet postwar period, such as the notorious coupon system for bread and other essentials and the never-ending concerns of rank-and-file citizens about their money and daily bread.

In Muzga, buried deep in the Soviet provinces, a high-school teacher and former participant in the Great Patriotic War, Dmitrii Lopatkin, has designed a machine for the fast and efficient casting of pipes—an invention that could have groundbreaking consequences for many branches of the Soviet heavy industry, military as well as civilian. In the meantime Lopatkin's principal opponents sit comfortably in a high-profile, well-equipped yet unproductive Moscow institute, the task of which is to design a machine such as the one created by Lopatkin. So far, however, they have achieved nothing. Jealously guarding their perks, the large crowds of engineers, department heads, celebrities, and has-beens at the institute view Lopatkin as an "unqualified" intruder. To them, the essence of his invention is of no interest. Any form of cooperation with creative people outside of the institute is anathema to them and a threat to their privileges. Thus, there is

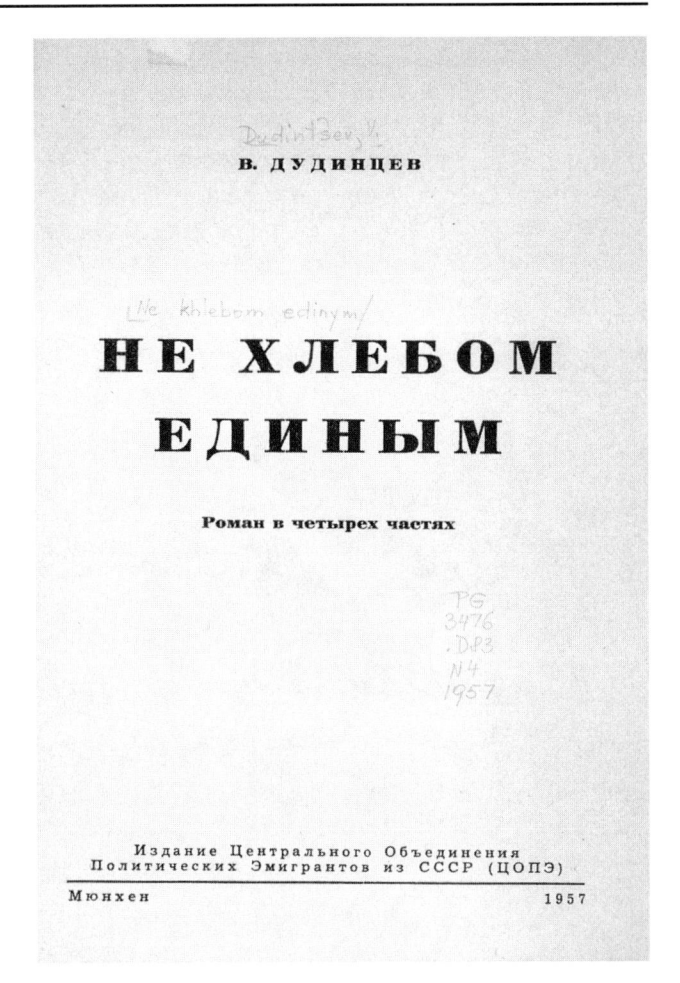

*Title page for* Ne khlebom edinym *(translated as* Not by Bread Alone, *1957), Dudintsev's first and most popular novel (Thomas Cooper Library, University of South Carolina)*

no willingness to compromise and work with Lopatkin even minimally. Instead, a sophisticated pecking order, vanity, and ignorance are the norm for the majority of the institute members. For a negligible minority, social incentives are replaced by an obsession with purely theoretical questions with little practical consequences.

Lopatkin was Dudintsev's greatest artistic challenge: the creation of a believable central character, a genuinely positive hero who at the same time—and in the riskiest aspect of the author's strategy—did not enjoy the support of the Communist Party. Riskier still, Lopatkin's selflessness is not politically motivated. Its roots lie deeper, although they are never explicitly discussed. Thus, religious underpinnings must be seen as motivating this character, whether Lopatkin is conscious of them or not. The negative characters of the novel—most convincing among them the influential bureaucrat Drozdov, whose wife falls in love with Lopatkin and eventually leaves her husband for the poor inventor—sense this gifted underdog's complete

*Title page for* Belye odezhdy *(The White Robes), Dudintsev's novel about genetics research during the reign of Joseph Stalin (William T. Young Library, University of Kentucky)*

lack of support by the system and therefore fight him fearlessly and ruthlessly. At crucial points in his struggle Lopatkin is saved by his few devotees: the loving Nadia Drozdova, the maverick scientist Professor Bus'ko, and a representative of the secret service, Galitsky. But his enemies, in particular the demonic pseudoinventor and powerful administrator Avdiev, score several major victories against the heroic Lopatkin that almost bring him down, and as a result of their slander, he even has to serve more than a year in prison. Lopatkin's triumph in the end comes at a heavy price, and almost all the forces that had been trying to destroy him continue to exercise power and occupy key positions in the Soviet scientific and industrial establishment. Thus, Dudintsev's diagnosis of the crux of Soviet misery is far from being simplistic, as some critics and literary historians later charged.

When the campaign against the novel and Dudintsev was in full force, the character Lopatkin was denounced by one critic as a "poser and self-indulgent martyr." The term "martyr" points to the fact that the system under attack accurately recognized the religious allusions of the novel. Those allusions are manifold, from its very title (a well-known biblical quotation) to the subconscious religious values that motivate several positive characters. One of the reasons why the significance of *Ne khlebom edinym* is more than a "document of de-Stalinization" or a "symbol of 1956" is that it implicitly reminded millions of baffled readers of the Christian-Orthodox foundation of Russian society even after its Soviet transformation. This referral to moral values not determined by considerations of "class" or other Communist schemes may to a certain extent explain the readers' passionate response to Dudintsev's book, as well as the continuing unease on the part of officialdom about it.

The debates surrounding *Ne khlebom edinym* were heated. Judging from later statements by Anastas Ivanovich Mikoian and other party officials, they reflected discussions within the Communist Party. Inside literary circles diverse writers such as Paustovsky, Vsevolod Viacheslavovich Ivanov, Vladimir Fedorovich Tendriakov, and Veniamin Aleksandrovich Kaverin backed the novel, whereas Konstantin Aleksandrovich Fedin, Aleksei Aleksandrovich Surkov, Mariia Pavlovna Prilezhaeva, Galina Iosifovna Serebriakova, Erenburg, Anatolii Vladimirovich Sofronov, Aleksandr Andreevich Prokof'ev, Nikolai Matveevich Gribachev, and Vasilii Aleksandrovich Smirnov—literary administrators for the most part—attacked it viciously. Dudintsev was maligned as an "American agent of influence" and a traitor. Shortly after the publication of the novel in *Novyi mir*, Simonov, the editor in chief of the journal and a seasoned political tactician, switched his position completely and was reprimanded in spite of this turn. He was removed from his post at the journal and sent "on assignment" to Tashkent for two years.

The public readings and discussions of literature in the 1950s were equivalent to a training ground for grassroots democracy in post-Stalinist society. Dudintsev contributed prominently to these debates. Whether he was naive or had a real lack of comprehension, he publicly defended his novel and in doing so cited the many newspaper articles that were pointing to the very phenomenon he had described in *Ne khlebom edinym*: the shelving by incompetent bureaucrats of important inventions and the harassment of the inventors by powerful officials who maligned and even jailed them. Dudintsev, who believed that such arguments could persuade his opponents, may well have been unaware that newspaper articles did not come close to the level of generalization that he had achieved in his fiction;

Lopatkin's story was about the destruction of creativity in the Soviet system as a whole. Nonetheless, some Soviet officials acknowledged that Dudintsev's bleak depiction was accurate, and his implied suggestions for corrective measures were to the point. On a later occasion, legendary Communist Party of the Soviet Union (CPSU) Politburo member Mikoian admitted that the novel in its basic assumptions coincided with the assessments and intentions of Party leadership.

The question of how a provocative work could get published in the first place is worth asking, but the "Thaw" does not suffice as an answer. One neglected aspect may be that, though socially astute and critical, Dudintsev's story revived an ancient Russian creed (and a Romantic motif)—namely, the myth of the inventor as a principally self-sustaining individual who can contrive a machine in a barn, without collegial support and with only the most primitive equipment at his disposal. Stalinist education propagated this belief as typical for the tsarist past, when talented Russians were neglected by society and their inventions suppressed and then ultimately forgotten. Dudintsev's application of the same myth to Soviet times made it both culturally recognizable and acceptable to a Russian audience (though much less so to foreigners). Party officials were split about the acceptability of *Ne khlebom edinym;* despite the harsh criticism directed at the novel, it was republished twice, during the so-called years of stagnation, in large editions and without omissions. Furthermore, *Ne khlebom edinym* did not fit the definition of a dissident text. Although Dudintsev never became a member of the Communist Party, he had written a deeply pro-Communist novel but from the point of view of "Communism with a human face." "A literary paradox underlies the novel: the author uses the apparatus of a literate Socialist Realism to discredit that which it would be expected to glorify," as Hongor Oulanoff writes in *Handbook of Russian Literature* (1985). The sharp turn in the official debate surrounding the novel can be explained by the fear of the Communist Party to repeat the uprising in Hungary in 1956. Still, the lashing out of the system against Dudintsev, harsh as it appeared at the time, was not as life-threatening as it no doubt would have been ten years earlier.

It took more than thirty years before Dudintsev was allowed to present his next novel, *Belye odezhdy* (1988, The White Robes), to Soviet readers. Artistically, it is more robust than *Ne khlebom edinym,* perhaps because Dudintsev could afford the time to rework it. The dramatic fight for the publication of *Belye odezhdy* in the journal *Neva* lasted for years. He spent two decades on studying its subject matter, the history of genetics and geneticists during the Stalin years. That the initial title of the novel was "Neizvestnyi soldat" (An

Cover of Mezhdu dvumia romanami, *the posthumous edition of Dudintsev's uncompleted last novel, published in 2000 with notes by his widow, Natal'ia Fedorovna Dudintseva (Jean and Alexander Heard Library, Vanderbilt University)*

Unknown Soldier) points to an idea that always remained dear to Dudintsev—namely, the inevitability of fighting for the truth once it was recognized by people of integrity. Although this title later was dropped (Dudintsev decided in favor of a biblical motif, based on Rev. 7:13), the idea remained the philosophical foundation of the novel. As in *Ne khlebom edinym,* the main forces opposing each other are the Party-led Soviet establishment and genuine scientists—that is, creators similar to Lopatkin.

The plot centers on real events in 1949, at the peak of the official campaign against genetics. The powerful and devious Kassian Damianovich Riadno, a hack in the Soviet Academy of Sciences (his real prototypes were scientists such as Lysenko, Lepeshinskaia, and Abakian), is mercilessly rooting out any remnant of genetics in Soviet institutes and laboratories. He initiates the public burning of books and replaces the scientists he chased from biological research with slavishly loyal dunces and informers. A ruthless and slick careerist, Riadno poses as a protective patriarch whose origins are in the very depth of the Russian people. He successfully manipulates politicians who trust his questionable theories, with their implied promises of miraculous harvests and the staged "discoveries" that are meant to prove his claims. But Riadno also tempts genuine scientists who have to make a hard moral choice that could cost them their lives.

*Belye odezhdy* won high praise from critics and writers. The Belorussian writer Vasil' Bykov, for one, called it an example of *sverkhliteratura,* a term signifying both supreme artistic and civic qualities. The novel appeared too late, however, to make a long-lasting impact and was outshone by Anatolii Naumovich Rybakov's *Deti Arbata* (1987, Children of the Arbat) and other light fare. Furthermore, its publication in the lesser-known journal *Neva*—instead of in *Novyi mir* or *Znamia* (Banner), with their circulation in the millions—made obtaining a copy of *Belye odezhdy* difficult prior to its appearance as a book. Dudintsev had insisted on publishing the work in *Neva* as a gesture of gratitude toward its editorial board.

In the last years of his life Dudintsev suffered from severe ailments and underwent cardiac surgery after several heart attacks. He died in Moscow on 22 July 1998. Two years after his death the notes for an autobiographical novel, titled "Ditia" (The Child), on which he worked in the mid 1980s, were published by his widow, Natal'ia Fedorovna, in 2000 as a separate book, *Mezhdu dvumia romanami,* with her own comments.

Dudintsev's passing occurred at a time when the systemic incorrigibility of Soviet society had become clear to almost everybody and when his idealism was challenged by a new type of cynicism, though—often by members of the same old establishment, now transformed into proponents of the so-called free market and democracy. Yet, he preferred to see himself beyond political labels. In his view he was a chivalrous fighter on battlefields created by universal polarizations such as good versus evil and truth versus lies. These poles also inform his narratives and their inherent worldview. A law-abiding citizen and father of four, he was entangled in endless financial predicaments caused by a lack of support from the literary establishment. Dudintsev's first novel gave him many friends in all social strata, however, many of whom helped him remained anonymous. These experiences strengthened his religious convictions even further.

Vladimir Dmitrievich Dudintsev justly can be called a civic writer of considerable talent, a genuinely professional author whose prose neither features nor claims artistic refinement but offers solid realistic narration, leading his readers toward a worthy cathartic goal. Both his great novels were completed when the time for them had come. While Dudintsev certainly had a keen ear for what Soviet society needed in any given moment and could respond to this need, his high personal ethical standards always outweighed career considerations. For example, as a man of dignity even under severe pressure, he refused to appear at the trial against Andrei Donatovich Siniavsky and Iulii Markovich Daniel', although he did not hold their artistry in high esteem. Dudintsev gave his society moral impulses. But the true and lasting power of his novels—the political and social conflicts of which are relevant no more—derives from his deep-held belief that the material sphere neither determines nor limits human consciousness.

**References:**

G. Avis, "Moskovsky Litearator and the Dudintsev Debate," *Journal of Russian Studies,* 18 (1969): 26–35;

Katerina Clark, *The Soviet Novel: History as Ritual* (Chicago & London: University of Chicago Press, 1985), pp. 217–220;

Aleksandr Dymshits, "Pravda zhizni i kraski khudozhnika," in *V velikom pokhode* (Moscow: Sovetskii pisatel', 1962);

Dmitrii Eremin, "Chem zhiv chelovek?" *Oktiabr',* 12 (1956);

Natal'ia Kriuchkova, "O romane 'Ne khlebom edinym,'" *Izvestiia,* 2 December 1956;

Irma Mamaladze, "Tsvet nashikh odezhd: Interv'iu s Vladimirom Dudintsevym," *Literaturnaia gazeta,* 33 (1988): 11;

Hongor Oulanoff, "Dudintsev," in *Handbook of Russian Literature,* edited by Victor Terras (New Haven: Yale University Press, 1985), p. 117;

Michael Pursglove, "Dudintsev, Vladimir Dmitrievich," in *The Modern Encyclopedia of Russian and Soviet Literatures,* volume 6, edited by Harry Weber (Gulfbreeze, Fla.: Academic International, 1982), pp. 89–91;

Mikhail Shkerin, "Shtrikhi k portretu Vladimira Dudintseva," *Literaturnaia gazeta,* 30 March 1988, p. 6;

Marc Slonim, *Soviet Russian Literature: Writers and Problems* (London, Oxford & New York: Oxford University Press, 1977), pp. 331–333;

Valerii Soifer, "Gor'kii plod," *Ogonek,* 1(1988): 26–29; 2 (1988): 4–7, 31;

Grigori Svirski, *A History of Post-War Soviet Writing: The Literature of Moral Opposition* (Ann Arbor, Mich.: Ardis, 1981), pp. 123–128;

Harold Swayze, *Political Control of Literature 1946–1959* (Cambridge, Mass.: Harvard University Press, 1962), pp. 164–169;

Irina Tosunian, "Vechnaia tema: Beseda s Vladimirom Dudintsevym," *Literaturnaia gazeta,* 51(1988): 7.

# Evgeniia Ginzburg
*(20 December 1904 – 25 May 1977)*

Jane Gary Harris
*University of Pittsburgh*

BOOKS: *Tak nachinalos' . . . zapiski uchitel'nitsy* (Kazan': Tatarskoe kn-vo, 1961);

*Krutoi Marshrut* (Milan: Mondadori, 1967; Frankfurt am Main: Possev, 1967); translated by Paul Stevenson and Max Hayward as *Journey into the Whirlwind* (New York: Harcourt, Brace & World, 1967; London: Collins Harvill, 1967); Russian version republished (New York: Possev-USA, 1985; Riga: Izdatel'stvo TSK KP Latvii "Kursiv," Tvorcheskaia fotostudiia Soiuza zhurnalistov LSSR, 1989);

*Krutoi Marshrut: Tiur'ma, lager', ssylka* (Milan: Mondadori, 1979); translated by Ian Boland as *Within the Whirlwind,* foreword by Heinrich Böll (New York: Harcourt Brace Jovanovich, 1981; London: Collins Harvill, 1981); Russian version republished as *Krutoi marshrut: Kniga vtoraia* (New York: Possev-USA, 1985).

**Edition:** *Krutoi marshrut: Khronika vremen kul'ta lichnosti* (Moscow: Sovetskii pisatel', 1990).

**Editions in English:** *Into the Whirlwind,* translated by Paul Stevenson and Manya Harari (London: Collins Harvill, 1967);

*Precipitous Journey,* translated by Andrew Jackson (London: Flegon Press, 1967).

SELECTED PERIODICAL PUBLICATIONS – UNCOLLECTED: "Edinaia trudovaia . . . ," *Iunost',* 11 (1965);
"Studenty dvadtsatykh godov," *Iunost',* 8 (1966);
"Iunosha," *Iunost',* 9 (1967).

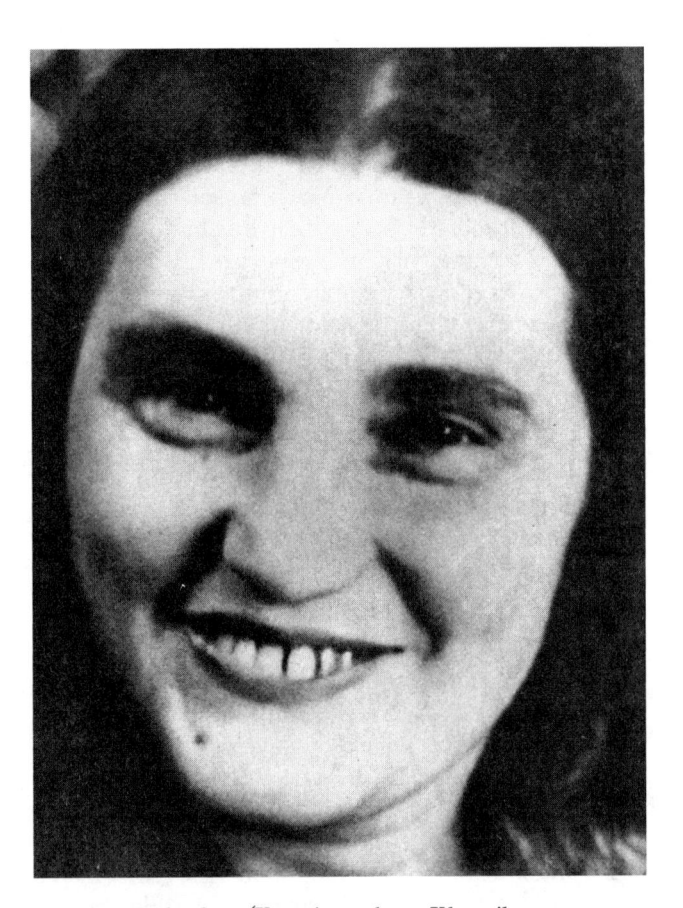

*Evgeniia Ginzburg (*Krutoi marshrut: Khronika vremen kul'ta lichnosti, *1990; Jean and Alexander Heard Library, Vanderbilt University)*

Evgeniia Semenovna Ginzburg's memoirs of her eighteen years in the gulag gained international renown both as the first female eyewitness account of the camps and as a literary masterpiece. Ginzburg was born on 20 December 1904 into a family of the Moscow Jewish intelligentsia; her father was a pharmacist. She spent her childhood and youth in Kazan', where she attended the University of Kazan' and then taught history and worked as a Communist Party activist. Later she went into journalism, becoming assistant head of the cultural department of the local newspaper, *Red Tartary*. She married Pavel Vasil'evich Aksenov, a high-ranking official in the Tartar Regional Communist Party Committee and chairman of the Kazan' city council. They had two children, Alesha and Vasilii.

In 1937 Ginzburg was arrested; her husband was arrested shortly afterward. A military tribunal sentenced Ginzburg under Article 58 of the Soviet Penal Code to ten years in solitary confinement for "participation in a counter-revolutionary Trotskyite terrorist organization." After two years in the Iaroslavl' women's prison, Ginzburg was sent to serve out the rest of her sentence in labor camps in the Kolyma region of northeastern Siberia. There she worked as a medical assistant and then as a nurse and met the man who was much later to become her second husband, Anton Walter, a devout Catholic of Crimean German origins. He was a fellow prisoner working as a camp doctor. Ginzburg's son Alesha died during the German siege of Leningrad in World War II without ever seeing his mother again. Her second son, Vasilii, was not allowed to join his mother until 1947, when she was living in exile. He became a famous dissident writer.

Ginzburg was released on 15 February 1947, with six years yet to serve in exile. She went to live in Magadan with Julia, a friend she had met in prison, to be as close as possible to Walter, who still had six years to serve. In 1949 Ginzburg was arrested again and sentenced to permanent exile. She and Walter were allowed to leave Kolyma in 1955; they went to Lvov, where Walter died in 1959. After her official rehabilitation in the 1960s, Ginzburg was granted an apartment in Moscow.

Ginzburg's earliest works are about growing up in Kazan'. Her memoirs of her childhood and of her youth in Kazan' appeared in the popular magazine *Iunost'* (Youth). Her novella "Iunosha" appeared there a year later. Her first novella, *Tak nachinalos'* (1961, This Is The Way It Began), is about her life as a teacher in Kazan'. "Edinaia trudovaia . . ." (The Coeducational Soviet School . . . , 1965) looks back at the beginning of the radical changes introduced in Soviet Russia from the perspective of Genia, a Kazan' high-school girl in the immediate postrevolutionary years. Its sequel discusses her life in the 1950s. The girl's point of view is mostly one of awe, excitement, and wonder at the changes transforming school life; but a retrospective narrator expresses misgivings about the girl's naive acceptance of events, foreshadowing the arbitrary and irrational nature of things to come. In the fall of 1918 Genia notices her teacher's unease with the new form of address as "comrades" replaces the more intimate "children"; the students themselves, however, feel grown-up when addressed as "Comrade" and their surnames. The retrospective narrative voice associates the new term of address with a significant social change: the end of the old single-sex Russian gymnasium and the beginning of the coeducational Soviet school system. Ginzburg's story of her initiation into the "new school" continues with the juxtaposition of her description of the children's happy relationship with their remarkable history teacher and the retrospective narrator's comments on his end: after defending his not being a Communist Party member by claiming that "A historian must be objective," he eventually does join—only to be caught up in the Stalinist purges. Recounting an incident of class warfare that almost gets out of hand, she notes that back then they "still did not know the word 'demagoguery,'" for they could still recognize the arbitrary and the wrong. Overall, however, Ginzburg emphasizes the positive changes brought about by the revolution. She recognizes the need for improvement in the lives of impoverished working-class children and downplays the signs of negative outcomes.

"Studenty dvadtsatykh godov" (Students of the Twenties, 1966) is narrated by Genia as a freshman at Kazan' University. Genia grows increasingly aware of problems in the society around her but maintains her enthusiasm about acquiring a Marxist education. In addition to the natural crises of the early 1920s—famine and bitterly cold winters—she describes ideological conflicts between the left-liberal humanitarian values of some of the professors and the dogmatic single-mindedness of the upholders of the new Communist ideology. As students in the Social Sciences Division, Genia and her best friend, Liuba, encounter a wide variety of views and teaching methods. Genia is praised for having "mastered concrete historical facts by applying the methods of Marxist analysis," even if they are only the "elementary methods." On the other hand, she worries that her middle-class background will hinder her capacity to become a good Communist. While Liuba is of proletarian origins, Genia thinks that she herself may be "truly doomed to ideological ambivalence because of my intelligentsia origins." She is torn between the need to help all suffering human beings and the Marxist-Leninist principle that aid is to be directed toward the betterment of the lower classes. She questions the rigidity of the disciplined, single-minded, ideological reasoning that is beginning to prevail in the 1920s and will be distorted into the cruel, merciless, and arbitrary formulations of the 1930s and 1940s.

Genia also observes disturbing contradictions between theory and reality: "While we were striving to resolve questions of theory, our city and the entire Volga region were starving." This realization affects her behavior in the most powerful section of the story, which describes her turn on duty at the Studpomgol—a student organization set up to provide food aid to starving students. She receives not only written instructions but also oral reminders to clarify eligibility for food parcels. The parcels are designated for students with typhus, but "all things being equal, it was necessary to give priority to those of proletarian origin." Genia's conscience torments her when an older student, just released from the hospital for kidney problems, begs for food; she finally gives the girl a parcel. It turns out that the student's father, long dead, had been a deacon. Genia is summoned before the student disciplinary board; the reserved, polite, and principled Franz Geys, a Volga German proud that his father was a master carpenter "not associated with the regional landowners," accuses her of "squandering the funds of the organization," and Sasha Ryabinin, an unruly, emotional, and sensitive proletarian, shouts that she is "an idiot" with "petty bourgeois sympathies." The passage ends ominously: "Life continued to rush ahead, constantly demanding action, and not what Vitka Goldman called 'psychologizing,' and what Professor Ditiakin called 'the tendency toward intelligentsia reflection.'" Nevertheless, the piece concludes with several anecdotes revealing Ginzburg's acceptance of the new ideology and her joy in being able to teach students who never before had a chance to learn.

Ginzburg spent her last years writing her masterpiece, the two-volume prison-camp memoir *Krutoi Marshrut* (Steep Journey). Her naive hopes for domestic publication of the first volume and of joining the Writers' Union were inspired by Nikita Khrushchev's anti-Stalinist rhetoric at the Twenty-Second Congress of the Communist Party in 1961 and by the publication of Aleksandr Solzhenitsyn's *Odin den' Ivana Denisovicha* (translated as *One Day in the Life of Ivan Denisovich*, 1963) in the periodical *Novyi mir* (New World) in 1963; they were dashed when the book was rejected by both Aleksandr Trifonovich Tvardovsky, the editor of *Novyi mir*, and Boris Nikolaevich Polevoi, the editor of *Iunost'*. After those rejections, the self-censorship she had imposed on volume one was abandoned in writing volume two. Circulated in the Soviet Union only in samizdat, volume one was first published in Italy and Germany in 1967 (translated as *Journey into the Whirlwind*, 1967); the second volume was published in Italy in 1979 (translated as *Within the Whirlwind*, 1981), two years after Ginzburg's death on 25 May 1977. Vasilii Pavlovich Aksenov, who had become a dissident novelist, was forced to leave the Soviet Union in 1980 after an abortive attempt to co-edit an uncensored literary miscellany, *Metropol'*. Publication of his mother's prison memoir in their homeland was not allowed until 1989, when the first volume appeared in Riga, Latvia, which was then still part of the Soviet Union; the two volumes were published together in one volume in Moscow in 1990.

*Krutoi Marshrut* spans more than two decades. The "steep journey" of the Russian title is a metaphor for initiation into a world beyond the realm of the normal imagination. Volume one depicts the naive narrator's gradual realization of the extent of the Terror and her own increasing feelings of guilt as a Communist Party member. In an optimistic introduction (the epilogue in the English translation), however, she concludes: "All that this book describes is over and done with. I, and thousands like me, have lived to see the Twentieth and the Twenty-Second Party Congresses." The book, which she believed at the time of writing could be published in the Soviet Union because of the self-censorship she had exercised, is offered to readers as "the story of an ordinary Communist woman during the period of 'the personality cult.'"

Volume one chronicles the years 1934 to 1939. The opening chapter demonstrates Ginzburg's skill at collapsing time and space in a terse display of historical understanding: she recognizes that Joseph Stalin's para-

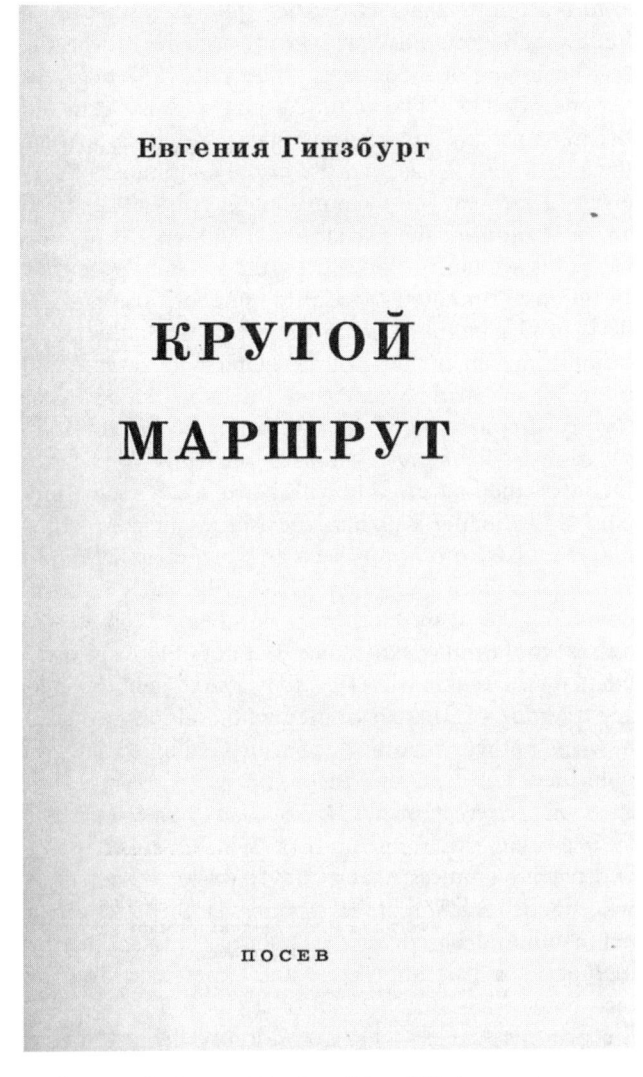

*Title page for the 1985 Russian edition of Ginzburg's prison-camp memoir first published in Germany and the United States in 1967 (translated as* Journey into the Whirlwind). *This volume, the first of two about her eighteen years in the gulag, covers the years 1934 to 1939 (William T. Young Library, University of Kentucky).*

noid reaction to the 1 December 1934 assassination of Leningrad Communist Party head Sergei Kirov was the real beginning of the purges: "The year 1937 began at the end of 1934." The volume begins with the chaos of the mass arrests, the arbitrary nature of the interrogations and mock trials, and the brutal conditions of solitary confinement and the punishment cells—all of which are revelations to the narrator of the extent of the Terror. This section is followed by the narrator's journey east on trains marked "Special Equipment," the camaraderie of Car Number 7, and the joy of the baths in the disinfection center at Sverdlovsk, interspersed with obituaries of the many women who perished en route or shortly after arriving at the camps; then come the transit camps, the convict steamer through the Sea of Okhotsk, the first meeting with hardened female criminals, and, finally, Kolyma, the Magadan camp infirmary, and the notorious women's camp in Elgen. In *Kolyma: The Arctic Death Camps* (1978), Robert Conquest points out the "disproportionate number of women witnesses" to the gulag experience. But not only were these women remarkable witnesses, they also upheld the literary tradition of Russian women who had long excelled in writing down what they had witnessed in private and published journals and memoirs, as Barbara Heldt notes in *Terrible Perfection: Women and Russian Literature* (1987). Like earlier memoirists, Ginzburg juxtaposes two narrative voices: that of the retrospective narrator who stands back and observes and even theorizes about her condition, based on the resources of her private memory, her past knowledge and experience, and the fact that she has survived; and the voice of the subject, the prisoner-witness who is constantly being initiated into the system as the suffering victim, the model Russian heroine who "endures." The identity and consciousness of the protagonist emerge through the events depicted and the anecdotes related, while her life and behavior are contemplated from a distance by the retrospective narrator.

Ginzburg illustrates the stages of her developing consciousness and conscience with poignant anecdotes, broadening her own self-definition within the universal context of human suffering. For example, recalling an incident in which younger prisoners laughed at an older illiterate peasant woman's confusion of "traitor," "tractor," and "terrorist" in the neologism "tractorist," Ginzburg feels twinges of guilt and remorse as she realizes that her own mother was only eight years younger than this woman: "I couldn't laugh. I was ashamed. When would I at last stop feeling ashamed and responsible for all this? After all, I was the anvil, not the hammer. But might I too have become a hammer?"

In *Return from the Archipelago* (2000) Leona Toker points out that the typical gulag memoir is structured in stages and that this "text division re-enacts the 'transport' stages of a Gulag prisoner's life"; she suggests that the experience is relived at the time of writing, "with the consciousness of calendar time replaced by vivid memories of place." For Ginzburg, each stage represents a new revelation, a deeper insight into her soul. Indeed, Ginzburg's memoirs epitomize life writing in that the retrospective narrating voice is ever conscious of her writer's function to survive and bear witness but is equally aware of aesthetic interest and human curiosity, the stuff of stories: "Each of us told story after story . . . not only about her own life, but about all she had seen and heard in prison." In drawing associations between literature and life, Ginzburg's account combines profound insights and eyewitness descriptions of sheer horror, evil, corruption, coarseness, wasting, and starvation with the loftiest outpourings of the private emotional and intellectual spirit.

In volume two the "journey" devolves into a more internalized "journey of the soul." No longer restrained by her "inner censor," Ginzburg recognizes the extent of her feelings of shame and remorse as a Communist Party member and offers an anguished "Mea Culpa." The chapter so titled concludes: "Mea culpa . . . and it occurs to me more and more frequently that even 18 years of hell on earth is insufficient expiation for the guilt."

Volume two begins with the winter of 1939–1940 and treats the anomalies of the World War II years and the paranoid fear of all Germans; it describes Ginzburg's work in the children's infirmary at the Elgen women's labor camp, the "light work" stints at the Taskan food processing plant, and the grotesque horrors of Izvestkovskaya, the "punishment camp to end all punishment camps." Some of the most poignant scenes include Ginzburg's efforts to create a haven of family life in Magadan after her release with Julia, Vasilii, an adopted baby named Tonya, and her second husband. It includes her fear of a second arrest, her release as a "permanent exile," and, finally, her rehabilitation and return to the "mainland" of European Russia. Although the style of volume two is much harsher, the humor blacker, and the narrator much more uncompromising toward herself than in volume one, the initial journey of growing historical and personal awareness evolves into a journey revealing "the heroine's spiritual evolution, the gradual transformation of a naive young Communist idealist . . . a cruel journey of the soul and not just the chronology of my sufferings. . . ."

If the first volume is sustained by the narrator's naive curiosity—"My thoughts were taken off my own suffering by the keen interest I felt in the unusual aspects of life and of human nature which unfolded around me"—then the second is sustained by an incredible love story and by profound inner moments of reprieve, as well as of remorse. Toker notes that one of the key elements of the gulag narrative is the alternation of suffering with such "moments of reprieve" that allow for the "rise and fall of emotional intensity." Ginzburg not only describes innumerable strategies of survival in an atmosphere intended to deprive people of their true identities but also refers to specific compensations at every stage of her eighteen-year journey through the gulag. Reprieve may come in the form of chance: "One had to be prepared for a lucky break, recognize it, and use it to best advantage." It also comes in the form of poetry, love, and friendship, in the sharing of unexpected joys as well as expected suffering. Ginzburg's phenomenal memory makes literary reprieve frequent in both volumes as the solace of poetry allows her to escape, if only momentarily, from harsh reality. But for Ginzburg poetry serves another purpose. She commits events to memory by associating them with lines of verse, ranging from Boris Pasternak's "1905" in volume one to poetry by Aleksandr Aleksandrovich Blok in volume two: "Blok had a premonition.... It fell to us to behold the reality.... More often than not it was Blok we recited: 'The last, the foulest age of all / Shall you and I behold.'"

In addition to poetry, the love Ginzburg shared with Walter helps to lyricize her narrative and to provide a symbol of hope for the future: "The jolly saint was to become my second husband. Our love grew amid the stench of putrefying flesh, against the darkness of the arctic night. For 15 years we marched together across all the abysses, through all the blizzards." She captures the bliss of their walk to Taskan through a blizzard on the day of her release from prison in 1947: "We marched side by side. We were heading for freedom.... Suddenly, I felt a paroxysm of happiness coursing through me. Not joy, not pleasure, but happiness. That irresistible uplift of the spirit ... you are borne upward as if you were holding the tail of the legendary Firebird. You have managed to grasp him at last!" She states her intention to use Walter's character as a symbol: "I wanted to show through his image that the victim of inhumanity can remain the bearer of all that is good."

Ginzburg's keen awareness of language, character, and story is expanded to include the fantasies, rumors, and dreams that helped to sustain people in the camps: "fantastic rumors circulated. These were pure invention—we called them 'hallucinations.' 'Have you heard? Kolyma's been sold to the Americans!' 'With or without inhabitants?'" This even led to violent arguments between those who "dreamed of being rescued at any price and those who—damn it—wanted to stay in their own country if it killed them." As Ginzburg's faith

*Ginzburg and her son, Vasilii Pavlovich Aksenov, in the early 1960s, about the time he became a professional writer (Krutio marshrut, 1990; translated as* Journey into the Whirlwind; *Jean and Alexander Heard Library, Vanderbilt University)*

in humanity is severely tested, she retains her faith with the support of poetry, humor, intelligence, love, and friendship. Of the latter she writes: "the feeling of prison kinship ... is perhaps the strongest of all human bonds." The conflicts between humanitarian values and the utopian Bolshevik ideals represented in the memoirs of her youth reemerge in her final literary masterpiece as the once naive young Communist idealist seeking to expiate her past provides a devastating moral indictment of the Communist system and its ideological principles gone wild.

Evgeniia Semenovna Ginzburg's place in Russian literary history as author of the first female eyewitness account of the Soviet women's labor camps has been compared to that of Solzhenitsyn, who first revealed the male experience of the gulag. Whie Ginzburg details the brutalized existence of women's lives in prison, labor camps, and exile, she also is able to call upon her strengths to illuminate the power of the human soul, which literally preserved her life. Her memoirs have been well received; in particular, they have been lauded for "infusing tragedy with dignity . . . the author's greatest achievement" (Heldt), for originality as a memoir (Toker), for embodying "so much of the Soviet experience" (Natasha Kolchevska), and for uncovering "the dynamic of women's hidden memories behind the hegemonic representations of a new Soviet woman" (I. Novikova).

**References:**

Vasilii Pavlovich Aksenov, *Ozhog* (Ann Arbor, Mich.: Ardis, 1980); translated by Michael Glenny as *The Burn* (Boston: Houghton Mifflin, 1984; London: Hutchinson, 1984);

Mark Altshuller and Elena Dryzhakova, *Put' Otrecheniia* (Tenafly, N.J.: Hermitage, 1985), pp. 277–282;

Edward J. Brown, "The Education of a Communist," *New Republic* (21 March 1981);

Robert Conquest, *Kolyma: The Arctic Death Camps* (London: Macmillan, 1978; New York: Viking, 1978);

Olga Cooke, "Evgeniia Semenovna Ginzburg," in *Reference Guide to Russian Literature,* edited by Neil Cornwell (London: Fitzroy Dearborn, 1998), pp. 320–322;

Barbara Heldt, *Terrible Perfection: Women and Russian Literature* (Bloomington: Indiana University Press, 1987);

Beth Holmgren, "For the Good of the Cause: Russian Women's Autobiography in the Twentieth Century," in *Women Writers in Russian Literature,* edited by Toby W. Clyman and Diana Greene (Westport, Conn.: Greenwood Press, 1994), pp. 127–148;

V. Iverni, "Kniga-zhizn'," *Kontinent,* 23 (1980): 286–292;

Natasha Kolchevska, "A Difficult Journey: Evgeniia Ginzburg and Women's Writing of Camp Memoirs," in *Russian Women and Russian Culture: Projections and Self-Perceptions,* edited by Rosalind Marsh (New York & Oxford: Berghahn, 1998), pp. 148–162;

Lev Zalmanovich Kopelev and Raisa Davydovna Orlova, *Tri Portreta* (Ann Arbor, Mich.: Ardis, 1983);

A. L. Litvin, ed., *Dva sledstvennykh dela Evgenii Ginzburg* (Kazan': Knizhnyi Dom Taves, 1994);

David Lowe, "E. Ginzburg's *Krutoi marshrut* and A. Aksenov's *Ozhog:* The Magadan Connection," *Slavic and East European Journal,* 27, no. 2 (1983): 200–210;

Iurii Vladimirovich Maltsev, *Vol'naia russkaia literatura 1955–1975* (Frankfurt am Main: Possev, 1976), pp. 235–242;

Roy Medvedev, "Meetings and Conversations with Aleksandr Tvardovskii," *Michigan Quarterly Review,* 28, no. 4 (1989): 604–638;

Raisa Davydovna Orlova and Lev Kopelev, "Evgeniia Ginzburg v kontse krutogo marshruta," in their *My zhili v Moskve 1956–1980* (Ann Arbor, Mich.: Ardis, 1988), pp. 311–344;

Grigorii Svirski, *A History of Post-War Soviet Writing: The Literature of Moral Opposition,* translated by Robert Dessaix and Michael Ulman (Ann Arbor, Mich.: Ardis, 1981);

Leona Toker, *Return from the Archipelago* (Bloomington: Indiana University Press, 2000);

Alexander Zholkovsky, "Three on Courtship, Corpses, and Culture: Tolstoy, 'Posle bala'–Zoshchenko, 'Dama s cvetami'–E. Ginzburg, 'Raj pod mikroskopom'," *Wiener Slawistischer Almanach,* 22 (1988): 7–24.

# Lidiia Iakovlevna Ginzburg

(5 March 1902 – 15 July 1990)

Jane Gary Harris
*University of Pittsburgh*

BOOKS: *Agentsvo Pinkertona* (Moscow: Molodaia gvardiia, 1932);

*Tvorcheskii put' Lermontova* (Leningrad: Khudozhestvennaia literatura, 1940);

*"Byloe i dumy" Gertsena* (Leningrad: Izd-vo khudozh. lit-ry, 1957);

*O lirike* (Leningrad: Sovetskii pisatel', 1964; revised and enlarged, 1974);

*O psikhologicheskoi proze* (Leningrad: Sovetskii pisatel', 1971; revised edition, Leningrad: Khudozh. lit-ra, 1977); translated by Judson Rosengrant as *On Psychological Prose* (Princeton: Princeton University Press, 1991);

*O literaturnom geroe* (Leningrad: Sovetskii pisatel', 1979);

*O starom i novom: Stat'i i ocherki* (Leningrad: Sovetskii pisatel', 1982);

*Literatura v poiskakh real'nosti: Stat'i, esse, zametki* (Leningrad: Sovetskii pisatel', 1987);

*Chelovek za pis'mennym stolom* (Leningrad: Sovetskii pisatel', 1989);

*Pretvorenie opyta,* edited by Nikolai Kononov (Riga: "Avots" / Leningrad: Assotsiatsiia "Novaia literatura," 1991);

*Zapisnye knizhki: Novoe sobranie* (Moscow: Zakharov, 1999);

*Zapisnye knizhki; Vospominaniia; Esse,* edited by Aleksandr Kushner (St. Petersburg: Iskusstvo-SPB, 2002).

**Editions in English:** "The 'Human Document' and the Formation of Character," in *The Semiotics of Russian Cultural History: Essays by Iurii M. Lotman, Lidiia Ia. Ginzburg, Boris A. Uspenskii,* edited by Alexander D. Nakhimovsky and Alice Stone Nakhimovsky, introduction by Boris Gasparov (Ithaca, N.Y. & London: Cornell University Press, 1985);

*Blockade Diary,* translated by Alan Myers, introduction by Aleksandr Kushner (London: Harvill Press, 1995);

"Selected Works: From *The Journals,*" translated by Jane Gary Harris, in *Russian Women Writers,* volume 2, edited by Christine Tomei (New York: Garland, 1999), pp. 1166–1178.

*Lidiia Iakovlevna Ginzburg (*Chelovek za pis'mennym stolom, *1989; Howard-Tilton Memorial Library, Tulane University)*

OTHER: "Viazemskii–literator," in *Russkaia proza,* edited by Boris Mikhailovich Eikhenbaum and Iurii Nikolaevich Tynianov (Leningrad: Academia, 1926), pp. 102–134; translated by Ray

Parrott as "Vyazemsky–Man of Letters," in *Russian Prose* (Ann Arbor: Ardis, 1985), pp. 87–108;

Introduction, Petr Andreevich Viazemsky, *Staraia zapisnaia knizhka,* edited by Ginzburg (Leningrad: Izd-vo pisatelei Leningrad, 1929), pp. 9–50;

"Puti detskoi istoricheskoi Povesti" (Directions for the Juvenile Historical Novella), in *Detskaia literatura* (Children's Literature), edited by A. V. Lunacharsky (Moscow & Leningrad: Goslitizdat, 1931), pp. 159–181;

Viazemsky, *Stikhotvoreniia,* edited by Ginzburg (Leningrad: Sovetskii pisatel', 1936);

Vladimir Grigor'evich Benediktov, *Stikhotvoreniia,* edited by Ginzburg (Leningrad: Sovetskii pisatel', 1939);

Vasilii Andreevich Zhukovsky, *Stikhotvoreniia,* edited by Ginzburg (Leningrad: Sovetskii pisatel', 1956);

*Poety 1820–1830–kh godov,* edited by Ginzburg (Leningrad: Sovetskii pisatel', 1961; enlarged edition, 2 volumes, edited by Ginzburg, Vadim Erazmovich Vatsuro, and V. S., Kiselev-Sergenin, 1972);

*Zarubezhnaia poeziia v russkikh perevodakh: Ot Lomonosova do nashikh dnei,* edited and translated by Ginzburg and Evgenii Mikhailovich Vinokurov (Moscow: Progress, 1968);

Louis de Rouvroy, duc de Saint-Simon, *Un espion chez le Roi-Soleil: Extrait des Mémoires de Saint-Simon,* edited by José Cabanis, introduction by Ginzburg (Paris: Gallimard, 1976);

"Tynianov-uchenyi," in *Vospominaniia o Tynianove: Portrety i vstrechi,* edited by Veniamin Aleksandrovich Kaverin (Moscow: Sovetskii pisatel', 1983), pp. 147–172;

"Zabolotskii kontsa dvadtsatykh godov," in *Vospominaniia o N. Zabolotskom,* edited by Adrian Vladimirovich Makedonov, Ekaterina Vasil'evna Zabolotskaia, and Nikita Nikolaevich Zabolotsky, second edition (Moscow: Sovetskii pisatel', 1984), pp. 145–156;

"Eshche raz o starom i novom (Pokolenie na povorote)," in *Tynianovskii sbornik: Vtorye Tynianovskie chteniia,* edited by Marietta Omarovna Chudakova (Riga: Zinatne, 1986), pp. 132–140;

"'I zaodno s pravoporiadkom,'" in *Tynianovskii sbornik: Tret'i Tynianovskie chteniia,* edited by Chudakova (Riga: Zinatne, 1988), pp. 218–230;

"Vspominaia Institut Istorii Iskusstv," in *Tynianovskii sbornik: Chetvertye Tynianovskie chteniia,* edited by Chudakova (Riga: Zinatne, 1990), pp. 278–288;

*Perepiska Borisa Pasternaka,* edited by Ginzburg, E. V. Pasternak, and Evgenii Borisovich Pasternak (Moscow: Khudozhestvennaia literatura, 1990);

Osip Mandel'shtam, *Kamen',* edited by Ginzburg (Leningrad: Nauka, 1990);

Nikolai Oleinikov, *Stikhotvoreniia i poemy,* edited by Ginzburg and Aleksandr Nikolaevich Oleinikov (St. Petersburg: Akademicheskii proekt, 2000).

SELECTED PERIODICAL PUBLICATIONS–UNCOLLECTED: "Akhmatova (Neskol'ko stranits vospominanii)," *Den' poezii* (1977): 216–217;

"Chelovek za pis'mennym stolom: Po starym zapisnym knizhkam," *Novyi mir,* 6 (1982): 234–245;

"Za pis'mennym stolom: Iz zapisei 1950–1960–x godov," *Neva,* 3 (1986): 112–139;

"Nikolay Oleinikov," *Iunost',* 1 (1988): 54–58;

"Zabluzhdenie voli," *Novyi mir,* 11 (1988): 137–154;

"Vybor budushchego: Iz zapisei 1920–1930–x godov," *Neva,* 12 (1988): 131–157;

"Iz zapisei 1950–1980–x godov," *Daugava,* 1 (1989): 96–108;

"Iz zapisei 1950–1980–x godov," *Rodnik,* 1 (1989): 22–27;

"Zapisi raznykh let," *Rodnik,* 3 (1990): 26–30;

"Dve vstrechi," *Russkaia mysl',* no. 3852 (2 November 1990);

"Zapisi 20–30–x godov (Iz neopublikovannogo)," edited by Aleksandr Kushner and Aleksandr Chudakov, *Novyi mir,* 6 (1992): 1–41;

"Iz dnevnikov Lidii Ginzburg," edited by Kushner, *Literaturnaia gazeta,* 41 (13 October 1993): 6.

Lidiia Iakovlevna Ginzburg is best known outside Russia for her theoretical writings and scholarly studies of nineteenth- and twentieth-century narrative prose and lyric poetry. Only in the 1980s did she begin to gain recognition as the most distinguished theorist of "life writing"–a field that encompasses autobiography, biography, letters, diaries, and memoirs–in Russian literary studies. Between 1982 and 1993 Ginzburg, and later her literary executor, Aleksandr Kushner, made large parts of her journal available for publication, revealing a master practitioner of the genres of life writing–what she first termed the "intermediary genres" and later the "direct conversation about life." While perfecting her mastery of the journal, including the entire gamut of life-writing genres–the essay, quasi-fictional prose, and even the art of conversation–Ginzburg simultaneously established new principles of analysis for materials not previously considered "aesthetic" and reassessed the aesthetic qualities of materials not previously considered "literature." Appreciation of both the processes by which life is transformed into literature and by which literary models influence codes of social behavior and society's self-consciousness dominates all of Ginzburg's writing, and her theories are an outgrowth of her literary practice and scholarship. In a 1988 interview Ginzburg explained her interest in the noncanonical genres as part of the evolving "literary process": "In contemporary prose the sense of the author's presence is developing apace.... You take up a pen for a conversation about life—not to write an autobiography, but to express directly your own life experience, your views on reality.... This is one of the paths of future literary development ... the path I prefer."

Ginzburg was born into a middle-class assimilated Jewish family of the Odessa intelligentsia on 5 March (Old Style 18 March) 1902. Her parents had met in Switzerland, where her father, Iakov, and his brother had been sent to study chemical engineering. Her father's death in 1910 left her uncle to become a second father to Lidiia and her brother, Viktor, who was ten years older than she. While Lidiia was still in school, he moved to Moscow and became a comic actor and theater director under the stage name Viktor Teapot. Lidiia maintained close relations with Viktor and his family until his death in 1960. Conversations recorded in her journal reveal his wit and document his interaction with Moscow literary circles.

In 1917 Ginzburg and her gymnasium schoolmates, heirs to the liberal social ideals of the Russian-Jewish intelligentsia, were caught up in the intellectual and emotional fervor of the Russian Revolution. In "Pokolenie na povorote" (1979, Turning Point of a Generation) she describes the power of those feelings: "there was acceptance, no looking back, no questions asked. That may be cause for surprise, but I am not surprised. We were all like that—at age 15. And something remains with us from our youth." She also observes that her generation's welcoming of the revolution reflected contemporary intellectual currents: "Revolution attracted the entire Russian avant garde. The Symbolists as early as 1905...." As for the postsymbolists, "Osip Mandelshtam's essays of the 1920s are incomprehensible without noting what he said in *Noise of Time* about reading the Erfurt Program at school, or the influence of the Narodnik movement on his best friend's family.... And Boris Pasternak in 'The Year 1905' ... and even [Anna Akhmatova] once told me, not without a hint of pleasure, how her mother had been acquainted with members of the Peoples' Will. 'Mama was very proud that she somehow gave Vera Figner a blouse of hers—it was needed for the conspiracy.'"

Ginzburg retained other indelible memories from her Odessa girlhood at the time of the revolution, including changes in language and dress and the unconcern with their own material well-being displayed by the teenagers in her circle: "Having been raised in material prosperity, we did not know its value or potential.... When the historical cataclysm arrived, it affected everyone.... We had been raised from childhood to be ashamed of our privileges, thus although we did not repudiate them ourselves, if history took them away, we did not lodge any complaints against history."

After graduating from the gymnasium in June 1920, Ginzburg went to Moscow to be near her brother. Housing was scarce, however, and she returned to Odessa. Two years later she moved to Petrograd, which became Leningrad in 1924; it was her beloved adopted city until her death, and over the next seven decades Ginzburg was associated with Leningrad's most significant intellectual and cultural phenomena. She captured the vitality of her student years at the Gosudarstvennyi institut istorii iskusstv (State Institute of History of the Arts) in her journal and in a 1986 interview in *Literaturnaia gazeta* (Literary Gazette):

> our teachers included the brilliant philologists and linguists Eikhenbaum, Tynianov, Tomashevskii, Zhirmunsky, and Vinogradov, among others. Our institute did not adhere to strictly pedagogical demands because the systematic communication of information was not taught there. Our teachers lectured about their current projects. It was as if they were sharing their ideas and their research. Ours was an education in scholarly thinking.... and it was up to us, the students, to learn what we had to from books, to fill in the gaps in our education.

The 1920s, Ginzburg claims in "'I Zaodno s pravoporiadkom'" (1988; translated as "At One with the Prevailing Order"), taught her circle of "young formalists" that they were "part of history in the making." Indeed, she defined her generation in terms of the epoch's literary and cultural alignments: "It seemed to us—and so it was for a short time—that we were the principal actors in a segment of culture that had just begun. But in the 1930s and 1940s, we became the passive property of the Stalinist epoch and the war years, with all that followed."

After graduating in 1926, Ginzburg worked as a *nauchnyi sotrudnik* (research fellow) and taught seminars in nineteenth-century Russian poetry at the institute. Her first scholarly publications—on Petr Andreevich Viazemsky as a litterateur, on Vladimir Grigor'evich Benediktov's literary life, and on the philosophical lyric—appeared under the institute's auspices. Ginzburg's journal provides tantalizing glimpses into the vibrant atmosphere at the institute, as well as her despair over the disintegration of collegial relationships and the destruction of the institute. In a 1930 entry published in *Chelovek za pis'mennym stolom: Esse, iz vospominanii, chetyre povestvovaniia* (1989, The Person Behind the Writing Desk: Essays, Memoirs, Four Tales) she says: "The results of 1929–30.... I'm working, I'm quarreling with people who have nourished me with their ideas; I've been called an idealist in the press, I've been firmly and politely refused publication—in a word, I now have all the qualifying signs of a literary professional." The institute was closed by the authorities in 1930.

In contrast to conventional thinking about the 1930s, Ginzburg emphasizes that the ever-present fear was countered by involvement in the "microhistorical" details of daily living. Thus, in rereading her journals of those years, she was not surprised to find records of many acts of heroism and examples of enthusiasm, creativity, and amusement. Despite confusion, frustration, and alienation, her circle viewed the "creative experience" as almost a human right, fulfilling an incorrigible need to be active even during the worst of times. On the other hand, the first of what she calls in "Dve vstrechi" (1990, Two Encounters) her two "direct encounters with the organs" of state security took place in 1933. She was detained in the "Big House," Leningrad's house of detention, as a case was developed against Viktor Maksimovich Zhirmunsky, the former director of the Section of Verbal Arts at the institute. She says that she was "so psychologically unprepared" that she burst out laughing when asked if she "knew Zhirmunskii to be a spy."

After the institute was closed, Ginzburg worked for a time at the children's publishing house Detgiz, along with the poets Nikolai Makarovich Oleinikov and Nikolai Alekseevich Zabolotsky, on Samuil Iakovlevich Marshak's children's magazines *Chizh* and *Ezh*. During that time she wrote a detective novel for adolescents, *Agentsvo Pinkertona* (1932, The Pinkerton Agency). In 1933–1934 she taught language and literature at the Rabfak (Workers' School) of the Civil Aeronautics Academy and the Post-Secondary School of the Labor Movement. Barred from teaching at institutions of higher education during the 1930s, she spoke on Russian literature for the Leningrad Municipal and Regional Public Lecture Service and the Section for Artistic Propaganda of the Leningrad branch of the Soviet Writers' Union. In contrast to her journal entries from the 1920s that record intense intellectual involvement and the taking of principled stands on a broad range of issues, entries from the 1930s describe bouts of severe depression, confusion, anxiety over issues of right and wrong, penance and remorse, contemplation of class privilege, and recognition of the impossibility of publishing her major article on Marcel Proust.

Paradoxically, the 1940s appeared "simpler," bringing psychological relief because of "the wartime convergence of private values with those of the state." Nevertheless, Ginzburg's powers of endurance were severely tested as she remained in Leningrad throughout the German siege of the city. She did not seek to be evacuated because she was sure that her mother, who was ill, would not survive the journey. Working as an editor in the literature and drama section of the state radio network, she says in *Literatura v poiskakh real'nosti* (1987, Literature in Search of Reality), she received two awards for valor as she "quietly corrected the broadcasts of other writers' war literature." After her mother died, during the first winter of the Blockade, Ginzburg took up residence at the radio station. Her "Zapiski blokadnogo cheloveka" (Notes from the Leningrad Blockade), which took her more than forty years to write, was begun during the winter of 1942. This highly acclaimed work derives in part from records in her journal of conversations overheard in bomb shelters, on breadlines, and at work. In the early 1960s, when Nikita Khrushchev's "Thaw" years seemed to promise some hope of publication, she began to revise her notes. Nothing could be published, however, until decades later. Part 1, predominantly narrative, appeared in the Leningrad magazine *Neva* in 1984 and was republished in *Chelovek za pis'mennym stolom;* part 2, comprising mainly conversations, appeared posthumously in her *Pretvorenie opyta* (1991, Transformation of Experience).

In "Zapisi raznykh let" (1990, In the Zapis, Notes) Ginzburg claims that for her, the immediate postwar years 1946 to 1953 were by far the most traumatic and degrading, because the moral and psychological "variant" used by the "creative intelligentsia" in the 1930s "no longer worked" and because they finally realized their own naiveté in failing to recognize the full horror of what had been taking place around them. She taught the history of Russian literature at the All-Russian Academy of Arts in Leningrad from 1944 to 1946, a time of vicious anti-intellectual and anti-Semitic attacks against "cosmopolitanism." She taught at the Karelo-Finnish University in Petrozavodsk in 1947, as it was safer for Jewish intellectuals to be employed outside the major cities; she continued to teach there until 1950.

Ginzburg's second encounter with state security occurred at the end of 1952. Unsuccessfully recruited in an endeavor to develop a case against her teacher and mentor, Boris Eikhenbaum, she was saved by Joseph Stalin's death. At this point she experienced her first feelings of renewal and hope, combined with a new sensation of being part of the "older generation."

In the late 1950s Ginzburg studied at the Leningrad Institute of Russian Literature, where she defended her dissertation on Aleksandr Herzen in 1958; she had defended her candidate's dissertation on Mikhail Iur'evich Lermontov at Leningrad University twenty years earlier. Later, however, she repudiated as repugnant her work of the postwar years, including her doctoral dissertation: "We had not even recognized how the common language had penetrated and contaminated our language . . . hence, the most difficult thing for me now is to re-read my work on Herzen's *Past and Thoughts* . . . no one escaped unscathed," she says in "'I zaodno s pravoporiadkom.'"

Ginzburg's most fruitful years began in the 1960s as sporadic publication was superseded by a new book or revised edition every two or three years. Her popular 1964 work *O lirike* (The Lyric) was republished in a revised and enlarged edition ten years later. *O psikhologicheskoi proze,* published in 1971, was revised and republished in 1977 (translated as *On Psychological Prose,* 1991). *O literaturnom geroe* (On the Literary Hero) appeared in 1979. Several volumes of collected writings appeared in the 1980s, including prose narratives; literary, philosophical, and memoiristic essays; and journal excerpts: *O starom i novom* (The Old and the New) in 1982, *Literatura v poiskakh real'nosti* in 1987, and *Chelovek za pis'mennym stolom* in 1989.

Ginzburg's editorial and textual work, begun in 1929 with her edition of Viazemsky's *Staraia zapisnaia knizhka* (Old Notebook), continued unabated until her death. As a member of the Osip Mandel'shtam Commission in the 1960s Ginzburg was instrumental in rehabilitating the poet's name and publishing his work, though her introduction to the Poet's Library edition of his selected poems was rejected by the authorities. Her various editions in the Poet's Library, Literary Heritage, and Literary Monuments series, and her contributions to the publication of such widely different authors as Benediktov, Viazemsky, Mandel'shtam, Lermontov, Herzen, Pasternak, Zabolotsky, Oleinikov, Aleksandr Pushkin, Aleksandr Blok, Eduard Bagritsky (Eduard Georgievich Dzyubin), and Iurii Tynianov testify to the esteem in which she was held as a scholar. Besides Russian literature, she edited with Evgenii Mikhailovich Vinokurov *Zarubezhnaia poeziia v russkikh perevodakh: Ot Lomonosova do nashikh dnei* (1968, Foreign Poetry in Russian Translation) and wrote introductions to "Memuary Sen Simona" in Saint-Simon's memoirs and *Frantsuzskaia romanticheskaia povest'* (1982, French Romantic Prose).

One of Ginzburg's major contributions to literary theory is her notion of the continuum of the aesthetic function and, hence, of genre. She posits the absence of absolute boundaries between aesthetically and historically determined "facts," because the various forms of historical material, organized in accordance with particular aesthetic principles, are all part of the literary process and comprise different correlates between history and belles lettres. Thus, she considers "boundaries" not as finite or absolute limits but as fluid and changing entities in the historical context and in the aesthetic continuum of genre, ranging from everyday "human docu-

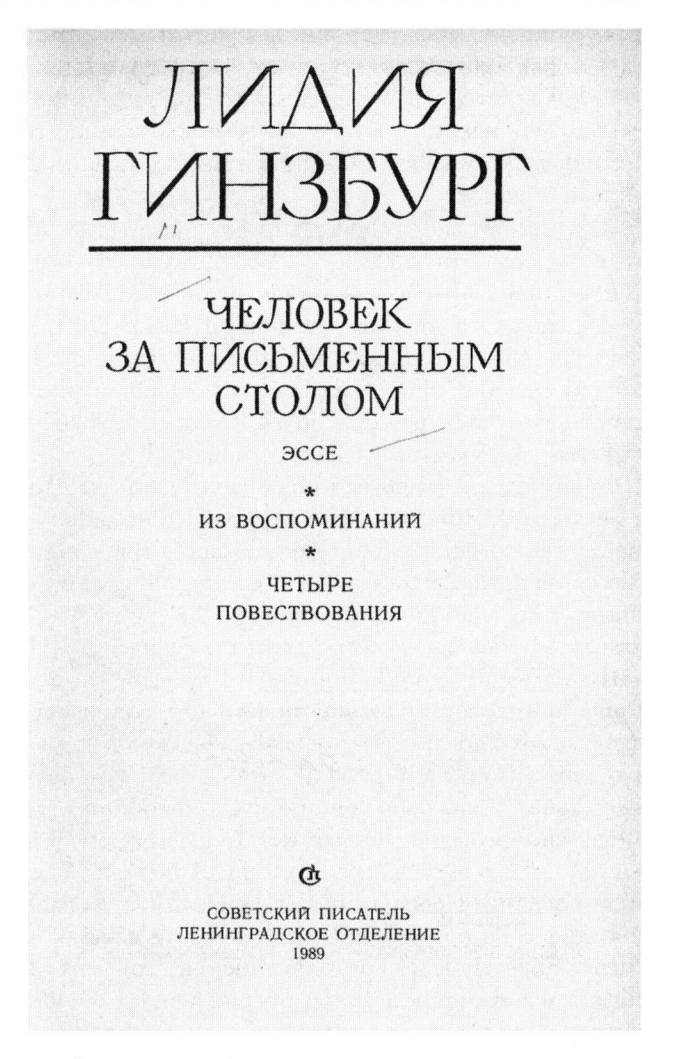

*Title page for Ginzburg's* Chelovek za pis'mennym stolom *(The Person Behind the Writing Desk: Essays, Memoirs, Four Tales), published the year before her death (Howard-Tilton Memorial Library, Tulane University)*

ments"—letters, anecdotes, gossip, journal entries, essays, and so on—to genres in which the aesthetic element predominates.

Ginzburg's consistent search for principles in literature and life by which to broaden her understanding of human behavior led her to focus on the perception of processes; on the "transformation" of life into art; on the correlates, as well as the distinctions, between literature and life; and on the reverse effects of art on life. Thus, she devoted a good portion of her literary scholarship to life writing and the processes of aesthetic genesis, transformation, and change. By keeping a journal she participated in the aesthetic and historical continuum on a regular and firsthand basis. In her essays on the behavior of the Russian intelligentsia in the Soviet cultural environment, she adapted techniques and ideas from both her scholarship and her journal. For example, Ginzburg's theory of the art of conversation emerges in her journals, quasi-narrative prose, and theoretical writings; in *O literaturnom geroe* conversation is treated as another means of formalizing and organizing human activities.

Ginzburg had begun keeping her journal in 1925, while writing a student essay on Viazemsky for the special seminar in Russian prose taught by Eikhenbaum and Tynianov at the State Institute of History of the Arts. In 1982, although she attributed the impulse behind her journal to Viazemsky, she claimed in *O starom i novom* to be working "in a different genre." Nevertheless, like Viazemsky, Ginzburg apparently regarded her journal as a serious and publishable enterprise and considered the time and care she expended on individual entries to be significant literary labor. She shared Viazemsky's declared goal of recording "the morals and manners and living expression of the community" associated with the *journal externe* of the eighteenth and early nineteenth centuries but decried his lack "of anything in the nature of authorial (diary) confession, self-analysis and abstract reasoning." Ginzburg's journal entries from the beginning through the 1930s deal with issues of self-definition and the formation of personal and professional character traits; that is, the entries evolve as a literary creation of the self. The interpretation of personality developed in her journal played a significant role in Ginzburg's formulation of a theory of psychological prose in which her concepts of historical and empirical personality and her ideas on life writing were advanced. In *O literaturnom geroe* she points out that people "constantly rework their lives through their internal and external speech"; thus, even "spontaneous oral speech contains the potential for scientific and poetic thought, and consequently, has a powerful creative potential." And finally, in theorizing about art as "interpretation" in a 1989 journal entry, Ginzburg reaffirms that all efforts to formalize and organize human activities and behavior are part of the continuing aesthetic process: "Art is the interpretation of experience, not of reality because only through experience do we know reality. Interpretation is aesthetic . . . latent in every activity, in every aspect of behavior."

Even the earliest entries exemplify the high value Ginzburg placed on writing—on literary style, structure, and strategy—and demonstrate that the journal was not merely a psychological outlet but a mode of aesthetic and intellectual cognition, a means of giving structure to her complex mental processes. Writing may also have served as a strategy of defiance, allowing her to oppose certain social, political, or cultural requirements or limitations. Thus, many entries include carefully designed parallelisms, juxtapositions, and paradoxes; express a kind of "double-voiced discourse"; and conclude with a witticism. This attentiveness to literary composition suggests Ginzburg's effort to seek an aesthetic solution to problems she was not otherwise able to resolve.

During the 1920s Ginzburg viewed herself as part of a collective intellectual project. Her journal entries reflect attempts to describe the personalities and behavioral patterns of her circle, to depict how people looked, talked, dressed, acted, and performed in official debates. As such, they provide another form of self-evaluation.

Ginzburg's journal also indicates how much she identified with her reading and sought out explanations for her private life in books and conversations not associated with her professional life. Her views on women's issues and sexuality emerge most directly here. Fluency in French made it possible for her to keep abreast of the literary and cultural scene abroad, including such causes célèbres as Andre Gide's *Corydon* (1924; translated, 1950) and Proust's *A la recherche du temps perdus* (1913–1927; translated as *Remembrance of Things Past*, 1981). In an early journal entry evaluating *Corydon* Ginzburg expresses her opinion on how homosexuality should be discussed and defended; her defense is based on her own lesbian-feminist perspective. On the other hand, in her praise of Proust, Ginzburg's defense of homosexuality moves beyond social, psychological, and political concerns to focus on aesthetics. Between 1927 and 1930 Proust was Ginzburg's model for reformulating and transforming her image both as a writer and as a human being; she says in a 1930 entry, "I will probably write until I take my last breath. . . . because for me to write means to live, to experience life. I not only cherish things per se, but conceptions of things, processes of perception (that is why Proust is the most significant writer for me)." Ginzburg evaluates her own writing in this context, recognizing her journal as her special mode of literary expression, the most "appropriate form for" her own "inclinations," even though she is "bothered by its being unprintable" and that "it is too easy for me to write."

If by 1930 Ginzburg's journal was the form best suited to her needs, the essay emerged as the preeminent genre of her mature years. Beginning in the 1940s she expanded occasional journal entries into topical or philosophical essays; and by the time of Stalin's death, when she first began to regard herself as part of the "older generation biologically," she was devoting major essays to the psychology and behavior of the Soviet intelligentsia. Her memoiristic essays "Pokolenie na povorote" and "'I zaodno s pravoporiadkom'" cite her own experiences not for autobiographical purposes but as a semiotic model of the behavior of the intelligentsia of her generation: "What can I say about my own case? Basically, that we should have no illusions, no one escaped unscathed.... For me, the mechanism of justification was the most weakly developed; my inborn analytical sense interfered. But the mechanism of indifference never ceased to operate."

Ginzburg gained recognition as a major public figure in the early 1980s. In 1982 conferences and readings in honor of her eightieth birthday were held in the Soviet Union and in the United States. In 1985, following publication of the first part of "Zapiski blokadnogo cheloveka," she was interviewed for the *Literaturnaia gazeta*. In 1988, after receiving the prestigious State Prize for Literature, Ginzburg eagerly accepted opportunities to be interviewed in the press and on television and declared her satisfaction with the spirit of glasnost (openness): "People have been stirred up to talk. That's the most important thing.... The curse that has hung over our society since the 1930s has been lifted.... The principle itself—that I can say what I think—is an event of enormous moral consequence," she said in a 1988 interview in *Literaturnaia Rossiia* (Literary Russia). In 1990, in "Zapisi raznykh let," she declared her allegiance to life writing as the most "contemporary" of literary forms; she concludes that "the direct conversation about life—in its various forms, and oblique forms also exist—is now the only genre that is contemporary."

Ginzburg died on 15 July 1990. The early 1990s brought the posthumous publication of more journal excerpts in *Novyi mir* and *Literaturnaia gazeta* and Ginzburg's last authorized volume, *Pretvorenie opyta;* the volume includes two essays on Mandel'shtam, whom she regarded as the seminal poet of the twentieth century.

Lidiia Iakovlevna Ginzburg's reputation as a literary theorist and critic has long been firmly established. In addition, she is now being recognized as a master of life writing. Indeed, Ginzburg's lifelong contemplation of the correlations between the reality of "lived experience" and literary creation provides the key to all her writing, above all, to her own wide-ranging art of the *zapis'* (journal entry), which included the vast range of genres of self-expression, from poignant self-analyses, simple anecdotes, recorded conversations, to lengthy philosophical and memoiristic essays. Ginzburg's focus on ongoing processes, on correlations as well as distinctions between literature and life, on the "transformation" of life into art and the reverse effects of art on life originates from her view that "boundaries" between life and art were not finite or absolute, but fluid and changing entities in history as well as in an ongoing aesthetic continuum. Thus, in writing about literature, she often chose to study the noncanonical genres of life writing and the processes of aesthetic genesis, transformation, and change. In keeping a journal, she chose to participate in the ongoing aesthetic and historical continuum on a regular, firsthand basis. And in her memoirs, especially those of 1979–1980, she chose to adapt modes of expression from both her scholarship and her journal to analyses of human culture, identifying and interpreting literary and cultural images returned to life in the form of consciously accepted historical facts and codes of human behavior.

**Interviews:**

A. Latynina, "Chtoby skazat' novoe i svoe, nado myslit' v izbrannom napravlenii," *Voprosy literatury*, 4 (1978): 182–197;

Victor Erlich, "Two Conversations with Lidiia Ginzburg," *Canadian American Slavic Studies,* special issue, "Lidiia Ginzburg's Contribution to Literary Criticism," 19 (Summer 1985): 193–195;

L. Titova, "Interv'iu," *Smena*, no. 262 (13 November 1988): 2;

I. Pankeev, "Interv'iu," *Literaturnaia Rossiia*, 51 (23 December 1988): 8–9.

**References:**

V. S. Bibler, "Lidiia Iakovlevna Ginzburg i sudby russkoi intelligentsii," *ARKhE: Kulturologicheskii ezhegodnik*, 1 (1993): 422–427;

*Canadian-American Slavic Studies,* special issue, "In Memoriam: Lidiia Ginzburg," edited by Jane Gary Harris, 28 (Summer 1994);

*Canadian-American Slavic Studies,* special issue, "Lidiia Ginzburg's Contribution to Literary Criticism," edited by Sarah Pratt, 19 (Summer 1985);

Caryl Emerson, "Bakhtin, Lotman, Vygotsky and Lydia Ginzburg," in *Self and Story in Russian History,* edited by Laura Engelstein and Stephanie Sandler (Ithaca, N.Y.: Cornell University Press, 2000), pp. 20–45;

Boris Gasparov and others, "Tvorcheskii portret L. Ia. Ginzburg," *Literaturnoe obozrenie,* 10 (1989): 78–86;

Iakov Gordin, "Mashtabnost' issledovaniia," *Voprosy literatury*, 1 (1981): 273–281;

Jane Gary Harris, "The Crafting of a Self: Lidiia Ginzburg's Early Journal," in *Gender and Russian Literature: New Perspectives,* edited by Rosalind Marsh (Cambridge: Cambridge University Press, 1996), pp. 263–282;

Harris, "'The Direct Conversation about Life': Lidiia Ginzburg's Journal as a Contemporary Literary Genre," in *Neoformalist Papers: Contributions to the Silver Age Jubilee Conference to Mark 25 Years of the Neo-Formalist Circle,* edited by Joe Andrew and Robert Reid, Studies in Slavic Literatures and Poetics, no. 32 (Amsterdam: Rodopi, 1998), pp. 45–64;

Harris, "Lidiia Ginzburg" and "Selected Works: From *The Journals*," in *Russian Women Writers,* volume 2, edited by Christine Tomei (New York: Garland, 1999), pp. 1157–1178;

Harris, "Lidiia Ginzburg: Images of the Intelligentsia," in *The Russian Memoir: History and Literature,* edited by Beth Holmgren (Evanston, Ill.: Northwestern University Press, 2003), pp. 5–34;

Harris, "Lidiia Iakovlevna Ginzburg," in *Reference Guide to Russian Literature,* edited by Neil Cornwell (London: Fitzroy Dearborn, 1998), pp. 322–324;

Holmgren, "Russian Women's Autobiography," in *Women Writers in Russian Literature,* edited by Toby Clyman and Diana Greene (Westport, Conn.: Greenwood Press, 1994), pp. 138–140;

Catriona Kelly, *A History of Russian Women's Writing, 1820–1992* (Oxford: Clarendon Press, 1994), pp. 370–371;

Aleksandr Kushner, ed., "Iz dnevnikov Lidii Ginzburg," *Literaturnaia gazeta,* 41 (13 October 1993): 6;

Iurii Mikhailovich Lotman, "The Decembrist in Daily Life: Everyday Behavior as a Historical-Psychological Category," in *The Semiotics of Russian Cultural History: Essays by Iurii M. Lotman, Lidiia Ia. Ginzburg, and Boris A. Uspenskii* (Ithaca, N.Y.: Cornell University Press, 1985), pp. 188–224;

Elena Nevzgliadova, "Na samom dele, mysl' kak gost' . . . O proze Lidii Ginzburg," *Avrora,* 4 (1989);

Boris Leonidovich Pasternak, "Stolet'e s lishnym–ne vchera," *Novyi mir,* 5 (1932): 67;

Pasternak, "Vysokaia bolezn'," *LEF,* 1 (1924): 1–18; revised, *Novyi mir,* 11 (1928): 18–20;

Irina Podol'skaia, "Lidiia Ginzburg. O lirike," *Izvestiia Akademii Nauk SSSR: Seriia literatury i iazyka,* 34 (January–February 1975): 81–83;

Pratt, "Lidiia Ginzburg and the Fluidity of Genre," in *Autobiographical Statements in Twentieth Century Russian Literature,* edited by Harris (Princeton: Princeton University Press, 1990), pp. 207–216;

Rosengrant, "Lidiia Ginzburg," in *Encyclopedia of the Essay,* edited by Tracy Chevalier (London: Fitzroy Dearborn, 2000), pp. 341–342.

# Anatolii Tikhonovich Gladilin
(21 August 1935 - )

Boris Lanin
*Russian Academy of Education, Moscow*

BOOKS: *Khronika vremen Viktora Podgurskogo: Sostavlennaia iz dnevnikov, letopisei, istoricheskikh sobytii i vospominanii sovremennikov* (Moscow: Sovetskii pisatel', 1958);

*Brigantina podnimaet parusa: Istoriia odnogo neudachnika* (Moscow: Sovetskii pisatel', 1959);

*Vechnaia komandirovka* (Moscow: Sovetskii pisatel', 1962);

*Idushchii vperedi: Povesti* (Moscow: Molodaia gvardiia, 1962);

*Pervyi den' Novogo goda: Povest' i rasskazy* (Moscow: Sovetskii pisatel', 1965);

*Evangelie ot Robesp'era: Povest o velikom frants. revoliuts* (Moscow: Politizdat, 1970);

*Prognoz na zavtra* (Frankfurt am Main: Possev, 1972);

*Sny Shlissel'burgskoi kreposti: Povest' ob Ippolite Myshkine* (Moscow: Politizdat, 1974);

*Dva goda do vesny: Roman, rasskazy* (Moscow: Sovetskii pisatel', 1975);

*Repetitsiia v piatnitsu: Povest' i rasskazy* (Paris: Tret'ia volna, 1978);

*The Making and Unmaking of a Soviet Writer: My Story of the "Young Prose" of the Sixties and After,* translated by David Lapeza (Ann Arbor, Mich.: Ardis, 1979);

*Parizhskaia iarmarka: Fel'etony, putevye zametki, literaturnye portrety* (Paris & Tel Aviv: Effect, 1980);

*Bol'shoi Begovoi Den'* (Ann Arbor, Mich.: Ardis, 1983); translated by Robert Paul Schoenberg and Janet G. Tucker as *Moscow Racetrack: A Novel of Espionage at the Track* (Ann Arbor, Mich.: Ardis, 1990);

*FSSR: Frantsuzskaia Sovetskaia Sotsialisticheskaia Respublika. Povest'* (New York: Effect, 1985);

*Kakim ia byl togda* (Ann Arbor, Mich.: Ardis, 1986);

*Menia ubil skotina Pell* (Moscow: Sov.-Britanskogo sovmestnogo predpriiatiia Slovo, 1991);

*Bespokoinik: Rasskazy raznykh let* (Moscow: Konets veka, 1992);

*Ten' vsadnika* (Moscow: Olimp, Astrel', Ast, 2000);

*Prognoz na zavtra: Povesti, rasskazy* (Moscow: AST/Olimp, 2001).

*Anatolii Tikhonovich Gladilin (from* Pervyi den' Novogo goda: Povest' i rasskazy, *1965; Thomas Cooper Library, University of South Carolina)*

**Edition in English:** "The Double," in Anatoly Vishevsky, *Soviet Literary Culture in the 1970s: The Politics of Irony. With an Anthology of Ironic Prose Translated by Michael Biggins and Anatoly Vishevsky* (Gainesville: University Press of Florida, 1993).

Anatolii Tikhonovich Gladilin was one of the founders of "youth prose," a movement in Soviet literature that began in the mid 1950s, after the "Thaw," and lasted for about twenty years. In contrast to the "positive hero" models of socialist realism, Gladilin's characters struggle for freedom and a chance to celebrate their individuality in opposition to the collective; they question the morality of their lives and seek ways to retain their integrity as they face moral choices and intellectual problems. By placing his characters in situations in which they must deal with representatives of an earlier generation, Gladilin presents a sensitive look at problems of the so-called generation gap. His style and methods of narration also defy the simplicity of the accepted models of socialist realism. Attacked by critics and censured by the political-literary establishment, Gladilin, like his heroes, fought for freedom of expression.

Gladilin was born in Moscow on 21 August 1935 to Tikhon Gladilin, an attorney, and Polina Taradeyko-Gladilina, a physician. He received a certificate from school N73 in Moscow in 1953 and entered the military academy of Air Fighters in Kazakhstan, where he remained for only a few months. His account in *The Making and Unmaking of a Soviet Writer: My Story of the "Young Prose" of the Sixties and After* (1979) of his brief stint in the military reveals his ironic tone and his sardonic view of the times in which he lived:

> A Soviet upbringing will show—even now I cannot give the exact address of the academy, I'm so used to keeping military secrets. However, in the city of N–, I ran up against the army face to face for the first time, and instantly all the romance disappeared. In the army, personalities were not needed, the army needed obedient automatons. And then I understood that my true calling wasn't flying anyway, it was writing.

Returning to Moscow too late to take competitive examinations for entrance into any of the institutes, Gladilin "got fixed up as an electromechanics student at . . . (so now this is a military secret too, even if the apparently peaceful enterprise made machine tools? . . . Damn them and their secrets!)." In the summer of 1954 he entered Gor'ky Literary Institute of the Union of Writers but did not graduate. He also worked for a time as an electrician. On 10 April 1955 he married Marii Taits, a technical editor; they have two children, Alla and Lisa.

Gladilin's first published work, the novella *Khronika vremen Viktora Podgurskogo: Sostavlennaia iz dnevnikov, letopisei, istoricheskikh sobytii i vospominanii sovremennikov* (A Chronicle of the Time of Viktor Podgurskii, Compiled from Diaries, Annals, Historical Facts, and Memoirs), appeared in the magazine *Iunost'* (Youth) in September 1956 and brought him immediate acclaim; it was published in book form in 1958. Gladilin's young nonconformist male characters were the first of their kind to appear in Soviet literature; thus, this novella, rather than the works of Vasily Aksyonov and Vladimir Nikolaevich Voinovich that appeared several years later, marks the birth of youth prose. In interviews at that time and subsequently Gladilin explained the ideology of his literary generation as a desire for truth and honesty.

In 1958 Gladilin was appointed head of the department of art and culture of the newspaper *Moskovskii komsomolets* (Moscow Communist Youth). By the spring of 1959 he was, he says in *The Making and Unmaking of a Soviet Writer,* "seized by . . . cursed restlessness," and he flew to Magadan in May to work in the gold mines. The work proved too strenuous for him, and he became a blacksmith's striker instead. When he returned to Moscow at the end of the year, he took a position as a writer at the newspaper *Komsomol'skaia Pravda* (Komsomol Truth).

Gladilin's novella "Dym v glaza" (Smoke in the Eyes), about the talented if arrogant footballer Igor' Serov seeking his own individuality, was published in *Iunost'* in 1959 and collected in Gladilin's *Idushchii vperedi* (Going Ahead) in 1962. It was harshly reviewed by some critics; although she found Gladilin's psychology superficial, however, the critic Inna Solov'eva, a supporter of youth prose, added: "The writer is capable of entering into polemics with banality in literature. He can find banality in life itself and can give this banality grotesque form. In this lies the nature of his gift" (*Novyi Mir* 4 [1963]).

In 1960 Gladilin became the youngest member of the Writers' Union. He was never part of the Soviet literary establishment, however, and was never elected a delegate to the Writers' Union congresses. Nevertheless, in 1961 membership in the group afforded him a trip to France as part of a delegation of writers.

Gladilin's short story "Kakim ia byl togda" (What I Was Like Then) was published in *Iunost'* in 1961 and in book form in 1986. The protagonist, Kolia Mikhailov, studies music as a child and dreams of becoming a great musician. When he realizes that he will never achieve that goal, he takes up mathematics so that he can enroll in a prestigious military academy. There he studies little and rises no higher than the rank of senior lieutenant, and his marriage breaks up. But he finds his own bearings and his own limits. He occasionally regrets the dashing of his childhood hopes, but he realizes that he has become a different person. Gladilin's young hero spoke for millions in the Soviet Union who were coming to terms with the fact that they would not become socialist heroes or models for schoolchildren to look up to, and, like millions of young people the world over, were reconciling themselves to their own ordinariness.

The short story "Poezd ukhodit" (The Train Leaves Forever), published in *Iunost'* in 1961 and collected in *Bespokoinik* (The Uneasy One) in 1992, is typical of the early period of Gladilin's career. The town in which the story takes place is nameless, as is the protagonist, an ordinary man locked in a loveless marriage and a humdrum career. Suddenly, "on the eighth day of the week," it is announced that "The Blue Express" train is leaving: "Anyone could take this train accompanied by whom he wants, his wife, girlfriend, a girl he didn't even know, or simply alone. This train made a person free in his love, made him free of all ties and binds, although they remained very slender, but not torn." The protagonist imagines the interesting new life and freedom from old problems offered by the train; but he does not reject his present life and remains in the town. "The Blue Express," which is departing only "for the first time during the two last millennia," leaves the station without him. Gladilin's typical hero resembles Anton Chekhov's: he is a young man who does not possess any particularly elevated ideals and has spent his early promise but is not a bad person.

Gladilin worked as a film editor at the Gorky studio in 1962–1963 and was an editor of the Moscow cinema journal *Fitil* from 1967 to 1969. In 1966 Gladilin signed a letter protesting the trial of writers Iulii Daniel' and Andrei Siniavsky, angering the authorities. He was subsequently excluded from the literary community and began sending his work to the West for publication. He was, however, ordered by Moscow to write two books about revolutionaries in 1970 and 1974.

Gladilin took the manuscript for his novel *Prognoz na zavtra* (Tomorrow's Forecast) to various publishing houses in the Soviet Union to no avail; it was published in West Germany in 1972. In *Prognoz na zavtra* Martynov, a professional meteorologist, makes uncannily accurate weather forecasts: he has unerring intuition and can "feel" the most unpredictable changes in the weather. But he cannot predict anything about his personal life. His wife, Natasha, is in a mental hospital, leaving Martynov to maintain the household and raise their daughter, Alyona. The only bright spot in his life is his mistress, Irina, whose love helps him to retain his self-confidence. His dilemma is that he cannot divorce Natasha while she is ill; but if she recovers, he wonders if he will be able to continue his relationship with Irina. He muses: "The only thing I can do, an ordinary Soviet worker, is to earn miserable money, do the shopping, do the housework, calm others down, bustle about here and there: I'm not strong enough for two families." In the end, Martynov stays with Natasha when she returns from the hospital. He is sustained by the hope that his long-term forecast of a bright future in science for himself will be realized.

After the publication of *Prognoz na zavtra,* Gladilin was summoned before the Central Committee of the Communist Party and told that the West was using him for political purposes. He protested that he had had no political motives in writing the novel. In a 2001 interview with Viacheslav Prokofiev in the newspaper *Trud* (Labor) Gladilin recalled encountering Iurii Valentinovich Trifonov in the Central House of Writers in Moscow and asking why Trifonov's controversial novel *Dom na naberezhnoi* (1976; translated as *The House on the Embankment,* 1983) had been allowed to be published in the Soviet Union when his own *Prognov na zavtra* could not find a publisher there. Trifonov replied that the authorities had found nothing criminal in Gladilin's book; they simply did not like his "stylistic tricks" and "formalistic intricacies." Soviet publishers, Trifonov said, wanted "normal prose."

When he became successful as a writer, Gladilin began betting on horse races in Moscow; he usually lost. He used his experiences in a novel that he began in 1976; in the middle of writing it he received the emigration visa for which he had applied, and he and his family left for Paris in 1976. There he became a successful journalist for the U.S. government–funded news service Radio Liberty. The work did not leave him much time for the novel; he did not complete it until 1981, and it was published two years later as *Bol'shoi Begovoi Den'* (Day of the Great Derby; translated as *Moscow Racetrack: A Novel of Espionage at the Track,* 1990). In the novel the KGB (Komissariat gosudarstvennoi bezopasnosti [State Security Committee]) hires successful horse players to bet at foreign races and put their winnings into the Soviet state budget; if they lose, they are immediately sent back to the Soviet Union.

Gladilin took four years, with no time off–not even weekends and holidays–to complete the novel *FSSR: Frantsuzskaia Sovetskaia Sotsialisticheskaia Respublika* (1985, The French Soviet Socialist Republic), his only work to date in the antiutopia genre; it also features elements of the detective novel. The outwardly charming "superman" antihero, colonel Boris Borisovich Zotov of the KGB, tells how he met his Waterloo as a spy when he helped to establish the Soviet system in France. After a minor miscalculation the KGB dismissed him and sent him into an honorable exile as director of a steamship company in a Russian provincial backwater, where he watches on television as French workers line up for fresh cabbage almost "like people back home." At the end of the novel he explains to a French communist imprisoned in a Soviet labor camp that serving a totalitarian regime is not the path to happiness. Gladilin explained in a 1991 interview that power is one of the main themes of the book:

Everybody–and men especially–is building a career–in academia, in literature or in business. Sometimes he tries to gain power–this is normal. If he is lucky he

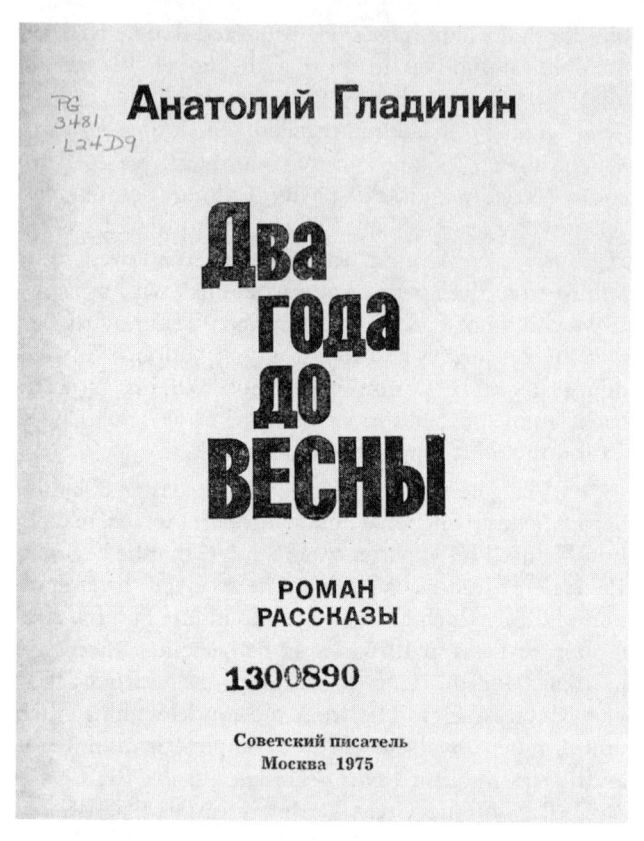

*Title page for* Dva goda do vesny *(Two Years Until Spring), Gladilin's collection published just after the Central Committee of the Communist Party informed him that he was being used by forces in the West for political purposes. The authorities deplored his "stylistic tricks" and "formalistic intricacies" (John C. Hodges Library, University of Tennessee-Knoxville).*

climbs higher and higher—as high as his talent allows. But sooner or later he falls. Only Politburo members managed to die naturally on the political Olympus. A new generation arrives and carries out its own agenda. A person who has tasted power feels himself betrayed. He remembers the new breed when they were just boys who were happy if he so much as cast a look at them. The history of famous people, from Julius Caesar to Gorbachev, proves I am right.

Gladilin was allowed to return to his home country after the fall of the Soviet Union. In 1991 he made a triumphal visit to Moscow, where he was interviewed by journalists, made many public appearances, and participated in television talk shows. His novel about Radio Liberty, *Menia ubil skotina Pell* (The Swine, Pell, Killed Me), was published that year. He did not move back to Russia, however, but continues to live in the Paris suburb of Maisons-Alfort.

"Bespokoinik," the title novella of Gladilin's 1992 collection, is a kind of updating of Leo Tolstoy's play *Zhivoi Trup* (1900; translated as *The Living Corpse: A Drama in Six Acts and Twelve Tableaux,* 1912) adapted to Soviet conditions. In a 2001 interview Gladilin called this novella "the first 'samizdat' of my literary generation." He had written it in 1957 in Novorossiisk and had never published it in Russian but later published it in German. The original manuscript was lost, and Gladilin restored the Russian version of the work through reverse translation from the German.

The "bespokoinik" is Nikolai Aleksandrovich Sergeev, who takes part in his own funeral, then sets out from the crematorium on foot to start his afterlife with another person's documents and money that he stole in a jewelry-store robbery. Living quite well after his fabricated "death," Sergeev evaluates his life and concludes that his moral death happened before his physical death from a second heart attack: he died as a moral being on the day he betrayed a friend by failing to support the latter's project at an important meeting. The hero's self-presentation is important for his confession: "I am a simple, ordinary man, educated in a particular system, and who can count the options available. From this point of view 1937 taught me a lot"; the reference is to the year of Joseph Stalin's "Great Terror." Sergeev visits his grave and corrects the year of death from 1958 to 1950—the year he betrayed his friend. Sergeev is sure of the topsy-turvy nature of the society in which he lives, one in which

> the foundations of our society contradict normal human life. We have got used to doing one thing, and saying another, what we do is the opposite of what we want, we stifle our impulses, we play the hypocrite in full realization that we are hypocrites, and no matter how much we may castigate ourselves we continue to lie. Our life is a fight against endless taboos.

But he does not agree with another character, who says that "better times—they will never come. Enough of slogans. And don't tell me about fight and sacrifices—I want to live in peace, and I don't mind the tears of other people. People who cannot earn money must feed themselves by telling tales about the bright future." Sergeev says that he is a happy man; but at the same time, he is a dead man.

Gladilin's novel *Ten' vsadnika* (Rider's Shadow), which he has called his best book, was completed in the spring of 2000 and published at the end of the year. In a story that spans two hundred years, the main character undergoes three incarnations: in his first life he is a leader of the French Revolution in 1794; in the second he is the king of Sweden; and in the third he is a twentieth-century professor of French history in love with a Russian woman who has immigrated to Los Angeles.

Anatolii Tikhonovich Gladilin's place in Russian literature rests on his status as one of the founders of youth prose, in which the "all-powerful narrator" of Socialist Realism is replaced by a fallible storyteller. Throughout his career Gladilin mainly has used first-person narrators, but the thoughts and opinions even of his third-person narrators are close to those of his protagonists. The hero's way of thinking is opened up to the reader and shown to be impulsive and even wrong; this right to make mistakes brings the protagonist closer to the reader. Youth prose was one of the most productive and popular trends in twentieth-century Russian literature.

**Interviews:**

T. Kulikova, "Svoboda luchshe nevoli," *Kuranty,* 20 November 1991;

"'Svoboda' kak osoznannaia neobkhodimost': Beseda s russkim pisatelem, zhivushchim v Parizhe, A. T. Gladilinym, Zapisala Iuliia Rakhaeva," *Novoe vremia,* 12 (1994): 44–46;

"A teper' zasiadu za 'Netlenku' (Beseda s pisatelem nakanune ego 60-letiia)," *Literaturnaia gazeta,* 6 September 1995;

Ol'ga Martynenko, "Podpolie v Parizhe: Kniga zhizni Anatoliia Gladilina," *Moskovskie novosti,* 6 March 2001;

Viacheslav Prokofiev, "Khronika vremen Anatolia Gladilina," *Trud,* 4 April 2001.

**References:**

Iurii Andreevich Andreev, "Chelovek i vremia," in *Problema kharaktera v sovremennoi sovetskoi literature* (Moscow & Leningrad: Nauka, 1962), pp. 105–106;

Vasilii Ivanovich Ardamatsky, "Vechnaia komandirovka," *Izvestiia,* 20 September 1962;

Irina Basova, "Chto nasha zhizn'?–Igra," *Grani,* 135 (1985): 344–348;

Deming Brown, *Soviet Russian Literature since Stalin* (Cambridge & New York: Cambridge University Press, 1978), pp. 204–206;

Nora Buhks, "Can You Win at Chess with a Marked Deck of Cards?" in *Under Eastern Eyes: The West as Reflected in Recent Émigré Writing,* edited by Arnold McMillin (London: Macmillan, 1991; New York: St. Martin's Press, 1992), pp. 84–90;

Marietta Omarovna Chudakova and Alexandr Pavlovich Chudakov, "Sovremennaia povest' i iumor," *Novyi mir,* 7 (1967): 229–231;

Arkadii Pavlovich El'iashevich, "O masterstve s'iuzhetoslozheniia," *Ural,* 1 (1960): 168–169;

El'iashevich, "Nerushimoe iedinstvo," *Zvezda,* 8 (1963): 191–192;

Evgenii Gromov, "V krivom zerkale paradoksov," *Smena,* 22 (1960): 11–22;

Lev Grigorievich Iakimenko, *Zhizn'. Geroi, Literatura* (Moscow: GIKhL, 1961): 391–395;

Boris Aleksandrovich Lanin, *Proza Russkoi Emigratsii* (Moscow: Novaia Shkola, 1997), pp. 73–83;

Mikhail Petrovich Lobanov, "Lichnost' istinnaia i lichnost' mnimaia," *Molodaia gvardiia,* 8 (1966): 283–289;

Priscilla Meyer, "Anatolii Gladilin and the Soviet Prose of the 1960s," *Critique* (Glasgow), 4 (1975): 88–95;

Valentin Dmitrievich Oskotsky, "Dobrogo puti," *Moskovskii komsomolets,* 3 November 1956;

Oskotsky, "Pered novym ekzamenom," *Moskva,* 4 (1960): 206–208;

Nikolai Davidovich Otten, "Novye o novom," *Literatura i zhizn',* 28 August 1960;

Eduard Shim, "Na obsuzhdenii rasskazov A. Gladilina," *Moskovskii literator,* 5 January 1952;

Victoria Shitova, "Urok zhizni i prosto urok," *Iunost',* 5 (1960): 74–78;

Boris Vadimovich Sokolov, "Gor'kaia ispoved'," *Nezavisimaia gazeta,* 26 August 1992;

Inna Solov'eva, "Material i priem," *Novyi mir,* 4 (1963): 258–262;

Feliks Grigorievich Svetov, "Dym v glaza," *Literaturnaia gazeta,* 3 March 1960;

Leonid Aramovich Terakopian, "Bitva s mel'nitsami," *Ural,* 10 (1963): 178–180;

Terakopian, "Pelionki naprokat," *Molodoi kommunist,* 4 (1965): 123–124;

Diana Tevekelian, "Geroiu semnadtsat' let," *Moskva,* 11 (1959): 202–207.

# Daniil Granin

(1 January 1918 –   )

Alexandra Smith
*University of Canterbury, New Zealand*

BOOKS: *Spor cherez okean: Povest'* (Moscow: Pravda, 1950);

*Iaroslav Dombrovskii* (Moscow: Molodaia gvardiia, 1951); republished as *General Kommuny: Iaroslav Dombrovskii. Povest'* (Moscow: Sovetskaia Rossiia, 1965);

*Novye druz'ia* (Moscow, 1952);

*Iskateli: Roman* (Leningrad: Sovetskii pisatel', 1955); translated by Robert Daglish as *Those Who Seek: A Novel* (Moscow: Foreign Languages Publishing House, 1955);

*V nashem gorode* (Leningrad: Lenizdat, 1958);

*Posle svad'by: Roman* (Leningrad: Sovetskii pisatel', 1959);

*Neozhidannoe utro* (Leningrad: Sovetskii pisatel', 1962);

*Idu na grozu* (Moscow: Sovetskii pisatel', 1964); translated by Daglish as *Into the Storm* (Moscow: Progress Publishers, 1965);

*Mesiats vverkh nogami* (Leningrad: Lenizdat, 1966);

*Primechaniia k putevoditeliu* (Leningrad: Sovetskii pisatel', 1967);

*Kto-to dolzhen: Povesti i rasskazy* (Leningrad: Sovetskii pisatel', 1970);

*Sad kamnei: Rasskazy i povesti* (Moscow: Sovremennik, 1972);

*Do poezda ostavalos' tri chasa: Povesti i rasskazy* (Leningrad: Sovetskii pisatel', 1973);

*Eta strannaia zhizn': Povest'* (Moscow: Sovetskaia Rossiia, 1974);

*Prekrasnaia Uta: Sbornik* (Moscow: Sovetskaia Rossiia, 1974);

*Vybor tseli* (Leningrad: Sovetskii pisatel', 1975);

*Klavdiia Vilor: Povest'* (Moscow: Sovetskaia Rossiia, 1977);

*Dozhd' v chuzhom gorode* (Leningrad: Khudozhestvennaia literatura, 1977);

*Obratnyi bilet: Povesti* (Moscow: Sovremennik, 1978)—comprises *Obratnyi bilet*, *Nash kombat*, and *Klavdiia Vilor*;

*Blokadnaia kniga*, by Granin and Ales' Adamovich (Moscow: Sovetskii pisatel', 1979); translated by Hilda

*From* Iskateli: Roman, *1955; Thomas Cooper Library, University of South Carolina*

Perham as *A Book of the Blockade* (Moscow: Raduga, 1983);

*Kartina: Roman* (Leningrad: Sovetskii pisatel', 1980);

*Mesto dlia pamiatnika: Povesti* (Moscow: Izvestiia, 1982)—comprises *Kto-to dolzhen*, *Povest' ob odnom uchenom i odnom imperatore*, *Mesto dlia pamiatnika*, *Nash kombat*,

*Obratnyi bilet, Dozhd' v chuzhom gorode,* and *Odnofamilets;*
*Dva kryla* (Moscow: Sovremennik, 1983);
*Tochka opory: Stat'i, besedy, portrety* (Moscow: Izdatel'stvo agenstva pechati "Novosti," 1983);
*Trinadtsat' stupenek: Povesti, esse* (Leningrad: Sovetskii pisatel', 1984);
*Eshche zameten sled: Povesti i rasskazy* (Leningrad: Sovetskii pisatel', 1985);
*Reka vremeni: Ocherki, stat'i, povesti* (Moscow: Pravda, 1985);
*Vybor tseli: Publitsistika, proza* (Leningrad: Sovetskii pisatel', 1986);
*Leningradskii katalog, Detskaia literatura* (Leningrad: Lenizdat, 1986);
*Neozhidannoe utro: Sbornik* (Leningrad: Lenizdat, 1987);
*Zubr: Povest'* (Leningrad: Sovetskii pisatel', 1987); republished as *Zubr: Povest' o N. V. Timofeeve-Resovskom* (Moscow: Profizdat, 1989); translated by Antonia W. Bouis as *The Bison: A Novel about the Scientist Who Defied Stalin* (New York: Doubleday, 1990);
*Miloserdie* (Moscow: Sovetskii pisatel', 1988);
*Chuzhoi dnevnik: Povesti i rasskazy* (Moscow: Sovremennik, 1988);
*Miloserdie: Ocherki* (Moscow: Sovetskaia Rossiia, 1988);
*O nabolevshem* (Leningrad: Sovetskii pisatel', 1988);
*Nash kombat: Povesti, rasskazy* (Moscow: Pravda, 1989);
*Nash dorogoi Roman Avdeevich* (Leningrad: Sovitturs, 1990);
*Zapretnaia glava: Povesti* (Leningrad: Sovetskii pisatel', 1991);
*Begstvo v Rossiiu* (Moscow: Novosti, 1995);
*Strakh* (St. Petersburg: Russko-baltiiskii Informartsionnyi tsentr BLITS, 1997);
*Chudesa liubvi* (St. Petersburg: Zhurnal "Neva," 2000);
*Vechera s Petrom Velikim: Soobshcheniia i svidetel'stva gospodina M* (St. Petersburg: Istoricheskaia Illiustratsiia, 2000);
*Tainyi znak Peterburga* (St. Petersburg: Logos, 2001);
*Neizvestnyi chelovek: Povest, rasskazy, esse, st.* (St. Petersburg: Neva, 2002);
*Kerogaz i vse drogie: Leningradskii Katalog* (Moscow: Tsentrpoligrof, 2003).

**Collections:** *Izbrannye proizvedeniia v dvukh tomakh*, 2 volumes (Leningrad: Khudozhestvennaia literatura, 1969);
*Sobranie sochinenii*, 4 volumes, introduction by V. Ozerov (Leningrad: Khudozhestvennaia literatura, 1978–1980);
*Obratnyi bilet; Odnofamilets; Dozhd' v chuzhom gorode; Kto-to dolzhen: Povesti* (Leningrad: Lenizdat, 1982);
*Idu na grozu: Roman; Klavdiia Vilor: Povest'* (Moscow: Sovetskaia Rossiia, 1989);
*Sobranie sochinenii v piati tomakh*, 5 volumes (Leningrad: Khudozhestvennaia literatura, 1989–1990).

OTHER: "A Personal Opinion," in *Bitter Harvest: The Intellectual Revolt behind the Iron Curtain*, edited by Edmund O. Stillman (New York: Praeger, 1959);
*Pobeda: Sbornik*, volume 1, edited by Granin and others (Leningrad: Lenizdat, 1970);
"The House on the Fontanka," translated by Margarete Orga, in *The House on Fontanka: Modern Soviet Short Stories*, edited by Orga (London: Kimber, 1970);
Ilya Gurevich, Galina Khodasevich, and Valeria Belanina, *Risen from the Ashes: Petrodvorets, Pushkin, Pavlosk*, introduction by Granin, translated by Graham Whittaker (Leningrad: Aurora Art, 1992).

SELECTED PERIODICAL PUBLICATIONS—
UNCOLLECTED: "Pobeda inzhenera Korsakova," *Zvezda*, 1 (1949);
"Malen'koe delo," *Zvezda*, 10 (1951): 46–52;
"Lunisha s dalekoi reki," *Leningradskii al'manakh*, 6 (1953): 386–388;
"Bespokoinye liudi," *Novyi mir*, 5 (1955): 20–27;
"Predolevaia trudnnosti," *Oktiabr'*, 7 (1955): 147–150;
"On uzhe zhivet sredi nas," *Druzhba narodov*, 1 (1959): 130–148;
"Ostrov molodykh," *Novyi mir*, 6 (1962): 190–215;
"Pervyi posetitel'," *Zvezda*, 4 (1964): 7–40;
"Rasskazy iz tsikla Molodaia voina," *Neva*, 5 (1965): 38–46;
"O vremeni i o cheloveka," *Oktiabr'*, 9 (September 1978): 184–196;
"The Responsibility of Art," *Soviet Literature*, 8 (1980): 137–143;
"Literature and the Scientific and Technological Revolution," *Soviet Literature*, 12 (1980): 124–131;
"Neobkhodimost'," *Literaturnaia gazeta*, 21 (20 May 1981): 3;
"Dostoevskii," *Soviet Literature*, 12 (December 1981): 83–84;
"Kuda dvizhetsia vremia'," *Literaturnoe obozrenie*, 10 (October 1987): 83–88;
"Serving His Country," *Soviet Literature*, 5 (1987): 128–135;
"Nash dorogoi Roman Andreevich: Povest," *Neva*, 11 (1990);
"On ne vernulsia iz boia," *Literaturnaia gazeta*, 25 (January 1995): 3;
"Dnevnik odnogo goda, ili monolog-67," *Zvezda*, 6 (1997): 186–201;
"Dva rasskaza," *Voprosy literatury*, 2 (March-April 1998): 219–222;

"Fenomen Likhacheva," *Neva,* 12 (December 1999): 143–148.

Daniil Granin published his first story in 1949 and became a professional writer in 1950. He rose to prominence during the period of the Soviet cultural Thaw in the 1950s, but his stories and novels of the post-Thaw period brought him fame. He continues to be productive in post-Soviet Russia.

Granin was born Daniil Aleksandrovich German on 1 January 1918 in Volyn in the Kursk region to Aleksandr Danilovich German, a forestry warden, and Anna Bakirovna German. He spent his childhood in the Novgorod and Pskov regions; in the 1920s the family moved to Leningrad, where Daniil German attended the secondary school formerly called the Tenishev School; among his teachers were famous professors who had taught at the school before 1917. In the 1930s Aleksandr German was arrested and sent to Siberia, and Anna German began working as a dressmaker. On his return from the camps Aleksandr German was not allowed to live in big cities, and the family had to settle in the countryside. Daniil German was not allowed to join the Komsomol (Communist Youth organization for members 14–28 years old) because of his father's arrest.

In 1939–1940, while studying at the Leningrad Polytechnic Institute, German wrote an historical novel about Jaroslaw Dombrowski that included references to the Polish revolt of 1863 and the 1871 Paris Commune. In 1940 he received a degree in electromechanics and went to work at the Kirov factory. During World War II he graduated from a military college and served as an officer in a tank regiment; he joined the Communist Party in 1942. After the war he worked as an engineer and researcher.

In 1948 German showed the manuscript of his novel about Dombrowski to the fiction writer Dmitrii Konstantinovich Ostrov, who advised him to write about his own experiences instead of attempting historical narratives. Adopting the pen name Daniil Granin, he responded with a 1931 story published in the journal *Rezets* about graduate students, "Variant vtoroi" (The Second Variant). Iurii Pavlovich German, an established Leningrad writer and an editor of *Zvezda* (The Star), published the story in the journal in 1949. Granin's novella *Spor cherez okean* (A Dispute across the Ocean) was published in *Zvezda* in the same year and in book form in 1950. Soviet critics found fault with the novella because of the author's admiration of Western technology and of the United States.

In 1954 Granin became a member of the board of the Soviet Writers' Union; he served as secretary of the Leningrad branch of the Writers' Union from 1954 to 1969. He wrote his first major novel, *Iskateli* (translated as *Those Who Seek,* 1955), while taking postgraduate studies in electrical mechanics at the Leningrad Polytechnic Institute; it was published in 1954 in *Zvezda* and in book form the following year. Andrei Lobanov, a talented inventor, struggles against bureaucrats and petty officials who lack Communist Party integrity and discipline. The network of researchers in the Soviet Union is depicted as full of mediocre, career-minded scientists; Professor Tonkov, the head of an important project, epitomizes the Soviet establishment: he is more concerned with power and fame than with science. A critique of Stalinism and the Soviet propaganda machine, which advocated science and technology as a means of gaining superiority over the United States, the novel tested the boundaries of the permissible in Soviet fiction. Nevertheless, the commercial success of *Iskateli* made Granin financially secure, and he ceased his studies at the polytechnic institute.

In his "Avtobiografia" (autobiography) Granin asserts that the Twentieth Congress of the Communist Party in February 1956, at which First Secretary Nikita Khrushchev denounced Stalinism, provoked his critical reevaluation of the past. That year he traveled abroad with the prominent writers Rasul Gamzatov and Konstantin Georgievich Paustovskii. His recollections of this trip and other travel experiences are included in essays and novellas that describe life in France, Germany, Turkey, Italy, Sweden, the United States, Japan, Australia, and Cuba. Also in 1956 he became a member of the Board of Writers of the RSFSR (Russian Socialist Federal Soviet Republic).

In Granin's short story "Sobstvennoe mnenie" (A Personal Opinion), published in the journal *Novyi mir* (New World) in 1956 and collected in *Sobranie sochinenii* (1978–1980), the young scientist Olkhovskii produces an invention that could provide huge savings in the amount of fuel used in Soviet industry. But Olkhovskii's discovery challenges a classic work in the field by the academician Stroev, whose influence in technology is comparable to that of Trofim Denis'evich Lysenko in Soviet biology. Minaev, the acting director of the Leningrad research institute where Olkhovskii works, is a mediocre scientist who envies Olkhovskii's independence and inner freedom; he recognizes the value of the invention but, hoping for a promotion to permanent director, refuses to support it. When Olkhovskii complains to the district committee, Minaev tells them that he is a troublemaker and is to be ignored. Olkhovskii then sends a description of his invention to the deputy minister, who passes it on to Minaev for assessment—a vicious circle. Even when Minaev becomes the permanent director of the institute, he makes no move to promote the invention he privately admired. Olkhovskii characterizes the Leningrad Communist Party city committee's attitude to his problem as "a corpse-like indifference to living thought." Loktev, an instructor at the city committee who epitomizes the most negative aspects of Soviet bureaucracy, is described as having "a dead, disused sort of face"; "because of his lack of talent, Loktev let no act of opposition to him go unpunished," and he demands Olkhovskii's dismissal from the institute and expulsion from the city to an outlying area. Minaev asks one of his assistants to prepare a final decision on Olkhovskii's case. Although the assistant is sympathetic to Olkhovskii, he prepares the sort of paper that is expected of him: he demolishes Olkhovskii. The assistant explains to Minaev: "I have written it as you want it so that one day I can write as I consider necessary." The story ends with Minaev in a railway carriage; he is traveling back to Leningrad from Moscow, where he has again betrayed Olkhovskii at the ministry because he needs Stroev's support for some developments in the institute. In his reflection in the window, Minaev sees three images of himself: the Minaev of his youth tells the present Minaev: "You are putting it off again; you are a useless wretch." Granin concludes, "There was a third Minaev, as well, who listened to the old Minaev, reassuring the young one. . . . He would always play tricks with himself and keep playing the same endless game, lacking the strength to tear himself free from the grasp of his own double-mindedness. He would always find some justification. He would always strive to be honest tomorrow." Soviet critics thought that Granin's pessimistic vision of Soviet bureaucracy in science and technology was too subversive, especially for a member of the Communist Party, and he received an official reprimand in 1957.

Granin's novel *Posle svad'by* (1959, After the Wedding) portrays an undeveloped collective farm that improves its operational function as soon as the rehabilitation of purge victims begins. His novel *Idu na grozu* (1964; translated as *Into the Storm*, 1965), first published in *Znamia* (The Banner) in 1962, is a veiled criticism of Lavrentii Pavlovich Beria's role as head of the Soviet atomic research program. Other issues treated in the work include anti-Semitism in the Soviet scientific establishment, the return of modernist literature, and new trends in motion pictures and music that are more exciting than socialist realism. In 1967 Granin joined the editorial board of the journal *Neva*.

The narrator of Granin's novella *Eta strannaia zhizn'* (1974, This Strange Life) presents himself as the biographer of the eccentric real-life biologist Aleksandr Aleksandrovich Liubishchev; his account of his friend's life is largely based on Liubishchev's private archive and the diaries that the scientist began in 1916. The work conveys Granin's admiration for a dedicated sci-

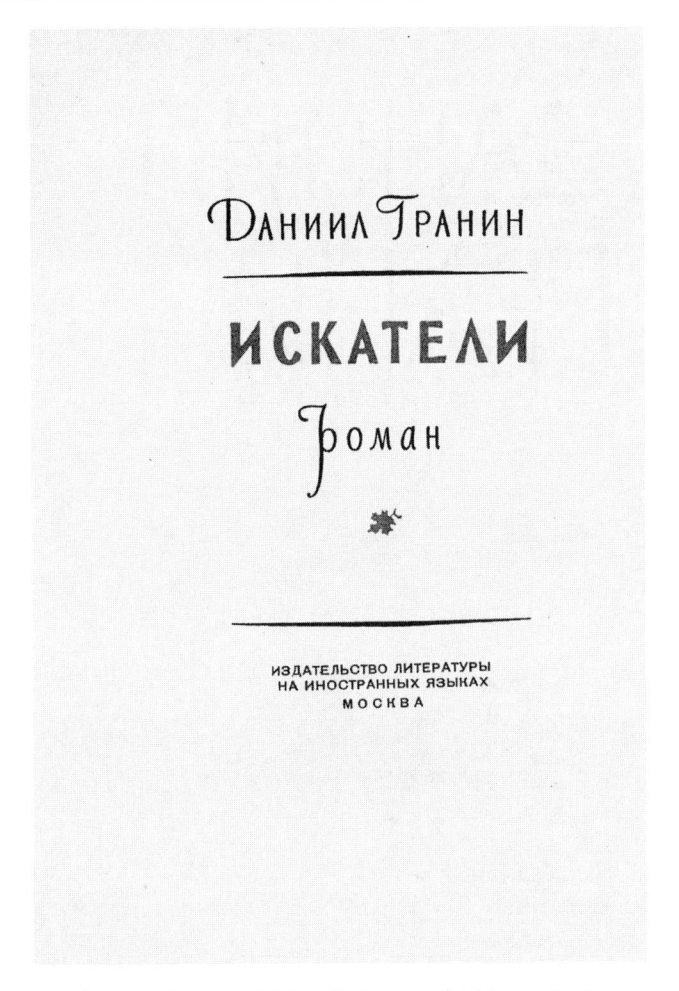

*Title page for Granin's* Iskateli: Roman *(1955; translated as* Those Who Seek, *1955), his first major work of fiction, in which he portrays a Soviet scientific establishment filled with career-minded bureaucrats (Thomas Cooper Library, University of South Carolina)*

entist who combined erudition with modesty and was interested in philosophy and classical studies. Granin presents Liubishchev as a hero and a role model for young scientists: "His life does not represent a heroic deed, but it represents something bigger than a heroic deed; it is a life that was well lived." Although he did not sacrifice his life "for the sake of the truth, or for the sake of his motherland," Liubishchev's incredible self-discipline resulted in many significant articles about insects. In the concluding lines of the work, Granin avoids the didactic style prevalent in Soviet literature, stating that he cannot advise his readers how to respond to his account of Liubishchev's life: "Because the author himself, still full of contemplative thoughts, is profoundly grateful to his hero, who made the author seriously question the cause of his own life."

In 1977 Granin published *Klavdiia Vilor;* based on many documents and interviews, the work won him the U.S.S.R. State Prize. Klavdiia Denisovna Burim, who assumed the name Vilor–an acronym for *Vladimir Il'ich Lenin*–volunteered in April 1942 to lecture on social science at a military college in the south of Russia. Sent to the army as a political instructor in charge of Communist propaganda, she participated in the battle of Stalingrad. She was captured and experienced tremendous hardships in the German camps but escaped and worked during the rest of the war helping local resistance units on various collective farms. Nevertheless, in 1948 she was expelled from the Communist Party for "behavior incompatible with the party membership, because she revealed to the Gestapo that she was a Communist Party member and she was serving in the Red Army." Vilor was reinstated after collecting letters to prove her integrity as a Communist. Once again, Granin reveals the Stalinist establishment's unjust treatment of an individual who deserves to be respected as a national hero. In 1979 Granin and the Belorussian writer Ales' Adamovich collaborated on *Blokadnaia kniga* (translated as *A Book of the Blockade*, 1983), a collection of essays and interviews on the siege of Leningrad.

Most of Granin's works of the 1960s through the 1980s deal with the new class of bureaucrats ruining the country; vividly portrayed for the first time in Vera Panova's novel *Kruzhilikha* (1947; translated as *The Factory*, 1949), the theme was one of the favorites of the postwar generation of Soviet writers. In his novel *Kartina* (1980, The Picture) Granin depicts the thoughtless planning and development practices of the Soviet state as a provincial Party official struggles to preserve a beautiful estuary and an old merchant's house that were immortalized in an avant-garde painting of the town; his superiors want to use the land for a computer factory.

The title novella of Granin's collection *Eshche zameten sled* (1985, A Trace Is Still Visible) is the story of Zhanna, a beautiful woman who had an affair with the narrator's friend Volkov before he died at the end of World War II. In the 1980s Zhanna discovers some letters from Volkov that had been hidden by her mother, who wanted her to marry another man. Zhanna's guilt over Volkov leads the narrator to reevaluate his own behavior, which has been based on compromising with his conscience. For example, he remembers that he took part in the construction of a factory with a faulty wiring system that resulted in an accident in which several people were severely injured. The narrator tries to justify his actions on the basis that he was never taken to court and, therefore, could not be guilty. "What can I do with this knowledge of the past, with this memory, if nothing can be done about it? This question kept haunting me, and the thoughts it evoked would not give me a sense of peace for a long time." In the concluding lines of the story, people walk along the main street of Leningrad, Nevsky Prospect, casting no shadows; Granin implies that they are all deluding themselves.

During the period of perestroika (economic, political, and social restructuring) under Communist Party General Secretary Mikhail Gorbachev, which began in 1987, Granin was one of the first organizers of charitable groups in the Soviet Union. In his essay "O miloserdii" (On Compassion), published in *Literaturnaia gazeta* (Literary Gazette) on 18 March 1987, he advocates humanist values and compassion and criticizes the materialism of Soviet society. That year he published *Zubr* (translated as *The Bison: A Novel about the Scientist Who Defied Stalin*, 1990), a fictionalized biography of the geneticist Nikolai Vladimirovich Timofeev-Resovskii, who immigrated to Berlin in 1925 and worked in Ger-

*Title page for the first volume of Granin's two-volume* Izbrannye proizvedeniia *(Selected Works; Thomas Cooper Library, University of South Carolina)*

many during World War II. The novel was severely criticized in Russia and was not allowed to be published in East Germany until 1989.

On a visit to the United States as the new head of the Soviet Writers' Union in late 1987, Granin promoted *glasnost'* (openness) and described the cultural thaw in the Soviet Union in storybook terms: "One fine day after Gorbachev came to power censorship was abolished. It's the first time in the history of Russia, not only the Soviet Union." In 1990 Granin published the satirical novella *Nash dorogoi Roman Avdeevich* (Our Dear Roman Avdeevich), about the former Leningrad Party boss of the Leonid Brezhnev era who was known for his lavish lifestyle and for disastrous development projects that led to severe ecological problems in the city. In 1994 he became a member of the Presidential Council established by Boris Yeltsin.

In the late 1990s Granin became disappointed with the political scene and began to advocate the independence of literature from politics. In an interview in the 15 September 1999 issue of *Argumenty i fakty* (Arguments and Facts) Granin asserted that literature should not be used for political goals and that it should function independently of any regime. The interviewer introduces Granin to the readers of *Argumenty i fakty* as a living classic.

In Granin's novel *Vechera s Petrom Velikim: Soobshcheniia i svidetel'stva gospodina M.* (2000, Evenings with Peter the Great: Reports and Accounts Presented by Mr. M.) an historian undergoing treatment for heart problems at a resort treats his friends each evening to vivid stories of Peter the Great's life that lead to lively discussions. Granin's Peter is a philosopher, or even an ordinary man with problems and weaknesses, rather than a great tyrant. In an interview Granin revealed his reasons for writing the work: "In my opinion, Peter the Great is the most enigmatic figure in Russian history. His name is surrounded with myths, stereotypes, and fiction. In my book I portray Peter the way I see him. My idea of him is quite different from the habitual one. . . . My novel is partly a documentary, partly fiction. The writer steps in where the researcher steps out. The author's fantasy is not only appropriate, but even necessary." The latter statement echoes Iurii Nikolaevich Tynianov's description of the method he employed in his historical fiction. Granin molds his protagonist as an ideal reformist ruler who turned Russia from a state "in the backyard of Europe" into a powerful empire and suggests that this kind of ruler is needed in today's Russia.

Daniil Granin is a member of the Union of Writers and of PEN. Among his honors from the Soviet period other than the U.S.S.R. State Prize for *Klavdiia*

*Granin in 1985, about the time he published his story collection* Eshche zameten sled *(A Trace Is Still Visible; from Lev Fink,* Neobkhodimost' Don Kikhota: Kniga o Daniile Granine, *1988; Jean and Alexander Heard Library, Vanderbilt University)*

*Vilor* are two Orders of Lenin, the Order of the Red Banner, the Red Star, two Orders for the Patriotic War, and the Order "For Achievements Concerning the Fatherland"; he was also a Hero of Socialist Labor. Granin has received two German awards: the Heinrich Heine Literary Prize and the State Cross for contributions to the development of cultural contacts and mutual understanding between Russia and Germany, and he is a member of the German Academy of Arts. He holds an honorary doctorate from the St. Petersburg University of Humanities and is president of the Menshikov Fund. He lives in St. Petersburg with his wife, R. M. Maiorova; the couple has a daughter, Marina Daniilovna Chernysheva, born in 1945.

**Interviews:**
Mariia Vardenga, "Daniil Granin: Vo chto ia veriu," *Argumenty i fakty,* 37 (15 September 1999): 1038;

L. Zherdeva, "Evenings with Peter the Great: A New Book by Daniil Granin" <www.vor.rv/culture/cultrach168_eng.html>;

Elena Kuznetsova, "Ostaetsia tol'ko liybet," *Kul'tura*, 1, no. 91 (20 April 2004).

**Bibliography:**

D. B. Aziattsev and others, *Daniil Granin: Bibliograficheskii ukazatel'*, Rossiiskaia national'naia biblioteka (St. Petersburg: Izdatel'stvo "Aleteiia," 2000).

**References:**

Keith Armes, "Daniil Granin and the World of Soviet Science," *Survey*, no. 90 (1974): 47–59;

N. Azhgikhina, "Put' k sebe," *Oktiabr'*, 6 (June 1990): 203–205;

Liutsiia Bartashevich, "Petr Velikii: Versiia Daniila Granina," *Neva*, 11 (November 2000): 179–183;

Vladimir Grigorievich Boborykin, "Vospitanie delom," *Voprosy literatury*, 6 (June 1984): 18–52;

L. Borich, "Bol' davnikh sledov," *Neva*, 4 (April 1986): 165–166;

Kharal'd Khartvig Epsen, "O zubrakh i sviatykh: 'Zubr' Daniila Granina," *Scando-Slavica* (Copenhagen), no. 40 (1994): 113–131;

Lev Fink, "Geroi nashikh dnei: Po stranitsam proizvedenii D. Granina," *Voprosy literatury*, 6 (1986): 11–31;

Fink, *Neobkhodimost' Don Kikhota: Kniga o Daniile Granine* (Moscow: Sovetskii pisatel', 1988);

Irina Nikolaeva Grekova (Elena Sergeevna Venttsel), "A Legendary Image," *Soviet Studies in Literature*, 24 (Fall 1988): 82–95;

Dmitrii Iur'evich Il'in, "Neprikasaemmaia literatura," *Nash sovremennik*, 6 (1989): 140–149;

Gagik Karapetyan, "Daniil Granin: 'Time to take off!,'" *Soviet Literature*, 10 (1988): 126–129;

L. Lazar' Il'ich Lazarev, "Eto bylo pri nás," *Voprosy literatury*, 9 (September 1984): 105–136;

Lazarev, "Neizgladimyi sled," *Literaturnoe obozrenie*, 9 (September 1984): 40–43;

Lazarev, "Sovest' ne zamerzaet," *Druzhba narodov*, 9 (September 1982): 255–258;

Boris Nikol'sky, "Ia khochu zdorovogo optimizma," *Neva*, 1 (January 1999): 113–122;

Valentin Oskol'tsky, "Chemu uchit istoriia," *Voprosy literatury*, 3 (May–June 2002): 176–204;

Oskol'tsky, 'Chetvert' veka spustia: Pochemu perechityvaiut 'Idti na grozu,'" *Neva*, 6 (June 1988): 152–160;

Oskol'tsky, "Ktoto dolzhen idti na grozu," *Voprosy literatury*, 7 (1977): 168–199;

Oskol'tsky, "Otkrytyi boi," *Literaturnoe obozrenie*, 11 (November 1980): 45–49;

Vitalii Mikhailovich Ozerov, "Geroi nravstvennogo podviga," *Oktiabr'*, 9 (September 1977): 197–205;

Boris Dmitrievich Pankin, "The Past That Is Always with You," *Soviet Studies in Literature*, 18 (Winter 1981–1982): 30–50;

A. Pavlovsky, "Rasskaz-dokument," *Neva*, 5 (May 1978): 183–187;

I. Petrovsky, "Iskatel': K 60-letiiu Daniila Granina," *Zvezda* (1979): 177–182;

Lev Abramovich Plotkin, *Daniil Granin: Ocherk tvorchestva* (Leningrad: Sovetskii pisatel', 1975);

Plotkin, "Gimn cheloveku," *Oktiabr'*, 9 (September 1976): 209–213;

Plotkin, "Novye povesti Daniila Granina," *Neva*, 5 (1977): 183–187;

Evgenii Sidorov, "Povest' o redkostnom cheloveke," *Znamia*, 6 (June 1987): 226–228;

Svetlana Leonidovna Skopkareva, *V poiskakh ideala: Kontseptsiia lichnosti b proze D. Granina 60–80-khkh gg.* (Moscow: Prometei, 1998);

Anatolii Nikolaevich Starkov, *Nravstvennye poiski geroev Daniila Granina* (Moscow: Khudozhestvennaia literatura, 1981);

Starkov, "Vybor sud'by," *Druzhba narodov*, 7 (July 1981): 231–241;

Aron Uzilevsky, "Vybor tseli: Variant vtoroi," *Neva*, 1 (1989): 197–202;

Ol'ga Sergeevna Voitinskaia, *Daniil Granin: Ocherk tvorchestva* (Moscow: Sovetskii pisatel', 1966);

"'Vremia–soiuznik ili vrag?': Dialogi o povesti D. Grannina 'Eta strannaia zhizn'," *Voprosy literatury*, 19, no. 1 (1975): 35–89;

A. G. Waring, "Science, Love and the Establishment in the Novels of D. A. Granin and C. P. Snow," *Forum for Modern Language Studies*, 14 (1978): 1–15;

Igor Zolotoussky, "Bez riska," *Literaturnoe obozrenie*, 11 (November 1980): 42–45.

# Irina Grekova
## (Elena Sergeevna Venttsel')
*(21 March 1907 – 15 April 2002)*

Nadya L. Peterson
*Hunter College, CUNY*

BOOKS: *Elementarnyi kurs teorii veroiatnostei v primenenii k zadacham strelby i bombometaniia,* as Venttsel' (Moscow: VVA, 1945);

*Elementy teorii priblizhennykh vychislenii,* by Venttsel' and Dmitrii Aleksandrovich Venttsel' (Moscow, 1949);

*Teoriia veroiatnosti,* as Venttsel' (Moscow, 1958);

*Elementy teorii igr,* as Venttsel' (Moscow: Gosudarstvennoe izdatel'stvo fiziko-matematicheskoi literatury, 1959); translated and adapted by Jerome Kristian and Michael B. P. Slater as *An Introduction to the Theory of Games* (Boston: Heath, 1963);

*Osnovnye poniatiia teorii informatsii,* as Venttsel' (Moscow, 1961);

*Sbornik zadach po issledovaniiu operatsii,* by Venttsel' and Lev Aleksandrovich Ovcharov (Moscow: VVIA, 1962);

*Elementy dinamicheskogo programmirovaniia,* as Venttsel' (Moscow: Nauka, 1964);

*Vvedenie v issledovanie operatsii,* as Venttsel' (Moscow: Sovetskoe radio, 1964);

*Kliuchi k programme v teorii veroiatnostei,* as Venttsel' (Leningrad: VVIA, 1966);

*Pod fonarem* (Moscow: Sovetskii pisatel', 1966)—includes "Za prokhodnoi," translated by Thomas P. Whitney as "Beyond the Gates," in *The Young Russians,* edited by Whitney (New York: Macmillan, 1972), pp. 61–104; and "Damskii master," translated by Larry Gregg as "The Ladies' Hairdresser," in *Ardis Anthology of Recent Russian Literature* (Ann Arbor, Mich.: Ardis, 1975), pp. 223–264;

*Rukovodstvo dlia pol'zovaniia programmirovannymi materialami po kursu "Teoriia veroiatnostei"* (Moscow: VVIA, 1966);

*Issledovanie operatsii,* as Venttsel' (Moscow, 1972); translated by Michael G. Edelev as *Operations Research* (Moscow: Mir, 1983);

*Serezhka u okna* (Moscow: Detskaia literatura, 1976);

*Ania i Mania* (Moscow: Detskaia literatura, 1978);

*Irina Grekova (from* Kafedra, *1980; Jean and Alexander Heard Library, Vanderbilt University)*

*Issledovanie operatsii: Zadachi, printsipy, metodologiia,* as Venttsel' (Moscow: Nauka, 1980);

*Kafedra* (Moscow: Sovetskii pisatel', 1980)—includes *Kafedra,* translated by Melinda Maclean as "The Faculty," with introduction by Alla Nikolaevna Latynina, *Soviet Literature,* no. 9 (1979): 3–107; no. 10 (1979): 16–128; "Khoziaika gostinitsy," translated by Michel Petrov as "The Hotel Manager," in *Russian Women: Two Stories*, with introduction by Maurice Friedberg (New York: Harcourt Brace Jovanovich, 1983);

*Metodicheskie ukazaniia k resheniiu teoretiko-veroiatnostnykh zadach zheleznodorozhnogo transporta,* as Venttsel' (Moscow: MIIT, 1981);

*Prikladnye zadachi teorii veroiatnosti,* by Venttsel' and Ovcharov (Moscow: Radio i Sviaz', 1983); revised and translated by Irene Aleksanova as *Applied Problems in Probability Theory* (Moscow: Mir, 1986);

*Vdovii parokhod* (Paris: Institut d'Etudes Slaves, 1983); translated by Cathy Porter as *The Ship of Widows* (London: Virago, 1985);

*Porogi* (Moscow: Sovetskii pisatel', 1986);

*Teoriia veroiatnostei i ee inzhenernye prilozheniia,* by Venttsel' and Ovcharov (Moscow: Nauka, 1988);

*Na ispytaniiakh* (Moscow: Sovetskii pisatel', 1990);

*Teoriia sluchainykh protsessov i ee inzhenernye prilozheniia,* by Venttsel' and Ovcharov (Moscow: Nauka, 1991);

*Svezho predanie* (Tenafly, N.J.: Hermitage, 1995).

**Editions in English:** *Lectures on Game Theory* (New Delhi: Hindustan, 1961);

*Elements of Game Theory,* translated by Vladimir Shokurov (Moscow: Mir, 1980);

"One Summer in the City," translated by Lauren G. Leighton, in *The Barsukov Triangle*, edited by Carl R. Proffer and Ellendea Proffer (Ann Arbor, Mich.: Ardis, 1984), pp. 245–274;

"Real Life in Real Terms," *Moscow News*, 24 (1987): 11;

"A Legendary Image," *Soviet Studies in Literature: A Journal of Translations,* 24 (Fall 1988): 82–95;

"No Smiles," translated by Dobrochna Dyrch-Freeman, in *The New Soviet Fiction, Sixteen Short Stories,* compiled by Sergei Zalygin (New York: Abbeville, 1989), pp. 79–110;

"A Summer in the City," translated by Sigrid McLaughlin, in *The Image of Women in Contemporary Soviet Fiction* (New York: Macmillan, 1989), pp. 18–48;

"Masters of Their Own Lives," translated by Dyrch-Freeman, in *Soviet Women Writing: 15 Short Stories,* edited by Jacqueline Decter (New York: Abbeville, 1990), pp. 85–105;

"Under the Street Lamp," translated by Dyrch-Freeman, in *Russia According to Women,* edited by Marina Ledkovsky (Tenafly, N.J.: Hermitage, 1991), pp. 45–66.

PLAY PRODUCTION: *Budni i prazdniki*, by Grekova and Aleksandr Arkad'evich Galich, Moscow Art Theater, 14 September 1967.

OTHER: *Sbornik zadach po teorii veroiatnostei,* compiled by Venttsel' (Moscow, 1942).

Irina Grekova (pseudonym of Elena Sergeevna Venttsel') ranks among the most prominent women writers in Soviet literature. She began writing fiction in the 1960s while still engaged in a successful career as a scientist and professor of mathematics. As Venttsel', she has published influential studies on game theory and probability, including *Issledovanie operatsii* (1972; translated as *Operations Research,* 1983) and *Teoriia veroiatnosti* (1958, Probability Theory). As Grekova, she has written stories and novels about women's lives in the former Soviet Union.

Grekova was born Elena Sergeevna Dolgintsova on 21 March 1907 in Reval (now known as Tallinn, the capital of Estonia) into a family of prerevolutionary intelligentsia. Dolgintsova's father, Sergei Dolgintsov, was a mathematician whose benevolent influence was apparently quite considerable. The affectionately drawn character N. N. Zavalishin in Grekova's novella *Kafedra* (first published 1978 in the journal *Novyi mir* [The New World], collected 1980; translated as "The Faculty," 1979) bears a noticeable resemblance to Sergei. Resolving to pursue the same professional path, his daughter entered the University of Leningrad in the mid 1920s and graduated in 1929 with a degree in mathematics. In the same year that she finished her university studies Dolgintsova married Dmitrii Aleksandrovich Venttsel', a scientist who specialized in ballistics. The couple eventually had three sons. Venttsel' became one of the few Soviet women scientists to receive a doctorate; later she obtained a full professorship at the Zhukovsky Air Force Academy in Moscow, where she taught together with her husband. After Dmitrii Aleksandrovich died in 1955, Venttsel' continued teaching at the academy until an incident connected with the appearance of one of her works, which she had published as Grekova, led to her resignation in 1967.

When she began publishing fiction, Venttsel' decided to use a pseudonym in order to protect her identity as a Soviet scientist with access to sensitive information. Professional and scientific training were not uncommon among Russian male writers. Vassily Aksyonov, Mikhail Afanas'evich Bulgakov, and Anton Pavlovich Chekhov all received training as doctors. Aleksandr Isaevich Solzhenitsyn was a teacher of physics and mathematics, while the poet Andrei Andreevich Voznesensky was educated as an architect. Rare, however, was the Russian woman scientist who combined her professional activities with a successful writing career. For Venttsel', writing fiction was a creative outlet that allowed her to analyze, and remark on, her society and its people—resulting in a commentary that was out of bounds for a scientist working in the field of pure mathematics. Even so, mathematics inspired her pen name: she derived "Grekova" from the Russian mathematical symbol for an unknown quantity, *igrek* (known as *Y* in Western mathematics).

Grekova's first work of published fiction, the short story "Za prokhodnoi," appeared in the prestigious journal *Novyi mir* in 1962 (collected 1966; translated as "Beyond the Gates," 1972), when she was fifty-five years old. "Beyond the Gates" is a story dedicated by Grekova to the "creators of the first space rockets" and is a description of a group of talented and enthusiastic young people who work in a classified lab. Grekova's friend, the writer and teacher Frida Abramovna Vigdorova, had shown the story to the poet Aleksandr Trifonovich Tvardovsky, then editor in chief of *Novyi mir*. He responded enthusiastically, and Grekova's career as a writer was successfully launched. In 1967 Grekova, together with Aleksandr Arkad'evich Galich, adapted "Za prokhodnoi" into a play, titled *Budni i prazdniki* (Work Days and Holidays) and staged that same year by the Moscow Art Theater. After the appearance of her second story, "Damskii master" (published 1963 in *Novyi mir*, collected 1966; translated as "The Ladies' Hairdresser," 1975), Tvardovsky urged Grekova to abandon science in favor of literature, but she refused. "Damskii master" tells the story of a maternal relationship between a middle-aged female mathematician and a young male hairdresser, whom Grekova presents as a true artist and a creative soul. His artistic endeavors are brought to a quick end, however, when the managers of the salon become intolerant of his talent and ambition and insist on treating him with condescension and rudeness. This tale of an up-and-coming man thwarted in his desire for self-improvement and high achievement offers a cautionary view of the fate of the young generation in Soviet Russia.

Among her early writings, perhaps Grekova's most socially pointed work was her novella *Na ispytaniiakh* (On Maneuvers), first published, amid great controversy, in 1967 in *Novyi mir*. A story of corruption and low morale in the Soviet armed forces, it is narrated from the point of view of an air force officer and depicts the work of a Red Army division that is conducting secret tests in a remote area of the country in 1952, one year before the death of Joseph Stalin. Women are virtually invisible in the male-populated scenes of this work, and conversations about women are full of censorious and arrogant comments.

This direct criticism of the army—and, by Grekova's implication, of Soviet society as a whole—did not pass unnoticed. The ruse of a pen name did not prevent the scientific community or the literary establishment from discovering Grekova's penchant for writing and publishing fiction. She was censured for providing a view of the armed forces that, in the opinion of her critics, was inappropriate for a woman and a military-academy professor to express. In addition, Tvardovsky's tenure at *Novyi mir* was coming to a close, and the journal, together with its editor, was attacked by conservatives for their liberal views. Although she ultimately received a vote of confidence from her colleagues, Grekova resigned from the Air Force Academy and subsequently took a position at the Moscow Institute of Railway Engineers, where she stayed until her retirement in 1981. (Her fictionalized account of this period can be found in her short story "Bez ulybok" [Without Smiles], written in 1970 but not published until 1986 in *Oktiabr'*.) At the same time that she was the target of criticism at the academy, a polemic about her style and language arose at the Institute of Russian Literature, where Kornei Chukovsky came to her defense and praised her language.

Besides making a theme out of the professional military in her novellas and stories, Grekova also wrote fiction about children and the people who devote themselves to improving the lives of children—ideas that occupy an important place in her literary legacy. Two works by Grekova for children are *Serezhka u okna*

*Title page for Grekova's collection* Kafedra. *The title novella, translated in 1979 as "The Faculty," includes a character based on Grekova's mathematician father, Sergei Dolgintsov (Jean and Alexander Heard Library, Vanderbilt University).*

(1976, Serezhka by the Window) and *Ania i Mania* (1978). A child orphaned in the siege of Leningrad is the protagonist of her story "Malen'kii Garusov" (Little Garusov, first published 1970 in *Zvezda* [The Star], collected 1980). The relationships between parents and children, a theme that is found in almost all of Grekova's published works, typically are portrayed as difficult and unrewarding. She mostly depicts the women who are in charge of rearing the new generation, and they manage because they rely—partly out of necessity, partly out of tradition—on other women around them.

The story "Khoziaika gostinitsy" (first published 1976 in *Zvezda,* collected 1980; translated as "The Hotel Manager," 1983) tells about a woman, Vera Platonovna Laricheva, who, finding herself at a crossroads after the death of her husband, discovers in her career an outlet for her need to mother. The death of her manipulative and difficult husband has released her from a painful relationship, in which she was a submissive dependent rather than an equal partner. The women around Vera—her mother, sister, best friend, adopted daughter, and roommate—provide the support necessary to make her search for relevance and autonomy successful. In *Skripka Rotshil'da* (1980, The Rothschild Violin), the title of which is the same as an 1894 story by Chekhov, Grekova provides an ironic portrait of a female teacher who is stunned to discover that class differences are not easily bridged and that contact with great literature (in this case Chekhov's story) does not lead necessarily to the spiritual awakening or intellectual improvement of her cleaning lady.

The dependence of women on other women is the primary source of emotional and material sustenance for Grekova's female protagonists. These relationships offer psychological insights, heal wounds, and allow the heroines to survive their misfortunes with some dignity. In *Vdovii parokhod,* which Grekova wrote a decade before it was finally published in 1981 in *Novyi mir* (published 1983 in book form; translated as *The Ship of Widows,* 1985), she describes the lives of five different women, bereft of their loved ones because of the war and forced by housing shortages to share a shabby communal apartment in Moscow. The multiple voices and points of view in this straightforward, realistic account illuminate the cultural and class roots of the tensions between these women. The intellectual Ol'ga, the former nurse Anfisa, the metal worker Panka, the deeply religious peasant woman Kapa, and the aging singer Ada are shown not only in their daily quests for food, work, and medical care but also in their search for love, dignity, and fulfillment. The war destroyed these women's lives, took away their husbands and children, and left them anchorless on this "ship of widows." Yet, by sharing the burdens of existence and by raising together the son born to one of them, these women become united in a common cause.

Men are mostly absent in the endeavor of raising children, but when they—such as Anfisa's husband and son—are present, they are tortured, brutish, and weak. Grekova points to the absence of male role models as the major reason for the failure of the women to raise sons who will fulfill their expectations. The end of the novella, nevertheless, offers a redemption of sorts for both the ship's widows and their adopted son. Anfisa's son is made to appreciate her sacrifice and understand his debt to his mother and the women around her. *Vdovii parokhod* provides a compendium of Grekova's themes, as well as a view of life that, while essentially pessimistic, is also accepting and somewhat hopeful. In Grekova's works the majority of the women protagonists and some of the male characters are thwarted in their attempts to find equilibrium and fulfillment in their daily existence. They have not been allowed by the circumstances of history, or gender, or both, to live their lives to the fullest.

Grekova was one of the first to offer Soviet readers a peek into the workings of the scientific community. The backdrop for *Porogi* (Thresholds, first published 1984 in the journal *Oktiabr'* [October], published 1986 in book form), for example, is a formerly inaccessible high-level scientific research institute. Grekova's women characters, nonetheless, are largely responsible for the attention she has received from critics and readers. These characters are made to exhibit all of the frustrations, anxieties, and pain that result from living in a society that not only is conventional in terms of gender roles but also is suffering the aftereffects of the Stalinist purges and a war in which millions of men perished. Consequently, in the majority of Grekova's stories men appear somewhat peripheral to her authorial concerns. Some of her male characters, such as V. A. Fliagin in *Kafedra* or B. M. Gan in *Porogi,* are capable of providing a nurturing and sympathetic presence, while others play important parts in plot development. But Grekova's women and their problems lie at the narrative core of her works: women are the ones who are called upon to cope with the hardships of postwar Soviet life, such as orphaned children, a lack of companionship, and poverty. Even Grekova's early fiction is immediately recognizable as the work of a mature woman who speaks of the challenges and delights of life with empathy for her characters and a confidence born of experience. Her women protagonists vary in age, class, and occupation; they include factory workers, actresses, teachers, accountants, and nurses—both young and old. These women have experienced the horrors of the purges, the devastation of World War II, the hopes of de-Stalinization, and the disappointments of the "period of stagnation" under Leonid Il'ich Brezhnev.

In giving frank and realistic glimpses into the lives that these Soviet women lead, Grekova departs considerably from the formulaic and predictable path of domestic and public heroism that typically is charted for women in the works of her Socialist Realist predecessors. By attempting to portray Soviet life without the gloss and manipulative embellishments of Socialist Realism, she inevitably ventures into a social critique that touches on—besides gender bias—the issues of class; racial and religious prejudice; the materialism and lack of spirituality among her fellow citizens; and the ineptitude of those in power. For example, *Svezho predanie* (In Recent Memory), written in 1962 but published only in 1995, offers a portrait of a Jewish family in Russia during the harsh years of Stalinism.

In addition to portraying the world of the Soviet scientific intelligentsia—which remained unexplored in Russian literature before the works of Grekova—she was one of the first Soviet writers to draw her readers' attention to the burdens imposed on Soviet women. Although in her style of narration she shuns experimentation, insisting on a dispassionate and transparent representation of reality around her, she was innovative in her selection of themes, in the directness of her "conversation" with the reader, and in her almost stoic acceptance of the difficulties of life. The men in Grekova's fiction are essentially superfluous in the hard work of survival. In her stories love is seen as a burden; dependence on men is bound to bring disappointment; and women must find—among themselves—sources for their emotional and physical support and comfort. Grekova's fatalistic outlook anticipates the views expressed in the work of Liudmila Stefanovna Petrushevskaia, Nina Nikolaevna Sadur, Galina Nikolaevna Shcherbakova, and other women writers of the 1980s and 1990s. The inner connection with the work of younger women authors was not missed by Grekova herself, even though she is uncomfortable with the notion of "feminine literature." Keenly aware of the developments in Russian fiction, she has provided critical commentary on authors whom she finds especially important.

In her long life Irina Grekova has fulfilled, with determination and passion, the roles she chose for herself. As a writer she points to areas of social concern that have been neglected by the literary establishment. As a scholar and teacher she is living proof of the intellectual equality of the sexes. As a literary critic she has shown her perceptiveness and sensitivity toward new trends. Her characters struggle with adversity and the limitations imposed on them by their society. Few, if any, are able to achieve the graceful combination of the intellectual, creative, and maternal pursuits in their lives. Grekova herself, however, has convincingly demonstrated that such a combination is possible and even necessary.

**Bibliography:**
Diane M. Nemec Ignashev and Sarah Krive, *Women and Writing in Russian and the USSR: A Bibliography of English Language Sources* (New York: Garland, 1992).

**References:**
Adele Barker, "Are Women Writing 'Women's Writing' in the Soviet Union Today?: Tolstaya and Grekova," *Studies in Comparative Communism*, 21, nos. 3–4 (1988): 357–364;

Barker, "Irina Grekova's 'Na ispytaniiakh': The History of One Story," *Slavic Review,* no. 48 (1989): 399–412;

Grigorii Abramovich Brovman, "Ploskoe bytopisatel'stvo i ego advokat," *Nash sovremennik,* 9 (1965);

Deming Brown, *Soviet Russian Literature since Stalin* (Cambridge: Cambridge University Press, 1978), pp. 163–167;

Edward J. Brown, *Russian Literature since the Revolution* (Cambridge, Mass.: Harvard University Press, 1982), pp. 321–322;

Efim Semenovich Dobin, "Khoziaika gostinitsy," *Literaturnoe obozrenie,* 10 (1977);

Barbara Heldt, *Terrible Perfection: Women and Russian Literature* (Bloomington & Indianapolis: Indiana University Press, 1987), pp. 150–151;

Viktor Kam'ianov, "Sluzhba pamiati," *Novyi mir,* 5 (1971);

Catriona Kelly, *A History of Russian Women's Writing, 1820–1992* (Oxford: Clarendon Press, 1994), pp. 350–372;

Vladimir Iakovlevich Lakshin, "Pisatel', chitatel', kritik," *Novyi mir,* 4 (1965): 222–240;

Sigrid McLaughlin, *The Image of Women in Contemporary Soviet Fiction* (New York: St. Martin's Press, 1989), pp. 18–20;

Elisabeth Menke, *Die Kultur der Weiblichkeit in der Prosa Irina Grekovas* (Munich: O. Sagner, 1988);

L. G. Mikhailova, "Puteshestvie za prokhodnoi," *Literaturnaia gazeta,* 13 September 1962;

N. Naumova, "The Modern Heroine," *Soviet Studies in Literature,* 15 (1979): 80–102;

Nikolai Nazarov, "About I. Grekova's Work," *Soviet Literature,* 5 (1986): 137–141;

I. A. Pitliar, "I. Grekova," in *Russkie pisateli 20 veka. Biograficheskii slovar',* edited by Pavel Alekseevich Nikolaev (Moscow: Randevu-AM, 2000);

Victor Terras, ed., *Handbook of Russian Literature* (New Haven: Yale University Press, 1985), p. 184;

Margareta Thompson, "Scientist and Mother: Portrait of the Heroine in I. Grekova's Fiction," in *International Women's Writing: New Landscapes of Identity,* edited by Anne E. Brown and Marjanne E. Gooze (Westport, Conn.: Greenwood Press, 1995), pp. 196–205.

# Fazil' Abdulevich Iskander
(6 March 1929 - )

Marina Kanevskaya
*University of Montana*

BOOKS: *Gornye tropy: stikhi* (Sukhumi: Abkhazskoe gosudarstvennoe izdatel'stvo, 1957);

*Dobrota zemli* (Sukhumi: Abkhazskoe gosudarstvennoe izdatel'stvo, 1959);

*Zelenyi dozhd'* (Moscow: Sovetskii pisatel', 1960);

*Deti Chernomor'ia* (Sukhumi: Abkhazskoe gosudarstvennoe izdatel'stvo, 1961);

*Molodost' moria* (Moscow: Molodaia gvardiia, 1964);

*Trinadtsatyi podvig Gerakla* (Moscow: Sovetskaia Rossiia, 1966);

*Zapretnyi plod* (Moscow: Molodaia gvardiia, 1966);

*Zori zemli* (Moscow: Detskaia literatura, 1966);

*Letnii les: stikhi* (Moscow: Sovetskii pisatel', 1969)—includes "Zmei," "Balada ob ukradennom kozle," "Balada ob okhote i zimnem vinograde," and "Detstvo";

*Derevo detstva* (Moscow: Sovetskii pisatel', 1970)—includes *Sozvezdie Kozlotura,* translated by Helen P. Burlingame as *The Goatibex Constellation* (Ann Arbor, Mich.: Ardis, 1975);

*Pervoe delo* (Moscow: Detskaia literatura, 1972; enlarged, 1978);

*Vremia schastlivykh nakhodok* (Moscow: Molodaia gvardiia, 1973);

*Sandro iz Chegema* (Moscow: Sovetskii pisatel', 1977; enlarged edition, Ann Arbor, Mich.: Ardis, 1979; enlarged edition, 3 volumes, Moscow: Moskovskii rabochii, 1989);

*Nachalo* (Sukhumi: Alashara, 1978);

*Pod sen'iu gretskogo orekha* (Moscow: Sovetskii pisatel', 1979);

*Novye glavy, Sandro iz Chegema* (Ann Arbor, Mich.: Ardis, 1981);

*Kroliki i udavy* (Ann Arbor, Mich.: Ardis, 1982); translated by Ronald E. Peterson as *Rabbits and Boa Constrictors* (Ann Arbor, Mich.: Ardis, 1989);

*Zashchita Chika: Prazdnik ozhidaniia prazdnika* (Moscow: Sovetskii pisatel', 1983);

*Bol'shoi den' bol'shogo doma* (Sukhumi: Alashara, 1986);

*Prazdnik ozhidaniia prazdnika: rasskazy* (Moscow: Molodaia gvardiia, 1986);

*Fazil' Abdulevich Iskander (*Zapretnyi plod, 1966;* Davidson College Library)*

*Podvig Chika* (Moscow: Pravda, 1987)—includes "Podvig Chika";

*Put'* (Moscow: Sovetskii pisatel', 1987);

*Kroliki i udavy: Proza poslednikh let* (Moscow: Knizhnaia palata, 1988);

*Povesti, rasskazy* (Moscow: Sovetskaia Rossiia, 1989);

*Stoianka cheloveka* (Moscow: Molodaia gvardiia, 1990);

*Poety i tsary* (Moscow: Ogonek, 1991);

*Stoianka cheloveka: Povesti i rasskazy* (Moscow: Pravda, 1991);

*Kroliki i udavy* (Moscow: Tekst, 1992);

*Detstvo Chika* (Moscow: Detskaia literatura, 1993)—includes "Chik idet na okhotu";

*Chelovek i ego okrestnosti* (Moscow: Olimp – PPP, 1993);

*Stikhotvoreniia* (Moscow: Moskovskii rabochii, 1993);

*Sofichka: povesti i rasskazy* (Moscow: Vagrius, 1997);

*Lastochkino gnezdo* (Moscow: Fortuna Limited, 1999);

*Rasskazy, povest', skazka, dialog, esse, stikhi* (Ekaterinburg: U-Faktoriia, 1999);

*Shkol'nyi val's, ili Energiia styda* (Moscow: Lokid, 1999);

*Siuzhet sushchestvovaniia* (Moscow: Podkova, 1999);

*Nochnoi vagon*, with introduction by Stanislav Rassadin (Moscow: Panorama, 2000).

**Editions and Collections:** *Izbrannoe* (Moscow: Sovetskii pisatel', 1988);

*Sandro iz Chegema* (Moscow: Vsia Moskva, 1990);

*Sandro iz Chegema*, 2 volumes (Moscow: Sovetskii pisatel', 1991);

*Sobranie sochinenii*, 4 volumes (Moscow: Molodaia gvardiia, 1991– );

*Chelovek i ego okrestnosti* (Moscow: Tekst, 1995);

*Stoianka cheloveka* (Moscow: Kvadrat, 1995);

*Sobranie sochinenii*, 6 volumes (Khar'kov: Folio, 1997);

*Sandro iz Chegema* (Moscow: EKSMO-Press, 1999);

*Abkhazskaia osen': stikhi, poemy, perevody, epigrammy shutki* (Moscow: Zebra E-Eksmo, 2003);

*Sobranie*, 2 volumes (Moscow: Vremia, 2003– ).

**Editions in English:** "Old Crooked Arm," translated by Robert Daglish, *Soviet Literature*, 6 (1968): 67–92;

"Old Crooked Arm," *Afro-Asian Writings*, 1 (1970): 95–115;

*Forbidden Fruit and Other Stories*, translated by Daglish (Moscow: Progress, 1972);

"Kolcherukii," translated by Marcia Satin, in *The Ardis Anthology of Recent Russian Literature*, edited by Carl R. Proffer and Ellendea Proffer (Ann Arbor, Mich.: Ardis, 1973), pp. 165–191;

"Belshazzar's Feasts," translated by Susan Brownsberger and Carl Proffer in *Contemporary Russian Prose*, edited by Proffer and Proffer (Ann Arbor, Mich.: Ardis, 1975), pp. 335–378;

"A Sexy Little Giant," translated by Carl Proffer, in *Metropol* (New York: Norton, 1982), pp. 322–358;

*Sandro of Chegem*, translated by Brownsberger (New York: Random House, 1983); republished as *The Gospel According to Chegem: Being the Further Adventures of Sandro of Chegem*, translated by Brownsberger (New York: Vintage, 1984);

*Chik and His Friends*, translated by J. C. Butler (Moscow: Raduga, 1985);

*The Thirteenth Labor of Hercules*, translated by Daglish and K. M. Cook-Horujy (Moscow: Raduga, 1989);

"The Goblet of State," *Russian Studies in Literature*, 29 (Fall 1993): 32–37;

"Who Are We?" translated by Catherine A. Fitzpatrick, in *Remaking Russia: Voices from Within*, edited by Heyward Isham (Armonk, N.Y.: M. E. Sharpe, 1995), pp. 37–49;

*The Old House under the Cypress Tree*, translation of *Put* (1987) by Butler (London & Boston: Faber & Faber, 1996).

PRODUCED SCRIPTS: *Vremia schastlivykh nakhodok*, by Iskander and Genrikh Gabai, motion picture, Mosfil'm, 1969;

*Chegemuri detektivi*, motion picture, Georgian Film, 1986;

*Vory v zakone*, by Iskander and Iurii Kara, motion picture, Gor'ky Film Studios, 1988;

*Dgesastsauli dgesastsaulis molodinshi*, by Iskander and Leila Gordeladze, motion picture, Qartuli Pilmi, 1989;

*Piry Val'tasara, ili Noch' so Stalinym*, motion picture, Gor'ky Film Studios, 1989;

*Rasstanemsya, poka khoroshiye*, by Iskander and Vladimir Motyl, motion picture, Mosfil'm, 1991;

*Malen'kii gigant bol'shogo seksa*, by Iskander, Aleksandr Borodyansky, and Nikolai Dostal, motion picture, Krug, 1993.

Fazil' Iskander began his literary career as a poet in the late 1950s but turned to prose soon after; he often appears in lists of notable "young writers" of the 1960s but does not strictly belong with writers such as Vassily Pavlovich Aksyonov, Anatolii Tikhonovich Gladilin, and Vladimir Nikolaevich Voinovich, who took Russian literature in a new direction. Like his contemporaries, Iskander writes short stories of ordinary people in ordinary circumstances, but his gentle humor and subtle, almost oblique, phrasing mask the bite of his satire. His masterpiece, *Sandro iz Chegema* (Sandro of Chegem, 1977), is a comic, sometimes satiric novel made up of stories of the narrator's legendary Abkhazian uncle, Sandro. This novel, as well as his many stories and novellas guarantee Iskander a place as one of Russia's greatest comic writers.

Fazil' Abdulevich Iskander was born on 6 March 1929 in Sukhumi, the capital of Abkhazia, which at that time was an autonomous republic within the Soviet Republic of Georgia. Iskander's maternal relatives were natives of a small Abkhazian mountain village. In his childhood he often visited his grandparents, and the impressions of these visits inspired his most important work, the epic cycle *Sandro iz Chegema*. Iskander's parents lived in Sukhumi with the extended family of his father, Abdul Ibragimovich Iskander. In 1939 Abdul Ibragimovich, who was of Iranian descent, fell victim to Joseph Stalin's genocide policy against the national minorities of the Caucasus. He was imprisoned and then deported to Iran, where he worked in a labor camp; he died in 1957. Iskander's mother, Leili Khasanovna Iskander, with the help of the family, was able to provide her two sons, Fazil' and Feredun, and her daughter, Giuli, with an education. The life of Iskander's big family and the habits and cultures of his multiethnic village formed the background for his second biggest cycle of long and short stories, which are about a boy named Chik, and a novel related to that cycle—*Shkol'nyi val's, ili Energiia styda* (School Waltz, or The Energy of Shame, 1999).

In 1948, after graduating from high school in Sukhumi, Iskander studied in Moscow at the Institute of Librarianship and, later, at the Maksim Gor'ky Literary Institute, from which he graduated in 1954. He began writing in the early 1950s. In 1954–1955 he worked in the Russian provincial city of Briansk for the local newspaper *Brianskii Komsomolets* (The Briansk Young Communist). In 1955–1956 he continued working as a journalist in Kursk for the newspaper *Kurskaia Pravda* (Kursk Truth). In 1956 he returned to Sukhumi and worked for the Abkhazian state publishing house. Nikita Sergeevich Khrushchev's ill-devised economic reforms of those years, in combination with Iskander's experience in the provincial press, served as the inspiration for the satirical novella *Sozvezdie Kozlotura* (1966; translated as *The Goatibex Constellation*, 1975). In 1960 Iskander married Antonina Mikhailovna Khlebnikova. Since 1962, when their daughter, Marina, was born, Iskander and his family have resided in Moscow. He and his wife also have a son, Aleksandr (Sandro), born in 1983.

Iskander began his literary career as a poet. Between 1957 and 1964 he published seven volumes of verse. His first book of poetry, *Gornye tropy* (Mountain Paths), appeared in Abkhazia in 1957, the same year that he joined the Union of Soviet Writers. At the end of the 1950s he began contributing to a popular, Moscow-based literary magazine, *Iunost'* (Youth). In 1959 and 1961 his second and third books of poetry—*Dobrota zemli* (Kindness of the Earth) and *Deti Chernomor'ia* (The Children of the Black Sea), respectively—were published, also in Abkhazia. His next four collections, *Zelenyi dozhd'* (Green Rain, 1960), *Molodost' moria* (The Youth of the Sea, 1964), *Zori zemli* (Dawns of the Earth, 1966), and *Letnii les* (Summer Forest, 1969), were released by prestigious Moscow publishing houses. Critics and fellow writers gave Iskander's poetry positive reviews.

In his verse Iskander uses traditional rhymes and realistic imagery. Most of his poems resemble compact novellas. In the poem "Zmei" (The Kite, 1969), for example, the narrator tells the story of a child whose worries about his kite (he is afraid that it will fly away) mingle with his worries about the grave troubles of his country. The child dreams of flying—a wish that, Iskander suggests, is inspired both by the ideological propaganda of Soviet aviation and by the longing to break away from the harsh life of adults. A great many of Iskander's poems are dedicated to the traditions and lore of the Abkhazian countryside. "Balada ob ukradennom kozle" (The Ballad of the Stolen Ram, 1969) romanticizes hospitality and the sharing of food, as well as the ancient right to slay a thief and wash away the insult with his blood. "Balada ob okhote i zimnem vinograde" (The Ballad of Hunting and Grapes in Winter, 1969) describes the hot pursuit of an ibex. Iskander presents hunting as an honorable preoccupation of men, but his hunter always remains an ardent protector of nature. In the autobiographical "Detstvo" (Childhood, 1969) he introduces the reader to his own past. This poem brings forth the impressions of a boy's last moments before he falls asleep. He vaguely overhears the hum of voices in the next room, where courtyard neighbors have gathered for a chat and a cup of tea with his family. In the child's mind these indistinguishable words merge into the melody of mutual sympathy. The poem ends with a eulogy—typical in Iskander's works—to the supposed obliviousness of childhood, which masks profound wisdom.

Although Iskander's first short story, "Pervoe delo" (My First Errand), appeared in the magazine *Pioner* (Pioneer) in 1956, not until 1966, when his first short-story collection, *Zapretnyi plod* (The Forbidden Fruit), was published, did genuine renown come to him. These stories, describing life in Abkhazia in the 1940s and 1950s, rapidly made him a well-known author among the vast Russian reading public. His talent naturally encompassed a felicitous constellation of artistic and social qualities that were congruent with the literary tastes and expectations of his contemporaries. Iskander's works received unusually wide attention from critics both in Russia and abroad.

Iskander's protagonist is usually a schoolboy who is still naive enough not to analyze Soviet reality; yet, he is sufficiently intelligent to express irony and even forebodings. His intuitive impressions and premonitions are imbued with the dreamy aura of childhood, for which the picturesque Caucasus Mountains and the warm Black Sea are the backdrop, a classical setting reminiscent of the myth of the Golden Age. The generally benevolent, humane tone of Iskander's narratives made his melancholic irony palatable to the Soviet reading public when his prose works were first published. Moreover, his witty repartee differed strikingly from the crude and ideological Soviet official rhetoric, and his genuine sense of humor and exquisite narrative style provided relief from such rhetoric for cultured Russian readers.

Equally, if not more, important was Iskander's national position. In the 1960s Soviet society faced the consequences of its imperialist national policy. The Russian "Big Brother" attitude toward the republics dealt a heavy blow to their economy and social development. The impact on national identity and culture proved similarly devastating. Regional artistic self-expression was forced to remain marginal vis-à-vis Russian culture and to follow the officially prescribed patterns of pseudofolk tradition invented for them by state-approved artists. Predictable artistic productions manufactured under such circumstances resulted in uniformly fake works. They revolted the freethinking intellectuals, on the one hand, and, on the other, bolstered the already existing sense of self-satisfied national superiority among the wide, brainwashed Russian reading circles.

Iskander successfully surmounted this difficult problem. That his writing reached the reader not in translation but in original Russian contributed enormously to its artistic merits and its social appeal. He represents a relatively small minority of Caucasus dwellers, the Abkhazians, whose existence had been unknown to the majority of Soviet citizens before the end of the 1980s and in the ensuing period of national clashes. There was tension between the Muslim Abkhazians and Christian peoples of the Caucasus. In the years before perestroika, among the largely atheistic Soviet society, the very idea of religious conflict between Muslims and Christians in a remote corner of the U.S.S.R. seemed exotic and entertaining. Thus, Iskander's ostensibly docile nationalism—one of an unthreatening provincial character—proved acceptable. At the same time, the exotic setting of his stories created a shelter of sorts for the writer and the reader, one in which they were able to "discuss" peacefully their ethical problems. These seemingly benign features of his creative work enabled Iskander to express his progressive nationalist conception yet keep it undetected by the ideological censorship.

Also at this time Iskander addressed his own "exotic" heritage with mild humor. He managed to resurrect the pure Romantic tradition of the noble savage by retelling the lore and describing the traditions of his ancestors. He succeeded in creating the utopian

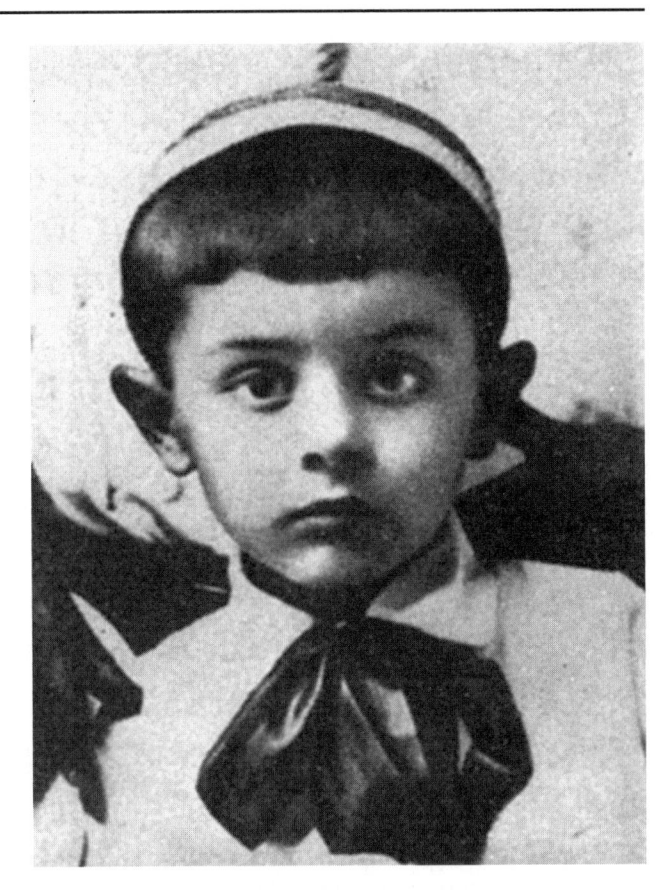

*Iskander, age seven (Natal'ia Ivanova,* Smekh protiv strakha, ili Fazil' Iskander, *1990; Jean and Alexander Heard Library, Vanderbilt University)*

world of a village, Chegem, that was more connected to the Romantic representations of the Caucasus in 1820s Russian literature than to life in the Soviet era. Without challenging directly the Russian chauvinist mythology of enlightenment, which Russians allegedly brought to the national minorities by conquering their lands and obliterating their customs, Iskander merely let his narrator record the destructiveness of this barbaric intrusion. Likewise, rather than resort to direct political accusations, he introduced the theme of great human loss, resulting from Stalin's terror and from World War II, through his depiction of the sufferings of the survivors. Tactful and wise, Iskander did not place the guilt for the devastation of the old way of life on Russians or on the authorities alone. He internalized the problem by showing the weaknesses and vices of those who were eager to "open the gates of the city" from within and thereby served the hostile forces in the dismantling of their own community.

Nevertheless, Iskander's stories always include concrete historical references that allow him to ground the eternal and universal themes of love, truth, fidelity, friendship, and honor. Historical concreteness and precision in the description of exotic life in Chegem or Mukhus (an anagram of Sukhumi) add much curiosity to Iskander's stories. His narrative rings true in contrast to the social realist depictions of life in the Soviet republics, which by the 1960s fell, by and large, on deaf ears. Iskander was a trustworthy and therefore informative author.

Furthermore, his debut took place in a broader context of rivalry between "village prose" and the urban trends of literature in the post-Thaw years. Village authors such as Fedor Aleksandrovich Abramov, Vasilii Ivanovich Belov, and Vasilii Markovich Shukshin captivated readers with their new, sincere tone of writing. While witty and colloquial dialogues and powerful descriptions of nature constituted the strong and appealing side of their creativity, their fascination with the Russian *Volksgeist* (national spirit) and innate anti-intellectualism precluded non-Russian, as well as some Russian, readers from identifying with their worldview. At the same time, urban writers such as Vassily Aksyonov, Iurii Valentinovich Trifonov, and Iurii Markovich Nagibin specialized in portraying the overwhelming skepticism and loss of ethical values among city dwellers, particularly against the background of the unresolved political problems that were endemic to the post-Thaw period. Iskander's artistic talent and his profoundly ethical nationalist position aided him in overcoming this rift as well.

Iskander's narrator treats his exotic compatriots with respect and fondness, though never shortchanging the advantages of his own education. Ever-present irony helps to maintain this narrative distance. A certain nostalgia rooted in the schoolboy narrator's image and the polished style of his self-expression, however, hints at a retrospective rendition of this boy's point of view rather than an attempt to mimic authentically a child's discourse. As Vickie Babenko has pointed out, "The little hero always has an adult counterpart who keenly analyzes his every action and feeling. In this respect, Iskander's narrator resembles Tolstoy's in the trilogy, *Detstvo* (Childhood), *Otrochestvo* (Adolescence), and *Iunost'* (Youth)."

Iskander's stories also differed from the children's literature being written at that time by popular authors, such as Evgenii Ivanovich Nosov, Viktor Iuzefovich Dragunsky, and Anatolii Georgievich Aleksin. Attracting genuinely talented writers, Soviet children's literature of the 1960s produced a great abundance of charming stories. The genre enjoyed unusual success among Soviet intellectuals; it permitted them to forge generational ties that had been shattered by Stalinism. While sharing a story with their young children, these intellectuals in effect made up for the gap that separated them from their own parents, whom they blamed for Stalin's repressions. Though linking himself superficially to this trend of literature, Iskander maintained his own distinctiveness by offering much more to the mind of an adult than was typical then of children's literature. His protagonist differs from the standard child character, in that he has a considerable amount of learned knowledge and life experience. As Helen P. Burlingame explains in her 1976 article for *The Russian Literature Triquarterly*, "the narrator of these stories is an adult looking back on the experiences of his childhood with adult eyes. And what he chooses to concentrate on is not so much the experiences themselves as his own reactions to them—how they affected him at the time and how they contributed to his growing maturity."

"Rasskaz o more" (A Story about the Sea), published in *Zapretnyi plod*, displays powerful descriptions of a boy's love for the sea. The lyrical aura of the story abruptly vanishes when the boy, who has been swimming near a pier, suddenly begins to sink. Noticing a young man on the pier, the boy attempts to signal his appeal for help with facial expressions. He is concerned that the nicely dressed man will not risk wetting his white shirt to save his life.

> "This is me, me!" I felt like shouting. "I have just swum by you, you must remember me!" I even tried to make a composed face for fear that my agitation and fright had so terribly disfigured it that the young man will not recognize me. But I saw that he recognized me and drowning seemed then not so sad, and I stopped resisting water which covered my head at that moment.

The persistent scrutiny of a facial expression, gesture, or body posture appears frequently in Iskander's narratives. He perseveres with these attempts at description and with explanations of momentary gestures until his analysis yields a deeper significance regarding this ostensibly trivial detail; he also uses this technique as a powerful comic device. In "Rasskaz o more" the young man on the pier sacrifices his nice costume, jumps into the water, and saves the boy.

The best-known story in *Zapretnyi plod* features the same boy who appeared in "Rasskaz o more." Iskander's young protagonist grows up in a Muslim family. The narrator explains that because of the multinational life led by Soviet Mukhus, many religious restrictions are not observed by the boy's family—with the exception of not eating pork. The story relates how the protagonist's sister eats a sandwich with pork fat at their neighbors' tea party. The next day, the boy tells their strict father on her. But contrary to the boy's expectations, the father turns his indignation against him, and he admonishes his son never to act as an informer. The moralizing narrator thus ends his tale: "Many years passed since that day. For many years I have been eating pork like everybody else around me but this did not make me any happier. My father's lesson, however, did not pass in vain. I have forever realized that no lofty goal can excuse lowliness and treachery. Treachery is a hairy caterpillar of envy no matter in what principles it shrouds itself."

Several stories in *Zapretnyi plod* form a nucleus for Iskander's future epic cycle *Sandro iz Chegema*. These stories include "Slovo" (The Word), "Petukh" (A Rooster), "Pervoe delo" (My First Errand), "Loshad' diadi Kiazyma" (Uncle Kiazym's Horse), and "Vecherniaia doroga" (Evening Journey). All of them have a boy as their protagonist; he narrates the stories as a reminiscing adult. (The title character of the cycle refers to the boy's Uncle Sandro.)

"Vecherniaia doroga" informs the reader that during World War II the boy's family, which resides in Mukhus, had to break up and join the households of their maternal relatives in the mountain villages. The narrator tells about this difficult period in his life. Separated from his mother and siblings, he—a "city boy"—had to learn new responsibilities:

> While I was still resolving where familial cooperation ends and exploitation begins, my uncle surreptitiously and without coercion made me take care of the goats . . . [The goats and I] communicated by two ancient and magical exclamations: "Kheit!" and "Jio!" These exclamations have multiple shades of meaning depending on how you pronounce them. The goats understood them perfectly, but sometimes when it suited them, they pretended that they confused the shades. These shades were really multiple. For example, if you pronounce with a drawl, with freedom and scope: "Kheit! Kheit!" that means: "Go, graze in peace, you are in no danger." If you pronounce with a kind of pedagogical reproach, it means: "I can plainly see where you are trying to turn." And if suddenly you say it very quickly and sharply: "Jio! Jio!"—it should be understood as "Danger! Come back!" The skillful combination of these exclamations produced many variants of educational value: an order, advice, warning, reproach. When hearing my voice, the goats would raise their heads as if trying to comprehend what exactly were they expected to do this time.

Through this ironic, double-voiced explanation, the adult narrator reveals the perplexity of a boy who does his best in coping with a new and confusing situation.

Suddenly, the boy receives the news that his wounded brother is in the hospital in Tbilisi (the capital of Georgia) and waiting for their mother to visit him. Although night is falling, he sets out for the distant village where his mother temporarily is residing. He has almost completed his long hike, when—in the middle of a dark cemetery—he tumbles into an open grave, only to find that a billy goat has fallen there before him. After overcoming his first fright, the boy clings to the billy goat's warm fur and praises the animal's companionship: "It licked my salty hand and I clung to its warm body and felt that even if at that moment a moon-light blue death face showed up at the edge of the grave I would only cling tighter to my billy-goat, and I almost stopped feeling afraid. For the first time I learnt what it meant when a living creature was next to you." Eventually, and not without a funny quid pro quo, a horseman extracts them both from the pit and brings the boy to his mother. This tale is echoed in another story from the cycle *Sandro iz Chegema*, "Kolcherukii" (Old Crooked Arm), which tells about the owner of the vacant grave.

The story "Loshad' diadi Kiazyma" introduces an attractive Chegemian—Uncle Sandro's brother Kiazym. Similar to "Vecherniaia doroga," this story is set in World War II and gives a simple and poignant account of Kiazym's love for his racing horse Kukla (which means "doll" in Russian). With admiration and fear, the boy describes Kukla's free spirit and Kiazym's high esteem for the animal. In the midst of the war, together with the rest of the village horses, Kukla is drafted for hard labor. Exhausting work and bad care soon break her haughty spirit. Kiazym is unable to replace his former adoration of the horse with compassion for the broken-spirited animal, and he sells Kukla to another village.

A central theme in "Loshad' diadi Kiazyma" is love. While the boy disapproves of Kiazym's rejection of Kukla, the adult narrator shows his understanding of Kiazym's course of action based on his own experience of the futility of substituting sympathy for love. Another theme of this story is love for one's work—be it horse riding, basket weaving, or writing. The peasant's love for his work turns it into art and at the same time attests to his own integrity. This theme is implied in the image of Kiazym and spelled out with reference to the boy's grandfather: "Only after many years I have realized that my grandfather remained his own self through the end of his life because he possessed the gift of the good peasants and great artists, the gift of deriving pleasure out of the work itself without expecting its often deceptive results." In these stories the world of Chegem emerges in its mythological significance and beauty.

In 1966, the same year that *Zapretnyi plod* came out, the journal *Novyi mir* (New World) published *Sozvezdie Kozlotura*, Iskander's best-known and most spirited short novel. It is about a propaganda campaign waged around a hybrid animal, the Kozlotur, pro-

*Front cover for* Zapretnyi plod *(Forbidden Fruit), Iskander's first short-story collection, which received international acclaim when it was published in 1966 (Davidson College Library)*

duced at an Abkhazian collective farm by crossing a goat with a buffalo. On an ideological plane, the novel lampoons certain aspects of Soviet society, such as Khrushchev's inept and devastating agricultural reforms, such as the replacement of cows with sheep, goats, and pigs. In the novel, ignoring the protests of the qualified "agrobiologists" and common sense itself, the Communist Party press exaggerates the importance of this new undertaking. Glorifying the Kozlotur's qualities in a paradoxical way, the party downplays the animal's useful qualities and praises its negative ones; for example, the hybrid animal has less meat and wool than a goat but greater jumping capacity. One of the Kozlotur's admirers suggests that the animal compete in the Olympic Games. The editor of a local newspaper, *Krasnye subtropiki* (Red Sub-Tropics—a jibe at the Soviet arrogance of attaching the political epithet "red" to a geographical term such as "subtropics"), which pioneered the campaign, proposes the Kozlotur as "a weapon for antireligious propaganda." The absurdity of the Kozlotur movement gains scope when the newspaper publishes a story, "Kozlotur i samodur" (Kozlotur and a Petty Tyrant); the folk chorus rehearses a "Song of Kozlotur," which has been composed by an accountant; and a café adopts the name "Kozlotur's Well." Someone even suggests a competition with the state of Iowa in raising Kozloturs, similar to the previous competition for corn growing (a satire of Khrushchev's famous declaration of competition with the United States in food production). The narrator of this story is a young reporter who is eventually fired from *Krasnye subtropiki* as a result of the failure of the Kozlotur campaign. Through the example of his own journalism and the work of his colleagues, he exposes the typical Soviet mechanisms for exaggerating successes and disguising failures.

Also in 1966 Iskander published his second collection of short stories, *Trinadtsatyi podvig Gerakla* (The Thirteenth Labor of Hercules), which includes the title story, "Vremia schastlivykh nakhodok" (A Time of Happy Discoveries), "Urok igry v shakhmaty" (Chess Lesson), "Dolzhniki" (Moochers), and "Detskii sad" (The Kindergarten). Most of these stories relate to Iskander's novel *Shkol'nyi val's, ili Energiia styda*. The year 1966 was also when the story "Sandro iz Chegema" appeared in the newspaper *Nedelia* (Week); Iskander returned to the character of Uncle Sandro periodically over the course of almost thirty years.

"Trinadtsatyi podvig Gerakla" gives a hilarious account of a boy's industriousness. Mortified by a fear of his math teacher, the boy ushers a group of medical nurses, who have a round of painful vaccination shots, into his class in order to prevent being called on to work on a math problem that he failed to solve for homework the day before. Despite his efforts to disrupt the class—or because of them—the teacher calls him to the blackboard, and in the last minutes of class time he gives the boy a failing grade. The teacher also secures for himself just enough time to explain to the students that normally the glorious deeds in the history of humankind have been inspired by courage, such as Hercules' mythological twelve labors. Yet, he tells his students, their classmate has performed right before their eyes the thirteenth glorious deed inspired not by valor but by cowardice.

Like "Trinadtsatyi podvig Gerakla," the story "Petukh" addresses courage and valor, also from a comical perspective. "Petukh" actually links the Chik cycle and the cycles *Sandro iz Chegema* and *Shkol'nyi val's, ili Energiia styda* through their young protagonist. The adult narrator retells an episode from his early childhood, when he spent a summer in the village. There an especially large and aggressive rooster, who grew to dislike him, watched the boy's every step. Admiring his awesome adversary, the boy comments on the rooster's prowess as a tyrant but also as a defender of his flock. Eventually, a clash between the boy and the rooster takes place—and the rooster wins. At that point the adults interfere and take justice into their hands: the rooster is decapitated and cooked for the family dinner. While helping his brother to chase the rooster through the yard, the boy feels the unfairness of this verdict: "It looked like he wanted to tell me: 'Yes, we had a feud. It was an honest war between two men, but I did not expect treachery from you.'" The narrator takes over by concluding that "it was a remarkable rooster . . . but to fight with humans is a lost cause."

In his stories Iskander often switches to the adult narrator's voice to make conclusions on the basis of the boy's observations. For example, in "Nachalo" (The Beginning), which appears in the collection *Derevo detstva* (1970, Tree of Childhood), the narrator actually retells an earlier story, "Detskii sad":

> There was a pear tree in the kindergarten yard. From time to time, an overripe pear would fall from the tree. The children picked them up and immediately devoured them. Once a boy picked up an especially big and handsome pear. He wanted to eat it up, but the teacher took it away from him and told him that it would go into the fruit stew for all of them. After certain hesitation, the boy consoled himself that his pear would enhance the collective dinner. On his way out, the boy saw the teacher. She was also going home. In her hand she was carrying a net shopping bag. In the bag he spotted his pear. The boy began to run because he was ashamed to look in his teacher's eyes.

Iskander transfers the didactic gist of "Detskii sad," a story he composed as a beginning writer, into "Nachalo," a much later narrative, as if inviting his readers to look into their own lives before jumping to conclusions about human deceptiveness. In "Nachalo" he restates his conclusion through irony. One of his many readers who sees this story as a humorous one bursts into laughter and offers his own interpretation: "If the kindergarten teacher took the pear home, then you can imagine what the kindergarten director must have taken." The narrator observes that there is not a single word in the story about the director. "The fact that you do not mention him makes it particularly funny because you imply him," the reader answers. In this "estranged" interpretation, the author conveys the difficulty of expressing his idea even in the most straightforward story. At the same time, he reveals that his ethical parables deal with age-old vices. He also shows that although the readers easily recognize these vices, they do not feel indignant but merely amused.

Besides "Nachalo," the other stories in the 1970 collection, *Derevo detstva*, include "Kolcherukii," "Pis'mo" (The Letter), "Dedushka" (Grandfather), "Moia militsiia menia berezhet" (My Police Look after Me), "Lov foreli v verkhov'iakh Kodora" (Trout Fishing on the Upper Kodor), "Anglichanin s zhenoi i rebenkom" (An Englishman with Wife and Child), "Letnim dnem" (On a Summer Day), "Poputchiki" (The Fellow-Travelers), "Moi kumir" (My Idol), and *Sozvezdie kozlotura*.

At the center of the narrative "Kolcherukii" is the title character, an old Abkhazian peasant whose main link in life is with the earth and everything that grows and lives on it. Therefore, even death itself proves powerless over him. One of his practical jokes consists in announcing his own death—for a trivial reason: he has recovered at a Mukhus hospital, and he wants his village to send a car for his ride home; he knows, however, that the village administrators provide transportation only for a dead body. This deceit—his pretense of death—does not stop him from arguing with his relatives over his decision to keep their funeral gifts. The fact that a grave pit has also been prepared for him does not bother him in the least. He saves the pit for the future and, meanwhile, plants peach trees around it. Into this grave tumbles the boy from the story "Vecherniaia doroga." Kolcherukii makes a political mistake when he plants a tung tree on his grave: the cultivation of the tung, an industrial plant, has been imposed on the collective farm by the authorities. The authorities read rebellious meaning into Kolcherukii's planting of the tung tree on his grave. The whole village collectively helps Kolcherukii to compose a letter of explanation in response to this dangerous accusation. In the letter he tells the story of his injured arm. Apparently, Kolcherukii was as unrestrained in his jokes in his younger years as he was in his old age. His joke about the local prince's sexual inadequacy cost him his arm. Although in reality Kolcherukii's wound has nothing to do with the political struggle, the insulted prince's aristocratic origin and the Marxist interpretation of this incident in an explanatory letter save Kolcherukii from arrest. Even on the brink of his real death, Kolcherukii plays a practical joke on his rival in horse breeding. Knowing that the horses are afraid of dead bodies, he asks his friend to jump over his coffin on horseback. The people at the funeral appreciate this joke when the horse backs away from the body. The narrator's ending summarizes the life-affirming message of the story: "When an old man dies, in our land the wake proceeds joyfully. People drink wine and tell funny stories . . . A man has completed his earthly journey, and, if he is of an old age, if he has lived, as

*Front cover for Iskander's 1970 collection of nine stories,* Derevo detstva *(Tree of Childhood), which includes his best-known novella,* Sozvezdie Kozlotura *(translated in 1975 as* The Goatibex Constellation*), about a propaganda campaign centered on a hybrid animal (Pollack Library, Yeshiva University)*

they say here, to the full of his time, then it means that the living can celebrate the victory of the man over his fate."

The juxtaposition of ideological clichés against the experience of life informs a humorous story, "Anglichanin s zhenoi i rebenkom." Here two worlds are pitted against each other–that of the Englishman, with his wholesome concept of personal freedom, and that of the protagonist, whose relations with this freedom are much more complicated. The humor of the situation arises from their mutual misunderstanding on all levels, including the level of language. Iskander pokes the greatest fun at preconceived notions. The protagonist keeps repeating that the Englishman looks anything but English. When he attempts to name what the Englishman reminds him of–Vikings or ancient Greeks–it turns out he has never seen either. For the protagonist, an Englishman constitutes no less an abstract and practically unverifiable concept than the representatives of the ancient world. The Englishman's wife and son also look different from what the narrator imagines. In trying to sort out his own feelings toward these foreigners, he recollects how people treated the German prisoners of war. At that time, at the end of the catastrophic war, compassion overcame animosity toward the defeated enemies; people began sharing their food and tobacco with the Germans. "Anglichanin s zhenoi i rebenkom" essentially sets forward the need to destroy intercultural "deafness."

This same theme figures prominently in the story "Letnim dnem." On a summer day, in a café at the Black Sea, the narrator meets a tourist from West Germany. After the obligatory praise of Soviet champagne–to which foreigners often resort–the German tells the story of his life. At the end of the war, he served at an important research institute. A secret-police agent approached him with the suggestion to work as an informer. The German firmly stood his ground, and his tormentor left him alone. The gist of the story, however, lies in the German's suspicion that his best friend collaborated with the secret police in this recruitment attempt. The suspicion proved wrong but their lifelong friendship suffered irreparable damage. Parallels between Stalinism and fascism stand out in "Letnim dnem," and they challenge the mainstream post-Thaw ideology. Iskander also overturns the Russian intellectuals' romantic concept of outright rebellion against tyranny. He maintains that the impractical and extremist requirement of rebellion undermines the value of consistent ethical behavior. He places this message into the German's comment: "The historical moment did not grant the right of choice to our generation. It would be unrealistic to demand from us anything exceeding the limits of decency . . . Under the conditions of fascism, the demands that an individual, especially a scientist, should heroically rebel against the regime would be wrong and even harmful." Iskander warns against a situation when the impossibility of open protest results in global cynicism and skepticism in regard to personal choices.

The collection *Pervoe delo* (My First Errand), published in 1972 and enlarged in 1978, had five previously published stories and three new ones, including the title story, "Dedushka," and a longer narrative, "Den' Chika" (Chik's Day). In "Pervoe delo," a story thematically close to "Vecherniaia doroga," a boy receives the task of transporting two sacks of corn to a far-off mill; he completes this errand successfully and returns home just before nightfall. This minimal plot permits the narrator to illuminate various aspects of the boy's emotions and thoughts. On the road the boy is not alone but travels with a donkey, who carries the heavy load of corn sacks and whose well-being the boy perceives as one of his responsibilities. As in a fairy tale, the road that lies ahead of the boy is full of both perils and joys. His companionship with the donkey grows strong through their nonverbal yet lyrical communication: "The donkey stretched out his furry face with big sad eyes and long sparse eye-lashes. He exhaled his warm breath into my palm and bit a whole handful of corn out of the cob. . . . In the dangerous places, I held the donkey by the tail. He got used to it and didn't feel offended. He would only step even slower and with more caution as if sensing that a human being has entrusted his life to him." The suspense of the narrative hangs on the reader's empathy with the boy's overwhelming feeling of responsibility. One feels gratitude toward a miller in the story; he temporarily relieves the boy of his duty and assumes the task of milling the corn himself. But even at this moment of respite, the boy is careful to check whether the corn gets the right grinding, as his aunt had instructed him. With his corn flour in his sacks and the sacks secured on the donkey's back, the boy sets out for the way home, now hastening to make this end of the trip before the sun falls. The story again shows its fairy-tale side by making a full circle of the boy's return. His uncle sets out with a lantern to meet him on the darkening road, and his aunt sews into the night to finish his new red shirt for the next school day. The story portrays the life of peasants, one in which love and care express themselves in the family's effort to perform one's best on a daily basis.

The story "Dedushka" is another lyrical variation on the theme of "Pervoe delo." Grandfather is an inspired artist of the peasant life. There is no discord between his beliefs and actions. The turbulent history of his generation has taught him the wisdom of remaining true to his work and his people: "The mysterious footprints of his very long life in the moments when I hoped they were leading to a war path of the *abrek* [a brigand] invariably lead to a stinky goat shed or corn field. But there is something in him that makes people respect him and this feeling of respect prevents them from living their lives the way they would like to, and they curse him often for that." To the boy's frustration, the grandfather tells stories about the *abreks* and the Abkhazian displacement to Turkey without any sense of excitement, in contrast to his animated remarks on how one should perform good work. The situation takes a comical turn when the boy realizes that the adults in the family are also annoyed by the grandfather's inexhaustible industriousness and love of work. At that point, however, the boy's vision changes and he feels a piercing tenderness toward this unappreciated old man.

In the story "Den' Chika," included in the collection *Pervoe delo,* Iskander introduces a protagonist, Chik, who recurs in many stories. Eventually, "Den' Chika" became the second part of the short novel *Den' i noch' Chika* (Chik's Day and Night), published in the collection *Pod sen'iu gretskogo orekha* (1979, Under the Walnut Tree). All together, the Chik cycle consists of this short novel and several short stories, such as "Vozmezdie" (Retribution), "Zashchita Chika" (Chik's Defense), "Chaepitie i liubov' k moriu" (Tea Drinking and the Love of the Sea), and "Zhivotnye v gorode" (Animals in the City)–all four of which appeared in *Zashchita Chika* (1983)–"Podvig Chika" (1987, Chik's Glorious Deed), and "Chik idet na okhotu" (1993, Chik Goes Hunting). The stories related to the short novel *Shkol'nyi val's, ili Energiia styda* and written in the first person also are inseparable from the Chik cycle. In addition, the stories about Chik are linked to the cycle *Sandro iz Chegema*: Chik's maternal relatives live in Chegem, and Sandro himself is the older brother of Chik's mother. There are other family and thematic connections among the stories because, as the narrator observes on several occasions, "Abkhazia is small." For example, in the story "Den' Chika," a girl Nika has recently lost her father, an outstanding dancer named Pata Patariia. He was the best soloist dancer in the Abkhazian folk ensemble. The rivalry between Uncle Sandro and Pata Patariia during a dance performance constitutes a subplot in the story "Piry Val'tasara" (Belshazzar's Feasts), which is a chapter in *Sandro iz Chegema*.

The collection of short stories *Vremia schastlivykh nakhodok* (A Time of Happy Discoveries), published in 1973, includes the title story (which previously appeared in 1966 in *Trinadtsatyi podvig Gerakla*), "Petukh," "Moi diadia samykh chestnykh pravil" (My Uncle–A Man of Highest Principles), "Moi pervyi shkol'nyi den'" (My First Day at School), "Dolgi i strasti" (Duties and Passions), "Mucheniki stseny" (The Martyrs of the Stage), "Vremia po chasam" (Telling Time by the Clock), "Trinadtsatyi podvig Gerakla," "Dom v pereulke" (House in the Alley), "Sviatoe ozero" (The Sacred Lake), and "Anglichanin s zhenoi i rebenkom."

"Vremia schastlivykh nakhodok" is similar in theme to *Shkol'nyi val's, ili Energiia styda*. The boy of the story tells about his suddenly discovered gift of finding lost objects. To complement this talent, he develops several clever techniques to amplify his reputation as a first-rate finder. For this purpose he even hides objects belonging to various people to rediscover and

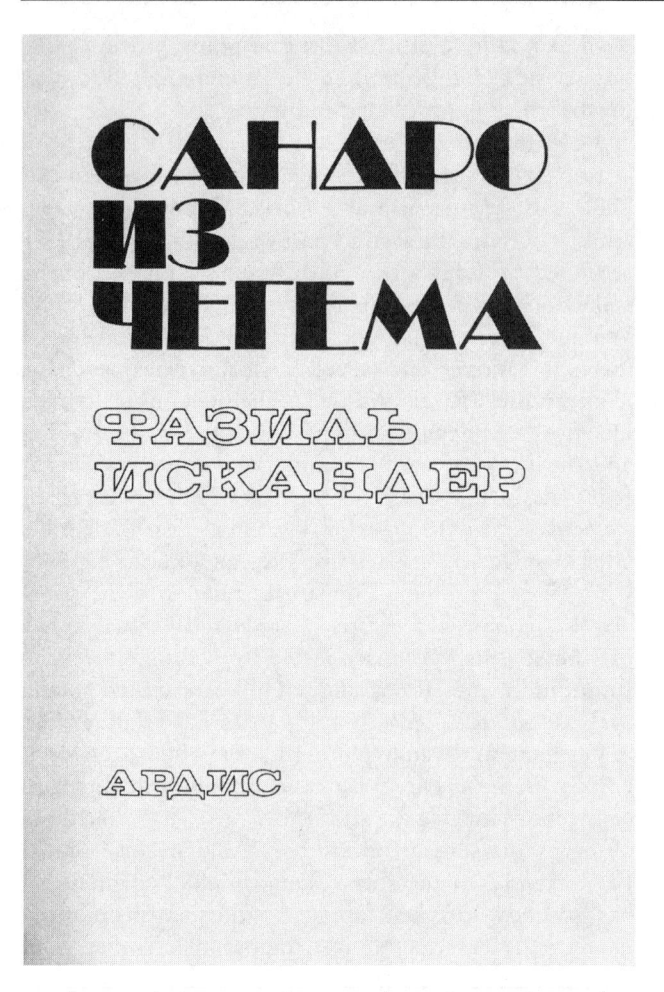

*Title page for* Sandro iz Chegema *(1977, Sandro of Chegem), Iskander's comic novel of stories about the narrator's Abkhazian uncle Sandro, regarded as Iskander's masterpiece (D. H. Hill Library, North Carolina State University)*

return them to their amazed owners. The story focuses, however, on the boy's inability to find an ancient Greek stela, which he had detected previously at the bottom of the sea. His history teacher does not lose faith—even after hours of fruitless diving and searching—that the boy will find the object. The problem of trust converts this funny story into an earnest discussion of mutual respect between the teacher and his pupil.

In "Sviatoe ozero" Iskander suggests that sympathy alone with the beauty of nature is not enough to protect nature. Years of living in Moscow have distanced the narrator from his folk traditions. When he finds himself in rural environs again, obstacles such as high altitude and the icy water of an enchanted lake challenge him rather than instill him with pious humility. Despite the belief of the local Svanetians that bathing in the lake brings misfortune, he succeeds in ascending the glacier and swimming in the lake. Later in the story, he visits a hospitable Svanetian household and learns its master's history. The man has three wives. Two of them still live in the house. But the third one, who cheated on him many years ago, lives in a separate house built by the husband; he visits her there "because he loves her but does not consider her his wife." As for the mystery of the sacred lake, the Svanetians react humorously when they learn that someone has bathed there. At the end of the story an old Svanetian tells the young man that they stopped fearing the spells of the lake long ago; they merely seek to protect its pristine beauty from the tourists. The protagonist thus learns lessons about remaining true to traditions without losing touch with one's emotions and sense of ethics. The significance of old beliefs, Iskander implies, is realized in individual choices.

In 1979 a collection of short novels, *Pod sen'iu gretskogo orekha,* was published. It includes *Den' i noch' Chika; Derevo detstva;* and *Morskoi skorpion* (Sea Scorpion, first published in 1976 in *Nash sovremennik* [Our Contemporary]). *Den' i noch' Chika* remains one of Iskander's most admired narratives. Chik lives at home with his family in their apartment, but his life also embraces the courtyard of their building. There he washes his dog Belochka and observes his neighbors converse, drink tea and coffee, quarrel, and make peace. There are also cats, chicken, horses, goats, and trees in this yard. As Natal'ia Borisovna Ivanova points out, "it is the Noah's ark of a courtyard," and a multilingual Babylon as well. The life of adults presents an educational spectacle for the perceptive boy. Instinctually, Chik perceives that "the ignorance makes children more independent and happy while the knowledge makes adults more vulnerable. Chik knew it. To be exact, he knew it but he did not know that he knew it." He also knows that the reverse side of vulnerability is hypocrisy. "When Chik was a young boy he used to hear that in the courtyard one adult would talk to another telling one thing while thinking another. Chik thought that it was a game of sorts. Chik also noticed that the other adult also thought something different from what he said, and therefore no one was deceiving the other. He only wondered why at the end they wouldn't laugh and congratulate each other on a nice game." The narrator's voice provides the commentary to Chik's immediate impressions. This duality of the narrative mode creates ethically meaningful discourse. "In any case, Chik knew that the part of his brain responsible for determining what was just and what was not worked very well. Chik wouldn't say the same about many adults." Still, Chik does not "expose" wrongdoings; he simply refuses to deceive himself about evil.

Chik is the acknowledged leader of the courtyard's younger generation. From the conversation of the adults, he learns that the legendary dancer Pata Patariia, the father of his friend Nika, has been arrested. Although this day is dedicated to a perilous expedition to pick pine tar, Chik never loses sight of Nika, who is worried about her father's fate. From his own experience of losing his father and uncles, Chik knows that people do not return from jails. He protects Nika from this knowledge. The image of children protecting each other at a time of trouble is a powerful picture of harmony, which is opposite to the world of injustice and cruelty.

A recurring artistic device in Iskander's narratives of childhood is the boy-protagonist's imaginary dialogues with an entity that normally does not speak, such as an animal or a plant. For example, a rough-and-tumble encounter with a puppy receives the following dramatization:

> The puppy suggested that they pretend that Chik was trying to grab his prey from him. What do you mean by "pretend," thought Chik, when you are hurting my leg so much. Chik bent forward and slightly slapped the puppy on his ear. "Don't distract me," the puppy snarled. "If you only knew what a tasty bone I am gnawing on."–"How can I not know that," thought Chik with irritation.

Chik carries on a similar dialogue with his dog Belochka: "Chik pretended that he was bending down to pick up a pebble, and then that he threw it at the dog. 'I don't believe you!' said Belka shaking her head. 'So, you don't believe me!' responded Chik out loud." Chik's imaginary penetration into the minds of animals widens his inner imaginative world. The optimistic unity of his consciousness provides the unity for this cycle.

In *Morskoi skorpion* Iskander departs from the world of his semi-autobiographical characters, although the events of the novel take place in the familiar setting of Sukhumi and the surrounding Black Sea resorts. The characters are tourists who arrive from Moscow to spend their vacations there. Iskander creates a psychological and moralistic narrative dedicated to contemporary family matters, love and jealousy, friendship and career, and the place of woman in society. Although the critics have extensively discussed this work in the press, it has failed to attract as much attention as his other writings.

In 1979 Iskander published a short story, "Malen'kii gigant bol'shogo seksa" (A Sexy Little Giant), in the underground almanac *Metropol'*. This subversive act made further publications in the Soviet Union considerably more difficult. Although he was not exiled from the U.S.S.R. or expelled from the Soviet Writers' Union–unlike some other participants in the almanac–Iskander still was subjected to censorship restrictions. "Malen'kii gigant bol'shogo seksa" is not one of the best short stories Iskander ever wrote. It tells about a young Abkhazian "Don Juan," who, because of his many sexual conquests, becomes a rival of Lavrentii Pavlovich Beriia, Stalin's formidable chief of the secret police. Although there are no political commentaries in the story, its satirical portrayal of Beriia challenges the official taboo of the time.

Also in 1979 *Sandro iz Chegema* was released by the American publishing house Ardis, which specialized in printing books prohibited in Russia. Iskander had been working on the cycle about Uncle Sandro ever since the 1966 publication of the story "Sandro iz Chegema" in *Nedelia*. The cycle first appeared in the journal *Novyi mir* in 1974 but, because of censorship, was excised heavily (roughly 240 pages were cut). The publication of *Sandro iz Chegema* by Ardis was the most complete version up to that point and also contributed to Iskander's reputation as a dissident. It was 800 pages long and included thirty-two short stories, or chapters. Most of them had appeared previously in literary periodicals and short-story collections. The 1979 edition was followed in 1981 by the supplementary volume *Novye glavy: Sandro iz Chegema* (New Chapters: Sandro of Chegem). From this point on, Iskander's critics and readers–as well as he himself–began referring to this work as a novel. In 1989, when the novel appeared in Russia for the first time, all the chapters–including "Piry Val'tasara," the most famous and most controversial section–were published in a three-volume edition. In its present form the novel begins with "Sandro iz Chegema" and ends with "Derevo detstva." Laura Beraha's dissertation, "Compilation in the Art of Fazil' Iskander as a Key to *Sandro iz Chegema*" (1992), provides a history of publication for each of the "Sandro" works.

The novel features hundreds of characters–Sandro's relatives, friends, and fellow villagers, as well as outsiders from "the valley" who bring in their languages and customs. These fictional characters interact freely with historical figures, from Nicholas I and Prince Oldenburg to Stalin and his retainers. Through the memories of the older generation, the narrative recounts the Abkhazian national tragedy of the 1840s to 1860s, when the "semi-voluntary" Turkish exile movement decimated the Abkhazian people and their culture. It also tells about the Russian Revolution and the Russian Civil War, as well as the devastation caused by both Stalin's terror and World War II.

The narrator in the novel has an Uncle Sandro, who embodies the very spirit of the utopian Chegem: "The nation that has Sandro will never cease to be."

*Andrei Bitov and Iskander in Moscow, late 1970s (Natal'ia Ivanova,* Smekh protiv strakha, ili Fazil' Iskander, *1990; Jean and Alexander Heard Library, Vanderbilt University)*

Iskander emphasizes the comical features both of his uncle and his people. Here the hilarious exists side by side with the tragic. In his foreword to the 1989 edition of the novel Iskander explains this paradox: "I conceived Sandro of Chegem as a comical narrative, as a parody of a picaresque novel. Gradually, however, the design grew more complex, sprawled with details. I strove to break through into the freedom of pure humor, but failed."

The chapter "Piry Val'tasara" enjoys international fame not only for its politicized subject matter but also for its exuberant humor. In it Uncle Sandro is shown at the peak of his career—he is youthful, talented, and charismatic. He serves as a chauffeur for the Abkhazian Party leader Nestor Lakoba and also performs in a folk song-and-dance ensemble-competition, in which the excellent dancer Pata Patariia also participates. The chapter culminates in the ensemble's performance in front of an assembly of Party leaders with Stalin at its head. Uncle Sandro manages both to impress the tyrant and to win the title of "first dancer" from Pata Patariia by performing a dangerous pas. He drapes his face with a *bashlyk* (an Abkhazian traditional hood) and, with his eyes closed, plunges forward to land on his knees at Stalin's feet. Taking a good look at Sandro's face, Stalin expresses his suspicion that he has met Sandro in the past. Without remembering this meeting and sensing the mortal danger of these recollections, Sandro bravely responds that their ensemble recently was filmed for a documentary and that Stalin must have seen him on this film. Absorbed in his sadistic intrigues of the moment, Stalin accepts Sandro's answer as truthful. Eventually, Sandro recalls that, as a boy, he met the young Stalin escaping from the police after one of his notorious burglaries and the murder of his partner. With the chase at his heels, Stalin spared the boy's life "for fear of losing speed."

In the last chapter of the novel, "Derevo detstva," Iskander uses the metaphor of a growing walnut tree to express both the potential of childhood and the living force of the nation. One may also observe in this image of a tree the metatextual emblem of the self-proliferation of the novel *Sandro iz Chegema:* "Taking a firm footing in the ground the tree bravely raises its branches to the sky." Similarly, the novel has deep roots in Abkhazian history and lore. At the end of the chapter this mythological world comes to a close. The legendary walnut tree dies, and the pristine spring that provided water for the whole village dries out. Chegem lies in ruins, and Chegemians are dispersed. Iskander does not describe any particular or distinct disaster that would have put an end to this village. Throughout *Sandro iz Chegema,* however, the reader witnesses the increasing erosion of optimism from Chegemian life, and without it, apparently, the myth must come to an end. Because of this rich layer of original mythology, intertwined with idiosyncratic interpretations of history, Boris Briker and Per Dal'gor place *Sandro iz Chegema* in the tradition of "magical realism," as launched by Gabriel García Márquez in his renowned *Cien años de soledad* (1967; translated as *One Hundred Years of Solitude,* 1970).

In Iskander's next novel, *Kroliki i udavy,* first published in 1980 in *Kontinent* (published in book form, 1982; translated as *Rabbits and Boa Constrictors,* 1989), a Paris-based émigré journal that was staunchly anti-Soviet, Iskander takes a harsh perspective on the notorious "resilience" of the nation. The anti-utopia of *Kroliki i udavy* is viewed as a political allegory of George Orwell's *Nineteen Eighty-Four* (1949) and other anti-utopian works. In his philosophical tale, Iskander sets forth the question of whether people are able to become free if they rid themselves of tyranny. At the time of publication, this question seemed to be premature; its full potential was realized only in the years of perestroika. Iskander warns his contemporaries that by eliminating Stalin's bloody methods of suppression, the government of the Stagnation period has widened its social base and turned the masses into volunteer slaves. When it was first published in Russia in 1988, *Kroliki i udavy* landed squarely in the center of the new debate about the future of the country. As Richard L. Chapple observes, the novel is a "fable-type allegory" based upon details of Soviet reality. It attacks dictatorship in general, underscoring themes such as international politics and external relations; the system's abuse of its subjects; motivation and self-interest; and political and cultural mythmaking.

Iskander's next short-story collections—*Zashchita Chika: Prazdnik ozhidaniia prazdnika* (1986, A Celebration of the Expectation of the Celebration); and *Detstvo Chika* (1993, Chik's Childhood)—include stories that are, for the most part, related to the Chik cycle. During the 1980s he also collected his old and new verse in *Put'* (1987, The Road). His poetry rings with the same ethical and civic pathos as his prose; his favorite subgenre, therefore, is the parable. In the poem "Bibleiskaia basnia" (Biblical Fable) Iskander confronts the essential question of how evil may be explained in a world created by God. The theme of the poem is Judas's betrayal of Jesus, and the speaker asks, "Why did not He create a miracle? While preaching Good he allowed evil to happen." Iskander suggests that Jesus lets the evil reveal itself, while his prevention of Judas's treachery would cause perpetuation of hypocrisy: "And He decided: 'There will be no Miracle. The Good shall remain the Good, and let Judas become a Judas. He wanted to save the world from Pharisees. Our world was so naive and young then."

A great many of Iskander's poems have the plot of a short story. For example, the poem "Liftersha" (Elevator Operator) reminds the reader of a concise and poignant story in the style of Anton Pavlovich Chekhov. In the poem, to the casual question of "How are you?" an old woman suddenly replies that her daughter has died. In the next few moments, while the elevator moves upward, her interlocutor experiences conflicting emotions—regret for asking the question, irritation that the woman did not answer in a less upsetting manner, and, finally, piercing sympathy for a fellow human who has been stricken with a tragedy. A short cycle of poems is titled "Portrety pisatelei" (Portraits of Writers), and the poem dedicated to Leo Tolstoy addresses him as the most outstanding Russian intellectual. Analyzing the problem of spiritual sovereignty, Iskander concludes that only Christianity endows personality with the freedom of inner growth.

In his 1989 collection, *Povesti, Rasskazy* (Short Novels. Stories), Iskander includes two short novels, *Sozvezdie kozlotura* and *Morskoi Skorpion,* as well as the stories "Slovo Mal'chik rybolov" (A Boy-Fisherman), "Remzik," and "Utraty" (The Losses). In "Remzik" the title character's mournful worldview contrasts with Chik's all-encompassing cheerfulness. Remzik and Chik are cousins and coevals. Their lives seem to share more or less similar impressions. Remzik, however, perceives life as unhappy and full of deceit. He fixes his attention on human deviousness and believes in atonement rather than forgiveness. Remzik's own act of treason weighs heavily on his conscience: on the night of his arrest, his father entered his room to kiss him farewell, and the terrified boy pretended to be asleep. He is witness to another deceit when his beautiful aunt goes to bed with her lover while her husband fights in the war. Remzik's indirect monologues mix his naive utterance with his earnest and responsible attitude to life, which creates a warm and humorous aura in the story. Gradually, notes of sadness emerge from the background and overwhelm the narrative. Remzik forbids himself to enjoy life and even to divert his attention from people's vices onto more-cheerful matters. He runs away from his aunt and arrives in Chegem, where his beloved grandparents live. Yet, even this return to the source of life turns into a search for the perfect place of death. While bathing a horse, Remzik semiconsciously drowns himself.

"The Losses" is one of the most important biographical stories among Iskander's works. The writer's alter ego, Zenon, arrives at his native Mukhus after his sister's death, a terrible loss that prompts him to reevaluate his life and profession. Zenon had left the mountains earlier for the "city of the valley," Mukhus, and eventually moved to Moscow, "the valley of the valleys." Although he has realized his artistic calling, the best and most valuable part of his life apparently has remained behind, in an Abkhazian mountain village. Thus, the descent from the mountains to the valley corresponds to the gradual compromising of life values. "Probably, every one who undertakes writing in earnest, thought Zenon, consciously or unconsciously promises the people to make them happier." Zenon believes that by just being a compassionate person his sister has fulfilled this task better than he: "The highest valor of intellect consists in living your life in such a way that everyone or almost everyone loves you. The surrender of intellect to the soul is the highest stage of intellect. The goal of a person is becoming a good person. There is no other goal and should not be."

Iskander's 1991 collection of short novels, *Stoianka cheloveka: Povesti i rasskazy* (A Human's Settlement: Novellas and Stories), includes the title novella, *Sozvezdie Kozlotura,* and *Shkol'nyi val's, ili Energiia styda.* The novel *Stoianka cheloveka* was written in 1979, the year that Iskander joined the ranks of the dissidents, and represents his most didactic piece of prose. Its main hero, Vladimir Maksimovich, is essentially a Romantic. Descended from exiled Russian aristocrats, he becomes a fighter pilot during World War II, then an engineer, and eventually a builder of the *makholet,* a flying machine similar to the winged contraptions of Leonardo da Vinci. Vladimir Maksimovich's behavior is invariably heroic, and his moral teaching constitutes a separate section of the novel. He dies during the experimental launching of his *makholet.* The theme of flight connects the novel to the classic avant-garde struggle to break away from the triviality of life into a harmonious world by means of airborne design. In an interview Iskander explained the relative schematicism of this image: "My other main characters derive from the power of their people while Vladimir Maksimovich is an essentially modernist human being: a naked man on naked earth. He depends on his moral uprightness for he has nothing else to rely upon." While the 1960s constitute the narrative present, Vladimir Maksimovich's memories connect the decade of the 1960s with life in provincial Mukhus between the wars, World War II, Stalin's terror before and after World War II, and, eventually, the disappointing aftermaths of Khrushchev's Thaw.

The 1995 collection *Chelovek i ego okrestnosti* (A Man and His Environment) presents a new phase in Iskander's writing. For the most part these stories bear dark and moralizing overtones—here belles lettres yield to the essay. Although the past shines brightly in these stories, its glow produces severe and ominous contrasts with the gloomy narrative of the present. The collection includes the stories "Lenin v Amre" (Lenin at Amra), "Rapira" (Rapier), "Lovchii iastreb" (A Hunting Hawk), "Sumrachnoi iunosti svet" (The Light of Gloomy Youth), "Krasota normy, ili Mal'chik zhdet cheloveka" (The Beauty of the Norm, or A Boy Is Waiting for the Man), "Zvezdy i liudi" (Stars and People), "Rukopis', naidennaia v peshchere" (A Manuscript Which Was Found in a Cave), "More oboianiia" (An Ocean of Charm), "Palermo-New York," "Lastochkino gnezdo" (Swallow's Nest), "Strakh" (Fear), "O, moi pokrovitel'!" (Oh, My Benefactor!), "Kutezh starikov nad morem" (The Old Men's Feast Over the Sea), and "Lenin i diadia Sandro" (Lenin and Uncle Sandro).

A profound pessimism resounds in the story "Lenin v Amre." Although laughter prevails in this hilarious tale of a maniac who imagines that he is Vladimir Lenin incarnate, the general aura of the story is sad. The narrator reveals the impenetrable absurdity in the maniac's arguments, as if reminding the reader that a similarly insane discourse ruled them for too long to be brushed away as an inconsequential nightmare.

"Rapira" presents the life story of a young athlete and philosopher, Iura Zvanba. Describing the fate of his generation, Iskander affirms that the worst of childhood premonitions have materialized. Late Stalinism and the ensuing Thaw have resulted in the public's loss of civic and personal mores. Although the author, together with the rest of the people, rejoices over Stalin's death, he hurries to point out the enormous spiritual devastation that the regime has left behind. According to Iskander, the hectic years of Khrushchev's reforms, followed by the stagnant era of Leonid Ilyich Brezhnev's rule, allow little hope that these deeply rooted evils will be eradicated in the observable future. The tragedy of Iura's life is that his spiritual world revolves around bookish values and ideas. Similar to most of Iskander's adult protagonists, Iura places his inner balance in the only realm that he can control—literary culture—as he shuns life.

In these stories the narrator's voice turns cheerful when he again addresses the theme of childhood.

Although in "Krasota normy, ili Mal'chik zhdet cheloveka" the protagonist is called simply "the boy," the reader recognizes Chik in him not only through his life story but also by his optimistic philosophy. This story brings forward one of the boy's uncles, Samad, who before the revolution was a gifted lawyer. The hardships of the civil war have broken his spirit, however, and he has become a drunkard–a shame to his family and a laughingstock to his friends. Yet, even this downtrodden position does not protect him from his arrest, which is the third time a member of his family is incarcerated. Before him, his two brothers, Riza and the boy's father, disappeared into jails. The circle of friends around the boy's family dwindles: many are arrested, and others are driven away by fear. Only an old peasant, Vartan, keeps visiting them regularly. In the distant past Samad won a case in court on Vartan's behalf, and the peasant expresses his undying gratitude by bringing fruit to Samad's family. After the uncle's arrest, the boy becomes concerned that Vartan will stop visiting. His wait for Vartan constitutes the plot of the story. Vartan does keep visiting, and gradually the boy perceives the true meaning of support in the face of overpowering evil.

In his collections published in 1999 Iskander combined old and new writings. For the first time he amassed his most important essays in the same volume. Critics have noted that his fiction has a considerable "essayistic" element, in terms of both its digressions and its observations on the characters. Iskander's essays largely develop ideas that are familiar to his readers from his short stories. In the essay "Popytka poniat' cheloveka" (1993, An Attempt to Understand a Human Being), Iskander expounds his unfavorable attitude toward the idea of progress. He argues that the evolution of civilization has failed to reflect the cultural and ethical growth of humans: "The philosophy of progress as expressed through the belief in the self-propelling movement to a certain goal undermines the struggle for virtue in a human being. People rely on the current of progress to bring them to their goal without the participation of their own will." Unengaged ethical sense, according to him, begets despair. He regards the revolutions as explosions of accumulated despair. Examining Andrei Platonovich Platonov's novel *Chevengur* (1972; translated, 1978), which is dedicated to the civil war period, he comments that its characters are "half-children and half-insane . . . [they] do not know what Communism means but they know that Communism has already liberated them from the bondage of responsibility for what happens around them." Iskander finds the answers to these complex questions in the Russian Orthodox faith.

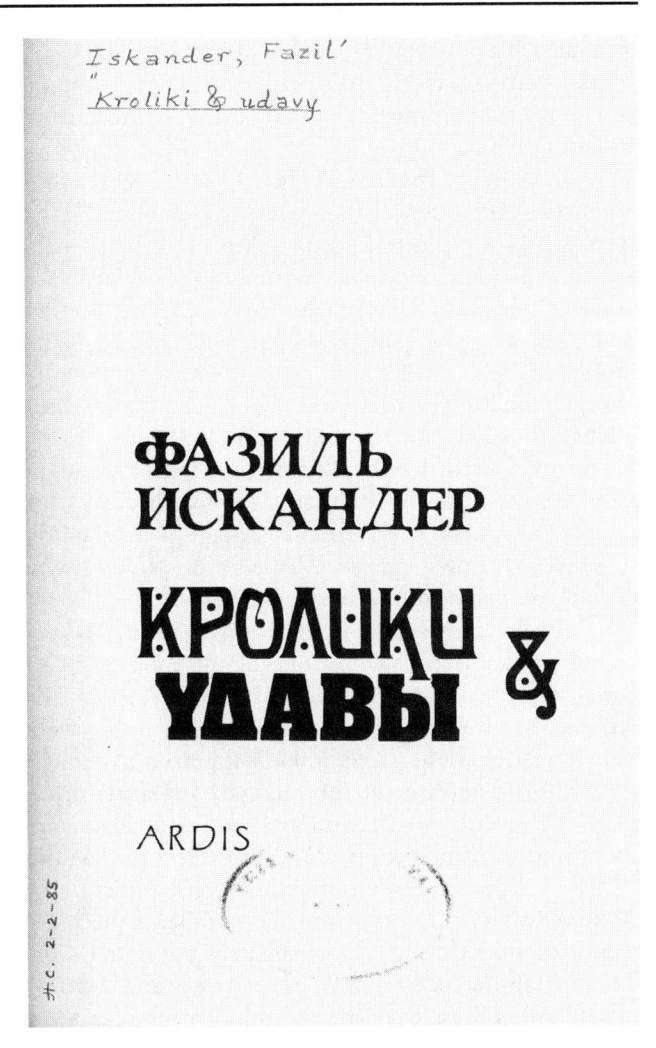

*Title page for* Kroliki i udavi *(1982) Iskander's anti-utopian novel translated in 1989 as* Rabbits and Boa Constrictors *(Jean and Alexander Heard Library, Vanderbilt University)*

A discussion of the nature of creative talent informs the essays "Motsart i Salieri" (1987, Mozart and Salieri, published in *Znamia* [The Banner]), "Slovo o Pushkine" (1997, Discourse on Pushkin), and "Iskrennost' pokaianiia porozhdaet energiiu vdokhnoveniia" (The Sincerity of Repentance Begets the Energy of Inspiration, published in *Literaturnaia gazeta* [The Literary Gazette], 1996). Following the Russian Romantic tradition, Iskander traces the features of the national artistic genius to Aleksandr Sergeevich Pushkin. He pinpoints the main theme of Pushkin's tragedy *Motsart i Salieri* (1830) as the problem of envy. Connecting this dramatic piece to contemporary Russia, he points to the role that genius plays in Russian culture. He expounds on the Romantic notion of the poet as the spirit of the people and maintains that a genius of Pushkin's dimension also plays a role as healer of the nation. Thus, Iskander interprets Mozart's acceptance of Salieri's poison as his selfless attempt to stir Salieri's conscience in order to save his soul.

In his essay "Stalin i Vuchetich" (1995, Stalin and Vuchetich) Iskander relates a conversation between the tyrant and the sculptor Evgenii Viktorovich Vuchetich, the creator of the enormous monument to Stalin in the city of Stalingrad. Here, Iskander once more profiles Stalin as a psychopath obsessed with death: "The immobile eternity of the huge monument apparently warmed the leader's heart." In this way he underscores Stalin's proclivity to mummify himself already during his lifetime. According to Iskander, the leader is caught between his insane craving for immortality and his ideological rejection of eternal life. Stalin is terrified by the idea of his own demise. This attitude explains why "death was his most industrious secretary."

As Burlingame points out, today Fazil' Abdulevich Iskander is considered one of the most talented Russian prose writers of the postwar generation. His writings are autobiographical, and most of his well-known stories are narrated in the first person. Although the author-narrator is the central figure in these stories, there are several other central and marginal characters that reappear from one story to the next, connecting the cycles of short stories into a comprehensive picture of Abkhazian life, as it was from the middle of the nineteenth century through approximately the mid 1960s. There is also a recurrence of place-names and even of events. All of these overlapping strands help to create a sense of unity and continuity. One can speak of Iskander's work as a single narrative—or, rather, as many separate narratives which, taken together, add up to a coherent whole, a colorful mosaic that encompasses not only the author's childhood and youth but also a large segment of Abkhazian life. He leaves to the reader, however, the construction of the actual pattern of this mosaic, since his stories do not appear in any chronological or thematic order, even within a single volume. According to Iskander's own statements in his essays and interviews, the essential message and focus of his artistic representation always concerns the moral and psychological development of his characters.

**Interviews:**

Tat'iana Mamaladze, "Ob ochage i dome," *Komsomol'skaia pravda,* 6 January 1977, p. 2;

E. Guseva, "Put' k schastlivym nakhodkam," *Turist,* 9 (1977): 24;

N. Uvarova, "Zhivite interesno," *Moskovskii komsomolets,* 17 January 1979, p. 4;

S. Lakoba, "Poeziei pronizannye stroki," *Sovetskaia Abkhaziia,* 13 September 1981, p. 3;

N. Nekrasova, "I chuvstvo sobstvennoi sud'by," *Smena,* 17 October 1982, p. 4;

D. Gvilava and L. Novozhenov, "Dushi vnezapnaia svoboda," *Moskovskii komsomolets,* 24 April 1983, p. 2;

I. Mazilkina, "Chelovek i sud'ba," *Moskovskii komsomolets,* 21 May 1984, p. 4;

N. Nazarov, "Udivitel'nyi mir Fazilia Iskandera," *Kommunist Tadzhikistana,* 14 November 1985, p. 4;

Grigorii Anisimov and Marina Bondariuk, "Korotko, no ne koroche istiny," *Literaturnoe obozrenie,* 11 (1985): 35–40;

Evgenii Shklovsky, "Potrebnost' ochishcheniia," *Literaturnoe obozrenie,* 8 (1987): 32–34;

Sergei Chuprinin, "Uroki gneva i liubvi," *Literaturnaia gazeta,* 3 February 1988, p. 4;

Oleg Dolzhenko, "Den'zhizni otlichat' ot nochi," in *Khronograf: Ezhegodnik 89* (Moscow: Moskovskii rabochii, 1989), pp. 41–54;

Elena Veselaia, "Esli ostanovimsia, nas poneset nazad," *Moskovskie novosti,* 12 March 1989, p. 16;

Petr Spivak, "Glotok kisloroda," *Moskovskii komsomolets,* 21 May 1989, p. 2;

Nadezhda Zheleznova, "Chitaem Solzhenitsyna: 'Dai mne uderzhat' shchit . . . ,'" *Literaturnoe obozrenie,* 2 (1991): 64–66;

Sally Laird, *Voices of Russian Literature: Interviews with Ten Contemporary Writers* (Oxford & New York: Oxford University Press, 1999): 1–22.

**Bibliography:**

Zoia Borisovna Mikhailova, *Fazil' Iskander: Bibliograficheskii ukazatel'* (Ul'ianovsk: Oblastnoi sovet profsoiuzov, 1982).

**References:**

Nikolai Atarov, "Korni talanta," *Novyi mir,* 1 (1969): 204–209;

Atarov, "Die Wurzeln des Talents von Fasil Iskander," translated by Vera Smirnoff, *Kunst und Literatur,* 17 (1969): 814–821;

Vickie Babenko, "Fazil Iskander: An Examination of His Satire," *Russian Language Journal,* 106 (1976): 131–142;

Laura Beraha, "Compilation in the Art of Fazil' Iskander as a Key to *Sandro iz Chegema*," dissertation, McGill University, 1992;

Boris Briker and Per Dal'gor, "Sandro iz Chegema i magicheskii realizm Iskandera," *Scando-Slavica,* 30 (1984): 103–115;

Helen P. Burlingame, "The Prose of Fazil Iskander," *Russian Literature Triquarterly,* 14 (1976): 123–165;

Richard L. Chapple, "Fazil Iskander's *Rabbits and Boa Constrictors:* A Soviet Version of George Orwell's

Animal Farm," *Germano-Slavica,* 5, nos. 1–2 (1985): 33–47;

Zhanna Dolgopolova, "Obrazy detstva: Viivi Luik i Fazil' Iskander," *Australian Slavonic and East European Studies,* 5, no. 2 (1991): 31–41;

Iakov El'sberg, "Diapazony tvorcestva," *Literaturnoe obozrenie,* 9 (1975): 26–29;

Margot Frank, "Fazil Iskander's View of Muslim Caucasia," *World Literature Today,* 60 (Spring 1986): 261–266;

Evgenii Fridman, "Nashei literature nedostaet sterzhnia . . . ," *Literaturnoe obozrenie,* 2 (1999): 100–103;

Kathleen Ann Haase, "Fazil' Iskander: An Analysis of His Prose," dissertation, Michigan State University, 1987;

Sergei Ivanov, "O 'maloi proze' Iskandera, ili Chto mozhno sdelat' iz nastoiashchei mukhi," *Novyi mir,* 1 (1989): 252–256;

Natal'ia Borisovna Ivanova, "Bestiarii Fazila Iskandera," *Literaturnaia Armeniia,* 5 (1989): 101–111;

Ivanova, "Smekh protiv strakha," *Znamia,* 3 (1988): 220–228;

Ivanova, *Smekh protiv strakha, ili Fazil' Iskander* (Moscow: Sovetskii pisatel', 1990);

Ivanova, "Stroi zanovo razbitoi zhizni zdan'e . . . 'Sandro iz Chegema': O tsene khudozhestvennykh obretenii v kontekste obshchestvennykh poter'," *Druzhba narodov,* 9 (1989): 245–261;

Marina Kanevskaya, "The Shortest Path to the Truth: Indirection in Fazil' Iskander," *Modern Language Review,* 99, 1 (January 2004): 131–149;

P. Kile, "Epos detstva," *Neva,* 2 (1984): 159–160;

A. Lebedev, "Smeshno skazat'," *Literaturnoe obozrenie,* 10 (1984): 53–56;

Mark Lipovetsky, "Usloviia igry," *Literaturnoe obozrenie,* 7 (1988): 46–49;

Lipovetsky, "Znamenitoe chegemskoe lukavstvo: Strannaia idilia Fazilia Iskandera," *Kontinent,* 103, no. 1 (2000): 280–291;

Valerii Lyshenko, "Toska po cheloveku pariashchemu," *Literaturnaia gazeta,* 1 November 1989, p. 4;

Stanislav Rassadin, *Posle potopa* (Moscow: Pravda, 1990);

Karen Ryan-Hayes, "Iskander and Tolstoj: The Parodical Implications of the Beast Narrator," *Slavic and East European Journal,* 32 (Summer 1988): 225–236;

Ryan-Hayes, "Soviet Satire after the Thaw: Tvardovskij, Solñenicyn, Vojnovi . . . and Iskander," dissertation, University of Michigan, 1986;

Benedikt Sarnov, "Chem glubze zacherpnut': Zametki o proze Fazilia Iskandera," *Voprosy literatury,* 7 (1978): 126–151;

Sarnov, "Gedanken zur Prosa Fasil Iskanders," *Kunst und Literatur,* 26 (1978): 1264–1282;

Irina Vasiuchenko, "Dom nad propast'iu," *Oktiabr',* 3 (1988): 199–202.

# Iurii Pavlovich Kazakov

*(8 August 1927 – 29 November 1982)*

Naum Leiderman
*Russian Academy of Science*

(Translated by Edward Alan Cole)

BOOKS: *Teddi* (Arkhangel'sk: Arkhangel'skoe knizhnoe izd-vo, 1957);

*Arktur–gonchii pes* (Moscow: Detgiz, 1958); translated by Anne Terry White as *Arcturus: The Hunting Hound, and Other Stories* (Garden City, N.Y.: Doubleday, 1968)–includes "Arcturus: The Hunting Hound";

*Man'ka* (Arkhangel'sk: Arkhangel'skoe knizhnoe izd-vo, 1958);

*Na polustanke* (Moscow: Sovetskii pisatel', 1959);

*Po doroge* (Moscow: Sovetskii pisatel', 1961);

*Tropiki na pechke* (Moscow: Detgiz, 1962);

*Krasnaia ptitsa* (Moscow: Gosudarstvennoe izdatel'stvo detskoi literatury, 1963);

*Goluboe i zelenoe* (Moscow: Sovetskii pisatel', 1963);

*Legkaia zhizn'* (Moscow: Pravda, 1963);

*Selected Short Stories* [in Russian], introduction and notes by George Gibian (Oxford: Pergamon / New York: Macmillan, 1963);

*Dvoe v dekabre*, introduction by Aleksandr Alekseevich Ninov (Moscow, 1964);

*Zapakh khleba* (Moscow: Sovetskaia Rossiia, 1965); translated by Manya Harari and Andrew Thomson as *The Smell of Bread, and Other Stories* (London: Harvill, 1965);

*Arktur–gonchii pes* (Moscow: Detskaia literatura, 1966);

*Rasskazy / Stories* [in Russian] (Letchworth, U.K.: Bradda, 1968);

*Osen' v dubovykh lesakh* (Alma-Ata: Zhazushi, 1969); translated by Bernard Isaacs as *Autumn in the Oak Woods* (Moscow: Progress, 1970)–includes "Adam and Eve" and "Autumn in the Oak Woods";

*Severnyi dnevnik* (Moscow: Sovetskaia Rossiia, 1973); enlarged as *Dolgie kriki: Severnyi dnevnik* (Moscow: Khudozestvennaia literatura, 1977);

*Selected Stories* [in Russian], edited by Alexander Pavlov (London: Bradda, 1975);

*Pervoe svidanie* (Letchworth, U.K.: Prideaux, 1977);

*Vo sne ty gor'ko plakal* (Moscow: Sovremennik, 1977);

*Olen'i roga* (Moscow: Detskaia literatura, 1980).

*Iurii Pavlovich Kazakov (* Iurii Kazkov: Nabroski k portretu, *1986; Jean and Alexander Heard Library, Vanderbilt University)*

**Editions and Collections:** *Dvoe v dekabre* (Moscow: Molodaia gvardiia, 1966);

*Goluboe i zelenoe; Nekrasivaia* (Copenhagen: Grafisk, 1972; London: Murray, 1972);

*Goluboe i zelenoe* (Paris: Institut d'Etudes Slaves, 1973);

*Arktur–gonchii pes* (Moscow: Sovetskaia Rossiia, 1980);

*Rasskazy,* introduction by Vladimir Turbin (Moscow: Izvestiia, 1983);

*Poedem'te v Lopshen'gu* (Moscow: Sovetskii pisatel', 1983);

*Osen' v dubovykh lesakh* (Moscow: Sovremennik, 1983);

*Izbrannoe,* introduction by Vladimir Gusev (Moscow: Khudozhestvennaia literatura, 1985);

*Dve nochi,* edited by Tamara Mikhailovna Sudnik and Igor' Sergeevich Kuz'michev (Moscow: Sovremennik, 1986);

*Tikhoe utro* (Moscow: Detskaia literatura, 1989);

*Plachu i rydaiu* (Moscow: Russkaia kniga, 1996);

*Vo sne ty gor'ko plakal* (Moscow: Sovremennik, 2000);

*Legkaia zhizn',* compiled by Igor' Kozmichev (St. Petersburg: Azbuka-Klassika, 2003).

**Editions in English:** *Going to Town, and Other Stories,* compiled and translated by Gabriella Azrael (Boston: Houghton Mifflin, 1964)—includes "Going to Town";

*Arcturus: The Hunting Hound, and Other Stories,* translated by Anne Terry White (Garden City, N.Y.: Doubleday, 1968);

"Adam and Eve," translated by H. T. Willetts, in *The Portable Twentieth-Century Russian Reader,* edited by Clarence Brown (New York: Penguin, 1985), pp. 507–509.

OTHER: "Zapakh khleba," "Ni stuku, ni griuku," and "V gorod," in *Tarusskie stranitsy,* 2 volumes, edited by Vladimir Koblikov, compiled by N. Otten (Kaluga, 1961);

Abdizhamil Nurpeisov, *Sumerki,* translated by Kazakov (Moscow: Molodaia gvardiia, 1966; Moscow: Khudozhestvennaia literatura, 1966);

Nurpeisov, *Krov' i pot* (Moscow: Izvestiia, 1969).

SELECTED PERIODICAL PUBLICATION—UNCOLLECTED: "'Zhili, sobstvenno Rossiei . . .': Iz naslediia Iuriia Kazakova," edited by Tamara Mikhailovna Sydnik and Igor' Sergeevich Kuz'michev, *Novyi mir,* 7 (1990): 114–139.

Iurii Kazakov revived and strengthened, even during the post-Stalin period of the Thaw, the bonds between contemporary literature and the tradition of classical realism. In his prose the Russian realistic tradition merged with the existentialist philosophy of Anton Pavlovich Chekhov, Ivan Alekseevich Bunin, Leonid Nikolaevich Andreev, and others, that were forcibly interrupted during the Stalinist period. By moving logically along this path and perfecting the chief instrument of realism—the art of psychological analysis that led him to a fine "micronized" acuteness and subtlety—Kazakov entered those spiritual spheres that had been only tentatively explored by classical realism. He was a person whose character bore the stamp of his time and whose lot lay within the realm of the most mundane human cares. In his prose he revealed the deepest drama of human consciousness.

Iurii Pavlovich Kazakov was born on 8 August 1927 in Moscow into a family of workers. In "Autobiography" he describes his origins: "As far as I know, there were no educated people in our clan, although there were many talented ones. Thus I am the first in our family who occupied himself with literary matters." Originally from Smolensk province, his parents—especially his mother—brought their country ways and customs to the city. His father, Pavel Gavrilovich Kazakov, was the son of a shoemaker and first got a job as an apprentice typesetter. He eventually gave up this profession, however, and held various positions, even working as a carpenter. He also served in the Red Army. In 1933 Pavel Gavrilovich was arrested for "failure to provide information." Kazakov's mother, Ustin'ia Andreevna Kazakova, first worked as a nanny and then studied to become a nurse. For her son she remained a source for the pure language of the "common folk."

Kazakov spent his childhood in conditions of serious need. He went through his adolescence during wartime. Impressions of those times—of 1941 and the bombing of Moscow—put their mark on the unfinished tale "Razluchenie dush" (Separation of Souls, posthumously published in *Dve noch i* [1986]). He spent his youth searching for a profession in the postwar years of famine. Kazakov's biography is one that is common to the *shestidesiatniki* (the generation of the 1960s). In his life there was, nevertheless, one particularity: he spent his childhood and youth on the Arbat in Moscow. He had the liveliest feelings for this legendary corner of the city. In his interview of 1979, he reconstructs the impressions of his youth and the specific mind-sets of simple Soviet boys from the Arbat:

> Gentlemen, how I love the Arbat! The Arbat—it is like a special city, even a different population. . . . When I was young, I loved to loaf along the Arbat. We didn't gather together as nowadays: there were no separate apartments or dachas, but *kommunalki* (communal apartments), where there was one room to a family. So we wandered about. . . . We thought that we were the best boys in the world! We had not only been born in Moscow, in the capital of our motherland, but also in "the capital of Moscow," the Arbat. We called one another countrymen.

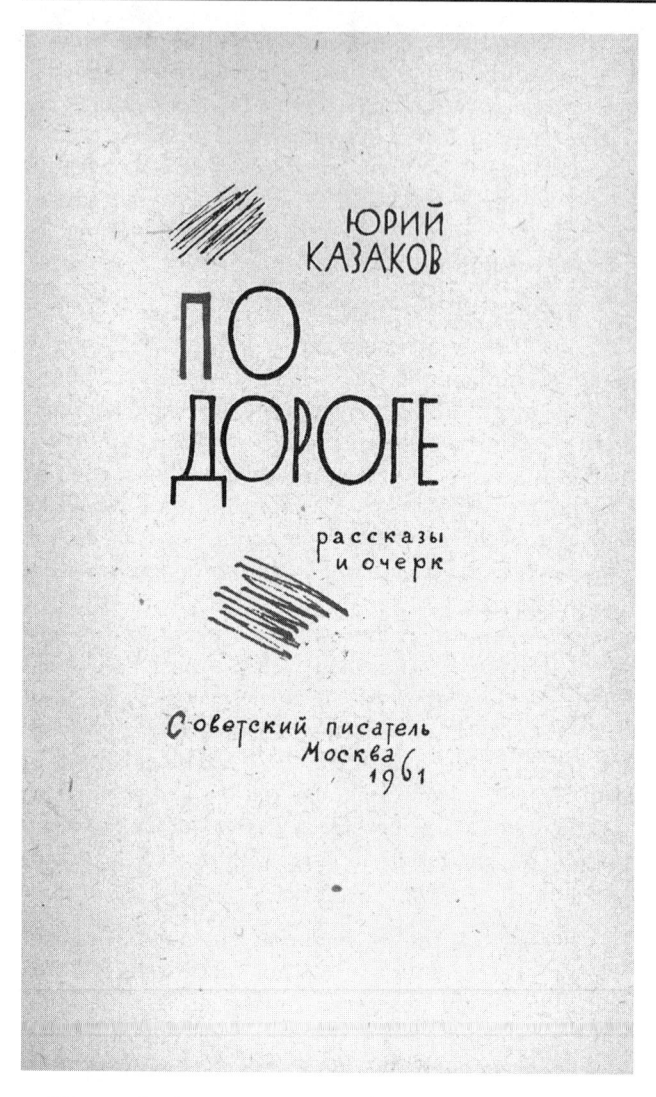

*Title page for Kazakov's story collection* Po doroge *(On the Way), which includes "Trali Vali" (Silly Billy) about a drunkard who is a remarkable singer. The story was criticized by the literary establishment because Kazakov "uncritically delineates the 'artistry'" of a hooligan (William T. Young Library, University of Kentucky).*

In 1944, after completing his elementary education, he entered the Moscow Architectural-Construction Technical College, where he spent two years. Right after the war, in 1946, he entered the Gnesin Music School, from which he graduated in 1951 as a double bassist. (He had commenced the study of music at age fifteen.) When he entered the music school he took cello lessons but soon realized that he had started too late to excel at the instrument. He also said that his fingers were not nimble enough for the cello. He then turned to the bass, but his role as a bass player in both symphonic and jazz orchestras did not provide a steady income. As a result, Kazakov took on all sorts of work–for example, as a stevedore in a candy factory and as a reporter for the news photo division of TASS (Soviet News Agency). By the late 1940s and early 1950s he was keeping a writer's diary, and by the mid 1950s he began to think of himself as a writer.

Kazakov gives two explanations for his entry into literature. First, he turned to writing because of his stuttering: "I stuttered a lot and was all the more shy because of this. I suffered wildly. And on that account I especially wanted to express on paper everything that had been accumulating" (interview, 1979). Second, he was enticed by dreams of "glory, of fame . . . I passionately desired to see my name on a poster, or in a newspaper or a journal" ("Autobiography"). Both explanations are half serious, half jocular. Whatever the tone of his remarks, Kazakov published a few sketches in 1953 in the magazine *Sovetskii sport* (Soviet Sport).

That same year he was accepted into the Litinstitut (Literary Institute), from which he graduated in 1958 with only average grades. Beginning as a correspondence student, he took a seminar led by the dramatist Boris Sergeevich Romashev. In 1954 he became a full-time student, with Nikolai Ivanovich Zamoshkin as his adviser; Zamoshkin later nominated Kazakov for membership in the Writers' Union. During the mid 1950s many seminars at the institute were taught by illustrious writers–among them, Konstantin Georgievich Paustovsky, Viktor Borisovich Shklovsky, Pavel Grigorievich Antokol'sky, and Vera Fedorovna Panova, with whom Kazakov carried on a lively correspondence. In spite of this array of teachers, however, Kazakov later recalled this period as largely nonproductive and seemed to regret the time he spent in formal training.

During his years at the institute, the story "Teddi" (published 1957 in a book of the same name) and the collection *Man'ka* (1958) came out in Arkhangel'sk. In addition, a modest collection of tales titled *Arktur–gonchii pes* (Arktur–Hunting Dog, 1958) was published in Moscow by Detgiz, the state publisher of books for children. In the mid to late 1950s his stories began to appear with some regularity in prestigious journals, including *Oktiabr'* (October), *Moskva* (Moscow), *Molodaia gvardiia* (The Young Guard), and *Znamia* (The Banner). Yet, publication in the premier literary journal *Novyi mir* (New World), the main editor of which was Aleksandr Trifonovich Tvardovsky, continued to elude him.

Tvardovsky reproached Kazakov in 1958 for pretending to act "experienced, weary, apparently having known 'the vanity of all earthly' bitterness and hopelessness of losses" ("Tvardovskii"). He advised Kazkov to recognize "that in art you don't go far on 'dew,' 'smoke,' etc." Even Aleksandr Isaevich Solzhenitsyn, in his memoirs *Bodalsia telenok s dubom: Ocherki literaturnoi zhizni* (The Oak and the Calf: Sketches of a Literary Life, 1975), wrote sharply, "And how strong and substantial Iurii Kazakov would be, if only he did not conceal the principal truth from himself." Yet, Solzhenitsyn and Kazakov understood the "principal truth" differently. For example, in "Adam i Eva" (translated as "Adam and Eve," 1962), the talented artist Ageev fulminates, "Critics cry out against the contemporary, but the contemporary they comprehend in a foul manner." Kazakov was completely determined not to accept a "foul" understanding of the contemporary, just as his hero asserts; or, put innocuously, he was determined not to accept a simplified, one-dimensional understanding that reduced all problems to the topic of the day.

Kazakov's "biography" is rendered in his stories, rather than in long autobiographical notes. Almost everything that his readers know about him they have learned from the thoughts and actions of his characters. Early in his life Kazakov developed an interest in hunting and nature (especially in the backwoods), and these two themes appear frequently in his works. He also enjoyed the freedom that travel allows. At the same time, his travels–in the 1950s and 1960s–provided him with insights into the minds and souls of the people he met wherever he went, and these insights mattered more than mere adventures. Like his heroes, Kazakov embarked on a spiritual, metaphysical, and philosophical quest that helped him describe in his works the complex psychological makeup of his heroes. He strove to express these emotions in the relationships among the characters of his stories as well as in their relationship to the world of nature.

The attempt to grasp the inner truth of natural feelings and conditions led the young Kazakov to write works that focus on animals and on children of nature. Two such stories are "Teddi" and "Arktur–gonchii pes" (the title story of the collection published in 1958; translated as "Arcturus: The Hunting Hound," 1968). In the first story Teddi is a big brown bear, an old circus performer accustomed to living in a cage and working in an arena. Kazakov depicts the world from the viewpoint of this bear, through his "consciousness." During a move to a new town Teddi runs out of his cage and finds himself free; he then follows the gradual process of returning to his natural habitat. In "Teddi," Kazakov presents the reader with subtle psychological prose in which the traditional device of "humanizing" an animal's psychology becomes a means for the closest possible observation of a process. He shows how a living being's connection with the place that gave rise to his nature is restored. Yet, "Teddi" provoked a negative reaction from Socialist-realist critics. Valerii Bushin raged in his review, "Well, what kind of echo might be found in the soul of a person building the happiest life on earth in a story about a bear who searches for 'bear paradise,' and upon finding it, plunges into hibernation?" (*Literatura Izhin,* 19 August 1939).

In "Arktur–gonchii pes" the title character, a dog, has been blind from birth, but he still has a feeling for the surrounding world. When Arcturus is taken to the woods, he cultivates a trust in his native instincts. He burns for the chase and is led by a passion for the hunt:

> The forest was his enemy, the forest beat him, whipped him on the snout, on the eyes, the forest threw him underfoot, the forest stopped him short. No, he could never catch up with his enemies, never sink his teeth into them! Only the smell, the wild, eternally exciting, inviting, unbearably beautiful and hostile smell, captured him; only one track among a thousand led him ever onward and onward. Having awakened from furious running, from a great daydream, how did he find the way home? Having awakened, completely weakened, beaten up, gasping for breath, having lost his voice somewhere many kilometers into the depth of the forest, with the rustling of the vegetation and the smell of damp gullies, what a feeling for space and topography, what a great instinct he needed in order to get himself home!

The nature that seethes within this blind dog's every cell seeks an escape. The life of Arcturus enters the lives of humans–his master, a doctor, and the hero-narrator. When Arcturus is lost in the woods and later found dead, life for these people loses its luster.

In his stories about animals Kazakov returns to the natural world–and, simultaneously, to natural speech. In place of the Soviet cultural *novoiaz* (news speak), which, for example, in the story "Goluboe i zelenoe" (published 1959 in *Na polustanke* [At the Railway Stop]), the boy from the Arbat uses to express himself, Kazakov's prose reflects an expansion of the normal literary style: his words ripen into form. Moreover, he is not enamored of special expressive devices and stylistic figures. His graphic quality is spontaneous; its essence lies in a descriptive precision, an appreciation of details, and an interest in nuances.

This predilection for the natural brought Kazakov to the image of the "natural man"–that is, a man who is free from generally accepted behavioral clichés. In the context of the times this image symbolized the condition of not being bound by the Soviet mind-set. Kazakov first turned to the phenomenon of the natural man in his "northern" tales–above all, in the story "Pomorka" (The Coast-Dweller, published 1958 in *Man'ka*).

*Title page for* Na polustanke *(At the Railway Stop), which Kazakov regarded as his first solid collection of stories. This book marked the beginning of ideological attacks on him and his work (Graduate Center Library, City University of New York).*

In those years the government often arranged travel opportunities for writers—creative missions described officially as a chance for them "to study material." Young literati liked to set off on exotic expeditions to what was called "the great construction sites of communism" or to see people of renown. During the holidays, as a Litinstitut student, however, Kazakov departed for the Russian North—then unprepossessing—and, from that time on, was "infected" by it for many years. These travels came at an opportune time. Although the city of Leningrad had enchanted him with the beauty of its setting and architecture, he was growing tired of living within the confines of a room situated on the Fontanka canal. Kazakov visited the Kola Peninsula, traveled via the Mariinskaia System and the Northern Dvina, went along the Arctic Ocean from the Barents Sea to the Laptev Sea, and visited Solovka. A consequence of these travels was a book of sketches—*Severnyi dnevnik* (Northern Diary)—written in 1960, published in the journal *Zelenoe* in 1961, and collected in *Goluboe i zelenoe* (1963). Subsequently, *Severnyi dnevnik* was enlarged, as Kazakov added new stories and sketches for the 1973 and 1977 editions. The Russian North was where he became a writer in reality, not only in aspiration, and "Pomorka" was one of the first works born of his experiences there.

In "Pomorka" the life of Kazakov's heroine, a ninety-year-old coast dweller named Martha, has been spent outside of socialist history and those temporal and social "landmarks" that seem obligatory, such as the year 1917, collectivization, and the Great Patriotic War (as the Soviets termed World War II). Martha's entire life has run in synchrony not with history but with eternity. The coordinates of eternity within which she lives finds concrete expression only in the sources of everyday existence, or the basic way of life for the *pomorki,* the inhabitants of the White Sea coast who eternally struggle with the freezing sea. In Kazakov's work the *pomorka* characters are surrounded by a heroic "aureole." These women are doomed to wait for their husbands and sons who are off to work in the cold sea and who do not always return. In this story a character description of a contemporary heroine summons up motifs of antiquity and of the *bylina,* the traditional Russian heroic poem. Martha's iconic face is striking: "She is so old that at times it is strange and terrifying for me [the narrator] to look at her—so ancient and dark is her face." Here the principal virtue of a heroine is that she "preserves the old order," and for that her fellow villagers respect her: "A good old lady, a holy one, in a word, a *pomorka!*"

In the 1958 story "Man'ka," published in the collection of the same name, Kazakov presents a different hypostasis of the natural man. In this narrative about an openhearted, young northern woman who works as a mail carrier, Kazakov describes the delicate but durable connection existing between the moody, psychic conditions of natural man and that which happens, flutters, and stirs in the surrounding world. No one knows what is the cause and what is the consequence—natural life or spiritual life, which are two interconnected vessels. Through this story Kazakov questions whether such a connection is the basis of the moral purity of natural man.

A change in the image of the natural man occurs in the story "Trali-vali" (published in 1961 in *Po doroge* [On the Way]; translated as "Silly-Billy," included in *Going to Town and Other Stories*). The hero of the story is Egor, a buoy keeper. In describing the effects of such a profession on Egor, Kazakov writes that "the work of the buoy keeper, easy and geriatric, had finally corrupted and spoiled him." He continues, "Egor is still young, but already a drunkard"—everything is "trali-vali" to him. Nonetheless, there exists within Egor a poetic side: he sings splendidly. For Kazakov, music is primarily formative. An understanding of it is linked to an understanding of beauty and harmony, and, consequently, in many of his novellas forms of music play a considerable role in the creation of an emotional ambience. In the story "Trali-vali," Kazakov, by his own admission, "attempted, professionally, as a musician, to describe a song" (1979 interview). Egor sings "in an antique Russian manner, drawling, almost reluctantly, almost hoarsely, just as in childhood he heard the elders singing":

> He sings an old song, a long one, with endless "oh-oh-oh's" and "ah-ah-ah's," drawn out with delight. He sings low, just playing, just flirting, but with so much strength and penetration in his quiet voice, so much that is genuinely Russian, as though from an ancient epic, that for a minute everything is forgotten: Egor's crudeness and silliness, his drunkenness and boastfulness, the journey and the fatigue, as if the past and the future had vanished at the same time and only an unusual voice rings, enters into, and clouds the head that wants to listen without end.

Such was the force of the talent with which Egor was endowed. The poetic in the natural man proves to be something unstable, however, and it begins to disturb and shatter the peace and balance in his soul. Indeed, Kazakov "catches" his hero on such occasions: "And sometimes he is seized, a strange tremor strikes and strange, wild thoughts get into his head. . . . Weary at heart, he wants something, wants to take off for someplace, wants a different life."

Egor cannot, nor does he know how to, explain to himself the sources of his heartache. In essence, his heart is disturbed by existence as such. His soul enters spheres where thought has no power to control and even the author-narrator is unable to help him. The narrator tries to mitigate Egor's existential torment with various romantic phrases: "And in a way that is vague and chilled to him, some kind of distant places call out to him, cities, noise, the world . . . a longing for work, for real labor, for mortal weariness unto happiness!" But the narrator gives up in the face of the protagonist's drama.

In the 1950s the story "Trali-vali" was published under the title "Otshchepenets" (The Renegade in Oktiabr 7 [1959]) to protect Kazakov from accusations of sympathy with the central character. This change did not save the story from the negative criticism it received, however, when it first appeared. Reviewing the work for Zvezda (The Star) in 1962, the critic Larisa Fomenko wrote that "Having rewarded his hero with miraculous talents, Kazakov uncritically delineates the 'artistry' of a disgracefully-acting hooligan." Some years passed, and then critics such as Igor' Georgievich Shtokman recognized in the character of Egor the predecessor for Vasilii Makarovich Shukshin's *chudaki* (oddballs).

Kazakov considered his first solid book to be the collection *Na polustanke*. At this time, from the late 1950s to the early 1960s, his stories began to be mentioned in critical surveys. Paustovsky evaluated them highly in an article published in *Literaturnaia gazeta* (The Literary Gazette); he even invited Kazakov to contribute to the almanac *Tarusskie stranitsy* (Pages from Tarusa, 1961), a miscellany that was subjected to harsh criticism in the official press. Kazakov's stories in *Tarusskie stranitsy*—"Zapakh khleba" (The Smell of Bread), "Ni stuku, ni griuku" (Neither a Knock nor a Bang), and "V gorod" (translated as "Going to Town," 1964)—were among those stigmatized.

As a result of the ideological attack on *Tarrusie stranitsy*, publishers and editorial boards of journals grew more wary of Kazakov, a development that, for him, meant further publishing complications. Yet, he did not make creative compromises. As Iurii Markovich Nagibin, one of the first critics to appreciate Kazakov's talent, recalls in his posthumously published diary, "He could never accommodate himself to the 'demands,' the style, or the ruling tastes, and furthermore, did not know what these were."

In the 1960s Kazakov settled on depicting heroes with agitated souls. His was a special anxiety that could not be defined either by social or by moral categories; as a troubled, inexpressible anxiety, it was a certain burdensome condition of the soul. If one subjects Kazakov's hero to the standard measure of the time, then one will notice nothing calamitous in his condition; he lives like everyone else—no worse but no better. He himself senses, however, that he does not live a so-called normal life, not the sort of life necessary for a man who wants to be an individual. He cannot even understand and explain to himself the cause of his restless aimlessness.

When the artist Ageev, the hero of the 1962 story "Adam i Eva," attempts somehow to express his agitation, his arguments border on stereotypes. His feelings are complex, profound, and tormented: "Bitter alienation, a sense of being cut off from the world, descended on him and he did not want to know anything or anyone. . . . He felt tired beyond measure, tired of himself, of thoughts, of a soul divided by doubts, of drunkenness, and he felt completely sick."

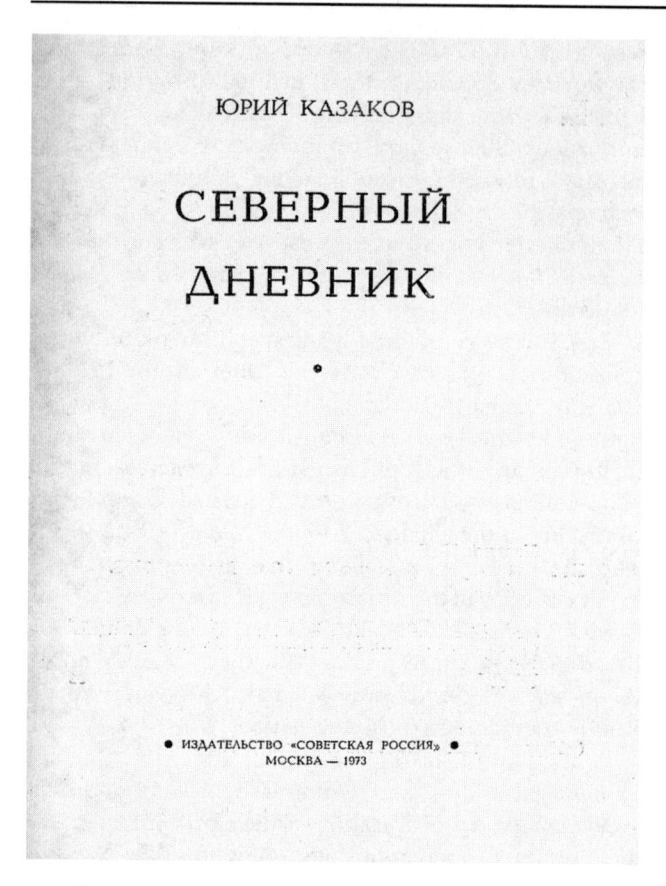

*Title page for the first edition of* Severnyi dnevnik *(Northern Diary), Kazakov's stories and travel sketches from his trip along the northern rim of the Soviet Union. He published an enlarged edition in 1977 (John C. Hodges Library, University of Tennessee-Knoxville).*

Imperceptibly, "signs of eternity" exert an influence on Ageev's process of tortured reflection and enter the range of his interests in the artistic world. These images, which include "an ancient, big church" and a bell tower, call forth a complex mood: details grow dim, and a person senses himself to be standing in the midst of the universe, feeling frozen, lonely, and somehow not right. Gazing upon the silent, level, and limitless expanse, where the old church rises, Ageev strives "to divine in the darkness that had for so many centuries lived its life, the real life of land, water, and people without him." But he does not succeed in divining anything in the darkness, and because of that incomprehensibility, he does not quiet his soul. This failure generates decisive moral consequences. For example, a loving woman becomes a sacrifice to the confusion in the hero's soul: Ageev had invited Vika here, to the North, but did not greet her; his inattention insulted her and crudely sent her packing. In addition, Ageev finds no way out into spiritual clarity.

In turning to this type of hero in "Adam i Eva," Kazakov had to decide how to treat new and difficult creative problems—how to capture this inexpressible confusion in the soul of a character and how to put into words the tortured process of outpouring feelings (and vacillating spiritual conditions). He arrives at an original poetics, which can be called the poetics of psychological parallelism, particularly between the state of a person and the state of nature. In this sense the end of "Adam i Eva" is instructive. The hero cannot find a way out of a psychological crisis. Yet, a sense of catharsis emerges in the story through an image of nature, or more precisely, by means of a depiction of nature—the northern lights that accompany the moment of Ageev's separation from Vika: "Suddenly in the sky something like a sigh flew by, and the stars flickered and trembled. The sky darkened, then flickered anew, and rose up flowing with a pale blue trembling light. Ageev turned to the north and instantly saw the source of the light. Out of the church, out of its silent darkness, radiating beams, the weak, pale blue and gold northern lights swayed, shrank, and swelled." This splendid picture, like a materialized metaphor, illuminates the soul of the hero with a consciousness of the developing tragedy:

> The earth rotated. In his legs and in his heart, Ageev suddenly felt how it turned, how it flew along with lakes, with cities, with people, and with their hopes. Surrounded by the lights, it turned and flew into a strange infinity, and on this land, on this island under the silent light, he remained, and she had left him. Eve departed from Adam, and this took place not sometime, but now. And this was like death, which one could regard with derision when far distant, but which was unbearable even to contemplate, if near.

The device of psychological parallelism was born in folklore—particularly in folk poetry. It gradually entered Russian prose from the time of Ivan Sergeevich Turgenev. Different from allegory, the peculiarity of this device is that it does not suggest a direct transference of a person's attributes to nature, or vice versa. It places images of the person and of nature together and arranges them in accordance with some sort of disturbing perceptive relationship. In this parallelism the form of the image from nature can represent that which is impossible to formulate logically or to explain in words. Because of Kazakov, the isolated device of psychological parallelism, familiar in folk poetry, became an integral stylistic principle in Soviet prose of the 1950s and 1960s.

Beginning with the 1960s, Kazakov enriched his nature motifs with new meanings. To the world of his stories he slowly introduced what can be termed the "mysticism of nature." In Boris Leonidovich Pasternak's *Doktor Zhivago* (1958; translated as *Doctor Zhivago*, 1958) it appears as an affirmation of the epic legality of "a miracle of life," not subject to any kind of speculative plans for the administration of existence. In Kazakov's prose the mysticism of nature is, above all, a lyric force; powerful and tender, it radiates warmth, calming and healing one's soul.

In a mystical contact with nature Kazakov's hero even meets with the reverse side of the great universe. In a most mysterious gloom, on the horizon of the bright radiant world of nature, there also lives and moves something so dark, frightening, and terrifying that a person does not realize its presence with his mind but, rather, senses it with his skin, spine, and tensed nerves. This dark and terrifying entity comes into Kazakov's artistic world for the first time in the 1960 story "Kabiasy" (published in 1961 in *Po doroge*), albeit in a somewhat comic scene. The hero, Zhukov, who has lived through several adventures described in the story, is a half-educated, highly insecure manager of a rural club. An old man, the night watchman Matvei, tells Zhukov about a presence of some kind, which Matvei describes as a mysterious "kabiasy"—devils, yet not devils, who are "black with some green"—that appears at night. After hearing Matvei's story, Zhukov ponders a bit and concludes that "my work with atheistic propaganda is just bad, that's what!"

When Zhukov has to return at night from the neighboring *kolkhoz* (collective farm), however, fears brought on by Matvei's account start to stir in him. The "latticed supporting masts" of the trees appear to Zhukov as "a line of gigantic silent creatures, abandoned by other worlds and going silently with upraised hands." The enigmatic dark spots among the empty fields begin to prick up their ears, which "may be bushes, and also may not be bushes." Zhukov grows more scared, as now every rustle, every sound in the dark, and every song of a nocturnal bird arouse terror in him. He even perceives little pine seedlings standing by the road to be those same terrifying "kabiasy" of which the watchman had spoken. There is no thought now of sermons aimed at strengthening atheistic propaganda: "'It's necessary to cross oneself!' thought Zhukov, feeling how they tried to catch him from behind with cold fingers. 'Oh Lord, into your hands. . . .'"

A sense of authorial irony suffuses the descriptions of the night fears that Zhukov, a fighter of superstitions, endures. Yet, the story concludes somewhat paradoxically. At home in his room Zhukov regains his wits, even though he begins to remember how the landscape frightened him: "He was almost asleep, when suddenly everything returned to him. . . . He commenced to relive the whole of his journey, his road, but this time, happily, with a warm feeling for the night, the stars, the aromas, the rustling, and the bird cries." In other words, a feeling for the secret, mysterious life of nature is born in the openhearted club manager, and the introduction—however brief—somehow enriches his soul.

The dark element—the fateful, spellbinding one that conceals itself in nature—appears with increasing frequency in Kazakov's prose of the 1960s and 1970s. The hero of the story "Osen' v dubovykh lesakh" (published 1969 in collection of same name; translated as "Autumn in the Oak Woods," 1970) says, "It's terrifying to go alone at night with a lantern." Darkness is "punctured, as if with a needle, by the buoys burning all along the river," and silence is described as "resonant." In Kazakov's stories, nature generates a certain current, which alerts and sometimes frightens a person, imperiously subduing his spiritual condition, as in the story "Na ostrove" (On the Island, published in 1965 in *Zapakh khleba* [The Smell of Bread]): "After Zabavin visited the cemetery, he got a strange feeling for this island. . . . And because of the mist, and the wild howls of the alouetta monkeys, and the sight of the immobile goats, he felt unwell and wanted conversation, people, and music." Similarly, something in the nature of the Far North seems troubled, compelling, and strange to the narrator in the story "Nestor i Kir" (Nestor and Kir censored in *Prostor* [1965]; full text in *Noygi Mir* [1990]): "So I didn't want to see any more of this gloomy wildness that even got to me."

There has been some speculation—by Vladimir Turbin, Sergei Fediakin, and Igor' Shotkman, for example, that, beginning in the late 1960s, Kazakov suffered a profound psychological and creative crisis. During the second half of this decade he was occupied with his translation of an epic trilogy by the Kazakh writer Abdizhamil Nurpeisov. The translation, titled *Krov' i pot* (Blood and Sweat), appeared in 1969. At the same time, Kazakov's own creative activity was on the wane.

Also during this decade Kazakov spent much time traveling. In the mid 1960s he visited the Baltic regions, the estuary of the Danube, the Pskov region, parts of Siberia, Kazakhstan, Transcarpathia, the Arctic, and satellite countries within the Soviet sphere of influence, such as Romania, Bulgaria, and East Germany. He also went abroad to India, Thailand, Spain, Norway, Holland, Switzerland, West Germany, and the United States. Of all these trips, one held special importance for him. In the spring of 1967 he and the writer Vladimir Alekseevich Souloukhin took an official three-week trip to Paris and Provence. In Paris, Kaza-

*A late photo of Kazakov (Igor' Sergeevich Kuz'michev,* Iurii Kazakov: Nabroski k portretu, *1986; Jean and Alexander Heard Library, Vanderbilt University)*

kov met with Boris Konstantinovich Zaitsev, the émigré writer and critic; in some measure, he was for Kazakov a living link to his idol, Ivan Alekseevich Bunin. During his time in Paris, Kazakov searched out Bunin's "haunts."

The critic Igor' Sergeevich Kuz'michev quotes Kazakov's wife, Tamara Mikhailovna Sudnik, who recalls the effect that Paris had on her husband, whom she married in 1965. For Kazakov, according to Tamara Mikhailovna, the architecture of Paris did not have the "painful" effect that the architecture of St. Petersburg had on him when he first saw it. Rather, he delighted in the offerings of the city–namely, "accessi-

bility and comfort, with its antiquities." Kazakov was smitten with Paris "and without fail wanted to go there again–especially since he had been invited to lecture there about Russian literature."

In the 1970s, when Kazakov was writing rarely, only two stories, which rank among his best, were published–"Svechechka" (A Little Candle) and "Vo sne ty gor'ko plakal" (In Sleep You Wept Bitterly); both first appeared in book form in 1977 in the collection *Vo sne ty gor'ko plakal*. "Svechechka," written not long after Kazakov's son, Aleksei (Alesha), was born in 1967, is constructed as a father's monologue addressed to a son. He reminisces about how things were when his son was still a child and in the process recalls the dark emotions and anguish that would overcome him at certain times, such as when he went for a walk with his son and the world was cast in a gloomy and sad light: "We went with you into the slate darkness of a November evening. . . . Bushes . . . touched our faces and hands, and the touches recalled the time with you, already irretrievable for us, when they bloomed and were always damp with dew." At one point in the story the father recounts a time when his boy wandered off, for a few steps into the darkness, and he became anxious with worry that his son might get lost in the forest. After the child came running back, a dispute broke out. The account of the incident–freshly retraced by the narrator and full of details–grows disturbing, creating the feeling that these events have just occurred. The father peruses each of his son's expressions, probes his painful reflection in the child's condition, and himself suffers the boy's torment.

Behind all the father's emotional reactions is his prayerful relationship to his son. Filled with secular religiosity, Kazakov's story centers on the deification of a child by his father. At the end of the story angelic rays proceed from the sleeping boy. In "Svechechka," Kazakov asserts that the supporting role belongs to the father. Although the father protects his son from all sorts of misfortunes lying in wait at every step, this fragile boy is the one who holds the man, his father, in this life. The son endows the father with a feeling of happiness, delivers him from the horror of mortal loneliness, and saves him from being doomed to vanish without a trace.

"Vo sne ty gor'ko plakal," which Kazakov wrote in 1977, is tied to "Svechechka" in both concept and structure. As in "Svechechka," there are two parts to "Vo sne ty gor'ko plakal," and the first part is filled with existential feelings–only this time they are not bound to the personal fate of the hero-narrator but, rather, to his reminiscences of a friend's suicide. The narrator questions why his friend, a person who really had a complete life—with a wife, children, and grandchildren—killed himself. He recalls his friend's mention of depression and the disappointments that come with the experience of growing old, when the sky ceases to be high and its light seems to have dimmed. The narrator supposes that the terrifying power of the dark and an acute feeling of fatal loneliness drove his friend to suicide.

The second part of "Vo sne ty gor'ko plakal" is about a son, similar to the one who appeared in "Svechechka"—only, the boy's angelic features are more explicit than in the earlier tale. The father remembers what his son looked like when he was a newborn, just home from the hospital: "You were radiant with whiteness, moved your thin little hands and feet, and solemnly regarded us with your big eyes of indeterminate gray-blue color. You were totally miraculous, and there was only one flaw in your appearance—a plaster bandage on your navel." The inner spiritual life of the infant is what concerns the narrator in "Vo sne ty gor'ko plakal." More precisely, the father senses that the infant is inwardly concentrating; he intuits that some kind of mysterious work is in process in the soul of his son. He constantly wants to grasp what the child really thinks and what he knows. He searches for the answer to the question: "thousands of years ago did they sense the mysterious superiority of children? What is it that exalts them above us? Is it innocence, or some kind of higher knowledge that becomes lost in maturity?" In essence, this search for an explanation is reminiscent of what takes place in "Svechechka"—the phenomena of a child's holiness, harmony, and purity.

Beginning in the late 1960s Kazakov lived mostly, as he himself said, "like an anchorite," at his dacha in the Aksakov homestead of Abramtsevo. In 1972 he began to complain of stenocardia and other illnesses. He survived a serious operation and in the autumn of 1982 was confined to a hospital near Moscow. In one of the last letters he wrote, he tells a friend of his medical woes, such as complications from diabetes, and discusses amputations and constant pain. In his last days he suffered from spasms in his brain and searing chest pains. In the early morning of 29 November 1982 Kazakov, suffering from a hemorrhage in the brain, died at age fifty-five. He is buried in a shady, wooded section of the old Bagan'kov Cemetery in Moscow.

During his lifetime Kazakov's works were translated and read in Hungary, Czechoslovakia, Poland, England, the United States, Yugoslavia, France, and Italy. He received recognition in Europe: in 1962, in France, he received the prize for the best book translated into French, and in 1970, he was awarded the Dante Prize. In his own country, however, his reputation remained controversial. Critics recognized in him "an excellent stylist possessing the art of the smooth, fully noble sentence" (Evgenii Osetov). Nevertheless, for a long time his name drew these comments from Stalinist critics: Kazakov is "given to abstract psychologism" and "cut off from the concrete social signs of the time" (Petr Nikolaev); his works are full of "contemplation, thoughtless love of nature" and provide a "doleful, gray, dispirited representation of life" (Larisa Fomenko); he is prone to "borrowed motifs" and "insurmountable stylistic views" (Oleg Mikhailov); and, finally, "despite the living truth of the contemporary Soviet person, always and everywhere he sees the frightfully lonely one, totally unengaged in any general, collective endeavor" (Valerii Bushin, *Literatura i zhizn'*).

For Iurii Pavlovich Kazakov, as he expressed in one of his last interviews (1979), "A good writer is, above all, a writer who thinks about the important questions." The questions that Kazakov considered in his writing concerned morality and the significance of life and death. Literature, he once wrote, should "depict the spiritual movements of a person, and in the main, not the trivial." For this reason he named Leo Tolstoy as the "chief figure. . . . The nobility, the landed gentry, serfdom—all are now gone, but you read him with the same enjoyment as they did a century ago. His description of the soul's impulses has not gone" (*Dve nochi*). The impulses of the soul constituted the main field of Kazakov's artistic analysis. In a quintessential and stubborn way he grasped this "holy of holies" in his heroes, moving from one psychological horizon to another, and at each horizon he opened new dramatic relationships between the person and the world. Kazakov's contributions as a writer are considered among the most significant in the history of mid- to late-twentieth-century Russian literature. A new generation of readers in the twenty-first century has discerned that his writings encompass a whole range of human feelings and emotional states—from delight and tenderness before a miracle of nature to horror and despair at its cruel and implacable laws. This discovery has meant the destruction of prejudiced and superficial judgments; a high regard for Kazakov's words; and a thoughtful penetration into his essence as a writer.

**Letters:**

"Kak liubliu ia liudei . . . Iz pisem Iuriia Kazakova," edited by Mikhail Mikhailovich Roshchin, *Literaturnoe obozrenie*, 8 (1986): 103–112;

"Paket iz Tarusy: Pis'ma Iuriia Kazakova A. I. Shemetovu," edited by Igor' Sergeevich Kuz'michev, *Neva,* 6 (1998): 177–182;

Am-Rus Literary Agency, *Records of the Am-Rus Literary Agency, 1927–1990.*

**Interview:**

Tatiana Aleksandrovna Bek and Oleg Afanas'evich Salynsky, "Dlia chego literatura i dlia chego ia sam?" *Voprosy literatury,* 2 (1979).

**References:**

Vasilii Pavlovich Aksenov [Vassily Aksyonov], "Ne otstavaia ot bystronogogo," *Literaturnaia gazeta,* 15 June 1961;

V. A. Apukhtina, "Russkii Sovetskii rasskaz v sovremennom literaturnom protsesse," *Vestnik Moskovskogo Universiteta. Seriia 9, Filologiia,* 2 (1979): 174–190;

Gundula Bahro, "Intention und Grenzen der lyrischen Prosa bei Juri Kasakow," *Weimarer Beitrage: Zeitschrift für Literaturwissenschaft, Asthetik und Kulturtheorie,* 212, no. 3 (1975): 115–124;

Fidelis Odun Balogun, "The Soviet Russian Short Story, 1950s–1970s," dissertation, University of Illinois, Urbana-Champaign, 1977;

Andrei Georgievich Bitov, "Priamoe vdokhnovenie," *Voprosy literatury,* 7 (1984);

Deming Brown, "The Rise of Short Fiction," in his *Soviet Russian Literature since Stalin* (Cambridge: Cambridge University Press, 1978), pp. 157–161;

Valerii Bushin, "Shtampy byvaiut raznye: Zametki o rasskazakh Iuriia Kazakova," *Literatura i zhizn',* 99 (19 August 1959);

Stephen Francis Carmody, "Influences of Xruščev's Liberalization on Selected Works of Abramov and Kazakov," M.A. thesis, University of Virginia, 1975;

Edward M. Davis, "Nature in the Short Stories of Jurij Kazakov," M.A. thesis, University of North Carolina at Chapel Hill, 1976;

L. Fomenko, "Iskosstvo maloi prozy," *Zvezda,* 3 (1960): 193–200;

Elena Sh. Galimova, *Khudozhestvennyi mir Iuriia Kazakova* (Arkhangel'sk: Izdatel'stvo Pomorskogo gosudarstvennogo pedagogicheskogo universiteta, 1992);

Roman Gershkovich, "Iurii Kazakov (1927–1982): Growth of the Writer's Consciousness," dissertation, Cornell University, 1992;

Gleb Aleksandrovich Goryshin, "Chestnost' zvan'ia svoego . . . ," *Literaturnaia gazeta,* 5 August 1987, p. 7;

Goryshin, "Snachala bylo slovo: Vospominaniia o Iuriie Kazakove," *Nash sovremennik,* 12 (1986): 157–173;

Aleksei Ivanov, "Toska po svetu: Vospominaia Iuriia Kazakova," *Literaturnaia gazeta,* 13 August 1997, p. 12;

Viktor Isaakovich Kamianov, "Moderne Literatur und Klassik im Vergleich," translated by Leon Nebenzahl, *Kunst und Literatur: Zeitschrift für Fragen der Aesthetik und Kunsttheorie,* 30, no. 6 (1982): 575–599;

Mikhail Kholmogorov, "Eto zhe smertel'noe delo! . . . ," *Voprosy literatury,* 3 (1994);

Viktor Viktorovich Konetsky, "Literaturnaia obstanovka kontsa 50-kh; Sovsem raznye pis'ma," in his *Nekotorym obrazom drama: Neputevye zametki, pis'ma* (Leningrad: Sovetskii pisatel', 1989), pp. 18–34, 209–241;

Konetsky, "Opiat' nazvanie ne pridumyvaetsia," *Neva,* 4 (1986): 65–107;

Isaak Naumovich Kramov, "Khleb i sol' zhizni: O rasskazakh Jurija Kazakova," *Nash sovremennik,* 14, no. 12 (1977): 170–178; translated by William Mandel as "The 'Bread' and 'Salt' of Life: On Iurii Kazakov's Stories," *Soviet Studies in Literature,* 15, no. 2 (1979): 3–27;

Valentin Iakovlevich Kurbatov, "Stikhiia i mera," *Literaturnoe obozrenie,* 3 (1987): 41–44;

Igor' Sergeevich Kuz'michev, *Iurii Kazkov: Nabroski k portretu* (Leningrad: Sovetskii pisatel'/Leningradskoe otdelenie, 1986);

Kuz'michev, *Mechtateli i stranniki: Literaturnye portrety* (Leningrad: Sovetskii pisatel'/Leningradskoe otdelenie, 1992);

Mikhail Lapshin, "Uroki idushchim vosled: Shtrikhi k portretu Iuriia Kazakova," *Moskva,* 10 (1987): 196–201;

Maria Arkad'evna Litovskaia, "'Ontologicheskaia proza' v otsenke 'gnoseologicheskoi' kritiki," in *Khudozhestvennaia literatura, kritika i publitsistika v sisteme dukhovnoi kul'tury* (Tiumen': Izdatel'stvo Tiumenskogo universiteta, 1997);

N. G. Makhinina, *Problema nravstvennykh tsennostei v tvorchestve Iu. P. Kazakova,* Avtoreferat dissertatsii . . . kandidata filologicheskikh nauk (Kazan': Kazanskii gosudarstvennyi universitet, 1997);

Nancy Ann McAuliffe, "Jurij Kazakov: A Study in Molodaja Proza," M.A. thesis, Brown University, 1966;

Aleksandr Alekseevich Mikhailov, "Dolgie kriki (Iurii Kazakov)," in his *Moia Giperboreiia: Stat'i o literature, vospominaniia* (Arkhangel'sk: Izdatel'stvo Pomorskogo gosudarstvennogo universiteta, 1999);

Iurii Markovich Nagibin, "Svoe i chuzhoe," *Druzhba narodov,* 7 (1959);

Pyotr Nikolaev, "Lichnost,' moral', literature," *Moskva*, 3 (1962): 167–175;

Fediakin Sergei Nikolaevich, "Nostal'gia," *Literaturnoe obozrenie*, 4 (1989): 91–95;

Aleksandr Alekseevich Ninov, "Iurii Kazakov," in his *Skvoz' tridtsat' let: Problemy, portray, polemika 1956–1986* (Leningrad: Sovetskii pisatel'/Leningradskoe otdelenie, 1987);

Aleksandr Ivanovich Ovcharenko, "V polemicheskom azarte," in his *Bol'shaia literatura: Osnovnye tendentsii razvitiia sovetskoi khudozhestvennoi prozy 1945–1985* (Moscow: Sovremennik, 1985);

Konstantin Georgievich Paustovsky, "Besspornye i spornye mysli," *Literaturnaia gazeta*, 20 May 1959;

Evgenii Aleksandrovich Shklovsky, "Dal'nii put' k blizkim: Zametki o proze Iuriia Kazakova," *Detskaia literatura*, 8 (1987);

Igor' Georgievich Shtokman, "Adam i Eva: Liubov', poiski schast'ia i geroi Iuriia Kazakova" and "Dolgoe ekho, chto ostavil nam Iurii Kazakov," in his *Zhizn' na miru* (Moscow: Kliuch, 1996), pp. 114–133, 134–139;

Mark Slonim, *Soviet Russian Literature: Writers and Problems (1917–1977)* (New York: Oxford University Press, 1977), pp. 348–350;

Inna Iosifovna Solov'eva, "Nachalo puti," *Novyi mir*, 9 (1959);

Timothy Preston Spengler, "The Motif of Love in the Works of Ju. P. Kazakov," M.A. thesis, Ohio State University, 1972;

Elena Tarasova, "On kazalsia togda po-nastoiashchemu schastlivym: Iurii Kazakov: Nachalo puti," *Nash sovremennik*, 8 (1997): 222–227;

Aleksandr Trifonovich Tvardovsky, "Iurii Kazakov. Rasskazy," in his *Sobranie sochinenii*, volume 6 (Moscow: Khudozhestvennaia literatura, 1980), pp. 291–292;

Tamara Zhirmunskaia, *My–schastlivye liudi* (Moscow: Latmes, 1995).

**Papers:**

The papers of Iurii Pavlovich Kazakov are kept by his widow, Tamara Mikhailovna Sudnik-Kazakova.

# Anatolii Kuznetsov
## (A. Anatoly)
### (18 August 1929 – 13 June 1979)

Jennifer Ryan Tishler
*University of Wisconsin–Madison*

See also the Kuznetsov entry in *DLB 299: Holocaust Novelists*.

BOOKS: *Prodolzhenie legendy: Zapiski molodogo cheloveka* (Moscow: Gosudarstvennoe izdatel'stvo detskoi literatury, 1958); translated by R. Bobrova as *Sequel to a Legend: From the Diary of a Young Man* (Moscow: Foreign Languages Publishing House, 1959); translated by William E. Butler as *The Journey* (Dobbs Ferry, N.Y.: Transnational, 1984);

*V solnechnyi den': Rasskazy,* by Kuznetsov, L. Vinogradov, and I. Vinogradova (Moscow: Sovetskaia Rossiia, 1960);

*Bienie zhizni: Rasskazy* (Moscow: Sovetskaia Rossiia, 1961);

*Selenga: Rasskazy* (Moscow: Sovetskii pisatel', 1961);

*Avgustovskii den': Rasskazy* (Moscow: Pravda, 1962);

*Moreplavateli* (Tula: Priokskoe knizhnoe izdatel'stvo, 1966);

*U sebia doma* (Moscow: Molodaia gvardiia, 1964);

*Babii Iar: Roman-dokument* (Moscow: Molodaia gvardiia, 1967); translated by Jacob Guralsky as *Babi Yar: A Documentary Novel* (New York: Dell, 1967; London: MacGibbon & Kee, 1967); uncensored and enlarged Russian edition, as A. Anatoly (Frankfurt am Main: Posev, 1970); translated by David Floyd as *Babi Yar: A Document in the Form of a Novel* (London: Cape, 1970; New York: Farrar, Straus & Giroux, 1970).

SELECTED PERIODICAL PUBLICATIONS—
UNCOLLECTED: "Artist mimansa," *Novyi mir,* no. 4 (1968): 58;

"Ogon'," *Iunost',* 3 (1969): 2–39; 4 (1969): 16–50;

"Kuznetsov Gives Account of Furor over Novel," *New York Times,* 7 August 1969, p. A1.

*Anatolii Kuznetsov (Sequel to a Legend [Moscow: Foreign Languages Publishing House, 1959]; Thomas Cooper Library, University of South Carolina)*

Classified by some critics as a dissident writer, yet condemned by his fellow dissidents for his complicity with the Komissariat gosudarstvennoi bezopasnosti (KGB, State Security Committee), Anatolii Kuznetsov is best known for his *Babii Iar: Roman-dokument* (1967;

translated as *Babi Yar: A Documentary Novel*, 1967), which tells the story of the Nazi massacre of Jews outside Kiev. As a whole, Kuznetsov's writings are remarkable more for their subject matter than for their literary form, and the quality of his literary output is likewise overshadowed by the details of his biography. Kuznetsov's fate as a writer illustrates the unsettled period in Soviet society known as the "Thaw," generally understood as a period of relative truthfulness and openness in Soviet literature. The period of the Thaw was ushered in soon after the death of Joseph Stalin on 5 March 1953 and was strengthened by Nikita Khrushchev's 1956 secret speech to the Twentieth Party Congress, in which he denounced the excesses of Stalin's "cult of personality." The Thaw was not a constantly progressive loosening of Communist Party control over literature but rather came in a series of waves. The publication histories of Kuznetsov's major works demonstrate a pattern by which writers' hopes and expectations for greater freedom of expression and greater truthfulness in literature were often met with a reactionary backlash.

Anatolii Vasil'evich Kuznetsov was born on 18 August 1929 to a working-class family in Kurenevka, on the outskirts of Kiev, Ukraine. His father, Vasilii Gerasimovich Kuznetsov, had joined the Communist Party in 1918 and fought on the side of the Reds in the Russian Civil War. His mother, Mariia Fedorovna Kuznetsova, was a grade-school teacher. Kuznetsov was twelve years old when the Nazis took Kiev in 1941; the German occupation was the formative event of his early years. At the age of fourteen he began to keep a diary, in which he recorded his experiences and observations of the occupation, including what he saw and heard of the mass killings at Babii Iar, a ravine not far from his home, where almost two hundred thousand people, mostly Jews but also Ukrainians and Roma, were killed during the two-year occupation.

Kuznetsov's first publications were short stories that appeared in 1946 in *Pionerskaia Pravda* (Pioneer Truth), the Communist Party newspaper for children. In 1952 he worked as a carpenter and bulldozer operator on the construction site of the Kakhovskaia hydroelectric power station on the Dnieper River. During this time he also published stories in the plant newspaper. Attending night school, he finished the tenth grade in 1954 and then enrolled at the Gor'ky Institute of Literature in Moscow. He was admitted to the Communist Party in 1955.

In 1956, while still enrolled at the Gor'ky Institute, Kuznetsov was sent by the recently founded journal *Iunost'* (Youth) to the construction site of the Irkutsk hydroelectric power station, where he worked mixing concrete. He wrote about this experience in his short novel for young readers, *Prodolzhenie legendy: Zapiski molodogo cheloveka* (1958; translated as *Sequel to a Legend: From the Diary of a Young Man*, 1959). The book takes the form of a diary written by the semi-autobiographical Tolia, a young man from Moscow who has just graduated from school with mediocre grades and no clear prospects. As the book opens, Tolia is on a train headed to Siberia in order to join a work crew. He ends up in Irkutsk, where he signs up as a concrete mixer at the power station. Through hard work and much contemplation, young Tolia finally breaks through the false optimism of his childhood and comes to see the contradictions of reality with the eyes of an adult.

When *Prodolzhenie legendy* first appeared in print, some critics dismissed it as a pleasant but not enduring book, noting the insignificance of Tolia's trials in relation to the importance of a major construction site and faulting Kuznetsov for not understanding the lives of young people. Favorable criticism of the book noted its timeliness, since it appeared during a period of debate about educational reform in Soviet society: how to make the transformation from school to work more coherent. Moreover, critics praised Kuznetsov's depiction of everyday life in the novel: Tolia's personal musings are accompanied by the noise and motion of large-scale construction and the diverse voices of workers who have come to the site from all over the Soviet Union. Kuznetsov was also praised for his positive depiction of physical labor as a key component in building character.

Through the confessional structure of the book, the young hero reveals not only his successes, but also his doubts, which reflects the candor in Soviet literature and life that was one of the hallmarks of the cultural Thaw. Moreover, *Prodolzhenie legendy* was among the works that heralded the new genre of *molodezhnaia povest'* (youth story). In the spirit of the *molodezhnaia povest'*, a young narrator such as Tolia would seem to be more honest and trustworthy than an older one. *Iunost'* was the pulpit for this youth trend in literature. In addition to Kuznetsov, young writers such as Vasily Pavlovich Aksyonov and Andrei Georgievich Bitov appeared in print, eager to express their distinctive outlooks. Kuznetsov not only published many of his works in *Iunost'* but later served on its editorial board for a brief time.

The legend in the title of the novel refers to Siberian lore about the Angara and Enisei Rivers, personified as a maiden and a warrior. In the novel a young mother tells her son a bedtime story about Angara and Enisei, but rather than ending the story at the point where the hero and heroine live happily ever after, she continues her tale. According to the mother's elaboration, Angara and Enisei experienced true happiness only when humans built dams on the rivers and harnessed the hydroelectric power. True happiness, the

*Front cover for the first English-language edition of the uncensored version of Kuznetsov's "document novel" about atrocities committed against Russian Jews during the German occupation of Kiev in 1941. The title refers to a ravine in the city where an estimated 100,000 people were slaughtered (Bruccoli Clark Layman Archives).*

book teaches its young readership, is never easy, but must be hard-won, often involving physical labor. Kuznetsov also polemicizes with the Soviet myth of human conquest of nature as embodied by the massive building projects of the 1930s, such as the Uralmash industrial complex. In contrast to the positive heroes of earlier Soviet literature, who never doubted in their abilities or in the worthiness of their goals, Kuznetsov's young narrator uses his participation in the construction project in order to test himself. His hard work does not merely have a social goal—the completion of a power plant—but is also the means to a greater self-awareness. Tolia, in contrast to the extraordinary literary heroes of the 1930s, demonstrates his humanity and physical limitations: he lands in the hospital when he pushes himself to work too hard.

In 1960 Kuznetsov completed his studies at the Gor'ky Institute of Literature. He published several collections of short stories, including *Selenga* (1961), *Bienie zhizni* (The Pulse of Life, 1961), and *U sebia doma* (At Home, 1964). None of these works received the same attention as *Prodolzhenie legendy*. Kuznetsov received renewed consideration, however, not all of it positive, with the publication of *Babii Iar*. *Babii Iar*, which documents the German occupation of Kiev during World War II, is Kuznetsov's most significant—and controversial—literary work. The book carries the subtitle *Roman-dokument* (Novel-document), which designates the integration of literary elements and factual records. To write the book, Kuznetsov not only drew upon his own wartime diary but also interviewed survivors of the occupation and studied newspapers and other written documents of that period. *Babii Iar* weaves together the direct, spontaneous language of Tolik, the young narrator, with documents from the time period, such as copies of Nazi proclamations, newspaper stories, and leaflets. Occasionally the narration shifts from that of Tolik in 1941–1943 to the adult author-narrator of the 1960s.

*Babii Iar* was highly problematic for the literary establishment for several reasons. First, Soviet authorities had long suppressed the fact that the Nazis singled out Jews for annihilation; official doctrine emphasized Soviet losses and sacrifices in World War II. While the poet Evgenii Aleksandrovich Yevtushenko had already broached the topic of the Jewish massacre in his 1961 poem "Babii Iar," Kuznetsov's novel probed further, addressing such forbidden topics as Russian and Ukrainian anti-Semitism, the fact that many Ukrainians initially welcomed the invading Germans as liberators, and the complicity of the local police force in carrying out the killings. Kuznetsov and Yevtushenko had studied together at the Gor'ky Institute in the 1950s, and Kuznetsov claimed that he had first given the poet the idea for "Babii Iar" when he brought Yevtushenko to see the site of the mass murders.

Kuznetsov faced many trials in seeing his book to print. He first attempted to publish the novel in *Iunost'*, where the editors accused him of being anti-Soviet. The writer was forced to remove approximately one-quarter of the text, including references to Stalin and the Great Terror of the 1930s, the retreat of the Red Army at the beginning of World War II, and discussions of official plans to excavate and flatten the ravine in order to prevent it from becoming a discomforting memorial site. In the autumn of 1966 *Iunost'* began to publish the censored text serially. As Kuznetsov later wrote, he was especially irked by a tiny footnote on the first page of the *Iunost'* publication that identified this publication of *Babii Iar* as a *zhurnal'nyi variant* (magazine version). The sole indication that this version of his novel had been censored, the phrase suggested that the work had been edited solely for length, not for content. A book, slightly more comprehensive than the magazine version, was published by

Molodaia gvardiia but then quickly recalled as a "mistake." Even in its censored form, the novel caused a sensation when it appeared in print.

Khrushchev had been removed from power in 1964. With Leonid Brezhnev taking over as first secretary of the Communist Party, there could be no question that the cultural Thaw had ended. In the atmosphere of neo-Stalinism cultivated under Brezhnev, writers once again became targets of searches, and Kuznetsov was no exception. Afraid to keep the unabridged manuscript of *Babii Iar* in his apartment, Kuznetsov found various hiding places for it, going so far as to seal pages of the manuscript in glass jars and bury them in the woods outside Tula. Nevertheless, the official literary establishment considered Kuznetsov reliable enough to promote him to the editorial board of *Iunost'* in May 1969, following the removal of three of the leading liberal writers: Yevtushenko, Aksyonov, and Viktor Sergeevich Rozov. Kuznetsov's name, however, appeared on the *Iunost'* masthead for only one issue of the journal.

Kuznetsov was already considering emigrating from the Soviet Union when he devised a plan for leaving: in preparation for the 1970 centennial celebration of Vladimir Il'ich Lenin's birth, Kuznetsov proposed to make an official research trip to London in order to collect material about Lenin's participation in the Second Congress of the Russian Social-Democratic Workers' Party, which took place in London in August 1903. The KGB approached Kuznetsov with a proposal: he would be issued a visa to exit the Soviet Union only if he first informed on his fellow writers to the secret service. Kuznetsov informed against his own friend, the poet Yevtushenko. He later claimed that he had fabricated his report on Yevtushenko—that the poet was involved in a conspiracy to publish an underground magazine—believing that this story was too outlandish for the authorities to believe and so would not do Yevtushenko any real harm.

On 24 July 1969 Kuznetsov departed for his official trip to London on an invitation from the Society for Cultural Relations with the U.S.S.R. On 30 July, Kuznetsov announced his defection and requested official permission to remain indefinitely in Great Britain, which the Home Office granted on 31 July. He never returned to the Soviet Union. He left behind his mother; his estranged wife, Irina Marchenko; and his nine-year-old son, Aleksei. On 31 July the Soviet Writers' Union expelled Kuznetsov for "betrayal of the homeland, for treason to the cause of socialism, and for political and moral double-dealing." Condemnation of Kuznetsov came not just from the authorities but also from Western writers and Soviet dissidents. The American playwright Lillian Hellman and American novelist William Styron also attacked Kuznetsov in the press, accusing him of cowardice for not remaining in the Soviet Union to oppose and reform the system, as other writers had done, and suggesting that those writers who had stayed behind would now be harmed by Kuznetsov's defection. Kuznetsov rejoined that people in the West were deluded about the true conditions in the Soviet Union and suggested caustically that Styron go live for a year in Kuznetsov's vacant Tula apartment before passing judgment. Andrei Alekseevich Amalrik, although defending Kuznetsov's right to leave the Soviet Union, chastised the writer in the Winter/Spring 1970 issue of *Survey: A Journal of Soviet and East European Studies* for his collaboration with the KGB and his "philosophy of impotence and self-justification." Kuznetsov, according to Amalrik, had chosen the external freedom of life in the West at the cost of the inner freedom of living according to one's moral values.

In London, Kuznetsov adopted the name A. Anatoly (or A. Anatol, according to some newspapers), renouncing those works written under the name Kuznetsov as having been distorted by political censors. The writer made several public statements to elaborate on the workings of Soviet literary censorship, including a detailed account about the publication and translation of *Prodolzhenie legendy*. According to Kuznetsov, when he had first submitted the manuscript to the editors of *Iunost'*, they informed him that the novel, despite its appeal, would not pass censorship because it did not depict life in Siberia in an adequately positive light. Then in 1961 Kuznetsov discovered that, without his permission, *Iunost'* had published his novel, reworked and edited by someone who had given the book an ideologically optimistic tone. The novel was a great success in the Soviet Union and was translated into several languages, among them a French version, published in 1958 under the title *L'Etoile dans le Brouillard* (The Star in the Mist). The translator, Paul Chaleil, was a Jesuit priest who had been a missionary in China, was turned over to the Soviets, was a forced laborer at the same Irkutsk work site that Kuznetsov had described, and was eventually rescued by the Red Cross. His translation, which eliminated or merely summarized the most optimistic passages of Kuznetsov's novel, was denounced in the Soviet Union as a distorted, unauthorized translation, and Kuznetsov filed a suit against the publishing house of the Roman Catholic Archdiocese of Lyons. A French court ruled against the translation and awarded Kuznetsov damages of Fr 1,000 (at the time, approximately $200). Once in London, Kuznetsov praised Chaleil for his insight in having guessed so well the author's true thoughts that he passed over the overly sunny sections. Kuznetsov revealed that the Soviet literary establishment had forced him to bring about the lawsuit, and so he asked the French courts to reconsider the case.

Kuznetsov found work typical for representatives of the so-called third wave of Soviet emigration, becoming a correspondent for Radio Liberty. He did not write any new works but published the full, uncensored version of *Babii Iar*, a microfilm copy of which he had smuggled out in his clothing. This new version included all the passages that censors had removed from the first edition, as well as new passages, which Kuznetsov, working under a principle of self-censorship, had not included in his original manuscript. This expanded version of the novel includes typographical clues, allowing the reader to trace its evolution. Sections in normal type were published by *Iunost'* in 1966, sections in italics were removed by the censor prior to the 1966 publication, and sections contained in brackets are additions written between 1967 and 1969.

In May 1979 a daughter, Maria, was born to Kuznetsov and his second wife, Jolana, a Polish journalist he had met in London. On 13 June, Kuznetsov died at Whittington Hospital in London after suffering a heart attack at his home. His first wife died in Kiev in 1995. Their son, Aleksei, is a correspondent for Radio Liberty in Moscow. Anatolii Kuznetsov's letters from London to his mother in Kiev were published by Aleksei in 2002. In the letters Kuznetsov avoids discussions of politics and literature; instead, he shares the small details of his new life in London, such as gardening, shopping, and travel.

The uncensored version of *Babii Iar* was not published in Russia until 1991. *Babii Iar* remains Anatolii Kuznetsov's most significant literary work. In its uncensored form, the novel notes the striking resemblance between the two totalitarian regimes of Stalin and Adolf Hitler. Some critics have made a connection between *Babii Iar* and Vasilii Semenovich Grossman's *Zhizn' i Sud'ba* (completed in 1960 but unpublished until 1980; translated as *Life and Fate*, 1985), which also demonstrated the ties between Soviet Communism and German Nazism at a time when few made that connection.

**Letters:**

*Mezhdu Grenvichim i Kurenëvkoi: Pis'ma Anatoliia Kuznetsova materi iz emigratsii v Kiev,* edited by Aleksei Kuznetsov (Moscow: Zakharov, 2002).

**References:**

Andrei Alekseevich Amalrik, "An Open Letter to Kuznetsov" and "I Want to Be Understood Correctly," *Survey: A Journal of Soviet and East European Studies,* 74/75 (Winter/Spring 1970): 95–102, 102–110;

Lady Falls Brown, "The White Hotel: D. M. Thomas's Considerable Debt to Anatoli Kuznetsov and Babi Yar," *South Central Review,* 2 (1985): 60–79;

John L. Hess, "French Reopen Literary Suit Won by Kuznetsov," *New York Times,* 8 August 1969, p. A3;

N. Makarova, "O bor'be 'protiv' i bor'be 'za'," *Znamia,* 9 (1958): 176–189;

Abraham Rothberg, "The Kuznetsov Case," in his *The Heirs of Stalin: Dissidence and the Soviet Regime, 1953–1970* (Ithaca, N.Y. & London: Cornell University Press, 1972), pp. 251–276;

Harrison E. Salisbury, "Kuznetsov Backs Soviet on China," *New York Times,* 24 August 1969, p. A20;

Israel Shenker, "Russian Defector Anatoly Vailyevich Kuznetsov," *New York Times,* 1 August 1969, p. A2;

"Soviet Writer Defends Publisher He Attacked in '61," *New York Times,* 7 August 1969, p. A14;

Victor Terras, "Anatolii Vasil'evich Kuznetsov," in *A Handbook of Russian Literature,* edited by Terras (New Haven & London: Yale University Press, 1985), p. 240;

"3 Soviet Liberals Lose Posts on Magazine Editorial Board," *New York Times,* 22 July 1969, p. A6;

Zoia Vatnikova-Prizelk, "Babii Iar A. Anatoliia (Kuznetsova): Novaia (sinkreticheskaia) forma memuarnoi literatury," *Russian Language Journal,* 106 (1976): 143–152;

James E. Young, "Holocaust Documentary Fiction: The Novelist as Eyewitness," in *Writing and the Holocaust,* edited by Berel Lang (New York: Holmes & Meier, 1988), pp. 200–215.

# Vladimir Emel'ianovich Maksimov

*(27 November 1930 – 26 March 1995)*

Peter Rollberg
*George Washington University*

BOOKS: *Pokolenie na chasakh* (Cherkessiia: Knigoizdatel'stvo, 1956);

*Zhiv chelovek* (Moscow: Molodaia gvardiia, 1964)—comprises *Zhiv chelovek,* translated by Anselm Hollo as *A Man Survives* (New York: Grove Press, 1963); and *My obzhivaem zemliu;*

*Povesti. Rasskazy* (Magadan: Magadanskoe izdatel'stvo, 1965);

*Pozyvnye tvoikh paralellei* (Moscow, 1965);

*Zhiv chelovek. Povesti. Rasskazy* (Magadan: Knigoizdatel'stvo, 1965);

*Zhiv chelovek. Drama* (Moscow, 1965);

*Shagi k gorizontu. Rasskazy* (Moscow: Pravda, 1966)—includes "Iskushenie" and "Dusia i nas piatero";

*Shagi k gorizontu. Povesti* (Moscow: Sovetskii pisatel', 1967);

*Dom bez nomera* (Moscow, 1969);

*My obzhivaem zemliu* (Moscow: Sovetskaia Rossiia, 1970);

*Sem' dnei tvoreniia* (Frankfurt am Main: Posev, 1971); translated as *The Seven Days of Creation* (London: Weidenfeld & Nicolson, 1974; New York: Knopf, 1975);

*Karantin* (Frankfurt am Main: Posev, 1973);

*Proshchanie iz niotkuda* (Frankfurt am Main: Posev, 1974; enlarged edition, Orange, Conn.: Antiquary, 1988); translated by Michael Glenny as *Farewell from Nowhere* (London: Harvill Press; Garden City, N.Y.: Doubleday, 1979);

*Saga o Savve* (Frankfurt am Main: Posev, 1975);

*Sobranie sochinenii,* 6 volumes (Frankfurt am Main: Posev, 1975–1979);

*Kovcheg dlia nezvanykh* (Frankfurt am Main: Posev, 1979); translated by Julian Graffy as *Ark for the Uncalled* (London & New York: Quartet, 1984);

*Zhiv chelovek* (Frankfurt am Main: Posev, 1979);

*Saga o nosorogakh* (Frankfurt am Main: Posev, 1981);

*Chasha iarosti* (Frankfurt am Main: Posev, 1982);

*Zaglianut' v bezdnu* (Paris & New York: CASE.-Tret'ia volna, 1986);

*Zvezda Admirala Kolchaka* (Minsk: Eridan, 1991);

*Izbrannoe* (Moscow: Terra, 1994);

*Vladimir Emel'ianovich Maksimov (from* Zaglianut' v bezdnu, *1986; Gabriel Library, University of the South)*

*Samoistreblenie* (Moscow: Golos, 1995);

*Dvor posredi neba* (Moscow: Progress, 1999).

**Edition:** *Kovcheg dlia nezvanykh. Zaglianut' v bezdnu* (Moscow: Voskresenie, 1994).

**Collection:** *Sobranie sochinenii,* 8 volumes (Moscow: Terra, 1991–1993).

OTHER: Midin Alybaev, *Razgovor s sovremennikom,* translated by Maksimov (Frunze: Kirgizgosizdat, 1958);

Mariiam Bulakieva, *Vernost'. Stikhi,* translated by Maksimov (Frunze: Kirgizgosizdat, 1958);

*Kontinent,* edited by Maksimov (New York: Arno, 1976).

Few Russian writers went through as many diverse life experiences as did Vladimir Maksimov. He traversed all strata of Soviet society, transforming himself from a lowly criminal outcast to a controversial member of the Moscow literary intelligentsia. His travels, whether by choice or mandatory, encompassed the vast Soviet Union and, after his forced emigration, the entire world. Many of these experiences became the raw material on which he later drew as a novelist. They informed his prose with a freshness, immediacy, and authenticity—even the works of a lesser artistic quality was absent.

In histories of Russian literature Maksimov often is referred to as an émigré author of the "third wave"—that is, as one of the many writers who left the Soviet Union during the years of Leonid Il'ich Brezhnev's rule. Maksimov's worldview and aesthetic peculiarities set him apart, however, from the émigré and dissident mainstream of that period, a fact that finally became obvious after the breakup of the U.S.S.R., when he recanted some of his earlier anti-Soviet statements. In hindsight his earlier abandonment of Communist Russia was symptomatic of a life filled with restless wanderings from its very beginning. Deprived of family comfort at the age of three, after which he was often a ward of the state, Maksimov always reacted with emotional sensitivity when his freedom and independence were threatened, whether such threats were Soviet and Communist in origin or, in his later years, "Western." This sensitivity toward external limitations to the individual formed a central theme that lies at the heart of most of his prose works—the painful incompatibility of individual emotional needs with societal pressures. In the stories *Zhiv chelovek* (1963; translated as *A Man Survives,* 1963) and "Saga o Savve" (1975, Legend of Savva), for example, the main hero is invariably a social outsider who has been brutally ostracized by his environment; he is Maksimov's alter ego in a world of criminals, hobos, and other dropouts. Maksimov knew the Soviet social underground intimately, and his testimony against Communism was rooted in that milieu of underdogs that includes former peasants and workers—in other words, precisely those classes that supposedly had been liberated by the Soviet system. As Arnold McMillin once described, Maksimov will be remembered as the "creator of subtle and complex novels which, for all their apocalyptically anti-Soviet content and seemingly over-simple Christian solutions, form an important part of Russian prose of the 1970s and 1980s, a powerful individual witness of the lower depths of Soviet society."

Maksimov was born Lev Alekseevich Samsonov on 27 November 1930 in Moscow (other sources indicate 9 December 1932 and Leningrad as, respectively, the date and place of birth) into the family of a former peasant. The name Vladimir Emel'ianovich Maksimov was given to him arbitrarily when he was confined to an orphanage after one of the many arrests of his father, Aleksei Samsonov. Maksimov's grandfather was an active revolutionary who, after the October Revolution, became a commissar in charge of railroads; he was later arrested, however, and sentenced to a term in the gulag. His life after his release from the camps ended in poverty. Maksimov's earliest childhood memories were overshadowed by the ordeal of fatherlessness. Samsonov, born in 1901, had fought in the Red Army. As a follower of Leon Trotsky (whose real name was Lev Davydovich Bronshtein and after whom Samsonov named his son), however, he was arrested several times between 1927 and 1938. He spent the subsequent years in Soviet camps and prisons. When Nazi Germany invaded the Soviet Union in June 1941, thus beginning the period of World War II known to Soviets as the Great Patriotic War, Samsonov volunteered for service; he died that year during a German bombardment. The young Maksimov was raised in orphanages and spent 1945–1950 in correctional institutions for juvenile delinquents, called "children's colonies." He then received a professional education as a construction worker and mason and was employed in factories and collective farms in various regions of the Soviet Union. As a young man he also participated in diamond expeditions in the Taimyr Mountains.

The 1950s were a turning point for Maksimov. In the early part of the decade he discovered literature as a medium of self-expression. In the late 1950s, particularly through the writings of Fyodor Dostoevsky, Nikolai Aleksandrovich Berdiaev, Pavel Aleksandrovich Florensky, and Sergei Nikolaevich Bulgakov, he came to see Christianity as a spiritual guide. These realizations proved crucial for the shaping of Maksimov as an artist and as a man. In his view writing and religious faith were inseparably linked. In 1952 he began to write poetry and prose; some minor pieces were published in journals (mostly in *Stalinskoe znamia* [The Banner of Stalin]) of the Kuban' region, where he was living at the time. What was meant to become his first book, a collection of early poetry, was destroyed, however, on administrative orders in 1954. Maksimov also worked as a radio journalist in Cherkessiia.

In 1956 Maksimov's first book publication appeared. *Pokolenie na chasakh* (A Generation on Guard) was a collection of verse, including long narrative poems, and came out after he had moved to Moscow to make a living as a freelance writer for newspapers and journals. He first gained renown with a work of prose fiction, the *povest'* (novella) *My obzhivaem zemliu* (We Make the Earth Feel Homey), which Konstantin Georgievich Paustovsky included in his 1961 almanac *Tarusskie stranitsy* (Pages from Tarusa). In 1963 Maksimov was admitted as a full member to the Soviet Writers' Union and his novella *Zhiv chelovek* was published in English. It won considerable recognition all over the Soviet Union and was successfully adapted by Maksimov for the stage by the Moscow Pushkin Drama Theater in 1965. The plot centers on the fate of a youth who becomes an outcast to society and thus is increasingly isolated. *Zhiv chelovek* fit in the atmosphere of the 1960s, with heightened interest during that time in the social and psychological problems of young people and a rediscovery of the individual, especially after a long period of unchallenged collectivism. Somewhat more unusual was Maksimov's short story "Iskushenie" (1966, The Temptation), which features a war invalid who is abandoned by his wife and escapes to a monastery. Soviet critics noted that other stories by Maksimov, such as "Dusia i nas piatero" (1966, Dusia and the Five of Us), focused on people with "scattered lives" but conceded that he nonetheless emphasized the idea of man's moral steadiness. What official critics were not free to mention (and what Maksimov himself could only hint at) were the actual roots of this steadiness—a spirituality beyond the Communist doctrine, one that was Christian in essence.

From October 1967 to August 1968 Maksimov served as a member of the editorial board of the literary journal *Oktiabr'* (October). He left his position in protest of the 1968 Soviet-led invasion of Czechoslovakia. This gesture suddenly turned him into an open dissident whose every step was watched closely by the Soviet authorities. He was incarcerated twice in psychiatric hospitals as a result of his political stance. Since most official publishing venues would not accept his work, Maksimov consequently turned to samizdat, the common practice of underground self-publishing by dissidents. For the next four years he was constantly harassed by the Komitet gosudarstvennoi bezopasnosti (KGB, State Security Committee) and repeatedly threatened with imprisonment. During those years, when Maksimov's name more and more symbolized resistance to Communist tyranny, he published the one work that has remained his best known to this day.

*Sem' dnei tvoreniia* (1971; translated as *The Seven Days of Creation*, 1974), a novel that had been rejected by Soviet publishers and widely circulated in samizdat editions, presents a radically negative depiction of fifty years of Soviet history from the point of view of one family. At the center is a disillusioned revolutionary, Petr Vasil'evich Lashkov, a widower and father of six. Lashkov is a retired functionary in his seventies who lives in the provincial town of Uzlovsk. Portrayed as the typical "decent" Communist—that is, an idealistic and selfless Communist—he would never think of exploiting his position to gain privileges, and his loyalty to the party is unshakable. Lashkov's youngest daughter, a severe alcoholic, is deeply unhappy in her private life. His other children, who left home long ago, are estranged from him; his brothers also are not close to him. Lashkov lost all interest in life after Mariia, his wife, died two decades earlier. He has become apathetic toward the disintegration of his family. Yet, when trying to understand what may have caused his daughter's condition, he takes a closer look at his family history. Since Mariia was an Orthodox believer, a perceived anomaly in Soviet Russia that he tolerated out of love for her despite his atheist convictions, Lashkov undertakes a revision of his own attitude toward the transcendental. These introspective parts dominate much of the novel. They convey a sense of Lashkov's spiritual growth, for at the end he undergoes an awakening that is described by Maksimov as based on divine inspiration.

The novel consists of seven parts, each of which is named after a day of the week and focused on a different character; "Sunday," the last section, is only a one-sentence announcement. In the first part, "Monday," Antonina Lashkova falls in love with her father's godson Nikolai, who has just been released from prison, where he served a sentence for beating a Soviet official. Although he views their relationship as undesirable, Lashkov lets his daughter marry for the sake of her happiness and even—quite uncharacteristically—uses his political connections to get Nikolai the necessary "clean documents." The next part, "Tuesday," is devoted to the life of Lashkov's brother Andrei whose wartime experiences turned him into a recluse, as he spends his days in the remote forests of Russia. The third brother, Vasilii, works as a janitor in Moscow and inhabits a communal apartment with vulgar, brutal, endlessly drinking tenants; his life is described in "Wednesday." "Thursday" portrays Lashkov's grandson, Vadim, a talented actor who is suffering in an ill-advised marriage and who ultimately is confined to a mental institution. In "Friday" Maksimov follows Lashkov's daughter Antonina and her husband, Nikolai, to one of the construction sites in the Central Asian steppe. Nikolai's outrage over a corrupt boss and the suicide of a decent colleague lead to a fight and another

*Title page for* Proshchanie iz niotkuda *(1974, translated as* Farewell from Nowhere, *1979), Maksimov's autobiographical novel about his life in orphanages and prison camps (William T. Young Library, University of Kentucky)*

prison term, thus ending Antonina's brief family happiness. "Saturday" describes Lashkov's efforts to obtain a passport for Vadim, who has been released from the psychiatric ward; Vadim decides to join his uncle Andrei in seclusion. Lashkov gives shelter to Antonina and her newborn upon their return from Central Asia. As a result of his thoughts, a deep inner cleansing occurs in him: he makes peace with former foes—among them ardent Christians—and finds a new, albeit vague, faith beyond his former Communist persuasions.

Each part of the novel possesses its own rhythm, tonality, and atmosphere. For example, the scenes of Andrei's evacuation of a cattle herd during World War II—though deeply symbolic on a philosophical level—are written like a dark adventure story set in beautiful, wild nature, whereas Vasilii's conflicts in Moscow unfold in the brooding atmosphere of spatial restriction. Antonina's and Nikolai's encounters at the construction site are full of dramatic social and psychological tension, while all sections devoted to Lashkov's inner growth are calm and introspective. In most scenes Maksimov prefers direct one-on-one confrontations between his characters; only in a few scenes do more than two characters interact. This structure, intended to support the overall didactic purpose of the novel, leaves little room for ambiguity.

*Sem' dnei tvoreniia* is unusual because of its milieu—namely, that of the Soviet working class, which Maksimov knew intimately and was able to describe with a harsh realism unmatched by his literary peers. Until the appearance of Maksimov's novel, the working class as a theme in Soviet fiction had been the domain of low-quality literary hacks who falsified it beyond recognition; this knowledge is essential to an appreciation of Maksimov's mastery of the milieu. To supply that sphere with a Christian subtext, while also providing all the realistic details that socialist realism kept under wraps, meant a fundamental challenge to the literary establishment. Despite a loosely episodic structure that is kept together largely by the procession from one day of the week to the next, several flashbacks enrich the temporal fabric considerably. As a result the officially claimed evolution of Soviet society toward the heights of communism appears like a never-ending degeneration.

To view literature as a means toward truth seeking and confession echoed the nineteenth-century Russian canon, and Maksimov consequently insisted on continuing that tradition and living up to its supreme moral standards. Faith and literature provided him with the stability that he otherwise missed throughout his life. For Maksimov, as for Dostoevsky and Leo Tolstoy, whose example he consciously and humbly emulated, the principles of creating art and the principles of life were subject to the same strict rules of Christian morality. *Sem' dnei tvoreniia* has remained Maksimov's magnum opus; all other works were written with varying degrees of professionalism but lacked the inspiration and verve of this novel. More than in any other work, in *Sem' dnei tvoreniia* Maksimov manages to distance himself from his own involved role in the subject matter, which allowed him to avoid the overly personal tone that is characteristic of his later works.

*Karantin* (1973, The Quarantine), Maksimov's next novel, is also informed by Christian values and motifs. He paints a sobering, at times shocking, collective portrait of a Soviet people lost in alcoholism, vulgarity, and cruelty. In *Karantin*—more so than in *Sem' dnei tvoreniia*—Maksimov attempts to achieve a representative cross section of the population, including intellectuals and peasants. From an aesthetic point of view, *Karantin* is arguably his most successful synthesis of personal vision and artistic realization. As in *Sem' dnei tvoreniia*, the concise structure is made possible by one overreaching plot element: a train full of passengers is quarantined because of a cholera epidemic. All the episodes of the novel descend from this single idea. The generally sardonic tone of narration curiously complements—without ever undermining—the historical pathos expressed through the utterances and thoughts of the main character, Boris Khramov, whose name and kin Maksimov traces back across one millennium (that is, all the way down to the Christian conversion of Russia).

*Proshchanie iz niotkuda* (1974; translated as *Farewell from Nowhere*, 1979) is a minimally fictionalized autobiography depicting Maksimov's life as a child in prison camps and orphanages. The brutality, starvation, and misery of such an environment, to which Maksimov introduces the reader, exceed those of his previous works. *Chasha iarosti* (1982, Cup of Fury), the sequel to *Proshchanie iz niotkuda*, is similarly autobiographical in nature and devoted to Maksimov's literary career from 1954 until the mid 1970s, when he was exiled.

The success of Maksimov's books in the West and his stubborn refusal to join the Soviet literary mainstream in opportunism and corruption increasingly made him a nuisance and even a risk factor in the eyes of the Communist establishment. The reaction was inevitable and in tune with the standards of political and cultural engagement in the time of the Cold War. On 26 June 1973 Maksimov was officially excluded from the Soviet Writers' Union. In a surprising move, on 12 February 1974—the same day that Aleksandr Isaevich Solzhenitsyn was forced to leave the U.S.S.R.—Maksimov was granted permission to spend one year outside the Soviet Union. He and his wife, Tat'iana Viktorovna, left the country on 1 March.) He was stripped of his Soviet citizenship the following year and thus could not return to Russia.

As an involuntary émigré, Maksimov first made his home (together with his wife and their two daughters) in Brussels, then in Paris. He published a volume of prose approximately every other year, usually with the Posev publishing house in Frankfurt am Main. Many of his novels were translated into English as well as into western European languages. But he remained a stranger in the West, never learning French; instead, he concentrated all his activities on attempts to effect change in the Soviet political system. Socializing almost exclusively with Russian émigrés, Maksimov's Paris apartment became a major center of dissident life. In Paris he founded the influential quarterly *Kontinent* (Continent), a political and cultural forum mostly for Soviet dissidents; Maksimov served as editor in chief of the quarterly until 1992. For some fifteen years *Kontinent*, the title of which had been suggested to Maksimov by Solzhenitsyn, arguably carried the most weight among all Soviet dissident publications—both in regard to its circulation (about four thousand, a sizable number for Russian-language dissident journals) and the quality of its contributions.

In the 1970s and 1980s Maksimov's energy was consumed largely by political and cultural activities; his literary output suffered noticeably as a consequence, not in quantity but in quality. Freed from Soviet censorship, Maksimov now could write whatever and however he pleased. Yet, like many fellow émigré authors, he also lacked vital feedback from a critical readership, which he had enjoyed in Russia. Because he felt that his personal experiences in the West were of no value to him as literary subject matter, he returned, time and again, to the familiar ground of his own past (his 1975 work *Saga o Savve* [Savva's Saga] is devoted to the life of an escaped prison inmate) and to historical themes.

Although Maksimov had included historical episodes as flashbacks in some of his earlier fiction, *Kovcheg dlia nezvanykh* (1979; translated as *Ark for the Uncalled*, 1984) became his first completely historical novel. Set in the Far East at the end of World War II, the narrative focuses on the colonization of the Kurile Islands. It features two central characters—one of them a criminal, the other a Christian—who pursue strangely parallel paths in life; at the conclusion of the novel, their similarity is undeniably disturbing. Through the genre of the historical novel Maksimov expresses a deep skepticism about human nature and the Russian mentality. In a noteworthy similarity to Solzhenitsyn's *V kruge pervom* (1968; translated as *The First Circle*, 1968), a senile, partly demented Joseph Stalin appears in person, resembling a victim of the system that he claims to rule.

Maksimov's next novel, *Saga o nosorogakh* (1981, The Saga of the Rhinoceroses), deviates in theme somewhat from his other works. It is an angry diatribe against Western leftists, whose eagerness to compromise with Communist dictatorships renders them blind to the consequences of such alliances. This text, together with Maksimov's open anti-Communism and his willingness to accept the support of German conservative publisher Axel C. Springer (who almost single-handedly financed *Kontinent*), alienated the writer from large groups of Western intellectuals, who viewed him as a "cold warrior" and reactionary. Thus, Maksimov found himself increasingly isolated in the West. Translations of his works did not appear as often as they did during the 1970s, and those works that were translated did not attract many readers.

In diagnosing the pathetic moral state of twentieth-century Russia and attempting to get to the very roots of this condition, Maksimov explored vital questions of Russian history and mentality, in particular during periods that were called *smuta* (times of trouble) and were distinctive because of their incredible brutality and lawlessness. Key to an understanding of his worldview is that statehood and state stability were fundamental positive values to Maksimov—mainly because in Russia the firmness of state structures often was lacking and was challenged internally as well as externally. In his historical fiction Maksimov explores the problem of statehood and its legitimacy as one of the main factors that led to the Communist fiasco. Through his narratives he also tried to predict what would happen to Russia in the near future by drawing analogies to events in the past. In historical novels such as *Zaglianut' v bezdnu* (1986, Looking into the Abyss), devoted to the renowned White Army leader Admiral Aleksandr Vasil'evich Kolchak and his futile attempts to create an anti-Bolshevik republic in the Far East, Maksimov laid out his peculiar "historiosophical" concept. In many ways Kolchak is the incarnation of Maksimov's ideal of a political leader: he is strong-willed yet emotional and sensitive; he is a born leader yet a humble Orthodox believer, a practitioner of social duty, and—at the same time—a tender, even sentimental lover. That such an outstanding figure is betrayed by his foreign allies, as well as by his Russian subordinates, marks a typical failure of the old order—namely, to understand the scoundrel rules of a new, modern world, the goal of which is (in Maksimov's view) to annihilate Russia as a nation led by an idea. Maksimov also informs this fictitious portrait of Kolchak with his own longing for a lasting, genuine home that neither he nor his historical hero were ever able to find, as well as a tiredness and hopelessness in the face of an insurmountable plot of evil. "Why can decent people not act in a decisive manner?" is a rhetorical question posed by Kolchak, who speaks on behalf of Maksimov.

In *Zaglianut' v bezdnu* Maksimov extensively employs comments of anticipation that are voiced by an omniscient narrator. Yet, as a result, the unfolding events acquire an air of inevitability, and the narrator becomes a hopeless doomsayer. In this late novel Konstantin Nikolaevich Leont'ev's assumption that Russia is an old nation approaching its final days serves as another justification to foretell doom, the metaphorical "abyss" of the title. At this point the entire twentieth century is seen as shaken by an outbreak of popular destructive energy, the revolt of the common man against order and authority. One noteworthy link to Maksimov's previous novels is the character of a rank-and-file soldier, Egorychev, whose conclusion boils down to a crude "I don't give a damn . . ."–an attitude of passive contempt for the vanity of the world that had saved other personae in Maksimov's fiction. Maksimov also signals his awareness, however, that such passiveness contributes to the agony of Russia, as part of a fatal cluster of betrayal, hypocrisy, indifference, and boundless selfishness.

*I Az Vozdam* (1987, I Shall Avenge) deals, in similar fashion, with the fate of the Russian Cossacks. An implied polemic against Mikhail Aleksandrovich Sholokhov's *Tikhii Don* (1928–1940, And Quiet Flows the Don), yet far from the artistic energy of its target, *I Az Vozdam* shows the Cossacks' downfall as part of the general historical defeat of Russia, for which all involved parties bear some responsibility. Explicit eschatological motifs, similar to those in *Zaglianut' v bezdnu*, abound in this text. The critical response to these novels was scarce, which is hardly surprising, given their characteristic anti-Western angle and limited relevance for non-Russian audiences. Both *Zaglianut' v bezdnu* and *I Az Vozdam* also reveal a shortage of thorough archival research, a flaw that Maksimov may have tried to disguise by introducing a variety of narrative devices. But he was not able to overcome the clumsiness and hastiness, or even lackluster quality, of their textual rendition in a persuasive manner. In these late historical novels he pays less attention than in his previous books to the creation of verisimilitude and atmosphere. Concrete cultural and everyday-life details are in short supply, to the extent that these late prose attempts approach novelistic essays at best.

Toward the end of his life Maksimov summarized his experiences of universal alienation in the novel *Kochevanie do smerti* (Nomadism until Death), first published in 1994 in *Kontinent*. Here, the lack of a guiding and loving father and a sheltering homeland constitute the initial trauma that causes sadness and despair. The novel features some brilliant chapters, including a satirical portrait of Eduard Limonov (pseudonym of Eduard Veniaminovich Savenko), but the overall impression of exhaustion and bitterness outweighs all of those achievements.

Even in his best works Maksimov was never completely successful in creating a coherent plot and a consistent tonality. The accusations leveled against him by some literary critics—for the "aesthetic unevenness" and "irregular treatment of time and space" in his works—do have merit. As integral elements within his favored realistic approach, the majority of Maksimov's novels and short stories embody rather diverse stylistic particles: "splinters" of criminal jargon, bureaucratese, or the vernacular of vulgar jokes. But the later mixture of text segments belonging to different genres such as biography, chronicle, newspaper article, letter, memoir, proceedings of interrogations, and diaries, all assembled under the most generous of genre notions, "novel," often does not function in itself, or in the service of realistic narration. When successful, Maksimov's narratives resemble artful mosaics; often, however, his inner aesthetic indecisiveness gives the impression of amorphous compilations, especially in his works of the 1980s. For an otherwise outspoken defender of the classical tradition, Maksimov's frequent deviations from the rules of chronology and spatiotemporal logic come as a surprise. But regardless of a missing consistency between his professed ideals and his own literary practice, the lack of plausibility in applying modernist narrative devices points to a more serious weakness. During a forty-year career Maksimov's literary skills did not undergo a genuine evolution. Only if interpreted psychologically—as a tormenting lack of integration (both internal and external), which he lamented on several occasions—the "shattered" form of his prose might also be legitimized.

As a public figure, Maksimov was and remained a staunch defender of Mikhail Sergeevich Gorbachev even after 1991, but he retained his skepticism regarding the prospects of perestroika in Russia and the good that could come of it for the Russian people. At one point he stated that "Too much resentment has accumulated in Russia." Yet, if nothing else, democratization and liberalization allowed him to return to his native country. On 10 April 1990 Maksimov was given official permission to enter the U.S.S.R. That same year he oversaw the transfer of operations for *Kontinent* to Moscow. (After 1992, he retained the position of "President of the Association of Friends of *Kontinent* Magazine".) His Soviet citizenship was reinstated in 1991, the year in which the Soviet Union ceased to exist. Then, novelist and publisher Petr Fedorovich Aleshkin nominated Maksimov for reinstatement as a member of the Writers' Union, from which he had been expelled twenty years earlier. The Writers' Union that he joined, however, was a transformed one and now was called Soiuz pisatelei Rossii (Union of Writers of Russia), the patriotic counterforce to the Russian section of PEN and other liberal organizations.

Together with Vladimir Konstantinovich Bukovsky and Eduard Kuznetsov, Maksimov had founded the organization "Resistance International" in the 1970s. Yet, the dissident movement, the various factions of which had been held together temporarily by their opposition to a common enemy, the Communist system, fell apart with the breakup of the Soviet Union. Maksimov mostly expressed somewhat evenhanded political views among representatives of the third wave of Soviet emigration and a willingness to compromise, which had allowed the emigre community to reach a

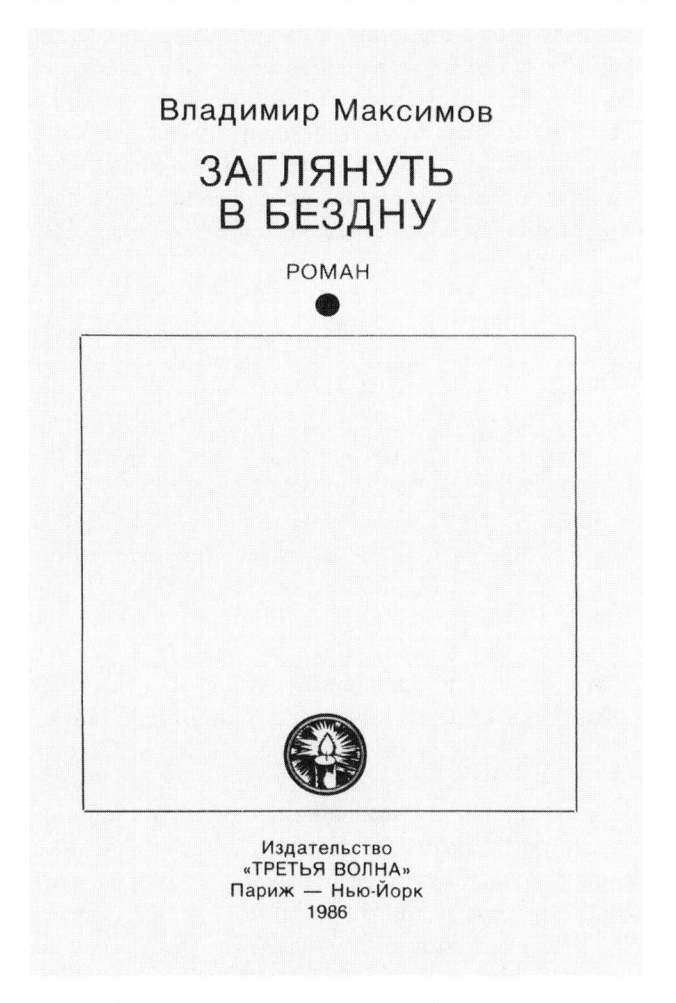

*Title page for* Zaglianut' v bezdnu *(Looking into the Abyss), Maksimov's novel about the pervasive mood of doom in the last years of the Soviet Union (Gabriel Library, University of the South)*

consensus and even syntheses of liberal and conservative values. Yet, after 1991 he gravitated more and more in the direction of the Russian patriotic conservatives, although his own view of the Russian people was far from idealization: whatever he proclaimed in public, the many scenes of arbitrary rancor and barbarism featured in many of his novels reveal a certain unease about the potential of his nation.

Maksimov, whose prominence as a literary and societal figure had waned in the West but grown in Russia, died of cancer on 26 March 1995 in Paris. "There is great symbolism in the fact that he died on the Day of the Adoration of the Holy Cross," said Nikita Struve. "He bore the burden of Russia's cross, and his own, throughout his entire life." Toward the end of Maksimov's life the basic dichotomy of Communism versus Christianity that had nourished his work was replaced by his belief in a global conspiracy against Russia, a conspiracy in which Russia played the role of a guinea pig in a diabolical sociopolitical experiment of unseen proportions. He described the West during these years as a "civilization of rats," while he, as the almost undisguised author-narrator, treated himself as an alien wherever he went. Shocking many, he expressed his disenchantment with the West and Western institutions precisely in those newspapers he had formerly attacked for their atheistic crusades. And *Pravda* (Truth), grotesquely patriotic and religiously "tolerant" in the early 1990s, returned the favor and wrote in its eulogy that Maksimov "cannot be imagined as an outsider to Russia, Russian literature and the Russian people." In another necrology the leaders of the Writers' Union praised him as a defender of "civilized patriotism," whose moral authority and independent positions did not need to be proven. However, in the final years of his life, Maksimov's political standpoint should be defined correctly as incoherent rather than pro-Soviet. On the one hand, he publicly supported Belorussian proto-Communist autocrat Aleksandr Lukashenka; on the other, he attacked former Communists and "democratic" turncoats such as Grigorii Iakovlevich Baklanov and Aleksandr Lukich Borshchagovsky. Since the scandals surrounding these publications have subsided, Maksimov's articles in the post-Soviet press, written in the aftermath of perestroika, are outcries of genuine despair and pessimism, not evidence of a pro-Communist conversion. They show that his isolation had become unbearable: stripped of an atheist Communist Party dictatorship to fight against, the dissident position proved obsolete and dissidents superfluous, and journals such as *Kontinent* acquired new functions (if they managed to survive at all).

Friends and colleagues remember Maksimov as a quiet, modest, and kind man with a benevolent demeanor, unskilled in literary schemes and rather defenseless when confronted with resentment and anger. Some accounts mention his uneven personality, which sometimes could astonish his colleagues—in the forms of uncontrolled outbursts and vicious attacks against people, especially writers, whom he despised. The liberal Soviet émigrés Andrei Donatovich Siniavsky and his wife, Mariia Rozanova, became a particular target of Maksimov's venom. But in his interviews and articles he often regretted such conflicts and offered reconciliation. On the other hand, his inability to maintain long-term friendships points to a deeper deficiency that tormented him throughout his life and became symptomatic in his extreme swings of attitude toward colleagues and political figures. Generous in his material and spiritual support of fellow dissidents, Maksimov helped many budding writers find their first publishers.

Born and raised in the Soviet lower depths, Vladimir Emel'ianovich Maksimov had faced the dark side of Communist reality in harsher ways than did the majority of his literary peers. To him the promises of a Marxist-Leninist utopia never held much appeal. As a writer he is most convincing when featuring barely fictionalized events from his own life. Although he worked in various genres—prose, poetry, and drama—his forte was narrative prose. He was not by nature an inventor of stories but a teller of what he himself had seen and heard. A direct outcome of Maksimov's confessional and sermonizing literary practice was the dominance of autobiographical material. The most successful and promising phase of his career as a professional *literator* (person of letters) were the 1960s and early 1970s. Already in the late 1970s symptoms of stagnation indicated that the raw material accumulated by him in the first three decades of his life had been depleted. Today, few of Maksimov's works are read or remembered other than by historians of literature. His prose has been characterized as "awkward yet powerful." Toward the end of his career Maksimov's fiction became more raw, his language increasingly crude, and the composition careless. The plots of his last novels involve a multitude of sudden transitions in time and space, not all of them motivated. This fact notwithstanding, the same weakness in craftsmanship informed his narratives with an atmosphere of painful disintegration and psychological authenticity—criteria that Russian geniuses such as Dostoevsky always held in higher esteem than elegance and aesthetic perfection. As Victor Terras has said, "The basic mood of Maksimov's art is somberly tragic, with a ray of light suggested by the hope of regeneration through Christian faith."

**References:**

Petr Aleshkin, "Kakim ia ego znal," *Literaturnaia Rossiia,* 31 March 1995, p. 7;

N. Antonov, "Krest i kamen': O romane V. Maksimova Karantin," *Grani,* 92–93 (1974): 295–310;

Anna Berzer, "Pobedil chelovek," *Novyi mir,* 4 (1963);

V. Bushin, "Spor veka," *Zvezda,* 4 (1963);

Gustaw Herling-Grudzinski, "Z Archipelagu na Kontynent (Rozm\wa s W. E. Maksimowem)," *Kultura,* 235 (1974): 84–88;

Geoffrey Hosking, "The Search for an Image of Man in Contemporary Soviet Fiction," in *Studies in Twentieth Century Russian Literature,* edited by Christopher J. Barnes (Edinburgh: Scottish Academic Press, 1976; New York: Barnes & Noble, 1976), pp. 61–77;

Anne C. Hughes, "The Significance of 'Stan' za chertu' in Vladimir Maksimov's Literary Development," *Journal of Russian Studies,* 36 (1978): 19–26;

Liudmila Ivanova, "Eshche raz o zle i dobre," *Znamia*, 3 (1963);

Violetta Iverni, "Kazhdyi raven svoemu vyboru," *Grani*, 116 (1980): 184–192;

Wolfgang Kasack, *Lexikon der russischen Literatur des 20. Jahrhunderts* (Munich: Otto Sagner, 1992), pp. 728–731;

Iurii Kovalenko, "Kontinent Vladimira Maksimova," *Izvestiia*, 28 March 1995, p. 7;

Elena Krasnoshchekova, "Nravstvennyi konflikt v sovremennoi povesti," in *Zhanrovo-stilevye skaniia sovremennoi sovetskoi prozy*, edited by Aleksandr Vasil'evich Ognev, N. N. Kiselev, and others (Moscow: Nauka, 1971), pp. 175–199;

Anatolii Emmanuilovich Krasnov-Levitin, *Dva pisatelia. Aleksandr Solzhenitsyn. Vladimir Maksimov* (Paris: Poiski, 1983);

Dzhemma Kvachevska, ed., *V literaturnom zerkale. O tvorchestve Vladimira Maksimova* (Paris & New York: Tret'ia volna, 1986);

Arnold McMillin, "Chronicler of the Lower Depths," *Guardian*, 13 April 1995, p. T15;

Andrei Nemzer, *Literaturnaia gazeta*, 17 April 1991;

Helen Prochazka, "Death as a Counterpoint to Life in Maksimov's Seven Days of Creation," *Modern Language Review*, 84 (October 1989): 885–893;

Prochazka, "Present Imperfect: An Analysis of Time in Maksimov's Sem' Dnei Tvoreniia," *Modern Language Review*, 87 (July 1992): 652–663;

Iurii Riabinin, "'Literatura tam, gde est' bol','" *Literaturnaia gazeta*, 9 March 1994, p. 5;

Leonid Rzhevsky, "Triptikh V. E. Maksimova: Algebra i garmoniia," *Grani*, 10 (1978): 229–266;

Adele Stachiw, "V. Maksimov's 'Quarantine,'" in *Russian Contributions II: Problemy perevoda*, edited by Roland Sussex (Melbourne: Russian Department of the University of Melbourne, n.d.), pp. 117–127;

Feliks Svetov, "'Vot i vyshel grazhdanin'," *Literaturnaia gazeta*, 10 August 1994, p. 4;

Victor Terras, ed., *Handbook of Russian Literature* (New Haven: Yale University Press, 1985), p. 270;

"Vladimir Maksimov's Visa: An Interview in London," *Encounter*, 42 (June), pp. 51–55.

# Nadezhda Iakovlevna Mandel'shtam

*(30 October 1899 – 29 December 1980)*

Beth Holmgren
*University of North Carolina–Chapel Hill*

BOOKS: *Moe zaveshchanie* (N.p., 1966); enlarged as *Moe zaveshchanie i drugie esse,* with foreword by Joseph Brodsky (New York: Sereberianyi vek, 1982)—includes "Motsart i Sal'eri," "Mandel'shtam v Armenii," "Stikhi o Gruzii," "Stikhi Mandel'shtama dlia detei," "Dva interv'iu s. N. Ia. Mandel'shtam," "Dva pis'ma k Ioannu San-frantsis-skomu," and "Al'bom fotografii";

*Vospominaniia* (New York: Chekhov, 1970); translated by Max Hayward as *Hope Against Hope,* with an introduction by Clarence Brown (New York: Atheneum, 1970);

*Vtoraia kniga* (Paris: YMCA-Press, 1972); translated by Hayward as *Hope Abandoned* (New York: Atheneum, 1974);

*Kniga tret'ia* (Paris: YMCA-Press, 1987);

*Snomeni,* edited by Georgi Borisov (Sofiia: Fakel Ekspres, 1999).

**Editions in English:** *Chapter 42,* translated by Donald Rayfield (London: Menard, 1973);

*Mozart and Salieri* (Ann Arbor, Mich.: Ardis, 1973).

OTHER: "Khlopot polon rot," "Ptichii professor," and "Kukolki," in *Tarusskie stranitsy,* edited by Vladimir Koblikov, compiled by N. Otten (Kaluga: Kaluzhskoe knizhnoe izdatel'stvo, 1961).

SELECTED PERIODICAL PUBLICATION–UNCOLLECTED: "[Ob Akhmatovoi,]" *Literaturnaia ucheba,* 3 (1989): 134–151.

Nadezhda Mandel'shtam earned her place in Russian literature as the foremost "widow of Russia," one of the female survivors of the Stalinist era who, in Carl R. Proffer's tribute, "preserved that genuine Russian culture which was locked up, blotted out, censored and unmentionable not only in the official press, but everywhere that the Party rules." Through her unceasing labors as an archivist and interpreter of the life and work of her husband, the great poet Osip

*Nadezhda Iakovlevna Mandel'shtam (in* Hope Against Hope, *1970, Richland County Public Library, Columbia, South Carolina)*

Emil'evich Mandel'shtam, labors that at last "surfaced" in the post-Stalin samizdat-tamizdat press and her own Moscow "salon," she emerged as a vital, compelling, and provocative source for her husband's work as well as for many figures of and trends in Soviet culture. The repressions and forced silences of the Stalinist period catalyzed and shaped her celebrated memoirs, *Vospominaniia* (1970, Recollections; translated as *Hope Against Hope,* 1970) and *Vtoraia kniga* (1972, Second Book; translated as *Hope Abandoned,* 1974), evoking what some critics applaud as unvarnished history and persuasive rhetoric and others deplore as lies and slander. *Vospominaniia* was welcomed by Soviet readers and is continually appreciated by audiences outside of Russia as a masterful commentary on her era. One should bear in mind another, less explored, influence on her work: her artistic and social formation in the bohemian Russian culture of the 1910s and 1920s. Her self-conception and public performance guardedly reflect the penchant of that milieu for audacious expression and social role play.

Nadezhda Mandel'shtam was born Nadezhda Iakovlevna Khazina in Saratov on 30 October 1899 (old style). She was the youngest of four children in an upwardly mobile, materially comfortable Jewish family. Her mother, Vera Iakovlevna Khazina, had trained in the first group of Russian women pursuing medical degrees; Nadezhda Mandel'shtam later mentions her mother's mobilization as a doctor to aid famine victims after the Bolshevik Revolution. Khazina's father, Iakov Arkad'evich Khazin, was the son of a *cantonist* (a soldier's son). He completed higher degrees in mathematics and law; worked as a barrister; read Greek tragedies in the original for pleasure; and impressed his daughter as a *barin* (a nobleman) because of his wide-ranging education and cultural sensitivity. Although the family's conversion to Christianity was clearly an act of political expedience rather than of religious conviction, Khazina's atheist father insisted on her respect for the Christian scriptures and for their devoutly Russian Orthodox cook, Daria.

Iakov Arkad'evich's quest for lucrative work moved the Khazins to Kiev, where Khazina learned German and English (courtesy of an English nanny); studied in the Kiev Women's Gymnasium, one of the few institutions to adopt a "male" program (that is, a program academically more rigorous than those usually instituted in Russian girls' schools); and fought repeatedly with her older brothers, Aleksandr and Evgenii. Nadezhda Mandel'shtam's memories of childhood, recorded late in life in three short sketches ("Otets" [Father], "Sem'ia" [Family], and "Devochki i mal'chik" [Girls and a Boy], published in *Kniga Tret'ia,* 1987) cherish her parents' loving indulgence and the family's rich diet. The revolutions of 1917 and the ensuing civil war destroyed this idyll. The Khazins were effectively dispossessed and threatened intermittently by White Army and Red Army pogroms. In "Sem'ia'," Nadezda Mandel'shtam notes that both her brothers enlisted in the White Army and thus summarizes their fate: "One [Aleksandr] disappeared, and the other [Evgenii] lived in Moscow until his 80th year, bound internally by his past in the White Guard."

For a brief time, Khazina flourished as a young painter and youth about town in a Kiev as yet undevastated by the civil war. Running with "a small herd of painters," as she wrote dismissively decades later in a reproving way, she worked in the studio of Aleksandra Ekster, a renowned avant-garde theatrical artist, painting sets and street posters and spending what she earned from her in-vogue "left-wing art" in coffeehouses, pastry shops, and nightclubs. Khazina's herd felt invigorated by their art, youth, and radical politics, and they cultivated a defiantly bohemian lifestyle. During this exhilarating, precarious period, the nineteen-year-old Khazina tumbled into what she presumed would be a short-term affair with Mandel'shtam, who had escaped to Kiev from the war-torn north. She dated their relationship from 1 May 1919, when they met in a Kiev nightclub called "Khlam" (The Junk Shop). Shortly thereafter, Kiev descended into a bloodbath of alternating White and Red Army occupations, and Mandel'shtam had to flee further south to the Crimea and circle north to Petrograd (formerly St. Petersburg); Khazina was separated from him for a year and a half. The two reunited in Kiev in March 1921 and left together several weeks later on a journey that ended with their relocation in Moscow. Nadezhda Mandel'shtam recalls that they registered for a marriage certificate before this (or some other) journey simply to placate the commandant of the train. Jane Gary Harris, a biographer of the poet Mandel'shtam, asserts that they were officially married in 1922.

Nadezhda Mandel'shtam's nonchalance about the registration for marriage typifies her abiding defiance of social conventions. The Mandel'shtams' marriage was neither conventional nor monogamous, although their interdependency was intense, enforced by political terror and their precarious livelihood. They coped with the constant disruption of moving, first to a series of apartments in Moscow in 1922–1924 and then to Leningrad (formerly Petrograd) and Tsarskoe Selo. They returned to Moscow in 1933, where Osip Mandel'shtam was arrested the next year for his defamatory poem about Joseph Stalin. In 1934–1937 they were exiled to Voronezh, and in 1937–1938, as former political exiles, they were confined essentially to the towns of Savelovo and Kalinin, located along a 105 kilometer perimeter of Moscow. The couple finally were separated when Osip Mandel'shtam was arrested on 1 May 1938 and

*Nadezhda Iakovlevna Khazina in 1922, the year she married poet Osip Emil'evich Mandel'shtam (Clarence Brown, Mandelstam, 1973; Richland County Public Library, Columbia, South Carolina)*

then disappeared in the camp prison system known as the gulag. Nadezhda Mandel'shtam learned only much later of her husband's death, which occurred in a transit camp on 27 December 1938.

Although she later read her marriage as a formative period devoted to the primary goal of her husband's creativity and the secondary value of their stormy but enduring love, Nadezhda Mandel'shtam's personal sacrifice for and intermittent dissatisfaction with her husband register in her own and others' memoirs of the couple. Preoccupied with Mandel'shtam's creative bursts or stagnancy, she gave up her painting and submitted to the role of her husband's beleaguered literary secretary. She took on pedestrian translating and editorial jobs (often those that Mandel'shtam refused to do) in order to make ends meet. Neither domestic nor practical, she nonetheless struggled with the essential tasks of a proscribed poet's caretaker, such as shopping, cooking, cleaning, and concealing manuscripts in their makeshift "homes." Yet, her hard life with Mandel'shtam also brought her into intimate contact with his extraordinary work, an experience she deeply cherished and later transcribed. Nadezhda Mandel'shtam inevitably was imbued with her husband's poetry, witnessing its creation and committing it either to paper or to memory. For many years her memory alone archived politically dangerous work such as Mandel'shtam's *Chetvertaia proza* (1966, Fourth Prose) and the poems he wrote during their exile in Voronezh.

Nadezhda Mandel'shtam thus functioned as the poet's de facto wife for nineteen years, always preferring to behave and be treated as Mandel'shtam's "girlfriend." Yet, for the forty-two years that she lived without him, she presented herself unequivocally as his widow and champion. She narrowly escaped Kalinin in May 1938 before the secret police, then known as the Narodnyi komissariat vnutrennikh del (NKVD, People's Commissariat of Internal Affairs), came to arrest her. She spent the next two decades concealing herself from the centers of Soviet power in various provincial towns. Before World War II she lived in Strunino, where she worked in a textile factory, and in Maloiaroslavets; after the war she lived in Ul'ianovsk, Chita, Cheboksary, and Pskov. Through the intervention of the poet Anna Andreevna Akhmatova, Nadezhda Mandel'shtam was evacuated during the war to the relatively safe haven of Tashkent. There she commenced, and eventually completed, a degree in English-language instruction and thereby secured a means of modest support. Sheltered by academia, she even produced a dissertation in the field of linguistics (on the accusative case in Anglo-Saxon) in 1951 and earned praise from her adviser, the distinguished scholar Viktor Maksimovich Zhirmunsky. She later claimed knowledge of twenty languages (most of them ancient). Yet, Nadezhda Mandel'shtam's main ambition in these fugitive years was, by her own admission, "to preserve [her husband's] poetry and to leave something in the nature of a letter telling of our fate."

The intermittent political thaws in the late 1950s facilitated Osip Mandel'shtam's partial rehabilitation; he was vindicated of the charges brought against him in 1938 but not those from 1934. Nadezhda Mandel'shtam first set about the business of his textual preservation during her Moscow "vacations" from teaching in the provinces. She negotiated with the Writers' Union to establish a literary heritage commission in Mandel'shtam's honor, collected his manuscripts, and collaborated with Nikolai

Ivanovich Khardzhiev on an edition of Mandel'shtam's work, to be published by Sovetskii pisatel' as part of its "Biblioteka poeta" (The Poet's Library) series. She began to gather information about all aspects of her husband's life, from his early years as an artist to his death in the camps. In this period of strictly limited liberalization she necessarily consulted human, not archival, sources; this group of people encompassed well-known cultural figures and recently returned prisoners from the gulag. Her passion for human contact, her instinct for a good story, and her uncensored curiosity about every facet of human behavior all aided Nadezhda Mandel'shtam in the quest to preserve her husband's work. She soon attracted others as a "source." Cultural luminaries, dissidents, and young people eager for the unofficial truth sought her out wherever she lodged with Moscow friends. One such pilgrim, Mikhail K. Polivanov, recalls that visitors had to wait in line to chat with her when she stayed in the tiny "guest" room of her friends the Shklovskys. In 1965 she finally obtained her own apartment in Moscow. She hosted there, almost until the end of her life, a highly informal salon, to which she cautiously invited foreign scholars interested in her husband's—and, eventually, her own—work. Her bohemian manners kept her from posing as a sanctimonious "poet's widow," the sort of holy oracle for the pre-Stalin past that Russians and foreigners were then eager to revere. Her visitors relished instead her salty language, uninhibited interests, strong opinions, and encouragement toward a freedom of thought and expression in her interlocutors.

This intensive social interaction paved the way for her own writing career. For a long time Nadezhda Mandel'shtam had been working with language—as a translator, a foreign-language teacher, and a linguist—but she had not conceived of herself as a writer, certainly not before she undertook the project of her memoirs. During the period of the "Thaw" her first writings were journalistic essays, published in the 1961 anthology titled *Tarusskie stranitsy* (Tarussa Pages), which commemorate, in a conventional way, local Tarussa workers; she writes about the collective farm manager, the old man who tended the aviaries, and the artisan-seamstresses. Nadezhda Mandel'shtam's autobiographical writing proved much less orthodox, for it drew from the persona that she was cultivating as an "authoritative" source. Her first volume of memoirs, *Vospominaniia*, may suggest her desired "letter" in its explicit awareness of its audience, yet she narrates and structures it as a series of trenchant monologues. The result is a riveting montage of anecdotes, analyses, and opinions undiluted by scholarly circumspection and unsweetened by a memoirist's censoring decorum. According to the recollections of her friends, she would type her memoirs nonstop and distribute already "finished" copy. While these recollections may not reflect Nadezhda Mandel'shtam's actual process of composition, they reinforce an important impression of similarity between her spoken and written monologues. In a surprising debut for a novice writer, Nadezhda Mandel'shtam succeeded in translating her strong voice and "source" material into written text.

Planned as her only book, *Vospominaniia* pursues several urgent agendas. She produces here her definitive version of Mandel'shtam's life story, asserting and demonstrating the poet as the prophetic voice and spiritual touchstone of his era. She implies that she, as Mandel'shtam's chosen life partner, was schooled to convey his vital art and model it to the world. She expands on this mission as she carries it out, extrapolating readings and judgments of the Stalinist system from Mandel'shtam's worldview and her own extensive conversations with "sources." Chapters such as "Maiskaia noch'" (A May Night) fashion a vivid, dramatic tale of martyrdom and touching human response; others, such as "Teoriia i praktika" (Theory and Practice), deliver semisociological analyses of the Stalin-era attitudes and practices in which, according to her, all Soviet citizens were victimized and complicit.

Circulated in samizdat and published in Russian and English tamizdat in 1970, Nadezhda Mandel'shtam's first book of memoirs awed readers the world over, including Aleksandr Trifonovich Tvardovsky, the editor of the influential Soviet journal *Novyi mir* (New World). He praised the power and concision of *Vospominaniia*, yet he would not risk publishing it. Critics welcomed her insights into Mandel'shtam's poetry, creative process, and persecution. Her interpretations of specific poems have since been contested by scholars and other eyewitnesses, but Mandel'shtam experts recognize his wife's great textual service in spotlighting him; they must acknowledge her work, in Charles Isenberg's words, as "the enabling condition, the virtual horizon, of Osip Mandelstam's." Other reviews hailed her foray into social analysis. She was credited with an astute dissection of ordinary life under Stalin and commended for her fearless criticism of the intelligentsia's capitulation to the Stalinist regime.

The success of *Vospominaniia* increased Nadezhda Mandel'shtam's "unofficial" and overseas celebrity and restored to her a late-Soviet facsimile of the bohemian milieu she had enjoyed in her youth, when she worked as a painter and lived as a free

*Title page for the American edition of* Vospominiia, *1970, in which Mandel'shtam explains her role in communicating what she describes as the vital art of her husband's poetry (Richland County Public Library, Columbia, South Carolina)*

spirit. By this point, writing had become her expressive medium. As she discovered, her first book launched—rather than completed—her work of uncensored remembering and retelling, an impulse that grew as cultural liberalization waned during the rule of Leonid Il'ich Brezhnev, a time known as the Stagnation. Nadezhda Mandel'shtam had published occasional introductions and commentaries to her husband's poems and was still waiting for the book edition of his work to appear; the snail-like pace and limited scope of his rehabilitation rankled her.

Akhmatova's death in 1966 specifically moved Nadezhda Mandel'shtam to compose the first variant of her second book of memoirs, "Ob Akhmatovoi," in 1967, an assay at Akhmatova's portrait that she opted not to circulate or publish. It first appeared in 1989 in the journal *Literaturnaia ucheba* (Literary Studies). Akhmatova, another persecuted poet and a close friend, proved to be a problematic, yet liberating, subject for Nadezhda Mandel'shtam. Her memories of Akhmatova invoke for her "everything personal and intimate"—what was "swept away" by Mandel'shtam's terrible fate—and this material builds a complex, sometimes ambiguous character analysis. Nadezhda Mandel'shtam could approve Akhmatova's poetry, bravery, and solidarity (with both Mandel'shtams) in times of trial; reflecting on what she as a woman shared with Akhmatova, Nadezhda Mandel'shtam even hypothesized women's greater strength. Yet, in contrast to her wholehearted endorsement of her husband's poetic work and life practice, she disapproved of Akhatmova's self-directed cult—her pose as a grande dame and a beautiful lady. Her selective celebration of Akhmatova extends to the poet's courageous, eloquent acts of witness and what Nadezhda Mandel'shtam chooses to perceive as Akhmatova's true personality, that of a "khuliganka i ozornitsa" (hooligan and mischief-maker).

Soon after she had drafted and abandoned "Ob Akhmatovoi," Nadezhda Mandel'shtam produced "Motsart i Sal'eri" (1973, Mozart and Salieri), her most "well-behaved" book of memoirs, which focuses on the poet's creative process. Her ambivalence toward Akhmatova lingers here in much fainter form, for the title points out her "correction" of Akhmatova's pseudo-academic "misreading" of Aleksandr Sergeevich Pushkin's "little tragedy," *Mozart i Salieri* (1832). Resisting a scholarly approach to her topic, Nadezhda Mandel'shtam instead writes in accordance with her husband's critical credo—that is, as the poet's human witness, reader, and interlocutor. Observing Mandel'shtam, Akhmatova, and Boris Leonidovich Pasternak in the act of creation, she argues that Mozart (the intuitive impulse) and Salieri (the exercise of control) inhere in all true poets. She also prescribes a fundamental consonance between the poet's art and life, a fusion she claims was achieved in Mandel'shtam's case but sometimes blocked in Akhmatova's. Akhmatova, unlike Nadezhda Mandel'shtam herself, could or would not transmit "the furious raging of [her] intonation and thought" on paper.

Nadezhda Mandel'shtam's own "raging" was fully unleashed in her last major work, *Vtoraia kniga*, which was the second variant of her second book of memoirs. Although her friends and associates recall her various plans for future books—for example, on Maksim Gor'ky, on the first lonely decades of her

*Title page for the American edition of Mandel'shtam's second memoir,* Vtoraia kniga *(1972), in which she angrily describes herself as "a crazy old woman who fears nothing and despises force" (Richland County Public Library, Columbia, South Carolina)*

widowhood, and on "Soviet education and Soviet washrooms"—*Vtoraia kniga* stands as the most extensive and complex indulgence of her urge to write everything that she had experienced and learned about her dreadful era. The tight dramatic structure of the first book expands here into broad, loosely organized sections. Into her established mix of illustrative anecdotes, concise character sketches, social analyses, and sharp judgments, she interjects philosophical digressions and extensive textological commentaries on her husband's poems.

Nadezhda Mandel'shtam narrates *Vtoraia kniga* on the basis of the authority that she felt she had accrued in her first volume; her subjective voice and viewpoint dominate the text. One of her stated goals is to ascertain the nature of that subjectivity, and her desultory self-definition aims to join implicitly contradictory concepts of a self in harmony with a spiritually sanctioned, responsibly free community and a self that is enormously willful and peremptory in its expression and judgment. Her sanctioning community embraces the great and humble (such as Mandel'shtam, Akhmatova, Nataliia Shtempel', Natasha Stoliarova, and a kindly cobbler and his wife); to varying degrees she learns from them both goodness and inner freedom. Her highly subjective judgment falls on an even more startling array of characters, who encompass many famous figures and onetime friends. In *Vtoraia kniga* the people with whom she "settles accounts" include Gor'ky, the "father of Soviet literature"; the Symbolist poet Viacheslav Ivanovich Ivanov; the Mandel'shtam textologists Khardzhiev and Sergei Borisovich Rudakov; the beloved expert on children's literature Samuil Iakovlevich Marshak; and the esteemed formalist critic Iurii Nikolaevich Tynianov.

In the moral terms of her book Nadezhda Mandel'shtam's frank "settling of accounts" carries out a kind of self-fulfillment and attests to her evolution from silent victim into "a crazy old woman who fears nothing and despises force." Yet, many readers of *Vtoraia kniga* thought and wrote otherwise. Her first book of memoirs won her universal critical acclaim and moral authority; her second book tested the limits of that authority and outraged primarily her Russian readers. The critic and memoirist Emma Grigor'evna Gershtein, who later divulged a more libelous exposé of the Mandel'shtams' sexual adventures, accused her of Stalinist-style demagoguery and slander. The liberal author Veniamin Aleksandrovich Kaverin, infuriated by Nadezhda Mandel'shtam's unkind portraits of revered figures, denied her the status of writer; he "demoted" her to Mandel'shtam's "shadow" in an open letter circulated in samizdat. Writing in her defense in his book *The Widows of Russia and Other Writings* (1987), Proffer attested that most of the objections lodged against her book were directed at "*opinions,* not facts" and that "every time we had been able to cross-check, it turned out *N. M. was right*" in her critical impressions. Whatever its excesses and untruths, *Vtoraia kniga* largely confirms Nadezhda Mandel'shtam's talents as a keen observer, an accomplished raconteur, and a plainspoken "source." It presents a narrative tour de force and a rich compendium of stories and theories—vehement table talk—about unofficial and official Stalinist culture.

The number of Nadezhda Mandel'shtam's visitors to her home declined after the circulation of *Vtoraia kniga,* but she never again suffered the utter isolation of her early widowhood. In the late 1970s she produced a few more sketches, primarily about her childhood in Kiev. Thereafter, heart trouble quite often confined her to her bed, and increasing senility prevented further projects. In her old age Nadezhda Mandel'shtam embraced Russian Orthodoxy and specified that she be buried according to Orthodox rites. She died on 29 December 1980. Although the authorities had not harassed her in her final decade, despite the forthright anti-Sovietism of her memoirs, they "deported" her body without a coffin to the morgue almost immediately after her death—presumably to forestall any dissident demonstration. Her friends succeeded in recovering her body and burying her as she wished, on 3 January 1981.

Over the course of her life Nadezhda Iakovlevna Mandel'shtam, once the unprepossessing, bohemian "girlfriend" of Osip Mandel'shtam, proved equal to the martyr's role of Soviet poet's wife. She acted as caretaker, transcribed, collected, memorized, and lobbied tirelessly for her husband's personal and artistic rehabilitation. She epitomized the post-Stalin phenomenon of the female survivor, the living link to a cultural heritage severed and repressed by political terror. This poet's wife, however, also evolved into a trenchant teller of her own and others' tales in an era when stories shared in confidence were devoured as the only truth. Nadezhda Mandel'shtam's memoirs demonstrate the premium placed on direct, uncensored communication in post-Stalin Soviet society. Her personalized analyses and anecdotes are as characteristic and reflective of post-Stalin sociocultural concerns and privileged modes of expression as realist novels were of Russian culture and society in the 1860s and the 1870s. Moreover, like other innovators in Russian literature, she deliberately exceeded the bounds of the genre that she was most famously responsible for creating. Nadezhda Mandel'shtam's two volumes of memoirs endure as a classic revelation of the "unofficial" passions, values, and poetics of her society.

**Letters:**

"192 pis'ma k B. S. Kuzinu," in Boris Sergeevich Kuzin, *Vospominaniia, proizvedeniia, perepiska* (St. Petersburg: Inapress, 1999), pp. 513–752.

**References:**

Eduard Grigor'evich Babaev, *Vospominaniia* (St. Petersburg: Inapress, 2000);

Joseph Brodsky, "Nadezhda Mandelstam (1899–1980): An Obituary," in his *Less Than One: Selected Essays* (New York: Farrar, Straus & Giroux, 1986), pp. 145–156;

Emma Grigor'evna Gershtein, "Nadezhda Iakovlevna," *Memuary* (St. Petersburg: Inapress, 1998), pp. 412–445;

Gershtein, *Novoe o Mandelstame* (Paris: Atheneum, 1986);

Frederick T. Griffiths and Stanley J. Rabinowitz, "Stalin and the Death of Epic: Mikhail Bakhtin, Nadezhda Mandelstam, Boris Pasternak," in *Epic and Epoch: Essays on the Interpretation and History of a Genre,* edited by Steven M. Oberhelman, Van Kelly, and Richard J. Golsan (Lubbock: Texas Tech University Press, 1994), pp. 267–288;

Beth Holmgren, "For the Good of the Cause: Russian Women's Autobiography in the Twentieth Century," in *Women Writers in Russian Literature,* edited by Toby W. Clyman and Diana Greene (Westport, Conn.: Greenwood Press, 1994), pp. 127–148;

Holmgren, "Stepping Out/Going Under: Women in Russia's Twentieth-Century Salons," in *Russia–*

*Women–Culture,* edited by Holmgren and Helena Goscilo (Bloomington & Indianapolis: Indiana University Press, 1996), pp. 225–246;

Holmgren, *Women's Works in Stalin's Time: On Lidia Chukovskaia and Nadezhda Mandelstam* (Bloomington & Indianapolis: Indiana University Press, 1993);

Charles Isenberg, "The Rhetoric of *Hope against Hope*," in *Autobiographical Statements in Twentieth-Century Russian Literature,* edited by Jane Gary Harris (Princeton: Princeton University Press, 1990), pp. 193–206;

Richard Pevear, "On the Memoirs of Nadezhda Mandelstam," *Hudson Review,* 24 (Autumn 1971): 426–440;

Mikhail K. Polivanov, "Introduction to Nadezhda Mandelstam's *Vospominaniia,*" *Iunost',* 8 (1988): 34–35;

Sarah Pratt, "Angels in the Stalinist House: Nadezhda Mandel'shtam, Lidiia Chukovskaia, Lidiia Ginzburg, and Russian Women's Autobiography," in *Engendering Slavic Literatures,* edited by Pamela Chester and Sibelan Forrester (Bloomington & Indianapolis: Indiana University Press, 1996), pp. 158–173;

Carl R. Proffer, "Nadezhda Mandelstam," in his *The Widows of Russia and Other Writings* (Ann Arbor, Mich.: Ardis, 1987), pp. 13–61;

Judith Robey, "Gender and the Autobiographical Project in Nadezhda Mandelstam's *Hope against Hope* and *Hope Abandoned,*" *Slavic and East European Journal,* 42 (Summer 1998): 231–253;

Natal'ia Shtempel', "Mandel'shtam v Voronezhe," *Novyi mir,* 10 (1987): 207–234;

Shtempel', "Pamiati Nadezhdy Iakovlevnoi Mandel'shtam," *Pod'em,* 6 (1989): 209–213.

**Papers:**

The papers of Nadezhda Iakovlevna Mandel'shtam are located at the Muzei Anny Akhmatovy v Fontannom Dome (The Anna Akhmatova Museum in the Fontannyi House) in St. Petersburg.

# Vladimir Rafailovich Maramzin
(5 August 1934 -    )

Lev Loseff
*Dartmouth College*

BOOKS: *Tut my rabotaem. Rasskazy cheloveka, ne vsegda absoliutno ser'ioznogo* (Leningrad: Detskaia literatura, 1966);

*Kto razvozit gorozhan. Ne sovsem ser'ioznye rasskazy, iz kotorykh, odnako, mozhno uznat' mnogo poleznogo* (Leningrad: Detskaia literatura, 1969);

*Blondin obeego tsveta* (Ann Arbor, Mich.: Ardis, 1975);

*Smeshnee chem prezhde* (Montgeron, France: Tret'ia volna, 1979);

*Tianitolkai* (Ann Arbor, Mich.: Ardis, 1981);

*Syn Otechestva* (Paris: Ekho, 2003).

SELECTED PERIODICAL PUBLICATIONS–UNCOLLECTED: "Andrei Platonovich Platonov: Bibliograficheskii ukazatel'," compiled by Maramzin, *Ekho,* 4 (1977); 8 (1980); 13 (1984);

"Vozvrashchenets," *Zvezda,* 5 (1999): 36–43.

During the politically turbulent period from the late 1950s through the mid 1970s–starting with Nikita Sergeevich Khrushchev's "Thaw" (de-Stalinization and moderate ideological liberalization policy) and ending with the stabilization of Leonid Il'ich Brezhnev's corrupt and oppressive regime–two distinct trends were developing in Russian literature. One may be characterized as a continuation of sociopsychological, sometimes satirical, realism in the style of Leo Tolstoy and Anton Pavlovich Chekhov. The majority of writers whose works belonged to this trend and who are sometimes categorized as authors of either *derevenshchiki* (Village Prose) or *gorodoskaic proza* (City Literature) lived in the provinces or in Moscow; considered the journal *Novyi mir* (The New World) their main tribune; and saw their works published–although often these publications were mutilated by censors and subsequently attacked by ideological watchdogs. The other trend was a resurgence of the modernist tradition, which had been completely trampled upon in Joseph Stalin's time. An experimentation with language and narrative techniques–implicit in the prose of Andrei Bely, Fedor Kuz'mich Sologub, Evgenii Ivanovich Zamiatin,

*Vladimir Rafailovich Maramzin (*Blondin obeego tsveta,
*1975; Collection of Christine Rydel)*

Mikhail Mikhailovich Zoshchenko, Boris Stepanovich Zhitkov, Konstantin Konstantinovich Vaginov, and Leonid Ivanovich Dobychin and rooted in the grotesque narratives of Nikolai Semenovich Leskov, Nikolai Vasil'evich Gogol, and Fyodor Mikhailovich Dostoevsky–was taken up by a group of young writers who lived in Leningrad (now St. Petersburg). Only occasionally did these writers have their less representative pieces published in the U.S.S.R., while their major works circulated in samizdat or were published abroad at the authors' peril. This group included Andrei Georgievich Bitov, Igor' Markovich Efimov, Viktor Vladimirovich Goliavkin, Rid Iosifovich Grachev (Vitte), Vadim Viktorovich Nechaev (Bakinsky), Valerii Georgievich Popov, German Vladimirovich Shef, and Boris Borisovich Vakhtin. A powerful artistic and political temperament, combined with an exceptional knack for the intricacies of the Russian language, made another person in this pleiad, Vladimir Maramzin, one of the most original writers of postwar Soviet literature.

Vladimir Rafailovich Maramzin was born in Leningrad on 5 August 1934. His father, Rafail Markovich, a factory worker, was killed in World War II; his mother, Vera Aleksandrovna (née Sokolova) was a schoolteacher. From earliest childhood through the age of eleven Maramzin lived in the small town of Kashin (Tver' region), where he was raised by his maternal grandmother, the widow of a Russian Orthodox country priest, who perished during the early Soviet onslaught against the church. After finishing high school in 1953, Maramzin studied at a prestigious engineering school, the Leningrad Institute of Electrical Technology, and upon graduation in 1957 worked at the electronic tubes factory, where he was employed until 1965. While still at the institute, he had begun writing short fiction pieces and attending literary clubs and workshops, where he met and befriended young writers, such as Bitov, Efimov, Grachev, and Vakhtin, bent on stylistic experimentation. Among their mentors were Viktor Semenovich Bakinsky, David Iakovlevich Dar, Gennadii Samoilovich Gor, and other survivors of the Stalinist ideological purges. These people in essence were writers and critics who provided a living link to the 1920s, the age of relative creative freedom and artistic experimentation.

In 1966 Maramzin became a full-time freelance writer. Like many of his peers, he followed in the footsteps of earlier "politically incorrect" authors: he supported himself mainly by writing for children. Drawing from his technical knowledge and engineering experience, he wrote many amusing stories for children's magazines, as well as two lively books in the "how-does-it-work" genre: *Tut my rabotaem. Rasskazy cheloveka, ne vsegda absoliutno ser'ioznogo* (1966, Here We Work: Tales Told by a Man Who Is Not Always Absolutely Serious) and *Kto razvozit gorozhan. Ne sovsem ser'ioznye rasskazy, iz kotorykh, odnako, mozhno uznat' mnogo poleznogo* (1969, Who Takes Townspeople Where They Want to Go: Not Quite Serious Stories, from Which, However, One Can Learn Many Useful Things). He also produced occasional essays and book reviews for literary magazines and moonlighted at a film studio, where he edited dialogue for foreign-language motion pictures that had been dubbed in Russian.

Two early stories that made Maramzin well-known to samizdat readers were "Ia s poshchechinoi v ruke" (1964, Me with a Slap in My Hands) and "Tianitolkai" (1966), the title of which refers to a character—a fantastic animal with heads on both ends of his body—from a popular children's story. Both stories feature Kafkaesque plots that are evidently rooted in Maramzin's own life experiences: an innocent, open-hearted hero falls victim to a bureaucratic machine, the modus operandi of which is mysterious.

At the beginning of "Ia s poshchechinoi v ruke," the protagonist, a young factory engineer, is insulted for no reason by a dowdy coworker. He suppresses his first impulse—to slap the boor in the face, an act that likely would have ended the conflict on the spot. The insult is followed by increasingly hostile treatment of the hero by the factory management. Once the hero's enemy has falsely reported his misbehavior to the authorities, he can do nothing to clear his name. Meanwhile, the undelivered slap becomes an object, which the hero has to carry around and hide from people. Finally, he tries to throw it away. The slap returns like a boomerang and hits him in the face. The satirical message of this parable-like story is that in an unjust society everyone is tainted. Even little acts of cowardly conformism strengthen the oppressive regime.

Another grotesque yet cautionary tale about the perils of conformism is "Tianitolkai." Here the hero is a young dissident writer who is taken from the street to the headquarters of the Kommitet gosudarstvennoi bezopasnosti (KGB, State Security Committee), where a secret police colonel and other officers perform an elaborate farce for him and gradually draw him into their play. Maramzin borrows parts of the plot for "Tianitolkai" from Aleksei Konstantinovich Tolstoy's satirical ballad "Counselor Popov's Dream" (1878). This connection gives Maramzin's satire a historical dimension: the more it changes, the more it remains the same. Both stories are genuinely funny. Maramzin's forte, already apparent at this early stage in his career, is his ear for poignant, dynamic dialogue—which is often hilarious because of the stylistic clashes between street jargon and officialese.

These and other early stories attest to Maramzin's nearly perfect linguistic pitch, comedic talent, and mastery of composition, but they were not entirely original: the stylistic hodgepodge in which his characters thought and expressed themselves was evidently learned from Zoshchenko, while Maramzin's plots were influenced by Franz Kafka and later absurdists such as Eugène Ionesco, who at the time was popular in Russia. In 1966 Maramzin found his own voice through the writing of *Sekrety* (Secrets), a collection of twenty-eight short stories. Some of these stories have simple anecdotal plots reminiscent of folktales, while others seem to be plotless sketches consisting of observed street scenes, quick portraits, or reported gossip. The comedy in these stories is muted, the majority of them are not overtly satirical, and the narrator strives for objectivity. Usually one person is carefully observed at the center of each miniature—a man or a woman from a different walk of life: a factory worker, a schoolboy, a single woman in a big city, a poor old widow in a provincial town, a young soldier, or a silly old professor. The combined effect of the twenty-eight "secrets" is more than any one of these unpretentious individual pieces might suggest: together they form a psychologically complex and, ultimately, lyrical portrait of a nation. The peculiar lyricism of *Sekrety* has as its hidden source Maramzin's deep sympathy for the "little man."

The "little man" as literary hero, a trope with origins in nineteenth-century Russian literature, was deemed obsolete by Soviet ideology and replaced with the "new Soviet man, builder of Communism." The "little man," a pathetic character who aspires not to construct a utopia but only to carve out for himself a niche of simple family happiness, was reincarnated in *Sekrety* and in three novellas, or *povesti*, written by Maramzin in the 1960s: *Nachal'nik* (The Boss, in *Continent*, 1964), *Istoriia zhenit'by Ivana Petrovicha* (The History of Ivan Petrovich's Marriage, in *Continent*, 1964), and *Chelovek, kotoryi veril v svoe osoboe naznachenie* (The Man Who Believed in His Special Predestination, in *Vremia i my*, 1967). The eponymous hero of the ironically titled *Nachal'nik* is a young family man who works as a low-rank factory supervisor. The novella tells about his daily routine as a series of lost and won little battles in the unending war for the preservation of his dignity. The opening paragraph of the work sets the tone: "On Thursday, his bath day, the boss went to the bathhouse. There were too many people there. The boss got upset: 'O.K., he thought, I'm going home; they'll be sorry.' But then he calmed down and took his place at the end of the line." The story of a man striving to be the boss of his own life continues in this same vein.

The two main characters of *Istoriia zhenit'by Ivana Petrovicha*—a young single man in search of a girlfriend and a starving young woman who has decided to sell herself—meander through the streets of a big city (Leningrad) until they meet each other. What started as a mere transaction in the sex trade turns into a relationship of extreme tenderness. The remarkable characteristic of this story is its dense, albeit somewhat infantile, eroticism. The title character Ivan Petrovich's sudden and prayerful outburst—"Lord! . . . What happiness is given to people between the legs! And what they do with it! How unpardonably badly they treat it!"—could be an epigraph to the third novella, *Chelovek, kotoryi veril v svoe osoboe naznachenie*, which describes the adventures of a Soviet-age Don Juan.

The gentle blend of humor, eroticism, and sentimentality that characterizes Maramzin's short stories and novellas of the 1960s gives way to a darker, Dostoevskian stream-of-consciousness narrative in the 1975 novella, *Blondin obeego tsveta* (A Fair-Haired Man of Both Colors). This confessional narrative is a monologue spoken by a bisexual Soviet artist, whose psyche is tortured by a triple compromise: his art is compromised by conformism, his conscience is compromised by contacts with the secret police, and his sexuality is compromised by his pretense at heterosexuality. A distant literary descendant of Dostoevsky's "Underground Man," he has a closer predecessor in Nikolai Kavalerov, the protagonist of Iurii Karlovich Olesha's *Zavist'* (1928; translated as *Envy*, 1947). Maramzin's Blondin lives by the same passion: he worshipfully envies someone who is unapproachable, the wholesome Nikolai the Painter, a master who never betrayed his talent. Secretly infatuated with him, Blondin tries to imitate Nikolai's art, and he marries Nikolai's former wife as a substitute for physical contact with the object of his passion.

However poignant is the story line of *Blondin obeego tsveta*, its most striking feature is its language. It differs qualitatively not only from the language found in Maramzin's earlier works but from almost anything else in Russian literature—with the possible exception of Osip Emil'evich Mandel'shtam's late poetry. Throughout *Blondin obeego tsveta* Maramzin avoids common usages and creates a powerful and disturbing effect by combining seemingly incompatible words or larger semantic blocks (which are, by and large, parts of colloquial or ideological set expressions). In the introductory chapter he explains that this apparently "a-grammatical" language reflects the "disintegration of the Russian consciousness." It is also an extreme experiment in expanding the semantic potential of spoken Russian. The very title of the novella is a triple-layered wordplay that employs a slangy expression and "a-grammaticality." That is, the slang term for a gay man is *goluboi* (the blue one); thus Maramzin's expression "of both colors" refers to the bisexuality of his protagonist-narrator. Furthermore, the blatantly ungrammatical *obeego* of the title is the feminine form of the Russian pronoun for "both"—instead of the masculine *oboego*, which would be correct. *Obeego* is a common mistake in the speech of the uneducated; its presence in the title immediately discloses the narrator's intellectual status. At the same time, this confusion of grammatical genders surreptitiously exacerbates the theme of Blondin's ambivalent sexual persona. This example is relatively simple, but most of Maramzin's linguistic innovations are nearly impossible to explain in a foreign language, let alone translate. Six monological short stories under the common title *Smeshnee chem prezhde* (1979, Even Funnier Than Before) are written in a similar manner.

In the years between his first publication and his forced removal from public life in 1974, Maramzin managed to publish in the Soviet Union just a dozen of his early "adult" stories, most of them short. His continuously frustrated attempts to have a collection of his stories released by one of the Leningrad state publishing houses led to an infamous episode in 1968, when the notoriously hot-tempered Maramzin, after an especially insulting reply to an inquiry about the production progress of his book, physically assaulted the Communist Party functionary who ran the publishing house. For that misdemeanor Maramzin was tried and given a one-year suspended sentence.

This first serious brush with authorities did not make Maramzin more cautious. He maintained wide contacts with dissident communities in Leningrad and Moscow and eagerly, almost recklessly, disseminated forbidden texts, particularly Russian books smuggled from abroad and homespun samizdat literature. Although he lacked formal philological training, Maramzin by now was an experienced researcher and editor, thanks to his deep interest in the work of Andrei Platonovich Platonov. He had discovered and prepared for publication some lost stories by Platonov and compiled a complete bibliography of Platonov's publications. (The bibliography appeared in *Ekho* [Echo], the Paris-based journal that Maramzin helped edit, from 1977 to 1984.)

In 1971 Maramzin undertook his own major samizdat project. He decided to collect and publish clandestinely a complete edition of the works of Joseph Brodsky, who at this time was already a mature, prolific, and widely popular poet—although only a handful of his poems had been officially published in the U.S.S.R. Brodsky was utterly unconcerned about the fate of his finished works: while some of his long and short poems reached émigré publishers and were released abroad, many more circulated in samizdat as individual pieces in unedited, often distorted, versions. There was a real risk that a large part of his early poetry might simply disappear. Maramzin's task was to collect, as comprehensively as possible, the poems that were scattered in dozens of private homes in Leningrad and Moscow; to establish authoritative texts with the help of the poet; and to provide basic annotation for each text.

Under the best of circumstances such a project would have required a long-term concerted effort by a

*Title page for* Blondin obeego tsveta *(1975, A Fair-Haired Man of Both Colors), the confessional narrative of a Soviet bisexual artist tortured by the compromise of his art, his conscience, and his sexuality (William T. Young Library, University of Kentucky)*

group of professional scholars and editors. Yet, in fewer than three years, Maramzin—almost single-handedly (some financial and editorial help came from other Brodsky enthusiasts)—compiled a virtually complete five-volume edition of Brodsky's poetry, for which Maramzin also wrote some useful commentary. In the process he collected and organized the poet's archive, which he managed to hide from inquisitive authorities in an ingenious and secure way after Brodsky's expulsion from the Soviet Union in 1972. Several dozen copies of the typewritten edition, nicknamed the "Maramzin collection," circulated in samizdat and eventually became the major source for all subsequent printed editions of Brodsky's poetry. In addition, Maramzin's commentary is now a standard reference source for students of Brodsky's work.

In the spring of 1974 the Leningrad branch of the KGB conducted searches in the apartments of Maramzin and Mikhail Ruvimovich Kheifets, a literary critic and historian who had written an introductory essay for the "Maramzin collection." Kheifets was arrested immediately, while Maramzin's arrest occurred three months later. After eight months of solitary confinement in a KGB prison, Maramzin was tried and given another suspended sentence. The relatively mild sentence can be explained by the interference of the central authorities: Moscow was displeased by the clumsy work of the Leningrad KGB. In these days of detente the Soviet government did not need from the West another wave of protests against the persecution of a writer. Like Brodsky three years earlier, Maramzin was pressed to leave the country after his release from prison.

Since 1975 Vladimir Rafailovich Maramzin has lived in Paris, where he runs a bureau of technical translation. Initially, he was active in the political and cultural life of the Russian émigré community in France. He submitted works that had remained unpublished in Russia, as well as works written while in emigration, to Russian-language newspapers and journals; these works also appeared in book form. Many of his short stories and novellas have been translated into French, English, German, and other European languages. In 1978–1986 he sponsored and co-edited (with Aleksei L'vovich Khvostenko) a quarterly journal, *Ekho*, which was more avant-garde in its orientation than other émigré literary magazines. Besides new prose and poetry, several early works by Maramzin's Leningrad peers were published initially in *Ekho*. A decade-long hiatus in Maramzin's literary activity lasted from the late 1980s until the late 1990s. Since 1999 new short stories and essays by him have been appearing in periodicals in Russia and abroad. In 1999 he married his fourth wife, Veronika. He has three children, one from each of his previous marriages.

**References:**

Valerii Nikolaevich Chalidze, ed., *Literaturnye dela KGB: Dela Superfina, Etkinda, Kheifetsa, Maramzina* (New York: Khronika, 1976), pp. 73–139;

Emile Kogan, "Vladimir Maramzine: Un jeune 'hyperréaliste' soviétique," *Le Monde,* 13 December 1974, p. 19;

Lev Vladimirovich Lifshits, "Proza Ivana Petrovicha," *Kontinent,* no. 10 (1976): 386–393;

Iurii Vladimirovich Mal'tsev, *Vol'naia russkaia literatura: 1955–1975* (Frankfurt am Main: Posev, 1976), pp. 107–115;

Natal'ia Rubinshtein, "Zametki o povesti V. Maramzina 'Blondin obeego tsveta,'" *Grani,* no. 100 (1976): 495–505;

Pietro Zveteremich, "Vachtin e i 'Gorozane'," in *Fantastico grotesco absurdo e satira nella narrativa russa d'oggi (1956–1980)* (Messina: Peloritana, 1980), pp. 43–46.

**Papers:**

Maramzin's papers, mostly related to publishing *Ekho* from 1977–1984, are in the archive of the Institute of East Europe, Bremen University, Bremen, Germany.

# Iurii Markovich Nagibin

(3 April 1920 – 17 June 1994)

Alexandra Smith
*University of Canterbury, New Zealand*

BOOKS: *Chelovek s fronta: Rasskazy* (Moscow: Sovetskii pisatel', 1943);

*Bol'shoe serdtse: Rasskazy* (Moscow: Sovetskii pisatel', 1944);

*Dve sily* (Moscow, 1944);

*Gvardeitsy na Dnepre* (Moscow: Molodaia gvardiia, 1944);

*Zerno zhizni: Rasskazy* (Moscow: Sovetskii pisatel', 1948);

*Gosudarstvennoe delo: Rasskazy* (Moscow: Pravda, 1950);

*Gospodstvuiushchaia vysota* (Moscow, 1951);

*Trubka: Rasskazy* (Moscow: Izd-vo Pravda, 1953);

*Rasskazy* (Moscow: Sovetskii pisatel', 1955);

*Zimnii dub: Rasskazy* (Moscow: TSK VLKSM, 1955);

*Na ozerakh: Rasskazy* (Moscow: Pravda, 1957);

*Skalistyi porog: Rasskazy* (Moscow: Molodaia gvardiia, 1958);

*Chelovek i doroga: Rasskazy* (Moscow: Sovetskii pisatel', 1958);

*Poslednii shturm* (Moscow: Voennoe izdatel'stvo, 1959);

*Pered prazdnikom: Rasskazy i povest'* (Moscow: Molodaia gvardiia, 1960);

*Rannei vesnoi: Rasskazy* (Moscow: Goslitizdat, 1961);

*Druz'ia moi, liudi: Rasskazy* (Moscow: Sovetskaia Rossiia, 1961);

*Chistye prudy: Rasskazy raznykh let. Povest'. Dorogi-vstrechi* (Moscow: Moskovskii rabochii, 1962);

*Stranitsy zhizni Trubnikova: Povest'* (Moscow: Sovetskaia Rossiia, 1963);

*Pogonia: Meshcherskie byli* (Moscow: Sovetskaia Rossiia, 1964);

*Trudnyi put' (predsedatel') literaturnyi stsenarii* (Moscow: Iskusstvo, 1965);

*Dalekoe i blizkoe: Povest' i rasskazy* (Moscow: Sovetskii pisatel', 1965);

*Na tikhom ozere i drugie rasskazy* (Moscow: Sovetskaia Rossiia, 1966);

*Nochnoi gost'* (Moscow: Fizkul'tura i sport, 1966);

*Zelenaia ptitsa s krasnoi golovoi* (Moscow: Moskovskii rabochii, 1966);

*Ne dai emu pogibnut'* (Moscow: Molodaia gvardiia, 1968);

*Iurii Markovich Nagibin, 1968 (from* Ne dai emu pogibnut', *Thomas Cooper Library, University of South Carolina)*

*Chuzhoe serdtse: Povesti i rasskazy* (Moscow: Molodaia gvardiia, 1969);

*Perekur: Povest' i rasskazy* (Moscow: Sovetskaia Rossiia, 1970);

*Pereulki moego detstva* (Moscow: Sovremennik, 1971);

*Nepobedimyi Arsenov: Rasskazy* (Moscow: Fizkul'tura i sport, 1972);

*Moia Afrika: Putevye ocherki* (Moscow: Nauka, 1973);

*V aprel'skom lesu: Povesti i rasskazy* (Moscow: Voennoe izdatel'stvo Ministerstva oborony SSSR, 1974);

*Ty budesh' zhit': Povesti i rasskazy* (Moscow: Sovremennik, 1974);

*Pik udachi: Izbrannye povesti* (Moscow: Sovetskaia Rossiia, 1975);

*Malen'kie rasskazy o bol'shoi sud'be* (Moscow: Sovetskaia Rossiia, 1976);

*Literaturnye razdum'ia* (Moscow: Sovetskaia Rossiia, 1977);

*Ostrov liubvi: Povesti i rasskazy* (Moscow: Molodaia gvardiia, 1977);

*Berendeev les: Rasskazy, ocherki* (Moscow: Sovetskii pisatel', 1978);

*Zabroshennaia doroga* (Moscow: Sovremennik, 1979);

*Tsarskosel'skoe utro: Povesti, rasskazy* (Moscow: Izvestiia, 1979);

*Ispytanie: Rasskazy* (Moscow: Fizkul'tura i sport, 1980);

*Kinotsenarii* (Moscow: Iskusstvo, 1980);

*Nauka dal'nikh stranstvii* (Moscow: Molodaia gvardiia, 1982);

*Dorozhnoe puteshestvie* (Moscow: Goskomizdata, 1983);

*Ne chuzhoe remeslo* (Moscow: Sovremennik, 1983);

*Dvory, pereulki i ves' mir: Povest' i rasskazy* (Moscow: Detskaia literatura, 1984);

*Reka Geraklita: Rasskazy i povesti* (Moscow: Sovremennik, 1984);

*Moskovskaia kniga* (Moscow: Moskovskii rabochii, 1985);

*Lunnyi svet: Povesti i rasskazy* (Minsk: Vysheishaia shkola, 1986);

*Muzykanty; Kniaz'; Iurka Golitsyn; Blestiashchaia i gorestnaia zhizn' Imre Kal'mana* (Moscow: Sovremennik, 1986);

*Poezdka na ostrova: Povesti i rasskazy* (Moscow: Molodaia gvardiia, 1987);

*Sil'nee vsekh inykh velenii: Povest'* (Moscow: Goskomizdata, 1987);

*Vremia zhit'* (Moscow: Sovremennik, 1987);

*Terpenie: Rasskazy, povesti* (Moscow: Izvestiia, 1987);

*Moskva, kak mnogo v etom zvuke–* (Moscow: Sovetskaia Rossiia, 1987);

*V dozhd': Rasskazy* (Moscow: Pravda, 1988);

*Vstan' i idi: Povesti i rasskazy* (Moscow: Khudozhestvennaia literatura, 1989);

*Vdali muzyka i ogni: Povesti i rasskazy* (Moscow: Sovremennik, 1989);

*Il'in den': Povest' i rasskazy* (Moscow: Sovremennik, 1990);

*Prorok budet sozhzhen: Novelly* (Moscow: Kniga, 1990);

*Rasskazy sinego liagushonka* (Moscow: Mosgorpechat, 1991);

*Buntashnyi ostrov: Povesti i rasskazy* (Moscow: Moskovskii rabochii, 1994);

*T'ma v kontse tunnelia; Moia zolotaia teshcha: Povesty* (Moscow: Nezavisimoe izdatel'stvo PIK, 1994);

*Liubov' vozhdei: Povesti, rasskazy* (Moscow: Nezavisimoe izdatel'stvo PIK, 1994);

*Dafnis i khloia epokhi kul'ta lichnosti, voliuntarizma i zastoia* (Moscow: Nezavisimoe izdatel'stvo PIK, 1995);

*Dnevnik* (Moscow: Knizhnyi sad, 1995; revised and enlarged, 1996);

*Iurii Nagibin*, 3 volumes (Moscow: Agraf, 1996);

*Vspoloshnyi zvon: O Moskve* (Moscow: Podkova/Dekont+, 1997);

*Nad propast'iu vo lzhi* (Moscow: Podkova, 1998);

*Ital'ianskaia tetrad'* (Moscow: Podkova, 1998);

*Uchitel' slovesnosti* (Moscow: Podkova, 1998);

*Predsedatel'* (Moscow: Podkova, 1998);

*Utrachennaia muzyka* (Moscow: Podkova, 1998);

*Vechnaia muzyka* (Moscow: Podkova, 1998);

*Belaia siren'*, by Nagibin and Andrei Sergeevich Mikhalkov-Konchalovskii (St. Petersburg: Fonda russkoi poezii/Tsentr Gumanitarnaia Akademiia, 2001);

*Pered tvoim prestolom* (Moscow: AST/VZOI, 2004);

*Chto skazal by Gamlet* (Moscow: AST/Tranzitkniga, 2004);

*Ulybka Dzhokondy* (Moscow: AST/VZOI, 2004).

**Editions and Collections:** *Izbrannye proizvedeniia*, 2 volumes (Moscow: Khudozhestvennaia literatura, 1973);

*Chistye prudy: Kniga dlia chteniia* (Moscow: Russkii iazyk, 1977);

*Sobranie sochinenii*, 4 volumes (Moscow: Khudozhestvennaia literatura, 1980–1981);

*Tsarskosel'skoe utro: Povesti, rasskazy* (Moscow: Sovetskii pisatel', 1983);

*Chelovek s fronta: Povest' i rasskazy* (Moscow: DOSAAF, 1988);

*Izbrannoe* (Moscow: TERRA, 1994);

*Izbrannoe*, 3 volumes (Moscow: AGRAF, 1996);

*Moskovskaia kniga* (Moscow: Podkova, 1997);

*Terpenie* (Moscow: Podkov, 1998);

*T'ma v kontse tunnelia* (Moscow: Podkova, 1998);

*Ostrov liubvi* (Moscow: AST/Olimp/Astrel', 2000);

*Dnevnik* (Moscow: AST/Olimp/Astrel', 2001);

*Ostrov libvi: Libvov' vozhdei; T'ma v kontse tonnelia; Moia zolotaia teshcha* (Moscow: OLMA-Press, 2004).

**Editions in English:** *Each for All* (London & New York: Hutchinson, 1945);

"Komarov," in *Short Stories by Soviet Authors*, volume 1, edited by R. Dixon (Moscow: Progress Publishers, 1951);

*The Pipe: Stories*, translated by V. Shneerson (Moscow: Foreign Languages Publishing House, 1955);

*Dreams: Short Stories* (Moscow: Foreign Languages Publishing House, 1958);

"The Night Guest," in *Short Stories of Russia Today*, edited by Yvonne Kapp (Boston: Houghton Mifflin, 1959);

"The Khazar Ornament," in *The Year of Protest, 1956: An Anthology of Soviet Materials*, edited by Hugh McLean and Walter N. Vickery (New York: Vintage, 1961);

*Selected Short Stories*, edited by D. J. Richards (Oxford: Pergamon Press / New York: Macmillan, 1963);

"The Green Bird with the Red Head," in *The Young Russians: A Collection of Stories about Them*, edited by Thomas P. Whitney (New York: Macmillan, 1972);

"A Light in the Window," in *Fifty Years of Russian Prose: From Pasternak to Solzhenitsyn*, volume 2, edited by Krystyna Pomorska (Cambridge, Mass.: MIT Press, 1973);

"In the April Forest," in *Spring Light: Short Stories*, translated by K. M. Cook (Moscow: Progress Publishers, 1974);

"The Newlywed," in *Soviet Short Stories*, edited by Avrahm Yarmolinsky (Westport, Conn.: Greenwood Press, 1975);

"An Old Turtle," in *Twelve Contemporary Russian Stories*, edited by Vytas Dukas (Rutherford, N.J.: Fairleigh Dickinson University Press, 1977);

"The Lilac," in *Soviet Russian Stories of the 1960's and 1970's*, edited by Iurii A. Bochkarev (Moscow: Progress Publishers, 1977);

*Island of Love*, translated by Olga Shartse (Moscow: Progress Publishers, 1982);

*The Peak of Success and Other Stories*, edited by Helena Goscilo (Ann Arbor, Mich.: Ardis, 1986);

*An Unwritten Story by Somerset Maugham: Novellas* (Moscow: Raduga, 1988);

*Arise and Walk*, translated by Catherine Porter (London: Faber & Faber, 1990);

"Discovering Our Past," translated by Dudley Hagen, in *Openings: Original Essays by Contemporary Soviet and American Writers*, edited by Robert Atwan and Valerii Vinokurov (Seattle: University of Washington Press, 1990);

"Peak of Success," in *Peak of Success: Tales of Fantasy by Modern Soviet Writers* (Moscow: Raduga, 1991).

PRODUCED SCRIPTS: *Gost's Kubani,* motion picture, Mosfil'm, 1956;

*Trudnoe schast'e,* motion picture, Mosfil'm, 1958;
*Nochnoi gost',* motion picture, Lenfil'm, 1958;
*Neoplachennyi dolg,* motion picture, Mosfil'm, 1959;
*Pod stuk koles,* motion picture, Lenfil'm, 1959;
*Pobeditel',* motion picture, Lenfil'm, 1960;
*Brat'ia Komarovy,* motion picture, Lenfil'm, 1962;
*Lichnoe pervenstvo,* motion picture, Mosfil'm, 1962;
*Samyi medlennyi poezd,* motion picture, Sverdloskaia kinostudiia, 1963;
*Bab'e tsarstvo,* motion picture, Mosfil'm, 1963;
*Trudnyi put',* motion picture, Mosfil'm, 1963;
*Predsedatel',* motion picture, Mosfil'm, 1964;
*Devochka i ekho,* motion picture, screenplay by Nagibin, Anatolii Charchenko, and Arunas Zhebriunas, Litovskaia kinostudiia, 1964;
*Chaikovskii,* motion picture, screenplay by Nagibin, Budimir Metal'nikov, and Igor' Talankin, Mosfil'm, 1969;
*Direktor,* motion picture, Mosfil'm, 1969;
*Goluboi led,* motion picture, screenplay by Nagibin and Tsezar Solodar, Lenfil'm, 1969;
*Zhdi menia, Anna,* motion picture, Belarusfil'm, 1969;
*Dersu Uzala,* motion picture, screenplay by Nagibin and Akira Kurosawa, Mosfil'm/Atelier 41/Daiei Studios, 1975;
*Sem'ia Ivanovykh,* motion picture, 1975;
*Tak nachinalas' legenda,* motion picture, 1976;
*Olsnienie,* motion picture, PRF Zespol Filmowy/Zespol Filmowy Profil, 1976;
*Élét muziskája–Kálmán Imre, Az,* motion picture, Hungarofilm/Mafil'm/Mosfil'm/Sovinfil'm, 1984;
*Detstvo Bembi,* motion picture, screenplay by Nagibin and Natalya Bondarchuk, Gorky Film Studios, 1985;
*Iunost' Bembi,* motion picture, screenplay by Nagibin and Bondarchuk, Gorky Film Studios, 1986;
*Sil'nee vsekh inykh velenii (Syuita na russkiye temy),* motion picture, Gorky Film Studios, 1987;
"Gardemariny, vperyod!" television, screenplay by Nagibin, Svetlana Druzhinina, and Nina Sorotokina, Gosteleradio/Mosfil'm, 1987;
*Vivat, Gardemariny!* motion picture, screenplay by Nagibin, Druzhinina, and Sorotokina, Mosfil'm/ Zhanr, 1991;
*Gardemariny III,* motion picture, screenplay by Nagibin and Sorotokina, CCC Filmkunst/Mosfil'm/ Zhanr, 1992;
*Il quarto re,* television, screenplay by Nagibin, Enzo De Caro, and Enrico Medioli, Mediaset/Taurus Film/ Titanus, 1998.

OTHER: "Knut: Pravdivoe gadan'e," in *Moskovskii al'manakh* (Moscow: Sovetskii pisatel', 1941);

Felix Salten, *Bembi: Lesnaia skazka,* translated and adapted by Nagibin (Moscow: Detskaia literatura, 1964);

"Gde-to vozle konservatorii," in *"Nash Sovremennik," izbrannaia proza zhurnala, 1964–1975,* edited by V. Petrov (Moscow: Sovremennik, 1975);

*Front cover for* Zimnii dub: Rasskazy *(1955, Winter Oak: Stories). The title story, about a schoolboy who introduces his teacher to the lessons of nature, was adapted as a television movie (George A. Smathers Libraries, University of Florida).*

"Vasia, chuesh'?" in *Veter veka: Sbornik rasskazov I ocherkov,* edited by Anatolii Mikhailovich Mednikov (Moscow: Sovetskii pisatel', 1976);

"Kvasnik i buzheniniva," in *Povest' 86,* edited by Iurii Stefanovich (Moscow: Sovremennik, 1987);

"Otechestvo vo vsekh ego predelakh," in *Vsled podvigam Petrovym...,* edited by G. I. Gerasimov, introduction by Leia Georgievna Kisliagina (Moscow: Molodaia gvardiia, 1988);

V. V. Gorbunov, *Ideia sobornosti v russkoi religioznoi filosofii: Piat' izbrannykh portretov,* introduction by Nagibin (Moscow: Feniks, 1994).

**SELECTED PERIODICAL PUBLICATIONS– UNCOLLECTED:** "Samaia vazhnaia vstrecha," *Voprosy Literatury,* 2 (1979): 191–198;

"O tom, chto trevozhit–v literature i zhizni," *Oktiabr',* 2 (February 1988): 194–200.

Iurii Nagibin was a prolific fiction writer whose stories and novellas touch on such themes as childhood, war, love, history, music, Moscow life, and nature. He is also known for his scripts for many successful movies, including the Japanese-Soviet *Dersu Uzala* (1975), co-written and directed by Akira Kurosawa, which received the American Academy Award for best foreign-language film in 1976. Nagibin's works have been translated into many languages. He traveled extensively in the Soviet Union and abroad, and his travel stories include lively descriptions of Japan, the Middle East, the United States, Europe, and Australia. According to Marc Slonim, Nagibin is "representative of a whole group of writers who have brought genuine emotions, psychological insight, humaneness, and a careful objective rendering of reality into contemporary Soviet literature."

Iurii Markovich Nagibin was born in Moscow on 3 April 1920, the only child of Kirill Aleksandrovich Nagibin, an economist, and Kseniia Alekseevna Konevskaia. Nagibin's father was apparently killed during the civil war of 1920. His mother began living with another man, Mark Iakovlevich Levental'. Though she and her son continued to go by her husband's last name, Nagibin took on the patronymic Markovich after his stepfather. The family lived near the Chistye prudy (Clear Ponds), and during his childhood Nagibin spent a great deal of time swimming and boating there. His reminiscences of those years are depicted in his collection of autobiographical stories, *Chistye prudy* (1962). Nagibin did not see much of his stepfather because of the latter's many business trips; occasionally he and his mother traveled to his stepfather's places of work in various provincial towns, steppes, and villages. Nagibin learned English from a Mrs. Colbert, an Englishwoman who taught him at home; he learned German at school.

Nagibin's mother and stepfather separated when he was eight; his mother married Iakov Semenovich Rykachov when he was in senior school. Rykachov was a writer, and Nagibin began to write under his new stepfather's influence. In 1938 he enrolled in medical school, where he studied for one semester. He then entered the Institute of Cinematography, where he took courses in writing scripts. His first published story, "Dvoinaia oshibka" (Double Mistake), appeared in 1940 in the periodical *Ogonek* (The Flame) and is collected in *Sobranie sochinenii* (1980–1981).

Nagibin's studies at the Institute of Cinematography were interrupted by World War II. Because of his fluency in German, he was assigned to an army counterpropaganda unit near the Volkhov front. He was involved in publishing a German newspaper and made frequent trips to the front with a mobile radio unit to make broadcasts in German to the enemy soldiers.

"Knut" (1941, Whip), one of Nagibin's early stories, is about a ten-year-old boy who is given a whip to control a flock of sheep; it reveals Nagibin's interest in violence and in child psychology. In 1942 Nagibin joined the Union of Writers on the recommendation of Aleksandr Aleksandrovich Fadeev. After an injury affected his hearing, he served in 1943–1945 as a war correspondent for the newspaper *Trud* (Labor) and traveled to Stalingrad, Leningrad, and Minsk, Vilnius, and Kaunas in Lithuania. His war stories are included in the collections *Chelovek s fronta* (1943, Person from the Front) and *Bol'shoe serdtse* (1944, Big Heart); they depict heroism, sense of duty, and humane qualities of ordinary Soviet soldiers. Among the best of these stories is "Sviazist Vasil'ev" (Radio Operator Vasil'ev), included in *Chelovek s fronta* (1988). Vasil'ev is the most experienced radio operator and engineer in a Soviet division engaged in heavy combat with German troops. Radio contact between the Soviet units has been lost; when two operators are killed attempting to repair the broken line, the commander of the communications unit has no choice but to send the overweight and clumsy Vasil'ev. Vasil'ev crawls to the area of the heaviest fighting, attaches the broken wire to a roll of unbroken wire, and pulls it to a safe place in the bushes. The narrator says, "It is difficult to describe his actions as a heroic deed. His behavior in this situation was based on a calculated and well-thought-out plan; this was the beauty of the job he did. In spite of the fire aimed at him, the operator acted as a pragmatic, clever master of his body, life, and strength." At the end of the story Vasil'ev reads letters from his wife. Nagibin avoids the depiction of epic scenes prevalent in Soviet novels of this period; ordinary people like Vasil'ev, Nagibin indicates, are the true heroes.

After the war, Nagibin worked as a journalist for the periodicals *Sotsialisticheskoe zemledelie* (Socialist Agricultural Science) and *Nash sovremennik* (Our Contemporary). On an assignment for *Sotsialisticheskoe zemledelie* in 1947 he visited the Kursk region, which had experienced a severe drought the year before; the tractor-repair stations were immobilized, and workers on most of the collective farms had to plow the fields with their cows. But Nagibin discovered a farm near the town of Sudzha where the workers were not experiencing hardships but were eating goose and freshly baked bread. The prosperity of the farm was the result of the good management and selfless labor of the chairwoman, Tat'iana Petrovna Diachenko. Nagibin wrote a story about this extraordinary woman that was broadcast on the radio. Later he turned the story into a screenplay for the 1963 motion picture *Bab'e tsarstvo* (A Woman's Kingdom). He then used the screenplay to create a tale with the same title. That story became the basis of the successful play *Sudzhanskie madonny* (The Sudzha Madonnas), which was staged by

*Front cover for* Chistye prudy *(1962, Clear Ponds), Nagibin's collection of autobiographical stories about his childhood (Kent State University Library)*

the Lenin Communist Youth Theater, and of the opera *Russkie zhenshchiny* (1969, Russian Women). Nagibin incorporated parts of the story into his novella *Stranitsy zhizni Trubnikova* (1963, Pages from the Life of Trubnikov), which he then turned into a screenplay for the motion picture *Predsedatel'* (1964, The Chairman). The movie was a great success, and the actor Mikhail Aleksandrovich Ul'ianov was awarded the 1966 Lenin State Prize for his performance in it.

From 1955 to 1965 Nagibin was a member of the editorial board of the literary journal *Znamia* (The Banner). His stories "Khazarskii ornament" (translated as "The Khazar Ornament," 1961) and "Svet v okne" (translated as "A Light in the Window," 1973) appeared in the second issue of the liberal anthology *Literaturnaia Moskva* (Literary Moscow) in 1956. These stories were severely criticized by Soviet reviewers. While "Khazarskii ornament" deals with intellectuals living during Joseph Stalin's time, "Svet v okne" exposes the legacy of Stalinism as manifested in the growing influence of Soviet bureaucrats in every sphere of life in the post-Stalin period. Nastia, the protagonist of "Svet v okne," is a maid in a rest home. She is told to keep an empty room clean and tidy in case an important official, "the big man," should decide to turn up. This practice was a common one: there were such rooms in every rest home and sanatorium, each of which had its own big men—Central Committee or District Committee secretaries, factory managers, or ministry officials. After a year of sweeping out the uninhabited room and thinking of the cramped living conditions most Soviet citizens endure, Nastia invites some friends and the janitor's children to watch television in the room set aside for "the big man." Her manager sees the light in the reserved room and reprimands Nastia in abusive language.

In the early postwar years Nagibin was a passionate hunter and fisherman; many of his stories are based on his intimate knowledge of the Meshchera region 120 miles southeast of Moscow, where he went duck hunting with his friends on Lake Pleshcheevo. The Meshchera region is featured prominently in his collection *Pogonia: Meshcherskie byli* (1964, The Chase: The Meshchera Region Tales). He stopped hunting when he developed the strong environmentalist convictions that are reflected in his stories "V rasputitsu" (1956, Impassable Roads), "Meshcherskie storozha" (1956, Wardens of the Meshchera District), "Na tikhom ozere" (1963, By a Quiet Lake), "Brakon'er" (1965, The Poacher), and "Na kordone" (1968, The Cordon). In "Brakon'er" he denounces not only the practice of poaching that was widespread in the postwar Soviet Union but also, and even more, industrial pollution. Petrishchev lives in a village but works as a loading-dock foreman at a textile factory in a nearby city. He earns "enough to live on, when you have a cow, a goat, chickens, geese, your own potatoes, and free fresh fish just about all year round." As the May Day holiday approaches, Petrishchev sets out to spear fish in the nearest lake at night so that he can sell them in town for vodka money. Spearfishing is illegal, and Petrishchev is caught. The authorities want to make an example of him to impress higher officials and the media and to send a message to other poachers. Khmet', one of the jurors at his trial, is a director of a large factory, "thanks to which the ancient and rather neglected town had gained a new, much higher status." The waste his plant discharges has left most bodies of water around the town biologically dead. "Only Kashchei Lake, with its powerful natural cleansing system, still somewhat resists the fate of its frightening neighbor, and nevertheless the more delicate fish such as smelt and burbot have died out in it." Thus, the man responsible for the pollution sits in judgment of a man who poaches a few fish a year. Furthermore, Khmet' is an adulterer who is having an affair with a young woman, the wife of one of his employees, who tutors his deaf child; the woman's "husband, a shy and ambitious young man with acne," is powerless to object because he is "completely dependent on . . . Khmet'." Petrishchev, on the other hand, is a faithful husband and a hard worker who drinks only when he is treated or has bonus money or earnings from fishing or hunting undertaken around holidays. The story ends with Petrishchev struggling with the bailiffs who are trying to put him in the paddy wagon as his distressed wife watches. Meanwhile, Khmet' leaves in his chauffeur-driven car, joyfully thinking about his mistress and a forthcoming weekend of fishing on Kashchei Lake.

Many of Nagibin's stories of the 1950s and 1960s deal with childhood. In "Zimnii dub" (translated as "Winter Oak," 1955), the title piece of a 1955 collection, the country boy Kolia Savushkin is scolded by his teacher, Anna Vasil'evna, for being late for school. But Kolia, who has an intimate knowledge of the forest near the school, is able to teach the young Anna Vasil'evna to appreciate nature. He takes her for a walk in the forest and shows her a winter oak: "The powerful tree, brimming with life, had gathered around itself so much vital warmth that the poor creatures couldn't have found themselves a better dwelling. Anna Vasil'evna was staring with joyous interest at the secret life of the forest, so unfamiliar to her." As a result of this experience Anna Vasil'evna, a recent graduate who teaches Russian language and literature, becomes anxious about the ability of language to capture reality:

> She remembered that day's class and all her other classes: how poor, how dry, and cold were her comments on the world, on language, on those things without which man, helpless in his feelings, is mute before the world—on their beautiful language, which was as fresh, beautiful, and rich as life was bounteous and beautiful. . . . And suddenly Anna Vasil'evna realized that the most wonderful thing in the forest wasn't the winter oak, but the small person in the worn felt boots and the patched cheap clothes, the son of a nurse and a soldier who had perished for his country—a marvelous and mysterious citizen of the future.

One of Nagibin's most popular stories, "Zimnii dub" was made into a television movie and was included in later editions of the fifth-grade reader *Rodnoi iazyk* (Native Language).

Nagibin's "Ekho" (1960, Echo), the title story of his 1964 collection, about Vitka, a girl who collects echoes, is another story of childhood; but it also marks the rebirth of the Russian modernist tradition. The metatextual qualities of literature became of interest to Nagibin during the period of the Soviet literary

"Thaw," 1954 to 1957. The story is set in Koktebel' and the surrounding countryside, which includes Mount Kara-dag and its rock, the Devil's Finger, famous for producing various types of echoes. Koktebel' is an important cultural landmark because of the poet and painter Maksimilian Aleksandrovich Voloshin's house, which was frequently visited at the beginning of the twentieth century by Russian modernist writers such as Marina Ivanovna Tsvetaeva, Anastasiia Ivanovna Tsvetaeva, and Osip Mandel'shtam. Nagibin adapted the story into the screenplay for the movie *Devochka i ekho* (1964, The Girl and the Echo), which won a special prize at the 1965 Locarno International Film Festival.

In one of the stories in his autobiographical collection *Chistye prudy*, "Zhenia Rumiantseva" (1962), Nagibin constructs a psychological profile of one of his schoolmates who became a war hero. During their last days of high school the narrator, Zhenia Rumiantseva, and some of their friends row a dinghy to an island in a Moscow park. When they are approached by a local bully, Zhenia chases him off. In the traditional vein of socialist realist narratives, Zhenia exhibits such qualities as courage, love of adventure, and self-sacrifice. She tells her friends over a glass of beer that she dreams of being a cosmonaut and is prepared to sacrifice her life for the sake of Soviet space exploration. Instead, the narrator tells the reader, Zhenia became a pilot and was killed in World War II. At the end of the story the narrator dreams of going to meet Zhenia at the Bolshoi Theater in Moscow at 8 P.M. on 29 May, ten years after their last meeting, as they had arranged; he thinks that if Zhenia were still alive, he could tell her that he has published a collection of stories and is working on another: "it is not the sort of books I would have liked to write, but I believe that one day I will write the books I wish to write." He implies that Zhenia was attracted to him, but at the time he was not interested in her. Ten years later, he regrets that he was so young and blind. The narrator presents himself as a young man who is far from ideal: he is a conformist who enjoys driving his German Opel car. The story thus has prominent Chekhovian elements that subvert the socialist realist mode of writing: it deals with the narrator's feelings rather than being the perfect biography of a positive hero.

In 1966 Nagibin signed a letter in support of the writers Andrei Siniavsky and Iulii Daniel', who were on trial for anti-Soviet activities. His cycle of stories "Rasskazy o Iurii Gagarine" (Stories about Iurii Gagarine), included in his collection *V aprel'skom lesu*, 1974, celebrates the Soviet cosmonaut Iurii Gagarin, who became the first man in space on 12 April 1961 and was killed in an airplane crash in 1968. In "Semeinyi spor" (Family Argument) Gagarin's parents

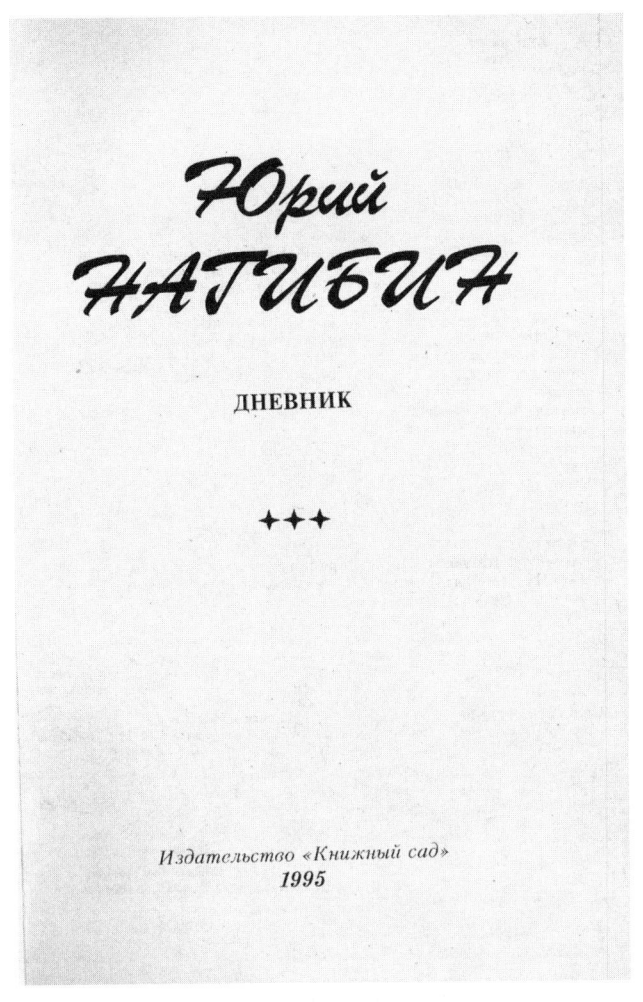

*Title page for* Dnevnik *(1995, Diary), Nagibin's somber, unflattering account of his adult life, submitted for publication the week before his death (Jean & Alexander Heard Library, Vanderbilt University)*

are involved in the preparations for the 250th anniversary of their hometown, which was renamed Gagarin in 1968 in honor of their late son; the father modestly suggests keeping the original name, Gzhatsk, on the badges and posters. Nagibin's account of Gagarin's life bears many of the traditional marks of Soviet narratives that celebrate the country's heroes. For example, in "V shkolu" (To School) the schoolboy Gagarin knows many poems about pilots and airplanes; in several stories young Iurii and his friends are presented as war heroes because they resisted the German occupation of the Smolensk region; and in "Zvezdy" (Stars) Gagarin's mother, Anna Trofimovna, recalls that her son was always fascinated by the stars. In the last story of the cycle, "Fotografiia" (Photograph), Nagibin pays homage not only to Gagarin but also to the Ukrainian-born engineer Sergei Pavlovich Korolev, who designed the rocket that put Gagarin into orbit but whose role as the

*Iurii Nagibin, 1994, the year of his death (from* Dnevnik; *Jean & Alexander Heard Library, Vanderbilt University)*

mastermind of the Soviet space program was revealed only after his death in 1966. Nagibin calls Korolev an invisible, forgotten hero.

In 1975 Nagibin was invited to join the board of the Union of Writers of the Russian Soviet Federated Socialist Republic, and in 1981 he became a member of the board of the Union of Writers of the Soviet Union. Nevertheless, he remained critical of various shortcomings of Soviet life. For example, his story "Terpenie" (Patience), included in his collection *Reka Geraklita* (1984, Heraclitus's River), brings to the fore the issues of the moral decay of the Soviet intelligentsia and the government's neglect of its war invalids. Aleksei and Anna Skvortsov, respected University of Leningrad scholars, take their children on a boat trip to the beautiful island Bogoiar. There Anna encounters the war invalid Pasha, her husband's best friend from before the war, with whom she was once in love. Aleksei had lied to Anna about Pasha's fate, telling her that he was dead. Anna offers to leave her husband if Pasha will come back to Leningrad and live with her, but Pasha refuses. On the way home Anna jumps from the boat and dies of heart failure in the attempt to swim back to the island. The most moving aspect of the story is the theme of war invalids, which was largely suppressed in Soviet narratives: the motherland for which they had fought abandoned them, leaving institutions such as the monastery on Bogoiar to provide for their care.

Historical themes are prominent in Nagibin's works of the 1970s to the 1990s. His story "Beglets" (1978, The Runaway, collected in *Ostrov liubvi* [Island of Love]) is a portrait of the eighteenth-century poet Vasilii Vasil'evich Trediakovsky, who also appears in "Shuty imperatritsy" (Jesters of the Empress), published in the collection *Liubov' vozhdei* (1994, Leaders' Love). In the late 1980s Nagibin's political views became more radical. He incorporates his memories of and reflections on Stalin's gulag in "Vstan' i idi" (1987, Arise and Go), an autobiographical narrative that explores the complex emotions of a son who reevaluates his unjustly imprisoned father.

Other historical works show the cruelty and injustice of those in power. "Shuty imperatritsy" is the tragic story of Prince Mikhail Alekseevich Golitsyn, who goes to Italy, converts to Catholicism, and marries an Italian girl. During the reign of the empress Anna Ioannovna, Golitsyn is recalled to Russia, stripped of his nobility and wealth because of his conversion, and made a jester in the empress's court. One day, for amusement, the empress marries him to the female jester Avdotia Ivanovna Buzheninova; Trediakovsky is forced to write a celebratory verse for the wedding, making his services comparable to those of the jesters. The newlyweds must spend their wedding night in a palace made of ice. Avdotia loves her husband, and he grows to love her, in spite of the difference in their social backgrounds. After the death of the empress, Golitsyn and his wife are freed and given a substantial sum of money to compensate for Golitsyn's lost wealth; they settle on a country estate near Moscow. After Avdotia dies of cancer, Golitsyn remarries but becomes depressed. The story concludes with Golitsyn trying to cure his melancholy by hiring some jesters to amuse him. In "Shuty imperatritsy" Nagibin remarks that some monarchs were more humane than others: they allowed their victims to be beheaded, rather than tortured and hanged. Another concern manifested in the narrative is the impossibility of adequately assessing the past. According to Nagibin, in his later years Golitsyn's contemporaries did not know the truth about him and did not care to learn it. He says: "Every historical event firstly becomes a legend (already among the contemporaries of this event); then it turns into an object of analysis; but the final version of an event comes alive in the shape of a new legend." The statement reveals some postmodernist tendencies in Nagibin.

A mixture of playful and disturbing images of the past can be found in *Liubov' vozhdei*. "Edinstvennyi i nepovtorimyi" (The Only One and Not Reproducible) depicts the aging Stalin's affair with Asia, a Bolshoi ballerina who is also a high-class call girl; Stalin improves his virility when he makes love to Asia by looking at a photograph of Adolf Hitler. In "Tsyganskoe kaprichchio" (Gypsy Capriccio) the Soviet spymaster Lavrentii Beria has sex with two teenage Gypsy girls, then sends them to the gas chamber because they were not virgins. Beria's bodyguard amuses himself by spying on his boss through a keyhole and indifferently obeys Beria's orders to dispose of the girls. "V angel'skom chine" (In the Rank of Angels) claims that Eva Braun's diary and rumors from knowledgeable sources suggest that Hitler's drive for power and military conquest was a sublimation of his sexual desires, which could not be satisfied normally because he did not have a penis. The narrator refers to himself as a person "who happens to have in his possession numerous facts to support the case described above, and therefore he asserts that the story is true." "Posledniaia liubov'" (Last Love) purports to reconstruct the final days of Communist Party general secretary and Soviet president Leonid Brezhnev who, according to the story, was kept alive by bodyguards equipped with the latest technology to make various parts of his body function; one bodyguard is given the code name "Spleen," another is "Phallus." The half-dead, robot-like Brezhnev finally expires while having simulated intercourse with a young female bodyguard: one of the generals cuts the blood supply to Brezhnev's heart so that he will die happy. The title of the story is a playful appropriation of that of Fedor Ivanovich Tiutchev's poem (written between 1851 and 1854) about the intensity of an old man's last love.

Nagibin was married six times; no information is available about these marriages except that his wife from 1962 to 1967 was Bella (Izabella Akhatovna) Akhmadulina, one of the most important poets of the postwar period, and that his last wife, Alla Grigor'evna, was a linguist. Nagibin died in Moscow on 17 June 1994.

A week before his death Nagibin had submitted for publication the diary he had kept for many years. The critic Viktor Toporev calls the posthumously published *Dnevnik* (1995, Diary) a "chernukha" (gloomy work) filled with unpleasant revelations about Nagibin and others. In one entry, for example, he admits:

> I did not just get in fights; I drank in disgustingly large quantities, smoked like a madman, never let a single woman pass by unnoticed, caused all sorts of debauchery, was constantly surrounded by friends, fellow drinkers, freeloaders and was repulsive to myself far more frequently than to those around me. In general, people do not find someone else's decay repulsive—so long as they get their piece, and I tossed money around like litter; I earned plenty from the movies. My apartment was alternately a cafe or a mess—and often combined these two institutions.

Deming Brown describes Iurii Nagibin's fiction as "psychologically sensitive and disciplined in the manner of Chekhov and Bunin, with clear, uncomplicated moral values tempered by a sense of irony and compassion." Nagibin's oeuvre as a whole awaits reassessment, however, because of the postmodernist tendencies that appeared in his writing in the 1990s. Although his place as a short-story author is secure, the diary significantly undermined his reputation in post-Soviet literary circles. Nevertheless, it also paved the way for the rise of subjectivist and exhibitionist tendencies that became a hallmark of Russian literature of the late 1990s.

**References:**
I. Aizenshtock, "Frontovye povesti Iuriia Nagibina," *Zvezda,* 6 (1961): 208–210;

Lev Alabin, "Taina zhizni I zgadka psevdonima," *Nash sovremennik,* 8 (1995): 222–224;

Irina Aleksandrovna Bogatko, *Iurii Nagibin: Literaturnyi portret* (Moscow: Sovetskaia Rossiia, 1980);

Nina Sergeevna Bolotnova, "Funkstionirovanie glagolov govoreniia v konstruktsiiakh s priamoi-rech'iu: Na materiale proizvedenii Iu. M. Nagibina," in *Klassy glagolov v funksional'nom aspekte,* edited by Eva Vasil'evna Kuznetsova, L. G. Babenko, Leonod Mikhailovich Vasil'ev, I. T. Vepreva, Liudmila Mikhailovna Maidanova, N. P. Potapova, and Anatolii Prokop'evich Chudnikov (Sverdlovsk: Ural'skii gosudarstvennyi universitet, 1986), pp. 53–60;

Maksim Borisov, "Fenomen Nagibina," *Literaturnaia gazeta,* 27 (3 July 1996): 4;

Deming Brown, *Soviet Literature since Stalin* (Cambridge: Cambridge University Press, 1978), pp. 154–157;

Vera Chaikovskaia, "Preemstvennost'," *Literaturnoe obozrenie,* 12 (1986): 51–53;

Chaikovskaia, "Puteshestvie s otsom," *Literaturnoe obozrenie,* 9 (1988): 39–40;

L. P. Cherkasova and E. P. Karpenko, "Tsvetopis' v proze Iu. Nagibina," *Russkaia rech',* 4 (July–August 1985): 65–68;

Sergei Chuprinin, "Prochtite Nagibina," *Literaturnaia gazeta,* 51 (16 December 1987): 4;

Ellen Joan Cochrum, "Jurij Nagibin's Short Stories: Themes and Literary Criticism," dissertation, Michigan State University, 1977;

Lidiia N. Fomenko, "Pobezhdaet khudozhnik," *Znamia*, 9 (1973): 221–231;

E. A. Frolova, "Gimn 'synu chelovecheskomu' v rasskaze Iu. Nagibina 'Komarov,'" *Russkii Iazyk v Shkole: Metodicheskii zhurnal*, 2 (March–April 2000): 74–78;

M. Grzeszczak, "Die kunstlerische Darstellung der Personlichkeitsentwicklung in der povest' 'Leto moego detstva' von Jurij Nagibin," *Wissenschaftliche Zeitschrift der Ernst Moritz Arndt-Universitat Greifswald*, 20, no. 1–2 (1971): 49–55;

A. Gur'ev, "My u nikh v dolgu: beseda s Iuriem Nagibinym," *Literaturnoe obozrenie*, 12 (1981): 33–35;

I. Gusarova, "Kniga, kotoraia vospityvaet serdtse," *Znamia*, 11 (1978): 247–250;

Gusarova, "Shestidesiatiletnie," *Znamia*, 11 (November 1981): 243–245;

R. Hager, "Die Evolution des literarischen Menschenbildes im Erzahlschaffen Sergej Antonovs, Jurij Nagibins und Vladimir Tendrjakovs de 50er Jahre," *Zeitschrift für Slawistik*, 20 (1975): 214–225;

V. Kardin, "'Po sushchestvu li eti voprosy'?" *Voprosy literatury*, 2 (1983): 91–118;

Valentina Khlopova, *Paradoks liubvi: Novelistika Iuriia Nagibina* (Moscow: Sovremennik, 1990);

A. Kogan, "Priznaniia izlomannoi dushi," *Literaturnoe obozrenie*, 4 (1996): 100–105;

Vladimir Ivanovich Korobov, "Shchedrost' mysli i chuvstva: Iuriiu Nagibinu–60 let," *Oktiabr'*, 4 (1980): 216–217;

Sergei Kostyrko, "Belletrist protiv pisatelia," *Novyi mir*, 11 (November 1995): 224–248;

Vladimir Alekseevich Lavrov, "'S otvrashcheniem chitaia zhizn' moiu . . . ,'" *Neva*, 9 (1995): 183–189;

Vladimir Vladimirovich Lopatin, "Korichnevyi chernotu, sinii v lilovost': O iazyke prozy Iu. Nagibina," *Russkaia rech'*, 3 (1980): 55–61;

E. L. L'vova, "Novo-obrazovaniia v proze Iu. M. Nagibina," *Russkaia rech'*, 1 (1980): 47–52;

Rafael' Mustafin, "Doroga I dozhd': Razmyshleniia po povodu rasskaza Iuriia Nagibina 'V dozhd','" *Literaturnoe obozrenie*, 10 (October 1985): 8–12;

M. Iu. Novikova, "Metafora v povesti Iu. Nagibina 'Perekur,'" *Russkaia rech'*, 4 (July–August 1986): 62–65;

Valentina Efremovna Ostrovskaia, "Russkii-sovetskii liriko-psikhologicheskii rasskazy 70-kh godov: Problematika i poetika (Iu. Nagibin, V. Konetskii, G. Semenov)," dissertation, Gosudarstvennyi Pedagogicheskii Institute imeni V. I. Lenina, 1984;

Oleg Pavlov, "Bessmertnaia ispoved'," *Oktiabr'*, 9 (September 1996): 184–185;

Lidiia Moiseevna Poliak, "Traditsii Chekhova v sovremennoi novellistike," in *Zhanrovo-stilevye iskaniia sovremennoi sovetskoi prozyi*, edited by Poliak and Vadim Evgen'evich Kovskii (Moscow: Nauka, 1971), pp. 232–265;

Michael Pursglove, "The Genre of Silence: Iurii Nagibin's Zamolchavshaia vesna," in *The Short Story: Structure and Statement*, edited by William J. Hunter (Exeter, U.K.: Elm, 1996), pp. 159–171;

M. M. Radetskaia, "Zhanrovo-stilevoe svoeobrazie pisatel'skoi khudozhestvennoi biografii v proze Iu. Nagibina 70-kh godov," *Voprosy Russkoi literatury*, 1, no. 51 (1988): 88–94;

Tat'iana Rasskazova, "Iurii Nagibin: 'Khudozhnik prezhde vsego teshit sobstvennogo besa,'" *Literaturnaia gazeta*, 50 (9 December 1992): 4;

Larisa Riazanova, *Nad strokoi pisatelia: Iurii Nagibin* (Leningrad: Izdatel'stvo LGPU imeni Gertsena, 1985);

Wendy Rosslyn, "Reverberations in Nagibin's 'Ekho,'" *Journal of Russian Studies*, 33 (1977): 19–26;

Earl D. Sampson, "The Poacher and the Polluter: The Environmental Theme in Nagibin," in *Studies in Russian Literature in Honor of Vsevolod Setchkarev*, edited by Julian W. Connolly and Sonia I. Ketchian (Columbus, Ohio: Slavica, 1986), pp. 222–232;

Harold K. Schefski, "Children and the Retreat from Collective Identity," *Scottish Slavonic Review*, 4 (Spring 1985): 99–106;

Munir Sendich, "Poetika belletrizovannykh biografii Iu. M. Nagibina," *Russkii iazyk za rubezhom*, 2 (1991): 94–100;

Evgenii Sergeev, "O cheloveka–dlia cheloveka," *Znamia*, 3 (March 1982): 225–232;

Iurii Shcheglov, "Pritcha o syne," *Znamia*, 8 (August 1988): 220–221;

Marc Slonim, *Soviet Russian Literature: Writers and Problems*, revised edition (New York: Oxford University Press, 1977), p. 350;

Jadwiga Szymak, "Opowiadania mysliwskie Jurija Nagibina," *Slavia Orientalis*, 16 (1967): 293–300;

Viktor Toporev, "Gibel' Nagibina," *Postskriptum: Literaturnyi zhurnal*, 3, no. 5 (1996): 266–280 (also at <http://vavilon.ru/metatext/ps5/toporov.html>);

Ivan Ukhanov, "Proshchanie s Nagibinym," *Molodaia gvardiia*, 11 (1994): 188–216.

# Viktor Platonovich Nekrasov
*(17 June 1911 – 3 September 1987)*

Michael Falchikov
*University of Edinburgh*

BOOKS: *V okopakh Stalingrada* (Moscow: Sovetskii pisatel', 1947; Moscow: Moskovskii rabochii, 1947); translated by David Floyd as *Front-Line Stalingrad* (London: Harvill, 1962);

*V rodnom gorode* (Moscow: Molodaia gvardiia, 1955);

*Pervoe znakomstvo; iz zarubezhnykh vpechatlenii* (Moscow: Sovetskii pisatel', 1960);

*Sudak* (Moscow: Khudozhestvennaia literatura, 1960);

*Vasia Konakov, rasskazy* (Moscow: Voennoe izdatel'stvo Ministerstva oborony SSSR, 1961);

*Kira Georgievna* (Moscow: Sovetskii pisatel', 1962); translated by Moura Budberg as *Kira* (London: Cresset, 1963);

*Po obe storony okeana* (Moscow: Novyi mir, 1962); translated by Elias Kulukundis as *Both Sides of the Ocean* (London: Cape / New York: Holt, Rinehart & Winston, 1964);

*Vtoraia noch'* (Moscow: Sovetskaia Rossiia, 1965);

*Puteshestviia v raznykh izmereniiakh* (Moscow: Sovetskii pisatel', 1967);

*V zhizni i pis'makh. Rasskazy* (Moscow: Sovetskii pisatel', 1971);

*Zapiski zevaki* (Frankfurt: Posev, 1976);

*Saperlipopet (esli by da kaby . . . )* (London: Overseas Publications Interchange, 1983);

*Po obe storony steny* (New York: Effect, 1984);

*Malen'kaia pechal'naia povest'* (London: Overseas Publications Interchange, 1986);

*Napisano karandashom,* compiled by Mikhail N. Parkhomov (Kiev: Dnipro, 1990);

*Tri vstrechi* (Moscow: Pravda, 1990);

*I zhiv ostalsia–,* compiled by V. A. Potresov (Moscow: Kniga, 1991);

*V samykh adskikh kotlakh pobyval–,* compiled by Potresov (Moscow: Molodaia gvardiia, 1991);

*Dom Turbinykh* (Kiev: Kii, 1998).

**Editions and Collections:** *V okopakh Stalingrada* (Moscow: Moskovskii rabochii, 1948);

*V okopakh Stalingrada* (Moscow: Voenizdat, 1948);

*V okopakh Stalingrada* (Moscow: Khudozhestvennaia literatura, 1951);

*Viktor Nekrasov (from* Po obe storony steny, *1984; Robert W. Woodruff Library, Emory University)*

*V okopakh Stalingrada* (Moscow: Sovetskii pisatel', 1952);

*Izbrannye proizvedeniia* (Moscow: Khudozhestvennaia literatura, 1962);

*Vasia Konakov* (Kiev: Dnipro, 1965);

*Puteshestviia v raznykh izmereniiakh* (Moscow: Sovetskii pisatel', 1967);

*V okopakh Stalingrada* (Moscow: Izvestiia, 1968);
*Viktor Nekrasov v zhizni i pis'makh* (Moscow: Sovetskii pisatel', 1971);
*Kira Georgievna* (Paris: Institut d'études Slaves, 1978);
*V okopakh Stalingrada* (London: Overseas Publications Interchange, 1988);
*V okopakh Stalingrada* (Moscow: Pravda, 1989);
*Malen'kaia pechal'naia povest'* (Moscow: Knizhnaia palata, 1990);
*V okopakh Stalingrada* (Moscow: Khudozhestvennaia literatura, 1990);
*V okopakh Stalingrada* (Leningrad: Lenizdat, 1991);
*V okopakh Stalingrada* (Moscow: Molodaia gvardiia, 1991);
*Zapiski zevaka* (Moscow: Slovo, 1991);
*Po obe storony steny* (Moscow: Khudozhestvennaia literatura, 1991);
*V okopakh Stalingrada* (Moscow: Russkaia kniga, 1995);
*V okopakh Stalingrada* (Moscow: Panorama, 2000).

**Editions in English:** *Kira Georgievna,* translated by Walter N. Vickery (New York: Pantheon, 1962);
"The Perch," translated by Vic Shneerson in *The Third Flare: Three War Stories* (Moscow: Foreign Languages Publishing House, 1963);
*Postscripts: Short Stories by Viktor Nekrasov,* translated by Michael Falchikov and Dennis Ward (London: Quartet, 1991);
"Forty Years Later," translated by Charles Allen, *Partisan Review,* 63 (Winter 1996): 54–64.

OTHER: "Epilogue," in Mikhail Afanas'evich Bulgakov, *The White Guard,* translated by Michael Glenny (London: Collins, 1971);
Vladimir Konstantinovich Bukovsky and Semen Gluzman, *A Manual on Psychiatry for Dissidents,* with introductory material by Nekrasov (London, 1976).

SELECTED PERIODICAL PUBLICATIONS—UNCOLLECTED: "Mesiats vo Franstsii," *Novyi mir,* 4 (1965): 102–163;
"Vzgliad i nechto," *Kontinent,* 10 (1976): 13–85; 12 (1977): 90–119; 13 (1977): 7–82.

In his old age in France, his adopted homeland, Viktor Nekrasov looked back on his eventful life and speculated on how it might have turned out had he pursued a different direction at certain crucial moments. As a Russian living through most of the twentieth century, Nekrasov's destiny was shaped by the great upheavals of war and revolution.

Viktor Platonovich Nekrasov was born in Kiev on 17 June 1911. There are many references, though scattered, to Nekrasov's childhood throughout his work. The younger of two sons in a family that belonged to the radical intelligentsia, he was taken to Paris as a child; he was just old enough to remember the early months of World War I and the zeppelins that floated over the city. The moving force behind this transfer to Paris—as indeed behind all his early years—was his mother, Zinaida Nikolaevna Nekrasova. She had completed her education in Switzerland, graduating with a degree in medicine from Lausanne University in 1906. When war broke out she was working in a Paris hospital. No doubt she could have remained there, but the pull of Russia in wartime drew the family back in 1915, with momentous consequences for all of them.

Nekrasov says little about the circumstances that led his mother to work abroad, except to state that in those days relocation was not unusual for educated Russians. Later, he wrote much about the three women—mother, aunt, and grandmother—who played a vital role in his upbringing but rarely made mention of his father. Nekrasov's father, Platon, lived mostly apart from the family and died of a heart attack in the summer of 1917. A passing comment in Nekrasov's writings attests that his father's side of the family was "pure Russian."

Nekrasov wrote extensively about the background of the maternal grandmother who helped to raise him. Of Swedish lineage, she was born Alina Von Ern (or Orn, in Russian transliteration). He points out that she had "no drop of Russian blood": her father was a Swede who rose to the rank of general in the Russian army (perhaps in the Finnish garrison, as Russia tended to appoint Swedes to high positions in the Grand Duchy of Finland), while her mother, Valeria Floriani, was Venetian in origin. By marriage, Nekrasov's grandmother was known as Alina Antonovna Motovilova. His writings provide no evidence as to what role, if any, members of his family played in the revolutions of 1917 and in the subsequent Russian Civil War (1918–1920), but he does mention what happened to his older brother, Nikolai (known as Kolya), in 1919. Sometime that year he was stopped by a patrol and found to be carrying French literature. Because of the paranoid atmosphere of the time, Kolya was taken for a foreign spy and shot by the Red Army.

With the end of the civil war in 1920 and the establishment of Vladimir Il'ich Lenin's New Economic Policy (NEP), Nekrasov's family remained in Kiev, where Zinaida Nikolaevna was much in demand as a doctor. Nekrasov's extended semi-autobiographical sketch "Dedushka i vnuchek" (Grandfather and Grandson), published in the collection *Viktor Nekrasov v zhizni i pis'makh* (1971, Viktor Nekrasov in Life and Letters), presents an interesting picture of life in Kiev at this time. He writes with great affection and vividness about the handsome city, circa 1923–1924, as it began to recover from years of war and neglect. Kiev was as yet unsullied by the soulless postwar tower blocks that Nekrasov, with his architect's eye, was later to deplore. The family lived in a communal flat, typically an accommodation for several families that has been carved out of a more spacious prewar apartment. Life was often difficult: the water was switched on only at night; Zinaida Nikolaevna, despite her professional status, had no phone of her own; and both Nekrasov and his mother frequently had to walk barefoot in the summer. Yet, the city was the boy's playground, and for a twelve-year-old, life was not too demanding. According to Nekrasov, the schools were busily throwing out old prerevolutionary syllabi and structures; thus, the schoolwork was light and the disciplinary actions mild. Communist Party youth organizations had still to penetrate Kiev, so the young Nekrasov joined the Boy Scouts instead. His interest in the cinema also began at this time and was fed by a staple fare of Charlie Chaplin comedies and adventure movies starring Douglas Fairbanks. Nekrasov is engagingly frank about his favorite reading matter—usually he preferred Tarzan's adventures to the Russian classics.

Despite his slightly atypical childhood, the young Nekrasov apparently adjusted well to the new order imposed by the Soviet regime. He reflects in "Dedushka i vnuchek" on his good fortune in having a mother who, as a doctor, was indispensable to the powers that be. He learned much, too, from his aunt, Sofiia Nikolaevna Motovilova, who worked quietly as a librarian but counted Lenin's wife, Nadezhda Konstantinovna Krupskaia, among her friends from youth. As he recounts in "Dedushka i vnuchek," Sofiia Nikolaevna introduced him to Harry M. Lydenberg of the New York Public Library, who came to Kiev in 1923 to exchange information on cataloguing systems.

Although Nekrasov completed his schooling at the end of the 1920s, at the time of the first Five-Year Plan, neither this major upheaval nor the subsequent purges of the late 1930s seems to have affected him directly. Initially, Nekrasov trained as an architect. Apart from his participation in a student project to redesign the Kiev railway station, however, he never practiced this profession. He did retain an excellent eye for buildings and a lifelong interest in cities throughout the world. After graduation he became involved in the theater and was a member of several small repertory groups that toured the country. This experience led to an audition in 1938 with an aging Konstantin Sergeevich Stanislavsky for the Studio Theater, which Stanislavsky headed. Nekrasov was unsuccessful in his audition, but already he had begun to question his commitment to the theater. Writing in later years about this period of his life, he expresses some guilt about the terrible suffering of the Russian people in the 1930s; he was spared such suffering, for the most part. He also acknowledges that, given their past history, he and his family had luck on their side in emerging unscathed from the purges. This outcome, he suggests, was possibly because his mother, though determinedly nonparty herself, had high-ranking secret-police officials among her patients.

World War II (or the Great Patriotic War, as it is designated in the Soviet Union) was the turning point in Nekrasov's life. He enlisted, and in the summer of 1942 the sapper battalion he commanded was brought up from the reserve to take part in the defense of Stalingrad. Throughout a long hot summer and into the following winter, the Red Army fought—yard by yard, block by block—to stave off the *Wehrmacht* (German armed forces) and hold the city. Defeat would have meant opening the way for the enemy to march on the Urals, where most of the industrial strength of the U.S.S.R. was centered. For Nekrasov, promoted to captain, the experience was formative, and he led his battalion with skill and courage. Moreover, the army gave him his first experience of comradeship with other young men of more humble origins. Like many of his contemporaries from the urban intelligentsia—and despite the avowedly classless society of the Soviet Union, Nekrasov "discovered" the Russian peasantry by fighting alongside them. After the successful defense of Stalingrad, he took part in the counteroffensive, and by the summer of 1944 his unit had reached Lublin in Poland. Here he was wounded and his active service came to an end, but from these two years of frontline action sprung a full-fledged writer.

Until his war service Nekrasov's literary activity had been confined to a few unfinished drafts and an amusing attempt at the age of eleven to write a series of mystery stories. Within two years after the end of the war, however, Nekrasov became the author of a best-seller. The work that brought him such rapid success was *V okopakh Stalingrada* (1947, In the Trenches of Stalingrad; translated as *Front-Line Stalingrad,* 1962). First published in the journal *Znamia* (The Banner) in 1946 and told in the first person by a Lieutenant Kerzhentsev, this semiautobiographical novel impressed readers with its unpretentious celebration of qualities such as duty, comradeship, and unforced patriotism, and its vivid, frank descriptions of the squalor, cruelty, and often sheer muddle of war. The title of the work when it appeared in *Znamia* was simply "Stalingrad," but when it was published in book form the following year, the editors added the reference to the trenches. This change was a sensible idea, since the work does

*Front cover for* Saperlipopet (esli by da kaby . . . ) *(1983, Saperlipopet [If Only I Had . . .]), published in London nine years after Nekrasov was permanently expelled from the Soviet Union*

not celebrate the battle for Stalingrad on an epic scale but, rather, depicts the defense of the city through intense battles fought on a modest scale by small groups over individual streets, courtyards, or factory sites. Such concentration on the everyday minutiae of war and the mundane concerns of ordinary soldiers (how to get a cigarette or read a letter from home between bursts of gunfire, for example) later attracted some criticism, particularly in the years when socialist realism "decreed" that all accounts of the war had to conclude with a hymn of praise for the wisdom of the Communist Party and the military genius of Joseph Stalin. But Nekrasov had submitted the manuscript of "Stalingrad" during a brief period of relaxation, before the country became engulfed in the Cold War and the paranoia of the aging dictator.

For the first ten years or so after the publication of *V okopakh Stalingrada,* Nekrasov led the life of a moderately successful Soviet writer. Much of his writing of the 1950s reworks and redefines the themes from his first novel, or it addresses the aftermath of war, including *V rodnom gorode* (In His Home Town, published in 1954 in *Novyi mir* [New World]), which appeared in book form in 1955. By the end of the decade, however, and in the aftermath of Nikita Sergeevich Khrushchev's speech to the Twentieth Party Congress of 1956, in which at least some of Stalin's crimes were revealed, new themes begin to appear in Nekrasov's work. His key publication during this period—the book with which his name began to be known in the West—was *Kira Georgievna* (published in 1961 in *Novyi mir;* translated as *Kira,* 1963). In this novella an outwardly successful sculptress approaching middle age (Nekrasov makes her the same age as the Soviet Union) is forced to look back on her life and reexamine her commitment to art. She engages in this process as a result of the return of her first husband, who had been arrested during the purges. In *Kira Georgievna,* Nekrasov asks some difficult questions—questions that accurately capture the atmosphere of the time among the creative intelligentsia as they attempted to respond to Khrushchev's ongoing "de-Stalinization" campaign. Nekrasov ponders how, with the knowledge of falsehoods in the past, a person can live one's life honestly. He asks how art, the purpose of which hitherto has been to celebrate the achievements of the regime, can respond adequately to tragedy and uncertainty. He provides no easy answers or happy endings in the novella. Although topics such as the reintegration of purge victims and the mild criticism of the limitations of socialist realism were no longer taboo, *Kira Georgievna* did attract some adverse comments for its "negative approach."

In 1957 Nekrasov traveled to Italy, making his first trip abroad in more than four decades. In the next few years after this trip he revisited Italy, spent a month in France, and paid his first visit to the United States. The freedom to travel abroad, even if still slightly circumscribed by the presence of party "vigilantes," was for him the fulfillment of a long hoped-for dream. Nekrasov was an unabashed Europhile, and this aspect of his character is reflected in his travel writing, which was a major part of his literary output for the rest of his life. The travel sketches that encompass *Po obe storony okeana* (published in *Novyi mir* and in book form, 1962; translated as *Both Sides of the Ocean,* 1964) cast him into serious trouble, however, for the first time in his career. A perceptive and humorous account of his travels in Italy and the United States, they illustrate the parameters of the tolerance of the Soviet regime for the mildly unorthodox. Following the appearance of the sketches in *Novyi mir,* Nekrasov was singled out for a venomous attack during a speech by Leonid Fedorovich Il'ichev, the cultural supremo of the Party. Il'ichev's main thrust seemed to be that Nekrasov had so much enjoyed his trip abroad that he had failed to produce a "balance of pluses and minuses," so as to bring out the negative side of life abroad when compared to the Soviet Union. Threatened with expulsion from the Writers' Union—which effectively would mean the loss of his livelihood—Nekrasov was defended by fellow writers. At this time in the U.S.S.R., peer-group solidarity continued to be successful in fighting the oppression of a writer.

Meanwhile, Nekrasov had attracted quickly the interest of translators, and the translations of his works in the West introduced him to a wider reading public. Not only did *Kira Georgievna* and *Po obe storony okeana* appear in English but so did *Front-Line Stalingrad,* somewhat belatedly in 1962. The reviewer for *The Times Literary Supplement* (*TLS;* 23 February 1962) detected certain political undertones in *Front-Line Stalingrad* that made the work problematic in a Soviet context. Nonetheless, he judged that for the average Western reader, the work was "just another better than average, but by no means outstanding, war novel." The following year, however, again in *TLS* (1 February 1963), in a piece titled "Ordinary Russian Chaps," the reviewer—writing about the Russian text of *Vasia Konakov* (1961), a work in which Nekrasov returns to the theme of war—encapsulated well the difficulties facing Nekrasov and those who thought like him in the Soviet Union: "A big question is whether this gentle humanist tradition so typical of Russia will inevitably come into conflict (as it has done in the past) with the official concept of 'Soviet Man', and whether the two can somehow go on co-existing." As the 1960s turned into the 1970s, this conflict came to have fateful consequences for Nekrasov.

From the mid 1960s onward, Nekrasov's writing became increasingly difficult to define in terms of a single genre. An engaging intermingling of fact and fiction and reminiscence and travelogue, it sometimes included digressions on, for instance, the differing roles of writer and actor. Thus, the idea of putting the past to rights, which is such a strong feature of *Kira Georgievna,* is taken several steps further in the somewhat unsettling fantasy that is "Sluchai na Mamaevom kurgane" (Incident on Mamai tumulus, published in 1965 in *Novyi mir*). In the story the author returns to Stalingrad in the postwar period, finds his old dugout, and is promptly transported back (in uniform) to the siege of 1942. He is called upon to defuse a mine and fears he has forgotten how; moreover, he is tormented by a terrible thought: he knows which of his comrades is to die in battle, but he cannot bring himself to tell him. There are cross-references here to another story from the 1950s, which Nekrasov reworked in 1967, titled *Tri vstrechi* (1990, Three Meetings). Here, Nekrasov discusses the differences between a hero in real life and the hero of a book or a motion picture. The background to this was the filming of *V okopakh Stalingrada,* in which much emphasis was placed on the character Private Valega, a minor figure in Nekrasov's real-life war story who had been made into a much more significant character in the eventual movie version of the book. The story is brought back into reality by the arrival of a letter from Valega, who apparently is still alive. During this period Nekrasov published two collections, *Puteshestviia v raznykh izmereniiakh* (Journeys in Various Dimensions, 1967) and *Viktor Nekrasov v zhizni i pis'makh*. The second collection recounts his early life in Kiev and in particular strikes an elegiac note.

By the end of the 1960s many of the hopes for a better, freer Soviet Union had come to nothing. A complacent and occasionally threatening leadership had achieved social quiescence with a mixture of material improvements, sporadic and targeted repressive actions against dissidents, and the grandiose celebration of landmark events, such as the centenary of Lenin's birth and the quarter century since the defeat of Nazism, both in 1970. In this atmosphere there was little scope for the "gentle humanism" of people such as Nekrasov. Aleksandr Isaevich Solzhenitsyn was effectively silenced at the Writers' Congress of 1967, and the Soviet invasion of Czechoslovakia in 1968 finally ended any thoughts of "socialism with a human face." These occurrences led most would-be reformers to abandon public activism and retreat into private concerns. Nekrasov's life changed at this point. He had never married; between his forays into the literary and artistic life of Moscow and his trips abroad, he continued to live with his mother and aunt in Kiev. After his mother's death he married a widow, Galina Nikolaevna Kondyreva, and became a stepfather to her son, Viktor Kondyrev.

Nekrasov clashed with the authorities again over their failure to erect a monument to the Jews who perished at Babii Yar. His friendships with Solzhenitsyn (although they were not particularly compatible personalities) and others who existed on the fringes of society, together with his unapologetically bohemian lifestyle, inevitably made Nekrasov a subject of interest for the Kommisariat gosudarstvennoi bezopasnosti (KGB, State Security Committee). Thus, in September 1974, in the wake of Solzhenitsyn's expulsion from the Soviet Union earlier that year, the KGB paid a visit to Nekrasov and his wife and instigated a lengthy search. The Nekrasovs were relatively fortunate, in that they were not put on trial or confined to a mental hospital (two consequences of dissidence), but—like others who were presumed to have contacts and support in the West—

they were given a one-way ticket out of the U.S.S.R. At the age of sixty-three, Nekrasov became an exile and settled in Paris, where he worked on the journal *Kontinent*, became a French citizen, and traveled with the vigor and keen eye of a man half his age. His destinations included Great Britain, Australia, and the United States.

A confirmed cosmopolitan such as Nekrasov found adjusting to life in exile less painful than many of his fellow citizens who had traveled the same road. He had been able to take out of the country with him the manuscript for another collection of sketches, *Zapiski zevaki* (Notes of a Bystander), published in 1976, and—with the addition of certain material that would have been impossible to publish in the U.S.S.R.—the collection became his first Western publication that year; it showed no diminishing of his powers. In the 1980s he published two more volumes of observations on life and literature, reminiscences, and the revisiting of old themes that did not show the constraint of Soviet censorship. In his final work, the short novel *Malen'kaia pechal'naia povest'* (A Sad Little Story, published 1986 in *Grani* [Grains]); Nekrasaov essentially reverts to fiction. The story is about three Leningrad friends—a dancer, a movie actor, and a cabaret artist—whose friendship over the years is put to the test by professional successes and failures, by marriage, and by emigration. Nekrasov sets the work in Leningrad—a new locale for him—and he writes in such a way that Leningrad seems to compete with Paris for his affections. The action takes place during a period of almost twenty years, starting in the mid 1960s, and the narrative ends on the eve of perestroika. *Malen'kaia pechal'naia povest'* is tinged with Nekrasov's nostalgia for the homeland and Leningrad that must have seemed inaccessible to him. In this work his "three musketeers" express a certain affection for the more unofficial aspects of the Soviet way of life.

*Malen'kaia pechal'naia povest'* turned out to be Nekrasov's literary farewell. The following year his health suddenly deteriorated, forcing the cancellation of a trip to Great Britain. He died on 3 September 1987 at the age of seventy-six. On his deathbed he apparently received a letter from the fellow soldier on whom he based his recurring character Valega. Before Nekrasov died there had been a rumor that the Soviet government, led by the newly installed Mikhail Sergeevich Gorbachev, had put out feelers to see whether the writer might like to reclaim his Soviet citizenship and return to his country. As much as he had wanted to see Russia again, however, Nekrasov was on record as saying that his life was now in France, and he would return only as a visitor to see familiar places and old friends. However, with glasnost underway, he was one of the first émigré writers to be "reclaimed" in his homeland—initially with a complete obituary, which was followed by the republication of almost his entire body of work.

Viktor Platonovich Nekrasov was not, perhaps, a writer of the first rank. Like one of his idols, Anton Pavlovich Chekhov, he did not belong to the tradition of the big, powerful novel. At just under three hundred pages long, *V okopakh Stalingrada* remains by far his longest work, and he remained supremely (and unjustifiably) modest about his abilities as a writer. Nekrasov's strength was his ability to capture particular moments in the life of his country and invest them with human interest and sympathy. He illuminated the minutiae of everyday existence with the warmth and sudden recognition of the familiar. He had a lively perception of cityscapes and city life the world over. His literary technique—particularly when he experimented with time shifts or blurred the distinction between fact and fiction—often was much more complex and sophisticated than it seemed at first sight. The technique stemmed from his broad cultural background. Above all, his curiosity and warmth toward his fellow man meant that he always had something perceptive, amusing, or unorthodox to say. He was much loved within a broad circle of friends and acquaintances and will be admired always for his tolerance, his universality, and his staunchness in adversity.

**Biography:**

Mikhail N. Parkhomov, comp., *O Viktore Nekrasove: Vospominaniia,* edited by E. I. Nikanorova (Kiev: Ukrainskii pys'mennyk, 1992).

**References:**

Grigorii Baklanov, "Iz neopublikvannogo," *Druzhba narodov,* 3 (1995): 25–58;

Anna Berzer, "Iz tsikla; Malen'kie portrety,'" *Druzhba narodov,* 8 (1988): 226–232;

Berzer, "Malen'kaia pechal'naia povest'," *Druzhba narodov,* 5 (1989): 107–152;

Iurii Vasil'evich Bondarev, "Molodost' chuvstv," *Literaturnaia gazeta,* 17 June 1962;

E. Breitbart, "Puteshestvie po vremeni Iipo sobstvennoi zhizni: Proza Viktora Nekrasova posle Rossii," *Grani,* 107 (1978): 175–188;

V. Bykov, "Byt' dostoinym nashego chitataelia," *Novyi mir,* 11 (1963);

Herman Carmel, "Victor Nekrasov: Pioneer of Renaissance in Post-Stalin Russian Prose," *Books Abroad,* 40 (1966): 381–385;

"Document: U.S.S.R.," *Survey,* 94–95 (1975): 179–199;

Michael During, "Mythos 'Stalingrad' in der Literatur: Anmerkungen zum Werk Vijtor Nekrasovs," in *Porta Slavica: Beitrage zur slavistischen Sprach- und Lite-*

*raturwissenschaft,* edited by Bettina Althaus, Friedemann Kluge, and Henrieke Stahl-Schwaetzer (Wiesbaden: Harrassowitz, 1999), pp. 85–98;

Michael Falchikov, "Art, Life and Truth in Viktor Nekrasov's 'Kira Georgievna'," *Forum for Modern Language Studies,* 1(1981): 26–38;

Anatolii Tikhonovich Gladilin, "Viktor Nekrasov: Beseda u mikrofona," *Literaturnaia gazeta,* 23 April 1997, p. 12;

Viktor Iukht, "Vremia poslednikh voprosov," *Literaturnoe obozrenie,* 1 (1992): 86–89;

V. Kardin, "Viktor Nekrasov i Iuii Kerzhentsev: O povesti 'V okopakh Stalingrada' i o ee avtore," *Voprosy literatury,* 4 (April 1989): 113–148;

Grigorii Kipnis, "Ivan Dziuba, kakim ia ego znaiu," *Voprosy literatury,* 2 (1993): 301–312;

Kipnis, "'Proshloe ne vycherknesh': Slishkom mnogo zhiznei i krovi ono stoilo," *Literaturnaia gazeta,* 28 October 1992, p. 6;

Grigorii Kipnis-Grigor'ev, "I tol'ko pravdy . . . : Kievskii sobkor 'LG' o Viktore Nekrasove," *Literaturnaia gazeta,* 18 October 1989, p. 6;

Lazar' Lazarev, "'Kto zhe spas, a kto prisutsvoval?': Neopublikovannaia rplika Viktora Nekrasova," *Literaturnaia gazeta,* 16 October 1996, p. 6;

A. K. Lojkine, "Nekrasov's Anapests," *Melbourne Slavonic Studies,* 9–10 (1975): 54–63;

Samuel F. Orth, "'V okopakh Stalingrada' i Dni i nochi': problematika stalingradskoj temy v poslevoennoj sovetskoj proze," *Russian Language Journal,* 110 (1977): 115–123;

Vladimir Poltoratzky, "The Battle of Stalingrad in the Works of Simonov and Nekrasov," *Dissertation Abstracts International,* 38 (1978): 4876A;

Kirill Privalov, "'Eto vam govoriu iz Parizha ia . . .'," *Literaturnaia gazeta,* 31 August 1988, p. 5;

Hilary Sternberg, "Being Earnest Isn't Always Enough," *Survey,* 104 (1978): 42–51;

B. Suris, "Sosed po frontu," *Neva,* 10 (1990): 198–202;

Igor' Ivanovich Vinogradov, "Na kraiu zemli," *Novyi mir,* 44, no. 3 (1968): 227–247;

Vladimir Nikolaevich Voinovich, "Tri portreta," *Voprosy literatury,* 4 (1993): 178–198;

Dennis Ward, "Reconstructions of Realities in Art–Viktor Nekrasov's 'Incident on Mamai tumulus'," *Poetics and Theory of Literature,* 4 (1979): 285–298.

# Vera Fedorovna Panova
(7 March 1905 – 3 March 1973)

Nadya L. Peterson
*Hunter College, CUNY*

BOOKS: *Sputniki: Povest'* (Moscow: Sovetskii pisatel', 1946); translated by Moura Budberg and Eve Manning as *The Train* (London: Putnam, 1948; New York: Knopf, 1949);

*Kruzhilikha: Roman* (Moscow: Sovetskii pisatel', 1948); translated by Budberg as *The Factory* (London: Putnam, 1949; Westport, Conn.: Hyperion, 1977);

*Iasnyi bereg: Povest'* (Leningrad: Molodaia gvardiia, 1950);

*Vremena goda; iz letopisei goroda Enska: Roman* (Leningrad: Sovetskii pisatel', 1954); translated by Vera Traill as *Span of the Year* (London: Harvill Press, 1957; Westport, Conn.: Hyperion, 1977);

*Serezha: Neskol'ko istorii iz zhizni ochen' malen'kogo mal'chika* (Leningrad: Sovetskii pisatel', 1955); translated as *Time Walked* (London: Harvill Press, 1957; Cambridge, Mass.: Arlington, 1959);

*Metelitsa: P'esa* (Leningrad: Iskusstvo, 1957);

*Il'ia Kosogor; V staroi Moskve; Metelitsa; Devochki* (Leningrad: Sovetskii pisatel, 1958);

*Sentimental'nyi roman* (Leningrad: Lenizdat, 1958);

*V staroi Moskve: Kartiny* (Leningrad: Iskusstvo, 1958);

*Provody belykh nochei* (Leningrad: Iskusstvo, 1961);

*Valya. Volodya* (Moscow: Gosudarstvennoe izdatel'stvo khudozhestvennoi literatury, 1961);

*Serezha. Sentimental'nyi roman. Valya. Volodya. Evdokiia. Metelitsa. Provody belykh nochei* (Moscow & Leningrad: Gosudarstvennoe izdatel'stvo khudozhestvennoi literatury, 1963);

*Troe mal'chishek u vorot: I Drugie rasskazy i povesti* (Leningrad: Lenizdat, 1964);

*Sestry: Rasskazy* (Moscow: Sovetskaia Rossiia, 1965);

*Rabochii poselok, Sasha, Rano utrom: Povesti* (Leningrad: Lenizdat, 1966);

*Liki na zare: Istoricheskaia povesti'* (Leningrad: Sovetskii pisatel', 1966);

*Skazanie ob Ol'ge* (Leningrad: Izdatel'stvo literatury, 1968);

*Pogovorim o strannostiiakh liubvi . . . : P'esy* (Leningrad: Sovetskii pisatel', 1968);

*Vera Fedorovna Panova (from A. Ninov, Vera Panova–Zhizn', tvorchestvo, sovremenniki, 1980; John C. Hodges Library, University of Tennessee–Knoxville)*

*P'esy* (Leningrad: Khudozhestvennaia literatura, 1970);

*Zametki literatora* (Leningrad: Sovetskii pisatel', 1972);

*O moei zhizni, knigakh i chitateliakh* (Leningrad: Lenizdat, 1975);

*Konspekt romana: Povesti i rasskazy* (Leningrad: Lenizdat, 1985);

*P'esy* (Leningrad: Iskusstvo, 1985);

*Istoricheskaia i avtobiograficheskaia proza* (Leningrad: Khudozhestvennaia literatura, 1989);

*Zhizn' Mukhameda,* by Panova and Iurii Borisovich Vakhtin (Moscow: Izdatel'stvo politicheskoi literatury, 1990).

**Editions and Collections:** *Sputniki. Kruzhilikha. Iasnyi bereg* (Moscow: Khudozhestvennaia literatura, 1951);

*Izbrannye sochineniia: V dvukh tomakh,* 2 volumes (Leningrad: Leningradskoe gazetno-zhurnal'noe knizhnoe izdatel'stvo, 1956);

*Sputniki, povest'* (Moscow: Khudozhestvennaia literatura, 1957);

*Sputniki. Kruzhilikha. Sentimental'nyi roman* (Moscow & Leningrad: Gosudarstvennoe izdatel'stvo khudozhestvennoi literatury, 1960);

*Sentimental'nyi roman* (Leningrad: Sovetskii pisatel', 1965);

*Sputniki. Iasnyi bereg. Serezha* (Moscow: Izvestiia, 1969);

*Liki na zare: Istoricheskie povesti* (Leningrad: Lenizdat, 1969);

*Sobranie sochinenii v piati tomakh,* 5 volumes (Leningrad: Khudozhestvennaia literatura, 1969–1970);

*Kruzhilikha. Roman–Sputniki. Povesti–Serezha: Neskol'ko istorii iz zhizni ochen' malen'kogo mal'chika* (Moscow: Sovremennik, 1972);

*Izbrannoe* (Moscow: Molodaia gvardiia, 1972);

*Kruzhilikha: Roman. Povesti. Rasskazy* (Leningrad: Sovetskii pisatel', 1973);

*Sputniki: Povest'* (Leningrad: Khudozhestvennaia literatura, 1973);

*Sputniki. Serezha. Skazanie ob Ol'ge. Kto umiraet* (Leningrad: Lenizdat, 1978);

*Izbrannye proizvedeniia v dvukh tomakh,* 2 volumes (Leningrad: Khudozhestvennaia literatura, 1980);

*O moei zhizni, knigakh i chitateliakh* (Leningrad: Sovetskii pisatel', 1980);

*Sentimental'nyi roman. Istoricheskie povesti* (Leningrad: Khudozhestvennaia literatura, 1980);

*Sputniki: povest'. Kruzhilikha: Roman. Serezha: povest'* (Leningrad: Khudozhestvennaia literatura, 1980);

*Vremena goda. Sentimental'nyi roman. Kotoryi chas?: Roman-skazka* (Leningrad: Khudozhestvennaia literatura, 1980);

*Konspekt romana: povesti, rasskazy* (Leningrad: Lenizdat, 1985);

*Sentimental'nyi roman: Roman, rasskazy* (Moscow: Sovetskaia Rossiia, 1985);

*P'esy* (Leningrad: Khudozhestvennaia literatura, 1985);

*Sputniki: Povest'. Kruzhilikha: Roman. Evdokiia: Povest'* (Leningrad: Khudozhestvennaia literatura, 1987);

*Povesti i rasskazy* (Leningrad: Khudozhestvennaia literatura, 1988);

*Serezha: Neskol'ko istorii iz zhizni ochen' malen'kogo mal'chika: Kniga dlia chteniia s kommentariem na angliiskom iazyke I slovarem* (Moscow: Russkii iazyk, 1988).

**Editions in English:** *Looking Ahead [Kruzhilikha: Roman],* translated by David Skvirsky (Moscow: Foreign Languages Publishing House, 1955);

*Yevdokia* ["Evdokiia"], translated by Julius Katzer (Moscow: Foreign Languages Publishing House, 1959);

*Serezha and Valya* (Oxford: Pergamon Press / New York: Macmillan, 1964);

*On Faraway Street [Serezha],* translated by Rya Gabel, adapted by Anne Terry White (New York: Braziller, 1968);

*Selected Works,* translated by Olga Shartse and Eve Manning (Moscow: Progress, 1976).

PRODUCED SCRIPTS: *Serezha,* motion picture, Mosfil'm, 1960;

*Evdokiia,* motion picture, 1961;

*Visokosnyi: Visokosnyi god,* motion picture, Mosfil'm, 1961;

*Vstuplenie,* motion picture, Mosfil'm, 1962;

*Rabochii poselok,* motion picture, Lenfil'm, 1965;

*Rano utrom,* motion picture, Kinostudiia, imeni Gorkogo, 1965;

*Mal'chik i devochka,* motion picture, Lenfil'm, 1966;

*Chetyre stranitsy odnoi molodoi zhizni,* Lenfil'm, 1967;

*Na vsyo ostavshuyusya zhizn',* screenplay by Panova, B. Bakhtin, and Pyotr Fomenko, motion picture, 1975.

OTHER: "It's Been Ages!" in *Contemporary Russian Drama,* selected and translated by F. D. Reeve from "Skol'ko let, skol'ko zim!" (New York: Pegasus, 1968).

SELECTED PERIODICAL PUBLICATION– UNCOLLECTED: *Sem'ia Pirozhkovykh, Prikam'e* (1944);

"Insomnia: A Play in Three Acts," translated by Clive Liddiard, *Soviet Literature,* 463, no. 10 (1986): 66–116.

One of the prominent writers of the post–World War II period in Soviet literature, Vera Panova gained fame and the esteem of Soviet readers for her short novel *Sputniki* (1946; translated as *The Train,* 1948). *Sputniki* offers a close and compassionate look at the people who manned a wartime hospital train during World War II and who, in Panova's view, symbolized the hope of the country for survival and victory. The majority of her subsequent stories, novels, and plays enjoyed a similar positive reception. Panova's enduring

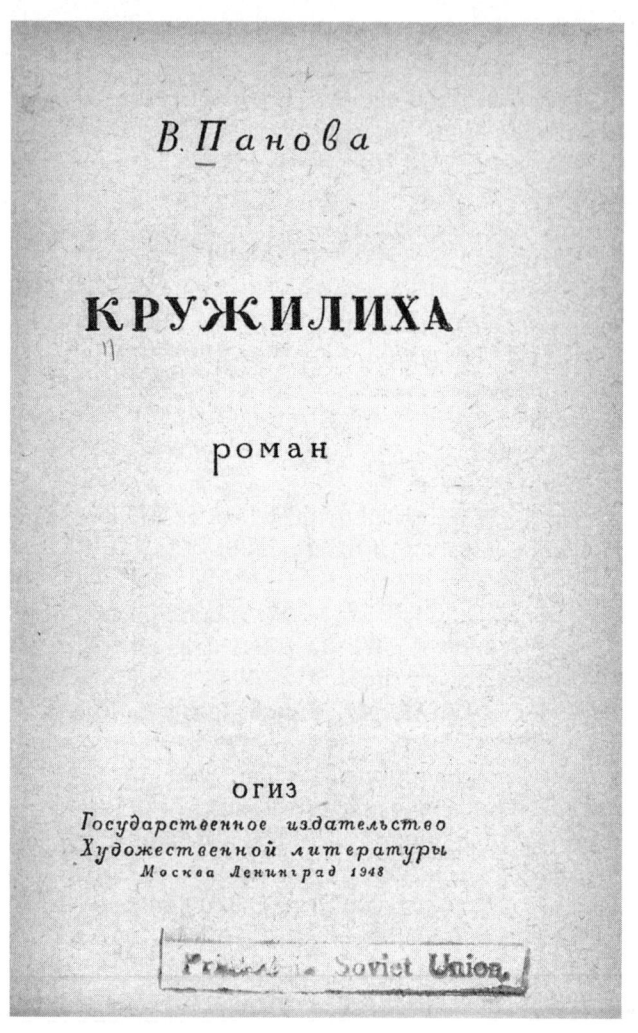

*Title page for the novel translated in 1949 as* The Factory, *about Russian family life in the Urals during World War II. It won the Stalin Prize for literature in 1948 (Perkins Library, Duke University).*

popularity, both with Soviet readers and the literary establishment, rests on her ability to portray the ordinary lives of her characters with great sympathy and some nuance. Even though the contours of Panova's works remain firmly rooted in the aesthetics of socialist realism, the subtlety with which her protagonists were drawn, as well as her fidelity to the issues of primary importance to the people of her country, resulted in works that deviated to a degree from the rigid prescriptions of the "leading method" of Soviet letters.

Vera Fedorovna Panova was born on 7 March 1905 in Rostov-on-Don, a city that she remembered later as "lively, exuberant, and rebellious, the city whose spirit was that of a worker and a wit." Panova's native city was cosmopolitan and multicultural, peopled with representatives of various ethnicities and faiths, such as Russians, Ukrainians, Armenians, Azeris, and Georgians.

Panova faced a series of adversities during her childhood. Her grandfather, a former serf, managed to succeed in the furniture manufacturing business. After his death, however, the family went bankrupt. Panova's father, Fedor Ivanovich Panov, a bank worker, drowned at the age of thirty, leaving the family in difficult circumstances. Her mother, Vera Leonidovna Ren'eri, the daughter of an impoverished music teacher, found a job as an office clerk. The burden of taking care of the household fell on the young daughter's shoulders. Panova never finished her formal education, having been removed from the gymnasium for lack of finances after two years of schooling.

Panova's talent for writing manifested itself early. She produced her first stories and poems at the age of eight. When she was ten, a poem of hers was printed—without her knowledge and to her profound embarrassment—in the children's journal *Zadushevnoe slovo* (The Sincere Word). Toward the end of World War I Panova became an active contributor to the Rostov student journal *Iunaia mysl'* (Young Thought). From the early 1920s up until World War II Panova worked as a journalist on several Rostov papers, such as *Trudovoi Don* (The Working Don), *Sovetskii iug* (The Soviet South), *Sovetskii pakhar'* (The Soviet Ploughman), and *Leninskie vnuchata* (Lenin's Grandkids). Panova's 1952 sketch "Vstrechi i sud'by" (Encounters and Fates) describes this period in her life.

As a journalist in Rostov, Panova was engaged in a variety of occupations related to her field, working as a correspondent, essayist, editor, and occasional writer of stories: experiences that were instrumental in shaping her as a writer. Under the pseudonym Vera Vel'tman she published short reports, essays, and sketches about the relevant issues of the day. Like many other Soviet journalists of the period, Panova found herself on the front lines of the emerging society, providing optimistic and inspirational reports about a wide range of issues and a broad spectrum of people. She wrote about factories and kindergartens, about the lives of young people in the cities, and of those who remained in the village. Panova's various journalistic assignments took her all over the Soviet Union and provided material for her later work. She met her first husband, the journalist Arsenii Vladimirovich Starosel'sky, in the 1920s in Rostov. Her first child, Natal'ia, was born there. Panova and Starosel'sky's marriage ended in divorce in 1927.

Panova eagerly shared in the literary life of the 1920s, taking part in the meetings of the Rostov branch of RAPP (The Russian Association of Proletarian Writers). Through her association with RAPP she met Aleksandr Aleksandrovich Fadeev, later a prominent Soviet writer. Yet, Panova appears not to have had an official affiliation with any literary organization until 1946, when she became a member of the Writers' Union and, eventually, the secretary of its Leningrad branch. She continued her work as a journalist in Rostov until the mid 1930s and during that decade also devoted some time to writing for the theater. *Il'ia Kosogor* (1939) is an historical play that deals with the events in the countryside on the eve of the Russian Revolution. *V staroi Moskve* (In the Old Moscow, 1958) is another historical piece about pre-Revolutionary life in Moscow, and *Devochki* (The Girls, written in the 1930s and published in 1945) focuses on the lives of two young sisters during World War II.

There are conflicting reports about Panova's whereabouts in the decade before the war. Without any reference to her place of residence after her departure from Rostov, Soviet biographers place her in Perm (in the Urals) in 1944. Some Western sources mention Panova's move to the village of Shishaki, near Poltava, shortly before the war and her subsequent move to Perm. More recent information published in the West provides additional data about Panova's life at the time. After her second husband, the journalist Boris Borisovich Vakhtin, was arrested in 1935, Panova apparently spent some time in Leningrad. Early in the war she appears to have been briefly detained as a refugee in Estonia. It is not clear whether Panova's three children—Natal'ia and two sons by Vakhtin, Boris (later a writer himself) and Iurii—were with her at the time. Panova wrote of her life during this time in *O moei zhizni, knigakh i chitateliakh* (About My Life, Books, and Readers) written shortly before her death in 1973 and published in 1975. Her play *Metelitsa* (The Blizzard), performed in 1956 and published in 1957, is also based on her experiences in the war. There are many parallels between Panova's autobiographical essays and the play; both deal with the Nazi occupation and describe the experiences of a refugee in Narva, Estonia, after an escape from the town of Pushkin (Tsarskoe selo), near Leningrad, early in the war. While in Shishaki, Panova felt compelled to hide the manuscript of *Metelitsa* as well as her diary, the source of the autobiographical essays.

After her arrival in Perm, Panova continued working as a journalist in local newspapers and on the radio. Here she met her third husband, the writer David Iakovlevich Dar. In 1944 she wrote her first long work, the novel *Sem'ia Pirozhkovykh* (The Pirozhkov Family), which was published in the almanac *Prikam'e*; she later used the novel as the basis for her 1959 story "Evdokiia" (translated as *Yevdokia*, 1959). Also in 1944 she began writing the novel *Kruzhilikha* (1948; translated as *The Factory*, 1949), which describes the lives of workers at an ammunition plant in the Urals during the war.

The turning point in Panova's literary career came in 1944, when the Perm section of the Writers' Union assigned her to ghostwrite a report about the work of a hospital train. Panova made four trips with a mobile hospital, interviewing the personnel between the stops made to collect the wounded from the front. Panova completed her assignment, but the brochure she wrote was never published. The only copy of the manuscript, which includes photographs of the people who served on the train, is among the exhibits of the Muzei sanitarnoi oborony (Museum of the Corps of Medicine), along with two cars from the train. Observations and impressions collected by Panova as a journalist on the hospital train formed the basis for *Sputniki*, which was first published in *Znamia* (Banner) in 1946. The novel, written in eight months, earned Panova a prominent place in Soviet letters and garnered her the 1947 Stalin Prize for literature.

In *Sputniki* Panova attempts to represent through her characters a microcosm of Soviet society. Seemingly unconnected, hailing from all walks of life—workers, peasants, orphans raised in children's homes, established physicians, a nurse from a family with a long pedigree in medicine, soldiers—the *sputniki* (fellow travelers) work together in unity, inspired by a shared mission and a sense of patriotic duty. To convey the complexity of their fates, Panova resorts to a plot configuration that has much in common with the way she structured her plays. When describing her approach to writing prose, and in response to the oft-cited criticism about the lack of coherent plots in her work, Panova mentioned the device of the "vrashchaiushchaiasia stsenicheskaia ploshchadka" (revolving stage) as her main principle of composition. The reader is offered an array of characters in orderly succession, each with his or her own history and personality.

With one exception, all of Panova's characters in the novel display their professionalism, resolve, optimism, and strength when faced with the challenges of the war. United by the shared purpose to do everything possible to help their country in its time of greatest need, Panova's protagonists still differ in the way they live their lives. *Sputniki* dwells with humor and sympathy on the triumphs and disappointments of love and on the need for people to experience happiness in the midst of the most painful adversity. Panova's women characters, unbending in their dedication to the motherland, spend a great deal of the narrative thinking about love and beauty.

Panova's representation of women in *Sputniki* fits in with the changes in women's roles that occurred in Stalinist Russia shortly before World War II. The revolutionary heroine of 1920s Soviet prose was austere, dedicated, intelligent, and contemptuous of sexual game-playing; she

*Title page for Panova's* Iasnyi bereg *(Bright Shore), about postwar reconstruction on a Soviet state farm. It won the Stalin Prize for literature in 1950 (Joint University Libraries, Nashville, Tennessee).*

demanded equal treatment from men and often forsook her motherly obligations to serve her country in more immediate and practical ways. In the 1930s female characters acquired features indicative of the new political reality and new social demands. In the official language of the time she was still an equal citizen and a loyal worker, but she was also depicted as a loving wife and mother. Panova's portraits of women in *Sputniki* are clearly indebted to this shift in the public articulation of women's roles. Her women characters are characterized by a high level of citizenship, selflessness, steadfastness, responsibility, and confidence in the correctness of their actions; yet, they also exhibit spiritual softness, emotion, and a desire to help, to ease other people's burdens, and to take care of and support men. The women on the hospital train act like dedicated professionals, but happiness for them is equated with the family and with the fulfillment of the maternal role.

Panova's attention to the personal lives of her characters is undoubtedly one of the features that made the book so popular with contemporary readers. The sense of an imminent return to normalcy, the feeling that life will prevail after the catastrophe experienced by the country—as well as the escapist flavor of Panova's romantic plotlines—provided needed relief to her readers. Touches of humor in the descriptions of some characters and situations add to the overarching feeling of optimism and hope.

Belief in the restoration of normal life is also supported in the novel by the introduction of the leader of the train, Commissar Danilov. A benevolent and highly conscious mentor to his people, whose peasant background and military service insure his political worthiness and reliability, Danilov is the moral anchor of the novel and a clear nod to the norms of socialist realism. His own path in life, as well as his interactions with the people on the train, represent faithful variations on the Socialist Realist master plot. Danilov stands for the inevitable awakening of every member of the Soviet society to its higher goals. His realization that the middle-aged, crippled woman who gives birth on the train is his long-lost love, Faina, and his awareness of the futility of this love and of his obligation to his wife and son, are the personal stages toward maturity that make Danilov into an ideal leader.

Danilov's recollections of the affair with Faina are a throwback to the literature of the 1920s. Faina, a selfless, dedicated, and sexually liberated teacher, does not belong in the new literary reality of "high Stalinism." The punishment for her emancipated ways (she flirts with the young Danilov, then has an affair with another man), as well as for her inability to recognize Danilov's potential when they first meet twenty years before, is quite harsh. Once beautiful and free-spirited, she is now a gray-haired widow who is disfigured for life. The future, according to Panova, is with those women who can be model workers and take care of their men as well. Danilov, on his part, finds personal redemption in the act of returning to his son and his submissive and nurturing wife.

Panova's subsequent works elaborate her approach to narrative structure and characterization developed in *Sputniki*. All of her writings are clearly indebted to the model of socialist realism; yet, her version of socialist realism is infused with humanity. *Kruzhilikha*, completed in Leningrad, where Panova lived after the war until the end of her life, is the story of those who participated in the war effort in the Urals. As in her previous novel, Panova offers the reader a panoply of characters, each quite memorable in his or her individuality. Women characters again combine the dedication of a loyal servant of the state with that of a perfect wife and mother. The plot is enlivened by the various love entanglements of its protagonists.

As in the 1930s, in the postwar period new public and professional roles for women were grafted onto their family and domestic roles. Middle-class notions of propriety and order, reintroduced in Joseph Stalin's time after the abandonment of early post-Revolutionary experiments with communal living and sexual liberation, continued to shape the attitudes of the Soviet people and their literary representations. In Panova's postwar novels, domesticity, the exclusive territory of women, competes with public life. Women characters in *Kruzhilikha* are invariably rewarded for their attention to their husbands, children, and households. They are in complete charge of family life but also amaze the world with their feats as *udarniki* (shock workers), or workers who exceed their production quotas.

Panova's central male character, the director of the plant, Listopad, is yet another strong and dedicated leader. Panova humanizes her protagonist by demonstrating that because of his complete dedication to the cause of winning the war and restoring the country, Listopad sometimes fails to address his own emotional needs or those of the people who work for him. Successful functioning of the plant is everything for Listopad; in the process he often abandons sensitivity to his workers' well-being, instead behaving with the arrogance of a determined bureaucrat. Panova hints at a possibility of an abuse of power inherent in such attitudes but promptly rehabilitates her character in the concluding chapters of the novel. As in *Sputniki*, the emotional lives of the characters occupy an important place in *Kruzhilikha*. All of the protagonists of the novel are shown to experience the ups and downs of emotional involvements; most find their happiness in the end. Like *Sputniki*, *Kruzhilikha* manages to create a feeling of prevailing optimism and hope for a better future. The novel was awarded the Stalin Prize for literature in 1948.

The orderly and selfless transition of the country to peace is the theme of Panova's next novel, *Iasnyi bereg* (1950, Bright Shore), another recipient of a Stalin Prize for literature. In this novel Panova describes a Soviet *sovkhoz* (state farm), focusing on the challenges of the postwar reconstruction in the village. Once more people are asked to contribute in a selfless and dedicated way, and again Panova assures her readers that the people in charge of this reconstruction are worthy of the faith the country places in them. As in other contemporary socialist realist works on the subject of postwar village life, the picture that emerges has little in common with the true devastation in the countryside after the war. Panova's protagonist, the director Korostelev—who also appears as the title character's stepfather in Panova's well-known short novel *Serezha: Neskol'ko istorii iz zhizni ochen' malen'kogo mal'chika* (1955, Serezha: A Few Histories from the Life of a Very Small Boy; translated as *Time Walked*, 1957)—is a variation on Listopad of *Kruzhilikha*, another dedicated official for whom the needs of his state farm overshadow everything else.

Panova's first post-Stalin novel, *Vremena goda; iz letopisei goroda Enska* (1954, The Seasons: From the Chronicles of the Town of Ensk; translated as *Span of the Year*, 1957), offers a noticeably darker view of contemporary Soviet society and was predictably attacked by Soviet critics on the grounds of its excessive pessimism. Panova once again turned her attention to the life of an industrial town and did not depart significantly from the way she portrayed her characters in previous novels. Yet, in the spirit of the Thaw to come, some of the negative characters in the novel now belong to the Party. Most of the respected leaders of the town are connected with criminals, and their families are destroyed by the revelations of these connections. The townspeople generally react with puzzlement and disappointment, although some of Panova's young characters act to foil the evil machinations of the corrupt leaders.

*Vremena goda* was followed by perhaps the most successful and charming of all Panova's works, *Serezha*. Like several other of her works, *Serezha* was made into a popular motion picture. The 1960 movie version, directed by Georgii Nikolaevich Daneliia, was awarded prizes at various festivals, including the 1960 Cannes festival. Written from the point of view of a five-year-old boy, the novel addresses the stages of maturation and acculturation experienced by its young protagonist. Throughout the work the focus remains on Serezha's interactions with his family and friends. His mother's marriage to Korostelev, the state farm director, is treated with sensitivity and discretion by everyone, and Serezha's life is enhanced by the presence of a caring and understanding male. Serezha is subtly shaped by Korostelev's nurturing guidance, but even before the new stepfather appears on the scene, the little boy is shown to have clear notions about what is right and what is wrong.

Serezha's life is full of events that test him as a human being and a future member of Soviet society. He faces separation from friends, illness, a death of a relative, and the threat of being temporarily left behind by his parents. Yet, the support of those around him enables Serezha to handle all of these difficulties. Panova hints at another crucial event of the time, the death of Stalin. From Serezha's perspective this historical moment is marked only by a change in radio music, from robust and happy to mournful and solemn. In the end Serezha's home is shown to be a place where all of the challenges of life, including the leader's death, can be met with strength and dignity.

Panova's next work, *Sentimental'nyi roman* (1958, Sentimental Novel), draws upon her experiences as a young Rostov journalist in the 1920s and is largely autobiographical. The novel focuses on the members of the Soviet intel-

*Panova in her study, Leningrad, 1962 (from A. Ninov,* Vera Panova–Zhizn', tvorchestvo, sovremenniki, *1980; John C. Hodges Library, University of Tennessee–Knoxville)*

ligentsia, on their participation in the creation of a new society, and, more narrowly, on their work at a provincial newspaper. As in her other novels, Panova pays especial attention to the process of emotional maturation of her protagonists. Sevast'ianov, a journalist and Panova's main character, loves the wrong woman. His eventual happiness is shown to be predicated on the realization and acceptance of this mistake. As in *Serezha,* personal fulfillment depends on inner strength and on the support of those around the characters.

The importance of family is again underscored in Panova's story "Evdokiia," a tale of a woman unable to bear children, who loves a former beau and has to decide whether to return to her old love or stay married to a man whose love for her and their adopted children is beyond doubt. Most of the characters in the story face a similar moral choice: either to seize immediate happiness or to overcome the impulse through self-control. Predictably, Evdokiia decides to return to her reliable husband. She chooses in favor of the family, since they provide the resources for her own emotional development, as well as the foundation for her adopted sons' and daughters' success in life. Society, in Panova's view, cannot function without such families, because they provide the strength on which its well-being depends. Panova's women characters make up the backbone of this life-affirming attitude.

Panova's stories "Valya" and "Volodya," both published in 1959, return to the writer's interest in young characters and trace the fates of children who lived through World War II. As in *Serezha,* the stories are told from the point of view of a child. The young people face displacement, loss of family, and destruction of their homes with courage. Panova is at pains to demonstrate the determination of Soviet people, no matter what age, to restore the country and to heal wounds inflicted by the war. In its attention to the personal lives of the Soviet people, in the writer's sympathetic view of her women characters, and in her focus on the direct challenges of living in postwar society, Panova's work appeared to her contemporary readers as fresh and even daring. Critics writing in the wake of the collapse of the Soviet Union, however, and in the context of the tremendous changes that have occurred in Russian literature since then, have tended to find her writing quite orthodox, if not mediocre.

Vera Fedorovna Panova died on 3 March 1973, just short of her sixty-eighth birthday, after a protracted illness that left her partially paralyzed. The literary establishment was shocked to discover that she left instructions to be buried according to the Russian Orthodox rite. As a result, no proper public recognition of Panova's contribution to Soviet literature took place immediately after her death. Her religious devotion, which, according to some accounts, was long-held, deep, and sincere, is not indicated in any of her writing. Also absent is anything that would undermine the reassuring certainty of the morally traditional and unequivocally patriotic outcomes of her fiction. Even if *Sputniki* or *Kruzhilikha* do not strike modern readers as particularly provocative or innovative, however, they offer excellent examples of a Soviet woman writer's attempts to push against the constraints of established literature, satisfying in the process the reader's nostalgic need for a return to the imagined past of optimism and hope–the staple of official Soviet literature.

**Biographies:**

Aleksandr Alekseevich Ninov, *Vospominaniia o Vere Panovoi: Sbornik* (Moscow: Sovetskii pisatel', 1988);

Serafima Iur'eva, *Vera Panova: Stranitsy zhizni: K biografii pisatel'nitsy* (Tenafly, N.J.: Ermitazh, 1993);

Iur'eva, *Poslednie stranitsy zhizni Very Panovoi* (N.p.: LIKK, 1997).

**References:**

Zoia Borisovna Boguslavskaia, *Vera Panova: Ocherk tvorchestva* (Moscow: Khudozhestvennaia literatura, 1963);

Deming Brown, *Soviet Russian Literature since Stalin* (Cambridge & New York: Cambridge University Press, 1978), pp. 177–178, 287–289;

Edward J. Brown, *Russian Literature since the Revolution* (Cambridge, Mass.: Harvard University Press, 1982), pp. 194–196;

Jurij Cernov, "Zazda sversenija," *Oktiabr': Literaturno-Khudozhestvennyi i Obshchestvenno-Politicheskii Zhurnal*, 2 (1975): 205–209;

Sarra Iakovlevna Fradkina, *V mire geroev Very Panovoi: Tvorcheskii portret pisatel'nitsy* (Perm': Permskoe knizhnoe izdatel'stvo, 1961);

Xenia Gasiorowska, *Women in Soviet Fiction, 1917–1964* (Madison: University of Wisconsin Press, 1968);

Juna Goff, "O Vere Fedorovne Panovoj: Besedy i perepiska," *Moskva*, 7 (1975): 203–206;

Nina Sergeevna Gornitskaia, *Kinodramaturgiia V. F. Panovoi* (Leningrad: Iskusstvo, 1970);

Gladys Horvath, "A Critical Analysis of Three Short Stories by Vera Panova," M.A. thesis, Kutztown State College, 1972;

Aleksandr Ivich, *Priroda, deti: Prishvin, Paustovsky, Dubov, Panova: Ocherki* (Moscow: Detskaia literatura, 1975);

Wolfgang Kasack, ed., *Dictionary of Russian Literature since 1917*, translated by Maria Carlson and Jane T. Hodges (New York: Columbia University Press, 1988);

Catriona Kelly, *A History of Russian Women's Writing, 1820–1992* (Oxford & New York: Clarendon Press, 1994);

Eduard Kolmanovsky, *Sovetskaia literatura nashikh dnei: Stat'i* (Moscow: Gosudarstvennoe izdatel'stvo khudozhestvennoi literatury, 1961);

Boris Kostelianets, *Tvorcheskaia individual'nost' pisatelia* (Leningrad: Sovetskii pisatel', 1960);

Ruth Kreuzer, "Panova, Vera," in *Russian Women Writers*, edited by Christine D. Tomei, 2 volumes (New York: Garland, 1999), II: 1009–1019;

Anna Krylova, "In Their Own Words? Soviet Women Writers and the Search for Self," in *A History of Women's Writing in Russia*, edited by Adele Marie Barker and Jehanne M. Gheith (Cambridge: Cambridge University Press, 2002), pp. 243–263;

L. Levin, "'Interesno, chto vy obo mne skazhite?'" *Voprosy Literatury*, 3 (March 1985): 185–194;

I. Nazarenko, "Idenost' i masterstvo," *Zvezda*, no. 11 (1954);

Aleksandr Alekseevich Ninov, "Gde nacinaetsja gorizont?" *Neva*, 10 (1966): 171–178;

Ninov, *Vera Panova: Ocherk tvorchestva* (Leningrad: Lenizdat, 1964);

Ninov, *Vera Panova–Zhizn', tvorchestvo, sovremenniki* (Leningrad: Sovetskii pisatel', 1980);

Ninov, "Vozvrashchenie v teatr: O sud'be dramaturgii Very Panovoi," *Zvezda*, no. 6 (1979): 188–203;

E. N. Obrazovskaia, "Tvorchestvo V. F. Panovoi," dissertation, University of Tomsk, 1952;

N. Ozernova-Panova, "'Kak zhe vse-taki nado pisat'?'" *Druzhba narodov: Nezavisimyi Literaturno-Khudozhestvennyi i Obshchestvenno-Politicheskii Ezhemesiachnik*, 5 (May 1985): 250–255;

Lev Abramovich Plotkin, "Dobryi talant: K shestidesiatiletiiu V. F. Panovoi," *Neva*, 10 (1965): 168–172;

Plotkin, *Tvorchestvo Very Panovoi* (Leningrad: Sovetskii pisatel', 1962);

L. Porokhina, "Vera Panova-I. A. Porokhin," *Neva*, no. 5 (1984): 191–200;

Marietta Sergeevna Shaginian, "Zametki o novom romane V. Panovoi," in her *Ob iskusstve i literature, 1933–1957: Stat'i i rechi* (Moscow: Moskovskii pisatel', 1958);

Evgeniia Shcheglova, "Pochemu ikh bylo interesno chitat'? O proze chisto 'sovetskoi' no vmeste s tem . . . ." *Neva*, 4 (1997): 179–188;

N. P. Soldatova, "Perechityvaia istoriiu Rossii: O tsikle istoricheskikh rasskazov Very Panovoi," *Vestnik Moskovskogo Universiteta. Seriia 9, Filologiia*, 9 (January–February 1986): 12–19;

E. Starikova, "Geroi Very Panovoj," *Novi Dni: Literaturno-Khudozhestvennyi i Obshchestvenno-Politicheskii Zhurnal*, 41, no. 3 (1966): 230–238;

Bosiljka Stevanovic and Vladimir Wertsman, *Free Voices in Russian Literature, 1950s–1980s: A Bio-Bibliographical Guide*, edited by Alexander Sumerkin (New York: Russica, 1987), pp. 315–316;

Eva Strauss, "The Choice of an A-level Set Book and Background Study," *Journal of Russian Studies*, 25 (1973): 28–38;

Victor Terras, ed., *Handbook of Russian Literature* (New Haven: Yale University Press, 1985);

Diana Vartkesovna Tevekelian, "'Everything Said Must Be True,'" *Soviet Literature*, 3 (1981): 141–152;

Tevekelian, *Vera Panova* (Moscow: Sovetskaia Rossiia, 1980);

Tevekelian, "You Describe Life as It Is," *Soviet Literature*, 10 (1986): 141–146;

Gennadii Trifonov, "D. Ia. Dar i V. F. Panova: Dve sud'by odnoi epokhi: Zametki literaturnogo sekretaria," *Voprosy literatury*, 2 (March–April 1996): 222–244;

D. Zolotnickij, "Istiny proverjajut zizn'," *Zvezda*, 44, no. 6 (1967): 204–211.

# Boris Pasternak
(29 January 1890 – 30 May 1960)

Karen Evans-Romaine
*Ohio University*

BOOKS: *Bliznets v tuchakh,* introduction by Nikolai Nikolaevich Aseev (Moscow: Lirika, 1914);

*Poverkh bar'erov* (Moscow: Tsentrifuga, 1917; revised, Moscow & Leningrad: Gosudarstvennoe izdatel'stvo, 1929; enlarged edition, Moscow & Leningrad: Ogiz, 1931);

*Sestra moia zhizn'* (Moscow: Grzhebin, 1922); translated by Olga Andreyev Carlisle as *My Sister Life and Other Poems* (New York: Harcourt Brace Jovanovich, 1976);

*Temy i variatsii* (Berlin: Gelikon, 1923);

*Karusel'* (Leningrad: Gosudarstvennoe izdatel'stvo, 1925);

*Rasskazy* (Moscow & Leningrad: Krug, 1925)—comprises "Detstvo Liuvers," "Il tratto di Apelle," "Pis'ma iz Tuly," and "Vozdushnye puti";

*Deviat'sot piatyi god* (Moscow: Gosudarstvennoe izdatel'stvo, 1927)—includes "Deviat'sot piatyi god" and "Leitenant Shmidt";

*Zverinets* (Moscow: Gosudarstvennoe izdatel'stvo, 1929);

*Okhrannaia gramota* (Leningrad: Izdatel'stvo pisatelei v Leningrade, 1931); translated by George Reavey as "Safe Conduct," in *Safe Conduct: An Autobiography and Other Writings* (New York: New Directions, 1958);

*Spektorsky* (Moscow & Leningrad: Gosudarstvennoe izdatel'stvo khudozhestvennoi literatury, 1931);

*Vtoroe rozhdenie* (Moscow: Federatsiia, 1932);

*Stikhotvoreniia* (Leningrad: Izdatel'stvo pisatelei v Leningrade, 1933);

*Vozdushnye puti* (Moscow: Gosudarstvennoe izdatel'stvo khudozhestvennoi literatury, 1933)—includes "Povest'";

*Na rannikh poezdakh* (Moscow: Sovetskii pisatel', 1943);

*Izbrannye stikhi i poemy* (Moscow: Gosudarstvennoe izdatel'stvo khudozhestvennoi literatury, 1945);

*Zemnoi prostor* (Moscow: Sovetskii pisatel', 1945);

*Izbrannoe* (Moscow: Sovetskii pisatel', 1948);

*Il Dottor Živago,* translated by Pietro Zveteremich (Milan: Feltrinelli, 1957); Russian version pub-

*Boris Pasternak (from* The Correspondence of Boris Pasternak and Olga Freidenberg, 1910–1954, *translated by Elliot Mossman and Margaret Wettlin, 1982; Collection of Patricia Hswe)*

lished as *Doktor Zhivago* (Milan: Feltrinelli, 1958; Ann Arbor: University of Michigan Press, 1958); first complete authorized edition, with introduction by Evgenii Borisovich Pasternak (Moscow: Knizhnaia palata, 1989); translated by Max Hayward and Manya Harari as *Doctor Zhivago* (London: Collins & Harvill, 1958; New York: Pantheon, 1958);

*Kogda razguliaetsia* (Paris: Izdatel'stvo liubitelei poezii B. L. Pasternaka, 1959);

*Sochineniia,* 4 volumes, edited by Gleb Struve and B. A. Filippov (Ann Arbor: University of Michigan Press, 1961)—comprises volume 1, *Stikhi i poemy,*

*1912–1932;* volume 2, *Proza 1915–1958. Povesti, rasskazy, avtobiograficheskie proizvedeniia;* volume 3, *Stikhi 1936–1959. Stikhi dlia detei. Stikhi, 1912–1957, ne sobrannye v knigi avtora. Stat'i i vystupleniia;* and volume 4, *Doktor Zhivago;*

*Stikhotvoreniia i poemy* (Moscow: Gosudarstvennoe izdatel'stvo khudozhestvennoi literatury, 1961);

*Stikhotvoreniia i poemy,* edited by Lev A. Ozerov, introduction by Andrei Donatovich Siniavsky (Moscow: Sovetskii pisatel', 1965)–includes "Nabroski";

*Slepaia krasavitsa* (London: Collins & Harvill, 1969; London: Flegon, 1969);

*Sonata for Piano,* edited by N. Bogoslovsky (Moscow, 1979);

*Vozdushnye puti. Proza raznykh let,* edited by Evgenii Pasternak and Elena Vladimirovna Pasternak (Moscow: Sovetskii pisatel', 1982)–includes *Liudi polozheniia;*

*Izbrannoe,* 2 volumes, edited by Evgenii Pasternak and Elena Pasternak (Moscow: Khudozhestvennaia literatura, 1985);

*Sobranie sochinenii,* 5 volumes, edited by Evgenii Pasternak, Elena Pasternak, Konstantin Mikhailovich Polivanov, and V. M. Borisov, introduction by Dmitrii Sergeevich Likhachev (Moscow: Khudozhestvennaia literatura, 1989–1992);

*Boris Pasternak ob iskusstve* (Moscow: Iskusstvo, 1990);

*Stikhotvoreniia i poemy,* 2 volumes, edited by Evgenii Pasternak and V. S. Baevsky, introduction by Vladimir N. Al'fonsov, Biblioteka poeta, Bol'shaia seriia (Leningrad: Sovetskii pisatel', Leningradskoe otdelenie, 1990);

*Boris Pasternaks Lehrjahre: Neopublikovannye filosofskie konspekty i zametki,* edited by Lazar Fleishman, Hans-Bernd Harder, and Sergei Dorzweiler, Stanford Slavic Studies, volume 11 (Stanford, Cal.: Department of Slavic Languages and Literatures, Stanford University, 1996);

*Polnoe sobranie sochinenii,* 2 [of 11 planned] volumes, edited by Evgenii Pasternak and Elena Pasternak, introduction by Fleishman (Moscow: Slovo, 2004–    ).

**Editions and Collections:** *Izbrannye stikhi* (Moscow: Uzel, 1926);

*Dve knigi. Stikhi (Sestra moia zhizn', Temy)* (Moscow: Gosudarstvennoe izdatel'stvo, 1927);

*Izbrannye stikhi* (Moscow: Pravda, 1929);

*Izbrannye stikhi* (Moscow: Sovetskaia literatura, 1933);

*Izbrannye stikhotvoreniia* (Moscow: Gosudarstvennoe izdatel'stvo khudozhestvennoi literatury, 1933);

*Poemy* (Moscow: Sovetskaia literatura, 1933);

*Izbrannye stikhotvoreniia* (Moscow: Gosudarstvennoe izdatel'stvo khudozhestvennoi literatury, 1934);

*Stikhi,* edited by Zinaida Pasternak and Evgenii Borisovich Pasternak, introduction by Kornei Ivanovich Chukovsky (Moscow: Gosudarstvennoe izdatel'stvo khudozhestvennoi literatury, 1966).

**Editions in English:** *Selected Writings* (New York: New Directions, 1949);

*Selected Poems,* translated by J. M. Cohen (London: Benn, 1958);

*Poems,* translated by Lydia Pasternak Slater, introduction by Hugh MacDiarmid (Fairwarp, U.K.: P. Russell, 1958; revised and enlarged, 1959);

*An Essay in Autobiography,* translated by Manya Harari, with introduction by Edward Crankshaw (London: Collins & Harvill, 1959);

*I Remember: Sketch for an Autobiography,* translated, with a preface, by David Magarshak (New York: Pantheon, 1959);

*The Last Summer,* translated by George Reavey (London: Peter Owen, 1959);

*The Poetry of Boris Pasternak, 1914–1960,* translated by Reavey (New York: Putnam, 1959);

*Poems,* translated by Eugene M. Kayden (Ann Arbor: University of Michigan Press, 1959);

*Prose and Poems,* translated and edited by Stefan Schimanski, introduction by Cohen (London: Benn, 1959);

*Poems, 1955–1959,* translated by Michael Harari (London: Collins & Harvill, 1960);

*Fifty Poems,* translated by Slater (London: Allen & Unwin, 1963);

*The Poems of Doctor Zhivago,* translated by Donald Davie (Westport, Conn.: Greenwood Press, 1965);

*The Blind Beauty,* translated by Max Hayward and Manya Harari (London: Collins & Harvill / New York: Harcourt, Brace & World, 1969);

*Collected Short Prose,* translated and edited by Christopher Barnes (New York: Praeger, 1977);

*My Sister–Life and A Sublime Malady,* translated by Mark Rudman with Bohdan Boychuk (Ann Arbor, Mich.: Ardis, 1983);

*Selected Poems,* translated by Jon Stallworthy and Peter France (New York: Norton, 1983);

*Pasternak on Art and Creativity,* translated and edited by Angela Livingstone (Cambridge & New York: Cambridge University Press, 1985);

*The Voice of Prose,* translated and edited by Barnes (Edinburgh: Polygon, 1986)–includes "Suboctave Story";

*The Year 1905,* translated by Richard Chappell (London: Spenser, 1989);

*Second Nature,* translated by Andrei Navrozov (London: Peter Owen, 1990);

*Selected Writings and Letters,* translated by Catherine Judelson (Moscow: Progress, 1990);

*People and Propositions,* translated and edited by Barnes (Edinburgh: Polygon, 1990);

*My Sister–Life,* translated by Rudman and Boychuk (Evanston, Ill.: Northwestern University Press, 1992).

OTHER: "Vassermanova reaktsiia," in *Rukonog* (Moscow: Tsentrifuga, 1914), pp. 33–38;

"Chernyi bokal," in *Vtoroi sbornik Tsentrifugi. Piatoe tuboizdanie* (Moscow: Tsentrifuga, 1916), pp. 39–44;

"Gorod. Otryvki tselogo," in *Liren'* (Moscow, 1920);

"V nashu prozu" [from "Deviat'sot piatyi god"], in *Polovod'e. Literaturnyi al'manakh* (Moscow & Leningrad: Molodaia gvardiia, 1926), pp. 160–161;

"Dvadtsat' strof s predisloviem," in *Pisateli–Krymu* (Moscow, 1928);

"Zametki k perevodam iz Shekspira," in *Literaturnaia Moskva* (Moscow: Gosudarstvennoe izdatel'stvo khudozhestvennoi literatury, 1956).

TRANSLATIONS: Johann Wolfgang von Goethe, *Tainy* (Moscow: Sovremennik, 1922);

Heinrich von Kleist, *Razbityi kuvshin, Prints Fridrikh Gomburgskii, Semeistvo Shroffenshtein,* and *Robert Giskar,* in his *Sobranie sochinenii,* 2 volumes, edited by Nikolai Stepanovich Gumilev and Vil'gelm Aleksandrovich Zorgenfrei (Moscow & Petrograd: Vsemirnaia literatura, 1923), pp. 19–148, 149–169;

Ben Jonson, "Al'khimik," in *Dramaticheskie proizvedeniia* (Moscow & Leningrad: Academia, 1931), pp. 301–564;

Vazha-Pshavela, *Zmeeed* (Tiflis: Zakgiz, 1934);

*Poety Gruzii* (Tbilisi: Zakgiz, 1935);

*Gruzinskie liriki* (Moscow: Sovetskii pisatel', 1935);

*Izbrannye perevody* (Moscow: Sovetskii pisatel', 1940);

William Shakespeare, *Gamlet, prints datskii* (Moscow: Gosudarstvennoe izdatel'stvo khudozhestvennoi literatury, 1941);

Kleist, *Razbityi kuvshin* (Moscow: Iskusstvo, 1941);

Shakespeare, "Zima," in *Ballady i pesni angliiskogo naroda,* edited by M. M. Morozov (Moscow & Leningrad: DETGIZ, 1942), pp. 48–50;

Shakespeare, *Romeo i Dzhul'etta* (Moscow: Vsesoiuznoe upravlenie po okhrane avtorskikh prav, 1943);

Shakespeare, *Antonii i Kleopatra* (Moscow: Gosudarstvennoe izdatel'stvo khudozhestvennoi literatury, 1944);

Shakespeare, *Otello–venetsianskii mavr* (Moscow: Gosudarstvennoe izdatel'stvo khudozhestvennoi literatury, 1945);

*Gruzinskie poety* (Moscow: Sovetskii pisatel', 1946);

Nikoloz Baratashvili, *Stikhotvoreniia* (Moscow: Pravda, 1946);

*Gruzinskie poety. Izbrannye perevody* (Tbilisi: Zaria vostoka, 1947);

Shakespeare, *Genrikh Chetvertyi* (Moscow: DETGIZ, 1948);

Sándor Petőfi, *Izbrannoe* (Moscow: Gosudarstvennoe izdatel'stvo khudozhestvennoi literatury, 1948);

Shakespeare, *Korol' Lir* (Moscow: Gosudarstvennoe izdatel'stvo khudozhestvennoi literatury, 1949);

Shakespeare, *V. Shekspir v perevode Borisa Pasternaka,* 2 volumes, edited by Morozov (Moscow: Iskusstvo, 1949);

Johann Wolfgang von Goethe, *Faust* (Moscow: Gosudarstvennoe izdatel'stvo khudozhestvennoi literatury, 1953);

Friedrich von Schiller, *Mariia Stiuart* (Moscow: Gosudarstvennoe izdatel'stvo khudozhestvennoi literatury, 1958);

*Stikhi o Gruzii. Gruzinskie poety. Izbrannye perevody* (Tbilisi: Zaria vostoka, 1958);

*Antologiia gruzinskoi poezii* (Moscow: Gosudarstvennoe izdatel'stvo khudozhestvennoi literatury, 1958);

Kleist, *Dramy. Novelly* (Moscow: Gosudarstvennoe izdatel'stvo khudozhestvennoi literatury, 1969);

*Ne ia pishu stikhi. Perevody iz poezii narodov SSSR,* edited by E. S. Levitina (Moscow: Sovetskii pisatel', 1991).

SELECTED PERIODICAL PUBLICATIONS–UNCOLLECTED: "Prelude," in "Boris Pasternak, the Musician-Poet and Composer," by Christopher Barnes, *Slavica Hierosolymitana,* 1 (1977): 330–335;

"Con moto" [1906], in "Boris Pasternak as Composer," by Barnes, *Performance,* 6 (1982): 14;

"From the *Zhivago* Cycle," translated by Barnes, *Russian Review,* 58, no. 2 (1999): 298–309.

Boris Pasternak ranks among the greatest writers of twentieth-century Russia. To native speakers of Russian he is perhaps best known and loved for his verse; nonnative speakers are rarely familiar with Pasternak's poetry because of the difficulties in translating it. Pasternak was the second Russian writer to win the Nobel Prize in literature–Ivan Alekseevich Bunin was the first–and he is known outside the Russian-speaking world primarily for his novel, *Doktor Zhivago* (1958; translated, 1958). European and American readers recall that he won the Nobel Prize in 1958 for his novel, but they often forget that the Nobel committee noted first his outstanding achievements in verse. He was cited "for his important achievement both in contemporary lyrical poetry and in the field of the great Russian epic tradition."

Pasternak scholars today are able to draw on a wealth of information provided by his biographers. Yet, because of his own autobiographical works, scholars at first faced a challenge in compiling such information. As Christopher Barnes, Boris A. Kats, and other scholars have pointed out, Pasternak led readers astray in his autobiographical essays, in the many autobiographical references found in his other works of prose as well as in his poetic works, and even in his voluminous correspondence. Despite his statement in the autobiographical essay *Okhrannaia gramota* (1931; translated as "Safe Conduct," 1958) against seeing life as "the life of the poet," Pasternak recounted his own life from the point of view of a writer. He embellished, omitted, and transposed events for the sake of the narrative or a point he wished to make. He told his life through metaphors, and if the events did not serve his metaphors, he altered those events. Therefore, only because of the scrupulous attention of his biographers is one able now to reconstruct the events of his life.

Boris Leonidovich Pasternak was born in Moscow on 29 January 1890 (10 February, new style). He was the first of four children born to artist Leonid Osipovich Pasternak and pianist Rozaliia Izidorovna (Kofman) Pasternak. Both parents were Jewish natives of Odessa, his father from a relatively poor family and his mother from a middle-class home. For professional reasons the couple decided to settle in Moscow and were married there on 14 February 1889. Their first apartment was on Tverskaia Street, near the old Triumphal Gate. The house remains standing to this day and bears a plaque commemorating Pasternak's birth. This working-class and lower-middle-class district is depicted in *Doktor Zhivago* as the neighborhood where Larisa (Lara) Gishar and Pasha Antipov live.

Pasternak's family lived frugally on what Leonid Osipovich made from the sales of his paintings and private painting lessons, as well as on Rozaliia Izidorovna's income from piano lessons. The family's financial circumstances improved when in 1894 Leonid Osipovich, despite his Jewish background, was invited to teach at the Moscow School of Painting, Sculpture, and Architecture. Pasternak once wrote (in a 1926 letter to poet and friend Marina Ivanovna Tsvetaeva) that his mother sacrificed a concert career for her children. But, according to Evgenii Borisovich Pasternak, his son and biographer, Rozaliia Izidorovna continued to practice for several hours a day and perform in solo and chamber recitals (in both private and public venues) for as long as her health permitted. After a scare in 1895, when Pasternak and his brother, Aleksandr, became gravely ill for a brief time, she stopped playing in public for ten years. Apparently, her decision to end her public concerts was a source of guilt for the children. Pasternak's image of his mother's sacrifice is one manifestation of a persistent theme throughout his work—that of women's difficult lot.

Art and music were a constant part of Pasternak's upbringing, and the careers that his siblings chose reflected this atmosphere. Aleksandr became an architect. Pasternak's sisters, Lidiia (later known as Lydia Pasternak Slater) and Zhozefina (later known as Josephine Pasternak) also wrote, but their literary achievements never approached those of their oldest brother. The careers of Pasternak's parents brought the family into contact with renowned artists, musicians, and writers of the period, including Leo Tolstoy and the poet Rainer Maria Rilke. Meetings with both writers are featured in Pasternak's literary autobiographies *Okhrannaia gramota* and *Liudi i polozheniia* (1982, People and Positions). Both Leonid Osipovich and Rozaliia Izidorovna encouraged the young Pasternak's early pursuits in various directions, including art and music. They wished their oldest son to be well educated, regardless of his future career path, and enrolled him in the Fifth Classical Gymnasium. Although they preferred to send him to a German school in Moscow, they knew that graduation with a gold medal (the equivalent of receiving an A in every subject) from a state gymnasium was a prerequisite for Jews to study at Moscow University without being subject to a 3 percent admissions quota. There was also a quota for Jews in the state schools, and because of this restriction Pasternak was unable to enroll until 1901—a year later than the typical age of enrollment at ten.

The summer of 1903 was momentous for Pasternak. He met composer Aleksandr Nikolaevich Skriabin, the family's neighbor in Obolenskoe, outside Moscow, where the Pasternaks rented a dacha in the summer. On 6 August, the Feast of the Transfiguration, Pasternak broke his leg in a fall from a horse; he had been imitating female bareback riders, whom his father was then painting. For Pasternak this incident signified the birth of music in him. In a prose fragment he wrote ten years later, he recalled that after the accident, in a delirium, he heard the three-beat syncopated rhythm of the gallop and fall. As Lazar' Fleishman discusses in his *Stat'i o Pasternake* (1977, Articles on Pasternak), fifty years later Pasternak combined the elements of the fall, the religious holiday, and the notion of death and resurrection in art in "Avgust" (August), a poem from *Doktor Zhivago*. Pasternak noted in *Liudi i polozheniia* that this injury kept him from being drafted; he did not mention directly, however, the resulting limp, which he had for the rest of his life and tried to conceal. In addition, two deaths and one near death occurred that summer, events reflected in his later writing: the accidental death or suicide of a man who fell onto the railroad tracks at Obolenskoe station; the death of a youth as he saved a

*Pasternak with his younger brother, Aleksandr, in Moscow, 1897 (from* The Correspondence of Boris Pasternak and Olga Freidenberg, 1910–1954, *translated by Elliot Mossman and Margaret Wettlin, 1982; Collection of Patricia Hswe)*

young woman from drowning; and the woman's attempt at suicide after learning of her savior's demise. The motif of drowning women appears in Pasternak's early work. The railroad death appears in *Doktor Zhivago* as the suicide of Andrei Zhivago, the father of the hero Iurii Zhivago, at the beginning of the novel.

Wanting to become a composer, Pasternak studied music seriously throughout his teens. Leonid Osipovich and Rozaliia Izidorovna were delighted with their son's ambition and arranged for private lessons in music theory and composition. Pasternak also studied piano, but he claimed that he never achieved the technical facility that would have allowed him to become a professional performer. Throughout these years he received a solid education, but his literary tendencies did not become apparent until he was nineteen.

Living in the center of Moscow, the Pasternak family witnessed the revolutionary wave that swept that city and St. Petersburg in 1905. Pasternak later conveyed the excitement he felt as a teenager at seeing the revolution in his own neighborhood in his long poem, written in 1925–1926 and titled simply "Deviat'sot piatyi god" (1927, The Year 1905). Concerned for the family's safety in the face of instability and the threat of pogroms, the Pasternaks left for Berlin, where both parents were able to carry on their professional pursuits. Arriving there in January 1906, they stayed in Germany for eight months. The sojourn gave the young Pasternak the chance to improve his German and to increase his familiarity with German literature.

Upon the family's return to Moscow, Pasternak continued his studies at the gymnasium, as well as his private lessons in music theory and composition. He graduated, with the necessary gold medal, from the gymnasium in 1908. He was admitted to Moscow University, where he decided to study law, as his father had done; this course of study was deemed easy enough to leave time for other pursuits more relevant to the young composer. Rozaliia Izidorovna resumed her concert career and gave public concerts from 1907 to 1911, when a heart condition forced her to stop performing outside the home. At some point during this period, probably in 1909, when Pasternak was in his first year at the university, he began to attend the meetings of the literary and artistic salon "Serdarda," where he first participated as a musician.

Also in 1909 Skriabin returned to Russia after a long stay in Switzerland. According to Pasternak's account in *Okhrannaia gramota,* Skriabin ironically played a key role in the young man's decision not to become a professional composer. Pasternak played his compositions for Skriabin and received his blessing, but he decided to "test fate." One of Pasternak's concerns about his musical abilities lay in his lack of perfect pitch. He decided that if Skriabin, who also did not have perfect pitch, was to admit this flaw, then the lack of perfect pitch would not matter, and Pasternak could pursue a musical career; if, on the other hand, Skriabin avoided reference to his own weakness and spoke of this deficit instead in Richard Wagner or Petr Il'ich Tchaikovsky, then the young man was destined not to become a composer. The latter happened, and Pasternak, disappointed in his idol, broke with music. Despite the dramatic account in *Okhrannaia gramota* of this final rupture, the break was actually more gradual, as Evgenii Pasternak and Boris Kats have pointed out. Pasternak's 1909 piano sonata was completed in June, several months after his February 1909 meeting with Skriabin. Moreover, there is evidence in his letters of a recurring desire to return to music even as late as 1916, three years after his graduation from the university. Throughout his life Pasternak's verse and prose demonstrated his profound love of music—thematically and, as scholars including Igor' Pavlovich Smirnov, Boris Gasparov, and Kats have written, sometimes structurally. Skriabin played a role in Pasternak's next life step as well. When the two men saw each other in February 1909, the composer advised Pasternak to abandon the study of law and pursue a degree in philosophy. In the 1909–1910 academic year Pasternak was admitted to the Faculty of History and Philosophy at the university.

Around this time, probably after deciding against a career as a composer, Pasternak began to write. His first fragments in verse and prose, which he hid from his friends and family, date from 1909. Pasternak's early verse and prose reflect his philosophical studies, his reading of Russian and French Symbolist works—as well as the works of German Romantics and Rilke—and his love for music. His first poems are conservative in form and tend toward dense, scholarly language that is reminiscent, as Barnes and others have noted, of the Russian Symbolist style. In a 1969 contribution to *Trudy po znakovym sistemam* (Studies in Semiotics) Iurii Mikhailovich Lotman shows in his studies of Pasternak's early verse fragments that he worked like a prose writer, building his poems around phrases that appealed to him and altering form to suit content.

Pasternak's early prose fragments, on the other hand, as Fleishman has discussed, constitute what Roman Jakobson called in a 1935 article for *Slavische Rundschau* (Slavic Review) a "poet's prose." More experimental than his early poetry, they generally are without plot and read like improvisations. Sentences tend to be either tremendously long or in enigmatic fragments. Characters with symbolic names walk the streets of Moscow, meditate on art and inspiration, and describe the natural world and urban landscape as an animated, personified universe. These prose fragments, first published in the 1970s and 1980s, provide the reader with valuable information about Pasternak's developing aesthetic system. The surrounding world that acts upon the writer, the notion of objects that have souls, the image of creativity as the splitting of oneself into two parts (one that dies off and another that comes alive and calls out to an unknown force)—all of these features remained with Pasternak, in more veiled and poetically sophisticated form, throughout his life.

Throughout his childhood and youth, Pasternak had had a close relationship with his cousin in St. Petersburg, Ol'ga Mikhailovna Freidenberg. Around 1910 this relationship reached its peak. He occasionally visited her and her family in St. Petersburg. Her rejection of his advances ended his hopes for romance, but their friendship endured. They continued to correspond until his death, and their letters, published in both Russian and English, reveal much about Pasternak's perception of literature, art, and the creative process.

In 1911 Pasternak's family moved to an apartment on Volkhonka Street, in a building (now partly demolished) located next to the Museum of Fine Arts; they occupied this apartment for the next two decades. At this time Pasternak finally settled into a writing career and was involved in several Moscow literary circles. Through the Serdarda salon, now transformed into a literary circle called "Lirika" (meaning lyric poetry or lyricism), Pasternak met the poet and critic Sergei Pavlovich Bobrov, with whom he had a close if difficult professional relationship during the next several years. Bobrov was an active organizer, though not a diplomatic person, and he played a role in launching Pasternak's career. In Moscow, at gatherings of the literary-philosophical circle associated with the publishing house Musaget, Pasternak met some of the leading writers and critics of the symbolist movement, which—though already beginning its decline—was still the reigning trend in Russian literature.

Disillusioned with the uninspiring way that philosophy was taught by some of his professors at Moscow University, Pasternak decided to study under Hermann Cohen, a leader of the neo-Kantian school, at Marburg University in the summer of 1912. During this time abroad Pasternak decided against philosophy as a profession. He writes openly of his rejection in *Okhrannaia gramota* and hints at it in his poem "Marburg" (published 1917 in *Poverkh bar'erov* [Over the Barriers]). In both works he also describes a concurrent unsuccessful proposal of marriage to a family acquaintance, Ida Vysotskaia, when she came to visit in June 1912. In both works he bids farewell to love and philosophy and embraces poetry; in "Marburg," in particular, the speaker appears to have made this decision in one fateful night. In fact, as Barnes and Evgenii Pasternak have disclosed in their respective biographies on the poet, events ran a more gradual and logical course. When Vysotskaia visited Pasternak in Marburg, he asked her to marry him; she refused, and he accompanied her and her sister to Berlin. Upon Pasternak's return to Marburg, Cohen—knowing the difficulties that Jews faced in their pursuits of academic careers in Russia—invited Pasternak to continue at Marburg University and complete a doctorate in philosophy. He declined, however; after completing his summer semester, he joined his family in Italy and then returned to Moscow. Thus, unlike his depiction of this period in his poetry and prose, Pasternak in actuality sensed only gradually in Marburg that he did not care for the life of an academic. (In a 19 July letter to his friend Aleksandr [Shura] Shtikh he referred to career academics as "beasts of intellectualism.") Although Pasternak completed his studies at Moscow University in 1912–1913, he began devoting himself to literature.

On 10 February 1913, at a Musaget meeting, Pasternak read a paper that became the first significant

*Pasternak in 1908, the year he graduated from the gymnasium (from* The Correspondence of Boris Pasternak and Olga Freidenberg, 1910–1954, *translated by Elliot Mossman and Margaret Wettlin, 1982; Collection of Patricia Hswe)*

statement of his aesthetic views. What remains of "Sivolizm i bessmertie" (Symbolism and Immortality) is only an abstract, but it effectively summarizes the philosophical approach that influenced his writing. Pasternak posits the notion of subjectivity as a generic element that exists outside the individual and lives beyond each person's death. The poet, in search of this "free subjectivity" outside and beyond himself, behaves like objects in the surrounding world. Thus, already in 1913 Pasternak articulated one of the fundamental aspects of his aesthetic system: the notion of the passive poet—someone who is a mere vessel of inspiration and at one with things around him or her.

In April 1913, just as he was completing his university studies, several of Pasternak's poems were published in the almanac *Lirika,* named after the literary group; this almanac, or miscellany, was the first publication by the group. Yet, *Lirika* drew little reaction; as Fleishman notes in *Boris Pasternak: The Poet and His Politics* (1990), there was an "epidemic of poetry" around 1910, and such publications were legion. That summer, just after graduation, Pasternak wrote the rest of the poems that composed his first complete book of poetry, *Bliznets v tuchakh* (1914, Twin in the Clouds). This collection of twenty-one poems reveals a voice of startling originality and, from the point of view of Pasternak's poetic predecessors, some eccentricity. His verse mixes stylistic registers and introduces colloquialisms, dialect, rarely used words, technical words, and foreign words—even in rhyming position. Aspects of Pasternak's mature style are evident in these poems, such as the notion of blending with the universe and the poet's tendency to be hidden behind objects and events in the surrounding world.

In autumn 1913 Pasternak moved to modest lodgings in Moscow, away from his parents' apartment. In January 1914 he, Bobrov, and Nikolai Nikolaevich Aseev formed a group called "Tsentrifuga" (Centrifuge). They announced to Lirika their break from them and became one of the Futurist alliances that rivaled the main Futurist group, the Cubo-Futurists, whose star poet was Vladimir Vladimirovich Maiakovsky. Tsentrifuga distinguished itself among Futurist groupings as the one whose poets most openly acknowledged their debts to literary tradition, both Russian and foreign. While the Cubo-Futurists issued a demand to cast out various poets from the "ship of modernity" in their famous manifesto, "Poshchechina obshchestvennomu vkusu" (A Slap in the Face of Public Taste), published in a miscellany of the same name in 1913, verses by Tsentrifuga poets featured prominent citations from the works of their literary ancestors. Valerii Iakovlevich Briusov noted this contrast in a 1914 article in *Russkaia mysl'* (Russian Thought), in which he was the first to call them Futurists.

Futurist politics were highly fractious, and Bobrov was eager to involve Tsentrifuga in the fray. In March 1914 he founded the Tsentrifuga publishing house and immediately published his essay "Liricheskaia tema" (The Lyric Theme) as a pamphlet. In April he published the almanac *Rukonog* (Brachiopod, in Vladimir Markov's translation), which included verse by Tsentrifuga and other poets. It also had three Futurist poems by Pasternak that never reappeared during his lifetime. More significant from the point of view of Futurist politics, however, was the publication in *Rukonog* of Pasternak's only truly polemical article, "Vassermanova reaktsiia" (The Wasserman Test), in which he attacked various Futurist rivals. Pasternak was later embarrassed by the tone of his article and never republished it. Yet, as Fleishman argues in a 1979 contribution to *Slavica Hierosolymitana* (Jerusalem Slavic Studies), this article is critical to an understanding of a key concept in Pasternak's work, clarified by Jakobson in his groundbreaking 1935 study of Pasternak's poetics, "Randbemerkungen zur Prosa des Dichters Pasternak" (Marginal Notes on the Prose of the Poet Pasternak, published in *Slavische Rundschau*). In "Vassermanova reaktsiia," Pasternak criticizes the Futurist poet

Vadim Shershenevich for using metaphors in his verse that are based on "sviaz' po skhodstvu" (associative connection by similarity), while only "sviaz' po smezhnosti" (connection by contiguity) is justifiable as a true metaphor. Jakobson decodes Pasternak's notion of "contiguity" as metonym and sees it as the defining trait of Pasternak's poetic system, in which things are associated with each other, can replace one another, and the part can represent the whole. This trait, he argues, distinguishes Pasternak's innovative poetics from that of the symbolists, whose primary literary device was metaphor. Thus, in his 1914 article Pasternak put forth a principle of fundamental importance to his work.

*Rukonog* also includes a Tsentrifuga "charter," written by Bobrov, which called all Futurists–except Maiakovsky and Velimir Khlebnikov–mediocrities, traitors, and cowards. This denunciation prompted a meeting, and several poets, including Maiakovsky, convened at a café. What happened the next day, after the meeting, was a turning point in Pasternak's career. By accident he met Maiakovsky at another café, and the Cubo-Futurist recited his long poem *Vladimir Maiakovsky. Tragediia* (1914, Vladimir Maiakovsky: A Tragedy) to Pasternak. After this episode Pasternak became an admirer of Maiakovsky and his work, and traces of Maiakovsky's verse were evident in Pasternak's poetry for at least the next five to ten years.

In the summer of 1914 Pasternak was invited to stay with the family of the poet Jurgis Baltrušaitis at their summer home and tutor their eleven-year-old son. Pasternak worked on a commission for Baltrušaitis–a translation of Heinrich von Kleist's play *Der zerbrochene Krug* (1811, The Broken Pitcher). Pasternak was fond of Kleist and in 1911 had written a paper on him that remained unfinished and unpublished during his lifetime. He wrote another article on Kleist to accompany his translation of the play, but it has been lost. The play, which Pasternak translated as *Razbityi kuvshin* and which appeared in the journal *Sovremennik* (The Contemporary) in 1915, was not staged, however, because the Moscow Chamber Theater refused to put on a German play–a refusal stemming from the political climate of the time.

As the prospect of war loomed, the mood that summer was grim. In July 1914 Pasternak was called to the draft office, but he was deemed unsuitable for active duty because of his shortened leg, a result of his 1903 riding accident. He reacted to World War I by writing about the nightmares of war in poems such as "Durnoi son" (Bad Dream), "Artillerist stoit u kormila . . ." (The artillery man stands by the helm . . .), and "Osen'. Otvykli ot molnii . . ." (Autumn. Unaccustomed to lightning . . .), all of which were first collected in 1917 in *Poverkh bar'erov*; another poem, "Sochel'nik" (Christmas Eve), hints at war.

In the winter of 1914–1915 Pasternak met the five Siniakova sisters through Maiakovsky and Aseev, and he fell in love with Nadezhda Mikhailovna Siniakova. Nadezhda and her sisters had a reputation as bohemians; they had come from Khar'kov to Moscow in order to pursue careers in the arts, and several of them became romantically involved with Futurist poets. According to Pasternak's commentators, many of his poems from the period 1914–1916 reflect his relationship with Nadezhda.

During that winter Pasternak wrote his first significant piece of prose fiction, a story titled "Il tratto di Apelle" (The Apelles Mark, first published in *Znamia truda. Vremmenik* [The Banner of Labor. Annals], 1918; published as "Apellesova cherta" in the book *Vozdushnye puti* [Aerial Ways], 1933). The name Apelles refers to a Greek painter who lived during the reign of Alexander the Great. In his commentary in volume four of the 1989–1992 *Sobranie sochinenii*, Evgenii Pasternak explains that the *cherta,* or mark, of the title is a thin brush stroke left by Apelles as a sign of his mastery in an artistic rivalry. The story is about a fictional character named Heinrich Heine and his meeting with an Italian poet, Emilio Relinquimini (in Russian, Relinkvimini), whose name, with an added *n* (Relinquiminni, as opposed to Reliquimini), appeared in Pasternak's early prose sketches. "Apellesova cherta," a story that addresses romantic and artistic rivalry and revenge, has been interpreted by scholars as a reflection of Pasternak's rivalrous relationship with Maiakovsky and his reckoning with the "Romantic manner," which he wrote against in *Okhrannaia gramota*. Scholars disagree about the identity of Pasternak's character Heine–whether he meant to portray his version of the real Heine, or whether the name was merely an emblem for the great German writer. As Heine biographer Jeffrey L. Sammons has written, the actual Heine considered his body of work the swan song of Romanticism and himself both its final representative and murderer. Heine was therefore important to Pasternak as a model for coping with his own literary ancestors. As Fleishman asserts in *Boris Pasternak: The Poet and His Politics,* however, this anti-Romantic polemic is not nearly as strong as it becomes in Pasternak's later work. Fleishman sees the story in part as an examination of the tenuous line between art and reality. For Evgenii Pasternak, writing in *Boris Pasternak: Materialy dlia biografii* (1989, Boris Pasternak: Materials for Biography), "Apellesova cherta" represents Heine as both the ordinary and the immortal, reflected in the everyday world of the twentieth century.

In 1915 Pasternak moved in with the family of a German manufacturer, Moritz Philipp, in order to tutor their son. In Moscow on 28 May of that year, in an anti-German pogrom, Pasternak's books and papers were destroyed, and some of his manuscripts were lost. Also in 1915 he wrote a second theoretical article, "Chernyi bokal" (The Black Goblet), for Bobrov's *Vtoroi sbornik Tsentrifugi* (Second Centrifuge Miscellany), published in 1916. The black goblet is the equivalent of the sign on cardboard boxes that reads, "this end up"—a call for caution with delicate materials. The essay is a call for art for art's sake and opposes those who bring art down to the level of temporary squabbles, who use art for political purposes both grand and petty. Pasternak aims criticism at, among others, Futurists in love with contemporaneity and speed. He argues instead for a poetry of eternity.

In January 1916 Pasternak took an office job in a chemical factory in Vsevolodo-Vil'va, located in the Ural Mountains. According to Barnes in volume one of *Boris Pasternak: A Literary Biography* (1989), the move was most likely an attempt to avoid the draft. Pasternak's friend Konstantin Loks wrote that although Pasternak would not have been called up because of his disability, he mistakenly thought he might, and he felt that work related to the war effort could delay or prevent conscription. Pasternak liked the change of scene, and impressions of his half year in the Urals appeared later in his writings. A brief trip to Ekaterinburg, for example, is reflected in the setting of his story "Detstvo Liuvers" (The Childhood of Liuvers, written 1917–1918, published 1922 in *Nashi dni* [Our Days]); other impressions appear in the parts of *Doktor Zhivago* that take place in the Urals. In this remote setting Pasternak began to miss music, and in February 1916, in a letter to his parents, he asked them to send sheet music. He settled down to write full-time in March but produced little. His efforts included several stunning landscape poems and an article on William Shakespeare, the manuscript of which has been lost. Pasternak returned to Moscow in June 1916 and began to gather poems written within the last two years for his next book of verse, *Poverkh bar'erov*. These poems show the influence of Maiakovsky and of Futurist poetics. *Poverkh bar'erov* received much more favorable critical attention than had his first book of verse. Most important to Pasternak, his father liked it; previously, Leonid Osipovich had expressed disapproval of his son's career choice and early writing efforts.

In October, Pasternak left Moscow again to take a job similar to the one in Vsevolodo-Vil'va. He traveled to a place called Tikhie gory (Quiet Mountains), on the river Kama, west of the Urals, and worked there in a chemical plant at a job arranged for him by an acquaintance he had met in the Urals, a biochemist named Boris Il'ich Zbarsky, who became a Socialist Revolutionary. Pasternak's job involved saving from conscription local workers whose civilian work was necessary for the war effort. In December 1916 he himself was permanently released from military service. That fall he worked on translations of verse and of a play, *Chastelard* (1865), by Algernon Charles Swinburne; however, he did not complete the project. During his stay in Tikhie gory, Pasternak also wrote several poems that appeared in his collection *Temy i variatsii* (1923, Themes and Variations), and fragments of longer poems titled "Gorod" (The City, published with subtitle "Otryuki tselogo" [Excerpts], 1920) and "Nabroski. Fantaziia o blizhnem" 1965, (Sketches. Fantasy about Someone Close). These long poems were never completed. In addition, he wrote an ecstatic review of Maiakovsky's poetry collection *Prostoe kak mychanie* (1916, Simple as Mooing), as well as a review of Nikolai Nikolaevich Aseev's *Oksana* (1916).

In the winter of 1916 Pasternak wrote (but did not finish) a story that recalled aspects of his life in Berlin ten years earlier, such as the romantic flights of fancy and horror in the tales he had read there and his experiences listening to organ music, a sound unfamiliar to most Russians. In "Istoriia odnoi kontroktavy" (translated as "Suboctave Story," in 1986), a peculiar Gothic piece that was not published in Pasternak's lifetime, an organist inadvertently murders his small son. The boy crawls inside the instrument and quickly gets entangled in its workings; he dies as his father, absorbed in the music, plays the organ, not realizing until too late what has happened. The narrator expresses sympathy for the father, an artist in a provincial town of philistines who reject him as a murderer and pariah. Later, Pasternak was so ashamed of the story that he tried to burn it. His son saved the manuscript, however, and published it in Israel in 1977, many years after Pasternak died, in the journal *Slavica Hierosolymitana*.

Pasternak went back to Moscow in March 1917, one month after the first of the two revolutions that year, as soon as he learned about the February uprising. Liberal reactions—including those of the Pasternak family—to the February Revolution were highly positive. The ecstatic reception of the first revolution and his relationship with a new beloved, Elena Vinograd, are reflected in Pasternak's third book of verse, *Sestra moia zhizn'* (1922; translated as *My Sister Life and Other Poems*, 1976). He had met Vinograd, the cousin of his close friend Shura Shtikh, in 1909. She was engaged to another acquaintance, Sergei Listopad (the son of philosopher Lev Shestov), who was killed in action. After

*Building in Marburg, Germany, where Pasternak lived in 1912 while studying philosophy at Marburg University under Hermann Cohen, a leader of the neo-Kantian school (from* The Correspondence of Boris Pasternak and Olga Freidenberg, 1910–1954, *translated by Elliot Mossman and Margaret Wettlin, 1982; Collection of Patricia Hswe)*

Listopad's death, a romance began between Pasternak and Vinograd.

*Sestra moia zhizn'* is Pasternak's most cohesive book of poetry and, by many accounts, his most successful. It consists of fifty poems divided into titled cycles, or chapters, of two to six poems each. The book describes his romance with Vinograd in Moscow, his visit to her in Saratov province, urban and rural landscapes in the spring and summer, and Moscow street demonstrations in favor of the regime led by Aleksandr Fedorovich Kerensky; the verses in this collection also examine the nature of poetry and the creative process. *Sestra moia zhizn'* was not published until 1922–primarily because of printing and other logistical difficulties stemming from the Russian Civil War. Reactions to the book were swift and ecstatic: it firmly established Pasternak's career. Yet, writers with more conservative tastes, such as the émigré poet Vladislav Khodasevich and the émigré critic Vladimir Weidlé, disliked its modernist complexity, which they perceived–like Pasternak himself later–as shallow mannerism. In addition, Communist critics in 1922 and afterward wrote disparagingly of Pasternak's apparent lack of political engagement in his work.

Pasternak conveyed the political situation of these years in an unfinished verse drama on which he worked in the summer of 1917. "Dramaticheskie otryvki" (Dramatic Fragments), published in *Znamia truda* in 1918, juxtaposes the revolutionary views of Maximilien Robespierre and the philosophical musings of Louis de Saint-Just, who sees revolution as a creative act of self-sacrifice. It is also a battle of reason and emotion. The reader can see Pasternak siding with Saint-Just and recoiling at the cold calculations of Robespierre. Barnes notes the importance of this unfinished work as a precursor of the political arguments in *Doktor Zhivago*.

During the years 1917–1921 Pasternak was busy writing poems (for his fourth book of verse, *Temy i variatsii*) and short prose works, some of which rank among his best. In the autumn of 1917 he wrote the story "Detstvo Liuvers" (The Childhood of Liuvers), about a girl's coming of age (*Liuvers* is the Russian rendering of the French and English word "louvers," referring to a type of window blind). Angela Livingstone writes in *Boris Pasternak: Doktor Zhivago* (1989) that this story is "generally regarded as Pasternak's prose masterpiece." It stands out because of the clarity of its language, vision, and moral message; its perceptiveness in the psychological portrayal of a sensitive girl on the edge of womanhood; and its modernist statements about the relationship of the word and the thing. The heroine, who has the androgynous name Zhenia Liuvers, matures in three different ways: intellectually, by matching things with their names; physically, when she experiences her first menstrual period; and emotionally, by becoming aware of the fates of other people—ranging from her mother, who miscarried after witnessing an accident, to a stranger, who was killed in that accident. The heroine of the story has many traits in common with Pasternak's sensitive male writer-heroes. In both verse and correspondence he wrote of his sympathy with "women's lot," and this story, which takes place in an overwhelmingly female world, is one of his most eloquent expressions of such empathy. The story continues the tradition of Russian narratives about childhood (by Tolstoy, for example) yet departs from it in its modernist sensibilities. "Detstvo Liuvers" is written in a language unusually clear for early Pasternak. It was well received by writers such as Iurii Nikolaevich Tynianov and Mikhail Alekseevich Kuzmin.

In his story "Pis'ma iz Tuly" (Letters from Tula, written 1918, published 1922 in *Shipovnik* [Wild Rose]), Pasternak explores the contrast between true art and imitation, or falsehood, through the letters of a poet who observes actors playing falsely in art and life. The poet-narrator realizes the moral significance of art and his obligation to be truthful to it and thus to himself. The same thing happens to an old actor in the second part of the story, who goes through his gestures, replaying an episode from his past, and realizes that he is only the medium for a higher force. Written in both epistolary and diary form, "Pis'ma iz Tuly" expresses Pasternak's views on inspiration: the writer plays a passive role and must therefore be receptive.

Another 1918 story, "Bezliub'e" (Lovelessness), originally a chapter from an unfinished novella and first published in the journal *Znamia truda*, is based on Pasternak's return from the Urals to Moscow in 1917, during which, at one point, he took a long sleigh ride to the train station in Kazan' together with the Socialist revolutionary Zbarsky. The story centers on the dedication of a revolutionary for whom the dream of revolution is dearer than his life. The revolutionary and his traveling companion are reflections of Zbarsky and Pasternak himself; as Barnes points out in *The Voice of Prose*, the characters serve as prototypes for the opposition of Antipov and Zhivago in his novel.

During this period Pasternak drafted one of his most often quoted essays on art, "Neskol'ko polozhenii" (Several Propositions), written in December 1918 and revised in 1922, the same year it was published in *Sovremennik*. In this essay he makes explicit his notion of the passive artist: art is a "sponge," not a "fountain"; a book is unaware of anything outside of itself. Pasternak compares the oblivion of art to a mating grouse, which is aware only of its need to reproduce and therefore to sing. He also writes on the role of conscience in art and of the unity of art across the ages. Proud of "Neskol'ko polozhenii," Pasternak had intended to make it the first in a collection of art essays, titled "Quinta essentia" (Fifth Essence), but this piece was the only one he finished.

The years 1918–1921 were extremely difficult for all Russians. Muscovites, including Pasternak, suffered many privations. *Temy i variatsii,* his next book of verse, includes poems that portray the difficulties, illnesses, and fears of this period. Evgenii Pasternak views *Sestra moia zhizn'* and *Temy i variatsii* as opposite sides of the same coin. If in the former, he asserts (in *Boris Pasternak. Materialy dlia biografii*), nature imagery is full of life, in the latter it is often rendered artificial or mechanical through settings such as a pleasure garden, or through metaphors such as a watch. One of the illnesses in this book is the revolution; the illness from which the poet suffers, as described in the cycle "Boleza'," is blended metonymically with that of the post-October regime in verse so difficult that the censors bypassed such references. In these years financial difficulties and the virtual impossibility of publishing creative work also forced Pasternak to turn to translation assignments for income; translation work supported him for the rest of his life.

Pasternak's parents and sisters left for Berlin in 1921, after the civil war had ended. Pasternak and his brother, Aleksandr, decided to stay and remained in two of the family's rooms in the apartment on Volkhonka; they gave the other rooms to acquaintances, rather than wait for them to be occupied by strangers during this era of communalization. That year Pasternak met Evgeniia (Zhenia) Vladimirovna Lur'e, who became his first wife; she had moved to Moscow from Petrograd (formerly St. Petersburg) to study art and establish her career. They were married in Petrograd in February 1922.

In 1922 Pasternak made two significant acquaintances: he met fellow poets Osip Emil'evich Mandel'shtam and Tsvetaeva. Mandel'shtam, a Petersburg poet, had moved to Moscow that year. Their acquaintance grew into a distant friendship, one based on mutual respect combined with an awareness of their strong personal and artistic differences. They continued to meet and correspond until Mandel'shtam was exiled to Voronezh in 1934. In 1922 Pasternak also received a copy of Tsvetaeva's collection *Versty: Stikhi* (1921, Mileposts: Poems) and was in awe of it. He and Tsvetaeva had met before only in passing. He wrote her to praise her work, but by this time she had left Moscow for Berlin. Soon afterward she read *Sestra moia zhizn'* and wrote the essay "Svetovoi liven'" (A Downpour of Light, published 1922 in the journal *Epopeiia* [Epos]), a work of art in its own right. Pasternak and Tsvetaeva struck up a correspondence that continued for a brief period, then intensified in 1926–1928 and lasted until 1935.

In August 1922 Pasternak and his wife left for Berlin. Pasternak took his manuscript for *Temy i variatsii* to Berlin, intending to publish it there; it came out, published by Gelikon, at the beginning of 1923. At this time Berlin was a center of Russian culture abroad, almost as vital as Paris. Many Russian writers lived in Berlin, and despite the shock of seeing its postwar conditions, the stay there was pleasant for Pasternak. He and his wife planned to stay for a year but left for Russia early, in March 1923, because of Evgeniia's pregnancy. Evgenii Pasternak was born in Moscow that September.

In 1924 Pasternak again turned to short prose fiction with his story "Vozdushnye puti" (published the same year in *Russkii sovremennik* [The Russian Contemporary]). As Rudova indicates in *Understanding Boris Pasternak* (1997), this story anticipates *Doktor Zhivago*, particularly in the way the 1917 Revolution is treated in the plot of the novel. Writing in *The Voice of Prose*, Barnes notes that in "Vozdushnye puti," however, Pasternak applies a greater harshness to his depiction of the Bolshevik era. The love triangle in the story also resembles the one at work in *Doktor Zhivago*, although the gender roles in this triangle are the opposite of those in Pasternak's novel. In this two-part story a woman's son is kidnapped. The heroine, Lelia, persuades her lover, Polivanov, that the child is his, and both he and her husband search for the boy, who is found. In the second part the boy, now grown, has been arrested by the Bolsheviks. Once again Lelia appeals to Polivanov, now a Red Army officer, to save him. But the appeal comes too late: her son has already been executed. The prose in this story is much more complex and elliptical than that of "Detstvo Liuvers" or "Pis'ma iz Tuly." As in a later story, "Povest'" (A Tale, first published in full in *Novyi mir* [The New World], 1929), the plot of "Vozdushnye puti" is difficult to follow, and the style is reminiscent of Pasternak's verse technique. The story shows his growing interest in the fate of the individual in history. According to Evgenii Pasternak in *Boris Pasternak. Materialy dlia biografii,* the original draft, which was longer, has been lost. Pasternak was asked to shorten the story for publication, and Barnes notes in volume one of his biography of the poet that it was also cut by censors.

Pasternak continued to write verse in the 1920s, though not at nearly the same rate as in the 1910s. He wrote some landscape poems, as well as verse dedicated to Tsvetaeva and Anna Andreevna Akhmatova. Mainly, however, his verse in the 1920s turned toward epic forms. In 1923 he wrote his first major long poem, "Vysokaia bolezn'" (Lofty Malady, first variant published 1924 in the journal *LEF*), about the linked illnesses of revolution and art. In this dark era writers such as Pasternak and Mandel'shtam could see that their age was over, and Pasternak writes in "Vysokaia bolezn'" of artists, including himself, depicting their own demise. He revised the poem substantially and published it anew in 1928 in the journal *Novyi mir:* there he describes Vladimir Ilyich Lenin, without naming him, in a manner that is at once ecstatic and frightening. A second epic poem of the 1920s is "Deviat'sot piatyi god," about his experiences as a teenager witnessing the 1905 Revolution. This work is not merely a memoir, however. In order to re-create the spirit of the events that occurred in 1905, Pasternak conducted research on materials from the era, and the poem is written in a style reminiscent of a documentary.

During this time, after a lapse of several years, Pasternak resumed his correspondence with Tsvetaeva. In late March 1926 he read in manuscript form her new "Poema kontsa" (Poem of the End), published that year in the miscellany *Kovcheg* (The Ark). On the same day that he received Tsvetaeva's poem, a letter from his father came, in which he wrote that Rilke had read and liked Pasternak's work. Pasternak wrote Rilke a letter thanking him and expressing his debt to the poet's own work. He asked Rilke to send a copy of his *Duineser Elegien* (1923, Duino Elegies) to Tsvetaeva, whose work Pasternak praised. Rilke did so, and a three-way correspondence among the poets developed. This exchange is one of the most extraordinary epistolary events in twentieth-century Russian literature. It provides a rich source of information on the poets' thoughts about art, their own and others' work, and the essence of creativity and its sources. It also reveals significant biographical information about Pasternak and Tsvetaeva. The extraordinary three-way correspondence was in part romantic: Pasternak and Tsvetaeva exchanged what could be considered love letters, and Tsvetaeva's letters to the already ailing Rilke were also passionate. After a period of intense correspondence, by September 1926, the writers had fallen into an awkward silence, and Pasternak and Tsvetaeva resumed writing to each other only after Rilke's death at the end of that year. Pasternak's and Tsvetaeva's letters from the period 1926–1928 include discussions of plans for him to visit her or even to join her in emigration, although the plans never came to fruition for various reasons, both personal and

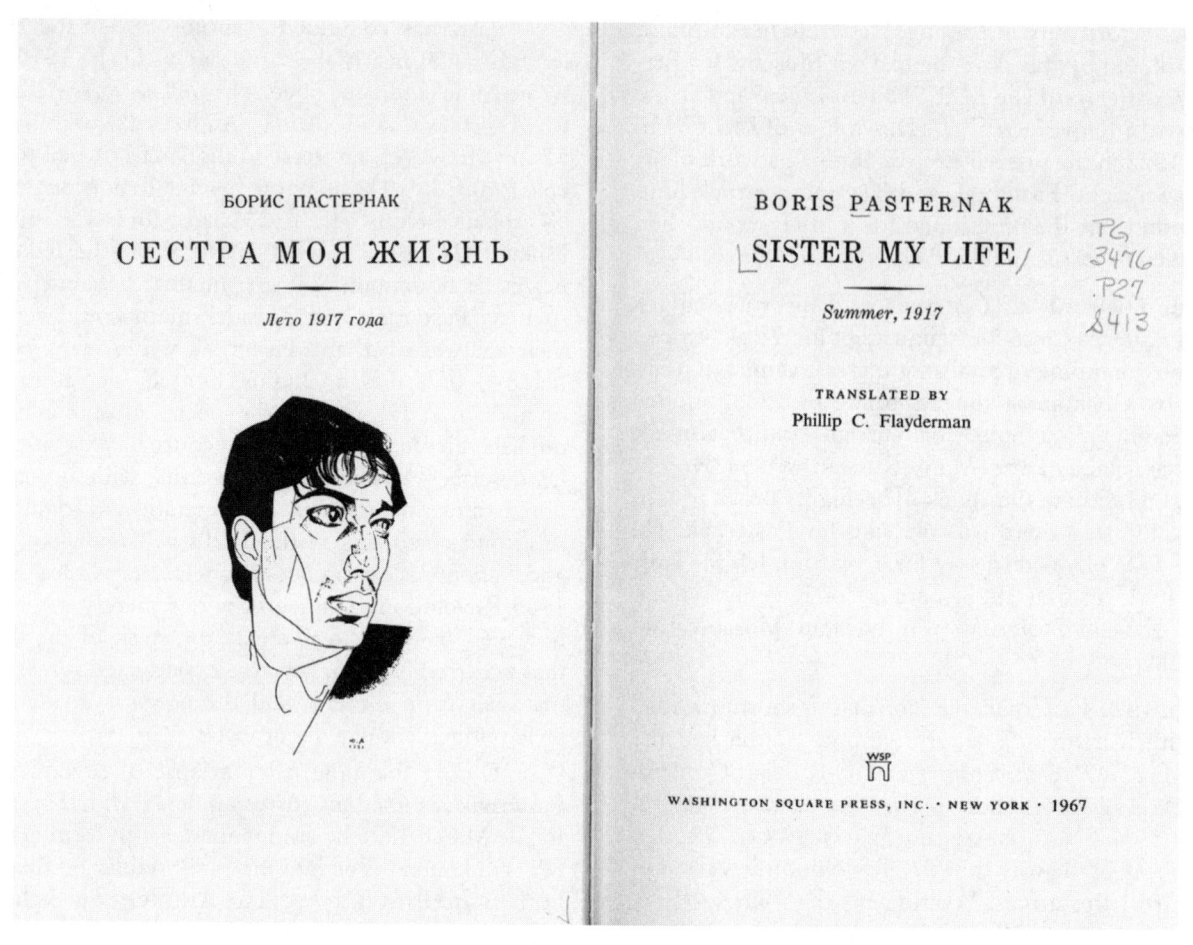

*Double title page for an English-Russian edition of Pasternak's 1922 collection of verse celebrating the success of the February revolution and his love for Elena Vinograd (Thomas Cooper Library, University of South Carolina)*

professional. The two poets continued to exchange letters, with decreasing intensity after 1928, until 1935.

In the summer of 1926 Pasternak's wife and son went to visit his family in Germany; Evgeniia also hoped to be cured of the tuberculosis she had contracted during the Russian Civil War. Their marriage, a stressful relationship between two artists, had been strained further by his correspondence with Tsvetaeva. Evgeniia returned to Moscow with their son in October 1926, and she and Pasternak resumed living together in their cramped quarters at the Volkhonka apartment.

Pasternak's next epic poem, "Leitenant Shmidt" (1927, Lieutenant Schmidt), recounts another event of 1905: a naval mutiny against the tsarist officer of a ship, led by the lieutenant of the title, who was tried and executed. Pasternak conducted research on this incident. He quotes extensively from some of the documents, as Iurii Levin and A. N. Lur'e assert in their scholarship. Pasternak's Schmidt, like his other revolutionary heroes, is of a philosophical turn of mind, and, in Christ-like fashion (expressed through a biblical quotation), he is prepared to sacrifice himself for the sake of his fellow men and a higher cause. Pasternak dedicated the work to Tsvetaeva; he wrote the dedication in verse, with her name in an acrostic. Yet, she was disappointed in the weakness of the protagonist. Once he learned of her low opinion of the poem, he asked to have the dedication removed. Furthermore, the acrostic had put him in political trouble, since the mention of Tsvetaeva's name was no longer permitted in Soviet publications.

Pasternak wrote a novel in verse, *Spektorsky,* from 1925 to 1931. It was published serially in various journals (*Krug* [The Circle], *Kovsh* [The Ladle], *Krasnaia nov'* [Red Virgin Soil], and *Novyi mir*) from 1925 to 1930 and subsequently came out in a separate edition in 1931. *Spektorsky* is closely related to his fragmentary poem "Dvadtsat' strof s predisloviem" (Twenty Stanzas with an Introduction, written 1925, published 1928), from which it developed, and to his unfinished work in prose works "Tri glavy iz povesti" (1922, Three Chapters from a Story), and "Povest'." The action of "Povest'" takes place during the gap of time left in *Spektorsky;* thus the two works can be considered interlocking. All three works have autobiographical elements. *Spektorsky* tells the story of a Moscow intellectual named Spektorsky, someone who would have been Pasternak's contemporary. The protagonist feels isolated in a changing world and in his romantic pursuits, including an affair with another character, Maria Il'ina—among whose prototypes, as Pasternak himself acknowledged, was Tsvetaeva. The poet recognized herself and certain settings in the story. As Fleishman notes in *Boris Pasternak: The Poet and His Politics,* the work emerges in fragmentary fashion; the plotline and the characterization of the hero are only vaguely defined. The plot of Pasternak's 1929 story "Povest'" is also vague. Its hero has the same name, Spektorsky. "Povest'" tells the story of a young writer who has romantic liaisons with two utterly different women: a Danish woman residing as a companion in the household where he works as a tutor and a prostitute named Sashka. His opposite, or foil, is a man of the new age named Lemokh. During the course of "Povest'" the protagonist works on his own story, which concerns an artistic hero named $Y_3$ (Igrek Tretii) who sells himself to the highest bidder in order to support the women, both enslaved in different ways. Here again Pasternak writes of the opposition between intellectual and revolutionary, developing a theme that became increasingly important to him—artistic martyrdom. This theme had appeared in earlier works, such as in *Temy i variatsii,* and it became more pronounced and persistent through the years.

At this time, with the writing of *Okhrannaia gramota,* which he had begun in 1927, Pasternak moved from the implicitly autobiographical to the explicitly autobiographical. In this long essay he formulates his professional coming-of-age in terms of his meetings with three mentors: first with Skriabin (music), then with Cohen (philosophy), and finally with Maiakovsky (literature). His 1900 meeting with Rilke, to whose memory he dedicated the work, serves as an introduction. As Evgenii Pasternak and his wife, Elena Vladimirovna Pasternak, note in the 1989–1992 *Sobranie sochinenii,* Pasternak had begun *Okhrannaia gramota* with the intention, conceived before Rilke's death in 1926, of writing an article about Rilke and had conducted research about the poet's life for this work. Rilke's death changed the focus of *Okhrannaia gramota,* but his work remained the original inspiration.

Although *Okhrannaia gramota* cannot be treated literally as an autobiography, it provides a path toward an understanding of Pasternak's emergence as a poet. He wrote it at the midpoint of his career—a time when, under tremendous societal pressure and internal strain, he was reassessing his work. From this work forward he declared open war on what he idiosyncratically labeled the "romantic manner." He explains this stance in *Okhrannaia gramota* as "the treatment of one's life as the life of a poet." He means, among other things, the self-consciousness and hyperbole of his own age, which includes his symbolist predecessors and his futurist contemporaries. Pasternak had fought for years against Maiakovsky's influence in his work, and his personal relations with Maiakovsky soured throughout the 1920s, as the Cubo-Futurist had become the poet of the October Revolution. Viktor Frankl has argued that Maiakovsky is one of the prototypes for the revolutionary Antipov in *Doktor Zhivago.* Like Antipov, Maiakovsky became a victim of crushed ideals. He realized by the late 1920s that he was falling out of step with the course of Soviet history, which caused him great despair. More personal issues led him to commit suicide in 1930.

Pasternak's critical reassessment of his writings prompted him in 1928, while working on *Okhrannaia gramota,* to revise many of the poems from his first two books, *Bliznets v tuchakh* and *Poverkh bar'erov.* He tried to shed them of "romantic" elements, including foreign words, openly autobiographical references, and hyperbolic intonation. Elena Pasternak argues in a 1970 contribution to *Russkoe i zarubezhnoe iazykoznanie* (Russian and Foreign Linguistics) that the poet sought to clarify his work with these 1928 revisions. Fleishman contends in *Boris Pasternak v dvadtsatye gody* (1981, Boris Pasternak in the 1920s), however, that Pasternak often made his poems more obscure. Both assessments are correct, if one looks at the revisions from different points of view. Pasternak does make his verse obscure or vague by omitting associative links, references to the lyrical "I," and other elements that might help the reader trace a line of thought; through opacity he distances himself from the reader. On the other hand, he saw the revisions as a clarification of his aesthetics, and from this point of view they accomplish the task of erasing the poetic "I," which he saw as a sign of the "romantic manner."

In 1930 Pasternak's personal life underwent a significant change. That summer his family rented a dacha close to those of his brother and sister-in-law and two couples who were family friends. One of these friends was the pianist Genrikh Gustavovich Neigauz and his wife, Zinaida Neigauz. Pasternak fell in love with Zinaida and that autumn in Moscow he confessed his love to her, her husband, and Evgeniia. Pasternak and Neigauz remained friends, but the marriages of both men broke up in 1931. In February 1931 Pasternak separated from Evgeniia, and in May he saw her and their son off to Germany, where his relatives took care of her. Later that month he traveled with a brigade of

*Pasternak with his first wife, Evgeniia, and their son, Evgenii, in Leningrad, 1924 (from* The Correspondence of Boris Pasternak and Olga Freidenberg, 1910–1954, *translated by Elliot Mossman and Margaret Wettlin, 1982; Collection of Patricia Hswe)*

writers to the Urals for about two weeks on an assignment to visit industrial sites, but he left before the end of the project and returned to Moscow in early June. In July he traveled to Georgia with Zinaida. Evgeniia returned with their son to Moscow at the end of 1931. Professional prospects in 1930s Germany were grim; she was in tight financial straits. Around this time Pasternak married Zinaida and in the spring of 1932, according to Evgenii Pasternak in *Boris Pasternak. Materialy dlia biografii,* settled with his new wife in a cramped apartment (then called the "Herzen House," now known as the Literary Institute), located on Tverskoi Boulevard. In September 1932 Evgeniia agreed to switch apartments, and Pasternak, Zinaida, and her children moved into the rooms on Volkhonka.

Pasternak's next major book of verse, his fifth to be published, reflected both personal and aesthetic changes. *Vtoroe rozhdenie* (Second Birth) was written in 1930–1932 and appeared as a book in 1932. In it he expresses his desire to re-create himself as a poet and simplify his work so that all his readers would be able to understand it. These poems are clearer in meaning than both his earlier poems and the 1928 revisions of his youthful verse. Yet, much in these poems remains obscure, though not to the extent of the riddles posed in his earlier work.

After this book Pasternak's poetic output declined sharply. The release of *Vtoroe rozhdenie* coincided with the formation of the Union of Soviet Writers (Writers' Union), which, Fleishman notes in *Boris Pasternak: The Poet and His Politics,* Pasternak did not celebrate with his colleagues. During the 1930s and in subsequent decades, he earned his living through translations. He turned his attention first to the work of Georgian poets, including his friends Titsian Tabidze and Paolo Yashvili. The translation of these poets' work was politically savvy on Pasternak's part; to the Russian public he was bringing poetry from the homeland of Joseph Stalin, the current Communist leader, and he had to translate odes to Stalin by Yashvili and Nikoloz Mitsishvili, in order to defend them from political criticism. His efforts on their behalf were in vain: they eventually perished in the Stalinist purges. The project also came from his sincere love of Georgia, its poets, and their verse. Pasternak made one more trip to Georgia in connection with his translations. He did not speak or read Georgian but worked with interlinear translations; in what is a fairly common practice in Russian poetic translating, Pasternak worked from a literal Russian translation (done by someone else) of the Georgian verses and turned them into poetic Russian. In 1935 *Poety Gruzii* (Poets of Georgia), translated into Russian by Pasternak and Nikolai Semenovich Tikhonov, was published. Their renderings of Georgian poetry received positive critical attention.

In May 1934 Mandel'shtam was arrested for composing an anti-Stalinist poem, which he recited to some trusted acquaintances, including Pasternak. After hearing the poem from Mandel'shtam in the autumn of 1933, Pasternak told him that the poem does not consist of literary fact but is a suicidal act—that he would consider that he had not heard it and that Mandel'shtam should never recite it to anyone else. After Mandel'shtam's arrest, at the request of his wife, Nadezhda Iakovlevna Mandel'shtam, Pasternak contacted the editor of the newspaper *Izvestiia* (News) and Politburo member Nikolai Ivanovich Bukharin, who had some influence with the regime. Mandel'shtam's sentence was commuted to an exile of three years, first in the provincial town of Cherdyn' and then in the larger city of Voronezh. Before the second decision to exile the poet in Voronezh, however, Stalin called Pasternak. As Evgenii Pasternak relates in *Boris Pasternak.*

*Materialy dlia biografii,* the leader assured Pasternak that Mandel'shtam would be all right and then asked Pasternak for his assurances that Mandel'shtam was a "master" of his art; Pasternak replied that the caliber of Mandel'shtam as an artist was not the point and that he would like to talk to Stalin further about life and death. Stalin hung up. According to Pasternak's son and biographer, Pasternak related the exact text of his phone conversation to Akhmatova and Nadezhda Mandel'shtam. Nadezhda Mandel'shtam and Akhmatova said his reaction was a "solid B+" performance; the latter interpreted Pasternak's response as coy professional jealousy. As Fleishman writes in his 1990 biography of the poet, however, these assessments are inadequate; there was nothing Pasternak could have said to ensure Mandel'shtam a better fate. Moreover, as Evgenii Pasernak notes in *Boris Pasternak. Materialy dlia biografii,* Pasternak attempted to turn the focus of the conversation away from Mandel'shtam. Irritated at the very nature of Stalin's question, he wanted to avoid answering questions about whether he knew of the existence of Mandel'shtam's poem in order not to incriminate his colleague.

The first Soviet Writers' Congress took place two months after Stalin's call to Pasternak, in August 1934, and Maiakovsky's and Pasternak's differing roles as literary models, positive or negative, were the subject of debate in speeches by various speakers, including Bukharin, Maksim Gor'ky, and Aleksei Aleksandrovich Surkov. The role of "premier Soviet poet" was bestowed posthumously on Maiakovsky the following year. Fleishman notes in his 1990 biography of the poet that for a few months after the Writers' Congress, Pasternak was optimistic with regard to the state and his position in the Soviet Union. This mood was to change, however, with the assassination on 1 December 1934 of Leningrad party chief Sergei Mironovich Kirov; this event signaled the beginning of the Stalinist terror, which peaked in 1935–1937. Writers had already been arrested, but the wave of arrests during the next several years frightened them into silence. By 1935 Pasternak was ill with depression and insomnia.

That year he was sent to Paris to attend the Congress of Writers in Defense of Culture as one of the leading Russian writers. The conference featured writers from all over the world who came to speak out against fascism and for peace. Although Pasternak was ill, he was forced to go, together with the writer Isaak Emmanuilovich Babel, because their Parisian hosts insisted on their presence and that of some other liberal writers. He and Tsvetaeva met briefly in what she called, in a 1935 letter to Anna Tesková, a "nonmeeting." By this time she was considering a return to the Soviet Union, although Pasternak tried to dissuade her by hinting at the current situation there. This trip was Pasternak's last one abroad. While he was able to visit his sister Zhozefina and her husband briefly as he went through Berlin, he could not visit his parents in Munich during the journey, and he was never to see them again. Leonid Osipovich and Rozaliia Izidorovna contemplated going back to Russia when, by 1936, the situation in Germany had become increasingly tense for Jews; they did not understand entirely Pasternak's coded attempts in his letters to prevent them from returning. In 1938 they resettled in Oxford, England, where his sister Lidiia and her husband were living. Rozaliia Izidorovna died there in 1939, and Leonid Osipovich died in 1945.

Somewhat recovered from his illness and feeling optimistic because of a general sense that liberalization was on the threshhold (an incorrect feeling, as Fleishman indicates in *Boris Pasternak: The Poet and His Politics*), Pasternak wrote two pro-Stalin verses at the end of 1935, published in *Izvestiia* on 1 January 1936: "Ia ponial–vse zhivo . . ." (I understand–everything is alive . . .) and "Mne po dushe stroptivyi norov . . ." (I like the stubborn character . . .). They are the first poems he had written since the appearance of *Vtoroe rozhdenie* and reflect his attempts at greater clarity and simplicity. Pasternak acknowledged that he wrote the poems at Bukharin's suggestion and as part of a sincere attempt to live with the times. The optimism of the period ended a few weeks later with the initiation of the antiformalism campaign, which started with an attack on the composer Dmitrii Dmitrievich Shostakovich. Although Pasternak included the latter poem in his cycle "Khudozhnik" (The Artist, published in *Na rannikh poezdakh* [On Early Trains], 1943), the former was never reprinted during his lifetime.

During this dark era, in which friends and colleagues of Pasternak were arrested and killed, he began work on what became his novel *Doktor Zhivago.* The exact year in which Pasternak started writing *Doktor Zhivago* is difficult to establish. Barnes gives the year 1932 (in volume two of *Boris Pasternak: A Literary Biography,* 1998), while Fleishman indicates that work began in the 1920s (in *Boris Pasternak: The Poet and His Politics*). Yet, Evgenii Pasternak and V. M. Borisov, who produced commentary about the novel for the 1989–1992 edition of Pasternak's collected works, approximate that *Doktor Zhivago* was started in the winter of 1917–1918, after the completion of *Sestra moia zhizn'.* According to their report, Pasternak responded in a 1919 questionnaire that he was working on a novel. In essence, works from the 1920s contributed to the novel; he began pieces such as "Detstvo Liuvers" as drafts to a larger work and themes from much of his

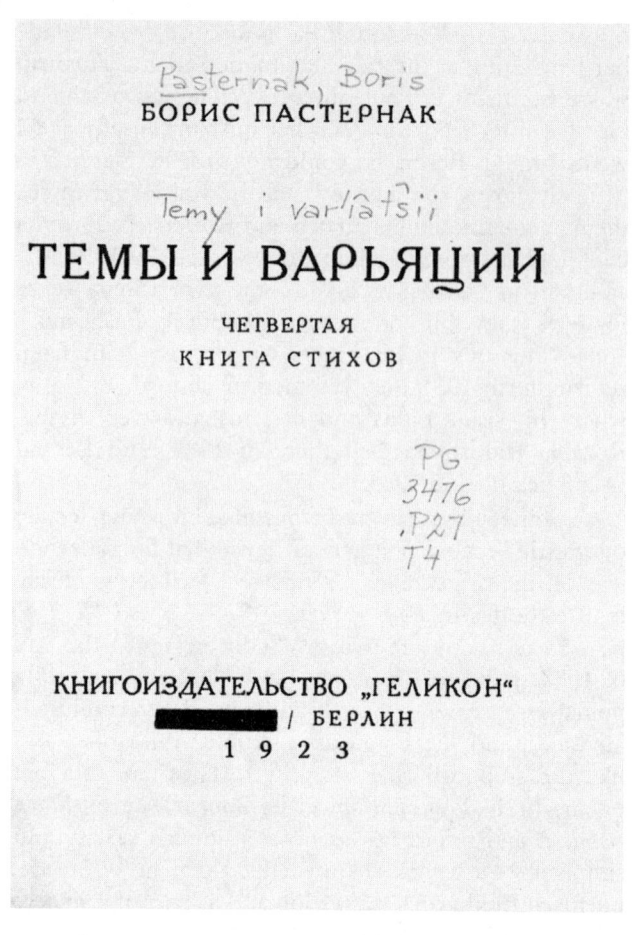

*Title page for* Temy i variatsii *(Themes and Variations), Pasternak's collection of verse and short prose works published in Berlin (Thomas Cooper Library, University of South Carolina)*

prose and verse from that decade appear in the novel. The novel was drafted at first in fragments—"notes" in which the characters were first forming and had names that later were to change; the first coherent set of notes, provisionally titled "Zapiski Patrika" (Patrick's Notes), date from 1936.

Despite the grim atmosphere of the antiformalism campaign and its aftermath, Pasternak wrote a few poems in the winter of 1936, followed in the summer by a dozen that he dedicated to his friends in Georgia. He wrote them at a dacha in the newly built writers' colony of Peredelkino, outside Moscow and reachable by commuter train. (He and his family were to move to another dacha there in 1939.) Peredelkino was to become his main residence for the rest of his life. This cycle of poems, titled "Iz letnikh zapisok" (From Summer Notes), was published in the October 1936 issue of *Novyi mir*. It reflects his new style and his desire to become a part of the world around him. Continuing a theme from *Vtoroe rozhdenie*—but with less of a sense of regret—the cycle shows an effort to depart from his tortured intellectual heroes. After the publication of "Iz letnikh zapisok," Pasternak wrote no verse for five years.

At midnight on 31 December 1936, on the verge of what was to be a terrible year, Pasternak's son with his wife, Zinaida, was born and named Leonid, after Pasternak's father. In 1937 the Pasternaks moved to a new apartment on Lavrushinsky pereulok. That year his closest Georgian friends, Tabidze and Yashvili, were victims of the terror; the former died in prison, and the latter committed suicide. On 31 December 1937 the first excerpts from Pasternak's nascent novel were published in *Literaturnaia gazeta* (The Literary Gazette).

In early 1939 Pasternak began to translate the dramas of Shakespeare, beginning with *Hamlet* (1604), which he completed at the end of that year. Pasternak's translations of Shakespeare's dramas are rendered in contemporary Russian in a style that reflects his classical restraint, begun in the 1930s, but clearly in his own manner. He also translated some of Shakespeare's sonnets; his rendering of Sonnet 66 was published together with his translation of *Hamlet* in the journal *Molodaia gvardiia* (Young Guard) in 1940. The translation of *Hamlet* appeared as a book in 1941. Pasternak continued to work on Shakespeare translations during the 1940s. His *Izbrannye perevody* (Selected Translations) appeared in 1940, and he gave public readings of his translations. Fleishman notes in his 1990 biography of Pasternak that such public contact inspired Pasternak, and he returned to writing poetry in the summer of 1940. He produced verse that was increasingly clear, with shorter lines and simpler metaphors and similes. The themes remained much the same as in his earlier work—nature, love, and art. Yet, his late verse possesses a calm reserve generally absent from his exuberant youthful work.

Tsvetaeva returned to Moscow in 1939, and Pasternak helped her find translation work. World War II began for the Soviet Union in June 1941. Pasternak spent the beginning of the war in Moscow, even serving guard duty on the roof of his apartment building, while his wife and son Leonid were evacuated to the writers' colony in Chistopol', in the Tatar Republic. Tsvetaeva also departed for Chistopol', against Pasternak's advice, and settled in the nearby town of Elabuga. There she was unable to find work as a writer or translator. On 31 August 1941 Tsvetaeva committed suicide. Pasternak, still in Moscow, found out about her death in early September. In October he left for Chistopol' to join his family, and in the winter of 1941–1942 he translated Shakespeare's *Romeo and Juliet* (1599). In 1943, after his return to Moscow, he wrote

'Pamiati Mariny Tsvetaevoi' (In Memory of Marina Tsvetaeva). Although he recited the poem in public at Moscow State University in 1946, it was not published until 1965, five years after his death.

In 1943 Pasternak published *Na rannikh poezdakh*. It consisted of the cycles "Voennye mesiatsy" (War Months), "Khudozhnik," "Putevye zapiski" (Travel Notes), and "Peredelkino." Barnes notes in volume two of *Boris Pasternak: A Literary Biography* that Pasternak was not proud of the book, which was of poor print quality; he had simply pulled together poems already published elsewhere. Pasternak was proud of the cycle "Khudozhnik," however, and the collection as a whole provides a general picture of his thoughts on nature, art, and war.

Throughout the 1940s Pasternak wrote essays on great artists and on his translations. These articles clarify aspects of his thought expressed in more obscure form in his earlier verse and prose, but they must be interpreted cautiously; his views on his work had changed by this time. "Zametki perevodchika" (Notes of a Translator, written 1943, published 1944 in *Znamia* [The Banner]) and "Zametki k perevodam iz Shekspira" (Notes on Shakespeare Translations, written 1946–1956, published 1956 in the miscellany *Literaturnaia Moskva* [Literary Moscow]) provide important explanations of his approach to translation, in light of his tendency to part from the original in order to convey (in his translations of Shakespeare's plays and of other works) what he considered their essence. Most significant among his articles on artists is his essay on Frédéric Chopin, simply titled "Chopin" (published 1945 in abridged form in the journal *Leningrad;* published 1965 in full in the newspaper *Literaturnaia Rossiia*), in which he defines realism in an idiosyncratic way: in essence, Pasternak labels "realist" the art of any epoch that he values highly, including the music of Johann Sebastian Bach and of Chopin. Romantic art, according to his measure, is second-rate and marked by falsehood, excess, or pretentiousness. These arguments continue his earlier thoughts against the "romantic manner" but do not concern traditional definitions of Romanticism.

The year 1946 was important in Pasternak's literary biography for two reasons: he was able to devote himself more fully to writing *Doktor Zhivago,* and he met Ol'ga Ivinskaia at the offices of the journal *Novyi mir,* where she was an assistant to editor in chief Konstantin Mikhailovich Simonov. In 1947 Pasternak and Ivinskaia began an affair that lasted until his death, their only extended time apart, before Pasternak died, was in 1949–1954, when she was imprisoned in a Soviet labor camp. She was one of the prototypes–the other was his second wife, Zinaida–for the heroine Lara in *Doktor Zhivago*. Starting in 1956, Ivinskaia also played intermediary between Pasternak and the Moscow publication world; her errands on his behalf allowed him to stay in Peredelkino and concentrate on his work.

*Doktor Zhivago,* on which Pasternak concentrated his efforts from 1946 to 1955, continues many of the themes he had been developing since his earliest prose sketches: the fate of a Russian intellectual in a changing world; the passive nature of the artist in his relations with others and in the face of events beyond his control; the relationship of art to history; and the connection between death and birth, particularly the concept of rebirth through art. *Doktor Zhivago* traces the life of Iurii Andreevich Zhivago, the orphaned son of a dissolute millionaire who has committed suicide. The opening scene is set during the funeral of Zhivago's mother, who has died of tuberculosis, a disease of the nineteenth century. His mother's brother, Nikolai Vedeniapin, takes him under his wing; when the uncle departs for Switzerland, he leaves the boy in the care of relatives, the Gromekos, a family of Moscow intellectuals. Brought up by Aleksandr Aleksandrovich Gromeko and his wife, Zhivago falls in love with, and marries, their daughter, Antonina (Tonia). He studies medicine and specializes in diseases of the eye. During World War I, Zhivago is drafted as an army doctor and goes to the front. When he returns to Moscow, his frightened infant son slaps him in the face, an act Zhivago takes to be an ill omen. During the Russian Civil War, he, Tonia, and their small son leave for the Urals in order to live off the land at the former estate of her mother's family, the Kruegers. Zhivago's mysterious and powerful half brother Evgraf, who comes to Moscow from his native Omsk and visits the young family, has advised them to move there. According to Livingstone in *Boris Pasternak Doctor Zhivago,* Evgraf is Zhivago's "deus ex machina."

Parallel to Zhivago's story is that of Lara, the daughter of an impoverished French widow who runs a sewing shop. She grows up in working-class Moscow. So does her future husband, Antipov, whose worker father was exiled for organizing a railway laborers' strike. Lara is seduced at the age of sixteen by her mother's paramour, a wealthy lawyer named Viktor Ippolitovich Komarovsky. She finds herself both attracted and repelled by his attention. In a fit of despair, determined to break off their relationship, Lara sneaks into a Christmas party that Komarovsky is attending and shoots him. Although her shot misses Komarovsky and he is not hurt, afterward he keeps his distance from her for fear of scandal. Eventually, she marries Antipov, and they set off to teach in the Urals town of Iuriatin, her birthplace. Their marriage

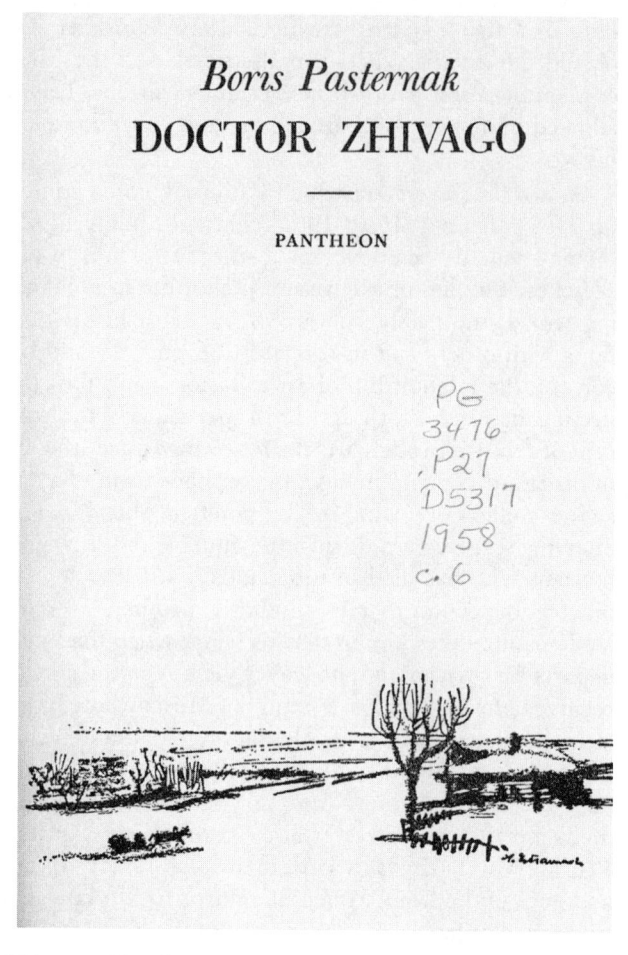

*Title page of first American English-language translation of Pasternak's* Il Dottor Zivago *(1957), published in 1958, the year he won the Nobel Prize for literature. Though this novel has proven to be his most enduring work, the Nobel Prize committee cited his outstanding achievement in verse (Thomas Cooper Library, University of South Carolina).*

becomes strained when she tells him of her past liaison with Komarovsky. Unable to bear the shadow of Lara's past and his own feelings of inadequacy, Antipov volunteers for the front, leaving her and their daughter, Katia.

Zhivago and Lara are brought together three times before their affair begins. He first sees her when Lara's mother attempts suicide out of a suspicion that Komarovsky is attracted to her daughter. Because of the attempted suicide, a neighbor is summoned while giving a concert, attended by Gromeko, Tonia, Zhivago, and a friend. Gromeko accompanies the neighbor to Lara's home. The young Zhivago goes along and sees both the sordid situation and the exchange of glances between Komarovsky and a schoolgirl who seems older than her years. The second meeting occurs at the Christmas party where Lara attempts to shoot Komarovsky; Zhivago and Tonia are among the attendees. (Before the shooting, on the way to the party Zhivago had passed the window of Antipov's room at the moment when he and Lara were deciding to marry; Zhivago saw the candle in the window and began to write a poem about it.) At the third meeting Lara and Zhivago are together for a longer period. Lara is a nurse on the front; she has volunteered for such work in order to find Antipov. Zhivago, now an army doctor, and Lara, known as Nurse Antipova, strike up a friendship. While on the front they begin to sense that something more than friendship is happening between them. They drop the subject, however, and he returns to Moscow.

The affair between Zhivago and Lara begins in the Urals, in the town of Iuriatin, near the Krueger estate, where the Zhivagos have settled. He rides regularly to the library, and one day he sees Lara there. He observes her pleasant effect on others, copies down her address from a library-book order slip, and visits her in town. They begin a romance that torments him with guilt. On his way home to confess to his wife, now pregnant with their second child, he is stopped by civil-war partisans and forced to serve them as a doctor. He is kept under guard for an extended period but finally escapes and returns by foot to Iuriatin. In Zhivago's absence Tonia and Lara meet: Lara assists at the delivery of Tonia's second child, a daughter named Mariia (Masha). Shortly thereafter, Tonia and her two children leave Iuriatin. When Zhivago returns, he moves in with Lara, who has remained in Iuriatin with her daughter. (Tonia and her family subsequently are deported, and they move to Paris.) Fearing for their lives—since he is now a deserter—Zhivago, Lara, and Katia go to the Krueger estate to hide for the winter. They pass an idyllic life for a brief period, during which he returns to writing poetry. Komarovsky finds them, however, and persuades Zhivago that he can take better care of Lara and her daughter, convincing him to let them go. Zhivago tricks Lara into leaving with Komarovsky by giving her the false impression that he will soon follow them. While Zhivago stays behind, Komarovsky, Lara, and her daughter head to the Russian Far East, where Komarovsky assumes a government position. Zhivago is left alone in despair. At this point Lara's husband, now called Strel'nikov and a non-Party Red Army commander, arrives. He had used the estate before as a hideout; in danger now that the civil war is coming to a close, he has come to hide again. The two men, who have met before, discuss Lara. That night Strel'nikov kills himself. Zhivago, with nothing else left and warned by

Strel'nikov that staying at the estate is dangerous, returns to Moscow by foot.

He moves into a spare room in a building managed by Markel, a former servant to the Gromekos. He soon takes Markel's daughter, Marina, a telegraph operator, as his common-law third wife. Zhivago no longer enjoys the company of his old friends, whom he now considers false and mannered. Evgraf again mysteriously steps in to help: he finds his brother a room where he can live alone and write. The room that Evgraf finds him is the same one in which Antipov and Lara decided to marry—the room in which Zhivago had seen a candle burning on the night of the Christmas party. Zhivago leaves Marina and their child and spends the rest of his life writing. One day, after getting off a bus, he dies of a heart attack on the street. After Zhivago's death, but not knowing that he has died, Lara returns to Moscow to enroll her daughter in a conservatory or theatrical academy. She visits her late husband Antipov's former room and wanders into Zhivago's funeral there by accident. She remains in Moscow to help Evgraf sort through Zhivago's papers, since she knows his work better than anyone else. She asks Evgraf's advice about finding a lost child. Not long afterward Lara disappears; the narrator assumes that she has been arrested.

On the front during World War II, Zhivago's friends Misha Gordon and Innokentii Dudorov meet a mysterious girl, Tania, who works as a laundress. A gregarious person, she tells them about her childhood. Her mother left her in the care of an acquaintance in order to protect her from a stepfather who disliked children; she promised to return but did not. Tania's guardian mistreated her, and she ran away and ended up among the bands of homeless children who wandered about Russia after the civil war. Gordon and Dudorov realize that Tania is Lara's and Zhivago's child, and they bring her to the attention of General Evgraf Zhivago, who looks after Tania. The novel ends five to ten years later, as Dudorov and Gordon recite Zhivago's poems together; in them they find comfort and a kind of transcendence. The collection of Zhivago's poems completes the novel.

The improved political climate following Khrushchev's secret speech in the spring of 1956 gave Pasternak hope that his novel might be published in the Soviet Union, and he submitted typescripts to two journals, *Novyi mir* and *Znamia*. His efforts came to no avail, however. In September 1956 it was rejected for publication by *Novyi mir*. Aware of the risk he was taking, he gave the manuscript to Italian publisher and Communist Giangiacomo Feltrinelli through his emissary, the Italian Communist Party journalist Sergio d'Angelo, who had gone to see Pasternak in May 1956. Barnes and the commentators to a scholarly edition of *Doktor Zhivago*, published in the 1989–1992 edition of Pasternak's collected works, assert that Pasternak released a typescript (not yet proofread) merely for examination. Under the impression that he would be able to revise the typescript he had submitted, Pasternak signed a contract with Feltrinelli in June 1956. In the meantime, despite the rejection by *Novyi mir*, the state publishing house Goslitizdat promised to publish it, and a contract was signed in January 1957. Although Pasternak permitted Feltrinelli, at the latter's request, to publish the novel in Italian translation, he warned that publication abroad prior to the planned appearance of the novel in the Soviet Union could have dire consequences for him. Religious poems from the novel appeared anonymously in the émigré journal *Grani* (Borders) in 1957, and excerpts from the novel were published in the Polish journal *Opinie* (Opinions), from a typescript Pasternak had given to the journal; the publication sparked Soviet criticism, and the journal closed. The Soviet authorities forced Pasternak to send a telegram to Feltrinelli instructing him to stop publication, but the writer sent a private letter contradicting the telegram. The entire novel appeared on 22 November 1957 in Italian translation and sold out that day. The frenzy of the Western press over this publication was countered by Soviet silence, and the promised edition of the novel did not appear in the Soviet Union. The publishing house Mouton brought out the first Russian edition; it appeared in the Netherlands in 1958 with the Feltrinelli imprint (at the insistence of the Italian publisher, who stopped the print run after fewer than one hundred copies). In January 1959 Feltrinelli released its own Russian edition without giving Pasternak the chance to correct it. Pasternak wrote his friend, the Slavist Jacqueline de Proyart, to whom he entrusted matters related to publication in the West, that he was deeply upset by the errors in it. Thus began her own efforts to have a corrected edition published from a clean manuscript Pasternak had given her in 1957.

Pasternak's fame abroad increased tremendously with the 1958 publication of *Doktor Zhivago* in Russian and with translations of the novel into major European languages. The novel remained unpublished in the Soviet Union until 1988, when it came out in four issues of *Novyi mir*—one of the landmark cultural events to occur during perestroika. Separate editions soon followed, including one published in the same year of its serial appearance; the textological difficulties of the work were resolved only with this book version. The scholarly edition appeared in 1990 as volume three of Pasternak's five-volume *Sobranie sochinenii* (1989–1992, Collected Works). The novel was adapted for motion

*First page of a letter that Pasternak wrote to Olga Freidenberg on 20 January 1953 (from* The Correspondence of Boris Pasternak and Olga Freidenberg, 1910–1954, *translated by Elliot Mossman and Margaret Wettlin, 1982; Collection of Patricia Hswe)*

```
RS87

MOSCOU 40 29 1027 =


ELT MR ANDERS ACADEMIE DE SUEDE STOCKHOLM =


EN VUE DU SENS QUE CETTE DISTINCTION SUBIT DANS LA
SOCIETE QUE JE PARTAGE JE DOIS RENONCER AU PRIX IMMERITE
QUI MA ETE ATTRIBUE NE PRENEZ PAS EN OFFENSE MON REFUS
VOLONTAIRE
        PASTERNAK
```

*The telegram, cabled on 29 October 1958 from Moscow to the Swedish Academy in Stockholm, in which Pasternak declined the Nobel Prize. It reads: "In view of the direction that this distinction has taken in the society I share, I must renounce the undeserved prize that has been awarded to me. Do not take offense at my voluntary refusal" (from Gerd Ruge,* Pasternak: A Pictorial Biography, *translated by Beryl and Joseph Avrach, 1959; Bruccoli Clark Layman Archives).*

pictures in 1965, in a production directed by David Lean, and was adapted as a miniseries for British television in 2003.

Scholarship on *Doktor Zhivago* is vast and varied—so vast that there are works and portions of works devoted to summarizing it. Notable among these overviews are those of Livingstone, Neil Cornwell, and Munir Sendich. Importantly, however, scholarship on the novel appeared entirely outside the Soviet Union until its 1988 publication in Russia. Some early Western studies criticized the novel for its lack of a logical progression of events, its inexplicable use of time, its unbelievable coincidences, and its monologic language in which only variants of Pasternak's own voice are present. Other critics noted that these are in fact features of Pasternak's poetic system: the inexplicable temporal shifts reflect ones that are present in his early poetry, and the coincidences reflect his view of the unity of all things. The monologic voice has been interpreted as the equivalent of a poet's lyrical "I." To Pasternak's defenders the novel makes sense if read as a kind of poem in prose and through the lens of Pasternak's earlier work and aesthetic statements. Many studies of *Doktor Zhivago* from the 1960s and 1970s focus on the philosophical and literary antecedents of the novel. Scholars have studied its formal and symbolic structure, including the relationship of prose to poetry in the work. More recent criticism on *Doktor Zhivago* has concentrated on its riddles: its references, use of dialect and folk motifs, and specific coincidences. Biographers and critics have also studied the connection of Pasternak's other works to the novel, juxtaposing it with his earlier poetry and prose in order both to clarify aspects of the novel and to show the unity of Pasternak's aesthetic system. Studies of the novel since it began receiving assessments have also examined prototypes for the main characters and subtextual sources, from its smallest details to its overall philosophy.

Shortly after Pasternak finished writing *Doktor Zhivago*, another burst of creativity came over him. In 1955 the state publishing house Goslitizdat approached him about compiling a collection of verse from his entire career. He wrote his second autobiographical essay, *Liudi i polozheniia*, in 1956 initially as an introduction to this proposed volume. He began to revise his earlier verse, following the criteria he had established for his late verse—brevity and simplicity.

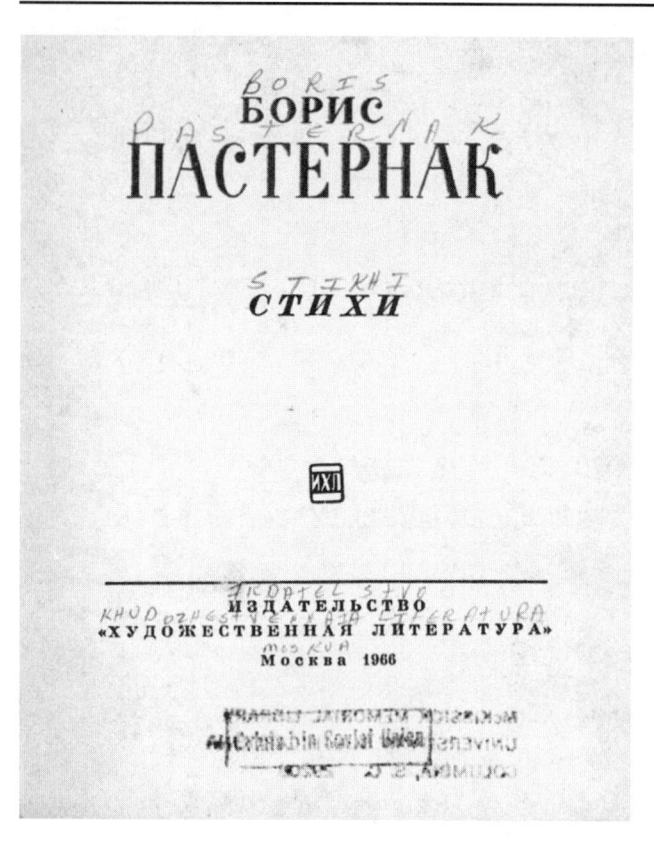

*Title page for* Stikhi *(Poems), a collection edited the year after Pasternak's death by wife and his son (Thomas Cooper Library, University of South Carolina)*

He also began to write new poems for the collection. What emerged was the beginning of a new book of poems, *Kogda razguliaetsia* (When the Weather Clears), completed in 1959 and published that year in Paris. *Liudi i polozheniia* is the memoir of a writer toward the end of his career who wishes to revise the record and examine his life from a literary distance. Pasternak attempts to correct what he now sees as aesthetic errors in his first autobiography. The essay is written in a different tone, with less emphasis on his painful breaks with his mentors and more focus on his connections to other writers, including Blok and Rilke. Pasternak continues his criticism of what he calls "romanticism" but from a more distanced point of view. Because he states a dislike for his work prior to 1940 and calls it mannered, the memoir is problematic if one takes it as an explanation of his entire body of work. Moreover, it is full of instances of poetic license with regard to biographical details. *Liudi i polozheniia* is interesting, nonetheless, both as an idiosyncratic account of his life and as a work of literature.

In October 1958, the same year that the first English translation of *Doktor Zhivago* appeared, Pasternak received the Nobel Prize, for which he had been nominated every year from 1946 to 1950 and again in 1957. At first he accepted the prize in a rapturously appreciative telegram. A vicious campaign began against him, however, and he was expelled from the Writers' Union. He was forced to reject the prize and did so regretfully in a second telegram; yet, the press campaign against him did not stop. He was advised to write a letter to Soviet leader Nikita Sergeevich Khrushchev, begging that he not be expelled from the country. Such a letter would prevent exile, according to Pasternak's friends, so he signed a letter to Khrushchev that had been written by Ivinskaia and others. In exchange for a second statement of contrition, also prepared by Ivinskaia and others and meant for publication in the newspaper *Pravda* (Truth), he was allowed to continue his correspondence with writers and readers in the West. Finally, at Ivinskaia's suggestion and with her help, he wrote Khrushchev another, more personal, letter asking to be allowed to resume professional translations and earn a living. In 1959 this work became possible again for Pasternak.

That same year Pasternak began writing his last work, a play titled *Slepaia krasavitsa* (1969, The Blind Beauty), which he was not able to finish. It is about the fate of peasants on a Russian estate in the middle of the nineteenth century, before and after emancipation. The "slepaia krasavitsa" of the title is a peasant girl, Lusha, who is blinded when a plaster bust is shattered by a shot that the master of the estate aimed at his valet, and bits of plaster hit her in the eyes. (According to Pasternak's plans, as related to Olga Andreyev Carlisle and published in her *Voices in the Snow: Encounters with Russian Writers* [1962], Lusha's son, a talented serf actor who would gain his freedom after the 1861 emancipation of the serfs, was to bring a great doctor from abroad to heal his mother.) Pasternak suggests that Lusha's blindness represents the blindness of Russia, a condition that potentially could be cured only with the emancipation of the serfs. Pasternak studied historical sources for the play, as he had for his epic poems and for *Doktor Zhivago*. Concerns for the fate of his country and a fascination with its history occupied him to the end of his life.

In the last years of his life Pasternak corresponded regularly with foreign writers and others interested in his work. He found such contact encouraging, although the writing of so many letters exhausted him physically. Soviet authorities, aware of the extent and value of this correspondence, used his right to receive mail from abroad as a means of control. During and after the scandal of the Nobel Prize, they alternately took away and returned his right to foreign correspondence. Accounts of his epistolary friendships, such as Renate Schweitzer's *Freundschaft mit Boris Pasternak* (1963, Friendship with Boris Pasternak), provide valuable information about his late-life aesthetic views: his letters are often clearer than his statements in verse or in belletristic prose.

Pasternak had another heart attack in May 1960, after which he was diagnosed with lung cancer. He died on 30 May 1960. His funeral in Peredelkino on 2 June was attended by hundreds, although there was no official announcement of it. He is buried in the cemetery at Peredelkino, and his dacha there is now a museum in his honor.

After Pasternak died, Ivinskaia—who had been arrested in 1949 and released in 1954, after Stalin's death—was arrested again and sentenced to eight years in a prison camp. She served a part of her sentence and was released in 1963. Prior to her arrest, agents of the Komitet gosudarstvennoi bezopastnosti (KGB, State Security Committee) seized from her the manuscript for Pasternak's *Slepaia krasavitsa*. Ivinskaia died in 1995.

Soon after the death of Boris Leonidovich Pasternak, the official attitude toward him once again took a liberal turn. In 1961 a collection of his poems came out, and in 1965 a scholarly edition of his collected verse was published in the "Biblioteka poeta" (Poet's Library) series, with an introduction by Andrei Donatovich Siniavsky. Also in 1961 the first complete edition of Pasternak's works was published by the University of Michigan Press, which was the authoritative edition until the appearance of his 1989–1992 *Sobranie sochinenii*. Scholarship on Pasternak flourished abroad and continued to grow in the West in the 1970s and 1980s. Several international congresses devoted to his work were held in Europe and the United States during these two decades, and proceedings from the conferences have appeared in multiple volumes. In the Soviet Union during this same period, before perestroika, Pasternak's position was ambiguous. In 1990 the coincidence of the freedoms permitted by perestroika and the centenary of Pasternak's death, however, produced a second boom of scholarship on him. Many superb studies on Pasternak appeared in the Soviet Union and abroad at this time. His work continues to attract considerable scholarly attention. A more complete scholarly edition of his writings, *Polnoe sobranie sochinenii* (Complete Collected Works), has started to be published; the first two volumes appeared in 2004.

**Letters:**

*Letters to Georgian Friends,* translated by David Magarshack (New York: Harcourt, Brace & World, 1968);

*Perepiska s Ol'goi Freidenberg* (New York: Harcourt Brace Jovanovich, 1980); translated by Elliot Mossman and Margaret Wettlin as *The Correspondence of Boris Pasternak and Olga Freidenberg, 1910–1954,* edited by Mossman (New York: Harcourt Brace Jovanovich, 1982); republished as *Pozhiznennaia priviazannost': Perepiska s Ol'goi Freidenberg,* edited by Evgenii Borisovich Pasternak and Elena Vladimirovna Pasternak (Moscow: Art-Fleks, 2000);

*A. Efron–B. Pasternaku. Pis'ma iz ssylki (1948–1957)* (Paris: YMCA-Press, 1982);

*Letters, Summer 1926,* by Pasternak, Rainer Maria Rilke, and Marina Ivanovna Tsvetaeva, translated by Wettlin and Walter Arndt, edited by Evgenii Pasternak, Elena Pasternak, and Konstantin Markovich Azadovsky (San Diego: Harcourt Brace Jovanovich, 1985); Russian version published as *Pis'ma 1926 goda* (Moscow: Kniga, 1990); enlarged as *Dykhanie liriki* (Moscow: Art-Fleks, 2000);

*Perepiska Borisa Pasternaka,* edited by Evgenii Pasternak and Elena Pasternak, introduction by Lidiia Iakovlevna Ginzburg (Moscow: Khudozhestvennaia literatura, 1990);

*Sobranie sochinenii,* volume 5, edited by Evgenii Pasternak and Konstantin Mikhailovich Polivanov (Moscow: Khudozhestvennaia literatura, 1992);

*Pis'ma B. L. Pasternaka k zhene Z. N. Neigauz-Pasternak,* edited by Polivanov (Moscow: Dom, 1993);

*Boris Pasternak i Sergei Bobrov: Pis'ma chetyrekh desiatetii,* edited by M. A. Rashkovskaia, Stanford Slavic Studies, volume 10 (Stanford, Cal.: Department of Slavic Languages and Literatures, Stanford University, 1996);

*Pis'ma k roditeliam i sestram,* edited by Evgenii Pasternak and Elena Pasternak, Stanford Slavic Studies, volumes 18–19 (Stanford, Cal.: Department of Slavic Languages and Literatures, Stanford University, 1998);

*Sushchestvovan'ia tkan' skvoznaia: Perepiska s Evgeniei Pasternak s dopolnitel'nymi pis'mami k E. B. Pasternaku i ego vospominaniiami* (Moscow: Novoe literaturnoe obozrenie, 1998);

*B. Pasternak: Biografiia v pis'makh,* edited by Evgenii Pasternak and Elena Pasternak (Moscow: Art-Fleks, 2000);

"Perepiska Pasternaka s Fel'trinelli," *Kontinent,* 107, no. 1 (2001): 278–316; 108, no. 2 (2001): 229–274.

**Bibliographies:**

Nikolai Aleksandrovich Troitsky, *Boris Leonidovich Pasternak 1890–1960. Bibliografiia* (New York: All-Slavic, 1969);

Grigorii Demianovich Zlenko and Natal'ia Nikolaevna Chernego, *Boris Pasternak. Bibliograficheskii ukazatel'*

(Odessa: Odesskaia gosudarstvennaia nauchnaia biblioteka imeni A. M. Gor'kogo, 1990);

Munir Sendich and Erika Greber, *Pasternak's* Doctor Zhivago: *An International Bibliography of Criticism (1957–1985)* (East Lansing, Mich.: Russian Language Journal, 1990);

Sendich, *Boris Pasternak: A Reference Guide* (New York: G. K. Hall, 1994);

N. G. Zakharenko, ed., *Russkie pisateli (Poety). Sovetskii period. Biobibliograficheskii ukazatel'* (St. Petersburg: Rossiiskaia natsional'naia biblioteka, 1995).

**Biographies:**

Gerd Ruge, *Pasternak: A Pictorial Biography,* translated by Beryl and Joseph Avrach (New York: McGraw-Hill, 1959);

Guy de Mallac, *Boris Pasternak: His Life and Art* (Norman: University of Oklahoma Press, 1981);

Ronald Hingley, *Pasternak: A Biography* (London: Weidenfeld & Nicolson, 1983);

Evgenii Borisovich Pasternak, *Boris Pasternak. Materialy dlia biografii* (Moscow: Sovetskii pisatel', 1989);

Elena Vladimirovna Pasternak and Evgenii Pasternak, "Pasternak, Boris Leonidovich," in *Russkie pisateli 1800–1917: Biograficheskii slovar',* 4 volumes, edited by Petr Alekseevich Nikolaev and V. N. Baskakov (Moscow: Bol'shaia sovetskaia entsiklopediia, 1989– ), IV: 544–549;

Christopher Barnes, *Boris Pasternak: A Literary Biography,* 2 volumes (Cambridge: Cambridge University Press, 1989, 1998);

Evgenii Borisovich Pasternak, *Boris Pasternak: The Tragic Years, 1930–1960,* translated by Michael Duncan, with poetry translated by Ann Pasternak Slater and Craig Raine (London: Collins & Harvill, 1990);

Lazar' Fleishman, *Boris Pasternak: The Poet and His Politics* (Cambridge, Mass.: Harvard University Press, 1990);

Evgenii Pasternak, *Boris Pasternak. Biografiia* (Moscow: Tsitadel', 1997);

Evgenii Pasternak and Elena Pasternak, *Zhizn' Pasternaka. Dokumental'noe povestvovanie* (St. Petersburg: Zvezda, 2004).

**References:**

*Acta Universitatis Szegediensis de Attila Jozseff Nominatae,* Dissertationes Slavicae, Sectio historiae litterarum Slavicae, no. 19 (Szeged: Jószeff Attila Tudományegyetem Összehasonlító Pító Irodalomtudományi Tanszéke, 1988);

Vladimir N. Al'fonsov, *Poeziia Borisa Pasternaka* (Leningrad: Sovetskii pisatel', Leningradskoe otdelenie, 1990);

Michel Aucouturier, ed., *Boris Pasternak 1890–1960. Colloque de Cérisy-la-Salle (11–14 septembre 1975)* (Paris: Institut d'études slaves, 1979);

Vadim Solomonovich Baevsky, *Boris Pasternak—lirik: Osnovy poeticheskoi sistemy* (Smolensk: Trast-Imakom, 1993);

Baevsky, *Pasternak* (Moscow: Izdatel'stvo Moskovskogo universiteta, 1997);

Christopher Barnes, "Biography, Autobiography, and 'Sister Life': Some Problems in Chronicling Pasternak's Early Years," *Irish Slavonic Studies,* 4 (1983): 48–58;

Barnes, "Boris Pasternak's Revolutionary Year," *Forum for Modern Language Studies,* 11 (October 1975): 334–348;

Per Arne Bodin, *Nine Poems from Doktor Zhivago. A Study of Christian Motifs in Boris Pasternak's Poetry* (Stockholm: Almqvist & Wiksell International, 1976);

Boris Iakovlevich Bukhshtab, "Lirika Pasternaka," *Literaturnoe obozrenie,* 46, no. 9 (1987): 106–112;

Olga Andreyev Carlisle, *Voices in the snow: Encounters with Russian Writers* (New York: Random House, 1962);

Edith W. Clowes, ed., *Doctor Zhivago: A Critical Companion* (Evanston, Ill.: Northwestern University Press, 1995);

Robert Conquest, *Courage of Genius: The Pasternak Affair* (London: Collins & Harvill, 1966);

Neil Cornwell, *Pasternak's Novel: Perspectives on "Doctor Zhivago"* (Keele, U.K.: Essays in Poetics, 1986);

Donald Davie and Angela Livingstone, eds., *Pasternak* (London: Macmillan, 1969);

Johanna Renate Döring, *Die Lyrik Pasternaks in den Jahren 1928–1934,* Slavistische Beiträge, volume 64 (Munich: Otto Sagner, 1973);

Sergej Dorzweiler and Hans-Bernd Harder, eds., *Pasternak-Studien. Beiträge zum Internationalen Pasternak-Kongress 1991 in Marburg* (Munich: Otto Sagner, 1993);

Victor Erlich, ed., *Pasternak: A Collection of Critical Essays* (Englewood Cliffs, N.J.: Prentice-Hall, 1978);

Karen Evans-Romaine, *Boris Pasternak and the Tradition of German Romanticism* (Munich: Otto Sagner, 1997);

Jerzy Faryno, "K probleme koda liriki Pasternaka," *Russian Literature,* 6 (January 1978): 69–101;

Faryno, *Poetika Pasternaka: "Putevye zapiski," "Okhrannaia gramota,"* Wiener Slawistischer Almanach, no. 22 (Vienna: Gesellschaft zur Förderung slawistischer Studien, 1989);

Lazar' Fleishman, *Boris Pasternak v dvadtsatye gody* (Munich: Wilhelm Fink, 1981);

Fleishman, *Boris Pasternak v tridtsatye gody* (Jerusalem: Magnes Press, Hebrew University, 1984);

Fleishman, "Fragmenty 'futuristicheskoi' biografii Pasternaka," *Slavica Hierosolymitana,* 4 (1979): 79–113;

Fleishman, "Ot 'Zapisok Patrika' k 'Doktoru Zhivago,'" *Izvestiia Akademii Nauk SSSR. Seriia literatury i iazyka,* 50, no. 2 (1991): 114–123;

Fleishman, "Problems in the Poetics of Pasternak," *PTL: A Journal for Descriptive Poetics and Theory of Literature,* 4 (1979): 43–61;

Fleishman, *Stat'i o Pasternake* (Bremen: K-Presse, 1977);

Fleishman, ed., *Boris Pasternak and His Times* (Berkeley, Cal.: Berkeley Slavic Specialties, 1989);

Fleishman, ed., *Poetry and Revolution: Boris Pasternak's My Sister Life,* Stanford Slavic Studies, volume 21 (Stanford, Cal.: Department of Slavic Languages and Literatures, Stanford University, 1999);

Fleishman, ed., *V krugu Zhivago. Pasternakovskii sbornik,* Stanford Slavic Studies, volume 22 (Stanford, Cal.: Department of Slavic Languages and Literatures, Stanford University, 2000);

*Forum for Modern Language Studies,* 26 (October 1990);

Anna Kay France, *Boris Pasternak's Translations of Shakespeare* (Berkeley: University of California Press, 1978);

Viktor Frankl, "Realizm chetyrekh izmerenij," *Mosty,* 2 (1959): 189–209;

Boris Gasparov, "Vremennoi kontrapunkt kak formoobrazuiushchii printsip romana Pasternaka 'Doktor Zhivago'," in *Boris Pasternak and His Times,* edited by Fleishman (Berkeley, Cal.: Berkeley Slavic Specialties, 1989), pp. 315–358; translated as "Temporal Counterpoint as a Principle of Formation in *Doctor Zhivago,*" in *Doctor Zhivago: A Critical Companion,* edited by Clowes (Evanston, Ill.: Northwestern University Press, 1995), pp. 89–114;

Mikhail Leonidovich Gasparov, Irina Iur'evna Podgaetskaia, and Konstantin Mikhailovich Polivanov, eds., *Pasternakovskie chteniia,* volume 2 (Moscow: Nasledie, 1998);

Henry Gifford, *Pasternak. A Critical Study* (Cambridge & New York: Cambridge University Press, 1977);

Erika Greber, *Intertextualität und Interpretierbarkeit des Texts. Zur frühen Prosa Boris Pasternaks* (Munich: Wilhelm Fink, 1989);

Olga Raevsky Hughes, *The Poetic World of Boris Pasternak* (Princeton: Princeton University Press, 1974);

Ol'ga Ivinskaia, *V pleny vremeni. Gody s Borisom Pasternakom* (Paris: Fayard, 1978); translated by Hayward as *A Captive of Time* (New York: Doubleday, 1978);

Roman Jakobson, *Noveishaia russkaia poeziia* (Prague: Politika, 1921);

Jakobson, "Randbemerkungen zur Prosa des Dichters Pasternak," *Slavische Rundschau,* 8 (1935): 357–374; Russian version translated by Ol'ga A. Sedakova as "Zametki o prose poeta Pasternaka," in *Raboty po poetike,* by Jakobson, edited by Mikhail Gasparov (Moscow: Nauka, 1987), pp. 324–328; translated as "Marginal Notes on the Prose of the Poet Pasternak," in *Language and Literature,* edited by Krystyna Pomorska and Stephen Rudy (Cambridge, Mass.: Belknap Press of Harvard University, 1987);

Boris A. Kats, *Muzykal'nye kliuchi k russkoi poezii* (St. Petersburg: Kompozitor, 1997), pp. 105–109;

Kats, ed., *Muzyka v tvorchestve, sud'be i dome Borisa Pasternaka. Sbornik literaturnykh, muzykal'nykh i izobrazitel'nykh trudov* (Leningrad: Sovetskii kompozitor, Leningradskoe otdelenie, 1991);

Iurii Levin, "O nekotorykh chertakh plana soderzhaniia v poeticheskikh tekstakh," in *Strukturnaia tipologiia iazykov,* edited by Ivanov (Moscow: Nauka, 1966), pp. 199–215;

*Literaturnoe obozrenie,* 2 (1990);

Angela Livingstone, *Boris Pasternak: Doktor Zhivago* (Cambridge & New York: Cambridge University Press, 1989);

Livingstone, "Some Affinities in the Prose of the Poets Rilke and Pasternak," *Forum for Modern Language Studies,* 19 (January 1983): 274–284;

Anna Ljunggren, *Juvenilia B. Pasternaka. 6 fragmentov o Relikvimini* (Stockholm: Almqvist & Wiksell International, 1984);

Konstantin Loks, "Povest' ob odnom desiatiletii (1907–1917 gg.)," *Voprosy literatury,* 2 (1990): 5–34; enlarged in *Minuvshee. Istoricheskii almanakh* (Moscow & St. Petersburg: Atheneum/Feniks, 1994), pp. 7–162;

Lev Loseff, ed., *Boris Pasternak 1890–1990: Centennial Symposium,* Norwich Symposia in Russian Literature and Culture, volume 1 (Northfield, Vt.: Russian School of Norwich University, 1991);

Iurii Mikhailovich Lotman, "Analiz dvukh stikhotvorenii," in *Tret'ia letniaia shkola po vtorichnym modeliruiushchim sistemam. Tezisy. Doklady* (Tartu: Tartu University Press, 1968), pp. 191–224;

Lotman, "Stikhotvoreniia rannego Pasternaka i nekotorye voprosy strukturnogo izucheniia teksta," in *Trudy po znakovym sistemam,* no. 4 (Tartu: Tartu University Press, 1969), pp. 206–238;

A. N. Lur'e, "Istoricheskaia osnova v poeme B. Pasternaka 'Leitenant Shmidt,'" *Filologicheskie nauki,* 4 (1976);

Anna Majmieskulow, ed., *Poetika Pasternaka: Pasternak's Poetics* (Bydgoszcz: Wydawnictwo Uczelniane wsp w Bydgoszcze, 1990);

Guy de Mallac, "Pasternak's Critical-Esthetic Views," *Russian Literature Triquarterly,* 6 (1973): 502–532;

Vladimir Markov, *Russian Futurism: A History* (Berkeley & Los Angeles: University of California Press, 1968);

Zoia Maslenikova, *Portret Borisa Pasternaka* (Moscow: Sovetskaia Rossii, 1990);

Elliot Mossman, "Pasternak's Prose Style: Some Observations," *Russian Literature Triquarterly*, 1 (1971): 386–398;

Mossman, "Pasternak's Short Fiction," *Russian Literature Triquarterly*, 2 (1972): 279–302;

Nils Åke Nilsson, "Life as Ecstasy and Sacrifice: Two Poems by Boris Pasternak," *Scando Slavica*, 5 (1959): 180–198;

Nilsson, ed., *Boris Pasternak: Essays* (Stockholm: Almqvist & Wiksell International, 1976);

Katherine Tiernan O'Connor, *Pasternak's 'My Sister Life.' The Illusion of Narrative* (Ann Arbor, Mich.: Ardis, 1988);

Aleksandr Leonidovich Pasternak, *Vospominaniia* (Munich & Vienna: Wilhelm Fink–Ferdinand Schöningh, 1983; enlarged edition, Moscow: Progress-Traditsiia, 2002); translated by Lydia Pasternak Slater as *A Vanished Present: The Memoirs of Alexander Pasternak*, edited by Pasternak Slater (New York & Oxford: Oxford University Press, 1984);

Elena Vladimirovna Pasternak, "Rabota Borisa pasternaka nad tsiklom 'Nachal'naia pora,'" *Russkoe i zarubezhnoe iazykoznanie*, 4 (1970): 124–141;

Pasternak and M. I. Feinberg, eds., *Vospominaniia o Borise Pasternake* (Moscow: Slovo, 1993);

Leonid Osipovich Pasternak, *Zapiski raznykh let*, edited by Zhozefina Pasternak (Moscow: Sovetskii khudozhnik, 1975); translated by Jennifer Bradshaw as *The Memoirs of Leonid Pasternak* (New York: Quartet, 1982);

Zinaida Nikolaevna Pasternak, *Vtoroe rozhdenie: Pis'ma k Z. N. Pasternak* (Moscow: GRIT/Dom-muzei B. Pasternaka, 1993);

Dale Plank, *Pasternak's Lyric. A Study of Sound and Imagery* (The Hague: Mouton, 1966);

Irina Iur'evna Podgaetskaia, E. F. Varlamova, Mikhail Gasparov, and Polivanov, eds., *"Byt' znametinym nekrasivo. . . ,"* Pasternakovskie chteniia, volume 1 (Moscow: Nasledie, 1992);

Krystyna Pomorska, *Themes and Variations in Pasternak's Poetics* (Lisse, Belgium: Peter de Ridder Press, 1975);

Jacqueline de Proyart, *Pasternak* (Paris: Gallimard, 1964);

Darlene Reddaway, "Pasternak, Spengler, and Quantum Mechanics: Constants, Variables, and Chains of Equations," *Russian Literature*, 26 (1992): 37–70;

Mary F. Rowland and Paul Rowland, *Pasternak's "Doctor Zhivago"* (Carbondale: Southern Illinois University Press, 1967);

Larissa Rudova, *Pasternak's Short Fiction and the Cultural Vanguard* (New York: Peter Lang, 1994);

Rudova, *Understanding Boris Pasternak* (Columbia: University of South Carolina Press, 1997);

Rima Salys, "Izmeritel'naia edinitsa russkoi zhizni: Pushkin in the Work of Boris Pasternak," *Russian Literature*, 9 (1986): 347–392;

*Sbornik statei, posviashchennykh tvorchestvu B. L. Pasternaka* (Munich, 1962);

Jean Marie Schultz, "Pasternak's 'Zerkalo'," *Russian Literature*, 13 (1983): 81–100;

Renate Schweitzer, *Freundschaft mit Boris Pasternak* (Vienna: Kurt Desch, 1963);

D. Segal, "Nabliudeniia nad semanticheskoi strukturoi poeticheskogo proizvedeniia," *International Journal of Slavic Linguistics and Poetics*, 9 (1968): 159–171;

Segal, "Pro Domo Sua: The Case of Boris Pasternak," *Slavica Hierosolymitana*, 1 (1977): 199–250;

Segal, "Zametki o siuzhetnosti v liricheskoi poezii Pasternaka," *Slavica Hierosolymitana*, 4 (1979): 174–192;

Irina Shevelenko and Andrei Ustinov, eds., *Themes and Variations: In Honor of Lazar' Fleishman*, Stanford Slavic Studies, volume 8 (Stanford: Department of Slavic Languages and Literatures, Stanford University, 1994);

Igor' Pavlovich Smirnov, *Porozhdenie interteksta: Elementy intertekstual'nogo analiza s primerami iz tvorchestva B. L. Pasternaka* (St. Petersburg: Sankt-Peterburgskii gosudarstvennyi universitet, 1995);

Smirnov, *Roman tain "Doktor Zhivago"* (Moscow: Novoe literaturnoe obozrenie, 1996);

Kiril Taranovsky, "On the Poetics of Boris Pasternak," *Russian Literature*, 9 (1981): 339–358;

Jane Taubman, "Marina Tsvetaeva and Boris Pasternak: Towards the History of a Friendship," *Russian Literature Triquarterly*, 2 (Winter 1972): 303–321;

Victor Terras, "Boris Pasternak and Romantic Aesthetics," *Papers on Language & Literature*, 3 (Winter 1967): 42–56;

Terras, "Boris Pasternak and Time," *Canadian Slavic Studies*, 2 (Summer 1968): 264–270;

Afiani Tomilina and N. G. Tomilina, *A za mnoiu shum pogoni: Boris Pasternak i vlast'. Dokumenty 1956–1972* (Moscow: ROSSPEN, 2001);

Marina Ivanovna Tsvetaeva, "Epos i lirika v sovremennoi Rossii," *Novyi grad*, 6–7 (1933);

Tsvetaeva, "Poety s istoriei i poety bez istorii," in her *Sobranie sochinenii*, volume 5 (Moscow: Terra, 1997), pp. 75–106;

Tsvetaeva, "Svetovoi liven'," *Epopeia*, 3 (1922);

Iurii Nikolaevich Tynianov, "Promezhutok," in his *Arkhaisty i novatory* (Leningrad: Priboi, 1929), pp. 541–580;

N. N. Vil'iam-Vil'mont, *O Borise Pasternake. Vospominaniia i mysli* (Moscow: Sovetskii pisatel', 1989);

Aleksandr Konstantinovich Zholkovsky, "Invarianty i struktura poeticheskogo teksta. Pasternak," in *Poetika vyrazitel'nosti: Sbornik statei,* by Zholkovsky and Iurii K. Shcheglov (Vienna: Institut für Slawistik der Universität Wien, 1980);

Zholkovsky, "Mesto okna v poeticheskom mire Pasternaka," *Russian Literature,* 6 (1978): 1–38; translated by Zholkovsky as "'Window' in the Poetic World of Boris Pasternak," in his *Themes and Texts: Toward a Poetics of Expressiveness,* edited by Kathleen Parthé (Ithaca, N.Y.: Cornell University Press, 1984).

**Papers:**
Most of Boris Leonidovich Pasternak's papers are in the Pasternak family archive in Moscow, under the care of Evgenii Borisovich Pasternak and Elena Vladimirovna Pasternak, and in the Pasternak Trust in Oxford, England. Elsewhere in Moscow, Pasternak's papers are archived at the Institute of World Literature (IMLI), fond 120; the Russian State Library (RGB) in the Department of Manuscripts, fond 386 (the Valerii Iakovlevich Briusov archive); the Russian State Archive of Literature and Art (RGALI), fond 379; the State Literary Museum (GLM), fond 143, *osnovnoi fond* (basic archive) 4840. In St. Petersburg, collections of Pasternak's papers can be found at the Russian National Library (RNB), fonds 474 and 60. They are also located at the Georgian Literary Museum in Tbilisi. In the United States, archives of Pasternak's papers are housed at the Houghton Library of Harvard University; at Sterling Memorial Library of Yale University; at Amherst College (in the Thomas P. Whitney Collection); and in the I. T. Holtzman Collection at the Hoover Institution Archive at Stanford University.

# Valentin Grigor'evich Rasputin

(15 March 1937 –    )

David Gillespie
*University of Bath*

BOOKS: *Krai vozle samogo neba* (Irkutsk: Vostochno-Sibirskoe knizhnoe izdatel'stvo, 1966);

*Kostrovye novykh gorodov* (Krasnoiarsk: Krasnoiarskoe knizhnoe izdatel'stvo, 1966);

*Chelovek s etogo sveta* (Krasnoiarsk: Krasnoiarskoe knizhnoe izdatel'stvo, 1967)–includes "Starukha";

*Den'gi dlia Marii* (Moscow: Molodaia gvardiia, 1968)–includes *Den'gi dlia Marii,* translated by Kevin Windle and Margaret Wettlin as *Money for Maria,* in *Money for Maria and Borrowed Time: Two Village Tales* (London & New York: Quartet, 1981), pp. 1–141; and "Vstrecha";

*Poslednii srok* (Irkutsk: Vostochno-Sibirskoe knizhnoe izdatel'stvo, 1970)–includes *Poslednii srok,* translated by Windle and Wettlin as *Borrowed Time,* in *Money for Maria and Borrowed Time: Two Village Tales* (London & New York: Quartet, 1981), pp. 145–374;

*Vniz i vverkh po techeniiu* (Moscow: Sovetskaia Rossiia, 1972);

*Zhivi i pomni* (Moscow: Sovremennik, 1975); translated by Antonina W. Bouis as *Live and Remember* (New York: Macmillan, 1978);

*Povesti* (Moscow: Molodaia gvardiia, 1976);

*Poslednii srok: Drama v 2-kh d.* (Moscow, 1977);

*Zhivi i pomni* (Moscow: Izvestiia, 1977)–includes "Proshchanie s Materoi," translated by Bouis as *Farewell to Matera* (New York & London: Macmillan, 1979);

*Zhivi i pomni: Drama v 2-kh akhtakh,* edited by V. Tsirniuk (Moscow: VAAP-inform, 1979); republished as *Zhivi i pomni. Roman* (Elista: Kalmytskoe knizhnoe izdatel'stvo, 1980);

*Vek zhivi – vek liubi* (Moscow: Molodaia gvardiia, 1982); translated by Alan Myers as *You Live and Love,* in *You Live and Love, and Other Stories* (London: Granada, 1985; New York: Vanguard, 1985);

*Povesti* (Khabarovsk: Khabarovskoe knizhnoe izdatel'stvo, 1984);

*Povesti i rasskazy* (Moscow: Sovremennik, 1984);

*Valentin Grigor'evich Rasputin (*Pozhar, *1990; William T. Young Library, University of Kentucky)*

*Izbrannye proizvedeniia,* 2 volumes (Moscow: Molodaia gvardiia, 1984);

*Vek zhivi – vek liubi [i drugie rasskazy]* (Moscow: Khudozhestvennaia literatura, 1984);

*Chto v slove, chto za slovom?* (Irkutsk: Vostochno-Sibirskoe knizhnoe izdatel'stvo, 1987);

*Vek zhivi – vek liubi: Rasskazy, ocherki, povest'* (Moscow: Molodaia gvardiia, 1988);

*Izbrannye proizvedeniia*, 2 volumes (Moscow: Khudozhestvennaia literatura, 1990);

*Sibir', Sibir' . . .* (Moscow: Molodaia gvardiia, 1991); translated by Gerald E. Mikkelson and Margaret Winchell as *Siberia, Siberia* (Evanston, Ill.: Northwestern University Press, 1996);

*Rossiia: Dni i vremena* (Irkutsk: Pis'mena, 1993);

*Sobranie sochinenii*, 3 volumes (Moscow: Molodaia gvardiia, 1994);

*Nezhdanno-neganno* (Moscow: Detskaia literatura, 1998).

**Editions and Collections:** *Poslednii srok* (Novosibirsk: Zapadno-Sibirskoe knizhnoe izdatel'stvo, 1971);

*Povesti* (Moscow: Sovetskaia Rossiia, 1978);

*Zhivi i pomni* (Irkutsk: Vostochno-Sibirskoe knizhnoe izdatel'stvo, 1978);

*Zhivi i pomni. Povesti* (Krasnoiarsk: Krasnoiarskoe knizhnoe izdatel'stvo, 1978);

*Zhivi i pomni. Povest'* (Moscow: Sovetskii pisatel', 1980);

*Chetyre povesti* (Leningrad: Lenizdat, 1982);

*Proshchanie s Materoi. Povesti i rasskazy* (Irkutsk: Vostochno-Sibirskoe knizhnoe izdatel'stvo, 1983);

*Povesti* (Minsk: Belarus', 1983);

*Poslednii srok; Proshchanie s Materoi; Pozhar* (Moscow: Sovetskaia Rossiia, 1986);

*Povesti* (Novosibirsk: Novosibirskoe knizhnoe izdatel'stvo, 1988);

*Povesti* (Moscow: Profizdat, 1990);

*Zhivi i pomni. Povesti* (Moscow: Golos, 1993).

**Editions in English:** "Vasilii and Vasilisa," translated by Susan Henderson, *Soviet Literature*, 3 (1980): 43–64;

"Downstream," translated by Valentina G. Brougher and Helen C. Poot, in *Contemporary Russian Prose*, edited by Carl R. Proffer and Ellendea Proffer (Ann Arbor, Mich.: Ardis, 1982), pp. 379–430;

"Rudol'fio," translated by Helen Burlingame, *Kenyon Review*, 5, no. 3 (1983): 28–40;

*Siberia on Fire: Stories and Essays*, translated by Gerald E. Mikkelson and Margaret Winchell (De Kalb: Northern Illinois University Press, 1989).

OTHER: Fedor Aleksandrovich Abramov, *Sobranie sochinenii*, volume 4, edited by Rasputin (St. Petersburg: Khudozhestvennaia literatura, 1993).

SELECTED PERIODICAL PUBLICATIONS–UNCOLLECTED: "Novaia professiia," *Nash sovremennik*, 7 (1998): 3–23;

"Izba," *Nash sovremennik*, 1 (1999): 3–20;

"Na Rodine. Rasskaz-byl'," *Nash sovremennik*, 6 (1999): 9–18;

"Mestnaia vlast' i mestnyi narod," by Rasputin and Boris Govorin, *Nash sovremennik*, 2 (2000): 3–10;

"Doch' Ivana, mat' Ivana, Povest'," *Nash sovremennik*, 11 (2003): 3–100.

Valentin Grigor'evich Rasputin made his name as one of the foremost writers of "village prose" with four novellas written in the late 1960s to the mid 1970s achieving particular prominence with "Proshchaniies Materoi" (translated as *Farewell to Matera*, 1979) in 1977. Whereas other *derevenshchiki* (writers of village prose) told about disappearing villages; the values and traditions nurtured there; and of European Russia in their works, Rasputin described the countryside of his own childhood on the banks of the Angara River in Siberia. Not only did he effectively bring village prose to an end, but he also enriched contemporary Russian literature with his use of the language and speech of native Siberians and with his research into the history and ethnography of Siberia. With the possible exception of Aleksandr Isaevich Solzhenitsyn, Rasputin is, according to Gerald E. Mikkelson in his introduction to *Siberia, Siberia* (1996), "the most gifted and influential prose writer of the last thirty years of the Soviet era."

Rasputin was born on 15 March 1937 in Ust'-Uda, about 180 miles from Irkutsk, and went to primary school in the village of Atalanka, about 30 miles away. His father, Grigorii Nikitich Rasputin, was a peasant farmer who fought in World War II and then fell afoul of the authorities, spending some years in prison in the postwar years. As a result Rasputin was raised largely by his mother, Nina Ivanovna Rasputina, and his paternal grandmother, Mariia Gerasimovna Rasputina. In 1948, at the age of eleven, he went to high school in Ust'-Uda, and in 1954 he entered Irkutsk State University. His ambition then was to become a schoolteacher. While a university student he was short of money and worked part-time at a local Irkutsk newspaper. Upon graduation in 1959 Rasputin began working in television in Irkutsk. Next he moved to Krasnoiarsk, traveling around Siberia on assignments and becoming acquainted with the vast construction projects taking place at that time—in particular, the construction of the Krasnoiarsk hydroelectric plant and the Abakan-Taishet railway. In the early to mid 1960s he succeeded in publishing two books and several short stories based on these experiences. In 1966 Rasputin returned to Irkutsk to become a professional writer. Several of his short stories and novellas appeared, and in 1975 he was invited to join the editorial board of the journal *Nash sovremennik* (Our Contemporary). That same year he also was accepted into the Writers'

*Title page for Rasputin's novella* Pozhar *(The Fire) about settlers driven from their homes by floods resulting from a hydroelectric dam project (William T. Young Library, University of Kentucky)*

Union. In 1989 he served as a people's deputy in the U.S.S.R. Supreme Soviet, and in 1990 he was brought into the Presidential Council of then Soviet leader Mikhail Sergeevich Gorbachev; Rasputin served in the council until 1991. Twice he was awarded the U.S.S.R. State Prize for Literature—in 1977 and 1987 (in the latter year he was also made a Hero of Socialist Labor). In 2000 he received the Solzhenitsyn Prize for Russian Writing, an award established in 1997. He still lives in Irkutsk with his wife, Svetlana. The couple have two children, Sergei and Mariia.

Rasputin's first work of fiction was the short story "Ia zabyl sprosit' u Aleshki" (I Forgot to Ask Aleshka), published in the Siberian journal *Angara* in 1961. (It was subsequently titled "Ia zabyl sprosit' u Leshki" in *Literaturnaia Rossiia* [Literary Russia], 10 September 1965). Inspired by the Thaw and de-Stalinization, it bears a striking resemblance to Vladimir Tendriakov's novella *Ukhaby* (Potholes), published in 1956. In Tendriakov's story a young man is injured in an accident at work, and the foreman in charge refuses to part with the only form of transport—a tractor—to take him to the hospital. The injured man eventually dies. In Rasputin's story seventeen-year-old Aleshka is an idealistic member of the Komsomol (Communist Youth League), doing his bit in the construction of socialism by helping lay a railroad. When a tree falls on him, he is seriously injured and in need of urgent hospital treatment. Yet, the hospital is thirty miles away. Because the foreman refuses to let them use a vehicle for transportation, Leshka's two friends must carry him on foot on a makeshift stretcher, and he dies on the way to the hospital. Like Tendriakov's novella, "Ia zabyl sprosit' u Leshki" is an angry attack on the moral decay of a society forced for too long to adhere to industrial priorities, to the exclusion of human values and decency.

In other short stories of the 1960s Rasputin explores the complexities of emotional relationships, and offers no easy solutions or sentimentality. In "Vstrecha" (1968, A Meeting) two former lovers, now both middle-aged, see each other for the first time in twenty years at a conference. Half-forgotten memories and perceived slights come to the surface, but they part as friends. In certain places the story "Rudol'fio" (first published 1966 in *Angara;* translated, 1983) reads like an inverted version of Vladimir Vladimirovich Nabokov's *Lolita* (1955), as sixteen-year-old Io becomes infatuated with happily married Rudol'f, who is almost twice her age. The relationship does not develop; Rudol'f breaks it off when he feels that she is getting too close, but Io is hurt by her first experience of the adult world. In "Vasilii and Vasilisa" (published 1967 in *Literaturnaia Rossiia;* translated by Margaret Wettlin, in *Soviet Literature,* 1969) the title characters live together but are estranged. For thirty years Vasilii has lived in the barn (although he comes into the house in the mornings for a cup of tea). He has been cooking for himself, but eventually he has a younger woman, Aleksandra, to come and look after him. Vasilii's wife is Vasilisa, with whom he had seven children. One night, two years before the outbreak of World War II, he was drunk and raised an ax to Vasilisa, who was pregnant, and she miscarried. Since that incident he has had to make his home in the barn. "Vasilii and Vasilisa" is a touching story about loss, for both Aleksandra and Vasilisa have lost children in the past, and about reconciliation with the past—Vasilisa comes to Vasilii as he lies dying, and she forgives him.

Vasilii is a man of the taiga, the evergreen Arctic forest, where he hunts and collects berries and nuts, or acts as guide to geologists from Moscow or Lithuania. Other stories also feature individuals who are at one with their natural surroundings, such as in "Chelovek s etogo sveta" (A Person from This World, first published 1967 in *Angara*), about an old woman who continues to hunt alone in the taiga. The old *shamanka* (female shaman) in "Starukha" (1967, The Old Woman) is the last of her kind, a repository of age-old wisdom and healing powers, and when she dies, so will this well of tradition.

Rasputin's keen interest in a centuries-old way of life, which is bound up with the natural world and the seasons and is now under threat in the modern age, comes across strongly in one of his earliest books, *Krai vozle samogo neba* (1966, The Land Next to the Sky). The book consists of a series of journalistic sketches about the Tofalars, a tiny Central Asian people of shamanistic beliefs who, numbering in the hundreds, inhabit the Saian Mountains to the southwest of Lake Baikal. The Tofalars are hunters and share their meat equally among themselves. Their culture is based on the rugged landscape around them, as they sing songs and tell folktales at night. Kind and simple, they not only are inseparably linked to the natural world but also provide a link with the past. As these sketches show, Rasputin has a deep respect for these people, a respect tinged with sadness that their way of life is threatened in the modern age. Significantly, the motifs of loss and endurance are as prominent in these sketches as in his other works of short fiction, with several characters also belonging to the older generation. The values represented by these people are revisited in Rasputin's subsequent works.

By way of contrast, Rasputin published *Kostrovye novykh gorodov* (Lights for Building New Cities) in the same year that *Krai vozle samogo neba* appeared. Yet, unlike Rasputin's writings about the Tofalars, the sketches that make up *Kostrovye novykh gorodov* praise industrial construction. He describes the building (between 1958 and 1965) of the Siberian Abakan-Taishet railway line, which stretches for more than 360 miles through mountains, swamps, ravines, and the taiga with tunnels, bridges, and viaducts. The construction is a monumental effort as well as a testament to Soviet man's much-trumpeted desire to conquer nature. The narrative reflects Socialist Realist aesthetics, whereby fathers and sons share a common cause, the war hero Aleksandr Matrosov inspires the younger generation with his dedication and effort, and the collectivist ethos is triumphant.

The railway is a potent symbol of progress and modernization and has often been viewed by Russian writers with foreboding and a sense of doom—as a disruptive force capable of destroying the soul of Russia. In Rasputin's book the railway is seen in positive and ideological terms. The same can be said of the sketches that address the construction of the Bratsk hydroelectric dam, a public display of industrial might and the political will behind it. Though of minor literary value, serving mainly as examples of upbeat and ideologically affirmative journalism, these sketches are significant in Rasputin's body of works as pieces written from the point of view of the builders—not, as his later work was, through the eyes of those affected by technological progress.

Rasputin came to national attention in 1967 with the publication in *Angara* of his first long prose work, *Den'gi dlia Marii* (Money for Maria, published in book form, 1968; translated as *Money for Maria,* 1981). It is set, as all of Rasputin's later works are, in a Siberian village. Though semiliterate, Maria is the manager of the village store. An external auditor finds that the store has lost 1,000 rubles, which Maria and her husband Kuz'ma must make good on. Otherwise, she will go to prison for embezzlement. That Maria has not stolen the money is obvious to everyone, even the auditor, but she simply has not been careful enough, or she has been too kindhearted to refuse credit to customers. The auditor gives Kuz'ma five days to make up the deficit.

The story is about the disruption to a small rural community by the intrusion of modern mores. Kuz'ma and his fellow villagers have never worried about money before, because they have been able to rely on each other, or been able to make things with their own hands that people nowadays buy in shops. This self-reliance is all the more important as the little money Maria and Kuz'ma earn is spent on their children (they have four boys). Never has there been any possibility of saving money for a rainy day, and now that rainy day is upon them. For the couple 1,000 rubles is a huge amount.

The story implicitly criticizes a draconian law that sends people to prison not because they have done wrong but because they have made mistakes. The story has some factual basis, since Rasputin's own father had spent time in prison after the war. Moreover, Rasputin treads a fine line between a wistful nostalgia for a never-never land, where people live in harmony with each other and make do with the bare essentials, and a tempered warning of the dangers that face a society, when its members do not pull together and pursue their own narrow, self-centered interests. Soon, Kuz'ma goes around the village asking each household to donate a few rubles each. The story opens with his dream of collecting the required sum from all the village without any difficulty, and he later dreams again that the whole

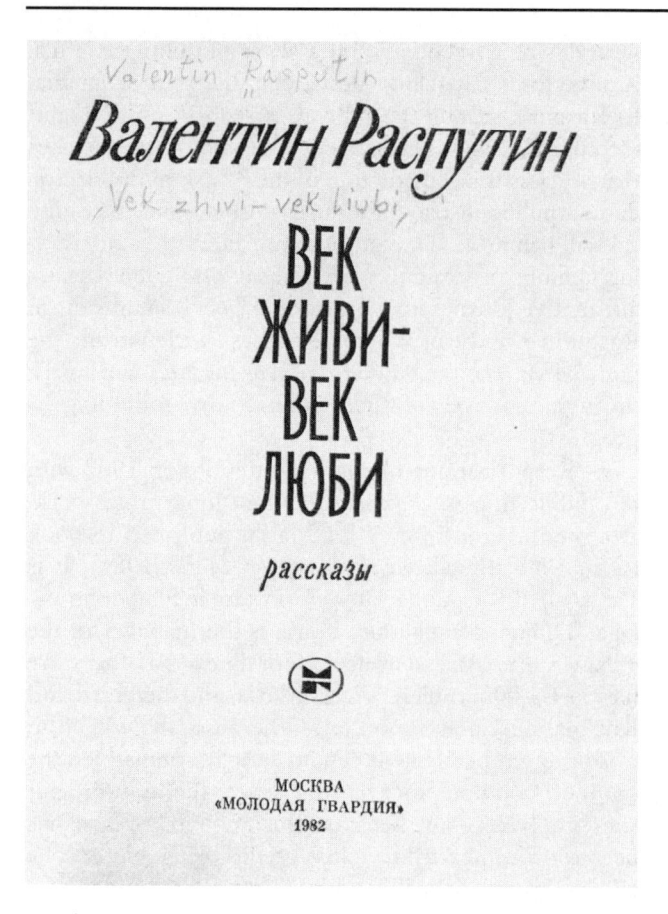

Title page for Vek zhivi – vek liubi, translated as You Live and Love, 1985, stories of people who either find a link to nature through spirituality or are isolated by their moral degradation (Howard-Tilton Memorial Library, Tulane University)

collective farm willingly provides the 1,000 rubles. Reality, however, is different.

As Kuz'ma makes his rounds, a gallery of peasant characters comes into play—all vivid and individualized and all representing some aspect of village life. But his efforts are in vain, as he cannot collect the total sum, and he is forced to travel out of the village to the town where his brother, Aleksei, lives. He and Aleksei have not seen each other in seven years, when their father died. Maria had visited Aleksei three years before, but Aleksei would not return to the village: "In the end, his brother should understand what's what, he wasn't a child. It was a mutual thing between the village and him: his brother gradually forgot his village, and consequently his own childhood, and the village gradually forgot that such a person had once lived there."

Kuz'ma has to travel to the town by bus and then train. On the train, too, he encounters a cross section of society that embodies various values and attitudes. Rasputin's style in this story shows his increasing maturity as a writer. Nature is represented not only in the passage of the seasons—so vital in the life of the rural community—but also as a comment on the narrative. As Kuz'ma travels by bus, a strong wind outside makes him aware of his own precarious situation: "Kuz'ma realized that this was how it should be, that the weather could not remain calm when he and Maria had been thrown into such turmoil." Rasputin also succeeds in using time shifts, dream sequences, and embedded narratives, which throw light on past events as essential elements that provide both psychological motivation and a moral framework. The story is narrated not chronologically but through Kuz'ma's eyes as he travels to the town. Thus, the reader's perceptions are informed by the protagonist's reactions and responses to events. There is also a significant religious dimension, not only in the use of the name "Maria" but also in the key moment when one brother must be the other's keeper to avert misfortune.

Narrative closure makes clear that the proof of the story is in its telling, not its resolution, as Rasputin ends the narrative just as Kuz'ma approaches Aleksei's door. The reader does not, therefore, know how he will be received by his estranged brother—whether Aleksei will lend Kuz'ma the rest of the money needed to keep Maria out of jail, or whether Maria will be sentenced. On the one hand, this work has a topical sociological resonance: Rasputin provides an unromantic snapshot of village life and a discouraging statement of town-village relations. On the other, it has a complex structure—even the minor characters are vivid creations—and it deliberately confounds the reader's expectations.

Rasputin's next major work was the novella *Poslednii srok* (1970; translated as *Borrowed Time*, 1981). Its central theme is death, and here the author follows in the famous footsteps of Leo Tolstoy, who covered much the same ground in his *Smert' Ivana Il'icha* (1886, The Death of Ivan Il'ich). The acceptance of death as the natural culmination of life manifested by Rasputin's eighty-year-old heroine, Anna, is reminiscent of the same resignation felt by many of Tolstoy's peasant characters. Another personal note is present in this story: Anna is based on Rasputin's own grandmother. As with *Den'gi dlia Marii,* the narrative takes place within a tightly enclosed period of time—three days. Anna takes to her bed and is obviously dying, and Mikhail, her youngest son, with whom she lives, calls the rest of the family together for one final meeting. Varvara, the eldest daughter, lives thirty miles away, while both Il'ia and Liusia live in cities. The youngest daughter, Tania, lives in Kiev and does not come to the gathering.

The arrival of Anna's children provides an opportunity for Rasputin to poke fun at their acquired ways and airs, an indication of how far they have traveled from the village. The first to arrive, Varvara collapses in feigned hysteria at her mother's bed but makes sure that Anna is comfortable. Mikhail meets Il'ia and Liusia at the ferry quay, and while he accompanies them to the house, they walk on the rickety wooden pavement, as he trundles alongside in the dried mud. Mikhail then wastes no time in berating Il'ia and Liusia for not visiting the village: "When you left that was it. Only Varvara pops in, when she needs some potatoes or whatever. But it's as if you don't exist." The family thus is split into rural and urban halves, and this split assumes a symbolic significance. In addition, the siblings are distinguished physically. Varvara is prematurely old, while Liusia has taken care, in her urbane fashion, to remain slim and looks younger than her years. Il'ia, short and bald, likes to clown around, while Mikhail, bearded and with thick, curly hair, can be frightening and aggressive when drunk. As they sit around the family table, the narrator remarks: "All of them, having lived apart, now barely resembled one another."

Rasputin takes an ironic attitude toward his characters that is enhanced as the narrative progresses. For example, far from receding into senselessness and death, Anna actually revives in the presence of her children. When they first arrive she is barely breathing, and they fear that she might not survive the night. Two days later she is sitting up in bed and has even walked outside. The children engage in a bitter dispute, as Mikhail especially bridles at continuing taunts from Liusia. He offers to give his mother away to any of the others, "who among you loves our mother the most," and even offers to throw in a cow—the cow can be sold for money, after all. The simpleminded Varvara replies that she would take her mother to live with her, but her daughter is expecting another baby and living space is limited; she would have room, however, for the cow. Varvara, Il'ia, and Liusia quickly decide that Anna has recovered, and the next day the three go their separate ways. The night after they leave, Anna dies.

Whereas Rasputin does not spare the children his anger and sarcasm, his portrayal of Anna is imbued with reverence. She represents an old and more harmonious way of life that is disappearing with her, and the only person with whom she has any meaningful contact is old Mironikha, another representative of the old ways. Only with Mironikha can Anna talk—as with a kindred spirit—and together they bemoan modern vices such as drunkenness and moral laxity. They are, they realize, the last of a dying breed in a world changing fast. Anna's instinctive relationship with the natural world can be seen in an episode during the lean postwar years, when the horse Igrenia collapsed from exhaustion, but Anna coaxed it back to its feet with kind words and caresses and led it home. In Rasputin's representation of Anna, the sun shines on her, it fills her room so she can reach out and touch it, and at night she dreams of church bells. As she looks upon her children she sees that they have drifted apart, but she appeals to them nevertheless to remain as a family even after she has gone. She wants them to visit their ancestral home, for a spiritual bond remains there that links the living and the dead.

Rasputin's next publication, *Vniz i vverkh po techeniiu* (1972, Upstream, Downstream), also focuses on a journey into the past and childhood memory. It is the most explicitly autobiographical of all his works. Viktor is a writer who returns to his native village after five years. The village has been transplanted to a site further downriver, since the original site was flooded and became part of the new bed for the Bratsk hydroelectric dam reservoir. As he travels upstream he sees remnants of the upheaval: abandoned stoves that were too heavy to carry, and trees grotesquely growing out of the water. They seem to groan as they rock in the waves caused by the steamer's passage.

Viktor's memories of childhood soon return. He recalls the Angara River as it used to thaw in the spring and the games he would play with other boys in the village. Like that of Rasputin, Viktor's childhood coincided with the years of World War II but still seemed to him a carefree and happy time. When he reaches the village, however, he feels himself an outsider almost immediately. His family seems alien to him, as do the surrounding houses and countryside. His memories of the past and the actual reality before him are starkly different, and although he hopes that with time he will get used to it, "days passed and nothing changed." Even the sky seems "different" and "alien." Viktor leaves after five days.

*Vniz i vverkh po techeniiu* is not ranked among Rasputin's greatest works, although it is of interest primarily in what it tells readers about Rasputin in his mid thirties. There are passages about Viktor's work as a writer that are obviously born of Rasputin's own experience, and he uses this semifictional format to reply to Soviet critics who had accused him of peering too deeply into the psychology of his characters and of not clearly dividing them into "positive" and "negative" heroes. He also uses Viktor as a mouthpiece through which to attack some existing literary practices, censorship and self-censorship, and the pervasive lie underpinning totalitarian art. Like nature, art has a moral value, and it should not be tainted by corruption.

Another story that relies heavily on Rasputin's childhood memories is "Uroki frantsuzskogo" (French Lessons, first published 1973 in *Literaturnaia Rossiia*), set

*Rasputin delivering a speech before the Order of Lenin and the Gold Star, Hero of Socialist Labor, 1987 (I. A. Pankeev,
Valentin Rasputin: Po stranitsam proizvedenii, 1990; Miami University Libraries, Oxford, Ohio)*

just after World War II. The first-person narrator is the central character of the story. He is a schoolboy who has to move to the nearest town, thirty miles away, to continue his education. Lonely and vulnerable, he is "adopted" by Lidiia Mikhailovna, the French teacher. Lidiia Mikhailovna's kindness toward the boy is misunderstood by the school principal, who sees it as commercial exploitation, and she loses her job. The lack of understanding between adults and children is a constant feature of Rasputin's prose and stands here as an indicator of greater social antagonisms.

*Zhivi i pomni* (1975; translated as *Live and Remember*, 1978) is set during the war and is the only one of Rasputin's major works that does not have a contemporary relevance. It is also the one work that was universally acclaimed by critics, with its clear good-versus-evil plot and absence of any topical polemics. It is, though, set in a remote Siberian village, and represents a clear development in Rasputin's treatment of landscape and symbolism.

The novella begins in the winter of 1945, when an ax disappears from the bathhouse of the Gus'kov family in the village of Atamanovka (a name reminiscent of Atalanovka, where Rasputin spent much of his childhood). The head of the household is Mikheich; his wife is Semenovna and their son is Andrei, who is away fighting at the front. Andrei's wife, Nastena, lost both her parents during collectivization a decade earlier. She soon finds herself in an impossible situation, for—as the narrative readily makes clear—the ax was taken by Andrei, who has deserted and made his way back home. He reveals himself only to her, insisting that no one, not even his parents, be informed of his return.

By deserting, Andrei has placed himself outside the law, and by confiding in Nastena, he has made her an accomplice. Yet, Rasputin's deserter is no coward or shirker. From the earliest days of the war, Andrei had been at the front. He fought in the battles of Moscow, Smolensk, and Stalingrad; suffered wounds and shell shock; and was decorated. In the summer of 1944 he was seriously wounded again and underwent operations. While recuperating—and with the encouragement of doctors and other patients—he had expected to be sent home on leave. For this very reason he had even discouraged Nastena from visiting him. On recovery, however, he was told to rejoin his unit. Initially he intended to go home just for a few days, in the hope that in the confusion of wartime nobody would notice his absence.

The journey takes longer than expected, however, and Andrei begins to realize the awful consequences of his actions. A few months later he could have become a war hero, but now he is a fugitive. He becomes increasingly self-centered. On his way home he lives for a month with Tania, a deaf-mute, who panders to his every need and asks for nothing in return. He leaves her without warning. When he sets himself up in a refuge on the other side of the Angara River from Atamanovka, his increasingly harsh demands on Nastena take no account of her precarious situation.

This situation becomes even more grave when she becomes pregnant. Andrei can move about only at night, but Nastena can visit him by walking across the ice on the river, at least during the winter. For a few months she is able to hide her pregnancy, but her mother-in-law is the first to notice the bulge in her belly. Nastena outrages the family and the village when she claims that she slept with a visitor from outside the village. The police are making inquiries, however, and Mikheich is suspicious. As the ice on the river melts and Nastena makes her way by boat to warn Andrei, she is followed. In despair, she jumps into the river, killing herself and her unborn child. This act is Andrei's final damnation.

*Zhivi i pomni* is Rasputin's least tendentious work and his most accomplished in purely aesthetic terms. Rasputin's natural images have their own active function in the narrative, and the river, the forest, and the seasons all play their own dramatic parts. He does not portray Andrei as an out-and-out villain but shows his inner torment and breakdown from inside. The deep love that has bound Nastena and Andrei through three and a half years of war is also emphasized, such as in the dream they both have of one another. Whereas Rasputin's earlier works encompass periods of only a few days, this one takes place over several months, thus allowing human destinies to be decided by the elements and the seasons.

Rasputin's best-known work is also the one commonly acknowledged to have brought canonical "village prose" to an end. Set in the present, "Proshchanie s Materoi" focuses on the modern destruction of land and home in the name of technological progress. The island village of Matera is symbolic in several respects: its very name (derived from *mat'*, the Russian word for "mother") suggests Mother Earth, and its fate can be seen as an allegory of the modern destruction of Mother Russia.

Matera, like Viktor's home village in *Vniz i vverkh po techeniiu,* is to be flooded to make way for a huge reservoir (the "sea"), which will service the hydroelectric dam further downriver. A sense of death and of the end of things is apparent in the title of the work, as well as in the opening lines of the novella: "And once again Spring came around in its never-ending cycle, but for Matera, the island and village that bore the same name, this was to be its last." The narrative follows the villagers as they gather in the last harvest, prepare their houses to be razed, and are relocated to a semiurban settlement downriver. The novel also shows the destruction of nature as trees are felled. The dam is a symbol of man's conquest of nature, and so is an affirmation of official ideology, but it also causes people to be uprooted from their homes and destroys a culture that had been flourishing for centuries.

Rasputin's heroes are the old men and women of the island who embody the values and traditions of the past, who will find resettlement difficult if not impossible, and who offer moral and philosophical resistance to the idea of material progress, if that progress uproots man from the land and destroys his home. The heroine of *Proshchanie s Materoi* is Dar'ia Pinigina, who, like Anna in *Poslednii srok,* is eighty years old. Her son, Pavel, is in charge of the operation to clear the island of its buildings and trees. Pavel's son, Andrei, is an eager young volunteer who wants to be "in the front line" of progress; he acts as the spokesman for official ideology that proclaims that "man is the Tsar of nature." Andrei may be young and naive, but his denial of the soul and of spirituality—of anything that cannot be seen or felt—is not born of youthful flamboyance but of ideological certainty. Still, other younger characters, such as Petrukha, who destroys his and his mother's home willingly, and Klavdiia Strigunova, who wants only to get out of the village as quickly as possible, are also viewed negatively by Rasputin. Klavdiia, in particular, is scorned by other villagers as she embodies the worst aspects of youth culture—lax morals and personal laziness.

The antilife forces of officialdom are contrasted with the people and creatures who celebrate life in all its forms. Rasputin gives his villagers colorful turns of phrase, carefully endowing them with Siberian words, pronunciation, and even grammar—a living language

*Rasputin with Archmandrite Innokenty at a holiday celebration of Slavic writing and culture in Novgorod (from I. A. Pankeev, Valentin Rasputin: Po stranitsam proizvedenii, 1990; Miami University Libraries, Oxford, Ohio)*

created from life on the land that is in stark contrast to the empty ideological phrases of the "outsiders." The villagers as a whole, and Dar'ia in particular, are linked with the spirit of the island, the Khoziain (Master), a small creature no larger than a cat, which humans cannot see and which knows every living thing on the island. Only Dar'ia sees the Khoziain, thus bringing herself within touching distance of myth.

Rasputin provides other symbols of man's profound link with nature. The largest tree on the island is called the "tsarskii listven'," or Tsar's larch, because of its majestic presence. Its roots, according to legend, tie the island to the riverbed. The tree has resisted all attempts to be cut down, hacked, sawed, or burned. The old "holy fool" Bogodul, who speaks only in obscenities and in a language that only he and the other old people can understand, walks around barefoot, and even snakes cannot bite into his tough skin. Thus, both he and the larch, along with Dar'ia, are part of the mythology of the island—the unseen but prescient link of nature and man.

Dar'ia, especially, both embodies and expresses this link, as she lies in the cemetery amid the smoke of the burning island and talks with her long-dead ancestors. The dead, too, are part of the island, for the living remember the dead, and at night "the living and the dead come together." This memory makes a man human, as Dar'ia realizes on the eve of the demise of the island: "Truth is in memory. He who has no memory has no life." This sentiment serves as a direct challenge to official ideological discourse, hell-bent on progress and destroying man's roots in the process.

The tragedy of Matera and those who live on the island is not played through in the narrative. The novella ends with the last of the old men and women stranded on the island, caught between the living and the dead, for the flooding is about to begin. A few lost souls, including Pavel, are adrift on the river in thick fog trying to locate and rescue the stranded. Strange shapes whirl and twist in the gloom, and strange sounds fill the air. Destruction by fire and water is the stuff of the Apocalypse, but the living and bountiful land of Matera is a metonym for Russia itself. Matera is threatened and ultimately destroyed by the forces of progress in the twentieth century.

*Proshchanie s Materoi* offers not only a culmination of the themes of village prose but also its catharsis. The genre did not die but, rather, transmuted into something more angry and more directly confrontational. In the mid to late 1980s the publication of controversial works by other village writers attacked all aspects of modernity, including the perceived influence of Jews in the country, emancipated women, urban decay and crime, and the general collapse of spiritual and moral values. Rasputin's novella *Pozhar* (1986, The Fire; first published 1985 in *Nash sovremennik*) was usually discussed alongside these works, although it is rather more muted and defiantly elegiac.

The reflective and occasionally mystical tone of *Pozhar* was prefigured in some of the short stories that Rasputin published in the early 1980s, which were his first works of fiction since the appearance of *Proshchanie s Materoi*. This five-year silence is partly because in March 1980 Rasputin was the victim of a vicious attack by street thugs; after the incident he needed several months of hospital treatment and recuperation. In addition, Rasputin clearly was moving away from fiction as a means of expressing his increasingly anguished concerns about man and his roots. In the late 1970s and early 1980s he was more interested in *publitsistika*, that particularly Russian, direct appeal to the audience on matters of topical urgency—in Rasputin's case, the environmental threats to Siberia. He has continued in this vein in the 1990s and into the next century.

Rasputin consistently asserts that he is not against change, but he calls for rational and measured development. In an essay titled "Tvoia i moia Sibir'" (Your Siberia and Mine, in *Povesti*, 1984) he made this opinion explicit, together with his undying faith in the natural beauty and richness of his native land:

> Rational utilization, comprehensive development, responsible treatment of Siberia's treasures large and small—now is the time for these principles of theoretical economics to finally become the law of life and action. *Sturm und Drang* in Siberia's development is no longer acceptable: otherwise the blushing bride, as people continue to regard Siberia, could easily turn into a feeble old woman. . . . Siberia is large, but we cannot allow a single meter of ground to be treated carelessly, and we cannot permit another tree in its forests to be felled without urgent need. Siberia is large, but we can claim no credit for its largeness. We will deserve credit if we preserve nature's primordial grandeur side by side with the grandeur of our own deeds [*Siberia on Fire*].

In a cycle of highly autobiographical short stories, Rasputin engages a mystical appreciation of the world and a connectedness with the depths of his own inner being, especially through dreams or the unconscious, such as in "Chto peredat' vorone?" (What Shall I Tell the Crow?) and "Natasha," both first published in 1982 in *Nash sovremennik*. To the narrator's despair, in *Vek zhivi – vek liubi* (1982; translated as *You Live and Love*, 1985) and "Ne mogu-u . . ." (I Can't Do It, first published 1982 in *Nash sovremennik*), the sad, lonely, and occasionally malicious world of real life breaks through. In these stories man is linked again to nature through his spirituality, or else he is isolated from it through the collapse of his personality, or its moral degradation. These twin themes are prominent in *Pozhar*.

*Pozhar* is set in Sosnovka, a new settlement on the banks of the Angara, used to house villagers who have been uprooted from their homes because of flooding from the hydroelectric dam project. *Pozhar* therefore can be seen as a sequel to *Proshchanie s Materoi* (especially since Sosnovka includes an inhabitant named Klavka Strigunova) and as a companion piece to *Vniz i vverkh po techeniiu*. Furthermore, in terms of its sheer clumsiness, it resembles the *poselok* (settlement) described in *Proshchanie s Materoi*: it was built in a hurry, without any landscaping, and lacks even proper roads and pavements, so that after it rains the streets are awash with mud. The settlement has no soul or roots, and its people are similarly removed from the land, working as itinerant loggers—symbolically destroying the natural landscape.

The fire of the title occurs in the food stores of the settlement, threatening the livelihood of the whole area. Whereas individuals help to put out the fire, most people descend to looting. It is a sad story of social breakdown and emphasizes the problems of drunkenness, arbitrary violence, corruption, and the devil-may-care attitudes of the young toward work and their elders. One of the few characters (from the older generation) who tries to put out the fire is murdered. So, as in *Den'gi dlia Marii*, a community is put to the test and its collective nerve fails. As in *Proshchanie s Materoi*, fire acts as the means of destruction, here as a kind of biblical retribution for a community that has cut itself off from nature. The main character, the honest and morally upright Ivan Petrovich, can see no future in a community without its sense of home and seeks solace and solitude in the world of nature. A work of strident social and also political criticism, *Pozhar* was one of the first to announce Gorbachev's policy of greater "openness" in the mid 1980s, and it reveals Rasputin's profound unease at the state of his nation.

This unease continued into the 1990s. On the one hand, Rasputin's fiction shows barely restrained outrage at what he sees as the loss of values in post-Soviet Russia, while in his historical and ethnographic writings on Siberia he has celebrated the richness and vitality of his native land. He writes in order to preserve memory and remind Siberians and Russians of spiritual values and traditions that are now, as he sees it, all but dead. Thus, the tone of his works alternates between anger, factual discourse, and sad lament.

In his writings about Siberia, for instance, Rasputin displays not only an historian's scrupulousness and attention to detail but also an ethnographer's burning desire to preserve the past. He has written at length about Siberian towns and cities—such as Tobol'sk and Irkutsk—as well as about other less well-known havens of tradition and history, such as Russkoe Ust'e and Kiakhta, and, of course, his beloved Lake Baikal. His vision of the historical past is steeped in a personal mysticism:

> One's sense of homeland is an amazing and inexpressible thing. . . . People cannot stand firmly or live confidently without this feeling, without a sense of closeness to the acts and destinies of their ancestors, without an inner comprehension of their responsibility for the place granted them in the vast, general continuum that allows them to be what they are.

For Rasputin the modern world increasingly bypasses the natural world, and the link with nature is lost; in his fiction the lament for the past is a consistent note. Stories such as "Sania edet" (Sania on the Move) and "Rossia molodaia" (Young Russia), both published in 1994 in *Moskva* (Moscow), are distinguished by their rejection of the modern world, youth, rock music, and the West. "V bol'nitse" (In the Hospital, first published

1995 in *Nash sovremennik*) similarly is an unrelieved picture of gloom, as the hospitalized Aleksei Petrovich condemns crime, corruption, permissiveness, television, and even the education system. "Izba" (The Wooden House, first published 1999 in *Nash sovremennik*) is a more ambitious work; it marks an attempt, not unlike that in *Proshchanie s Materoi,* to present a history of Russia through the history of a community—here, a single house and its occupiers. Rasputin carefully relates how the house was put together more than fifty years ago, how the roof and stove were installed, and how it remained empty after its owner, Agaf'ia, died. Her spirit continues nevertheless to look after it, even though life all around has "crashed to the ground" and "become crippled as never before."

Valentin Grigor'evich Rasputin remains a somewhat controversial figure in the post-Soviet period because of his perceived allegiances to nationalist and extremist groups. Yet, his concerns have been consistent: since his early writings about the Tofalars, he has affirmed the link of nature and man, and the spiritual nourishment it provides. He also has lamented the loss of this link and the consequent collapse of value systems in the modern world. He remains, though, a writer of imposing importance in the Russia of the late twentieth and early twenty-first centuries.

**Bibliography:**
Susan K. Burks, "A Bilingual Bibliography of Works by and about Valentin Rasputin," *Russian Literature Triquarterly,* 22 (1988): 327–336.

**References:**
Lewis Bagby, "A Concurrence of Psychological and Narrative Structures: Anamnesis in Valentin Rasputin's 'Upstream, Downstream,'" *Canadian Slavonic Papers,* 22 (1980): 388–399;

Galina Belaia, *Khudozhestvennyi mir sovremennoi prozy* (Moscow: Nauka, 1983), pp. 123–151;

Deming Brown, *The Last Years of Russian Soviet Literature: Prose Fiction 1975–1991* (Cambridge: Cambridge University Press, 1993), pp. 81–86;

Brown, "Valentin Rasputin: A General View," in *Selected Papers from the Second World Congress for Soviet and East European Studies: Russian Literature and Criticism,* edited by Evelyn Bristol (Berkeley, Cal.: Berkeley Slavic Specialties, 1982), pp. 27–35;

Edward J. Brown, *Russian Literature since the Revolution* (Cambridge, Mass. & London: Harvard University Press, 1982), pp. 305–311;

R. A. Budagov, "Kak napisan rasskaz Valentina Rasputina 'Uroki frantsuzskogo,'" *Russkaia rech',* 6 (1982): 37–41;

John P. Dunlop, "Valentin Rasputin's *Proshchanie s Materoi,*" in *Selected Papers from the Second World Congress for Soviet and East European Studies: Russian Literature and Criticism,* edited by Bristol (Berkeley, Cal.: Berkeley Slavic Specialties, 1982), pp. 63–68;

A. A. Dyrdin, "Dialektika pamiati (Chelovek i vremia v povesti V. Rasputina 'Zhivi I pomni')," in *Sovremennyi sovetskii roman: filosofskie aspekty,* edited by V. A. Kovalev (Leningrad: Nauka, 1979), pp. 178–193;

L. Gerasimova, "Trevozhnaia sovest' Valentina Rasputina," *Literatura v shkole,* 4 (1979): 4–13;

David Gillespie, *Valentin Rasputin and Soviet Russian Village Prose* (London: Modern Humanities Research Association, 1986);

Geoffrey Hosking, *Beyond Socialist Realism: Soviet Fiction since "Ivan Denisovich"* (London: Granada, 1980; New York: Holmes & Meier, 1980), pp. 70–81;

N. Ianovsky, "Zaboty i trevogi Valentina Rasputina: Problemy nravstvennosti," *Sever,* 2 (1979): 106–116;

B. M. Iudalevich, "'Dialektika dushi' v rannikh proizvedeniiakh Valentina Rasputina," in *Ocherki literatury i kritiki Sibiri (XVII–XX vv.),* edited by Iu. S. Postnov (Novosibirsk: Nauka, 1976), pp. 255–273;

Iudalevich, "Priroda konflikta v povesti V. Rasputina 'Poslednii srok,'" in *Problemy zhanra v literature Sibiri,* edited by Postnov (Novosibirsk: Nauka, 1977), pp. 139–150;

Violetta Iverni, "Smert'iu – o zhizni," *Kontinent,* 15 (1978): 291–312;

N. D. Khmeliuk, "Kharaktery i obstoiatel'stva v povestiakh V. Rasputina," *Voprosy russkoi literatury,* 2 (1980): 66–73;

Nikolai Nikolaevich Kotenko, "Prezhde vsego – tochnost': o tvorchestve V. Rasputina," *Literaturnaia ucheba,* 4 (1978): 127–133;

Kotenko, "Put' k cheloveku. Zametki o proze V. Rasputina," *Nash sovremennik,* 1 (1972): 113–117;

Kotenko, *Valentin Rasputin: Ocherk tvorchestva* (Moscow: Sovremennik, 1988);

V. Ia. Kurbatov, *Valentin Rasputin: Lichnost' i tvorchestvo* (Moscow: Sovetskii pisatel', 1992);

Feliks Feodos'evich Kuznetsov, *Samaia krovnaia sviaz'. Sud'by derevni v sovremennoi proze* (Moscow: Prosveshchenie, 1977), pp. 119–126;

A. F. Lapchenko, "'Pamiat'' v povestiakh V. Rasputina," *Vestnik Leningradskogo universiteta. Istoriia, iazyk, literatura,* 3 (1983): 50–54;

Irena Maryniak, *Spirit of the Totem: Religion and Myth in Soviet Fiction, 1964–1988* (London: Modern Humanities Research Association, 1995), pp. 49–72;

Gerald E. Mikkelson, "Religious Symbolism in Valentin Rasputin's Tale *Live and Remember*," in *Studies in Honor of Xenia Gasiorowska*, edited by Lauren G. Leighton (Columbus, Ohio: Slavica, 1983), pp. 172–187;

I. A. Pankeev, *Valentin Rasputin: Po stranitsam proizvedenii* (Moscow: Prosveshchenie, 1990);

B. Pankin, "Proshchaniia i vstrechi s Materoi. Zametki o proze V. Rasputina," *Druzhba narodov*, 2 (1978): 236–248;

Kathleen F. Parthé, *Russian Village Prose: The Radiant Past* (Princeton: Princeton University Press, 1992);

N. Podzorova, "Raznozvuchie: zlobodnevnoe i vechnoe v proze V. Rasputina," *Nash sovremennik*, 10 (1978): 180–186;

Teresa Polowy, *The Novellas of Valentin Rasputin: Genre, Language and Style* (New York: Peter Lang, 1989);

Robert Porter, *Four Contemporary Russian Writers* (Oxford: Berg, 1989), pp. 11–51;

Porter, "The Mother Theme in Valentin Rasputin," *Canadian Slavonic Papers*, 28 (1986): 287–303;

"Proza Valentina Rasputina (Po materialam obsuzhdeniia za 'kruglym stolom' v redaktsii zhurnala *Voprosy literatury*)," *Voprosy literatury*, 2 (1977): 3–81;

G. Semenova, *Valentin Rasputin* (Moscow: Sovetskaia Rossiia, 1987);

V. Shaposhnikov, *Valentin Rasputin* (Novosibirsk: Zapadno-Sibirskoe knizhnoe izdatel'stvo, 1978);

N. N. Shneidman, *Russian Literature 1988–1994: The End of an Era* (Toronto: Toronto University Press, 1995);

Shneidman, *Soviet Literature in the 1970s: Artistic Diversity and Ideological Conformity* (Toronto: Toronto University Press, 1979), pp. 75–87;

V. K. Sigov, "Avtor i geroi v povesti V. Rasputina 'Poslednii srok,'" in *Zhanrovo-stilevye problemy sovetskoi literatury*, edited by A. V. Ognev (Kalinin: Kalininskii gosudarstvennyi universitet, 1982), pp. 91–105;

Sigov, "Vnutrenniaia rech' v povesti V. Rasputina 'Zhivi i pomni,'" in *Zhanrovo-stilevye problemy sovetskoi literatury*, edited by Ognev (Kalinin: Kalininskii gosudarstvennyi universitet, 1982), pp. 115–127;

E. Starikova, "Zhit' i pomnit': Zametki o proze V. Rasputina," *Novyi mir*, 11 (1977): 236–248;

Vsevolod Alekseevich Surganov, *Chelovek na zemle: Tema derevni v russkoi sovetskoi proze 50–70-kh godov. Istoki. Problemy. Kharaktery* (Moscow: Sovetskii pisatel', 1981), pp. 550–579;

Nadezhda Stepanovna Tenditnik, "'Iskusstvo – sluchivshaiasia real'nost': Voprosy khudozhestvennogo tvorchestva v publitsistike V. Rasputina," *Sibir'*, 1 (1980): 124–136;

Tenditnik, *Otvetstvennost' talanta: O tvorchestve Valentina Rasputina* (Irkutsk: Vostochno-Sibirskoe knizhnoe izdatel'stvo, 1978);

Tenditnik, "Starukha Anna i ee deti," *Sibir'*, 5 (1971): 99–105;

Tenditnik, *Valentin Rasputin: Kolokola trevogi* (Moscow: Golos, 1999);

Tenditnik, *Valentin Rasputin: Ocherk zhizni i tvorchestva* (Irkutsk: Irkutskoe universitetskoe knizhnoe izdatel'stvo, 1987);

Leonid Terakopian, "Blagodarnaia pamiat'. Povesti V. Rasputina," *Molodaia gvardiia*, 6 (1977): 250–271;

Terakopian, *Pafos preobrazheniia: Tema derevni v proze 50–70-kh godov* (Moscow: Khudozhestvennaia literatura, 1978);

V. Vasil'ev, "Radi istiny i dobra. Povesti V. Rasputina," *Nash sovremennik*, 6 (1976): 160–168;

Margaret Winchell, "'Live and Love': The Spiritual Path of Valentin Rasputin," *Slavic and East European Journal*, 31 (1987): 533–547;

P. V. Zabelin, "Russkii chelovek v proze V. Rasputina," in his *Literaturnyi raz"ezd (Razmyshleniia o tvorchestve irkutskikh pisatelei)* (Irkutsk: Vostochno-Sibirskoe knizhnoe izdatel'stvo, 1974), pp. 62–86;

R. S. Zueva, "Leksiko-stilisticheskii analiz povesti V. Rasputina 'Proshchanie s Materoi,'" in *Issledovaniia iazykovogo masterstva pisatelia*, edited by Kh. Kh. Makhmudov (Alma-Ata: Kazakhskii gosudarstvennyi universitet, 1984), pp. 80–93.

# Anatolii Naumovich Rybakov
*(14 January 1911 – 23 December 1994)*

Boris Lanin
*Russian Academy of Education, Moscow*

(Translated by Christine A. Rydel)

BOOKS: *Kortik: Povest'* (Moscow & Leningrad: Gosudarstvennoe izdatel'stvo Detskoi literatury, 1948); translated by David Skvirsky as *The Dirk: A Story* (Moscow: Foreign Languages Publishing House, 1954);

*Voditeli: Roman* (Moscow: Sovetskii pisatel', 1950);

*Ekaterina Voronina: Roman* (Moscow: Sovetskii pisatel', 1955);

*Bronzovaia ptitsa: Povest'* (Moscow: Gosudarstvennoe izdatel'stvo Detskoi literatury Ministerstva Prosveshcheniia RSFSR, 1957); translated by Skvirsky as *The Bronze Bird* (Moscow: Foreign Languages Publishing House, 1958);

*Kanikuly Krosha: Povest'* (Moscow: Detgiz, 1960);

*Prikliucheniia Krosha: Povest'* (Moscow: Detgiz, 1962);

*Leto v Sosniakakh: Roman* (Moscow: Sovetskii pisatel', 1965);

*Zapiski Krosha* (Moscow: Sovremennik, 1971)—comprises *Prikliucheniia Krosha*, *Kanikuly Krosha*, and *Neizvestnyi soldat*;

*Vystrel: Povest'* (Moscow: Detskaia literatura, 1976);

*Tiazhelyi pesok* (Moscow: Sovetskii pisatel', 1979); translated by Harold Shukman as *Heavy Sand* (London: Allen Lane, 1981; New York: Viking, 1981);

*Deti Arbata: Roman* (Moscow: Sovetskii pisatel', 1987); translated by Shukman as *Children of the Arbat* (Boston: Little, Brown, 1988; London: Hutchinson, 1988);

*Strakh: Tridtsat' piatyi i drugie gody. Roman* (Moscow: Sovetskii pisatel', 1990); translated by Antonina W. Bouis as *Fear* (Boston: Little, Brown, 1992; London: Hutchinson, 1993);

*Prakh i pepel: Roman* (Moscow: Terra, 1994); translated by Bouis as *Dust and Ashes* (Boston: Little, Brown, 1996; London: Hutchinson, 1996);

*Roman-vospominanie* (Moscow: Vagrius, 1997).

**Editions and Collections:** *Kortik; Bronzovaia ptitsa* (Alma-Ata: Kazuchpedgiz, 1960);

*Anatolii Naumovich Rybakov (from* Fear, *1992; Richland County Public Library, Columbia, South Carolina)*

*Voditeli; Ekaterina Voronona* (Moscow: Khudozhestvennaia literatura, 1964);

*Prikliucheniia Krosha; Kanikuly Krosha* (Moscow: Molodaia gvardiia, 1966);

*Povesti*, introduction by Ekaterina Vasil'evna Starikova (Moscow: Khudozhestvennaia literatura, 1969);

*Ekaterina Voronina: Roman*, introduction by Starikova (Moscow: Molodaia gvardiia, 1970);

*Voditeli; Ekaterina Voronina, Prikliucheniia Krosha, Kanikuly Krosha, Neizvestnyi soldat. Romany i povesti* (Moscow: Sovetskii pisatel', 1971);

*Voditeli; Ekaterina Voronina: Romany. Neizvestnyi soldat: Povest'* (Moscow: Voenizdat, 1972);

*Izbrannye proizvedeniia,* 2 volumes, introduction by Mikhail Matveevich Kuznetsov (Moscow: Khudozhestvennaia literatura, 1978);

*Sobranie sochinenii,* 4 volumes (Moscow: Sovetskaia Rossiia, 1981–1982);

*Kortik; Bronzovaia ptitsa* (Moscow: Stroiizdat, 1983);

*Prikliucheniia Krosha* (Moscow: Detskaia literatura, 1984)–comprises *Prikliucheniia Krosha, Kanikuly Krosha,* and *Neizvestnyi soldat;*

*Kortik; Bronzovaia ptitsa; Vystrel* (Moscow: Detskaia literatura, 1987);

*Sobranie sochinenii v semi tomakh,* 7 volumes (Moscow: Terra, 1995);

*Kortik; Bronzovaia ptitsa; Vystrel: Povesti* (St. Petersburg: Lenizdat, 1996);

*Sochineniia v dvukh tomakh,* 2 volumes (Moscow: Terra-knizhnyi Klub, 1998);

*Deti arbata: Trilogiia,* 3 volumes (Moscow: Terra, 1998)–comprises volume 1, *Deti Arbata;* volume 2, *Strakh;* and volume 3, *Prakh i pepel.*

PRODUCED SCRIPTS: *Ekaterina Voronina,* motion picture, adapted by Rybakov and Isidor Annensky from Rybakov's novel, Moskovskaia kinostudiia khudozhestvennykh fil'mov imeni, Gor'kogo, 1957;

*Priklyucheniya Krosha,* motion picture, Gorky Film Studio, 1961;

*Kortik,* television miniseries, adapted by Rybakov from his novel, 1973;

*Poslednee leto detstva,* television, adapted by Rybakov from his novels *Kortik* and *Bronzovaia ptitsa,* Belarusfil'm, 1974;

*Bronzovaya ptitsa,* television miniseries, adapted by Rybakov from his novel, Belarusfil'm/Soyuztelefil'm, 1974;

*Kanikuly Krosha,* television miniseries, adapted by Rybakov from his novel, Ekran, 1980;

*Neizvestnyj soldat,* television miniseries, adapted by Rybakov from his novel, Ekran, 1984;

*Voskresenye, polovina sedmogo,* television miniseries, Ekran, 1988.

OTHER: "Dlia detei i dlia vzroslykh," in *Vslukh pro sebia,* edited by A. I. Vislov and Fanni E. Ebin (Moscow: Detskaia literatura, 1975), pp. 324–349;

*Oslo Conference: The Anatomy of Hate,* contributions by Rybakov (New York: Elie Wiesel Foundation for Humanity, 1991).

SELECTED PERIODICAL PUBLICATIONS– UNCOLLECTED: "O vidennom i prochitannom," *Literaturnaia gazeta,* 7 (June 1950): 3;

"O rabote nad romanom 'Voditeli' i prodolzheniem povesti 'Kortik.' Otvet na anketu," *Literaturnaia gazeta,* 4 (January 1951): 4;

"Pisatel' i redaktor," *Literaturnaia gazeta,* 19 April 1956;

"Ne nado uspokaivat'!" *Literaturnaia gazeta,* 10 (May 1956): 4;

"O liudiakh, vkusakh i borodatykh studentakh," *Komsomol'skaia pravda,* 12 (April 1958): 4;

"Ostav' geroiu serdtse," *Voprosy literatury,* 1 (1972): 25–33.

Anatolii Naumovich Rybakov's major novel, *Deti Arbata* (1987; translated as *Children of the Arbat,* 1988), waited twenty years to be published in the era of *glasnost'* (openness). It appeared at a time when horrible truths about Russia's recent past were capturing the reading public, which had grown weary of the official propaganda that had made up much of Soviet Russian literature. An eyewitness to his age, Rybakov combines historical narrative with psychological portraiture to try to unravel the motives and consequences of Joseph Stalin's actions. Though some critics consider him not to be a writer of the first rank, Rybakov will be remembered as a witness to the horrors of the Great Terror and Stalin's cult of personality.

Rybakov was born on 14 January 1911 in Chernigov, Ukraine, to Naum Borisovich Aronov, a manager of distilleries, and Dina Avraamova Aronov. In his posthumously published memoir, *Roman-vospominanie* (1997, Novel-Reminiscence), Rybakov describes his father as a stern, unloving disciplinarian who left the family for a time; his memories of his mother are more tender and affectionate. But Rybakov's fondest recollections are of his maternal grandfather, Avraam Isaakovich Rybakov, an elder in the synagogue and a kind and generous man who loved to help people who were in trouble. He adopted his grandfather's surname as his own after *Kortik* was published in 1948.

In 1919 the family moved to Moscow, where the father became an important Soviet engineer; they lived in an apartment in building 51 on the Arbat, a street that was the center of a bohemian and literary district. Rybakov and his sister, Raisa, learned French from two teachers who lived with the family at different times; Rybakov then attended the Khvorostovskaia Gymnasium and, for his final two years, an experimental demonstration commune-school run by the noted Soviet pedagogue Moisei Mikhailovich Pestrak. After completing his schooling, Rybakov worked as a loader and then as a driver at the Dorogomilovsky Chemical Plant. In the fall of 1930 he enrolled at the Moscow Transportation Economic Institute (formerly the Moscow Institute of Transport Engineers).

*Rybakov in 1933, the year he was expelled from the Moscow Transportation Economic Institute and arrested for engaging in counter-revolutionary activities (*Roman–vospominanie, *1997; Eckstrom Library, University of Louisville)*

On 5 November 1933 Rybakov was expelled from the institute and arrested for engaging in counterrevolutionary activities; his "crimes" seem to have been the publishing of humorous antiworker poems in the school paper. In 1934 he was sentenced by the Special Commission of the NKVD (Narodnyi komissariat vnutrennykh del [People's Commissariat for Internal Affairs]) under political statute 58-10 (counterrevolutionary agitation and propaganda) to three years in Siberia. After completing his sentence he was forbidden to live in any of the one hundred largest Soviet cities; he traveled from town to town and supported himself with jobs such as driving trucks and teaching ballroom dancing. While in exile he wrote stories about the French Revolution and reminiscences of his childhood on the Arbat and of his school years; he never published them.

In 1940 Rybakov married Anastasia (Asia) Alekseevna Tysiachnikova in Riazan. Their son, Aleksandr, was born soon afterward. As the German army approached Moscow in October 1941, Rybakov's wife, son, and parents were evacuated to Dzhambul in the Kazakh Soviet Socialist Republic. Rybakov served in the Eighth Army of the Guards under Marshall Vasilii Ivanovich Chuikov, taking part in battles from the defense of Moscow to the capture of Berlin in 1945. On 19 October 1945 a military tribunal expunged his criminal record. Having entered the army as a private, he was demobilized in 1946 with the rank of major after serving as chief of the army automobile service. In *Roman-vospominanie,* Rybakov confesses to having been unfaithful to his wife during the war with his "true love," a "beautiful blue-eyed brunette" named Marina, whom he met in Saratov just before he was sent to fight at Stalingrad. After leaving the army Rybakov moved back in with his parents on the Arbat in 1946, placing his wife and son in an apartment in the Fili district of Moscow; in his memoirs Rybakov says that he had grown tired of Marina and wanted his freedom. He continued to see her after they parted, but they never married. Rybakov continued to support his wife and son, and Aleksandr spent summers with him in Peredel'kino, the writers' colony near Moscow where he wrote most of his books.

Rybakov was always an avid reader; his favorite authors were Aleksandr Pushkin, Mikhail Lermontov, Nikolai Gogol', Leo Tolstoy, Anton Chekhov, Vladimir Maiakovsky, Sergei Esenin, Honoré de Balzac, Stendahl (Marie-Henri Beyle), and Guy de Maupassant. In 1946 he bought an Olympia typewriter and began to write the *povest'* (novella) *Kortik* (translated as *The Dirk: A Story,* 1954); he finished it in 1947, and it was published in 1948. Beginning with *Kortik,* all of Rybakov's works are distinguished by their dynamic plots. He says in *Roman-vospominanie:* "In prose, the plot is not the revelation of a secret, but a joining of fates, circumstances of life; the interrelationships of the characters, the development of character, an internal yearning, which does not allow the reader to lay aside the book." *Kortik* is an adventure story for children set in the 1920s in which twelve-year-old Misha Poliakov and two fellow members of the Communist youth group Young Pioneers solve the mystery of a secret message hidden in the handle of a dagger belonging to a Red Army officer. Rybakov adapted the novel as a 1973 television miniseries.

In 1950 Rybakov published *Voditeli* (Drivers), a typical Soviet "industrial novel" that demonstrates his understanding of automobiles and reflects his experiences as a driver. Compared to other production novels it stands out because of the charming, intelligent, and energetic hero, Mikhail Poliakov, the grown-up protagonist from *Kortik.* The work received many laudatory reviews, and Rybakov was nominated for the Stalin Prize for it. During the deliberations of the prize committee it was revealed that Rybakov had been "repressed"–arrested and exiled–but thanks to the intervention of the poet Aleksei Aleksandrovich Surkov and the novelist Aleksandr Aleksandrovich Fadeev, who were on the prize committee, Rybakov was awarded the Stalin Prize.

In 1950 Rybakov met twenty-one-year-old Tat'iana Markovna; her father had been an assistant to the Communist Party official and Soviet statesman Anastas Mikoyan but had been "liquidated" during the Stalinist purges. Thus, Tat'iana was considered the daughter of "an enemy of the people." When the two met again in Moscow in 1953, Tat'iana was the wife of poet Yevgenii Mikhailovich Vinokurov and the mother of a two-year-old girl. When they met yet again, this time in the Crimea, more than twenty years after their first encounter, Tat'iana became Rybakov's wife, companion, critic, and adviser.

In 1955 Rybakov wrote a novel with the working title "Odinokaia zhenshchina" (Lonely Woman); it was published the same year as *Ekaterina Voronina*. The title character is a young widow who becomes the captain of a Volga River steamboat. A movie version, with a screenplay by Rybakov and the director, Isidor Annensky, appeared in 1957; it was broadcast nationwide on Russian television for the first time in 2002.

In 1956 Rybakov published *Bronzovaia ptitsa* (translated as *The Bronze Bird*, 1958), a sequel to *Kortik*, in the magazine *Ionust'* (Youth); it appeared in book form in 1957. The idea for the work came from a marble inkstand decorated with a bronze bird that stood on Rybakov's desk; the stand broke when he was moving to a new residence, and he saw that the bird was hollow. The thought occurred to him that the bird would be a good hiding place. In this work Misha Poliakov has become a Young Pioneer leader.

Rybakov was officially fully "rehabilitated" from his alleged crimes of the 1930s on 19 January 1960. In the 1960s and early 1970s he wrote a popular series of works for children and youths about Sergei Krasheninnikov, nicknamed "Krosh": *Prikliucheniia Krosha* (1962, Krosh's Adventures), *Kanikuly Krosha* (1960, Krosh's School Holidays), and *Neizvestnyi soldat* (Unknown Soldier), which was first published in *Iunost'* in 1970 and collected in the volume *Prikliucheniia Krosha* (Krosha Sketches) in 1971. Rybakov's novel *Leto v Sosniakakh* (Summer in Sosniaki) was published in the magazine *Novyi mir* (New World) in 1964 and in book form the following year; it deals with the moral conflict between two protagonists, Kolchin and Angeliuk. He returned to the 1920s and the Arbat in the novella *Vystrel* (1976, The Shot).

Rybakov wrote *Tiazhelyi pesok* (translated as *Heavy Sand*, 1981) between 1975 and 1977; it was first published in the journal *Oktiabr'* (October) in 1978 and appeared in book form in 1979. The novel portrays several generations of a Ukrainian Jewish family from 1910 through 1943, culminating during the Holocaust; the author's maternal grandfather is the prototype for one of the main protagonists, Avraam Rakhlenko. Forced into a ghetto, the Jews stage an uprising, and some of the insurrectionists survive and escape. Avraam's forty-nine-year-old mother, Rakhil' Rakhlenko, remains behind with those who are too emaciated and enfeebled to leave. She saves four hundred people, but she herself

> disappeared, melted, dissolved into air in the pine forest near the little town where she was born, lived her life; where she loved and had been loved; where, in spite of all adversities, she had been happy, gave birth to her children, raised her grandsons, witnessed their horrible ends; she bore what no single human heart could withstand. But her heart bore it, and in the very last moments of her life, she could become a mother for all of the unfortunate and deprived people, and set them on the path of battle and a worthy death.

Over the communal grave of those shot by the Nazis a black granite obelisk is placed, on which are inscribed in Hebrew letters words roughly taken from the Bible: "Everything is forgiven, but those who have shed innocent blood will never be forgiven." Another inscription is in Russian: "Eternal memory to those sacrificed by the German-Fascist invaders." Because of government anti-Semitism, Soviet critics were cautious in their assessments of the novel. Discussing it in 1988, Kaleriia Ozerova does not even use the phrase "Jewish people," substituting instead "dannaia natsional'naia obshchnost'" (a given ethnic community).

The work that brought Rybakov worldwide praise was the novel *Deti Arbata,* the first volume in a trilogy; Rybakov had originally intended to write seven novels tracing the fates of seven childhood friends from the Arbat and covering the period from 1934 to the Twentieth Communist Party Congress in 1956 at which Stalin was denounced; the novels were to be linked by the presence of the autobiographical character Sasha Pankratov. He chose 1934 as the starting point because for him that year, which began with the party "Congress of Victors"—the majority of whom were repressed in 1937–1938—and ended with the murder of Leningrad party leader Sergei Mironovich Kirov that Stalin used as the pretext for launching the Great Terror, signified the moment of moral choice for his characters: they could uphold the values they received in their Arbat childhood or betray those values and enter the service of those in power. Rybakov wanted to show the psychological mechanism of such a choice.

*Deti Arbata* was twice accepted for publication during the Leonid Brezhnev era: in July 1966 the cover of *Novyi mir* announced that it would be published in 1967, and *Oktiabr'* promised that it would appear in 1979; but both times it was withdrawn. The serialization of the novel in the April, May, and June 1987 issues of *Druzhba narodov* (Friendship of Nations) was a major step in the final de-Stalinization of the Soviet Union. Although Aleksandr Solzhenitsyn's *Arkhipelag GULag, 1918–1956* (1973–1975; translated as *The Gulag Archipelago, 1918–1956: An Experiment in Literary Investigation,* 1974–1978), Georgii Nikolaevich Vladimov's *Vernyi Ruslan: Istoriia karaul'noi sobaki* (1975; translated as *Faithful Ruslan: The Story of a Guard Dog,* 1979), and Vasilii Semenovich Grossman's *Zhizn' i sud'ba* (1980; translated as *Life and Fate,* 1985) had already been published, *Deti Arbata* was for many Russians the first revelation of the Great Terror because it first appeared in a popular literary journal.

*Deti Arbata* is set entirely during 1934 and is structured as the moral opposition of two main protagonists: Sasha Pankratov and Joseph Stalin. In a 1987 interview Rybakov told Nadezhda Zheleznova:

> In this novel it was important for me to stylize the narration as a documentary chronicle of the time: on the one hand, concrete signs of the character and life of Moscow under renewal (recall how they removed the tram cars from the Arbat and that the "Moscow" hotel was under construction? . . .); on the other hand, the natural forces of history, the natural forces of character, in which will, love of honor, and passion for unlimited power took on monstrous, ugly forms. I tried to have unexpected "montage-like junctions" appear in the seemingly self-contained plot and stylistic layers of the novel: Moscow and the little village of Mozgova, the study in the Kremlin and the godforsaken wilderness of the forest, into which my hero Sasha Pankratov falls to escape his sorrow and lack of faith in the future. . . . In the conflict, in the clashes and "exchange of messages" among the most disparate characters, there were to have appeared rings of fateful years which had tightened around the throat of our common lot.

Like his creator, Sasha Pankratov is a student at the Moscow Transport Economic Institute who is arrested for a school newspaper prank and some other minor acts of insubordination and sentenced to three years of exile in Siberia. In Sasha, Rybakov creates a hero who is a real person, not just a mouthpiece for the author's ideas: he believes in God and sins, falls in love and becomes disenchanted, studies, works, drinks, has fun, travels, and fights. Through Sasha's eyes, provincial Russia opens up to the reader.

The real revelation for Russian readers at the time of the publication of the novel was the character of Stalin. Two generations had not lived under Stalin's rule; after decades of an underground struggle for the rehabilitation of Stalin's image, the widespread view was that Stalin was a great historical figure who occasionally made mistakes: the builder of the metro system, the victor in World War II, the creator of the atomic bomb. Before *Deti Arbata* no history textbook, novel, or movie existed that portrayed Stalin as the paranoid, megalomaniacal tyrant that he was or that could help people imagine the horror and lawlessness of his reign. To give a sense of the awe in which Stalin was held, he uses all-capital letters for all pronouns referring to the dictator, as is usually done in Russian only in the case of God.

One of the most successful scenes in the novel is Stalin's conversation with his dentist:

> Lipman remained silent.
> "Did they forbid you to speak?" Stalin grinned ironically.
> Lipman remained silent.
> "Who forbade you?"
> Lipman remained silent.
> "Tovstukha?"
> Lipman nodded in a barely noticeable way.
> "So here's the way it is," said Stalin impressively, "just bear this in mind: one MAY tell Comrade Stalin everything, one MUST tell Comrade Stalin everything, it is IMPOSSIBLE TO HIDE ANYTHING from Comrade Stalin. Sooner or later Comrade Stalin will know the truth."

To expose the state of mind behind Stalin's monstrous actions, Rybakov uses interior monologue:

> For this millions perished—history will forgive this. He even accomplished a second revolution—he put Russia on the path of productive, industrial growth; he transformed her into a contemporary, industrial, mighty military government. He transformed her with a high cost, many lives were lost for [this cause]—even for this will history forgive Comrade Stalin; but history would not forgive him had he kept Russia weak and helpless before the face of her enemies. Now he must create a new, special apparatus of power. And destroy the old. Destruction of the old apparatus must begin with those who have already come out against HIM,—with Zinov'ev, Kamenev; they are more vulnerable, they have fought against the Party; and they have already admitted so many of their mistakes that they will admit even more, they will admit to whatever is necessary. And no one will dare to defend them, even Kirov will not dare.

When the April issue of *Druzhba narodov* came out, more than sixty publishing houses around the world bid for the right to publish translations of *Deti Arbata*. In the Soviet Union the initial pressrun for the book version, published the same year, totaled 1.5 million copies.

The publication of *Deti Arbata* elicited a wide range of reactions. Lev Aleksandrovich Anninsky said in *Oktiabr'* for October 1987 that Rybakov had struck the "nerve of the spiritual process that is going on in people now, at the end of the twentieth century"; in the same

*Frontispiece and title page of Rybakov's* Deti Arbata *(1987), translated in 1988 as* Children of the Arbat. *This first novel in his acclaimed trilogy is set in 1934, beginning with the Communist "Congress of Victors" and ending with the murder of Kirov, signalling the beginning of the Great Terror (Eckstrom Library, University of Louisville).*

issue Anatolii Georgievich Bocharov claimed that the author succeeded in portraying not only historical figures but the general mood of the period; in the June 1988 issue of *Literaturnoe obozrenie* (The Literary Review) Igor' Zolotussky exclaimed, "we are all children of the Arbat." On the other hand, Alla Nikolaevna Latynina wrote in *Znamia* (The Banner) for December 1987: "The fate of things shaded with ideology will not survive the test of time. The sharpness of the problems may turn out to be taken as simple circumstance; the ideas that today seem to be new, tomorrow will become commonplace.... The characters of Rybakov's novel are not sufficiently full-blooded to have pretensions for a long life in the reader's consciousness." Critics of the "populist" bent came out harshly against the novel. Valerii Khatiushin voiced the pro-Stalinist position in *Molodaia gvardiia* (The Young Guard) for February 1989, claiming that the children of the Arbat were "the center of the circle of intellectualizing do-nothings, torn from life and from the people, who, calling themselves nonconformists, have lost faith in everything: in Russia, in the people, in themselves."

The second novel in the *Deti Arbata* trilogy, *Strakh: Tridtsat' piatyi i drugie gody* (1990; *Fear: The Thirty-fifth and Other Years*, translated as *Fear*, 1992) divides its focus among Sasha in exile, his mother and friends in the Arbat, and Stalin's conduct of the Great Terror. The third volume, *Prakh i pepel* (1994; translated as *Dust and Ashes*, 1996) carries Sasha from exile in a provincial town to rehabilitation as a tank commander in World War II.

In his final years Rybakov became disenchanted with Mikhail Gorbachev because of what he perceived as disparities between the words and actions of the Soviet president. Rybakov's son, Aleksandr, who had became a journalist after graduating from Moscow University and marrying the literary critic Natal'ia Borisovna Ivanova, died of liver failure in 1994 at the age of fifty-three. Rybakov died in New York City, where he lived for the last two years of his life, on 23 December of the same year. He is buried in Moscow, and a memorial plaque hangs on the facade of his former home on the Arbat.

In his *Roman-vospominanie,* published posthumously in 1997, Rybakov presents himself as a basically happy person but, at the same time, as a tragic figure: his major book could have done much to change the consciousness of the people twenty years earlier than it did, had it been published when first scheduled. The memoir goes beyond his personal life to provide valuable information about the technical aspects of his literary creations, his work on well-known pieces, his problems with censors, and many previously unknown events that touched on the publication of some of his works. No less important are his musings on the historical fate of Russia, human nature, and the psychology and philosophy of the craft of writing.

For Anatolii Naumovich Rybakov the highest human value was integrity, and the highest human virtue was truthfulness. In his works Rybakov brings to judgment the leaders who, in his view, led Russia to destruction. Rybakov called for honesty in an era when honesty had lost much of its meaning.

**Interviews:**

Leonid Vladlenovich Bakhnov, "Pamiat' i vymysel," *Voprosy literatury,* 5 (1980): 102–124;

John Schillinger, "Interview with Anatolij Rybakov," *Russian Language Journal,* 41 (1987): 191–201;

Nadezhda Leopol'dovna Zheleznova, "Eto, soglasites', postupok," *Literaturnoe obozrenie,* 9 (1987): 38–43;

A. Zotikov, "Interv'iu posle poezdki: Rabotat' na perestroiku," *Literaturnaia gazeta,* 49 (7 December 1988): 7;

Leonid Bakhnov, "U menia net drugogo vykhoda," *Druzhba narodov,* 9 (1989): 262–270;

Irina Rishina, "Zarubki na serdtse: Poslednee moskovskoe interv'iu," *Druzhba narodov,* 3 (1999): 173–181;

Solomon Volkov, "Razgovor s Anatoliem Rybakovym," *Druzhba narodov,* 1 (2000): 191–206.

**Bibliography:**

Zinovii Samoilovich Papernyi, "Anatolii Rybakov," *Russkie pisateli i prozaiki, Bibliograficheskii ukazatel',* 4 (1966): 240–255.

**References:**

Lev Aleksandrovich Anninsky, "Pochva, vozdukh, sud'ba," *Novyi mir,* 1 (1983): 248–258;

Aleksandr Borisovich Aronov, "The Arbat of the Fathers: Comments on Anatolii Rybakov's New Novel," *Soviet Studies in Literature: A Journal of Translations,* 25 (Winter 1988–1989): 42–54;

Aleksandr Adol'fovich Bek, "O pravde," *Voprosy literatury,* 1 (1972): 33–40;

Bek, "Po sledu ottsov," *Novyi mir,* 12 (1970): 254–257;

Anna Samoilovna Berzer, "Taina Kortika i pobeda Krosha," *Oktiabr',* 1 (1961): 120–121;

Iurii Boldyrev, "Bol'she chem professiia: Chelovek, trud, vremia v proizvedeniiakh Anatoliia Rybakova," *Oktiabr',* 2 (February 1983): 192–198;

Grigorii Abramovich Brovman, "Vazhnaia zadacha sovremennogo romana," in *Russkaia Sovetskaia Literatura 1954–1955 gg. Materialy nauchnykh sessii Instituta mirovoi literatury imeni A. M. Gor'kogo* (Moscow: Akademii nauk SSSR, 1956), pp. 376–385;

"Chitatel'skaia konferentsiia po knige A. Rybakova *Voditeli,*" *Sovetskii voin,* 11 (1951): 19–22;

Nina Ivanovna Dikushina, "Neskol'ko zamechanii i romane A. Rybakova i povesti S. Georgievskoi," in *Russkaia Sovetskaia Literatura 1954–1955 gg. Materialy nauchnykh sessii Instituta mirovoi literatury imeni A. M. Gor'kogo* (Moscow: Akademii nauk SSSR, 1956), pp. 386–390;

M. Eidelman, "Indestructibility: A Review of Anatolii Rybakov's Novel *Heavy Sand,*" *Soviet Studies in Literature,* 15, no. 4 (1979): 91–98;

Iakov Efimovich El'sberg, *O besspornom i spornom* (Moscow: Sovetskii pisatel', 1959), pp. 160–161;

Vladimir Vladimirovich Ermilov, *Izbrannye raboty, v trekh tomakh,* volume 3 (Moscow: Goslitizdat, 1956), pp. 317–319;

Ermilov, "Novoe v nashei zhizni i literatura," *Pravda,* 4 November 1950;

Leonid Fink, "Stoit li soglashattsa? (Otkrytoe pis'mo A. Rybakovu)," *Voprosy literatury,* 1 (1972): 20–25;

"Free Thought and Free Action," *Soviet Literature,* 8 (1988): 10–16;

I. Gommlikh, "Spor vokrug romana 'Deti Arbata' v zerkale sovetskoi literaturnoi kritiki," *Zeitschrift für Slawistik,* 35, no. 3 (1990): 395–402;

David Gurewich, "Glasnost, Ho!" *New Criterion,* 7 (September 1988): 77–81;

Adel' Alekseevna Ivanova and V. K. Pukhiikov, "Problema chelovecheskogo sushchestvovaniia v romane A. Rybakova *Deti Arbata,*" *Voprosy filosofii,* 12 (1988): 97–112;

Nataliia Borisovna Ivanova, "Ottsy i deti epokhi," *Voprosy literatury,* 11 (1987): 50–83;

Ivanova, *Tochka zreniia: O proze poslednikh let* (Moscow: Sovetskii pisatel', 1988);

Ivanova, "Vol'noe dykhanie," *Voprosy literatury,* 3 (1983): 179–213;

Vladimir V. Kavtorin and Vadim V. Chubinsky, "Roman i istoriia (dialog v pis'makh)," *Neva,* 3 (1988): 156–175;

Zoia S. Kedrina, "O nekotorykh voprosakh sovremennogo literaturnogo protsessa," in *Russkaia Sovetskaia Literatura 1954–1955 gg. Materialy nauchnykh sessii Instituta mirovoi literatury imeni A. M. Gor'kogo* (Moscow: Akademii nauk SSSR, 1956), pp. 364–365;

Vadim Valerianovich Kozhinov, "Pravda i istina," *Nash sovremennik,* 4 (1988): 160–175;

Mikhail Matveevich Kuznetsov, "Ekaterina Voronina i drugie," *Komsomol'skaia pravda,* 15 June 1955, p. 4;

Anatolii Petrovich Lanshchikov, "My vse gliadim v Napoleony," *Nash sovremennik,* 2 (1988): 106–142;

Alla Nikolaevna Latynina, "Luchshii vymysel-pravda," *Literaturnaia gazeta,* 10 September 1997, p. 11;

Latynina, "Vzgliad iz segodnia: Zametki po povodu romana Anatoliia Rybakova 'Tridtsat' piatyi i drugie gody,'" *Literaturnaia gazeta,* 14 December 1988, p. 4;

Latynina, *Za otkrytym shlagbaumom* (Moscow: Sovetskii pisatel', 1991), pp. 171–179;

Genrikh Morisovich Lenobl', "Geroika povsednevnogo truda," *Novyi mir,* 10 (1950): 241–244;

Rosalind Marsh, *Images of Dictatorship: Portraits of Stalin in Literature* (London & New York: Routledge, 1989);

Sigrid McLaughlin, "Rybakov's *Deti Arbata:* Reintegrating Stalin into Soviet History," *Slavic Review,* 50 (Spring 1991): 90–99;

Vazif Meilanov, "Who'd Like to Speak?" *Index on Censorship,* 17 (October 1988): 19–21;

Igor' Pavlovich Motiashov, "Interesnee vsiakoi skazki (Zametki o sovremennoi detskoi literature)," *Sibirskie ogni,* 2 (1962): 185–187;

Andrei Semenovich Nemzer, "Vremia kadrovoi revoliutsii," *Oktiabr',* 1 (January 1989): 202–205;

Galina Evgenievna Nikolaeva, "Sovetskii chelovek 1950 goda," *Literaturnaia gazeta,* 4 November 1950;

Armen Oganesian, "Samaia bol'shaia tsennost'—pravda," *Literaturnaia Armeniia,* 2 (February 1988): 65–72;

Kaleria Nikolaevna Ozerova, *Sovetskie pisateli-prozaiki (kratkie biografii)* (Moscow: Russkii iazyk, 1988), pp. 227–234;

Zinovii Samuilovich Papernyi, "Krosh rasskazyvaet," *Znamia,* 3 (1961): 204–207;

Papernyi, "Zhizn' v trude," *Znamia,* 6 (1950): 179–186;

Lev Emmanuilovich Razgon, "Anatolii Rybakov: 'Neizvestnyi soldat' (K sporam o novoi povesti A. Rybakova)," in *Knigi—detiam: Sbornik materialov v pomoshch' uchiteliam, bibliotekariam i pionerskim vozhatym,* edited by V. IA. Meerzon and G. V. Patynskaia (Moscow: Detskaia literatura, 1972), pp. 59–66;

Boris Sergeevich Riurikov, *Literatura i zhizn'* (Moscow: Sovetskii pisatel', 1963), pp. 162–172;

Riurikov, "Schastie tvorchestva," *Pravda,* 15 July 1950, p. 4;

Gary Rosenshield, "Socialist Realism and the Holocaust: Jewish Life and Death in Anatoly Rybakov's *Heavy Sand*," *PMLA: Publication of the Modern Language Association,* 111, no. 2 (1996): 240–255;

Natalya Rubinshtein, "Glasnost Bestseller," *Index on Censorship,* 17 (October 1988): 18–19;

Evgenii Shklovsky, "Samoe glavnoe," *Literaturnoe obozrenie,* 11 (1987): 20–21;

O. L. Smaryl, "Stalin's Revolution," *Encounter,* 72 (March 1989): 34–36;

Vera Vasil'evna Smirnova, "Sbyvaettsa mechta detstva: O Rybakove i ego knigakh," *Detskaia literatura,* 1 (1971): 18–22;

Ekaterina Vasil'evna Starikova, *Anatolii Rybakov, ocherk tvorchestva* (Moscow: Detskaia literatura, 1977);

Starikova, "Muzhestvo profesii: Anatoliiu Rybakovu—70 let," *Oktiabr',* 1 (January 1981): 215–218;

Starikova, "Tvorcheskii put' Anatoliia Rybakova," in Rybakov, *Povesti* (Moscow: Sovetskii pisatel', 1969), pp. 3–20;

Starikova, "V piatnadtsat' let," *Novyi mir,* 1 (1961): 250–252;

Ireneusz Szarycz, "The Red Avalanche: Anatolii Rybakov's *Children of the Arbat* and Alexander Weissberg's *The Accused*," *Germano-Slavica,* 7, no. 2/8, no. 3 (1992/1993): 83–95;

Leonid Aramovich Terakopian, "Zavershenie spora, ili Vse snachala," *Literaturnoe obozrenie,* 1 (1996): 39–47;

Iurii Valentinovich Trifonov, "Zrelost' talanta," *Literaturnaia Rossiia,* 5 February 1971, p. 9;

Andrei Mikhailovich Turkov, "'Chtoby plyt' v revoliutsiiu dal'she'," *Literaturnaia gazeta,* 6 July 1987, p. 4;

Shamil' Gamidovich Umerov, ed., *S raznykh tochek zreniia: Deti Arbata Anatoliia Rybakova* (Moscow: Sovetskii pisatel', 1990);

Andrei Upit, "Roman A. Rybakova Voditeli," *Oktiabr',* 3 (March 1951): 182–184;

Dmitrii Mikhailovich Urnov, "Peremeny i mneniia," *Voprosy literatury,* 8 (1988): 26–47.

**Papers:**

Letters of Anatolii Naumovich Rybakov are in the records of the Am-Rus Literary Agency, a literary agency for Soviet writers seeking publication or theatrical production in the United States in affiliation with the Copyright Agency of the Union of Soviet Socialist Republics (Vsesoiuznoe agentstvo po avtorskim pravam [VAAP]), 1927–1990, in the Manuscript Division of the Library of Congress.

# Varlam Tikhonovich Shalamov
*(18 June 1907 – 17 January 1982)*

Janet Tucker
*University of Arkansas*

BOOKS: *Ognivo* [censored edition] (Moscow: Sovetskii pisatel', 1961);

*Shelest list'ev* (Moscow: Sovetskii pisatel', 1964);

*Doroga i sud'ba* (Moscow: Sovetskii pisatel', 1967);

*Kolymskie rasskazy,* with an introduction by Mikhail Geller (London: Overseas Publication Interchange, 1978); translated by John Glad as *Kolyma Tales* (New York: Norton, 1980); republished as *Graphite,* translated by Glad (New York: Norton, 1981);

*"Such'ia" voina: Ocherki prestupnogo mira* (Moscow: Pravda, 1989);

*Chetvertaia Vologda,* compiled, with an introduction, by Valerii V. Esipov (Vologda: Grifon, 1994);

*Neskol'ko moikh zhiznei* (Moscow: Respublika, 1996).

**Editions and Collections:** *Doroga i sud'ba* (Moscow: Sovetskii pisatel', 1967);

*Moskovskie oblaka* (Moscow: Sovetskii pisatel', 1972);

*Tochka kipeniia* (Moscow: Sovetskii pisatel', 1977);

*Shokovaia terapiia* (London: Overseas Publications Interchange, 1978; Khabarovsk: Khabarovskoe knizhnoe izdatel'stvo, 1990);

*Kolymskie rasskazy* (Paris: YMCA-Press, 1982);

*Kolymskie rasskazy* (Paris: YMCA-Press, 1985);

*Voskreshenie listvennitsy* (Paris: YMCA-Press, 1985);

*Stikhotvoreniia* (Moscow: Sovetskii pisatel', 1988);

*Levyi bereg* (Moscow: Sovremennik, 1989);

*Vishera. Antiroman* (Moscow: Orbita, 1989);

*Voskreshenie listvennitsy,* 2 volumes (Moscow: Khudozhestvennaia literatura, 1989);

*Vishera. Antiroman . . . Butyrskaia tiur'ma . . . Perchatka, ili KR-2* (Moscow: Orbita, 1990);

*Kolymskie rasskazy* (Cheliabinsk: Iuzhno-Ural'skoe knizhnoe izdatel'stvo, 1991);

*Kolymskie rasskazy* (Moscow: Russkaia kniga, 1992);

*Kolymskie tetradi* (Moscow: Versty, 1994);

*Shalamovskii sbornik* (Vologda: Izdatel'stvo Instituta povyshenniia kvalifikatsii i perepodgotovski pedagogicheskikh kadrov, 1994– );

*Varlam Tikhonovich Shalamov (from* Voskreshenie listvennitsy, *1989; Jean and Alexander Heard Library, Vanderbilt University)*

*Sobranie sochinenii,* 4 volumes (Moscow: Khudozhestvennaia literatura / Moscow: Vagrius, 1998).

**Edition in English:** *Kolyma Tales,* 2 volumes, translated by John Glad (London & New York: Penguin, 1994).

OTHER: "Varlam Shalamov: Proza, stikhi. Publikatsiia i podgotovka teksta I. P. Sirotinskoi," *Novyi mir,* 6 (June 1988): 106–151;

"Vospominaniia. Podgotovka teksta i publikatsiia I. Sirotinskoi," *Znamia,* 4 (April 1993): 114–170;

"Iz zapisnykh knizhek. Publikatsiia, vstupitel'naia zametka i primechaniia Iriny Sirotinskoi," *Znamia*, 6 (June 1995): 134–175.

In his code of belief, his sufferings as a prisoner, and his prosaic and poetic references to his overwhelming experiences, Varlam Shalamov was the archetypical representative of the terrifying events that were endemic in the Soviet Union during the rule of Joseph Stalin. He left fictionalized accounts of what ranks as one of the most horrific series of events to blight the twentieth century: the Great Terror in the Soviet Union, with millions sentenced to prison camps in the gulag (an acronym for Glavnoe Upravlenie ispravitel'no-trudovykh Lagerei [Prison Camp system]). Because, as one of its most thorough and faithful witnesses, Shalamov was able to record firsthand the enormity of the terror, his work–especially the short stories for which he is renowned–is central to a knowledge and understanding of the abhorrent excesses of Soviet rule, particularly during Stalin's hegemony. Shalamov is the author of six cycles of short stories–under the collective title *Kolymskie rasskazy* (1978; translated as *Kolyma Tales*, 1980)–which are about his seventeen years spent in the gulag and, subsequently, in exile. The cycles are not differentiated by any clear-cut themes, and the titles that Shalamov gave them appear to be arbitrary. The cycles of these approximately 150 stories (in essence miniature sketches that are distinct from one another yet, at the same time, related) are titled: "Kolymskie rasskazy" (Kolyma Tales) "Levyi bereg" (translated as "The Left Bank"), "Artist lopaty" (translated as "The Artist of the Shovel"), "Ocherki prestupnogo mira" (translated as "Sketches of the Criminal World"), "Voskreshenie listvennitsy" (translated as "The Resurrected Larches"), and "Perchatka, ili KR-2" (translated as "The Glove, or KR-2").

In addition to his short stories and his only play, *Anna Ivanovna* (1989, *Teatr*), Shalamov also wrote lyric poetry and literary criticism–important vehicles for understanding his principal work, which was prose fiction (although in actuality he considered himself primarily a poet). While a good portion of his work remained unpublished in the Soviet Union during his lifetime, a four-volume edition of his collected works, including his prose fiction, plays, poetry, correspondence, and essays, finally appeared in Moscow in 1998.

The last of five children, Varlam Tikhonovich Shalamov was born on 18 June 1907 in the northern Russian city of Vologda, traditionally a place of exile. He was the son of Tikhon Nikolaevich Shalamov, an Orthodox priest who had performed missionary work in Alaska, and Nadezhda Aleksandrovna Shalamova, a schoolteacher. Shalamov was much closer to his mother than to his father, a complex and difficult individual whom the son closely resembled in character. A rebel who railed against transgressions, much in the manner of the seventeenth-century archpriest Avvakum Petrovich, Tikhon Nikolaevich fought unreservedly against the "sins" of the day, against alcoholism, the excesses of the flesh, and even anti-Semitism, engaging thereby in the sorts of mutinous and unpopular actions that set an example for his son to follow later in adult life. The complex pattern of independence, rebelliousness, and subsequent martyrdom, which had an esteemed pedigree in Russian cultural life reaching back to Avvakum's life and work, constituted an ultimate model for the father and, especially, for the son.

Shalamov displayed an avid interest in literature from his earliest childhood. He was drawn to widely different Russian authors, such as the peasant poet Nikolai Alekseevich Kliuev and the ego-futurist Igor Severianin, and to Western writers, such as Alexandre Dumas, Jules Verne, James Fenimore Cooper, and Arthur Conan Doyle. During his youth he also wrote critical essays on the symbolist poets Konstantin Dmitrievich Bal'mont and Aleksandr Aleksandrovich Blok, demonstrating thereby a keen interest in avant-garde contemporary literary movements and in poetry as well as in prose. The rebelliousness that Shalamov took from his father and his precocious fascination with literature constituted the twin poles of his adult life and later found intense expression in his short stories and verse. Shalamov's broad reading and his appreciation of both Western and Russian authors provided him with important literary models for his own future career as a writer, while his horrifying experiences in the camps furnished him with the subject matter.

In his late teens, after completing secondary school, Shalamov decided to leave Vologda. He opted to go to Moscow, then the center of contemporary Russian life, and he moved there in 1926. He immersed himself in the political and cultural activities of the capital. Building on his earlier literary efforts, he prepared himself for his coming career–and much-anticipated future glory–as a prose writer and poet. He was especially interested in the work of the cubo-futurists and the constructivist poets but was also attracted to the verse of Boris Leonidovich Pasternak, particularly after reading *Sestra moia zhizn'* (1922; translated as *My Sister Life and Other Poems*, 1976). Years later the two even developed a relationship when Shalamov was once again free to live on the "mainland."

Later in 1926, during a period of open enrollment, Shalamov matriculated in the Department of Soviet Law at Moscow State University. He studied not only law but also literature, and he was considered to have much promise as a writer. Disappointed and dis-

*Shalamov, age one. He was the youngest of his parents' five children (from* Chetvertaia Vologda, *1994; Jean and Nathan Heard Library, Vanderbilt University).*

mayed by the petty squabbles infesting the literary groups that dominated Moscow during the 1920s, Shalamov attempted instead to play a significant role in the events of the time, and he switched to actual political organizations to channel his energies. In 1927–1929 he made the unwise choice of joining an underground Trotskyist cell, consisting of Komsomol (Communist Youth) members. Such participation was incredibly dangerous during this period; Stalin was in the process of consolidating his rule, and Leon Trotsky had already fallen from power. Shalamov even took part in a political demonstration in November 1927 on Manezhnaia ploshchad' in Moscow and was placed under arrest for the first time on 19 February 1929. He was interrogated for a month. On 13 April 1929, as Shalamov later contended, he then was sent for three years to a labor camp in Vishera, although contrary evidence suggests that he went into administrative exile during that same period. No confirmation for either claim can be found.

During these years, following in the footsteps of his father, Tikhon Nikolaevich, who himself had engaged in unpopular activities, Shalamov demonstrated a romantic attraction to rebellion and the inevitable punishment that followed in its wake. He seemed keen on seeking the spotlight through seditious and—in the context of his time—unwise political behavior. The sorts of actions that were merely risky and unsound in the case of the father proved potentially deadly in the case of the son.

While in Moscow, Shalamov was exposed to one of the important phenomena of the 1920s, known as *literatura fakta* (literature of fact), which emphasizes literature as an accurate record of seminal contemporary and near-contemporary events. *Literatura fakta* typically focused on the Russian Civil War, fought between the Red Army and the White Army in the aftermath of the October Revolution of 1917. Shalamov later wrote *Kolymskie rasskazy* as his own version of the literature of fact. The tales were his idiosyncratic accounts of actual incidents and his excoriation of the worst excesses of the Soviet system. For Shalamov the literature of fact represented an attempt to rewrite the "official" historical record; by casting actual events in narrative fiction—that is, by providing fictional accounts of events for which he had served as an immediate and accurate eyewitness—he exposed the falsehood of the "official" record. That he frequently altered what he had experienced and even had conflicting narrative descriptions of the same camps in different stories was a mark of his transformation of raw material into art, rather than evidence of deliberate inaccuracies on his part. His judicious changes lend the events he witnessed a universality that transcends the bounds of the camps and, moreover, condemn the fallen state of his country during this period. Official governmental reports about the camps—certainly until the advent of glasnost—could never be trusted, and official information on the excesses of Soviet rule were in any case scanty at best. For some years Shalamov's versions, certainly until the publication of Aleksandr Isaevich Solzhenitsyn's *Arkhipelag GULag 1918–1956: Opyt knudozhestvennego issledovaniia* (1973–1975; translated as *The Gulag Archipelago, 1918–1956: An Experiment in Literary Investigation,* 1974–1978), served as the only source for this dark period in Russian history. Not only did his stories represent an alternative "history" of camp life, they also signified an attempt to wrest control of intellectual and cultural life—of the Word itself—back from the false authority of the state. The literature of fact resonated in Shalamov's stories decades after his first exposure to it during the 1920s.

Coupled with his reliance on various narrators in the course of his stories, the tremendous breadth of

Shalamov's settings in terms of both time and space—his chronotope—helped to assure that his fiction was read as a successful attempt to comprehend the incomprehensible in Soviet Russian life and history. The narrator's complete autonomy over the text is readily apparent in his stories, such as, for example, at the conclusion of "Pervyi zub" ("First Tooth," from the cycle "Artist lopaty"). Here Sazonov, the ostensible narrator of the piece, wrestles with variant endings, trying each one out on his listener "I," who is identified with Shalamov himself. The listener rejects not only Sazonov's original ending but also the three variants that follow it. "Then I'll stick with the first one," Sazonov decides. "If you write it down, then you can forget." Yet, the story suggests that the last thing Shalamov wants his readers to do is forget any of the terrifying details and incidents woven into the fabric of the collection in its entirety; the device of variant endings is another way of adding to this heap of details. That the narrator exercises total control over a given text gives him, in this case, the enormous power of ethical authority that functions as a counterweight to the unethical authority of the state. Hence, Shalamov follows a time-honored tradition in Russian literature, in which the writer functions as the ultimate authority figure as a counterweight to state oppression.

Shalamov submitted works of poetry to the journals *Krasnaia nov'* (Red Virgin Soil) and *Krasnaia niva* (Red Grainfield), but his early efforts were not accepted. At a time of intense stylistic experimentation in Russian poetry, characterized by Russian modernist movements such as cubo-futurism and constructivism, Shalamov's verse was formally conservative. He never altered his adherence to traditional rhyme and metric schemes, however, even after his release from prison. The inability to publish his poetry came as a tremendous disappointment to him and anticipated a similarly frustrating situation decades later when he had difficulty securing the publication of his work and finding an appreciative audience for it. Throughout the course of his bifurcated literary career, which was brutally interrupted by his arrests in the late 1920s and the 1930s, followed by his subsequent imprisonments in the camps, Shalamov was always cut off from the literary and cultural mainstream. This process started early on, at the beginning of his literary activity, and it persisted in spite of his great initial promise as a writer. Although during the 1920s he established literary contacts—including his acquaintance with the cubo-futurist poet Vladimir Vladimirovich Maiakovsky, one of the most renowned and significant writers of the period—Shalamov nevertheless tended to hold himself aloof from the literary circles linked with Russian modernism. (These circles dominated Russian literature from the 1890s through the first decades of the twentieth century and extended into the early years of Soviet rule.) Because of his independent spirit, he remained apart from contemporary groups. His behavior recalled his father's independent and unpopular stances and foreshadowed his own later autonomy and distance from the typical societal values of Stalinist times, from Soviet society as a whole and, eventually, from dissident circles after Stalin's death. Shalamov, however, refused to consider himself marginalized. He instead seemed to position himself, as well as the narrators in his stories, as people at the focal point of the most seminal events of his time.

Shalamov's rebellious and remote nature made him a natural suspect in Soviet society, dominated as it was by collective values after the consolidation of Stalin's power. Shalamov's immediate problems were enormously compounded by the excesses of a vicious and corrupt regime. Although his independent stance proved extremely dangerous, he was able, nevertheless, to maintain a moral high ground during the difficult years of prison and exile. This autonomy is reflected in his later narrators in the *Kolymskie rasskazy*. Loosely identified much of the time with the author himself, these narrators display a strength that enables them to hold themselves apart from the horrors of camp life, even to stand up to the perpetrators of these same horrors. These narrators are the ones who pass judgment on their fellow prisoners in the deadly drama of camp life and who relate the separate yet related incidents—the miniature sketches—that together constitute *Kolymskie rasskazy*. Thus, Shalamov's later idiosyncrasies and strengths, characteristics that colored *Kolymskie rasskazy* and contributed to his later difficulties in life, had already emerged by this early point in his career. The later Shalamov—the author of *Kolymskie rasskazy*—thus evolved quite naturally from the young Moscow rebel. The link between his life and work that marked his later writing was, therefore, forged from the beginning of his literary activity.

Shalamov's early prison experiences inspired his first serious prose work dating from this same period. *Vishera. Antiroman,* begun in 1970 (The Vishera. Antinovel, first published in 1989) is a descriptive piece and anticipated his later, more famous tales. *Vishera* is essentially memoir-like prose—actually a collection of short pieces similar to *Kolymskie rasskazy*—with specific details related to his experiences during the late 1920s and the beginning of the 1930s. The very title incorporates Shalamov's independent position against accepted norms (in this case, literary ones) by positing the work as an "anti-work" and himself as an "anti-writer." The designation "anti" helps to place him in the modernist tradition: it designates him as a rebel and relates him

*Shalamov's father, Tikhon Nikolaevich Shalamov, an Orthodox priest, in 1905 (from* Chetvertaia Vologda, *1994; Jean and Nathan Heard Library, Vanderbilt University)*

specifically to the cubo-futurists and their dictum, "épater les bourgeoisie"–that is, to offend public taste and aggressively undermine contemporary aesthetic norms.

The first short piece in this cycle is "Butyrskaya tiur'ma" ("Butyr Prison"), dating from 1929. It constitutes a pointedly factual account of his arrest on 19 February of that year and of his actual time in Butyr Prison. This series of events in effect constituted a warm-up (though a fairly innocuous one) for the later terrors of the 1930s. *Vishera* itself can be regarded as a dress rehearsal for Shalamov's later prose work. He had by then established a connection between his political persecution–an inspiration for his art–and literary creation. While his arrest and his term in Vishera were clearly negative events, setting the stage for later persecution, Shalamov managed at this time to create his persona of the political martyr, a figure who later occupies a central position in *Kolymskie rasskazy*. For Shalamov, the writer was now synonymous with the political rebel. He had, in fact, become a nonperson even in the context of these earlier times, a nonperson who later was persecuted more actively, during the terror.

While Shalamov was in Vishera, he met his first wife, Galina Ignat'ievna Gudz', whom he married in 1939 (the relationship foundered later under the adverse conditions of separation, and they divorced at his behest to end her ten-year exile in Chardzho). Following his release, Shalamov stayed on in the Vishera region until 1932, when he ventured back to Moscow. Now married and eager to avoid political involvement and stay out of trouble, he definitively turned his back on the study of law, which he had commenced prior to his first arrest. Choosing literature as his venue for achieving fame and a lasting legacy, he was drawn at this time to prose. (He did not write poetry again until 1949.) In 1935 his short story "Gans" (Hans) was published in *Leningradskaia pravda* (Leningrad Truth), and his first child, a daughter named Elena Varlamovna Shalamova, was born. "Gans" was followed in 1936 by his novella *Tri smerti Doktora Austino* (Doctor Austino's Three Deaths), published in the journal *Oktiabr'* (October), and his short story "Vozvrashchenie" (The Return) in *Vokrug sveta* (Round the World). His prize-winning story "Pava i drevo" (The Peahen and the Tree) appeared in *Literaturnyi sovremennik* (Literary Contemporary) in March 1937, not long after Shalamov's second arrest. This last piece had gone to press too late for publication to be stopped in time. His literary career, which had started to flourish in the 1930s, was brutally interrupted by his subsequent arrest and imprisonment.

With excitement Shalamov anticipated that at Vishera he would be thrown in with former members of the outlawed Socialist Revolutionary Party, a party that both he and his father held in high esteem. He was, however, greatly disillusioned by his fellow inmates and, in general, by his experiences in Vishera, which were far more mundane and less romantic than he had anticipated. In the 1920s he had behaved as if he were looking actively for ways to force arrest and a prison sentence. Now he seemed anxious about avoiding further political persecution and was much more circumspect in the stories he wrote during this period, the early to mid 1930s. His attempts to stay out of political trouble at this time were in vain, however, and he was entrapped along with countless other intellectuals.

Not all of Shalamov's work from the 1930s, however, endures. Because of the dangerous political climate of the time, his wife Galina, his sister Galina Tikhonovna Shalamova, and his wife's sister Marina Ignat'evna Gudz' took no chances: they destroyed between 150 to 200 poems, as well as personal letters written during this period. Shalamov's circumspection, however, did not spare him from future adversity. He was arrested once again during the night of 11–12 January 1937. He may have been suspect because of his earlier Trotskyist activities; his previous arrest in 1929 made him a "natural" candidate for this second arrest and subsequent incarceration. That his father was a priest did not stand Shalamov in good stead. He himself maintained that one of his personal letters, read by the authorities, was an overriding cause. The very nature of the terror, with intellectuals the principal targets in a dragnet operation, virtually guaranteed the arrest of a man like Shalamov, one who long had been suspect for his openly hostile and independent stance.

Shalamov's arrest in 1937 ruined his family life. He subsequently was estranged from both his wife and his daughter. Charged with "Counterrevolutionary Trotskyist Activity," of which he no doubt had been guilty during the latter part of the 1920s, Shalamov was initially incarcerated in Butyrskaya (Butyr) Prison in Moscow, where he refused to confess. He was not beaten and was allowed access to the prison library; while there he was able to read forbidden authors such as Mikhail Afanas'evich Bulgakov and Boris Pil'niak. Shalamov's exposure to Bulgakov and Pil'niak enabled him to access the works of Russian writers whose careers had flourished during the period of prose experimentation in the 1920s and provided him with models for his own future work. Shalamov was also thrown in with the Socialist Revolutionary terrorist Aleksandr Georgievich Andreev, who was a member of a political party that Shalamov had admired but not encountered—much to his bitter disappointment—during his initial incarceration at Vishera. Andreev's presence (which constituted a reminder that a political opposition of sorts could still be considered a palpable threat even twenty years after the October Revolution) inspired Shalamov during this period and even later, once he actually had been sent to the camps. His earlier experiences as a writer gave him a special mission, even a purpose for living, as an accurate recorder of events. He juxtaposed his own truthful accounts of the suffering brought about by political persecution to the inevitable lying and grandiose propaganda statements that were endemic in the corrupt Soviet system, especially under Stalin.

Shalamov was sentenced to five years in corrective labor camps in Kolyma in the Far East and, in a move typical for this time, deprived of the right of correspondence. His sentence was short, given that ten-year and even twenty-five-year sentences were quite commonplace, but Shalamov stayed in the camps far longer than his five-year sentence. Here he survived precariously, at times getting by only thanks to the intervention of others, for the next fourteen years. Because he effectively was cut off from subsequent developments in Soviet literature during the latter part of the 1930s and beyond, he was not exposed to the official dicta of socialist realism that prevailed from the 1930s until after the death of Stalin on 5 March 1953. His work can be seen as part of a continuum that bypassed socialist realism and represented a continuation of the prose traditions of the 1920s, as practiced by writers such as Nikolai Alekseevich Zabolotsky, Isaak Emmanuilovich Babel, and Mikhail Mikhailovich Zoshchenko. Like Pasternak and the acmeist poet Anna Andreevna Akhmatova, Shalamov was a literal and literary survivor from another time. This situation was exacerbated by his long years out of circulation. He had completely bypassed not only the worst political and literary excesses of the 1930s and of postwar fiction in the years immediately before the death of Stalin but also the relatively more relaxed atmosphere of the war period.

As part of his sentence Shalamov was sent off to the gold mines at Partizan on 20 August 1937. He spent approximately three months laboring under what turned out to be fairly humane conditions. His experiences during this period are recounted in several stories, including one of his most striking tales, "Zaklinatel' zmei" ("The Snake Charmer"), a piece from the cycle "Kolymskie rasskazy" that would have been equally at home in Shalamov's cycle "Ocherki prestupnogo mira." His relatively comfortable circumstances (for camp-life standards) soon changed abruptly for the worse—Shalamov narrowly escaped execution during this period. In his early exposure to the hellish life of the camps, he rapidly came to the conclusion that forced labor coupled with near starvation destroyed one's moral fiber and the ability to survive physically. Shalamov's views—central to *Kolymskie rasskazy*—thus place him diametrically opposite Fyodor Dostoevsky and Shalamov's own contemporary, Solzhenitsyn, both of whom subscribed to the conviction that "useful" labor ennobled prisoners in the camps and strengthened them both morally and psychologically. Few characters in Shalamov's own stories retain any ethical standards whatsoever. Instead, they frequently sell out their fellow prisoners for personal gain, and their actions reflect what his friends and he himself witnessed in those years. He was careful to record individual acts of brutality, cowardice, and heartlessness and to posit his personae as counterweights to the negative characters of the stories, principally the camp authorities and the criminal element. Brutalized by their camp experiences, his protagonists differ markedly from the characters in Dostoevsky's or Solzhenitsyn's works. In "Sgushchennoe moloko," ("Condensed Milk" from the cycle "Kolymskie rasskazy"), the condensed milk of the title is a bribe for a fabricated escape attempt, a sham

*The gymnasium in Vologda where Shalamov began his schooling (from* Chetvertaia Vologda, *1994; Jean and Nathan Heard Library, Vanderbilt University)*

venture enabling one of Shalamov's many scoundrels to try to improve his circumstances at the expense of others. So pervasive is the depravity of the camp system that even the political prisoners themselves, such as Shestakov from "Sgushchennoe moloko," are corrupted in the end. Shalamov–savvy, able to take care of himself, and wise to the machinations of others–modeled the narrator of this tale on himself. His frequently ironic endings, such as at the conclusion of "Sgushchennoe moloko" or "Detskie kartinki" (A Child's Drawings) from the "Kolymske rasskazy" cycle, suggest a world that has lost its bearings. The tales recall Babel's stories and demonstrate that the destruction visited on the microcosm of the prisoners' lives and, by extension, on the macrocosm of the country as a whole is moral as well as physical.

Pessimistic to a great extent about human morality–with a few exceptions–Shalamov also examined the natural world and made ample use of the "pathetic fallacy" (John Ruskin's term for describing the attribution of human traits to nature and inanimate objects). Thus, a small tree in "Stlanik" (The Dwarf Cedar), a story that first was published in the journal *Sel'skaya molodezh* (Rural Youth) in 1965 and then later appeared as part of the cycle "Kolymskie rasskazy," becomes a "prisoner" who knows how to keep its "head" down under adverse conditions. Even the cedar's wary behavior fails to save it from victimization. Stripped of its needles, which are boiled up into a noxious liquid and served to the prisoners as a supposed preventative for scurvy, the tree suffers the common fate of all those caught in the monstrous web of the camps. Plants are not the only sacrifice. In the story "Medvedi" ("The Bears," from the cycle "Levyi bereg") a he-bear, infinitely superior to most of the humans the narrator has encountered, saves his mate at the cost of his own life. In conflicts between man and the natural world, nature is routinely victimized, with a clear line connecting victims and the brutalized political prisoners. Shalamov's own experiences are reflected here. The same kind of human brutality that underscores "Medvedi" also figures prominently in "Utka" (The Duck, from the cycle "Artist lopaty"), in which a hunter's pitiless pursuit ends in the death of an exhausted and beleaguered bird. In all three instances victims in nature are identified with the political prisoners. Shalamov's horrid memories in the camps during this period shaped his essentially negative view of humanity; only a few exceptions to this view stand out in the tales. Human cruelty, particularly the gratuitous kind, is especially vivid in contrast to the relative purity of the natural world, as can be seen not only from "Utka" and "Medvedi" but also from the story "Sententsiia" (Sententiousness, from the cycle "Levyi bereg"). Here the narrator prevents a topographer from shooting a small bird just for sport and is rewarded by the return of language and sensitivity (that is, humanity) after long, numbing years of the most infernal existence imaginable.

Shalamov was unbroken by his rearrest and his incarceration in the Far East, and like the few positive characters in his stories, he continued to stand up against injustice. He was transferred to Magadan prison in December 1938 as punishment for writing a complaint a year earlier on behalf of one of his fellow prisoners. From there he went to a transfer camp and subsequently landed in quarantine for typhus, an experience that inspired the title for one of his later stories, "Tifoznyi karantin" (The Typhus Quarantine, from the cycle "Kolymskie rasskazy"). A theme running throughout the stories as a whole is that of the camps themselves representing a sort of quarantine, with prisoners constituting the "infected" elements of society who must be isolated from it.

By April 1939 Shalamov was in the coal-prospecting camp of Chernoe ozero (Black Lake), where his physical and psychological states improved considerably. Some of his acquaintances from this period figure later in stories such as "Tifoznyi karantin," "Esperanto" (from "Levyi bereg"), "Trianguliatsiia III klassa" (Triangulation of the Third Class, from "Perchatka, ili KR-2"), and "Apostol Pavel" (The Apostle Paul, from the cycle "Kolymskie rasskazy"). At this time Shalamov's classification as an invalid allowed him to take on comparatively light work as a boiler operator and topographer's aide. His fluctuating fortunes in the camps are reflected in his fiction, in which salvation from near-death situations is seen frequently as unexpected and almost miraculous, a "gift" from those few prisoners who still retain a moral center.

Shalamov returned to the gold mines when coal mining proved unworkable, and he actually came to prefer work in the mine shafts, where temperatures were warmer than the frigid conditions that prevailed on the surface. In addition, these mines were shunned by the authorities because of a fear of accidents. Conditions improved slightly during the war, with an increase in the bread ration, but Shalamov's five-year sentence did not end on schedule. He was sent to the Dzhelgala camp in December 1942. Within months, in May 1943, he was rearrested, and his conviction (ten more years in the camps) followed on 3 July 1943. One possible cause for the rearrest may have been Shalamov's praise of the great émigré writer Ivan Alekseevich Bunin, although his comments on Bunin have not been corroborated. Typically, Shalamov romanticized the events connected with his arrest, as well as with his experiences in Moscow, Vishera, and, later, in the camps of Kolyma. His re-creation of himself as a heroic martyr (a legacy from his father) is linked, in *Kolymskie rasskazy*, with the persona of the narrator, a prominent figure in the text. Shalamov commenced his sentence with a month in a frigid punishment cell, where he subsisted on small quantities of bread and water. Until this rearrest he had been anticipating release at the end of the war, and the additional ten-year sentence came as a terrific shock to him. He continued to accumulate impressions for his later work. Shalamov did not shy away from relating pertinent events from his own life, particularly when demonstrating the devastating toll that the camps took on "normal" family life. For example, during this period he wrote a letter to his wife suggesting that she begin a new life without him, and in response she sent him a photograph of the two of them–a photograph that was stolen from Shalamov while he was in the camps. This episode is central to the tale "Smytaia fotogragiia" ("The Washed Photograph," from "Voskreshenie listvennitsy").

Events from this period are also recast in Shalamov's memoirs, as well as in his story "Perchatka" ("The Glove," from "Perchatka, ili KR-2"). The characters who recount their own experiences as well as those they witnessed strongly resemble the narrator in Babel's collection *Konarmiia* (1926, Red Cavalry), and echoes of Babel's stories can be found in some of the events of *Kolymskie rasskazy*. Babel was enormously popular during the 1920s, particularly in Moscow while Shalamov lived there. Thus, the title of Babel's story "Moi pervyi gus'" (My First Goose), from *Konarmiia*, resonates in that of Shalamov's tale "Pervyi zub." Moreover, both works are essentially about a rite of moral passage; a main difference is that Shalamov reverses the fall of Babel's narrator through his own narrator's heroic defense of a fellow prisoner. That Shalamov echoes Babel so closely attests to a negative assessment of the revolution, about which Babel himself was so equivocal. Both writers distort the events they witnessed: Babel does so by playing with time and historical accuracy, while Shalamov–through the choppy effect of extremely short sketches–distorts the past by suggesting a loss of temporal and moral integrity. The end result in both stories is a world in which the narrator is unable to perceive any center, an inability that evidences an acute sense of lost values in the wake of Soviet hegemony. Echoing the time-honored role of the Russian writer in competition and conflict with an immoral state, the narrator himself becomes the moral center.

Shalamov spent the summer of 1943 in the hospital in Belich'ia, where he had been sent to recover from dysentery, a condition worsened by his near starvation. He had been deprived of food as a punishment for poor production norms, a practice that brought about a

*Title page for the first English-language translation, in 1980, of* Kolmskie rasskazy, *Shalamov's collected works. In 1981 the volume was republished as* Graphite *(Thomas Cooper Library, University of South Carolina).*

vicious circle: less food meant less energy to work. During his stay he met Dr. Petr Semenovich Kalembet and the medical assistant and prisoner Boris Nikolaevich Lesniak, both of whom took Shalamov into their care. Shalamov, who intensely disliked physical labor, was glad of the respite. He "rewarded" Lesniak by giving him a significantly positive role in the story "Perchatka." Shalamov's experiences in Belich'ia, after his readmission to receive treatment for pellagra (a disease caused by a niacin deficiency), also are recorded in "Perchatka"; the story alludes to his unsubstantiated assertion that pellagra had caused the skin of his hands to shed intact, like gloves coming off. This claim underscores Shalamov's willingness to stretch the truth or even to fabricate events, taking artistic license and muddying the facts for the sake of intensity or for the enhancement of his romantic image as a martyred victim of the state. As a result, his assertion that he was sent to the gold mines at Spokoinyi in 1943 has been disputed. Shalamov himself undermines his own allegation when referring to his continued stay in Belich'ia in 1944. Furthermore, Lesniak's assertion that the camp at Spokoinyi was not even in operation until 1945 casts further doubts on Shalamov's claims. In short, Shalamov shapes the facts of his past in order to force them into conformity with the fictionalized version of his life that is presented in his tales. The story "Lesha Chekanov, ili odnodel'tsy Kolymy" ("Lesha Chekanov, or the Kolyma Sharp Dealers," from "Perchatka, ili KR-2"), for instance, is a record in narrative fiction of his request for a transfer; Shalamov wanted to get away from a work-brigade head who had recognized him from their time in Butyrskaia prison and subsequently had tormented him.

The experiences that Shalamov had in the camp at Kliuch almaznyi (The Diamond Source) form the basis, in turn, for his story of the same name from the "Artist lopaty" cycle, in which he recalls his flight to Yagodnyi, where he believed that he could better his chances of survival. His feverish illness at a transit camp at Susuman, while en route to Indigirka, are recorded in the story "Taiga zolotaia" ("The Golden Taiga") from the "Kolymskie rasskazy" cycle, with the details altered only slightly from the actual events. Typically, all of these stories focus either on individual acts of kindness that miraculously save the narrator of a given tale or, conversely, on acts of cruelty that make survival precarious and further erode his faith in human nature.

Shalamov's experiences in various hospitals in 1946 enabled him to pass the necessary examinations that allowed him to work as a medical assistant. He could now leave hard labor and his most horrible experiences behind and stay in hospitals in a professional capacity. The surgical ward of the Central Hospital for Prisoners at Debin, on the left bank of the Kolyma River, was his first assignment. He witnessed abortive escapes at this time, recording them in the stories "Zelenyi prokuror" (The Green Procurator) from the "Artist lopaty" cycle and "Poslednyi boi maiora Pugacheva" (Major Pugachev's Last Battle) from the "Levyi bereq" cycle. During this same period at Kliuch almaznyi he felt strong enough to write the poetry that later became part of his *Kolymskie tetradi* (The Kolyma Notebooks, 1994). For Shalamov, who early on had considered poetry a vital component of moral and even physical survival, the opportunity to write his own verse once again after a long hiatus marked a distinct turning point in his years spent in camp. *Kolymskie tetradi* eventually consisted of six notebooks—hence, the title—and continued to expand until 1956, three years after the end of Shalamov's sentence. The poems of this collection, which were written from 1937 to 1956, coincide quite closely with his actual term in the camps. Like the stories of *Kolymskie rasskazy,* the lyrics that make up *Kolymskie tetradi* are short. Occasionally, in the third volume of Shalamov's *Sobranie sochinenii* (1998, Collected Works), several poems appear on the same page. Like the poems themselves, the actual lines of verse are brief. Images from nature recur throughout, just as they do in Shalamov's prose fiction. His allusions to Babel's stories, his fictionalized account of the poet Osip Emil'evich Mandel'shtam's death, and the poem "Barantynsky"–a reference to the important early-nineteenth-century poet Evgenii Abramovich Baratynsky–all place Shalamov within the mainstream of Russian literature. He is at once the martyred but unbowed witness to the terrors of the gulag, an exemplar of moral rectitude (hinting at the legacy of his father), and a legitimate heir to a great literary and cultural tradition.

Shalamov was in close contact with criminals not only in the camps but also in the camp hospitals, where they often would languish with fraudulent claims of illness and tormented or even killed their fellow patients, who typically were political prisoners. Shalamov considered the criminals he encountered brutal, and because he witnessed horrific incidents during his long term in the camps, he gave them considerably negative roles in his stories. Criminals play prominent parts in several stories from *Kolymskie rasskazy;* the cycle "Ocherki prestupnogo mira" focuses entirely on them. In order to assure that his negative assessment of criminals is unmistakably clear to the reader and to support his case against their positive treatment by other writers, Shalamov begins "Ocherki prestupnogo mira" with the essay "Ob odnoi oshibke khudozhestvennoi literatury" (Concerning One Mistake of Belles-Lettres). His view of his fellow prisoners was, with few exceptions, unremittingly pessimistic. In this sense he was responding to Dostoevsky, who considered his time in the camps–so crucial for the development of his later prose works–as intrinsically valuable. Dostoevsky's sentence in Siberia inspired his own later, partially successful attempt to overcome the rift between his own social class and the serfs.

In contrast, Shalamov's own experience was at the opposite pole. Whereas Dostoevsky sought a bond, even a shared cause, with the common criminals of his time as representatives of the serfs, Shalamov viewed the common criminals of the Stalinist camps, who brutally terrorized the political prisoners–the intellectuals–with contempt and regarded them as a symbol, even a tool, of a lawless and repressive political regime. Nowhere are these negative assessments of criminal prisoners more pointedly illustrated than in his short story "Zaklinatel' zmei" (Snake Charmer, from "Kolymskie rasskazy"). Here, in a reworking of the Scheherazade motif that occasionally appeared in Soviet literature of the 1920s and later, the narrator Platonov prostitutes his gifts as a screenwriter in order to entertain hardened murderers. Platonov's very name echoes the prominent Soviet writer Andrei Platonovich Platonov, whose novel *Kotlovan* (1969, The Foundation Pit) was a searing indictment of the Soviet system. In this exemplary story Shalamov clearly identifies the common criminals in the camps with the murderers who are running the Soviet Union. His stories about criminals in the gulag reflect an overwhelming cynicism toward human nature and constitute an almost universally negative assessment of man's evil tendencies.

Shalamov's sufferings continued after the end of the war. Rare acts of kindness provided a counterweight, however, to random instances of extreme cruelty. He took pains to record these positive experiences, and such acts of kindness are central to "Domino" (The Domino) later published in the "Kolymskie rasskazy" cycle. In 1946 he was assigned to the USVITL (administration of the North East Corrective Labor Force) Hospital near the Magadan region. It was here that he reestablished relations with Dr. Fedor Efimovich Loskutov, who supplied material that later resurfaced in *Kolymskie rasskazy*. The presence of different narrators (in, for example, "Zaklinatel' zmei") may point to different points of view or instead may serve as a literary device. Iakov Mikhailovich Umansky, whom Shalamov first met during this period, figures in the tales as one of Shalamov's only benevolent characters.

While serving in the Central Hospital for Prisoners on the left bank of the Kolyma River at Debin, he made several longtime friends, including Arkadii Zakharovich Dobrovol'sky, the poet Valentin Valentinovich Portugal'sky, the physicist and engineer Georgii Georgievich Demidov, and Galina Aleksandrovna Voronskaia and her husband, Ivan Stepanovich Isaev, both of whom had studied at the Gor'ky Institute of World Literature in Moscow. Voronskaia and Isaev provided Shalamov with literary contacts, enabling him to resume the career he had to abandon at the time of his second arrest in 1937.

With his fellow medical assistants and others, Shalamov revived his literary activities and recited his poetry at literary evenings. He remained in the gulag, however, serving from 1950 until 1952 as a senior medical assistant in the hospital receiving room at Debin. During this period Shalamov had his works of poetry and prose smuggled out of the camps, including the prose collection "Siniaia tetrad'" (The Navy-Blue Notebook) later included in the "Kolymskie rasskazy" cycle. He attached a personal note to Pasternak, who responded with his own letter to Shalamov. "Siniaia tetrad'" encompassed many of the stories that later

*Nadezhda Mandel'shtam, widow of the renowned poet Osip Mandel'shtam, and Shalamov, whose collected works include a fictionalized account of the poet's death (from* Graphite, *Thomas Cooper Library, University of South Carolina)*

appeared in *Kolymskie rasskazy*. On 13 October 1951 Shalamov's sentence finally came to an end; because of extra work hours he was a year ahead of schedule. Still in exile, he was forced to remain in Kolyma and continued to work as a medical assistant, first in Baragon and then in Kiubiuma, near Oimiakon. At this time, prior to his release to the mainland on 30 September 1953, approximately six months after the death of Stalin, Shalamov composed a great deal of poetry.

After returning to the mainland and its relative freedoms, he considered writing his most important duty. He wrote fictionalized accounts of the horrifying events that he and others had witnessed, and he described the dehumanized officials and criminals with whom he had come into contact or about whom he had been apprised. In marked contrast to the official cult of optimism that continued to prevail under socialist realism, he shared an abrasively bitter pessimism with writers of the new generation such as Iuz Aleshkovsky (pseudonym of Iosif Efimovich Aleshkovsky), Vladimir Georgievich Sorokin, and Aleksandr Aleksandrovich Zinoviev. Shalamov maintained that the tragic Soviet experience was not an isolated one and that the unimaginable suffering of Stalin's time was part of an overall pattern of human baseness. This realization fed his overwhelming pessimism, in marked contrast to the optimism encountered elsewhere—as in, for example, Solzhenitsyn's *Odin den' Ivana Denisovicha* (1962; translated as *One Day in the Life of Ivan Denisovich,* 1963), with its underlying message of the essential goodness, indeed possible perfectibility, of man. Shalamov's own assessment of human nature can be seen as more deeply, intrinsically anti-Soviet (even anti-Soviet Marxist); it runs counter to the official view of man and society, which, in accordance with Soviet Marxism, perpetually soar upward toward perfection. Occasionally, however, his stories powerfully depict those few individuals of sufficient moral fiber who stand up to overwhelming evil, as in "Poslednii boi Maiora Pugacheva."

Shalamov's camp experiences were only one probable cause of his cynicism, for both his wife and daughter turned their backs on him. They continued to live on the "mainland," instead of joining him in exile, and offered no support for what had become the principal goal of his life: recording his experiences in Kolyma. Literature was now all that he had left. Because so little of his work was actually published before his death, Shalamov increasingly felt that his potential as a great writer was going unrealized because of all the time he had lost in the camps. Coming full circle, in a sense, with his early self-image as a rebel-writer, he now regarded himself as a writer-martyr who was destined to write for the sake of a higher good. He began identifying himself with all the writers and intellectuals who had been victimized by the Soviet system. His story "Sherri-Brendi" (Sherry-Brandy), about the death of the martyred Acmeist poet Mandel'shtam, himself a victim of the camps, can be considered one segment of this overarching pattern.

Because Shalamov's family life fell apart upon his release, he actually never returned "home." He severed ties with his wife and daughter in 1956. Pasternak admired Shalamov's work, and his warm encouragement of the writer during this same period helped ease Shalamov back into literature. Yet, Pasternak's contacts with Shalamov were limited by the latter's exile from the capital, which continued until 10 October 1956, the month he married; they divorced on 30 May 1966.

At this time Shalamov worked apace on *Kolymskie rasskazy*. He virtually had completed "Kolymskie rasskazy," the first of the seven cycles, while living in a workers' dormitory. He wrote most of the cycle "Ocherki prestupnogo mira" during the year 1959, while "Levyi bereg," "Artist lopaty," and "Voskreshenie listvennitsy" were drafted in the mid 1960s. The cycle "Perchatka, ili or KR-2" followed in the early 1970s. These stories not only reflect his pessimistic view of human nature, particularly that of "homo sovieticus," but also stress his important contention that the Soviet Union had been turned into one vast labor camp. Although he had planned to write approximately 200 tales, he managed to complete only about 150 of them—with several stories left unfinished—before he died. In the 1970s Shalamov decided to return to poetry, his first literary love.

Shalamov's sour views of humanity were reflected not only in his stories but also in his personal relationships. Never easy to get along with, he had become (albeit understandably) much more difficult by the time he returned from exile. He severed relationships with many of his former friends, keeping his ties with only two, Iakov Davydovich Grodzensky and Aleksandr Il'ich Gustiatinsky, who proved especially tolerant of his difficult and eccentric behavior. After Shalamov's sister Galina found him in 1955, even she considered her relationship with him difficult to maintain, at least in part because of her continued contact with his wife and daughter. He had known Pasternak's mistress, Ol'ga Vsevolodna Ivinskaia, from Moscow in the 1930s and, after his release from the camps, was able to revive their former relationship, although it did not take the romantic turn he was hoping for. During the summer of 1956 he frequently visited Ivinskaia at her dacha in Peredel'kino, but this contact, too, was soon severed.

Through Ivinskaia, however, Shalamov met the woman who became his second wife, Ol'ga Sergeevna Nekliudova. He married Ol'ga Sergeevna in October 1956 (following his rehabilitation on 18 July 1956), and because she was a Muscovite, Shalamov was able to obtain permission to live in Moscow once again. He settled there with his new wife and stepson, Sergei. He also was fortunate to find work in Moscow as a writer, and he produced essays on the history of culture, art, and science for the journal *Moskva* (Moscow). This employment lasted only until late 1957, when many writers at *Moskva* were fired at the end of the first Thaw period. Shalamov was in shock and anticipated a return to the terror of the 1930s. He began at that time to suffer from Menière's disease, followed almost simultaneously by liver and heart trouble. He was not given the invalid status that should have enabled him to retire on a pension. Forced to continue to work, he translated poetry until 1970. At the same time, he was a reader for the journal *Novyi mir* (New World). In part because of his poor health, coupled with the acute stress he had endured while in the camps, Shalamov began to display extremes of behavior; he would save food until it spoiled, and he isolated himself even from his few remaining friends. Although he had relished having his own home again, his marriage was not able to survive the continued stress from his difficult personality and situations. He and Ol'ga Sergeevna divorced on 30 May 1966.

Yet, also during this period, Shalamov began to enjoy a sense of literary accomplishment, especially with the circulation of his poetry in samizdat. The influence of Pasternak, who encouraged Shalamov's efforts, was crucial at this time. In the early 1950s, mainly because of Pasternak's special efforts, twenty of Shalamov's stories from *Kolymskie rasskazy* also began to make the rounds in samizdat. Shalamov wished to be remembered through his verses; he considered himself a poet who had acquired wisdom through the "martyrology" of his camp experiences. His prose fiction served as the backdrop against which his poetry could be read. While Shalamov wanted his poetry to appear in Moscow, he also had a special interest in seeing it published in two other venues—his hometown of Vologda and Magadan, the principal city of the Kolyma region. In 1956 he began sending out his verse to publishers but met with rejection from the journal *Neva*. The journal

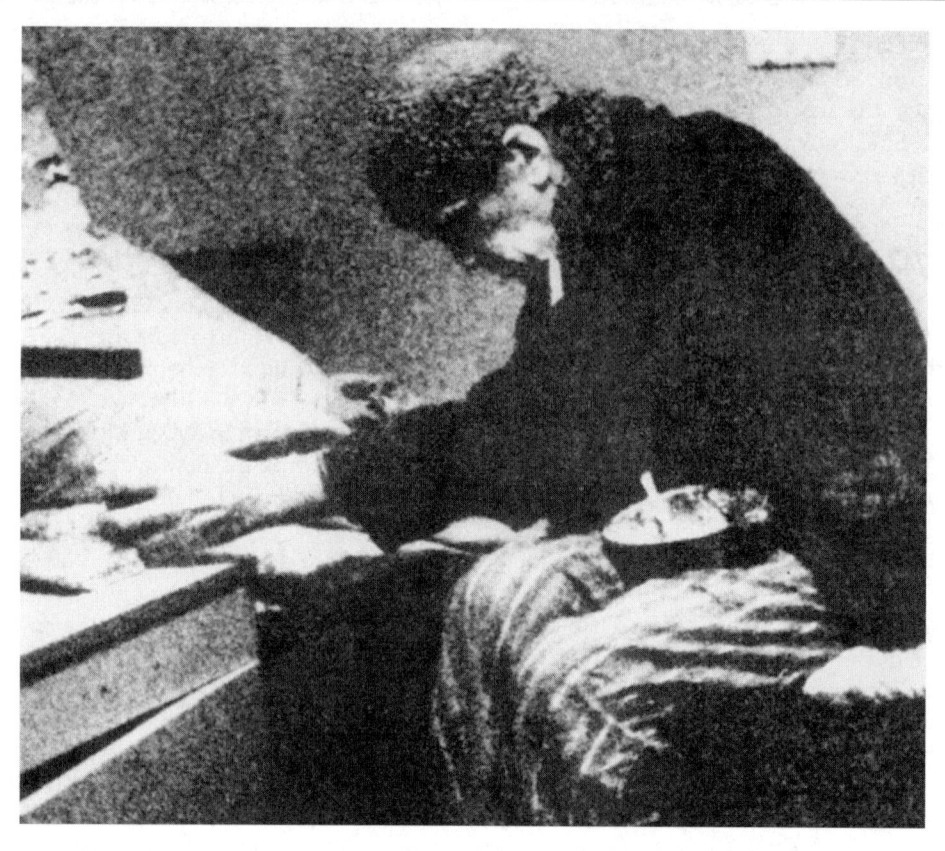

*Shalamov in the Home for Chronic Mental Patients No. 32 near the end of his life (from* Kolymske rasskazy, *1985; Jean and Alexander Heard Library, Vanderbilt University)*

*Na severe dal'nem* (In the Far North) and several other journals, including *Znamia* (The Banner), accepted some of his poetry, but only *Znamia* actually published it. The appearance of his poetry in *Znamia* in 1957 was his first time in print. His poems met with mixed success; some were dismissed as "insufficiently musical," an assessment that ran counter to Pasternak's own. *Moskva* ran five poems in 1958, and *Moskovskii komsomolets* (The Moscow Young Communist) followed with a publication in 1960. The publishing house Sovetskii pisatel' brought out a highly censored form of his first book of verse, *Ognivo* (Kindling Steel), in 1961 in a small publication of only two thousand copies. Between 1964 and 1968 Shalamov continued to publish poetry in the journals *Den' poezii* (The Day of Poetry), *Voprosy literatury* (Questions of Literature), and *Znamia,* as well as in the newspaper *Literaturnaia gazeta* (The Literary Gazette). He brought out his second book of verse, *Shelest' list'ev* (The Rustle of Leaves), in 1964, followed in 1967 by the collection *Doroga i sud'ba* (The Road and Fate). His modest successes in Moscow were not matched elsewhere. Initially, his hometown of Vologda slighted him completely. Although he was asked to contribute to *Antologiia poetov russkogo severa* (An Anthology of the Poets of the Russian North) in Vologda, he decided to refuse. One reason for Shalamov's limited success lay in his formal conservatism, for he adhered to classical form in his poetry during a period of stylistic experimentation and was considered a holdover from the past. As a result his verse was much more conservative formally than his prose. Nominated (in spite of his own general lack of enthusiasm) to join the Writers' Union in 1968, Shalamov refused.

He did not, however, cut back on his literary activities. During this same period he developed a friendship of sorts with Nadezhda Iakovlevna Mandel'shtam, the widow of the poet. Both had suffered through the Great Terror and attempted to preserve a record of the times—he through his tales and poetry, she through a two-volume edition of her memoirs. Nadezhda Mandel'shtam met frequently with Shalamov and read various cycles of his stories, including "Kolymskie rasskazy," "Artist lopaty," and "Levyi bereg." She had high praise for these pieces and, because she recognized their value, provided encouragement at the beginning of Shalamov's much belated career. He greatly appreciated her attention and dedicated the story "Sententsiia" to her. In addition, he became acquainted with various members of the intelligentsia at her home, including Natal'ia Vladimirovna Rozhanskaia, who surreptitiously sent copies of "Kolymskie rasskazy" and "Voskreshenie listvennitsy" to the West for publication in 1975; they were published in London in 1978. Through Nadezhda Mandel'shtam's good efforts, Clarence Brown and Olga Andreeva-Carlisle took four cycles of Shalamov's stories abroad in 1966. Another group of stories was smuggled out to West Germany, where they were published by Verlag in a well-received German translation in 1967. Shalamov's ties with Nadezhda Mandel'shtam, however, did not endure long, in spite of her assistance during this crucial period.

Shalamov's greatest significance lies in the short-story cycles that compose his *Kolymskie rasskazy*. Typically brief, sometimes abbreviated in the manner of the sketch, the stories of *Kolymskie rasskazy* are so short that they can be considered virtually plotless observations of camp life in general. They also characterize a pristine natural world victimized by a negative human presence, suggesting an indictment, by extension, of Soviet Marxism. In their brevity these sketches are actually closer to poetic prose–to Shalamov's own brand of poetry–than they are to the traditional short-story form. Through *Kolymskie rasskazy* he provides a conclusion to Babel's work, supplying the final frame of the violent revolutionary experience that intensely captured his predecessor's imagination. Shalamov's fictionalized records of his camp experiences are linked not only with Babel's own earlier fiction, however, but also with his father's feisty battles against a "fallen" society. While several of his pieces underscore this vacuum, none does so more poignantly than the story "Detskie kartinki," which recounts the discovery of a child's notebook, including sketches, on a garbage heap. The child's only world is the world of the camps: barbed wire, guards, and guard dogs. In this story Shalamov transforms the fairy tales of childhood into the terrifying world of the camps; he equates the lost innocence of childhood with the destruction of an entire culture. His role as a crucial witness of the camps placed him in direct competition with Solzhenitsyn, who was regarded in the West as the most celebrated recorder of camp experiences in Russian literature and culture–a sort of "semi-official historian" of the gulag.

The two men had met in 1962 in the offices of the journal *Novyi mir*, and Solzhenitsyn eventually proved to be one of Shalamov's most important associates. Because of widely differing views of the camps–Solzhenitsyn's positive assessment irritated Shalamov–their relationship turned out to be a tumultuous one. Shalamov criticized Solzhenitsyn's *Odin Den' Ivana Denisovicha* for what he considered its naive optimism. In addition,

*Front cover for* Chetvertaia Vologda *(1994, Fourth Vologda), published in Shalamov's hometown twelve years after his death (Jean and Nathan Heard Library, Vanderbilt University)*

Solzhenitsyn had achieved enormous success at a time when Shalamov's own career continued to languish. Solzhenitsyn had made friendly overtures toward Shalamov, particularly when he sought the latter's expert assistance–even his collaboration–on the renowned *Arkhipelag GULag, 1918–1956,* to help smooth over their tense relationship. The resentful Shalamov assumed that Solzhenitsyn's success had more to do with the contemporary political climate than with his actual literary merits. Matters came to a head in 1966, and the two broke off relations at this time. In part, Shalamov disapproved of Solzhenitsyn's constant involvement in political activities; but, in addition, he also considered himself the "true" witness of camp life in the late 1930s, in the 1940s, and in the early years of the 1950s. While Shalamov was first arrested back in 1929 and suffered the full brunt of the terror during the 1930s, Solzhenitsyn meanwhile was not arrested until 9 February 1945, when World War II was almost over. For his part, Shalamov felt that his younger rival had not had to endure the worst experiences of camp life during the late 1930s and most of the war period.

Shalamov, who definitively left politics behind late in the 1920s, decided to avoid overt political activities after Stalin's death, and he remained aloof from the evolving dissident movement that gained momentum at the time of Leonid Il'ich Brezhnev's hegemony, during the period of so-called *zastoi* (Stagnation). Shalamov was unable to get his poetry published, however, because of official government anger over the Western editions of *Kolymskie rasskazy*. His poetry collection *Moskovskie oblaka* (Moscow Clouds), for instance, was supposed to be published in the late 1960s but instead was kept on indefinite hold. Losing hope that this book would ever appear in print, at least in part because so many of his *Kolymskie rasskazy* had already appeared in the West in defiance of the authorities, he made an enormous sacrifice and decided to dissociate himself from his beloved stories. On 23 February 1972 he wrote a disclaimer in the form of a letter that was published in *Literaturnaia gazeta*. In the letter he denounced the Western publication of *Kolymskie rasskazy*, a move almost certainly undertaken to ease the domestic publication of his poetry, which was now more important to him than his prose. On 17 April 1972 *Moskovski oblaka* finally was permitted to be published, followed by the appearance of Shalamov's verse in the journals *Znamia*, *Den' poezii*, and *Iunost'* (Youth), all in 1977. That same year another verse collection, titled *Tochka kipeniia* (Boiling Point), appeared. The publication of his poetry continued in *Den' poezii* and *Iunost'*.

Throughout this period Shalamov's health continued to worsen. In addition to suffering from Menière's disease and liver and heart problems, he had poor vision and hearing. He was suffering from a premature general physical decline, a typical fate for camp survivors. His addiction to the anti-insomniac drug Nembutal further complicated his health problems. These difficulties increasingly interfered with his ability to maintain the few personal relationships he still enjoyed, and he found himself more isolated than before. In 1972 he was forced to move to a communal apartment, where he completed the final stories of *Kolymskie rasskazy*, as well as *Vishera* and a short story "Fyodor Raskol'nikov" in 1973. From this point onward Shalamov was finished with prose fiction and concentrated instead on poetry, criticism, and his memoirs. His rapidly and dramatically deteriorating health resulted in near blindness and deafness, handicaps that, in 1979, forced him to enter a nursing home. The nursing home was sufficiently horrific to remind him of his experiences in the camps. During this period, in 1981, a cycle of his poems appeared abroad in *Vestnik russkogo khristianskogo dvizheniia* (The Messenger of the Russian Christian Movement). This publication of his poetry in the West brought new troubles for Shalamov, who was now declared "officially senile"—a sign of the new turn that political oppression had taken.

Shalamov died of pneumonia on 17 January 1982 at the Home for Chronic Mental Patients #32. While his difficult life blighted a promising literary career, he nonetheless attained posthumous distinction for his moving vignettes of prison-camp life and for his unfailing courage under hellish conditions.

**Letters:**

"Perepiska Varlama Shalamova i Nadezhdy Mandel'shtam," *Znamia*, 2 (1992): 160–177;

"Iz perepiski. Publikatsiia i primechaniia I. Sirotinskoi," *Znamia*, 5 (May 1993): 110–160.

**References:**

Francziszek Apanowicz, *"Nowa proza" Warlama Szałamowa: problemy wypowiedzi artystyczney* (Gdansk: University of Gdansk Press, 1996);

Valéry Arzoumanov, *In Memoriam Warlam Schalamow: Mikrooper in 7 Szenen für Bariton und Violoncello* (Hamburg: H. Sikorski, 1991);

Maria V. Bourlatskaya, "Soviet Prison-Camp Literature: The Structure of Confinement," dissertation, University of Pennsylvania, 1999;

Michael Brewer, "Varlam Shalamov's *Kolyma Tales*: The Problem of Ordering," M.A. thesis, University of Arizona, 1995;

Andrzej Drawicz, "Szatamowowskie pukanie od dotu," *Dialog*, 34 (October 1989): 82–86;

Irina Emel'ianova, *Legendy Potapovskogo pereulka: B. Pasternak, A. Efron, V. Shalamov: vospominaniia i pis'ma* (Moscow: Ellis Lak, 1997);

Valerii Esipov, *Provintsial'nye spory v kontse XX veka* (Vologda: Grifon, 1999);

Vladimir Frenkel', "V kruge poslednem: Varlam Shalamov i Aleksandr Solzhenitsyn," *Daugava*, 4 (April 1990): 79–82;

John Glad, "Art out of Hell: Shalamov of Kolyma," *Survey: A Journal of East & West Studies*, 107 (1979): 45–50;

Michal Heller, "Smierc' Szatamowa," *Kultura*, 4, no. 145 (1982): 135–138;

Gustav Herling-Grudzitski, "Piętno: Ostatnie opowiadanie Kotymskie," *Kultura*, 6, no. 417 (1982): 37–41;

Geoffrey A. Hosking, "The Ultimate Circle of the Stalinist Inferno," *New Universities Quarterly*, 34 (Spring 1980): 161–168;

Elena Iakovich, "Demidov i Shalamov: Zhitie Georgiia na fone Varlama," *Literaturnaia gazeta*, 11 April 1990, p. 7;

Viacheslav Vsevolodovich Ivanov, "Avvakumova dolia: Segodnia Varlamu Shalamovu ispolnilos' by 90 let," *Literaturnaia gazeta*, 18 July 1997, p. 12;

Laura Anne Kline, "'Novaja proza': Varlam Šalamov's 'Kolymskie rasskazy,'" dissertation, University of Michigan, 1998;

Boris Nikolaevich Lesniak, "Moi Shalamov," *Oktiabr'*, 4 (April 1999): 111–129;

Elena Mikhailik, "Varlam Shalamov: V prisutstvii d'iavola: Problema konteksta," *Russian, Croatian and Serbian, Czech and Slovak, Polish Literature*, 47, no. 2 (15 February 2000): 199–219;

Mikhailik, "Varlam Shalamov v kontekste literatury i istorii," *Australian Slavonic and East European Studies*, 9, no. 1 (1995): 31–64;

Christian Mouze, "Eclats des années vingt," *La Quinzaine littéraire*, 478 (16–31 January 1987): 5–7;

Matt F. Oja, "Shalamov, Solzhenitsyn, and the Mission of Memory," *Survey: A Journal of Soviet and East European Studies*, 29 (Summer 1985): 62–69;

Valery Petrochenkov, "State-Sponsored Persecution as Violence: Varlam Shalamov's *Kolyma Tales*," in *The Image of Violence in Literature, the Media, and Society*, edited by Will Wright and Steven Kaplan (Pueblo, Colo.: Society for the Interdisciplinary Study of Social Imagery, University of Southern Colorado, 1995), pp. 491–497;

Anna Raźny, "Kotyma–biegun śmierci," *Slavia Orientalis*, 41, no. 1 (1992): 57–66;

Raźny, *Literatura wobec zniewolenia totalitarnego: Warlama Szałamowa żwiadectwo prawdy* (Kraków: Uniwersytetu Jagiellozńskiego, 1999);

Evgenii Shklovsky, "Nenapisannyi rasskaz Varlama Shalamova," *Literaturnoe obozrenie*, 8 (1989): 8–14;

Shklovsky, "Pravda Varlama Shalamova," *Druzhba narodov*, 9 (1991): 254–263;

Iu. Shreider, "Granitsa sovesti moei," *Novyi mir*, 12 (December 1994): 226–229;

Shreider, "Iz tvorcheskogo naslediia," *Literaturnoe obozrenie*, 1 (1989): 99–104;

Shreider, "Predopredelennaia sud'ba," *Literaturnoe obozrenie*, 7, no. 1 (1989): 57–60;

Shreider, "Varlam Shalamov o literature," *Voprosy literatury*, 5 (May 1989): 225–248;

Evgenii Iur'evich Sidorov, "O Varlame Shalamove i ego proze," in *Varlam Shalamov, Voskreshenie listvennitsy* (Moscow: Khudozhestvennaia literatura, 1989), pp. 487–492;

I. P. Sirotinskaia, "Iz perepiski," *Znamia*, 5 (May 1993): 110–160;

Sirotinskaia, "Iz zapisnykh knizhek," *Znamia*, 6 (June 1995): 134–175;

Sirotinskaia, "Literaturnaia nit'," *Literaturnaia gazeta*, 28 (8 July 1987): 6;

Sirotinskaia, "O Varlame Shalamove," *Literaturnoe obozrenie*, 10 (1990): 103–112;

Sirotinskaia, "Ob avtore," in Shalamov, *Artist lopaty* (Moscow: Sovremennik, 1989), pp. 555–557;

Sirotinskaia, "Ot sostavitelia," in Shalamov, *Kolymskie tetradi* (Moscow: Versty, 1994), pp. 3–4;

Sirotinskaia, "Perepiska Varlama Shalamova i Nadezhdy Mandel'shtam," *Znamia*, 2 (1992): 160–177;

Sirotinskaia, "Varlam Shalamov: Proza, stikhi," *Novyi mir*, 6 (June 1988): 106–151;

Sirotinskaia, "Vospominaniia," *Znamia*, 4 (April 1993): 114–170;

Sirotinskaia and others, *Tezisy dokladov i soobshchenii: Mezhdunarodnye shalamovskie chteniia* (Moscow: Respublika, 1997);

Leona Toker, "Documentary Prose and the Role of the Reader: Some Stories of Varlam Shalamov," in *Commitment in Reflection: Essays in Literature and Moral Philosophy*, edited by Toker (New York: Garland, 1994), pp. 169–193;

Toker, "Stories from Kolyma: The Sense of History," *Hebrew University Studies in Literature and the Arts*, 17 (1989): 188–220;

Toker, "A Tale Untold: Varlam Shalamov's 'A Day Off,'" *Studies in Short Fiction*, 28 (Winter 1991): 1–8;

Toker, "Testimony as Art: Varlam Shalamov's 'Condensed Milk,'" in *Critical Ethics: Text, Theory and Responsibility*, edited by Dominic Rainsford and Tim Woods (Basingstoke, U.K.: Macmillan / New York: St. Martin's Press, 1999), pp. 241–256;

Elena Vasil'evna Volkova, *Tragicheskii paradoks Varlama Shalamova* (Moscow: Respublika, 1998);

Volkova, "Udar tseklebnogo kop'ia: Dva lika Varlama Shalamova," *Literaturnaia gazeta*, 24 April 1996, p. 5.

**Papers:**

The papers of Varlam Tikhonovich Shalamov, including the original manuscripts for *Kolymskie rasskazy*, are located in Moscow at the Russian State Archive of Literature and Art (RGALI), fond 2596.

# Vasilii Makarovich Shukshin
*(25 July 1929 – 2 October 1974)*

John Givens
*University of Rochester*

BOOKS: *Sel'skie zhiteli: Rasskazy* (Moscow: Molodaia gvardiia, 1963);

*Zhivet takoi paren': Kinostsenarii* (Moscow: Iskusstvo, 1964);

*Liubaviny: Roman* (Moscow: Sovetskii pisatel', 1965); enlarged as *Liubaviny: Roman (kniga pervaia i vtoraia)* (Moscow: Knizhnaia palata, 1988);

*Tam, vdali: Rasskazy, povest* (Moscow: Sovetskii pisatel', 1968);

*Zemliaki: Rasskazy* (Moscow: Sovetskaia Rossiia, 1970);

*Kharaktery: Rasskazy* (Moscow: Sovremennik, 1973);

*Ia prishel dat' vam voliu: Roman* (Moscow: Sovetskii pisatel', 1974);

*Besedy pri iasnoi lune: Rasskazy* (Moscow: Sovetskaia Rossiia, 1974);

*Kinopovesti* (Moscow: Iskusstvo, 1975; enlarged edition, edited by Viktor F. Gorn, Barnaul: Altaiskoe knizhnoe izdatel'stvo, 1986);

*Do tret'ikh petukhov: Povesti, rasskazy* (Moscow: Izvestiia, 1976);

*Nravstvennost' est' Pravda,* introduction by Lev Anninsky (Moscow: Sovetskaia Rossiia, 1979);

*Tochka zreniia: Rasskazy, povesti* (Barnaul: Altaiskoe knizhnoe izdatel'stvo, 1979);

*Voprosy samomu sebe,* introduction by Anninsky (Moscow: Molodaia gvardiia, 1981);

*Povesti dlia teatra i kino* (Moscow: Izvestiia, 1984);

*Ia prishel dat' vam voliu: Roman; Publitsistika,* edited by Gorn (Barnaul: Altaiskoe knizhnoe izdatel'stvo, 1991);

*Sobranie sochinenii v piati tomakh,* 5 volumes, commentaries by Anninsky, G. Kostrova, and Lidiia Fedoseeva-Shukshina, "Literaturnoe nasledie" series (Moscow: Panprint, 1996).

**Editions and Collections:** *Brat moi* (Moscow: Sovremennik, 1975);

*Izbrannye proizvedeniia v dvukh tomakh* (Moscow: Molodaia gvardiia, 1975);

*Sobranie sochinenii v trekh tomakh,* 3 volumes, commentaries by Lev Anninsky and Lidiia Fedoseeva-Shukshina (Moscow: Molodaia gvardiia, 1984–1985).

*Vasilii Makarovich Shukshin (Gor'ky Film Studio Museum)*

**Editions in English:** *I Want to Live: Short Stories,* translated by Robert Daglish (Moscow: Progress, 1973);

*Snowball Berry Red and Other Stories,* edited by Donald M. Fiene, translated by Fiene, Boris Peskin, Geoffrey A. Hosking, George Gutsche, George Kolodziej, and James Nelson (Ann Arbor, Mich.: Ardis, 1979)–includes Michel Heller, "Vasily Shukshin: In Search of Freedom," translated by George Gutsche, pp. 13–33;

*Roubles in Words, Kopeks in Figures and Other Stories,* translated by Natasha Ward and David Iliffe (London & New York: Marian Boyars, 1985);

*Articles,* in Eduard Yefimov, *Vasily Shukshin,* translated by Avril Pyman (Moscow: Raduga, 1986);

*Short Stories,* translated by Andrew Bromfield, Robert Daglish, Holly Smith, and Kathleen Mary Cook (Moscow: Raduga, 1990);

*Stories from a Siberian Village,* translated by Laura Michael and John Givens (De Kalb: Northern Illinois University Press, 1996).

PRODUCED SCRIPTS: *Iz Leb'iazhego soobshchaiut,* motion picture, Gor'ky Film Studio, 1960;

*Zhivet takoi paren',* motion picture, Gor'ky Film Studio, 1964;

*Vash syn i brat,* motion picture, Gor'ky Film Studio, 1966;

*Strannye liudi,* motion picture, Gor'ky Film Studio, 1969;

*Pechki-lavochki,* motion picture, Gor'ky Film Studio, 1972;

*Prishel soldat s fronta,* motion picture, based on stories by Sergei Antonov, Mosfil'm, 1972;

*Kalina krasnaia,* motion picture, Mosfil'm, 1974;

*Zemliaki,* motion picture, Mosfil'm, 1975;

*Pozovi menia v dal' svetluiu,* motion picture, Mosfil'm, 1977.

OTHER: "Makar Zherebtsov," translated by Marguerite Mabson, in *The Barsukov Triangle, The Two-Toned Blond, and Other Stories,* edited by Carl R. Proffer and Ellendea Proffer (Ann Arbor, Mich.: Ardis, 1984), pp. 149–155.

SELECTED PERIODICAL PUBLICATIONS–UNCOLLECTED: "Stories," translated by Ralph Parker, *Soviet Literature,* 5 (1964): 82–114;

"Inner Content," translated by Avril Pyman, *Soviet Literature,* 6 (1968): 138–145;

"The Obstinate One," translated by Natasha Johnstone, *Soviet Literature,* 10 (1974): 3–17;

"Short Stories," translated by Robert Daglish, Hilda Perham, H. Perham, and Keith Hammond, *Soviet Literature,* 9 (1975): 3–56;

"The Red Guelder Rose," translated by Daglish, *Soviet Literature,* 9 (1975): 56–122;

"The Odd-Ball," translated by Margaret Wettlin, *Soviet Literature,* 10 (1976): 130–138.

A director of five award-winning movies, a popular and prizewinning actor in more than twenty motion pictures in just sixteen years, and a writer with more than 130 short stories, 12 works for stage and screen, and 3 full-length novels to his credit, Vasilii Makarovich Shukshin was the most visible and prolific Soviet Russian artist of the 1960s and early 1970s. His works reached more people in more media than perhaps any other artist in the two decades following Joseph Stalin's death. Indeed, Shukshin's synthesis of his three creative personae–actor, director, and writer–not only made him a cultural phenomenon in his day but also blurred the boundary between his fiction and movies, an outcome that had a genre-shaping effect on Soviet literature and cinema. His dialogue-driven short stories–as lively, laconic, and luminous as the movies–revitalized that genre in Soviet literature, while his movies, bearing the unmistakable imprint of their creator's triple artistic contributions and betraying their literary origins, helped revive auteur cinema in the Soviet Union. Shukshin's central heroes–human beings in transition, most often rural folk fleeing from the mismanaged and marginalized collective farms to the urban centers in search of better lives–struck a vibrant chord with Soviet readers and moviegoers. His concern with the problems of adaptation, alienation, and accommodation in Soviet society and their effect on one's moral principles made Shukshin the spokesman for a whole generation of physically and spiritually displaced people. Testimony to Shukshin's importance in this regard is his almost universal popularity: he was praised by such diverse individuals as the writer Aleksandr Solzhenitsyn and the former Soviet premier Leonid Brezhnev. His eccentric (sometimes aberrant), soul-searching, and rebellious misfits and their metaphysical quandaries are not only emblematic of his own times but also anticipate the themes and protagonists of the writers whose appearance in the late 1980s marked the end of Soviet fiction and the rebirth of Russian literature. In many ways Shukshin prepared the thematic and stylistic ground in both fiction and motion pictures that others after him worked with greater success. His cri de coeur "What is happening to us?" in one of his last short stories reverberates through the final two decades of the Soviet Union and well into post-Soviet Russian culture.

Shukshin was born on 25 July 1929 in the village of Srostki, several hundred miles southeast of Novosibirsk in the western Siberian region known as the Altai. Shukshin's family on his father's side belonged to a class of well-to-do peasants known as *starozhily,* while his mother came from one of the poorest families in the village. Indeed, Makar Leont'evich Shukshin's decision to marry the lowly Mariia Sergeevna Popova earned him his family's disfavor, although it did not spare him the wave of purges carried out by Communist Party activists sent from Moscow to eliminate the *starozhily* as a class. While they had been tolerated during Vladimir Il'ich Lenin's New Economic Policy of limited private ownership and free markets that lasted from 1921 to

1928, the *starozhily* were branded kulaks and perished during Stalin's policy of collectivization, which began the year Shukshin was born.

The concurrence of Shukshin's birth and the advent of forced collectivization constitute a significant fact in the writer's literary biography. The destruction of a way of life and the uprooting of families through inclusion in collective farms *(kolkhozy)* or migration to the cities haunt the histories of Shukshin's characters. Four years into collectivization, Makar Shukshin was arrested and executed for allegedly either "sabotage" in the *kolkhoz* or "inciting an uprising." Shukshin's mother was not only faced with the task of raising him and his sister alone but also had to cope with a stigma peculiar to the advent of Communist power: that of being the widow of an "enemy of the people." Labeled by their neighbors *sebulonki* (a neologism meaning "wives of Siberian camp inmates"), Mariia Sergeevna and other purge widows were ostracized both socially and within the work collective and were often the last in line for such things as communal farming implements and horses. Shukshin's mother even went back to her maiden name in an attempt to rid her children of the stigma of their father's fate. Thus, until he turned sixteen and applied for his internal passport, Shukshin was Vasilii Makarovich Popov, an experience that left an indelible mark on the writer. Shukshin's decision to reclaim his father's name marks an important moment in the writer's psychological development: by assuming the name of an enemy of the people, he was also rejecting the pall of illegitimacy—political as well as paternal—that hung over him.

A few years after Makar's death, Mariia Sergeevna married Pavel Nikolaevich Kuksin, and the family moved to the neighboring town of Biisk. To these village dwellers the provincial backwater was "the big city," and for Shukshin this first encounter with "city life" was a formative one. Shukshin's stepfather hoped to learn a trade so that the family could improve its fortunes; but when Nazi Germany invaded the Soviet Union in 1941, Kuksin was drafted into the army. He died in battle a year later. Meanwhile, Mariia Sergeevna moved her family back to Srostki, where she could turn to relatives for help and support. Shukshin finished his compulsory seven-year schooling in 1943, and his mother sent him to apprentice with his uncle, Pavel Sergeevich Popov, as a bookkeeper in Ogundai in the nearby Gorno-Altaisk district. The results were disastrous, and Shukshin was enrolled in the Biisk vocational technical school, where he began to write stories and submit them to a Moscow journal around the age of sixteen. None made it into print, nor did Shukshin ever graduate from the vocational school. He was either forced to leave on academic grounds because he failed engine mechanics or was expelled for swearing at his teachers. He returned to Srostki, worked for a while on the collective farm, and in 1946 left the Altai.

For two to three years Shukshin wandered around central Russia taking odd jobs as a metalworker, scaffolder, painter's apprentice, and longshoreman and living in workers' dormitories or sleeping on park benches at industrial sites in and around Moscow. In August 1949 he was drafted into the navy. Discharged in February 1953 because of severe stomach ulcers, he returned to Srostki and earned his high-school equivalency diploma in the fall. After a brief stint as the head of a village night school and a short-lived marriage in 1954 to Mariia Shumskaia, Shukshin went to Moscow to study at the Gor'ky Institute of World Literature. Arriving too late to take the entrance examinations there, he applied (against the rules) simultaneously to the Historical Archives Institute and to the Cinematography Institute (VGIK). The Historical Archives Institute accepted him into its night degree program, and VGIK accepted him into its movie director's department. On his mother's advice, Shukshin enrolled at VGIK in August 1954.

It was Shukshin's good fortune to find himself in Mikhail Il'ich Romm's directing studio at VGIK. Romm was part of the largely ignored second generation of Soviet directors who appeared at the end of the "Golden Age" of Russian cinema in the late 1920s, when sound was about to transform the industry. He lived through Stalin's monopolization of cinema in the 1930s and 1940s and emerged in the Thaw period after Stalin's death as an open-minded and original movie theoretician. His studio at the cinematography institute produced famous and strikingly different directors, among them Grigorii Naumovich Chukhrai, Andrei Arsen'evich Tarkovsky, Andrei Konchalovsky, Larissa Efimovna Shepitko, and Shukshin himself. From Romm, Shukshin learned the value of artistic independence (one of the central concerns of artists during the Thaw) and the importance of good intellectual preparation. Romm encouraged Shukshin to be true to his rural roots and helped him fill in the "blank spots" of his inferior, uneven rural education. He taught Shukshin the importance of economy, whether of form, style, or content, a lesson that applied equally to literature and cinema. Indeed, Shukshin's apprenticeship as a writer took place at the institute, when he began writing short stories as an outgrowth of assignments in his teacher's studio. By Shukshin's fourth year at the institute Romm was impressed enough with his progress to advise him to submit his work to the capital's journals. In 1958 his first publication, "Dvoe na telege" (Two on a Cart), appeared in the journal *Smena* (Change).

*Shukshin in the movie made from his* Pechki-lavochki *(1972, Not Worth Attention), his first "cine-novel," about the differences between city and country life (Gor'ky Film Studio Museum)*

That same year, while still studying directing at VGIK, Shukshin debuted to critical acclaim in his first acting role in Marlen Martynovich Khutsiev's *Dva Fedora* (The Two Fedors). Thus, Shukshin's three creative impulses were confirmed early on. His final project at the institute—his "diploma movie" *Iz Leb'iazhego soobshchaiut* (1960, Report from Lebyazhe)—was written by Shukshin himself, who also played the main role. "I began to write under the influence of the cinema and to make films under the influence of literature," Shukshin later affirmed in an interview ("Edin v trekh litsakh," *Moscovskii komsomolets*, 11 March 1973, p. 3). These three muses beckoned Shukshin all of his short creative life, producing as much a division as a synthesis within the artist. Although his prose is at its core performative and benefited from the insights Shukshin brought to it as an actor, reading other people's lines in other directors' movies interfered with his writing. Similarly, though Shukshin's movies brought his stories to the screen and thus to a broader audience, the time, energy, and bureaucratic red tape involved took their toll on the artist, who complained bitterly at the end of his life that he had not sufficiently devoted himself to literature.

From the beginning Shukshin's career moved in zigzag fashion among the three spheres of his creative activity. Though writing was his consuming passion, he heavily invested himself in his movie careers. In the five years following his debuts as an actor and a writer he appeared in eight movies, published nineteen stories in major literary journals, saw his first collection of stories appear in book form, and wrote and directed his first feature-length motion picture. This breakneck pace of artistic activity hardly abated throughout his career and probably contributed to his death at forty-five.

Shukshin's first collection of stories and first feature movie had the same enthusiastic reception that had greeted his acting debut. *Sel'skie zhiteli* (1963, Country Folk) was praised for its authentic character speech, its laconic style, and the rural Siberian setting of many of its stories. Though Shukshin included few of these tales in later collections, the anthology anticipates much of his mature work both in its heroes and in its central polemic. Unlike the writers of village prose, who focused on the old men and women of a vanishing Russian peasant culture, Shukshin celebrates mobile, technically inclined young men in step with the newly mechanized collective farms: truck drivers, mechanics, and tractor drivers—occupations relatively new to the village. Simple and frequently undereducated, Shukshin's heroes are often also jesters, poets, even philosophers at heart, as sensitive to deep feeling as they are incapable of expressing it. These characters are psychologically suspended between the city and the village, neither committed to life in the countryside nor able to make the transition to urban living. In these early works, however, the conflicted identity of Shukshin's heroes rarely rises to the level of crisis. Most of the stories in the collection are fairly typical Siberian "slice of life" narratives: warm, often amusing tales celebrating life in the Siberian village, they lie somewhere between canonical village prose and exotica literature.

Based in part on two stories from this first collection, Shukshin's debut as a feature motion-picture writer and director, *Zhivet takoi paren'* (1964, A Guy Like That), was also an instant critical success, largely because of its winning central character. Pasha Kolokol'nikov, played by the actor Leonid Kuravlev, is a prankster and a dreamer with a quick wit and a heart of gold and one of Shukshin's most successful literary and cinematic creations. Driving his truck in picaresque fashion from village to village along the Siberian Chuiskii Tract in search of his "ideal"—the perfect woman—Pasha alternates comic stunts with good deeds, ultimately failing in his quest but charming audiences and critics in the process. Like *Sel'skie zhiteli*, the movie is as much a celebration of Shukshin's birthplace and its people as the story of Pasha Kolokol'nikov, a fact underscored in the opening shot of a map of the Chuiskii Tract showing all of the villages along its winding roadway. Pasha was a new hero for Soviet cinema, one whose simplicity did not mask an inner complexity. He was just simple through and through, Siberian bred and country savvy, and this simplicity made him the perfect agent of authenticity for Soviets weary of dissimulation and insincerity. The movie garnered the grand prize at the All-Union Film Festival in 1964; it resonated with foreign audiences, as well, earning Shukshin the Golden Lion Award at the 1964 Venice Film Festival.

Buoyed personally and professionally by the success of the movie, Shukshin was, nevertheless, disappointed that it was viewed as a comedy. Perhaps in response to this misperception, he conceived, scripted, and directed his next movie as a much more serious treatment of his central theme of physical and psychological displacement. *Vash syn i brat* (1966, Your Son and Brother) premiered only eighteen months after the release of *Zhivet takoi paren'*, an indication of both the frenetic pace at which Shukshin worked and the urgency of his artistic program. Based on the stories "Ignakha priekhal" (translated as "Ignakha's Come Home," 1996), "Stepka" (translated as "Styopka," 1996), and "Zmeinyi iad" (Snake Poison), all published in the journal *Novyi mir* (New World) in 1963–1964, the movie treats the problem of the exodus of youth from the village. Of the four sons of Voevodin, the patriarch of a peasant household, only Vas'ka seems willing to follow in his father's footsteps and remain in the village: Ignakha has moved to Moscow, married, and works as a circus wrestler; Maksim is a student at one of the capital's institutes of higher learning and is unlikely to return home, where his degree would be useless; and Stepka has been in a correctional labor camp for nearly five years. The movie is a meditation on the two homecomings that occur—those of Ignakha and Stepka—each of which is in its own way a failure. Stepka has escaped with only three months of his prison term remaining because of his irresistible need to walk down the main street of his home village in the springtime. The joy and celebration his return evokes, however, are cut short by the swift arrival of the police, who will add two more years to his sentence. Instead of Stepka's festive stroll, the viewer watches Stepka's deaf sister stumbling home from the police station, crying inconsolably. She is a symbol of the pain of the village, whose sons and brothers are being taken away. Ignakha's visit home also falls flat. He has grown boastful and condescending, has forgotten all of the old village songs, and refuses to get drunk with his father. Wounded by the change in his son and hoping to prove the superiority of the countryside in a contest of strength, Voevodin keeps insisting that Ignakha wrestle Vas'ka. Neither the wrestling match nor any reconciliation—either between father and son or city and village—materialize, though the movie ends on a positive note: Vas'ka, the son faithful to his roots, leaves with his work collective to another day of fruitful labor in the village.

Though well received, the movie provoked controversy in its thinly veiled criticism of city life, which is particularly pronounced in an episode in which Maksim rushes from pharmacy to pharmacy in Moscow looking for medication that his mother needs back home in Siberia. He encounters indifference and hostility; only connections, not compassion, he learns, can procure the prescription. Critics faulted Shukshin for promoting a village idyll and for creating characters who are insufficiently ideologically aware. The criticism was so shrill in some quarters that Shukshin was asked to explain himself at a roundtable discussion called by the Union of Cinematographers on 8 April 1966. His appearance led to a series of essays in which he staked out his positions in the debate over the changing village and the relationship between the city and the countryside. These essays—"Voprosy samomu sebe" (1966, Questions to Myself) and "Monolog na lestnitse" (1967, Monologue on the Staircase), and "Tol'ko e to ne budet ekonomicheskaia stat'ia" (1967, Only This Won't be an Economics Article) published in *Nravstvennost' est' Pravda* (Moscow: Sovetskaia Rossiia, 1979)—reveal Shukshin's feelings of guilt over having left the village like so many others but also establish him as an artist with a significantly different philosophy and theme from the village-prose writers with whom he is often associated. For Shukshin, change in the village is inevitable and should be welcomed, especially if it takes the form of new libraries, schools, and hospitals. What is wrong, Shukshin argues, is not the exodus of youth from the village, but that in the city these youths "lose themselves . . . their personality, their character" (*Nravstvennost' est' Pravda*). Worse still, they become indifferent, even nihilistic, about their rural heritage and seek not culture but consumer goods and cozy careers in the city.

The root cause of the rift between the city and the village, Shukshin decided, must be sought in the changes brought about in the Russian countryside by the arrival of Soviet power. Shukshin's first novel, composed while he was writing the short stories of his first collection and making his first movie, reflects his desire to explore the history of his native region as a way of better understanding the reasons for the current problems faced by his fellow Siberian peasants. *Liubaviny* (1965, The Liubavin Family) is set in the 1920s in the remote Siberian village of Baklan' and treats the clash of politics, culture, and tradition that ensues when Communist Party activists sent from Moscow battle the wealthy kulak families of the village, including the Liubavins, in an attempt to establish the Soviet rule of law. The novel develops two main plotlines: the trials and tribulations of the Liubavin patriarch and his four sons as they try to preserve their wealth and ward off change introduced from outside; and the mission of the two party activists to exterminate a band of outlaws and former White Army officers and appropriate local grain harvests for redistribution. Schematic in structure and lacking philosophical and historical depth, the novel was neither a critical success nor a serious exploration of the consequences of Soviet agricultural reforms in Siberia. Rather, it describes in episodic fashion the conflicted relationships of a relatively small cast of characters. At its best, it offers a series of lively character sketches. At its worst, it betrays its author's cinematic training in its heavy reliance on dialogue and multiple plot twists. The main character, however, the violent Liubavin son, Egor, marks the earliest appearance in Shukshin's prose of a line of social outcasts and mavericks who occupy an important place in his works.

No more important rebel engaged Shukshin's thoughts and artistic ambition than the one to whom he turned next: the Cossack Sten'ka Razin, who led an uprising against Tsar Aleksei Mikhailovich Romanov from 1667 to 1671. Shukshin conceived of a movie about Razin as early as 1965, and in March 1966 he submitted to Gor'ky Film Studio a proposal for a two-part work based on the life of the legendary ataman. He completed the first draft of the screenplay in September. But with Tarkovsky's medieval epic *Andrei Rublev* mired in controversy and budgetary overruns at Mosfil'm, no studio was willing to undertake another expensive and potentially controversial subject.

Besides budgetary concerns, studio executives had objections to Shukshin's artistic conception of Razin. Neither the class-conscious revolutionary leader of Soviet history books who anticipates the Russian Revolution, nor the colorful legendary hero of Russian folklore who flings a beautiful princess overboard because she has come between him and his men, Shukshin's Razin is the embodiment of an individual's quest for *volia* (freedom) from all that encumbers him physically, spiritually, and psychologically. Instead of the tsar, his corrupt regional governors, and the oppressive class of landowning boyars, Razin struggles against the insidious power of an impersonal centralized bureaucracy whose consequences are self-satisfied materialism, slavish complacency, and crass careerism. In this conflict Shukshin's present-day audience could scarcely fail to see a reflection of their own Soviet reality. Razin himself was also a hero with whom Shukshin's contemporaries could easily identify: someone chafing against the constraints of an autocratic authority who must make difficult decisions and compromise his beliefs and ultimately fails in his quest for freedom. Shukshin worked for the next decade to win approval for his project at Gor'ky Film Studio and later at Mos'film, submitting proposals, revising his scenario, and currying favor with studio executives by fulfilling acting assignments and agreeing to smaller-budget movie projects in exchange for permission to continue preparations for his Razin epic. Permission came a month before his death and only because of the spectacular success of his fifth and final movie, *Kalina krasnaia* (1974, Red Kalina Berry), which was produced as one of Mosfil'm's conditions for considering his Razin proposal. Never appearing on Soviet movie screens, *Ia prishel dat' vam voliu* (I Have Come to Give You Freedom) remained the great unfulfilled passion of his life. The screenplay appeared in 1968 and won the top prize that year at the All-Union Competition of Movie Scripts, while the novel version appeared serially in the journal *Sibirskie ogni* (Siberian Fires) in 1971.

Shukshin married Lidiia Nikolaevna Fedoseeva in 1966; they had two children: Mariia, born on 23 May 1967, and Ol'ga, born on 29 July 1968. Shukshin had also fathered a child out of wedlock: Ekaterina, born on 12 February 1965 to Viktoriia Anatol'evna Sofronova. Between 1966 and 1970 he acted in four movies, wrote and directed another, and wrote forty-five short stories and a novella; twenty-one of the stories were collected in 1968 and published together with the novella, which

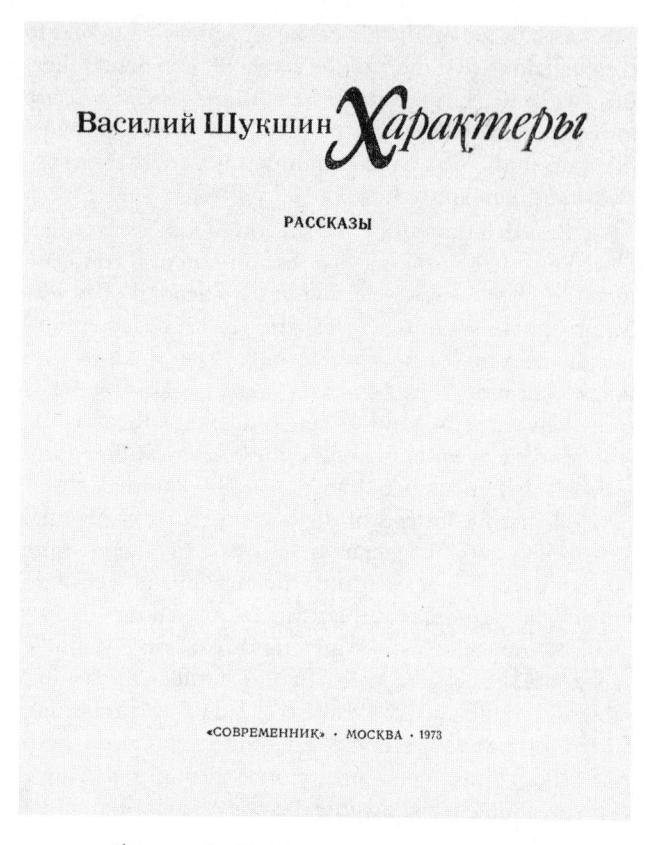

*Title page for Shukshin's* Kharaktery: Rasskazy *(Types: Stories), twenty stories that secured his reputation as a master of the short form (Northern Illinois University Libraries)*

lent the volume its title: *Tam, vdali* (There, in the Distance). Another collection followed in 1970, although half of the twenty-one stories that comprise *Zemliaki* (Fellow Countrymen) were reprinted from *Tam, vdali*. Together with the movie *Strannye liudi* (1969, Strange People), these stories mark a new stage in the development of Shukshin's hero. The titles tell the story: these protagonists are eccentrics and rugged individualists *(strannye liudi)* who live at a great remove from the urban centers *(tam, vdali)* and are bound together by a common rural heritage *(zemliaki)*. Shukshin's best-known appellation for them was *chudik,* from his 1967 story of that title (translated as "Oddball," 1996). The word can be translated as "quirky," "crank," "weirdo," "crackpot," or "nut," though "oddball" seems best to capture the whimsical and essentially harmless nature of these eccentrics. They have various nervous tics and a propensity for acting on their impulses, often wind up in ridiculous predicaments, or inadvertently bring trouble and misfortune crashing down around their heads. As Shukshin puts it in "Chudik": "Oddball possessed one peculiarity: things were always happening to him. He didn't desire this, he'd suffer because of it, but time and time again he'd get into scrapes—minor ones, it's true, but vexing ones all the same."

The rural eccentric as a colorful protagonist has a long history in Russian literature, from Ivan Turgenev's *Zapiski okhotnika* (1852, Hunter's Sketches; translated as *Russian Life in the Interior; or, The Experiences of a Sportsman,* 1855) through Mikhail Sholokhov's country jesters in *Podniataia tselina* (Virgin Soil Upturned, 1932; translated as *The Soil Upturned,* 1934) to the various iconoclasts in the works of Iurii Pavlovich Kazakov, an important and influential contemporary of Shukshin's. Shukshin's oddballs, however, have a wholeness and depth that is lacking in the eccentrics of other writers. The oddness or foolishness of his characters is invariably symptomatic of a much more serious, often spiritual, striving and questioning. Whether masked by annoying but harmless fixations or hidden deep at the core of their impulsive natures, this need to find a higher meaning in life lifts Shukshin's oddballs out of the merely aberrant or curious and transports them into the realm of the philosophical. Even Pasha Kolokol'nikov's search for the perfect woman in *Zhivet takoi paren'* is but the reflection of this desire to find a deeper significance to an otherwise mundane daily life; in this regard, Pasha is an important early incarnation of Shukshin's mature hero.

Broadly speaking, all of Shukshin's oddballs suffer from a similar complaint: a wronged soul. The seriousness of the slights they receive, or their consequences, vary from suicide and prison in the worst-case scenarios to alarmed and aching souls in the best. The eccentricity of many characters, such as Oddball himself in "Chudik," is simply the manifestation of a deep-seated innocence—what Iurii Smelkov called a "hypertrophy of conscience"—that comes into conflict with the harsh outside world, revealing, in the collision between real and ideal, the souls of all involved. Thus, Oddball is taken for a country bumpkin by everyone he encounters on a trip from the village to the big city to visit his brother. At every step his essentially open and guileless nature is opposed by prosaic, closed-minded people lacking the spiritual freedom latent in all of Shukshin's *chudiki*. Eventually, his brother's wife—a transplanted villager herself who has acquired all of the negative traits of urban life, including an obsession with material goods and a contempt of her rural roots—sends him packing back home for painting her baby carriage with country motifs. A more dire outcome occurs in "Suraz" (1969; translated as "The Bastard," 1978), in which another Shukshinian fool commits suicide when his attentions to a young teacher lead to a humiliating beating by her husband. For Spir'ka it is not the physical punishment that matters so much as the psychic wound it inflicts, a wound that prevents him from living in his accustomed free and easy manner. A life thus constrained and stigmatized, Spir'ka believes, is not worth living.

For Shukshin, to "live for one's soul" is to cast off all that compromises one and ties one to the mundane world—the daily grind of work; worry over making ends meet; an unsympathetic spouse; the hostility of friends, neighbors, or strangers; an unhealthy attachment to material things; or a prosaic approach to life. As the priest tells Maksim in "Veruiu!" (1970; translated as "I Believe!" 1978): "Your soul aches? Good. Good! You've at least begun to stir, damn you! Or else it'd be impossible to drag you with all of your spiritual inertia off your berth on the stove." These heroes show others how to rid themselves of their own "spiritual inertia." Shukshin writes: "It's necessary to bring out their beauty in such a way that the satisfied philistine won't want to scoff at their 'strangeness.' On the contrary, so that he will bitterly feel his own good-for-nothingness and at least for a little while be alarmed" ("Kommentarii" to "Esli by Znat" in *Voprosy samomu sebe*). Shukshin is referring to his "strange" heroes' ability to expose the shallow, petty aspects of daily life and, in so doing, to indict the triviality of an outlook tied too strongly to the temporal and worldly.

But Shukshin was asserting the value of the atypical and the individual in an age of the orthodox and the collective, and some critics faulted Shukshin's third collection for seemingly celebrating eccentricity for eccentricity's sake. Conspicuous in this regard are Bron'ka Pupkov in "Mil' pardons, madam!" (1968; translated as "Mille pardons, Madame!" 1978), who insists on repeating his outlandish tale of his secret mission to assassinate Adolf Hitler despite abuse from his wife and threats from the village council to report him to the authorities for "distorting history"; Aleksandr Kozulin in "Daesh' serdtse!" (1970; translated as "Let's Conquer the Heart!" 1996), who fires two rifle shots into the air in the middle of the night to celebrate the news of the first successful human heart transplant in South Africa and is arrested for disturbing the peace; and Andrei Erin in "Mikroskop" (1969; translated as "The Microscope," 1996), who spends a month's salary on a microscope so that he can destroy all of the microbes that keep human beings from living as long as they should. While such stories are amusing, critics charged, there is little to emulate in these heroes. The critics were right from the point of view that Soviet philosophy expected from its citizens, but Shukshin is more concerned with something else: celebrating nonconformity, rebelling against the stagnation of the human personality, and affirming the right of his heroes to be different, to be themselves—to be individuals. One of the main functions of Shukshinian eccentricity and buffoonery is to provide an outlet for nonconformity while masking it as harmless deviation. The provincial location of many of his stories helps to conceal the challenge implicit in the eccentric deeds and obsessions of his oddballs: they are backwater freaks who behave the way they do out of a lack of culture, education, and sophistication.

Shukshin's third motion picture strengthens this perception of his hero both in its title—*Strannye liudi*—and in its subject matter: the stories "Chudik" and "Mil' pardons, Madam!" figure prominently in it. By displaying his "oddball" character types on the wide screen in movie theaters across the country, Shukshin was announcing loudly and clearly his allegiances as an artist. Provocative in its protagonists, the movie was also experimental in form. Rather than combine and adapt different stories to form one unified plot as he did in *Zhivet takoi paren'* or stitch separate stories together into "episodes" as in *Vash syn i brat*, in *Strannye liudi* Shukshin attempts a pure anthology movie: three separate stories are told that do not relate to each other at all. Indeed, each story is given its own title and acting credits, with only an opening and closing sequence providing any sense of unity. In each "story" the audience meets a different kind of oddball: the innocent *chudik* in the first part; the ridiculous assassin, Bron'ka Pupkov, in the second; and the village chairman Matvei Riazantsev and the folk sculptor Vaseka in the last. These quirky heroes are meant to highlight, in amusing yet poignant fashion, the wondrous whimsicality of the human race and to give partial expression to the endless variety of human foibles and virtues. Unlike his previous two movies, however, *Strannye liudi* failed at the box office; audiences walked out before it was over. Shukshin blamed the form, not the content, of the work for the flop. Never again, he decided, would he experiment so radically in his medium; in fact, never again would he bring his short stories to the screen. From this point onward he resolved to write longer works meant explicitly for the movies. Thus were born Shukshin's so-called *kinopovesti* (cine-novellas), a cross between a screenplay and a traditional novella.

Shukshin's first venture in the genre was *Pechki-lavochki* (1972, Not Worth Attention), written as a screenplay in 1969 and as a *kinopovest'* in 1972. Though its hero is another of Shukshin's country-bumpkin *chudiki*, *Pechki-lavochki* is a more serious treatment of the gulf separating the city from the countryside; as such, it is an outgrowth of the themes of several of the stories in *Tam, vdali* and *Zemliaki*. "I razygralis' zhe koni v pole" (1967, O See the Horses Frolic in the Fields; translated as "See the Horses Gallop," 1973), "V profil' i anfas" (1967; translated as "In Profile and Full Face," 1978), "Dva pis'ma" (1967, Two Letters), and the title pieces of the collections feature heroes who are torn between the rural landscapes of their childhood and the urban centers of their adult years that hold out the promise of a better life. The choice is always cast as a loyalty test, and Shukshin's characters frequently fail it. In "I razygralis' zhe koni v pole" and "Dva pis'ma," former villagers who are now making their way in the big city are haunted by memories of their homes and long to return there, if only briefly. "Zemliaki" depicts one such return: Grin'ka Kvasov, who never came back to his village after the war, travels there shortly before he dies to see his long-forgotten home and the brother who had not heard from him since he left. The novellas "Tam, vdali" and "V profil' i anfas" portray restless young men of the postwar generation born into the newly mechanized countryside, men whose roots are no longer in the soil and who are more likely to leave for the city than stay in the village. For them, as for many of these heroes, the peasant's eternal worry about his daily bread is no longer the driving force of their lives. Unlike their parents and grandparents, they are not satisfied with living "just for their stomachs." Ivan, a truck driver in "V profil' i anfas," gives voice to their complaint: "I don't know what I'm working for. . . . Is it really just so I can stuff my face? Well, I've stuffed it. Now what?" Thus, like their *chudiki* counterparts, these rootless heroes adrift between the city and the village are in search of a higher meaning in life–one that is sometimes mysteriously inscribed into the landscape itself. Petr Ivlev in "Tam, vdali," for instance, views these open expanses as the physical embodiment of his own conflicted desires:

> They had come to the outer limits of the village, beyond which opened up a great distance, hilly, forested, but unimaginably broad, and limitless. It seemed to Petr that he had to go into this unknown, unbounded distance. It was unfamiliar, a little frightening, but he already wondered what it would be like there, in the distance. And it was precisely that which was unfamiliar and unknown and so astoundingly immense that beckoned and bid him go thither.

Most of the action of the movie *Pechki-lavochki* is situated in this landscape separating the city and the village: it takes place on board the train transporting Ivan Rostorguev and his wife, Niura, from Siberia to Moscow and then on to the Black Sea on a trip Ivan has earned through his exemplary labor. Along the way they experience various adventures and misadventures in their encounters with an arrogant city slicker, a thief, and a Moscow linguistics professor–only to be told by the director of the Black Sea resort that Ivan has illegally brought his wife along on vacation documents issued to him alone. The movie's title is an untranslatable phrase Ivan often mutters whose original meaning–"living together in friendship and harmony"– reflects the significance of the *pechka* (stove) in the peasant home as a source of warmth, where meals were cooked and grandparents slept, and the *lavochki* (benches) on all sides of the main dining table, where meals were taken in common. In contemporary usage the phrase refers to petty concerns, humorous trivialities, things not worth paying attention to. Shukshin plays on both meanings in his movie, which, for all of its almost slapstick humor, is a serious study in cultural mobility cast as a modern-day folktale: until 1976 rural dwellers in the Soviet Union were not allowed to have the internal passports that were routinely issued to urbanites; thus, the movie, which relates the journey of Ivan and Niura, neither of them possessing internal passports and only one of them carrying official permission papers, celebrates a freedom normally denied those who live in the village–freedom of movement in their own country. Shukshin, of course, was keenly aware of this irony, and the whole movie is a commentary on the disparity between life in the city and life in the country.

The picture is also an important fictional reflection of the writer's own journey from Siberia to Moscow, for Shukshin himself never felt that he had fully made the transition to city living. "It's a terribly uncomfortable position," he wrote in *Nravstvennost' est' Pravda*. "It's not even like trying to straddle a fence. It's more like having one foot on shore and the other in a boat. You can't avoid shoving off, but the thought's a bit frightening." In *Pechki-lavochki*, Shukshin expresses this discomfort through his "fish-out-of-water" protagonist Ivan, who admires the culture and conveniences of life in Moscow but cannot keep from thinking about what must be happening back home in Siberia. Shukshin's skillful interpolation of shots of Siberia at various points throughout the Moscow sequences reinforces the underlying dialectic between Ivan's comic country backwardness so abundantly on display during his journey and the real backwardness of the documentary-like shots of life in the village that open the movie and are glimpsed throughout. In this way the comic folktale about leaving the safety and harmony of one's *pechki-lavochki* on a journey fraught with danger, meetings with villains, disruptions, and deceptions (as in many a folktale about journeys) is also a cutting critique of contemporary Soviet reality, where the phrase *pechki-lavochki* no longer points to "something not worth paying attention to" but, rather, to real social inequality. *Pechki-lavochki* is one of the first honest depictions in Soviet cinema of the bleak conditions of the Soviet countryside, akin to Konchalovsky's *Istoriia Asi Kliachinoi, kotoraia liubilia, da ne vyshla zamuzh* (The Story of Asia

Kliachina, Who Loved but Did Not Marry), produced in 1967 but not released until 1987, the documentary style of which was a direct influence on Shukshin when he saw it at a private studio screening.

*Pechki-lavochki* marked another milestone for Shukshin: for the first time since his diploma project he combined his skills as writer, director, and actor by playing the lead role of Ivan Rostorguev—a feat he repeated in his next and final movie, *Kalina krasnaia*. The "self-collaboration" was highly successful and further solidified his reputation in all three fields. Though it was cut and censored at every step of the production process and received poor distribution, *Pechki-lavochki* was praised by critics. The only bad reviews came from Shukshin's homeland, where he was accused of depicting his fellow Siberians as hicks and faulted—as he was for *Vash syn i brat*—for not noticing the changes that had taken place in the contemporary village. Letters from the Altai complaining about the movie were even written to the Supreme Soviet. Shukshin responded in print with the essay "Priznanie v liubvi" (1973, A Declaration of Love, published as "Slovo o maloi rodine" in *Nravstvennost' est' Pravda*), in which he confronts his conflicted identity and confesses his guilt over having left Siberia: "For people who had to leave home (whatever the reason), and there are very many such people, there is always an involuntary residue of loss, a feeling of guilt and sadness. With the years, the sadness grows less but it doesn't pass altogether. . . . I would like to get to the bottom of all this. Is it mine—the place where I was born and grew up?"

Shukshin's question was no rhetorical one, for by the fall of 1972, when *Pechki-lavochki* was released, the artist scarcely resembled the ambitious, undereducated rural son who had left the village some twenty years previously with the hope of studying in the capital. Though Shukshin vowed that he would eventually return to Siberia, the last five years of his life show a deepening commitment to his movie careers—an outcome of his relentless pursuit of his Razin project—even as he continued to write at an unprecedented pace. Between 1970 and his death four years later, Shukshin acted in nine movies, including his own *Pechki-lavochki* and *Kalina krasnaia,* while writing sixty stories, three novellas, two cine-novellas, two screenplays based on his own stories and one based on those of Sergei Petrovich Antonov, and putting the finishing touches on his novel about Razin. By 1974 Shukshin was known, in the words of Ia.E. El'sberg, as "the most professional, that is, the most regularly appearing 'storyteller' in Soviet literature." Though some critics wondered whether he was rushing unpolished stories into print, Shukshin's fourth anthology, the last that appeared in his lifetime, was his greatest critical success.

*Front cover for the enlarged 1991 edition of Shukshin's collection of fiction* Ia prishel dat' vam voliu *(I Have Come to Give You Freedom; Baylor University Libraries)*

*Kharaktery* (1973, Types) had a print run nearly half that of *Zemliaki* and a fraction of that of *Tam, vdali;* yet, it is the collection that secured Shukshin's place as a master of the short form. The twenty stories were hailed as a major event in fiction and were the object of sharp critical discussions. *Kharaktery* also marks a noticeable turning away from his favorite character type, the village misfit. As reviewers noted, Shukshin was distancing himself from his strange heroes, who in this collection are not so much endearing oddballs and rootless seekers as types: the incarnation of social ills subject to the writer's increasingly satiric pen. Indeed, in many of these stories it is impossible to find a sympathetic character; both protagonist and antagonist are equally subject to the narrator's censure. In "Srezal" (1970; translated as "Cutting Them Down to Size," 1996), a village know-it-all engages a neighbor's visiting son and his wife, two freshly minted *kandidaty* (the equivalent of the American Ph.D.), in a contest of wits and thoroughly humiliates them–not because he is smarter than they are but because the *kandidaty* insist on trying to answer his ridiculous questions in a way that will show off their newly acquired erudition. The title character of "Neprotivlenets Makar Zherebtsov" (1969, Nonresister Makar Zherbtsvo; translated as "Makar Zherebtsov," 1984) is a village postman and busybody who pokes his nose into everyone's business and forces his unwanted advice on anyone unlucky enough to meet him on his rounds, even though this practice sometimes provokes violent reactions. Nikolai Shurygin in "Krepkii muzhik" (1970; translated as "Tough Guy," 1996) hopes to make a name for himself by demolishing an old village church but earns not the admiration of his neighbors but their contempt. In "Svoiak Sergei Sergeevich" (1969, Brother-in-Law Sergei Sergeevich). Andrei Kochugano's wife's sister's husband, a braggart and a showoff, makes Andrei give him a piggyback ride to show gratitude for an expensive gift. A drunken *muzhik* in "Biletik na vtoroi seans" (1971, A Ticket to the Second Showing) mistakes his visiting father-in-law for St. Nicholas and confesses all sorts of abominable things to the man, including his true opinion of his wife and in-laws. In these stories and many of those others of this collection and the next, the posthumously published *Besedy pri iasnoi lune* (1974, Conversations under a Clear Moon), which Shukshin assembled shortly before his death, his heroes often resemble the cast of the amateur village actors in "Krysha nad golovoi" (1970; translated as "A Roof Over Your Head," 1996) in *Kharaktery*: they are petty, small-minded people, frozen into the roles they have assumed, and are themselves to blame for many of the unpleasant things that happen to them.

This state of affairs is particularly apparent in Shukshin's four satiric novellas written in such a way that they could be staged. His last major works–two were published after his death–these novellas confirm his turn to satire and typification in the last years of his life and also attest to his late interest in the theater: two were written explicitly to be staged, and all have been performed repeatedly in Russia. In each work Shukshin uses satire to demythologize and deconstruct present-day Soviet reality in a search for authenticity, and he chooses highly symbolic Soviet settings through which to refract his satire. "Tochka zreniia" (Point of View), conceived as a screenplay in 1966 but reworked as a "fairy-tale novella" in 1974 and published in the journal *Zvezda* in July 1974, for instance, is set in a communal apartment; Shukshin depicts village matchmaking from the points of view of an Optimist and a Pessimist, two "offstage" embodiments of the false viewpoints of Soviet socialist propaganda. The cooperative apartment of the leader of a group of black marketers is the setting of Shukshin's next novella, "Energichnye liudi" (Energetic People), published in *Povesti dlia teatra i kino* (1984), in which everything from the failures of the Soviet command economy to the bankruptcy of socialist morality is exploited satirically and held up to ridicule. The play version was just on the ragged edge of what the censorship would allow and created a minor sensation when it premiered under Georgii Aleksandrovich Tovstonogov's direction at the Leningrad Gor'ky Drama Theater in the summer of 1974. "Do tret'ikh petukhov" (Till the Cock Crows Thrice), published in installments in *Literaturnaia Rossiia* on 7, 14, and 21 June, 1974 and begins in the "sacred space" of a Soviet library from which Ivan the Fool of Russian folklore is sent on a quest for a "certificate of wisdom" by other characters from Russian literature; if he does not obtain it, he faces expulsion from his place in Russian culture. The quest is purely bureaucratic and thoroughly Soviet: it is not important whether Ivan is truly wise, only that he have the proper document. Throughout his quest Ivan battles not supernatural villains from Russian fairy tales but the petty tyrants of modern Soviet society. Finally, in the unfinished "A poutru oni prosnulis'" (And They Woke up in the Morning), published in the January 1975 issue of *Nash sovremennik*, Shukshin chooses his most debased setting of all–a drunk tank–in which to reflect the outside world of Soviet society, whose citizens, the audience learns, are no better and in certain instances are much worse than the hapless inmates awaiting their sentences. In this play Shukshin's bitter laughter reaches its apex.

While these novellas chart important and understudied territory for Shukshin, the greatest triumph of his tripartite career came with the sensational success of his last film, *Kalina krasnaia*, released in March 1974. For many critics it is his defining work. Not only did the tragic and controversial story of recidivist-thief Egor Prokudin's attempt to go straight and return to the rural home of his childhood draw more than sixty million people to theaters across the country; it also generated public debate over the themes of the movie on a scale unprecedented in Soviet cinematic history. Nearly killed by the censorship, *Kalina krasnaia* was approved for wide release only through the intervention of Premier Brezhnev, who was reportedly moved to tears at a private screening. Shukshin wrote, directed, and starred in the movie and is best known as an actor for his award-winning performance as Egor Prokudin. The role is any actor's dream come true. A bit of the folk buffoon, Egor is constantly changing masks and mischievously shamming even as he is engaged in a life-and-death search for his true identity. As he tries on one role after another–repeat offender, village *muzhik*, man about town, sly rogue, clown–he interrogates to humorous effect a whole host of social and socialist stereotypes, only to die at the hands of his former gang members. Like *Pechki-lavochki,* the movie is a study in contrasts, a modern-day folktale that depicts a familiar contemporary reality. On the one hand, the colorful hero sings folk ditties, talks to birch trees, and plays the fool, looking like more of a folk hero than a former convict. On the other hand, Egor is a recognizable product of Stalin's social and agricultural policies that uprooted thousands of Soviets like him, setting them adrift between the village and the city and leading many of them into and out of lives of petty crime. For most Russian viewers and for Shukshin himself, however, the important story being told was that of the return of the prodigal son to his native parts. In the tale of why one can never go home again Shukshin's own private anguish is clearly visible.

Shukshin's death from a heart attack on 2 October 1974, six months after the release of the movie, augmented the already strong resonance the picture had with audiences. As the nation mourned, Egor Prokudin's death was reenacted each night on the movie screen. Within months of Shukshin's death a handful of previously unpublished works appeared and new collections with print runs in the hundreds of thousands were hastily prepared, both a reflection of the writer's popularity and of the level of his support from the authorities, who allowed him to become somewhat of a cult figure after his death. Only one work was kept back: the sequel to his first novel, *Liubaviny;* it was one of the first works to be published during Mikhail Gorbachev's policy of *glasnost'* (openness), appearing in the same 1987 issue of *Druzhba narodov* (Friendship of Nations) as the more sensational delayed debut of Anatolii Naumovich Rybakov's novel *Deti Arbata* (translated as *Children of the Arbat,* 1988) and in book form the following year. In book 2 Shukshin describes the fate of the next generation of the Liubavin family, which is coming of age just after Stalin's death. At the same time he attempts to construct something akin to a fictional treatment of his own biography. Shukshin accomplishes this feat by investing the conflicting tensions of his own life in two interacting fictional alter egos: Ivan Liubavin, the uncompromised "true" village son, whose permanent return to his Altaian homeland is the centerpiece of the book, and Petr Ivlev, the son of an "enemy of the people" who, nevertheless, pursues a successful career and membership in the Communist Party even as he tries to understand the role of the party in his parents' disappearance in the rural purges. As such, the novel offers insights into Shukshin's own split identity–peasant/intellectual, son of a purged kulak/Communist Party member, citified Siberian/maladjusted Muscovite, provincial outsider/establishment artist–even as it fails ultimately to resolve Shukshin's inner divisions. In this way art resembles life, for Shukshin, like his most famous hero, Egor Prokudin, was destined to die without overcoming the problems of his own conflicted identity.

Since Vasilii Makarovich Shukshin's death, his success has been interpreted in diametrically opposed ways: either as the triumph of natural or "folk" talent over the cultural constraints of the Brezhnev era or as the victory of an anti-intellectual and rural bigot. Ultimately, however, Shukshin should be seen as a latecomer to the world of art who all of his life felt a great inferiority complex over his rural origins. At the same time, while grateful to the city for his education and artistic success, he resented the fact that the city was depleting the village of its greatest resource: talented youth. In his life and works Shukshin told the story of an important stratum of Soviet society on the move between city and country and gave voice to its sense of physical and spiritual dislocation and protest. In the end, however, his movies and stories are much more than chronicles of demographic displacement, for they achieved a profundity of theme and universality of character that are both broadly appealing and of enduring value. His threefold creative persona and his equally original works–so unlike much of what appeared during the Brezhnev era–have earned him the distinction of being one of the most talented and innovative artists to come out of the Thaw period of Soviet culture.

**Letters:**

*Shukshinskie chteniia: Stat'i, vospominaniia, publikatsii,* edited by Viktor Gorn (Barnaul: Altaiskoe knizhnoe izdatel'stvo, 1984);

"'Odno znaiu–rabotat'...': Pis'ma Vasiliia Shukshina k Vasiliiu Belovu," *Literaturnaia Rossiia* (21 July 1989): 6–7;

Tamara Ponomareva, "On prishel izdaleka," *Altai,* 2 (1989): 3–79.

**Bibliographies:**

Geoffrey Hosking, "Vasily Shukshin: A Preliminary Bibliography," in Shukshin, *Snowball Berry Red and Other Stories,* edited by Donald M. Fiene, translated by Fiene, Hosking, Boris Peskin, George Gutsche, George Kolodziej, and James Nelson (Ann Arbor, Mich.: Ardis, 1979), pp. 237–249;

M. L. Bortsova and others, *Vasilii Makarovich Shukshin (1929–1974): Bibliograficheskii ukazatel'* (Barnaul: AO Poligrafist, 1994).

**References:**

Aristarkh Andrianov, "Eshche raz o 'strannykh' geroiakh Vasiliia Shukshina," *Molodaia gvardiia,* 10 (1973): 308–312;

Lev Anninsky, "Kommentarii," in Shukshin, *Sobranie sochinenii,* 3 volumes (Moscow: Molodaia gvardiia, 1984–1985), I: 683–701;

Anninsky, "Put' pisatelia," in *O Shukshine: Ekran i zhizn'*, edited by Lidiia Fedoseeva-Shukshina and R. D. Chernenko (Moscow: Iskusstvo, 1979), pp. 113–139;

Anninsky, "'Shukshinskaia zhizn'," *Literaturnoe obozrenie*, 1 (1974): 50–55;

Anninsky, "Volia. Put'. Rezul'tat," *Novyi mir*, no. 12 (1975): 262–264;

V. A. Apukhtina, *Proza V. Shukshina* (Moscow: Vysshaia shkola, 1986);

V. I. Ashcheulov and Iu. G. Egorov, eds., *On pokhozh na svoiu rodinu: zemliaki o Shukshine* (Barnaul: Altaiskoe knizhnoe izdatel'stvo, 1989);

Galina Belaia, "Paradoksy i otkrytiia Vasiliia Shukshina," in her *Khudozhestvennyi mir sovremennoi prozy* (Moscow: Nauka, 1983), pp. 93–118;

Vasilii Ivanovich Belov and Anatolii Dmitrievich Zabolotsky, *Tiazhest' kresta: Shukshin v kadre i za kadrom* (Moscow: Sovetskii pisatel', 2002);

L. Belova, "Tri rusla odnogo puti: O tvorchestve Vasiliia Shukshina," in *Voprosy kinoiskusstva*, volume 17 (Moscow: Nauka, 1976), pp. 136–162;

N. A. Bilichenko, "Shukshin's Hero through the Eyes of the Critics," *Soviet Studies in Literature*, 17 (Winter 1980–1981): 45–69;

Galina Pavlovna Binova, *Tvorcheskaia evoliutsiia Vasiliia Shukshina* (Brno: Univerzita J. E. Purkyne v Byrne, 1988);

Anatolii Georgievich Bocharov, "Counterpoint: The Common and the Individual in the Prose of Iuryi Trifonov, Vasilii Shukshin, and Valentin Rasputin," *Soviet Studies in Literature*, 20 (Winter 1983–1984): 21–48;

Evgenii Chernosvitov, *Proiti po kraiu: Vasilii Shukshin. Mysli o zhizni, smerti i bessmertii* (Moscow: Sovremennik, 1989);

Nicole Christian, "Manifestations of the Eccentric in the Works of Vasilii Shukshin," *Slavonic and East European Review*, 75 (April 1997): 202–203;

Christian, "Vasilii Shukshin and the Russian Fairy Tale: A Study of *Until the Cock Crows Thrice*," *Modern Language Review*, 92 (April 1997): 392–400;

A. Chuvakin, ed., *Iazyk i stil' prozy V. M. Shukshina* (Barnaul: Altaiskii gosudarstvennyi universitet, 1991);

Chuvakin and others, eds., *Tvorchestvo V. M. Shukshina: Opyt entsiklopedicheskogo slovaria-spravochnika* (Barnaul: Altaiskii gosudarstvennyi universitet, 1997);

Chuvakin and others, eds., *Tvorchestvo V. M. Shukshina: Poetika, stil', iazyk* (Barnaul: Altaiskii gosudarstvennyi universitet, 1994);

V. V. Desiatov and others, eds., *Tvorchestvo V. M. Shukshina: Opyt entsiklopedicheskogo slovaria-spravochnika,* (Barnaul: Altaiskii gosudarstvennyi universitet, 1997);

L. I. Emel'ianov, *Vasilii Shukshin: Ocherk tvorchestva* (Leningrad: Khudozhestvennaia literatura, 1983);

Raul' Eshel'man, "Epistemologiia zastoia: O postmodernistskoi proze V. Shukshina," *Russian Literature*, 35 (1994): 67–92;

Lidiia Fedoseeva-Shukshina and R. D. Chernenko, eds., *O Shukshine: Ekran i zhizn'* (Moscow: Iskusstvo, 1979);

Donald M. Fiene and Boris N. Peskin, "The Remarkable Art of Vasily Shukshin," *Russian Literature Triquarterly*, 11 (1975): 174–178;

V. I. Fomin, *Peresechenie parallel'nykh* (Moscow: Iskusstvo, 1976);

L. Geller, "Opyt prikladnoi stilistiki: Rasskaz V. Shukshina kak ob'ekt issledovaniia s peremennym fokusnym rasstoianiem," *Wiener Slawistischer Almanack*, 4 (1979): 95–123;

John Givens, *Prodigal Son: Vasilii Shukshin in Soviet Russian Culture* (Evanston, Ill.: Northwestern University Press, 2000);

Viktor F. Gorn, *Vasilii Shukshin: Lichnost', knigi* (Barnaul: Altaiskoe knizhnoe izdatel'stvo, 1990);

Gorn, ed., *Shukshinskie chteniia: Stat'i, vospominaniia, publikatsii*, 2 volumes (Barnaul: Altaiskoe knizhnoe izdatel'stvo, 1984, 1989);

V. Grishaev, *Shukshin, Srostki, Piket* (Barnaul: Altaiskoe knizhnoe izdatel'stvo, 1994);

Geoffrey Hosking, *Beyond Socialist Realism: Soviet Fiction since Ivan Denisovich* (London: Granada, 1980);

N. N. Ianovsky, ed., *Stat'i i vospominaniia o Vasilii Shukshine* (Novosibirsk: Novosibiskoe knizhnoe obozrenie, 1989);

Diane Nemec Ignashev, "The Art of Vasilij Šukšin: Volja through Song," *Slavic and East European Journal*, 32 (1988): 415–427;

Ignashev, "Song and Confession in the Short Prose of Vasilij Makarovič Šukšin: 1929–1974," dissertation, University of Chicago, 1984;

Ignashev, "Vasily Shukshin's *Srezal* and the Question of Transition," *Slavonic and East European Review*, 66 (1988): 337–356;

Valentina Ivanovna Kaplina and Viktor Vasil'evich Biukhov, eds., *S vysoty Shukshinskogo Piketa* (Barnaul: OAO, 1998);

Valentina Karpova, *Talantlivaia zhizn': Vasilii Shukshin, prozaik* (Moscow: Sovetskii pisatel', 1986);

Veniamin Aleksandrovich Kaverin, "Shukshin's Stories," *Soviet Studies in Literature*, 14, no. 3 (1978): 47–60;

Vladimir Korobov, *Vasilii Shukshin: Veshchee slovo* (Moscow: Molodaia gvardiia, 1999);

Svetlana Mikhailovna Kozlova, *Poetika rasskaza V. M. Shukshina* (Barnaul: Altaiskii gosudarstvennyi universitet, 1993);

Kozlova, "Sud'ba narodnoi pesni v proze V. M. Shukshina," in *Kul'turnoe nasledie Altaia,* edited by T. M. Stepanskaia (Barnaul: Altaiskii gosudarstvennyi universitet, 1992);

Kozlova, ed., *V. M. Shukshin: Filosof, istorik, khudozhnik* (Barnaul: Altaiskii gosudarstvennyi universitet, 1992);

Kozlova, V. A. Chesnokova, and Chuvakin, eds., *Rasskaz V. M. Shukshina "Srezal": Problemy analiza, interpretatsii, perevoda* (Barnaul: Altaiskii gosudarstvennyi universitet, 1995);

Kozlova and others, eds., *Tvorchestvo V. M. Shukshina: Metod, poetika, stil'. Mezhvuzovskii sbornik statei* (Barnaul: Altaiskii gosudarstvennyi universitet, 1997);

Kozlova and others, eds., *Tvorchestvo V. M. Shukshina: Problemy, poetika, stil'* (Barnaul: Altaiskii gosudarstvennyi universitet, 1991);

Aleksandr Ivanovich Kuliapin and Ol'ga Gennadievna Levashova, *V. M. Shukshin i russkaia klassika* (Barnaul: Altaiskii gosudarstvennyi universitet, 1998);

V. A. Kuz'muk, "Vasilii Shukshin and the Early Chekhov (An Essay in Typological Analysis)," *Soviet Studies in Literature,* 14, no. 3 (1978): 61–78;

Stephen le Fleming, "Vasily Shukshin: A Contemporary Scythian," in *Russian and Slavic Literature: Selected Papers in the Humanities from the First International Slavic Conference,* edited by R. Freeborn, R. Milner-Gulland, and Charles A. Ward (Cambridge, Mass.: Slavica, 1977), pp. 449–466;

Aleksandr Lebedev, *Tsvety zapozdalye: Zhenshchiny v zhizni Vasiliia Shukshina* (Moscow: Podmoskov'e, 1999);

Levashova, *V. M. Shukshin i traditsii russkoi literatury XIX v. (F. M. Dostoevskii i L. N. Tolstoi)* (Barnaul: Altaiskii gosudarstvennyi universitet, 2001);

Levashova and others, eds., *V. M. Shukshin: Problemy i resheniia* (Barnaul: Altaiskii gosudarstvennyi universitet, 2002);

Robert Mann, "St. George in Vasilij Shukshin's *Kalina krasnaja*," *Slavic and East European Journal,* 28, no. 4 (1984): 445–454;

Lyndall Morgan, "Shukshin's Women: An Enduring Russian Stereotype," *Australian Slavonic and East European Studies,* 1, no. 2 (1987): 137–146;

Morgan, "The Subversive Sub-text: Allegorical Elements in the Short Stories of Vasilii Shukshin," *Australian Slavonic and East European Studies,* 5, no. 1 (1991): 59–76;

Boris Pankin, "Shukshin about Himself: Notes on the Collection Morality is Truth," *Soviet Studies in Literature,* 17, no. 1 (1980–1981): 28–44;

Pankin, "Vasilii Shukshin and His 'Cranks,'" *Soviet Studies in Literature,* 14, no. 2 (1978): 16–37;

Tamara Alekseevna Ponomareva, *Potaennaia liubov' Shukshina* (Moscow: Algoritm, 2001);

"Reality and the Writer's Vision [*Voprosy literatury* roundtable on *Kalina krasnaia*]," translated by Margaret Wettlin, *Soviet Literature,* 9 (1975): 123–138;

Vladimir Sigov, *Russkaia ideia V. M. Shukshina* (Moscow: Intellekt-tsentr, 1999);

Iu. Tiurin, *Kinematograf Vasiliia Shukshina* (Moscow: Iskusstvo, 1984);

Nina Tolchenova, *Slovo o Shukshine* (Moscow: Sovremennik, 1982);

Evgenii Vertlib, *Vasilii Shukshin i russkoe dukhovnoe vozrozhdenie* (New York: Effect, 1990);

Ida Aleksandrovna Vorob'eva, *Slovar' dialektizmov v proizvedeniiakh V. M. Shukshina* (Barnaul: Altaiskii gosudarstvennyi universitet, 2002);

Yuri Vorontsov and Igor Rachuk, *The Phenomenon of the Soviet Cinema* (Moscow: Progress Publishers, 1980);

Eduard Yefimov, *Vasily Shukshin,* translated by Avril Pyman (Moscow: Raduga, 1986);

Neya Zorkaya, *The Illustrated History of Soviet Cinema* (New York: Hippocrene Books, 1989), pp. 275–279.

**Papers:**

The bulk of Vasilii Marakovich Shukshin's manuscripts and papers are in the possession of his widow, Lidiia Fedoseeva-Shukshina. Some archival materials are at the Altai Regional Museum of the History of Literature, Art, and Culture and the Shukshin Center at Altai State University in Barnaul, as well as the Gor'ky Film Studio Museum and the Mosfil'm Studio in Moscow.

# Konstantin Simonov
(15 November 1915 – 28 August 1979)

Marina Balina
*Illinois Wesleyan University*

BOOKS: *Pavel Chernyi: Poema* (Moscow: Sovetskii pisatel', 1938);

*Ledovoe poboishche: Poema* (Moscow: Pravda, 1938; Moscow: Goslitizdat, 1941);

*Nastoiashchie liudi: Kniga stikhov* (Moscow: Goslitizdat, 1938);

*Dorozhnye stikhi* (Moscow: Sovetskii pisatel', 1939);

*Luganchane: Kniga stikhov i prozy,* by Simonov and Mikhail L'vovich Matusovskii (Moscow: Sovetskii pisatel', 1939);

*Suvorov: Poema* (Moscow & Leningrad: Detizdat, 1940);

*Stikhi tridtsat' deviatogo goda* (Moscow: Sovetskii pisatel', 1940);

*Iz frontovogo bloknota* (Moscow: Sovetskii pisatel', 1941);

*Pobeditel': Stikhi* (Moscow: OGIZ Voenizdat, 1941);

*Paren' iz nashego goroda: P'esa v chetyrekh deistviiakh, desiati kartinakh* (Moscow: VUOAP [Vsesoiuznoe upravlenie po okhrane avtorskikh prav], 1941);

*Syn artillerista: Stikhi* (Moscow: Voenizdat, 1941);

*Stikhotvoreniia, 1936–1942 gg.* (Moscow: Khudozhestvennaia literatura, 1942);

*Lirika* (Moscow: Molodaia gvardiia, 1942);

*Ot Chernogo do Barentseva Moria: Zapiski voennogo korrespondenta,* 4 volumes (Moscow: Sovetskii pisatel', 1942–1945);

*Russkie liudi: P'esa v trekh deistviiakh, deviati kartinakh* (Moscow: VUOAP, 1942; translated by Gerard Shelley and adapted by Sir Tyrone Guthrie as *The Russians,* in *Four Soviet War Plays* (New York & London: Hutchinson, 1944), pp. 118–175;

*Moskva* (Moscow: Voenizdat, 1942); translated as *Moscow* (Moscow: Foreign Languages Publishing House, 1943);

*Zhdi menia: P'esa v trekh deistviiakh, vos'mi kartinakh* (Moscow: VUOAP, 1943);

*Lager' unichtozheniia* (Moscow: Voenizdat, 1944); translated as *The Lublin Extermination Camp* (Moscow: Foreign Languages Publishing House, 1944; London: Daily Worker League, 1944);

*Tak i budet: P'esa v trekh deistviiakh, shesti kartinakh* (Moscow: VUOAP, 1944);

*Konstantin Simonov (from* Friends and Foes: A Book of Poems, *1951; Thomas Cooper Library, University of South Carolina)*

*Dni i nochi: Povest* (Moscow: Sovetskii pisatel', 1944); translated by Joseph Barnes as *Days and Nights* (New York: Simon & Schuster, 1945);

*Voina: Stikhi, 1937–1943 goda* (Moscow: Sovetskii pisatel', 1944);

*Iugoslavskaia tetrad'* (Moscow: Sovetskii pisatel', 1945);

*Stikhotvoreniia i poemy* (Moscow: Khudozhestvennaia literatura, 1945);

*Frontovye stikhi* (Moscow: Pravda, 1945);

*Russkoe serdtse* (Moscow: Pravda, 1945);

*Pis'ma iz Chekhoslovakii* (Moscow: Voenizdat, 1945);

*Ser'eznyi Razgovor* (Moscow: Voenizdat, 1945);

*Rasskazy* (Moscow: Sovetskii pisatel', 1946);

*Pod kashtanami Pragi: Drama v chetyrekh deistviiakh, piati kartinakh* (Moscow: VUOAP, 1946);

*Stikhi* (Moscow: Pravda, 1946);

*Russkii vopros: P'esa v 3-kh deistviiakh, 7 kartinakh* (Moscow: VUOAP, 1946); translated by George Leonof as *The Russian Question* (Shanghai: Epoch, 1947);

*Rasskazy* (Smolensk: Smolgiz, 1947);

*Ot nashego voennogo korrespondenta* (Moscow: Voenizdat, 1948);

*Druz'ia i vragi: Kniga stikhov* (Moscow: Sovetskii pisatel', 1948); translated by Irina Zhukovitskaia as *Friends and Foes: A Book of Poems* (Moscow: Foreign Languages Publishing House, 1951);

*P'esy: Russkii vopros. Chuzhaia ten'* (Moscow: Khudozhestvennaia literatura, 1949);

*Chuzhaia ten': Drama v 4 deistviiakh, 6 kartinakh* (Moscow: Iskusstvo, 1949);

*Stikhi. P'esy. Rasskazy* (Moscow: Khudozhestvennaia literatura, 1949);

*Aleksandr Sergeevich Pushkin: doklad na torzhestvennom zasedanii v Bol'shom Teatre Soiuza SSR 6 iiunia 1949 goda* (Moscow: Sovetskii pisatel', 1949);

*Srazhaiushchiisia Kitai* (Moscow: Sovetskii pisatel', 1950);

*V eti gody: Publitsistika 1941–1950 gg.* (Moscow: Khudozhestvennaia literatura, 1951);

*Pekhotnitsy: Rasskazy* (Moscow: Voenizdat, 1953);

*Tretii adiutant: Rasskaz* (Moscow: Voenizdat, 1953);

*Stikhi 1954 goda* (Moscow: Sovetskii pisatel', 1954);

*Tovarishchi po oruzhiiu* (Moscow: Molodaia gvardiia, 1954);

*Istoriia odnoi liubvi: P'esa v trekh deistviiakh, chetyrekh kartinakh* (Moscow: VUOAP, 1954);

*Novye stikhi* (Moscow: Pravda, 1955);

*Stikhi i poemy, 1936–1954* (Moscow: Goslitizdat, 1955);

*Na literaturnye temy: Stat'i 1937–1955* (Moscow: Khudozhestvennaia literatura, 1956);

*Dym otechestva* (Moscow: Sovetskii pisatel', 1956);

*Norvezhskii dnevnik* (Moscow: Sovetskii pisatel', 1956);

*Liudi s kharakterom: Zametki pisatelia* (Tashkent: Goslitizdat UzSSR, 1958);

*Ivan da Mar'ia* (Moscow: Pravda, 1958);

*Zhivye i mertvye* (Moscow: Goslitizdat, 1960); translated by R. Ainsztein as *The Living and the Dead* (Garden City, N.Y.: Doubleday, 1962); translation republished as *Heroes and Victims* (London: Hutchinson, 1963);

*Front: Ocherki i rasskazy, 1941–1945* (Moscow: Voenizdat, 1960);

*Shtrikhi epopei* (Tashkent: Gospolitizdat, 1961);

*Vo imia druzhby: izbrannye stikhotvoreniia* (Moscow: Gosudarstvennoe izdatel'stvo detskoi literatury, 1961);

*Chetvertyi: Drama* (Moscow: Iskusstvo, 1962);

*Iuzhnye povesti* (Moscow: Sovetskii pisatel', 1962);

*Stikhi, poemy, volnye perevody, 1936–1961* (Moscow: Sovetskii pisatel', 1962);

*Paren' iz nashego goroda: P'esa: Novaia stsenicheskaia redaktsiia* (Moscow: Iskusstvo, 1963);

*Ne zabluzhdaites! Zametki pisatelia* (Moscow: Politizdat [Politicheskaia literatura], 1964);

*Tri tetradi: Stikhi, poemy* (Moscow: Voenizdat, 1964);

*Soldatami ne rozhdaiutsia*, 4 volumes (Moscow: Sovetskii pisatel', 1964);

*Stikhi, poemy, vol'nye perevody, 1936–1961* (Moscow: Sovetskii pisatel', 1964);

*Tam, gde my byvali: Povesti i rasskazy* (Moscow: Moskovskii rabochii, 1964);

*Inozemtsev i Ryndin: (Iz bumag Lopatina)* (Moscow: Sovetskaia Rossiia, 1964);

*Druz'ia ostaiutsia druz'iami (Staraia fotografiia). Komediia v shesti kartinakh,* by Simonov and V. Dykhovichnyi (Moscow: VUOAP, 1965);

*Kazhdyi den'–dlinny: Iz voennykh dnevnikov 1941–1945 gg.* (Moscow: Sovetskaia Rossiia, 1965);

*Iz zapisok Lopatina* (Moscow: Sovetskaia Rossiia, 1965);

*Ostaius' zhurnalistom: putevye ocherki, zametki, reportazhi, pis'ma (1958–1967)* (Moscow: Pravda, 1968); translated as *Always a Journalist* (Moscow: Progress, 1989);

*Dvadtsat' piat' stikhotvorenii i odna poema* (Moscow: Sovetskii pisatel', 1968);

*Voennaia lirika: 1936–1956* (Moscow: Sovetskaia Rossiia, 1968);

*Daleko na Vostoke: Khalkhingol'skie zapisi* (Moscow: Sovetskii pisatel', 1969);

*Razgovor s tovarishchami. Razgovor s tovarishchami. Vospominaniia. Stat'i. Literaturnye zametki. O sobstvennoi rabote* (Moscow: Sovetskii pisatel', 1970);

*Zapiski molodogo cheloveka: Kniga v dvukh chastiakh* (Moscow: Molodaia gvardiia, 1970);

*Poslednee leto: Roman* (Moscow: Sovetskii pisatel', 1971);

*V'etnam, zima semidesiatogo . . .* (Moscow: Sovremennik, 1971);

*Tridtsat' shestoi-sem'desiat pervyi: Stikhotvoreniia i poemy* (Moscow: Khudozhestvennaia literatura, 1972);

*Murmanskoe napravlenie* (Murmansk: Murmanskoe knizhnoe izdatel'stvo, 1972);

*Dvadtsat' dnei bez voiny. Iz zapisok Lopatina. Povest'* (Moscow: Sovremennik, 1973);

*Ot Khalkhin-Gola do Berlina* (Moscow: DOSAAF, 1973);

*V svoi vosemnadtsat let: Razmyshleniia o podvige komsomol'tsa A. Merzlova* (Moscow: Sovetskaia Rossiia, 1973);

*Nezadolgo do tishiny: Zapiski 1945 g. mart-apr.-mai* (Moscow: Sovetskaia Rossiia, 1974);

*Segodnia i davno: Stat'i. Vospominaniia. Literaturnye zametki. O sobstvennoi rabote* (Moscow: Sovetskii pisatel', 1974);

*Raznye dni voiny: Dnevnik pisatelia* (Moscow: Molodaia gvardiia, 1975);

*Druz'iam na pamiat'* (Baku: Azerneshr, 1975);

*Piat tysiach strok* (Moscow: Sovetskii pisatel', 1975);

*Povesti i rasskazy* (Moscow: Moskovskii rabochii, 1976);

*Shel soldat . . .* (Moscow: DOSAAF, 1976);

*Iaponiia 46* (Moscow: Sovetskaia Rossiia, 1977);

*My ne uvidimsia s toboi (Iz zapisok Lopatina): Povest'* (Moscow: Khudozhestvennaia literatura, 1978);

*Tak nazyvaemaia lichnaia zhizn': (Iz zapisok Lopatina). Roman v trekh povestiakh* (Moscow: Moskovskii rabochii, 1978);

*Soldatskie memuary: Dokumental'nye stsenarii* (Moscow: Iskusstvo, 1985);

*Glazami cheloveka moego pokoleniia: Razmyshleniia o I. V. Staline*, edited by Lazar' Il'ich Lazarev (Moscow: Agenstvo Pechati Novosti, 1988); translated by Hilda Perham, Barbara Ellis, Diana Turner, Patricia Donegan, and Clive Liddiard as *Through the Eyes of My Generation: Meditations on I. V. Stalin*, with introduction and notes by Lazarev, *Soviet Literature*, 4, no. 493 (1989): 25-104; 5, no. 494 (1989): 30-112;

*Sto sutok voiny* (Smolensk: Rusich, 1999);

*Konstantin Simonov*, edited by A. F. Zaivansky (St. Petersburg: Diamant, Zolotoi vek, 2000).

**Editions and Collections:** *Lirika* (Moscow: Molodaia gvardiia, 1942);

*S toboi i bez tebia: Iz liricheskogo dnevnika* (Moscow: Pravda, 1942);

*Izbrannoe* (Moscow: Sovetskii pisatel', 1948);

*P'esy* (Moscow & Leningrad: Goslitizdat, 1948);

*P'esy* (Moscow: Sovetskii pisatel', 1950);

*Izbrannye stikhi* (Moscow: Sovetskii pisatel', 1951);

*Stikhi i poemy* (Moscow: Molodaia gvardiia, 1952);

*Sochineniia v 3-kh tomakh*, 3 volumes (Moscow: Goslitizdat, 1952-1953);

*P'esy* (Moscow: Iskusstvo, 1954);

*Povesti i rasskazy* (Moscow: Goslitizdat, 1956);

*Lirika* (Moscow: Khudozhestvennaia literatura, 1956);

*Izbrannye stikhi* (Moscow: Goslitizdat, 1958);

*Izbrannye stikhotvoreniia* (Tashkent: Goslitizdat UzSSR, 1960);

*Sobranie sochinenii*, 6 volumes (Moscow: Khudozhestvennaia literatura, 1966-1970);

*Stikhotvoreniia*, edited by K. Platonova (Moscow: Khudozhestvennaia literatura, 1967);

*Izbrannaia lirika* (Moscow: Molodaia gvardiia, 1969);

*Zhivye i mertvye. Roman. V trekh knigakh* (Moscow: Sovetskii pisatel', 1972);

*Stikhotvoreniia i poemy* (Perm': Knizhnoe izdatel'stvo, 1974);

*Poemy* (Moscow: Sovetskaia Rossiia, 1975);

*Sobranie sochinenii*, 10 volumes, edited by Lazar' Il'ich Lazarev (Moscow: Khudozhestvennaia literatura, 1979);

*Esli dorog tebe tvoi dom . . . : Poemy, stikhotvoreniia, povest'* (Moscow: Molodaia gvardiia, 1982);

*Stikhotvoreniia i poemy* (Moscow: Pravda, 1982);

*Stikhotvoreniia i poemy*, edited, with an introduction, by Lazarev, notes by Tat'iana Aleksandrovna Bek (Moscow: Sovetskii pisatel', 1982);

*Povesti* (Moscow: Sovetskaia Rossiia, 1984);

*Sofia Leonidovna: Povest'* (Moscow; Sovetskii pisatel', 1985); translated by Alex Miller as *Sofia Leonidovna*, edited by Lazarev, *Soviet Literature*, 7, no. 448 (1985): 3-92;

*Stikhotvoreniia i poemy*, edited by Lazarev, notes by Bek, Biblioteka poeta, malaia seriia (Leningrad: Sovetskii pisatel' Leningradskoe otdelenie, 1990);

*Stikhotvoreniia*, edited by Lazarev (Moscow: Slovo, 1996).

**Editions in English:** *On the Petsamo Road: Notes of a War Correspondent* (Moscow: Foreign Languages Publishing House, 1942);

*Stalingrad Fights On: Articles*, translated by D. L. Fromberg (Moscow: Foreign Languages Publishing House, 1942);

*No Quarter* (New York: L. B. Fischer, 1943);

*Friendship Is the Most Important Thing in the World*, translated by Bernard Koten (San Francisco: American Russian Institute, 1946?);

*Field Marshall Kutuzov*, in *Seven Soviet Plays*, edited by Henry Wadsworth Longfellow Dana (New York: Macmillan, 1946);

*The Whole World Over: A Comedy in Two Acts*, adapted by Thelma Schnee Moss from Simonov's play *Tak i budet* (New York: Dramatists Play Service, 1947);

"I Write about What I Know," *Soviet Studies in Literature*, 15, no. 4 (1979): 82-90;

*In One Newspaper: A Chronicle of Unforgettable Years*, by Simonov and Ilya Ehrenburg, translated by Anatol Kagan (New York: Sphinx, 1985).

PLAY PRODUCTIONS: *Istoriia odnoi liubvi*, Moscow, Lenin Komsomol Theater, December 1940;

*Paren' iz nashego goroda*, Moscow, Lenin Komsomol Theater, March 1941;

*Russkie liudi*, Moscow, Moscow Art Theater, 1942;

*Russkii vopros,* Moscow, Mossovet Theater, 1946;
*Chetvertyi,* Moscow, Sovremennik Theater, 1961.

PRODUCED SCRIPTS: *Paren' iz nashego goroda,* motion picture, script by Simonov and Aleksandr Ptushko, Tsentral'naia kinostudiia khudozhestvennykh fil'mov, Alma-Ata, 1942;

*Zhdi menia,* motion picture, Tsentral'naia kinostudiia, khudozhestvennykh fil'mov, Alma-Ata, 1943;

*Dni i nochi,* motion picture, Mosfil'm, 1945;

*Russkii vopros,* motion picture, script by Simonov and Mikhail Il'ich Romm, Mosfil'm, 1947;

*Bessmertnyi garnizon,* motion picture, Mosfil'm, 1956;

*Normandiia-Neman,* motion picture, script by Simonov, Charles Spaak, and El'sa Triolet, Mosfil'm, Al'kam Film, France/London Film, 1960;

*Zhivye i mertvye,* motion picture, script by Simonov and Aleksandr Borisovich Stolper, Mosfil'm, 1963;

*Esli dorog tebe tvoi dom,* motion picture, script by Simonov and Evgenii Vorob'ev, Mosfil'm, 1967;

*Sluchai s Polyninym,* motion picture, script by Simonov and Aleksei Sakharov, Mosfil'm, 1970;

*Dvadtsat' dnei bez voiny,* motion picture, Lenfil'm, 1976.

Konstantin Simonov was one of the most celebrated and decorated writers in Soviet literature during World War II and after. The government awarded him the State (former Stalin) Prize for Literature six times (in 1942, 1943, 1946, 1947, 1949, and 1950), and in 1967 Simonov received the highest honor given by the Soviet Union to its writers, the Lenin Prize for achievements in literature. During his lifetime he held key positions in Soviet literary administration: he served as an editor in chief of the most popular Soviet "thick" journal, *Novyi mir* (New World), from 1946 to 1950 and from 1954 to 1958, and of *Literaturnaia gazeta* (Literary Gazette) from 1950 to 1953. He was elected as a deputy of the Supreme Soviet of both the Russian Federation and the Soviet Union; he also served as secretary of the Union of Soviet Writers and in 1974 was finally awarded the highest honor in the Soviet system, the title of Hero of Soviet Labor. He was known to his contemporaries as a poet, dramatist, prose writer, and journalist.

Celebrated by the government as the official promoter of Soviet values, Simonov nevertheless enjoyed enormous popularity among diverse circles of Soviet readership. His literary works on World War II were equally popular among workers and intelligentsia, for they were perceived as honest reflections of the tragedy of the war. His documentary series on the war for Soviet cinema and television brought him recognition in virtually every Soviet household. These documentaries, which focus on the war experiences of ordinary soldiers, provided a striking contrast to the self-promoting war memoirs of Soviet political leaders. Labeled as a government collaborator by Western scholars and neglected by post-Soviet literary scholars because of his reputation as a government collaborator, Simonov reflects in his life and works some of the major intellectual and moral conflicts a creative person faced within the Soviet totalitarian system. During World War II his work was well received; his war poems, especially "Zdi menia i ia vernus'" (Wait for Me and I'll Return), were particularly popular. His experience as a war correspondent provided the basis for his postwar fiction and documentary prose. In these works Simonov portrays war as a national, as well as personal, tragedy.

*Front cover for one of the four volumes of* Ot Chernogo do Barentseva Moria *(1942–1945, From the Black to the Barents Sea), Simonov's travel essays written during World War II (William T. Young Library, University of Kentucky)*

Kirill Mikhailovich Simonov was born on 15 November 1915 in Petrograd. Later he decided to change his name to Konstantin because of a speech defect that left him unable to pronounce *r* or *l*. He was born into a family of noble origin. His mother, Princess Aleksandra Leonidovna Obolenskaia, became a widow in early 1917. Information on the life of Simonov's father, Mikhail Simonov, is varied and incomplete. Lazar' Il'ich Lazarev, in *Konstantin Simonov: Ocherk zhizni i tvorchestva* (1985, Konstantin Simonov: A Sketch of His Life and Works), states that he was killed during World War I and that Simonov did not have any recollections of his birth father. Aleksandr Vasil'evich Karaganov, in his book *Konstantin Simonov–Vblizi i na rasstoianii* (1987, Konstantin Simonov–Close and at a Distance), mentions that Simonov's father was an officer in the tsar's army.

Simonov was raised and heavily influenced by his stepfather, Aleksandr Grigorievich Ivanishchev, a colonel in the tsarist army and later a military instructor and officer of the Red Army. Decorated many times for his personal courage during the Russo-Japanese War and World War I, Ivanishchev was for Simonov the embodiment of honor and responsibility. Lev Adol'fovich Fink, in his *Konstantin Simonov: Tvorcheskii put'* (1983, Konstantin Simonov: Creative Path), asserts that Ivanishchev's upbringing of the boy and the atmosphere of the small military communities in which Simonov spent his formative years contributed to his interest in military themes as a writer.

Simonov spent the early years of his life in Saratov, a large provincial town, among families of military personnel of the infantry school where his stepfather taught tactics. In 1930 he finished school and decided not to continue his formal education but rather to pursue a profession. He enrolled in a vocational school in Saratov and continued his professional education in Moscow, where his family moved soon thereafter. He then became a lathe hand. Why Simonov decided to break so abruptly with his comfortable childhood remains unknown. He was conscious of the disappointment his parents felt over his decision not to continue his education. He may have been influenced by the excitement over industrialization throughout the country, as well as the prestige that was given to workers in the new Soviet society. His break with his family's past had a positive result for his future career in literature: for years he was looked upon as a poet who had joined Soviet literature directly from the workshop.

In 1932 Simonov started to work as a turner, first at an aviation plant in Moscow and shortly after that at the mechanical shop of a film factory. He also began writing poetry at about this time. His first publication, fragments from his poem "Belomorzy" (Workers of the White Sea Canal), is dated 1934 and appeared in a collection of young poets, *Smotr sil* (A Review of Forces). He was able to spend a month on the White Sea construction site under the auspices of Goslitizdat (the State Publishing House of Literature). Simonov was placed under the creative supervision of another worker-poet, Vasilii Vasilievich Kazin, but in the same year, 1934, he was accepted as a student at the Gor'ky Literary Institute. His poetry started to appear in periodicals such as *Molodaia gvardiia* (Young Guard) and *Oktiabr'* (October). Simonov completed his education at the Gor'ky Institute in 1938, the same year his *Pavel Chernyi: Poema* (Pavel Chernyi) was published as a separate book. In this poem Simonov presents the popular Soviet tale of the moral conversion of a former criminal into a conscientious builder of the new society. His main protagonist, a former thief from Odessa, Pavel Chernyi, is raised in a prerevolutionary orphanage. As a child and youth he experienced only criminal life, but the revolution gives him a second chance. Instead of being kept in the prison he is sent to the construction of the White Sea Canal, where, inspired by the collective efforts of people around him, he changes into a productive laborer and challenges his former criminal peers.

The plot of *Pavel Chernyi* became an overused model in the literature of the 1930s. Further, Simonov's poetic style was highly imitative of Vladimir Vladimirovich Maiakovsky and Eduard Georgievich Bagritsky. Simonov's overwhelming use of criminal jargon, long descriptive passages, and plain metaphors are the most obvious shortcomings of the poem. Simonov himself understood the limitations of this work and never included it in his subsequent volumes of poetry. Nevertheless, the publication of this poem helped launch his literary career by gaining him access to the Union of Soviet Writers, which he joined in 1938 after graduating from the Gor'ky Institute.

Galina Andreevna Belaia writes in *Istoriia russkoi sovetskoi literatury* (1971, History of Russian Soviet Literature) that Simonov's poetry in general is highly influenced by the social and political journalism of his time. He apparently constantly searched the newspaper headlines for heroic topics. He wrote about the Spanish Civil War in the poem "General," published in 1937 in the journal *Znamia* (Banner), and about sailors and fliers who conquered polar regions in "Murmanskie Dnevniki" (Murmansk Diaries), first published in *Molodaia gvardiia* in 1938. He also turned to the topic of the past of Russia and commemorated the most glorious moments of her military history.

Simonov chose to write on two popular military leaders of Russian history, Prince Aleksandr Nevsky and General Aleksandr Vasil'evich Suvorov. His *Ledovoe poboishche: Poema* (1938, Battle on the Ice: Poem) celebrates the Russian victory over invading German knights in 1242. Led by Nevsky, the Russians completely destroyed the more experienced German troops on the ice of Lake Chud (Peipus). Simonov later explains his interest in this particular episode in his introductory notes to *Sobranie sochinenii* (1966–1970, Collected Works): "I felt that the war with German fascism would start soon. My poem was not a simple reflection on history, it was an anti-fascist pamphlet."

In his poem *Suvorov,* which was first published in fragmentary form in *Literaturnaia gazeta* (16 October 1938) and in full in *Znamia* that same year before appearing in book form in 1940, Simonov chose as his protagonist one of the most celebrated figures in Russian military history, the head of the Russian army during the reigns of Catherine II and her son Paul. Suvorov's victories over Prussia and Turkey, as well as his troubled relationship with the Russian imperial court, helped to promote the image of him as a popular "soldiers' general," hated by the rulers, despite his noble origin. In his poem Simonov concentrates on the three last years of Suvorov's life. Having been banished to his estate in February 1797 because of a dispute with the new emperor, Paul, Suvorov is nevertheless called upon to lead the Russian army against France in 1799. His retreat through the French-occupied Swiss Alps is considered one of the greatest feats of military history; yet, he died in solitude because of his opposition to the court. Simonov's choice of Suvorov as the main protagonist of his new poem was a questionable one in 1938, when Joseph Stalin's Great Purges were at their greatest intensity. Simonov returned to the issues this poem raises in his last work, the posthumously published *Glazami cheloveka moego pokoleniia: Rasmyshleniia o I. V. Staline* (1988; translated as *Through the Eyes of My Generation: Meditations on I. V. Stalin,* 1989).

The end of the 1930s and the early 1940s marked a productive time in Simonov's life. After graduating from the Gor'ky Institute, he entered the Institut istorii, filosofii, i literatury im. N. G. Chernyshevskogo (N. G. Chernyshevsky Institute of History, Philosophy, and Literature), where he pursued a graduate degree. He took exams at the end of the academic year but did not go on with his studies. In 1939 he became a war correspondent for *Geroicheskaia Krasnoarmeiskaia'* (Heroic Red Army Newspaper). He also worked for the Department of Propaganda of the Red Army and traveled on assignments to the battlefields of the Far East, where the Soviet Union was fighting with Japanese troops on the Mongolian and Manchurian borders. This so-called small war was a prelude to World War II and was carried on under the premises of support for communist movements in Asia, namely in China and Mongolia. This policy led to military conflicts with Japan on Soviet borders near Lake Khasan in 1938 and on the river Khalkhin-Gol, where Simonov traveled in August 1939. He also took a two-month course at the Frunze Academy to train as a war correspondent, and then in the fall of 1940 he continued his training at the Voenno-politicheskaia Akademiia (Military-Political Academy). After he finished his courses there in mid

*Simonov during World War II, when he was a Soviet soldier serving as a war correspondent (from In One Newspaper, 1983; Thomas Cooper Library, University of South Carolina)*

June 1941, he received the rank of quartermaster, second class. He immediately applied for membership in the Communist Party and was accepted the following year.

Simonov's literary life also flourished during this period. He published the poetry collections *Nastoiashchie liudi: Kniga stikhov* (Real People: A Book of Poems) in 1938, *Dorozhnye stikhi* (Travel Poems) in 1939, and *Stikhi tridtsat' deviatogo goda* (Poems from the Year 1939) in 1940. He was trying to find his own subjects for poetic expression; however, he also wanted to write on the most popular as well as the most politically acceptable themes in the life of his country. Simonov published his first love poem, "Piat' stranits: Liricheskaia poema" (Five Pages: A Lyric Poem), in *Znamia* in 1938; with this poem he made a conscious effort to move away from the descriptive mode of his previous poems toward deeper analyses of his own feelings. In "Piat' stranits" Simonov creates a somber mood as he depicts the separation of two lovers. His descriptions are unusually candid for Soviet literature of the time; in his depiction of the relationship between the lovers Simonov was not afraid to talk about sex as a normal part of human relations. Although his treatment of intimate details seems extremely modest to contemporary readers, Simonov was accused of "naturalism."

"Piat' stranits" and another poem, "Pervaia liubov" (First Love), published in *Znamia* in 1941, on which he worked from 1936 to 1941, were met with negative comments by contemporary critics, who accused Simonov of paying too much attention to personal feelings while neglecting "the achievements of our great and unrepeatable epoch," in the words of critic Tamara Iur'evna Khmel'nitskaia in the journal *Leningrad* (1940). Natal'ia Pushnova, in her book *Valentina Serova: Krug otchuzdeniia* (2001, Valentina Serova: Circle of Alienation), attributes Simonov's intensity of feeling in his love poetry to his personal circumstances: in 1940 he met and fell in love with Valentina Vasil'evna Serova, actress and widow of the celebrated pilot Anatolii Konstantinovich Serov. The details of Simonov's personal life remain murky; the dates of his marriages and of the births of his children are generally not known. He lived with Natal'ia Viktorovna Tipot as his first wife, but they were never officially married and separated after a short time. In 1940 Simonov left his second wife, Evgeniia Samoilovna Laskina, and son, Aleksei, who was born in 1939 in Moscow. He subsequently entered into an intense relationship with Serova. In the summer of 1943 Simonov and Serova married and had a daughter, Masha. Although they divorced in 1953, during the war years Serova was Simonov's poetic muse. His war experience in Mongolia served as the basis for a group of fifteen poems, *Sosediam po iurte* (To the Neighbors in My Yurt), eight of which appeared in *Molodaia gvardiia* in 1940. In these lyrics Simonov for the first time successfully combines his narrative style with a lyrical voice. He focuses his attention not on heroic battles but rather on the feelings and singular experiences of the participants in those events.

Simonov's work as a newspaper correspondent freed him to explore literary genres other than poetry. In 1940 he completed his first play, *Istoriia odnoi liubvi* (Story of One Love), which first appeared in print in the collection *P'esy* (1949, Plays). At the center of the plot is a love triangle: Aleksei Markov and his wife, Katia, love each other, but after the loss of their son they become estranged. Katia turns for help and sympathy to their former classmate, Vaganov, a successful administrator. Manipulating Katia's feelings, Vaganov makes every effort to separate the couple. Markov passively waits for Katia to make her decision; he never offers her any support and never shows his true feelings for her. A talented engineer, he volunteers for the army to fight at the Mongolian border and leaves his wife alone to decide with whom she wants to stay. After his departure Katia figures out that she loves her husband and does not respect the career-oriented Vaganov. When Markov comes for a short stay between the battles, Katia greets her husband warmly, signaling that she has rejected Vaganov. This play was met with mixed reviews, and Simonov was again criticized for paying too much attention to personal drama and for isolating his protagonists from their social experiences. The play was staged with relative success at the end of 1940.

The importance of *Istoriia odnoi liubvi* lies in Simonov's creation of a prototype for relations between the sexes that recurs in his works. With few exceptions, his love stories involve a love triangle in which a character waits patiently for his or her partners and offers security, warmth, and understanding. Pushnova's book on Serova attests to the relevance of such female protagonists to Simonov's relationship with her: their life together was full of breakups and reconciliations, infidelities and widespread rumors about Serova's many involvements. Serova was not only the writer's inspiration; she also performed all the leading roles in the productions of his plays in a variety of Moscow theaters, as well as in movie adaptations.

Creating an image of a perfect woman who is capable of the intense loyalty to her man that wartime separation requires became a personal task for Simonov. His male protagonists are virile soldiers who go about their business knowing that the home front is protected and preserved by their women. In his work for the theater of this period Simonov did not create complicated characters that were driven by controversial feelings. Rather, he employed stark contrasts between his main characters, as with Markov and Vaganov in *Istoriia odnoi liubvi*.

Simonov's next play, *Paren' iz nashego goroda* (1941, A Fellow from Our Home Town) enjoyed more success than *Istoriia odnoi liubvi*. The play was first staged in March 1941 and was produced in several theaters during the early days of World War II; in 1942 it was made into a motion picture. *Paren' iz nashego goroda* presents different stages in the life of a young officer and member of a tank crew, Sergei Lukonin. He develops from a mischievous, carefree young boy into a dedicated soldier. Simonov finally succeeded in creating a character that pleased his contemporaries because he subordinated personal happiness to common goals. Lukonin participates in all the major battles of his time. He volunteers to take part in the civil war in Spain; he fights in Mongolia; and he is ready to fight against Nazi Germany. His wife, Varia, a successful actress, leaves behind her chances for work in a theater in the capital and follows her husband. She continues to perform in the small theater of the military town where Sergei's unit is stationed and devotedly waits for his return. The characters in the play are simply drawn in order to embody simple values such as trust, honesty, responsibility, love, and dedication.

*Paren' iz nashego goroda* has no opposing characters: there are no villains, only heroes. Varia's passive and indecisive brother, medical doctor Arkadii Burmin, could be considered a counterpart of the active and willful Lukonin. Burmin comes to represent humanity and compassion, however, when he dies trying to provide medical help to an enemy solder, who in turn kills him. In *Paren' iz nashego goroda* Simonov's usual black-and-white oppositions between characters are abandoned, as characters unite to defend their homeland against the common enemy invading its borders.

Simonov began the Great Patriotic War, as the Russians called World War II, as a correspondent for the West Front newspaper *Krasnoarmeiskaia Pravda* (Red Army Truth). Several months later he was transferred to another army newspaper, *Krasnaia Zvezda* (Red Star), where he remained until the fall of 1946. During the war his publications appeared in the pages of leading Soviet newspapers such as *Izvestiia* (News) and *Pravda* (Truth). Simonov was known to his contemporaries for his personal courage and the honesty of his newspaper reports. He participated in many military actions and completed the war as a highly decorated officer. During the war, in 1942, he became a member of the Communist Party, which he and many other Soviet citizens viewed as the ultimate leader in the universal struggle against fascism.

Simonov's poetry became enormously popular during the war. It was quoted in letters and diaries and recited from the stage and on radio. The features of his style that had previously been attacked by critics—the plainness of his metaphors, the sketchiness of his images, the schematic juxtaposition of his characters—were celebrated by readers. His most popular war poem, "Zdi menia i ia vernus'," was written at the end of 1941, during a short return to Moscow from the front, and first published in *Pravda* on 14 January 1942. Once again Simonov's love for Serova inspired the poem. When he first offered it to one of the army newspapers, it was rejected by the editors with a brief explanation that in the time of struggle "there was a desperate demand for heroic poetry and not such intimately lyric digressions." Simonov himself recalled that he was completely surprised when two editors of *Pravda*, Petr Nikolaevich Pospelov and Emelian Mikhailovich Iaroslavskii, decided to publish it. In this poem Simonov explains the catastrophe of the war not only as a national tragedy but also as a personal one for all people. In place of the abstract demand to fight for the motherland that the government required in wartime literature, Simonov writes in "Zhdi menia i ia vernus'" about the less glorious but much more concrete power of love between two people that provides a sustaining force.

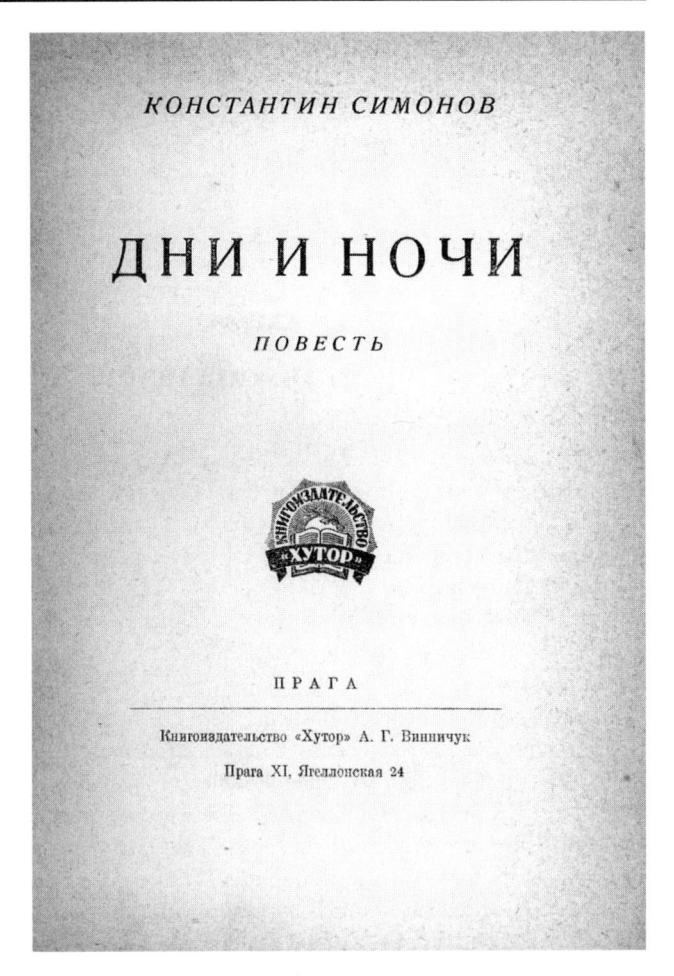

*Title page for* Dni I nochi *(1944; translated as* Days and Nights, *1945), Simonov's novella based on characters drawn from his journalism (Davis Library, University of North Carolina at Chapel Hill)*

Through this poem Simonov provided an alternate scale for measuring the future victory in the war: survival of a loved one. The message of the poem stresses the importance of a single life in contrast to the official war propaganda that glorified self-sacrifice at all costs. The popularity of the poem led to the creation of a play under the same title that the writer later converted into a motion-picture script. The movie was released in 1943, and its emotional message reflected the feelings of many of the Soviet people. In the screen version Serova played the leading female character, Lisa Ermolova, who embodied Simonov's favorite female protagonist—a faithful woman, waiting and believing in the return of her beloved. The motion picture was popular mainly because of the performances of the leading actors and its emotional appeal to the moment, but its popularity was short lived.

In his lyric poetry Simonov was instrumental in attaching a human face to every event and every battle about which he was writing. Thus, in such poems as "Ty pomnish, Alesha, dorogi Smolenshchiny" (Do You Remember, Alesha, the Roads of Smolensk) and "Maior privez mal'chishku na lafete" (The major brought the boy to the top of the gun carriage), both of which appeared in a group of poems under the heading "S toboi i bez tebia" (With You and Without You) in *Novyi mir* in 1941, the lyrical narrator becomes an eyewitness who presents his own experiences. The poet himself sees the ten-year-old boy with his head full of gray hair; he reminds his fellow journalist of the marching along village roads that is "measured by tears more often than by miles." Simonov's war was not the war of heroes but rather a prosaic task that one needed to accomplish as best one could; and he, the poet, was there together with the rest of his people. His inspiration was based not on the beauty and glory of heroic actions, but rather on the sweat and blood of his comrades in arms.

If Simonov's contemporaries looked upon the poem "Zhdi menia i ia vernus'" as a magic spell and map for survival, the soldiers themselves viewed another of his poems, "Ubei ego" (Kill Him), as a rationalization for the cruelty of the war. It was first published 18 July 1942 in the newspaper *Krasnaia Zvezda*; later it was recited on the radio and was distributed on all fronts in the form of leaflets. Karaganov writes that this poem sounded like a direct order in verse form, and the phrase "ubei ego" "became a password of righteous hate, a call for no-mercy to the enemy." Simonov starts the poem with a direct appeal to every soldier at the front:

Tak ubei zhe khot' odnogo!
Tak ubei zhe ego skorei!
Skol'ko raz uvidish' ego,
Stol'ko raz ego i ubei!

(Kill him, at least kill one of them!
Kill him as soon as you can!
As many times as you see him,
So many times kill him!)

In the next stanzas Simonov creates images of the house that will be destroyed, the old mother who will be humiliated, the old father whose portrait on the wall will be destroyed, and finally the loved one who will be raped if the enemy is not killed. Such intensification of hate for the enemy leads to only one possible conclusion:

Znai: nikto ee ne spaset,
Esli ty ee ne spasesh'.

Znai: nikto ego ne ub'et,
Esli Ty ego ne ub'esh'.

(Know that nobody can save her [the motherland],
If you will not save her.
Know that nobody will kill him [the enemy],
If you will not kill him).

With these two poems Simonov was instrumental in creating a code of moral behavior for the Soviet soldiers during the tragic days of World War II: they were supposed to be fearless protectors and defenders of their homeland. They must be firm in the belief in their righteous cause. The characters in Simonov's prose also act in accordance with those moral norms.

Wartime prepared Simonov for his future work as a prose writer; however, his immediate postwar popularity was attributed mostly to his poetry and his work for the theater. The play *Russkie liudi* (Russian People), on which Simonov started to work in December 1941, testifies to the writer's success in expressing the feelings of the nation at that period. The play first appeared in *Znamia* and immediately went into production in several theaters, both in Moscow (Moscow Art Theater) and in other places (such as the Baltic Navy Theater). The plot concerns a small detachment led by Captain Boris Feoktistovich Safonov. Although they were isolated and separated from the main army, the men nevertheless continued to fight against the German troops and became the vanguard for future counterattacks by the Soviet army. Supporting Safonov in his fight, a group of ordinary people organize themselves into a partisan movement to support the efforts of the military. Among those who fight alongside the detachment are his bride, Valia, and his mother, whom Safonov sacrifices to the Nazi occupiers, thus transcending his personal feelings for the sake of victory.

In contrast to *Zhdi menia* and *Paren' iz nashego goroda,* this play has a more complicated structure. The scenes change often to show different people under different circumstances; in addition, his characters are much more psychologically complex. A medical attendant, Globa, first appears in the play as a womanizer, a man without high moral principles; nevertheless, he does not hesitate for a moment to sacrifice his life for the common victory. Although he knows that he will not survive, Globa walks fearlessly into a village occupied by the Nazis to fulfill his order to destroy the enemy. In this play, for the first time, Simonov moved away from depicting his protagonists in black and white colors; he even created a different image of the enemy: not just cruel and determined, but also intelligent.

The play has a melodramatic tone, expressed in the love story of Captain Safonov and Valentina Anoshchenko (Valia). They subordinate their profoundly strong feelings for one another to their greater love for their motherland. In this play Simonov markedly departs from his traditional interpretation of the female character. Captain Safonov sends the woman he loves into enemy territory and now waits for his beloved's return. He must protect her from death through his love. This interpretation of gender roles opened the door for the parade of his female characters who would fight next to their men. *Russkie liudi* demonstrates the need for every person, men and women, to join the fight against Nazi Germany, to commit to victory at whatever cost for the sake of the motherland.

As a war correspondent, Simonov had accumulated rich materials that he was able to convert into a larger narrative of the battle of Stalingrad. In the winter of 1943–1944 Simonov began a new project, a prose novella *Dni i nochi* (1944, Days and Nights). Behind almost every character stands a real person whom Simonov met and had written about in his numerous newspaper articles. Some of his characters, like the soldier Koniuchov, retain their real names in the novel; some, like Colonel Utlenko, have barely disguised last names (the real name was Utvenko). Scholars such as Fink, Irina L'vovna Vishnevetskaia, and Lazarev write about the strong influences Leo Tolstoy's *Voina i mir* (1864–1869, War and Peace) had on Simonov's war narrative. Following the Tolstoyan device of mingling fictional characters with real-life heroes, Simonov creates a realistic depiction of the war. The critic Karaganov states that in this novel "observation and imagination merged as closely as possible. The events described in the novel were always verified with war diaries and numerous notebooks."

The main character, Saburov, continues the line of Simonov's male warriors: dry, rational, and unable to show his real emotions, specifically his love for fellow soldier Ania Klimenko. Saburov, who was trained as a history teacher and not a military commander, teaches his soldiers how to survive in the war. He measures his personal victory by the rate of survival of his men, not by the number of the dead; by their ability to deal with the everyday trials of wartime, not by heroic sacrifice. Saburov teaches that the purpose of war is to prepare the way for a satisfying life after war.

Among the many works Simonov wrote during World War II is his travel prose, later published under the collective title *Ot Chernogo do Barentseva Moria* (1942–1945, From the Black to the Barents Sea), *Iugoslavskaia tetrad'* (1945, Yugoslav Notebook), and *Pis'ma iz Chekhoslovakii* (1945, Letters from Czechoslovakia). These publications served as the bases for his future fiction. Two volumes of his poetry were published between 1942 and 1945: *S toboi i bez tebia* (With You and Without You) and *Voina: Stikhi, 1937–1943 goda* (The War:

*Title page for* Zhivye I mertvye *(1960; translated as* The Living and the Dead, *1962), the first volume of the trilogy that was Simonov's most important work (John C. Hodges Library, University of Tennessee–Knoxville)*

Poems from 1937 to 1943). Simonov also completed two plays, *Tak i budet* (So It Will Be) in 1944 and *Pod kashtanami Pragi* (1946, Under the Chestnut-trees of Prague) in 1945. In both of these plays he focuses his attention on the problems of postwar life and the possibilities of a new beginning for those who suffered so many losses and were eyewitnesses to so many human tragedies. Neither play has particular literary merit; rather, they served the demands of the moment, and their life onstage was relatively short.

Simonov started World War II as a known poet and author of two plays; he completed the war as a highly decorated war correspondent and famous playwright. Twice during World War II his work was awarded the Stalin (State) Prize (1942 and 1943). His popularity was legendary; he represented the Soviet Union on many occasions at home and abroad where the Soviet government used his image and reputation for propaganda. Boris Dmitrievich Pankin, in *Chetyre "Ia" Konstantina Simonova: Roman-biografiia* (1999, The Four "I's" of Konstantin Simonov: A Biographical Novel), writes that during the first years after the war Simonov was possessed by the feeling of duty to his people and country. Simonov also represented creative intelligentsia in his meetings with the government. His contacts with Stalin further strengthened his reputation as the "court writer."

Several factors contributed to Simonov's reputation as an apologist for the Soviet regime. He never gave up his support for the military and its mission. He also belonged to that generation of true believers in the Communist ideal, a generation that maintained the enthusiasm of the industrialization of the 1930s. The victory of the Soviet Union in World War II strengthened the tradition of the past glory of Russia. Therefore, it is not surprising that Simonov continued to serve the communist cause without visible reservations. Only later, in *Glazami cheloveka moego pokoleniia,* could one understand the complexity of his personal compromise. He stated that even through the early postwar years he continued to identify himself as a war correspondent; however, now he was simply observing and reporting a different type of war, the Cold War. Simonov viewed his assignments in the West in the same light as his correspondences from the front line during World War II.

Simonov's social status and his position as a celebrated Soviet writer often shadow the recognition of his literary merit in the West. In *Soviet Russian Literature: Writers and Problems* (1964) Marc Slonim states that "Simonov later adjusted to the policy of the Party by producing trivial and melodramatic plays and tendentious travelogues." Johannes Holthusen, in *20th Century Russian Literature: A Critical Study* (1972), talks about Simonov's "almost naive attachment to truth and the directness of his interpretations and evaluations." In her entry on Simonov in *Handbook of Russian Literature* (1985), Helen Segall characterizes Simonov as a "skillful, officially approved writer in tune with the spirit of his time." These statements convey much truth; however, they still limit Simonov as a one-sided literary phenomenon.

Simonov's life from the 1950s until his death in 1979 and his work during those years serve as direct proof of the difficult choices, both forced and self-imposed, that surrounded the personal and professional lives of creative individuals in the Soviet Union. He attempted to address in allegorical form the nature of compromise in his play *Chetvertyi* (1962, The Fourth), first published in *Teatr* (Theater) in 1961. Simonov says in the introduction to his collected works (1966–1970) that he felt that it was his direct responsibility to be "in tune with his time," that is, to serve the Soviet cause. He believed that in his work he reacted directly to the most important events of history.

Often written as an immediate reaction to political demands of his time, his plays serve as direct evidence of the destructive nature of Soviet control over the creative abilities of a talented individual. For example, his play *Russkii vopros* (Russian Question), first published in *Zvezda* (Star) in 1946, is a commentary on the beginning of the Cold War. The main character, American journalist Gary Smith, is a former war correspondent who once wrote friendly and positive reports about Soviet soldiers. He is asked to write a book to serve as an advertisement for the new anti-Soviet political campaign in the United States. Smith accepts the assignment, but under the influence of his own experience in Russia, he decides to present a different "truthful" picture about the peace-loving Soviet Union. His rebellion against his bosses, publishers McPherson and Gould, destroys his life: he loses his job, his wife, and his house. This play was a specific governmental assignment to explain to the Soviet people the negative attitude of the Soviet Union toward the West.

The poetry volume *Druz'ia i vragi* (1948; translated as *Friends and Foes,* 1951) belongs to the same category of open propaganda for the government. The quality of poetry in this volume is much lower than in the verses Simonov wrote during the war. The highly emotional style that was the poet's trademark became declarative, often resembling a political speech. His novella *Dym otechestva* (1956, Smoke of Our Native Land) and his play *Chuzhaia ten'* (1949, The Foreign Shadow) serve as examples of Simonov's commitment to his politically charged responsibilities; they show little literary merit. His novel *Tovarishchi po oruzhiiu* (1954, Comrades in Arms) stands apart from his work in the late 1940s and early 1950s. Here Simonov returns to the events of the "small war" of 1939 and describes the battle at Khalkin-Gol, where Soviet and Mongolian armies were fighting with Japan. He reexamines those events as a prelude to the long and exhausting World War II. By revisiting the military theme, Simonov returns to the territory where he felt most secure. His diary entries helped him to re-create real events and characters. This novel is also important to Simonov's subsequent work since it introduces the characters of his trilogy, *Zhivye i mertvye* (1960; translated as *The Living and the Dead,* 1962). In the earlier work Simonov introduces the character Commander Schmelev, who is the first to express his concern over the war propaganda that describes glorious bloodless victories that were absolutely incongruent with actual war events. He states: "The war that requires little blood is possible only in theory; in practice it is rather difficult to accomplish." This theme of personal responsibility for human life by the commanding officers was later developed in Simonov's favorite character of *Zhivye i mertvye,* General Serpilin.

After World War II Simonov fulfilled many administrative duties, editing *Novyi mir* and *Literaturnaia gazeta.* During those years he assumed the highly celebrated position as one of the secretaries of the Union of Soviet Writers. His life as a Soviet bureaucrat was full of controversies. He supported and facilitated the publication of Vladimir Dmitrievich Dudintsev's controversial "Thaw" novel *Ne khlebom edinym* (1957; translated as *Not by Bread Alone,* 1957); on the other hand, he supported and participated in the government-orchestrated attacks on Mikhail Mikhailovich Zoshchenko and Boris Leonidovich Pasternak.

One particular event in Simonov's life as a writer in many ways explains his reception by his contemporaries as well as by his critics abroad. On 18 March 1953, only thirteen days after Stalin's death, Simonov published in *Literaturnaia gazeta* the lead article dedicated to Stalin. He called on the Soviet literary establishment to fulfill the most important task of Soviet literature: "to create in all of its fullness the image of Stalin–the greatest genius of all times and all nations." According to his diaries, Simonov had taken Stalin's death as a personal loss. He was not alone; the majority of Soviet people reacted in a similar fashion. For them Stalin had been an irreplaceable, fearless leader, a great victor, and a god-like, mythological figure. In *Glazami cheloveka moego pokoleniia* Simonov directly addresses the topic of the people's idealization of Stalin. Only after the Twentieth Party Congress in 1956, when Nikita Khrushchev publicly denounced Stalin for his crimes against the Party and revealed many previously hidden facts, did Simonov force himself to reevaluate his feelings toward Stalin and his legacy.

In the second half of the 1950s Simonov himself became a victim of attacks from both the Left and the Right. He was viewed as a loyal Stalinist; however, at the same time he was criticized for his liberal editorial politics at *Novyi mir.* Simonov was forced to leave his post as the editor in chief in 1958; he also resigned from all his administrative duties and went to the Central Asian Republic of Uzbekistan as special correspondent for the newspaper *Pravda.* This assignment for a writer with Simonov's credentials can be interpreted as political and literary exile. During his time in Tashkent, Simonov turned to what became the major work of his life–his trilogy, *Zhivye i mertvye.*

The new political climate that emerged after the Twentieth Party Congress and Khrushchev's public denunciation of Stalin's cult of personality offered Simonov the opportunity to present the past history of the Great Patriotic War from a different perspective. In *Zhivye i mertvye* he revisits his own observations of Russia's struggle against Nazi Germany and tells of unknown heroes. The first volume of the trilogy is without doubt Simonov's most significant contribution to the corpus of Russian literature. It focuses on the events of 1941 and tells the story of the defeats of the Soviet army in the first days of the war. Nineteen chapters of the novel seem to be relatively freestanding, and each of them centers on one particular episode; all of the chapters are, however, connected through the same set of characters.

The narrator describes events from the point of view of an eyewitness, the newspaper correspondent Ivan Sinzov, providing further unity to seemingly disconnected episodes. Individual characters such as Sinzov, Serpilin, and Klimovich emerge in this novel as spokesmen for millions of people who found themselves in the whirlpool of the national tragedy of the war. Simonov uses every opportunity to stress that the opinions, observations, and thoughts of his characters reflect those of their contemporaries. Thus, Simonov writes about Sinzov, who marched along with him on the war roads: "He was not a coward but like millions of other people he was not ready to witness what was happening around him." In this novel Simonov produces a collective portrait of the nation in the time of its greatest national tragedy by telling the stories of individuals.

The novel has three central characters: the war correspondent Sinzov, General Serpilin, and the narrator, who presents the main events of the novel from the perspective of historical distance. The main characters provide psychological evaluations of the events of the war and give them a human dimension. One of the most interesting of Simonov's characters, Serpilin is a victim of Stalin's repressions. He arrives at the front directly from the prison where he had been kept for four years. In spite of the bitterness he feels because of his mistreatment at the hands of the government, Serpilin willingly shoulders his responsibility as a military commander: to save his people and to fight against the enemy.

In 1957 Simonov published two short novellas in the journal *Moskva,* "Panteleev" and "Eshche odin den'" (One More Day), which develop themes important to the trilogy. Both novellas describe the military defense of the Crimean Peninsula and the city of Odessa in 1941. These works offer images of the military leaders who had found themselves to be so frightened by Stalin's prewar repression that they were not able to report truthfully about the situation on the battlefield. After the publication of these novellas, Simonov was accused in *Literaturnaia gazeta* of creating images of cowards and

*Simonov near the end of his life (from Lev Fink,* Konstantin Simonov: Tvorcheskii put', *1983; O'Neill Library, Boston College)*

idiots; both stories were labeled as a "discredit to the people who are serving now or have served before in our army." A polemic around these stories took place in *Literaturnaia gazeta* beginning on 11 July, continuing on 8 August, and concluding with remarks from the editors and a rebuttal from Simonov on 31 August.

Fear and its paralyzing effects provide another all-pervading theme to the narrative, which Simonov first introduces in "Panteleev." Prior to the start of the war, one of the characters, Colonel Baburov, was the subject of an investigation of a wholly invented plot. He survived the accusations but became frightened and lived in fear for the rest of his life. An experienced soldier who lived through the civil war in Russia and who was decorated for his personal courage, Baburov remains completely paralyzed by fear of possible future false accusations. Unable to shoulder the responsibility for his military actions, he shoots himself through the heart after he witnesses the death of his soldiers. Baburov chooses suicide rather than protest. This type of military leader, who allows himself to be destroyed by the fear and suspicion rampant during the Stalinist Purges of the late 1930s, is depicted in the trilogy, as well, and assumes several names, such as General L'vov or Colonel Baranov.

Another important topic the trilogy explores is how personally painful it was to try to believe in Stalin and trust him as the leader of the country. During the course of the defeats of 1941, many characters from various social groups ask themselves and others one question: "How did it happen that the country was so unprepared for the war?" Simonov's narrator shows how frightened those different classes of people were to question the political leadership and to doubt Stalin. They do not fear possible repressions; Simonov's characters are participating in the war and, in any case, they face constant peril at every turn. Rather, they fear the loss of belief in the values that now they must protect with their lives. While Simonov was depicting this psychological turn in the mass consciousness, he forced himself to reconsider his own system of values and beliefs.

The second part of the trilogy, *Soldatami ne rozhdaiutsia* (One Is Not Born a Soldier), was published in 1964. The same major characters remain the focus of the narrative, which depicts the events of 1943, a decisive year in the history of World War II. On 2 February the Soviet military won the battle of Stalingrad, and the army of German general Friedrich Paulus surrendered to the Red Army. Simonov expands his narrative beyond the borders of the war battles. In this volume, he portrays the lives of civilians evacuated from their cities, which had been occupied by the Germans, alongside descriptions of the military events. Left without homes and placed into temporary accommodations, millions of people channeled all of their efforts into the struggle for the coming victory. One of the most striking devices in this volume is Simonov's attempt to re-create Stalin's thoughts and present them in a narrative form.

An important question in this volume is who takes responsibility for human life in wartime. Serpilin, Simonov's most important character, personifies for the writer the best qualities in leadership: he feels responsible for every life he touches with his decisions. In his conversation with Maksimov, the head of the political bureau of the army, Serpilin argues: "Wait, Maksimov, do not rush this! These are not branches of firewood. They are real people. They should not be sent to a pointless death." In opposition are such commanders as General Batiuk, for whom human life does not have any value.

While the depiction of military events is vivid, their psychological effects remain the focus of the trilogy; yet, the personal lives of Simonov's characters off the battlefield are awkwardly drawn. The love story of Sinzov, who had lost his daughter and wife in the war, and the medical doctor Tatiana Ovsiannikova is artificial and overly complicated. At times it seems as if Simonov does not know what to do with these characters: their daughter dies, and Tatiana returns to the front, where she feels she belongs more than she does at home. At the end of the third part of the trilogy, *Poslednee leto* (1971, Last Summer), Simonov brings back to life Sinzov's late wife, who had supposedly been killed while fighting with the partisans. This love plot does not have a resolution in the story. Equally unclear is the personal life of Simonov's other main character, General Serpilin. His wife died from cancer while he was fighting, and he could not leave his army to bid her a final farewell. His new love, the surgeon Baranova, is the wife of his former colleague whose cowardly suicide he witnessed while retreating from the front, an event that occurs in the first part of the trilogy. These women are soldiers, and they fulfill their duty to the country rather than to a man. Still, Simonov remained true to his depiction of love as a painful experience. His love stories are never happy.

Simonov's novellas *Zhena priekhala* (The Wife Has Arrived; first published in *Moskva*, 1964) and *Sluchai s Polyninym* (The Polynin Incident; first published in *Znamia* in 1969) resurrect female character types from his early poems: both Kseniia, Lopatin's wife, and the actress Galina are incapable of fidelity; therefore, both embody the most painful betrayal of the wartime love story. A more complicated female character type appears in Simonov's novellas *Dvadtsat' dnei bez voiny* (1973, Twenty Days without War), first published in *Znamia* in 1972, and in *My ne uvidimsia s toboi* (We Will Not See Each Other Again), which first appeared in *Znamia* in 1978. Nika, the woman in the life of the war correspondent Lopatin, is dedicated to her man but nevertheless deceives him under pressure of personal trouble. Ashamed of her deception, Nika refuses to see Lopatin again rather than lie to him.

*Poslednee leto* demonstrates Simonov's strength as a World War II historian. In this volume Serpilin reaches the highest level of his strategic achievements, but the author does not know what to do with his character and kills him off at the end of the book. Some of the most interesting character studies, however, unfold in the last part of the narrative in the portrayals of General L'vov and Commissar Bastrukov. L'vov is a military leader who embodies the destructive power of a calculating military bureaucrat. Courageous but distrustful, L'vov does not like people and sees them as numbers rather than human beings. Bastrukov is responsible for the soldiers' political spirit. As commissar he communicates the party's will; however, he is the one who abandons his soldiers in the Crimea. A coward, he is concerned only with his own career, which he values above everything else. Even seasoned war generals fear him because he has the capability to turn things upside down and "take you through every possible military court that exists," as one of the generals states. Bastrukov and L'vov share the same empty bureaucratic approach to human life in a time of great human tragedy. Simonov chooses these two characters—one who represents the ultimate voice of military authority and the other who commands the highest political authority in this volume—to be the agents of the most inhuman behavior in the war. In the final analysis, the trilogy *Zhivye i mertvye* revitalized the genre of *roman-epopeia*—the epic novel—in Soviet literature. Exceptionally well received by the readers, the trilogy was later made into a two-part motion picture under the same title.

In 1975 Simonov published his war diaries under the title *Raznye dni voiny* (Different Days of the War); in 1978 his collection of novellas *My ne uvidimsia s toboi (Iz zapisok Lopatina)* (A So-called Private Life [From Lopatin's Notes]) appeared and included some previously published stories, such as "Panteleev." The stories in this collection are thematically connected to *Zhivye i mertvye*. His journalistic past led him into documentary moviemaking, and he has co-authored several documentaries. The documentary *Esli dorog tebe tvoi dom* (1967, If You Treasure Your Home), made with E. Vorob'ev and V. Ordynsky, depicts the story of the battle over Moscow and was based on the memoirs of the battle participants and clips from Soviet and German war chronicles. The documentary *Grenada, Grenada, Grenada moia* (1968, Grenada, Grenada, My Grenada), which Simonov made with R. Karmen, re-creates the history of the Spanish Civil War and the participation of Soviet volunteers in this conflict. In 1973 Simonov's poetry served as an inspiration for the documentary *Chuzhogo goria ne byvaet* (Everybody's Sorrow), about the war in Vietnam. In 1975 and 1976 Simonov, together with the producer Marina Babak, created two documentary motion pictures dedicated to the everyday life of simple soldiers during World War II, *Shel soldat . . .* (The Soldier Was Marching . . .) and *Soldatskie Memuary* (Soldier's Memoirs). Both documentaries were based on actual clips from war chronicles and soldiers' reminiscences.

Konstantin Mikhailovich Simonov remained true to the theme of World War II in his life and work. His dedication to this theme allowed him to remain both an historian of the war as well as its chronicler. Simonov was passionately committed to keeping this war alive in the memory of his people, and he succeeded admirably in this task. The difficult times of the war remained the best years of his life as a human being and as a creative individual. He died on 28 August 1979. His widow,

Larisa Alekseevna Zhadova-Simonova; his son Aleksei (with his second wife); his stepdaughter Katia; and his daughters Masha (with Serova) and Aleksandra (with Zhadova) fulfilled Simonov's wishes when, in accordance with his will, they scattered his ashes on the Buinichev field near Mogilev, where in July 1941 he witnessed the Soviet soldiers burning thirty-nine German tanks. His war novels established an important place for Simonov in twentieth-century Russian literature.

**Letters:**

*Pis'ma o voine (1943–1979)* (Moscow: Sovetskii pisatel', 1990).

**Bibliographies:**

Dagmara Andreevna Berman and Bella Mikhailovna Tolochinskaia, *K. M. Simonov: Bibliograficheskii ukazatel'* (Moscow: Kniga, 1985);

*K. Simonov i Krym: k 75-letiiu so dnia rozhdeniia: Bibliograficheskii ukazatel'*, edited by O. A. Pavlova, T. L. Shostak, and L. A. Shamruk (Simferopol': Krymskaia oblastnaia universal'naia nauchnaia biblioteka im. I. A. Franko, 1990).

**Biography:**

*Konstantin Simonov v vospominaniiakh sovremennikov*, compiled by Larisa Alekseevna Zhadova, Sof'ia Grigor'evna Karaganova, and Evgeniia Aleksandrovna Katseva (Moscow: Sovetskii pisatel', 1984).

**References:**

G. I. Alaeva, "Zhanrovaia spetsifika trilogii K. Simonova 'Zhivye i mertvye'," *Vestnik Moskovskogo Universiteta. Seriia 9, Filologiia*, 4 (July–August 1982): 3–10;

George Avis, "Moskovsky literator and the Dudintsev Debate," *Journal of Russian Studies*, 18 (1969): 26–35;

Vladimir Sergeevich Barakhov, "V zerkale pisatel'skoi memuaristiki: K voprosu o ee roli i ideino-khodizhesvennom svoeobrazii," *Russkaia literatura*, 1 (1984): 90–106:

Galina Andreevna Belaia, "Istorizm kak nravstvennaia i khudozhestvennaia pozitsiia pisatelia," in *Zhanrovo-stilevye iskaniia sovremennoi sovetskoi prozy* (Moscow: Nauka, 1971), pp. 93–119;

Belaia, "K. M. Simonov," in *Istoriia russkoi sovetskoi literatury*, volume 4 (Moscow: Nauka, 1971), pp. 348–365;

Valerie Mercedes Benito-Nedel, "Konstantin Simonov and Soviet Ideology," dissertation, San Diego State University, 1983;

Natal'ia Bianki, *K. Simonov, A. Tvardovskii v "Novoi mire": Vospominaniia* (Moscow: VIOLANTA, 1999);

Edward James Brown, *Russian Literature since the Revolution* (Cambridge, Mass.: Harvard University Press, 1982);

Lev Adol'fovich Fink, *Konstantin Simonov: Tvorcheskii put'* (Moscow: Sovetskii pisatel', 1983);

Fink, "Simonov, Konstantin Mikhailovich," in *Russkie pisateli 20 veka: Biographicheskii slovar'*, edited by Pavel Alekseevich Nikolaev (Moscow: Nauchnoe izdatel'stvo Bol'shaia Rossiiskaia Entsiklopediia, 2000), pp. 638–640;

Sarra Iakovlevna Fradkina, *Tvorchestvo Konstantina Simonova* (Moscow: Izdatel'stvo Nauka, 1968);

Yuri Yakovlevich Glazov, "Stalin's Legacy: Populism in Literature," in *The Search for Self-Definition in Russian Literature*, edited by Ewa M. Thompson (Houston: Rice University Press, 1991), pp. 92–105;

T. S. Glebova, "Khudozhevtvennyi obraz voiny v povestiakh i romanakh K. Simonova," *Russkaia rech'*, no. 3 (1975): 10–17;

Glebova, "Ranniaia voennaia proza K. Simonova v sviazi s ego poslednimi romanami," *Izvestiia Akademii Nauk, Seriia Literatury i Iazyka*, 26 (1967): 333–343;

Glebova, "Tragicheskie sluchainosti i neobkhodimost' na voine v proizvedeniiakh K. M. Simonova," *Izvestiia Akademii Nauk, Seriia Literatury i Iazyka*, 45, no. 5 (September–October 1986): 390–401;

Glebova, "Tri redaktsii povesti K. M. Simonova 'Dni i nochi'," *Izvestiia Akademii Nauk, Seriia Literatury i Iazyka*, 47, no. 1 (January–February 1988): 75–88;

Nina Pavlovna Gordon, "Various Days of Konstantin Simonov: Diary Notes," *Soviet Studies in Literature*, 19, no. 1 (Winter 1982–1983): 3–41;

Johannes Holthusen, *20th Century Russian Literature: A Critical Study*, translated by Theodore Huebener (New York: Ungar, 1972), pp. 152, 177, 179–181, 279;

Natal'ia Borisovna Ivanova, "Konstantin Simonov glazami cheloveka moego pokoleniia," *Znamia*, 7 (July 1999): 192–207;

Aleksandr Vasil'evich Karaganov, *Konstantin Simonov– Vblizi i na rasstoianii* (Moscow: Sovetskii pisatel', 1987);

Tamara Iur'evna Khmel'nitskaia, "Voennye stikhi Simonova,'" *Leningrad*, 13/14 (1940): 27–28;

Lazar' Il'ich Lazarev, "Dolg i muzhestvo: Zametki o poezii Konstantina Simonova," *Novyi mir*, no. 1 (1982): 232–245;

Lazarev, "Dolgaia byla voina . . . : Zametki o voennykh dnevnikhax Konstantina Simonova i nekotorykh problemakh memuarnoi literatury," *Oktiabr'*, no. 1 (1975): 185–201;

Lazarev, *Dramaturgiia Konstantina Simonova* (Moscow: Iskusstvo, 1952);

Lazarev, "Duty and Courage: Notes on the Poetry of Konstantin Simonov," *Soviet Studies in Literature*, 19, no. 1 (Winter 1982-1983): 42-76;

Lazarev, "For His Whole Life: Notes on Konstantin Simonov's Novel *So-Called Private Life*," *Soviet Studies in Literature: A Journal of Translations*, 17, no. 2 (Spring 1981): 3-30;

Lazarev, "Glavnaia tsel': Iz pisem Konstantina Simonova," *Voprosy literatury*, 5 (May 1985): 182-227;

Lazarev, "I ispoved', i propoved'," *Voprosy literatury*, no. 12 (1978): 97-117;

Lazarev, *Konstantin Simonov: Ocherk zhizni i tvorchestva* (Moscow: Khudozhestvennaia literatura, 1985);

Lazarev, "Na vsiu zhizn': Zametki o romane Konstantina Simonova *Tak nazyvaemaia lichnaia zhizn'*," *Voprosy literatury*, no. 11 (1979): 33-58;

Lazarev, "'Nothing Stands between the Friendship of Our Countries': Correspondence between Ernest Hemingway and Konstantin Simonov," *Soviet Literature*, 1, no. 454 (1986): 130-137;

Lazarev, *Voennaia proza Konstantina Simonova* (Moscow: Khudozhestvennaia literatura, 1974);

Lazarev, "Voennye romany K. Simonova," *Novyi mir*, no. 8 (1964): 238-252;

Lazarev, ed., "Iz pisem Konstantina Simonova," *Voprosy literatury*, 5 (May 1982): 102-149;

Naum Lazarevich Leiderman and Mark Naumovich Lipovetsky, "Trilogiia K. Simonova 'Zhivye i mertvye,'" in *Sovremennaia russkaia literatura*, volume 1, *Literatura Ottepeli' (1953-1968)* (Moscow: URCC, 2000), pp. 129-140;

Arkadii L'vovich L'vov, *S Simonovym naedin: Neizvestnye fakty vpervye–dostoianie chitatelia* (Odessa: OKFA, 1994);

Samuel Francis Orth, "'V okopax Stalingrada' i 'Dni i nochi': Problematika stalingradskoj temy v poslevoennoj sovetskoj proze," *Russian Language Journal*, 110 (1977): 115-123;

Orth, "The War Novels of Konstantin Mikhailovich Simonov," dissertation, New York University, 1969;

Boris Dmitrievich Pankin, *Chetyre "Ia" Konstantina Simonova: Roman-biographiia* (Moscow: Voskresen'e, 1999);

Zinovii Samoilovich Papernyi, "Stikh i sud'ba: Lirika Konstantina Simonova," *Znamia*, 5 (May 1981): 240-247;

Vladimir Poltoratzky, "The Battle of Stalingrad in the Works of Simonov and Nekrasov," dissertation, Vanderbilt University, 1977;

G. I. Ponomarev, "O traditsiiakh L. Tolstogo v tvorchestve K. Simonova: Na materiale romana *Zhivye i mertvye*," *Voprosy Russkoi literatury*, 1, no. 35 (1980): 11-21;

Oleg Petrovich Presniakov, "Slovo i siuzhet v drame K. Simonova *Russkie liudi*," *Voprosy Russkoi literatury*, 1, no. 25 (1975): 22-28;

Natal'ia Pushnova, *Valentina Serova: Krug otchuzhdeniia* (Moscow: AST, 2001);

George Reavey, *Soviet Literature To-Day* (New York: Greenwood Press, 1969), pp. 74-75, 88-89;

Helen Segall, "Simonov," in *Handbook of Russian Literature*, edited by Victor Terras (New Haven & London: Yale University Press, 1985), pp. 418-419;

Vera Sergeevna Sinenko, *Trilogiia K. Simonova "Zhivye I mertvye": Monograficheskoe issledovvanie* (Ufa: Bashkirskoe knizhnoe izdatel'stvo, 1986);

Marc Slonim, *Soviet Russian Literature: Writers and Problems* (New York: Oxford University Press, 1964);

Pavel Maksimovich Toper, "Poiski voennoi prozy," *Zhanrovo-stilevye iskaniia sovremennoi sovetskoi prozy* (Moscow: Nauka, 1971), pp. 43-92;

Sergei Petrovich Varshavsky, "'Zhdi menia': Moia vstrecha so stikhotvoreniem Simonova," *Voprosy literatury*, 3 (March 1985): 47-56;

Irina L'vovna Vishnevetskaia, *Konstantin Simonov: Ocherk tvorchestva* (Moscow: Sovetskii pisatel', 1966);

Evgenii Zakharovich Vorob'ev, "Samaia trudnaia dolzhnost'," *Novyi mir*, no. 2 (1983): 221-237.

**Papers:**

Konstantin Simonov's papers are in the Russian State Archive of Literature and Art (RGALI, fond [archive] 1814; formerly TsGALI, Central State Archives of Literature and Art).

# Andrei Siniavsky
# (Abram Tertz)
(8 October 1925 – 25 February 1997)

Catharine Theimer Nepomnyashchy
*Barnard College*

BOOKS: *On Socialist Realism,* as Abram Tertz, translated by George Dennis (New York: Pantheon, 1960); Russian version published as "Chto takoe sotsialisticheskii realizm," in *Fantasticheskii mir Abrama Tertsa* (New York: Inter-language Literary Associates, 1967);

*Pikasso,* by Siniavsky and Igor' Naumovich Golomshtok (Moscow: Znanie, 1960);

*The Trial Begins,* translated by Max Hayward (New York: Pantheon, 1960); Russian version published as *Sud idet,* as Tertz (Munich? 1960);

*Fantasticheskie povesti,* as Tertz (Paris: Instytut literacki, 1961); translated by Hayward and Ronald Hingley as *Fantastic Stories* (New York: Pantheon, 1963);

*Lyubinov,* as Tertz (Washington: B. Filipoff, 1964); translated by Manya Harari as *The Makepeace Experiment* (London: Collins & Harvill, 1965; New York: Pantheon, 1965);

*Poeziia pervykh let revoliutsii: 1917–1920,* by Siniavsky and Andrei Nikolaevich Men'shutin (Moscow: Nauka, 1964);

*Mysli vrasplokh* (New York: Rausen, 1966); translated by Harari as *Unguarded Thoughts* (London: Collins & Harvill, 1972);

*Golos iz khora,* as Tertz (London: Stenvalli, 1973); translated by Hayward and Kyril FitzLyon as *A Voice from the Chorus* (New York: Farrar, Straus & Giroux, 1976);

*Progulki s Pushkinym,* as Tertz (London: Overseas Publications Interchange, 1975); translated by Catharine Theimer Nepomnyashchy and Slava I. Yastremski as *Strolls with Pushkin* (New Haven: Yale University Press, 1993);

*In the Shadow of Gogol; V teni Gogolia,* as Tertz (London: Overseas Publications Interchange, 1975);

*Kroshka Tsores,* as Tertz (Paris: Sintaksis, 1980); translated by Larry P. Joseph and Rachel May as *Little*

*Andrei Siniavsky (from* On Trial: The Case of Sinyavsky [Tertz] and Daniel' [Arzhak], *1967; Jean and Alexander Heard Library, Vanderbilt University)*

*Jinx* (Evanston, Ill.: Northwestern University Press, 1992);

*"Opavshie list'ia" V. V. Rozanova* (Paris: Sintaksis, 1982);

*Spokoinoi nochi,* as Tertz (Paris: Sintaksis, 1984); translated by Richard Lourie as *Goodnight!* (New York: Penguin, 1989);

*La civilisation soviétique,* translated by Annie Sabatier and Catherine Prokhoroff (Paris: Albin Michel, 1988); English version published as *Soviet Civilization: A Cultural History,* translated by Joanne Turnbull, with the assistance of Nikolai Formozov (New York: Little, Brown, 1990); Russian version published as *Osnovy sovetskoi tsivilizatsii* (Moscow: Agraf, 2001);

*Ivan-durak: Ocherk russkoi narodnoi very* (Paris: Sintaksis, 1991).

**Editions and Collections:** *Chto takoe sotsialisticheskii realizm,* as Tertz (Paris: Sintaksis, 1988);

*Sobranie sochinenii,* 2 volumes (Moscow: SP Start, 1992);

*Spokoinoi nochi* (Moscow: Zakharov, 1998);

*Puteshestvie na chernuyu rechku i drugie proizvedeniia* (Moscow: Zakharov, 1999);

*Pkhents i drugie* (Moscow: Agraf, 2003).

**Editions in English:** *For Freedom of Imagination,* translated by Laszlo Tikos and Murray Peppard (New York: Holt, Rinehart & Winston, 1971);

*A Voice from the Chorus,* translated by Kyril FitzLyon and Max Hayward, introduction by Siniavsky (New Haven: Yale University Press, 1995);

*The Russian Intelligentsia,* translated by Lynn Visson (New York: Columbia University Press, 1997).

OTHER: "A. M. Gor'ky" and "Eduard Bagritsky," in *Istoriia russkoi sovetskoi literatury,* volume 1 (Moscow: Izdatel'stvo Akademiia nauk SSSR, 1958);

"Ob khudozhestvennoi strukture romana 'Zhizn' Klima Samgina,'" in *Tvorchestvo M. Gor'kogo i voprosy sotsialisticheskogo realizma,* edited by Boris Vasil'evich Mikhailovsky (Moscow: Izdatel'stvo Akademiia nauk SSSR, 1958);

"Literatura perioda velikoi otechestvennoi voiny," in *Istoriia russkoi sovetskoi literatury,* volume 3 (Moscow: Izdatel'stvo Akademiia nauk SSSR, 1961);

"Akmeizm" and "M. A. Voloshin," in *Kratkaia literaturnaia entsiklopediia* (Moscow: Sovetskaia entsiklopediia, 1962);

"Poeziia Pasternaka," in Boris Leonidovich Pasternak, *Stikhotvoreniia i poemy,* Biblioteka poeta, Bol'shaia seriia (Leningrad: Sovetskii pisatel' [Leningradskoe otdelenie], 1965).

Andrei Siniavsky, one of the most complex and controversial Russian literary and cultural figures of the latter half of the twentieth century, first came to prominence in the late 1950s as a liberal voice during the period of the Thaw, following Joseph Stalin's death in 1953. In 1966, however, Siniavsky achieved a much greater notoriety both within the Soviet Union and abroad: he was placed on trial by the authorities for writing literary works that had been smuggled out of the country and published beyond the bounds of Soviet censorship under the pseudonym Abram Tertz. Despite protests by prominent Soviet intellectuals—protests that many viewed as the beginning of the Soviet dissident movement—Siniavsky and his codefendant, Iulii Markovich Daniel', were convicted of anti-Soviet activity and sentenced to terms in labor camps. While imprisoned, Siniavsky wrote (as Tertz) his most controversial work, *Progulki s Pushkinym* (1975; translated as *Strolls with Pushkin,* 1993), in the form of letters that he sent from the labor camps to his wife, Mar'ia Vasil'evna Rozanova. After his release, he emigrated with his family from the Soviet Union and settled in France, where he lived out his life, teaching Russian literature at the Sorbonne and continuing to write and publish under both his real name and his pseudonym. His unorthodox writings and opposition to mainstream political and aesthetic positions placed him at the center of émigré, Soviet (during the glasnost years), and, finally, post-Soviet literary and political polemics.

Siniavsky's reputation is inseparable from the aesthetic position embodied in his literary persona Tertz. The pseudonym, at first a necessary cover for his illicit publishing activities, later evolved into a metaphor for Siniavsky's literary method, which he termed Fantastic Realism. He first elaborated the concept in the concluding paragraphs of his essay, "Chto takoe sotsialisticheskii realizm" (first published as *On Socialist Realism,* 1960; Russian version published 1967). The pseudonym was inspired by the title character—a Jewish pickpocket—in a thieves' song. Throughout his literary career, he returned to, and elaborated on, the idea of the writer as outsider and criminal, inextricable from the texture of his own "exaggerated prose" and from his vision of literature. In the corpus of his works—and, most especially, of the works he wrote as Tertz—he argues for the autonomy of literature and its freedom from the tyrannies of politics and mimesis; he declares the right of literature to be playful, inventive, and transgressive. Yet, just as Siniavsky began his career as Tertz by invoking the "metamorphoses of God," so his later works, in particular, for all their irreverence toward worldly powers, make clear the debt that his conception of the "play" of literature owes to the tradition of Russian religious thought.

Andrei Donatovich Siniavsky was born on 8 October 1925 in Moscow. He grew up in a communal apartment there and spent summers at the home of his maternal grandmother in Rameno. Siniavsky's mother, Evdokiia Ivanovna (Torkhova) Siniavskaia, was a teacher who later worked in the Lenin Library. Siniavsky father, Donat Evgen'evich Siniavsky, graduated from a mining institute before the 1917 Revolution. A leftist Socialist Revolutionary, he was imprisoned

*Siniavsky's wife, Masha, in the 1950s (from* On Trial: The Case of Sinyavsky [Tertz] and Daniel' [Arzhak], *1967; Jean and Alexander Heard Library, Vanderbilt University)*

three times during his life: once during 1912–1913 under the tsarist regime and twice during the Soviet period, the first time in the 1920s and the second time in the late Stalin years. While he worked at many jobs during his life, including as an engineer and at a village theater (in an attempt to "go to the people") in the 1920s, Donat Evgen'evich aspired unsuccessfully to be a writer. Siniavsky devotes the third and central chapter of his autobiographical novel *Spokoinoi nochi* (1984; translated as *Goodnight!* 1989) to a detailed portrayal of his relations with Donat Evgen'evich, which he casts in the tradition of the generational divide between "fathers and sons": "He grew from the year 1909 as I did from 1948. Each person has his point of orientation." Donat Evgen'evich came from a noble family and was a nineteenth-century kind of revolutionary—a firm believer in a positivist, rationalist approach to reality.

During World War II, Siniavsky was evacuated to Rameno. After he finished high school there, he was drafted in 1943 and sent to a military training school. He served out the last year of the war in the Red Army as a radio technician at an airfield outside of Moscow. After his demobilization, he entered Moscow State University to study literature. Upon graduation he contin-

ued at the university to obtain his candidate degree (the equivalent of a Ph.D.) in 1952 after defending his dissertation on Maksim Gor'ky's four-volume novel *Zhizn' Klima Samgina* (1927–1937, The Life of Klim Samgin). Siniavsky did not remain untouched by the rigors and intrigues of late Stalinist political culture. His father was arrested in 1950 in a final purge of surviving members of rival parties of the Bolsheviks and after nine months of imprisonment and interrogation in Butyrki Prison in Moscow was sent into exile at the family home in Rameno, where he was forced to remain until after Stalin's death. In the "Father" chapter of *Spokoinoi nochi,* Siniavsky relates how, while visiting his father in exile and walking with him in the same woods where they had hunted in his childhood, he realizes that his father has been scarred by his incarceration; he believes that a listening device was implanted in his father's brain while he was in prison. In his literary autobiography this realization—that he can no longer speak freely even to his father and even in the safety of the forest—symbolizes another step in his evolution as a writer. Siniavsky's mother, Evdokiia Ivanovna, died in 1955, while Donat Evgen'evich died in 1960.

Also during this period, Siniavsky became embroiled in a plot by the secret police organization Narodnyi komissariat vnutrennykh del (NKVD, People's Commissariat for Internal Affairs), which later led to accusations of collaboration, but also presented him, paradoxically, with the means to smuggle his works abroad for publication. Despite the closed society and xenophobia of the late Stalin era, the daughter of the French military attaché, Helene Peltier, studied in the philological department of Moscow State University while Siniavsky was a student there. Siniavsky was ordered by the NKVD to lure the unsuspecting foreigner into marriage with him in order to compromise her father. In the fifth and final chapter of *Spokoinoi nochi,* Siniavsky recounts how, after agonizing over what to do, he finally blurted out to Helene the plot, and she agreed to play out an elaborate farce in which she pretended to be insulted by his advances in order to throw off the security forces. The two emerged unscathed from the episode, and Helene later aided Siniavsky in spiriting his manuscripts out of the U.S.S.R.

Siniavsky began to publish works of literary history and scholarship while he was still in graduate school. His first published article, "Ob estetike Maiakovskogo" (On Maiakovsky's Aesthetics), appeared in *Vestnik Moskovskogo universiteta* (Moscow University Herald) in 1950 and was followed shortly thereafter by the article "Osnovnye printsipy estetiki V. V. Maiakovsko-go" (Basic Principles of V. V. Maiakovsky's Aesthetics), which appeared in *Znamia* (Banner). Siniavsky devoted his first publications to the works of the avant-garde, revolutionary poet Vladimir Vladimirovich Maiakovsky during the same period as he was writing his dissertation on Gor'ky, the realist prose writer and canonical "father of socialist realism." Siniavsky later pointed out that, because of his acceptable status in the official Soviet pantheon of writers, Maiakovsky served as a cover and a mode of library access to the early-twentieth-century modernist tradition in Russian poetry as a whole; Siniavsky's interest in Maiakovsky lasted until the end of his life. Gor'ky, on the other hand, was a writer for whom Siniavsky later professed little empathy.

After completing his candidate degree, Siniavsky took up a post as a research fellow at the prestigious Gork'y Institute of World Literature (IMLI) and began to teach as an adjunct both at Moscow State University and at the Studio School of the Moscow Art Theater, where Vladimir Semenovich Vysotsky, who became one of the most celebrated bards of the Soviet Union, was among his students. At the university Siniavsky taught a large lecture course on the history of Soviet literature and, later, a seminar on Russian poetry. In January 1955 Siniavsky met his future wife. Mar'ia Vasil'evna worked nearby, just off Red Square, and would sometimes sit in on Siniavsky's lectures. In 1958, in the wake of the Soviet political uproar that followed both the Western publication of the novel *Doktor Zhivago* and the subsequent awarding of the Nobel Prize in literature to Boris Leonidovich Pasternak, Siniavsky was forced out of his teaching position at Moscow State University. He was already writing a lengthy article on Pasternak for the series *Istoriia russkoi sovetskoi literatury* (History of Russian Soviet Literature), which could not be included in the volume because of the controversies surrounding the poet. Moreover, Siniavsky refused to condemn Pasternak for publishing his work abroad.

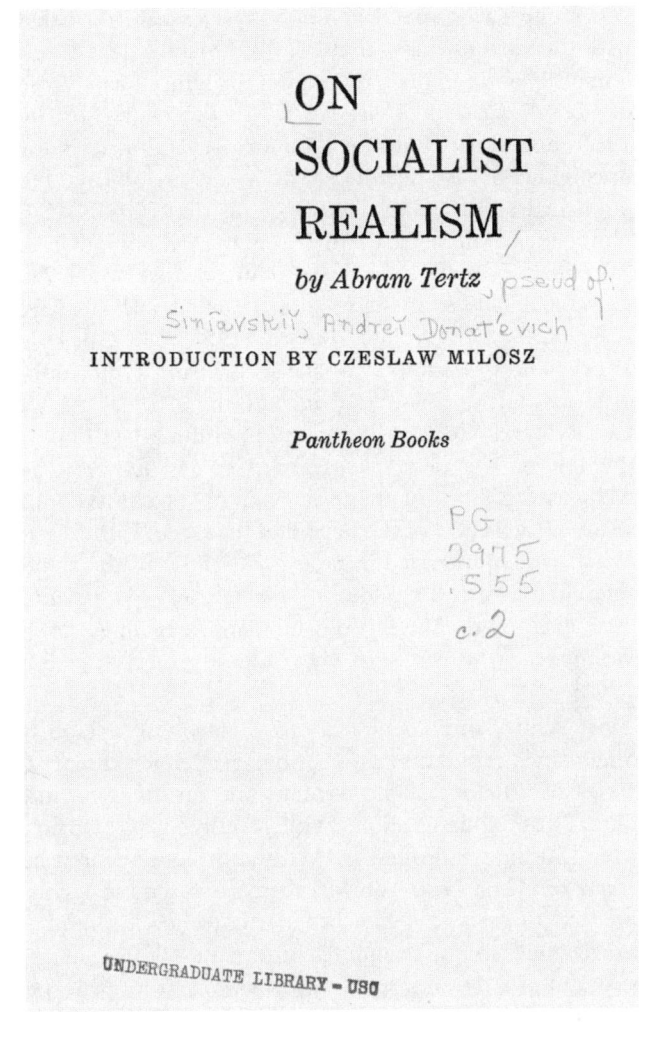

*Title page for Siniavsky's first book (1960), initially published in English, in which he described the literary method he called Fantastic Realism. For works published abroad to avoid Soviet censors, he adopted the pseudomym Abram Tertz, from a traditional song about a Jewish pickpocket (Thomas Cooper Library, University of South Carolina).*

The early years of Siniavsky's career coincided with the various thaws that followed Stalin's death, and Siniavsky soon made a reputation for himself as a voice of liberal ideas in Soviet letters. In the course of the 1950s and early 1960s he produced several articles for prestigious Soviet reference works and periodicals. He published an article distilled from his dissertation, "Ob khudozhestvennoi strukture romana 'Zhizn' Klima Samgina'" (On the Artistic Structure of the Novel *The Life of Klim Samgin*) in the volume *Tvorchestvo M. Gor'kogo i voprosy sotsialisticheskogo realizma* (1958, M. Gor'ky's Works and Questions of Socialist Realism). Other publications during this period include the articles "A. M. Gor'ky" and "Eduard Bagritsky" in volume 1 (1958) of the reference series *Istoriia russkoi sovetskoi literatury*, as well as "Literatura perioda velikoi otechestvennoi voiny" (Literature of the Period of the Great Fatherland War), which appeared in volume 3 (1961) of the same reference work. In addition, his entries "Akmeizm" (Acmeism) and "M. A. Voloshin" appeared in *Kratkaia literaturnaia entsiklopediia* (A Short Literary Encyclopedia, 1962).

While these publications helped to establish Siniavsky's reputation as a serious academic scholar, a series of articles that he wrote–some on his own and others in collaboration with Andrei Nikolaevich Men'shutin, a colleague at IMLI–and that appeared in *Novyi mir* (The New World), then the foremost Soviet literary journal, gave him broader currency in popular intellectual circles. Beginning in the late 1950s, Siniavsky published ten articles in *Novyi mir* that can be divided roughly into three complementary critical strains: those devoted to the reconsideration, or rehabilitation, of figures hitherto banned or marginalized in official Soviet literature; those emphasizing the literary, as opposed to political, evaluation of contemporary Soviet literary works; and those taking to task establishment writers for their hackneyed, politically tainted works. In the first group were articles on Pasternak, Robert Frost, and Anna Andreevna Akhmatova, respectively: "Poeticheskii sbornik B. Pasternaka." (1962, B. Pasternak's Poetry Collection), "'Poidem so mnoi . . .'" (1964, Come with Me . . . ), and "Raskovannyi golos (k 75-letiyu A. Akhmatovoi)" (1964, Unfettered Voice [For A. Akhmatova's Seventy-Fifth Birthday]). In the second strain were articles on contemporary poetry: "Den' russkoi poezii" (1959, Day of Russian Poetry), written in collaboration with Men'shutin; "Poeziia i proza Ol'gi Berggolts" (1960, The Poetry and Prose of Ol'ga Berggolts); and, also written with Men'shutin, "Za poeticheskuiu aktivnost' (zametki o poezii molodykh)" (1961, For Poetic Activism [Notes on Poetry by Young Writers]). Finally, the last group included "Davaite govorit' professional'no" (1961, Let's Talk Professionally), in collaboration with Men'shutin; "O novom sbornike stikhov Anatoliia Sofronova" (1959, On Anatolii Safronov's New Collection of Verse); and "Pamflet ili paskvil'?" (1964, Pamphlet or Lampoon). An article on the poetry of Yevgeny Yevtushenko was slated to be published in the September 1965 issue of *Novyi mir*, but the article, titled "The Defense of the Pyramid," was removed and the issue delayed when Siniavsky was arrested. All of these articles, in one way or another, furthered the goal of stretching the limits of what was permissible in Soviet letters while at the same time staking out for literature a cultural space distinct from the sphere of politics. In articles published in other periodicals Siniavsky discussed, within the parameters allowable in the Soviet Union at the time, fantastic literature, which was a defining preoccupation of his parallel creative-writing career. He published the article "Bez skidok (o sovremennom nauchno-fantasticheskom romane)" (No Discount [On the Contemporary Science Fiction Novel]) in *Voprosy literatury* (Questions of Literature) and "Realizm fantastiki" (The Realism of the Fantastic) in *Literaturnaia gazeta* (The Literary Gazette), both in January 1960 as he was making his debut in the West as Tertz.

In this context Siniavsky also co-authored with the art historian Igor' Naumovich Golomshtok a monograph simply titled *Pikasso* (1960). Primarily designed to introduce Pablo Picasso to a Soviet audience unfamiliar with Western avant-garde art, the work demonstrates Siniavsky's interest in painting, which resurfaces in significant contexts in his later writings. In its positive evaluation of Picasso's aesthetic, the work also gives expression to a vision of art more compatible with the literary activities of Siniavsky's illicit alter ego, Tertz.

What might be termed Siniavsky's official Soviet career culminated in the publication of two substantive works of literary historical revisionism. The first, the book-length study on which Siniavsky collaborated with Men'shutin, *Poeziia pervykh let revoliutsii: 1917–1920* (Poetry of the First Years of the Revolution), came out in 1964. Here, adopting the same strategy he had since the beginning of his scholarly activities, he set new standards for the serious literary reexamination of poetry of the revolutionary period by focusing his analyses on the "acceptable" poets Maiakovsky and the symbolist Aleksander Aleksandrovich Blok. The second publication, "Poeziia Pasternaka" (The Poetry of Pasternak), was arguably bolder and ultimately ill-fated. The extended analysis of Pasternak's poetry was published as the introduction to *Stikhotvoreniia i poemy*, the Biblioteka poeta (Poet's Library) edition of Pasternak's verse, which finally came out–after repeated delays–in August 1965. This volume constituted the first substantive edition of Pasternak's poetry since the virulent campaign of harassment directed at him upon the publication of *Doktor Zhivago*. The book sold out virtually immediately. Siniavsky, who (along with Daniel') had borne the coffin lid at Pasternak's funeral five years before, was instrumental in getting the Biblioteka poeta edition of Pasternak's verse published, an act that was true to his mission of reclaiming Russian twentieth-century poetry from politics and from public oblivion. Yet, Pasternak's *Stikhotvoreniia i poemy* came out only two weeks before Siniavsky's arrest, after which the volume was recalled and destroyed. At this point Siniavsky's official publishing career in the U.S.S.R. ended. His works were not published again in Russia until the late glasnost period.

Beginning in the mid 1950s, Siniavsky surreptitiously had embarked on a parallel, pseudonymous writing career beyond the borders of his homeland in *tamizdat* (literally, publication "there," meaning abroad). With the help of Helene, now known as Helene Peltier Zamoyska, he managed to smuggle his own manuscripts and those of three other writers—most notably Daniel'—out of the U.S.S.R. for publication in the West. The first of Siniavsky's works to be published abroad was the essay "Chto takoe sotsialisticheskii realizm," which appeared anonymously in French translation in the journal *Esprit* in February 1959; the Russian version was collected in *Fantasticheskii mir Abrama Tertsa* (The Fantastic World of Abram Tertz) in 1967. The essay was followed in May 1960 by the publication of the novella *Sud idet* (translated as *The Trial Begins*, 1960) in the Paris-based Polish émigré journal *Kultura* (Culture). Both the essay, which at once is an exorcism of the past and a manifesto for the future, and the novel, which performs the fundamental principles of "Chto takoe sotsialisticheskii realizm" in the form of the "phantasmagoric art" anticipated by the essay, represented the debut of Siniavsky's alter ego, Tertz.

"Chto takoe sotsialisticheskii realizm" is considered by many to be Siniavsky's most important work. It deconstructs in a bold stroke the reigning Soviet aesthetic of the time and remains one of the most astute analyses of socialist realism. In the tradition of such classics of the Russian critical canon as Leo Tolstoy's *Chto takoe iskusstvo?* (1898, What is Art?), the essay confutes Soviet artistic policy and practice by placing them within a philosophical framework of universalizing historical sweep. Siniavsky's essay is divided into three parts. In the first he elaborates a cyclical theory of history in relation to a sequence of teleologies:

> There are periods in history when the presence of the Goal becomes evident, when trivial passions are swallowed up by the striving toward God. And He begins to call mankind openly to Himself. Thus arose Chris-

*Siniavsky (front) and Iulii Daniel' carrying Boris Pasternak's casket from his house at Peredelkino during his funeral in 1960 (from* On Trial: The Case of Sinyavsky [Tertz] and Daniel' [Arzhak], *1967; Jean and Alexander Heard Library, Vanderbilt University)*

tian culture, which caught the Goal, perhaps, in its most inaccessible sense. Then the epoch of individualism proclaimed the Free Personality and began to bow down to it as the Goal, with the help of the Renaissance, humanism, the superman, democracy, Robespierre, service and many other prayers. Now we have entered the era of a new universal system—that of socialist purposefulness.

History thus is driven by the rise to ascendancy, institutionalization, and degeneration of goal after goal—each of which makes dangerous claims to exclusivity and each of which eludes realization, doomed by the imperfect means employed to bring into being the ideal end.

In the second section of "Chto takoe sotsialisticheskii realizm," Siniavsky turns to the subject of literary genealogy. He challenges the claim of socialist realism as the continuation and heir to the nineteenth-century Russian realist tradition by contrasting the goal-directed positive hero of the socialist realist novel with the superfluous man of the nineteenth century, who was consumed with striving toward a goal precisely because he lacked one. In the third section of the essay the narrator claims that the true literary forebear of socialist realism is the classical tradition of eighteenth-century Russian literature, devoted to the glorification of empire. He draws the conclusion that socialist realism fails on aesthetic grounds, because it tries to combine what cannot be combined: "A socialist, i.e., goal-directed, religious art cannot be created using the means of that nineteenth-century literature that was called Realism."

The essay concludes with two paragraphs that were written a couple of years after the rest of the essay was completed; these paragraphs were smuggled separately out of the U.S.S.R. to the West. They represent both the solution to the dilemma of socialist realism posed in the essay and a manifesto for the writings of Tertz:

> In the given case, I place my hopes on a phantasmagoric art with hypotheses instead of a purpose and grotesque in place of realistic descriptions of everyday life. It would correspond more fully to the spirit of our day. Let the exaggerated images of Hoffmann, Dostoevsky, Goya, and the most socialist of them all Maiakovsky and of many other realists and nonrealists teach us how to be truthful with the help of absurd fantasy.
>
> In losing our faith, we did not lose our ecstasy at the metamorphoses of God which take place before our eyes, at the monstrous peristalsis of his intestines—the convolutions of the brain. We don't know where to go, not having understood that there is nothing to be done, we begin to think, to construct conjectures, to suggest. Perhaps we will think up something amazing. But it will no longer be socialist realism.

Yet, while the essay generally has been read primarily as an exposé of socialist realism, it is a consummate "Tertz work," in that it blurs the bounds between the literary and the critical text. The essay is narrated by an *eiron,* who professes to speak in defense of socialist realism, but who, in the course of the essay, acknowledges that he has caught himself falling into irony, the very device he identifies as the mode of the nineteenth-century superfluous man: "Irony is the unfailing companion of unbelief and doubt; it disappears as soon as faith, which does not permit blasphemy, appears." In the end the ambiguous semantic space staked out by the narrator's irony poses the most biting challenge to the semiotic hegemony of socialist realism. In this regard "Chto takoe sotsialisticheskii realizm" is a tour de force of ironic discourse in the mode of Jonathan Swift's *A Modest Proposal* (1729) as well as an example of Tertz's technique of courting "blasphemy" by destabilizing language that has been totalized and made rigid and conventional.

*Sud idet* enacts the basic argument of "Chto takoe sotsialisticheskii realizm" in fictional form. The tale opens with a phantasmagoric conflation of literature as social command, with a vision of the writer as a prophet called by God. The writer-narrator is ordered by an apparitional figure, called "Khoziain" (Master, a term commonly applied to Stalin), to write a work glorifying the Moscow municipal prosecutor Vladimir Petrovich Globov, who, in a thinly veiled reference to the Doctor's Plot, is charged with prosecuting the case of an abortionist named Rabinovich—which is the name of the stock character and common punch line of Russian "Jewish jokes." In the course of the novel Globov's family life unravels: his son, Serezha, is arrested for anti-Soviet agitation; his wife, Marina, has an abortion, apparently performed by the very culprit he is prosecuting; and she has an affair with the defense attorney Iurii Karlinsky. The narrator is arrested for writing the manuscript and at the end of the novel finds himself in a labor camp with Rabinovich and Serezha. In the terms elaborated in "Chto takoe sotsialisticheskii realizm" Marina represents the aging Goal, Globov the positive hero, and Serezha the youthful Romanticism of the ideal before it has reified into classicism. Karlinsky, who fantasizes about blowing up the monument to Aleksandr Sergeevich Pushkin, located in the center of Moscow, voices the irony of lost faith. Together these characters play out the drama of the Goal destroyed by the means employed to realize it. Midway through the text the writer-narrator, confronted by his sponsor Khoziain, lays bare the metaphor on which hinges the novel, as an allegory of the act of writing:

> Court is in session *[sud idet],* court is in session throughout the whole world. And it is no longer Rabinovich, exposed by the city prosecutor, but all of us, as many as there are taken all together, who daily, nightly, are taken to trial and questioning. And this is called history.
>
> The bell rings. "Your surname? Given name? Date of birth?"
>
> That's when you begin to write.

In the course of the next five years, eight more works by Siniavsky appeared in the West under his pseudonym Tertz. These include the stories of *Fantasticheskie povesti* (1961; translated as *Fantastic Stories,* 1963): "V tsirke" (translated as "At the Circus"), "Ty i ia" (translated as "You and I"), "Grafomany" (translated as "Graphomaniacs"), "Kvartiranty" (translated as "Tenants"), and "Gololeditsa" (Icy Weather; translated as "The Icicle"). The novella *Lyubimov* (1964; translated as *The Makepeace Experiment,* 1965) also came out during this period. In addition, a collection of aphorisms titled *Mysli vrasplokh* (1966; translated as *Unguarded Thoughts,* 1972) was published in the West only after the trial of Siniavsky and Daniel' had ended, as was the sixth and probably best-known early story by Tertz, "Pkhents" (1967). "Pkhents" actually was the first of the "fantastic tales" that Siniavsky wrote, but it could not be released until after his arrest, because he had shown it to his friend Sergei Grigor'evich Khmelnitsky—on whom the character Serezha, in the final chapter of *Spokoinoi nochi,* is based—and realized that his identity would be betrayed if "Pkhents" appeared abroad.

While Siniavsky strove, with the writings he published under his own name in the U.S.S.R., to work within the system to stretch the limits of what could be published and to attempt to reaffirm aesthetic rather than political standards for Soviet literature, the works he wrote as Tertz were transgressive in their very conception—they crossed geographical, political, and aesthetic bounds of acceptability. From the outset Siniavsky knew that they were not publishable in the Soviet Union. At heart the issue lay in what he later termed "stylistic differences," which emanated from Siniavsky's idea of literature as it was embodied in the writings and figure of Tertz—as the pseudonym that marked the place of the writer transformed into text.

Like *Sud idet,* Siniavsky's stories, while yielding surface interpretations that point to the writer's immediate political context at the time of their writing, are amenable to more-profound metaliterary readings as well. This is particularly evident in the two earliest stories, "V tsirke" and "Pkhents," in which the protagonist functions not only as an artist figure but also as a figure of the artistic sign. Moreover, in both stories the act of creation begins with a crime. In "V tsirke" an electrician named Kostia is inspired to become a pickpocket when he sees a magician called the Manipulator perform at the circus. Kostia's initial theft of a wallet is both a transformation and an appropriation of identity; it becomes a paradigm of the artist's self-transformation into text. Kostia, who then goes by the name Konstantin Petrovich, has a lucrative career as a thief until he is persuaded to take part in an apartment robbery—in the course of which he is surprised by the Manipulator and murders him. Kostia is caught and put in a labor camp, and the story ends as he performs the ultimate circus feat, a *salto-mortale,* just as he is shot dead attempting to escape. While the story evokes Siniavsky's masquerade as Tertz and his risky, illicit career as an underground writer, it also suggests an allegory for the artistic act sui generis.

The central character and first-person narrator of "Pkhents" also presents himself as a fugitive from the law. The story takes the form of his notes, in which he translates himself into a foreign language. He claims to be an alien being who resembles a cactus and lives on water. Traveling as an intergalactic tourist decades earlier, he crashed to earth when his spacecraft had an accident that killed all the others onboard. Forced to take up a fictitious identity in order to survive, he masquerades as a human being; for years he has been living in a communal apartment in Moscow. When the story opens, the narrator hopes that he finally has found another like himself—another being from his own planet who also is disguised as a hunchback. He soon learns to his dismay, however, that the other man is nothing but an ordinary hunchback. Unlike the narrator, the man does not understand the word "Pkhents," which thereby comes to represent the impossible ideal of perfect communication through language, while at the same time echoing Siniavsky's pseudonym Tertz. Now more alone than ever, the aging creature feels his powers waning and fears that he may not be capable of maintaining his disguise much longer. He briefly contemplates revealing himself to the authorities, but he is brought up short before the prospect of his untranslatable condition:

> How can they understand me when I myself in their language can in no way express my unhuman essence. I do nothing but dodge all over the place and make do with metaphors, but as soon as it comes to what is most important—I fall silent. And I only see the solid, low GOGRY, I hear the swift VZGLYAGU, and the indescribably beautiful PKHENTS overshadows my trunk. Ever fewer and fewer of these words remain in my fading memory. The sounds of human speech can only approximately convey their construction. And if linguists crowd around and ask what it means, I will say only GOGRY TUZHEROSKIP and make a helpless gesture.

This passage captures perhaps better than any other in Tertz's prose the existential problem of the writer caught in a language in which metaphor is the only form of referentiality, the only bridge between reality and writing. Overwhelmed by the impossibility of communication, the narrator resolves to return to the site of the crash and, after living out a final summer in the north country, to immolate himself and his notes.

Like "Pkhents," Siniavsky's other early stories center on failed communication and the potent but inevitably inadequate power of metaphor to bridge the gap between word and deed, between reader and text.

The motif of the double recurs in the story "Ty i ia," which is structured around a fatal confrontation between the first-person narrator, who claims omniscience, and a character who bears Gogol's name and patronymic, Nikolai Vasil'evich, and to whom the narrator addresses alternating sections of the story, using the familiar second-person pronoun "ty." As the story progresses, the narrator and his subject are locked in a struggle that is played out in misdirected gazes and misconstrued intent and that ends with Nikolai Vasil'evich committing suicide. "Ty i ia" has been interpreted as a representation of the struggle between two halves of a diseased consciousness—it reads like a contest for control between an author and his character.

The same motif structures the story "Grafomany," which tells about an unsuccessful and bitter Soviet hack writer named Pavel Ivanovich Straustin, who believes that his aspiration to literary celebrity is being thwarted by a conspiracy of editors and writers who have plagiarized his work. Here, the play on literary theft becomes a biting satire of the clichéd nature of Soviet official prose, in which stock phrases reappear in text after text. In the wake of an argument with his wife, precipitated by the rejection of his most recent manuscript, Straustin takes refuge with an avant-garde poet and samizdat "publisher" named Galkin, who holds court for a motley group of underground writers. Straustin dismisses them all as "graphomaniacs," while Galkin proudly professes a gospel of graphomania and preaches to his followers an apocalyptic vision of the earth overrun by writers covering the planet with their scribblings. Straustin leaves Galkin's apartment even more embittered and, as he walks through the streets of Moscow named after famous writers, he castigates canonical writers for blocking his way to literary fame and fortune. Suddenly he realizes that he is merely a writing instrument in another's hand and addresses himself to the sky, "Hey you, graphomaniac! Quit working! Everything you write is no good. Everything you've composed is devoid of talent. It's impossible to read you." His rebellion against God exhausted, he returns home and promises his wife never to write again. Behind her back as the story ends, however, he encourages his son, whom he earlier had feared as a rival, to write and himself vows to keep writing. Not only does "Grafomany" lampoon the creative bankruptcy of the Soviet literary establishment and its empty lionization of the canon of nineteenth-century Russian realist authors, but it questions the very essence of literary authority.

"Kvartiranty" also features a writer figure but one who is relegated to silence as the interlocutor in a dialogue in which the first-person narrator, who claims to be a *domovoi* (house spirit), does all the talking. The narrator portrays the world of the communal apartment as populated by creatures from folklore, united in a conspiracy to silence him and the writer who might tell his tales to the world. The pointed satire of Soviet reality again penetrates beyond the surface of the plot to interrogate the nature of narrative, in which continued failure to communicate spurs the narrator on to ever more daring realizations of metaphor.

The final and longest of Siniavsky's "fantastic tales," "Gololeditsa," opens with a most poignant image of the tenuous relationship between reader and text. The first-person narrator, whose name the reader never learns, presents the tale he is about to tell as akin to a message in a bottle from a castaway flung into the sea of time, in the hopes that fate will somehow carry it to its destined reader. As he claims in the course of the story, one day—without warning or explanation—he finds himself endowed with the ability to see into his future, as well as the past and future of others. This gift of fate soon proves to be a curse, when he sees that his girlfriend, Natasha, is destined to be killed by a falling icicle on a specific date and at a specific time. His desperate attempts to stave off fate, to save her from doom, end in failure because of a series of misunderstandings that lead to his arrest by the security police. The narrator loses his peculiar omniscience at the end, but not before he is vouchsafed visions of past and future incarnations that, on the one hand, undercut Marxist pretensions to historical inevitability and, on the other, reveal that he himself is caught in continual, paradigmatic failures of time and language—failures that repeatedly part him from his love. Like the image of the message in a bottle, however, the narrative leaves open the possibility of finding the ideal reader in the future, whether that person incarnates the narrator's love of Natasha or of the narrator himself.

Of the early works that Siniavsky wrote as Tertz, *Lyubimov* is the longest and walks the same precarious tightrope between political satire and metaliterary meditation. On the surface the novel represents a thinly veiled satire on the Soviet experiment and thus parallels "Chto takoe sotsialisticheskii realizm" and "Gololeditsa," especially in its subversion of Marxist pretensions to historiographical hegemony. At the center of the story stands Lenia Tikhomirov (in the English translation, Lenny Makepeace), a bicycle mechanic who, driven by his infatuation with the local librarian, Serafima Petrovna Kozlova, acquires the power to impose his own will telepathically on his fellow citizens in the town of Liubimov. He takes over from the local authorities in a mind-control coup d'état and sets about instituting a utopian society in the city. When his powers become overextended, however, his reign over the town collapses as Soviet troops close in on the renegade state.

The novel closes with the penniless Lenia fleeing town in disgrace. This bitingly comical put-down of Soviet pretensions toward building a communist utopia, however, is complicated by an elaborate narrative frame in which two narrators—the town librarian Savelii Kuz'mich Proferansov and the spirit of his prerevolutionary ancestor Proferansov—vie for control of the narrative, which itself ends up a proscribed, underground manuscript. As in other works by Siniavsky during this early period, realized metaphor becomes the motive force of the plot: it constitutes the fundamental principle of Lenia's translation of thought into deed—of utopia into reality.

That the Soviet authorities took some five years to track down the culprit behind Tertz serves as eloquent testimony to the effectiveness of Siniavsky's literary mask. Almost from the beginning, the opinion was prevalent in the West that these works by Tertz could not be the writings of a Soviet author, and rumors circulated that Tertz was the pseudonym of a Polish writer or of a Russian émigré. Siniavsky and his wife even aided in the spread of disinformation by disseminating false speculations about the identity of Tertz among the writer's colleagues at the IMLI. Even after Siniavsky's arrest, Aleksander Trifonovich Tvardovsky, who edited the liberal journal *Novyi mir* (in which Siniavsky had published pieces virtually simultaneously with the appearance of his work as Tertz in the West), refused to believe that Siniavsky could possibly have committed so unpatriotic an act.

On 8 October 1965 Siniavsky was arrested on the street on his way to teach a class at the Studio School of the Moscow Art Theater and was held for interrogation, first at the Lubyanka Prison and then at Lefortovo in central Moscow. As rumors circulated in Moscow and beyond, and eventually made their way to the West, that the IMLI professor of literature had been unmasked as the literary fugitive Tertz, intellectuals both within and beyond the borders of the U.S.S.R. mobilized in his support. A rally, calling for an open trial for Siniavsky and Daniel', who had been arrested a few days after Siniavsky, was held on Pushkin Square in Moscow on 5 December 1965. This protest marked the first large public demonstration against government policy of the post-Stalin period and is widely considered to have marked the beginning of the dissident movement as a serious force in Soviet politics and culture.

The trial of Siniavsky and Daniel' began on 10 February 1966 and lasted for four days. Entrance to the trial was strictly controlled, and the courtroom was packed largely with official figures, although Siniavsky's students and other supporters gathered outside the courthouse throughout the proceedings. Others were allowed passes for the trial, issued by the Writers'

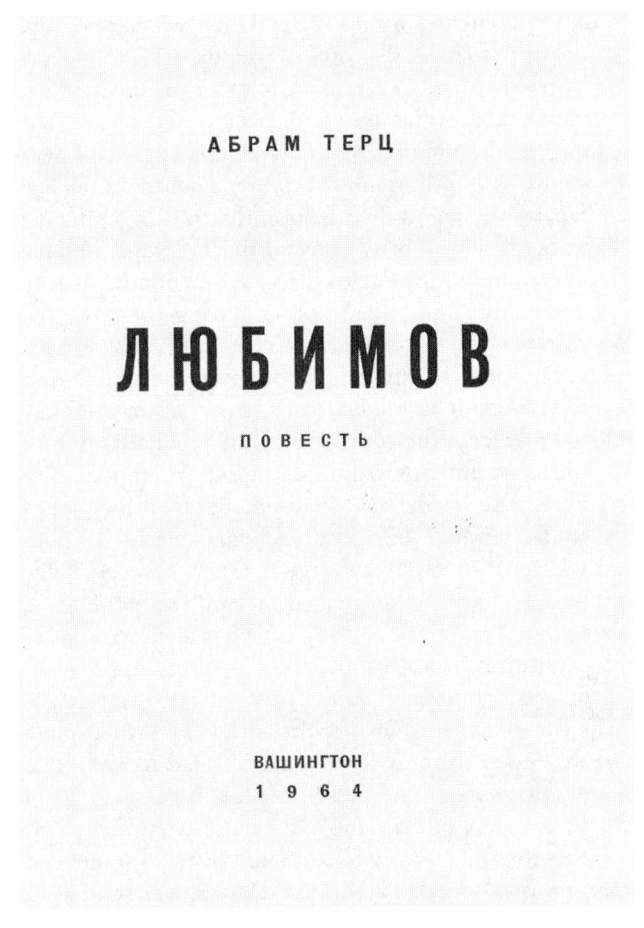

*Title page for* Lyubinov, *1964, Siniavsky's thinly veiled satire on the Soviet government, first published in Washington, D.C., and translated into English in 1965 as* The Makepeace Experiment *(John C. Hodges Library, University of Tennessee–Knoxville)*

Union, for a single day, with the exception of the Leningrad writer Boris Vakhtin, who argued successfully for a two-day pass because he had traveled from a distance. Despite the authorities' precautions, Siniavsky's wife, Mar'ia Vasil'evna, and Vakhtin managed to compile a transcript of the proceedings, which was collected along with letters and other documents relating to the arrest and trial, such as commentary by the dissident editor Aleksandr Ginzburg, who himself was imprisoned for his role in preparing and circulating the *Belaia kniga* (White Book).

The proceedings were conceived as a show trial in the Stalinist mode. In this vein it was preceded by a virulent national press campaign in which Siniavsky and Daniel' were accused of being "turncoats" who had betrayed the motherland by selling out to foreigners and maligning the Soviet Union in their works. Since virtually no one had read the works in question, which could be circulated by the defendants' wives and supporters only to a small group of friends before the trial, the overblown rhetoric and scare tactics could find no contradiction among the populace at large. But the authorities, despite their virtually complete control over the media within the country, soon encountered the legacy left by the cultural relaxation that occurred during Nikita Sergeevich Khrushchev's rule. The most notable difference came in the refusal of the defendants to confess their guilt and recant, either during their pretrial incarceration or during the trial itself. Siniavsky especially, both in his responses throughout the trial and in his final statement to the court, not only steadfastly refused to accept the court's foregone condemnation of his works as anti-Soviet but also took the opportunity to elaborate in his defense the fundamental principles of his understanding of literature, particularly as concerned the distinction between literary and legal discourse: "The artistic image is always polysemic. Even I, the author, have difficulty saying what it means. I consider juridical trials of the literary text impossible. Because it is impossible to define juridically unambiguously the meaning of an artistic work." The trial, nonetheless, ended the way it was orchestrated to end. The defendants were found guilty of violating article 70 of the Criminal Code of the Russian Soviet Federated Socialist Republic (R.S.F.S.R.). Siniavsky was sentenced to seven years of hard labor, and Daniel' was sentenced to five years.

The harshness of the sentences was a wake-up call for those who had hoped that Stalinism was an evil that had receded irrevocably into the past. The trial marked the intensification of the cultural crackdown that brought a final end to the Thaw and ushered in the Stagnation that defined the years of Leonid Il'ich Brezhnev's governance. Yet, the creative intelligentsia, which now had a taste of freedom, was unwilling to accept the trial verdict without a fight. The most significant protest—one that was to shape and define the cultural geography of official Soviet literature for the remainder of its existence—was a petition signed by sixty-three Moscow writers, calling on the government for clemency. The most notable among these writers were Bella Akhatovna Akhmadulina, Lidiia Korneevna Chukovskaya, Vladimir Nikolaevich Voinovich, Lev Zinov'evich Kopelev, Bulat Shalvovich Okudzhava, and Kornei Ivanovich Chukovsky. The need to adopt a position with regard to the trial and its verdict—to hold the line against a return to Stalinism—forced the cream of the Soviet intelligentsia to make hard choices and to take a public stand, in sharp contrast to an older generation's treatment of Pasternak less than a decade earlier.

Despite expressions of consternation and outrage from intellectuals at home and abroad, the Soviet authorities did not move to mitigate the results of the trial. Siniavsky was transported to a labor camp in Mordovia, where, despite continued protests, he served out almost six years of his seven-year sentence. While in the camp, Siniavsky continued to write. He was allowed to write one letter to his wife every two weeks. He describes his strategy in the work that resulted from this correspondence, *Progulki s Pushkinym*:

> I realized that I had to come up with something, and I thought up the idea of incorporating my writing into letters. Letters are usually written at one sitting, and in this I was aided by a misfortune. There was a restriction on letters—you could mail only two letters a month. Fortunately, there was no restriction on their length. Of course it was forbidden to send a very long letter, but you could write twenty pages in tiny but very neat handwriting, so that it would be easier for the censor to read.

In this fashion, while incarcerated and under strict surveillance by the authorities, Siniavsky wrote *Progulki s Pushkinym*, which turned out to be his most controversial work. He also completed the first chapter of *V teni Gogolia* (1975, *In the Shadow of Gogol; V teni Gogolia*). Moreover, after his release and with the help of his wife, Siniavsky collected other excerpts from his letters in *Golos iz khora* (1973, *A Voice From the Chorus*).

Whatever their differences in subject and scope, a consideration of Siniavsky's books on Pushkin and Gogol as complementary parts of the same project is appropriate. Just as Siniavsky began his publishing careers in the U.S.S.R. and beyond, preoccupied with the "founding fathers" of Soviet letters, Gor'ky and Maiakovsky, so his labor-camp works, which initiated his émigré publishing career, grappled with the patriarchs of nineteenth-century Russian literature, Pushkin and Gogol. *Progulki s Pushkinym* and *V teni Gogolia*, however, were written outside of the Soviet publishing establishment, giving Siniavsky the freedom to pursue Tertz's more idiosyncratic stylistic agenda. The former work, in particular, plays itself out in a series of dazzling metaphors reminiscent of the lamentation of the narrator in "Pkhents," affirming metaphor as the sole, albeit imperfect, bridge between reality and linguistic sign. Yet, if Siniavsky's early works as Tertz are preoccupied with what appears to be the virtually inevitable failure of the encounter between text and reader to produce meaningful signification, the later works—beginning with *Progulki s Pushkinym*—adumbrate a more optimistic vision of the reading process, with metaphor as a form of ultimately sacred play as its focal point.

Like *Sud idet*, moreover, *Progulki s Pushkinym* has at its core the figure of a joke, the Pushkin of "anecdotes." He is an empty, carnivalesque figure of fun whom

Siniavsky-Tertz poses as his traveling companion as he "strolls" through the poet's life and works, an irreverent guide who will punctuate the inflated pretensions of the official Pushkin canonized by the Soviet scholarly establishment. In the simplest terms, the joke Pushkin stands for everyone and therefore no one, as in the stock example of a denial of responsibility cited in the text:

"Who'll pay?"

"Pushkin!"

"Who do you take me for—Pushkin—that I'm supposed to be responsible for everything?"

"Pushkinspieler! Pushkinstein!"

He's our Charlie Chaplin, a contemporary ersatz Petrushka, who spiffed himself up and got the hang of strutting his stuff in rhyme.

This central metaphor of Pushkin, not as a great national poet but as a figure of emptiness and not as absence, comes in the course of the narrative to depict the complementary openness of Pushkin's texts—they resist being commandeered to the exclusive service of simple and single-minded ideological or aesthetic platforms—and the uncontrollable nature of the reader. In the end the author's concession of the reader's freedom becomes an ethical counterbalance to the utilitarian imperative placed on art by the Russian radical and Soviet critical traditions. Here the pessimism of Tertz's earlier writings, regarding the possibility of reaching an empathetic reader, is transformed into a principled renunciation of authorial control. The deft lightness of the text is exemplified by its most famous—or infamous—passages. Thus, Tertz describes Pushkin's debut as a poet: "Pushkin ran into great poetry on thin erotic legs and created a commotion." By the same token, critics of the work were incensed by Tertz's likening of Pushkin's protean artistic persona to a vampire. The bold attempt embodied in *Progulki s Pushkinym* to reclaim Pushkin from gray Soviet academic clichés proved to be Tertz's most controversial work.

The aesthetic position declared in *Progulki s Pushkinym* is elaborated in the much lengthier *V teni Gogolia*. Divided into five substantial chapters, this work follows the trajectory of Gogol's life and goes chronologically backward, in order to arrive at the sources of his creativity. It opens with Gogol's death, or rather with the legend that Gogol was buried alive. Just as emptiness becomes the prevailing metaphor of *Progulki s Pushkinym*, suggesting precisely the openness of the literary sign, so death in life defines the central metaphorical cluster of *V teni Gogolia*. It signifies the author's failed and misguided attempts to control his readers through his texts, which figuratively and literally attempt the impossible: to resurrect himself in his readers. In essence Siniavsky argues that Gogol completely misconstrued the spiritual significance both of his own particular talent and of art per se. By trying to use his later writings to dictate his readers' religious beliefs and behavior, Gogol rendered his texts closed, reified, dead. His earlier writings, on the other hand—which came back to haunt him in the form of what he considered readers' misinterpretations, figured as his own characters coming back to haunt him—were redemptive precisely because they prompted laughter at the imperfect world. Through this sacred laughter Gogol's early texts gave indication of an ideal reality beyond.

АБРАМ ТЕРЦ

ПРОГУЛКИ
С
ПУШКИНЫМ

OVERSEAS PUBLICATIONS INTERCHANGE
*in association with*
COLLINS - LONDON

*Title page for* Progulki s Pushkinym, *1973, published under the pseudonym Tertz and translated in 1976 as* A Voice from the Chorus. *Siniavsky wrote this, his most controversial work, in prison and sent it out in the form of letters to his wife (Cornell University Library).*

In his books on Pushkin and Gogol, Siniavsky in essence transforms the writers into complex metaphorical systems figuring what amounts to the performance of an aesthetic theory. In *Golos iz khora,* however, he broaches the same issues in a markedly different generic form. While, given the context of its genesis (letters that Siniavsky wrote from the labor camp to his wife), *Golos iz khora* must be viewed in the long tradition of Russian prison writing, it nonetheless departs from its predecessors. The meditations that compose the work register not the physical rigors of imprisonment—typically described in prison writing and yet absent from this text—but, rather, the writer's life of the mind, allowing him to transcend his immediate surroundings. Siniavsky again transforms external constraints placed on his writing, in this case the prison censorship, into an act of aesthetic transcendence. Unable to write about the hardships of camp life in his letters to Mar'ia Vasil'evna, he made use of the opportunity to explore and record the life of the mind. *Golos iz khora* also defies generic classification. Siniavsky maintained that unlike *Progulki s Pushkinym,* which he conceived as a book as he was writing it in the camp, *Golos iz khora* was concocted from his letters only after his release. The text consists of a diverse array of fragments, ranging from aphoristic utterances and longer meditations on art to snippets of overheard conversation and Chechen folk songs.

As in the texts on Pushkin and Gogol, the play of metaphor is the organizing principle of *Golos iz khora,* and the central metaphor is inscribed in the title of the work: the voice from the chorus. The voice, or the narrating "I," jostles with other voices in the text—whether those of the other inmates or citations from literary and other kinds of texts, all of which constitute the chorus. The text, like the camp, becomes a place of meeting between the voice and the chorus, the self and others, and the writing and its readers. The ideal reader of the text, moreover, is inscribed in the actual mode of the production of the text as letters to the author-prisoner's wife. The correspondence between husband and wife thus becomes a figure of the possibility of perfect communication based on intimacy and trust. In the end *Golos iz khora,* like the books about Pushkin and Gogol, enacts an allegory of reading. The text created in communion with the ideal reader goes out into the world to be read by the "random" reader, who will give the text new life by responding as much to its gaps and silences as to the words that make it up. Art becomes the surrender of self. Above all, the text, which escaped the bounds of the camp in letters, becomes an emblem of art as the transcendence of confining boundaries.

Siniavsky was released from prison on 8 June 1971, after serving five years and nine months of his term. He was freed apparently because Mar'ia Vasil'evna made known to the Kommitet gosudarstvennoi bezopasnosti (KGB, State Security Committee) that Siniavsky had written another book while in the camp and that if he were not released early, she would arrange to have it published in the West on the day he completed his term. Reluctant to provoke another international outcry, the authorities let Siniavsky out of prison shortly before the end of his sentence. In 1973 Siniavsky, his wife, and son, Egor, were allowed to emigrate. They settled in France, where Siniavsky had been offered a position teaching Russian literature at the Sorbonne. The Soviet authorities allowed the writer and his family to leave, supposedly because they knew that his continued residence in the Soviet Union would cause only further embarrassment. In emigration Siniavsky continued to publish under both his own name and his pseudonym; from the beginning he played an active role in émigré intellectual life.

In this latter stage of his career, when the pseudonym Tertz no longer served the practical function of hiding Siniavsky's true identity from the Soviet authorities, the deeper, fundamentally aesthetic implications of the distinction between Siniavsky and Tertz inevitably came to the fore. In the simplest sense Siniavsky affixed his own name to works of a predominantly political nature or to works that fit more or less comfortably into conventional generic categories of literary scholarship or criticism. He attributed to Tertz, on the other hand, works that might be defined broadly as literary but which might be characterized better as ones that challenge straightforward axiological definition. In a more profound sense, however, Tertz became tantamount to an extended metaphor played out (through all of the texts by Tertz) for Siniavsky's vision of art—the artist transformed into text. This significance of the pseudonym, implicit even in Siniavsky's early works as Tertz, became inescapable when Siniavsky chose to publish his first books after emigration, those he had written while imprisoned, under the pseudonym—that is, *Golos iz khora, Progulki s Pushkinym,* and *V teni Gogolia.* Despite the substantive differences between texts written by Tertz and those written by Siniavsky (and between the writing and scholarly careers of Tertz and Siniavsky), discord and controversy were to pursue Siniavsky in both these incarnations to the end of his life.

In this respect Siniavsky's involvement with émigré periodicals is telling. Initially, he participated in mainstream émigré publishing activities and, like most major émigré writers of the time, was allied with the Munich-based journal *Kontinent,* the major Russian literary journal published in Europe. He published the article "Literaturnyi protsess v Rossii" (The Literary Process in Russia), a dissection of mechanisms driving

*Double title page for the English-Russian version of* V teni Gogolia *(1975), which Siniavsky wrote in prison. The work begins with Nikolai Gogol's death and moves backward chronologically in an attempt to discover the source of his creativity (Jean and Alexander Heard Library, Vanderbilt University).*

contemporary Soviet Russian letters comparable in scope to his seminal essay on socialist realism, in the inaugural issue of the journal in 1974. He published two more articles in *Kontinent,* the second appearing in the fifth issue in 1975, before breaking with the journal over disagreements with its editor, Vladimir Emel'ianovich Maksimov, and its most visible contributor, Aleksandr Isaevich Solzhenitsyn, concerning émigré politics.

Siniavsky's break with *Kontinent* was emblematic of the stance he was to take in the émigré community for the rest of his life. He challenged attitudes that he considered conservative and authoritarian and took up the role of Socratic gadfly with regard to émigré shibboleths. Mar'ia Vasil'evna shared and encouraged Siniavsky's status as a renegade. In 1978 she founded the journal *Sintaksis* (Syntax), and shortly thereafter a publishing house of the same name was formed. Both the journal and the publishing concern operated out of the Siniavsky home in the Paris suburb of Fontenay aux Roses. The journal, initially conceived as an outlet solely for Siniavsky's own writings, from the beginning attracted like-minded contributors, both émigré and Soviet. It developed into a counterforce to *Kontinent* and other "institutions" of establishment émigré life. Both manifestations of *Sintaksis* welcomed writers who were politically or aesthetically unorthodox from the point of view of Soviet and mainstream émigré culture. In the partisan politics of emigration, Siniavsky–together with Mar'ia Vasil'evna–used *Sintaksis* the journal as a forum. He argued against dangerously anti-Semitic Russian chauvinism and aesthetic conservatism, which were invested in a realist and utilitarian view of literature; he identified this outlook with the Russophile camp of the emigration, who claimed Maksimov and Solzhenitsyn as their standard-bearers. Siniavsky concluded his 1987 article "Chtenie v serdtsakh" (Reading Angrily), for instance, with an impassioned outburst against Solzhenitsyn and others, whom he saw as trying to impose their own, exclusive claim on Russian culture:

Who gave you the right to appropriate Pushkin, to usurp Russia? And religion, morality, art? Exclusively for yourself and those who think like you. Yes, we've heard this all before: anti-patriotism! Anti-patriotism! As if they were the only ones who could express the will of the people. And whoever is not with us is a traitor to the Motherland. After all is said and done, what a diabolic faith in one's own saintliness one must carry in one's soul in order to deprive other people who don't agree with you of the ordinary right–to love one's country.

Until the end of his life *Sintaksis*, both the journal and the publishing house, remained the primary outlet for the Russian editions of Siniavsky's works.

As Siniavsky and his supporters repeatedly pointed out, the reaction to *Progulki s Pushkinym*, his second book-length work by Tertz and released in emigration, was reminiscent of the slander campaign orchestrated, more than a decade earlier, by the Soviet press to accompany and harness public sentiment for the trial of Siniavsky and Daniel'. Furthermore, this outcry spanned generations of the Russian emigration. Roman Borisovich Gul', editor of the New York–based émigré journal *Novyi zhurnal* (New Review) and an émigré of the First Wave (after the 1917 Revolution), accused Siniavsky of committing "blasphemy" against Russian culture in his irreverent portrayal of Pushkin; Gul' used the same word that had been leveled at Siniavsky by the judge in his Soviet trial. In his article ". . . Koleblet tvoi trenozhnik" (. . . Shakes Your Sacrificial Altar) Solzhenitsyn–who was forced to leave the U.S.S.R. during the Third Wave of emigration (in the 1970s)–presents a detailed analysis of *Progulki s Pushkinym*, in which he portrays the work as a dangerous attack on Russian culture and implicitly compares Siniavsky to the philistine crowd in the famous 1830 Pushkin lyric "To the Poet," a line from which Solzhenitsyn's article borrows its title.

In the early 1980s Siniavsky published the two remaining major works as Tertz that were to appear during his lifetime, *Kroshka Tsores* (1980; translated as *Little Jinx*, 1992) and *Spokoinoi nochi*. The former work began as part of the latter but eventually outgrew it to become an autonomous text. As a result, a strong kinship of images and concerns exists between the two texts, which conventionally may be termed novels.

*Kroshka Tsores* takes as its starting point E. T. A. Hoffmann's 1819 story *Klein Zaches genannt Zinnober* (Little Zaches, Surnamed Zinnober). In Hoffmann's tale the central character is an ugly dwarf with no redeeming features. To exact political revenge, however, a fairy casts a spell, the result of which is that Zaches is given credit for any good deed or valiant act that is accomplished in his vicinity. At the end the nasty impostor Zaches is unmasked, and he drowns in his own chamber pot. In Tertz's short novel, the situation is reversed. The title character, Tsores (alternatively referred to as Siniavsky in the text), no matter how hard he strives to be a good son and citizen, is always blamed by those around him for anything bad that happens, including the deaths–one after the other–of his five stepbrothers. In this strange and fantastic tale Siniavsky's autobiography is conflated with the history of the Soviet Union. The title character, at the age of five, gives up his ability to love to a fairy, in the guise of a pediatrician, in order to stop stuttering. This exchange, which takes place in 1934, the same year in which socialist realism was proclaimed the sole acceptable mode of writing in the U.S.S.R., figures Tsores's calling as a writer. Subsequent events suggest strongly, however, that his very attempts to be a good Soviet writer doom Soviet history, which is in the guise of his stepbrothers. The first stepbrother dies in an accident in 1936; the second falls victim to the Stalin purges in 1938; the next perishes in 1943 at the height of World War II; the death of the fourth one corresponds to the Doctor's Plot (circa mid 1950s); and the last stepbrother apparently expires as a result of Khrushchev's policy of de-Stalinization. At the end of the book, when Tsores returns from a stint in the camps (where his father had disappeared before him), the fairy reappears and vouchsafes him a vision in which he hears that he is the one who has died, while his brothers are still alive and blame themselves for his death.

Based on the biblical story of Cain and Abel as much as on Hoffmann's tale, *Kroshka Tsores* constitutes a parable of guilt–particularly that of the writer who dooms society in trying to save it. Yet, the tale introduces the concept of redemptive sin *(grekh vo spasenie)* as a metaphor for art: "We try to justify ourselves, we strive, while the evil committed by us keeps growing and growing. Would it not be better to repent to begin with? To say honestly, looking truth in the eye: I have never met anyone worse than myself. Would not then the long sought after sin for the sake of salvation, at which people have so laughed, appear like a guiding light?" Tsores himself, marked by his name and fate as a source of human ills, appears to be redeemed at the end when he asks for and receives his stutter back, accepting his human imperfection and thereby, one can assume, regaining his ability to love.

What is probably Siniavsky's most important work written in emigration, *Spokoinoi nochi*, is also concerned with the relationship between art and ethics. A complicated combination of autobiography and fantasy, *Spokoinoi nochi* is not easily classifiable by genre, although Siniavsky himself felt it simply should be labeled a novel. *Spokoinoi nochi* is divided into five parts, each of which is grounded in a particular time period from the author's past and roughly arranged in reverse chronological sequence, so that the work essentially moves backward through Siniavsky's life–from the moment of his arrest to the stirrings of his alter ego Tertz in his aesthetic disenchantment with high Stalinism. The first chapter, "Perevertysh" (Turncoat), which draws its title from one of the more vicious articles that came out during the press campaign before the 1966 trial, opens with Siniavsky's arrest and focuses on his pretrial imprisonment and interrogation. The second chapter, "The House of Assignation," intersperses Tertz's evasion of the Soviet authorities' pursuit before his arrest with accounts of his wife's conjugal visits to him in the camp. Chapter 3, "Otets" (Father), focuses on Siniavsky's relationship with his father, particularly their meeting in the woods after Donat Evgen'evich's release from prison into exile in the early 1950s. The fourth chapter, "Dangerous Liaisons," has at its center the day of Stalin's death–5 March 1953, which, according to Siniavsky's portrayal of himself, the writer spent in the Lenin Library reading about the Time of Troubles. The binding force of the chapter becomes the parallels it draws between the interregnum precipitated by Stalin's death and the time of dynastic confusion that preceded the Romanov family's ascension to power as tsars. The final chapter–the section that generated the most controversy–is titled "In the Belly of the Whale" and structured around a drama played out by figures identified as S., or Serezha, and Helene; the former is an aesthete turned informer, modeled on Khmelnitsky, and the latter is a French woman allowed to study literature at Moscow University in the late Stalin years, modeled on Helene Peltier Zamoyska. Khmelnitsky himself was largely responsible for precipitating the uproar around Siniavsky's account of the attempt by the NKVD to recruit him, since he wrote an article in which he revealed his own identity as S. and accused Siniavsky of collaborating with the secret police.

Not unlike Siniavsky's other works that drew political fire, in the case of *Spokoinoi nochi* the distracting surface "scandal" overlays a profound examination of the nature of the artist caught between ethics, aesthetics, and politics. In sum, the book–balanced between the opposing poles of the literary criminal Tertz and S., the dangerous artist in life–addresses the question of the compatibility of artistic genius and evil posed by Pushkin in his *malen'kaia tragediia* (little tragedy) *Motsart i Sal'eri* (1832, Mozart and Salieri). *Spokoinoi nochi*, a powerful account of the writer's emergence from the horrific night of high Stalinism, resolves itself into a peaceful night beneath an open sky, with which the novel concludes.

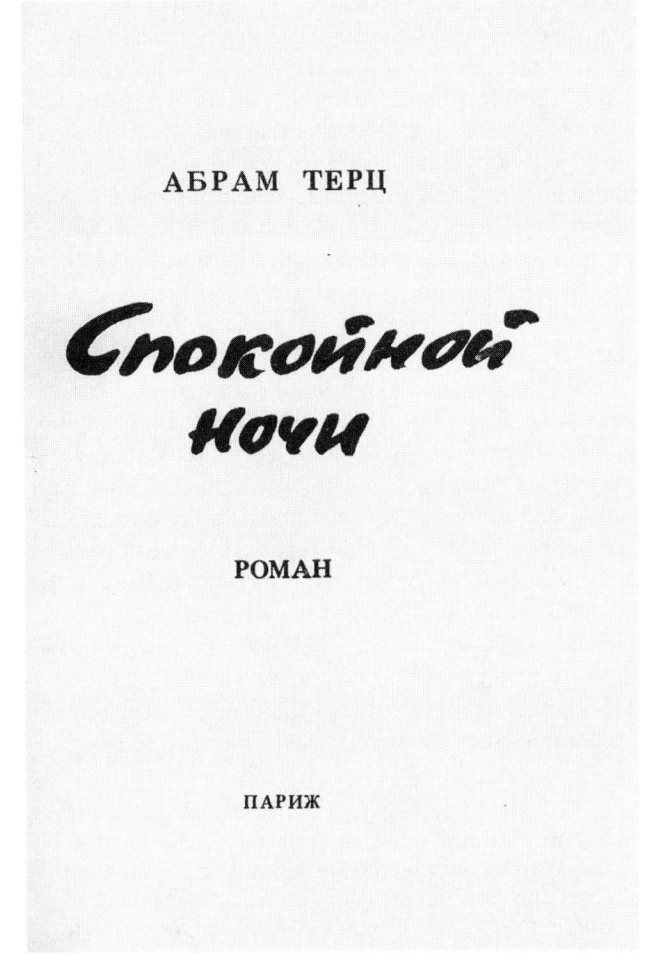

*Title page for* Spokoinoi nochi, *1984, published in Paris under the pseudonym Abram Tertz and translated into English as* Goodnight! *in 1989. A combination of autobiography and fantasy, this work is regarded as Siniavsky's most important publication written after his immigration to France in 1973 (Ralph Brown Draughon Library, Auburn University).*

During the émigré period of his career, Siniavsky also published a series of books under his own name, all compiled (with the help of Mar'ia Vasil'evna) from his lecture notes for courses he taught at the Sorbonne. This series comprises *"Opavshie list'ia" V. V. Rozanova* (1982, V. V. Rozanov's "Fallen Leaves"), *La civilisation soviétique* (1988; translated as *Soviet Civilization: A Cultural History,* 1990; Russian version published as *Osnovy sovetskoi tsivilizatsii* [The Foundations of Soviet Civilization], 2001), and *Ivan-durak: Ocherk russkoi narodnoi very* (1991, Ivan the Fool: An Essay on Russian Popular Belief).

*"Opavshie list'ia" V. V. Rozanova* presents a clear example of what distinguishes the works that Siniavsky

wrote as himself from those he attributed to Tertz. First, that the works based on Siniavsky's class lectures are attributed to his professorial persona is appropriate. Second, while Siniavsky wrote about the canonical authors Pushkin and Gogol as the convention-flouting Tertz, his adoption of a more traditionally scholarly stance in his book on the eccentric late-nineteenth-century writer Vasilii Vasil'evich Rozanov is fitting. Yet, despite the difference in authorial stance, there is a clear resonance and continuity between the works by Siniavsky and Tertz. Thus, on the one hand, Tertz's *Mysli vrasplokh* and *Golos iz khora* might have been inspired by Rozanov's aphoristic writings–particularly his own *Opavshie list'ia* (1913–1915). On the other hand, Siniavsky's analysis of Rozanov's *Opavshie list'ia* illuminates Tertz's writings both intellectually and formally, in that Siniavsky explores the inextricable interconnection between form, or rather formlessness, and content in Rozanov's writing. Siniavsky draws conclusions that appear to apply, as well, to his own writings as Tertz. Viewing *Opavshie list'ia* as "Apofeoz besformennosti" (The Apotheosis of Formlessness), the title of the seventh chapter, Siniavsky holds the fragmentary form of the book as an exemplary strategy for representing the self:

> Aphorisms–as a genre, as a literary form–free the author from the necessity of laying out his thoughts consecutively and gradually, in the form of some system or doctrine, in the form of cohesive narrative. Aphorisms, as a genre, presuppose discontinuity. Aphorisms presuppose as it were that the author's 'I' is multi-faceted and many faced. It is impossible to write aphorisms entirely on one theme. Aphorisms are always characterized by a diversity of thoughts, a diversity of subjects.

That is, Siniavsky's reading of Rozanov suggests a model for a representation of the self in the literary text that is compatible with Siniavsky's own fragmented works. Thus, Siniavsky, in commenting on Rozanov, also illuminates the formal strategy and model of the discontinuous authorial self embodied in the figure of Tertz.

*La Civilisation Soviétique,* which Mar'ia Vasil'evna compiled from Siniavsky's lectures at the Sorbonne, was geared toward his Western students. The English translation, *Soviet Civilization,* preceded the Russian version, *Osnovy sovetskoi tsivilizatsii,* by more than a decade. *La Civilisation Soviétique* appeared just as the Soviet Union it sought to analyze was about to collapse. Yet, if this unfortunate timing seemed at first to threaten the work with irrelevance, it has been recognized by some in the West as an insightful postmortem on the system. Describing his approach in the preface, Siniavsky claims that he is studying the "metaphysics" of Soviet civilization through the symbols that are given form in its literature, for symbols, he maintains, are "the Soviet epoch's majestic and enduring monuments." The "symbols" that he addresses in the book include the revolution, Vladimir Il'ich Lenin, Stalin, and what he terms the "Soviet Way of Life" and "Soviet Language." Echoing his argument in "Chto takoe sotsialisticheskii realizm," Siniavsky here follows the poet Blok in the distinction he draws between culture and civilization–the former a "primal force" and the latter "the cold, dead crust that congeals on the surface of life and culture, stifling them." He writes that "History is a series of elemental bursts and explosions, like volcanic eruptions after which the outer crust again begins to congeal, to mold a lifeless civilization." Following this paradigm for history, the elemental aspiration of the revolution to create heaven on earth ends in the Lenin Mausoleum, in "the worship of a corpse." The pivotal figure in this evolution is "Stalin: The State Church," as Siniavsky titles his central chapter. Stalin, Siniavsky contends, was an artist, a magician, who created a cult around his own person by realizing metaphors in life and fatally transgressing the boundaries between life and art. Here, Siniavsky once more adumbrates in a scholarly work issues that Tertz played out in figures, most notably in the final chapter of *Spokoinoi nochi.*

*Ivan-durak* is the product of Siniavsky's enduring interest in Russian folk religion. In the introduction he points out that he came into contact with manifestations of this popular belief on trips that he and his wife made to the Russian North in the late 1950s and early 1960s and later among his fellow inmates in the labor camp. Indirectly indicating again, moreover, the connection between the works he wrote as Siniavsky and those as Tertz, he also reveals that folklore "long served me as a point of aesthetic orientation." Echoes and illuminations of Siniavsky's nonscholarly writings are found throughout *Ivan-durak,* not least of all in the title itself. For Siniavsky, the fool is a sort of magician related to the thief–also a folktale hero–and to the sorcerer. Here one recognizes the primary metaphors for the artist that recur throughout the writings by Tertz and are embodied in the pseudonym itself. They correspond as well to the nature and origins of the folktale as Siniavsky understands them, creating a continuum between, on the one hand, folklore and religion and between, on the other, Siniavsky's excursus on popular beliefs and his vision of art as a whole. The folktale does not mirror but, rather, transforms reality, responding to the "common human passion for the bright and shimmering" and resonating with both magic and religion in that it "draws the soul out of the body." As the book progresses, moving from folklore to manifestations of popular belief to a consideration of Old Believer sects, the link between folklore, religion, and the negation of the self runs throughout as a leitmotiv. Siniavsky concludes *Ivan-durak* with an image of human beings transformed into books and of sectarians imprisoned in the camps who have each memorized a section of the Apocalypse. In this fashion, just as the human being becomes the text, so the written word is preserved by its transformation back into the oral, and the circle is closed between the religion of the book and the people who preserve culture.

Of Siniavsky's most notable articles published in emigration, a foremost place must be assigned to "Literaturnyi protsess v Rossii," the substantive essay he published in *Kontinent* shortly after emigrating from the U.S.S.R. In that article he gives a most memorable expression to the metaphor of the writer as Jew inscribed in the Tertz pseudonym and echoed in Little Tsores's Yiddish name. Asserting that "The Jew is an objectification of Russia's original sin, of which it constantly tries to purge itself and cannot," he concludes that "Every writer of Russian (origin) who does not want at the present time to write by decree is a Jew. He is a monster and an enemy of the people. I think that if now (finally) they were to begin to slaughter Jews in Russia, first of all they would massacre writers, members of the intelligentsia not of Jewish origin, who somehow do not fall under the rubric of 'one of us.'" Like the motif of the artist as pariah, the perception of true literature as transgression occurs repeatedly in Siniavsky's émigré articles. In this context he cautions more than once against the danger of confusing life and art. While in "Stalin–geroi i khudozhnik stalinskoi epokhi" (Stalin–Hero and Artist of the Stalin Era) he locates the origins of the Stalinist terror in the dictator's propensity to impose the rules of art on real life, in "Otechestvo. Blatnaia pesnia" (The Fatherland. A Thieves' Song) he notes that art cannot be bound by the same criteria of morality as is reality:

> People will say gloatingly: you would sing a different tune if you were in the place of the victim. I agree. I would sing a different tune. But it would no longer be a song, but a sad fact of my biography or, more broadly, a "social calamity," "morality," "the police," "the struggle with crime," a "special juridical case," and so on and so on, which has no direct relation to poetry, and sometimes even irresolvably contradicts it. This does not mean at all that art is "asocial" or "amoral." It's simply that its social and moral criteria are evidently somewhat different than in normal life, perhaps broader.

In his articles as in his longer works, Siniavsky returns again and again to the problem of the representation of the self. Perhaps his most interesting article in this respect is "'Ia' i 'oni': O krainikh formakh obshcheniia v usloviiakh odinochestva" ("I" and "They": An Essay on Extreme Forms of Communication under Conditions of Human Isolation). In this article he suggests the breakdown in communication between prisoners and their guards as a model for contemporary artistic expression. By the same token, in "Dostoevsky i katorga" (Dostoevsky and Hard Labor) he argues that Dostoevsky, drawing on his own experience in a tsarist labor camp, originated a revolutionary model of the self fragmented into discontinuous states.

Along with his articles devoted to issues that might in a broad sense be termed aesthetic or literary, Siniavsky throughout his émigré years continued to write articles in which he took principled stands on political issues. His most constant concern in writings such as "Russophobia" and "Russian Nationalism" and in repeated interviews with the press was what he considered the dangerously intolerant Russian chauvinism of the émigré and Soviet cultural establishments.

Siniavsky was able to return to his native land only in the final stages of Mikhail Sergeevich Gorbachev's policy of glasnost. His return also meant that his works would be published openly in the U.S.S.R. Whatever his notoriety as a defendant in the watershed 1966 trial, Siniavsky was relatively little known as a writer in his homeland, since the works he wrote as Tertz had never been published in the Soviet Union and had been available only in samizdat to a limited number of people. Moreover, writing densely troped, primarily apolitical and metaliterary texts, he had never aspired to mass-audience appeal. The first of his works to appear in the U.S.S.R. thus passed largely without comment, lost in the flood of "returning" literature and blockbuster political exposés. Yet, such was not the case with *Progulki s Pushkinym*. Thanks to the efforts of admirers on the editorial board of the Soviet journal *Oktiabr'* (October), a four-page excerpt from *Progulki s Pushkinym* appeared in the April 1989 issue of the journal. Even this short piece quickly drew fire and, in the course of the months after it appeared, became a touchstone of sorts for the polarization between progressive reformers and conservative nationalists in the Writers' Union. In 1990, not long after the excerpt was published, Siniavsky traveled to the Soviet Union for the first time since his exile. Though anathema to the Russophile camp, he was lionized by reformers for his symbolic significance to the dissident movement, acknowledged as a literary forebear by more-experimental younger writers, and welcomed back as a respected senior scholar. These varying responses serve as an eloquent testimony to the complexity of his legacy.

Two-page title for Siniavsky's Kroshka Tsores, *published in Paris in 1980 under the pseudonyum Abram Tertz and translated into English in 1992 as* Little Jinx *(John C. Hodges Library, University of Tennessee–Knoxville)*

Siniavsky had retained his Russian citizenship, and for the remainder of his life, while he continued to reside in France, he returned regularly to Russia and participated actively in Russian intellectual life. He served as head of the jury for the first Russian Booker Prize in 1992. On 8 October 1992, on the occasion of his sixty-seventh birthday, the first Russian edition of his collected works was presented to him at a conference held at the Russian State Humanities University in Moscow. At least one documentary on the Siniavsky and Daniel' trial was made for, and shown on, Russian television. Siniavsky's work appeared frequently in Russian periodicals, while he retained *Sintaksis* as his primary publication outlet.

During the post-Soviet years he espoused a stance unpopular even in those circles most sympathetic to him. Believing that the intelligentsia should serve as a loyal opposition to the government, he expressed concern over what he viewed as the overly uncritical support of Boris Nikolaevich Yeltsin among Russian intellectuals. In October 1993, in the wake of the bombing of the Russian Belyi dom (White House), occupied by recalcitrant members of the Duma who were challenging Yeltsin's power, Siniavsky spoke out publicly against the bombing. He also cosigned a letter of protest with his longtime ideological opponent Maksimov, hoping to demonstrate in the spirit of the détente of the time in the Middle East that people of goodwill could rise above political differences in the interests of peace and democracy. In February 1996, at the Harriman Institute at Columbia University, he further elaborated his position in a series of lectures, later published as *The Russian Intelligentsia* (1997). In the same vein he once more dismayed the mainstream of the Russian liberal establishment by giving interviews to the Communist newspapers *Pravda* (Truth) and *Zavtra* (Tomorrow). What Siniavsky considered a principled act in affirmation of the freedom of speech in post-Soviet Russia was yet another example of the extent to which he unnerved opponents and supporters alike by challenging simple political bipolarities.

Until the end of his life Siniavsky continued writing as both Siniavsky and Tertz. During his last years he made significant progress on a book about Maiakovsky and on a compendium of travel sketches, neither of which, however, he was able to complete. In this category should be included Siniavsky's extensive lectures and other notes on major Russian poets; these materials are included in his archive at the Hoover Institution at Stanford University.

The last work Siniavsky published in *Sintaksis* during his lifetime was "Puteshestvie na chernuiu rechku" (Journey to the Black River), a work that, while not a continuation of *Progulki s Pushkinym,* nonetheless marks a return to Pushkin. In the earlier work the aimless movement of strolling constitutes the primary metaphor for the movement and structure of the text. As the title of the later work suggests, "Puteshestvie na chernuiu rechku" presents itself as a journey to the site of Pushkin's fatal duel—that is, as a journey that follows a route leading to the author's death. Thus, in his last article for *Sintaksis* Siniavsky interweaves an examination of Pushkin's novel *Kapitanskaia dochka* (The Captain's Daughter) with the events leading up to Pushkin's duel and with episodes from Siniavsky's own life, such as the outraged response to *Progulki s Pushkinym* from émigré and Soviet readers. In the context of that bitter experience, the duel becomes a metaphor for the showdown between reader and writer, in which the author inevitably dies, killed by the reader's incomprehension or ill will. The author counters, on the other hand, with an image of himself as reader-critic, resurrecting the classics: "I imagine myself as a light shade at night in the cemetery, the extended Elysian Fields of the history of world literature. What would I do there? They've already been mourned for a hundred years. No, I'd run from gravestone to gravestone and whisper in the ear of each one individually: 'Wake up! Your time has come!'"

On 25 February 1997, not long after retiring from teaching full-time at the Sorbonne, Siniavsky died of cancer at his home in Fontenay aux Roses. On 28 February, after a service at the Russian Orthodox church Sergievskoe Podvor'e in Paris, he was buried in the Municipal Cemetery in Fontenay aux Roses. In a gesture laden with symbolic significance the poet Andrei Andreevich Voznesensky (one of the few attendees at the funeral who had managed to travel from Russia) threw into the grave a handful of earth he had brought from Pasternak's grave in the cemetery at Peredel'kino, the writers' colony outside of Moscow.

At the time of his death Siniavsky had completed all but the final editing on a novel titled *Koshkin dom* (The Cat's House), which he wrote as Tertz and which first appeared in the journal *Znamia* in 1998; his wife and a family friend, Natal'ia Rubinshtein, prepared the work for publication. Titled after Samuil Iakovlevich Marshak's classic children's story, *Koshkin dom*—like Siniavsky's earlier works—challenges the boundaries of conventional genres. Thus, in a narrative fragment, attributed to "some Siniavsky" and interpolated roughly into the center of the novel, the author announces: "I always wanted to write a novel about nothing." *Koshkin dom* is a response to such an aspiration. As suggested in the works that Siniavsky wrote as Tertz years before, especially in *Progulki s Pushkinym,* the figure of emptiness or nothingness is fraught with significance. It denotes the openness of the text to interpretation and misinterpretation and the concomitant self-abnegation of the author in transforming himself into a text. In this sense the author's loss of self through magical transformation becomes the central structural trope of the phantasmagoric *Koshkin dom,* in which texts are embedded within texts, including the inserted manuscript attributed to Siniavsky himself at the center of the novel, which was written by Tertz.

*Koshkin dom* is narrated by multiple personae of a character enigmatically referred to as "koldun" (sorcerer). He is being sought by a "literary detective," a retired schoolteacher named Donat Egorovich Balzanov, who bears the name of Siniavsky's father and a patronymic that recalls the name of Siniavsky's son, Egor. Balzanov likes to rummage about in deserted houses. He finds his way into a cat's house, where he comes across a trove of manuscripts, a find that sets him off in hot pursuit of a literary evildoer, Inozemtsev (the foreigner), also known as "koldun." In the course of the narrative the reader learns that Inozemtsev is capable of reincarnating himself—or at least the villainous essence that constitutes the drive to write—in others; in the process of reincarnation he destroys the souls of the bodies he occupies. The pursuit reaches its climax when "koldun" takes over the body of Balzanov's friend "Super" and flees abroad. He summons Balzanov to California for a final meeting, however, before he expires, apparently for good and all, in his presence. The cat's house thus becomes Siniavsky's final metaphor for the encounter among reader, writer, and text. The dogged critic and the villainous author appear to be locked in a complex relationship of mutual dependency.

After Andrei Donatovich Siniavsky's death, his widow, Mar'ia Vasil'evna, ceased publishing *Sintaksis* regularly but brought the journal back for a commemorative issue, which began appropriately with a selection of articles under the rubric, "Ura i uvy–Siniavskomu!"

(Hurrah and Alas–for Siniavsky!). The issue also includes two pieces, one attributed to Tertz and the other to Siniavsky; they constitute the beginning of a stock of unpublished manuscripts that Mar'ia Vasil'evna continues to prepare for publication. Yet, Siniavsky's continual challenge to conventional boundaries–whether linguistic, generic, professional, or political–also make difficult the codification and classification of his works in a literary pantheon that itself is in the process of fundamental redefinition. There can be no doubt, however, that he earned an enduring place for himself as a writer, thinker, and literary theoretician in the history of Russian literature and thought.

**References:**

Margaret Dalton, *Andrei Siniavskii and Julii Daniel': Two Soviet "Heretical" Writers* (Würzburg: Jal-Verlag, 1973);

Evgenii Gollerbakh, *Trepetnyi provokator* (St. Petersburg, 1993);

Max Hayward, ed. and trans., *On Trial: The Soviet State versus "Abram Tertz" and "Nikolai Arzhak"* (New York: Harper & Row, 1967);

Walter F. Kolonsky, *Literary Insinuations: Sorting Out Sinyavsky's Irreverence* (Lanham: Lexington Books, 2003);

Richard Lourie, *Letters to the Future: An Approach to Sinyavsky-Tertz* (Ithaca, N.Y.: Cornell University Press, 1975);

Catharine Theimer Nepomnyashchy, *Abram Tertz and the Poetics of Crime* (New Haven: Yale University Press, 1995);

*Russian Studies in Literature,* special Siniavsky issue, 28 (Winter 1991–1992);

*Siniavskii i Daniel' na skam'e podsudimykh* (New York: Interlanguage Literary Associates, 1966);

*Slavic and East European Journal,* special Siniavsky issue, 42 (Fall 1998).

# Vladimir Alekseevich Soloukhin
*(14 June 1924 – 4 April 1997)*

Alexandra Smith
*University of Canterbury, New Zealand*

BOOKS: *Dozhd' v stepi: Stikhi* (Moscow: Molodaia gvardiia, 1953);
*Rozhdenie Zernograda: Ocherk* (Moscow: Pravda, 1955);
*Zolotoe dno: Ocherki* (Moscow: Sovetskii pisatel', 1956);
*Razryv-trava: Stikhi* (Moscow: Molodaia gvardiia, 1956);
*Za sin'-moriami* (Moscow: Molodaia gvardiia, 1956);
*Vladimirskie proselki* (Moscow: Molodaia gvardiia, 1958); translated by Stella Miskin as *A Walk in Rural Russia* (London: Hodder & Stoughton, 1966; New York: Dutton, 1967);
*Ruch'i na asfal'te: Stikhi* (Moscow: Sovetskii pisatel', 1958);
*Zhuravlikha* (Moscow: Moskovskii rabochii, 1959);
*Stepnaia byl'* (Moscow: Molodaia gvardiia, 1959);
*Kolodets: Stikhi* (Moscow: Pravda, 1959);
*Veter stranstvii: Ocherki* (Moscow: Sovetskii pisatel', 1960);
*Kaplia rosy* (Moscow: Molodaia gvardiia, 1960);
*Otkrytki iz V'etnama* (Moscow: Molodaia gvardiia, 1961);
*Kak vypit' solntse: Stikhi* (Moscow: Sovetskii pisatel', 1961);
*Liricheskie povesti* (Moscow: Moskovskii rabochii, 1961);
*Imeiushchii v rukakh tsvety* (Moscow: Sovetskii pisatel', 1962);
*Karavai zavarnogo khleba: Rasskazy* (Moscow: Biblioteka Ogon'ka Pravda, 1963);
*Svidanie s Viaznikakh* (Moscow: Molodaia gvardiia, 1964);
*Zhit' na zemle: Stikhi* (Moscow: Sovetskii pisatel', 1965);
*S liricheskikh pozitsii* (Moscow: Sovetskii pisatel', 1965);
*Slavianskaia tetrad': Bul'gariya; izbrannye etiudy* (Moscow: Sovetskaia Rossiia, 1965);
*Mat'-machekha: Roman* (Moscow: Sovetskii pisatel', 1966);
*Rabota* (Moscow: Sovetskaia Rossiia, 1966);
*Rodnaia krasota: Dlia chego nado izuchat' i berech' pamiatniki stariny* (Moscow: Sov. khudozhnik, 1966; London: Iskander, 1969);
*Pis'ma iz russkogo muzeia* (Moscow: Sovetskaia Rossiia, 1967);
*Ne priach'tes' ot dozhdia: Stikhi* (Moscow: Pravda, 1967);

*Vladimir Alekseevich Soloukhin (frontispiece, Zimnii den', 1969; Thomas Cooper Library, University of South Carolina)*

*Sorok zvonkikh kapelei—Osennie list'ia* (Moscow: Molodaia gvardiia, 1968);
*Tret'ia okhota: Grigorovy ostrova* (Moscow: Sovetskaia Rossiia, 1968);
*Zimnii den': Rasskazy* (Moscow: Sovetskii pisatel', 1969)—includes "Chernye doski," translated by Paul S. Falla as *Searching for Icons in Russia* (London: Har-

vill Press, 1971; New York: Harcourt Brace Jovanovich, 1971);

*Zakon nabata: Rasskazy* (Moscow: Sovremennik, 1971);

*Argument: Stikhi* (Moscow: Sovetskii pisatel', 1972);

*Olepinskie prudy* (Moscow: Sovremennik, 1973);

*Po griby* (Moscow: Reklama, 1974);

*Lirika* (Moscow: Sovetskaia Rossiia, 1975);

*Venok sonetov* (Moscow: Molodaia gvardiia, 1975);

*Prekrasnaia Adygené: Povesti i rasskazy* (Moscow: Sovetskii pisatel', 1976);

*Slovo zhivoe i mertvoe* (Moscow: Sovremennik, 1976);

*Kameshki na ladoni* (Moscow: Sovetskaia Rossiia, 1977);

*Sedina: Novaia kniga stikhov* (Moscow: Sovetskii pisatel', 1977);

*Med na khlebe: Povesti i rasskazy* (Moscow: Molodaia gvardiia, 1978); translated as *Honey on Bread: Short Stories* (Moscow: Progress Publishers, 1982);

*Pisatel' i khudozhnik: Proizvedeniia russkoi klassicheskoi literatury v illiustratsüakh Il'i Glazunova*, by Soloukhin and Il'ia Sergeevich Glazunov (Moscow: Izobrazitel'noe iskusstvo, 1979);

*Vremia sobirat' kamni: Ocherki* (Moscow: Sovremennik, 1980); translated by Valerie Z. Nollan as *A Time to Gather Stones: Essays* (Evanston, Ill.: Northwestern University Press, 1993);

*Stikhi . . . ; Liricheskie povesti* (Moscow: Khudozhestvennaia literatura, 1983);

*Prekrasnaia Adygene: Povest; Tret'ia okhota; Grigorovy ostrova; Trava: Etidy o prirode* (Moscow: Khudozhestvennaia literatura, 1984);

*Bedstvie s golubiami: Rasskazy, ocherki* (Moscow: Sovetskii pisatel', 1984);

*Prodolzhenie vremeni* (Moscow: Sovetskii pisatel', 1984);

*Sozertsanie chuda: Ocherki* (Moscow: Sovetskaia Rossiia, 1984);

*Dary prirody: Travy, iagody, griby*, by Soloukhin, S. L. Oshanin, and others (Moscow: Izdatel'stvo Ekonomika, 1984);

*Smekh za levym plechom* (Frankfurt am Main: Posev, 1988; Moscow: Sovremennik, 1989); translated by David Martin as *Laughter over the Left Shoulder* (London: Peter Owen, 1990);

*Lugovaia gvozdichka* (Moscow: Sovetskaia Rossiia, 1989);

*Chitaia Lenina* (Frankfurt am Main: Posev, 1989);

*Severnye berezy: Stikhotvoreniia* (Moscow: Molodaia gvardiia, 1990);

*Vozvrashchenie k proshlomu: Liricheskaia povest' i roman* (Moscow: Sovremennik, 1990);

*Rasstavanie s idolom* (New York: Posev-USA, 1991);

*Drevo* (Moscow: Molodaia gvardiia, 1991);

*Pri svete dnia* (Moscow: V. Soloukhin, 1992);

*Solënoe ozero* (Moscow: AO Khakasinter-Servis, 1994);

*Posledniaia stupen': Ispoved' nashego sovremennika. Roman* (Moscow: Delovoi tsentr, 1995).

**Editions and Collections:** *Liricheskie povesti: Rasskazy* (Moscow: Khudozhestvennaia literatura, 1964);

*Mat'-machekha: Roman. Rasskazy* (Moscow: Moskovskii rabochii, 1969);

*Izbrannaia lirika* (Moscow: Molodaia gvardiia, 1970);

*Kaplia rosy: Povest'* (Ufa: Bashkirskoe knizhnoe izdatel'stvo, 1971);

*Slavianskaia tetrad': Pis'ma iz Russkogo muzeia. Chernye doski* (Moscow: Sovetskaia Rossiia, 1972);

*Izbrannye proizvedeniia*, 2 volumes (Moscow: Khudozhestvennaia literatura, 1974);

*Derevo nad vodoi: Poeticheskie perevody* (Moscow: Sovetskaia Rossiia, 1979);

*Chernye doski* (San Francisco: Globus, 1980);

*Stikhotvoreniia* (Moscow: Sovremennik, 1982);

*Kaplia rosy: Povest' i rasskazy* (Leningrad: Lenizdat, 1983);

*Sobranie sochinenii v chetyrekh tomakh*, 4 volumes (Moscow: Khudozhestvennaia literatura, 1983);

*Kameshki na ladoni* (Moscow: Sovremennik, 1988);

*Smekh za levym plechom: Kniga prozy* (Moscow: Sovremennik, 1989);

*Stikhotvoreniia* (Moscow: Sovetskaia Rossiia, 1990);

*Pis'ma iz Russkogo muzeia; Chernye doski; Vremia sobirat' Kamni* (Moscow: Molodaia gvardiia, 1990);

*Sobranie sochinenii v desiati tomakh*, 10 volumes (Moscow: Golos, 1995);

*Izbrannoe* (Moscow: Ast / Rostov-na-Donu: Feniks, 1999);

*Tret'ia okhota* (Moscow: Armada-Press, 2002);

*Ne priach'tes' ot dozhdia: Rasskazy raznykh let* (Moscow: Sovremennik, 2003).

**Editions in English:** *White Grass*, translated by Margaret Wettlin (Moscow: Progress Publishers, 1971)—comprises "Twenty Years Later," "Bread," "Serafima," "Swindlers," "A Golden Lily," "Speak the Stars," "Our Lady," "Lesson in Telepathy," "Revenge," "Frustration," "White Grass," "Pickled Apples," "The Law of the Tocsin," "Varvara Ivanovna," "The Icy Heights of Civilisation," and "Autumn Leaves";

"The Chased Gold," *Soviet Literature*, no. 5 (1979): 172–179;

*Scenes from Russian Life*, translated by David Martin (London: Peter Owen / Chester Springs, Pa.: Dufour Editions, 1989)—comprises "Sentenced," "Tittle-Tattle," "Under One Roof," "The Fortieth Day," "A Winters Day," "The Guests Were Arriving at the Dacha," and "A Little Girl by the Edge of the Sea";

"Stepanida Ivanovna's Funeral," in *The New Soviet Short Fiction*, edited by Sergei Zalygin (New York: Abbeville Press, 1989).

**RECORDING:** *Russian Poet Vladimir Soloukhin Reads Four of His Poems*, Archive of World Literature on Tape, Library of Congress, 1989.

OTHER: "Olepinskie prudy," in *Vozvrashchenie: Proza kontsa 40-kh-nachala 50-kh godov,* edited by Arkadii Stavitsky, Valentin Ivanovich Korovin, and Andrei Platonovich Platonov (Moscow: Sovetskaia Rossiia, 1984);

"Pri svete dnia," in *Pod "kryshei" mavzoleia* (Tver': Polina, 1998).

Vladimir Alekseevich Soloukhin is a flamboyant representative of Soviet village-prose writing, who became prominent in the 1960s. His literary output included novels, short novels, stories, poems, and essays. He began his writing career as a poet and produced collections of poetry throughout his life. In his poetry Soloukhin expresses his reflections on personal life, Russian history, and nature; in his essays he presents himself as a monarchist and nationalist and criticizes Communist ideology. Soloukhin's views derive from his childhood experience of the collectivization Joseph Stalin imposed on the Russian peasantry in the 1920s and 1930s, and most of his essays and stories include strong autobiographical overtones. The beginning of Soloukhin's career coincides with the post–World War II economic recovery of the countryside, to which Soviet authorities expected writers to contribute. In response, Soloukhin and such authors as Valentin Vladimirovich Ovechkin, Iurii Pavlovich Kazakov, and Vladimir Fedorovich Tendriakov resurrected mythical images of rural Russia, pointing to the suppressed memories and values of the past. In his works of the early 1960s Soloukhin challenges the concepts of utopian vision and modernity that were defined during Stalinism. Soloukhin's interest in the relationship between human beings and nature might be compared to that of Leo Tolstoy.

Soloukhin was born on 14 June 1924 in the village of Alepino (called Olepino in some of Soloukhin's works) in the Vladimir region to Aleksei Alekseevich and Stepanida Ivanovna Soloukhin. He had five older sisters and two brothers. He graduated from Vladimir Technical College in 1942. During World War II he served in the army unit guarding the Kremlin. His first poems appeared in *Komsomol'skaia pravda* (Komsomol Truth) in 1946, the same year he started his studies at the Gorky Literary Institute in Moscow, from which he graduated in 1951. In the late 1940s Soloukhin married Roza Iavren't'evan Zasedateleva. They had two children, Elena and Olga.

In the early 1950s Soloukhin worked as a feature writer for the magazine *Ogonek* (The Flame). He joined the Communist Party in 1952. His first collection of poetry, *Dozhd' v stepi* (Rain on the Steppe), was published in 1953. His collection of essays about the exploration of virgin lands in the Soviet Union, *Rozhdenie*

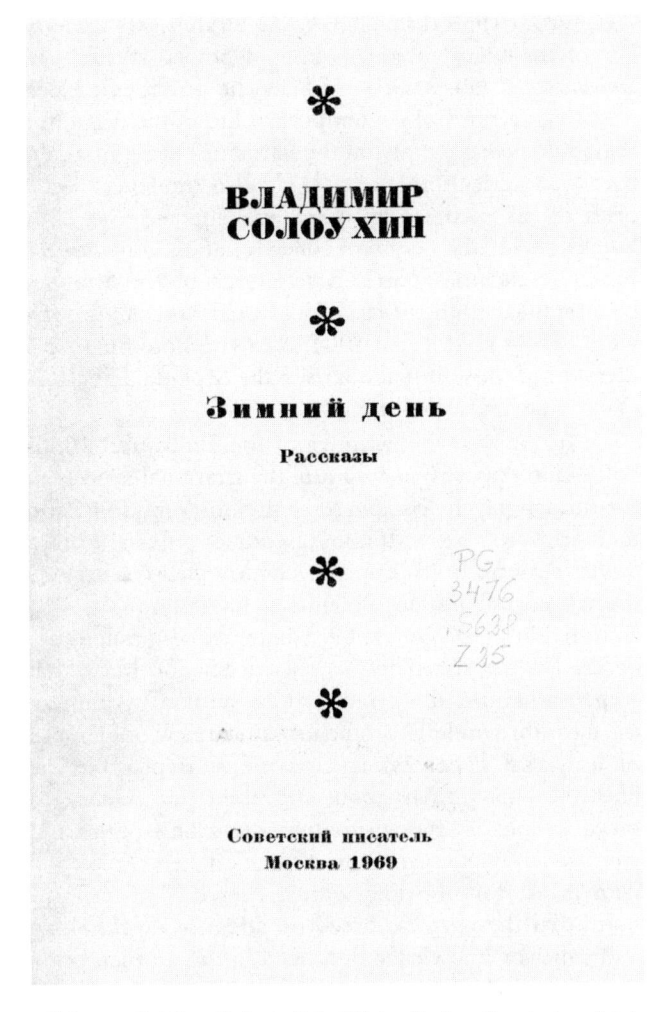

*Title page for* Zimnii den', *Soloukhin's collection of stories translated as* Searching for Icons in Russia *in 1971 (Thomas Cooper Library, University of South Carolina)*

Zernograda (The Birth of Zernograd), appeared in 1955, followed by *Zolotoe dno* (Golden Bottom) in 1956 and his first long narrative, *Vladimirskie proselki* (Vladimir Region Roads; translated as *A Walk in Rural Russia,* 1966), in 1958. In *Vladimirskie proselki,* Soloukhin describes walks in the Vladimir region with his wife, Roza, painting a romanticized picture of the traditional Russian village. The wonders of nature, in Soloukhin's eyes, are more appealing than the technological advantages of Soviet modernity: "the cow remains, as before, a more valuable aggregate than, for example, a jet plane." Soloukhin praises the craftsmen—icon makers, artists, carpenters, and lace makers—who preserve the traditions of the region; his admiration extends to ancient churches, wooden houses with carved window frames, and the expressive language of villagers. *Vladimirskie proselki* was dangerously inclined toward pre-revolutionary values, but Communist Party officials were willing to allow such sentiments in village prose.

From 1959 through 1975 Soloukhin was a member of the board of the Union of Soviet Writers. In *Kaplia rosy* (1960, A Drop of Dew) he provides a kaleidoscopic account of contemporary life in the Vladimir region, focusing mainly on the hardships brought about by Soviet agricultural policies. He also resurrects memories of his own family members who were seen as kulaks during the period of collectivization. Soloukhin's narrative includes poetic descriptions of the Russian countryside. Both *Vladimirskie proselki* and *Kaplia rosy* were widely read. From 1964 to 1981 Soloukhin was a member of the editorial board of the Molodaia gvardiia (Young Guards) publishing house.

In many of his writings of the 1950s and 1960s Soloukhin opposes his vision of the irrational aspects of the human psyche composed of dreams, emotions, and memories to the scientific discourse prevalent in a Soviet society. In "Ledianye vershiny chelovechestva" (translated as "The Icy Heights of Civilisation," 1971), collected in *Zimnii den'* (1969, Winter's Day), Soloukhin challenges the statement in a science-fiction book that "The human mind is capable of everything." Although the narrator would like to believe that a new golden age of universal happiness and harmony is possible, he illustrates his doubts about the ability of science to serve people in every situation by telling of an old woman whose son committed suicide when threatened with arrest for brawling with a friend. The narrator notes that the paradise based on advanced technology and superior knowledge described in the utopian book would not help him to stop crying and comfort the old woman. "Why," he asks, "cannot we, who have learned everything possible, do one important and necessary thing—console the heart of the distressed mother?" The story incorporates the ancient pagan chants that the old woman repeats while visiting the grave of her son. At the end Soloukhin draws a dystopian image of a distant future when robots will attempt to analyze books and people, trying to understand such concepts as "happiness, doubts, light melancholy, heavy depression, banal boredom." At first they will try to comprehend these phenomena and will argue about them, but eventually the "poor iron robots" will give up and call such unexplainable things "surreal."

Soloukhin's collection of philosophical essays *Pis'ma iz russkogo muzeia* (1967, Letters from the Russian Museum) reflects the growing interest in cultural heritage among the Soviet population in the mid 1960s. For example, officially sanctioned "*Rodina*" (Motherland) clubs were established in 1964, and in 1965 the All-Russian Society for the Preservation of Historical and Cultural Monuments was founded. In *Pis'ma iz russkogo muzeia* Soloukhin calls for the reinstatement of forgotten values essential to Russian identity. He draws readers' attention to the many churches that were demolished by the Communists in Moscow and other areas, as well as to the important collection of icons kept in the cellars of the Russian Museum in Leningrad.

In the 1960s and 1970s Soloukhin journeyed far from Moscow. His travels almost appear to be journeys into the past, because his reports on these distant places revive images of rural prerevolutionary Russia and are permeated with Slavophile overtones. In the story "Uroki telepatii" (1964; translated as "Lesson in Telepathy," 1971) a Moscow poet on his way to the Arctic Ocean stops in an ancient Russian city and visits local churches and monasteries; in "Tri Belosnezhnye khrizantemy" (Three Snow-White Chrysanthemums), collected in his *Olepinskie prudy* (1973, The Olepin Ponds), Soloukhin describes his visit to the grave of the singer Fedor Ivanovich Shaliapin in the Russian cemetery in Paris, which he compares to a cemetery in his native village of Alepino. In "Zolotoe zerno" (Golden Wheat), also collected in *Olepinskie prudy,* he recounts his visit to a Russian Orthodox cathedral in Novgorod accompanied by another well-known singer, Ivan Semenovich Kozlovsky, who sang a hymn in a voice "flowing as gold and unbearable light" that awakened the stones of the cathedral.

Soloukhin is not blind to shortcomings of Russian provincial life. In yet another piece in *Olepinskie prudy,* "Kumys" (1970, Horse-Milk Drink), he criticizes the manager of a resort in a town south of Moscow where patients with lung problems were formerly treated with a central Asian horse-milk drink. A family in the area was related to Genghis Khan, and the recipe for the drink was a family secret. A twenty-year-old woman, the only remaining member of the family, made the drink for the resort, but the manager fired her because he regarded her as a threat to his authority. The resort continues to produce an approximation of the drink, but it is inferior to the real one. The narrator tries to persuade the manager that he should promote talented people, not get rid of them. In the title story of *Olepinskie prudy* the narrator sadly reflects on war veterans celebrating Victory Day with their families by picnicking on vodka and fish from the local ponds instead of wearing their medals and parading around the village to set an example for the younger generations. They have also forgotten that the pressing need in their village is to clean the ponds, which have been neglected for years. The story reflects the writer's preoccupation with the lack of personal responsibility and moral values in 1970s Soviet society.

Like other authors of village prose, Soloukhin prefers characters who are eccentrics and misfits in Soviet society, especially those who have preserved traditional values of the Russian peasantry or who have character traits that conflict with Communist ethics. The title character of the story "Pasha," collected in *Prekrasnaia Adygené* (1976, Marvelous Adygené), is such an eccentric. Pasha is an old woman in Alepino who dreams of having her own cottage. She has never worked on a collective farm, only in a Moscow factory; she cannot understand the collective-farm practice of calculating salaries at the end of the year on the basis of actual workdays, which means that the workers are never sure how much money they will be paid in a given year. Pasha rejects the narrator's suggestion that she live in an old people's home, because there everything proceeds according to a schedule, including meals, and the residents are deprived of their individuality and their pension money. That is, the old people's home is run on the same basis as the collective farm in the village. Soloukhin thus uses a woman in her seventies, whose ideas can be dismissed as whimsical and eccentric, to make a veiled and indirect criticism of the Soviet collective-farm system.

In his collection of meditative essays *Kameshki na ladoni* (1977, Pebbles on my Palm) Soloukhin advocates the revival in Russia of a religious worldview that can appeal to individual emotions and needs. He challenges scientific discourse with a rhetorical question: "Does this high reason know about me, and does it care about me at all?" Criticized in the journal *Kommunist* and reprimanded by party officials of the Russian Soviet Federated Socialist Republic Writers' Union, Soloukhin was forced to make a public affirmation of his atheism.

In the title story of the collection *Med na khlebe* (1978; translated as *Honey on Bread: Short Stories*, 1982) the narrator laments that today's honey and bread do not taste as good as the ones prepared by his grandfather. This poetic treatise on bees and the healing powers of honey expresses nostalgia for a way of life based on spiritual values that have vanished. In 1979 Soloukhin was awarded the State Prize for Literature (the Gorky Prize). In the title piece of *Vremia sobirat' kamni: Ocherki* (1980; translated as *A Time to Gather Stones: Essays*, 1993) he lovingly describes the monastery Optina pustyn' near Kozel'sk.

In the freer intellectual climate created by Soviet president Mikhail Gorbachev's policy of *perestroika* (restructuring), Soloukhin attacked Stalin and Vladimir Il'ich Lenin as the authors of policies that were profoundly damaging to the Russian peasantry and to the spiritual life of the Russian people. In works such as his autobiography, *Smekh za levym plechom* (1988; translated as *Laughter over the Left Shoulder*, 1990), and *Chitaia Lenina* (1989, Reading Lenin) Solukhin presents himself as a Russian nationalist and a critic of Marxism-Leninism. In *Chitaia Lenina*, for example, he writes: "Genocide, especially one as thorough as that conducted for decades in Russia, deprives a people of ability to blossom, it deprives them of the fullness of life and spiritual growth. . . . Genetic damage cannot be undone, and this is the most tragic result of the event which we, sobbing with joy, call the Great October Socialist Revolution."

*Smekh za levym plechom* is a hybrid narrative with an awkward mixture of genres and moods; it subverts the childhood-narrative structure of canonical village prose because Soloukhin's anxious and self-righteous adult voice dominates. His egocentrism and tendency both to praise and blame himself for his actions go against the grain of mainstream village-prose narratives, which focus on village life and customs. Throughout the book he places value on family, local identity, the purity of rural life, Christian beliefs, folk customs, and the glorious past, and he stresses his strong sense of roots and of belonging to a family with traditions by making constant references to his grandfather. He finds significance in the fact that he himself was born on the Day of the Holy Spirit, which occurs on the day after Holy Trinity Sunday. He claims that the teaching of his mother was more lucid and impressive than the lessons of the professors and writers he encountered later in life. His mother told him to please the angel on his right shoulder, who would "smile with joy" each time he performed a good or kind action, and warned him against Satan, the Cunning Angel standing on his left shoulder, who would "gloat and giggle" if he did something wrong: "That night as I lay awake I promised to myself that my angel would always be laughing and full of joy, while the Cunning One at my left would be left writhing about and gnashing his teeth." At evening gatherings with other seven- and eight-year-old boys near the church, Soloukhin often developed "an irresistible urge to go to the church and remain there for the night. . . . I had the feeling that there, inside the nocturnal church, someone loved me very much and was waiting eagerly for me. . . . There I am loved very much and eagerly awaited, but I cannot go there, I have to be here, with the boys." He remembers with bitterness the order by the chairman of the collective farm that the bells be removed from the church tower so that the metal could be used to make guns. He criticizes the Soviet officials who replaced the centuries-old names of villages in the Vladimir region with Soviet-style names such as Champion, Red Communist Avant-garde, The Road to Socialism, Forward, and Pace-setter. He remembers with disgust that the District Education Department ordered the Alepino school in the 1930s to process "children's brains and souls," so that after lessons "all four classes found themselves together, learning songs" about Five-Year-Plan achievements, factories, and tractors. He and his schoolmates lived double lives: at

*Front cover for Soloukhin's* Solënoe ozero *(1994, Salty Lake), in which he "demythologizes" popular children's writer Arkadii Petrovich Gaidar as a Bolshevik sadist who terrorized the Khakasiia region of Siberia in the 1920s (University of Massachusetts at Amherst Libraries)*

school the teachers "concentrated on stupefying and cluttering up our brains," while at home their parents continued to educate them in accordance with traditional values. Soloukhin's mother recited nineteenth-century poems to him; but his parents did not interfere with his socialist upbringing, because they "clearly understood that I would have to live my whole life surrounded by Soviet power." As a result, "I began to put together a 'Lenin Corner' at home and fixed a mass of photographs of Lenin to the wall." Soloukhin suggests that when he was worshiping Lenin, the Cunning Angel on his shoulder was gloating and snickering.

The overall tone of Soloukhin's description of the past is bitter and self-critical. He is filled with guilt over his early romanticized descriptions of Soviet collective farms. His revised narrative of his childhood includes details that were omitted in his earlier autobiographical work, *Kaplia rosy,* in which he says that since he was six years old at the time he did not remember the details of the effects of collectivization on his village. In *Smekh za levym plechom,* however, he describes his parents' anxieties during the early 1930s: they had the biggest house in the village and were afraid of being labeled kulaks at the beginning of Stalin's collectivization campaign. They lost the use of one floor of their house when it was occupied by two officials who had been sent to the village to carry out the new government policies. Soloukhin asserts the superiority of the more prosperous peasants over the poor ones, noting with pride that in the 1920s his father would go to the city of Vladimir during Lent to buy the tastiest food. In *Smekh za levym plechom,* Soloukhin reinvents himself as a writer who has preserved traditional Christian values. His description of his childhood does not lead to self-discovery or psychological insight but offers a sentimental and calculating discourse on his own identity. Because of his negative comments on the Soviet regime, the book was first published in West Germany.

In 1994 Soloukhin published the controversial documentary novel *Solënoe ozero* (Salty Lake) in the journal *Nash sovremennik* (Our Contemporary); it appeared in book form the same year. In this work he demythologizes the image of Arkadii Petrovich Gaidar (real name: Golikov), one of the most popular Soviet writers for children, as a Red Army officer and hero of the Civil War. Soloukhin presents Gaidar as a sadist who was sent to the Khakasiia region of Siberia at the beginning of the 1920s to terrorize a population that was strongly opposed to the introduction of Bolshevik rule. According to Soloukhin, Gaidar was threatened with execution for his excessive use of violence but was instead sent to a mental hospital; after his release he embarked on his career as children's writer.

Soloukhin's autobiographical novel/essay *Poslredniaia stupen': Ispoved' nashego sovremennika* (1995, The Last Stair: A Contemporary's Confession) offers a revisionist view of the term *Slavophilism,* which, in his view, has been wrongly used by cultural historians as a pejorative word. He regards the Slavophile outlook as "the original thinking" that was distorted and debased. In this emotional account of his intellectual and spiritual evolution Soloukhin provides critical perspectives on the Bolshevik Revolution that have anti-Semitic and extremist overtones. He mourns the deaths of millions during Soviet times, including the last tsar, Nicholas II, and the tsar's family. In his 1990s cycle of poems *Druziam* (My Friends, in *Severnye berezy*), Soloukhin fashions himself in the complex image of an observer and participant in Russia's tragic history, touching on the traditional theme of the artist's moral responsibility. He sums up his role in contemporary Russian history as a holder of collective memory and appeals to his friends to keep

Russia alive: "Russia is not dead yet / It remains alive as long as we, my friends, are alive."

Vladimir Alekseevich Soloukhin died of cancer in Moscow on 4 April 1997 and is buried in Alepino. With the reawakening of nationalism in post-Soviet Russia, his work enjoys considerable popularity among readers who are interested in Russian spiritual life, popular art, and folklore.

**Interview:**

John Glad, *Vladimir Soloukhin*, videocassette 1 of his *Interviews with 17 Russian Émigré Writers*, Washington, D.C., Birchbark Press, 1986.

**References:**

Natal'ia Artemova, "Konechno v olepine," *Literaturnaia gazeta*, 29 July 1981, p. 6;

John B. Dunlop, "Ruralist Prose Writers in the Russian Ethnic Movement," in *Ethnic Russia in the U.S.S.R.: The Dilemma of Dominance*, edited by Edward Allworth (New York: Pergamon, 1980), pp. 80–87;

Isabelle Esmein, "Le premier roman de Vladimir Soloukhine: Le Tussilage," *Table ronde*, 226 (1966): 137–139;

Mikhail Viktorovich Gorbanevsky, "Pomidornaia liubov'," *Russkaia rech'*, 2 (March–April 1990): 37–40;

Sergei Kharlamov, "VspominaiaVladimira Solukhina" <http://www.voskres.ru/gosudarstvo/heald/solouhin.htm>;

Aleksandr Kuznetsov, "Vspominaia o russkom pisatele" <http://www.voskres.ru/gosudarstvo/heald/soloukhin.htm>;

Kuznetsov, "Vzoshedshii na vershinu" <http://zavtra.ru/cgi/veil//data/zavtra/99/291/61.html>;

Alla Laskina, "Pora perchitat' napisannoe," *Literaturnaia gazeta*, 27 April 1983, p. 6;

Viacheslav Morozov, "Nakaz Vladimira Solukhina," *Nash sovremennik*, 7 (1997): 238–240;

E. A. Morozova and G. A. Tsvetov, "Razvernutaia metafora v stikhakh Vl. Soloukhina," *Russkaia rech'*, 2 (1975): 76–80;

Elzbieta Mozdzierska, "Narrator w reportazach artystycznych Wladimira Solouchina," *Slavia Orientalis*, 30, no. 3 (1981): 321–329;

Valerie Z. Nollan, "Reinterpreting the Soviet Period of Russian History: Vladimir Soloukhin's Poetic Cycle Druzi'am," *Slavonic and East European Journal*, 41, no. 1 (1997): 74–93;

Evgenii Ivanovich Ostrov, "Solntse v kaple rosy," *Literaturnaia gazeta*, 14 June 1989, p. 7;

Aleksandr Ivanovich Ovcharenko, "Podvedenie itogov," *Novyi mir*, 7 (July 1985): 239–245;

Kathleen F. Parthé, *Russian Village Prose: The Radiant Past* (Princeton: Princeton University Press, 1992);

V. D. Piatnitskii, "Gribnaia okhota," *Russkaia rech'*, 4 (1972): 36–40;

Liana Polukhina, "Sobesedniki na pominkakh," *Literaturnaia gazeta*, 25 November 1992, p. 5;

S. Rybak, "Granitsy vol'nosti," *Druzhba narodov*, 3 (1981): 259–263;

El'vina A. Shugaeva, "Idti po svoei trope," *Literaturnaia gazeta*, 30 May 1990, p. 4;

Andrei Mikhailovich Turkov, "Energy and Talent," *Soviet Literature*, 6 (1984): 103–106;

Sergei Vasil'evich Vikulov, "Sila slova neravnodushnogo," *Moskva*, 6 (1974): 209–214;

Oleg Volkov, "Suetnost' odnogo reportazha," *Literaturnoe obozrenie*, 10 (1975): 39–41;

Igor' Petrovich Zolotusskii, "'Ia nadeius' na medlennyi protsess . . .': V gostiakh u Vladimira Soloukhina," *Literaturnaia gazeta*, 24 August 1994, p. 5.

# Aleksandr Solzhenitsyn
*(11 December 1918 – )*

Edward E. Ericson Jr.
*Calvin College*

and

Alexis Klimoff
*Vassar College*

BOOKS: *Odin den' Ivana Denisovicha* (Moscow: Sovetskii pisatel', 1963); authorized, unexpurgated edition published in *Odin den' Ivana Denisovicha. Matrenin dvor* (Paris: YMCA-Press, 1973)–includes "Matrenin dvor"; translated by Ralph Parker as *One Day in the Life of Ivan Denisovich* (New York: Dutton, 1963), and by Ronald Hingley and Max Hayward as *One Day in the Life of Ivan Denisovich* (New York: Bantam, 1963); authorized edition translated by H. T. Willets (New York: Farrar, Straus & Giroux, 1991);

*Izbrannoe* (Chicago: Russian Language Specialties, 1965);

*Rakovyi korpus* [part one] (Milan: Mondadori, 1968; complete edition, Frankfurt: Posev, 1968); translated by Rebecca Frank as *The Cancer Ward* (New York: Dial, 1968);

*V kruge pervom* (New York: Harper & Row, 1968); enlarged edition, volumes 1 and 2 of *Sobranie sochinenii*, 20 volumes (Vermont & Paris: YMCA-Press, 1978–1991); translated by Thomas P. Whitney as *The First Circle* (New York: Harper & Row, 1968);

*Sobranie sochinenii*, 6 volumes (Frankfurt: Posev, 1969–1970);

*Avgust chetyrnadtsatogo* (Paris: YMCA-Press, 1971); translated by Michael Glenny as *August 1914* (New York: Farrar, Straus & Giroux, 1972): part one of the multivolume *Krasnoe koleso: Povestvovanie v otmerennykh srokakh*, in *Sobranie sochinenii*, volumes 11–20 (Vermont & Paris: YMCA-Press, 1983–1991)–comprises volumes 11–12, *Uzel I. Avgust chetyrnadtsatogo;* followed by volumes 13–14, *Uzel II. Oktiabr' shestnadtsatogo;* volumes 15–18, *Uzel III. Mart semnadtsatogo;* and volumes 19–20, *Uzel IV. Aprel' sem-*

*Aleksandr Solzhenitsyn (photograph by Viktor Akhlomov; Collection of Christine Rydel)*

*nadtsatogo;* translated by Willetts as *August 1914* (New York: Farrar, Straus & Giroux, 1989);

*Nobelevskaia lektsiia po literature 1970 goda* (Paris: YMCA-Press, 1972); translated by F. D. Reeve as *Nobel*

*Lecture* [bilingual edition] (New York: Farrar, Straus & Giroux, 1972);

*Arkhipelag GULag, 1918–1956: Opyt khudozhestvennego issledovaniia*, 3 volumes (Paris: YMCA-Press, 1973–1975); translated by Whitney and Willetts as *The Gulag Archipelago, 1918–1956: An Experiment in Literary Investigation*, 3 volumes (New York: Harper & Row, 1974–1978);

*Pis'mo vozhdiam Sovetskogo Soiuza* (Paris: YMCA-Press, 1974); translated by Hilary Sternberg as *Letter to the Soviet Leaders* (New York: Index on Censorship in association with Harper & Row, 1974);

*Solzhenitsyn: A Pictorial Autobiography* (New York: Noonday, 1974);

*Prusskie nochi* (Paris: YMCA-Press, 1974); translated by Robert Conquest as *Prussian Nights* (New York: Farrar, Straus & Giroux, 1977);

*Lenin v Tsiurikhe* (Paris: YMCA-Press, 1975); translated by Willetts as *Lenin in Zurich* (New York: Farrar, Straus & Giroux, 1976);

*Bodalsia telenok s dubom: Ocherki literaturnoi zhizni* (Paris: YMCA-Press, 1975; enlarged edition, Moscow: Soglasie, 1996)–includes "Nevidimki"; translated by Willetts as *The Oak and the Calf: Sketches of Literary Life in the Soviet Union* (New York: Harper & Row, 1980);

*A World Split Apart* [bilingual edition], translated by Irina Alberti (New York: Harper & Row, 1978);

*Sobranie sochinenii*, 20 volumes (Vermont & Paris: YMCA-Press, 1978–1991);

*Rasskazy* (Moscow: Sovremennik, 1989);

*Kak nam obustroit' Rossiiu? Posil'nye soobrazheniia* (Paris: YMCA-Press, 1990); translated by Alexis Klimoff as *Rebuilding Russia: Reflections and Tentative Proposals* (New York: Farrar, Straus & Giroux, 1991);

*"Russkii vopros" k kontsu XX veka* (Moscow: Golos, 1995); translated by Yermolai Aleksandrovich Solzhenitsyn as *"The Russian Question" at the End of the Twentieth Century* (New York: Farrar, Straus & Giroux, 1995)–includes "Address to the International Academy of Philosophy";

*Po minute v den'* (Moscow: Argumenty i fakty, 1995);

*Publitsistika*, 3 volumes (Iaroslavl': Verkhne-Volzhskoe knizhnoe izdatel'stvo, 1995–1997);

*Na izlomakh: Malaia proza* (Iaroslavl': Verkhniaia Volga, 1998);

*Rossiia v obvale* (Moscow: Russkii put', 1998);

*Proterevshi glaza* (Moscow: Nash dom–L'Age d'Homme, 1999)–includes *Dorozhen'ka* and *Liubi revoliutsii;*

*Dvesti let vmeste, 1795–1995,* 2 volumes (Moscow: Russkii put', 2001, 2002);

*Armeiskie rasskazy* (Moscow: Russkii put', 2001);

*Stolypin i Tsar'* (Ekaterinburg: U-FAKTORIIA, 2001);

*Lenin. Tsiurikh – Petrograd* (Ekaterinburg: U-FAKTORIIA, 2001);

*Nakonets-to revoliutsiia,* 2 volumes (Ekaterinburg: U-FAKTORIIA, 2001).

**Editions and Collections:** *Arkhipelag GULag,* 3 volumes (Moscow: Sovetskii pisatel', 1989);

*Rakovyi korpus* (Moscow: Khudozhestvennaia literatura, 1990);

*V kruge pervom* (Moscow: Khudozhestvennaia literatura, 1990);

*Krasnoe koleso. Povestvovanie v otmerennykh srokakh,* 10 volumes (Moscow: Voenizdat, 1993–1997);

*Izbrannoe* (Moscow: Molodaia gvardiia, 1993);

*Sobranie sochinenii,* 9 volumes (Moscow: Terra, 1999–2000);

*Na kraiakh* (Moscow: Vagrius, 2000);

*Odin den' Ivana Denisovicha; Matrenin dvor; Sluchai na stantsii Kochetovka* (Moscow: Progress-Pleiada, 2000).

**Editions in English:** *We Never Make Mistakes: Two Short Novels,* translated by Paul W. Blackstock (Columbia: University of South Carolina Press, 1963);

*The First Circle,* translated by Michael Guybon (London: Collins-Harvill, 1968);

*Cancer Ward,* translated by Nicholas Bethell and David Burg (New York: Farrar, Straus & Giroux, 1969);

*Stories and Prose Poems,* translated by Michael Glenny (New York: Farrar, Straus & Giroux, 1971);

*The Nobel Lecture on Literature,* translated by Thomas P. Whitney (New York: Harper & Row, 1972);

*Candle in the Wind,* translated by Keith Armes with Arthur G. Hudgins (Minneapolis: University of Minnesota Press, 1973);

*East & West: The Nobel Lecture on Literature, A World Split Apart, Letter to Soviet Leaders, and an Interview with Aleksandr Solzhenitsyn by Janis Sapiets,* translated by Alexis Klimoff, Irina Alberti, and Hilary Sternberg (New York: Harper & Row, 1980);

*The Mortal Danger: How Misconceptions about Russia Imperil America,* translated by Michael Nicholson and Klimoff (New York: Harper & Row, 1981);

*The Gulag Archipelago, 1918–1956* [authorized abridgment], edited by Edward E. Ericson Jr., translated by Whitney and H. T. Willetts (New York: Harper & Row, 1985);

*Three Plays: Victory Celebrations, Prisoners, The Love-Girl and the Innocent,* translated by Bethell, Burg, Helen Rapp, and Nancy Thomas (New York: Farrar, Straus & Giroux, 1986);

*Invisible Allies,* translated by Klimoff and Nicholson (Washington, D.C.: Counterpoint, 1995);

*November 1916,* translated by Willetts (New York: Farrar, Straus & Giroux, 1999).

OTHER: *Iz-pod glyb,* edited by Solzhenitsyn (Paris: YMCA-Press, 1974); translated as *From Under the*

*Rubble,* edited by Michael Scammell (Boston: Little, Brown, 1975);

*Russkii slovar' iazykovogo rasshireniia,* compiled by Solzhenitsyn (Moscow: Nauka, 1990).

SELECTED PERIODICAL PUBLICATIONS–UNCOLLECTED: "*Golyi god* Borisa Pil'niaka," *Novyi mir,* no. 1 (1997): 195–203;

"*Smert' Vazir-Mukhtara* Iuriia Tynianova," *Novyi mir,* no. 4 (1997): 191–199;

"*Peterburg* Andreia Belogo," *Novyi mir,* no. 7 (1997): 191–196;

"Iz Evgeniia Zamiatina," *Novyi mir,* no. 10 (1997): 186–201;

"Priemy epopei," *Novyi mir,* no. 1 (1998): 172–190;

"Chetyre sovremennykh poeta," *Novyi mir,* no. 4 (1998): 184–195;

"Ivan Shmelev i ego *Solntse mertvykh,*" *Novyi mir,* no. 7 (1998): 184–193;

"Ugodilo zernyshko promezh dvukh zhernovov: Ocherki izgnaniia," *Novyi mir,* no. 9 (1998): 47–125; no. 11 (1998): 93–153; no. 2 (1999): 67–140; no. 9 (2000): 112–183; no. 12 (2000): 97–156; no. 4 (2001): 80–141; no. 11 (2003): 31–97;

"Okunaias' v Chekhova," *Novyi mir,* no. 10 (1998): 161–182;

"Feliks Svetov–*Otverzi mi dveri,*" *Novyi mir,* no. 1 (1999): 166–173;

"Panteleimon Romanov–rasskazy sovetskikh let," *Novyi mir,* no. 7 (1999): 197–204;

"Aleksandr Malyshkin," *Novyi mir,* no. 10 (1999): 180–192;

"Iosif Brodskii–izbrannye stikhi," *Novyi mir,* no. 12 (1999): 180–193;

"Evgenii Nosov," *Novyi mir,* no. 7 (2000): 195–199;

"Dvoen'e Iuriia Nagibina," *Novyi mir,* no. 4 (2003): 164–171;

"David Samoilov," *Novyi mir,* no. 6 (2003): 171–178;

"Dilogiia Vasiliia Grossmana," *Novyi mir,* no. 8 (2003): 154–169;

"Leonid Leonov–'Vor,'" *Novyi mir,* no. 10 (2003): 165–171;

"Vasilii Belov," *Novyi mir,* no. 12 (2003): 154–169;

"Georgii Vladimov–'General i ego armiia,'" *Novyi mir,* no. 2 (2004): 144–151.

The life and literary career of Aleksandr Solzhenitsyn are nothing short of extraordinary. He is a veteran of frontline duty during World War II and a survivor of eleven years of Soviet prisons, forced-labor camps, and internal exile. Solzhenitsyn also endured a near-fatal bout with cancer before achieving world fame in 1962. That year his short novel *Odin den' Ivana Denisovicha* (translated as *One Day in the Life of Ivan Denisovich,* 1963) was published in the journal *Novyi mir* (The New World). Other works soon followed, including *V kruge pervom* (1968; translated as *The First Circle,* 1968) and *Rakovyi korpus* (1968; translated as *The Cancer Ward,* 1968), both of which could be published only in the West because of the increasingly hostile attitude of the Soviet regime toward Solzhenitsyn, a defiantly independent writer. In 1970 he was awarded the Nobel Prize in literature, raising the ire of the regime further still; a 1971 plot by the Komitet gosudarstvennoi bezopasnosti (KGB, State Security Committee) to assassinate Solzhenitsyn was discovered after the fall of the Soviet Union. In the mid 1970s he was on the verge of achieving even greater renown with the publication, again in the West, of *Arkhipelag GULag, 1918–1956: Opyt khudozhestvennego issledovaniia* (1973–1975; translated as *The Gulag Archipelago, 1918–1956: An Experiment in Literary Investigation,* 1974–1978), a massive indictment of the Soviet penal system. The regime retaliated by arresting Solzhenitsyn and charging him with treason; he was expelled from the U.S.S.R. in 1974. He spent the next two decades in the West. At first he made many high-profile public appearances but mostly worked on *Krasnoe koleso: Povestvovanie v otmerennykh srokakh* (The Red Wheel: A Narrative in Discrete Periods of Time, 1983–1991), a cycle written partially in the tradition of the historical novel; it traces the descent of Russia into the revolutionary chaos of 1917. He returned to post-Communist Russia in 1994 and has continued to speak out on important public issues while adding to his corpus of writings, which includes fiction, poetry, drama, and nonfiction. Many of Solzhenitsyn's literary works are autobiographical. They provide authoritative information about, in particular, the first thirty years of his life, and for that reason a discussion of his works in the order of the autobiographical events as they occurred is necessary.

As a writer and a public figure, Solzhenitsyn has evoked strong reactions–although one must add that the ideological sympathies of the commentators have often shaped the opinions expressed. Accordingly, responses have ranged from crude abuse to uncritical adulation; rarely have they risen above a perfunctory or tendentious analysis of the nonpolitical core of Solzhenitsyn's message. Beyond the predictable political commentary, however, lies a more fundamental philosophical issue that has caused discerning critics to agree or disagree with the author. Solzhenitsyn is a committed adherent of the Russian literary tradition that took shape in the nineteenth century, and as such he rejects the idea of a discontinuity between literary art and the world of moral values. Therefore he is unapologetic about presenting many issues in what might be called an ethically absolute manner–with the urgency and power characteristic of his talent. This stance is at odds with the tendency toward moral relativism that permeates modern thought and is incompatible with the belief of postmodernist critics, who dismiss all absolutist convictions in principle.

Aleksandr Isaevich Solzhenitsyn was born on 11 December 1918 in Kislovodsk, a resort town in the Caucasus. Both parents came from peasant families but were educated. His father, Isaakii Semenovich Solzhenitsyn, served with distinction as an artillery officer in World War I but died as a result of a hunting accident six months before Solzhenitsyn was born. Following this tragedy, his mother, Taissia Zakharovna (Shcherbak) Solzhenitsyna, the daughter of a prosperous Ukrainian farmer, was forced by circumstances to seek employment in Rostov-on-Don; she left her son in the care of her sister, Mariia, and sister-in-law, Irina Shcherbak. The latter, a feisty and deeply religious woman with literary interests, influenced the young Solzhenitsyn's love for the Russian classics and his appreciation of Russian Orthodoxy. At age six he was reunited with his mother in Rostov, where, destitute, the two lived for the next twelve years in a rickety shack without plumbing. The boy often spent summer vacation at the home of his Aunt Irina.

Solzhenitsyn relates several episodes from this period of his youth in *Dorozhen'ka*, a long autobiographical poem written in 1947–1952 (published in 1999). In each case he emphasizes his inability at the time to draw conclusions from the ominous scenes he happened to witness. These scenes include the brutal intimidation of his mother and visiting grandfather by the political police, as well as the arrest of his best friend's father and of the most popular and brilliant boy at the school Solzhenitsyn attended. (In 1926 Solzhenitsyn entered the former Pokrovsky College, referred to as the Malevich Gymnasium, after its headmaster. The school was considered the best in Rostov.) Despite such portents, the well-orchestrated and all-pervasive Soviet propaganda succeeded in winning him over by the time he was a teenager. A chapter in *Dorozhen'ka*, titled "Mal'chiki s luny" (Boys from the Moon), describes a leisurely boat ride taken by the autobiographical protagonist and his equally indoctrinated friend down the Volga River; the two idealists remain blithely insensitive to the implications of the sights around them, from the throngs of cowed prisoners to the visible injury to rural life wreaked by collectivization.

Solzhenitsyn's literary ambitions manifested themselves early, and some surviving juvenilia show that he was composing short stories already at age nine. The years when Solzhenitsyn finished at the gymnasium and when he entered secondary school are not known, but by 1936 he had graduated from the latter.

*Solzhenitsyn in 1946, after he had been sentenced to eight years of forced labor in the GULag for "malicious slander" (courtesy of the Solzhenitsyn family)*

That year he undertook his first serious attempt to write on what he considered the greatest event in modern history, the Bolshevik Revolution of 1917. The epic scale of his intentions required months of historical research into the antecedents of the revolution, starting with the catastrophic defeat of the Russian army in Eastern Prussia at the outset of World War I. These early writings have survived, and Solzhenitsyn has said that several decades later he was able to incorporate much of it into his *Avgust chetyrnadtsatogo* (1971; translated as *August 1914*, 1972), the first part—what he called an *uzel*, or knot—of the multivolume *Krasnoe koleso*.

Although Solzhenitsyn wished to pursue literary studies, this option was not available at Rostov University, where he had enrolled in 1936 in order to stay close to his ailing mother. He majored in mathematics and physics, choices that in time were providential; later, during his imprisonment in the labor camps, this specialty was his ticket out: it enabled him to enter an institution that housed technically trained prisoners. While studying the exact sciences at Rostov University, he nevertheless was also able to take up literary studies through a correspondence course offered by the prestigious Moscow Institute of Philosophy, Literature, and History (MIFLI). At this time, too, Solzhenitsyn began seeing a fellow student, Natal'ia Alekseevna Reshetovskaia, a chemistry major with strong musical interests; in 1940 they married. He graduated with distinction in 1941 and resolved to apply for admission to advanced study at MIFLI.

The Nazi invasion of the Soviet Union on 22 June 1941, however, put an end to these plans. When Solzhenitsyn attempted to enlist, he was unexpectedly rejected for medical reasons. Yet, four months later he was called up and assigned to a horse-drawn transport unit far from the front lines. In an autobiographically based short novel, *Liubi revoliutsii* (Love the Revolution)—originally conceived as a sequel to *Dorozhen'ka*, written mostly in 1948, and published as an unfinished work in 1999—Solzhenitsyn describes the shame and humiliation of the protagonist when he is turned away by the military in his attempt to volunteer. He is mortified even more when he finds himself attached to an enormous train of horse-drawn wagons and surrounded by middle-aged men who have no interest in the revolutionary ideals he holds sacred and who are amused by the protagonist's inability to handle horses. After much effort, he is able to transfer to artillery school. *Liubi revoliutsii* includes a chapter describing the protagonist's phantasmagoric trip through a war-torn country afflicted by disrupted rail schedules and general chaos.

Solzhenitsyn's mathematical training landed him in an accelerated course in sound ranging—also known as instrumental reconnaissance, a technique whereby dispersed microphones are used to pinpoint enemy gun emplacements. By early 1943 he was commanding his own battery and was soon engaged in frontline action. As in his schooling, in the army Solzhenitsyn compiled a record of excellence, earning decorations for heroism and a promotion to captain. At the same time, there were serious moral challenges to his convictions, but his overall faith in Marxist dogma appears to have survived intact throughout the war. *Dorozhen'ka* makes clear, nonetheless, that he was shaken to learn of the existence of Russian military units fighting against the Soviet forces alongside the Germans. In addition, he was deeply troubled by a chance meeting with members of a Soviet unit made up of political prisoners deliberately employed in an operation in which survival was unlikely, and the wild rampage that characterized the Soviet advance through German territory in early 1945 repelled him. The latter theme is developed at some length in a chapter of *Dorozhen'ka*. Published separately as *Prusskie nochi* (1974; translated as *Prussian Nights*, 1977), the work emphasizes the protagonist's anguished remorse at his participation in the rape and pillage of a Germany left defenseless by its collapsed army.

Another work directly based on Solzhenitsyn's wartime experience is *Pir pobeditelei* (written 1951; published 1981 in *Sobranie sochinenii*, translated as *Victory Celebrations*, 1986), a drama in verse. Subtitled *Komediia* (A Comedy), it started as a chapter in *Dorozhen'ka*. Set in early 1945, the bitterly satirical work centers on the unexpected appearance of Gridnev, a representative of a military counterintelligence directorate known as SMERSH (short for the Russian expression "smert' shpionam" [death to spies]), at a feast prepared by a group of Soviet army officers in celebration of their victorious advance through Eastern Prussia. The SMERSH man poisons the festivities by voicing suspicions about a beautiful girl who has been invited to the party (and who has resisted his amorous advances), as well as about the "social provenance" of the officer Gleb Nerzhin—the name used for the autobiographical hero here as well as in *Dorozhen'ka* and in two later works, *Plenniki* (written 1953, published 1981 in *Sobranie sochinenii*, translated as *Prisoners*, 1986) and *Respublika truda* (The Republic of Labor, written 1954, published 1981). Solzhenitsyn's goal in *Pir pobeditelei* is to show the tension between the visceral dislike that Gridnev generates and the sinister power over everyone that he nevertheless wields. The tension is resolved when the Germans launch a sudden counterattack and Gridnev, instead of remaining to keep an eye on Soviet troops, reveals his cowardice by fleeing.

Solzhenitsyn's military career ended disastrously. He and Nikolai Vitkevich, the true-believing Rostov friend with whom he had sailed down the Volga some years earlier and who was now serving in the military at a neighboring section of the front, began to exchange correspondence that included disparaging comments on Joseph Stalin's leadership. More dangerous to their reputations was the platform they drafted for a reform-minded and "purely Leninist" political party. Their letters were intercepted by military censors, and arrests of the two men followed. In *Dorozhen'ka* and the first volume of *Arkhipelag GULag*, Solzhenitsyn describes how he was seized by SMERSH operatives in February 1945 and taken under guard to Moscow, where, after he spent months in prison, a perfunctory investigation was followed by a foreordained guilty verdict. For "malicious slander" and setting up a "hostile organization," Solzhenitsyn was sentenced to eight years of forced-labor camp, followed by "perpetual exile" to a remote area of the U.S.S.R. He was entering the world of the gulag, a term that originates from GULag, the acronym for the Soviet prison-camp system (Glavnoe upravlenie ispravitel'no-trudovykh lagerei, or Chief Administration of Corrective Labor Camps).

In a sense Solzhenitsyn completed his education in the GULag. His faith in Marxism, to some degree already mitigated by his wartime experiences, was taxed now by his new learning, and it collapsed completely. He was impressed by the fortitude and personal decency of fellow prisoners who held views radically unlike his earlier convictions, as in the case of the quiet but unshakable commitment to democratic values exhibited by his Estonian cell mate Arnold Susi or the Christian beliefs fervently argued by Boris Gammerov, a young Moscow intellectual.

An early work that communicates some of the intellectual tumult that Solzhenitsyn experienced during the initial period of his incarceration is the drama *Plenniki*. The play is a mixture of poetry and prose, a stylistic feature that appropriately echoes the jumble of ideologies voiced in the text. The action takes place in a Soviet prison in mid 1945 and is based on Solzhenitsyn's experience of being thrown together with a diverse group of individuals when he was first incarcerated. His fellow prisoners included Soviet soldiers and officers liberated from German POW camps and then promptly rearrested as alleged security risks; men who had fought with the Wehrmacht-directed Russian Liberation Army; Russian émigrés snatched from the streets of Western Europe; devout Christians; and a few diehard Communists. The arguments among these men are presented as a cacophonous montage in which everyone's opinions clash. But *Plenniki* also diverges in a significant way from the autobiographical tendency of Solzhenitsyn's early works. The most prominent character in the play is not the familiar Gleb Nerzhin but a former colonel in the tsarist army named Georgii Vorotyntsev, who is in prison for fighting, on the German side, against the Soviet Union. Years later Vorotyntsev returns as a character when Solzhenitsyn makes him the protagonist of the *Krasnoe koleso* epic. Thus, *Plenniki* was the earliest hint of the way Solzhenitsyn was visualizing *Krasnoe koleso*, and it served as an epilogue to the still unwritten cycle (which Solzhenitsyn was to set during the ancien régime). (In the play Vorotyntsev refuses a chance to commit suicide in order to escape the gallows that await him, arguing that the responsibility for his death must fall on his executioners, not on him.)

Solzhenitsyn experienced forced labor soon after his sentence was pronounced. He spent almost a year in camps of the "mixed" type, so designated for holding political prisoners together with common criminals. In the second volume of *Arkhipelag GULag* he relates some of the difficulties and moral quandaries that bewildered and humiliated him during this period. Much of this experience has been condensed into a play titled *Respublika truda*. (The "republic of labor" is an ironic echo of the supposed workers' paradise.) It is about a recently arrested frontline officer, Gleb Nerzhin, who is unexpectedly placed in a position of authority and tries to undo some of the flagrantly corrupt, unfair, and unsafe practices that characterize the operation of the camp. (Prison camps played an important role in the Soviet economy, and the authorities cared only about maximizing productivity.) Nerzhin's attempts at reform are shown to be hopelessly naive, and by challenging many vested interests he generates so much hostility that he is demoted and marked for transportation to a far more lethal camp. He is saved from this fate by the intervention of a girl with whom he has fallen violently in love, but she is able to help only by a self-sacrificing act: she agrees—without Nerzhin's knowledge—to join the "harem" of the camp doctor, who has many connections. Like most writers who employ the realistic mode to project images related to actual fact, Solzhenitsyn has selected, condensed, rearranged, and highlighted data stemming from his own experiences. In *Respublika truda* his aim is to depict the utter helplessness and demoralization of the protagonist in the face of the bottomless corruption he encounters in the camp system. While there is no reason to question the psychological veracity of that central theme in terms of the author's real-life attitude, the plot—in the narrow sense of the term—remains a fictional construct.

Many years later, in the wake of the publication of *Odin den' Ivana Denisovicha*, Solzhenitsyn hoped to receive permission to stage *Respublika truda*. For this purpose he prepared a politically toned-down version, titled *Olen' i shalashovka* (written 1962, published 1969 in the journal *Grani* [Facets]; translated as *The Love-Girl and the Innocent*, 1986); he also renamed the protagonist Rodion Nemov. The latter change presumably was made to avoid drawing attention to the link between the play and the novel *V kruge pervom*, in which the central character is once again named Gleb Nerzhin.

*V kruge pervom* reflects the radically changed circumstances in which Solzhenitsyn found himself in mid 1946, when he entered a closed prison institute, or *sharashka*. As had been the case in his wartime transfer to the artillery, his mathematical training was the reason why he was plucked out of the regular camp system and brought into the institute, which was then engaged in developing a telephone encryption device. The novel is based on his four years at the Marfino *sharashka*, located outside Moscow. Just as the "first circle" in the *Inferno* section of Dante's *La Commedia* (1472; translated as *The Divine Comedy*, 1802) housed virtuous pagans who were spared the torments of the lower circles of hell, so the inmates of the prison research institute received relatively privileged treatment—such as better

*Marfino, the closed prison research institute where Solzhenitsyn worked as a prisoner for four years, beginning in 1946, developing a telephone message encryption device. Marfino is the setting for Solzhenitsyn's novel* The First Circle *(from Lev Kopelev,* Utoli moia pechali, *1981).*

working conditions, enough food, and access to books. The novel represents Solzhenitsyn's first use of what he has called the "polyphonic" principle of construction: in this approach sections of the work, typically a chapter or group of chapters, are presented from the point of view—and often in the language—of a particular character, not necessarily a major protagonist; all the while the third-person format of the basic account is retained. The technical term for this type of narrative mode is *erlebte Rede* (experienced speech, in the sense of a represented discourse or a narrated monologue), and the polyphonic aspect points to the presence of several individual viewpoints and voices within the text. This technique is highly effective for bringing out the fundamental worldview of each character.

The action covers only four days, the symbolically charged period of Christmastide, 24–27 December 1949, which followed the extravagant celebrations of Stalin's seventieth birthday (21 December 1949). The gallery of characters in the work is huge. It cuts across the whole of Soviet society and ranges from a portrait of the *sharashka*'s humble janitor to a study of the aging Stalin, a prisoner of his megalomania. Among other historical personages appearing in fictionalized guise are Viktor Semenovich Abakumov, the minister of state security during this period, and Eleanor Roosevelt, who is caricatured by the prisoners as the prototype of a blind Western "do-gooder"—she is easily misled by the mendacious facade erected for her benefit at a prison she visits.

Solzhenitsyn began working on *V kruge pervom* in the mid 1950s and brought it to completion in 1968. But after the success of publishing *Odin den' Ivana Denisovicha,* he pruned the ninety-six-chapter work down to eighty-seven chapters, readjusting the plotline and "softening" various parts of the book in the hope that it, like *Odin den' Ivana Denisovicha,* might slip past the censors. The Moscow journal *Novyi mir* accepted the novel in its shortened version in 1964, but publication proved impossible. In 1968 the author allowed a similarly "lightened," eighty-seven-chapter version to circulate privately, and it soon appeared abroad, in Russian as well as in translation. The full ninety-six-chapter Russian version, including late emendations, was published only in 1978 in Solzhenitsyn's twenty-volume *Sobranie sochinenii* (Collected Works, 1978–1991); it remains untranslated into English.

The most significant difference between the definitive and the "lightened" versions of *V kruge pervom* concerns the character Innokentii Volodin, a Soviet diplomat with a conscience, whose action at the beginning sets the plot in motion. In the definitive version Volodin telephones the United States embassy in Moscow in an unsuccessful attempt to warn of an impending Soviet espionage operation in New York involving nuclear-bomb technology. (A similar phone call actually was made in the fall of 1949 by a Soviet diplomat about to be posted in Canada.) The "lightened" version replaces this overtly anti-Soviet act with the diplomat's decent gesture of attempting to caution a doctor acquaintance against sharing an experimental drug with Western colleagues, since the authorities, in their paranoia, would consider this act a betrayal of Soviet science. In both versions the phone call is monitored and recorded, and the Marfino prison institute is charged with identifying the caller. In addition, the complete *V kruge pervom* touches on several other politically sensitive issues, including the long-held suspicion that Stalin had been a double agent for the tsarist secret police.

These differences, however, are eclipsed by the thematic continuities between the two versions. The most important continuity entails the complex interrelationships among three prisoners, Gleb Nerzhin, Lev Rubin, and Dmitrii Sologdin, each of whom is based on an actual person—Solzhenitsyn, Lev Zinov'evich Kopelev, and Dimitrii Mikhailovich Panin, respectively. (Kopelev and Panin have published accounts of their friendship with Solzhenitsyn; through these memoirs the process whereby Solzhenitsyn transmutes real life into fictional representation can be traced.) The overarching theme of what being human means comes into fullest play through the characterizations of these three figures. Rubin, a committed Marxist who remains loyal to the official collectivist ideology of the state even after he enters the camps, is, however, also a man of genuinely humane instincts, and these contradictory tendencies give rise to utopian visions. Thus, in order to imbue citizens of an atheist society with traditional morality, Rubin proposes to institute compulsory attendance at "civic temples," which, despite his denials, are essentially "Christian temples without Christ." Sologdin, Rubin's main ideological adversary, delights in challenging his opponent by reciting the evils of the Soviet system. But in what is probably an exaggeration of the real Panin's views (embellished for the sake of highlighting philosophical differences), Solzhenitsyn has presented Sologdin as a spokesman of radical individualism. Nerzhin, apparently much like Solzhenitsyn during his time in the *sharashka*, takes a middle ground between the philosophical antipodes represented by his two friends. Refusing to adopt either of their positions, he sets out to develop his own personal point of view, which to him is "more precious than life itself." As he asserts, "Everyone keeps shaping his inner self year after year. One must try to temper, to cut, to polish one's soul so as to become *a human being*." As if to distinguish his position from Sologdin's proud elitism, however, Nerzhin immediately adds, "And thereby become a tiny particle of one's own people." Nerzhin's personalism thus places the individual within a community while remaining free of both monolithic collectivism and isolated individualism.

Of the many subsidiary themes in the novel, a particularly noteworthy one concerns language. The Marfino prisoners study the physical properties of speech in their work on a voice scrambler and through their efforts to perfect a reliable method of voice recognition. Sologdin labors to purify the Russian by inventing substitutes for foreign words. Rubin seeks to buttress Marxist theory through comparative etymology. Stalin attempts to write an essay on linguistics but is stymied by his failing mind. In addition, Volodin's failed attempt to transmit a warning by telephone; the lies that are told at every turn by prisoners and Soviet officials alike; and the inability of a husband and wife to establish an understanding in the sharply limited time allotted to them by prison rules are all examples of ideology-spawned obstacles that disrupt and pervert normal communication.

For Solzhenitsyn, the four-year stay at the Marfino *sharashka* provided the opportunity for profound self-examination. Temporarily shielded from the physical hardships and psychological stresses of the camps, he now began reevaluating his past and constructing a new worldview upon the ruins of his former Marxist convictions. During this time he began writing the narrative poem *Dorozhen'ka,* its prose sequel, *Liubi revoliutsiiu,* and several poems.

In the spring of 1950 Solzhenitsyn's relatively privileged existence came to an abrupt end when a conflict with authorities at the *sharashka* caused him to be expelled from Marfino. He was cast back into the labor-camp system. Two years earlier Stalin had decreed that political prisoners (deemed much more dangerous than thieves and murderers) be segregated in so-called Special Camps with a particularly harsh regime, and Solzhenitsyn was transported accordingly to Ekibastuz, a huge new prison camp for "politicals" located in the arid steppe of central Kazakhstan. He was destined to finish out his term there and to try his hand at several physical tasks—from laying bricks to working at the foundry. His experience is distilled in *Odin den' Ivana Denisovicha* (titled in manuscript "Shch-854," a prison identification number of the protagonist), although Solzhenitsyn chose to distance the narrative from any direct autobiographical reference.

He has stated that he conceived the idea of the story on a dreary workday in the winter of 1950–1951.

*Solzhenitsyn in prisoner garb soon after he was released from Ekibastuz prison camp in 1953 to begin serving his perpetual exile in Kok-Terek (photograph courtesy of the Solzhenitsyn family; from* Solzhenitsyn: A Pictorial Autobiography, *1974)*

When he sat down to write the work in 1959, he reports, it "simply gushed out with tremendous force" (quoted in volume ten of the 1978–1991 *Sobranie sochinenii*) and was done in forty days. The central character is a peasant, Ivan Denisovich Shukhov. His name and mannerisms were derived from a soldier who had served in Solzhenitsyn's military unit (and who was never in prison); the soldier's biography was typical of the vast majority of inmates in the Special Camps—they were innocent of any real crimes. In the narrative Ivan Denisovich is charged with being a German spy (he had fallen briefly into German hands during the war and had managed to escape). Many of the other characters are modeled on specific camp acquaintances.

The story follows Ivan Denisovich and his fellow *zeks* (derived from *z/k,* an abbreviation for prisoners), from reveille to taps, in a single day in early 1951. The narrative structure is a "monophonic" version of the *erlebte Rede* mode employed by Solzhenitsyn in *V kruge pervom,* with a third-person account presented as if through Ivan Denisovich's eyes and in his peasant idiom. This method allows Ivan Denisovich's subjective outlook to be expressed in an unmediated and understated form, perhaps the most affecting aspect of the story. Ivan Denisovich and his labor brigade spend the long workday laying cinder blocks in the bitter cold. Though devoid of loyalty to his overlords, he takes such pride in his work that he risks punishment by staying beyond quitting time in order to finish laying one last row of bricks in a way that will affirm his sense of self-worth as a skilled craftsman. All his other small successes of that day are cast in physical terms as well: he keeps his boots in good repair, sneaks through inspection a blade that he can make into a knife, finagles an extra portion of gruel, and buys tobacco.

But deeper issues of a spiritual nature underlie the response to physical hardships, and these matters come into clearest focus in the critically important conversation between Ivan Denisovich and Alyoshka, a fellow prisoner arrested for his Baptist faith. While some innate yet unarticulated life force allows Ivan Denisovich to survive with his humanity intact despite the merciless and degrading pressures of camp life, Alyoshka's serene faith in God provides a vocabulary that Ivan Denisovich lacks for understanding the triumph of the human spirit. Even though Ivan Denisovich is not prepared to embrace Alyoshka's view of the world, the sympathetic hearing he gives to the Baptist's arguments points toward the implicit religious foundation of Solzhenitsyn's moral vision.

In *Odin den' Ivana Denisovicha* Solzhenitsyn aspires to depict camp life in the way it was commonly experienced by the majority of prisoners; as a result, he has deliberately eschewed any direct identification of the main protagonist with himself. Autobiographical information on his experiences in the Ekibastuz camp is given in *Arkhipelag GULag,* including a vivid account of the trip from the Moscow area to the new destination and a portrayal of the spirit of defiance that began to take hold of the political prisoners in the Special Camps. This spirit gathered strength rapidly, leading first to the systematic assassination of camp informers and, in early 1952, culminating in a general strike, which at first was met with concessions on the part of the authorities but soon was crushed with repressive measures. (This episode, together with a much more serious mid-1954 uprising that occurred in the nearby Kengir camp, is reflected in Solzhenitsyn's screenplay *Znaiut istinu tanki* [Tanks Know the Truth, written 1959, published 1981 in *Sobranie sochinenii*].) Although he had participated in the 1952 strike, Solzhenitsyn escaped retribution because at the time when the authorities were reestablishing control, he underwent an emergency operation for what apparently was abdominal cancer. According to Solzhenitsyn, he lay in a postoperative haze in the recovery room of the hospital, and one of the doctors, Boris Nikolaevich Kornfel'd, sat on his bed and spoke fervently of his recent conversion to Christianity. The doctor was murdered by unknown assailants that same night, probably on suspicion that he had been an informer, and his ardent words at Solzhenitsyn's bedside–the last words he said in his life–weighed upon the writer "as an inheritance." Solzhenitsyn states that this extraordinary sequence of events precipitated his conscious return to a belief in God, formally marked by a poem written in 1952, in which the writer rededicates himself to the faith in which he was brought up.

Solzhenitsyn was released from the Ekibastuz camp in early 1953, but he was now compelled to begin his "perpetual" exile in Kok-Terek, a small settlement in southern Kazakhstan, where he supported himself by teaching mathematics and physics in a local secondary school. Every moment free of pedagogical duties was spent writing the works that he had accumulated in his head during the preceding years, beginning with what he had composed in verse and committed to memory: the narrative poem *Dorozhen'ka,* the two plays that grew out of specific chapters of that work, *Pir pobeditelei* and *Plenniki,* as well as many poems.

In late 1953 Solzhenitsyn became seriously ill–the abdominal swelling that had necessitated the earlier operation had returned–and terminal cancer was diagnosed. He was permitted to travel to Tashkent, a major city some three hundred miles away, and there he underwent massive radiation treatment, which succeeded in shrinking the tumor. Once again Solzhenitsyn transmuted his personal experience into art and wrote about the period of treatment in a novel-length "tale" *(povest')* titled *Rakovyi korpus.* He says that this work was conceived on the day he left the Tashkent clinic after being pronounced cured.

The main protagonist of *Rakovyi korpus* is Oleg Kostoglotov, who, like Solzhenitsyn, has known war, prison, and cancer but can be viewed as an authorial alter ego only in part. As in *V kruge pervom,* the narrative is presented in the *erlebte Rede* mode and in a polyphonic setting, and the gallery of characters is large and diverse. Cancer patients are necessarily in extremis, and the prospect of dying, while universal, has an unavoidable immediacy for each of them. In some cases the cancer seems to "match" the patient–a malignancy is diagnosed in the breast of a sexy girl and in the tongue of a liar–but the mystery of suffering is the dominant theme. A noisy patient, Podduev, reads Leo Tolstoy's story "Chem liudi zhivy" (1882; translated as "What Men Live By," 1901) and is jolted into an awareness that he has lived unworthily. When he asks others what they think men live by, he receives shallow answers: rations, air, water, one's pay, one's professional skill, one's homeland. To the physical suffering that afflicts these cancer patients is added the deformity of character produced and magnified by an aggressively ideological system. This deformation is seen most clearly in Rusanov, a self-important and mean-spirited government functionary whose Communist faith leaves him with insufficient resources to cope with the prospect of death. Rusanov serves as a foil to Oleg Kostoglotov, the only ward mate who, amid the individualized responses to suffering, achieves philosophical depth in meditating upon death. Rough-hewn and uneducated, Kostoglotov has learned in the camps that survival "at any price" is an unsatisfactory way to live. Seemingly cured and free to make a new life at age thirty-five, he discovers that his hormone treatments will render him impotent. He fathoms his cruel plight just as two attractive women, the vivacious nurse, Zoia, and the ethereal doctor, Vera, reciprocate his interest in them. Both women offer him a place to stay when he leaves the hospital, but instead of imposing his sexual limitations upon either of them, Kostoglotov chooses renunciation as the only honorable path to follow and heads off to his place of exile. By an act of will, he transcends despair and achieves spiritual liberation, and the undeviating focus on moral values that animates Solzhenitsyn's fiction again is confirmed.

The years 1956 and 1957 are particularly significant in Solzhenitsyn's life. In February 1956 Nikita Sergeevich Khrushchev delivered an address to the Twentieth Congress of the Communist Party of the Soviet Union (CPSU) in which he denounced Stalin's excesses. This speech marked the beginning of the "Thaw," a cultural liberalization that proved to be short-lived and lacking in clear guidelines. Nevertheless, it was a major departure from the stifling rigidity of the Stalinist era, and profound political changes followed almost immediately. In April 1956 Solzhenitsyn's sentence of "perpetual exile" was annulled, and at the end of the school year he moved to Mil'tsevo, a Russian village about a hundred miles east of Moscow. His day job continued to be school teaching, but he continued what became his lifelong habit of pouring every free moment into his writing. Mil'tsevo supplied the setting for his celebrated short story "Matrenin dvor" (first published 1963 in *Novyi mir;* translated as "Matryona's Home," 1963). In early 1957 he was officially "rehabilitated," which meant that the 1945 charges against him were formally erased from his record. This change of status was followed by his remarriage to Natal'ia Alekseevna, who had divorced Solzhenitsyn in the early 1950s to protect herself (by severing her ties to an

*Contents page for the issue of* Novyi mir *that first published Solzhenitsyn's* One Day in the Life of Ivan Denisovich *(Collection of Edward E. Ericson Jr. and Alexis Klimoff)*

"enemy of the people"). The couple then moved to Riazan', a provincial city south of Moscow, where he again taught school.

In 1958–1960 Solzhenitsyn wrote seventeen prose poems. Titled "Krokhotki" (miniature stories) and first published in the émigré journal *Grani* in 1964, the poems range in length from a dozen lines to a page and a half and display exquisite attention to rhythmic structure. They also reveal his pensive, even gentle side. Typically, they move from a single episode or observation to a broad philosophical insight. Among the values embraced by these prose poems are joy in the beauty of nature, recognition of the life force at all levels, respect for simple peasant life, and an attachment to the old Russian towns and domed churches that dot the rural landscape. Although he scrupulously avoids romanticizing old Russian ways, he does use them as a yardstick for judging the sterility of modern Soviet society, which has desecrated the land of the nation and despiritualized the life of its people. A particularly memorable prose poem, "My-to ne umrem" (translated as "'We Will Never Die'" in *Stories and Prose Poems*, 1971), shows the materialist ideology of Marxism sharply at odds with the natural rhythms of life and death that faith allows religious persons to accept.

"Matrenin dvor," written in 1959, is Solzhenitsyn's best-known short story; some commentators consider it his most accomplished literary production. It is also autobiographical. The narrator is a former prisoner (referred to only by his patronymic, Ignatich) who has returned to European Russia after forced residence in Central Asia and tries to obtain lodging in a backwoods village. He yearns to find peace by losing himself in the Russian heartland, but his melancholy discovery is that most of the villagers, including a bearded elder of dignified and imposing appearance, turn out to be greedy, quarrelsome, and petty. The one exception is Matrena, a poor and sickly middle-aged widow in whose house Ignatich has lodged. With a work ethic not unlike that of Ivan Denisovich but combined with an altruism that is all her own, she helps neighbors with their tasks whenever she is asked. Moral but not observably religious, Matrena has had a life filled with tragedy and suffering but has not become bitter. She accepts injustices with equanimity and does no one harm. With an unreflective natural piety, she respects the life-giving earth and loves animals, especially her lame cat. Her grasping relatives, needing wood for a construction project, dismantle part of her log cabin. The cart carrying the wood gets stuck on the railroad crossing, and a train kills Matrena, who, characteristically, had been trying to help. The story concludes by describing her as "that one righteous person without whom, as the saying goes, no city can stand." The saying is based on a biblical text: Abraham's entreaty to God to spare the city of Sodom in Genesis 18.

In 1960 Solzhenitsyn wrote a play titled *Svecha na vetru* (written 1960, first published 1969 in *Grani*; translated as *Candle in the Wind*, 1973), published in the West in 1973. It is the only belletristic work by him that is not set in Russia—it has instead a vaguely international setting. In the opinion of both Solzhenitsyn and the critics, the play was not a successful work.

Khrushchev's de-Stalinization campaign peaked with the Twenty-Second Congress of the CPSU in October 1961. The denunciations of Stalinism that were sounded there emboldened Solzhenitsyn to risk submitting some of his writing for publication. The manuscript for *Odin den' Ivana Denisovicha* made its way from the author to Kopelev, Solzhenitsyn's old friend from their *sharashka* days, then through other intermediaries, and on up to Aleksandr Trifonovich Tvardovsky, editor in chief of *Novyi mir*. Solzhenitsyn, meanwhile, suffered serious misgivings about the possible consequences of coming out of hiding as a writer.

Tvardovsky's strategy for seeking permission to publish the work was to pass it on to Khrushchev, a personal acquaintance with peasant roots like his own, and to suggest that the premier could use the book in his de-Stalinization campaign. While the book can be seen as anti-Stalinist, it is a protest against any dehumanization wherever perpetrated. Khrushchev had copies of the manuscript made for each member of the Politburo; he asked them to declare at the next meeting whether they were in favor of, or opposed to, publication. Those in favor he counted as political supporters, and those in opposition, he viewed as foes. Thus, the first public use of a Solzhenitsyn work was as a political tool. *Odin den' Ivana Denisovicha* was published in November 1962 in a huge overrun of *Novyi mir*. Within months it was reprinted in *Roman-gazeta* (a monthly periodical that specialized in publishing entire short novels), a mass-circulation magazine, and then in book form. Reader response to it was enormously positive, and published translations followed promptly. Solzhenitsyn immediately passed from anonymity to global fame.

By authorizing the publication of *Odin den' Ivana Denisovicha*, Khrushchev had set the terms for its initial reception, and establishment Soviet publications slavishly followed the leader's instrumental approach. In contrast, Tvardovsky gave priority to the literary quality of the work, including the moral force of its truthful account of human nature. The profuse Western responses to the book were enthusiastic, and generally they followed the Tvardovsky approach of highlighting its aesthetic and moral achievements. A decade later the tables turned, however, and the politicizing approach of Khrushchev became, willy-nilly, the more common approach among Western critics—and the bane of Solzhenitsyn's reception ever since.

Whereas Khrushchev had hoped to satisfy readers that the Stalinist terror was a thing of the past, he and his entourage were not prepared for, nor were they pleased by, the explosive reaction to *Odin den' Ivana Denisovicha*. In the West, Solzhenitsyn was hailed as a champion of freedom who revealed hitherto-unknown truths about Soviet atrocities. The domestic response was even more significant. Few Soviet citizens had been spared the disappearance of a family member into the gulag, but only with the publication of this story was official silence about camp life challenged by a forthright account. Letters flooded in to Solzhenitsyn, and many of them described personal experiences of the camps. This correspondence led in 1963–1964 to his meetings with hundreds of former *zeks*, who agreed to be interviewed about their experience. At one point he had set aside as overly ambitious the idea of writing a history of the gulag system, but now he was receiving detailed material of the sort that he needed for this project. These eyewitness accounts returned him to his task, and many of them made their way into *Arkhipelag GULag*.

This period of lessened restraint in the press did not last long. Two months after *Novyi mir* published *Odin den' Ivana Denisovicha*, it featured "Matrenin dvor" and another short story, "Sluchai na stantsii Krechetovka" (translated as "Incident at Krechetovka Station," 1963). The latter is about a military officer and his humane impulses, which are overridden by his Soviet indoctrination when, in an excess of vigilance, he orders the arrest of an innocent man. Later in 1963

*Novyi mir* ran a rather long story by Solzhenitsyn, "Dlia pol'zy dela" (translated as *For the Good of the Cause*, 1964), which he and the critics have come to consider as inferior. The only other works by him published in the Soviet Union before his expulsion were a 1965 essay on language and the story "Zakhar-Kalita" (published 1966 in *Novyi mir;* translated as "Zakhar the Pouch," in *Stories and Prose Poems*, 1971). Then the Soviets stopped allowing the publication of his works.

In 1964 Solzhenitsyn was nominated for the Lenin Prize, but his candidacy was sabotaged by the deliberately false, last-minute charge that he had collaborated with the Nazis during the war. In retrospect, however, the rejection was probably good fortune, for winning the prize would have pressured him toward more-compliant behavior. Khrushchev fell prey to a coup and was removed from office in October 1964, and a hardening of the party line followed. This tightening of measures, together with the failure of his efforts to get the "lightened" version of *V kruge pervom* published at home, moved Solzhenitsyn to have a copy of the novel smuggled out of the country for safekeeping, though not yet for publication. The unauthorized appearance abroad of other works by him, however, also began in 1964, starting with the publication of the miniature stories "Krokhotki." During the mid 1960s, as more and more of his activities transpired in the public arena—where the KGB could track them—he kept strictly secret the composition of his most dangerous book, *Arkhipelag GULag*. (He later revealed this story of secrecy in "Nevidimki" [first published in English as *Invisible Allies*, 1995; published in Russian in book form, 1996].)

Direct harassment began in 1965 when the KGB raided the apartments of two of Solzhenitsyn's friends and took possession of a large trove of his notes and unpublished manuscripts. Included in this haul were early plays such as *Pir pobeditelei*, in which Solzhenitsyn's opposition to the regime was undisguised. Soon the authorities added selective references from the confiscated material to their ongoing effort to discredit Solzhenitsyn. He responded by resorting to samizdat, that is, distributing typed copies of protests, statements, or entire works through an informal network of fellow dissenters. The first work that he knowingly allowed to circulate in samizdat was *Rakovyi korpus*. His increasingly combative public statements were now usually published in the West and then broadcast over Radio Liberty.

Solzhenitsyn spared no effort in his attempts to get *Rakovyi korpus* published at home. Like *V kruge pervom* before it, *Rakovyi korpus* was accepted by the editorial board of *Novyi mir* and awaited clearance by the censors. In late 1966 Solzhenitsyn met with the prose section of the Moscow branch of the Writers' Union to discuss the manuscript. These writers showered the novel and the novelist with praise; Solzhenitsyn expressed his gratitude and his willingness to consider making recommended revisions. No movement toward publication ensued, however, and in May 1967 he wrote an open letter to the upcoming Fourth Congress of the Soviet Writers' Union. In the letter he chastised the Union for its servility before the regime—especially its cringing assent to the persecution of hundreds of writers—and its similarly silent acquiescence to the draconian censorship. He also appealed to the union leadership to respond to his repeated entreaties to support the publication of *Rakovyi korpus* in the Soviet Union. It was his first major act of public defiance, but the congress was not permitted to discuss these general topics. Denunciation of Solzhenitsyn soon became the prevailing note, and in the wake of this episode he believed that a record of his version of his conflict with the regime would be necessary, in case action was taken against him. Thus began the autobiographical accounts that eventually appeared in 1975 as *Bodalsia telenok s dubom: Ocherki literaturnoi zhizni* (translated as *The Oak and the Calf: Sketches of Literary Life in the Soviet Union*, 1980).

In 1968 Solzhenitsyn completed *Arkhipelag GULag* and arranged for a copy of it to reach the West for safekeeping. Also in that year *V kruge pervom* and *Rakovyi korpus* were published in the West within weeks of each other, both in Russian and in translation, although Solzhenitsyn had authorized publication of only *V kruge pervom*. The two novels received a warm welcome from Western reviewers; high praise in the vein of that lavished upon *Odin den' Ivana Denisovicha* continued to be the norm, with disagreement among reviewers largely limited to which work was the greater, *V kruge pervom* or *Rakovyi korpus*. In addition, world opinion was running strongly in his favor, and his public-relations successes gave him a relative sense of invulnerability from any initiatives against him by the regime.

In 1969 Solzhenitsyn turned to the work that as a youth he had projected to be his magnum opus. He began intensive work on *Avgust chetyrnadtsatogo*, the first installment of the literary rendering of the events that took place before the Bolshevik Revolution. *Avgust chetyrnadtsatogo* was published in Paris in 1971 and the next year in English translation. A greatly enlarged version in original Russian appeared in 1983, but not until 1989 did an edition of this version come out in English. Despite the severe distractions that interrupted his work on this ambitious project in the late 1960s and early 1970s, he never wavered from his commitment to it. One such distraction occurred on 12 November 1969: the Riazan' local branch of the Writers' Union expelled Solzhenitsyn for "antisocial behavior." A technically unemployed writer was subject to arrest for "parasitism," but the vociferous protests in his defense by Western writers made clear that, at least for the time being, the author was safe from more-energetic measures.

In 1970 Solzhenitsyn was awarded the Nobel Prize in literature "for the ethical force with which he has pursued the indispensable traditions of Russian literature." His name appeared in the headlines of newspapers around the world, and sympathetic attention from the West bolstered his position. As the Soviet press hotly protested the selection of Solzhenitsyn for the prize, he was faced with the likely prospect that if he traveled to Sweden, he would not be allowed to return home. The Swedish government, wishing to avoid the wrath of the Soviet Union, refused to permit the award to be presented publicly at its embassy in Moscow. Solzhenitsyn then made an attempt to have the ceremony held at the Moscow flat of Moscow mathematician Natal'ia Dmitrievna Svetlova, but the Soviet regime denied an entry visa to the secretary of the Swedish Academy, who had agreed to make the presentation in this context; this event, too, had to be cancelled. The text of the lecture was first published in 1972 in the Nobel Foundation yearbook, *Les Prix Nobel en 1971,* but was never delivered orally. In December 1974, by which time Solzhenitsyn was already living abroad, he traveled to Stockholm and received the Nobel insignia in person from King Carl XVI Gustaf of Sweden at the formal presentation ceremony.

The Nobel address, published in book form as *Nobelevskaia lektsiia po literature 1970 goda* (1972; translated as *Nobel Lecture,* 1972), is Solzhenitsyn's most sustained statement on the meaning and function of literature. The lecture opens with a contrast between two kinds of writers—a comparison that at the start reveals Solzhenitsyn's spiritual orientation: one writer "imagines himself the creator of an independent spiritual world," while the other "acknowledges a higher power above him and joyfully works as a common apprentice under God's heaven." The artist of the second kind will not allow literature to be strictly self-referential but will seek to relate literature to life. In a world riven by irreconcilably conflicting worldviews, Solzhenitsyn hopes that perhaps beauty can move and persuade when goodness and truth no longer suffice and that through aesthetic instrumentation beauty might even cultivate goodness and truth and in that sense "save the world." Because literature is capable of transmitting "condensed and irrefutable human experience" from generation to generation and from nation to nation, Solzhenitsyn thinks of world literature as "the one great heart that beats for the cares and misfortunes of our world."

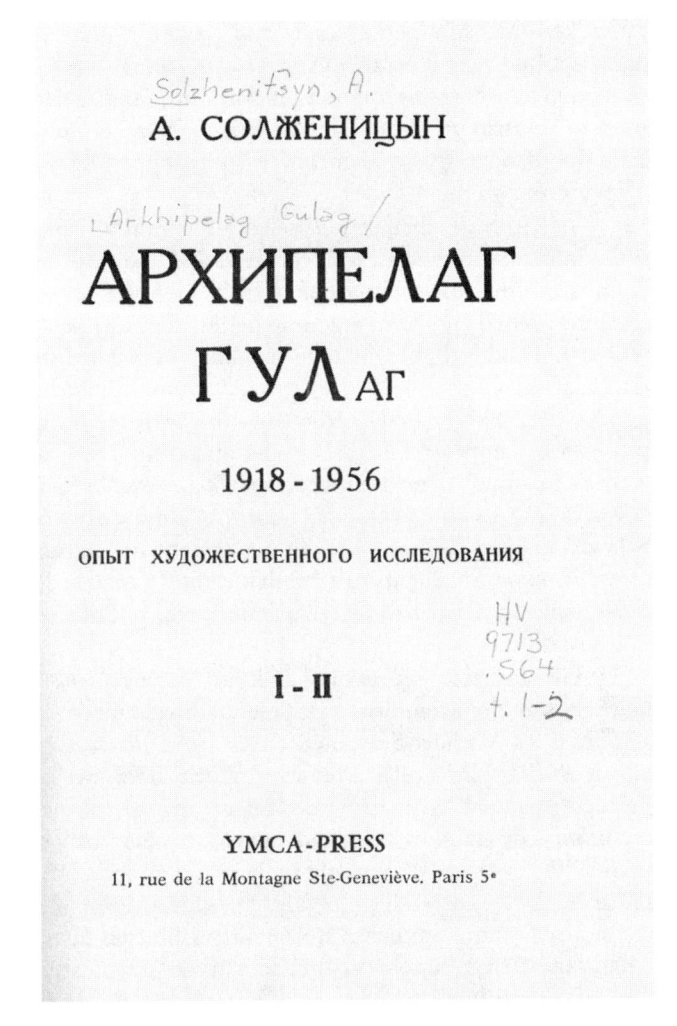

*Title page for Solzhenitsyn's* Arkhipelag GULag, 1918–1956 *(1973–1975; translated as* The Gulag Archipelago, 1918–1956, *1974–1978), his internationally acclaimed indictment of the Soviet penal system that caused his expulsion from the Soviet Union after it was published in 1973 (Thomas Cooper Library, University of South Carolina)*

The years 1970–1972 mark the period of the most intense conflict between Solzhenitsyn and the Soviet authorities, especially the KGB. The nuclear physicist Andrei Dmitrievich Sakharov, who had developed reservations about the Soviet role in the world, and Solzhenitsyn were thrown into an alliance as the two leading dissenters in the land. Each of these men has described the significant differences of perspective that made their alliance a somewhat uneasy one, with Solzhenitsyn challenging Enlightenment principles to which Sakharov was committed; for the most part, however, mutual respect characterized their relationship. While Western support provided crucial cover for both men, official harassment of each turned physically threatening in 1971; in Solzhenitsyn's case KGB agents ransacked his summer cottage and severely beat a friend of his; visited Solzhenitsyn's birthplace in search of compromising information about him; and even tried to assassinate him. (The last episode is recounted by a KGB operative and included in an appendix to "Nevidimki.")

In 1972 Solzhenitsyn's religious commitments came into clear public view. To Patriarch Pimen of the Russian Orthodox Church he wrote an open letter (first published 1972 in the newspaper *Russkaia mysl'* [Russian Thought]), in which he challenged the collaboration of the Church with the atheistic regime. In addition, a 1962 prayer that Solzhenitsyn had written as a prose poem appeared in 1972 in the magazine *Time,* as well as in other Western magazines; it begins, "How easy for me to live with you, Lord, / How easy to believe in you!" Also, the first version of *Avgust chetyrnadtsatogo,* Solzhenitsyn's emphatically Russian and most explicitly Christian piece of fiction, was published in translation.

The guarded reception of *Avgust chetyrnadtsatogo* marked the first significant decline of Solzhenitsyn's standing. As Michael Scammell observes in his *Solzhenitsyn: A Biography* (1984), reviews of the book were decidedly mixed, and its appearance "disrupted the unanimity of opinion that had enveloped his earlier works." A few highly favorable reviews did appear, but more reviews expressed ambivalence, with a dominating note of disappointment. Solzhenitsyn himself later dated "the schism among my readers" and "the steady loss of supporters" (quoted in *The Oak and the Calf: Sketches of Literary Life in the Soviet Union*), both at home and abroad, with the appearance of this book. Mary McCarthy, writing for *The Saturday Review* in 1972, gave the most plainspoken explanation for the defections: Solzhenitsyn was "rude and unfair" toward "the 'liberals' and 'advanced circles' of 1914." Confident that she knew her audience, she added, "He has it in for those people, just as he would have it in for you and me, if he could overhear us talking."

During this time Solzhenitsyn's marriage was in trouble. He and Natal'ia Alekseevna had been drifting apart for several years. The radical alteration in his worldview since their marriage in 1940 and his increasingly complicated life in open confrontation with the regime did not suit her. He began a relationship with Natal'ia Dmitrievna Svetlova; Solzhenitsyn's wife made a failed attempt at suicide. Though initially turned down by the authorities, a divorce petition was finally granted in early 1973. The KGB-controlled press agency Novosti offered to help Natal'ia Alekseevna write a memoir about her former husband. Published in 1975, *V spore so vremenem* (translated as *Sanya: My Husband Aleksandr Solzhenitsyn,* 1975) was intended to damage Solzhenitsyn's reputation. Yet, he did not try to exculpate himself from blame for the break-up of his marriage; both parties were responsible. In his second wife he found a woman with a capacity for work and an intensity of spirit equal to his own.

An ominous development in the campaign against Solzhenitsyn came in mid 1973 with the arrest of Elizaveta Denisovna Voronianskaia, who was prominent among his "invisible allies," in that she had typed many of his manuscripts. Against his express order to destroy all copies of the typescript for *Arkhipelag GULag* in her possession, she kept one copy—in the event that all the other copies were destroyed. After five days of nonstop interrogation, she broke down and told the interrogators where her copy was located. Soon after this incident she died, either by suicide or, as Solzhenitsyn has guessed, by murder. With a copy of this work in the possession of the KGB, Solzhenitsyn's hand was forced. Through a Swiss lawyer, he sent word to publish the work in the West. The first volume in Russian appeared in Paris by the end of 1973 and translations of all parts of the work followed shortly thereafter. Solzhenitsyn's name again made front-page headlines.

Few books rival *Arkhipelag GULag* for its impact on the consciousness of its contemporary readers. To begin with, Solzhenitsyn introduced the word *gulag,* which became a universally recognized linguistic emblem of the horrors of twentieth-century totalitarianism. The image of archipelago in the title suggests that the network of prisons and camps that dotted the Soviet Union—but were cut off from outside life by barbed wire—resembled a multitude of islands surrounded by an alien element. Against official efforts to deny the very existence of the gulag universe, this nonfiction work aims to reveal its reality and its horrendous impact on Soviet history. Spanning eighteen hundred pages, the book consists of seven parts divided into three volumes. In an effort to come as close as he could to an exhaustive treatment of a vast subject matter, Solzhenitsyn collected testimonies from more than two hundred former *zeks*. Combining factual information with interpretive commentary, he built an overwhelming "case" against a state that had liquidated millions of its own citizens and against the ideology that drove it to do so. (Estimates of the number of victims vary widely; for the book Solzhenitsyn borrowed an émigré demographer's figure of sixty-six million.)

The concept of "literary investigation" asserted by the subtitle of the work, *Opyt khudozhestvennego issledovaniia,* is an unusual phrase and accurately expresses Solzhenitsyn's intention of bringing the methods of literary art to bear on the task of revealing an officially nonexistent but looming reality. Metaphors such as the archipelago of the title, the comparison of the camps with a sewerage system, or the pervasive animal imagery—employed to suggest dehumanization—are some obvious examples. But the main feature borrowed from literary art is the ever-present authorial voice with its impressive repertoire of rhetorical strategies. This voice holds together the huge text, in which masses of facts are presented with a running commentary that is by turns lively, outraged, sarcastic, bitterly ironic, or sorrowful. The tone shifts constantly, disturbing, challenging, or startling the reader; as a result, preserving the stance of an uninvolved observer, in the face of the facts and images marshaled by Solzhenitsyn, is made difficult. For example, the voice explains the transportation of *zeks* to the camps in a sentence that parodies logic and deflates hope for a compensating factor, which is teasingly implied by the structure: "They don't heat the car, they don't protect the other prisoners from the thieves, they don't give you enough to drink, and they don't give you enough to eat—but on the other hand they don't let you sleep either." A chapter on forced collectivization opens with a deliberately misleading understatement: "This chapter will deal with a small matter. Fifteen million souls. Fifteen million lives." The chapter on children narrates some particularly vile episodes of child torture, then concludes, "And let any country speak up that can say it has loved its children as we have ours!" The brisk and energetic language of Solzhenitsyn's voice is at a far remove from the usual idiom of scholarship. Filled with parentheses and dashes, given to authorial asides, frequently elliptical in the extreme, and everywhere enriched with camp slang and folk speech, it is a mix that is designed to counter, and sometimes to ridicule, the stilted idiom of Marxist-influenced Russian.

The organization of *Arkhipelag GULag* poses its own problems. Structuring the material according to chronology or a similarly straightforward principle might impose rational order on a methodically perverse and nightmarish world. The chapters that do trace the historical development of the gulag from 1918 to 1956 are interspersed with sections devoted to Solzhenitsyn's personal experiences or to generalized accounts of typical progression through the harsh world of prisons and camps: arrest, interrogation, transport, backbreaking labor, and death. Other chapters describe disparate groups, such as guards, thieves, women, children, and religious believers. Sometimes a series of consecutive chapters elucidates a single theme, such as escape. Overall, *Arkhipelag GULag* moves from a long recitation of misery and grief to a climactic celebration of hope. Solzhenitsyn's characteristic ending on a note of hope—a constant feature of his essays and speeches—is an organic by-product of his religious convictions.

While *Arkhipelag GULag* might invite analysis in political terms, Solzhenitsyn emphatically warns against that approach: "Let the reader who expects this book to be a political exposé slam its covers shut right now." He proceeds to explicate the moral vision that governs all of his writing, including this book. In a passage of central importance he writes of "the line dividing good and evil" and states that this division passes not between good and bad classes of people, as Marxists and other ideologues prefer, but "through the heart of every human being." Solzhenitsyn fingers ideology as the ultimate culprit. (For him, "ideology" is likely not a neutral term synonymous with "worldview" but represents a sociopolitical program rooted in utopianism and committed to social engineering.) In classic literature villains generally recognize the immoral nature of their acts, he explains, but ideology can justify evil and allow the evildoer to "believe that what he's doing is good" and to receive praise and honors. The moral vision of the work reaches its clearest expression in the chapter titled "The Ascent." Although prison corrupts many, others grow through suffering, and Solzhenitsyn is not alone in coming to say *"Bless you, prison"* for having opened his eyes to moral reality. This seeming apotheosis is, however, immediately followed by an acknowledgment of the extraordinary fortune that allowed him to reach this quintessentially Christian conclusion—and to be able to tell about it: "But from the burial mounds I hear a response: 'It's very well for you to say that—you who've come through alive.'" This qualification is an archetypal example of Solzhenitsyn's resolutely unsentimental view of the world as well as of the inner dialogue that energizes the entire text.

At the time of its publication Solzhenitsyn predicted that *Arkhipelag GULag* was destined to affect the course of history. He cited with relish responses in Western newspapers recognizing the historical significance of the work, such as a 1974 editorial statement from the *Frankfurter Allgemeine*: "The time may come when we date the beginning of the collapse of the Soviet system from the appearance of *Gulag*." Reviewing *Arkhipelag GULag* that year for *The Atlantic Monthly*, Harrison Salisbury predicted of Solzhenitsyn that "one hundred years from now all the world (including the Russian world) will bow to his name when most others have been forgotten." Western enthusiasm for *Arkhipelag GULag* approached that for *Odin den' Ivana Denisovicha* of more than a decade earlier. Although much of the basic information about Soviet prison camps had already appeared in scholarly studies and various memoirs, this work broke through a shell of skepticism and imprinted upon Western consciousness the enormity of the atrocities perpetrated by the Soviet regime upon its own citizens. The image that had been painstakingly

*Solzhenitsyn after receiving the 1970 Nobel Prize in literature from King Carl XVI Gustaf of Sweden (far right), Stockholm, December 1974. When the prize was announced, Solzhenitsyn refused to leave Russia, and authorities blocked attempts to present the award in Moscow. The official ceremony took place after Solzhenitsyn was expelled from the Soviet Union (Nobel Foundation).*

cultivated by the regime received a blow from which it never fully recovered, and accounts of the subsequent demise of the Soviet Union regularly mention *Arkhipelag GULag* and *Odin den' Ivana Denisovicha* as contributing factors. In France a whole generation of young intellectuals abandoned Marxism upon reading the book. Thus, not by coincidence did former Marxists in France eventually produce *Le livre noir du communisme: Crimes, terreur, répression* (1997; translated as *The Black Book of Communism: Crimes, Terror, Repression*, 1999), a collection that corroborates much of what Solzhenitsyn first revealed. *Arkhipelag GULag* has been translated into thirty-five languages, and more than thirty million copies of the book have been sold.

The publication of *Arkhipelag GULag* was the immediate cause of Solzhenitsyn's expulsion to the West. On 12 February 1974 a sizable cadre of KGB operatives came to his apartment to arrest him. They took him to Lefortovo prison, where he endured the manifold indignities that he had described in "Arest" (Arrest), the opening chapter of *Arkhipelag GULag*. He was charged with treason and stripped of his citizenship. The next day he was put on a plane bound for West Germany; he learned where he was going only when he saw the airport sign for Frankfurt am Main. The Western press carried daily installments of the drama of his exile. Upon his departure Solzhenitsyn left behind for the public a brief statement, "Zhit' ne po lzhi" (published 14–16 February in several émigré newspapers; appeared in translation as "Live Not by Lies," in *The Daily Express* [London], 1974). In his lexicon "the lie" is a synonym for ideology.

Accolades were heaped upon Solzhenitsyn when he arrived in the West, and they ran to superlatives. For example, on 15 February 1974, in *The Times* of London, he was called "the man who is for the moment the most famous person in the western world." This adulatory mood was not to last, for as he arrived in the West he was plagued by what may be called "the Solzhenitsyn question." This phrase refers to the controversies aroused by his essays, speeches, and interviews exploring nonliterary themes. The first significant episode virtually coincided with the date of his banishment and involved *Pis'mo vozhdiam Sovetskogo Soiuza* (1974; translated as *Letter to the Soviet Leaders*, 1974). Solzhenitsyn had sent the letter privately to the Kremlin on 5 September 1973; receiving no reply, he then released it to the public shortly before his arrest. Thus, Western readers had two new publications to consider—the massive *Arkhipelag GULag* and the brief letter.

In the letter Solzhenitsyn, turning practical in the modest hope that his advice will be taken to heart, recommends that Soviet leaders retain their power but abandon Marxist ideology. This suggestion, offered in the spirit of compromise as the first stage of a post-Soviet scenario, dovetails with his suggestion to the citizenry in "Zhit' ne po lzhi" to leave the falsehoods of ideology behind. Once rid of the mandates of an ideology of world revolution, the leaders could attend to domestic reforms, and to that end Solzhenitsyn offers such proposals as husbanding natural resources according to the insights of the then-prominent Club of Rome (an international think tank of scientists, economists, business professionals, civil servants, and politicians); developing the underpopulated northeastern region of Russia; and reducing Soviet military might to the level needed only for defense against possible Chinese encroachments. The leaders could afford to turn their attention inward, he explained, because the West, having lost its spiritual moorings, had become too weak in will to take Cold War advantage of a Soviet shift to domestic priorities. The explicitly political suggestions of the letter are moderate and gradualist in nature—reformist rather than revolutionary. Without the prop of ideology, Solzhenitsyn suggests, totalitarianism will give way to authoritarianism, serving as an intermediate arrangement during the course of increasing liberation for individuals and social institutions.

Shortly after *Pis'mo vozhdiam Sovetskogo Soiuza* appeared, Solzhenitsyn explained that he foresaw an era of transition and that his real audience consisted of leaders to come—that is, after the "stagnation" of Leonid Il'ich Brezhnev's rule. At the time that the letter was published, however, his suggestions shocked many Western readers. William Safire, writing on 18 February 1974 in *The New York Times*, announced himself "the first on my block to feel misgivings" about the newcomer, and he correctly predicted that the hero worship of the moment was mere trendiness and would soon dissipate. Liberals unaccustomed to defending the United States expressed resentment at Solzhenitsyn's disparagements at the moral fiber of their country. Many commentators fixed their attention more on what the letter did not say than on what it did say—for example, it did not urge democracy upon the Soviet leaders. The Western reception of the text caused issues of genre (pamphlet) and audience (Soviet leaders) to be overlooked. As a result, at the very time when Solzhenitsyn was being lauded for *Arkhipelag GULag*, he was rebuked for *Pis'mo vozhdiam Sovetskogo Soiuza*. Moreover, in an incongruous twist, reaction to the modest pamphlet outweighed the reception for *Arkhipelag GULag* in determining subsequent Western attitudes toward the author of both. In a 1974 piece for *The Columbia Journalism Review*, human-rights activist Jeri Laber, who earlier had written appreciatively about Solzhenitsyn's fiction, now asserted that "he is not the 'liberal' we would like him to be." That Solzhenitsyn was not a liberal was a judgment that many commentators came to repeat with only slight variations in wording. Laber added, "Reactionary, authoritarian, chauvinistic—hardly adjectives that sit comfortably with the typical image of a freedom-fighter and Nobel Prize winner." Other commentators underwent much the same shift and supplemented Laber's list of adjectives: Solzhenitsyn was theocratic, fundamentalist, messianic, monarchist, medieval, utopian, and fanatical. These reevaluations were in the process of merging into a negative consensus that later became conventional wisdom among molders of Western opinion. This new climate provided the context for Secretary of State Henry Kissinger's decision to recommend against welcoming Solzhenitsyn to the White House for a visit.

Also in 1974 Solzhenitsyn edited a collection of articles titled *Iz-pod glyb* (translated as *From Under the Rubble*, 1975). His intention with this publication, which comprises eleven essays by seven contributors—one of them Solzhenitsyn, who wrote three pieces—was to set forth a vision of spiritual renewal for Russia. It was designed to update two well-known collective manifestos published in the prerevolutionary and immediately postrevolutionary periods, *Vekhi: Sbornik statei o russkoi intelligentsii* (1909; translated as *Landmarks: A Collection of Essays on the Russian Intelligentsia*, 1977) and *Iz glubiny: Sbornik statei o russkoi revoliutsii* (1918; translated as *Out of the Depths=De Profundis*, 1986). Members of each of the groups had journeyed from socialist convictions to spiritual beliefs. Just as the contributors to *Vekhi* and *Iz glubiny* endeavored to spare Russia the ideology-induced calamities looming on the horizon, so did their heirs in the late Soviet period seek to point the way out of the misfortunes that had befallen their homeland. The 1974 collection includes Solzhenitsyn's "Raskaianie i samoogranichenie kak kategorii natsional'noi zhizni" (translated in *From Under the Rubble* as "Repentance and Self-Limitation in the Life of Nations"). By his own reckoning it is one of his most important essays, in

*Solzhenitsyn at Harvard University, 8 June 1978 (© Bettmann/CORBIS)*

which the universal moral principles widely seen as applicable to individuals are applied to whole nations.

Not long after his exile began, Solzhenitsyn settled in Zurich, Switzerland, where his wife and their family—which by now included sons Yermolai, Ignat, and Stephan—soon were allowed to join him. (Natal'ia Dmitrievna's son by a previous marriage and her mother also were part of the household.) Two years later, in 1976, Solzhenitsyn purchased a chalet on fifty wooded hillside acres outside the village of Cavendish, Vermont, and there the family lived for the next eighteen years. This location brought the advantages of substantial privacy; access to rich American library holdings; and for his sons—as Solzhenitsyn pointed out repeatedly—exposure to a major world language. He had a chain-link fence put up around the property to keep out hunters and snowmobilers; Natal'ia Dmitrievna later semiplayfully added journalists to the list. (This fence evoked press speculation about Solzhenitsyn's alleged need for prison-like enclosures.)

Invitations for interviews and public appearances flooded in, and, relishing his newfound freedom to speak out, Solzhenitsyn at first consented to many of them. Although heretofore he had written almost exclusively about his homeland, on these occasions he satisfied his hosts' curiosity to know what he thought about the West. In 1975 he participated in a symposium for French television, spoke in Washington and New York under the auspices of the AFL-CIO (the leading labor organization in the United States), and addressed the United States Congress. In 1976 he made two appearances on British television and radio. Also in 1976 he gave a speech at the Hoover Institution of Stanford University, which had designated him an honorary fellow and provided him access to its rich archives for his research; for this occasion he and his wife drove across the United States. These and other public events brought him considerable attention but a decidedly mixed reception. Among Solzhenitsyn's views that were perceived as contentious were his unremitting enmity toward Marxist ideology, his belief that United States foreign policy of détente toward the Soviet Union was based on illusion, his judgment that moral laxity and shaky political courage characterized Western political behavior, and his accusation that the West sometimes failed to implement its vaunted principles of democracy and freedom of speech. Generally lost in the largely defensive reactions of Western auditors were the nuances in his arguments and his expressions of broad appreciation of Western ways. His frequently combative tone also impaired the persuasiveness of his message; in particular, it obscured the fundamental moderation that has characterized his political views. The writer who had been honored for his revelations about Soviet realities was mostly rebuffed when he turned his attention to Western issues. He soon retired from the field of public pronouncements and turned his attention to the main work of his life, the historical cycle that had commenced with *Avgust chetyrnadtsatogo*.

Despite the distractions accompanying his status as a celebrity, Solzhenitsyn kept his attention trained on Russian themes. In 1975 *Bodalsia telenok s dubom*, a personal account of his running battle with the Soviet authorities, was published. The title comes from a Russian proverb about a calf who tries in vain to butt down a great oak tree. The title is not only self-deprecating but also implicitly tongue-in-cheek, in that Solzhenitsyn did not consider his odds of success as hopeless as the proverb suggests. He avoids calling these reminiscences "memoirs," supplying instead the subtitle *Ocherki literaturnoi zhizni*. Several sections of *Bodalsia telenok s dubom* were written intermittently from 1967 onward, and the book ends with a rousing section on his 1974 arrest and forced departure from the U.S.S.R. There is also a large appendix of invaluable documentary materials, including many letters. Taken together and described by Solzhenitsyn as an "agglomeration of lean-tos and annexes," these reminiscences cover the years 1961–1974.

*Bodalsia telenok s dubom* is the essential source of information about key events such as the publication of *Odin den' Ivana Denisovicha*, the efforts to follow up that success with other approved publications, the ceaseless rounds of struggle between Solzhenitsyn and literary and political authorities, and his ongoing work on major projects, including *Arkhipelag GULag* and *Krasnoe koleso* (which was first called "R-17"). Throughout, Solzhenitsyn is acutely conscious of his mission as a truth-telling writer. He is equally aware that one false step vis-à-vis officialdom could imperil his mission and even his life. Not infrequently, he resorts to military imagery to convey his sense of being locked in mortal combat with an implacable foe. Even as he justifiably revels in his impressive successes, he is unsparing about his missteps and humiliating failures. The dual nature of such self-analysis is most clearly on display in his account of the climactic event of the plotline of *Bodalsia telenok s dubom*—his arrest and expulsion from the Soviet Union in early 1974. He pitilessly describes the "state of witless shock" that left him confused and unsteady when KGB officers arrived at his door to take him away. He regains control of himself soon enough, however, and the prevailing tone during this crisis is one of defiance toward the authorities.

Another prominent focus of this work is Tvardovsky, the editor of *Novyi mir* and Solzhenitsyn's first and most important publisher. Solzhenitsyn was delighted by the peasant core of Tvardovsky's personality, encouraged by his support, and thrilled by his exquisite literary taste. Yet, Tvardovsky's inability to shake free of his loyalty to the Party frustrated Solzhenitsyn; the editor's alcoholic excesses also bewildered him. Despite the complications and conflicts in the friendship, their mutual admiration was genuine. The general culture of *Novyi mir* was another matter. Despite the reputation of the journal for liberalism, the petty office intrigues and what Solzhenitsyn considered exaggerated caution created an atmosphere that he found stifling. By the time *The Oak and the Calf* was published in 1980, the Western reception of it—which fell along predictable ideological lines—was mixed. One common reason for disapproval was Solzhenitsyn's allegedly excessive harshness toward Tvardovsky. For the most part, however, the book won Western reviewers over with its lively style; some critics placed it near the top of Solzhenitsyn's canon.

In 1975 Solzhenitsyn published *Lenin v Tsiurikhe* (translated as *Lenin in Zurich*, 1976), a classic example of how he subsumes history into literature. In this volume he collocates the series of chapters on Lenin, eleven chapters in all, from three "knots," or fascicles, of *Krasnoe koleso*. Solzhenitsyn published *Lenin v Tsiurikhe* when he did because the appearance of the complete *Krasnoe koleso* was then still years away, and the idea of coming to terms with Lenin was part of the conversation about the nature of the Soviet system that Solzhenitsyn was trying to foster. With the completion of the historical cycle, these chapters have been restored to their rightful places and can be read in their contexts. As four consecutive chapters of *V kruge pervom* had rendered a portrait of Stalin, so the chapters in *Lenin v Tsiurikhe* depict the character of Lenin. For both portrayals Solzhenitsyn relied on extensive research and tried to render a faithful account of both the external events and the inner lives of his controversial subjects. In these works he uses internal monologue as a means to reveal the essence of each man. The portrait of Lenin is fuller than the portrait of Stalin—as befits Lenin's more multifaceted personality and Solzhenitsyn's view of his greater historical importance. Solzhenitsyn's Lenin is a fully realized, three-dimensional character with believable motives who bears moral responsibility for bringing much evil into the world; in his case the line dividing good and evil is pushed far to one side.

In 1977 Solzhenitsyn announced the establishment of the Russian Memoir Library, conceived as a depository of unpublished materials that would keep alive the truth of modern Russian history in the face of ongoing Soviet efforts to distort or erase factual evidence. Many Russian émigrés sent in their memoirs, letters, and photographs. Solzhenitsyn eventually funded the publication of more than a dozen book-length manuscripts considered to be of the greatest interest.

On 8 June 1978 Solzhenitsyn came out of seclusion to present the commencement address at Harvard University. Press coverage was enormous, and the speech was destined to become the best-known of his many public addresses in the West. In the speech, after a brief preface of congratulations to the graduates and a characterization of himself as a friend of the West, Solzhenitsyn launches into a critique of the current moral condition of the West, taking issue with such epiphenomena as commercial advertising, "TV stupor," "intolerable" popular music, excessive litigiousness, and a lack of energetic resistance to crime and terrorism. He rebukes both the press and the intelligentsia—the former for its hasty and superficial judgments, the latter for its loss of willpower and decline of courage. After an extensive cataloguing of the problems of the West, the peroration of the address reveals Solzhenitsyn's religious cast of mind, in that he proposes remedies to the problems in overtly spiritual terms. Specifically, he urges the West to move beyond the "autonomous irreligious humanistic consciousness" that it embraced at the time of the Enlightenment and to reach "a new level of life," in which both physical and spiritual aspects of human existence can be cultivated equally.

The denunciation of secular humanism at Harvard, a citadel of enlightened thought, did not curry favor with an audience that had gathered for the purpose of celebration. A clamor of responses to Solzhenitsyn's address, most of them sharply negative, ensued. Most reviews conceded his personal greatness but passed quickly into argumentation against various of his points. Few of the respondents acknowledged that his criticisms of Western weakness were offered in friendship to help the West strengthen its resolve, and scant attention was paid to the climactic concluding paragraphs of the speech. This event marks a defining moment in the Western elites' rejection of Solzhenitsyn.

In 1978 the text of the commencement speech in English was published in a bilingual edition titled *A World Split Apart;* the speech in original Russian, featured in this edition, is called "Raskolotyi mir." Two years later *Solzhenitsyn at Harvard* was published. It has a series of early reviews, and appended are six longer reflections, which were written later and are less defensive, more appreciative, and considerably more nuanced than the reviews. The organization of the book suggests that the press had been hasty and superficial in its reaction to the speech, but the damage to Solzhenitsyn's reputation had been done. His writings have continued to attract sympathetic readers in substantial numbers, but antipathy, in varying degrees, informs most Western journalistic commentary about him.

During the 1980s Solzhenitsyn permitted himself relatively few interruptions from his work on *Krasnoe koleso*. In 1980 he wrote a long essay titled "Chem grozit Amerike plokhoe ponimanie Rossii" (published that year in *Vestnik R. Kh. D.;* translated in *Foreign Affairs* as "Misconceptions about Russia Are a Threat to America," 1980) for the journal *Foreign Affairs*. In 1981 the essay came out in book form as *The Mortal Danger: How Misconceptions about Russia Imperil America*. This highly critical foray into the field of Russianist scholarship in the American academy did not help his reputation among Sovietologists. In 1983 Solzhenitsyn received the Templeton Prize for Progress in Religion and traveled to London to give an acceptance speech. This speech succinctly summarizes Solzhenitsyn's fundamental understanding of the distinctive nature of the twentieth century as a whole. Great disasters befell Russia, he declares, because "men have forgotten God." Moreover, the same "flaw of a consciousness lacking all divine dimension" affects the world as a whole and is the "principal trait" of the century.

In the second half of the 1980s the Soviet Union underwent momentous changes as Mikhail Sergeevich Gorbachev rose to power. The new policy of glasnost paved the way for renewed attention to Solzhenitsyn. In 1988 one Moscow periodical urged that the treason charges against him be dropped and his citizenship restored. Other Soviet publications explored the possibility of publishing his works. *Novyi mir* arranged with him to publish selections from *Arkhipelag GULag* in 1989, with *V kruge pervom* and *Rakovyi korpus* to follow. Literary gatherings were scheduled to celebrate his seventieth birthday in 1988; the Politburo interfered with these plans, however, and several events were simply canceled. Permission to publish any part of *Arkhipelag GULag* was also denied.

Yet, the foundations of the Soviet edifice were already weak, and *Arkhipelag GULag,* though not legally published in the Soviet Union, already had played a part in the process of undermining them. In 1989 Soviet hegemony over large parts of Eastern and Central Europe came to an end, with the fall of the Berlin Wall in November most visibly symbolizing the demise. In the wake of these events the U.S.S.R. itself disintegrated into its constituent parts, and on Christmas Day of 1991 the red flag over the Kremlin was lowered for the last time. Whether Gorbachev should be credited for liberalizing the society over which he

*Solzhenitsyn with his sons, Ignat, Yermolai, and Stephan, in Vermont, circa 1978 (courtesy of the Solzhenitsyn family)*

governed or faulted for ineffectuality in pursuing his announced goal of reforming the state system remains debatable. Similarly, how much credit for the breakup of the Soviet Union should go to the pressures for change that emanated from Western governments is an open question. A strong contributing factor, perhaps a governing one, is that the Soviet Union suffered from a loss of faith, even among its leaders, in the ideology that had justified its vast social experiment. Solzhenitsyn had made exactly this point long before, in *Pis'mo vozhdiam Sovetskogo Soiuza*. As for the role of *Arkhipelag GULag* in bringing down the Soviet Union, American diplomat George Kennan's 1974 remarks about the work sounded like fulfilled prophecy in 1991: "It is too large for the craw of the Soviet propaganda machine. It will stick there, with increasing discomfort, until it has done its work."

Foreseeing as few did that the collapse of the Soviet Union was imminent, Solzhenitsyn wrote an essay on the reconstruction of Russia. It appeared in September 1990 in the Moscow-based periodicals *Komsomol'skaia pravda* and *Literaturnaia gazeta* and was published in book form as *Kak nam obustroit' Rossiiu? Posil'nye soobrazheniia* (1990; translated as *Rebuilding Russia: Reflections and Tentative Proposals,* 1991). With the Soviet system crumbling, Solzhenitsyn offered advice about how to avoid being crushed beneath the rubble. The essay must be seen as a sequel to the 1973 *Pis'mo vozhdiam Sovetskogo Soiuza* in its sketch of a pragmatic political program, but the audience now addressed not the leaders but, as with "Zhit' ne po lzhi," the citizenry at large. The two halves of the essay address short-term and long-term needs, respectively. Solzhenitsyn makes clear his commitments to democracy (developed from the ground up, rather than imposed by fiat from above); a free market (but with a social safety net); and private ownership of land (introduced gradually). He devotes considerable attention to post-Soviet relationships between Russians and non-Russians. He recommends that Russia develop by stages its own indigenous form of democracy, rather than borrow procedures directly from the modern West, by drawing on such historically embedded elements as the nineteenth-century zemstvo system, in which the populace chose its local leaders. The picture that emerges is similar to early American republicanism, with local leaders selecting their best members for the next largest unit of government, all the way up to the central government. Throughout, the tone of the essay is solicitous and earnest, as befits the moderate positions it espouses. The range of responses to the essay fell along predictable lines, predetermined by the commentators' political views and their attitudes toward the author—though with the balance this time tipping toward respectfulness, somewhat more so in Russia than in the West.

Solzhenitsyn's concern with the manifold losses suffered by Russia in the twentieth century extends to language in the technical sense, and he is renowned for leavening his writing with words outside the familiar lexical terrain as a way to counteract what he considers the radical impoverishment of the Russian vocabulary. Apart from items that he himself has formed in accordance with the inherent rules of Russian word formation, Solzhenitsyn has diligently collected what he calls "unjustly forgotten" words culled from special dictionaries and various literary works, with his favorite source being Vladimir Ivanovich Dal's four-volume *Tolkovyi slovar' zhivogo velikorusskogo iazyka* (Dictionary of the Living Great Russian Language, 1863–1866). In 1990 Solzhenitsyn published his collection in the form of an alphabetical compilation that included some thirty-five thousand items, under the title *Russkii slovar' iazykovogo rasshireniia* (Russian Dictionary of Lexical Augmentation). It joins several other statements on language, notably Solzhenitsyn's essay "Nekotorye grammaticheskie soobrazheniia" (Select Observations on Grammar, published 1983 in his *Sobranie sochinenii*).

The fall from power of the Soviet leaders cleared the way for Solzhenitsyn to send to press those parts of *Bodalsia telenok s dubom* that he had initially held back to protect the identities of various individuals. These missing parts bore the title "Nevidimki" and appeared in late 1991 in two issues of *Novyi mir* and thereafter in translation. A 1996 edition of *Bodalsia telenok s dubom* incorporates "Nevidimki" as a "fifth supplement."

"Nevidimki" comprises fourteen sketches, each focused on an individual or a group who had been part of the secret network of helpers involved in all phases of Solzhenitsyn's work. The network expanded to include foreigners—among them journalists, who also maintained the trust. The manifold tasks undertaken on Solzhenitsyn's behalf included typing texts; transporting and hiding manuscripts; retyping texts (before the advent of computers) to accommodate the nearly endless flow of revisions and emendations; keeping track of the manuscripts and their various locations; destroying caches of outdated material; and transmitting finished works to their intended recipients in the West. The literary element of characterization, a strength in Solzhenitsyn's fiction, is on full display in these sketches. Most of the helpers were women. The longest sketch describes the author's right-hand intimate, Elena Tsezarevna Chukovskaia, granddaughter of Kornei Ivanovich Chukovsky, a well-known writer of children's literature. Through collaboration they came to the painful realization that their worldviews were in serious conflict. In another sketch the reader learns that one of the helpers became the author's second wife; the highly discreet narration of the love story between Solzhenitsyn and Natal'ia Dmitrievna is among the most memorable sections of the book. Some of the personages are the real-life prototypes for fictional characters such as Potapov of *V kruge pervom* and the Kadmins of *Rakovyi korpus*. Others are old gulag friends, most notably Arnold Susi and Georgii Tenno, who helped provide Solzhenitsyn with a safe haven in Estonia for writing *Arkhipelag GULag*. The story of the furtive work on this book is highly dramatic. At his Estonian "Hiding Place" during the winters of 1965–1966 and 1966–1967, Solzhenitsyn wrote at a feverish pace. The cumulative 146 days of labor—in typical fashion he gives an exact figure—marked for him "the highest point in my feelings of victory and of isolation from the world." Not once as he composed did he have the whole manuscript on his desk. At one time all copies of the work were in the same place, and had the KGB confiscated that cache, he declares, he could never have reconstructed the whole work. The main character in these sketches is, of necessity, the author himself. Despite the high stakes of his underground life, he relishes the conspiratorial game. The exhilaration of outwitting deadly but lumbering foes creates a rare camaraderie among all of his intimates.

At this time, as the U.S.S.R. verged on collapse, Solzhenitsyn's prerequisites for returning to his homeland were soon met. All of his works were published; the charge of treason was dropped; and his citizenship was restored. Nothing remained but the trip home. His popularity in Russia soared. One poll in St. Petersburg (formerly Leningrad) listed him as the runaway first choice to become the president of the new Russia: 48 percent were for him (with Boris Nikolaevich Yeltsin as a runner-up at 18 percent). Yet, Solzhenitsyn delayed his return to Russia, and impatience with him grew. One reason for the delay is that he had no interest in pursuing political office. More important, however, was that he was closing in on the completion of *Krasnoe koleso*. What he considered the chief work of his life had to be finished before he became ineluctably caught up in the public life of the nation. The widespread perception in both the West and the East about the timing of Solzhenitsyn's move to Russia is that he missed his magic moment and waited too long.

In 1993, with the work on *Krasnoe koleso* behind him, Solzhenitsyn gave speeches and interviews of farewell to the West. All but one of these interviews were delivered in Europe rather than in the United States, his home for eighteen years; in his view the American elites had shown little interest in listening to him. His travels in Europe that year included a visit to France, the country where his impact on intellectual life was felt most strongly; in the Vendée region he spoke to an audience of thirty thousand. He had an hour-and-a-half-long audience with Pope John Paul II. His most important address on this trip was delivered to the International Academy of Philosophy, a Roman Catholic institution in Liechtenstein. This speech reiterates several of the themes presented in his 1978 address at Harvard, with the criticism of the Enlightenment now focused on the doctrine of progress and the divorce of morality from politics. In terms of political themes in the speech, he praises the West for its stable rule of law. If the end of the Cold War had rendered obsolete some of his earlier warnings to the West, it also had vindicated, in his opinion, his understanding of the twentieth century as a whole. In addition, the speech shows to a certain degree a shift away from the political and toward the personal. Instead of the stridency that irked some commentators about his earlier speeches, a softened, measured tone prevails on this occasion.

Two months before his departure for Russia, Solzhenitsyn wrote his last work in exile, *"Russkii vopros" k kontsu XX veka* (published in *Novyi mir,* 1994; published in book form, 1995; translated as *"The Russian Question" at the End of the Twentieth Century,* 1995). Whereas *Krasnoe koleso* took nearly six thousand pages to cover four years (1914–1917), the new book allots a little more than a hundred pages to cover four centuries of Russian history. The purpose of this historical sketch is to explain how Russia arrived at what Solzhenitsyn terms its third "Time of Troubles"—the early seventeenth century and the year 1917 are the two occasions that precede "the Great Russian Catastrophe of the 1990s." In his view the resources for coping with the crisis were so severely limited that the Russian question now was, "Shall our people *be* or *not be*?" If Russia is to survive as a people, he concludes, "We must build a *moral* Russia, or none at all—it would not then matter anyhow."

In May 1994 Solzhenitsyn returned home to Russia. He reentered through the "back door" of the country: rather than using the standard portal of Sheremet'evo airport in Moscow, he flew across the Pacific Ocean. Some reporters believed that in using a different route, he was snubbing Moscow, but all were struck by his dramatic gesture of landing first in Magadan, the capital of the Kolyma region, where the harshest prison camps had been located—thus the symbolic capital of the gulag. The next stop was Vladivostok, the main Pacific port city in Russia. There he received a hero's welcome from four thousand citizens, who had been standing in the rain for hours waiting to hear him speak. This public address was his first ever to a large audience of fellow Russians. He then launched a fifty-five-day train trip westward across Russia, with frequent stops to talk with citizens. When possible, he reminisced with other former *zeks*. A crew from the British Broadcasting Company went along and filmed the whistle-stop tour. He filled his notebook with statements by the people, and he promised to deliver their words to the leaders once he reached Moscow. A turnout estimated at ten thousand to fifteen thousand people met Solzhenitsyn's train as it pulled into Yaroslavsky Station in Moscow. In contrast to the warmth expressed toward him by most ordinary citizens, his ensuing reception by the Moscow intelligentsia tended toward the negative, in this sense mirroring the viewpoint of Western intellectuals. After a trip to his former home territory in southern Russia, Solzhenitsyn and his wife settled on the outskirts of Moscow.

During his first year back on Russian soil, Solzhenitsyn maintained a relatively high profile. In the first month he gave a speech in which he used the word *oligarkhiia* (oligarchy) to describe the real power structure in the new Russia. In the late summer and early fall of 1994 he made another tour—to Mil'tsevo, Riazan', and Rostov to visit his old haunts. In October 1994 he addressed the Duma. He scolded the leaders for sham reforms and an absence of authentic democracy—in short, for pursuing the worst possible path out from under the rubble of communism; the legislators were tepid in their reactions. He met privately with President Yeltsin, began appearing in a fortnightly television program on issues he considered crucial, and continued giving public addresses. He condemned the privatization scheme devised by Deputy Prime Minister Anatolii Borisovich Chubais for allowing insiders to snap up property that should have been distributed equitably to citizens, gave strong support to the principle of local governance at a Moscow conference for regional leaders, and pursued the same theme at a similar conference held in Samara. Within a year of his return home, Solzhenitsyn lost the limelight of public attention, but not until he had made nearly a hundred public appearances. In October 1995 his television program was dropped; the stated reason for the cancellation was not his sharp criticism of the authorities but the allegedly low ratings. (The texts of Solzhenitsyn's talks on television have been collected in *Po minute v den'* [A Minute a Day, 1995].) Whereas earlier the intellectual elites at home and abroad had commonly consid-

*Solzhenitsyn in Vermont, circa 1978, at a worktable he built himself (courtesy of the Solzhenitsyn family)*

ered Solzhenitsyn misguided, after his homecoming they increasingly pronounced him irrelevant.

Solzhenitsyn did continue to participate in public life, though with decreasing frequency. A certain decline in health, starting with a 1997 hospitalization for heart trouble, constrained his activities. In May 1997 he was elected to the Russian Academy of Sciences, to which he gave a speech in September of that year. In October 1997 he established an annual literary prize to honor contemporaries who were contributing to the preservation and development of the Russian literary tradition. The prize came from the worldwide royalties for *Arkhipelag GULag*; the same source funds a large program of assistance to thousands of needy survivors of the gulag. As another example of his selective public appearances, he spoke on the occasion of the unveiling of a monument honoring Anton Pavlovich Chekhov at the Moscow theater that bears the playwright's name. In 1998 Solzhenitsyn's eightieth birthday was publicly celebrated in several events, including a theatrical adaptation of *V kruge pervom* by director Iurii Liubimov and a concert given by cellist and conductor Mstislav Leopol'dovich Rostropovich, an old and valued friend. President Yeltsin offered Solzhenitsyn the Order of St. Andrei, the highest honor awarded to civilians in Russia, but the octogenarian, in a sharply worded rebuke, declined on grounds that there was little to celebrate in contemporary Russia.

That Solzhenitsyn continued to write abundantly is noteworthy, given his public activities and the inevitable burdens of old age, including serious back trouble. Returning to the genre of the short story, he experimented with a format he has called a "binary tale" *(dvuchastnyi rasskaz)*. This term refers to narrative structures divided into two distinct parts that are only tenuously connected in terms of plot; instead they are linked on the level of theme or thematic contrast. "Abrikosovoe varen'e" (Apricot Jam, published 1995 in *Novyi mir*) is the most interesting example of this genre among the eight binary tales that appeared in Russian periodicals in 1995–1996. In this text, part 1 consists of a letter from a deported and terminally ill former kulak, who describes the suffering experienced by him and his family after they are driven from their homestead. He also mentions in passing the apricot jam his mother used to make from the fruit of a tree that was cut down during the forced collectivization process. Part 2 juxtaposes this tale of misery and loss to the luxurious life of the recipient of the letter, an unnamed Writer (capitalized in the text); he can be identified easily with Aleksei Nikolaevich Tolstoi, a former aristocrat who managed to reach the summits of success, Soviet style, by writing extravagantly mendacious hosannas to Stalin and his regime. The story depicts the Writer mouthing some of Tolstoy's notorious statements while enjoying tea with apricot jam—the clarity and beautiful amber color of which, he suggests, would make a good model for literary language. He plans to make use of the lexical turns of phrase from the letter he has received, but he obviously has no intention of responding to the kulak's desperate plea for help.

Two stories of a different type evolved from unused material originally prepared for *Krasnoe koleso*. Published in *Novyi mir* in 1995, "Ego" (Ego) and "Na kraiakh" (On the Edge) both concern the so-called Antonov Rebellion of 1920–1922, the last significant armed resistance to Bolshevik hegemony in Russia. Two further stories, "Zheliabugskie Vyselki" (1999) and "Adling Shvenkitten" (1999), are based on Solzhenitsyn's wartime reminiscences. The first of these is a binary tale, with the frontline episode of part 1 juxtaposed with a visit to the same area in 1995.

Another genre to which Solzhenitsyn returned in his later years is the prose poem. He had written seventeen "Krokhotki" between 1958 and 1960. In the 1990s he wrote thirteen more of them, nine of which appeared in *Novyi mir* in 1997. In the foreword to the poems Solzhenitsyn stated, "It was only when I got back to Russia that I found I could write them again; living abroad–I simply couldn't do it." These reflections–mostly on journeys, landscapes, and natural phenomena–are imbued with a contemplative, even elegiac tone.

Solzhenitsyn continued as well to write sustained works of nonfiction. *Rossiia v obvale* (Russia in Collapse, 1998) conveys his view of post-Soviet conditions in Russia. It can be seen as the closing bookend to the 1990 work *Kak nam obustroit' Rossiiu,* in which he laid out advice for Russia to follow (advice that was not heeded). *Rossiia v obvale* is filled with alarm, bordering on despair, at the frightening decline in those spheres of life without which civilized existence becomes impossible, such as education and medical care.

Between 1997 and 2004 Solzhenitsyn published thirteen essays of literary commentary on modern Russian authors ranging from Chekhov to Joseph Brodsky, all under the series title "Literaturnaia kollektsiia" (Literary Miscellany) in the journal *Novyi mir*. In some instances Solzhenitsyn comments on multiple works of a particular writer–stories by Chekhov or poems by Brodsky; at other times he focuses on a single literary production, such as Andrei Bely's avant-garde 1913 novel *Peterburg* (translated as *Petersburg,* 1959). In a brief preface to the first installment of the series Solzhenitsyn explains that what he is offering are notes he had made for himself as he reread selected Russian authors and works in the late 1980s and early 1990s. He states that although he originally had not intended these remarks for print, he changed his mind when he became aware of the extent to which the very memory of some outstanding Russian literary works had faded among his countrymen. He agreed to have these notes published on the condition that he would not have to make revisions, and this provision explains the fragmentary appearance of some of his texts. That Solzhenitsyn has chosen to allot considerable attention to the purely lexical aspect of the works surveyed–to the point of including lists of words and expressions that in his opinion enrich the Russian lexicon–is also quite consistent with his concerns about what he sees as the ongoing impoverishment of the Russian vocabulary. The most pervasive feature of the series is Solzhenitsyn's focus on the cognitive and informational aspect of the works he has chosen to examine. Of specific interest to him is the depiction of physical conditions or historical events that have not received a full portrayal elsewhere, as well as an evaluation of attitudes that, in his opinion, have played a significant role in Russian history. An example of the latter is his often-repeated objection to what he considers the hackneyed manner in which many authors have chosen to present prerevolutionary life. One of Solzhenitsyn's essays, a negative evaluation of Brodsky (he criticizes the poet for a lack of emotion and an excessive reliance on irony) has aroused considerable controversy.

Solzhenitsyn then turned his attention to the longstanding troubled relationship between Russians and Jews and produced *Dvesti let vmeste, 1795–1995* (Two Hundred Years Together, 1795-1995), a two-volume investigation of the theme published in 2001-2002. As Solzhenitsyn writes in his foreword, the emotion that guided him throughout was "a quest for all points of common understanding, and all possible paths into the future, cleansed from the acrimony of the past." In the chapters that take the story up to the mid nineteenth century he essentially follows the established mainline accounts of the subject, though never allowing himself to forget the abrupt and catastrophic twist in Russian history (the 1917 Revolution) addressed in the first volume. For this reason he laments the unperceptive, heavy-handed, and often maddeningly obtuse government policies toward the Jews–an approach that ultimately contributed to the 1917 Revolution. The study adopts a more independent, original approach as the narrative enters the late nineteenth and early twentieth centuries. Solzhenitsyn has for several decades immersed himself in the prehistory of the Russian Revolution (his research is reflected in the ten-volume *Krasnoe koleso*), and his unparalleled knowledge of the interplay of social, political, and ideological forces during this period allows him to show persuasively how the Jewish theme fits into the general context. In the second volume Solzhenitsyn traces the vicissitudes of Russian-Jewish relations during the seven decades of Soviet rule. In researching this period, he inevitably needed to confront the multitude of bitter charges and countercharges that had accumulated in the collective memory of both groups, doing so with a genuine effort to be fair but, predictably enough, without satisfying the extremists on either side. Apart from the intrinsic value of the material presented in the book, this work also holds interest as the product of an author who has been accused of anti-Semitic tendencies–a manifestly unfair charge in a debate that nonetheless shows no sign of ending.

Solzhenitsyn also undertook the serial publication of "Ugodilo zernyshko promezh dvukh zhernovov: Ocherki izgnaniia" (The Little Grain Managed to Land Between Two Millstones: Sketches of Exile), which came out in seven installments in 1998–2003 in *Novyi mir*. It consists of his reminiscences of persons and experiences encountered during his years in the West. This work

*Solzhenitsyn with his wife, Natal'ia Dmitrievna, in Moscow, October 1995 (photograph by Viktor Akhlomov; Collection of Christine Rydel)*

has the same verve and immediacy as *Bodalsia telenok s dubom* and "Nevidimki," the memoir-like sketches of his preexile years in the Soviet Union. With an abundance of vivid details that are based on notes made immediately after the events described, Solzhenitsyn relates his reception in Germany after his expulsion from the Soviet Union; his move to Switzerland and the complications encountered there; his American speeches and the search for a place to settle; the move to Cavendish; the tide of criticism that followed the Harvard speech; and the various travels he undertook during these years—whether for public appearances (in England, Spain, Japan, and Taiwan), research (at Stanford University), or personal interest (in Russian Old Believer communities on the West Coast of the United States). Throughout "Ugodilo zernyshko promezh dvukh zhernovov" he provides rich commentary on his own work and on a variety of current affairs, often presented with humor and startling candor.

As with the title *Bodalsia telenok s dubom,* the title "Ugodilo zernyshko promezh dvukh zhernovov" is a Russian proverb. To the extent that the earlier title evokes youthful naiveté (a silly calf butting a mighty oak in the futile hope of bringing it down), the later title emphasizes helplessness and bad luck. In both works the autobiographical protagonist who is implied in the titles—whether "calf" or "little grain"—is stylized as a distinct underdog, an image contradicted by the energetic and combative figure who emerges from these pages.

Standing apart from the many publications of Solzhenitsyn's own texts that have appeared since his return to Russia, but of greatest relevance to the story of his confrontation with the regime in the 1960s and 1970s, is a collection of formerly top-secret Soviet documents detailing the highly sensitive reactions of the Communist leadership to everything related to Solzhenitsyn. The volume, titled *Kremlevskii samosud* (an idiomatic rendering is "A Kangaroo Court in the Kremlin"), was published in Moscow in 1994 and appeared the following year in a slightly abridged English-language translation as *The Solzhenitsyn Files.* These materials provide a final proof of the absolute incompatibility of Solzhenitsyn's message with Soviet ideology. At the same time, it offers some fascinating glimpses into the inner workings of an increasingly sclerotic regime, one that Solzhenitsyn had presciently described—in a 1965 conversation monitored by the KGB and duly reported to the Central Committee of the Communist Party—as hopelessly moribund. In terms of Solzhenitsyn's "oak and calf" image, the "oak" was rotten to the core, and the energetic buttings of the "calf" were unquestionably a factor in its ignominious downfall.

Solzhenitsyn has stated repeatedly that he viewed his writings on the camp theme as a fulfillment of a moral obligation to the millions who disappeared into the world of the gulag. Eventually he considered this immense duty completed, and in *Bodalsia telenok s dubom* he speaks metaphorically of *Arkhipelag GULag* (and the works that preceded it) as a huge boulder that he was able to roll aside in order to return, at last, to the chosen "main task" of his life: a fundamental reexamination of the Russian Revolution. This labor yielded a cycle of works that bears the collective title *Krasnoe koleso* and consists of ten volumes published from 1983 to 1991 as part of his twenty-volume *Sobranie sochinenii.* Yet, even the massive assemblage of *Krasnoe koleso* represents only part of the vast original conception. As Solzhenitsyn explains in a note appended to the last volume of the series, he had earlier envisaged writing twenty "knots," or installments, each one dealing with a specific historical period between 1914 and 1922, further supplemented by five epilogues that were to follow the story up to 1945. Contingencies of time forced Solzhenitsyn to cut short this ambitious plan after completing four *uzly,* or knots: *Uzel I. Avgust chetyrnadtsatogo* (Knot I. August 1914); *Uzel II. Oktiabr' shestnadtsatogo*

(Knot II. October 1916, 1984); *Uzel III. Mart semnadtsatogo* (Knot III. March 1917, 1986–1988); and *Uzel IV. Aprel' semnadtsatogo* (Knot IV. April 1917, 1991). The last volume also has a separately paginated section with a 135-page outline of the original plan based on twenty knots. The net effect of not reaching the month of the Bolshevik coup is to focus intently on the period during which, in Solzhenitsyn's opinion, events as they actually unfolded led ineluctably to the success of Lenin's power grab.

The cycle bears the subtitle *Povestvovanie v otmerennykh srokakh,* or "A Narrative in Discrete Periods of Time." Just as in the case of Solzhenitsyn's descriptive subtitle for *Arkhipelag GULag,* his wording here points to the basic method employed in structuring the series. The strategy consists of concentrating on brief and sharply demarcated segments of historical time rather than presenting the full sequence of historical events, which would mean filling in the gaps between these discrete periods. The text allocated to each temporal segment is referred to as a knot, or *uzel,* a term derived from the mathematical concept of "nodal point" and used to refer to historical moments when many forces intersect in ways that display their potential for significant consequences.

The first knot in the series, *Avgust chetyrnadtsatogo,* (enlarged edition, 1983), is in essence a study in the manifold weaknesses of the ancien régime of Russia. Its main focus is on the catastrophic destruction of an entire army corps in Eastern Prussia at the outset of World War I owing to inadequate planning, bungled operations, and a willful disregard of orders. Whereas many military and civilian leaders are depicted as simply irresponsible, others, notably General Samsonov, have their good intentions stymied by ineffectuality and ignorance of their situation. Chief among the actors in the tragedy is Tsar Nicholas II, a well-meaning but severely limited man whose family and court matters blind him to urgent issues of state. Related to the general theme of the tragic inability of the regime to safeguard the people of Russia is the painful account of the 1911 assassination of Prime Minister Petr Arkad'evich Stolypin. In Solzhenitsyn's view Stolypin's death deprived Russia of the only major political figure experienced and forceful enough to see the state through the critical years that lay just ahead. Here, as elsewhere in his narrative, Solzhenitsyn dwells bitterly on the unrealized hopes and missed opportunities that have figured with heartrending frequency in twentieth-century Russian history. To a considerable extent this palpable frustration is personified in a fictional (and recurrent) character named Vorotyntsev, a luminously intelligent colonel in the Russian army. Presented as a witness to many of the attitudes and events contributing to the drift of the country toward a revolutionary precipice, Vorotyntsev is an invented literary figure superimposed on actual historical circumstances. He thus remains incapable of affecting the real events Solzhenitsyn depicts—and deplores.

With the second knot of the work, titled *Uzel II. Oktiabr' shestnadtsatogo,* Solzhenitsyn suggests that it need not encompass high action to serve as a nodal point. (The date October 1916 is in accordance with the Julian calendar; conversion to the Gregorian calendar, the calendar in use in Russia since 1917, renders the date as November 1916.) This particular month is a period in which little happens, but Solzhenitsyn uses this knot to describe the listlessness and foreboding that accompany the anticipation of disaster. Squeezed by war abroad and revolutionary ferment at home, Russia needs action in its defense, but no one takes the requisite initiative. With little plot to trace, in this volume Solzhenitsyn undertakes what he does best—namely, characterization. The volume is also strong in capturing a sense of atmosphere, particularly the oppressive stagnation, without which the revolution would not have occurred. The selection of this month also allows Solzhenitsyn to argue that the revolution was not inevitable. Inactivity has its consequences, too; the action needed to save Russia was not taken, but it could have been.

*Krasnoe koleso,* like *Arkhipelag GULag* before it, eludes ready classification in terms of genre. While the sections involving Vorotyntsev fit the pattern of an historical novel, much of the text cannot be accommodated within the novelistic tradition. Several sections concern historical figures without any reference to Vorotyntsev; these figures include Stolypin, Lenin, Tsar Nicholas II and his strong-willed wife, and dozens of political actors of the day who are all presented in terms of what might be appropriately called dramatized history. These sections, moreover, have no fictive intent whatever; the actions, words, and thoughts of the individuals depicted in each case are grounded in the prodigious research that had occupied Solzhenitsyn for decades. Yet, even this mode proves incapable of absorbing the immense amount of material that he wishes to present, and he repeatedly digresses into densely written third-person excursuses on historical and political circumstances that he considers crucial to an understanding of the state of affairs. Finally, there is the telling fact that in the massive four-volume third knot, titled *Uzel III. Mart semnadtsatogo,* the fictional characters introduced in the earlier knots become peripheral to the narrative. The general movement away from all fictional constructs is consistent with the approach stated in Solzhenitsyn's subtitle: the unconnected gaps in time between the various knots are in fundamental conflict with the literary demands of character develop-

> Здесь помещены мои произведения
> тюремно-лагерно-ссыльных лет.
>
> Они были моим дыханием и
> жизнью тогда. Помогли мне выстоять.
>
> Они тихо, ненавязчиво пролежали
> 45 лет. Теперь, когда мне за 80,
> я счёл, что время их и напечатать.
>
> Трилогия "1945 год" (пьесы
> "Пир победителей", "Пленники"
> и "Республика труда"), тоже напи-
> санная в эти годы, — уже
> напечатана мною двадцатью
> годами раньше и сюда не входит.
>
> А. Солженицын
> 1999

*Solzhenitsyn's facsimile preface in the nine-volume 1999 publication of his early works,* Sobranie sochinenii
*(Collection of Edward E. Ericson Jr. and Alexis Klimoff)*

ment. Solzhenitsyn never minimizes the potency of individuals' actions to produce good or evil social consequences. But because he set himself the goal of tracing the ill-starred convolutions that had shaped twentieth-century Russian history, the focus of his narrative is ultimately not on individual fates but on the greater tragedy that engulfed the nation.

In stylistic terms *Krasnoe koleso* exhibits the characteristic features developed in Solzhenitsyn's earlier work as well as many new literary devices. A prominent example of the former is the polyphonic technique, whereby individual characters are given the opportunity to carry the narrative point of view in the section of the text in which they are the principal actors. This device is used throughout the historical cycle, with an entire chapter typically devoted to a particular character. The technique is especially striking in *Uzel III*, in which shifts of perspective follow one another in rapid succession because of the brevity of most chapters. The result is to accentuate the rising tide of disruption and chaos, key ingredients in Solzhenitsyn's vision of revolutionary turmoil.

Among the stylistic innovations, the most significant is the manner in which Solzhenitsyn intersperses his prose with diverse materials that are visually set off from the main text—documents in boldface, historical retrospectives in eight-point font, collages of excerpts from the press of the time set in a variety of styles and sizes, "screen sequences" arranged in columns of brief phrases intended to mimic actual cinematic effects, and Russian proverbs printed entirely in capital letters. His frequent recourse to proverbs, in this as in his other works, demonstrates a fondness for pithy verbal constructions that convey wry wisdom. Some chapters of *Krasnoe koleso* conclude with freestanding proverbs, which provide a succinct commentary on the preceding text. Solzhenitsyn grants proverbs a privileged position among the many voices of his fiction; proverbs represent an authoritative "folk judgment" and serve a function not unlike that of the chorus in Greek tragedy. Together with the cinematic sequences, they provide further evidence of the deep mark that the principles of drama have made on Solzhenitsyn's prose.

Central to the cycle *Krasnoe koleso* is the question of whether one loves Russia. On one side are those whose sense of organic connection to the land and people causes them to take an active role in helping and defending their increasingly enfeebled homeland, whether on the level of Stolypin's valiant struggle as prime minister to institute desperately needed systemic reforms or in such instinctive acts as the decision of a would-be pacifist to enlist at the outset of World War I because he feels "sorry for Russia." On the other side are individuals obsessed by ideology-induced hatred or blinded by self-interest, who willingly or unwittingly contribute to the Russian catastrophe. The further the cycle progresses, the less resistance is offered to the surging forces of chaos and demolition, which Solzhenitsyn links to the title image of a wheel rolling or rotating in a frightening or threatening way. In the end, the life of the Russian people is violently disrupted by a revolution fomented in the name of those very people, and Lenin, who—more than anyone else—hates Russia, comes to power. The revolution, like a wheel broken loose from a careening carriage, unleashes in its furious energy the totalitarian horrors that become the hallmark of twentieth-century life.

Despite its tragic coloration *Krasnoe koleso* is in an important sense a great monument to hope. Solzhenitsyn has acknowledged that a long time will be needed for scholars to focus on a cycle that is at least four times the length of Leo Tolstoy's *Voina i mir* (War and Peace, 1868–1869). He has devoted the prime of his life to this cycle. In 2001 three separate selections of chapters from the cycle were published: *Stolypin i Tsar'* (Stolypin and the Tsar), which includes chapters from *Avgust chetyrnadtsatogo*; *Lenin: Tsiurikh – Petrograd* (Lenin in Zurich and Petrograd), featuring chapters from all four knots; and *Nakonets-to revoliutsiia* (The Revolution at Last), a two-volume compendium of chapters from *Mart semnadtsatogo*. In each case Solzhenitsyn presents only chapters that bear on historical figures and events. In this way he underlines the primacy of his educational and restorative mission: to reassert and disseminate the long-suppressed truth about the events leading up to 1917.

Solzhenitsyn has frequently been described as a grim, Jeremiah-like figure, but he has always thought of himself as an optimist. Beyond the personality trait of optimism lies hope as a habit of his being; his writings, both literary and nonliterary, almost always conclude on a note of hope. Along with faith and love, hope is one of the classic Christian virtues, and Solzhenitsyn's hope is an integral aspect of his religious worldview, in which humanity stands poised on the intersection between time and eternity.

Throughout a long life packed with high drama, Aleksandr Isaevich Solzhenitsyn has remained vitally engaged with the central issues of his era. Like his great nineteenth-century predecessors Tolstoy and Fyodor Dostoevsky, he has focused predominantly on Russia, while also addressing concerns and raising questions that resonate far beyond any national boundary. Fiercely independent and possessed of legendary determination and perseverance, he has been in conflict either with the powers that be or with conventional wisdom, frequently with both at once. The political dimension of his worldview, while not to be neglected, has unduly preoccupied the majority of commentators. The political controversies will fade with the passage of time. What will abide is Solzhenitsyn's sheer literary power. This quality gained the attention of the world, and it will ultimately determine the degree to which he attains the status of an enduring classic author.

**Bibliographies:**

Donald M. Fiene, *Alexander Solzhenitsyn: An International Bibliography of Writings by and about Him, 1962–1973* (Ann Arbor, Mich.: Ardis, 1973);

*Solzhenitsyn Studies: A Quarterly Review,* 1–2 (1980–1981);

Michael Nicholson, "Solzhenitsyn in 1981: A Bibliographic Reorientation," in *Solzhenitsyn in Exile: Critical Essays and Documentary Materials,* edited by John B. Dunlop, Richard S. Haugh, and Michael Nicholson (Stanford, Cal.: Hoover Institution, 1985), pp. 351–412;

N. G. Levitskaia, *Aleksandr Solzhenitsyn: Biobibliograficheskii ukazatel', avgust 1988–1990* (Moscow: Sovetskii fond kul'tury, 1991).

**Biographies:**

David Burg and George Feifer, *Solzhenitsyn: A Biography* (New York: Stein & Day, 1972);

Leopold Labedz, ed., *Solzhenitsyn: A Documentary Record* (Bloomington: Indiana University, 1973);

Natal'ia Alekseevna Reshetovskaia, *V spore so vremenem* (Moscow: Agentsvo pechati Novosti, 1975); translated by Elena Ivanoff as *Sanya: My Husband Aleksandr Solzhenitsyn* (Indianapolis: Bobbs-Merrill, 1975);

Michael Scammell, *Solzhenitsyn: A Biography* (New York: Norton, 1984);

Reshetovskaia, *Otluchenie: Iz zhizni Aleksandra Solzhenitsyna. Vospominanie zheny* (Moscow: MGAP "Mir knigi," 1994);

A. V. Korotkov, S. A. Melchin, and A. S. Stepanov, *Kremlevskii samosud: Sekretnye dokumenty Politburo o pisatele A. Solzhenitsyne* (Moscow: Rodina, 1994); translated by Catherine A. Fitzpatrick and others as *The Solzhenitsyn Files,* edited by Scammell (Chicago: Edition q, 1995);

D. M. Thomas, *Alexander Solzhenitsyn: A Century in His Life* (London: Little, Brown, 1998; New York: St. Martin's Press, 1998);

Vladimir Glottser and Elena Chukovskaia, *Slovo probivaet sebe dorogu: Sbornik statei i dokumentov ob A. I. Solzhenitsyne, 1962–1974* (Moscow: Russkii put', 1998);

Joseph Pearce, *Solzhenitsyn: A Soul in Exile* (Grand Rapids, Mich.: Baker Books, 2001);

Nikolai Ledovskikh, *Vozvrashchenie v Matrenin dom, ili Odin den' Aleksandra Isaevicha* (Riazan': Poverennyi, 2003).

**References:**

Sergei Alekseevich Askol'dov, Petr Berngardovich Struve, and others, *Iz glubiny: Sbornik statei o russkoi revoliutsii* (Moscow: Russkaia mysl', 1918); translated by William F. Woehrlin as *Out of the Depths=De Profundis,* edited by Woehrlin, with introduction by Bernice Glatzer Rosenthal (Irvine, Cal.: C. Schlacks Jr., 1986);

Francis Barker, *Solzhenitsyn: Politics and Form* (New York: Holmes & Meier, 1977);

Nikolai A. Berdiaev, S. N. Bulgakov, M. O. Gershenzon, and others, *Vekhi: Sbornik statei o russkoi intelligentsii* (Moscow: Kushnerev, 1909); translated by Marian Schwartz as *Landmarks: A Collection of Essays on the Russian Intelligentsia,* edited by Boris Shragin and Albert Todd (New York: Karz Howard, 1977);

Ronald Berman, ed., *Solzhenitsyn at Harvard: The Address, Twelve Early Responses, and Six Later Reflections* (Washington, D.C.: Ethics and Public Policy Center, 1980);

Harold Bloom, ed., *Aleksandr Solzhenitsyn,* Modern Critical Views (Philadelphia: Chelsea House, 2001);

Edward J. Brown, "Solzhenitsyn and the Epic of the Camps," in his *Russian Literature since the Revolution* (Cambridge, Mass.: Harvard University, 1982), pp. 251–291;

John B. Dunlop, Richard Haugh, and Alexis Klimoff, eds., *Aleksandr Solzhenitsyn: Critical Essays and Documentary Materials* (New York & London: Collier Macmillan, 1975);

Dunlop, Haugh, and Michael Nicholson, eds., *Solzhenitsyn in Exile: Critical Essays and Documentary Materials* (Stanford, Cal.: Hoover Institution, 1985);

Edward E. Ericson Jr., *Solzhenitsyn: The Moral Vision* (Grand Rapids, Mich.: Eerdmans, 1980);

Ericson, *Solzhenitsyn and the Modern World* (Washington, D.C.: Regnery Gateway, 1993);

Kathryn Feuer, ed., *Solzhenitsyn: A Collection of Critical Essays* (Englewood Cliffs, N.J.: Prentice-Hall, 1976);

M. M. Golubkov, *Aleksandr Solzhenitsyn* (Moscow: MGU, 1999);

Alexis Klimoff, *One Day in the Life of Ivan Denisovich: A Critical Companion* (Evanston, Ill.: Northwestern University Press, 1997);

Andrei Kodjak, *Alexander Solzhenitsyn* (Boston: Twayne, 1978);

Lev Kopelev, *Utoli moia pechali* (Ann Arbor, Mich.: Ardis, 1981); translated by Antonina W. Bouis as *Ease My Sorrows: A Memoir* (New York: Random House, 1983);

Michael Lydon, "Alexander Solzhenitsyn," in his *Real Writing: Word Models of the Modern World* (New York: Patrick Press, 2001), pp. 183–251;

Daniel J. Mahoney, *Aleksandr Solzhenitsyn: The Ascent from Ideology* (Lanham, Md.: Rowman & Littlefield, 2001);

Mahoney, "Solzhenitsyn on Russia's 'Jewish Question,'" *Society* (November–December 2002): 104–109;

Rufus W. Mathewson Jr., "Solzhenitsyn," in his *The Positive Hero in Russian Literature,* second edition (Stanford, Cal.: Stanford University Press, 1975), pp. 279–340;

Mary McCarthy, "The Tolstoy Connection," *Saturday Review* (16 September 1972): 79–96;

*Modern Fiction Studies,* special Solzhenitsyn issue, 23 (Spring 1977);

Christopher Moody, *Solzhenitsyn* (New York: Barnes & Noble, 1976);

Georges Nivat, *Soljénitsyne* (Paris: Seuil, 1980);

Nivat and Michel Aucouturier, eds., *Soljénitsyne* (Paris: L'Herne, 1971);

Dimitri Panin, *The Notebooks of Sologdin,* translated by John Moore (New York: Harcourt Brace Jovanovich, 1976);

James F. Pontuso, *Solzhenitsyn's Political Thought* (Charlottesville: University of Virginia Press, 1990);

Robert Porter, *Solzhenitsyn's* One Day in the Life of Ivan Denisovich (London: Bristol Classical, 1997);

David Remnick, "The Exile Returns," *New Yorker* (14 February 1994): 64–83;

Abraham Rothberg, *Aleksandr Solzhenitsyn: The Major Novels* (Ithaca, N.Y.: Cornell University, 1971);

Mariia Shneerson, *Aleksandr Solzhenitsyn: Ocherki tvorchestva* (Frankfurt & Moscow: Posev, 1984);

Dora Shturman, *Gorodu i miru: O publitsistike A. I. Solzhenitsyna* (Paris & New York: Tret'ia volna, 1988);

Leona Toker, *"The Gulag Archipelago"* and "The Gulag Fiction of Aleksandr Solzhenitsyn," in her *Return from the Archipelago: Narratives of Gulag Survivors* (Bloomington: Indiana University Press, 2000), pp. 101–121, 188–209;

Dariusz Tolczyk, "A Sliver in the Throat of Power," in his *See No Evil: Literary Cover-Ups and Discoveries of the Soviet Camp Experience* (New Haven & London: Yale University Press, 1999), pp. 253–310;

*Transactions of the Association of Russian-American Scholars in the U.S.A.,* special Solzhenitsyn issue [partially], 29 (1998): 183–315;

A. V. Urmanov, *Tvorchestvo Aleksandra Solzhenitsyna: Uchebnoe posobie* (Moscow: Flinta/Nauka, 2003);

Urmanov, ed., *"Matrenin dvor" A. I. Solzhenitsyna: Khudozhestvennyi mir. Poetika. Kul'turnyi kontekst* (Blagoveshchensk: BGPU, 1999);

Urmanov, ed., *"Odin den' Ivana Denisovicha" A. I. Solzhenitsyna: Khudozhestvennyi mir. Poetika. Kul'turnyi kontekst* (Blagoveshchensk: BGPU, 2003);

*Zvezda,* special Solzhenitsyn issue (June 1994).

# Arkadii Natanovich Strugatsky
*(28 August 1925 – 12 October 1991)*

and

# Boris Natanovich Strugatsky
*(15 April 1933 –   )*

Alexandra Smith
*University of Canterbury, New Zealand*

BOOK (BY ARKADII STRUGATSKY): *Pepel Bikini* (Moscow: Detgiz, 1958).

OTHER: *Tridtsat' pervoe iiunia: Sbornik iumoristicheskoi fantastiki,* edited by Arkadii Strugatsky, introduction by E. Parnova (Moscow: Izdatel'stvo Mir, 1968);
*Skazanie o Esitsune,* translated by Arkadii Strugatsky (Moscow: Khudozhestvennaia literatura, 1984).

SELECTED PERIODICAL PUBLICATION–UNCOLLECTED: "Cherez nastoiaschee–v buduschee," *Voprosy literatury,* 8 (August 1964): 73–76;
"O chem ne pishut fanatsy?" *Znanie–sila,* 6 (June 1965): 40–41;
"What Stars Gleam in Science Fiction," by Arkadii Strugatsky, Dmitri Bilenkin, and Igor' Bestuzhev-Lada, *Soviet Studies in Literature,* 14, no. 4 (1978): 3–26; translated from *Literaturnoe obozrenie,* 8 (1977);

PRODUCED SCRIPT (BY BORIS STRUGATSKY): *Pis'mo mertvogo cheloveka,* motion picture, by Boris Strugatsky, Konstantin Lopushansky, and Viacheslav Rybakov, Lenfil'm, 1988.

OTHER: "Five Spoons of Elixir: A Film Script," *Soviet Literature,* 12 (1986): 3–35;
*Fantastika: Chetvertoe pokolenie,* edited by Boris Strugatsky (St. Petersburg: IIK Severo-Zapad: Biblioteka Zvezdy, 1991);
*Kinostenarii* (Moscow: Act, 1998).

BOOKS (BY ARKADII STRUGATSKY AND BORIS STRUGATSKY): *Strana bagrovykh tuch* (Moscow, 1959; Moscow: Detskaia literatura, 1960);

*Arkadii and Boris Strugatsky (from* Izbrannoe, *1989; Jean and Alexander Heard Library, Vanderbilt University)*

*Put' na Amalteiu* (Moscow: Molodaia gvardiia, 1960); translated by Leonid Kolesnikov as "Destination: Amaltheia," in *Destination: Amaltheia* (Moscow: Foreign Languages Publishing House, 1962);
*Shest' spichek* (Moscow: Detgiz, 1960); translated by R. Prokofieva as "Six Matches," in *The Heart of the Serpent* (Moscow: Foreign Languages Publishing House, 1960);

*Stazhery* (N.p., 1962);
*Vozvrashchenie (Polden'. 22 vek)* (Moscow: Detgiz, 1962); republished as *Polden', 22 vek (Vozvrashchenie)* (Moscow: Detskaia literatura, 1967); translated by Patrick L. McGuire as *Noon, 22nd Century* (New York: Macmillan, 1978);
*Dalekaia Raduga. – Trudno byt' bogom* (Moscow: Molodaia gvardiia, 1964)—comprises *Dalekaia Raduga*, translated by A. G. Myers as *Far Rainbow* (Moscow: Mir, 1967); and *Trudno byt' bogom*, translated by Wendayne Ackerman as *Hard to be a God* (New York: Seabury, 1973);
*Khishchnye veshchi veka* (Moscow: Molodaia gvardiia, 1965); translated by Leonid Renen as *The Final Circle of Paradise* (New York: DAW, 1976);
*Ponedel'nik nachinaetsia v subbotu* (Moscow: Detskaia literatura, 1965);
*Tridtsat' pervoe iiunia* (Moscow: Mir, 1968);
*Obitaemyi ostrov* (Moscow: Detgiz, 1971);
*Gadkie lebedi* (Frankfurt am Main: Posev, 1972); translated by Alice Stone Nakhimovsky and Aleksandr Nakhimovsky as *The Ugly Swans* (New York: Macmillan, 1979);
*Ulitka na sklone* (Frankfurt am Main: Posev, 1972); translated by Alan Meyers as *The Snail on the Slope* (London: Gollancz, 1980);
*Atomvulkan Golkonda* (Munich: W. Heyne, 1974);
*Polden', 22 vek. – Malysh* (Leningrad: Detskaia literatura, 1975);
*Ponedel'nik nachinaetsia v subbotu* (Leningrad: Detskaia literatura, 1979);
*Zhuk v muraveinike* (Fidzhi: Nostal'giia, 1979); translated by Bouis as *Beetle in the Anthill* (New York: Macmillan, 1980);
*Nenaznachennye vstrechi* (Moscow: Molodaia gvardiia, 1980);
*Les* (Ann Arbor, Mich.: Ardis, 1981);
*Otel' u pogibshego al'pinista* (Moscow: Znanie, 1982);
*Zona* (New York: Adventa, 1983);
*Vtoroe nashestvie marsian* (New York: Adventa, 1983);
*Prishelets iz preispodnei* (New York: Adventa, 1984);
*Za milliard let do kontsa sveta* (Moscow: Sovetskii pisatel', 1984);
*Zhuk v muraveinike* (Riga: Liesma, 1986);
*Volny gasiat veter* (Haifa: Keshet Book Shop, 1986);
*Khromaia sud'ba* (Stavropol': BAAM, 1987);
*Peregruzki* (Melbourne: Artol, 1987);
*Den' zatmeniia*, by Arkadii Strugatsky, Boris Strugatsky, and Petr Kadochnikov (Addis Ababa: Menelik, 1988);
*Otiagoshchiennye zlom, ili sorok let spustia* (Moscow: Prometei, 1989);
*Grad obrechennyi* (Leningrad: Khudozhestvennaia literatura, Leningradskoe otdelenie, 1989);

*Vtoroe nashestvie marsian: Zapiski zdravomysliashchego* (Leningrad: Smart, 1990);
*Strugatskie fantasticheskie povesti* (Moscow: Kniga, 1990);
*Strugatskie o sebe, literature i mire. 1959–1966,* edited by Valerii Kononov (Omsk, 1991);
*Kuda zhe nam plyt' sbornik publitsistiki* (Volgograd: Liudny-Volgakonu, 1991);
*Zamok s prevrashcheniiami* (Moscow: Fizkul'tura i sport, 1993);
*Strugatskie o sebe, literature i mire. 1967–1975,* edited by S. Bondarenko (Omsk, 1993);
*Strugatskie o sebe, literature i mire. 1982–1984* (Omsk, 1994);
*Strugatskie o sebe, literature i mire. 1985 i prochee* (Omsk: Liiudeny, 1994);
*Paren' iz preispodnei; Bespokoistvo; Zhuk v muraveinike; Volny gasiat veter* (St. Petersburg: Terra Fantastica, 1996);
*Diavil sredi liudei; Podrobnosti zhizni Nikity Vorontsova; Poisk prednaznacheniia* (Moscow: EKSMO-Press, 1997);
*Obitaemyi ostrov; Zhuk v muraveinike* (Moscow: TEKST/EKSMO-Press, 1997);
*Kinostsenarii* (Moscow: Act, 1998).

**Editions and Collections:** *Strana bagrovykh tuch* (Moscow: Detskaia literatura, 1969);
*Trudno byt' bogom* (Baku: Azerbaidzhanskoe izdatel'stvo, 1981);
*Otel' u pogibshego al'pinista* (Moscow: Detskaia literatura, 1983);
*Put' na Amal'teiu* (Tel Aviv: Orfei, 1985);
*Stazhery* (Tel Aviv: Orfei, 1985);
*Ponedel'nik nachinaetsia v subbotu: Skazka dlia nauchnykh rabotnikov mladshego vozrasta* (Minsk: Iunatsva, 1986);
*Za milliard let do kontsa sveta* (Leningrad: Lenizdat, 1988);
*Izbrannoe* (Moscow: Moskovskii rabochii, 1989);
*Poseshchenie* (Moscow: Iurid. literatura, 1989);
*Stazhery* (Moscow: Detskaia literatura, 1991);
*Trudno byt; Bogom* (Moscow: Profizdat, 1991);
*Sobranie sochinenii,* 10 volumes (Moscow: Tekst, 1991–1994);
*Izbrannoe,* edited by Mark Grigor'evich Shalimov (St. Petersburg: Neva, 1992);
*Gadkie lebedi* (St. Petersburg: Terra Fantastika, 1993);
*Za milliard let do kontsa sveta; Piknik na obochine; Gadkie lebedi* (St. Petersburg: Al'ians: Pozisoft, 1993);
*Ponedel'nik nachinaetsia v subbotu; Skazka o troika* (Moscow: Tekst, 1995);
*Sochineniia,* 3 volumes (Moscow: TEKST, 1996);
*Khromaia sud'ba; Otiagoshchiennye zlom* (Moscow: TEKST/EKSMO-Press, 1997);
*Strana bagrovykh tuch* (Moscow: AST, 1999);
*Khishnye veshchi veka; Chrezvychainye proisshestviia; Polden', XXII vek* (Moscow: AST, 1999);

*Gadkie lebedi* (St. Petersburg: Iunimet, 2000).

**Editions in English:** *Monday Begins on Saturday,* translated by Leonid Renen (New York: DAW, 1977);

*Prisoners of Power,* translated by Helen Saltz Jacobson, introduction by Theodore Sturgeon (New York: Macmillan, 1977);

*Roadside Picnic; Tale of the Troika,* translated by Antonina W. Bouis (New York: Macmillan, 1977);

*Definitely Maybe: A Manuscript Discovered under Unusual Circumstances,* translated by Bouis (New York: Macmillan, 1978);

*Far Rainbow; The Second Invasion from Mars,* translated by Bouis and Gary Kern (New York: Macmillan, 1979);

*Space Apprentice,* translated by Bouis (New York: Macmillan, 1981);

*Escape Attempt,* translated by Roger De Garis (New York: Macmillan, 1982);

*Aliens, Travelers, and Other Strangers,* translated by De Garis (New York: Macmillan, 1984);

*The Time Wanderers,* translated by Bouis (New York: Richardson & Steirman, 1986).

PRODUCED SCRIPTS: *Stalker,* by Arkadii Strugatsky, Boris Strugatsky, and Andrei Arsen'evich Tvarkovsky, motion picture, Mosfil'm/Zweites Deutsches Fernsehen, 1979;

*Hukkunud alpinisti hotell,* motion picture, Tallinnfil'm, 1979;

*Charodei,* television, Gosteleradio/Odessa Film Studios, 1982;

*Dni zatmeniia,* by Arkadii Strugatsky, Boris Strugatsky, Iurii Arabov, and Petr Kadochnikov, motion picture, Lenfil'm, 1988;

*Iskushenie B.,* motion picture, Goskino/Laterna Film, 1990.

SELECTED PERIODICAL PUBLICATIONS—UNCOLLECTED: "Izvne," *Tekhnika molodiezhi,* 1 (1958): 26–30;

"Spontannyi refleks," *Znanie-sila,* 8 (1958): 24–28;

"Shest'spichek," *Znanie-sila,* 3 (1959): 32–37;

"Izobretatel' 'SKR'," *Izobretatel' i ratsionalizator,* 7 (1959): 38–42;

"Zabytyieksperiment," *Znanie-sila,* 8 (1959): 34–39;

"Chastnye predpolozheniia," *Znanie-sila,* 8 (1959): 40–43;

"Belyi Konus Alaida," *Znanie-sila,* 12 (1959): 36–40;

"Noch'iu na Marse," *Znanie-sila,* 6 (1960): 32–36;

"Ot chego ne svobodna fantastika," *Literaturnoe obozrenie,* 8 (1976): 107–108;

"The Desire Machine," translated by Monica Whyte, *Soviet Literature,* 2 (1984): 6–35;

"Zhidy goroda Pitera, ili neveselye besedy pri svechakh: Komediia," *Neva,* 9 (1990): 92–115;

Boris Stragatski, "'nashe televidenie obvinilo Leni Rifenshtal' v otsutstvie pokaianiia a pochemu my ne kaemsia," *Pelo, St. Petersburg,* 35 (15 September 2003): 3.

Arkadii Strugatsky and Boris Strugatsky are well known within and outside Russia as authors of acclaimed works of science fiction. Together they wrote short stories, novels, and screenplays. Their novel *Piknik na obochine* (first published in 1972 in *Avrora;* translated as *Roadside Picnic,* 1977) was the basis for the 1979 movie *Stalker,* directed by Andrei Arsen'evich Tvarkovsky (with whom they also collaborated on the script). From the 1960s through the 1980s, most of the works by the Strugatsky brothers are strongly satirical in tone and were written in a disguised form of fantasy in order to avoid Soviet censorship. The brothers received several awards for their most popular works, including the Second Award of the Ministry of Education in 1959 for their novel *Strana bagrovykh tuch* (1959, Land of Crimson Clouds); the Aelita Prize (1981) for *Zhuk v muraveinike* (1979; translated as *Beetle in the Anthill,* 1980); the European Science Fiction Society Award; the Jules Verne Society of Sweden Award; a John W. Campbell Award; and the 1987 World Science Fiction Conference Award.

Arkadii Natanovich Strugatsky was born in Batumi, Georgia, on 28 August 1925. Eight years later, on 15 April 1933, his brother, Boris Natanovich Strugatsky, was born in Leningrad, where the family had settled in the late 1920s. Their mother, Aleksandra Ivanovna Strugatskaia, was a teacher. Their father, Natan Zinov'evich Strugatsky, was an art historian and an active member of the Communist Party; he died of starvation during the siege of Leningrad in 1942. Aleksandra Ivanovna and Boris, who had been weakened by the privations of wartime, were unable to evacuate the city, but they nonetheless survived the siege.

While alive Natan Zinov'evich, who had received a degree in fine arts from Leningrad State University, instilled in Arkadii a serious interest in the works of Jules Verne, H. G. Wells, and Arthur Conan Doyle. In 1943–1945 Arkadii served in the Soviet army as a senior lieutenant. He studied English and Japanese at the Military Institute for Foreign Languages in Moscow, from which he graduated in 1949. In 1955 he married Elena Oshanina, who had a daughter from a previous marriage. He worked as a technical translator and editor for the Institute for Technical Information, known as Goslitizdat, in 1959–1961. In 1961–1964 he was an editor at Detgiz, the state publishing house for children's literature. From 1964 onward he worked as a freelance writer and a translator of English and Japanese. Arkadii died on 12 October 1991.

Boris studied astronomy in the Department of Mathematics and Mechanics at Leningrad State University from 1950 to 1955. He earned his Ph.D. at the State Observatory of the Academy of Sciences of the USSR in Pulkovo, near Leningrad, in 1958. He continued there as an astronomer and computer mathematician until 1964. During this period, in 1957, he married Adelaida Karpeliuk, with whom he had a son. In his last year at the observatory Boris began a career as a freelance writer.

The first stories by the Strugatsky brothers appeared in 1957 and 1958. One of them, published as "Spontannyi refleks" (1958, Spontaneous Reflex, in *Znanie-sila*, 1958), is about a sophisticated robot that one day develops a spontaneous reflex and decides to go on a walkabout. The combination of Boris's scientific knowledge and Arkadii's familiarity with the genre of science fiction (through the works of authors such as Verne) helped the brothers produce novels and stories on a par with Western science-fiction writing. Arkadii and Boris praised the achievements of science and technology in their early works, which therefore were palatable to Soviet authorities, who wanted to discourage writers from focusing on themes such as the gulag (Soviet system of labor prison camps) and the legacy of Stalinism. Thus, for example, their novel *Vozvrashchenie (Polden'. 22 vek)* (first published 1961 in *Ural* [The Urals], published 1962 in book form; translated as *Noon, 22nd Century*, 1978) is about optimistic cosmonauts and their outer-space explorations. The protagonists, Anton Bukov, Vladimir Iurovsky, and Ivan Zhilin, fly to Venus for uranium and have an adventure on one of the moons of Jupiter. They are courageous, but eventually they grow old and Iurovsky dies.

The fiction that the Strugatsky brothers wrote in the 1960s and 1970s has strong satirical overtones that did not please Soviet censors. A representative work of this period, *Vtoroe nashestvie marsian* (The Second Coming of the Martians, first published in *Baikal*, 1 [1961], published 1983 in book form), builds on some of the science-fiction themes of Wells. Yet, it also includes some distinctly ironic contemporary references to both Western and Soviet societies. In the story the Martians come back after their defeat with more sophisticated weapons such as bribes and propaganda; one of their posters reads, "Drugs are a poison and the shame of the nation!" and "We will punish severely those who circulate drugs!" Establishing a totalitarian rule, the Martians accuse the locals of terrorist attacks and of instigating arrests. They arrest Minotaur, the chief engineer responsible for the sewage system in the city described in the novel, and promise to repair the sys-

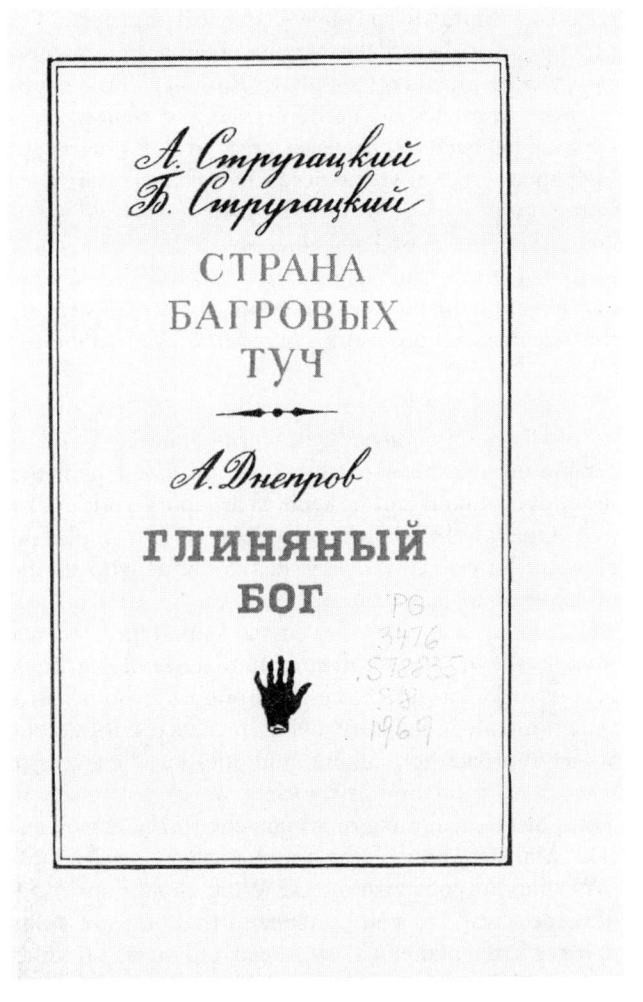

*Title page for* Strana bagrovykh tuch *(1959, Land of Crimson Clouds), the Strugatskys' first novel, which won the Second Award of the Soviet Ministry of Education (Thomas Cooper Library, University of South Carolina)*

tem themselves. They introduce new items (blue bread, for example) and reassure the local population described in the story that they will take care of the defense system of the nation. The Martians appear to be rich because of their ability to take care of the most profitable activities in the country and to ensure demilitarization. The story alludes to the growing role of the military industry in the Soviet Union in the 1960s. In one interview the Strugatsky brothers admitted, "What attracts us about science fiction is the fact that it is the ideal, and for the moment the only, literary means which allows us to broach the most important problems of today."

In 1964 the Strugatsky brothers published their short novel *Dalekaia Raduga* (translated as *Far Rainbow*, 1967), in which they mix fantasy not only with realistic descriptions of contemporary Russia but also with a serious warning of possible ecological disasters. The protagonist Robert Skliarov is involved in several laboratory experiments on the planet Raduga. These experiments are related to both physics and biology, and they are believed to enable scientists to shift objects at a high speed over any distance. The scientists portrayed in the novel are well aware that their tests could create an energy wave of enormous strength, which could lead to an energy imbalance in the universe. That disastrous event happens, and the entire planet is destroyed; the scientists whose work caused the catastrophe are killed.

*Dalekaia Raduga* addresses the moral responsibility of all scientists engaged in works that might endanger life on a planet—be it Earth or any other planet in the universe—and can be seen as an apocalyptic narrative. One of the characters central to the book, the physicist Leonid Gorbovsky, has to decide who should be allowed to leave the planet Raduga and who will have to stay—and thus die. At the same time, *Dalekaia Raduga* shows how contemporary technology helps people make moral choices. Through the novel, in a veiled manner, the Strugatsky brothers criticize the Soviet approach to planning and question the status of science in contemporary society as a new religion. Thus, at the beginning of a magnetic storm, a biologist asks Maliaev, one of the top managers on Raduga: "What about your guarantees? What about your beautiful speeches? Do you understand that you are going to leave half a planet without bread and meat?" Raduga is described as "a planet colonized by science and a testing ground for experiments in physics, for which the whole of humankind is waiting." This definition can be seen as a parody of 1960s Soviet propaganda, which presents the U.S.S.R. as a superpower headed for a communist future. Likewise, in the style of official Soviet discourse, Gorbovsky asserts, "The most valuable thing we have is our future." In the view of Rosalind Marsh, *Dalekaia raduga* "is a parable of the negative consequences of scientific progress such as the creation of nuclear weapons and, perhaps, also a warning of the price which must be paid for all man's scientific and historical experiments."

One of the Strugatsky brothers' most acclaimed works of the mid 1960s is the dystopian novel *Trudno byt' bogom* (1964; translated as *Hard to be a God,* 1973). It describes a group of historians who personify a technologically advanced future. They travel from Earth to a medieval planet to conduct their research. Anton, who goes by the name Don Rumata on this planet, is one of the historians. He stays in the city of Arkanar and eventually witnesses the growing tension there resulting from the actions of Don Reba, the ever more influential minister for security who spreads terror among the members of the intelligentsia through his pogroms. The king increasingly loses his power to Don Reba. When Don Reba finally attains complete power and takes over Arkanra, he establishes a tyranny and initiates a systematic purging of the people, expecting his subordinates to be obedient and loyal to him. His Grey Soldiers are eager to execute all intellectually superior citizens. Anton uses advanced technology in order to save some of these citizens. He thinks that he must oppose the directive of noninterference, put forth by the Historical Institute, so he helps several dissidents to escape from Arkanar. He witnesses the death of the king, who was poisoned, and the destruction of his heir. While Don Reba's terror progresses, Anton loses his mistress, Kira; eventually, he kills Don Reba and is sent back to Earth. Anton's assumed identity as the god-like figure Don Rumata appears to be a temporary escape into a pragmatic objectivity. His true human nature oscillates between various emotions, to the effect that at times he sees himself as a creature resembling a beast, rather than as a superman. One of the major concerns of the authors is the role of culture in educating people to think critically. Anton asks himself many Dostoevskian questions; he ponders, for example, whether man can be a god, or whether god should permit evil.

*Trudno byt' bogom* presents a hybrid of the fantastic tale and the medieval romance, but its philosophical touch exposes the hope of the Strugatsky brothers that scientists, scholars, and artists will be able to survive totalitarian conditions and create a more advanced society. In a Dostoevskian vein they assert that human nature cannot be transformed by science alone. The medieval city of Arkanar symbolizes pragmatic discourse based on an unquestionable belief in progress. It argues that the shortcut for many utopian transformations of society lies in a totalitarian regime. Arkanar, as presented in the novel, resembles Plato's vision of the ideal state; the image of the road of history, featured at both the beginning and the end of *Trudno byt' bogom,* alludes to the utopian notion of history, which appears to be conceived as a predetermined chain of events leading to its own negation. Anton seems not to be a god after all, since he is powerless to control the course of history.

A major theme in the work of the Strugatsky brothers during this period is a strong opposition to bourgeois consumerism and a philistine mentality, particularly as highlighted in their novel *Khishchnye veshchi veka* (1965, Predatory Things of the Age; translated as *The Final Circle of Paradise,* 1976). It depicts a "Country of Fools," whose inhabitants are overwhelmed with consumer goods. Their addiction to an artificial stimulant makes them stupid and passive. As the authors emphasize, *Khishchnye veshchi veka* can be read as an allegorical portrayal of the spiritual death that bourgeois ideology brings to man. This theme is one of the most prevalent in Soviet literature of the 1960s. The growth of materialism within the Soviet Union was associated at this time with the goal of Soviet scientific and technological revolution—to improve material conditions of life. Yet, many Soviet writers were concerned with spiritual and intellectual development. In "Kruglyi stol: Novye chelovecheskie tipy" (New Human types), an article published in *Voprosy literatury* in 1976, Arkadii reflected on the technological revolution in the U.S.S.R. and stated that the new type that was created by this revolution might be characterized as "the well-fed uneducated man of the masses."

In the mid 1960s the Strugatsky brothers shifted from utopian science fiction to fantastic writing of a philosophical kind, a trend affirmed especially by their novel *Trudno byt' bogom*. Soviet readers learned to decipher their symbols and their allegories of the triumph of evil over man in terms of references to Soviet reality. As a result, their popularity in the Soviet Union increased rapidly. A 1966 survey in the journal *Fantastika* (Science Fiction) listed the brothers as the most popular writers of science fiction, together with the Polish author Stanisław Lem and the American writer Ray Bradbury. As their work developed from the purely scientific toward a social fantasy, the Strugatskys created imaginary worlds, with recognizable elements of contemporary reality, so that readers could be estranged from their presence and assess their immediate environment in a critical way.

One of the brothers' fearless gestures is their use of the word *troika* in the title of their story "Skazka o troike" (Tale of a Troika), which appeared—after several periodicals rejected it for publication—in 1968 in the provincial Irkutsk journal *Angara*. It is a fable in which the world is represented by a skyscraper, where the sewer cleaners have seized power. Prior to the publication of the story, *troika* was used in Soviet prison-camp literature as a denunciatory term referring to groups of special-commission prosecutors. When the story was published, the issues of *Angara* in which they appeared were taken out of circulation, and the editors of the journal were dismissed for political subversion.

In "Skazka o troike" the authors disguise the description of real prosecutions as something fantastic and present their characters as heroes of a wonder tale. For example, they describe the execution of an old inventor: "The first case was announced, that of old Edelveis Zakharovich, the inventor. They dealt with him quickly. 'Death,' roared Lavr Fedotovich." The other victims of this merciless ritual include Konstantin, "who came from another planet"; Kuzka the pterodactyl; and the lizard Lizka, "who had refused to leave his lake, forcing the commission to go to Cow's Bog." Such an act was seen as a terrorist act: "The commission had been attacked by insects and the commandment was found guilty of preparing a terrorist act." In this wonder tale the absurdity of the Soviet legal system and of policing is the real object of the authors' criticism. Some passages of "Skazka o troike" make fun of highly dogmatic Soviet officials, who were continuing to support totalitarian rule. The central characteristic of Khlebovodov—one of the members of the Troika, as the prosecuting commission is called in the story—"is his great social adaptability and ability to survive, based on stupidity as a matter of principle and on a constant striving to be more orthodox than the orthodox." Khlebovodov's speech is full of Communist Party rhetoric and clichés, such as "whoever does not work, does not eat," "mistakes were made," "people are not saints," and "even old ladies make mistakes; even a horse with four legs stumbles." The speech of Lavr Fedotovich Vuniukov, who presides over the Troika, resembles the way many Soviet government officials of the 1960s used to address Soviet citizens. He uses phrases such as "we are obliged to announce," "we are obliged to emphasize," "we are obliged to assure you," "the people will thank us," and "the people will not forgive us if we will not carry out this task more energetically."

*Ulitka na sklone* (first published 1968 in *Baikal*, published 1972 in book form; translated as *The Snail on the Slope*, 1980), a philosophical work by the Strugatsky brothers, is even more subversive than their previous writings, because it challenges the Marxist-Leninist theories of progress and asserts that no form of knowledge can be the ultimate truth. When the work was initially published in the provincial journal *Baikal*, it was removed from circulation, and the editors were reprimanded and dismissed. *Ulitka na sklone* is about a giant forest that is being studied by a state security agency. The tall building at the edge of the woods represents the Directorate, personified by ignorant managers of the forest. The atmosphere is so oppressive that even the machines want to escape. Perets, one of the inhabitants of the forests, dreams of escape because the reality in the totalitarian state around him does not make any sense to him. In explaining the estrangement from his immediate environment, he says, "I live in a world which someone has invented, which I long to comprehend. I am sick with the longing to comprehend." Either by mistake, or because he won by chance the race organized by the Directorate, Perets is appointed as a new director. As soon as he assumes power, he orders his subordinates to eradicate themselves. The rulers of the fantastic state are sewer diggers who, as is

*Front cover for* Obitaemyi ostrov *(1971, The Inhabited Island), the Strugatskys' anti-utopian novel about a young pilot struggling to change a planet governed by tyranny (Thomas Cooper Library, University of South Carolina)*

observed by one of the positive characters, have no morals.

The anti-utopian narrative *Obitaemyi ostrov* (1971, The Inhabited Island) tells about a planet governed by tyranny and the attempts of a young idealistic pilot to change the society. The novel alludes to Soviet bureaucracy at the end of the 1960s, with its suppression of freedom of speech and reliance on technology to sustain its power. It expresses the authors' environmental concerns regarding scientific progress and pollution. The Strugatsky brothers' imaginary island is full of dirty factories, radioactive rivers, ugly houses, and dangerous robots. Their social fantasy might be seen as a warning to contemporary Soviet society about the ugly developments that might be associated with the technological progress and urbanization that could be prevented.

Another anti-utopian novel, rejected by Soviet editors and circulated in samizdat, appeared in Germany in 1972. Because of the publication of *Gadkie lebedi* (translated as *The Ugly Swans*, 1979) and of other works in the West, the Strugatsky brothers lived as semi-outcasts until the advent of glasnost in 1985. In *Gadkie lebedi,* a sluggish intelligentsia loses its role as a critical counterforce, and the new generation decides to leave the old world behind. The novel is infused with despair, and—in comparison with the brothers' previous works—the story line is more absurd than fantastic. In this short novel a mayor decides to put all the citizens who wear spectacles in a special leprosarium. There is revolt in the leprosarium: the rebels are joined by children who escaped their homes. The spectacle-wearers win against the old state, represented by officials, philistines, and the army. There is a desire to save children from the influence of the corroded old world. One of the rebels appeals to parents: "Look at yourselves! You brought them into the world and now are molding them after your own image and likeness." In a Romantic manner the novel urges the resurrection of antimaterialistic values and spirituality. *Gadkie lebedi* can be seen as a playful appropriation of "The Pied Piper of Hamelin," the German legend about the rat catcher and the children whom he took away from their parents, for it features a contemporary musician and poet, Viktor Banev, who recites his revolutionary verse in youth clubs while accompanying himself on his banjo. Banev gradually degenerates, however, from a talented poet to a cynic who likes women and likes to drink. He grows more tolerant of the oppressive regime in his city, thinking to himself: "Destroying the old world and building a new one on its bones is a very old idea and it has never led to the desired results. One cannot eradicate cruelty by cruelty."

The message of the novel—that violence cannot end violence—can be read as a compromise by the Strugatsky brothers to ensure their own semilegal existence in the Soviet Union. *Gadkie lebedi* depicts Banev's disillusionment with the new government of the spectacle-wearers, since the new bosses of the city have turned all alcohol into water. He deems the idea of progress as something that kills joy. "The newer the rule," he states, "the worse it is, as everyone knows." This pessimistic worldview reveals the authors' profound understanding of the impact of the totalitarian regime on the population of the country, in which, as one of the characters notes, half the population drinks and gets drunk. The talented poet Banev also personifies the aspirations of the authors during the Thaw period; they developed underground literature, because the official channels for publication of their works had ceased to exist. The novel includes some important discussions on literature that can be seen as the Strugatskys' attempt to subvert the established framework of the socialist realist mode of writing.

*Piknik na obochine,* which was adapted for motion pictures as *Stalker,* is one of the most popular novels written by the Strugatsky brothers. It tells about a group of scientists involved in studying various places, visited by aliens, where several important artifacts and picnic rubbish from aliens can be found. Some of the objects are believed to be able to revolutionize the science and technology of humankind. Military specialists become interested in these objects, too, as well as some people involved in the black market. The protagonist of the novel is Redrick Schuhart, a stalker who smuggles the space objects from the zone and offers them for sale to the black-market dealers. In spite of his involvement in this illegal trade, Redrick is portrayed with sympathy because of his humane qualities.

*Piknik na obochine,* like most eastern European science fiction, is not so much preoccupied with suspense or technology; rather it meditates on the sociological implications of both advanced technology in the context of fascist politics and the bureaucratically stagnant world of communist societies. Toward the end of the novel Redrick develops a transcendent vision of universal love, which derives from his own aesthetic and ethical worldview. He lives a criminal life in a frontier city near the zone, trying to support his wife and child, who is strangely mutated. After imprisonment for trafficking in stolen alien goods, Redrick agrees to one last expedition—to the very heart of the mysterious zone, where a magical sphere can be found; it is capable of granting any wish to the one who reaches it. While others have succumbed to the dangers of the zone, Redrick is successful in getting to the sphere and feels truly unworthy of the universe-shaping role that his wish will have. In the concluding lines of the novel he thinks of his own prayer to some divine forces of the universe, or some abstract god. He says to himself: "I am an animal. . . . I cannot think because these scoundrels did not teach me to think." His love for people overwhelms him, and he states his wish: "Let everyone be happy for free, and let no one leave this place humiliated."

In the short novel *Za milliard let do kontsa sveta* (A Billion Years Before the End of the World, published in *Zhanie-sila,* 9–12 [1976–1977]; translated as *Definitely Maybe: A Manuscript Discovered under Unusual Circumstances,* 1978) scientists witness strange events, which they perceive as attempts by some aliens to obstruct their scientific work that might lead to an imbalance of energy in the universe. The scientist fear that the faceless threat from above will disrupt the whole world order, which wants to keep its secrets. All but one of the scientists give up. The rebel mathematician Vecherovsky does not submit to the situation but continues to do research. This story is one of suspense, with a strong focus on the psychological profile of scientists who work in a totalitarian regime that turns them into conformists. The narrator is a mathematician specializing in astronomy and physics. At the end of the novel—thinking that he needs to protect his wife and child out of concern that his research project might undermine his family happiness—he brings his unfinished manuscript, which describes a highly important invention, to his friend Vecherovsky. In the concluding line of this novel the narrator thinks of Aleksandr Sergeevich Pushkin, whom he perceives as morally superior to himself, since the poet had something to die for and did not wish to settle for a mediocre existence. *Za milliard let do kontsa sveta* is reminiscent of Daniil Aleksandrovich Granin's novels, which feature Soviet scientists who often must make moral choices because of the restrictive environment and conditions of their work.

Most of the science-fiction novels created by the Strugatsky brothers suggest no easy solutions to contemporary problems. Their body of works demonstrates that some form of control is needed in order to prevent potentially useful yet undesirable and harmful consequences of scientific development. Their works also convey, however, a deep concern with the individual who must develop his true identity and come to terms with his surroundings. The Strugatskys are preoccupied with outcasts and the marginalized groups of Soviet society, revealing some of the fears and insecurities of those who do not conform to the established way of life. In this respect, their comedy "Zhidy goroda Pitera, ili neveselye besedy pri svechakh" (The Jews of St. Petersburg, or Unhappy Candlelit Conversations), published in the journal *Neva* in 1990, provides some useful psychological insights into the mentality of people who have suffered anti-Semitic attacks. It features some neighbors in a St. Petersburg block of apartments who are visited by a mysterious black person; he distributes telegrams urging the residents to come to various locations in the city, from which they will be taken away to unknown destinations. This episode alludes to Joseph Stalin's anti-Semitic campaigns and purges. The references to local residents include phrases such as "all Jews of St. Petersburg," "all rich residents of St. Petersburg," and "all promiscuous residents of St. Petersburg." The image of a mysterious stranger alludes to the black person who appears in the tormented imagination of the narrator in Sergei Aleksandrovich Esenin's well-known narrative poem "Chernyi chelovek" (Black Person; published posthumously in *Novyi Mir,* 1 [1926]). In addition, there are humorous references to Russian contemporary songs, radio programs, and to the absurdity of 1990s Russian life in general.

Although Arkadii Natanovich Strugatsky and Boris Natanovich Strugatsky stayed within the bounds of Soviet writing, never going into exile, they managed to publish highly experimental and innovative fiction, both in the Soviet Union and abroad. Their works are deeply rooted in the culture of the Thaw period, when fundamentally utopian questions were reinforced and brought into question. Their novels challenge the ideological foundations of the Soviet Union and pose significant questions that remain highly relevant to post-Soviet readers.

**Interviews:**

Suzanne Plog-Bontemps, "Interview mit Arkadij Strugazkij im November 1981 in Moskau," in *Science-Fiction in Osteuropa: Beiträge zur russischen, polnischen und tschechischen phantastischen Literatur*, edited by Wolfgang Kasack (Berlin: Spitz, 1984), pp. 70–78;

"A Talk with Arkadi Strugatsky," *Soviet Literature*, 12 (1986): 36–40;

Alla Bossart, "Interview with the Strugatskys," translated by Mary Meyer, *Foundation: The Review of Science Fiction*, 50 (Autumn 1990): 61–75;

Vladimir Gopman, "Science Fiction Teaches the Virtues Civic: An Interview with Arkadii Strugatsky," translated by Mark Knighton, *Science-Fiction Studies*, 18 (March 1991): 1–10;

B. Vishevsky, "Interview with Boris Strugatsky," *Vesti, Tel-Aviv*, 1 January 2004, pp. 22–23.

**References:**

Raphael Aceto, "The Ambiguous Miracle in Three Novels by the Strugatsky Brothers," *Science-Fiction Studies*, 11 (November 1984): 291–303;

Mark Amusin, *Brat'ia Strugatskie: Ocherk tvorchestva* (Jerusalem: Beseder, 1996);

Amusin, "Daleko li do budushchego?" *Neva*, 2 (1988): 153–160;

Amusin, "Illiuzii i doroga," *Oktiabr'*, 6 (June 1989): 204–206;

Amusin, "V zerkalakh budushchego," *Literaturnoe obozrenie*, 6 (1989): 37–39;

Maksim Borisov, "I vse-taki-Strugatskie," *Literaturnaia gazeta*, 3 April 1999, p. 4;

Istvan Csicsery-Ronay Jr., "Kafka and Science Fiction," *Newsletter of the Kafka Society of America*, 7 (June 1983): 5–14;

Csicsery-Ronay, "Towards the Last Fairy Tale: On the Fairy-Tale Paradigm in the Strugatskys' Science Fiction 1963–72," *Science-Fiction Studies*, 13 (1986): 1–41;

Aleksandr Fedorov, "Arkadi Strugatsky: 'Man Must Always be Man,'" *Soviet Literature*, 9, no. 426 (1983): 113–123;

Leonid Filippov, "Umnyi ne skazhet . . . : O proizvedeniiakh Strugatskikh voobshche i o fantastike v chastnosti," *Neva*, 8 (1998): 188–198;

Vladimir Gakov, "A Test of Humanity: About the Work of the Strugatsky Brothers," *Soviet Literature*, 1, no. 406 (1982): 154–161;

Elana Gomel, "Escape from Science Fiction," *Science-Fiction Studies*, 22 (November 1995): 438–444;

Gomel, "The Poetics of Censorship: Allegory as Form and Ideology in the Novels of Arkady and Boris Strugatsky," *Science-Fiction Studies*, 22 (March 1995): 87–105;

Diana Greene, "Male and Female in 'The Snail on the Slope' by the Strugatsky Brothers," *Modern Fiction Studies*, 32 (Spring 1986): 97–108;

Yvonne Howell, *Apocalyptic Realism: The Science Fiction of Arkady and Boris Strugatsky* (New York: Peter Lang, 1994);

Howell, "When the Physicians Are Lyricists: Translating the Strugatskys' Science Fiction," in *Essays in the Art and Theory of Translation*, edited by Lenore A. Grenoble and John M. Kopper (Lewiston, Me.: Edwin Mellen Press, 1997), pp. 165–196;

Wojciech Kajtoch, *Bracia Strugaccy: Zarys twórczołti* (Kraków: Universitas, 1993);

Evgenii Konchukov, "Mezhdu proshlym i budushchim," *Literaturnoe obozrenie*, 9 (1988): 25–29;

Konchukov, "Priem i mirovozzrenie," *Literaturnoe obozrenie*, 5 (1990): 37–42;

Eugene Kozlowski, "Comic Codes in Strugatskys' Tales 'Monday Begins on Saturday' and 'Tale of the Troika,'" dissertation, Ohio State University, 1991;

Kozlowski, "Multiple Comic Coding: Comedy, Satire and Parody in the Strugatskys' Tale 'Monday Begins on Saturday,'" in *Twentieth-Century Russian Literature: Selected Papers from the Fifth World Congress of Central and East European Studies: Warsaw 1995*, edited by Karen L. Ryan and Barry P. Scher (Basingstoke, U.K.: Macmillan / New York: St. Martin's Press, 2000), pp. 228–238;

Tanja Kudrjavtseva, "A Fracture in Time: On the Chronotope of Colonisation in a Science Fiction Novel," *Nordlit: Arbeidstidsskrift i litteratur*, 8 (Fall 2000): 149–164;

Vladimir Larianov, "'Iubileiny i god Borisa Strugatskoo," *Biblio-globus*, 8 (2003): 56–57;

Stanisław Lem, "About the Strugatskys' 'Roadside Picnic,'" translated by Elsa Scheider, *Science-Fiction Studies*, 10 (November 1983): 317–332;

Mikhail Lemkhin, "Tri povesti brat'ev Strigatskikh," *Grani*, 41, no. 139 (1986): 92–119;

Byron Lindsey, "On the Strugatskii Brothers' Contemporary Fairy Tale: 'Monday Begins on Saturday,'" in *The Supernatural in Slavic and Baltic Literature: Essays in Honor of Victor Terras*, edited by Amy Mandelker (Columbus, Ohio: Slavica, 1988), pp. 290–304;

Rosalind J. Marsh, *Soviet Fiction Since Stalin: Science, Politics, and Literature* (London: Croom Helm, 1986), pp. 228–231;

Patrick McGuire, "Future History, Soviet Style: The Work of the Strugatsky Brothers," in *Critical Encounters II: Writers and Themes in Science Fiction*, edited by Tom Staicar (New York: Ungar, 1982);

Elena Mikhailovna, "Brat'ia Strugatskie: 'Zhizn' ne uvazhat' nel'zia'," *Daugava: Literaturnyi Zhurnal*, 8 (1987 August): 98–109;

John Moore, "Miracle Stalker: Personal and Social Transformation in Arkady and Boris Strugatsky's 'Roadside Picnic,'" *Foundation: The International Review of Science Fiction*, 71 (Autumn 1997): 63–76;

Tatyana Moskvina, "A Billion Years Before the End of Cinema," in *Russian Critics on the Cinema of Glasnost'*, edited by Andrew Horton and Michael Brashinsky (Cambridge: Cambridge University Press, 1994), pp. 116–120;

Alice Stone Nakhimovsky, "Soviet Anti-Utopias in the Works of Arkady and Boris Strugatsky," in *Alexander Lipson: In Memoriam*, edited by Charles Gribble (Columbus, Ohio: Slavica, 1994), pp. 143–153;

Mikhail Nekhoroshev, "Nepoznannyi literaturnyi ob'ekt," *Neva*, 4 (1995): 199–202;

Christopher Pike, "Change and the Individual in the Work of the Strugatskys," in *Science Fiction, Social Conflict and War*, edited by P. J. Davies (Manchester, U.K.: Manchester University Press, 1990), pp. 85–97;

Stephen W. Potts, *The Second Marxian Invasion: The fiction of the Strugatsky Brothers* (San Bernadino, Cal.: Borgo, 1991);

V. Serebinenko, "Tri veka skitanii v mire utopii," *Novyi mir*, 5 (May 1989): 242–255;

A. Shabanov, "V griadushchikh 'sumerkakh morali,'" *Molodaia gvardiia*, 2 (February 1985): 282–289;

Erik Simon, "Der Zerfall der Zukunft: Die kommunistische Utopie im Werk der Strugazkis," in *Streifzuge ins Ubermorgen: Science Fiction und Zukunftsforschung*, edited by Klaus Burmeister and Karlheinz Steinmuller (Weinheim: Beltz, 1992), pp. 145–161;

Salvestroni Simonetta, "The Science-Fiction Films of Andrei Tarkovsky," *Science-Fiction Studies*, 14 (November 1987): 294–306;

George E. Slusser, "Structures of Apprehension: Lem, Heinlein and the Strugatskys," *Science-Fiction Studies*, 16, no. 1 (1989): 1–37;

Halina Stephan, "The Changing Protagonist in Soviet Science Fiction," in *Fiction and Drama in Eastern and Southeastern Europe: Evolution and Experiment in the Postwar Period*, edited by Henrik Birnbaum and Thomas Eekman (Columbus, Ohio: Slavica, 1980), pp. 361–378;

Andrei Stoialrov, "Peizazh posle bitvy," *Neva*, 7 (1994): 274–281;

D. Suvin, "Criticism of the Strugatsky Brothers' Work," *Canadian-American Slavic Studies*, 2 (Summer 1972): 286–307;

Suvin, "The Literary Opus of the Strugatsky Brothers," *Canadian-American Slavic Studies*, 3 (Fall 1974): 454–463;

Irina Vasiuchenko, "Otvergnuvshie voskresen'e: Zametki o tvorchestve Arkadiia i Borisa Strugatskikh," *Znamia*, 5 (May 1989): 216–225.

# Vladimir Fedorovich Tendriakov

*(5 December 1923 – 3 August 1984)*

Alexandra Smith
*University of Canterbury, New Zealand*

BOOKS: *Sredi lesov: Povesti i ocherki* (Moscow: Sovetskii pisatel', 1954);

*Ne ko dvoru: Povest'* (Moscow: Khudozhestvennaia literatura, 1956);

*Son-in-law: A Story* (Moscow: Foreign Languages Publishing House, 1956);

*Ukhaby* (Moscow: Molodaia gvardiia, 1957);

*Tugoi uzel* (Kirov: Kirovskoe knizhnoe izd-vo, 1958);

*Chudotvornaia: Povest'* (Moscow: Molodaia gvardiia, 1958);

*Za begushchim dnem: Roman* (Moscow: Molodaia gvardiia, 1960);

*Sud: Povest'* (Moscow: Sovetskii pisatel', 1961);

*Povesti* (Moscow: Moskovskii rabochii, 1961);

*Chrezvychainoe; Sud: Povesti* (Moscow: Moskovskii rabochii, 1962);

*Korotkoe zamykanie: Povest'* (Moscow: Sovetskaia Rossiia, 1962);

*Mednyi krestik* (Moscow: Detgiz, 1963);

*Svidanie s Nefertiti: Roman* (Moscow: Molodaia gvardiia, 1965);

*Nakhodka* (Moscow: Sovetskaia Rossiia, 1966);

*Podënka–vek korotkii: Povest'* (Moscow: Sovetskii pisatel', 1967);

*Podenka–vek korotkii; Chudotvornaia; Chrezvychainoe; Korotkoe zamykanie; Onega* (Moscow: Molodaia gvardiia, 1969);

*Svidanie s Nefertiti; Nakhodka; Kostry na s negu: Roman, povest', rasskazy* (Moscow: Sovetskii pisatel', 1970);

*Padenie Ivana Chuprova: Povesti* (Perm: Permskoe knizhn. izd-vo, 1971);

*Perevertyshi: Povesti* (Moscow: Sovremennik, 1974);

*Noch' posle vypuska* (Paris: Institut d'Etudes Slaves, 1975);

*Grazhdane goroda solntsa: Povesti* (Moscow: Molodaia gvardiia, 1977);

*Rasplata: Povesti* (Moscow: Sovetskii pisatel', 1982);

*Apostol'skaia komandirovka* (Moscow: Sovetskaia Rossiia, 1984);

*Shest'desiat svechei: Roman, povesti* (Moscow: Izvestiia, 1985);

*Zatmenie: Povesti* (Moscow: Sovremennik, 1986);

*Vladimir Fedorovich Tendriakov (from* Svidanie s Nefertiti; Nakhodka; Kostry na s negu: Roman, povest', rasskazy, *1970; Thomas Cooper Library, University of South Carolina)*

*Pokushenie na mirazhi: Roman; povesti; rasskazy* (Moscow: Sovetskii pisatel', 1986);

*Pokushenie na mirazhi; Chistye vody Kitezha* (Moscow: Khudozhestvennaia literatura, 1987);

*Liudi ili ne liudi: Povesti i rasskazy* (Moscow: Sovremennik, 1990);

*Okhota* (Moscow: Izdatel'stvo Pravda, 1991);

*Neizdannoe: Proza, publitsistika, dramaturgiia,* edited by N. Asmolovoi-Tendriakovoi (Moscow: Khudozhestvennaia literatura, 1995).

**Editions and Collections:** *Izbrannye proizvedeniia v dvukh tomakh,* 2 volumes (Moscow: Gosudarstvennoe izdatel'stvo khudozhestvennoi literatury, 1963);

*Three Novellas,* edited by J. G. Garrard (Oxford & New York: Pergamon Press, 1967)—comprises "Ukhaby," "Troika, semerka, tuz," and "Sud";

*Noch' posle vypuska* (Moscow: Sovetskaia Rossiia, 1976);

*Sobranie sochinenii,* 4 volumes (Moscow: Khudozhestvennaia literatura, 1978–1980);

*Sobranie sochinenii v piati tomakh,* 5 volumes (Moscow: Khudozhestvennaia literatura, 1987–1989);

*Pokushenie na mirazhi: Roman, povest', rasskazy* (Moscow: Sovetskii pisatel', 1988);

*Sud = The Trial,* edited by Peter Doyle (Oxford & Cambridge, Mass.: Blackwell, 1990).

**Editions in English:** *Three, Seven, Ace and Other Stories,* translated by David Alger, Olive Stevens, and Paul Falla, foreword by Max Hayward (New York: Harper & Row, 1973; London: Harvill Press, 1973)—comprises "Three, Seven, Ace," "Justice," and "Creature of a Day";

*A Topsy-Turvy Spring: Stories,* translated by Alex Miller and Avril Pyman (Moscow: Progress Publishers, 1978)—comprises "The Trial," "The Find," and "A Topsy-turvy Spring";

"On the Blessed Island of Communism," translated by Michael Duncan, in *Dissonant Voices: The New Russian Fiction,* edited by Oleg Chukhontsev (London: Harvill Press, 1991), pp. 76–102;

"Donna Anna," translated by Lila H. Wangler and Helena Goscilo, in *The Wild Beach: An Anthology of Contemporary Russian Short Stories,* edited by Goscilo (Ann Arbor, Mich.: Ardis, 1992), pp. 191–217.

PLAY PRODUCTION: *Tri meshka sornoi pshenitsy,* Leningrad, Bol'shoi Dramaticheskii Teatr, 1975.

PRODUCED SCRIPTS: *Chuzhaia rodnia,* motion picture, Lenfil'm, 1955;

*Sasha vstupayet v zhizn,* motion picture, Ministry of Culture of the USSR/Mosfil'm, 1956;

*Chudotvornaya,* motion picture, 1960;

*49 dnej,* screenplay by Tendriakov, Grigori Baklanov, and Iurini Bondarev, motion picture, Mosfil'm, 1962;

*Vesenniye perevyortyshi,* motion picture, Lenfil'm, 1974.

OTHER: *Pozhar,* in *Teatr pisatelei,* edited by O. R. Miroshnichenko (Moscow: Sovetskaia Rossiia, 1986);

"Na blazhennom ostrove kommunizma," in *Svet i teni "velikogo desiatiletiia": N. S. Khrushchev i ego Vremia,* edited by Lev Andreevich Kirshner and Svetlana Alekseevna Prokhvatilova (Leningrad: Lenizdat, 1989).

SELECTED PERIODICAL PUBLICATION–UNCOLLECTED: "Den', vytesnivshii zhizn'," *Druzhba narodov,* 1 (1985): 31–67.

Vladimir Fedorovich Tendriakov was one of the most popular and prolific of the liberal-minded writers who emerged in the Soviet Union after the death of Joseph Stalin in 1953. His works reveal his concerns about the moral and spiritual values of post–World War II Soviet society and provide psychological insights into the mentality of his fellow citizens, and many of them triggered lively debates and attracted negative criticism. His writings include a strong anti-Stalinist stance and a severe critique of the actions of the Soviet bureaucracy in both urban and rural areas. He wrote novels, short stories, plays, screenplays, and essays, but his favorite genre was the novella. His early works in this form are set in remote rural areas, but his later writings include urban life, education, and political and philosophical meditations.

Tendriakov was born in the village of Makarovskaia in Vologda province, three hundred miles northeast of Moscow, on 5 December 1923; his father was a civil servant who sometimes served as a judge. After completing his schooling in Podosinovets in Kirov province in 1941, Tendriakov joined the army; he served as a radio operator in the battles of Stalingrad and Khar'kov until he was wounded and invalided out in 1943. He then worked as a military instructor at his former school in Podosinovets and served as secretary of the District Committee of the Komsomol (Kommunisticheski Soiuz Molodezhi [Communist Union of Youth]). In 1945 he moved to Moscow, where he studied at the Institute of Cinematography and then at the Gor'ky Literary Institute. He joined the Communist Party in 1948.

Tendriakov graduated from the Gor'ky institute in 1951. He worked as a journalist for the Soviet news agency TASS and for the magazine *Ogonek* (Little Light) until 1953, when he became a full-time author. During the Soviet cultural "Thaw" from 1954 to 1957 Tendriakov's uncompromising works attracted the attention of a considerable Soviet readership. In 1958 he became editor of the journal *Literaturnaia Moskva* (Literary Moscow).

Tendriakov's early stories were popular for their criticism of Stalinist mismanagement of collective farms and the consequent demoralization of the Soviet peasantry. In "Padenie Ivana Chuprova" (The Fall of Ivan Chuprov), first published in the journal *Novyi mir* (New World) in 1953 and collected in Tendriakov's *Povesti*

(1961, Stories), the title character is a collective-farm manager who deceives state officials to protect his farm; his motive is noble, but as a result of his lie he degenerates morally. In "Ukhaby" (Potholes), which was published in the magazine *Nash sovremennik* (Our Contemporary) in 1956 and became the title piece in a collection the following year, the truck driver Vasilii Dergarchev is illegally transporting passengers in his company vehicle for money on a nearly impassable rural road: "Oh, what a road, what a road! It was the eternal bane of the whole Gustoi Bor district. Generation after generation of cars obsolesced on it before their time, destroyed by the ruts and potholes and the engulfing mud." Vasilii dozes off at the wheel; the truck overturns, crushing a young man beneath it. He can be saved if he can be towed on a sled by a tractor through the mud to the hospital, but Kniazhev, the manager of the nearby machinery and tractor station, tells Vasilii: "I cannot possibly let you use the state property for purposes for which it is not meant." A tractor is finally procured elsewhere, but it is too late: the youth dies on his way to the hospital. At the end the surgeon, after hearing Vasilii's account, calls Kniazhev a "bureaucrat who has grown into a murderer." "Sasha otpravliatetsia v put'" (Sasha Embarks on His Journey), published in *Novyi mir* in 1956 and republished as "Tugoi uzel" (A Tight Knot) in the 1958 collection of that title, explores the complex psychology of Communist Party secretary Pavel Mansurov, who puts his career above everything else and expects his subordinates to demonstrate economic achievements based on unreal expectations. *Chudotvornaia* (1958, The Miracle-Making Icon) urges the resurrection of the Christian spiritual values suppressed under Stalin's rule.

Tendriakov's short novel *Sud* (1961; translated as "The Trial," 1978) reveals his desire to break away from the constrictive dictates of socialist realism. The work touches on themes that are found in Soviet "village prose": writers in this genre exalt the relatively unspoiled countryside, especially in the northern parts of Russia and Siberia, as the repository of Russian cultural traditions and moral values. *Sud* is set in the forests of Vologda province. Three men go on a bear hunt: Semen Teterin, an experienced hunter; Konstantin Dudyrev, the manager of a construction site; and Vasilii Mitiagin, a young engineer. Dudyrev is "a most powerful person" whose wood-processing factory will change the village of Dymki forever. By contrast, Mitiagin is neither handsome nor powerful: "no one except old ladies respect him." The hunters discover that in addition to a bear, they have accidentally shot and killed a young man who was playing an accordion on his way to visit his girlfriend. The investigators believe Mitiagin to be responsible for the accident, but Teterin finds a bullet in the bear's carcass that points to Dudyrev as the killer of the young man. He hides the evidence, because he does not want the truth to come out about Dudyrev, on whom the future of the village depends. Mitiagin is cleared at the trial, and the truth is never revealed. Dudyrev, who is destroying the traditional environment with his bulldozers, represents the aggressive advancement of modernity; in his constant "hunting" for new areas to develop, the narrator says, he "stopped being a normal man and turned into a wild animal himself—malign, bloodthirsty, patient." The contrast between the beastly and pragmatic newcomer Dudyrev and his victim, a young man in love and a musician, a person full of creativity and vigor, symbolizes the clash between the technologically advanced modern world and the old world. At the end of the story Teterin meditates on the events and concludes that engineers such as Dudyrev make life much more complicated, confusing and disorienting people by distracting them from their roots and their natural environment: "It is possible to build an industrial complex in three or four years, but the human character needs years to mature. It is not enough to set the industrial complex going, to build a road, to shift people into modern buildings. It is necessary, but it is not everything. It is necessary to teach them how to live." Teterin is overwhelmed by guilt for not revealing the actual killer of the young man; the novel ends with the statement "There is no heavier judgment than the judgment of one's own consciousness." Thus, the traditional hunting story of nineteenth-century Russian narratives is appropriated to comment on the flaws in the Soviet legal system and on the shortcomings of utopianism.

In the 1960s and 1970s Tendriakov was an official in the Writers' Union of the Union of Soviet Socialist Republics. In 1963 he was reprimanded by the authorities for the play *Belyi flag* (White Flag), which he co-authored with Kamil Ikramov.

In the essay "Den' na rodine" (1964, A Day in the Native Town), first published in the journal *Nauka i religiia* (Science and Religion), Tendriakov's childhood reminiscences are interwoven with myths, fishing stories, and family legends and juxtaposed with a detailed description of the present-day collective farm in the village. The collective-farm scenes parody the style of the Soviet "production novel" with its clichéd images of roads, trucks, and tractors. Tendriakov conveys his sympathy for eccentric old peasants who have preserved their individuality; nevertheless, he admits that the collective farmers lead contented lives: they receive monthly salaries, buy motorcycles, brew beer, and continue to celebrate religious holidays such as Trinity Sunday and Easter. In May 1967 Tendriakov co-signed the critical letter of Aleksandr Solzhenitsyn sent to the Presidium of the Fourth Soviet Writers' Congress.

The search for identity is one of the most prevalent motifs in Tendriakov's works. In his short novel "Apostol'skaia komandirovka" (The Apostolic Business Trip), first published in 1969 in *Nauka i religiia* and published in book form in 1984, a popular science writer suddenly becomes dissatisfied with turning out propaganda and goes into the countryside to seek his roots. In the novella "Zatmenie" (Eclipse), published in 1977 in the magazine *Druzhba narodov* (The People's Friendship) and collected in *Zatmenie: Povesti* (1986), Tendriakov also touches on individual psychology and explores moral and spiritual issues. Pavel, a bacteriologist, is in love with Maia, who is stricken with melancholy. One night on the prairie, during an eclipse of the moon, she meets the mysterious stranger Gorsha and goes off with him; Pavel kills Gorsha in a jealous rage and afterward is tormented by guilt.

In 1973 Tendriakov received the Distinguished Award Badge for his contributions to Soviet literature. From 1973 to 1980 he served on the governing board of the Writers' Union. His novels and stories of the 1970s show a growing concern with the ethical aspects of Soviet education and propaganda. In "Vesennie perevertyshi," collected in his *Perevertyshi* (1974) and translated as "A Topsy-Turvy Spring" in *A Topsy-Turvy Spring: Stories* (1978), the mathematics teacher Vasilii Vasil'evich Vasil'ev believes that everyone has a hidden talent, including thirteen-year-old Diushka Tiagunov. But it is Diushka's friend Levka Gaizer, a fifteen-year-old interested in science, not the teacher, who sparks in Diushka a passion for mathematics and physics. The theme of education also runs through the novella "Tri meshka sornoi pshenitsy" (Three Sacks of Bad Wheat), published in the same volume, in which Tendriakov compares innocent teenagers to their fathers, whose worldview is shaped by the corrupt administration of the Soviet state. Some of Tendriakov's most outspoken criticism of the way Soviet schooling promoted the interests of the state rather than those of the students appears in "Noch' posle vypuska" (The Night after Graduation), published in the September 1974 issue of *Novyi mir*. It centers around a speech delivered by Iulechka Studentseva, the best student at an urban secondary school. Iulechka admits that even though her education has prepared her for a brilliant future, her school has not provided her with the ability to think critically and creatively: "School made me know everything, except one thing—what I like and what I love.... It expected top grades from me, so I obeyed.... Now I look around, and I realize that I love nothing and nobody. Except my mom, my dad, and my school. I have a thousand roads in front of me, and they all look the same to me. Do not think that I am happy. I am frightened. Very frightened." The speech suggests that the conventions adopted in Soviet schools foster conformity and discourage students from being individuals. Publication of the story shocked the Soviet establishment and provoked lively debates among educators; it was criticized for ideological shortcomings and deviations from socialist realism, since it provoked fundamental questions but failed to deliver solutions.

Other works of Tendriakov's of the 1970s and 1980s were also criticized in official Soviet circles for their pessimism and negativity. Yet, they provided a model for the new literary discourse of the perestroika years in the 1980s and for subsequent political transformations.

*Title page for* Zatmenie: Povesti *(Eclipse: Stories), Tendriakov's 1986 collection. In the title novella a jealous man murders his girlfriend's lover, whom she met during an eclipse of the moon (Olin Memorial Library, Wesleyan University).*

Tendriakov died in Moscow on 3 August 1984; he was survived by his widow, N. Asmolova-Tendriakova. Some of his most outspoken writings were published posthumously in the March 1988 issue of *Novyi mir* and collected in the volume *Okhota* (1991, Hunting). In these autobiographical stories, written between 1969 and 1971, Tendriakov shows the effects of collectivization on people in his home village. In "Para gnedykh" (A Pair of Bay Horses) the narrator reflects on the actions of his father, who, as a civil servant in the summer of 1929, had to implement the new policies of the Soviet government that discriminated against rich peasants. As a boy the narrator admired some of the kulaks and was perplexed that any peasant with two horses could be declared "an enemy of the people." In "Khleb dlia sobaki" (Bread for a Dog) the narrator recalls watching, along with other boys, as the victims of collectivization were transformed from relatively prosperous peasants into homeless and starving "bark-eaters" in 1933: "There was no horror so great that it could stifle tremendous—almost inhuman—curiosity. Frozen with fear and disgust, exhausted by the panic-filled sense of pity that we kept well-hidden, we watched the bark-eaters." The railway stationmaster kills himself after being driven to madness by observing the living corpses each day. One man, dying from hunger on the road, asks a passing official why he is being victimized: "Is it really because I had two horses?" The official, Dybakov, responds affirmatively in a detached and indifferent manner. The child's view of collectivization expressed in Tendriakov's stories subverts the myth of happy childhood prevalent in socialist realist narratives. "Parania," another story from this cycle, is set in the summer of 1937. Influenced by Communist antireligious propaganda, the children in the village tease the "holy fool" Parania for being a bride of Jesus until the day she asserts that she is betrothed to Stalin himself. She begins accusing some of the townspeople of being enemies of Stalin; the charges lead to their arrests. Finally, she is killed by one of those she has accused. Tendriakov incorporates documentary materials into the text.

In the words of N. N. Shneidman, Vladimir Fedorovich Tendriakov's posthumously published works "bear witness to his constant struggle with censors, with editors, and with himself." They also expose Tendriakov's struggle throughout his literary career with the dictates of socialist realism.

**Interview:**

Aleksandr Viktorovich Fedorov, "To Think about Life: A Talk with Vladimir Tendriakov," *Soviet Literature,* 444, no. 3 (1985): 147-151.

**Bibliography:**

Emma Aristarkhovna Volkova and L. A. Smirnova, *Vladimir Fedorovich Tendriakov: Bibliograficheskii ukazatel'* (Vologda: Vologodskaia obl. biblioteka im. I.V. Babushkina, 1993).

**References:**

Vladimir Il'ich Amlinsky, "Perechityvaia Vladimira Tendrikova: 'I vse-taki ia budu iskat' . . . ,'" *Literaturnaia gazeta,* 2 April 1986, p. 5;

Kh. Auersval'd, "Proportsii chastichnykh tekstov v 'Nochi posle vypuska' V. Tendriakova i v 'Zhivi i pomni' V. Rasputina i ikh kachestvenno-funktsional'naia interpretatsiia," in *VI Internationaler Kongress der Internationalen Assoziation der Lehrkrafte der russischen Sprache und Literatur, Budapest-UVR 11–16 August,* edited by Ludwig Wilske (Potsdam: Pedagogische Hochschule Karl Liebknecht, 1986), pp. 9–15;

L. Bartashevich, "Mirazhi i deistvitel'nost'," *Oktiabr'* (January 1988 ): 197–200;

Bartashevich, "Na puti poter' i obretenii," *Oktiabr'* (November 1988): 196–199;

Willi Beitz, "Epochenwidersproche und Konfliktgestaltung bei Tendrjakow, Trifonow und Granin," *Weimarer Beitrage,* 31, no. 5 (1985): 795–813;

D. S. Berestovskaia, "Geroicheskoe i tragicheskoe v sovremennoi proze o Velikoi Otechestvennoi voine," *Filologicheskie nauki,* 3 (1989): 3–9;

Galina Berkenkopf, "Zwei Schulgeschichten aus der Sowjetunion," *Neue Sammlung: Vierteljahres-Zeitschrift für Erziehung und Gesellschaft,* 22 (1982): 201–220;

Richard Chapple, "A Begrudging Testament: The Christ Who Would Not Go Away (on Tendriakov's 'An Attempt at Mirages')," *Australian Slavonic and East European Studies,* 2, no. 1 (1988): 55–67;

Vladimir Dmitrievich Dudintsev, "V labirinte protivorechii," *Literaturnoe obozrenie,* no. 12 (1977): 54–58;

Isabelle Esmein, "Polemique autour des oeuvres d'Axionov we de Tendriakov," *La Table Ronde,* 215 (1965): 175–179;

John G. Garrard, "Vladimir Tendriakov," *Slavic and East European Journal,* 9, no. 1 (1965): 1–18;

Daniil Granin, "Vladimir Tendriakov: The Bell of Memory," *Soviet Literature,* 450, no. 9 (1985): 3–4;

Rudolf Gregor, "Betrachtungen zu Fragen des ästhetisch-ethischen Anspruchs in Werken V. F. Tendrjakovs," *Wissenschaftliche Zeitschrift der Ernst Moritz Arndt- Universität Greifswald: Gesellschaftswissenschaftliche Reihe,* 35, nos. 1–2 (1986): 63–64;

Regina Hager, "Die Aktivierung des Gewissens der Helden (V. Tendrjakow: 'Sud')," *Wissenschaftliche Zeitschrift der Friedrich-Schiller-Universität Jena: Gesellschafts- und sprachwissenschaftliche Reihe,* 25 (1976): 255–261;

Hager, "Die Evolution des literarischen Menschenbildes im Erzahlschaffen Sergej Antonovs, Jurij Nagibins und Vladimir Tendrjakovs de 50er Jahr," *Zeitschrift für Slawistik,* 20 (1975): 214–225;

Hager, "'Er schlagt den Menschen die Wahrheit ins Gesicht!': Das moralische Urteil des Vladimir Tendjakow," in *Was kann den nein Dichter auf Erden: Betrachtungen über moderne sowjetische Schriftssteller,* edited by Anton Hirsche and Edward Kowalski (Berlin: Aufbau, 1982), pp. 410–427;

Hager, "Zur Bedeutung des Grossen Vaterlandischen Krieges für die Gestaltung des literarischen Menschenbildes in Tendrjakovs Erzahlung 'Tri meka sornoj pnicy,'" *Zeitschrift für Slawistik,* 21 (1976): 72–76;

Klaus Holtmeier, *Religiöse Elemente in der sowjetrussischen Gegenwartsliteratur: Studien zu V. Rasputin, V. Ukin und V. Tendrjakov* (Frankfurt am Main & New York: Peter Lang, 1986);

Geoffrey Hosking, "Vladimir Tendriakov," in his *Beyond Socialist Realism: Soviet Fiction since* Ivan Denisovich (London: Granada, 1980; New York: Holmes & Meier, 1980), pp. 84–100;

Kamil Ikramov, "Dukhovnyi predel Krokhaleva," *Literaturnoe obozrenie,* no. 12 (1977): 58–60;

Irene Jablonski, "Nebenperson und ihre Funktion: Adrian Fomi Gluev in Tendrjakovs Tri meka sornoy penicy," in *Colloquium Slavicum Basiliense: Gedenkschrift für Hildegard Schroeder,* edited by Heinrich Riggenbach and Felix Keller (Bern: Peter Lang, 1981), pp. 205–235;

Carola Jurchott, "Kultureller Kontext und verschiedene Strategien bei der Übersetzung von Vladimir Tendriakovs 'No posle vypuska,'" in *Translators' Strategies and Creativity,* edited by Ann Beylard-Ozeroff, Jana Kralova, and Barbara Moser-Mercer (Amsterdam: Benjamins, 1998), pp. 41–51;

Klaus Kantorczyk, "Zur Spezifik der Konfliktgestaltung in Werken der Neuesten sowjetischen Kriegsprosa," *Wissenschaftliche Zeitschrift der Universität Rostock,* 25 (1976): 277–282;

V. Kardin, "Neischerpaemo, nevospolnimo," *Novyi mir,* no. 9 (1985): 262–266;

Birgit Karlsson, "O sootnoeniiax polnyi i kratkix prilagatel'nyx v predikativnoj funkcii v romane V. Tendrjakova 'Svidenie s Nefertiti,'" *Scando-Slavica,* 16 (1970): 123–128;

Hyun Taek Kim, "Three Soviet Writers and the New Testament: Iurii Dombrovskii, Vladimir Tendriakov and Chingiz Aitmatov," dissertation, University of Kansas, 1990;

Boris Nikiforovich Kliusov, *Na perednei linii: Ocherk tvorchestva V. Tendriakova* (Minsk: Izd-vo Ministerstva vysshego, srednego spetsial'nogo i professional'nogo obrazovaniia BSSR, 1963);

Elena Aleksandrovna Krasnoshchekova, "Nravstvennyi konflikt v sovremennoi povesti," in *Zhanrovostilevye iskaniia sovremennoi sovetskoi prozy,* edited by Vadim Evgen'evich Poliak and Lidiia Moiseevna Kovsky (Moscow: Nauka, 1971), pp. 175–199;

E. P. Kravchenko, "Tipologiia kharakterov v tvorchestve V. F. Tendriakova," *Voprosy Russki Literatury,* 24, no. 2 (1974): 40–44;

Carl-Erik Lindberg, *Text and Content: A Textlinguistic Interpretation of a Major Aspect of "Content" in Vladimir Tendrjakov's Novella "Rezvyajnoe"* (Stockholm: Almqvist & Wiksell International, 1983);

Aleksandr Alekseevich Ninov, "Vladimir Tendryakov," *Soviet Literature,* 6 (1969): 162–165;

Gennadii Novikov, "Tendriakov na Baikale," in his *Zona dlia geniev* (St. Petersburg: Russko-Baltiiskii informatsionnyi tsentr BLITS, 1999);

Vladimir Novikov, "Ucha-uchimsia," *Literaturnoe obozrenie,* no. 7 (1981): 43–46;

Novikov, "Wladimir Tendrjakow," *Kunst und Literatur: Zeitschrift für Fragen der Aesthetik und Kunsttheorie,* 30, no. 5 (1982): 549–555;

Lidia Samukowicz Pacira, "Vladimir Tendryakov, a Survey and Analysis of His Works," dissertation, University of Michigan, 1975;

Boris Pankin, "Alongside the Obelisk," *Soviet Studies in Literature,* 17 (Fall 1981): 32–38;

Viktor Ksenofontovich Pankov, "Lykov, Slegov i drugie," *Znamia,* 38, no. 10 (1968): 236–244;

Fan Parker, "Vladimir Tendriakov: A First Appraisal," *Books Abroad,* 39 (1965): 36–37;

Kathleen Parthé, "Rereading Tendriakov," in her *Russian Village Prose: The Radiant Past* (Princeton: Princeton University Press, 1992), pp. 113–119;

V. Piskunov, "Evangelie ot komp'utera," *Literaturnoe obozrenie,* no. 1 (1988): 43–47;

N. Rubtsov, "Kak chelovekom byt'," *Literaturnoe obozrenie,* no. 12 (1989): 45–47;

Anne-Katrin Schentschischin, "Die Gestaltung der Lehrer-Schuler-Beziehung in V. F. Tendrjakovs povest' 'Rasplata,'" *Wissenschaftliche Zeitschrift der Ernst Moritz Arndt-Universität Greifswald: Gesellschaftwissenschaftliche Reihe,* 37, no. 1 (1988): 68–70;

Schentschischin, "Etisch-moralische Fragestellung im Schaffen V. F. Tendrjakovs," *Wissenschaftliche Zeitschrift der Ernst Moritz Arndt-Universität Greifswald: Gesellschaftswissenschaftliche Reihe,* 33, no. 1 (1984): 28–29;

V. Serdiuchenko, "V krugu 'vechnykh' voprosov," *Oktiabr'* (November 1983): 189–194;

G. Shaumani, "Progress i nravstvenost' o romane V. Tendriakova 'Pokushenie na mirazhi,'" *Zeitschrift für Slawistik,* 35, no. 3 (1990): 382–387;

N. N. Shneidman, "Soviet Schools and Society in the Prose of Vladimir Tendriakov," *Journal of Ukranian Studies,* 14 (Summer–Winter 1989): 1–2;

Shneidman, "Vladimir Tendriakov," in his *Soviet Literature in the 1980s: Decade of Transition* (Toronto, Buffalo, N.Y. & London: University of Toronto Press, 1989), pp. 84–93;

Michael Stanley Shylanski, "Vladimir Fëdorovich Tendrjakov: Artist and Social Critic," M.A. thesis, Ohio State University, 1975;

Evgenii Iur'evich Sidorov, "Muzhestvo pravdy," *Oktiabr'* (January 1978): 211–220;

E. Starikova, *Poeziia prozy: stat'i* (Moscow: Sovetskii pisatel', 1962);

Starikova, "Shagi komandora: O rasskazakh Vladimira Tendriakova," *Znamia* (February 1989): 223–231;

R. Stockl, "Das motivierte Wort in Autorenrede und Personenrede der sowjetischen kunstlirischen Prosa," *Wissenschaftliche Zeitschrift der Friedrich-Schiller-Universität Jena: Gesellschafts- und sprachwissenschaftliche Reihe,* 29 (1980): 205–213;

Vladimir Subkin, "Attestatsiia zrelosti," *Literaturnoe obozrenie,* no. 4 (1976): 97–104;

Iurii Valentinovich Trifonov, "Twenty Years Later," translated by Eve Manning, *Soviet Literature,* 401, no. 8 (1982): 3–4;

Andrei Turkov, "Srashchennyi provod: O rasskazakh Vladimira Tendriakova," *Literaturnaia gazeta,* 1 June 1988, p. 4;

I. Vladimirova, "Molodoi Sovremennik," *Neva,* 9 (1969): 175–178;

Lila Hilda Wangler, "The moral and religious themes in the works of Vladimir Tendriakov, 1956–1976," dissertation, University of Michigan, 1977;

Walter James Weeks, "Vladimir Fëdorovich Tendrjakov," M.A. thesis, Brown University, 1964.

# Iurii Valentinovich Trifonov
*(28 August 1925 – 28 March 1981)*

David Gillespie
*University of Bath*

BOOKS: *Studenty: Povest'* (Moscow: Molodaia gvardiia, 1951); republished as *Studenty: Roman* (Omsk: Omskoe oblastnoe knizhnoe izdatel'stvo, 1954); translated by Margaret Wettlin and Ivy Litvinova as *Students: A Novel* (Moscow: Foreign Languages Publishing House, 1953);

*Pod solntsem* (Moscow: Sovetskii pisatel', 1959);

*V kontse sezona* (Moscow: Fizkul'tura i sport, 1961);

*Utolenie zhazhdy* (Moscow: Goslitizdat, 1963);

*Kostry i dozhd'* (Moscow: Sovetskaia Rossiia, 1964);

*Otblesk kostra* (Moscow: Sovetskii pisatel', 1966);

*Neterpenie: Povest' ob A. Zheliabove* (Moscow: Politizdat, 1973; revised, 1974); translated by Robert Daglish as *The Impatient Ones* (Moscow: Progress, 1978);

*Drugaia zhizn'* (Moscow: Sovetskii pisatel', 1976); translated by Michael Glenny as "Another Life," in *Another Life; The House on the Embankment* (New York: Simon & Schuster, 1983);

*Obmen* (Moscow: VAAP, 1977);

*Starik* (Moscow: Sovetskii pisatel', 1980); translated by Jacqueline Edwards and Mitchell Schneider as *The Old Man* (New York: Simon & Schuster, 1984);

*Dom na naberezhnoi* (Ann Arbor, Mich.: Ardis, 1983); translated by Glenny as "The House on the Embankment," in *Another Life; The House on the Embankment* (New York: Simon & Schuster, 1983);

*Sobranie sochinenii*, 4 volumes, edited by Sergei Alekseevich Baruzdin (Moscow: Khudozhestvennaia literatura, 1985–1987)–includes volume 4, *Otblesk kostra; Rasskazy; Vremia i mesto; Stat'i*;

*Vremia i mesto* (Moscow: Izvestiia, 1988)–includes *Ischeznovenie*, translated by David Lowe as *The Disappearance* (Ann Arbor, Mich.: Ardis, 1991);

*Oprokinutyi dom* (Moscow: Panorama, 1999).

**Editions and Collections:** *Fakely nad Flaminio* (Moscow: Fizkul'tura i sport, 1965);

*Kepka s bol'shim kozyr'kom* (Moscow: Sovetskaia Rossiia, 1969);

*Igry v sumerkakh* (Moscow: Fizkul'tura i sport, 1970);

*Iurii Valentinovich Trifonov (from Sobranie sochinenii, volume 1, 1985; Jean and Alexander Heard Library, Vanderbilt University)*

*Rasskazy i povesti* (Moscow: Khudozhestvennaia literatura, 1971);

*Dolgoe proshchanie* (Moscow: Sovetskaia Rossiia, 1973);

*Prodolzhitel'nye uroki* (Moscow: Sovetskaia Rossiia, 1975);

*Povesti* (Moscow: Sovetskaia Rossiia, 1978);

*Izbrannye proizvedeniia*, 2 volumes (Moscow: Khudozhestvennaia literatura, 1978);

*Drugaia zhizn'* (Moscow: Izvestiia, 1979);

*Utolenie zhazhdy* (Moscow: Profizdat, 1979);

*Starik* (Moscow: Sovetskii pisatel', 1980)–includes Drugaia zhizn';

*Teatr pisatelia. Tri povesti dlia teatra* (Moscow: Sovetskaia Rossiia, 1982);

*Neterpenie. Starik* (Moscow: Izvestiia, 1983);

*Izbrannoe. Roman, povesti* (Minsk: Vysheisha shkola, 1983);

*Vechnye temy. Romany, povesti* (Moscow: Sovetskii pisatel', 1984)–includes *Vremia i mesto, Oprokinutyi dom*;

*"Kak slovo nashe otzovetsia . . ."* (Moscow: Sovetskaia Rossia, 1985);

*Predvaritel'nye itogi* (Kishinev: Literatura artistike, 1985);

*Iadro pravdy: Stat'i, interv'iu, esse* (Moscow: Pravda, 1987);

*Moskovskie povesti* (Moscow: Sovetskaia Rossiia, 1988);

*Otblesk kostra; Starik; Ischeznovenie* (Moscow: Moskovskii rabochii, 1988);

*Otblesk kostra. Ischeznovenie* (Moscow: Sovetskii pisatel', 1988);

*Otblesk kostra; Starik* (Moscow: Izvestiia, 1989);

*Beskonechnye igry: O sporte, o vremeni, o sebe* (Moscow: Fizkul'tura i sport, 1989);

*Ischeznovenie; Vremia i mesto; Starik* (Moscow: Sovremennik, 1989);

*Dom na naberezhnoi; Starik* (Alma-Ata: Zhasushy, 1989);

*Dolgoe proshchanie; Drugaia zhizn'; Dom na naberezhnoi; Vremia i mesto; Oprokinutyi dom* (Moscow: Slovo, 1999);

*Rasskazy. Povesti. Roman. Vospominaniia. Esse* (Ekaterinburg: U-Faktoriia, 1999);

*Dom na naberezhnoi; Vremia i mesto* (Moscow: ACT i dr., 2000);

*Dom na naberezhnoi. Roman, dnevniki* (Moscow: EKSMO-Priz, 2000).

**Edition in English:** *The Long Goodbye: Three Novellas*, translated by Helen P. Burlingame and Ellendea Proffer (Ann Arbor, Mich.: Ardis, 1978)–comprises "The Exchange," "Taking Stock," and "The Long Goodbye."

SELECTED PERIODICAL PUBLICATION–UNCOLLECTED: "Iz dnevnikov irabochikh tetradi," *Druzhba narodov*, 5 (1998): 94–122; 6 (1998): 96–124; 10 (1998): 96–126; 11 (1998): 54–84; 1 (1999): 81–114; 2 (1999): 89–113; 3 (1999): 94–135.

Iurii Trifonov achieved public prominence in the early 1970s with his cycle of novellas that described, often in withering satirical detail, the lives, loves, and moral anxieties of the Moscow intelligentsia. As a writer who concentrated on *byt* (the minutiae of everyday life), he was both celebrated and criticized in the Soviet periodical press, while Western scholars knew him as a writer who pushed back the borders of what was permissible–at a time when Soviet dissidents were being jailed or exiled, and many writers were not being published at all. But Trifonov's body of work cannot be reduced simply to several novellas (the "Moscow cycle," as critics have called them) written between 1969 and 1975, for he also wrote historical novels, travel sketches, and "stream of consciousness" narratives, trying to come to terms with the turbulent century in which he lived.

Iurii Valentinovich Trifonov was born on 28 August 1925 in Moscow. His father was Valentin Andreevich Trifonov, a prominent Bolshevik during the revolution and civil war who had helped organize the Red Army and then held various diplomatic posts abroad in the 1920s. Like so many of the Old Bolsheviks, Valentin Andreevich perished in Joseph Stalin's purges. Trifonov was eleven years old at the time; by no accident does the motif of a childhood disrupted recur in his fiction. His mother, Evgeniia Abramovna Lur'e-Trifonova, was arrested a few months later and sentenced to eight years in the gulag (the abbreviation for the Soviet camp system) and in exile.

The family had lived in the "house on the embankment" reserved for government officials and stalwarts of the Communist Party–a building that assumes a symbolic, even metonymic, function in Trifonov's writings of the 1970s and 1980s. He and his sister, Tat'iana (born in 1927), were adopted by their maternal grandmother, Tat'iana Aleksandrovna Slovatinskaia in about 1938, and lived toward the outer reaches of suburban Moscow until 1941, when they were evacuated to Tashkent with the outbreak of war. Trifonov returned to Moscow in 1942, when, at the age of sixteen, he began working at various manual jobs. He sent some short stories and poems to the Gor'ky Literary Institute and was accepted. He enrolled in 1944 and graduated in 1949.

Some of Trifonov's short stories and sketches appeared in the periodical press in 1947–1948, but he caused a sensation with *Studenty* (translated as *Students*, 1953), which appeared in 1950 in *Novyi mir* (New World), the leading literary journal in the country; *Studenty* was published as a book in 1951. That issue of *Novyi mir* sold out immediately, and the novella pleased the critics. As a result, at the age of twenty-six, in 1951, Trifonov was awarded the Stalin Prize. Soon afterward he became a full-time writer, although he had problems receiving acceptance into the Writers' Union: his father, an "enemy of the people," had been executed, and Trifonov had lied about his parentage on his application for membership. Despite winning the Stalin Prize, he was accepted into the Writers' Union only in 1957.

Trifonov's first novel is about a group of students training to become teachers, their academic and emotional lives, and the values by which they profess to live. In *Studenty* individualism is at sharp odds with the collective, and those who insist on going their own way without reference to the collective are brought to task. These students are bright young people building the Communist future; they toast the victory of Communism at New Year parties and share an ideological commitment with Koreans, Albanians, and exiled Spaniards. On Victory Day all the students gather together on Red Square—a symbolic affirmation of the solidarity and unity of the proletariat of all countries. At the same time, the novel celebrates the middle-class values of Stalin's gilded youth: the students worry about fashions and ways of being seen (whether girls should wear brooches or necklaces) and are taken around Moscow in chauffeur-driven cars. Their link with the working class is cemented when they participate in a "day of voluntary labor," helping to lay gas pipelines and taking part in literary discussions in a factory. In the end even the most recalcitrant egotists can be reintegrated into the collective, for, as described by one character, without the collective it is impossible to live.

When it was published, *Studenty* was a model of Stalinist socialist realism, with clearly identifiable narrative outcomes and the clear division between "forward-looking" and "backward-looking" elements. Yet, from the outset of the novella Trifonov emphasizes Moscow as the locale: he details the streets, bridges, and embankments as his characters experience the city. Moscow is also growing, bustling, and developing, "pushing outwards, spreading beyond its former boundaries, and not only westward but in all directions." It most definitely is the hub of the socialist world.

In 1951 Trifonov married into the established metropolitan intelligentsia: his bride, Nina Alekseevna Nelina, was a singer at the Bolshoi Theater; her father, Amshei Markovich Niurenberg, was an artist who had known Marc Chagall in the 1920s. Trifonov's daughter, Ol'ga, was also born in 1951. (Nelina died in 1966. In 1972 Trifonov entered into a short-lived marriage with Alla Pavlovna Pastukhova, divorcing her in 1979; later he married Ol'ga Romanovna Miroshnichenko in 1979, who gave birth to his son, Valentin, in the same year.) He experimented with writing plays but without success. He also tried to devote himself to the cause of socialist construction but was unlucky in that the cause he had trumpeted—the Great Turkmenistan Canal—was, after Stalin's death in 1953, declared unviable and had to be closed down. By 1954 Trifonov was in a creative crisis.

Since the early 1950s he had been traveling to Turkmenistan in order to write about the canal, and throughout that decade he continued to visit Central Asia. His travels culminated in a series of short stories about the area that clearly identified the tensions inherent in modernizing what was, by European standards, a backward culture. More important, his travel experiences led to the novel *Utolenie zhazhdy* (1963, The Quenching of Thirst). To say that Trifonov the writer was born in Turkmenistan is no exaggeration, for in this novel—as well as in the stories of the 1950s—he first engages the literary devices of metaphor and symbolism, develops imagery and characterization within a plot driven by melodrama and occasional intrigue, and confronts the political issues of the day, such as Stalinism and its legacy. The obvious parallel Trifonov makes in *Utolenie zhazhdy* is that of the barren desert of Turkmenistan and the sterile world of Stalinism, now being irrigated and civilized by the tyrant's successors. By marrying the thematics of the Socialist realist construction novel with the ideological imperatives of de-Stalinization, Trifonov managed to appease both aesthetics and politics in a way that served him well in subsequent years.

The Turkmenistan desert is the setting for the construction of the Kara-Kum canal, more than six hundred miles of which was built in the 1950s. The changing times are indicated by the cast of characters in the novel and their backgrounds. The main character is a journalist, Koryshev, who—like Trifonov—is the son of an "enemy of the people," a fact that he has to hide while looking for work. Other characters have spent time in the Kolyma camps or been separated from their families by war and prison camps. Koryshev recalls his childhood years, during which he waited for news or tried to deliver food parcels for his father outside the Matrosskaia Tishina prison in Moscow.

De-Stalinization is also in evidence in the cultural climate. The characters in *Utolenie zhazhdy* talk about the literary situation: the 1956 publication in *Novyi mir* of Vladimir Dmitrievich Dudintsev's novel *Ne khlebom edinym* (Not by Bread Alone) and the appearance of the second volume of the literary-artistic miscellany *Literaturnaia Moskva* (1956, Literary Moscow)—both of which caused political controversy; the Picasso exhibition in Moscow; and Il'ia Grigor'evich Erenburg's novel *Ottepel'* (1954, The Thaw), which became the term used to describe the initial years of the post-Stalin period. Furthermore, Stalinists and "democrats" are battling each other in print, denouncing work methods and philosophies in the local press ("these days we're all brave in print," one character caustically remarks), and others engage in heated polemics about "truth" and "justice." The conflict between the past and the present is not only an ideological dilemma but also a national one. Some of the more enlightened and forward-looking Turkmenians support the canal project in the knowledge that irrigation will bring progress and greater material comfort for the population as a whole, but the old ways of thinking still persist. For example, one young man is killed for refusing to pay the "bride money" traditionally demanded by the bride's family—another instance of the "war between the desert and the canal."

Trifonov's second novel is worthy of note in its depiction of everyday life in Turkmenistan and the customs of the local population. In addition, he vividly evokes the desert at night. He also places emphasis on the meetings and conversations that take place randomly—the seemingly inconsequential exchanges that make up the content of an individual's normal day. Moreover, there is a rather astonishing lack of sexual coyness, which indicates a significant shift away from the starchy proprieties of the Stalinist period. People engage in casual affairs, use a friend's hotel room for a clandestine tryst, and enjoy extramarital relationships, and there are out-of-wedlock pregnancies.

The novel remains firmly, however, within the bounds of permitted socialist realism. At the end everyone comes together to seal a breach in a dam that may be catastrophic for the canal project; all the workers, managers, and local people toil heroically for two days and nights without rest or sleep. Out of pure necessity, all nationalities and all sections of the population show solidarity and clear purpose. As he returns to Moscow, looking down on the completed canal from his airplane passing overhead, Koryshev expresses his hopes for the future:

> I saw the bare and boundless expanse of sand, as old as the earth itself, its death-like pallor of a thousand years hence, when we and our descendants, and everything that has lived on this earth and has yet to live on it will become part of this light and insubstantial gray-yellow sand. Billions and billions of grains of sand will cover the land surface, will swallow up forests, towns and atomic power stations, will cover the whole of our small globe, and each grain will contain an extinguished life. That is what will happen if man gives in, if he doesn't have the strength to defeat the desert.

In the mid 1960s Trifonov's career took a different turn with "Otblesk kostra" (The Glow of the Campfire), first published in the journal *Znamia* (Banner) in 1965. The subsequent book version, also titled *Otblesk kostra,* came out in 1966; for this edition Trifonov significantly expanded the original material with added documentary evidence and personal testimony from the public. As Solzhenitsyn does in *Arkhipelag GULag, 1918–1956: Opyt knudozhestvennego issledovaniia* (1973–1975; translated as *The Gulag Archipelago, 1918–1956: An Experiment in Literary Investigation,* 1974–1978), Trifonov attempts to show in *Otblesk kostra* the truth of the past not only through archival searches and the presentation of hard historical fact but also through the lives of individuals who "bear the reflection of history." The work is an exercise in historical inquiry that again involves the search for justice—in this case, the "truth" about his own father's role in the revolution and civil war. It is an intensely personal work, but one that also seeks to establish the fate of an entire generation. As Trifonov says:

> Father has been dead a long time now, Litke also disappeared somewhere, and the old field notebooks were almost lost, too, books that had absorbed that distant, tumultuous life that some of us find so difficult to grasp today. So why do I turn the pages now? They excite me. And not only because they are about my father and about people I knew, but also because they are about a time when everything began. When we began.

Trifonov's account of the life of his father, Valentin Andreevich, and his uncle, Evgenii Andreevich Trifonov, is a rediscovery of his own roots among the Don Cossacks and his identity as the son of one of the creators of the new world. He makes clear that Stalin and his cohorts, such as Viacheslav Mikhailovich Molotov and Klimentii Efremovich Voroshilov, were the ones who destroyed the Old Bolsheviks in the 1930s—although, in addition, he cleverly blames Leon Trotsky for the excesses of the Reds during the Russian Civil War. *Otblesk kostra* is, therefore, in line with the new ideological orthodoxy of the Thaw, whereby the values of the revolution were usurped and corrupted by Stalin and his cronies; but it also features other, more subversive material.

One of the major figures in *Otblesk kostra* is Fillip Kuz'mich Mironov, a Don Cossack commander who fought with the Reds during the civil war and was then shot by them in 1921 for supposed treason. Mironov was officially rehabilitated in 1960. Yet, his fate is a reflection of the Bolsheviks' mistrust of the Cossacks and of their implementation of terror and mass coercion as a key weapon during the civil war. Mironov is important, above all because he was a man of the people, a leader of men who shared his men's blood and allegiances; he was killed by the Bolsheviks exactly because they feared in him a potential figurehead for Cossack separatism. There is here no more than a hint, then, that the civil war was won through sheer force and wanton brutality, and that the Bolsheviks then, as now, could not tolerate dissidence or difference.

In these years Trifonov also published some short stories that showed his increasing interest in the lives of the Moscow intelligentsia, an interest that became more fully developed in his "Moscow cycle" of the late 1960s and early 1970s. The story "Obmen" (The Exchange, published in 1969 in *Novyi mir*) lays bare in unflinching terms the moral compromises and eventual betrayal forced on an otherwise decent individual if he is to improve his family's material standard of living. Viktor Dmitriev, his wife, Lena, and daughter, Natasha, live in one room of a communal apartment and have to share washing and toilet facilities with other families; his mother, Kseniia Fedorovna, lives alone in another room in a different flat. Lena devises a plan whereby they all can move in together and be entitled to a two-bedroom apartment, a convenient arrangement since Kseniia Fedorovna has been diagnosed with terminal cancer. Dmitriev is thus coaxed into using his mother's imminent death in order to secure better living quarters, and he eventually agrees to Lena's plan.

Within this sordid story of manipulation and moral capitulation—the stuff of soap opera and melodrama—there is another, more symbolic battle taking place. Dmitriev's family has considerable revolutionary lineage: his uncles took part in the Red Terror, and his grandfather was imprisoned by the tsar and then cast into exile in Switzerland before the revolution (he is, in Lena's words, "a well-preserved monster"). Lena's family are fixers, people with connections who manage to get things done and improve the material quality of life (such as repairing the sewage system in the dacha colony where Dmitriev and Lena spend their summers). As Kseniia Fedorovna disapprovingly observes, they "know how to live."

Trifonov crafted a well-observed story of changing values and priorities, in which the apparent idealism and abstract values of the past are forced to make way for the new pragmatics of urban life. Dmitriev's family exhibits a blatant snobbery toward Lena and her parents, which they, in turn, regard as "hypocrisy" mixed with thinly veiled contempt. Minor characters serve as either contrasts or mirrors, so that what emerges is a picture of a society breaking with past values. New priorities are emerging, and the result is a worrisome moral and spiritual vacuum.

In his next major novella, *Predvaritel'nye itogi* (Preliminary Stocktaking, published in 1970 in *Novyi mir*), Trifonov returned to Turkmenistan as a setting and to characters who are both impractical and ruthlessly pragmatic. Like "Obmen," *Predvaritel'nye itogi* is written as a form of confession by the central character, Gennadii Sergeevich, who details the mishaps and disharmony of his family life. This picture of Moscow life, though, is much darker than Dmitriev's account in "Obmen." In *Predvaritel'nye itogi* the protagonist has an exploitative and acquisitive wife who may be cheating on him, cynical friends, and a semidelinquent son who consorts with black marketers.

From Turkmenistan, where he is translating the work of a local poet, Gennadii Sergeevich relates a depressing account of his dysfunctional family, his own lack of moral guidance, and his constant capitulation. Whereas in *Utolenie zhazhdy* the desert of Turkmenistan represents both the historical and political past, which has to be overcome for the sake of the future, here the warmth, vitality, simplicity, and kindness of the Turkmeni people and the rich fauna of the country stand in

*Title page for* Vremia i mesto *(Time and Place), the first separate publication of Trifonov's 1981 metafictional novel about a writer struggling to master his craft in an environment dominated by the literary bureaucracy (Mugar Memorial Library, Boston University)*

marked contrast to the venality and sterility of Moscow life. There are few Muscovites who deserve the reader's sympathy; outraged condemnation is reserved for all those (almost everyone in the novella) who lie, cheat, exploit, and ultimately commit betrayals.

Just as Dmitriev's personal drama in "Obmen" worked out historical processes and the "exchange" of past values for those more suited to the modern world, here Gennadii Sergeevich's barren, amoral world is offset by its specific spiritual and cultural context. His wife, Rita, likes to obtain rare editions by writers such as the religious thinkers and philosophers Nikolai Aleksandrovich Berdiaev and Konstantin Nikolaevich Leont'ev, and she decorates their apartment with prints of works by Pablo Picasso. Her friend (and probable lover), Gartvig, is a polyglot academic who specializes in the religions of the Middle East; a man of prodigious learning, he nevertheless makes a fool of himself by confusing Mikhail Iu'revich Lermontov with Ivan Sergeevich Turgenev. Rita and Gartvig both make trips to the centers of Russian Orthodoxy–Suzdal', Zagorsk (Sergiev Posad), and Sviaty Gory–in order to obtain icons. Gennadii Sergeevich is a professional translator, and he is close to the hub of creative activity. All the while reference is made to literary paradigms, such as the motif of the unhappy family in Russian literature; in particular, Leo Tolstoy's *Anna Karenina* (1878) and the Chekhovian themes of individual alienation and the unattainable nature of personal happiness are all too evident. The most obvious allusion, though, is to religion. Several times Gennadii Sergeevich berates his wife for her "pseudoreligiosity": "the first precept of any religion–especially the Christian faith–is love for those close to you." That there is not much Christianity in this family is fitting for a husband such as Gennadii Sergeevich, who abandoned his first wife, Vera, which is the Russian word for "faith."

While in "Obmen" Dmitriev betrays the historical values of the past and in *Predvaritel'nye itogi* Gennadii Sergeevich betrays the cultural heritage, Grisha Rebrov, the central character of *Dolgoe proshchanie* (published in 1971 in *Novyi mir*; published in book form, 1973; translated as *The Long Goodbye*, 1978), tries to rescue these criteria and integrate them into his life. Stylistically, this work was Trifonov's most accomplished to date. It shows the maturing of both his vision and his abilities in these years.

The story is mostly narrated by Lialia, as she recalls her relationship with Rebrov eighteen years earlier. Rebrov was then a struggling writer, interested in historical themes, and despised by Lialia's mother for not bringing in a regular income. Lialia's career as a theater actress, however, is thriving. Rebrov spends hours in libraries and archives researching little-known figures from the nineteenth century, such as the dramatist Ivan Gavrilovich Pryzhov or the nihilist thinker and activist Sergei Gennadievich Nechaev, or, of particular interest, the secret police double agent Nikolai Vasil'evich Kletochnikov. As he declares: "The soil I work on is the experience of history, all that Russia has gone through!"

Rebrov is based largely on Trifonov himself. The character undoubtedly reflects Trifonov's own lack of success as a playwright in the 1950s, but, more importantly, the two men have the same historical interests. In addition, through Rebrov, Trifonov is working out his own view of history as the unity and interaction of all sorts of factors–sociopolitical as well as cultural. This unity is most explicitly stated to Rebrov himself by the aging theatre director Sergei Leonidovich:

> "You see, the rub is this. For you the year 1880 is Kletochnikov, the Third Department, bombs, trying to kill the Tsar, while for me it is Ostrovskii, 'Women Slaves' in the Malyi Theatre, Ermolova in the role of Evlaliia, Sadovskii and Musil . . . Yes, yes, yes! Lord, how cruelly intertwined everything is! You see, the history of a country is a wire with many strands, and when we pull out one strand we don't get anywhere. The truth about a time is in its unity (*slitnost'*), everything together: Kletochnikov, Musil. . . . Oh, if only we could depict on the stage this flow of time that carries everyone, indeed everyone, along!"

The "flow of time" is exactly what Trifonov tries to show, for the reader knows that the action takes place eighteen years previously, and when the narrative closes, the reader learns what has become of the various characters whose lives and loves were experienced in the text. Rebrov, for instance, finally achieves fame and success as a writer, although he thinks back to his difficult earlier period as the "happiest" years of his life. His archenemy and rival for Lialia's affections, Smolianov, gives up writing and is able to survive by renting out his dacha during the summer months.

Trifonov's portrayal of the creative intelligentsia is not a kind one. The theater where Lialia works has its fair share of self-seeking opportunists, demagogues, and careerist hacks; sexual favors are traded for promotion; and Rebrov is denounced to the police by a neighbor for not having a full-time job. These negative aspects are offset by paragons of virtue and humility, reminders that the values of the past are not dead. Moreover, there are no black-and-white delineations, as Trifonov provides telling details about each character's personality that enable the reader to see him or her in a new light at a particular point in the narrative.

Trifonov has also developed his own particular set of images, beginning with the water as the "flow of time" in both *Utolenie zhazhdy* and *Dolgoe proshchanie* and then moving on to the dacha as a symbol of the past, which is being destroyed in the modern world. In "Obmen" Dmitriev's dacha must be leveled to make way for a soccer field, and the dahlia garden of Lialia's father, Petr Aleksandrovich, must be bulldozed as part of urban development.

A key moment in Trifonov's creative evolution, *Dolgoe proshchanie* brings together his exploration of Russian history–it is even in the foreground with Rebrov's interest in the nineteenth century and the lives of the Moscow intelligentsia. Trifonov provides a gallery of sharply differentiated characters; some romantic and some darker political intrigues; and a particular vision of the individual's role and place in history. It is at once a summation of his concerns as an "urban prose" writer and a hint at his subsequent historical searches.

Trifonov's next major work, *Neterpenie: Povest' ob A. Zheliabove* (1973, Impatience: A Novella about A. Zheliabov; translated as *The Impatient Ones,* 1978), was his only excursion into the nineteenth century–and is of considerable interest within his canon, since it overlaps with much of *Dolgoe proshchanie* and offers an original take on the Soviet historical novel. Trifonov approached his subject matter with the scrupulousness and attention to detail of a professional historian, investigating hundreds of primary and secondary sources (diaries, letters, and trial transcripts), and the intellectual curiosity of a novelist. He did the actual research in 1969-1971, when he was publishing his "Moscow cycle," and completed the writing in 1972.

*Neterpenie* is about the terrorist organization "People's Will" and its clandestine activities over a three-year period, which culminated in the assassination of Tsar Alexander II in 1881. The main character is Andrei Zheliabov, the leader of the organization. The reader is given his life story in some detail, as well as a history of the "People's Will"–its development into a party espousing terror and its relationships with other, less extremist radical groups of the time. As in the "Moscow cycle," Trifonov tries to show life in Russia at this time in all its complexity and interrelatedness, within a totality of historical perception. Thus, terrorists in the "People's Will" are likened to the Irish Fenians, and Zheliabov sees himself as a Russian version of the Irish nationalist Charles Stewart Parnell. In *Neterpenie* space is further contracted with scenes in Paris, Vienna, Geneva, and parts of England–all are places where the political emigres discuss their plans and ideas. Moreover, here he attempts to convey the historical process from the point of view of those involved–those who show "impatience" with gradual reform and who decide to "give history a push," in order to "teach history what to do." The process is also seen from above, through the eyes of Clio, the Muse of History, who puts these events, profoundly significant as they were for Russia, within the context of the flow of time in general.

One of the most striking aspects of the novel is its sheer accumulation of detail about the period. Trifonov includes detailed discussions of various radical and populist political programs, the daily life of men and women devoted to terrorism (including the repressive apparatus at the disposal of the police), the constant dangers from spies and informers, and the conditions in Tsarist jails, where beatings and the rape of women prisoners are common. Intellectuals and radicals debate on whether the struggle to improve the life of ordinary people is enough, or whether the system itself should be dismantled. Thus, that émigré critics saw *Neterpenie* as a pointed allegory for the dissident movement in the Soviet Union in the 1970s (and the historical inevitability of its failure) is hardly surprising.

Trifonov's canvas of life in Russia one hundred years earlier includes many of the actual players of the period. Besides Zheliabov and his lover, Sof'ia Perovskaia, other historical figures include Tsar Alexander II and his son and heir, the future Alexander III; the government minister Count Petr Aleksandrovich Valuev; the procurator of the Holy Synod Konstantin Petrovich Pobedonostsev; and chief of police Count Mikhail Tarnelovich Loris-Melikov. Among the revolutionaries are Georgii Valentinovich Plekhanov, Sergei Nechaev, Vera Nikolaevna Figner, Stepan Nikolaevich Khalturin, and Vera Ivanovna Zasulich. In addition, the writings of Tolstoy, Fyodor Dostoevsky, Vladimir Sergeevich Solov'ev, Afanasii Afanasievich Fet, and Aleksandr Ivanovich Herzen are discussed. Actual events are also part of the narrative fabric, such as the funeral of Dostoevsky in January 1881, as well as peasant riots in the provinces in 1880 and the assassination of policemen and prosecutors. A broad cross section of Russian society–including soldiers, sailors, students, prostitutes, policemen, landowners, city workers, and peasants, in locations ranging from Ukraine to Moscow to St. Petersburg–makes up the rest of Trifonov's canvas. With seeming familiarity, he takes the reader through the streets, shops, stores, and taverns of nineteenth-century Odessa and St. Petersburg. But Trifonov is not content with just giving the reader a "feel" for the period. He enters the mind and thought processes of characters in order to explore the meaning of history and why events happened. He portrays the main characters through the eyes of others, too, so that the reader attains a rounded and fairly complete picture, especially of Andrei Zheliabov and his motives.

With the appearance of *Drugaia zhizn'* (first published in 1975 in *Novyi mir;* published in book form, 1976;

translated as "Another Life," 1983), Trifonov returned to the milieu of the Moscow intelligentsia, but the historical theme is never far from the surface. Although the narrative is related by Ol'ga Vasil'evna, the central character is her late husband, Sergei Troitsky, a professional historian searching for "truth" but running into the brick wall of "historical expediency." The novella demonstrates Trifonov's increasing interest in stream-of-consciousness narrative, as Ol'ga Vasil'evna's recollections are conveyed without chronological progression, and incidental characters appear and disappear as her memories move on. There is also the theme of art and, as with the historian, the difficulty of being true to one's calling and craft.

Ol'ga's stepfather is Georgii Maksimovich, an artist who had known Chagall and Amadeo Modigliani, and who had lived in Paris before the revolution. On returning to the Soviet Union, he had to destroy and renounce his best pictures in order to survive and earn a living as a hack artist and illustrator. Troitsky refuses to compromise his studies or to curry favor with those who are higher up, and he gets nowhere with his thesis on the Moscow secret police in February 1917 (itself a risky topic, given the persistent rumors that Stalin himself was a police spy). A hard drinker, womanizer, and rabble-rouser, Troitsky dies of a heart attack at the age of forty-two.

Ol'ga Vasil'evna's memories are an attempt to understand the man with whom she spent seventeen years of her life. The title refers not only to her new life without him but also to the fact that Troitsky did not live like others around him. He was consumed with passion for his subject, filling in notebook after notebook and sitting in archives and libraries every day from morning until night, but he was unable to get official approval for his research and so could not complete it. He also had a personal connection to his work: he discovered that the father he lost during the war was also active in uncovering spies in 1917 (and therefore similar to Valentin Andreevich, Trifonov's father).

Ol'ga Vasil'evna tries, above all, to understand what drove her husband to his early grave and why he was so obsessed with notions of history. She sees history as a succession of dates, events, and personalities—all kept in order by the historian, "like a policeman, who on days when a film opens, keeps order at the Progress cinema box-office." For Troitsky, though, history involved the link between past and present, as well as a Pasternakian belief in the immortality of the individual. The meaning of history is not discerned in what happens or when but in how it affects the individual and how the individual influences history.

In *Drugaia zhizn'* Trifonov again portrays his characters as contrasts and mirror images. Troitsky is at one end of the ethical spectrum, while his cynical nemesis Gennadii Vital'evich Klimuk (Genital'ich to his friends), an academic secretary, is at the other, with still other characters such as Georgii Maksimovich somewhere in between them. Fedia Praskukhin is a clear-minded and honest soul, but he is killed in a car crash. The future belongs to Klimuk, who becomes deputy director of the institute where he and Troitsky work, and to the man who replaces him as academic secretary, Sharipov, a young upstart with all the right connections. *Drugaia zhizn'* has been seen as the final installment in the "Moscow cycle," and undoubtedly it is the most pessimistic. It posits the impossibility of a man of honor and integrity realizing his own potential in an academic environment of craven duplicity and moral corruption. Escape into "another life" is the only solution.

*Dom na naberezhnoi* (translated as "The House on treh Embankment," 1983), which first appeared in 1976 in *Druzhba narodov* (People's Friendship) and was first published abroad in 1983, is another critical exploration of the mechanics of compromise and upward mobility. It is set in a contemporary period but retrospectively relates events of the late 1940s. Like *Studenty,* the novel takes place in an academic institution and concerns the political intrigues that lead to a professor's dismissal (in which his students also have played a part). Very much a rewrite of *Studenty, Dom na naberezhnoi* is armed with the moral certainties of the post-Stalin age, which are conveyed through Trifonov's ironic distancing from his characters and his story.

The novel was also Trifonov's most ambitious work to date, in that he organized it on two parallel temporal levels: the present, or at least the early 1970s, and past, or the late 1940s (for in the narrative the protagonist Glebov recalls his student days). Glebov's recollections are sparked by a chance encounter with a former childhood friend, Levka Shulepnikov, on a hot August day in 1972. Levka refuses to recognize him at first but then rings him up later that night; he is drunk and simply wants to insult him. Glebov reaches back in his memory, but there are significant events in his past that he refuses to remember, and the narrator fills in the blanks.

Glebov's childhood is an impoverished one. He is full of envy for Levka, or "Shulepa," as he called him, who lives in the luxurious "house on the embankment"—Levka's stepfather obviously is connected with the security services. In this world schoolteachers encourage children to inform on one another, and Levka's unnamed stepfather forces the twelve-year-old Glebov to inform on the boys (called "bandits" in the novel) that beat up his stepson. Those who go in and out of the "large house" are under constant surveillance and subject to "interrogations and reinterrogations" by the men who operate the elevators. (The phrase "bol'shoi dom," or large house, is a euphemism for the local secret police building in Russian towns and cities.) As a child Glebov hates his life, because he is ashamed of his poverty. He has no personal courage or integrity with which to win over friends—unlike Levka, who refuses to be cowed by his new "father." Nor, unlike Anton Ovchinnikov (who subsequently dies in the war), does Glebov possess any great talent. His lack of scruples, though, will serve him well later in life.

In 1947 he and Shulepnikov are both students at the Gor'ky Literary Institute. Levka is even more affluent than before the war: he has acquired his own personal car (a BMW), an American leather jacket, an Italian wife (whom he is no longer with), and one of the few television sets in Moscow. In addition, he has a new stepfather, also from the security services, but he has kept the surname Shulepnikov; Levka's former stepfather killed himself. As for Glebov, he now has his eyes on Sonia Ganchuk, with whom he also went to school; she is the daughter of Nikolai Vasil'evich Ganchuk, an eminent professor at the institute. Glebov begins visiting the Ganchuks and becomes the professor's valued assistant, as well as Sonia's lover.

Only Iuliia Mikhailovna, Sonia's mother, sees through Glebov's opportunism. She makes barbed comments about his interest in the relative affluence of their lifestyle and tries to get him to put forward a personal opinion. Glebov, though, refuses to commit himself on anything, even when Ganchuk himself—a hero of the civil war, a participant in the cultural debates of the 1920s, and a corresponding member of the Academy of Sciences with more than 180 publications to his name—comes under attack at the institute during the "anti-cosmopolitan" campaign against foreign influences (his wife, Iuliia Mikhailovna, is of German descent). The narrator provides a character sketch of the boy he knew in childhood as Vad'ka Baton, who is now Ganchuk:

> He was a complete nonentity, Vad'ka Baton. But this, I realised later, is a rare gift: to be a nonentity. People who have the brilliant ability to be nonentities go far. The whole point is that those who have anything to do with them have no background to work on and have to fill in the blanks with their imagination or paint their own character sketch, based on what their fears and desires tell them. Nonentities always get their own way.

Glebov is encouraged to spy on the Ganchuks and then invited to participate at a public meeting that has been called to discuss Ganchuk's future. Though asked to speak out against the old professor and in favor of him, in the end Glebov does neither. He fails to show up because his grandmother has died. Yet, he does not remember the second meeting that was organized, and this "blank" is one that the narrator fills in for the reader; he does not recall denouncing Ganchuk either: "Glebov did not know that there would come a time when he would try not to remember everything that occurred to him in those minutes, and, consequently, he did not know that he was living a life that had not happened." He does not remember the subsequent contempt of his friends toward him, and he tries afterward to forget accidental meetings with Ganchuk and Sonia.

The end of the story takes place two years after Glebov's initial meeting with Levka and relates what has happened to the surviving characters. Sonia and her mother are dead, Ganchuk is still alive at the age of eighty-six, and Levka is a drunken wreck, reduced to being the caretaker of the cemetery where Sonia is buried. Only Glebov has prospered. At the close of the novel he is on his way to Paris for an international conference, but inside he feels dead. *Dom na naberezhnoi* returns Trifonov's readers to the world of *Studenty*, his Stalin Prize–winning novel, but tears away the veneer of glittering prizes and enviable prospects. The "revision" replaces the false optimism of the earlier work with a world of envy, poverty, and fear bordering on terror—a world in which human actions are motivated purely by selfish urges, and only the mediocre "nonentities" prosper. In terms of structure, the novel is also Trifonov's most complex. It combines several voices and several pairs of eyes that give the reader different views of the same action, often interwoven so that at times one is unaware of who is narrating. Glebov's soul is laid bare, and the price of compromise and moral vacuity is that for the rest of his life he feels as if he is "living death."

Trifonov employs the same structure in his next novel, *Starik* (first published in 1978 in *Druzhba narodov*; published in book form, 1980; translated as *The Old Man*, 1984), praised in the West on its publication as his "boldest and most original work" (Herman Ermolaev). In *Starik* he attempts to blend past and present in the consciousness of an individual. Pavel Evgrafovich Letunov, the old man of the title, delves deeply into his own past for the answer to a question of profound importance. He recalls the bloodthirsty days of the Russian Civil War and his relationship with Sergei Migulin, a Cossack leader who fought with the Reds and who was shot for treason in 1920. Some years ago Letunov had written an article about Migulin. He has received a letter from Asia, Migulin's wife, in which she expresses surprise that Letunov, of all people, should be rehabilitating Migulin. Letunov himself is taken aback by

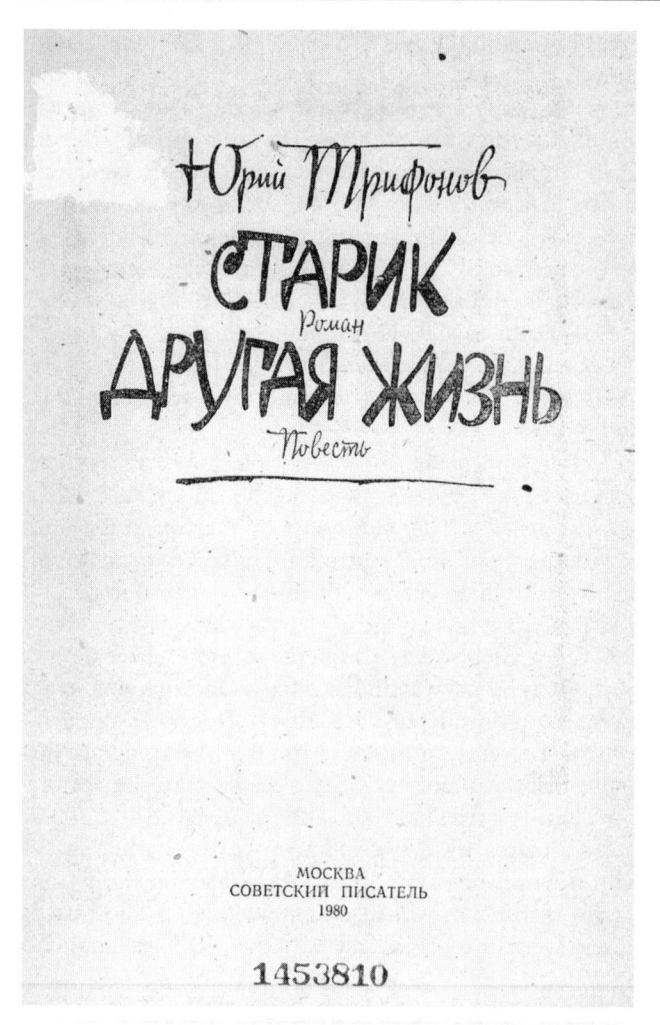

*Title page for* Starik, *translated in 1984 as* The Old Man, *Trifonov's last novel published during his lifetime, about a man whose failed memories of events fifty years in the past have allowed him to overcome his guilt over betrayal of a friend (John C. Hodges Library, University of Tennessee–Knoxville)*

Asia's surprise, as he always regarded Migulin as a friend. He had forgotten, though, as had Glebov in *Dom na naberezhnoi,* a key moment in the past—that he had given evidence against Migulin at his 1920 trial, thereby sealing his friend's fate. In *Starik* Trifonov is going over much the same ground that he covered in *Otblesk kostra*—Migulin is obviously based on the figure of Fillip Kuz'mich Mironov—but he presents it in a fictional framework. The question that Letunov would like answered after more than fifty years is why Migulin disobeyed orders and sent his cavalry out to meet the enemy—an act that sparked fears that he was about to defect to the Whites.

Letunov's memories are, in effect, an attempt to forget, or rather not to acknowledge his own guilt. At the center of his recollections is the year 1919, although he also provides a vivid picture of the revolutionary year 1917 and the feeling of exhilaration that gripped Petrograd (formerly St. Petersburg). People in the streets were talking about freedom and elections before General Lavrentii Georgievich Kornilov's abortive assault on the city, an attack that was meant to establish military rule. The year 1919, however, is an exceptionally bloody year, marked by the Bolsheviks' policy of "de-Cossackization" *(raskulachivanie)* on the Don, based on the decision of the Bolsheviks' Central Committee, which feared Cossack secession and called for "their extermination to a man." The flow of time and historical analogies are never far from the surface in *Starik*. For example, the Bolsheviks justify their policy of terror against the Cossacks by referring to the excesses carried out by the National Convention against the Vendée during the French Revolution. Other historical parallels mentioned in the work are the reign of Ivan the Terrible and the massacre of the Huguenots, which Trifonov employs to comment on Stalin's rule. Historical figures also make an appearance under their own names, such as Trotsky and Kornilov, as well as the Cossack leaders Petr Nikolaevich Krasnov and Anton Ivanovich Denikin. In addition, in *Starik* Trifonov introduces his own father under the name of Shura Danilov, a wise and farsighted Bolshevik who can see the significance of the moment within the greater flow of time. Undoubtedly idealized in this respect, Danilov is otherwise impotent in preventing the wanton terror against the Cossacks, nor can he save Migulin.

Letunov's life as he experiences it in the 1970s is far from comfortable. Regarded by his children as senile and living on his memories, he is still grieving over the death of his wife some years ago and has little contact with people. He notes with sadness the increasing alcoholism of his son Ruslan and the increasing strain on the marriage of his daughter Vera and her husband Nikolai Erastovich (he has forced her to have several abortions). The temporal present in *Starik* can be characterized by greed and cynicism. Nowhere is it better exemplified than in the figure of Oleg Kandaurov, a Foreign Ministry official in his forties who, solely for his own gain, manipulates all who cross his path. He keeps physically fit, can charm and cajole to get what he wants, has a mistress twenty years younger, and covets a recently vacated dacha in the same settlement as Letunov's.

*Starik* was Trifonov's last work of fiction to be published while he was alive. He died unexpectedly in Moscow after a kidney operation on 28 March 1981. His posthumous publications include the cycle of short stories *Oprokinutyi dom* (The Overturned House, first published in 1981 in *Novyi mir*); the novel *Vremia i mesto* (Time and Place, first published in 1981 in *Druzhba naro-*

*dov;* published in book form, 1988); and the unfinished novel *Ischeznovenie* (first published 1987 in *Druzhba narodov,* published 1988 in book form; translated as *The Disappearance,* 1991), which could be published only under the conditions of glasnost.

In his writing career when Trifonov turned to short stories, it usually indicated a change of thematic direction for him–whether toward the theme of construction in the Turkmenistan desert in the late 1950s or the theme of everyday Muscovite life in the 1960s. In *Oprokinutyi dom,* an intensely personal collection, he recounts his travels in various countries—such as Finland, Italy, the United States, and France—and also confronts his past. He reflects on the history, culture, and habits of these lands, as well as their links with Russia and with himself, for his father had served on the Trade Mission in Helsinki in 1926–1928; Trifonov even meets an old Russian woman who recalls working with Valentin Andreevich in those years. The most personal of the stories is "Nedolgoe prebyvanie v kamere pytok" (A Short Stay in the Torture Chamber), published separately only during glasnost but included in subsequent collections. The story is set in 1964 and tells of Trifonov's sudden meeting with a former colleague at the literary institute who, in 1950, had spoken up at a gathering that had been called in order to decide Trifonov's fate; Trifonov had lied about his father (in that he did not list him as an "enemy of the people") and was faced with expulsion. As he and "N." confront each other in a medieval torture chamber in a castle outside Salzburg, Austria, where Trifonov is reporting on the Winter Olympics, the past comes back–but not with any clear definition. As with his creations Glebov and Letunov, Trifonov cannot remember the crucial detail: he insists that N.'s words were instrumental in the expulsion to be given (later rescinded), but N. insists that his speech actually saved him. As the author reflects: "Yes, I had forgotten, I couldn't remember, I was confused, everything had disappeared into darkness. He proffered me an uncertain hand, and I uncertainly shook it."

In *Vremia i mesto* Trifonov comes as close as any Soviet writer to metafiction. About a writer, closely modeled on Trifonov himself, it focuses on the writer's craft, his struggles against the literary bureaucracy, and the process of writing. *Vremia i mesto* draws attention to itself as a work of literature, particularly to its devices of artifice and representation and to its own status as a work of "fiction." There is much that is nonfictional in the novel as well, since it is based upon many of Trifonov's own memories of his childhood and of working in a factory and as a part-time fireman in Moscow during the war. The characters in the book are similar to characters from earlier works, and the writer Kiianov is based on Aleksandr Aleksandrovich Fadeev, an actual Soviet writer. Kiianov, too, is called upon to rewrite a novel and commits suicide after the death of Stalin. Trifonov himself can be discerned in both the protagonist Antipov and the unnamed first-person narrator, who knew Antipov as a boy and who eventually meets him only when both are well into middle age, in 1979.

The novel spans all of Antipov's life, from his childhood in the 1930s to the late 1970s, and re-creates the major events of the day: the purges and the stifling atmosphere of suspicion and denunciation (Antipov is denounced to the police by a neighbor simply for reading the works of the "émigré" Ivan Alekseevich Bunin), the war, and the death of Stalin in 1953. The last episode assumes particular importance, as Antipov looks down on the surging, hysterical crowds in the streets below as Stalin is buried. He sees the chaos that leads to hundreds of people being crushed to death, yet this circumstance is of lesser importance than what is happening in the next room, where his wife is undergoing an illegal abortion. After Stalin's death, prisoners start returning from the camps and confronting those who, they feel, have wronged them. The prisoners' release is analogous to the people who disappear from Antipov's life, only to reemerge decades later. The narrative teems with the names of minor characters, all of whom are important to Antipov in some context, however small and passing. In *Vremia i mesto* Trifonov shows a world as seen not just by Antipov and the narrator but also by other characters such as Kiianov and old Elizaveta Gavrilovna, an unrepentant revolutionary who despises human weakness and affirms above all self-sacrificing commitment to the cause.

Trifonov includes in *Vremia i mesto* an "embedded novel," titled "Sindrom Nikiforova" (The Nikiforov Syndrome) and written by Antipov. It is a series of mirrors, with Nikiforov writing about another writer, who himself is writing a novel about a writer, and so on, "mirrors, stretching across almost two centuries." Whole pages from this "novel" are incorporated into Trifonov's own novel, which becomes a meditation on the relationship of the writer to his times and on the status of the work he produces. Antipov does not achieve great fame as a writer but remains a professional failure, just like his "creation" Nikiforov; both Antipov and Nikiforov have lived "a life that has not worked out." Antipov's novel does not succeed, because he suffers from the same "syndrome": the failure to confront life and accept its pain, for only through pain can real literature be created.

In *Ischeznovenie* Trifonov again revisits his past, and the figure of Valentin Andreevich assumes greater importance than in any of Trifonov's other works. Here the young Trifonov is called Igor' (nicknamed

Gorik) Baiukov, and his father is named Nikolai Grigor'evich. Although the novel begins in 1942, with the sixteen-year-old Gorik boarding a train in Tashkent to return to Moscow (and losing his suitcase when he changes trains in Kuibyshev), much of the novel is set in 1937 and concentrates on Nikolai Grigor'evich and his increasing fears about the fate of the revolution, to which he had dedicated his life. Like Danilov in *Starik*, Nikolai Grigor'evich has the ability to see the importance of the moment in the grander scheme of things and assess the flow of time. After his meeting with the secret police official Florinsky, he knows that his days are numbered. As he surveys his past life, he realizes that the revolution has deprived him of a sense of home: he has neglected his family for the cause, and he sees all around him fellow comrades thrown out of their jobs, sent to the gulag, or worse.

*Ischeznovenie* has a relatively straightforward narrative structure. It lacks the multiple viewpoints, flashbacks, and twin temporal planes—or metafictional aspects—of Trifonov's later works. It clearly was written in an earlier period (Trifonov's widow thinks 1968). Still, the themes of history and fatherhood place it in the later period, even if it is without the author's controlling overview and attempt at artistic synthesis. Trifonov kept faith in the values that his father held dear and that typified his generation. Even in his private notebooks he wrote: "The old guard was self-sacrificing, but with ambition, it was irreplaceable as a moral force." Clearly, when they died, so did the values of the revolution.

By the time of his death Trifonov had achieved widespread success and acclaim. His career began with the award of the Stalin Prize, but during the Stagnation he did everything in his power as a published writer to distance himself from that system. Still, there is no evidence in his written works that he was against the values of the revolution and the "self-sacrificing" idealism that brought it about. In his fiction and nonfiction he criticized the "impatience" of terrorists of the nineteenth and twentieth centuries who tried to move history along at their own pace; and there is a clear line of descent between the ideas and methods of the "People's Will" and the murderous Bolsheviks of *Starik*. In the end these values triumphed, and future society was built on them.

In his stories about Moscow life Iurii Valentinovich Trifonov also showed himself to be a great observer of the exuberance, potential, betrayals, and hypocrisies that are part of city life. But his characters are organized as types, with contrasts and mirror images; those who prosper end up following, or at least paying lip service to, the prevailing ideology, while those who go nowhere, or perish, are victims of "historical expediency." The female characters in Trifonov's works are sadly underwritten. They function either as materialistic harridans bound to frustrate the more spiritual values of their men, or as weak and innocent victims of intrigue. Even the most prominent of them, Ol'ga Vasil'evna in *Drugaia zhizn'*—perhaps the only one depicted sympathetically—can find the strength and will to face "another life" only with another man. Trifonov came as close as any Soviet writer, living and working in an extremely repressive age, to expressing the "truth" of his times, with complex narrative strategies, viewpoints, and syntax that undoubtedly served to confuse ideological watchdogs, as well as add to the textological richness of his writing. He tried to understand his times, the relationship between the past and the future, and the "time and place" to which the individual is assigned in this life.

**References:**

Mikhail Agursky, "Polemika s dissidentami Iuriia Trifonova," *Russkaia mysl'*, 27 September 1979, p. 6;

Sergei Akchurin, "Zvonite v liuboe vremia (Iz vospominanii o Iu. V. Trifonove)," *Literaturnaia ucheba*, 6 (1982): 230–233;

V. Amlinsky, "O dniakh edinstvennykh," *Literaturnoe obozrenie*, 1 (1982): 42–45;

Lev Aleksandrovich Anninsky, "Intelligenty i prochie," in his *Tridsatye-semidesiatye. Literaturno-kriticheskie stat'i* (Moscow: Sovremennik, 1977), pp. 199–227;

Anninsky, "Neokonchatel'nye itogi. O trekh povestiakh Iu. Trifonova ('Obmen', 'Predvaritel'nye itogi', 'Dolgoe proshchanie')," *Don*, 5 (1972): 183–192;

Anninsky, "Ochishchenie proshlym," *Don*, 2 (1977): 157–160;

Anninsky, "Rassechenie kornia. Zametki o publitsistike Iuriia Trifonova," *Druzhba narodov*, 3 (1985): 239–246;

Paul M. Austin, "From Helsingfors to Helsinki: Jurij Trifonov's Search for his Past," *Scando-Slavica*, 32 (1986): 5–15;

Sergei Alekseevich Baruzdin, "Neodnoznachnyi Trifonov," *Druzhba narodov*, 10 (1987): 255–262;

Galina Andreevna Belaia, *Khudozhestvennyi mir sovremennoi prozy* (Moscow: Nauka, 1983), pp. 151–184;

Fiona Björling, "Jurij Trifonov's *Dom na naberezhnoi*: Fiction or Autobiography?" in *Autobiographical Statements in Twentieth Century Russian Literature*, edited by Jane Gary Harris (Princeton: Princeton University Press, 1990), pp. 172–192;

Björling, "Morality as History: An Analysis of Jurij Trifonov's Novel *Starik*," in *Text and Context: Essays in Honor to Nils Åke Nilsson*, edited by P. A. Jensen and B. Lönnqvist (Stockholm: Almqvist & Wiksell International, 1987), pp. 154–169;

Anatolii Georgievich Bocharov, "Kontrapunkt: Obshchee i individual'noe v proze Iu. Trifonova, V. Shukshina, V. Rasputina," *Oktiabr'*, 7 (1982): 190–199;

Deming Brown, *The Last Years of Soviet Literature: Prose Fiction, 1975–1991* (Cambridge: Cambridge University Press, 1993), pp. 20–24;

Edward J. Brown, *Russian Literature since the Revolution* (Cambridge, Mass. & London: Harvard University Press, 1982), pp. 313–319;

Sally Dalton-Brown, "Creating a Sense of Time: Some Aspects of Style in Iurii Trifonov's Mature Prose," *Modern Language Review*, 88 (1993): 706–717;

Carolina De Maegd-Soëp, *Trifonov and the Drama of the Russian Intelligentsia* (Ghent: Ghent State University, 1990);

Evgenii Dobrenko, "Siuzhet kak 'vnutrennee dvizhenie' v pozdnei proze Iu. Trifonova," *Voprosy russkoi literatury*, 1 (1987): 44–50;

Iu. Druzhnikov, "Sud'ba Trifonova," *Vremia i my*, 108 (1990): 247–278;

Andrew Durkin, "Trifonov's 'Taking Stock': The Role of Cexovian Subtext," *Slavic and East European Journal*, 28 (1984): 32–41;

I. Efimov, "Pisatel', raskonvoirovannyi v istoriki," *Vremia i my*, 71 (1983): 139–153;

A. El'iashevich, *Gorizontali i vertikali: Sovremennaia proza – ot semidesiatykh k vos'midesiatym* (Moscow: Sovetskii pisatel', 1984), pp. 255–366;

S. Eremina and V. Piskunov, "Vremia i mesto prozy Iu. Trifonova," *Voprosy literatury*, 5 (1982): 34–65;

Herman Ermolaev, "Proshloe i nastoiashchee v 'Starike' Iuriia Trifonova," *Russian Language Journal*, 128 (1983): 131–145;

Ermolaev, "The Theme of Terror in *Starik*," in *Aspects of Modern Russian and Czech Literature: Selected Papers of the Third World Congress for Soviet and East European Studies*, edited by Arnold McMillin (Columbus, Ohio: Slavica, 1989), pp. 96–109;

Boris Galanov, "Nachalo puti," *Znamia*, 1 (1951): 171–174;

David Charles Gillespie, *Iurii Trifonov: Unity through Time* (Cambridge: Cambridge University Press, 1992);

Inna Anatol'evna Goff, "Vodianye znaki: Zametki o Iurii Trifonove," *Oktiabr'*, 8 (1985): 94–106;

V. S. Golovskoi, "Nravstvennye uroki trifonovskoi prozy," *Russian Language Journal*, 128 (1983): 147–161;

V. Gusev, "Prostranstvo slova: o dvukh stilevykh tendentsiiakh sovremennoi prozy," *Literaturnoe obozrenie*, 6 (1978): 24–27;

Geoffrey Hosking, *Beyond Socialist Realism: Soviet Fiction since 'Ivan Denisovich'* (London & New York: Granada, 1980), pp. 180–195;

Anne C. Hughes, "*Bol'shoi mir* or *zamknutyi mirok:* Departure from Literary Convention in Iurii Trifonov's Recent Fiction," *Canadian Slavonic Papers*, 22 (1980): 470–480;

Natal'ia Borisovna Ivanova, *Proza Iuriia Trifonova* (Moscow: Sovetskii pisatel', 1984);

V. Kardin, *Obretenie: Literaturnye portrety* (Moscow: Khudozhestvennaia literatura, 1989), pp. 6–67;

Lev Efimovich Kertman, "Mezhdustroch'ia bylykh vremen (Perechityvaia Iuriia Trifonova)," *Voprosy literatury*, 5 (1994): 77–103;

Nina Kolesnikoff, "Jurij Trifonov as a Novella Writer," *Russian Language Journal*, 118 (1980): 137–144;

Kolesnikoff, "The Temporal and Narrative Structure of Trifonov's Novel *Starik*," *Russian Literature*, 28, 1 (July 1990): 23–32;

Kolesnikoff, "Trifonov's *Vremja i mesto:* Compositional and Narrative Structure," *Russian Language Journal*, 140 (1987): 167–174;

Kolesnikoff, *Yury Trifonov: A Critical Study* (Ann Arbor, Mich.: Ardis, 1991);

Vadim Valerianovich Kozhinov, "Problema avtora i put' pisatelia," in *Kontekst–1977*, edited by Nikolai Konstantinovich Gei (Moscow: Nauka, 1978), pp. 23–47;

N. Kuznetsova, "I komissary v pyl'nykh shlemakh," *Kontinent*, 53 (1987): 391–396;

Julian L. Laychuk, "Yury Trifonov's Male Protagonists in the 'Test of Life,'" *New Zealand Slavonic Journal* (1989–1990): 109–125;

A. A. Lebedev, *Stat'i* (Moscow: Sovetskii pisatel', 1980), pp. 193–246;

Mikhail Lemkhin, "Zheliabov, Nechaev, Karlos i drugie," *Kontinent*, 49 (1986): 359–369;

Lev Levin, "Vosem' stranits ot ruki," *Voprosy literatury*, 3 (1988): 183–198;

G. S. Levinskaia, "'Dom' v khudozhestvennom mire Iuriia Trifonova," *Filologicheskie nauki*, 2 (1991): 3–11;

S. Markish, "K voprosu o tsenzure i nepodtsenzurnosti: gorodskie povesti Iu. Trifonova i roman F. Kandelia 'Koridor,'" in *Odna ili dve russkikh literatury?* edited by Georges Nivat (Lausanne: L'Age d'Homme, 1981), pp. 145–155;

Sigrid McLaughlin, "Antipov's *Nikiforov Syndrome:* The Embedded Novel in Trifonov's *Time and Place*," *Slavic and East European Journal*, 32 (1988): 237–250;

McLaughlin, "Iurii Trifonov's *Dom na naberezhnoi* and Dostoevskii's *Prestuplenie i nakazanie*," *Canadian Slavonic Papers*, 25 (1983): 275–283;

McLaughlin, "Jurij Trifonov's *House on the Embankment*: Narration and Meaning," *Slavic and East European Journal,* 26 (1982): 419–433;

McLaughlin, "Literary Allusions in Trifonov's 'Preliminary Stocktaking,'" *Russian Review,* 46 (1987): 19–34;

McLaughlin, "A Moment in the History of Consciousness of the Soviet Intelligentsia: Trifonov's Novel *Disappearance*," *Studies in Comparative Communism,* 21 (1988): 303–311;

Iurii Mikhailovich Okliansky, *Iurii Trifonov: Portret-vospominanie* (Moscow: Sovetskaia Rossiia, 1987);

Valentin Dmitrievich Oskotsky, "Nravstvennye uroki 'Narodnoi Voli'. Zametki o romane Iu. Trifonova 'Neterpenie,'" *Literaturnoe obozrenie,* 11 (1973): 55–61;

B. Pankin, "Po krugu ili po spirali? O povestiakh Iu. Trifonova 'Obmen', 'Predvaritel'nye itogi', 'Dolgoe proshchanie', 'Drugaia zhizn',' 'Dom na naberezhnoi,'" *Druzhba narodov,* 5 (1977): 238–253;

Colin Partridge, *Yury Trifonov's The Moscow Cycle: A Critical Study* (Lewiston, N.Y.: Edwin Mellen Press, 1990);

Tat'iana Patera, *Obzor tvorchestva i analiz moskovskikh povesti Iuriia Trifonova* (Ann Arbor, Mich.: Ardis, 1983);

Stuart Paton, "The Hero of His Time," *Slavonic and East European Review,* 64 (1986): 506–524;

G. Rogova, "Itogi i razdum'ia," *Pod"em,* 11 (1982): 135–138;

P. Rostin, "Pisatel', chitatel', tsenzor," *Poiski i razmyshleniia,* 1 (1982): 84–89;

Robert Russell, "Old Men in Kataev and Trifonov," in *Words and Images: Essays in Honour of Professor (Emeritus) Dennis Ward,* edited by Michael Falchikov, Christopher Pike, and Robert Russell (Nottingham, U.K.: Astra Press, 1989): 155–163;

Russell, "Time and Memory in the Works of Yury Trifonov," *Forum for Modern Language Studies,* 24 (1988): 37–52;

V. Sakharov, *Obnovliaiushchii mir. Zametki o tekushchei literature* (Moscow: Sovremennik, 1980), pp. 173–196;

Raisa Safullovna Satretdinova, *Turkmenistan v tvorchestve Iu. V. Trifonova* (Ashkhabad: Ylym, 1984);

Ralf Schröder, "'Moi god eshche ne nastupil . . .': Iz besed s Iuriem Trifonovym," *Literaturnoe obozrenie,* 8 (1987): 96–98;

Thomas Seifrid, "Trifonov's *Dom na naberezhnoi* and the Fortunes of Aesopian Speech," *Slavic Review,* 49 (1990): 611–624;

K. Shenfel'd, "Iurii Trifonov – pisatel' chastichnoi pravdy," *Grani,* 121 (1981): 112–118;

Aleksandr Pavlovich Shitov, *Iurii Trifonov: Khronika zhizni i tvorchestva, 1925–1981* (Ekaterinburg: Izdatel'stvo Ural'skogo universiteta, 1997);

Evgenii Aleksandrovich Shklovsky, "Samoe glavnoe," *Literaturnoe obozrenie,* 11 (1987): 25–34;

Shklovsky, "V potoke vremeni. Tema detstva v tvorchestve Iu. Trifonova," *Detskaia literatura,* 8 (1983): 17–22;

N. N. Shneidman, "The New Dimensions of Time and Place in Iurii Trifonov's Prose of the 1980s," *Canadian Slavonic Papers,* 27 (1985): 188–195;

Shneidman, *Soviet Literature in the 1970s: Artistic Diversity and Ideological Conformity* (Toronto: Toronto University Press, 1979), pp. 88–105;

Shneidman, *Soviet Literature in the 1980s: Decade of Transition* (Buffalo: University of Toronto Press, 1989), pp. 74–84;

M. Sinel'nikov, "Poznat' cheloveka . . . poznat' vremia . . . O 'Starike' Iu. Trifonova," *Voprosy literatury,* 9 (1979): 26–52;

Sinel'nikov and V. Sokolov, "Obsuzhdaem novye povesti Iu. Trifonova," *Voprosy literatury,* 2 (1972): 31–62;

Sally Thompson, "Reflections of America in Trifonov's *Oprokinutyi dom,*" in *The Waking Sphinx: South African Essays on Russian Culture,* edited by Henrietta Mondry (Johannesburg: The Library, University of Witwatersrand, 1989), pp. 23–39;

Ol'ga Romanovna Miroshnichenko-Trifonova, "'Pisat' na predele vozmozhnogo': Iz zapisnykh knizhek Iu. V. Trifonova," *Iunost',* 10 (1990): 4–6;

Andrei Mikhailovich Turkov, *Vechnye temy* (Moscow: Sovremennik, 1984), pp. 123–140;

Valentina Aleksandrovna Tvardovskaia, "Po povodu publikatsii pisem Iu. Trifonova," *Voprosy literatury,* 2 (1988): 192–195;

J. Venturi, "Kakim byl roman Trifonova do tsenzury," *Russkaia mysl',* 2 May 1986, p. 10;

Josephine Woll, *Invented Truth: Soviet Reality and the Literary Imagination of Iurii Trifonov* (Durham, N.C. & London: Duke University Press, 1991);

Woll, "Trifonov's *Starik*: The Truth of the Past," *Russian Literature Triquarterly,* 19 (1986): 243–258;

James B. Woodward, "The 'Dotted Line' of Jurij Trifonov's Last Novel," *Die Welt der Slaven,* 36 (1991) (neve Folge 15): 330–346;

Igor' Petrovich Zolotussky, "Vozvyshchaiushchee slovo," *Literaturnoe obozrenie,* 6 (1988): 23–32.

**Papers:**

The papers of Iurii Valentinovich Trifonov are held by his widow, Ol'ga Romanovna Miroshnichenko-Trifonova.

# Aleksandr Valentinovich Vampilov
## (A. Sanin)
### (19 August 1937 – 17 August 1972)

J. Alexander Ogden
*University of South Carolina*

BOOKS: *Stechenie obstoiatel'stv: Iumoristicheskie rasskazy,* as A. Sanin (Irkutsk: Vostochno-Sibirskoe knizhnoe izdatel'stvo, 1961);

*Printsy ukhodiat iz skazok: Sbornik ocherkov,* by Vampilov, Iurii Sergeevich Skop, and Viacheslav Maksimovich Shugaev (Irkutsk: Vostochno-Sibirskoe knizhnoe izdatel'stvo, 1964);

*Proshchanie v iiune* (Moscow: VUOAP, 1966); translated as *Farewell in June* (Arlington, Va.: Distributed by Theatre Research Associates, 1980);

*Starshii syn* (Moscow: Iskusstvo, 1970); translated by Alma H. Law as *The Elder Son* (Arlington, Va.: Distributed by Theatre Research Associates, 1980);

*Istoriia s metranpazhem* (Moscow: Iskusstvo, 1971); revised as part of *Provintsial'nye anekdoty,* in *Proshchanie v iiune: P'esy;* revision translated by Kevin Windle as *Provincial Anecdotes,* in *Farewell in June: Four Russian Plays* (St. Lucia: University of Queensland Press, 1983);

*Proshlym letom v Chulimske* (Moscow: VUOAP, 1973); translated by Margaret Wettlin as *Last Summer in Chulimsk,* in *Nine Modern Soviet Plays,* edited by Victor Komissarzhevsky (Moscow: Progress, 1977), pp. 467–542;

*Izbrannoe* (Moscow: Iskusstvo, 1975; revised and enlarged, 1984);

*Dvadtsat' minut s angelom* (Moscow: VAAP, 1975); revised as part of *Provintsial'nye anekdoty,* in *Proshchanie v iiune: P'esy;* revision translated by Windle as *Provincial Anecdotes;*

*Proshchanie v iiune: P'esy* (Moscow: Sovetskii pisatel', 1977)—includes *Utinaia okhota,* translated and adapted by Law as *Duck Hunting* (New York: Dramatists Play Service, 1980);

*Belye goroda: Rasskazy, publitsistika* (Moscow: Sovremennik, 1979);

*Dom oknami v pole: P'esy; Ocherki i stat'i; Fel'etony; Rasskazy i stseny,* compiled by Anastasiia Prokop'evna

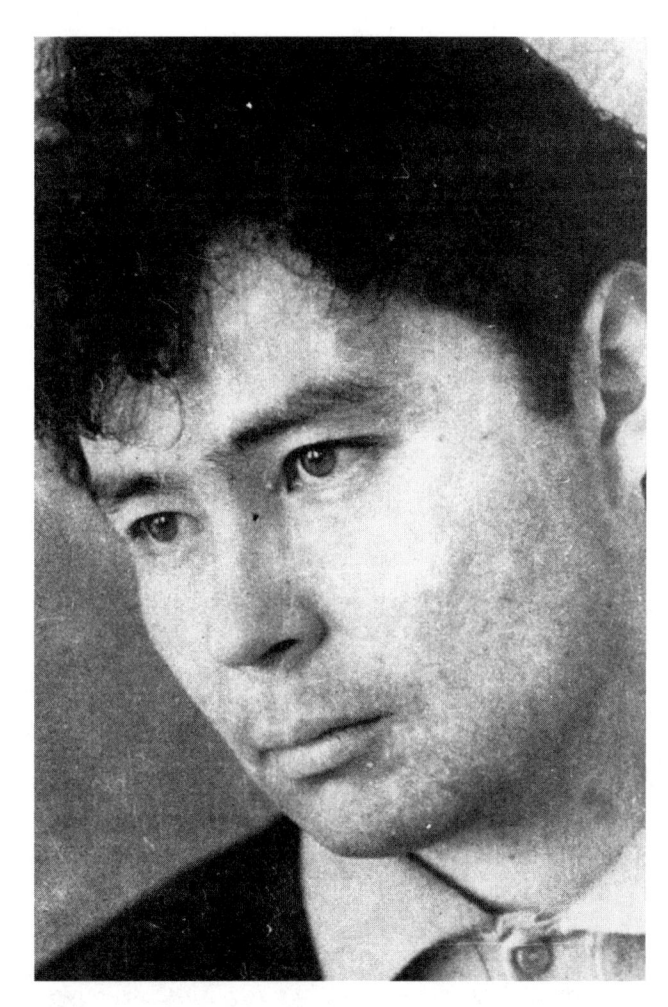

*Aleksandr Valentinovich Vampilov (from* Stechenie obstoiatel'stv, *1988; Collection of J. Alexander Ogden)*

Vampilova-Kopylova and L. V. Ioffe (Irkutsk: Vostochno-Sibirskoe knizhnoe izdatel'stvo, 1981)—includes *Dom oknami v pole,* translated as *The House with a View in the Field,* in *Soviet Literature,* no. 3 (1980): 138–148;

*Stechenie obstoiatel'stv: Rasskazy i stseny; Fel'etony; Ocherki i stat'i* (Irkutsk: Vostochno-Sibirskoe knizhnoe izdatel'stvo, 1988)—includes *Voron'ia roshcha* and *Uspekh;*

*Zapisnye knizhki* (Irkutsk: Irkutskii universitet, 1997).

**Editions and Collections:** *Starshii syn: [P'esy],* compiled by Anastasiia Prokop'evna Vampilova-Kopylova (Irkutsk: Vostochno-Sibirskoe knizhnoe izdatel'stvo, 1977);

*Bilet na Ust'-Ilim: Publitsistika,* compiled by Ol'ga Mikhailovna Vampilova (Moscow: Sovetskaia Rossiia, 1979);

*Utinaia okhota: P'esy,* compiled by Valentin Grigor'evich Rasputin (Irkutsk: Vostochno-Sibirskoe knizhnoe izdatel'stvo, 1987);

*Solntse v aistovom gnezde* (Moscow: Sovetskaia Rossiia, 1988);

*Ia s vami, liudi* (Moscow: Sovetskaia Rossiia, 1988);

*Uspekh: Odnoaktnye p'esy, stsenki, monologi, rasskazy* (Moscow: Sovetskaia Rossiia, 1990);

*Finskii nozh i persidskaia siren': Rasskazy i ocherki* (Irkutsk: Irkutskii universitet, 1997);

*Izbrannoe,* compiled by Ol'ga Mikhailovna Vampilova (Moscow: Soglasie, 1999).

**Editions in English:** *Farewell in June: Four Russian Plays,* translated by Kevin Windle and Amanda Metcalf (St. Lucia: University of Queensland Press, 1983);

*The Major Plays,* translated and edited by Alma Law (Luxembourg: Harwood Academic Publishers, 1996).

PLAY PRODUCTIONS: *Proshchanie v iiune,* Lithuania, Klaipedskii Dramatic Theater, December 1966; Moscow, K. S. Stanislavsky Dramatic Theater, 28 October 1972; Leningrad, Oblastnoi Theater of Drama and Comedy, 18 November 1972;

*Starshii syn,* Irkutsk, Okhlopkov Dramatic Theater, 18 September 1969; revised as *Svidaniia v predmest'e,* Leningrad, Oblastnoi Theater of Drama and Comedy, August 1970; as *Starshii syn,* Moscow, M. N. Ermolova Theater, 3 November 1972;

*Dva anekdota,* Leningrad, little stage of M. Gor'ky Bol'shoi Dramatic Theater, 30 March 1972; revised as *Provintsial'nye anekdoty,* Moscow, Sovremennik Theater, May 1974;

*Proshlym letom v Chulimske,* Krasnoiarsk, A. S. Pushkin Dramatic Theater, May 1973; Moscow, M. N. Ermolova Theater, 3 January 1974; Leningrad, M. Gor'ky Bol'shoi Dramatic Theater, 1 March 1974;

*Utinaia okhota,* Riga, State Academic Dramatic Theater of the Latvian SSR named for A. Upit, 25 April 1976 (in Latvian); Riga Theater of Russian Drama, 20 October 1976; Moscow, Moscow Art Theater, 10 January 1979.

Aleksandr Vampilov wrote only a handful of plays, but they defined his era sufficiently that "Vampilovian theater" and "the Vampilov hero" became standard phrases. In his life and his writing he expressed the hopes and frustrations of a generation that came to maturity during the "Thaw" that followed the death of Joseph Stalin. In drawing on traditional classics—critics often compare him to Anton Pavlovich Chekhov, Nikolai Vasil'evich Gogol, Ivan Sergeevich Turgenev, and Fyodor Dostoevsky—Vampilov was at the same time innovative for the theater of his day. He chose subjects that were not monumental or conventionally significant but, rather, that focused sharply on the irony, absurdity, and illogical "trifles" of inner life and the immense moral choices of day-to-day existence. Like Chekhov, Vampilov started his publishing career with humorous short stories, and they, like all his subsequent work, show a tolerance for, and even delight in, individual idiosyncrasies. He found the wryly humorous in everything. Even at his darkest, as when confronting stark, existential horror in his play *Utinaia okhota* (performed 1976, published 1977; translated as *Duck Hunting,* 1980), in which the main character is a depressed, suicidal, and incompetent womanizer, Vampilov undergirds his work with a dark sense of comedy as well as a nuanced combination of caustic criticism and tremendous sympathy for all fellow human beings. The Soviet artistic bureaucracy was perplexed by Vampilov's work, and only at the end of his short life did his plays begin to receive the widespread stagings and recognition they deserved.

Aleksandr Valentinovich Vampilov was born on 19 August 1937 in the city of Cheremkhovo, Irkutsk region, to two schoolteachers, Anastasiia Prokop'evna Vampilova-Kopylova and Valentin Nikitich Vampilov. His father, a Buriat whose grandfather had been a Buddhist lama, was denounced by a colleague and arrested by the Narodnyi komissariat vnutrennykh del (NKVD, People's Commissariat for Internal Affairs), when Vampilov was five months old, at the height of the Stalinist Terror. Accused of belonging to a "pan-Mongol counterrevolutionary diversionary-insurgent organization," Valentin Nikitich was sentenced to the conventional "ten years without the right of correspondence" but in fact was shot on 9 March 1938. Vampilov grew up in the settlement of Kutulik, a regional center and a stop on the Trans-Siberian Railroad.

For university Vampilov left Kutulik for Irkutsk, where he studied from 1955 to 1960 in the

Philological Faculty of Irkutsk State University. Several members of Vampilov's close circle of university friends have written memoirs, including the poet Andrei Grigor'evich Rumiantsev. The group was not known for particular devotion to academics and put most of their energies into practical jokes, "acting out" scenes of famous paintings, singing, and discussing literature. Vampilov emerged as a natural leader among his peers. His guitar playing was quite accomplished and always in demand, and he particularly enjoyed singing traditional romances. One setting composed by Vampilov of a poem by Sergei Aleksandrovich Esenin was in the repertoire of the university orchestra. At the university Vampilov was one year behind the writer Valentin Grigor'evich Rasputin; the two subsequently became friends, and after Vampilov's death Rasputin became one of the chief overseers of Vampilov's legacy.

The late 1950s were a time of openness and hope after the political and cultural repression of the Stalin years. Vampilov and his friends avidly took advantage of the opportunity to rediscover Russia's literary heritage as well as newly available riches of world culture. As Rumiantsev recounts, their favorite Russian reading included the works of Isaak Emmanuilovich Babel', Andrei Platonovich Platonov, Il'ia Il'f and Evgenii Petrov, and Daniil Ivanovich Kharms. Foreign selections included works by Ernest Hemingway, Erich Maria Remarque, Antoine de Saint-Exupéry, and Franz Kafka. Vampilov also discovered O. Henry, who became his favorite writer.

Vampilov put much of his time at university into writing. Throughout his life he carried notebooks with him, jotting notes that he subsequently reworked in his fiction and drama. Early in his university years Vampilov wrote poetry, but he soon switched to prose. He and his friends quickly joined a literary society that the university formed in the fall of 1957. His first publication, the story "Stechenie obstoiatel'stv" (A Coincidence), appeared in the campus newspaper *Irkutskii universitet* on 4 April 1958 under the pseudonym A. Sanin (formed from his nickname Sania). By that summer Vampilov's stories were appearing in other newspapers, including the Irkutsk edition of *Sovetskaia molodezh'* (Soviet Youth), where—by the fall of 1959—he had become a member of the staff.

Vampilov's employment at *Sovetskaia molodezh'* lasted five years (1959–1964), during which time he continued to publish stories and also wrote short journalistic pieces on a range of current issues. Increasingly, however, he showed an interest in drama; he started with a focus on dialogues, monologues, and brief scenes and later moved on to one-acts and then full-length comedies and dramas. Vampilov left *Sovetskaia molodezh'* to devote himself full-time to his own writing. In time he began participating in nationwide seminars for young writers, and in 1965–1967 he studied writing in Moscow. As his career progressed, his material circumstances changed little; his second wife, Ol'ga Mikhailovna Vampilova, in her preface to Vampilov's works published in *Zvezda*, 8 (1981), gives the following description of his surroundings: "A suitcase, table, bentwood chair, guitar, and lots of books, heaped right on the floor for lack of bookcases—those were the surroundings Vampilov lived in. . . . Over the years, little changed. . . . Life was poor, but happy. Everyone was young and talented, and poverty was not a vice."

*Front cover of Vampilov's first book,* Stechenie obstoiatel'stv, *(1961,* A Coincidence*) which was published under the pseudonym A. Sanin (Collection of J. Alexander Ogden)*

Vampilov's first publication as a dramatist came in 1964, when both *Sovetskaia molodezh'* and the national journal *Teatr* (Theater) published his one-act comedy *Dom oknami v pole* (translated as *The House with a View in the Field*, 1980). All action in the play takes place in the house of Liliia Vasil'evna Astaf'eva, the young and attractive director of a village dairy farm.

As the play opens, Astaf'eva is bustling about with her ironing; clearly nervous, she is expecting a visitor. When he shows up, the audience quickly learns that Vladimir Aleksandrovich Tret'iakov, the village geography teacher for the past three years, has reached the end of his assignment and is about to return to city life. Tret'iakov, in the honesty of this parting moment, admits that he has not been without feelings for Astaf'eva and wonders what might have happened the previous May, had things been different. Not letting him depart with these few light remarks, and playfully resentful that Tret'iakov has appeared only after making farewells throughout the whole village, Astaf'eva protests that it is too late at night for him to be seen leaving her house. The remainder of the play reveals the increasing tension between life in the closed, traditional world of the village and escape to the city, where, as Astaf'eva imagines, "everyone is young, everyone is proud, and no one knows what you're thinking about." But Tret'iakov protests that life in the city is stifling, empty, and boring. As he stands, both literally and figuratively, on the threshold and confronts his time in the village with the newly clear eyes of someone departing, he realizes that he envies the silly youth who will show up with a new globe to take his place and be loved by the people of the village. In spite of the waiting bus driver, he decides in the final moments that he will go nowhere, at least for today.

Even in this brief play, with only two onstage characters, Vampilov focuses on many of the concerns seen more fully in his later drama. The contrasts between old and new and between city and country are underlined here by the communal, ever-present voice of village opinion in the form of an offstage chorus singing traditional songs throughout the play. In this brief play with little outward action, Vampilov skillfully develops not only the relationship between the two characters but also each personality individually. Tret'iakov comes across as a slow-moving and appealing but self-centered and not introspective man, with little motivation or conviction. Astaf'eva, though, has a clear picture of her world; her small personal concerns and private emotions and dreams form the center of the play. Indirectly, Vampilov shows that the canned phrases and mind-set of Soviet official life are irrelevant to these concerns. When Tret'iakov expresses surprise that Astaf'eva—a "farm director, activist, and forward-looking woman"—would tell him that she and the other villagers are backward and prejudiced, with some irony she responds, "Why are you surprised? Here on the farm things are bad with the cultural mass-organizing work. Didn't you read about it in the paper?"

Also in 1964 Vampilov finished his first multi-act play, *Proshchanie v iiune* (first called "Iarmarka" [The Fair], 1966; translated as *Farewell in June,* 1980), a bittersweet two-act comedy about the adventures of Kolia Kolesov and his friends and associates in the spring of their university graduation. Kolesov, a charming bon vivant and a known prankster, has the misfortune to fall in love with Tania, the daughter of the university rector Repnikov. As far as Repnikov is concerned, Kolesov's utter unsuitability is epitomized by his arrest for disorderly conduct. He works off his time doing manual labor with Zolotuev, a gardener and veteran of the gulag (Soviet prison-camp system) who has been arrested this time for digging up an orchid; together they are supposed to remove the fence of a cemetery so a streetcar line can pass through.

The play presents several dilemmas: Repnikov forces Kolesov to choose between Tania and reinstatement in the university in time to get his diploma; Tania must confront her idealized view of her father and later of her first love. Zolotuev, meanwhile, has been on a quixotic quest for confirmation of his view of human nature ever since his inability to pay a large bribe landed him in the gulag for ten years. He strives to amass money and pay 20,000 rubles to the inspector responsible for his sentence, simply for the satisfaction of hearing the inspector admit he is a bastard who sent a man to prison for nothing.

While addressing issues ranging from compromise and lost innocence to the lure of outward respectability and authority, Vampilov captures the little comedies, absurdities, and dreams of everyday life in his characters' exchanges, whether flirtatious banter, or tense father-daughter exchanges, or the variously rowdy, officious, drunken, and loquacious voices at a wedding banquet. For convenience he gives many of the secondary student characters "speaking names," such as Veselyi (Jolly), Ser'eznyi (Serious), Komsorg (Communist Organizer), and Krasavitsa (Beauty). Yet, the "real" names of his leads are equally significant and range from the freewheeling Kolesov (from *koleso,* "wheel"), to Zolotuev, who is searching for gold (*zoloto*), and to Repnikov, who is rooted in his authority and mediocrity like a turnip (*repa*).

*Proshchanie v iiune* was first staged in 1966 in Lithuania, at the Klaipedskii Dramatic Theater, and was followed by productions in several other regional theaters. The conspicuous absence of a production in Moscow, however (until October 1972, two months after the playwright's death), established a pattern of exclusion from the main stages of the country that plagued Vampilov for his entire career. The long-awaited Moscow premiere of *Proshchanie v iiune* was heralded in *Sovetskaia kul'tura* (Soviet Culture) in a 6 November 1972 announcement: "The name of the Irkutsk dramatist A. Vampilov, whose plays are well known to the country's audiences, has appeared for the first time on the playbill of theaters in the capital."

Vampilov wrote his first version of the play ultimately known as *Starshii syn* (The Elder Son) in 1965. First published in excerpt as *Zhenikhi* (Suitors) in 1965 in *Sovetskaia molodezh'*, the play evolved into *Predmest'e* (The Suburb, published 1968 in the almanac *Angara*) and received its final title in 1969, when its national premiere took place in Irkutsk with the playwright's direct involvement in the production. Productions eventually were staged in Leningrad (as *Svidaniia v predmest'e* [Suburban Meetings], 1970) and Moscow (November, 1972).

The main protagonist of the play, Vladimir Busygin, becomes the "elder son" of the title, when he is mistaken for the previously unknown oldest child of Andrei Sarafanov. At the start of the play Busygin and Sil'va, a fellow reveler, are unceremoniously shut out on a late, cold spring evening by the young women they have escorted home. Left behind—they have missed the last commuter train—and shivering, they see Sarafanov's name on a mailbox and talk their way into his apartment, convincing his teenage son, Vasen'ka, that they know his father. The mistaken-identity ruse is completely unpremeditated: Busygin's high-flown appeal for sympathy on the grounds that all men are brothers is misinterpreted by Sil'va, and when he announces to Vasen'ka, "he's your blood brother," both Vasen'ka and Busygin are equally surprised.

The play centers on the resulting transformations in the life of the Sarafanov household as well as in Busygin's own. Twenty-one years ago Sarafanov was fighting in World War II and had a brief liaison with a seamstress, so after some initial suspicion he joyfully welcomes his new son. Life for Sarafanov has not lived up to his youthful dreams and ambitions: an underemployed musician, long divorced and often drunk, he thinks his two children do not realize that he long ago was fired from the philharmonic and now plays only at funerals and dances. His daughter, Nina, is about to marry a pilot and move to Sakhalin; Vasen'ka, rejected in his infatuation for an older neighbor who treats him like a puppy, is also preparing to leave. Busygin's appearance out of the blue brings new hope and a sense of completion for all of them. "Where have you been? Why didn't you show up sooner?" asks Nina to the elder brother she never

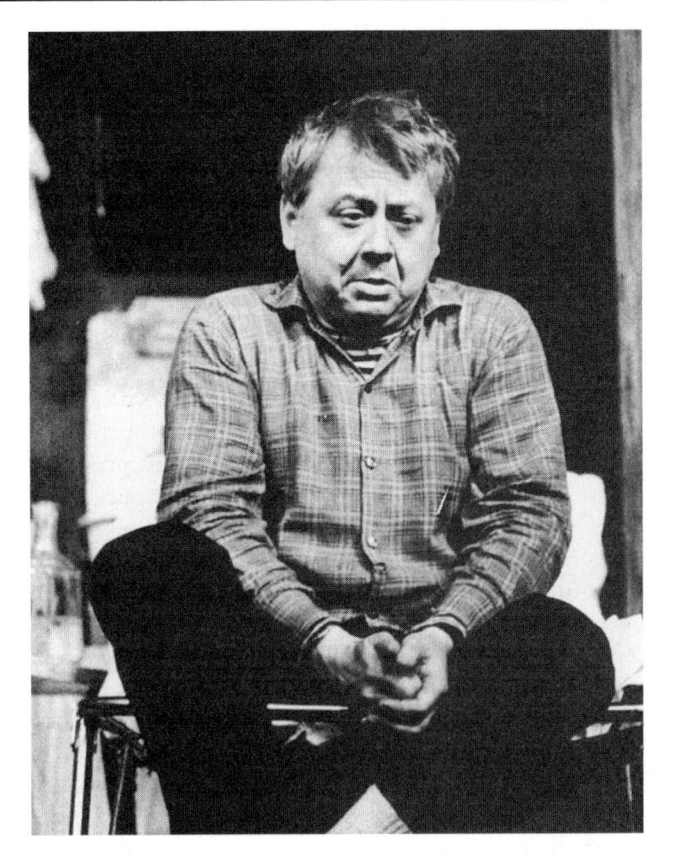

*Famed stage and movie actor Oleg Tabakov playing the role of Anchugin in the Moscow premiere production of Vampilov's* Provintsial'nye anekdoty *(Provincial Anecdotes) at the Sovremennik Theater, 1974 (from* Stechenie obstoiatel'stv, *1988; Collection of J. Alexander Ogden)*

had, whose intelligence, good looks, and concern for family make her suddenly defensive about her choice of fiancé.

Like Khlestakov, from Gogol's *Revizor* (1836, The Inspector General), Busygin reveals much about the disfunction, everyday frustrations, and intrinsic humor of life by showing up and being taken for someone he is not. To penetrate the uncaring veneer of modern society is not easy: "People have a thick skin, and breaking through it isn't so easy. You have to tell lies up and down—only then will people believe you and sympathize with you," he says to Sil'va at the beginning. But Busygin, like Kolesov in *Proshchanie v iiune,* is a great talker who can spin a story and get his listeners to dream along with him. And Busygin truly believes his assertion about the connections among all people; he comes to care deeply for his new family. Sarafanov, too, is a sensitive person somewhat perplexed by life—a "blessed fool," as his former wife called him in letters written before she ran off with someone more practical and successful. He has been writing an oratorio or cantata called "All Men Are

Brothers," although in a lifetime of work he has written only a page. As had happened with *Proshchanie v iiune,* party-line reviewers disapproved of the combination of whimsy, emotion, and philosophical questioning found in *Starshii syn.* Writing about a touring version of the Irkutsk premiere production, a critic for *Sovetskaia kul'tura* wrote (17 August 1971): "a trivial anecdotal mess underlies the plot and the production."

If in *Starshii syn* Vampilov gave a poignantly comic spin to life issues such as disillusionment and belonging, he used much darker tones in *Utinaia okhota.* Here he directly confronts social problems (infidelity, marital breakdown, suicide) and problematic mental states (alienation, depression, paranoia). The play presents the life of thirty-year-old Vitia Zilov as it spins out of control: though charming and surrounded by friends, he sinks into apathy, self-destructive behavior, and increasing isolation. Zilov, while compulsively flirting with other women, shuts himself off from his wife, Galina; she eventually leaves him, saying, "You don't need me." The play culminates in a gala dinner that Zilov holds to introduce friends and colleagues to his new girlfriend, the student Irina. Zilov, who becomes drunk, insults everyone with outrageous accusations and unfounded suspicions, driving them all away. The next day, the depressed Zilov nearly commits suicide, influenced by the mock funeral wreath that his erstwhile friends have sent in response to his behavior the night before, as well as by his father's recent death.

In Zilov, Vampilov creates a character who has achieved conventional, Soviet happiness, then loses it. Married and employed, he and Galina celebrate a housewarming in their new apartment and soon even have a telephone (as seen in a series of flashbacks). Yet, Zilov is indifferent toward his achievements, although he shows a nearly crazed jealousy and possessiveness when he fears that others will steal either the women or the things in his life. He has little self-respect; he trusts no one and truly cares about nothing. Duck hunting is the exception: throughout the play Zilov's attention is focused on an upcoming hunting trip in the fall, even as his life falls apart around him.

Like much of Vampilov's work, *Utinaia okhota* confronts the torment of memory and the lure of dreams of a different, better life. Galina is "deadened by work, by life with a capricious husband, and by the burden of unrealized hopes." In one attempt at reconciliation, Zilov starts reenacting an exchange from their courtship, but falters, forgetting his most important lines. Creating a new life is not as easy as a friend suggests when he says, "if you don't like your life, fine—live differently! Who's stopping you?" Most of the plot of the play is revealed in Zilov's remembrances of earlier events; Vampilov uses lighting, musical effects, and a revolving stage to set off these remembrances—as well as Zilov's imaginings—from the scenes that frame them. In its juggling of time and theatrical effects, *Utinaia okhota* is Vampilov's most formally inventive play, as well as his longest and the only one in three acts. The play was completed in 1967 and first published in *Angara* in 1970. It did not receive Soviet stagings until 1976 (in Riga), with Moscow premieres at both the Moscow Art Theater and the Ermolova Dramatic Theater in 1979. *Utinaia okhota* received numerous stagings as Vampilov's posthumous reputation grew in the late 1970s. However, as Iulii Smelkov wrote at the time in "Zigzagi sud'by Zilova: *Utinaia okhota:* Kak staviat? Kak stavit'?" (The Zigzags of Zilov's Fate: *Utinaia okhota:* How Is It staged? How to Stage It?), theaters were often not ready to confront Vampilov's "fundamentally new" kind of play writing and therefore spectacularly successful stagings were few.

During the late 1960s and early 1970s, as a period of "Stagnation" under Brezhnev increasingly stifled artistic expression in the country, many playwrights were having problems getting their works staged, and for Vampilov the problem was particularly bad, since his plays dealt with complex characters and situations and provided no easy answers. Surveying the state of contemporary drama in the Soviet Union, A. Kitainik wrote in a 20 October 1970 article for the newspaper *Sovetskaia kul'tura* that getting to know Vampilov's plays (some of which were available in published form) would convince readers "of the indubitable gifts of this author, of his ability to construct a plot pointedly, dynamically, and enticingly. But where are his plays showing? Nowhere."

For nearly a decade Vampilov rewrote two of his earliest theatrical pieces, eventually uniting them under the title *Provintsial'nye anekdoty* (Provincial Anecdotes) in 1971. Originally sparked by his work in dramatists' seminars in 1962, the two halves of *Provintsial'nye anekdoty* were first published separately, appearing as the one-act plays *Dvadtsat' minut s angelom* (1967, Twenty Minutes with an Angel, published in *Sovetskaia molodezh'*) and *Istoriia s metranpazhem* (Incident with a Paginator, finished in 1968 and published as a separate edition in 1971). *Provintsial'nye anekdoty* received its first performance in March 1972 under the title *Dva anekdota* on the little stage of the M. Gor'ky Bol'shoi Dramatic Theater. Both plays are set in the provincial hotel "Taiga," and both are united by a common premise (one they share with *Starshii syn*): an outsider appears out of nowhere and provokes others into a realization of their insecurities, cynicism, greed, and eagerness to think the worst of others. Vampilov emphasizes the Gogolian nature of the outsider—as well as of the absurdity that results—with an epigraph from Gogol's story "Nos" (1836, The Nose).

The first anecdote, *Istoriia s metranpazhem,* uses a series of absurd misunderstandings to reveal the stories and lies people tell others and themselves. The action occurs entirely in the hotel room of Viktoriia, a young woman whose evening is disrupted first by an ardent soccer fan, Potapov, in search of a room with a working radio and then by the hotel manager Kaloshin, who assumes the worst in this compromising situation of a man and woman together in a hotel room late at night. After sending Potapov back to his room, Kaloshin begins to worry that he has offended an important guest: as the inconvenienced Viktoriia asks with some satisfaction, "And if he's someone in charge, then what?" The situation does not improve when Potapov turns out to be a paginator; no one that Kaloshin asks knows what a paginator is or does. As infidelities and secrets, both imagined and real, emerge, Kaloshin is forced to confront a life spent skipping from job to job, fearing superiors, and always being insecure about his ignorance. He realizes, "My life has gone to waste . . . to waste . . . And who's to blame? . . . Is the paginator to blame?" Almost scared to death by worry about his behavior toward the paginator, Kaloshin welcomes his impending demise, and only when he learns that he will live is he truly perplexed, wondering how to lead his life and resolving to start on a new course the following day.

In *Dvadtsat' minut s angelom,* the other anecdote, two business travelers—a driver and a dispatcher who ships toilets—have spent their last kopek partying in their hotel room. In a joking way they yell out the window for a gift of one hundred rubles; improbably, an unassuming agronomist named Khomutov turns up at their door offering the money. This simple offer—an affront to everything the travelers or their hotel neighbors believe about human nature—leads them to suspect Khomutov is a radical, a religious lunatic, a hooligan, a thief, or worse. Meanwhile, they come to blows and display extreme suspiciousness, distrust, and cynicism. Khomutov, even before he finally is forced to admit a plausible motivation, makes both his listeners and the audience question what, in a crazy world, defines normal, or crazy, or angelic behavior.

Vampilov's correspondence, dating from 1965 to 1972, with Elena Leonidovna Iakushkina, the literary director of the Ermolova Theater in Moscow, bears witness to his increasing frustration with the theatrical censors in Moscow, who refused to see anything positive in his plays and demanded impossible and idiotic changes to his scripts. In a letter of late February 1969 he wrote: "I've become accustomed to a lot, but even so I didn't expect such a turn of events. The grievances that they bring forward against *Starshii syn* are especially far-fetched, and, clearly, we're talking about a conscious and now already systematic attitude to all my plays as a whole. Judge for yourself." Later that year his letters threatened that if things did not improve he would give up writing altogether. Iakushkina's responses constantly try to reassure and encourage the young playwright; in a letter from 16 February 1971 she says, "It's as if you've become the most popular dramatist in Moscow, even though you've never been staged. Over you, as once over the beautiful Helen, all the theaters of Moscow are arguing."

Vampilov's final completed play was written under the title "Valentina" in 1970 and revised the following year as *Proshlym letom v Chulimske* (Last Summer in Chulimsk, first published 1972 in the almanac *Sibir'* [Siberia]). Events take place during one day and the following morning outside a village tearoom-café. The play is about a village girl, Valentina, who works at the café, and her three suitors. These include Pashka, an awkward, angry young man and the son of the café manager; Vladimir Shamanov, a thoughtful but cynical police investigator; and Innokentii Mechetkin, a straightforward and unimaginative bookkeeper. In *Proshlym letom v Chulimske,* as in many of Vampilov's works for the stage, much is revealed about the characters during the course of the play, but ultimately little changes outwardly in their lives by the end of it. Vampilov leaves his audience with a scene in which Valentina and Eremeev, an old Evenk hunter, yet again repair the planks of a dilapidated fence around the front garden of the café—something Valentina has done throughout the play. In emphasizing this caretaker role of mending something that is broken, Vampilov ascribes great importance to these characters' sense of responsibility and sense of place. While all of his plays owe something to Irkutsk and the Siberian life that he knew best, *Proshlym letom v Chulimske* is the first one since *Dom oknami v pole* that stresses the features and details of an unchanging, old-fashioned village way of life (for example, the houses feature gingerbread fretwork, and electricity comes only from a generator that has to be turned off at night). Valentina, unlike all the other young people who leave the village for the city, is firmly committed to staying in her place, just as Eremeev loves his taiga and the natural world. Vampilov here shares several

*Monument to Vampilov on Lake Baikal near the spot where he drowned in 1972 (photograph by J. Alexander Ogden, 2000)*

concerns with Rasputin and other writers of "Village Prose," including the permanence of village life and its rootedness in nature and tradition; an attention to commitments kept and doing the right thing; and a sense of stewardship toward both the environment and the past.

Reviews of the Moscow premiere of *Proshlym letom v Chulimske* (two years after Vampilov's death) praised both the play and the staging. N. Leikin, in a 10 January 1974 review in *Moskovskaia pravda* (Moscow Truth), wrote of the director, V. Andreev, that, "in the personal and local love stories of A. Vampilov's drama, he keenly saw . . . that 'life of the human spirit' which, indubitably, has general significance." A review by Z. Vladimirova in *Vecherniaia Moskva* (Evening Moscow, 5 February 1974), while commending much about the play and many of the performers, also criticizes the play for nostalgia and a descent into melodrama.

On 17 August 1972 Vampilov drowned in a boating accident in Lake Baikal. A monument near Listvianka, where the Angara River flows out of the lake, marks the spot. His friend Rumiantsev quotes a phrase from one of Vampilov's ubiquitous notebooks that in hindsight seems prophetic: "the sepulchral, black darkness of water."

Vampilov's reputation spread tremendously after his premature death. In his native Irkutsk region, festivals and stagings are held often, and in August 1997 many events marked the sixtieth anniversary of his birth and twenty-fifth anniversary of his death. The Vampilov Foundation in Irkutsk has published several series of books related to the writer's legacy and continues to promote his work. His plays have received frequent performances in Russia and worldwide. At times, audiences in Britain and the United States have found relating to his characters difficult; Zilov, from *Utinaia okhota,* for instance, is seen as simply unsympathetic. Sometimes, though, Vampilov's approach has resonated with similar concerns in Western theater; Judith Martin, reviewing an Arena Stage production of *Duck Hunting* for *The Washington Post* on 19 May 1978, noted, "American theater is now in the throes of exploring the great personal, vague, anti-social depression, and here is an example of how that kind of thing can be done well, with great symbolic birds overhead, a chorus of figures demonstrating how sad acceptance is, and a great fireworks of torment in the center." Vampilov's plays, while grounded in 1960s Soviet reality, ultimately focus on eternal issues of morality, trust, and human foibles, and as such continue to find audiences and enthusiastic supporters.

**Letters:**

Valentin Rasputin and others, "Emu bylo by nynche piat'desiat . . . : Perepiski A. Vampilova s E. Iakushkinoi," *Novyi mir,* 9 (September 1987): 209–226;

I. S. Grakova and others, "Pis'ma Vampilova," *Zvezda,* 8 (1997): 133–138.

**Bibliographies:**

E. D. Elizarova, *Aleksandr Valentinovich Vampilov: Bibliograficheskii ukazatel'* (Irkutsk: Redaktsionno-izdatel'skii otdel Uprpoligrafizdata, 1989); continued by T.D. Zhikhareva as *Aleksandr Valentinovich Vampilov: Bibliograficheskii ukazatel',* edited by L. A. Kazantseva (Irkutsk: Izdatel'stvo Irkutskoi oblastnoi publichnoi biblioteki im I. I. Molchanova-Sibirskogo, 2000).

"Bibliography" and "Further Reading" in Vreneli Farber, *The Playwright Aleksandr Vampilov* (New York: Peter Lang, 2001), pp. 207–219.

**Biographies:**

Dmitrii Ivanovich Sergeev, "Vstrechi s A. V. Vampilovym," *Neva,* 7 (July 1984): 163–169;

"Zhizn' Aleksandr Vampilova v sobytiiakh i datakh: Biograficheskaia khronika," *Avrora,* 10 (1987);

Andrei Grigor'evich Rumiantsev, *Aleksandr Vampilov: Studencheskie gody. Vospominaniia, maloizvestnye stranitsy A. Vampilova* (Irkutsk: Vostochno-Sibirskoe knizhnoe izdatel'stvo, 1993);

Radnai Andreevich Sherkhunaev, *Korni i vetvi: Slovo o predkakh i roditeliakh vydaiushchegosia dramaturga Aleksandra Vampilova* (Ulan-Ude: Soel, 1994);

Liana Polukhina, "Vot ia ves' pered vami . . .: Moskovskie vstrechi s Aleksandrom Vampilovym," *Literaturnaia gazeta,* 28 (12 July 1995): 5;

M. Sergeev, "Zhenit'ba Vampilova," *Zvezda,* 8 (1997): 139;

Sergeev, "Vokrug *Utinoi okhoty,*" *Zvezda,* 8 (1997): 141–144;

*Venok Vampilovu: Stikhi, iz vospominanii, iz pisem* (Irkutsk: Izdatel'stvo Irkutskogo universiteta, 1997).

**References:**

I. V. Aleksandrova, "Osobennosti vyrazheniia avtorskoi pozitsii v p'ese A. Vampilova 'Utinaia okhota': Intonatsionnoe svoeobrazie dialoga i remarki," *Voprosy russkoi literatury,* 2 (56), (1990): 96–103;

James Edgar Bernhardt, "Alexander Vampilov: The Five Plays," dissertation, University of Pittsburgh, 1980;

L. V. Besprozvannyi, comp., *Vampilov na liubitel'skoi stsene: Narodnye teatry Priangar'ia* (Irkutsk: Izdatel'stvo Irkutskogo universiteta, 1997);

Sergei Ivanovich Borovikov, "Estestvennost' i teatral'nost'; Dramaturgiia Aleksandra Vampilova," *Nash sovremennik,* 15, no. 3 (1978): 162–177;

F. Farber and others, "P'esy Aleksandra Vampilova v kontekste amerikanskoi kul'tury (Elementy teatra absurda)," *Sovremennaia dramaturgiia,* 2 (1992): 158–164;

Vreneli Farber, *The Playwright Aleksandr Vampilov: An Ironic Observer,* Middlebury Studies in Russian Language and Literature, volume 25 (New York: Peter Lang, 2001);

Farber, *The Prose of Aleksandr Vampilov* (New York: Peter Lang, 2003);

M. I. Gromova, "Chekhovskie traditsii v teatre A. Vampilova," *Literatura v shkole,* 2 (1997): 46–56;

Elena Gushanskaia, *Aleksandr Vampilov: Ocherk tvorchestva* (Leningrad: Sovetskii pisatel', Leningradskoe otdelenie, 1990);

L. V. Ioffe and others, *Mir Aleksandra Vampilova: Zhizn'. Tvorchestvo. Sud'ba* (Irkutsk: Irkutskaia oblastnaia tipografiia No. 1, 2000);

V. Kamyshev, "Neobkhodimost' Vampilova," *Russkaia mysl'/La pensée russe,* 4200 (1997): 12; 4201 (1997): 12;

Nikolai Nikitich Kiselev, "Sluchainost' v strukture deistviia p'es A. Vampilova," *Problemy metoda i zhanra,* 19 (1997): 266–279;

Vladimir Klimenko, "Zhazhda dobra: Zametki o tvorchestve Aleksandra Vampilova," *Nash sovremennik,* 6 (June 1983): 163–169;

Iurii Petrovich Liubimov and others, "O Vampilove," *Zvezda,* 8 (1997): 140;

V. M. Loginov, "'Dionisiiskii chelovek' v tvorchestve Korolenko i Vampilova," in his *O Korolenko i literature* (Moscow, 1994), pp. 124–141;

M. G. Merkulova, "Teatr Leonida Leonova i Aleksandra Vampilova: (Opyt sravnitel'nogo analiza)," in *Vernost' Chelovecheskomu* (Moscow: Nasledie, 1992), pp. 102–116;

Merkulova, "Vremia v dramaturgii A.Vampilova," *Problemy evoliutsii russkoi literatury XX-ogo veka,* 2 (1995): 130–131;

V. P. Muromsky, "'Sokhranit' i preumnozhit' chelovecheskoe v cheloveke. . . .' K 60-letiiu so dnia rozhdeniia A. Vampilova," *Literatura v shkole,* 5 (1997): 78–85;

Aleksandr Ivanovich Ovcharenko, "Dramaturgicheskaia saga: P'esy Aleksandra Vampilova," *Molodaia gvardiia,* 6 (June 1985): 248–257;

Igor' Konstantinovich Petrov, *Slovo s muzykoi sol'etsia* (Irkutsk: Izdatel'stvo Irkutskogo universiteta, 1997);

A. M. Pronin, "Odnoaktnye p'esy v tvorchestve Aleksandra Vampilova," *Filologicheskie nauki*, 6, no. 144 (1984): 3–9;

Konstantin Lazarevich Rudnitsky, "Po tu storonu vymysla: Zametki o dramaturgii A. Vampilova," *Voprosy literatury*, 10 (1976): 28–75;

Iulii Sergeevich Smelkov, "Zigzagi sud'by Zilova: Utinaia okhota: Kak staviat? Kak stavit'?" *Literaturnoe obozrenie*, 12 (1979): 90–93;

S. O. Smirnov, ". . . Mat' synochka nikogda': Nedopetaia pesnia A. Vampilova i V. Shukshina," *Literatura v shkole*, 5 (1997): 86–89;

Anatolii Samuilovich Sobennikov, "'Chaika' A. P. Chekhova i 'Proshlym letom v Chulimske' A. Vampilova: K tipologii siuzheta," *Chekhovskie chteniia v Ialte: Chekhov i XX vek*, 9 (1997): 54–62;

E. I. Strel'tsova, *Plen utinoi okhoty* (Irkutsk: Irkutskaia oblastnaia tipografiia no. 1, 1998);

Strel'tsova, "Ruzh'e ili telefon?: O simvolike p'esy 'Utinaia okhota' A. Vampilova," *Russkaia rech'*, 4 (July–August 1988): 44–50;

Boris Filippovich Sushkov, *Aleksandr Vampilov: Razmyshleniia ob ideinykh korniakh, problematike, khudozhestvennom metode i sud'be tvorchestva dramaturga* (Moscow: Sovetskaia Rossiia, 1989);

Nadezhda Stepanovna Tenditnik, *Aleksandr Vampilov* (Novosibirsk: Zapadno-Sibirskoe knizh. Izd-vo, 1979);

Tenditnik, *Pered litsom pravdy: Ocherk zhizni i tvorchestva Aleksandra Vampilova* (Irkutsk: Izdatel'stvo Zhurnala "Sibir'" sovmestno s Tovarishchestvom "Pis'mena," 1997);

Ol'ga Mikhailovna Vampilova, "Neizdannyi Vampilov," *Zvezda*, 8 (1997): 120–122;

Tat'iana Zhilkina, "Rodilsia geniem," *Grani*, 69, no. 172 (1994): 163–208;

Zhilkina, ed., "Proveriaetsia pamiat'iu: Aleksandr Vampilov, khudozhnik i chelovek," *Literaturnoe obozrenie*, 8 (1983): 107–112;

Vitalii Innokent'evich Zorkin, *Ne uiti ot pamiati* (Irkutsk: Izdatel'stvo Irkutskogo universiteta, 1997).

# Georgii Vladimov
(19 February 1931 – 19 October 2003)

Svetlana McMillin
*University College London*

BOOKS: *Neman–Volga–Dunai,* by Vladimov and Petr Vasil'evich Sevast'ianov (Moscow: Voennoe izdatel'stvo, 1961);

*Bol'shaia ruda* (Moscow: Sovetskaia Rossia, 1962); translated by J. Kurago as *Striking It Rich* (Moscow: Foreign Languages Publishing House, 1963);

*Iunost' komissara,* by Vladimov and Evstafii Ivanovich Pozdniakov (Moscow: Voennoe izdatel'stvo, 1962);

*Vernyi Ruslan: Istoriia karaul'noi sobaki* (Frankfurt am Main: Posev, 1975); translated by Michael Glenny as *Faithful Ruslan: The Story of a Guard Dog* (London: Cape, 1979; New York: Simon & Schuster, 1979);

*Tri minuty molchaniia* (Moscow: Sovremennik, 1976; uncensored edition, Frankfurt am Main: Posev, 1982); translated by Glenny as *Three Minutes' Silence* (London & New York: Quartet, 1985);

*Ne obrashchaite vnimanie, maestro* (Frankfurt am Main: Posev, 1983); translated by Roger Keys as "Pay No Attention, Maestro," *Literary Review,* 59 (1983): 39–55;

*General i ego armiia* (Moscow: Knizhnaia palata, 1997);

*Sobranie sochinenii v chetyrekh tomakh,* 4 volumes (Moscow: NFQ/2Print, 1998);

*Roman, povest', rasskazy, p'esa* (Ekaterinburg: U-Faktoriia, 1999).

**Editions in English**: "The Ore," translated by Andrew R. MacAndrew, in his *Four Soviet Masterpieces* (Toronto & New York: Bantam, 1965);

"A General and His Army," excerpt, translated by Arch Tait, *Glas: New Russian Writing,* 11 (1996): 169–182.

SELECTED PERIODICAL PUBLICATION–UNCOLLECTED: *Shestoi soldat, Grani,* 121 (1981): 5–106.

Georgii Vladimov belonged to the 1960s generation of writers, which also included his close friends Vladimir Nikolaevich Voinovich and Vassily Aksyonov. The first generation to begin their careers after the death of the dictator Joseph Stalin, they brought to Russian literature new themes and intonations and a critical attitude to official ideology that made them outcasts during the Leonid Brezhnev period. Vladimov was a critic and an editor before beginning to write his own fiction; he also played a direct role in dissident affairs and human-rights activities. The two prizes he received reflect these two aspects of his career: in 1995 he was awarded the Russian Booker Prize for his novel *General i ego armiia* (1997, The General and His Army), first published in incomplete form in the magazine *Znamia* (The Banner) in 1994, and in 2001 he received the Andrei Sakharov Prize for Civic Courage for his activities in defense of human rights.

Vladimov was born Georgii Nikolaevich Volosevich in Khar'kiv on 19 February 1931. His parents, both of whom were teachers of literature, divorced when Vladimov was barely a year old. In 1941, during World War II, Vladimov was evacuated to Kyrgyzstan, where he studied and also worked on a collective farm. In 1942 he moved to Saratov, where his mother was teaching at a military medical school. At twelve, deciding that it was time for him to join the fighting, he ran away from home and made his way to the battlefront on skis but was picked up by a tank crew and returned to his badly shaken mother. This episode led his mother to enroll him in the Suvorov Military School of Frontier Troops, which had recently opened in Kutaisi, Georgia; she got a job teaching Russian language and literature in the Suvorov school system, and she and her son continued to live together. Meanwhile, Vladimov's father had found himself in German-occupied territory and been sent to a labor camp in Germany, where he probably died during a bombing raid in 1943. Vladimov later undertook many unsuccessful attempts to learn the circumstances of his father's death.

At first Vladimir enjoyed the military school; he quickly made many friends, with one of whom he began writing a utopian science-fiction novel; but, as he

*Georgii Vladimov (from* Bol'shaia ruda, *1962; John C. Hodges Library, University of Tennessee–Knoxville)*

said in an unpublished interview, "since nothing much interesting happened in this ideal society we soon got fed up with it." The teachers at the school were former officers, many of whom had been obliged to leave the fighting because of their wounds. They shared with the children their experiences in the war, which were quite different from the heroic picture created by Soviet propaganda. Vladimov believed that this exposure helped the children to develop a critical attitude to official ideology and to approach the statements of the government and the press with caution.

In 1946, during the government campaign against the poet Anna Andreevna Akhmatova and the satirist Mikhail Mikhailovich Zoshchenko, Vladimov and two friends from school visited Zoshchenko, whose work Vladimov admired, to give him moral support. "We were also writing our novel and therefore regarded ourselves as his colleagues and thought that he had been treated cruelly and unjustly," Vladimov said in the unpublished interview. This childish act of solidarity led to a great scandal in the school. The boys were almost expelled, but the administrators were so fearful for their jobs that they made the teenagers agree to a false version of events: that the visit to Zoshchenko occurred before Stalin's cultural spokesman Andrei Aleksandrovich Zhdanov's speech denouncing him and Akhmatova. Nevertheless, the incident brought Vladimov to the attention of the NKVD (Narodnyi komissariat vnutrennykh del [People's Commissariat for Internal Affairs]) and its successor, the MVD (Ministerstvo vnutrennykh del [Ministry of Internal Affairs]), at an early age. His mother began to be persecuted, and a Communist Party inquiry was made about her; typically for the time, the inquiry soon became a criminal one. In 1953 his mother was tried for criticizing the Communist Party's national policy: she had made no secret of her views on the anticosmopolitanism campaign that was raging at that time and had publicly blamed MVD head Lavrentii Beria for the atrocities that were taking place. And although Beria himself had been shot as a spy and a traitor by the time of his mother's trial, she nonetheless received a sentence of ten years in the camps, "because," as the judge put it, "she expressed doubts at a time when the party trusted him, and consequently considered herself more right than the party."

At that time Vladimov was studying law at Leningrad University, which he had entered in 1948. Evicted from his apartment and obliged to support himself, Vladimov transferred to the extramural section of the university and took jobs as a provincial journalist, stevedore, and steeplejack. Having dealt with his mother, the state security organs turned to Vladimov himself. One of his friends was approached to report on him and, while lacking the courage to refuse, at least had the decency to inform Vladimov. Vladimov proposed that they write the denunciations together, producing a picture of Vladimov that would not be incriminating: "I created for myself the image of a Soviet Ché Guevara," Vladimov explained in the unpublished interview. Eventually the MVD left him in peace, complaining, his friend told Vladimov, about the "immaturity of your mate."

Vladimov made his debut in print in 1954 with a long review in the journal *Teatr* (Theater) of Aleksei Nikolaevich Arbuzov's play *Gody stranstvii* (Years of Travel). He went on to write as a critic and reporter for *Teatr* and the journals *Novyi mir* (New World) and *Literaturnaia gazeta* (Literary Gazette). In 1955 his mother, who had been blinded in an accident in the camp, was amnestied and returned to Leningrad. She was, however, refused rehabilitation and, as a result, was denied both a place to live and a pension. In 1956 Vladimov moved to Moscow to work as an editor in the prose section of *Novyi mir*.

Vladimov considered his most considerable achievement as an editor to be the publication in *Novyi mir* in 1956 of Vladimir Dmitrievich Dudintsev's novel *Ne khlebom edinym* (1957; translated as *Not by Bread Alone*). In 1957 he achieved his mother's rehabilitation, with difficulty and only through the intervention of Konstantin Mikhailovich Simonov, the editor of *Novyi mir*. In 1958 he married the critic Larisa Teodorovna Isarova, whom he had met at a congress of young writers in Moscow two years earlier; their daughter, Marina, was born in 1961.

At the end of the 1950s the firm Voennoe izdatel'stvo (Military Publishers) invited Vladimov and other young writers to edit and polish the memoirs of World War II veterans for publication. In 1960 Vladimov began collaborating with General Petr Vasil'evich Sevast'ianov, whose memoirs were published in 1961 under the title *Neman–Volga–Dunai* (From the Neman to the Volga to the Danube). The work with Sevast'ianov gave Vladimov the idea for *General i ego armiia*.

Also in 1960 Vladimov visited the Kursk Magnetic Anomaly (KMA) as a correspondent for *Literaturnaia gazeta*. There he conceived his first novel, *Bol'shaia ruda* (1962, The Great Ore; translated as *Striking It Rich*, 1963). In 1961, to collect material for a second novel, Vladimov spent several months as a member of the crew of a fishing trawler in the Barents Sea; he pretended to be trying to save money to buy a car.

*Bol'shaia ruda* was published in *Novyi mir* in 1961 and in book form in 1962. Viktor Proniakin goes to work in a quarry at the KMA with the goal of making as much money as possible; he is also looking for a job in food distribution for his wife, who is to join him. His enthusiasm for work and money is badly received by his fellow workers, and his relations with them quickly become strained. In his pursuit of his dream of escaping from poverty, Proniakin ignores the safety rules, goes out to the quarry in the rain, and is killed when his truck tips over the edge. The newspapers—both Communist Party organs and the press generally—praise Proniakin as the hero of the Kursk quarry, who gave his life for the Fatherland and its people. Although the novel is set in one of the "socialist building projects" that were being given special ideological weight in the propaganda of the time, Vladimov's description of life at the quarry is quite different from the "industrial novels" that were prominent in Stalin's time and the period immediately following his death. The hero of *Bol'shaia ruda* is, by Soviet standards, more of an antihero: a clever, cunning young man who knows the value of economic independence, Proniakin is remote from the romantic Soviet stereotypes that dominated the genre. The novel received more than one hundred positive reviews and was also popular with the reading public. On this wave of enthusiasm Vladimov bypassed the many usual formalities and was accepted into the Soviet Writers' Union in the fall of 1963.

In 1965, after divorcing his first wife, Vladimov married the journalist and critic Natal'ia Evgen'evna Kuznetsova. His first public statement on human rights appeared in a letter he wrote in 1966 with other young writers in support of the authors Andrei Siniavsky and Iulii Daniel', who were being tried for anti-Soviet activities. Vladimov also publicly defended Aleksandr Solzhenitsyn, who wrote an open letter denouncing censorship to the Fourth Writers' Congress in 1967.

Vladimir's second novel, *Tri minuty molchaniia* (1976; translated as *Three Minutes' Silence*, 1985), severely disfigured by the censor's excisions, was first published in *Novyi mir* in 1969. It begins in Murmansk, the main northern fishing port of European Russia and a city filled with sailors, prostitutes, speculators, and vagrants—homeless alcoholic former sailors who live by begging and stealing from their erstwhile colleagues. Senia Shalai, who has saved a considerable sum from several voyages, plans to leave the city and settle with his future wife somewhere in the south. In taking leave

*Front cover for* Bol'shaia ruda, *translated in 1963 as* Striking It Rich, *Vladimov's popular first novel that led to his acceptance into the Soviet Writers' Union (John C. Hodges Library, University of Tennessee–Knoxville)*

of the fleet with a wild binge in a restaurant, however, he squanders nearly all of his money and is obliged to undertake another fishing expedition. The trawler is seriously damaged, but the careerist captain decides to carry on, and only by a miracle is the ship saved from sinking. In this extreme situation the trawler crew helps some Norwegian sailors who are also on the verge of drowning. The novel paints a completely unorthodox picture of Soviet reality, depicting poverty, homelessness, drunkenness, speculation, tragic women's lives, the struggle for the most elementary standard of living, careerism, bureaucracy, Stalinist repressions, the harsh conditions of life at sea, and the lack of professional clothing and instruments on the fishing boats—all of which were suppressed in official ideology. The novel aroused exceptional interest from readers: the issues of

*Novyi mir* quickly disappeared from newsstands, and libraries had long waiting lists for the journal. But unlike *Bol'shaia ruda,* the new novel drew a stream of negative reviews from the official critics and served as a pretext for the purging of *Novyi mir* editor Aleksandr Trifonovich Tvardovsky. *Tri minuty molchaniia* was banned from publication for the next seven years; when it was finally brought out by the Sovremennik (Contemporary) publishing house after the appearance in the West of Vladimov's third book, *Vernyi Ruslan: Istoriia karaul'noi sobaki* (1975; translated as *Faithful Ruslan: The Story of a Guard Dog,* 1979), the text was still distorted by a vast number of censorial cuts and changes. The full text of *Tri minuty molchaniia* was first published in 1982 by the Posev firm in Frankfurt am Main.

Vladimov wrote several versions of *Vernyi Ruslan,* which deals with Stalin's prison camps. The first version was a satirical short story about a "camp guard in a dog's skin"; but Tvardovsky, whose opinion Vladimov valued, told him: "You are making the hound into police shit, but the dog has its own tragedy." Accordingly, Vladimov reworked the story into a tragic novella. In 1970 Posev offered to publish the work, and Vladimov began a final revision. In that same year he also wrote a lyrical play about love, fate, and war, *Shestoi soldat* (1981, The Sixth Soldier), which had been ordered by the Theater of the Soviet Army and Fleet. When the play was nearly ready for performance, the military censor banned it for "pacifism." In 1972 Vladimov took the theater to court, won, and received compensation. That same year he became acquainted with the political dissident and physicist Sakharov, with whom he wrote an anonymous letter to the government on the fiftieth anniversary of the Soviet state advocating abolition of the death penalty and an amnesty for political prisoners.

In 1974 Vladimov sent *Vernyi Ruslan* to Posev, and the book came out the following year. Tvardovsky's prophecy after reading the final version, that "this dog will run around the world," came true with extraordinary rapidity: the novella was translated into German almost immediately and subsequently into many other languages. It circulated in samizdat in the Soviet Union, but the majority of Russian readers only got to know it in 1989, when it was published in the journal *Znamia.* By the common consent of readers and critics, *Vernyi Ruslan* is Vladimov's best book and one of the masterpieces of Russian literature of the second half of the twentieth century.

The work is set in the early post-Stalin years, when the Soviet camp system was being dismantled. Ruslan is a Central Asian sheepdog trained in a camp school to be a guard dog. The camp is the only world that Ruslan knows, and his service seems to him to be of great importance. But the camp is being closed, and Ruslan's handler, a young guard given early retirement, is ordered to shoot the dogs, who are no longer needed. He, however, feels that new times are beginning and no longer has any desire to fulfill the orders of his bosses, so he releases all the dogs to run free.

But the dogs, having been brought up in the camp regime, cannot adapt to a life of freedom. Refusing to take food from strangers, they nearly starve; if they see three people chatting, they disperse the "crowd"; they march alongside May Day processions and lines of workers going to day and night shifts at the factory as though they are herding prisoners; and they wait on the station platform for trains that they hope will bring new parties of prisoners for them to lead "in fine, straight columns" to the wonderful world of the camp. But the zeal to serve wanes in the demoralized, hungry dogs, and they become integrated into the surrounding society. The transition is hardest for Ruslan: loyal by nature, he accepted the camp rules as a great and just gospel whose commandments he was happy to carry out, even when they were not entirely clear to his dog brain. Life without service is impossible for Ruslan, and he looks for a new object to guard. With impeccable instinct he discovers a former prisoner among the population of the settlement and enters voluntary "service" in guarding his new master. The Shabby One, as he thinks of the man, understands what the dog is doing and, drained by years of captivity and inner "unfreedom," accepts the fearsome game. Refusing to take food from the "prisoner," Ruslan begins to hunt, using his animal instincts to support himself in the expectation of a return to his real destiny.

And one day the long-expected train arrives. Out of it pours a merry crowd of volunteers who have come to build a new plant. Onto the platform from all sides run Ruslan and his former comrades, ready to form this disorderly mass into a convoy. But strangely for the dogs, none of the camp guards comes to the platform to explain the rules to the new arrivals, such as that "any step to one side is regarded as an attempt to escape and the guards will fire without warning." Instead of forming in columns, the young Communists joyfully run to the nearest beer stall—something the dogs cannot allow. A desperate and bloody fight breaks out between the dogs and the young people; in the course of the battle Ruslan's spine is broken, and he dies. His death is the logical culmination of his disfigured life; the abnormal world of the camp has been destroyed, and a guard dog cannot adapt and survive in normal life. Ruslan represents the image of an idealist of the Soviet prison-camp system—*canis sovieticus*. The book is written mostly from the perspective of an animal incapable of reflection or analysis but full of life and love of humanity; sometimes Vladimov brings in the author's narrative voice and a human picture of what is going on, underlining the artificiality of the canine viewpoint and underlining the main theme of the novella: the murderous political manipulation of living beings, people and animals alike, and the complete distortion of all spiritual and human values under Stalinism. Vladimov has written about the "canine" tragedy of Ruslan: "Dogs had made an agreement with men that they had to love their master and defend him, even with their own life, but the idea of 'guarding two-legged sheep' was not there, but cunningly added later." Ruslan is an involuntary tormentor and the victim of a monstrous system. The fate of the unfortunate dog as depicted in Vladimov's novella is one of the most vivid and precise portrayals of Stalinist totalitarianism produced in twentieth-century Russia.

In October 1977 Vladimov took a step unheard of in the history of the Soviet Writers' Union: he voluntarily left the organization. The last straw for him came when the union performed an act of demeaning sabotage by not allowing him to attend the Frankfurt Book Fair. In an open letter he explained his unprecedented step, citing the arbitrariness of the authorities, the censorship, and the courts; the dim-witted bureaucracy of the organization; and the repression of writers by the union, which took upon itself punitive police powers. As a result, Vladimov said, he refused to take part in the shameful activities of such an organization. By turning in his union member's ticket he became an exile from the world of official Soviet literature. In the same year he was elected chairman of the Moscow branch of Amnesty International. State repression began immediately: a militiaman appeared, demanding to see financial documentation of how a writer whose work was not being published was living. Clearly not caring for the state security organs that had sent him, the militiaman explained in a friendly way to Vladimov what to write to avoid the accusation of "parasitism," an offense that could lead to prison. The same militiaman appeared every year and, after a cup of tea, took away with him Vladimov's standard explanation. Another method of isolating him was disconnecting his telephone and suddenly reconnecting it when "voices of the people" called to mock and threaten the rebellious writer and his wife.

The atmosphere around Vladimov at this time, the behavior of the KGB (Komissariat gosudarstvennoi bezopasnosti [State Security Committee])—the successor to the MVD—and the hostility between the KGB and the militia are reflected in the story *Ne obrashchaite vnimanie, maestro* (1983; translated as "Pay No Attention, Maestro," 1983). Three secret-police agents install themselves in the apartment of a Jewish family to put under surveillance a writer who lives opposite. To the touchingly naive head of the household the boorish behavior of the agents seems so incompatible with the reputation of the KGB that he begins to suspect that criminals have moved into his home, and he reports them to the militia. Enraged by the agents' mockery of and anecdotes about the militia related to them by the Jewish man, the militiamen decide to break up the secret operation and teach a lesson to the KGB officers, whom they see as parasites who earn incomparably more money than they do and enjoy privileges inaccessible to them. Seizing the apartment with the "criminals" and giving a few black eyes to the bewildered secret agents, the militiamen consider that they have had their revenge and, with some insincere apologies, withdraw. The story combines acute satire and subtle irony in raising serious questions about the loss of human dignity and elementary respect for others that were characteristic of Soviet society.

Vladimov's situation was becoming more and more threatening, with KGB interrogations of him and his wife, threats, blackmail, and police searches. In 1983, during which he was again elected head of the Moscow branch of Amnesty International, the KGB suggested that he leave the country. The alternative was a court case against the writer and his wife, followed by prison camp. Vladimov did not want to leave, but the threat that not only he but also Natal'ia Kuznetsova would end up behind bars decided the matter for him. After receiving an invitation from the University of Cologne, Vladimov departed for Germany with his wife and mother-in-law on 26 May 1983. On 1 July he was deprived of his Soviet citizenship. Receiving political asylum in Germany, he began the life of an exile in that country.

In Germany, Vladimov immediately received two offers of employment: one from Radio Svoboda, the Russian-language station of the United States government-funded Radio Free Europe, and another from the NTS (National Labor Union) to become editor of its Russian-language journal, *Grani,* published by the Posev firm. The radio offer carried much more favorable financial conditions and, after a few years, a grant of American citizenship. The writer Lev Zinov'evich Kopelev, who had organized Vladimov's departure from the Soviet Union and helped him greatly in emigration, advised him to accept the job. But radio journalism would be a completely new field for the writer, while *Grani* would give him the opportunity to resume the editorial work he knew and loved and would enable him to have an influence on Russian literature. Kopelev was afraid that Vladimov would be hindered in his work by the political ideology of NTS, but Vladimov thought that he could count on the decency and friendship of the leadership of NTS and Posev. He believed that their support during his difficult last years in Moscow was a sufficient guarantee of their honesty and their favorable attitude toward him.

In 1984 Vladimov moved to Niederhausen and began editing *Grani.* The issues produced under his editorship stand out for the unusually high level of the literary and critical pieces. That year Vladimov's mother died; despite requests to the Soviet embassy, Vladimov did not receive the permission or the necessary visa to say farewell before her death or to attend her funeral.

Vladimov had been with *Grani* for only a year when conflict arose with NTS, which thought that his activities as an editor went against the party's interests

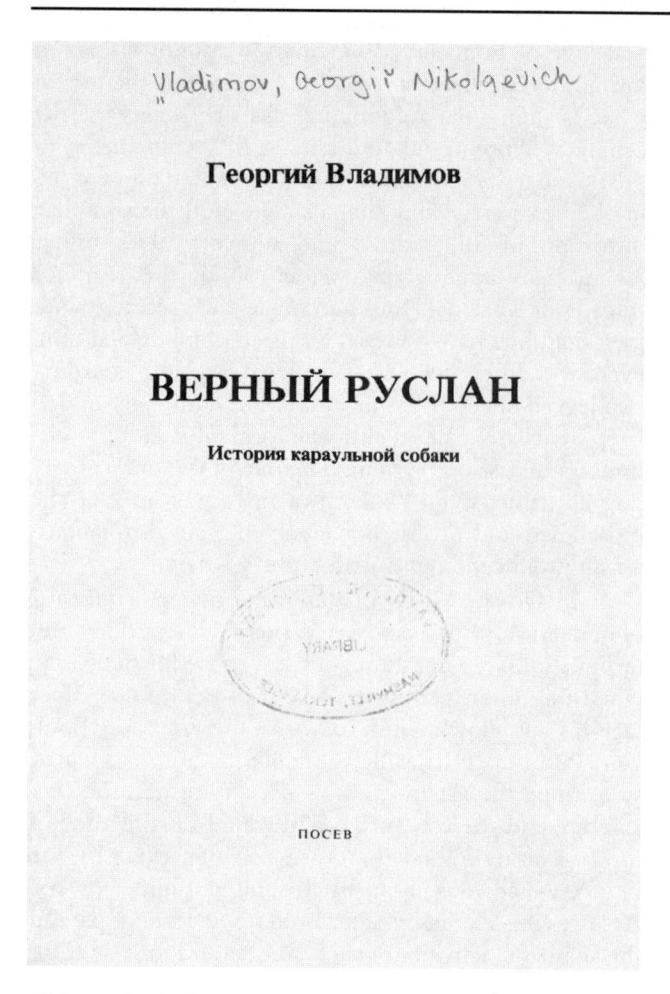

Title page for the first edition of Vernyi Ruslan: Istoriia karaul'noi sobaki, *initially published in Germany in 1975 and translated in 1979 as* Faithful Ruslan: The Story of a Guard Dog. *This satirical novel, about the difficulty of abandoning vicious habits developed during the Terror, is regarded by Russian critics as one of the most important fictional works of the post-Stalin era (Central Library, Vanderbilt University).*

and the spirit of the organization. Calls began to be made for the publication of artistically weak but ideologically sound works; there was also talk that under Vladimov the journal had become "Russian but not russophone"–a veiled reference to the Jewish authors whose work he published. He began to experience pressure and interference in his work and was subjected to increasingly offensive personal behavior by leading members of NTS. In 1986 Vladimov received a letter informing him that he was no longer the editor of *Grani,* and his wife's contract was canceled at the same time. The Vladimovs' attempt to take NTS to court came to nothing. In their new situation as émigrés the couple had had no idea how weak and dishonorable their contracts had been; they had no right to challenge the NTS's decision or to obtain elementary financial compensation. The episode was deeply traumatic for the couple.

In 1987–1988 Vladimov made regular broadcasts for Radio Svoboda. Nonetheless, his difficult financial situation and his isolation in Germany made the period a difficult one for Vladimov. With the advent of Soviet president Mikhail Gorbachev's policy of *perestroika* (restructuring), however, the situation began to change. In 1989 the journal *Znamia* published *Vernyi Ruslan;* soon afterward the Molodaiia Gvardiia (Young Guard) publishing house brought it out in book form in the "Manuscripts Do Not Burn" series. The publication of his masterpiece marked the return of Vladimov's literary work to its fatherland.

During the next few years Vladimov worked hard on *General i ego armiia*. In 1994 four chapters of the novel were published in *Znamia* and quickly nominated for the Russian Booker Prize, which Vladimov was awarded in 1985. When he went to Moscow to receive the prize, he saw his daughter, Marina, for the first time in more than two decades. His renewed relationship with Marina did much to brighten his life after the death of his wife from cancer on 26 February 1997.

In 1997 the Knizhnaia Palata publishing house brought out a complete version of *General i ego armiia*. The novel aroused fiercely negative criticism from Vladimir Osipovich Bogomolov for some supposed historical inaccuracies; Vladimov replied in a long article. A large number of reviewers entered into passionate debates that were mainly about technical military details rather than the literary merits of the work, which was warmly received by the public and by leading critics such as Natal'ia Borisovna Ivanova and Lev Aleksandrovich Anninsky.

In *General i ego armiia* fictional characters appear alongside historical figures such as Nikita Khrushchev, Georgii Zhukov, Nikolai Fedorovich Vatutin, Heinz Wilhelm Guderian, and other Soviet and German commanders. World War II, as depicted in the novel, takes place on three fronts: the real one in which the Soviet and German armies are fighting; the secret one in which SMERSH (Smert' Shpionam [Death to Spies]), the Russian military secret service, is operating; and the intrigues and corruption of generals' offices, where neither personal honor nor respect for human lives is taken into account. The novel is full of existential symbolism. The main character, General Kobrisov, is based on Nikandr Evlampievich Chibisov, who commanded the Thirty-eighth Army during the capture of Kyiv. Chibisov's Thirty-eighth Army is about to storm Predslavl' (Kyiv), the capital of Ukraine; as is reflected in its name, which literally means "before glory," Predslavl' might bring Kobrisov his long-awaited military triumph. But for the general it is a matter not just of military victory but also of liberation from his personal nightmare: Kobrisov has come to the war straight from an NKVD prison where, having been accused of an attempt on Stalin's life, he was tortured for several months. He was tormented not only by the physical pain and the humiliation but also by despair at the impossibility of defending himself in a grotesque inquisition. An exemplary soldier, he had suddenly found himself in a surreal world in which truth, sense, logic, honor, and dedication were completely devalued. But with the outbreak of war, the "terrorist" was set free and sent to defend the Fatherland and its tyrant. Memories of his incarceration and interrogation haunt Kobrisov, and as he looks at the mystical symbol of his liberation, the golden dome of Predslavl' cathedral with its black angel and cross hovering in the sky above it, he feels that his honor and dignity will soon be restored. Such, however, is not the way of the Soviet military and ideological machine. Intrigue, envy, petty calculation, indifference to loss of human life, and betrayal intervene, and the decision is made that a Ukrainian rather than a Russian commander should take the city. Kobrisov is told to attack the small town of Myriatin. Unable to bear yet another humiliation, foreseeing heavy and unnecessary casualties, and no longer willing to be used as a puppet, Kobrisov refuses to carry out the order and is recalled to Moscow. On his way to the capital, however, he learns that his troops have captured Myriatin and that he has been awarded a medal as a Hero of the Soviet Union and promoted. The shaken and inebriated Kobrisov decides to return to the front, where he is not expected. A SMERSH officer orders his car to be attacked; Kobrisov survives by pure luck, though his retinue is slain. The concluding chapter of the novel depicts the last day of the dying general, who was broken by the power of an inhuman system.

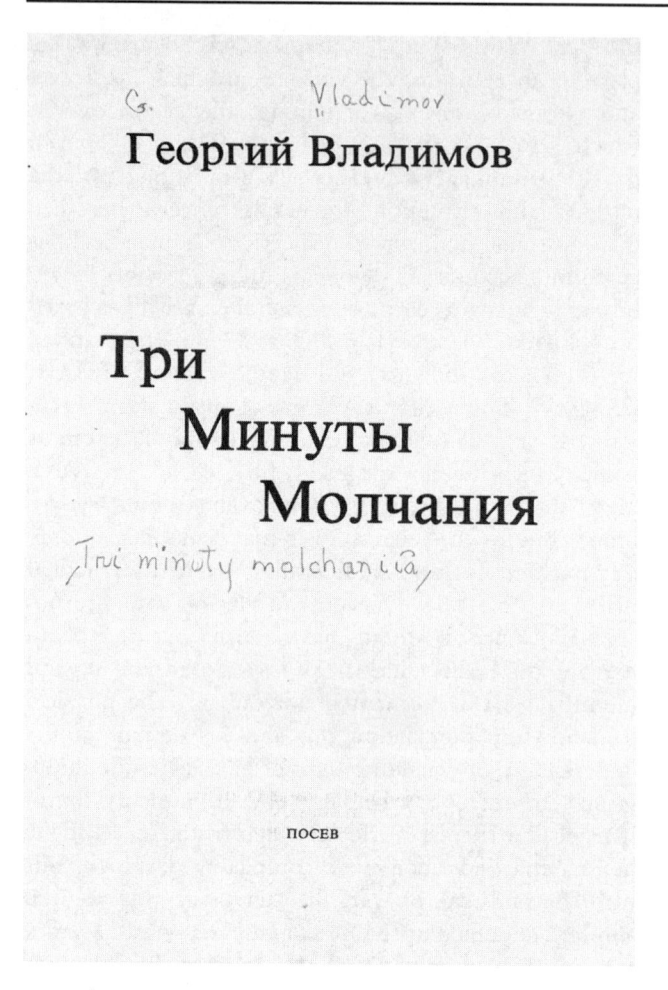

*Title page for the unexpurgated 1982 edition of Vladimov's* Tri minuty molchaniia, *first published, heavily censored, in Russia in 1976 and banned for the next seven years because official critics objected to his unorthodox portrayal of the Russian underclass. The novel was translated in 1985 as* Three Minutes' Silence *(Howard-Tilton Memorial Library, Tulane University).*

The novel touched on painful themes that had been almost completely ignored in Soviet war literature, among them the political domination of SMERSH, which had replaced the military wing of the NKVD, and the impotence of all ranks in the face of the secret police; the hundreds of thousands of Russians who had gone over to the enemy and fought with the German army; the role of General Andrei Andreevich Vlasov in the attack on Moscow in 1942; the lack of professionalism and personal honor among the opportunist Soviet command; the generals' scorn for the lives of their soldiers; and the NKVD divisions that followed the regular Soviet troops, shooting any soldiers who retreated under fire. Written in a concise and factual style, with vividly detailed descriptions and precise psychological portraits, Vladimov's novel combines deep irony with melancholy pathos and by common consent marked a new and important stage in the attempt of Russian literature to come to terms with the events of World War II. The book, which had taken years to write, was enthusiastically received by readers.

In 1997 Vladimov, still living in Niederhausen, received a telephone call from a Moscow businessman, E. Goldman, proposing to sponsor the publication of Vladimov's collected works in Moscow. His aim, he explained, was to return Vladimov not only to his readers but physically to his homeland. A four-volume edition of Vladimov's works appeared in 1998. Vladimov's return, however, took place several years later. When the Vladimovs left Moscow, they had been forced to abandon their apartment; attempts to obtain accommodations from the authorities as compensation for the lost flat were unsuccessful, and financial difficulties prevented Vladimov from buying an apartment in Moscow. But in 1999 the Literary Fund allotted him a flat in the writers' colony at Peredelkino so that he could fulfill his dream of living in two countries: Russia, to which he was connected by literary, cultural, and emotional ties, and Germany, where his wife and mother-in-law were buried. That same year he met the actress Evgeniia Alekseevna Sabel'nikova, who was living in Germany. They were married in Moscow in August 2000. Also in 2000 Vladimov received German citizenship, and on 29 April his Russian citizenship was returned to him.

In 2001 Vladimov received the Don Quixote Prize "for the honor and worthiness of his talent," as well as the Andrei Sakharov Prize for Civic Courage awarded by the journal and society *April*. He had been working since 1996 on an autobiographical novel, "Dolog put' do Tippereri" (It's a Long Way to Tipperary), but it remained incomplete when he died of cancer in Germany on 19 October 2003. He is buried in the Novodevich'e cemetery in Moscow.

Throughout his career Georgii Vladimov remained, in the best moral traditions of the Russian intelligentsia, an irreproachable knight (as his friends called him) in defense of justice and legality. His writing, in the tradition of Tolstoyan realism and addressed to the most important and painful questions of the Russian past and present, represents a significant contribution to postwar Russian literature.

**References:**

Lev Aleksandrovich Anninsky, "Spasti Rossiiu tsenoi Rossii . . . ," *Novyi mir*, no. 10 (1994): 214–221;

Aleksandr Nikolaevich Arkhangel'sky, "Strogost' i iasnost?" *Novyi mir*, no. 7 (1989): 262–264;

V. Cherniavsky, "Gibel' geroev: O tvorchestve Georgiia Vladimova," *Grani*, 106 (1977): 204–218;

Frank Ellis, "Georgii Vladimov's *The General and His Army:* The Ghost of Andrei Vlasov," *Modern Language Review*, 69, no. 2 (2001): 437–449;

Svetlana Geisser Schnittmann, "Glazami sobaki (O povesti Georgija Vladimova *Vernyj Ruslan*," in *Schweizerische Beiträge zum XI Internationalen Slavistenkongress in Bratislava 1993* (Bern: Peter Lang, 1994), pp. 41–56;

Geoffrey Hosking, *Beyond Socialist Realism: Soviet Fiction since* Ivan Denisovich (London: Granada, 1980; New York: Holmes & Meier, 1980), pp. 154–161;

Natal'ia Borisovna Ivanova, "Dym otechestva," *Znamia*, 7 (1994): 183–193;

A. A. Kots, "Khudozhestvennoe svoeobrazie prozy G. Vladimova," *Uchenye zapiski Permskogo universiteta*, 241 (1970);

Barry Lewis, "War on Two Fronts: Georgi Vladimov's *The General and His Army*," *World Literature Today* (Winter 1999): 29–36;

J. Mozur, "Georgii Vladimov: Literary Path into Exile," *World Literature Today*, 59 (1985): 21–26;

Mozur, "Vladimov's *Three Minutes of Silence* and the Soviet Production Novel," in *Oregon Studies in Chinese and Russian Culture*, edited by Albert Leong (New York: Peter Lang, 1990), pp. 277–292;

A. Nemzer, "V poiskakh utrachennoi chelovechnosti," *Oktiabr'*, 8 (1989): 184–194;

Robert Porter, *Four Contemporary Russian Writers* (Oxford: Berg, 1989), pp. 129–170;

Mary Seton-Watson, *Scenes from Soviet Life: Soviet Life through Literature* (London: BBC Publications, 1986);

Svetlana Shnitman-McMillin, "The Troika on the Road to Loneliness and Dishonour (Aspects of Georgii Vladimov's Novel *A General and His Army*)," *Canadian-American Slavic Studies*, 33, nos. 2–3 (1999): 293–305;

Abram Terts, "Liudi i zveri: Po knige G. Vladimova *Vernyi Ruslan (Istoriia karaul'noi sobaki)*," *Voprosy literatury*, 1 (1990): 61–86;

E. Tudorovskaia, "Sekret shedevra," *Strelets*, 8 (1985): 22–24.

# Vladimir Nikolaevich Voinovich

(26 September 1932 - )

Helen Segall
*Dickinson College*

BOOKS: *My zdes' zhivem: Povest'* (Moscow: Sovetskii pisatel', 1963);

*Povesti* (Moscow: Sovetskii pisatel', 1972)–comprises "My zdes' zhivem," "Dva tovarishcha," and "Vladychitsa";

*Stepen' doveriia: Povest' o Vere Figner* (Moscow: Politizdat, 1972);

*Zhizn' i neobychainye prikliucheniia soldata Ivana Chonkina: Roman-anekdot v piati chastiakh* (Paris: YMCA-Press, 1975); translated by Richard Lourie as *The Life and Extraordinary Adventures of Private Ivan Chonkin* (New York: Farrar, Straus & Giroux, 1977; Harmondsworth, U.K.: Penguin, 1978); Russian version republished as *Litso neprikosnovennoe: Zhizn' i neobychainye prikliucheniia soldata Ivana Chonkina* (Paris: YMCA-Press, 1981);

*Ivan'kiada, ili rasskaz o vselenii pisatelia Voinovicha v novuiu kvartiru* (Ann Arbor, Mich.: Ardis, 1976); translated by David Lapeza as *The Ivankiad, or the Tale of the Writer Voinovich's Installation in His New Apartment* (New York: Farrar, Straus & Giroux, 1977; London: Cape, 1978);

*Putem vzaimnoi perepiski* (Paris: YMCA-Press, 1979)–comprises "Kem ia mog by stat'," "Rasstoianie v polkilometra," "Putem vzaimnoi perepiski," "V krugu druzei," "Diadia Volodia," "Maior Dogadkin," "Kapitan Kurasov," and "Starshii leitenant Pavlenko"; translated by Lourie as *In Plain Russian: Stories* (New York: Farrar, Straus & Giroux, 1979; London: Cape, 1980)–comprises "What I Might Have Been," "A Distance of Half a Kilometer," "From an Exchange of Letters," "A Circle of Friends," "Skurlatsky, Man of Letters," "Autobiographical Stories," and "Four Open Letters";

*Pretendent na prestol: Novye prikliucheniia soldata Ivana Chonkina* (Paris: YMCA-Press, 1979; Ann Arbor, Mich.: Ardis, 1979); translated by Lourie as *Pretender to the Throne: The Further Adventures of Private Ivan Chonkin* (New York: Farrar, Straus & Giroux, 1981; London: Cape, 1981);

*Vladimir Nikolaevich Voinovich (courtesy of the author)*

*Tribunal: Sudebnaia komediia v trekh deistviiakh* (London: Overseas Publications, 1985);

*Antisovetskii Sovetskii Soiuz* (Ann Arbor, Mich.: Ardis, 1985); translated by Lourie as *The Anti-Soviet Soviet Union* (San Diego: Harcourt Brace Jovanovich, 1986);

*Moskva 2042* (Ann Arbor, Mich.: Ardis, 1987); translated by Lourie as *Moscow 2042* (San Diego: Harcourt Brace Jovanovich, 1987; London: Cape, 1988; republished with a new afterword by Voinovich, San Diego: Harcourt Brace Jovanovich, 1990);

*Shapka* (London: Overseas Publications Interchange, 1988); translated by Susan Brownsberger as *The Fur Hat* (San Diego: Harcourt Brace Jovanovich, 1989; London: Cape, 1990);

*Delo No. 34840: Sovershenno nesekretno: Nachato 11 maia 1975 goda, okoncheno 30 maia 1993 goda: Zakryto ne zakryto* (Moscow: Tekst, 1994);

*Zamysel: Avtobiograficheskii roman* (Moscow: Palata, 1995);

*Monumental'naia propaganda: Roman* (Moscow: Izograf/EKSMO-Press, 2000); translated by Andrew Bromfield as *Monumental propaganda* (New York: Knopf, 2004);

Vladimir Voinovich, *Antologiia satiry i iumora XX veka*, volume 7 (Moscow: EKSMO-Press, 2000);

*Portret na fone mifa* (Moscow: EKSMO-Press, 2002);

*Obrazy i slova: Katalog Zhivopisnykh Rabot* (Moscow: EKSMO-Press, 2003);

*Chonkin i dr.* (Ekaterinburg: U-Faktoriia, 2003).

**Editions and Collections:** *Zhizn' i neobychainye prikliucheniia soldata Ivana Chonkina: Roman-anekdot v piati chastiakh* (Ann Arbor, Mich.: Ardis, 1985);

*Khochu byt' chestnym: Povesti* (Moscow: Moskovskii rabochii, 1989)—comprises "Khochu byt' chestnym," "Rasstoianie v polkilometra," "Putem vzaimnoi perepiski," "Ivan'kiada, ili rasskaz o vselenii pisatelia Voinovicha v novuiu kvartiru," "Shapka," and "Otkrytye pis'ma";

*Zhizn' i neobychainye prikliucheniia soldata Ivana Chonkina: Roman-anekdot v piati chastiakh* (Moscow: Knizhnaia palata, 1990);

*Nulevoe reshenie*, Biblioteka "Ogonek," no. 14 (Moscow: Pravda, 1990);

*Moskva 2042* (Moscow: Vsia Moskva, 1990);

*Maloe sobranie sochinenii v 5 tomakh*, 5 volumes (Moscow: Fabula, 1993–1995)—comprises volume 1, *Povesti i rasskazy;* volume 2, *Zhizn' i neobychainye prikliucheniia soldata Ivana Chonkina;* volume 3, *Moskva 2042; Shapka; Ivan'kiada;* volume 4, *Antisovetskii Sovetskii Soiuz; Skazki; Mezhdu zhanrami; P'esy;* and volume 5, *Zamysel; Delo no. 34840;*

*Putem vzaimnoi perepiski*, edited by Robert Porter (London: Bristol Classical Press, 1996);

*Skazki dlia vzroslykh* (Moscow: Vagrius, 1996)—comprises *Moskva 2042* and *Skazki;*

*Zapakh shokolada: Povesti i rasskazy* (Moscow: Vagrius, 1997);

*Antisovetskii Sovetskii Soiuz* (Moscow: Materik, 2002);

*Shapka* (Moscow: Izograf/EKSMO Press, 2002).

**Editions in English:** "I'd Be Honest if They'd Let Me," in *Four Soviet Masterpieces*, translated by Andrew R. MacAndrew (New York: Bantam, 1965);

"In a Sleeping Compartment," translated by Christine Rydel, *Russian Literature Triquarterly*, 5 (Winter 1973): 303–306;

"In the Compartment," translated by Peter Reddaway, in *Russian Writing Today*, edited by Robin Milner-Gulland and Martin Dewhirst (Harmondsworth, U.K.: Penguin, 1977), pp. 264–268;

"A Distance of Half a Kilometer," translated by Donald M. Fiene, *Chicago Review*, 29 (Autumn 1977): 5–21;

"Appeal on Behalf of Sakharov," *New York Times*, 29 January 1977, p. A2;

"The Oxen and the Yoke," *Guardian Review*, 24 January 1981, p. 23;

"I Am Not a Dissident," *New York Times*, May 1981;

"Etude," translated by Liza Tucker, *Triquarterly*, 55 (1982): 130–133;

"Shut Up and Eat," *New Republic* (9 August 1982): 27–29;

"Moscow's Best Seller List," translated by Catherine A. Fitzpatrick, *New York Times*, September 1983, p. A23;

"The Zero Option," *Soviet Analyst*, 12 (26 October 1983): 2–3;

"The Trouble with Truth," translated by Tamara Glenny, *New Republic* (28 November 1983);

"Sidelights on Soviet Censorship," *Survey*, 28 (Autumn 1984): 221–226;

"The Life and Fate of Vasily Grossman," *Index on Censorship*, 14 (October 1985): 9–10;

"The Bald and the Hairy," *Guardian*, 28 December 1987, p. 13;

"Through Glasnost', Darkly," translated by Richard Lourie, *New York Times*, 11 December 1989;

"Left Hand, Right Hand," *Guardian*, 24 January 1991, p. 23;

"Incident at the Metropole," translated by David Chavchavadze, *Kontinent*, 2 (1992): 1–43;

"Have a Miserable Day," *Guardian*, 15 May 1992, p. 19;

PLAY PRODUCTIONS: *Khochu byt' chestnym*, Moscow, Moscow State University Student Theater, 1967;

*Dva tovarishcha*, Moscow, Teatr sovetskoi armii, March 1968;

*Tribunal: Sudebnaia komediia v trekh deistviiakh*, Kiev, 1988;

*Kot domashnii, srednei pushistosti*, by Voinovich and Grigorii Gorin, adapted from Voinovich's *Shapka*, Moscow, Moskovskii teatr Sovremennik, 1989;

*Neobychainye prikliucheniia soldata Ivana Chonkina—Spektakl'—anekdot v 2 chastiakh*, Kuibyshev, Kuibyshevskii teatr dramy im. M. Gor'kogo, 1989;

*Putem vzaimnoi perepiski,* Norilsk, Dramaticheskii teatr, 1990.

PRODUCED SCRIPT: "Fiktivnyi brak," radio, BBC, 1982.

OTHER: "Budushchee russkoi literatury v emigratsii: Pisateli za kruglym stolom," in *The Third Wave: Russian Literature in Emigration, Conference of Russian Writers in Emigration, 14–16 May, 1981 at U.C.L.A.,* edited by Olga Matich and Michael Heim (Ann Arbor, Mich.: Ardis, 1984), pp. 138–146, 272;

"Tri vida tsenzury v SSSR," in *Proceedings of the Fourth International Sakharov Hearing, Lisbon: October 1983* (London: Overseas Publications Interchange, 1985), pp. 137–143;

"Spasibo, ia uzhe poobedal," in *Volki ne pitaiutsia travoi: Publitsistika etikh dnei* (Moscow: Pressa, 1996), pp. 52–53;

"Vladimir Voinovich," in *Pisateli Rossii: Avtobiografii sovremennikov,* edited by V. A. Brun'ko (Moscow: Zhurnalistskoe agentstvo Glasnost', 1998), pp. 104–108;

"Ballada o kholodil'nike, Druzheskaia parodiia na Bellu Akhmadulinu, Posviashchennaia ei zhe," in *Literaturnaia parodiia,* Antologiia satiry i iumora XX veka, volume 9, edited by Arkadii Arkanov and others (Moscow: EKSMO-Press, 2000).

SELECTED PERIODICAL PUBLICATIONS–UNCOLLECTED: "Poka idet pis'mo," *Literaturnaia gazeta,* 30 May 1961, pp. 1–2;

"Propisan postoianno," *Literaturnaia gazeta,* 29 August 1961, p. 2;

"Zhizn' kak ona est' . . . ," *Literatura i zhizn',* 9 (December 1963);

"Pisaatel', geroi, molodezh," *Moskovskii komsomolets,* 11 December 1964, p. 4;

"V kupe: Stsenka," *Novyi mir,* no. 2 (1965): 69–71;

"Dva tovarishcha," *Novyi mir,* no. 1 (1967): 85–152;

"Vladychitsa," *Nauka i religiia,* 4 (1969): 84–91; 5 (1969): 60–71;

"V redaktsiiu *Literaturnoi gazety,*" *Literaturnaia gazeta,* 14 October 1970, p. 4;

"Master," *Trud,* 28 November 1971;

"O ritme khudozhestvennoi prozy," *Voprosy literatury,* 7 (1973): 100;

"Proisshestvie v 'Metropole.' Byl', pokhozhaia na detektiv," *Kontinent,* no. 5 (1975): 51–97;

"Voina protiv pisatelei," *Ekho,* 3 (1980): 142–145;

"V maske krolika: stsenka," *NRL-Almanach* (1981): 57–58;

"Brezhnevu: Gospodin Brezhnev," *Russkaia mysl',* 31 July 1981, p. 3;

"Da eto zhe Sakharov!" *Russkaia mysl',* 6 August 1981, pp. 6–7;

"O literature razreshennoi i nerazreshennoi bez razesheniia," *Kontinent,* 37 (1983): 439–445;

"Edinstvenno pravil'noe mirovozzrenie," *Strana i mir,* April 1984, pp. 92–96;

"Sovetskaia antisovetskaia propaganda," *Strana i mir,* May 1984, pp. 44–48;

"Esli vrag ne sdaetsia . . . ," *Strana i mir,* October 1984, pp. 52–63;

"Kak ia pisal 'Gimn Sovetskikh Kosmonavtov'," *Strana i mir,* March 1987, pp. 138–144;

"Viktor Platonovich Nekrasov," *Strana i mir,* May 1987, pp. 129–134;

"Pis'mo L. I. Brezhnevu," "V Sekretariat Moskovskogo otdeleniia soiuza pisatelei RSFSR," and "Zhizn' i sud'ba Vasiliia Grossmana i ego romana," *Knizhnoe obozrenie,* 27 January 1989, pp. 8–9;

"Na anketu *Inostrannoi literatury* otvechaiut pisateli russkogo zarubezh'ia," *Inostrannaia literatura,* 2 (1989): 245–247;

"Literator Skurlatskii," *Nedelia,* 20–28 February 1989, pp. 14–15;

"Kul'tura: Lichnoe mnenie," *Nedelia,* 25 (1989): 22;

"Vsia moia bol' ostaetsia zdes'," *Knizhnoe obozrenie,* 24 March 1989, p. 4;

"Proshchai Chonkin," *Ogonek,* no. 35 (1989);

"Otrezannyi lomot," *Ogonek,* no. 43 (1989): 7–8;

"Kak eto delalos'," *Iskusstvo kino,* 8 (1989): 128–133;

"Epizody iz zhizni proraba Petra Prokopenko," *Teatr,* 8 (1989): 135–139;

"S chego vse nachalos'; Epizody tvorcheskoi sud'by," *Studencheskii meridian,* 9 (1989): 48–49;

"V krugu druzei," *Evropa i Amerika,* 1 (1991): 112–122, 143;

"Idoly smutnogo vremeni," *Novoe vremia,* 3 (1991): 46–47;

"Vseobshchee pomeshatel'stvo na valiute," *Trud,* 29 March 1991, p. 3;

"Komu kogo chemu uchit'," *Moskovskie novosti,* 19 May 1991, p. 3;

"Lev Konson i ego rasskazy," *Nedelia,* 24 (1991): 14;

"U mikrofona–Vladimir Voinovich," *Soiuz,* 29 (July 1991): 13–14;

"Mechta Lenina nakonets sbylas'," *Literator,* 20 (1991): 7–8;

"U vymeni mertvoi korovy: nezavisimoe mnenie po chestnostiam podpisannogo manifesta," *Soiuz,* 41 (1991): 6;

"Intellektual'nyi peizazh–92: Klad pod sosnoiu," *Moskovskie novosti,* 5 January 1992, pp. 22–23;

"Dva mira, dva Shapiro," *We/My,* 3 (April 1992): 4;

"Sila protiv nasiliia," *Izvestiia,* 4 June 1992, p. 3;

"Vsego vam plokhogo," *Trud,* 16 July 1992, p. 6;

"Kak iskrivit' liniiu partii," *Krokodil,* 12 October 1992, p. 10;

"Sovest' naroda?" *Kul'tura,* 12 December 1992, p. 3;

"O Sergee Dovlatove," *Bestseller,* 1 (1993): 6–7;

"Mai-iun' 1941," *Literaturnaia gazeta,* 17 February 1993, p. 5;

"Tri portreta," *Voprosy literatury,* 4 (1993): 178–198;

"Pisateli mira o Sergee Dovlatove," *Zvezda,* 3 (1994): 171–173;

"Opiat' viezli," *Moskovskie novosti,* 1994, p. 5;

"Militseiskii 'bespredel' ili 'bytovukha'?" *Trud,* 22 December 1994, p. 7;

"Ia byl ves' v kolebaniiakh," *Literaturnaia gazeta,* 11 January 1995, p. 4;

"My ne zasluzhili takogo dolgogo nakazaniia za to, chto Adam i Eva s"eli iabloko," *Vechernii Klub,* 31 August 1995, p. 1;

"Zachem golodnomu svobodu?" *Trud,* 13–19 October 1995, p. 8;

"Populisty v opasnykh kolichestvakh," *Trud,* 20–26 October 1995, p. 5;

"Novye russkie," *Argumenty i fakty,* no. 44 (1995): 8; no. 45 (1995): 8; no. 46 (1995): 8; no. 48 (1995): 8; no. 49 (1995): 11; no. 50 (1995): 11; no. 51 (1995): 8; no. 52 (1995): 8; no. 2 (1996): 8; no. 3 (1996): 8; no. 4 (1996): 8; no. 5 (1996): 8; no. 7 (1996): 8; no. 8 (1996): 8;

"Zhizn' i perezhivaniia Vovy V.," *Andrei: Russkii zhurnal dlia muzhchin,* 6 (1995): 20–27, 124–128;

"O romantikakh, tsinikakh i pragmatikakh," *Trud,* 3–9 November 1995, p. 4.

Novelist, short-story writer, dramatist, scenarist, memoirist, poet, painter, and "publicist," Vladimir Nikolaevich Voinovich is one of the best-known contemporary Russian writers and a brilliant satirist of the post–Joseph Stalin period. Since the fall of the Soviet Union in 1991, he has become a public figure whose frequent appearances on Russian television and radio are eagerly watched and heard by Russians of all ages and walks of life.

Voinovich was born on 26 September 1932 in Stalinabad, Union of Soviet Socialist Republics (now Dushanbe, the capital of Tadzhikistan), to Nikolai Pavlovich Voinovich, a journalist, and Roza Kliment'evna Voinovich (née Gaikhman), a schoolteacher. In 1937 his father was arrested and exiled to hard labor, and the family moved to Zaporozh'e. When World War II broke out, his father was released and sent to the front; Voinovich was staying with his father's sister, Anna Pavlovna Voinovich, in Zaporozh'e while his mother was in Leninabad taking her teacher-certification examinations. He remained with his aunt for two years. When he was eleven, Voinovich began working as a shepherd on a collective farm. In 1944 his sister, Faina, was born. From 1946 to 1948 he studied at the Remeslennoe uchilishche No. 8, Goroda Zaporozh'e (Trade School No. 8 of the City of Zaporozh'e); in his ironically titled "Polnyi avtobiografichesky ocherk" (Complete Autobiographical Sketch) in volume seven of the series Antologiia satiry i iumora Rossii XX veka (2000, Anthology of Twentieth- century Russian Satire and Humor), Voinovich writes that he finished only five grades of the ten-year school: "first, fourth, sixth, seventh and tenth." He then found employment as a carpenter, construction worker, locksmith, airplane mechanic, and railroad worker. He served as a private in the army from 1951 to 1955 and was stationed in the Soviet Union and in Poland. During this time he began writing poetry and songs.

In 1957 Voinovich enrolled at the Moscow Pedagogical Institute. That year he married Valentina Vasil'evna Boltushkina; their daughter, Marina, who grew up to become a chemist, was born in 1958. Also in 1958, while still a student, he spent three months in Kazakhstan working on the *tselina,* the virgin lands that Soviet premier Nikita Khrushchev was trying to cultivate. He left the institute in 1959, during his second academic year. From 1960 until February 1961 he worked as an editor at the Vsesoiuznoe (All-Union) Radio Service in Moscow. In 1960 he wrote a poem about Soviet cosmonauts that began "Na pyl'nykh tropinkakh dalekikh planet / Ostanutsia nashi sledy . . ." (On dusty paths of distant planets / Our footprints will remain . . ."); it was soon set to music, and Khrushchev sang the song while standing on the Lenin Mausoleum in Red Square to welcome Iurii Gagarin back from the first manned flight into space in April. It became the unofficial "Anthem of Soviet Cosmonauts" and brought Voinovich immediate recognition.

In the early 1960s Voinovich turned to prose, but he never completely abandoned poetry: most of his works include songs, poems, and jingles. The short stories he wrote during the 1960s are based on his work and military experiences; they are brutally realistic representations of the bleak, shabby, and shoddy conditions he observed in rural and provincial Russia in the 1950s and 1960s. He depicts the loneliness, physical and intellectual poverty, and boredom of young military men and others living on the *tselina* and in collective farms, remote villages, and provincial towns. His characters are uneducated and often speak substandard Russian or Ukrainian; Voinovich has a keenly observant eye and ear: he describes settings and people in minute detail and captures the subtleties and accents of the characters' speech, including their mistakes, nuances, and intonations. Aleksandr Aleksandrovich Tvardovsky, the editor of *Novyi mir* (New World), published Voinovich's early stories in his journal.

"My zdes' zhivem" (1961, We Live Here) takes place in Popovka, Kazakhstan, "a population point"

*Voinovich and his wife, Irina, Moscow, 1979 (photograph by E. Gladkov; Collection of Helen Segall)*

that is the site of a future village. The name is related to *pop* (priest), but the inhabitants of the village are atheists; it also suggests *pup* (navel), implying that the village is the center of the universe for the inhabitants. Goshka, the main character, is a hardworking, honest young man who, unlike others in the village, refuses to cheat, even slightly, in order to help himself. "My zdes' zhivem" received enthusiastic reviews. Vladimir Fedorovich Tendriakov wrote in the 25 February 1961 issue of *Literaturnaia gazeta* (Literary Gazette), "Svezhy golos est'!" (There is a fresh voice!). In 1962 Voinovich and his wife had a son, Pavel, who is today an architect in Moscow.

In Voinovich's story "Rasstoianie v polkilometra" (1963; translated as "A Distance of Half a Kilometer," 1977) Ochkin dies when his head falls into a bowl of pea soup. Even though Ochkin has lived in faraway places—in prison and in exile at hard labor—intellectually, spiritually, and emotionally he never left the half-kilometer-long village where he was born and died. Voinovich's names are parodic and loaded with meaning; they often satirize the place or person named. "Ochkin" is related to *ochi* (eyes) and *ochki* (eyeglasses) and it implies vision and perspective, with which the protagonist certainly has not been blessed. In Klimashevka people eat, drink, have children, work, and die; they believe that in Moscow all good things happen and everything is available. Nikolai Merzlikin and Timofei Kon'kov, both of whom once went to Moscow, spend their days arguing about whether the Bolshoi Theater has six or eight columns. When Timofei gets a postcard with a picture of the theater and sees that it has eight columns, he tears it up; he would have nothing to argue about with Nikolai were he to reveal the truth.

"Khochu byt' chestnym" (1963, I Want to Be Honest) was published in *Novyi mir* with deletions demanded by the censor. The theme is how one must behave to be able to live with oneself. Samokhin, the supervisor of a construction site, is pressured by his superiors and promised a promotion if he completes a building on schedule before the holidays, but he refuses to certify completion because he knows that the construction is shoddy. Voinovich's original title, "Kem ia mog by stat'" (translated as "What I Might Have Been," 1979), was restored in the 1979 *tamizdat* (works clandestinely circulated abroad, as opposed to samizdat, those circulated in the Soviet Union) collection *Putem vzaimnoi perepiski* (From An Exchange of Letters; translated as *In Plain Russian,* 1979).

Voinovich's marriage ended in divorce in 1965; that year he married Irina Danilovna Braude, a schoolteacher. The 1965 arrest and 1966 trial of Andrei Siniavsky and Iulii Daniel' for the "crime" of publishing in *tamizdat* shocked the literary community, which reacted with letters of protest; Voinovich signed some of them.

In Voinovich's story "Dva tovarishcha" (Two Comrades), published in *Novyi mir* in 1967, high-school friends Valery and Tolik enlist in the army and meet again much later. Valery comes from a background in which education and honesty are valued above all else; he recites poetry and writes a story about flying. Tolik comes from a working-class home, and his father is a sometimes violent alcoholic from whom he has learned to lie and steal. He, like Valery, becomes a poet—not, however, because of an inner need or because he has something to say but because he hopes that writing will bring him money. His poems are unoriginal, cliché ridden, and ingratiating in their praises of the general he serves as an orderly. At the end of the story the leader of a gang orders him to beat up Valery; to protect himself, Tolik does so and thereby betrays his friend.

"Vladychitsa" (Sovereign), written in 1968 and published in Voinovich's *Povesti* (Novellas) in 1972, is set in a village that is a microcosm of Soviet society. It is ruled by Afanas'ich, a tyrannical white-bearded elder; he is aided by a nurse, Matrena, who acts as his informer, and the hunchback Timokha, who keeps the people in check with brute force. Falsehood and hypocrisy permeate this world. The teenager Man'ka is selected to be the *Vladychitsa* of the village; in return, she has to give up the possibility of love. But Man'ka is in love with another teenager, Grin'ka, an antihero and prankster. He is beaten by the villagers, twice expelled from the village, and finally murdered; when the *Vladychitsa* insists on telling the truth about her relationship with him, she is buried alive.

At the beginning of the 1970s Voinovich wrote letters and signed others protesting the persecution of the writer Aleksandr Solzhenitsyn and the dissident physicist Andrei Sakharov. In 1972 Politizdat (Political Press) published Voinovich's biographical novella *Stepen' doveriia: Povest' o Vere Figner* (A Degree of Trust: A Novella about Vera Figner). Educated in Switzerland, the nineteenth-century revolutionary Vera Nikolaevna Figner initially joins the Narodniki (Populist Movement) but soon becomes convinced that the group is too moderate to bring about radical change. She then joins Narodnaia Volia (People's Will), a revolutionary group led by Andrei Ivanovich Zheliabov that aims at eliminating the autocracy and its institutions, establishing a democracy, and granting all land to the peasants. Narodnaia Volia assassinates Tsar Alexander II in 1881. The leaders of the group are executed, and Vera is sentenced to twenty years in solitary confinement. Released in 1904, she feels numb; her lust for life has died in her prison cell. Several months after her release, she writes: "My freedom is like a wooden apple, which is artificially made to look like a real one only on its exterior: my teeth bite into it, but feel something which does not at all resemble a fruit." Vera dies in 1942 at the age of ninety.

In 1973 Voinovich wrote an open letter to Boris Dmitrievich Pankin, head of the recently formed VAAP (Vsesoiuznoe agentstvo Po avtorskim pravam [All-Union Copyright Agency]), protesting the establishment of the organization and accusing it of engaging in "criminal" activities, promulgating commands from the government, appropriating copyrighted materials, and limiting who among Soviet writers might publish. He also wrote more letters in defense of Solzhenitsyn. In February 1974 Solzhenitsyn was expelled from the Soviet Union, and Voinovich was expelled from the Union of Soviet Writers.

Persecution by the KGB (Komissariat gosudarstvennoi bezopasnosti [State Security Committee]) began immediately. Voinovich's telephone was disconnected; his wife was fired from her teaching position; and their daughter, Olga, who had been born on 5 October 1973, lost her nanny, who was afraid to continue working for them. With a few exceptions, such as Benedikt Mikhailovich Sarnov and his wife Slava Petrovna, Boris Isaakovich Balter and his wife Galina Fedorovna, Bella Akhatovna Akhmadulina, and Irina Il'inichna Erenburg, most of Voinovich's former friends and colleagues turned away from him and even ceased to greet him when they encountered him on the street. Between 1974 and 1980 at least two to four KGB operatives followed him wherever he went. They tried to intimidate visitors to his apartment and harassed him with such petty actions as flattening his car tires. Voinovich's parents were also harassed; in 1978 they were told that their son had disappeared. Soon after hearing this false report, his mother, who had a heart condition, died.

Voinovich's best-known and most popular novel, *Zhizn' i neobychainye prikliucheniia soldata Ivana Chonkina* was written over a fifteen-year period during the 1960s and 1970s. In 1969 the first part was published, without the author's permission, in the émigré journal *Grani* (Facets). Tvardovsky planned to publish it in *Novyi mir* but was removed as editor in 1970. Realizing that the book could not be published in the Soviet Union, Voinovich, with the help of foreign friends, sent the manuscript abroad to be published in *tamizdat*. The first two parts were published by the YMCA-Press in Paris in 1975 as *Zhizn' i neobychainye prikliucheniia soldata Ivana Chonkina: Roman-anekdot v piati chastiakh* (Life and Extraordinary Adventures of Private Ivan Chonkin: A Novel-Anecdote in Five Parts) and in English translation in 1977 as *The Life and Extraordinary Adventures of Pri-*

vate Ivan Chonkin. Parts 3 and 4 came out in Paris in 1979 as *Pretendent na prestol: Novye prikliucheniia soldata Ivana Chonkina* and were translated into English as *Pretender to the Throne: The Further Adventures of Private Ivan Chonkin* in 1981. Translations into other languages followed.

Ivan Chonkin is a Red Army private who, like the hero of the Czech writer Jaroslav Hašek's *Osudy dobrého vojáka Švejka za svetové války* (1921–1923; translated as *The Good Soldier Švejk and His Fortunes in the World War,* 1973), has a series of adventures and misadventures. Chonkin is also a parody of Tvardovsky's popular epic poem, *Vasily Terkin* (1940–1945), the title character of which was a perfect World War II hero because of his brave acts and cheerful disposition. Chonkin is the antithesis of a hero: he is an antihero and an antisoldier, and Voinovich's "war novel" is the antithesis of the Soviet model.

The novel begins not long before and ends shortly after the German invasion of the Soviet Union on 22 June 1941. The setting is somewhere south of Moscow in the village of Krasnoe (Red), which before the revolution had been called Griaznoe (Dirty) and is now part of the unproductive collective farm Krasnyi Kolos (Red Sheaf), and in the nearby provincial town of Dolgovo. These locations are a microcosm of Soviet society. Chonkin, a peasant conscript in his last year of service, is short and bowlegged and has big red ears. His puttees are forever falling down, and in all his years in the army he has not learned to salute properly. His only friend is his horse. This expendable soldier is sent to Krasnoe to guard a disabled airplane until a new motor can be delivered. Arriving at his post, he meets Niurka, a twenty-seven-year-old peasant girl whom nature has not blessed with beauty but who has a warm heart, her own house, a garden plot, a hog named Bor'ka, and a cow called Krasotka (Little Beauty); she is also the village postmistress. Chonkin helps Niurka with her gardening, and that evening he moves in with her and begins to lead a normal life on the fringes of the collective farm Krasnyi Kolos.

The simple, honest, unsophisticated peasant Chonkin, like the proverbial Russian fairy-tale hero Ivanushka Durachek (Ivan the Fool), sees objects in their primary, unsophisticated state, and the reader views life on the collective farm through his eyes. The chairman of the farm, Golubev, who has had to falsify his production quotas, drinks himself into oblivion. Gladyshev is a self-styled scientist, a "Michurinite" biologist who is developing a plant called PUKS (Put k sotsializmu [The Road to Socialism]) that is supposed to be a tomato on top and a potato below. In bed, the ardent Communist Aglaia Revkina cannot sleep and says to her husband, Andrei, the first secretary of the district committee of the Communist Party:

> "Andrei . . . tell me, as one Communist to another, are you by any chance having unwholesome thoughts . . ."?'

> Her question made Revkin thoughtful. He put out one cigarette and lit up another. "Yes, Glashka," he said, finished with his thinking. "It looks like you're right. I really am having unwholesome thoughts."

> Again they both fell silent.

> "Andrei," Aglaia said softly and inexorably, "if you yourself feel these unwholesome thoughts in you, then you should make a clean breast of it to the Party."

> "Yes, I should," agreed Andrei. "But what's going to happen to our son? He's only seven, after all."

> "Don't you worry. I'll raise him to be a true Bolshevik. He'll even forget what your name was."

> She helped her husband pack his suitcase but refused to spend the rest of the night in the same bed with him, out of ideological considerations.

Thus Voinovich shows how the perverted "morality" of Soviet dogma affected even the most personal relationships, such as those between husband and wife. Similarly, when Chonkin sees a girl playing with the hog, Bor'ka, he asks her:

> "Whose little girl are you?"
> "I am the Kilins'. And whose are you?"
> "I'm my own." Ivan grinned.
> "And I'm my papa's and mama's," boasted the little girl.
> "And who do you love more, papa or mama?"
> "Stalin," said the little girl, then ran away embarrassed.

The novel also parodies Soviet language and is permeated with the clichés and propaganda slogans that filled official speeches and radio broadcasts. Party organizer Kilin announces that "Fascist Germany" attacked the Soviet Union and rapidly drifts into "familiar word patterns":

> Kilin's tongue was babbling away all by itself, like a separate and independent part of his body. "We shall stand our ground, we shall return blow for blow, with heroic labor we shall meet . . ."

> At this point the weeping from the crowd had ceased. Kilin's words had shaken their eardrums but had not

reached through to their souls. People's thoughts were returning to their ordinary concerns.

Many episodes in the novel are based on mistaken identity. Miliaga, a local agent of the NKVD (Narodnyi komissariat vnutrennykh del [People's Commissariat for Internal Affairs], predecessor of the KGB), suspects that Chonkin is the leader of a fascist gang and sets out to arrest him; but Chonkin and Niurka tie him up and put him in Niurka's cellar. During the first days of the war, Red Army leaders assign a whole division to attack "Chonkin and his gang," thinking that they are Germans; the division is defeated by Chonkin with Niurka's help. At the end of part 2 Miliaga escapes but is captured by a Red Army officer. The Russian, believing that he has captured a German, interrogates Miliaga in broken German; Miliaga, believing that he has been captured by the Germans, answers in broken German and, trying to ingratiate himself with his captors, keeps saying "Heil Hitler, Stalin kaput!" He is finally shot by the Russians, who are convinced that he is a German SS officer.

*Pretendent na prestol* is more bitter, somber, and grotesque in tone than the first two parts of the novel. Chonkin is held prisoner first by the Germans and then by the Soviets; his treatment by the two sides does not differ. The book suggests that there is no significant difference between Stalin and Adolf Hitler, between the NKVD and the Gestapo, or between Soviet citizens and fascist Germans. In part 4, Hitler sends a division to rescue Chonkin, thinking that he is an important member of German intelligence.

Dreams play a major role throughout the novel; all of them are phantasmagoric and surreal. Chonkin's dreams are usually about Niurka. He is jealous of Niurka's hog, whom she loves, and in one of his dreams he finds himself at a wedding feast where Bor'ka is Niurka's groom and all of the guests are pigs who demand that he "oink" with them in chorus. In *Pretendent na prestol*, Chonkin keeps falling asleep during his trial by the Soviet military tribunal; his dreams about Stalin are frightening, and those about Niurka are erotic and lyrical: she is a mermaid who beckons him into the water to swim and play. Like the poor protagonist Evgeny in Aleksandr Pushkin's narrative poem *Mednyi vsadnik* (The Bronze Horseman, 1837), who dreams of marrying his beloved Parasha, Chonkin dreams about a peaceful life with Niurka in a little house with a garden—an ordinary picture of a happy life.

*Ivan'kiada, ili rasskaz o vselenii pisatelia Voinovicha v novuiu kvartiru* (1976; translated as *The Ivankiad, or the Tale of the Writer Voinovich's Installation in His New Apartment,* 1977) is a thinly fictionalized account, including real dates and names of people and places, of Voinov-

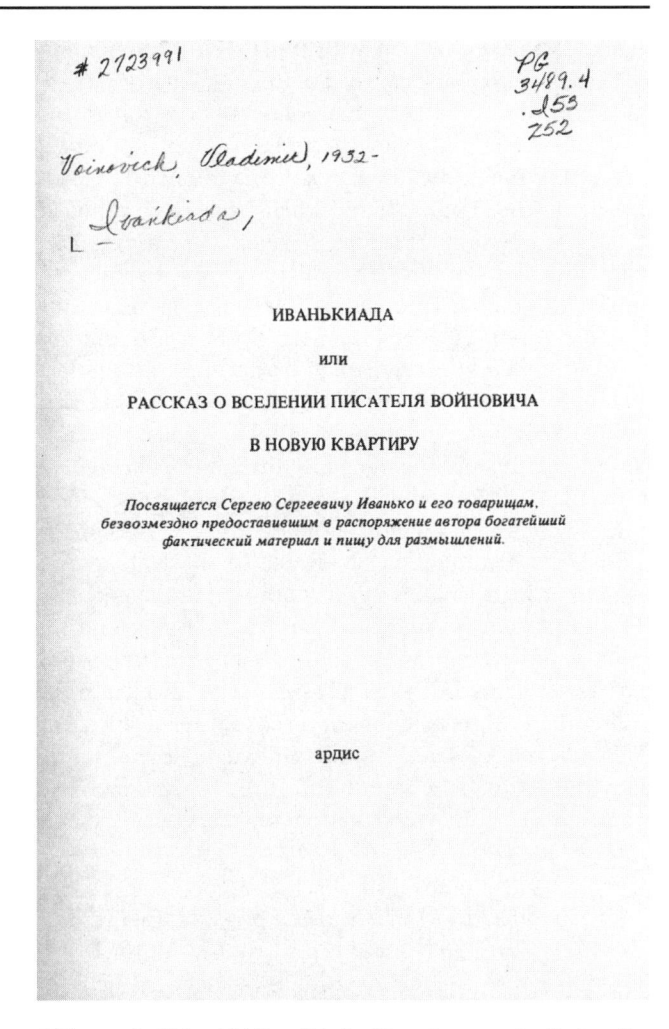

Title page for Voinovich's Ivan'kiada, ili rasskaz o vselenii pisatelia Voinovicha v novuiu kvartiru, *1976, translated in 1977* as The Ivankiad, or the Tale of the Writer Voinovich's Installation in His New Apartment *(University of South Carolina Aiken Library)*

ich's tribulations in obtaining a larger apartment from the Moscow Writer's Housing Cooperative near the Aeroport Metro station. The events described occurred in 1973, the year before Voinovich was expelled from the Union of Soviet Writers. Voinovich and his wife are living in a one-room apartment and for several consecutive years have applied to the cooperative for a two-room apartment. This time the need is particularly urgent, because Irina is pregnant. Voinovich is placed on the list and informed that the next two-room apartment to be vacated will be his. When the minor writer Andrei Klenov (pseudonym of Aaron Il'ich Kupershtock) in apartment 66 receives permission to leave for Israel, his apartment becomes available. But Ivan'ko, an untalented party apparatchik who holds an important position in the writers' union, is somehow associated with the KGB, and already has a three-room apartment, demands that he be given a room from the adjoining apartment 66 because he has accumulated many possessions, including a blue diamond-studded toilet, for which he needs the extra space. He cannot move to a larger apartment, because appliances and furnishings he bought in the United States when he was working at the United Nations are built in. Ivan'ko pressures and bribes members of the Assembly of the Shareholders to persuade Voinovich to accept a lesser apartment. But Voinovich refuses to give up his right to apartment 66. When letters and petitions fail, he becomes a squatter: he moves a couch into the empty apartment and begins to live there. One night the wall to the apartment collapses, and Ivan'ko charges in "through the breach in the wall, astride an improbably blue, diamond-studded toilet," shouting, "'I'll crush you-ou-ou-ou!'" This phantasmagoric nightmare is believable in the Kafkaesque world in which Voinovich finds himself. In the end, the General Assembly votes in Voinovich's favor, and he receives official permission to move into apartment 66. Ivan'ko is angry but is soon assigned to another position at the United Nations for a six-year term. Ivan'ko, with his murky background and vague connections with the KGB, is a symbolic figure, "*homo sovieticus*," who represents the whole system and serves as a metaphor for it.

In 1979 Voinovich published a collection of stories under the title *Putem vzaimnoi perepiski*. In the title story the poor, lonely, uneducated soldier Altinnik corresponds with women he has never met. When he finally does meet one of them, Liudmila Sirova, a medic at the Kirzavod railway station, he discovers that she has lied to him about almost everything: her age, her intentions, and her teenage son. She had sent him a photograph of herself taken at least seventeen years previously; she is much older than he is. Nevertheless, he eats dinner with her, drinks too much vodka, and sleeps with her. The next day, with her mother's approval and the help of her brother, Liudmila gets Altinnik so drunk that without realizing what he is doing, he goes to the registry office and marries her. Altinnik had dreamed of going to school and becoming someone important, but he abandons his ambitions and settles for a job as a watchman at the crossing barrier at Kirzavod Station. He turns into a henpecked alcoholic; the last the reader sees of him, Liudmila is dragging him away by the collar and pounding him on the head with her fist.

In another story in the collection, "V krugu druzei" (translated as "A Circle of Friends"), Kremlin leaders are having a wild party in Stalin's private quarters "on the eve of the shortest night of the year," 21 June 1941, which is also the eve of the German invasion of the Soviet Union. The reader meets Stalin in his secret room in the Kremlin and then sees him in his "official" uniform as Comrade Koba with his "friends," members of his Politburo whose names and behavior are parodied in verbal caricatures: the fictional Leonty Aria, Nikola Borshchev, Efim Vershilov, Lazar Kazanovich, Zhorzh Merenkov, Opanas Mirzoian, Mocheslav Molokov, and Antosha Zhbanov are toadies who sing, dance, and drink on command. At the end the reader finds himself in a surreal environment where the "friends" are afraid to tell Stalin that "Dolph" (Hitler) has invaded. Stalin himself is in his bedroom shooting at the "old pock-marked man" in the mirror. *Putem vzaimnoi perepiski* also includes several autobiographical stories based on the author's experiences in the army and in a workers' dormitory, and four open letters written during the 1970s.

In 1980, after Sakharov was exiled to the town of Gorky, Voinovich sent a letter defending the physicist to the newspaper *Izvestiia* (News) in which he expressed his "deep repulsion to all offices, labor collectives," and other Soviet institutions. As a result of this act, the KGB ordered him to leave the country. Shortly before his departure in December his mother-in-law died of a heart attack; his father-in-law went into shock and died the same day. Sponsored by the Bavarian Academy of Fine Arts, Voinovich settled in Stockdorf, a village near Munich, Germany, with his wife and their daughter. In 1981 he was declared an "enemy of the people" and stripped of his Soviet citizenship.

During his exile Voinovich traveled throughout Europe, as well as to the United States. While teaching Russian literature at Princeton University in 1982–1983, he wrote *Fiktivnyi brak: Vodevil' v odnom deistvy* (Fictitious Marriage: A Vaudeville in One Act), a situation comedy in which Nadia marries Otsebiakin so that she will have a place to live. He was a much sought-after speaker at American colleges and universities and before Russian émigré groups, clubs, and associations; his presentations included readings from his works and talks on the Soviet Union, Russian literature, and the role of the writer. His popularity resulted in regular appearances on Radio Free Europe.

In 1985 Voinovich published *Tribunal: Sudebnaia komediia v trekh deistvüakh* (The Tribunal: A Judicial Comedy in Three Acts). In the audience with his wife at a play set in a courtroom, Podoplekov begins to converse with one of the "judges" on the stage. Gradually the play transforms into reality—Soviet reality, that is—in which the theater becomes a courtroom and an innocent man is accused and convicted of a crime he never committed.

*Antisovetskii Sovetskii Soiuz* (1985; translated as *The Anti-Soviet Soviet Union,* 1986) consists of essays, stories, parables, vignettes, and anecdotes. Included are "Rasskazy o komunistakh" (Stories about Communists); an essay on Vasily Semenovich Grossman and his *Zhizn' i sud'ba* (1960, Life and Fate); articles about Russian literature, writers, and censorship; a discussion of the absurdity of Soviet life; and transcriptions of talks about Voinovich's visit to the United States. The reader is left with insights into life in the Soviet Union in the 1960s and 1970s and a Russian's perception of the United States and Europe in the 1980s. Almost everything and everyone is presented in the humorous manner characteristic of Voinovich.

In Voinovich's dystopian novel *Moskva 2042* (1987; translated as *Moscow 2042,* 1987) the exiled writer Kartsev, who is modeled on the author, travels through time and returns to his native Moscow in 2042, after the Great August Revolution (which bears eerie similarities to what actually happened in August 1991). Moscowrep (The Moscow Republic) is all that remains of the former Soviet Union; institutions, streets, and buildings have new names, but nothing has really changed. The successor to the Soviet Union is a bankrupt, demoralized, and disintegrated country where nothing works. The novel includes a parodic portrait of Solzhenitsyn, whom Voinovich caricatures for his anti-Western attitudes, reactionary views, and monarchist longings as Sim Simych Karnavalov. At the beginning of the work Karnavalov is on his Canadian estate, far removed from civilization, engaging in the antiquated practice of self-flagellation, eating simple Russian food, attempting to purge the Russian language of foreign words, and rehearsing for his entry into Moscow. At the end Karnavalov, dressed all in white, shining sword in hand, rides triumphantly into the city on the white stallion of victory, followed by his entourage. As Tsar Seraphim, he will return Moscowrep to a monarchy wedded to the Russian Orthodox Church and its patriarchal customs.

In 1988 Voinovich published the novella *Shapka* (translated as *The Fur Hat,* 1989), which provides insights into *homo sovieticus* in general and the Soviet writer in particular. Efim Rakhlin is a hack who writes adventure stories about explorers who are "decent people" and "positive" heroes. His dull books have been published regularly for more than eighteen years, and his five-room apartment is packed with goods from all over the world. He is "always groveling," regardless of whether the thing for which he grovels is important or not; and when the Union of Soviet Writers announces that it will bestow fur hats on its members and that the quality of the fur will correspond to that of the writer's art, Efim is horrified to learn that he will receive a hat of cat's fur. He becomes obsessed, runs from one office to another to appeal the decision, has a stroke, and dies. Like Nikolai Gogol in *Shinel'* (1842; translated as "The

*Voinovich, January 1978, in the home of Boris Balter in Vertoshino, near Maleevka, U.S.S.R., where he stayed to escape harassment from the KGB after he was expelled from the Union of Soviet Writers in 1974 (Collection of Helen Segall)*

Overcoat," 1923), Voinovich uses clothing as a status symbol and form of identity.

Voinovich returned to the United States as a fellow of the Kennan Institute in Washington, D.C., in 1989–1990. With the exception of the two long stays in the United States, Voinovich resided during his exile in Stockdorf and in Munich itself. His *Nulevoe reshenie* (Zero Decision), a satirical presentation of Soviet-American summit negotiations, came out in 1990. Also in 1990 Voinovich and Grigorii Gorin adapted *Shapka* as a play, *Kot domashnii, srednei pushistosti* (The House Cat of Medium Fluffiness), which enjoyed a long run at the Sovremennink (Contemporary) Theater in Moscow.

In 1990 Soviet president Mikhail Gorbachev restored Voinovich's citizenship and assigned him an apartment in the center of Moscow. The writers' union sent him an official apology. Since his return to Russia, his works, most of which first appeared abroad, have been republished in his home country both in journals and in book form.

In *Delo No. 34840: Sovershenno nesekretno: Nachato 11 maia 1975 goda, okoncheno 30 maia 1993 goda: Zakryto ne zakryto* (1994, Case Number 34840: Totally Not Secret: Begun 11 May 1975, Finished 30 May 1993: Closed but Not Closed) Voinovich, supported by documents from recently opened KGB files, recounts his interrogations in the Lubianka prison and at the Metropole Hotel in May 1975. He claims that while questioning him at the hotel, the KGB attempted to kill him with a poisoned cigarette. In 1994 he published five issues of the magazine *Russkoe bogatstvo: Zhurnal odnogo avtora* (The Russian Treasure: A Journal by One Author), in which he reprinted articles, essays, and stories previously published in other collections and editions.

In his best-selling *Zamysel: Avtobiograficheskii roman* (1995, Inkling: An Autobiographical Novel) Voinovich intertwines the fictitious autobiography of Luiza Barskaia, who details her sexual experiences, with the story of his own life. He transports the reader to his childhood and youth in Central Asia, with chapters devoted to his parents and grandparents, and then to Moscow, where he was a construction worker, a writer, and a dissident. He relates his persecution by the KGB and his heart-bypass surgery in a German hospital in 1988. At the end of the novel all of the characters gather at a bus stop and board a bus; Voinovich takes the driver's seat, and the bus rises from the ground. Together with everyone he loves—father, mother, sister, and favorite fictitious characters—the author flies away into the unknown.

Voinovich's *Maloe sobranie sochinenii v 5 tomakh* (1993–1995, Small Collection of Works in 5 Volumes) includes in volume four "Skazki" (Fairy Tales), a group of eight stories that were first published in the spring of 1992 in the Simferopol magazine *Krymsky komsomolets* (Crimean Young Communist). Written over a ten-year period, the pieces are satires of the political and social changes that took place in the former Soviet Union. The first three, which form a collection within the collection under the title "Skazki o parokhode" (Tales about the Steamship), are set aboard a vessel that is going nowhere—a metaphor for the period of *zastoi* (stagnation) in the Soviet Union under the leadership of Leonid Brezhnev. Besides their setting, the three tales are unified by the *zloi koldun* (evil sorcerer) Karla Marla and the persona of the narrator. The other tales are "Skazka o Nedovol'nom" (A Tale about a Malcontent), "My luchshe vsekh" (We Are the Best of All), "Skazka o glupom Galilee" (A Tale about Stupid Galileo), "Novaia skazka o golom korole" (A New Tale about the Naked King), and "Tsob-Tsob–skazka byl'" (Sob-Sob–a True Tale). Songs, poems, and jingles interspersed throughout the tales parody the normal Soviet tone of optimism. By choosing the genre of *skazki*, Voinovich debunks the mythological image of the Soviet Union and its leaders that was promulgated over an eighty-year period. In 1997 Voinovich published another collection of short stories, *Zapakh shokolada* (The Smell of Chocolate).

Since Voinovich's return to Russia, *Zhizn' i neobychainye prikliucheniia soldata Ivana Chonkina* has become one of the most popular novels in the country; all four parts are now published in one volume, with parts 1 and 2 renamed "Litso neprikosnovennoe" (The Untouchable Person) and parts 3 and 4 retaining the old title, "Pretendent na prestol." Voinovich had planned to write a fifth part in which Chonkin would settle on a farm in the United States; but he seems to have abandoned the project. The appeal of the work lies in the simplicity of its characters and plot and its ability to make readers laugh. The phenomenal success of the work can be illustrated by an incident that occurred in St. Petersburg in the mid 1990s. On Nevsky Prospekt, near the monument of Catherine the Great, a woman was selling homemade male dolls dressed in the uniform of a Red Army private. When Voinovich's friend Slava Petrovna Eremko Sarnova asked who it was, the vendor answered indignantly: "Don't you know? It's Chonkin!"

Voinovich has become a radio and television personality in Russia, and his weekly column appeared in the daily *Izvestiia* in 2000–2001 and continues to be published in *Novye izvestiia* (New News). He has his own website (www.voinovich.ru). His plays and his other works that have been adapted for the theater are performed in Moscow and in provincial theaters. *Zhizn' i neobychainye prikliucheniia soldata Ivana Chonkina* has been adapted for the stage several times, as well as for the screen and, in 2001, as a musical.

Voinovich's novel *Monumental'naia propaganda* (2000; translated as *Monumental propaganda*, 2004) is set in Dolgovo, where much of the action of *Zhizn' i neobychainye prikliucheniia soldata Ivana Chonkina* takes place. The staunch Communist Aglaia Revkina sacrificed her husband during the war when she blew up a building with him inside. After the war, she took his former position as secretary of the Regional Committee of the party and later reassumed control of the local kindergarten. Through her loyal Stalinist eyes the reader views events in Russia between 1956 and 2002, including the Twentieth Communist Party Congress, the policy of de-Stalinization, the years of *zastoi* and of glasnost, and the fall of the Soviet Union, in the aftermath of which she participates in Communist demonstrations and attempts to return to power. Voinovich describes the economic difficulties in post-Soviet Russia for pensioners such as Aglaia, and the enormous

*Voinovich in the Asti Gallery, Moscow, at his first exhibit, 1996 (courtesy of the author)*

wealth accumulated by the Russian oligarchs, one of whom helps the whole town by funding the kindergarten. A huge metal monument to Stalin is the main symbol of the novel. The statue stood in the center of town until it was removed during the period of de-Stalinization; since then, Aglaia has kept it in her apartment. When the statue is about to be returned to its pedestal in the center of town, a crippled veteran of the war in Afghanistan who produces and deals in weapons of mass destruction blows up the town, along with Aglaia and her home; thus, she perishes in the company of her idol and the symbol of her beliefs.

Voinovich and Solzhenitsyn had been introduced to Russian readers at almost the same time in the early 1960s through publication of their early prose stories in *Novyi mir*. From the day Voinovich signed his first letter in defense of Solzhenitsyn, the two were linked. After years of thinking about Solzhenitsyn, defending him, writing about him, and ridiculing him in *Moskva 2042*, Voinovich wrote the biography *Portret na fone mifa* (2002, A Portrait on a Mythical Background), in which he attempts to show how Solzhenitsyn changed over the years and how Voinovich's attitude toward him reflected these changes. The major task is to separate reality from a myth created partly by Solzhenitsyn himself but mostly by his friends and admirers.

Voinovich's first encounter with Solzhenitsyn occurred through the latter's prose. The book opens on a December evening in 1961, when Tvardovsky came to a friend's apartment with a manuscript that he read aloud to Voinovich and the others gathered there. It was Solzhenitsyn's *Odin den' Ivana Denisovicha* (1963; translated as *One Day in the Life of Ivan Denisovich*, 1963). Voinovich describes the pleasure and excitement he felt after hearing the work, which he recognized as not only a literary phenomenon but also as "a political and historic event." From that moment and for the next thirteen years Solzhenitsyn was "the strongest impression in my life" and his idol. As Solzhenitsyn's fame grew, the Soviet government became more and more nervous about him, and in 1969 Solzhenitsyn was expelled from the writers' union. Voinovich supported Solzhenitsyn, signing letters and making public statements praising him as a great writer. But Voinovich's doubts began to grow, especially after he read *Arkhipelag GULag, 1918–1956* (1973–1975; translated as *The Gulag Archipelago, 1918–1956*, 1974–1978). The typescript for *Arkhipelag GULag* was confiscated; Solzhenitsyn made statements in the foreign press, was arrested on 13 February 1974, and sent abroad the next day. On 20 February, Voino-

*Front cover of* Obrazy i slova, *a catalogue of Voinovich's paintings. The cover illustration is* With Pushkin and Gogol on a Friendly Footing *depicting, from left to right, Voinovich, Aleksandr Pushkin, and Nikolai Gogol (courtesy of Vladimir Nikolaevich Voinovich).*

vich received notice that he had been expelled from the Union of Soviet Writers. After the incident at the Metropole Hotel in May 1975, Voinovich asked Solzhenitsyn for help from abroad, but the latter did nothing. Similarly, Solzhenitsyn declined to assist Varlam Tikhonovich Shalamov in publishing his stories about the Kolyma death camps. Voinovich notes that the editors of the journal *Neva,* who had begged him for the rights to publish *Moskva 2042,* refused to do so after reading the manuscript because Voinovich was "besmirching the deeds of a heroic person." Voinovich calls this type of worship "bolezn' kumirotvoreniia" (idol-making disease) and considers it unhealthy and dangerous. After *Moskva 2042* was published, Voinovich says, Solzhenitsyn's friends, including the writers Viktor Platonovich Nekrasov and Lidiia Korneevna Chukovskaia and her daughter, Liudmila Tsesarevna Chukovskaia, were angry with Voinovich. A sharp exchange of letters between the Chukovskaias and Voinovich and his wife is quoted in the book; the Voinoviches fault Solzhenitsyn for his selfishness, arrogance, and failure to recognize his friends once he was abroad and no longer needed them. Furthermore, the International Literary Center, which purchased books for distribution in countries behind the Iron Curtain, did not buy *Moskva 2042* because of the parody of Solzhenitsyn. In sum, Voinovich criticizes Solzhenitsyn for conceit, hypocrisy, sanctimoniousness, self-satisfaction, lack of self-criticism, anti-Semitism, racism, xenophobia, and Russian chauvinism.

Shortly after Vladimir Putin came to power as president of the Russian Federation early in 2000, Voinovich wrote new words for the Russian National Anthem that begin:

Raspalsia na veki Souz nerushimyi
Stoit na rasput'e velikaia Rus' . . .

(Collapsed forever the inviolable Union,
Great Rus' now at the crossroads stands. . . .)

The song goes on to cite major historical events such as the October Revolution, the execution of the tsar, and the burial of the tsar's bones in St. Petersburg after the fall of the Soviet Union. Voinovich predicts the return of Vladimir Il'ich Lenin and Stalin as symbols of Communism, the execution of the "corrupters," and return to life as it was before the fall of the Soviet Union. This parodic anthem has not been published, but it circulates freely.

In the mid 1990s Voinovich, who has had no formal training in art, began to paint on cardboard and canvas, and for more than two years he devoted most of his time to this activity. Since 1995 he has had several exhibitions of his paintings, including one devoted solely to his work at the Asti Gallery in Moscow in 1996. In 2003 he published a catalogue of his paintings, *Obrazy i slova: Katalog Zhivopisnykh Rabot* (Images and Words: A Catalogue of Paintings). The works are arranged in thematic groups; reproductions of paintings are often accompanied by commentary and narrative and, in one case, a poem. The texts are sometimes only loosely connected to the paintings they accompany, and many are humorous. For example, the painting *Vozvrashchenie pisatelia Voinovicha na rodinu na belom kone* (The Return of the Writer Voinovich to His Motherland on a White Stallion) portrays the artist riding a white horse, with a rooster perched on his left shoulder; a description of a visit the poet, bard, and prose writer Bulat Shalvovich Okudzhava paid Voinovich in Stockdorf and a poem inspired by Okudzhava, "Domoi na belom kone" (Homeward on a White Stallion), accompany the painting.

Voinovich's paintings are representational, and, like some of his prose works, they are stylistically primitive. He sees the world in a fresh and naive way, as through the eyes of a child. His subjects are simple and taken from his surroundings: houses, villages, flowers, landscapes, chickens, roosters, and fish. He has painted still lifes depicting room interiors, tables with bottles, teapots and cups, and apples and pears. Many of his works are portraits of his wife, who died on 4 January 2004; of his daughter Olga, who teaches German at the University of Munich; of his parents; of his friends, including the painter Boris Georgievich Birger and the poet Tatiana Aleksandrovna Bek; and of his favorite writers: Gogol, Leo Tolstoy, and Aleksandr Pushkin. In addition, there are several self-portraits, including *Portrait of the Left Foot*.

Voinovich has received many honors, both in Russia and in the West. They include awards from the Bavarian Academy of Fine Arts in 1993 and from the Znamia (Banner) Foundation in 1994; the Mondello Prize for *Shapka* and the Triumf' Literary Prize "for a lifetime of achievement in Russian Letters" in 1996; an award from the Soros Foundation in 1998; the German Prize from the Deutsch-Russisches Forum (German-Russian Forum) "for outstanding contributions to German-Russian Relations" and the State Prize of the Russian Federation (formerly the Stalin Prize) in 2000; honorary degrees from Middlebury College in Vermont and Nottingham University in England in 2001; and the Andrei D. Sakharov Prize "for civic courage in literature" in 2002. He is an elected member of the Soiuz Pisatelei Rossii (Union of Russia's Writers), the Bavarian Academy of Fine Arts, the Serbian Academy of Arts and Sciences, and the American Mark Twain Society. In addition, Voinovich has become a regularly invited juror at the annual film festival in Sochi.

As a writer Voinovich is an iconoclast. Most of his prose works satirize, parody, and attack sacred cows, whether Soviet apparatchiks or "New Russians"; he does not even spare Solzhenitsyn, the idol of many conservative Russians. The power and effectiveness of his fiction greatly depends on his use of language: he has a remarkable ear for spoken Russian, capturing the language used in the far north and in the south, peasant speech and dialect, and the colloquial Russian heard on the street in urban workers' districts. He reproduces all of the shades, nuances, and implications of his characters' speech and slang. His texts include newspaper and political jargon, sayings, tongue twisters, and songs sung at births, weddings, and funerals.

In one of his paintings Vladimir Nikolaevich Voinovich suggestively depicts himself sitting at a table with Pushkin and Gogol. As he seems to imply, he has earned his place in the canon of Russian literature alongside those authors. A brilliant satirist, he uses parody and the grotesque to portray his characters and situations. He gives his readers an accurate picture of the world through a distorted, exaggerated, and skewed vision. He strips pretensions and verbal falsehoods from words and presents things as they really are. His work is distinguished by moral integrity, honesty, and unwillingness to compromise his beliefs. Voinovich will be remembered for his insistence on telling the truth and for creating Chonkin and other characters who help readers laugh at the absurdities of the world around them.

**Interviews:**

Zbigniew Podgorzec, "O sovremennosti i istorii," *Rossiia*, 2 (1975): 228–235;

Richard Boston, "An Interview with Vladimir Voinovich: The Newly-Exiled Russian Novelist Is Interviewed in Paris," *Quarto*, 1 (April 1981): 7–9;

Aleksander Gleizer, "Interv'iu s Vladimirom Voinovichem," *Strelets*, 1 (1988): 24–30;

Benedikt Sarnov, "Ia vse eti gody zhil nadezhdoi," *Iunost'*, 10 (1988): 81–83;

Andrei Vasil'ev, "Zavedomo iuzhnye izmyshleniia," *Moskovskie novosti,* 13 (1989): 14;

"Staraius' sokhranit' sebia," *Teatr,* 8 (1989): 129–139;

Anatolii Shikman, "A vy znaete, kakoi on?" "Otkrytye pis'ma," "Nulevoe resheniie," and "Vmesto predisloviia," *Sovetskaia Bibliografiia,* 4 (1989): 43–55;

Viktor Matizen, "Na pyl'nykh tropinkakh dalekikh planet," *Sovetskii ekran,* 10 (1989): 28–29;

Denis Gorelov, "V 64-om *Moskovskii komsomolets* iz-za menia chut' ne razognali," *Moskovskii komsomolets,* 17 May 1990, p. 4;

Irina Rishina, "Ia vernulsia by . . . ," *Literaturnaia gazeta,* 20 June 1990, p. 8;

I. Khurgina, "O moem neputevom bludnom syne," *Iunost',* 1 (1990): 76–78;

T. Akopian, "Smeius' nad lzhegeroiiami," *Kommunist,* 29 June 1990, p. 4;

V. Sisnev, "Luchshe pozdno," *Trud,* 18 August 1990, p. 3;

B. Iarkov, "Za tri mesiatsa do proshcheniia," *Gudok,* 11 September 1990, p. 4;

IU. Sigov, "Ia ne vernus' v Rossiiu postoronnim," *Argumenty i fakty,* 43 (1990): 6–7;

Ivan Shukhof, "Korabl' izmofrenikov: vzgliad izdaleka," *Moskovskii komsomolets,* 7 December 1990, p. 4;

Kabanov, "Russkaia literatura vsegda edina," *Rossiiskaia gazeta,* 16 (16 February 1991): 3;

Ol'ga Dubinskaia, "U cheloveka ne dolzhno byt' oshchushcheniia, chto on zhivet v dyre," *Ekran i stsena,* 25 April 1991, p. 15;

Efim Bershin, "Tainy professora chernoi magii," *Literaturnaia gazeta–Dos'e,* 5 (1991): 6;

V. Sisnev, "Velikaia avgustovskaia ne udalas'," *Trud,* 31 August 1991, p. 3;

Tat'iana Bek, "Iz russkoi literatury ia ne uezzhal nikuda," *Druzhba narodov,* 12 (1991): 245–261;

I. Kruglinskaia, "Voskresnye zagadki dlia Vladimira Voinovicha," *Izvestiia,* 27 December 1991, p. 5;

Kruglinskaia, "Ia khochu zdes' zhit' i ia budu zdes' zhit'," *Zhizn',* 1 (1992): 10–11;

M. Starush, "Shestidesiatniki devianostykh," *Rossiia,* 3 (1992): 12;

T. Kulikova, "Potomstvenny dissident," *Kuranty,* 10 April 1992, p. 8;

Iuliia Tereshchenko, "Ia vernulsia ne ves," *Baltiiskaia gazeta,* 15 (June 1992): 7;

S. Berestov, "Esli Chonkin pomret, tuda emu i doroga!" *Komsomol'skaia pravda,* 22 October 1992, p. 4;

I. Mil'shtein, "U nas eshche v zapase chetyrnadtsat' minut, . . . Vladimir Voinovich opiat' vernulsia domoi," *Ogonek,* 42–43 (1992): 30–31;

John Glad, ed., *Conversations in Exile: Russian Writers Abroad. Interviews,* translated by Richard Robin and Joanna Robin (Durham, N.C.: Duke University Press, 1993), pp. 85–97;

S. Vasil'eva, "Ia staralsia ne predskazyvat', a preduprezhdat'," *Smena,* 14 (April 1993): 8;

Anatolii Strepianyi, "Verkhom na tigre," *Trud,* 28 July 1993, p. 3;

Valerii Perevozchikov, "Liubliu zhizn' v epokhu reform," *Sibirskaia gazeta,* 36 (September 1993): 16;

I. Vinnik, "Stroili samolety po chertezham . . . parovoza," *Argumenty i fakty,* 42 (1993): 1, 5;

A. Borin, "Ne doveriat' druz'iam pozornee, chem byt' imi obmanutym," *Literaturnaia gazeta,* 23 November 1993, p. 12;

O. Martinenko, "Nesekretnoe 'delo' Vladimira Voinovicha," *Moskovskie novosti,* 6 (1994): B2–B3;

S. Fonarov, "Ia umeiu smeiatsia," *Kuranty,* 12 March 1994, p. 8;

G. Vasil'eva, "Ia dushevno pripisan k Rossii," *Izvestiia,* 8 June 1994, p. 7;

Nikolai Andreev, "Russkomu narodu pomogal i pomozhet iumor," *Narodnaia gazeta,* 9 July 1994, p. 1;

Vasilii Aksenov, "Govoriat nashi gosti," *Kul'tura,* 27 (July 1994): 8–9;

Pavel Sirkes, "Ot Fashizma privivki net," *Iskusstvo kino,* 10 (1994): 44–48;

Iurii Mar'iamov, "My bol'she ne vlastiteli dum, slava Bogu," *Vek,* 47 (1994): 10;

M. Maksimov, "Vladimira Voinovicha ne prel'shchaiut lavry topolia i Sim Simycha," *Smena,* 4 August 1995, p. 4;

I. Khrama, "Chonkin i Voinovich poshli po miru," *Komsomol'skaia pravda,* 19 (October 1995): 4;

Ch. Shevelev, "Lirik zhizni," *Nezavisimaia gazeta,* 29 February 1996, p. 7.

**References:**

Laura Beraha, "The Fixed Fool: Raising and Resisting Picaresque Mobility in Vladimir Vojnovič's Čonkin Novels," *Slavic and East European Journal,* 40 (Fall 1996): 475–493;

Deming Brown, "Soviet Russian Fiction: Changes, Challenges, and Frozen Propositions," in *Contemporary European Novelists,* edited by Siegfried Mandel (Carbondale: Southern Illinois University Press, 1968), pp. 3–38;

Brown, *Soviet Russian Literature since Stalin* (Cambridge: Cambridge University Press, 1978), pp. 187–192, 370–372;

Edward J. Brown, *Russian Literature since the Revolution* (Cambridge, Mass. & London: Harvard University Press, 1982), pp. 365–370;

Sergei Dovlatov, "Ne tol'ko Brodskii," *Literaturnaia gazeta,* 1 January 1992, p. 4;

John B. Dunlop, "Vladimir Voinovich's *Pretender to the Throne*," in *Russian Literature and American Critics: In Honor of Deming B. Brown,* edited by Kenneth N. Brostrom (Ann Arbor: University of Michigan Press, 1984), pp. 23–33;

Rachel S. Farmer, "Vladimir Voinovich—a Stupid Galileo?" *Canadian-American Slavic Studies,* 33, no. 2–4 (1999): 279–291;

M. D. Fletcher, "Voinovich's 'Consumer' Satire in *2042*," *International Fiction Review,* 16 (Summer 1989): 106–108;

Evgenii Gollerbakh, "Neprilichnyi anekdot: O proze Vladimira Voinovicha," *Novyi zhurnal,* 184–185 (September–December 1991): 324–343;

Geoffrey A. Hosking, *Beyond Socialist Realism: Soviet Fiction since Ivan Denisovich* (New York: Holmes & Meier, 1980), pp. 136–154, 243–246;

Natal'ia Ivanova, "Sezon skandalov: Voinovich protiv Solzhenitsyna," *Znamia,* 11 (November 2002): 186–198;

Wolfgang Kasack, "Vladimir Voinovich and His Undesirable Satires," in *Fiction and Drama in Eastern and Southeastern Europe: Evolution and Experiment in the Postwar Period,* edited by Henrik Birnbaum and Thomas Eekman (Columbus, Ohio: Slavica, 1980), pp. 259–276;

Halimur Khan, "Folklore and Fairy-Tale Elements in Vladimir Voinovich's Novel *The Life and the Extraordinary Adventures of Private Ivan Chonkin*," *Slavic and East European Journal,* 40 (Fall 1996): 494–518;

Anton Kuznetsov, "Ia ne khochu 'tishe-tishe'—ia khochu 'gromche-gromche'," *Voprosy literatury,* 1 (January–February 1997): 188–205;

Barry E. Lewis, "Homunculi Sovetici: The Soviet 'Writers' in Voinovich's *Shapka*," *Australian Slavonic and East European Studies,* 10, no. 1 (1996): 17–28;

Lewis, "Vladimir Voinovich's Anecdotal Satire: *The Life and Extraordinary Adventures of Private Ivan Chonkin*," *World Literature Today,* 52 (1978): 544–550;

Dragan Milivojevic, "The Many Voices of Vladimir Voinovich," *Rocky Mountain Review of Language and Literature,* 33 (1979): 55–62;

Andrei Nemzer, "V poiskakh utrachennoi chelovechnosti," *Oktiabr',* 8 (August 1989): 184–194;

Tatyana Novikov, "The Poetics of Confrontation: Carnival in Voinovich's *Moscow 2042*," *Canadian Slavonic Papers/Revue Canadienne des Slavistes,* 42 (December 2000): 491–505;

Viktor Obukhov, "Sovremennaia rossiskaia antiutopia," *Literaturnoe obozrenie,* 3, no. 269 (1998): 96–98;

Natalia Olshanskaya, "Anti-Utopian: Vladimir Voinovich Rewriting George Orwell," *Forum for Modern Language Studies,* 36 (October 2000): 426–437;

Evgenii Ovanesian, "Gde ishchet pochestei glumlivoe pero?: O 'pokhozhdeniiakh' soldata Chonkina v SSSR," *Molodaia gvardiia,* 5 (1990): 272–288;

Peter Petro, "Hašek, Voinovich, and the Tradition of Anti-Militarist Satire," *Canadian Slavonic Papers,* 22 (1980): 116–121;

Robert C. Porter, "Animal Magic in Solzhenitsyn, Rasputin, and Voinovich," *Modern Language Review,* 82 (July 1987): 675–684;

Porter, *Four Contemporary Russian Writers* (Oxford: Berg, 1989), pp. 87–128;

Porter, "Vladimir Voinovich and the Comedy of Innocence," *Forum for Modern Language Studies,* 16 (1980): 97–108;

Daniel Rancour-Laferriere, "From Incompetence to Satire: Voinovich's Image of Stalin as Castrated Leader of the Soviet Union in 1941," *Slavic Review,* 50 (Spring 1991): 36–47;

Irina Rishina, "Vladimir Voinovich: O tom o sem i okolo," *Literaturnaia gazeta,* 15 January 1997, p. 10;

Karen Ryan-Hayes, "Decoding the Dream in the Satirical Works of Vladimir Vojnovič," *Slavic and East European Journal,* 34, no. 3 (1990): 289–307;

Ryan-Hayes, "Vojnovič's *Moskva 2042* as Literary Parody," *Russian, Croatian and Serbian, Czech and Slovak, Polish Literature,* 35 (15 November 1994): 453–480;

Benedikt Mikhailovich Sarnov, "Simvoly vremeni," in his *Esli by Pushkin zhil v nashe vremiia* (Moscow: AGRAF, 1998), pp. 211–264;

D. Stok, "Vybor puti: O tvorchestve V. Vojnoviěa," *Grani,* 104 (1977): 150–170;

Grigorii Svirsky, *A History of Post-War Soviet Writing: The Literature of Moral Opposition,* translated and edited by Robert Dessaix and Michael Ulman (Ann Arbor, Mich.: Ardis, 1981), pp. 377–385;

Mary Ann Szporluk, "Vladimir Voinovich: The Development of a New Satirical Voice," *Russian Literature Triquarterly,* 14 (1976): 99–121;

Irina Vasiuchenko, "Chtia vozhdia i armeiskii ustav," *Znamia,* 10 (October 1989): 214–216;

Kevin Windle, "From Ogre to 'Uncle Lawrence': The Evolution of the Myth of Beria in Russian Fiction from 1953 to the Present," *Australian Slavonic and East European Studies,* 3, no. 1 (1989): 1–16.

# Sergei Pavlovich Zalygin
*(6 December 1913 – 19 April 2000)*

Jennifer Ryan Tishler
*University of Wisconsin–Madison*

BOOKS: *Rasskazy* (Omsk: Omgiz, 1941);

*Severnye rasskazy* (Omsk: Omgiz, 1947);

*Zerno: Rasskazy* (Omsk: Omskoe oblastnoe gosudarstvennoe izdatel'stvo, 1950);

*Os'kin argysh: Rasskazy dlia detei* (Omsk: Omskoe oblastnoe gosudarstvennoe izdatel'stvo, 1950);

*Na Bol'shuiu zemliu; Rasskazy* (Moscow: Molodaia gvardiia, 1952);

*Utrennii reis: Rasskazy dlia detei* (Omsk: Omskoe knizhnoe izdatel'stvo, 1953);

*Ocherki i rasskazy* (Moscow: Molodaia gvardiia, 1955);

*V nashi gody* (Novosibirsk: Knizhnoe izdatel'stvo, 1956);

*Obyknovennye dni: Povest', rasskasy i ocherki* (Moscow: Molodaia gvardiia, 1957);

*V strane druzei: Ocherki* (Moscow: Molodaia gvardiia, 1958);

*Probuzhdenie velikana* (Novosibirsk: Novosibirskoe knizhnoe izdatel'stvo, 1959);

*20 rasskazov* (Novosibirsk: Novosibirskoe knizhnoe izdatel'stvo, 1959);

*Prostye liudi: Rasskazy* (Tiumen': Knizhnoe izdatel'stvo, 1960);

*Krasnyi klever: Rasskazy* (Moscow: Sovetskii pisatel', 1961);

*O nenapisannykh rasskazakh: Literaturno-kriticheskie stat'i* (Novosibirsk: Novosibirskoe knizhnoe izdatel'stvo, 1961);

*Tropy Altaia* (Novosibirsk: Novosibirskoe knizhnoe izdatel'stvo, 1962);

*Bliny: Rasskazy* (Moscow: Pravda, 1963);

*Na Irtyshe* (Moscow: Sovetskii pisatel', 1965);

*Solenaia pad'* (Moscow: Sovetskii pisatel', 1968);

*Sibirskie rasskazy* (Moscow: Sovetskaia Rossiia, 1968);

*Cherty professii: Sbornik statei* (Moscow: Sovetskaia Rossiia, 1970);

*Interv'iu u samogo sebia: Stat'i* (Moscow: Sovetskii pisatel', 1970);

*Moi poet: O tvorchestve A. P. Chekhova* (Moscow: Sovetskaia Rossiia, 1971);

*Literaturnye zaboty* (Moscow: Sovremennik, 1972);

*Sergei Pavlovich Zalygin (from Igor' Aleksandrovich Dedkov, Sergei Zalygin: Stranitsy zhizni, stranitsy tvorchestva, 1985; Jean and Alexander Heard Library, Vanderbilt University)*

*Iuzhnoamerikanskii variant* (Moscow: Sovremennik, 1974); translated by Kevin Windle as *The South American Variant* (St. Lucia: University of Queensland Press, 1979);

*Komissiia* (Moscow: Molodaia gvardiia, 1976); translated by Vladimir Talmy as *The Commission, Soviet Literature,* 1, no. 346 (1977): 3–101; 2, no. 347 (1977): 69–125; 3, no. 348 (1977): 36–76;

*Sannyi put': Roman, povest', rasskazy* (Moscow: Sovetskaia Rossiia, 1976);

*Festival': Rasskazy* (Moscow: Sovetskii pisatel', 1980);

*Nashi loshadi: Povest'* (Moscow: Pravda, 1980);

*Sobesedovaniia* (Moscow: Molodaia gvardiia, 1982);

*Posle buri,* 2 volumes (Moscow: Sovetskii pisatel', 1982, 1986);

*Rasskazy ot pervogo litsa* (Moscow: Molodaia gvardiia, 1983);

*Kritika, publitsistika* (Moscow: Sovremennik, 1987);

*Povorot* (Moscow: Mysl', 1987);

*Pozitsiia* (Moscow: Sovetskaia Rossiia, 1988);

*V predelakh isskusstva: Razmyshleniia, fakty* (Moscow: Sovetskii pisatel', 1988);

*Svoboda vybora* (Moscow: Panorama, 1998).

**Editions and Collections:** *Izbrannye proizvedeniia,* 2 volumes (Moscow: Khudozhestvennaia literatura, 1973);

*Sobranie sochinenii,* 4 volumes (Moscow: Molodaia gvardiia, 1979–1981);

*Na bol'shuiu zemliu roman, povest', rasskazy* (Moscow: Molodaia gvardiia, 1985);

*Tri punkta bytiia: Roman, povest', rasskazy* (Moscow: Molodaia gvardiia, 1988);

*Sobranie sochinenii,* 6 volumes (Moscow: Khudozhestvennaia literatura, 1989–1991);

*Proza, Publitsistika* (Moscow: Molodaia gvardiia, 1991).

**Edition in English:** *The Commission,* translated by David Gordon Wilson (De Kalb: Northern Illinois University Press, 1993).

OTHER: *The New Soviet Fiction: Sixteen Short Stories,* compiled by Zalygin (New York: Abbeville Press, 1989);

Eremei Aipin, *Khanty, ili, Zvezda utrennei zari,* introduction by Zalygin (Moscow: Molodaia gvardiia, 1990).

SELECTED PERIODICAL PUBLICATIONS–UNCOLLECTED: "Vesna nyneshnego goda," *Novyi mir,* no. 8 (1954): 3–55;

*Ekologicheskii roman, Novyi mir,* no. 12 (1993): 3–106;

"Klub vol'nykh dolgozhitelei," *Novyi mir,* no. 4 (1998): 111–124.

A writer of prose, as well as a literary critic, editor, and outspoken defender of the environment, Sergei Zalygin had a long and prolific career. Zalygin wrote short stories, essays, novellas, and novels. Although Zalygin is best known for the clear, analytical realism with which he explored the watershed events of Soviet history, he also experimented with fantasy as a literary technique. In the period of glasnost, Zalygin became editor in chief of the prestigious journal *Novyi mir* (New World), the first person to hold that post who was not a member of the Communist Party. As editor of *Novyi mir,* Zalygin championed the publication of literary works that had been banned under the Soviet system of censorship.

Sergei Pavlovich Zalygin was born on 6 December (23 November) 1913 in the village of Durasovka, in the province of Ufa. Zalygin's father, Pavel Ivanovich, was born into a peasant family. He graduated from the gymnasium and enrolled at Kiev University. He did not finish his university education because he was twice imprisoned for political activities he carried out as a Menshevik. Pavel Ivanovich was then exiled from Kiev to the province of Ufa, where he worked as a salesclerk in bookstores. Zalygin's mother, Liubov' Timofeevna Apkina, who took the last name Zalygina after marriage, came from the middle class. Upon receiving her secondary education, she studied in Petersburg at the Higher Courses for Women but did not finish her higher education because she followed her husband into exile. Sergei was their only son. The family moved frequently around the Ural Mountains region; in 1920 they settled in Barnaul, in the Altai Mountains. In 1928 Zalygin enrolled in the Barnaul Agricultural Technical College, from which he graduated in 1932. He worked as an agronomist on the Enisei River in central Siberia, where he witnessed the complex and often tragic process of collectivization. He left the field of agronomy, because, as he recalled with understated irony in an interview published in 1995, "there were too many bosses involved." Changing his area of specialization to hydrology and land improvement, Zalygin enrolled at the Omsk Agricultural Institute. Through his formal study, he furthered his interest in the problems of ecology and responsible land use, themes he later explored in his creative writing. In 1935, while still a student at the Omsk Agricultural Institute, Zalygin began to publish short stories and essays about student life and scientific questions in the student newspaper *Za bol'shevktskie kadry* (For the Bolshevik Cadres) and in the city newspaper *Omskaia pravda* (Omsk Truth).

In 1939 Zalygin earned his degree as a hydrotechnical agricultural engineer from the Omsk Agricultural Institute. While at the institute he courted a fellow student, Liubov' Sergeevna Bashkirova, whom he married in 1939; she kept her maiden name in the marriage. They had one daughter, Galina Sergeevna. In 1941 his first book of short stories, *Rasskazy* (Stories), was published in Omsk. During World War II, Zalygin worked as a hydrologist along the northern Ob' River in north-

*Frontispiece and title page for Zalygin's* Solenaia pad' *(Salt Valley), a novel set in Siberia during the Russian Civil War. The work won the State Prize in 1968, the year of its publication (Joint University Libraries, Nashville, Tennessee).*

western Siberia. His book *Severnye rasskazy* (1947, Northern Stories), published in Omsk, received the attention of the Writer's Union in Moscow, which discussed it during a special session on young authors in 1949. Having returned to the Omsk Agricultural Institute for graduate study, Zalygin defended his dissertation in 1948 on the topic of planning irrigation systems. He became a professor at that same institute, where he served as the chairman of the Department of Hydrotechnical Land Improvement until 1955. In addition to his research and teaching responsibilities, Zalygin continued to devote time to his creative writing, which bore the features of precise scientific analysis.

In 1954 Zalygin published a series of essays, "Vesna nyneshnego goda" (The Spring of the Present Year), in the journal *Novyi mir*. The critical tone of the essays, which question collective farm leadership and the interference of the authorities into the lives of the peasants, was characteristic for this first period of the "Thaw" in literature. Zalygin left Omsk in 1955, when he became a senior research fellow at the western Siberian division of the Academy of Sciences of the U.S.S.R. in Novosibirsk, a post he held until 1964. In the summer of 1958 Zalygin joined an expedition to map vegetation in the Altai Mountains, an experience that formed the center of his first novel, *Tropy Altaia* (1962, Altai Paths). Combining fiction, sketches, and editorials, *Tropy Altaia* weaves together various stories about the scientists on the expedition through the commentary of the main character, Riazantsev, who expresses the author's own views on the need for foresight in managing natural resources. Although hailed as an environmentalist, Zalygin criticized as misguided those environmentalists who advocated an ethic of human noninterference. In both his literary works and his public statements, he called for a rational land-use policy that would consider human beings as the most active component of the natural world.

Zalygin considered his true arrival into Russian literature to be the publication of his novella *Na Irtyshe* (On the Irtysh), which was first published in *Novyi mir* in 1964 and in book form the following year. Zalygin's book addressed for the first time in Soviet letters the forced drive for collectivization in the Siberian countryside. The story takes place in 1931, in the small Siberian village of Krutye Luki. The main character is Stepan Chauzov, a strong, intelligent peasant and leader of his community. Chauzov recognizes the bond between the land and those who work it, but he is also loyal to the Soviet system, having fought against the Whites in the Civil War. *Na Irtyshe* depicts his moral and psychological struggle as he becomes caught between his desire to support the Soviet regime and his love for his land; he is ultimately exiled. Zalygin's novel, which reveals the inhumanity and senselessness involved in the process of collectivization, provoked conflicting reactions when it first appeared. Viktor Andreevich Chalmaev, for example, writing in *Literatura i sovremennost' 1964–1965* (1965, Literature and Contemporaneity 1964–1965), praised Zalygin's realistic portrayal of the peasants but faulted the author's portrayal of the regional authorities, who insist on Chauzov's blind acceptance of official decrees, as an exaggerated parody. Chalmaev argues that Zalygin, in his portrayal of collectivization, faults those in power simply for being in power; he creates an unfair and subjective opposition between the *vlast' t'my* (power of darkness) below and the *t'ma vlasti* (mass of power) above. The critic V. Survillo, writing in *Novyi mir* in 1969, condemned Chauzov as an expression of classless, petit bourgeois, abstract humanism. Coming to the defense of Zalygin's novel was no less a figure than Aleksandr Solzhenitsyn, who praised *Na Irtyshe* as "one of the best things to appear in the fifty years of Soviet literature." *Na Irtyshe* is often read along with Mikhail Aleksandrovich Sholokhov's *Podniataia tselina* (1932; translated as *The Soil Upturned*, 1934), long considered the authoritative literary work on the triumphs of collectivization. In contrast to Sholokhov, Zalygin demonstrates that Russian peasants perceived the policy of forced reeducation and collectivization as entirely alien to their way of life.

Zalygin's novel *Solenaia pad'* (1968, Salt Valley) earned him the State Prize in 1968. Set in Siberia, the novel involves a partisan detachment in the Russian Civil War (1918–1921), an event that Zalygin had witnessed as a young boy. Although the author conducted historical research for the novel over the course of five years, the result cannot be called an historical novel per se, as it is filled with fictional characters and events. Zalygin chose a time period that official Soviet fiction had celebrated as it affirmed the historical inevitability of the October Revolution and the heroic outcomes of the Russian Civil War. *Solenaia pad'*, in contrast, portrays the war as a tragedy of the Russian people and the deaths of innocent people as unjustifiable by any doctrine. Zalygin poses a conflict between the two main characters: the popular leader Meshcheriakov and Brusenkov, an inhuman, fanatical, dogmatic Communist who punishes and slanders those who waver in their support for the revolution. In his portrayal of Brusenkov, Zalygin questions the morality of revolutionary means, which official Soviet literature had portrayed as beyond reproach.

In 1970 Zalygin moved from Novosibirsk to Moscow in order to pursue his writing full-time. His newly adopted city was the setting for his novel *Iuzhnoamerikanskii variant* (1974; translated as *The South American Variant*, 1979). Turning away from the historical themes and the realistic technique of his earlier works, Zalygin examines the inner world of Irina Viktorovna Mansurova, a forty-five-year-old contemporary Muscovite who, having achieved success in her family, home, and career, realizes that she longs for passionate love and happiness. The "variant" of the title refers to the life not lived, the path not taken: Irina had once turned down a proposal of marriage from a man who later moved to South America as a diplomat. Zalygin attempts to probe the feminine nature, which, he argued, should be at the core of all humans, male and female, but which all too often is ignored in contemporary life. This attempt to explore the feminine was appreciated neither by the official literary critical establishment nor by Zalygin's readership. Some criticized the novel as an insult to Soviet women or viewed it as a parody of Leo Tolstoy's *Anna Karenina* (1875–1877). More-moderate critics noted that Zalygin's use of fantasy was not a rejection of earlier realistic traits but rather a variation on a theme. Common to all of Zalygin's works, they argue, are characters struggling to create a new world, whether this world exists in the post-revolutionary Siberian countryside or in the inner realm of fantasy and imagination.

In *Komissiia* (1976; translated as *The Commission*, 1977), Zalygin returns to traditional realism and historical material. The novel opens in the autumn of 1918, during the period of chaotic uncertainty between revolution and all-out civil war, when Siberia, lacking a central authority, was a patchwork of various provisional governments and local administrators. Peasants in the fictional Siberian village of Lebiazhka establish a forest commission, first to protect the forest riches from illegal acquisition and then to reconstruct village life as a whole. The members of the commission include the chairman, Petr Kalashnikov, who is good but indecisive; Nikolai Ustinov, the most respected person in Lebiazhka; the foolish Ignakha Ignatov; the aggressive Deriabin; and the quiet, ordinary Polovinkin. Rather than offering a unified interpretation of historical events, Zalygin uses the historical setting of his novel in order to discuss wider philosophical questions, such as how political power should be applied. Zalygin considered the possibility of power that truly originated with the people, without outside interference. The story line of Komissiia weaves in Siberian stories and legends, resulting in what one critic termed an "encyclopedia of Russian peasant life."

Zalygin worked for ten years on *Posle buri* (1982, 1986, After the Storm), a sweeping, two-volume novel that covers the Civil War, the program of War Communism, and Vladimir Lenin's New Economic Policy (NEP), a period of controlled capitalism meant to rebuild an economy that had been destroyed by revolution and civil war. Against this historical background, *Posle buri* grapples with issues of a person's self-definition and the danger of losing one's sense of self, of personal responsibility, and of the power of circumstances. The hero of the book, Petr Nikolaevich-Vasil'evich Kornilov, is a philosopher, a former university lecturer who must come to terms with the new realities of living with the NEP. He fights against Kaiser Wilhelm's army in World War I, later becomes a captain in Aleksandr Vasil'evich Kolchak's White forces, and is taken prisoner by the Reds. Kornilov escapes, using the documents of a man with the same first and last name but a different patronymic. His former self now dead, the intellectual Kornilov sets himself up to profit from the NEP, thanks to an inheritance meant for his namesake and alias. Images of splitting and the divided or fragmented world dominate the novel; the hero thinks: "This year is not a year and not a time, but only a fragment of time." The motif of fragmentation is manifested not only in the theme of the book and its motif of the dual patronymic, but also in its form. Zalygin tells his story in separate stories rather than a cohesive, finished plot, even going so far as to create a second finale to the novel: an epilogue in which the hero finally stops obeying the author and begins to draw moralistic and philosophical conclusions from his own life. Although some critics disparaged the diffuse and episodic narration of the novel, others praised Zalygin for provoking the reader to consider philosophical and historical questions and to address the painful aspects of Russian history. The novel was also praised for its contemporary relevance for the Soviet Union in the period of perestroika.

In the 1970s and 1980s Zalygin published essays and articles about the writers Anton Pavlovich Chekhov, Nikolai Vasil'evich Gogol', and Andrei Platonovich Platonov, as well as contemporary prose writers such as Valentin Grigor'evich Rasputin and Vasilii Makarovich Shukshin. He also wrote essays about the theoretical problems of contemporary artistic and technical works.

Zalygin, who had been trained as a specialist in agriculture and hydrology, led campaigns against two massive Soviet projects to reshape the natural environment. In 1963 he spoke out against the flooding of the northwest Siberian lowlands by the lower Ob' River Hydroelectric Station. In 1985–1986 he mobilized writers to stand in opposition to the ecologically unsound plan to redirect the great northern rivers of Siberia to the parched cotton-growing regions of Central Asia. Zalygin and his allies won that battle; General Secretary Mikhail Gorbachev, who was then waging his own campaign to weaken the rigid central-planning system, tabled the plan to reroute the rivers. Zalygin discussed the potentially disastrous environmental impact of the river diversion scheme in his book *Povorot* (1987, Turning Point).

In August 1986 Zalygin was appointed editor in chief of *Novyi mir*. In that capacity he published works that had previously been forbidden in the Soviet

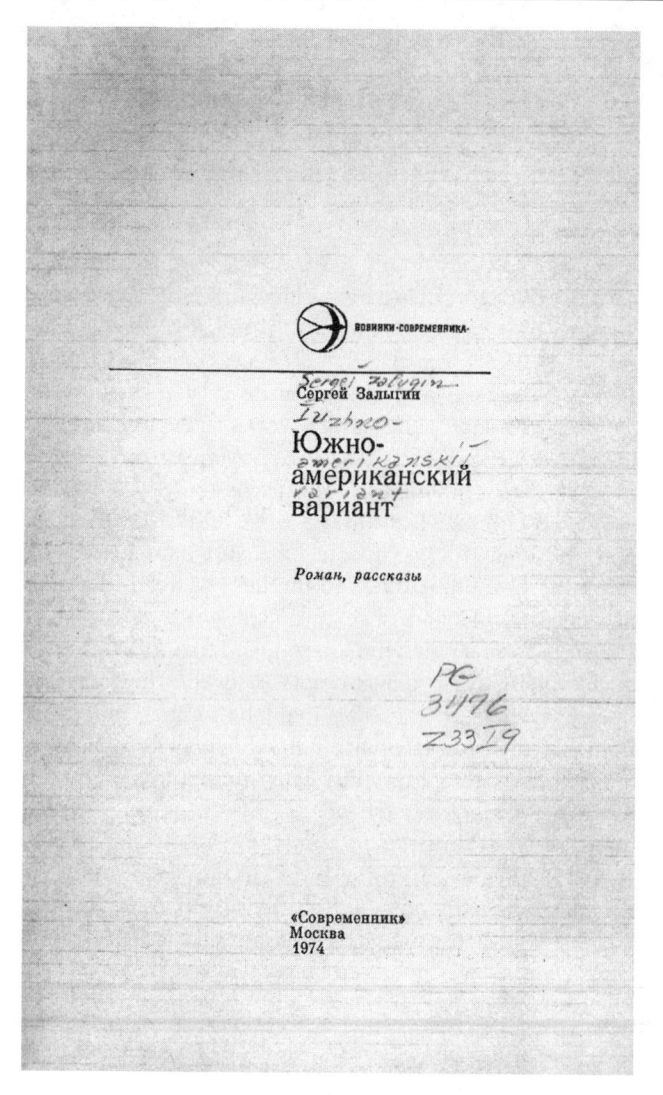

Title page for Zalygin's Iuzhnoamerikanskii variant, *translated in 1979 as* The South American Variant, *his first novel after he moved to Moscow to pursue writing full-time (San Diego State University Library)*

Union, such as Boris Leonidovich Pasternak's *Doktor Zhivago* (1957; translated as *Doctor Zhivago,* 1958), Solzhenitsyn's *Arkhipelag GULag* (1973–1975; translated as *The Gulag Archipelago,* 1974–1978), and the poetry of Iosif Aleksandrovich Brodsky. In the case of *Arkhipelag GULag,* an epic on Joseph Stalin's labor camps, Zalygin met personally with Gorbachev in order to secure permission for the 1990 publication. The reclamation and publication of repressed literary works was one of the most significant events of the period of glasnost, and Zalygin was widely viewed as an editor in the spirit of Aleksandr Tvardovsky, who had published Zalygin's stories in the 1960s. During his tenure as editor in chief, Zalygin continued to write and publish. He left the post of editor in March 1998 at the age of eighty-four.

In his later years, Zalygin continued to be involved in ecological and political activism. He was active in the Writers' Union and in 1989 was elected to the first semifree Soviet parliament, the Congress of People's Deputies, as a nominee of the union. He was a candidate to the Russian Duma from the environmentalist party Kedr (Cedar), but in 1995 withdrew his candidacy and left Kedr, citing differences of opinion with the leading party members.

Environmental issues are at the center of *Ekologicheskii roman* (Ecological Novel), published in *Novyi mir* in 1993. The autobiographical hero, the hydrologist Golubev, tries all his life to protect nature as the most necessary and most defenseless thing on the planet. Despite his worthwhile achievements in his profession, Golubev feels that he is unable to touch another person's soul on a profound level; he never taught another person to open his eyes and change his way of thinking. The novel ends with a hint of optimism, however: after the death of his son, Golubev must care for his two young grandsons, who need his protection and human warmth.

Zalygin's collection *Svoboda vybora* (1998, Freedom of Choice) is a summary of the writer's thoughts about the dramatic recent years of Russian history. In addition to the novel that gives the collection its name, the book includes shorter works first published in *Novyi mir* in the 1990s and a confessional essay, "Moia demokratiia" (My Democracy), published in *Novyi mir* in 1996. In the author's opinion, "Democratism is first and foremost a way of life; it is the relationship of people to one another, the ability of an individual personality to be democratic. It is . . . the experience which allows one to distinguish ability from inability, the word from verbiage, trust from mistrust." The novel *Svoboda vybora* first appeared in *Novyi mir* in June 1996 at the time of the Russian presidential elections, when the Russian people were made to choose between the

*Zalygin, circa 1977 (from* The Commission, *1993; Thomas Cooper Library, University of South Carolina)*

"democratic" Boris Yeltsin and the Communist Gennadii Andreevich Ziuganov. At the center of the work is Nelepin, an elderly writer who is collecting material for a book about Nikolai II, the last tsar of Russia. Nelepin brings the chief figures of twentieth-century Russian history to trial; the book also includes a fictitious dialogue between Nikolai II and Stalin. The extensive plot includes both the Russian war with Japan, which began the twentieth century, and its war with Chechnya, which marked the end of the century.

One of Zalygin's last works is the piercing "Klub vol'nykh dolgozhitelei" (1998, The Voluntary Old-Timers' Club). The hero of the story is a retired general, Zhelnin. Unable to come to terms with the idea he must eventually cede control of his own life to sickness, a foreign invader, Zhelnin organizes a club of like-minded elderly men who agree to commit suicide at the point they decide to stop living.

Sergei Pavlovich Zalygin's achievements were recognized during the Soviet period and in post-Soviet Russia. In 1988 he was granted the title "Hero of

Socialist Labor" for his literary and public work. In March 2000 Russian president Vladimir Putin awarded Zalygin a Presidential Prize for Literature and the Arts. Zalygin died in Moscow on 19 April 2000. Obituaries in Russian newspapers eulogized Zalygin not only as a scientist, author, publicist, and editor, but also as a man of conscience and courage who spoke out against ecologically unsound plans and who, through his work as a writer and editor, promoted free speech in Russia. Noted the poet Konstantin Aleksandrovich Kedrov in *Novye Izvestiia* (The New News, 22 April 2000): "Sergei Zalygin defended nature from the madness of man, and man from the madness of his nature."

**Interviews:**

Gunar Priede, "Edinstvo," *Daugava*, 3 (1985): 73–75;

I. Vasil'eva, "'Dozhivem do zabastovki? . . . ,'" *Literaturnaia gazeta*, 25 April 1990, p. 7;

Elisabeth Rich and David Smith, "Sergei Zalygin," *South Central Review: The Journal of the South Central Modern Language Association*, 3-4 (1995): 120–126.

**Biographies:**

Nikolai Nikolaevich Ianovsky, *Sergei Zalygin* (Kemerovo: Knizhnoe izdatel'stvo, 1965);

Galina Alekseevna Kolesnikova, *Sergei Zalygin: Tvorcheskaia biografiia* (Moscow: Sovetskii pisatel', 1969);

Leonid Aramovich Terakopian, *Sergei Zalygin: Pisatel' i geroi* (Moscow: Sovetskaia Rossiia, 1973);

Andrei Aleksandrovich Nuikin, *Zrelost' khudozhnika: Ocherk tvorchestva Sergeia Zalygina* (Moscow: Sovetskii pisatel', 1984);

Igor' Aleksandrovich Dedkov, *Sergei Zalygin: Stranitsy zhizni, stranitsy tvorchestva* (Moscow: Sovremennik, 1985);

Aleksei Valerievich Gorshenin, *Sergei Zalygin* (Novosibirsk: Knizhnoe izdatel'stvo, 1986).

**References:**

Iurii Andreev, "Zreslost' mastera," *Neva*, 12 (1973): 172–178;

Galina Andreevna Belaia, "Istorizm kak nravstvennaia i khudozhestvennaia pozitsiia pisatelia," in *Zhanrovo-stilevye iskaniia sovremennoi sovetskoi prozy*, edited by L. M. Poliak and Vadim Evgen'evich Kovsky (Moscow: Nauka, 1971), pp. 93–119;

Viktor Andreevich Chalmaev, "Raspakhannoe pole," in *Literatura i sovremennost' 1964–1965* (Moscow: Khudozhestvennaia literatura, 1965), pp. 91–119;

Igor' Aleksandrovich Dedkov, "'My khotim vruchit' svoi mysli,'" *Druzhba narodov*, 11 (1983): 259–262;

David Gillespie, "Sergei Pavlovich Zalygin," in *Reference Guide to Russian Literature*, edited by Neil Cornwell (London & Chicago: Fitzroy Dearborn, 1998), pp. 906–908;

Ann Hughes, "Sergey Zalygin and the 'Zhenskiy Vopros,'" *Journal of Russian Studies*, 50 (1986): 38–44;

Konstantin Aleksandrovich Kedrov, "Russkaia ideia Sergeia Zalygina," *Novye Izvestiia*, 22 April 2000, p. 4;

Pavel Alekseevich Nikolaev, "Sergei Pavlovich Zalygin," in *Russkie pisateli 20 veka: Biograficheskii slovar'*, edited by Nikolaev (Moscow: Bol'shaia rosskiiskaia entsiklopediia, 2000), pp. 280–282;

Svetlana Ilinichna Piskunova and Vladimir Maksimovich Piskunov, "Mezhdu byt' i ne byt'," *Novyi mir*, no. 5 (1986): 238–246;

N. N. Schneidman, "A New Approach to Old Problems: The Contemporary Prose of Sergei Zalygin," *Russian Language Journal*, 106 (1976): 115–130;

Evgenii Sergeev, "'Poisk schastliveishego sluchaia': Zametki o tvorchestve S. P. Zalygina," *Znamia*, 3 (1986): 205–215;

Aleksandr Sindel', "Oproverzhenie stilem," *Literaturnoe obozrenie*, 3 (1980): 47–50;

Ol'ga Aleksandrovna Slavnikova, "Staryi russkii: Pozdniaia proza Sergeia Zalygina," *Novyi mir*, no. 12 (1998): 204–221;

Aleksandra Spal', "Bremia sud'by i nadezhdy," *Oktiabr'*, 3 (1986): 201–203;

Vsevolod Alekseevich Surganov, "Voskhozhdenie: Proza Sergeia Zalygina i sovremennaia literatura," *Nash sovremennik*, 11 (1983): 176–184;

V. Survillo, "Zvenit truba Meshcheriakova: O tvorchestve S. P. Zalygina," *Novyi mir*, no. 6 (1969): 216–239;

T. M. Vakhitova, "Sergei Pavlovich Zalygin," in *Russkie pisateli: XX vek. Biobibliograficheskii slovar' v dvukh chastiakh*, volume 1, edited by N. N. Skatov (Moscow: Prosveshchenie, 1998), pp. 511–515;

David Gordon Wilson, "Fantasy in the Fiction of Sergei Zalygin," dissertation, University of Kansas, 1988;

E. I. Zakharova, "Novaia vstrecha a pisatelem Sergeem Zalyginym," *Vestnik Moskovskogo Universiteta: Seriia 9, Filologiia*, 5 (1981): 69–71.

**Papers:**

Part of Sergei Pavlovich Zalygin's archive—mainly what he wrote before the 1980s—is at the Institute of Russian Literature (Pushkin House) in St. Petersburg. The rest remains with his widow, Liubov' Sergeevna, and with his granddaughter, Mariia Savel'evna Mushinskaia.

# Aleksandr Aleksandrovich Zinov'ev
*(29 October 1922 –   )*

Boris Lanin
*Russian Academy of Education, Moscow*

(Translated by Christine A. Rydel)

BOOKS: *Filosofskie problemy mnogoznachnoi logiki* (Moscow: Izdatel'stvo Akademii nauk SSSR, 1960); revised edition, edited and translated by Guido Küng and David Dinsmore Comey as *Philosophical Problems of Many-Valued Logic* (Dordrecht, Holland: Reidel, 1963);

*Logika vyskazyvanii i teoriia vyvoda* (Moscow: Izdatel'stvo Akademii nauk SSSR, 1962);

*Osnovy logicheskoi teorii nauchnykh znanii* (Moscow: Nauka, 1967); revised and enlarged edition, translated by T. J. Blakeley as *Foundations of the Logical Theory of Scientific Knowledge (Complex Knowledge)* (Dordrecht, Holland: Reidel, 1973);

*Kompleksnaia logika* (Moscow: Nauka, 1970);

*Logika nauki* (Moscow: Mysl', 1971);

*Logicheskaia fizika* (Moscow: Nauka, 1972); translated by O. A. Germogenova as *Logical Physics,* edited by Robert S. Cohen (Dordrecht, Holland & Boston: Reidel, 1983);

*Ziiaiushchie vysoty* (Lausanne: L'Âge d'Homme, 1976); translated by Gordon Clough as *The Yawning Heights* (New York: Random House, 1979; London: Bodley Head, 1979);

*Svetloe budushchee* (Lausanne: L'Âge d'Homme, 1978); translated by Clough as *The Radiant Future* (New York: Random House, 1980; London: Bodley Head, 1981);

*Zapiski nochnogo storozha* (Lausanne: L'Âge d'Homme, 1979);

*Bez illiuzii* (Lausanne: L'Âge d'Homme, 1979);

*V preddverii raia* (Lausanne: L'Âge d'Homme, 1979);

*Zheltyi dom: Romanticheskaia povest' v chetyrekh chastiakh, s predosterezheniem i nazidaniem,* 2 volumes (Lausanne: L'Âge d'Homme, 1980); translated by Michael Kirkwood as *The Madhouse* (London: Gollancz, 1986);

*My i Zapad: Stat'i, interv'iu, vystupleniia 1979–1980 gg.* (Lausanne: L'Âge d'Homme, 1981);

*Aleksandr Aleksandrovich Zinov'ev (from Claude Schwab,* Alexandre Zinoviev: Résistance et lucidité, *1984; William Smith Morton Library, Union Theological Seminary)*

*Kommunizm kak real'nost'* (Lausanne: L'Âge d'Homme, 1981); translated by Charles Janson as *The Reality of Communism* (New York: Schocken, 1984; London: Gollancz, 1984);

*Gomo sovetikus* (Lausanne: L'Âge d'Homme, 1982); translated by Janson as *Homo Sovieticus* (London: Gollancz, 1985; Boston: Atlantic Monthly Press, 1985);

*Moi dom—moia chuzhbina* (Lausanne: L'Âge d'Homme, 1982);

*Nashei iunosti polet: Literaturno-sotsiologicheskii ocherk stalinizma* (Lausanne: L'Âge d'Homme, 1983);

*Ni svobody, ni ravenstva, ni bratstva: Stat'i, publichnye vystupleniia i otryvki iz vystuplenii v 1980–1981 gg.* (Lausanne: L'Âge d'Homme, 1983);

*Evangeli dlia Ivana/L'evangile pour Ivan,* bilingual edition, French translation by Wladimir Bérélowitch (Lausanne: L'Âge d'Homme, 1984);

*Die Diktatur der Logik: Über den gesunden Menschenverstand u.d. sowjetische Gesellschaft,* translated by Alexander Rothstein (Munich: Piper, 1985);

*Idi nà Golgofu* (Lausanne: L'Âge d'Homme, 1985);

*Para bellum* (Lausanne: L'Âge d'Homme, 1986);

*Der Staatsfreier* (Zurich: Diogenes, 1986);

*Die Macht des Unglaubens: Anmerkungen zur Sowjetideologie* (Munich: Piper, 1986);

*Gorbachevizm* (New York: Liberty, 1988);

*Zhivi!* (Lausanne: L'Âge d'Homme, 1989);

*Mon Tchekhov* (Brussels: Complexe, 1989);

*Il superpotere in URSS: It comunismo e'veramente tramontato?* (Milan: Sugar Co Edizioni, 1990);

*Les Confessions d'un Homme en trop* (Paris: Orban, 1990);

*Katastroika: Povest' o perestroike v Partgrade* (Lausanne: L'Âge d'Homme, 1990); translated by Janson as *Katastroika: Legend and Reality of Gorbachevism* (London: Claridge, 1990);

*Tsarville* (Paris: PLON, 1992);

*Smuta* (Moscow: Kelvori, 1994);

*Zapad: Fenomen zapadnizma* (Moscow: Tsentrpoligraf, 1995);

*Russkii eksperiment* (Moscow: Nash dom–L'Âge d'Homme, 1995);

*Postkommunisticheskaia Rossiia: Publitsistika 1991–1995 gg.* (Moscow: Respublika, 1996);

*Global'nyi cheloveinik* (Moscow: Tsentrpoligraf, 1997);

*O Rossii, o Zapade, o zagranitse, i o sebe . . .* (Moscow: ISPI RAN, 1998);

*Russkaia sud'ba: Ispoved' otshchepentsa* (Moscow: Tsentrpoligraf, 1999);

*Kommunizm. Evrokommunizm. Sovetskii stroi,* by Zinov'ev, Antonio Fernandes Ortis, and Sergei Georgievich Kara-Murza (Moscow: ITRK, 2000);

*Na puti k sverkhobshchestvu* (Moscow: Tsentrpoligraf, 2000);

*Zateiia* (Moscow: Tsentrpoligraf, 2000);

*Gibel' russkogo kommunizma* (Moscow: Tsentrpoligraf, 2001).

**Editions and Collections:** *Ziiaiushchie vysoty,* 2 volumes (Moscow: Nezavisimoe izdatel'stvo PIK, 1990);

*Gomo sovetikus; Moi dom, moia chuzhbina* (Moscow: KOR-INF, 1991);

*Gomo sovetikus; Moi dom, moia chuzhbina* (Moscow: Proizvodstvenno-izdatel'stvo predpriiatie, 1991);

*Gomo sovetikus; Parabellum* (Moscow: Moskovskii rabochii, 1991);

*Kommunizm kak real'nost'; Krizis kommunizma* (Moscow: Tsentrpoligraf, 1994);

*Sobranie sochinenii v desiati tomakh,* 10 volumes (Moscow: EvrAziia+, 1999–2000);

*Ziiaiushchie vysoty* (Moscow: Tsentrpoligraf, 2000);

*Svetloe budushchee* (Moscow: Tsentrpoligraf, 2000);

*Zheltyi dom* (Moscow: Tsentrpoligraf, 2000);

*Gomo sovetikus* (Moscow: Tsentrpoligraf, 2000);

*Zapad* (Moscow: Tsentrpoligraf, 2000);

*Global'nyi cheloveinik* (Moscow: Tsentrpoligraf, 2000);

*Global'noe sverkhobshchestvo i Rossiia* (Moscow & Minsk: AST/Kharvest, 2000);

*Russkaia sud'ba: Ispoved' otshchepentsa* (Moscow: Tsentrpoligraf, 2000);

*Sobranie sochinenii v desiati tomakh,* edited by L. I. Grekov, O. M. Zinov'eva, and others (Moscow: Tsentrpoligraf, 2000).

**Edition in English:** *Non-Standard Logic and Its Applications (Several Lectures in Oxford)* (Oxford: Willem A. Meeuws, 1983).

SELECTED PERIODICAL PUBLICATIONS–UNCOLLECTED: "Za chto borolis', na to i naporolis," *Sintaksis,* 3 (1979): 6–17;

"Predosterezhenie iz budushchego (Mir posle tretiei mirovoi voiny)," *Kontinent,* 40 (1984): 12–28;

*Ruka Kremlia: Komediia o mirnom sushchestvovanii dvukh sistem, Kontinent,* 47 (1986): 137–184;

"Propushchennaia mirovaia voina i krizis kommunizma," *22,* 65 (1989): 138–145;

"Manifest sotsial'noi oppozitsii," *Slovo,* 11 (1990): 68–73;

"O sotsial'nom statuse marksizma," *Raduga,* 5 (1990): 24–28.

Aleksandr Aleksandrovich Zinov'ev began his academic career as a philosopher, but political events of the 1960s in Russia led him instead to a different path: that of a belletrist. Forced to emigrate for his radical views and criticism of the existing regime, he returned to Russia after the onset of glasnost and perestroika. Disinclined to accept the new form of government, he continued on his course of criticism, this time of Mikhail Gorbachev and the folly of the president's "reforms." Zinov'ev generally resorts to biting satire, especially in his anti-utopian works. Once a staunch anti-Stalinist, he now views the past with a certain nostalgia that endears him to the more-chauvinistic elements in Russian society. Though difficult to decipher because of their complex structure and lexical peculiarities, his novels nevertheless reward those who persevere with a distinctive view of a disillusioned and often disgruntled Russian intellectual of the twentieth century.

Zinov'ev was born in Pakhtina, a village not far from Chukhloma (now the Chukhlomskoi raion Kostromskoi oblasti), on 29 October 1922. His mother, Appolinariia Vasil'evna, née Smirnova, was a peasant; his father, Aleksandr Iakovlevich, was a painter. Zinov'ev was the sixth of eleven children. He learned to read and write from a teacher who gave lessons in exchange for living in the Zinov'evs' home. Thus, when he entered school he was already literate and started his formal education in the second grade. He distinguished himself by his extraordinary memory: he could recall entire pages of textbooks word for word and was able to multiply large numbers in his head. In school he especially liked the works of Mikhail Iur'evich Lermontov, Victor Hugo, and Knut Hamsun. Zinov'ev was taught well in the village school, and reading became his preferred form of leisure activity. Later his reading tastes grew to include Aleksandr Sergeevich Griboedov, Mikhail Evgrafovich Saltykov, Nikolai Semenovich Leskov, and Anton Chekhov.

When Zinov'ev was twelve, he composed a sentimental story about a boy brought to Moscow to be educated. The story was written under the influence of Chekhov's tale "Van'ka" (1886), but Zinov'ev's ending is optimistic: Pioneers and *komsomol'tsy* (Communist Youth) help the hero of the story. Between the ages of fifteen and seventeen he wrote poetry in which he imitated the half-forgotten nineteenth-century Russian poet Dmitrii Dmitievich Minaev.

In 1939 Zinov'ev finished school with a gold certificate, which entitled him to first choice of universities. He entered the philosophy department of the Moscow Institute of Philosophy, Literature, and History, or MIFLI. While at the institute, he began to write for a *stengazeta* (wall newspaper) and drew caricatures for the satire and humor sections. He also became adamantly anti-Stalinist, as he explains in his book *Nashei iunosti polet: Literaturno-sotsiologicheskii ocherk stalinizma* (1983, The Flight of Our Youth: A Literary-Sociological Sketch of Stalinism), in which he produces an ideological interpretation of the epoch of Joseph Stalin:

> My anti-Stalinism emerged as a reaction to the difficult conditions of life of the people around me. All evil in life I personified in the character of Stalin.... When I was about seventeen, my personal hatred of Stalin reached its apogee. I was ready to kill him at the cost of my own life. Simultaneously I began to suspect that the causes of evil took root not merely in the person of Stalin, but also in the social structure. At the times of my wanderings around the country in 1939 and 1940, my suspicion grew into certainty. In me arose an intellectual curiosity about the very social structure of the country, as well as a desire to understand its mechanisms that were begetting evil.

On one occasion Zinov'ev carelessly shared with his comrades his impressions of his life in the countryside. He was arrested after one of his friends informed on him. While in jail, for the first time in his life he ate three meals a day and had his own bed; but these conditions did not make up for the oppressive atmosphere of the prison, and he escaped. Zinov'ev became the object of a countrywide manhunt. For a while he lived with false identification documents. Eventually he let his whereabouts become known and was subsequently recruited to work in the North. On 29 October 1940 he began his military service. He participated in World War II as a soldier in the cavalry, as a tank driver, and as a strafing pilot (the image of a pilot frequently appears in his works).

In 1942–1943 Zinov'ev composed "Ballada ob aviatsionnom studente" (Ballad about an Aviation Student), which is saturated with satirical political motifs. His model was Aleksandr Trifonovich Tvardovsky's long narrative poem, *Vasilii Terkin* (1942–1945). Although his friends advised him to destroy the ballad, Zinov'ev preserved the text, which he completely rewrote in 1975 and included in his *Ziiaiushchie vysoty* (1976; translated as *The Yawning Heights*, 1979); he published a fuller version in his *V preddverii raia* (1979, On the Threshold of Paradise). In 1943 he married Nina Kalinina, with whom he had a son, Valerii. In 1945 he finished writing "Povest' o predatel'stve" (A Tale of Treachery). Having returned from the war with a "suitcase full of manuscripts," Zinov'ev retyped the work but gave it the new title "Povest' o dolge" (A Tale about a Debt). He gave the manuscript to Konstantin Mikhailovich Simonov, who praised it but advised him to destroy it as soon as possible. This setback in his literary career plunged Zinov'ev into despair. He decided to commit suicide, but a meeting with his brother Vasilii changed his plans.

In 1946 Zinov'ev resumed his studies, this time at Moscow State University. After receiving his degree with distinction from the Department of Philosophy in 1951, he entered graduate school on the recommendation of the academic council. He dedicated his candidate's dissertation (roughly the equivalent of a Western doctoral dissertation) to the "method of ascent from the abstract to the concrete based on Karl Marx's *Das Kapital*." When Zinov'ev completed the dissertation, however, the academic council did not give its permission for a defense. Mark Semenovich Donskoi, a member of the body, appealed to the head of the propaganda section of the Central Committee of the Communist Party of the Soviet Union, G. F. Aleksandrov. In consequence, the academic council immediately reversed its decision.

In spite of his successful dissertation defense, Zinov'ev was not awarded his candidate of philosophy degree for about four years. His dissertation was removed from the open catalogue of both the Lenin and the university libraries, mainly because of the delicate nature of its subject matter; one needed a special permit to read it. In 1953 Zinov'ev became a candidate for membership in the Communist Party and thereafter was associated with that organization. Later he called this action one of the biggest mistakes of his life. In 1954 he received a position in the Institute of Philosophy of the Academy of Sciences of the Union of Soviet Socialist Republics, first as a typist and some time later as a research fellow.

In 1951 Zinov'ev married Tamara Filat'eva, who had been his classmate at the university. Their daughter, Tamara, was born in 1954. Two years later his wife managed to get them a one-room apartment with a living space of eight square meters. This dwelling was Zinov'ev's first real "private" home. The couple and their invalid daughter (who needed special care and physical therapy) lived in this room until 1960, when Zinov'ev once more abandoned his family.

In 1960 Zinov'ev published *Filosofskie problemy mnogoznachnoi logiki* (Philosophical Problems of Polysemantic Logic). Promptly translated into English (as *Philosophical Problems of Many-Valued Logic*, 1963), German, and Polish, the book made him well known internationally. In 1962 Zinov'ev earned his doctor of philosophy degree and became a professor, as well as a member of the editorial board of the learned journal *Voprosy filosofii* (Questions of Philosophy). Later he became chairman of the Department of Mathematical Logic at Moscow State University. In 1967 he finally procured his first separate one-room apartment.

At that time Zinov'ev also became a part of a group that included Aleksandr Evgen'evich Bovin, a journalist, speechwriter for Leonid Brezhnev, and the first Russian ambassador to Israel; the future dissidents and émigrés Boris Iosifovich Shragin, Aleksandr Moiseevich Piatigorsky, and Naum Moiseevich Korzhavin (Mandel'); Ivan Timofeevich Frolov, later an academician, aide to Gorbachev, and member of the Politburo of the Central Committee; Vasilii Vasil'evich Davydov, a leading pedagogue and future director of the Institute of Psychology; Eval'd Vasil'evich Il'enkov and Iurii Kariakin, who later became well-known philosophers; and the sculptor Ernst Iosifovich Neizvestny. In addition, in 1965 Zinov'ev became acquainted with a nineteen-year-old coworker at the Institute of Philosophy, Ol'ga Sorokina, whom he married two years later. From 1968 through 1976 he taught in schools and in universities, combining teaching and research. In 1974 he was elected to the Finnish Academy of Sciences.

Early in these years of success and recognition, however, came the decisive moment in Zinov'ev's intellectual life. On the night of 21 August 1968, armed forces of the Warsaw Pact invaded Czechoslovakia and forcibly suppressed the promising Communist reform movement known as the Prague Spring. The event had a profound effect on Zinov'ev, who was led to make a gesture of protest by resigning from the editorial board of *Voprosy filosofii*. The authorities reacted swiftly, stripping him of his departmental chairmanship at Moscow State University and also of his position on the higher examination board of the USSR Council of Ministers but leaving him in possession of his professorship. In the wake of this rebuke, Zinov'ev's interests began to move away from purely academic questions and toward journalism.

During the period from 1971 to 1973 Zinov'ev wrote a series of articles on various topics that were published not in the Soviet Union but in Poland and Czechoslovakia. He was already moving from journalism to a serious interest in creating satiric fiction, however. Throughout 1974 and 1975 he was mainly preoccupied with the project that became the novel *Ziiaiushchie vysoty*. He sent the manuscript in sections to France, with the intention of having it published *tamizdat'* (abroad). It was published in 1976, instantly establishing Zinov'ev's reputation as a writer.

In *Ziiaiushchie vysoty* Zinov'ev takes a position as a perpetuator of socialist realism, but in his own, idiosyncratic interpretation of that artistic ideology. Although many readers of *Ziiaiushchie vysoty* perceived it to be a sociological novel—an opinion not unlike Zinov'ev's own critique—it is nevertheless a distinctive work of art. The city of Ibansk (Fuckers) and such personages as Boltun (Chatterer), Shizofrenik (Schizophrenic), Klevetnik (Slanderer), Khriak (Hog), Mazila (Dauber), Zaiban (Superfucker), Myslitel' (Thinker), Pretendent (Claimant), Sotsiolog (Sociologist), Pravdets (Truth-teller), and Krikun (Shouter, or Bawler) all have allegorical significance. One can also, however, see in the work the real-life counterparts of the characters: the poet Raspashonka (Baby's Loose Jacket) is Yevgenii Yevtushenko; Khoziain (Landlord) is Stalin; Khriak is Nikita Khrushchev; Zaiban is Brezhnev; Mazila is Ernst Neizvestny; Myslitel' is the philosopher Merab Mamardashvili; Sotsiolog is Iurii Aleksandrovich Zamoshkin; and Pravdets is Aleksandr Solzhenitsyn. Several of the characters—including Krikun, Shizofrenik, Klevetnik, and Boltun—are arguably based on Zinov'ev himself.

Shizofrenik devises a sociological theory that explains Soviet society. Other characters try to apply this theory; they carve it in marble, then, having squandered all on drink, sell it. Thus, the unifying element of *Ziiaiushchie vysoty* is the advancement of the basic theory. The characters sometimes seem almost peripheral and from time to time disappear, only to be resurrected unexpectedly later. The book is broken up into titled fragments. Michael Kirkwood (1993) singles out at least twenty-seven different plotlines, which make up almost 400 of these 598 fragments. To add to the confusion, the book includes various genres and carnivalesque elements based on blasphemy and degradation, human excretory functions, eroticism, and a cynical sensibility.

The Soviet authorities reacted by punishing and rebuking the author of *Ziiaiushchie vysoty*. Even before its publication, they dismissed Zinov'ev from his university position and excluded him from the Soviet Philosophical Society—of which he had never been a member. After 26 August 1976, when radio stations announced the publication of his novel, he was stripped of his job, of his doctoral degree, and of his professor's rank. His daughter, Tamara; his son, Valerii; and even his brother Vasilii, who was thrown out of the army, all found themselves without employment. Some two years later Zinov'ev lived in de facto house arrest and, according to rumor, had been spared a worse fate only through the protection advanced by Politburo member Iurii Andropov. A person who helped him financially was Petr Leonidovich Kapitsa, a renowned physicist and an avid fan of *Ziiaiushchie vysoty*. Increasingly, however, Zinov'ev could not avoid the option of emigration. When in 1978 the rector of the University of Munich proffered an invitation for Zinov'ev to come to Germany as a visiting professor, the authorities seized on the invitation as a pretext for his exile. As soon as he arrived in Europe, they stripped Zinov'ev of his Soviet citizenship.

In rapid succession Zinov'ev published a series of books that seem in style, organization, and content to have been written as part of the *Ziiaiushchie vysoty* project. Of these books, *Svetloe budushchee* (1978; translated as *The Radiant Future*, 1980) and *Gomo sovetikus* (1982; translated as *Homo Sovieticus*, 1985) received considerable attention in the West and in the dissident culture of the Soviet Union. *Svetloe budushchee* is set in the elite world of the Academy of Sciences, which is shown to be basically the same sort of institution as the city of Ibansk in *Ziiaiushchie vysoty*. *Gomo sovetikus* endeavors to present both the Soviet Union and the West through the eyes of an émigré; as in the case of the other satires, the comic effect is intense and rather dark. In addition to these books, Zinov'ev proceeded to write prolifically, proving that he really had found a vocation as a writer. In particular, two of his titles, *Gorbachevizm* (1988, Gorbachevism) and *Katastroika: Povest' o perestroike v Partgrade* (1990; translated as *Katastroika: Legend and Reality of Gor-*

*Front cover for* Gorbachevizm *(1988), Zinov'ev's critique of the Russian president in which he argues: "Gorbachev's intentions are Stalinist, but his resources are Brezhnevian" (Thomas Cooper Library, University of South Carolina)*

*bachevism*, 1990), stand out because they address questions of particular interest not only to the troubled Soviet Union of the Gorbachev period but also to a Western world that was transfixed by the events unfolding in Zinov'ev's homeland.

*Gorbachevizm* appeared at a time when the West was enchanted by the personality of the first Soviet president, Mikhail Gorbachev. Zinov'ev explains Gorbachev's popularity as a universal "fraud" and "self-deception," but his historical role he describes aphoristically: "Gorbachev's intentions are Stalinist, but his resources are Brezhnevian."

*Katastroika*, whose title is a combination of *catastrophe* and *perestroika*, is as brilliantly written as Zinov'ev's best works, though it is more grotesque. New motifs appear; for example, the author recalls with nostalgia the epoch officially called "developed socialism": "the standard of living was raised to a level one could not even dream of in the pre- and post-war years. A separate apartment for a single family became the norm. Every family had a television and a refrigerator. Many provided themselves with motorcycles and automobiles; they built *dachas* (country homes). They began to dress better. . . . Thus they would have continued to live until now, if only they had not been planning *perestroika* in Moscow."

To Zinov'ev's surprise, in 1990 the moribund Soviet regime restored his citizenship and so brought his émigré life to an end. He had received many literary awards in the West: the Prix Medicis (1978) for *Svetloe budushchee;* the Prix Tocqueville (1982) for *Kommunizm kak real'nost'* (1981; translated as *The Reality of Communism,* 1984); and the Premio Internationale Tevere (1992) for his novel *Zhivi!* (1989, Live!).

Zinov'ev was welcomed home and soon elected vice president of the Russian Academy of Literature. His popularity grew, particularly among those disaffected by the realities of post-Soviet Russia, and in the elections of 2000 his run for the presidency of the Russian Republic was derailed only by a technicality. As a writer, his return to Russia marked a new phase of his career.

To the themes of his last works in emigration Zinov'ev added a deepening critique of the new Russia and its attempts at reform. For example, the action of the novel *Smuta* (1994, The Time of Troubles) is transferred to "Partygrad," and the artistic element is completely subordinated to unrestrained criticism of Russia under reform. *Zapad: Fenomen zapadnizma* (1995, The West: The Phenomenon of Westernism) is a large sociological essay devoted to the Western world and to perspectives on the growth of humanity in the Western context. In his terminology, one of the meanings of the term *Westernism* is what in the West is called "globalism" or "globalization." Aleksandr Donde (the pseudonym of Aleksandr Sergeevich Kustarev, the main editor for BBC literary programs), writing in *Ex libris NG* (29 January 1998), judged *Zapad* to have failed as an explanation of the distinctiveness of the West because somehow Zinov'ev consistently missed "the essence of the matter" at hand.

Another novel in this vein is *Global'nyi cheloveinik* (1997, Global Person-Hill); the title is a play on the word *muraveinik* (anthill). The action takes place in the fictional Great West and in West City–a typical town of the future in which Westernism, in Zinov'ev's idiosyncratic use of the term, has triumphed. Those who live in this society are called *zapadoidy* (westernoids). The contemporary trend of globalization has prevailed, and all lifestyles, except the Western, have perished. Some *zapadoidy* realize, however, that they have not only created a powerful civilization but in the same measure also have become the source of suffering and evil for the entire world.

Zinov'ev's unabashed nostalgia, not for what had been but for what could have been, saturates not only his novels but also his many speeches and articles. The evolution of his political views made him the favorite author of the Communist and nationalist-chauvinistic presses. During Soviet times, anti-Stalinism was the basis for his worldview; in 1997, however, Zinov'ev firmly announced in an article published in the journal *Sovetskaia Rossiia* (Soviet Russia) that "Stalinist democracy" was "a creation of the people," and its oft-reviled "apparatus of repression" was actually "the apparatus of preservation . . . the apparatus of growth."

In spite of the Stalinist nostalgia of his last years, Zinov'ev will probably be remembered mainly as a dissident writer. He was not a dissident in the conventional Western sense, however. In fact, he was not part of the dissident culture in its formative years. Not until the 1976 publication of *Ziiaiushchie vysoty* did he meet well-known dissidents such as Roy Medvedev, Vladimir Nikolaevich Voinovich, or Iurii Orlov. Although he paid his respects to Solzhenitsyn and Andrei Sakharov, his own views were not in harmony with either of theirs.

In many ways, Zinov'ev's dissidence was as much emotional as intellectual. In 1991, the last year of the Soviet Union, he said as much in an interview with John Glad. Zinov'ev remarked that while his head was full of thoughts, his heart was so overburdened with emotions that it had to find release. With reference to the Soviet authorities who had harassed him his entire life, he stated: "I simply wanted to punch THEM, THEM in capital letters, right in the snout." Those readers who shared this desire saw him as a dissident. Zinov'ev remained a true believer, however. Insofar as he had a philosophy of history in his dissident years, it was Marxist, in the sense that he believed that all historical paths lead to communism. He was even able to see in the high Stalinist period of the 1930s and 1940s a society in which a man could live most comfortably and simply, protected by all sorts of social blessings. He also saw, however, that this society had been degraded and ruined by the generation of bureaucrats who had inherited, rather than built, socialism.

In the final analysis, insofar as it was intellectual, Zinov'ev's dissidence was existential. His friend, the philosopher Karl Iakovlevich Kantor, concluded that Zinov'ev "was neither 'for' nor 'against' the existing regime," and that he was "only 'for' truth, and 'against' falsehood." Consequently, in an age of politicization, he was condemned to be misunderstood and unappreciated. In fact, his style and his unsystematic method of writing seem to take no notice of his readers. Critics have noted that his narrative approach is so idiosyncratic that it fails to serve satire; it is so self-referential that even his peers and contemporaries found it incomprehensible.

Aleksandr Aleksandrovich Zinov'ev will be remembered for his literary creativity. His novels are distinguished by narrative play with masks and styles, profound psychological analyses, and juxtaposition of adventure fantasies with the scabrous and the vulgar. He introduces jeering elements of elevated philosophizing, degrading and forbidden scatological themes, carnal debauchery, crude gutter language, sociological tracts, and anecdotes. Zinov'ev continued the satiric line in Russian literature, but complicated it with social grotesquerie, experiences of a personal character, and a distinctly autobiographical mode. The originality of his aesthetic lies in its essayistic quality and in its goal of quick publication. Although one cannot call Zinov'ev's style elegant, it is balanced with unexpected similes and bright images. At the basis of his narrative technique one finds a preference for the anecdote, for real (or most likely probable) events. The fragmentary quality of his composition is usually strengthened by his personal, journalistic asides to the reader. The paradoxical quality of his thought and his characteristic disagreement with the prevalent mood in society at any given moment give Zinov'ev an inimitable and irreplaceable position in Russian literature and aesthetics.

**Interviews:**

"Zhdu, kogda mne predlozhat izdat'sia," *Knizhnoe obozrenie,* 7 January 1988;

Evgenii Arshakovich Ambartsumov, "Odnu tebia liubliu, moia suzhenaia seraia zemlia," *Gorizont,* 12 (1989): 47–64;

Karl Iakovlevich Kantor, "Ia–eto gosudarstvo," in Zinov'ev, *Ziiaiushchie vysoty,* volume 2 (Moscow: Nezavisimoe izdatel'stvo PIK, 1990), pp. 306–309;

Ambartsumov, "Ne krivil dushoi, ne prisposablivalsia," in Zinov'ev, *Ziiaiushchie vysoty,* volume 2 (Moscow: Nezavisimoe izdatel'stvo PIK, 1990), pp. 310–315;

Vladimir Grigorievich Bondarenko, "Kakim vidit sovremenyi mir pisatel' i filosof Alexander Zinoviev," *Slovo,* 11 (1990): 67;

Feliks Nikolaevich Medvedev, "Padenie s ziiaiushchikh vysot," *Rodina,* 8 (1990): 21–25;

Wolfgang Kassak, "Formy inoskazaniia v sovremennoi russkoi literature/Odna ili dve russkikh literatury?" in *Mezhdunarodnyi simpozium, sozvanniy fakul'tetom slovesnosti Zhenevskogo universiteta i Shveitsarskoi Akademiiei slavistiki. Zheneva. 13–15 aprelia 1978,* edited by Georges Nivat (Lausanne: L'Âge d'Homme, 1991);

John Glad, *Conversations in Exile: Russian Writers Abroad,* translated by Richard Robin and Joanna Robin (Durham, N.C.: Duke University Press, 1993);

Aleksandr Andreevich Prokhanov, "Ia nikogda ne ronial chesti russkogo cheloveka," *Zavtra,* no. 24 (June 1994);

Vitalii Iliich Amursky, "Ia–odinochka vo vsem," in his *Zapechatlennye golosa: Parizhskie besedy s russkimi pisateliami i poetami* (Moscow: MIK, 1997), pp. 118–123;

Viktor Stefanovich Kozhemiako, "Iskanie istiny," *Sovietskaia Rossiia,* 22 November 1997;

Vladimir Vladimirovich Poliakov, "Spustivshis' s 'Ziiaiushchikh vysot,'" *Literaturnaia gazeta,* 33 (2001).

**References:**

German Andreev, *A. Zinoviev's "Waffende Hohen": Im Land der alogischen Gesetzmässigkeit* (Cologne: Bundesinstitut für Ostwissenschaftliche und Internationale Studien, 1978);

Libor Brom, *Alexander Zinoviev's Concept of the Soviet Man* (Munich & Hartford, Conn.: Comenius World Council, 1991);

Edward J. Brown, "Zinoviev, Aleshkovsky, Rabelais, Sorrentino, Possibly Pynchon, Maybe James, and Certainly *Tristam Shandy*: A Comparative Study of a Satirical Mode," *Stanford Slavic Studies,* 1 (1987): 307–325;

Aleksandr Donde, "Sovok i zapania: O zabluzhdeniakh i prozreniakh Aleksandra Zinovieva," *Ex libris NG,* 29 January 1998;

Fabrice Fassio, *Alexandre Zinoviev: Les fondements scientifiques de la sociologie* (Paris: Pensée Universelle, 1988);

Fassio, *La nature du communisme selon Alexandre Zinoviev* (Lion-sur-mer: Arcane-Beaunieux, 1991);

Philip Hanson and Michael Kirkwood, eds., *Alexander Zinoviev as Writer and Thinker: An Assessment* (Basingstoke, U.K.: Macmillan, 1988; New York: St. Martin's Press, 1988);

Michael Heller, "The Soviet Swift," *Survey,* 3 (Summer 1977–1978): 11–20;

Karl Iakovlevich Kantor, "Siiaiushchaia vysota slovesnosti," *Oktiabr',* 1 (1991): 32–33;

Michael Kirkwood, *Alexander Zinoviev: An Introduction to His Work* (Basingstoke, U.K.: Macmillan, 1993);

Kirkwood, "Alexander Zinoviev: Seer or Scientist?" in *Ideology in Russian Literature,* edited by Richard Freeborn and Jane Grayson (New York: St. Martin's Press, 1990);

Kirkwood, "Elements of Structure in Zinoviev's *Zheltyi dom*," *Essays in Poetics*, 7 (1982): 86–118;

Kirkwood, "On Translating Zinoviev," *Essays in Poetics*, 20 (1995): 102–132;

Kirkwood, "Osnovy zinon'evizma," *Journal of Russian Studies*, 46 (1983): 39–48;

Kirkwood, "*Ziiaiushchie vysoty* and Its Serialization in *Oktiabr'*," *Slavonic and East European Review*, 70, no. 3 (1992): 420–452;

Boris Aleksandrovich Lanin, *Proza russkoi emigratsii: Tret'ia volna: Posobie dlia prepodavatelei literatury* (Moscow: Novaia shkola, 1997), pp. 114–136;

Lanin, *Russkaia literaturnaia antiutopiia* (Moscow: Open University of Russia, 1993), pp. 107–124;

Lanin, "Vniz po rechke po Ibanke," *Khronika*, 8 (1992);

Gennadii Vasil'evich Osipov, Valentin Nikolaevich Ivanov, and M. I. Kodin, *Akademiia sotsial'nykh nauk: stenogrammy sesii 1997 g.* (Moscow: Institut sotsial'no-politicheskikh issledovanii Rossiiskoi akademii nauk, 1998);

P. Petro, "A. Zinoviev's *The Yawning Heights* as an Anatomy," *Canadian Slavonic Papers*, 23 (March 1981): 70–76;

Elizabeth Maclean Pollock, "A Comic Time, a Cosmic Joke," dissertation, Columbia University, 1992;

Nataliia Rubinshtein, "Skazanie o zemle Ibanskoi," *Vremia i My*, 16 (1977): 143–161;

Claude Schwab, *Alexandre Zinoviev: Résistance et lucidité* (Lausanne: L'Âge d'Homme, 1984);

"Sovetskoe obshchestvo i sovetskii chelovek–tochka zreniia Aleksandra Zinovieva (Materialy 'kruglogo stola': Tolstykh V. I., Mezhuev V. M., Liubomirova N. V., Fedina A. M., Kordonskii S. G., Pantin I. K., Kantor K. M.)," *Voprosy filosofii*, 11 (1992): 3–50;

Lucjan Suchanek, *Homo sovieticus: Swietlana przyszlosc, gnijacy Zachód: Pisarstwo Aleksandra Zinowiewa* (Kraków: Wydawn. Uniwersytetu Jagiellońskiego, 1999);

Valentin Ivanovich Tolstykh, "Vy chto, boites' Zinov'eva?" *Nezavisimaia gazeta*, 19 September 1992;

Petr Vail' and Aleksandr Genis, "Vselennaia bez mozzhechka," *Vremia i My*, 39 (1979): 147–158;

Vail' and Genis, "Zagovor protiv chuvstv: Besedy s Zinovievym," *Kontinent*, 24 (1980): 401–423.

# Checklist of Further Readings

Aleksandrova, Vera. *A History of Soviet Literature, 1917–1964: From Gorky to Solzhenitsyn,* translated by Mirra Ginsburg. Garden City, N.Y.: Anchor/Doubleday, 1964.

Allain, Annie. *Problemes d'écriture dans la littérature soviétique des annees trente.* Paris: Aux Amateurs de Livres, 1986.

Anderson, Roger and Paul Debreczeny, eds. *Russian Narrative and Visual Art: Varieties of Seeing.* Gainesville: University Press of Florida, 1994.

Barnes, Christopher J., ed. *Studies in Twentieth Century Russian Literature: Five Essays.* Edinburgh: Scottish Academic Press / London: Chatto & Windus, 1976.

Barta, Peter I., ed. *Metamorphosis in Russian Modernism.* Budapest & New York: Central European University Press, 2000.

Billington, James. *The Icon and the Axe: An Interpretive History of Russian Culture.* New York: Knopf, 1966.

Blair, Katherine Hunter. *A Review of Soviet Literature.* [London]: Ampersand, [1967].

Blake, Patricia and Max Hayward, eds. *Dissonant Voices in Soviet Literature.* New York: Pantheon, 1964.

Blake and Hayward, eds. *Half-way to the Moon: New Writing from Russia.* New York: Holt, Rinehart & Winston, 1964.

Blum, Jacob. *Image of the Jews in Soviet Literature: The Post-Stalinist Period.* New York: St. Martin's Press, 1990.

Bochkarev, Yuri, ed. *Soviet Russian Stories of the 1960s and 1970s.* Moscow: Progress Publishers, 1977.

Brainina, Berta Iakovlevna and Evdoksiia Fedorovna Nikitina, eds. *Sovetskie pisateli, avtobiografii,* 2 volumes. Moscow: Khudozhestvennaia literatura, 1959–1969.

Brown, Deming. *The Last Years of Soviet Russian Literature: Prose Fiction, 1975–1991.* Cambridge: Cambridge University Press, 1993.

Brown. *Soviet Russian Literature Since Stalin.* Cambridge & New York: Cambridge University Press, 1978.

Brown, Edward J. *Major Soviet Writers: Essays in Criticism.* London & Oxford: Oxford University Press, 1973.

Brown. *Russian Literature Since the Revolution.* New York: Collier, 1963; revised, 1969; revised and enlarged edition, Cambridge, Mass. & London: Harvard University Press, 1982.

Carlisle, Olga Andreyev. *Under a New Sky: A Reunion with Russia.* New York: Ticknor & Fields, 1993.

Choldin, Marianna Tax and Maurice Friedberg, eds. *The Red Pencil: Artists, Scholars, and Censors in the USSR.* Boston: Unwin Hyman, 1989.

Clark, Katerina. *The Soviet Novel: History as Ritual.* Chicago: University of Chicago Press, 1981.

Conquest, Robert. *The Great Terror: A Reassessment.* New York & Oxford: Oxford University Press, 1990.

Conquest. *The Harvest of Sorrow: Soviet Collectivization and the Terror–Famine.* New York & Oxford: Oxford University Press, 1986.

Conquest. *Kolyma: The Arctic Death Camps.* New York: Viking, 1978.

Conquest. *Tyrants and Typewriters: Communiqués in the Struggle for Truth.* London: Hutchinson, 1989.

Courtois, Stéphane, Nicolas Werth, Jean-Louis Panné, Andrzej Paczkowski, Karel Bartošek, and Jean-Louis Margolin. *The Black Book of Communism: Crimes, Terror, Repression,* translated by Jonathan Murphy and Mark Kramer; consulting editor, Mark Kramer. Cambridge, Mass.: Harvard University Press, 1999.

Crowley, Edward L. and Max Hayward, eds. *Soviet Literature in the Sixties: An International Symposium.* New York: Praeger, 1964.

Crozier, Brian. *The Rise and Fall of the Soviet Empire.* Rocklin, Cal.: Forum, 1999.

Danilov, Alexander A., Michael M. Gorinov, Sergei V. Leonov, Ekaterina P. Lugovskaya, Alexander S. Senyavski, and Alexander P. Naumov. *The History of Russia: The Twentieth Century,* translated by Galina Ustinova; translated and edited by Vincent E. Hammond. Mayflower, Ark.: Heron Press, 1996.

Dement'ev, E. G., ed. *Istoriia russkoi sovetskoi literatury,* 3 volumes. Moscow: Akademiia nauk: USSR, 1958–1961.

Dewhirst, Martin and Robert Farrell, eds. *The Soviet Censorship.* Metuchen, N.J.: Scarecrow Press, 1973.

Dobrenko, Evgenii Aleksandrovich. *The Making of the Soviet Writer: Social and Aesthetic Origins of Soviet Literary Culture,* translated by Jesse M. Savage. Stanford, Cal.: Stanford University Press, 2001.

Dunham, Vera S. *In Stalin's Time: Middleclass Values in Soviet Fiction,* with an introduction by Jerry F. Hough. Cambridge: Cambridge University Press, 1976.

Dziewanowski, M. K. *A History of Soviet Russia and Its Aftermath,* fifth edition. Upper Saddle River, N.J.: Prentice Hall, 1997.

Eng-Liedmeier, Jeanne van der. *Soviet Literary Characters: An Investigation into the Portrayal of Soviet Men in Russian Prose, 1917–1953,* translated from the Dutch by B. Timmer. The Hague: Mouton, 1959.

Erlich, Victor. *Modernism and Revolution: Russian Literature in Transition.* Cambridge, Mass. & London: Harvard University Press, 1994.

Erlich, ed. *Twentieth-Century Russian Literary Criticism.* New Haven: Yale University Press, 1975.

Field, Andrew, ed. *Pages from Tarusa: New Voices in Russian Writing.* London: Chapman & Hall, 1964.

Frank, Joseph. *Through the Russian Prism: Essays on Literature and Culture.* Princeton: Princeton University Press, 1990.

Freeborn, Richard. *The Russian Revolutionary Novel: Turgenev to Pasternak.* Cambridge: Cambridge University Press, 1982.

Freeborn and Jane Grayson, eds. *Ideology in Russian Literature.* New York: St. Martin's Press, 1990.

Friedberg, Maurice. *A Decade of Euphoria: Western Literature in Post-Stalin Russia, 1953–1964*. Bloomington: Indiana University Press, 1977.

Friedberg. *Russian Classics in Soviet Jackets*. New York: Columbia University Press, 1962.

Garrard, John and Carol Garrard. *Inside the Soviet Writers' Union*. New York: Free Press, [1990].

Gasiorowska, Xenia. *Women in Soviet Fiction, 1917–1962*. Madison: University of Wisconsin Press, 1968.

Gasparov, Boris [and others]. *Russian Literature in Modern Times*. Berkeley: University of California Press, 1995.

Gibian, George. *The Interval of Freedom: Soviet Literature During the Thaw, 1954–1957*. Minneapolis: University of Minnesota Press, 1960.

Gillespie, David. *The Twentieth Century Russian Novel: An Introduction*. Oxford & Washington, D.C.: Berg, 1996.

Glad, John. *Extrapolations from Dystopia: A Critical Study of Soviet Science Fiction*. Princeton: Kingston Press, 1982.

Glad. *Literature in Exile*. Durham: Duke University Press, 1990.

Guerney, Bernard Guilbert, ed. *An Anthology of Russian Literature in the Soviet Period from Gorki to Pasternak,* translated and annotated by Guerney. New York: Vintage, 1960.

Gutsche, George. *Moral Apostasy in Russian Literature*. De Kalb: Northern Illinois University Press, 1986.

Harris, Jane Gary, ed. *Autobiographical Statements in Twentieth Century Russian Literature*. Princeton: Princeton University Press, 1990.

Hayward, Max. *Writers in Russia, 1917–1978,* edited, with an introduction, by Patricia Blake. San Diego: Harcourt Brace Jovanovich, 1983.

Hayward and Leopold Labedz, eds. *Literature and Revolution in Soviet Russia, 1917–1962*. London: Oxford University Press, 1963.

Heller, Mikhail and Aleksandr Nekrich. *Utopia in Power: The History of the Soviet Union from 1917 to the Present,* translated by Phyllis B. Carlos. New York: Summit Books, 1986.

Hingley, Ronald. *Writers and Soviet Society, 1917–1978*. New York: Random House, 1979.

Holmgren, Beth. *Women's Works in Stalin's Time*. Bloomington & Indianapolis: Indiana University Press, 1993.

Holthusen, Johannes. *Twentieth Century Russian Literature: A Critical Study*. New York: Ungar, 1972.

Hosking, Geoffrey. *Beyond Socialist Realism: Soviet Fiction Since Ivan Denisovich*. New York: Holmes & Meier, 1980.

Jackson, Robert Louis. *Dostoevsky's Underground Man in Russian Literature*. The Hague: Mouton, 1958.

Kelly, Catriona, Michael Makin, and David Shepherd, eds. *Discontinuous Discourses in Modern Russian Literature*. New York: St. Martin's Press, 1989.

Kornblatt, Judith Deutsch. *Cossack Hero in Russian Literature: A Study in Cultural Mythology*. Madison: University of Wisconsin Press, 1992.

Lachmann, Renate. *Memory and Literature: Intertextuality in Russian Modernism*, translated by Roy Sellers and Anthony Wall, with a foreword by Wolfgang Iser. Minneapolis: University of Minnesota Press, 1997.

Lipovetskii, Mark Naumovich. *Poetika literaturnoi skazki: na materiale russkoi literatury 1920–1980-kh godov*. Sverdlovsk: Izdatelstvo Ural'skogo universiteta, 1992.

Litvinov, Pavel. *The Demonstration in Pushkin Square*, translated by Manya Harari. Boston: Gambit, 1969.

Lomidze, Georgii Iosifovich and Sofiia Mosesovna Khitarova. *Sovetskii roman: novatorstvo, poetika, tipologiia*. Moscow: Nauka, 1978.

Losev, Lev. *On the Beneficence of Censorship: Aesopian Language in Modern Russian Literature,* translated by Jane Bobko. Munich: Verlag Otto Sagner in Kommission, 1984.

Lourie, Richard. *Russia Speaks: An Oral History from the Revolution to the Present*. New York: Edward Burlingame, 1991.

Lowe, David Allen. *Russian Writing Since 1953: A Critical Survey*. New York: Ungar, 1987.

Malia, Martin. *The Soviet Tragedy: A History of Socialism in Russia, 1917–1991*. New York: Free Press, 1994.

Marsh, Rosalind J. *History and Literature in Contemporary Russia*. New York: New York University Press, 1995.

Marsh. *Soviet Fiction Since Stalin: Science, Politics and Literature*. Totowa, N.J.: Barnes & Noble, 1986.

Marsh, ed. *Women and Russian Culture: Projections and Self-Perceptions*. New York: Berghahn, 1998.

Mathewson, Rufus Wellington, Jr. *The Positive Hero in Russian Literature*. New York: Columbia University Press, 1958.

Matsuev, Nikolai Ivanovich. *Russkie sovetskie pisateli: Materialy dlia biograficheskogo slovaria 1917–1967*. Moscow: Sovetskii pisatel', 1981.

McLean, Hugh and W. N. Vickery, eds. *The Year of Protest: 1956,* translated by McLean and Vickery. New York: Random House, 1961.

McMillan, Priscilla Johnson. *Khrushchev and the Arts: The Politics of Soviet Culture, 1962–1964*. Cambridge, Mass.: MIT Press, 1965.

Moore, Harry Thornton and Albert Parry. *Twentieth-Century Russian Literature,* with an introduction by Moore. Carbondale: Southern Illinois University Press, 1974.

Muchnic, Helen. *From Gorky to Pasternak: Six Writers in Soviet Russia*. New York: Random House, 1966.

Nag, Martin. *Sovjetlitteraturen: 1917–1967*. Oslo: Cappelen, 1967.

Nikolaev, P. A. [and others], ed. *Russkie pisateli 20 veka. Biograficheskii slovar'*. Moscow: Nauchnoe izdatel'stvo "Bol'shaia rossiiskaia entsiklopediia," 2000.

Paperno, Irina and Joan Delaney Grossman, eds. *Creating Life: The Aesthetic Utopia of Russian Modernism*. Stanford, Cal.: Stanford University Press, 1994.

Parthé, Kathleen F. *Russian Village Prose: The Radiant Past*. Princeton: Princeton University Press, 1992.

Porter, Robert C. *Four Contemporary Russian Writers*. Oxford & New York: Berg, 1989.

Proffer, Carl R. and Ellendea Proffer, eds. *The Ardis Anthology of Recent Russian Literature*. Ann Arbor, Mich.: Ardis, 1973.

Proffer and Proffer, eds. *The Barsukov Triangle, The Two-Toned Blond, and other Stories*. Ann Arbor, Mich.: Ardis, 1984.

Proffer and Proffer, eds. *Contemporary Russian Prose*. Ann Arbor, Mich.: Ardis, 1982.

Reddaway, Peter, ed. *Uncensored Russia: Protest and Dissent in the Soviet Union*, translated, with a commentary, by Reddaway. New York: American Heritage Press, 1972.

Reeve, F. D., ed. *Great Soviet Short Stories*, with an introduction by Reeve. New York: Laurel Edition, Dell, 1962.

Reilly, Alayne P. *America in Contemporary Soviet Literature*. New York: New York University Press, 1971.

Riasanovsky, Nicholas Valentine. *A History of Russia*. New York & Oxford: Oxford University Press, 2000.

Roberts, Spencer E. *Soviet Historical Drama: Its Role in the Development of a National Mythology*. The Hague: M. Nijhoff, 1965.

Rogers, T. F. *Superfluous Men and the Post-Stalin Thaw: The Alienated Hero in Soviet Prose During the Decade 1953–1963*. The Hague & Paris: Mouton, 1972.

Rothberg, Abraham. *The Heirs of Stalin: Dissidence and the Soviet Regime, 1953–1970*. Ithaca, N.Y. & London: Cornell University Press, 1972.

Rühle, Jüngen. *Literature and Revolution: A Critical Study of the Writer and Communism in the Twentieth Century*, edited and translated by Jean Steinberg. New York: Praeger, [1969].

Ryan-Hughes, Karen. *Contemporary Russian Satire: A Genre Study*. Cambridge & New York: Cambridge University Press, 1995.

Segel, Harold B. *Twentieth-Century Russian Drama: From Gorky to the Present*. New York: Columbia University Press, 1979.

Seyffert, Peter. *Soviet Literary Structuralism: Background, Debate, Issues*. Columbus, Ohio: Slavica, 1983.

Shneidman, N. N. *Soviet Literature in the 1970s: Artistic Diversity and Ideological Conformity*. Toronto: University of Toronto Press, 1979.

Sicher, Efraim. *Jews in Russian Literature after the October Revolution: Writers and Artists Between Hope and Apostasy*. Cambridge & New York: Cambridge University Press, 1995.

Simmons, Ernest J. *Continuity and Change in Russian and Soviet Thought*. Cambridge, Mass.: Harvard University Press, 1955.

Simmons, ed. *Through the Glass of Soviet Literature: Views of Russian Society*. New York: Columbia University Press, 1953.

Slonim, Marc. *Soviet Russian Literature: Writers and Problems*. New York: Oxford University Press, 1964; revised, 1977.

Stites, Richard. *Russian Popular Culture: Entertainment and Society since 1900*. Cambridge & New York: Cambridge University Press, 1992.

Struve, Gleb. *Russian Literature under Lenin and Stalin, 1917–1953*. Norman: University of Oklahoma Press, 1971.

Surkov, A. A., ed. *Kratkaia literaturnaia entsiklopedia,* 9 volumes. Moscow: Sovetskaia entsiklopediia, 1962–1975.

Svirski, Grigori. *A History of Post-War Soviet Writing: The Literature of Moral Opposition,* translated and edited by Robert Dessaix and Michael Ulman. Ann Arbor, Mich.: Ardis, 1981.

Swayze, Harold. *Political Control of Literature in the USSR, 1946–1959.* Cambridge, Mass.: Harvard University Press, 1962.

Terras, Victor. *A History of Russian Literature.* New Haven & London: Yale University Press, 1991.

Terras, ed. *Handbook of Russian Literature.* New Haven & London: Yale University Press, 1985.

Thompson, Ewa Majewska. *Imperial Knowledge: Russian Literature and Colonialism.* Westport, Conn.: Greenwood Press, 2000.

Thompson, Terry L. and Richard Sheldon, eds. *Soviet Society and Culture: Essays in Honor of Vera S. Dunham.* Boulder, Colo.: Westview Press, 1987.

Toker, Leona. *Return from the Archipelago: Narratives of Gulag Survivors.* Bloomington: Indiana University Press, 2000.

Tolczyk, Dariusz. *See No Evil: Literary Coverups and Discoveries of the Soviet Camp Experience.* New Haven: Yale University Press, 1999.

Vilensky, Simeon, ed. *Till My Tale is Told: Women's Memoirs of the Gulag.* Bloomington: Indiana University Press, 1999.

Von Geldern, James and Richard Stites, eds. *Mass Culture in Soviet Russia: Tales, Poems, Songs, Movies, Plays, and Folklore, 1917–1953.* Bloomington: Indiana University Press, 1995.

Wolffheim, Elsbeth. *Die Frau in der Sowjetischen Literatur: 1917–1977.* Stuttgart: Klett, 1979.

Yarmolinsky, Avrahm, ed. *Soviet Short Stories.* New York: Doubleday, 1960.

Zekulin, Gleb. "Aspects of Peasant Life as Portrayed in Contemporary Soviet Literature," *Canadian Slavic Studies* (Winter 1967): 552–565.

Zekulin. "The Contemporary Countryside in Soviet Literature: A Search for New Values," in *The Soviet Rural Community: A Symposium,* edited, with an introduction, by James R. Millar. Urbana: University of Illinois Press, 1971, pp. 376–404.

Zholkovsky, Alexander. *Text Counter Text: Rereadings in Russian Literary History.* Stanford, Cal.: Stanford University Press, 1994.

Ziolkowski, Margaret. *Hagiography and Modern Russian Literature.* Princeton: Princeton University Press, 1988.

# Contributors

Marina Balina . . . . . . . . . . . . . . . . . . . . . . . . . . . . . . . . . . . . . . . . *Illinois Wesleyan University*
Edward E. Ericson Jr. . . . . . . . . . . . . . . . . . . . . . . . . . . . . . . . . . . . . . . . . *Calvin College*
Karen Evans-Romaine . . . . . . . . . . . . . . . . . . . . . . . . . . . . . . . . . . . . *Ohio University*
Michael Falchikov . . . . . . . . . . . . . . . . . . . . . . . . . . . . . . . . . . *University of Edinburgh*
Sibelan Forrester . . . . . . . . . . . . . . . . . . . . . . . . . . . . . . . . . . . *Swarthmore College*
Jefferson Gatrall . . . . . . . . . . . . . . . . . . . . . . . . . . . . . . . . . . . . . *Columbia University*
David Gillespie . . . . . . . . . . . . . . . . . . . . . . . . . . . . . . . . . . . . . . *University of Bath*
John Givens . . . . . . . . . . . . . . . . . . . . . . . . . . . . . . . . . . . . . . *University of Rochester*
Erika Haber . . . . . . . . . . . . . . . . . . . . . . . . . . . . . . . . . . . . . . . *Syracuse University*
Jane Gary Harris . . . . . . . . . . . . . . . . . . . . . . . . . . . . . . . . . . . *University of Pittsburgh*
Beth Holmgren . . . . . . . . . . . . . . . . . . . . . . . *University of North Carolina–Chapel Hill*
Marina Kanevskaya . . . . . . . . . . . . . . . . . . . . . . . . . . . . . . . . *University of Montana*
Alexis Klimoff . . . . . . . . . . . . . . . . . . . . . . . . . . . . . . . . . . . . . . . . . *Vassar College*
Konstantin V. Kustanovich . . . . . . . . . . . . . . . . . . . . . . . . . . . . . *Vanderbilt University*
Boris Lanin . . . . . . . . . . . . . . . . . . . . . . . . . . . . . *Russian Academy of Education, Moscow*
Naum Leiderman . . . . . . . . . . . . . . . . . . . . . . . . . . . . . *Russian Academy of Science*
Lev Loseff . . . . . . . . . . . . . . . . . . . . . . . . . . . . . . . . . . . . . . . . . *Dartmouth College*
Jonathan Z. Ludwig . . . . . . . . . . . . . . . . . . . . . . . . . . . . . . . . . . . . *Rice University*
Svetlana McMillan . . . . . . . . . . . . . . . . . . . . . . . . . . . . . . . . . *University College London*
Catharine Theimer Nepomnyashchy . . . . . . . . . . . . . . . . . . . . . . . . . . *Barnard College*
J. Alexander Ogden . . . . . . . . . . . . . . . . . . . . . . . . . . . . . . . *University of South Carolina*
Nadya L. Peterson . . . . . . . . . . . . . . . . . . . . . . . . . . . . . . . . . . . *Hunter College, CUNY*
Peter Rollberg . . . . . . . . . . . . . . . . . . . . . . . . . . . . . . . . . *George Washington University*
Helen Segall . . . . . . . . . . . . . . . . . . . . . . . . . . . . . . . . . . . . . . . . *Dickinson College*
Cynthia Simmons . . . . . . . . . . . . . . . . . . . . . . . . . . . . . . . . . . . . . . *Boston College*
Alexandra Smith . . . . . . . . . . . . . . . . . . . . . . . . . . *University of Canterbury, New Zealand*
Benjamin M. Sutcliffe . . . . . . . . . . . . . . . . . . . . . . . . . . . . . . . . *University of Pittsburgh*
Jennifer Ryan Tishler . . . . . . . . . . . . . . . . . . . . . . . . . . . *University of Wisconsin–Madison*
Janet Tucker . . . . . . . . . . . . . . . . . . . . . . . . . . . . . . . . . . . . . . *University of Arkansas*

# Cumulative Index

*Dictionary of Literary Biography,* Volumes 1-302
*Dictionary of Literary Biography Yearbook,* 1980-2002
*Dictionary of Literary Biography Documentary Series,* Volumes 1-19
*Concise Dictionary of American Literary Biography,* Volumes 1-7
*Concise Dictionary of British Literary Biography,* Volumes 1-8
*Concise Dictionary of World Literary Biography,* Volumes 1-4

# Cumulative Index

**DLB** before number: *Dictionary of Literary Biography,* Volumes 1-302
**Y** before number: *Dictionary of Literary Biography Yearbook,* 1980-2002
**DS** before number: *Dictionary of Literary Biography Documentary Series,* Volumes 1-19
**CDALB** before number: *Concise Dictionary of American Literary Biography,* Volumes 1-7
**CDBLB** before number: *Concise Dictionary of British Literary Biography,* Volumes 1-8
**CDWLB** before number: *Concise Dictionary of World Literary Biography,* Volumes 1-4

## A

Aakjær, Jeppe 1866-1930 ............... DLB-214
Aarestrup, Emil 1800-1856 ............. DLB-300
Abbey, Edward 1927-1989 ........ DLB-256, 275
Abbey, Edwin Austin 1852-1911 ....... DLB-188
Abbey, Maj. J. R. 1894-1969 .......... DLB-201
Abbey Press ........................... DLB-49
The Abbey Theatre and Irish Drama, 1900-1945 ........................... DLB-10
Abbot, Willis J. 1863-1934 ............. DLB-29
Abbott, Edwin A. 1838-1926 ........... DLB-178
Abbott, Jacob 1803-1879 ......... DLB-1, 42, 243
Abbott, Lee K. 1947- .................. DLB-130
Abbott, Lyman 1835-1922 .............. DLB-79
Abbott, Robert S. 1868-1940 ......... DLB-29, 91
Abe Kōbō 1924-1993 .................. DLB-182
Abelaira, Augusto 1926- .............. DLB-287
Abelard, Peter circa 1079-1142? .... DLB-115, 208
Abelard-Schuman ...................... DLB-46
Abell, Arunah S. 1806-1888 ............ DLB-43
Abell, Kjeld 1901-1961 ................ DLB-214
Abercrombie, Lascelles 1881-1938 ...... DLB-19
   The Friends of the Dymock Poets ........................... Y-00
Aberdeen University Press Limited ..... DLB-106
Abish, Walter 1931- ............ DLB-130, 227
Ablesimov, Aleksandr Onisimovich 1742-1783 .......................... DLB-150
Abraham à Sancta Clara 1644-1709 ..... DLB-168
Abrahams, Peter 1919- ......... DLB-117, 225; CDWLB-3
Abramov, Fedor Aleksandrovich 1920-1983 ......................... DLB-302
Abrams, M. H. 1912- .................. DLB-67
Abramson, Jesse 1904-1979 ............ DLB-241
*Abrogans* circa 790-800 ............... DLB-148
Abschatz, Hans Aßmann von 1646-1699 ......................... DLB-168
Abse, Dannie 1923- ............. DLB-27, 245
Abutsu-ni 1221-1283 .................. DLB-203
Academy Chicago Publishers .......... DLB-46

Accius circa 170 B.C.-circa 80 B.C. ....... DLB-211
Accrocca, Elio Filippo 1923-1996 ....... DLB-128
Ace Books ............................. DLB-46
Achebe, Chinua 1930- ...... DLB-117; CDWLB-3
Achtenberg, Herbert 1938- ............ DLB-124
Ackerman, Diane 1948- ............... DLB-120
Ackroyd, Peter 1949- ............. DLB-155, 231
Acorn, Milton 1923-1986 ............... DLB-53
Acosta, Oscar Zeta 1935?-1974? ......... DLB-82
Acosta Torres, José 1925- ............ DLB-209
Actors Theatre of Louisville ............. DLB-7
Adair, Gilbert 1944- .................. DLB-194
Adair, James 1709?-1783? .............. DLB-30
Aðalsteinn Kristmundsson (see Steinn Steinarr)
Adam, Graeme Mercer 1839-1912 ....... DLB-99
Adam, Robert Borthwick, II 1863-1940 .......................... DLB-187
Adame, Leonard 1947- ................ DLB-82
Adameşteanu, Gabriel 1942- ........... DLB-232
Adamic, Louis 1898-1951 ............... DLB-9
Adams, Abigail 1744-1818 ......... DLB-183, 200
Adams, Alice 1926-1999 ......... DLB-234; Y-86
Adams, Bertha Leith (Mrs. Leith Adams, Mrs. R. S. de Courcy Laffan) 1837?-1912 ........................ DLB-240
Adams, Brooks 1848-1927 .............. DLB-47
Adams, Charles Francis, Jr. 1835-1915 .... DLB-47
Adams, Douglas 1952-2001 ........ DLB-261; Y-83
Adams, Franklin P. 1881-1960 .......... DLB-29
Adams, Hannah 1755-1832 ............. DLB-200
Adams, Henry 1838-1918 ........ DLB-12, 47, 189
Adams, Herbert Baxter 1850-1901 ....... DLB-47
Adams, James Truslow 1878-1949 ................... DLB-17; DS-17
Adams, John 1735-1826 ........... DLB-31, 183
Adams, John Quincy 1767-1848 ......... DLB-37
Adams, Léonie 1899-1988 .............. DLB-48
Adams, Levi 1802-1832 ................ DLB-99
Adams, Richard 1920- ................ DLB-261
Adams, Samuel 1722-1803 ........... DLB-31, 43
Adams, Sarah Fuller Flower 1805-1848 .......................... DLB-199

Adams, Thomas 1582/1583-1652 ....... DLB-151
Adams, William Taylor 1822-1897 ....... DLB-42
J. S. and C. Adams [publishing house] ..... DLB-49
Adamson, Harold 1906-1980 ........... DLB-265
Adamson, Sir John 1867-1950 .......... DLB-98
Adamson, Robert 1943- .............. DLB-289
Adcock, Arthur St. John 1864-1930 ..... DLB-135
Adcock, Betty 1938- ................. DLB-105
   "Certain Gifts" .................... DLB-105
   Tribute to James Dickey .............. Y-97
Adcock, Fleur 1934- .................. DLB-40
Addison, Joseph 1672-1719 ............. DLB-101; CDBLB-2
Ade, George 1866-1944 ............ DLB-11, 25
Adeler, Max (see Clark, Charles Heber)
Adlard, Mark 1932- .................. DLB-261
Adler, Richard 1921- ................. DLB-265
Adonias Filho 1915-1990 .............. DLB-145
Adorno, Theodor W. 1903-1969 ........ DLB-242
Adoum, Jorge Enrique 1926- ......... DLB-283
Advance Publishing Company .......... DLB-49
Ady, Endre 1877-1919 ....... DLB-215; CDWLB-4
AE 1867-1935 ............. DLB-19; CDBLB-5
Ælfric circa 955-circa 1010 ............ DLB-146
Aeschines circa 390 B.C.-circa 320 B.C. .... DLB-176
Aeschylus 525-524 B.C.-456-455 B.C. ................... DLB-176; CDWLB-1
*Aesthetic Papers* ........................ DLB-1
Aesthetics
   Eighteenth-Century Aesthetic Theories ....................... DLB-31
African Literature
   Letter from Khartoum ............... Y-90
African American
   Afro-American Literary Critics: An Introduction ................. DLB-33
   The Black Aesthetic: Background ....... DS-8
   The Black Arts Movement, by Larry Neal ................... DLB-38
   Black Theaters and Theater Organizations in America, 1961-1982: A Research List ............... DLB-38
   Black Theatre: A Forum [excerpts] .... DLB-38
   *Callaloo* [journal] .................... Y-87

447

Community and Commentators:
   Black Theatre and Its Critics..... DLB-38

The Emergence of Black
   Women Writers............. DS-8

The Hatch-Billops Collection....... DLB-76

A Look at the Contemporary Black
   Theatre Movement ........... DLB-38

The Moorland-Spingarn Research
   Center ..................... DLB-76

"The Negro as a Writer," by
   G. M. McClellan ............. DLB-50

"Negro Poets and Their Poetry," by
   Wallace Thurman ............ DLB-50

Olaudah Equiano and Unfinished Journeys:
   The Slave-Narrative Tradition and
   Twentieth-Century Continuities, by
   Paul Edwards and Pauline T.
   Wangman ................. DLB-117

PHYLON (Fourth Quarter, 1950),
   The Negro in Literature:
   The Current Scene ........... DLB-76

The Schomburg Center for Research
   in Black Culture ............. DLB-76

Three Documents [poets], by John
   Edward Bruce ............... DLB-50

After Dinner Opera Company ........... Y-92
Agassiz, Elizabeth Cary 1822-1907...... DLB-189
Agassiz, Louis 1807-1873 .......... DLB-1, 235
Agee, James
   1909-1955 ....... DLB-2, 26, 152; CDALB-1

The Agee Legacy: A Conference at
   the University of Tennessee
   at Knoxville................... Y-89

Aguilera Malta, Demetrio 1909-1981 .... DLB-145
Agustini, Delmira 1886-1914 .......... DLB-290
Ahlin, Lars 1915-1997............. DLB-257
Ai 1947- ...................... DLB-120
Aichinger, Ilse 1921- .......... DLB-85, 299
Aickman, Robert 1914-1981.......... DLB-261
Aidoo, Ama Ata 1942- ....DLB-117; CDWLB-3
Aiken, Conrad
   1889-1973........ DLB-9, 45, 102; CDALB-5
Aiken, Joan 1924- .............. DLB-161
Aikin, Lucy 1781-1864 .......... DLB-144, 163
Ainsworth, William Harrison
   1805-1882 ...................... DLB-21
Aistis, Jonas 1904-1973 ..... DLB-220; CDWLB-4
Aitken, George A. 1860-1917 .......... DLB-149
Robert Aitken [publishing house]........ DLB-49
Aitmatov, Chingiz 1928- ............. DLB-302
Akenside, Mark 1721-1770 .......... DLB-109
Akhmatova, Anna Andreevna
   1889-1966 ................... DLB-295
Akins, Zoë 1886-1958............. DLB-26
Aksakov, Ivan Sergeevich 1823-1826.....DLB-277
Aksakov, Sergei Timofeevich
   1791-1859................ DLB-198
Aksyonov, Vassily (Vasilii Pavlovich Aksenov)
   1932- ....................... DLB-302
Akunin, Boris (Grigorii Shalvovich
   Chkhartishvili) 1956- ........... DLB-285
Akutagawa Ryūnosuke 1892-1927........ DLB-180

Alabaster, William 1568-1640 ........ DLB-132
Alain de Lille circa 1116-1202/1203 ..... DLB-208
Alain-Fournier 1886-1914............ DLB-65
Alanus de Insulis (see Alain de Lille)
Alarcón, Francisco X. 1954- ........ DLB-122
Alarcón, Justo S. 1930- ............ DLB-209
Alba, Nanina 1915-1968............ DLB-41
Albee, Edward 1928- ... DLB-7, 266; CDALB-1
Albert, Octavia 1853-ca. 1889 ........ DLB-221
Albert the Great circa 1200-1280 ...... DLB-115
Alberti, Rafael 1902-1999........... DLB-108
Albertinus, Aegidius circa 1560-1620 .... DLB-164
Alcaeus born circa 620 B.C..........DLB-176
Alcoforado, Mariana, the Portuguese Nun
   1640-1723................... DLB-287
Alcott, Amos Bronson
   1799-1888............... DLB-1, 223; DS-5
Alcott, Louisa May 1832-1888
   ... DLB-1, 42, 79, 223, 239; DS-14; CDALB-3
Alcott, William Andrus
   1798-1859.................... DLB-1, 243
Alcuin circa 732-804................ DLB-148
Alden, Henry Mills 1836-1919 ......... DLB-79
Alden, Isabella 1841-1930........... DLB-42
John B. Alden [publishing house] ....... DLB-49
Alden, Beardsley, and Company ....... DLB-49
Aldington, Richard
   1892-1962 ............DLB-20, 36, 100, 149
Aldis, Dorothy 1896-1966 ............ DLB-22
Aldis, H. G. 1863-1919............. DLB-184
Aldiss, Brian W. 1925- .......DLB-14, 261, 271
Aldrich, Thomas Bailey
   1836-1907...............DLB-42, 71, 74, 79
Alegría, Ciro 1909-1967 ............ DLB-113
Alegría, Claribel 1924- ........ DLB-145, 283
Aleixandre, Vicente 1898-1984......... DLB-108
Aleksandravičius, Jonas (see Aistis, Jonas)
Aleksandrov, Aleksandr Andreevich
   (see Durova, Nadezhda Andreevna)
Alekseeva, Marina Anatol'evna
   (see Marinina, Aleksandra)
Aleramo, Sibilla (Rena Pierangeli Faccio)
   1876-1960................. DLB-114, 264
Aleshkovsky, Petr Markovich 1957- ... DLB-285
Alexander, Cecil Frances 1818-1895..... DLB-199
Alexander, Charles 1868-1923 ......... DLB-91
Charles Wesley Alexander
   [publishing house] ............. DLB-49
Alexander, James 1691-1756 ......... DLB-24
Alexander, Lloyd 1924- ............ DLB-52
Alexander, Sir William, Earl of Stirling
   1577?-1640................... DLB-121
Alexie, Sherman 1966- ......DLB-175, 206, 278
Alexis, Willibald 1798-1871 .......... DLB-133
Alfred, King 849-899 .............. DLB-146
Alger, Horatio, Jr. 1832-1899 .......... DLB-42
Algonquin Books of Chapel Hill ....... DLB-46

Algren, Nelson
   1909-1981 ...... DLB-9; Y-81, 82; CDALB-1
Nelson Algren: An International
   Symposium .................... Y-00
Aljamiado Literature.................. DLB-286
Allan, Andrew 1907-1974 ............. DLB-88
Allan, Ted 1916-1995 ............... DLB-68
Allbeury, Ted 1917- ............... DLB-87
Alldritt, Keith 1935- .............. DLB-14
Allen, Dick 1939- ................ DLB-282
Allen, Ethan 1738-1789................ DLB-31
Allen, Frederick Lewis 1890-1954 .......DLB-137
Allen, Gay Wilson 1903-1995 .....DLB-103; Y-95
Allen, George 1808-1876 ............. DLB-59
Allen, Grant 1848-1899 ......... DLB-70, 92, 178
Allen, Henry W. 1912-1991 ............ Y-85
Allen, Hervey 1889-1949 ........... DLB-9, 45
Allen, James 1739-1808................ DLB-31
Allen, James Lane 1849-1925 .......... DLB-71
Allen, Jay Presson 1922- ............ DLB-26
John Allen and Company............. DLB-49
Allen, Paula Gunn 1939- ..............DLB-175
Allen, Samuel W. 1917- ............. DLB-41
Allen, Woody 1935- ................ DLB-44
George Allen [publishing house]......... DLB-106
George Allen and Unwin Limited ...... DLB-112
Allende, Isabel 1942- .......DLB-145; CDWLB-3
Alline, Henry 1748-1784............. DLB-99
Allingham, Margery 1904-1966 ........ DLB-77
   The Margery Allingham Society ........ Y-98
Allingham, William 1824-1889.......... DLB-35
W. L. Allison [publishing house] ........ DLB-49
The Alliterative Morte Arthure and the Stanzaic
   Morte Arthur circa 1350-1400 ... DLB-146
Allott, Kenneth 1912-1973 ........... DLB-20
Allston, Washington 1779-1843 ...... DLB-1, 235
John Almon [publishing house] ........ DLB-154
Alonzo, Dámaso 1898-1990........... DLB-108
Alsop, George 1636-post 1673 ......... DLB-24
Alsop, Richard 1761-1815............. DLB 37
Henry Altemus and Company ......... DLB-49
Altenberg, Peter 1885-1919 ........... DLB-81
Althusser, Louis 1918-1990 ........... DLB-242
Altolaguirre, Manuel 1905-1959........ DLB-108
Aluko, T. M. 1918- ..................DLB-117
Alurista 1947- ................... DLB-82
Alvarez, A. 1929- ............. DLB-14, 40
Alvarez, Julia 1950- .............. DLB-282
Alvaro, Corrado 1895-1956 .......... DLB-264
Alver, Betti 1906-1989 ..... DLB-220; CDWLB-4
Amadi, Elechi 1934- ................DLB-117
Amado, Jorge 1912-2001 ............ DLB-113
Amalrik, Andrei 1938-1980 .......... DLB-302
Ambler, Eric 1909-1998 ............. DLB-77
The Library of America ............ DLB-46

The Library of America: An Assessment
  After Two Decades ................. Y-02
America: or, A Poem on the Settlement
  of the British Colonies, by Timothy
  Dwight ....................... DLB-37
American Bible Society
  Department of Library, Archives, and
  Institutional Research ............ Y-97
American Conservatory
  Theatre ...................... DLB-7
American Culture
  American Proletarian Culture:
    The Twenties and Thirties ....... DS-11
Studies in American Jewish Literature ....... Y-02
The American Library in Paris ........... Y-93
American Literature
  The Literary Scene and Situation and...
    (Who Besides Oprah) Really Runs
    American Literature? ............ Y-99
  Who Owns American Literature, by
    Henry Taylor ................. Y-94
  Who Runs American Literature? ....... Y-94
American News Company ............ DLB-49
A Century of Poetry, a Lifetime of Collecting:
  J. M. Edelstein's Collection of Twentieth-
  Century American Poetry ............ Y-02
The American Poets' Corner: The First
  Three Years (1983-1986) ............ Y-86
American Publishing Company ......... DLB-49
*American Spectator*
  [Editorial] Rationale From the Initial
  Issue of the American Spectator
  (November 1932) ................ DLB-137
American Stationers' Company ......... DLB-49
The American Studies Association
  of Norway ..................... Y-00
American Sunday-School Union ........ DLB-49
American Temperance Union .......... DLB-49
American Tract Society ............. DLB-49
The American Trust for the British Library .. Y-96
American Writers Congress
  The American Writers Congress
    (9-12 October 1981) ............. Y-81
  The American Writers Congress: A Report
    on Continuing Business ........... Y-81
Ames, Fisher 1758-1808 .............. DLB-37
Ames, Mary Clemmer 1831-1884 ....... DLB-23
Ames, William 1576-1633 ............ DLB-281
Amiel, Henri-Frédéric 1821-1881 ....... DLB-217
Amini, Johari M. 1935- ............. DLB-41
Amis, Kingsley 1922-1995
  ..... DLB-15, 27, 100, 139, Y-96; CDBLB-7
Amis, Martin 1949- ............. DLB-14, 194
Ammianus Marcellinus
  circa A.D. 330-A.D. 395 .......... DLB-211
Ammons, A. R. 1926-2001 .......... DLB-5, 165
Amory, Thomas 1691?-1788 .......... DLB-39
Anania, Michael 1939- ............. DLB-193
Anaya, Rudolfo A. 1937- ..... DLB-82, 206, 278
*Ancrene Riwle* circa 1200-1225 ......... DLB-146
Andersch, Alfred 1914-1980 .......... DLB-69
Andersen, Benny 1929- ............. DLB-214

Andersen, Hans Christian 1805-1875 .... DLB-300
Anderson, Alexander 1775-1870 ....... DLB-188
Anderson, David 1929- ............. DLB-241
Anderson, Frederick Irving 1877-1947 .... DLB-202
Anderson, Margaret 1886-1973 ........ DLB-4, 91
Anderson, Maxwell 1888-1959 ...... DLB-7, 228
Anderson, Patrick 1915-1979 .......... DLB-68
Anderson, Paul Y. 1893-1938 ......... DLB-29
Anderson, Poul 1926-2001 ........... DLB-8
  Tribute to Isaac Asimov ............ Y-92
Anderson, Robert 1750-1830 ......... DLB-142
Anderson, Robert 1917- ............ DLB-7
Anderson, Sherwood
  1876-1941 ..... DLB-4, 9, 86; DS-1; CDALB-4
Andreae, Johann Valentin 1586-1654 .... DLB-164
Andreas Capellanus
  flourished circa 1185 .............. DLB-208
Andreas-Salomé, Lou 1861-1937 ........ DLB-66
Andreev, Leonid Nikolaevich
  1871-1919 .................... DLB-295
Andres, Stefan 1906-1970 ........... DLB-69
Andresen, Sophia de Mello Breyner
  1919- ........................ DLB-287
Andreu, Blanca 1959- ............. DLB-134
Andrewes, Lancelot 1555-1626 ..... DLB-151, 172
Andrews, Charles M. 1863-1943 ........ DLB-17
Andrews, Miles Peter ?-1814 .......... DLB-89
Andrews, Stephen Pearl 1812-1886 ...... DLB-250
Andrian, Leopold von 1875-1951 ....... DLB-81
Andrić, Ivo 1892-1975 ...... DLB-147; CDWLB-4
Andrieux, Louis (see Aragon, Louis)
Andrus, Silas, and Son .............. DLB-49
Andrzejewski, Jerzy 1909-1983 ........ DLB-215
Angell, James Burrill 1829-1916 ........ DLB-64
Angell, Roger 1920- ........... DLB-171, 185
Angelou, Maya 1928- ....... DLB-38; CDALB-7
  Tribute to Julian Mayfield ........... Y-84
Anger, Jane flourished 1589 .......... DLB-136
Angers, Félicité (see Conan, Laure)
*The Anglo-Saxon Chronicle*
  circa 890-1154 .................. DLB-146
Angus and Robertson (UK) Limited ..... DLB-112
Anhalt, Edward 1914-2000 ........... DLB-26
Anissimov, Myriam 1943- .......... DLB-299
Anker, Nini Roll 1873-1942 .......... DLB-297
Annenkov, Pavel Vasil'evich
  1813?-1887 .................... DLB-277
Annensky, Innokentii Fedorovich
  1855-1909 .................... DLB-295
Henry F. Anners [publishing house] ..... DLB-49
*Annolied* between 1077 and 1081 ....... DLB-148
Anscombe, G. E. M. 1919-2001 ........ DLB-262
Anselm of Canterbury 1033-1109 ...... DLB-115
Anstey, F. 1856-1934 ............ DLB-141, 178
Anthologizing New Formalism ........ DLB-282
Anthony, Michael 1932- ............ DLB-125

Anthony, Piers 1934- ............... DLB-8
Anthony, Susanna 1726-1791 ......... DLB-200
Antin, David 1932- ................ DLB-169
Antin, Mary 1881-1949 .......... DLB-221; Y-84
Anton Ulrich, Duke of Brunswick-Lüneburg
  1633-1714 ..................... DLB-168
Antschel, Paul (see Celan, Paul)
Antunes, António Lobo 1942- ........ DLB-287
Anyidoho, Kofi 1947- .............. DLB-157
Anzaldúa, Gloria 1942- ............ DLB-122
Anzengruber, Ludwig 1839-1889 ....... DLB-129
Apess, William 1798-1839 ........ DLB-175, 243
Apodaca, Rudy S. 1939- ............ DLB-82
Apollinaire, Guillaume 1880-1918 ...... DLB-258
Apollonius Rhodius third century B.C. ... DLB-176
Apple, Max 1941- ................. DLB-130
Appelfeld, Aharon 1932- ............ DLB-299
D. Appleton and Company ........... DLB-49
Appleton-Century-Crofts ............. DLB-46
Applewhite, James 1935- ............ DLB-105
  Tribute to James Dickey ............ Y-97
Apple-wood Books ................. DLB-46
April, Jean-Pierre 1948- ............. DLB-251
Apukhtin, Aleksei Nikolaevich
  1840-1893 ..................... DLB-277
Apuleius circa A.D. 125-post A.D. 164
  ......................... DLB-211; CDWLB-1
Aquin, Hubert 1929-1977 ............ DLB-53
Aquinas, Thomas 1224/1225-1274 ..... DLB-115
Aragon, Louis 1897-1982 ......... DLB-72, 258
Aragon, Vernacular Translations in the
  Crowns of Castile and 1352-1515 .... DLB-286
Aralica, Ivan 1930- ................ DLB-181
Aratus of Soli
  circa 315 B.C.-circa 239 B.C. ....... DLB-176
Arbasino, Alberto 1930- ............ DLB-196
Arbor House Publishing Company ...... DLB-46
Arbuthnot, John 1667-1735 .......... DLB-101
Arcadia House ................... DLB-46
Arce, Julio G. (see Ulica, Jorge)
Archer, William 1856-1924 .......... DLB-10
Archilochus
  mid seventh century B.C.E. ........ DLB-176
The Archpoet circa 1130?-? ........... DLB-148
Archpriest Avvakum (Petrovich)
  1620?-1682 .................... DLB-150
Arden, John 1930- ............ DLB-13, 245
*Arden of Faversham* ................. DLB-62
Ardis Publishers ................... Y-89
Ardizzone, Edward 1900-1979 ........ DLB-160
Arellano, Juan Estevan 1947- ........ DLB-122
The Arena Publishing Company ....... DLB-49
Arena Stage ...................... DLB-7
Arenas, Reinaldo 1943-1990 ......... DLB-145
Arendt, Hannah 1906-1975 .......... DLB-242
Arensberg, Ann 1937- .............. Y-82

Arghezi, Tudor 1880-1967............ DLB-220; CDWLB-4

Arguedas, José María 1911-1969 ....... DLB-113

Argueta, Manlio 1936- ............. DLB-145

Arias, Ron 1941- .................. DLB-82

Arishima Takeo 1878-1923........... DLB-180

Aristophanes circa 446 B.C.-circa 386 B.C. ................DLB-176; CDWLB-1

Aristotle 384 B.C.-322 B.C. ................DLB-176; CDWLB-1

Ariyoshi Sawako 1931-1984........... DLB-182

Arland, Marcel 1899-1986 ............. DLB-72

Arlen, Michael 1895-1956 .......DLB-36, 77, 162

Armah, Ayi Kwei 1939- ...DLB-117; CDWLB-3

Armantrout, Rae 1947- ............. DLB-193

Der arme Hartmann ?-after 1150 ....... DLB-148

Armed Services Editions............... DLB-46

Armitage, G. E. (Robert Edric) 1956- ............. DLB-267

Armstrong, Martin Donisthorpe 1882-1974................. DLB-197

Armstrong, Richard 1903- ........... DLB-160

Armstrong, Terence Ian Fytton (see Gawsworth, John)

Arnauld, Antoine 1612-1694............. DLB-268

Arndt, Ernst Moritz 1769-1860........... DLB-90

Arnim, Achim von 1781-1831........... DLB-90

Arnim, Bettina von 1785-1859 ........... DLB-90

Arnim, Elizabeth von (Countess Mary Annette Beauchamp Russell) 1866-1941 .... DLB-197

Arno Press ...................... DLB-46

Arnold, Edwin 1832-1904 ............. DLB-35

Arnold, Edwin L. 1857-1935............DLB-178

Arnold, Matthew 1822-1888 ......... DLB-32, 57; CDBLB-4

Preface to *Poems* (1853)............. DLB-32

Arnold, Thomas 1795-1842 ........... DLB-55

Edward Arnold [publishing house]...... DLB-112

Arnott, Peter 1962- ................. DLB-233

Arnow, Harriette Simpson 1908-1986 ..... DLB-6

Arp, Bill (see Smith, Charles Henry)

Arpino, Giovanni 1927-1987............DLB-177

Arrebo, Anders 1587-1637 ............. DLB-300

Arreola, Juan José 1918-2001 ........... DLB-113

Arrian circa 89-circa 155................DLB-176

J. W. Arrowsmith [publishing house] .... DLB-106

Art

John Dos Passos: Artist ............... Y-99

The First Post-Impressionist Exhibition....................DS-5

The Omega Workshops ............. DS-10

The Second Post-Impressionist Exhibition ..................DS-5

Artaud, Antonin 1896-1948 ........... DLB-258

Artel, Jorge 1909-1994 ............. DLB-283

Arthur, Timothy Shay 1809-1885 ........DLB-3, 42, 79, 250; DS-13

Artmann, H. C. 1921-2000............. DLB-85

Artsybashev, Mikhail Petrovich 1878-1927.................... DLB-295

Arvin, Newton 1900-1963 ............ DLB-103

Asch, Nathan 1902-1964 ............ DLB-4, 28

Nathan Asch Remembers Ford Madox Ford, Sam Roth, and Hart Crane .... Y-02

Ascham, Roger 1515/1516-1568........ DLB-236

Aseev, Nikolai Nikolaevich 1889-1963 ................. DLB-295

Ash, John 1948- ................. DLB-40

Ashbery, John 1927- ........DLB-5, 165; Y-81

Ashbridge, Elizabeth 1713-1755 ........ DLB-200

Ashburnham, Bertram Lord 1797-1878 ................. DLB-184

Ashendene Press.................. DLB-112

Asher, Sandy 1942- .................. Y-83

Ashton, Winifred (see Dane, Clemence)

Asimov, Isaac 1920-1992 ..........DLB-8; Y-92

Tribute to John Ciardi .............. Y-86

Askew, Anne circa 1521-1546 .......... DLB-136

Aspazija 1865-1943 ........ DLB-220; CDWLB-4

Asselin, Olivar 1874-1937............. DLB-92

The Association of American Publishers ..... Y-99

The Association for Documentary Editing.... Y-00

The Association for the Study of Literature and Environment (ASLE) ..... Y-99

Astell, Mary 1666-1731................ DLB-252

Astley, Thea 1925- ................ DLB-289

Astley, William (see Warung, Price)

Asturias, Miguel Ángel 1899-1974.........DLB-113, 290; CDWLB-3

Atava, S. (see Terpigorev, Sergei Nikolaevich)

Atheneum Publishers ................ DLB-46

Atherton, Gertrude 1857-1948 .....DLB-9, 78, 186

Athlone Press .................... DLB-112

Atkins, Josiah circa 1755-1781........... DLB-31

Atkins, Russell 1926- ............. DLB-41

Atkinson, Kate 1951- ............. DLB-267

Atkinson, Louisa 1834-1872 ........... DLB-230

The Atlantic Monthly Press .......... DLB-46

Attaway, William 1911-1986 ........... DLB-76

Atwood, Margaret 1939- ........ DLB-53, 251

Aubert, Alvin 1930- ................ DLB-41

Aubert de Gaspé, Phillipe-Ignace-François 1814-1841 .................. DLB-99

Aubert de Gaspé, Phillipe-Joseph 1786-1871 .................. DLB-99

Aubin, Napoléon 1812-1890............. DLB-99

Aubin, Penelope 1685-circa 1731 ............. DLB-39

Preface to *The Life of Charlotta du Pont* (1723)................. DLB-39

Aubrey-Fletcher, Henry Lancelot (see Wade, Henry)

Auchincloss, Louis 1917- ......DLB-2, 244; Y-80

Auden, W. H. 1907-1973 .......... DLB-10, 20; CDBLB-6

Audio Art in America: A Personal Memoir ... Y-85

Audubon, John James 1785-1851 ........ DLB-248

Audubon, John Woodhouse 1812-1862 .................... DLB-183

Auerbach, Berthold 1812-1882.......... DLB-133

Auernheimer, Raoul 1876-1948 ........ DLB-81

Augier, Emile 1820-1889 ............. DLB-192

Augustine 354-430 ................ DLB-115

Aulnoy, Marie-Catherine Le Jumel de Barneville, comtesse d' 1650/1651-1705...................DLB-268

Aulus Gellius circa A.D. 125-circa A.D. 180?...... DLB-211

Austen, Jane 1775-1817 ...... DLB-116; CDBLB-3

Auster, Paul 1947- ................ DLB-227

Austin, Alfred 1835-1913 ............. DLB-35

Austin, J. L. 1911-1960............. DLB-262

Austin, Jane Goodwin 1831-1894....... DLB-202

Austin, John 1790-1859................ DLB-262

Austin, Mary Hunter 1868-1934 ........ DLB-9, 78, 206, 221, 275

Austin, William 1778-1841 ............. DLB-74

Australie (Emily Manning) 1845-1890 ................ DLB-230

Authors and Newspapers Association ... DLB-46

Authors' Publishing Company......... DLB-49

Avallone, Michael 1924-1999................Y-99

Tribute to John D. MacDonald ........ Y-86

Tribute to Kenneth Millar ........ Y-83

Tribute to Raymond Chandler ........ Y-88

Avalon Books...................... DLB-46

Avancini, Nicolaus 1611-1686 ........ DLB-164

Avendaño, Fausto 1941- ........... DLB-82

Averroës 1126-1198 ................ DLB-115

Avery, Gillian 1926- ............. DLB-161

Avicenna 980-1037 ................ DLB-115

Ávila Jiménez, Antonio 1898-1965....... DLB-283

Avison, Margaret 1918-1987............ DLB-53

Avon Books ...................... DLB-46

Avyžius, Jonas 1922-1999............. DLB-220

Awdry, Wilbert Vere 1911-1997 ........ DLB-160

Awoonor, Kofi 1935- ................DLB-117

Ayckbourn, Alan 1939- .......... DLB-13, 245

Ayer, A. J. 1910-1989 ............. DLB-262

Aymé, Marcel 1902-1967 ............. DLB-72

Aytoun, Sir Robert 1570-1638 ........ DLB-121

Aytoun, William Edmondstoune 1813-1865 ............. DLB-32, 159

# B

B.V. (see Thomson, James)

Babbitt, Irving 1865-1933............... DLB-63

Babbitt, Natalie 1932- ............. DLB-52

John Babcock [publishing house] ........ DLB-49

Babel, Isaak Emmanuilovich 1894-1940 ...................DLB-272

Babits, Mihály 1883-1941....DLB-215; CDWLB-4

Babrius circa 150-200 .................DLB-176

Babson, Marian 1929- ................DLB-276

Baca, Jimmy Santiago 1952- .........DLB-122
Bacchelli, Riccardo 1891-1985.........DLB-264
Bache, Benjamin Franklin 1769-1798......DLB-43
Bachelard, Gaston 1884-1962 .........DLB-296
Bacheller, Irving 1859-1950............DLB-202
Bachmann, Ingeborg 1926-1973.........DLB-85
Bačinskaitė-Bučienė, Salomėja (see Nėris, Salomėja)
Bacon, Delia 1811-1859.............DLB-1, 243
Bacon, Francis
  1561-1626.....DLB-151, 236, 252; CDBLB-1
Bacon, Sir Nicholas circa 1510-1579 .....DLB-132
Bacon, Roger circa 1214/1220-1292 .....DLB-115
Bacon, Thomas circa 1700-1768.........DLB-31
Bacovia, George
  1881-1957 ...........DLB-220; CDWLB-4
Richard G. Badger and Company.......DLB-49
Bagaduce Music Lending Library ......... Y-00
Bage, Robert 1728-1801................DLB-39
Bagehot, Walter 1826-1877 ............DLB-55
Baggesen, Jens 1764-1826............DLB-300
Bagley, Desmond 1923-1983............DLB-87
Bagley, Sarah G. 1806-1848?............DLB-239
Bagnold, Enid
  1889-1981 ..........DLB-13, 160, 191, 245
Bagryana, Elisaveta
  1893-1991 ........DLB-147; CDWLB-4
Bahr, Hermann 1863-1934 ........DLB-81, 118
Bailey, Abigail Abbot 1746-1815 ........DLB-200
Bailey, Alfred Goldsworthy 1905- ......DLB-68
Bailey, H. C. 1878-1961................DLB-77
Bailey, Jacob 1731-1808................DLB-99
Bailey, Paul 1937- ............. DLB-14, 271
Bailey, Philip James 1816-1902 .........DLB-32
Francis Bailey [publishing house].......DLB-49
Baillargeon, Pierre 1916-1967 ..........DLB-88
Baillie, Hugh 1890-1966 ...............DLB-29
Baillie, Joanna 1762-1851..............DLB-93
Bailyn, Bernard 1922- ...............DLB-17
Bain, Alexander
  *English Composition and Rhetoric* (1866)
  [excerpt] ....................DLB-57
Bainbridge, Beryl 1933- ........DLB-14, 231
Baird, Irene 1901-1981 ...............DLB-68
Baker, Augustine 1575-1641 ...........DLB-151
Baker, Carlos 1909-1987 ..............DLB-103
Baker, David 1954- ..................DLB-120
Baker, George Pierce 1866-1935 ........DLB-266
Baker, Herschel C. 1914-1990 ..........DLB-111
Baker, Houston A., Jr. 1943- .........DLB-67
Baker, Howard
  Tribute to Caroline Gordon ........... Y-81
  Tribute to Katherine Anne Porter....... Y-80
Baker, Nicholson 1957- ........ DLB-227; Y-00
  Review of Nicholson Baker's *Double Fold:
  Libraries and the Assault on Paper* ...... Y-00
Baker, Samuel White 1821-1893........DLB-166
Baker, Thomas 1656-1740 ............DLB-213

Walter H. Baker Company
  ("Baker's Plays")..................DLB-49
The Baker and Taylor Company ........DLB-49
Bakhtin, Mikhail Mikhailovich
  1895-1975 .....................DLB-242
Bakunin, Mikhail Aleksandrovich
  1814-1876 .....................DLB-277
Balaban, John 1943- ................DLB-120
Bald, Wambly 1902- .................DLB-4
Balde, Jacob 1604-1668 ..............DLB-164
Balderston, John 1889-1954............DLB-26
Baldwin, James 1924-1987
  ......DLB-2, 7, 33, 249, 278; Y-87; CDALB-1
Baldwin, Joseph Glover
  1815-1864 ............... DLB-3, 11, 248
Baldwin, Louisa (Mrs. Alfred Baldwin)
  1845-1925 .....................DLB-240
Baldwin, William circa 1515-1563 .......DLB-132
Richard and Anne Baldwin
  [publishing house].................DLB-170
Bale, John 1495-1563.................DLB-132
Balestrini, Nanni 1935- ........ DLB-128, 196
Balfour, Sir Andrew 1630-1694.........DLB-213
Balfour, Arthur James 1848-1930 .......DLB-190
Balfour, Sir James 1600-1657..........DLB-213
Ballantine Books .....................DLB-46
Ballantyne, R. M. 1825-1894 ...........DLB-163
Ballard, J. G. 1930- ........ DLB-14, 207, 261
Ballard, Martha Moore 1735-1812.......DLB-200
Ballerini, Luigi 1940- ..............DLB-128
Ballou, Maturin Murray (Lieutenant Murray)
  1820-1895 ............... DLB-79, 189
Robert O. Ballou [publishing house] ......DLB-46
Bal'mont, Konstantin Dmitrievich
  1867-1942.......................DLB-295
Balzac, Guez de 1597?-1654............DLB-268
Balzac, Honoré de 1799-1855 .........DLB-119
Bambara, Toni Cade
  1939-1995 ........DLB-38, 218; CDALB-7
Bamford, Samuel 1788-1872............DLB-190
A. L. Bancroft and Company ..........DLB-49
Bancroft, George 1800-1891 ...DLB-1, 30, 59, 243
Bancroft, Hubert Howe 1832-1918 ...DLB-47, 140
Bandelier, Adolph F. 1840-1914.........DLB-186
Bang, Herman 1857-1912.............DLB-300
Bangs, John Kendrick 1862-1922......DLB-11, 79
Banim, John 1798-1842 ...... DLB-116, 158, 159
Banim, Michael 1796-1874...........DLB-158, 159
Banks, Iain (M.) 1954- ........ DLB-194, 261
Banks, John circa 1653-1706 ...........DLB-80
Banks, Russell 1940- ......... DLB-130, 278
Bannerman, Helen 1862-1946..........DLB-141
Bantam Books ......................DLB-46
Banti, Anna 1895-1985 ...............DLB-177
Banville, John 1945- ........ DLB-14, 271
Banville, Théodore de 1823-1891 .......DLB-217
Baraka, Amiri
  1934- ....DLB-5, 7, 16, 38; DS-8; CDALB-1

Barańczak, Stanisław 1946- ..........DLB-232
Baranskaia, Natal'ia Vladimirovna
  1908-..........................DLB-302
Baratynsky, Evgenii Abramovich
  1800-1844.....................DLB-205
Barba-Jacob, Porfirio 1883-1942 .......DLB-283
Barbauld, Anna Laetitia
  1743-1825 ..........DLB-107, 109, 142, 158
Barbeau, Marius 1883-1969............DLB-92
Barber, John Warner 1798-1885 .........DLB-30
Bàrberi Squarotti, Giorgio 1929- .....DLB-128
Barbey d'Aurevilly, Jules-Amédée
  1808-1889 ....................DLB-119
Barbier, Auguste 1805-1882 ..........DLB-217
Barbilian, Dan (see Barbu, Ion)
Barbour, John circa 1316-1395 .........DLB-146
Barbour, Ralph Henry 1870-1944 .......DLB-22
Barbu, Ion 1895-1961 ...... DLB-220; CDWLB-4
Barbusse, Henri 1873-1935 ............DLB-65
Barclay, Alexander circa 1475-1552......DLB-132
E. E. Barclay and Company ............DLB-49
C. W. Bardeen [publishing house].........DLB-49
Barham, Richard Harris 1788-1845......DLB-159
Barich, Bill 1943- ..................DLB-185
Baring, Maurice 1874-1945 ............DLB-34
Baring-Gould, Sabine 1834-1924....DLB-156, 190
Barker, A. L. 1918- .............DLB-14, 139
Barker, Clive 1952- ................DLB-261
Barker, Dudley (see Black, Lionel)
Barker, George 1913-1991.............DLB-20
Barker, Harley Granville 1877-1946 .......DLB-10
Barker, Howard 1946- ..........DLB-13, 233
Barker, James Nelson 1784-1858 ........DLB-37
Barker, Jane 1652-1727 ............DLB-39, 131
Barker, Lady Mary Anne 1831-1911.....DLB-166
Barker, Pat 1943- .................DLB-271
Barker, William circa 1520-after 1576 ....DLB-132
Arthur Barker Limited.................DLB-112
Barkov, Ivan Semenovich 1732-1768......DLB-150
Barks, Coleman 1937- ................DLB-5
Barlach, Ernst 1870-1938............DLB-56, 118
Barlow, Joel 1754-1812 ................DLB-37
  *The Prospect of Peace* (1778) ............DLB-37
Barnard, John 1681-1770 ..............DLB-24
Barnard, Marjorie (M. Barnard Eldershaw)
  1897-1987 .....................DLB-260
Barnard, Robert 1936- ..............DLB-276
Barne, Kitty (Mary Catherine Barne)
  1883-1957 ....................DLB-160
Barnes, Barnabe 1571-1609 ...........DLB-132
Barnes, Djuna 1892-1982 ....DLB-4, 9, 45; DS-15
Barnes, Jim 1933- ..................DLB-175
Barnes, Julian 1946- ...........DLB-194; Y-93
  Notes for a Checklist of Publications .... Y-01
Barnes, Margaret Ayer 1886-1967.........DLB-9
Barnes, Peter 1931- ...........DLB-13, 233

# Cumulative Index

Barnes, William 1801-1886 ............ DLB-32
A. S. Barnes and Company ........... DLB-49
Barnes and Noble Books ............. DLB-46
Barnet, Miguel 1940- ............... DLB-145
Barney, Natalie 1876-1972 ........ DLB-4; DS-15
Barnfield, Richard 1574-1627 ........... DLB-172
Richard W. Baron [publishing house] .... DLB-46
Barr, Amelia Edith Huddleston
　1831-1919.................. DLB-202, 221
Barr, Robert 1850-1912 ........... DLB-70, 92
Barral, Carlos 1928-1989 ............ DLB-134
Barrax, Gerald William 1933- .... DLB-41, 120
Barrès, Maurice 1862-1923.......... DLB-123
Barreno, Maria Isabel (see The Three Marias:
　A Landmark Case in Portuguese
　Literary History)
Barrett, Eaton Stannard 1786-1820...... DLB-116
Barrie, J. M.
　1860-1937...... DLB-10, 141, 156; CDBLB-5
Barrie and Jenkins.................. DLB-112
Barrio, Raymond 1921- ............. DLB-82
Barrios, Gregg 1945- ............... DLB-122
Barry, Philip 1896-1949 ............DLB-7, 228
Barry, Robertine (see Françoise)
Barry, Sebastian 1955- ............. DLB-245
Barse and Hopkins.................. DLB-46
Barstow, Stan 1928- .........DLB-14, 139, 207
　Tribute to John Braine................ Y-86
Barth, John 1930- ............. DLB-2, 227
Barthelme, Donald
　1931-1989 ...........DLB-2, 234; Y-80, 89
Barthelme, Frederick 1943- ..... DLB-244; Y-85
Barthes, Roland 1915-1980........... DLB-296
Bartholomew, Frank 1898-1985....... DLB-127
Bartlett, John 1820-1905.......... DLB-1, 235
Bartol, Cyrus Augustus 1813-1900.... DLB-1, 235
Barton, Bernard 1784-1849........... DLB-96
Barton, John ca. 1610-1675........... DLB-236
Barton, Thomas Pennant 1803-1869 .... DLB-140
Bartram, John 1699-1777 ............ DLB-31
Bartram, William 1739-1823.......... DLB-37
Barykova, Anna Pavlovna 1839-1893 ....DLB-277
Basic Books....................... DLB-46
Basille, Theodore (see Becon, Thomas)
Bass, Rick 1958- ..............DLB-212, 275
Bass, T. J. 1932- .................... Y-81
Bassani, Giorgio 1916-2000 .... DLB-128, 177, 299
Basse, William circa 1583-1653 ........ DLB-121
Bassett, John Spencer 1867-1928...... DLB-17
Bassler, Thomas Joseph (see Bass, T. J.)
Bate, Walter Jackson 1918-1999......DLB-67, 103
Bateman, Stephen circa 1510-1584...... DLB-136
Christopher Bateman
　[publishing house] ..................DLB-170
Bates, H. E. 1905-1974 ........ DLB-162, 191
Bates, Katharine Lee 1859-1929 ........ DLB-71

Batiushkov, Konstantin Nikolaevich
　1787-1855 .................. DLB-205
B. T. Batsford [publishing house]....... DLB-106
Battiscombe, Georgina 1905- ........ DLB-155
The Battle of Maldon circa 1000........... DLB-146
Baudelaire, Charles 1821-1867.......... DLB-217
Baudrillard, Jean 1929- ............. DLB-296
Bauer, Bruno 1809-1882............... DLB-133
Bauer, Wolfgang 1941- ............... DLB-124
Baum, L. Frank 1856-1919 .......... DLB-22
Baum, Vicki 1888-1960 ............. DLB-85
Baumbach, Jonathan 1933- ........... Y-80
Bausch, Richard 1945- ............. DLB-130
　Tribute to James Dickey .............. Y-97
　Tribute to Peter Taylor ............... Y-94
Bausch, Robert 1945- ............. DLB-218
Bawden, Nina 1925- .........DLB-14, 161, 207
Bax, Clifford 1886-1962...........DLB-10, 100
Baxter, Charles 1947- ............. DLB-130
Bayer, Eleanor (see Perry, Eleanor)
Bayer, Konrad 1932-1964 ............ DLB-85
Bayle, Pierre 1647-1706...............DLB-268
Bayley, Barrington J. 1937- .......... DLB-261
Baynes, Pauline 1922- ............... DLB-160
Baynton, Barbara 1857-1929.......... DLB-230
Bazin, Hervé (Jean Pierre Marie Hervé-Bazin)
　1911-1996 .................. DLB-83
The BBC Four Samuel Johnson Prize
　for Non-fiction ..................... Y-02
Beach, Sylvia
　1887-1962.................. DLB-4; DS-15
Beacon Press..................... DLB-49
Beadle and Adams ............. DLB-49
Beagle, Peter S. 1939- ................. Y-80
Beal, M. F. 1937- .................... Y-81
Beale, Howard K. 1899-1959 ........... DLB-17
Beard, Charles A. 1874-1948 ........... DLB-17
Beat Generation (Beats)
　As I See It, by Carolyn Cassady ..... DLB-16
　A Beat Chronology: The First Twenty-five
　　Years, 1944-1969................ DLB-16
　The Commercialization of the Image
　　of Revolt, by Kenneth Rexroth... DLB-16
　Four Essays on the Beat Generation .. DLB-16
　in New York City ................ DLB-237
　in the West..................... DLB-237
　Outlaw Days ................... DLB-16
　Periodicals of .................. DLB-16
Beattie, Ann 1947- .........DLB-218, 278; Y-82
Beattie, James 1735-1803 ............ DLB-109
Beatty, Chester 1875-1968 ............ DLB-201
Beauchemin, Nérée 1850-1931......... DLB-92
Beauchemin, Yves 1941- ............ DLB-60
Beaugrand, Honoré 1848-1906 ......... DLB-99
Beaulieu, Victor-Lévy 1945- ......... DLB-53

Beaumont, Francis circa 1584-1616
　and Fletcher, John
　1579-1625............. DLB-58; CDBLB-1
Beaumont, Sir John 1583?-1627 ........ DLB-121
Beaumont, Joseph 1616-1699.......... DLB-126
Beauvoir, Simone de 1908-1986.....DLB-72; Y-86
　Personal Tribute to Simone de Beauvoir ... Y-86
Beaver, Bruce 1928- .............. DLB-289
Becher, Ulrich 1910-1990 ............. DLB-69
Becker, Carl 1873-1945 ..............DLB-17
Becker, Jurek 1937-1997 ..........DLB-75, 299
Becker, Jurgen 1932- ............. DLB-75
Beckett, Samuel 1906-1989
　.......... DLB-13, 15, 233; Y-90; CDBLB-7
Beckford, William 1760-1844 ....... DLB-39, 213
Beckham, Barry 1944- ............. DLB-33
Bećković, Matija 1939- ............. DLB-181
Becon, Thomas circa 1512-1567........ DLB-136
Becque, Henry 1837-1899............. DLB-192
Beddoes, Thomas 1760-1808 .......... DLB-158
Beddoes, Thomas Lovell 1803-1849 ..... DLB-96
Bede circa 673-735 ................ DLB-146
Bedford-Jones, H. 1887-1949 .......... DLB-251
Bedregal, Yolanda 1913-1999 .......... DLB-283
Beebe, William 1877-1962 ............DLB-275
Beecher, Catharine Esther
　1800-1878.................. DLB-1, 243
Beecher, Henry Ward
　1813-1887.................. DLB-3, 43, 250
Beer, George L. 1872-1920............ DLB-47
Beer, Johann 1655-1700 ............. DLB-168
Beer, Patricia 1919-1999 ............. DLB-40
Beerbohm, Max 1872-1956 .........DLB-34, 100
Beer-Hofmann, Richard 1866-1945 ...... DLB-81
Beers, Henry A. 1847-1926 ........... DLB-71
S. O. Beeton [publishing house] ........ DLB-106
Begley, Louis 1933- ............. DLB-299
Bégon, Elisabeth 1696-1755 ........... DLB-99
Behan, Brendan
　1923-1964 ......... DLB-13, 233; CDBLB-7
Behn, Aphra 1640?-1689 ......... DLB-39, 80, 131
Behn, Harry 1898-1973 ............. DLB-61
Behrman, S. N. 1893-1973 ...........DLB-7, 44
Beklemishev, Iurii Solomonvich
　(see Krymov, Iurii Solomonovich)
Belaney, Archibald Stansfeld (see Grey Owl)
Belasco, David 1853-1931 ............ DLB-7
Clarke Belford and Company ......... DLB-49
Belgian Luxembourg American Studies
　Association...................... Y-01
Belinsky, Vissarion Grigor'evich
　1811-1848 .................. DLB-198
Belitt, Ben 1911- ................... DLB-5
Belknap, Jeremy 1744-1798..........DLB-30, 37
Bell, Adrian 1901-1980................ DLB-191
Bell, Clive 1881-1964...............DS-10
Bell, Daniel 1919- ................. DLB-246

Bell, Gertrude Margaret Lowthian
    1868-1926 . . . . . . . . . . . . . . . . . . . . . . . DLB-174

Bell, James Madison 1826-1902. . . . . . . . . . DLB-50

Bell, Madison Smartt 1957- . . . . . . DLB-218, 278

    Tribute to Andrew Nelson Lytle. . . . . . . . Y-95

    Tribute to Peter Taylor. . . . . . . . . . . . . . Y-94

Bell, Marvin 1937- . . . . . . . . . . . . . . . . . . . .DLB-5

Bell, Millicent 1919- . . . . . . . . . . . . . . . . . . DLB-111

Bell, Quentin 1910-1996 . . . . . . . . . . . . . . .DLB-155

Bell, Vanessa 1879-1961. . . . . . . . . . . . . . . . DS-10

George Bell and Sons. . . . . . . . . . . . . . . . . . .DLB-106

Robert Bell [publishing house]. . . . . . . . . . . .DLB-49

Bellamy, Edward 1850-1898 . . . . . . . . . . . . . DLB-12

Bellamy, Joseph 1719-1790 . . . . . . . . . . . . . .DLB-31

John Bellamy [publishing house] . . . . . . . . DLB-170

*La Belle Assemblée* 1806-1837 . . . . . . . . . . . .DLB-110

Bellezza, Dario 1944-1996 . . . . . . . . . . . . . .DLB-128

Belli, Carlos Germán 1927- . . . . . . . . . . . .DLB-290

Belli, Gioconda 1948- . . . . . . . . . . . . . . . . .DLB-290

Belloc, Hilaire 1870-1953 . . . . DLB-19, 100, 141, 174

Belloc, Madame (see Parkes, Bessie Rayner)

Bellonci, Maria 1902-1986 . . . . . . . . . . . . . DLB-196

Bellow, Saul 1915- . . . . . . DLB-2, 28, 299; Y-82;
    DS-3; CDALB-1

    Tribute to Isaac Bashevis Singer . . . . . . . . Y-91

Belmont Productions . . . . . . . . . . . . . . . . . .DLB-46

Belov, Vasilii Ivanovich 1932- . . . . . . . .DLB-302

Bels, Alberts 1938- . . . . . . . . . . . . . . . . . .DLB-232

Belševica, Vizma 1931- . . .DLB-232; CDWLB-4

Bely, Andrei 1880-1934. . . . . . . . . . . . . . . .DLB-295

Bemelmans, Ludwig 1898-1962. . . . . . . . . . DLB-22

Bemis, Samuel Flagg 1891-1973 . . . . . . . . . . DLB-17

William Bemrose [publishing house] . . . . .DLB-106

Ben no Naishi 1228?-1271? . . . . . . . . . . . . .DLB-203

Benchley, Robert 1889-1945 . . . . . . . . . . . . .DLB-11

Bencúr, Matej (see Kukučin, Martin)

Benedetti, Mario 1920- . . . . . . . . . . . . . . .DLB-113

Benedict, Pinckney 1964- . . . . . . . . . . . . .DLB-244

Benedict, Ruth 1887-1948 . . . . . . . . . . . . . .DLB-246

Benedictus, David 1938- . . . . . . . . . . . . . . DLB-14

Benedikt Gröndal 1826-1907 . . . . . . . . . . . DLB-293

Benedikt, Michael 1935- . . . . . . . . . . . . . . . .DLB-5

Benediktov, Vladimir Grigor'evich
    1807-1873. . . . . . . . . . . . . . . . . . . . . . . DLB-205

Benét, Stephen Vincent
    1898-1943 . . . . . . . . . . . . . DLB-4, 48, 102, 249

    Stephen Vincent Benét Centenary . . . . . . Y-97

Benét, William Rose 1886-1950. . . . . . . . . . DLB-45

Benford, Gregory 1941- . . . . . . . . . . . . . . . . Y-82

Benítez, Sandra 1941- . . . . . . . . . . . . . . . .DLB-292

Benjamin, Park 1809-1864. . . . . DLB-3, 59, 73, 250

Benjamin, Peter (see Cunningham, Peter)

Benjamin, S. G. W. 1837-1914 . . . . . . . . . .DLB-189

Benjamin, Walter 1892-1940 . . . . . . . . . . . .DLB-242

Benlowes, Edward 1602-1676 . . . . . . . . . . .DLB-126

Benn, Gottfried 1886-1956 . . . . . . . . . . . . . .DLB-56

Benn Brothers Limited. . . . . . . . . . . . . . . . .DLB-106

Bennett, Arnold
    1867-1931 . . . .DLB-10, 34, 98, 135; CDBLB-5

    The Arnold Bennett Society . . . . . . . . . . . Y-98

Bennett, Charles 1899-1995. . . . . . . . . . . . . DLB-44

Bennett, Emerson 1822-1905. . . . . . . . . . . DLB-202

Bennett, Gwendolyn 1902-1981 . . . . . . . . . . DLB-51

Bennett, Hal 1930- . . . . . . . . . . . . . . . . . . DLB-33

Bennett, James Gordon 1795-1872. . . . . . . . DLB-43

Bennett, James Gordon, Jr. 1841-1918. . . . . DLB-23

Bennett, John 1865-1956 . . . . . . . . . . . . . . . DLB-42

Bennett, Louise 1919- . . . . DLB-117; CDWLB-3

Benni, Stefano 1947- . . . . . . . . . . . . . . . . .DLB-196

Benoit, Jacques 1941- . . . . . . . . . . . . . . . . .DLB-60

Benson, A. C. 1862-1925. . . . . . . . . . . . . . . DLB-98

Benson, E. F. 1867-1940. . . . . . . . . .DLB-135, 153

    The E. F. Benson Society . . . . . . . . . . . . . Y-98

    The Tilling Society . . . . . . . . . . . . . . . . . . Y-98

Benson, Jackson J. 1930- . . . . . . . . . . . . .DLB-111

Benson, Robert Hugh 1871-1914. . . . . . . . .DLB-153

Benson, Stella 1892-1933. . . . . . . . . . .DLB-36, 162

Bent, James Theodore 1852-1897 . . . . . . . .DLB-174

Bent, Mabel Virginia Anna ?-? . . . . . . . . . DLB-174

Bentham, Jeremy 1748-1832 . . . DLB-107, 158, 252

Bentley, E. C. 1875-1956 . . . . . . . . . . . . . . . DLB-70

Bentley, Phyllis 1894-1977. . . . . . . . . . . . . .DLB-191

Bentley, Richard 1662-1742 . . . . . . . . . . . .DLB-252

Richard Bentley [publishing house] . . . . . .DLB-106

Benton, Robert 1932- and
    Newman, David 1937- . . . . . . . . . . . . DLB-44

Benziger Brothers. . . . . . . . . . . . . . . . . . . . . .DLB-49

*Beowulf* circa 900-1000 or 790-825
    . . . . . . . . . . . . . . . . . . . . . . .DLB-146; CDBLB-1

Berent, Wacław 1873-1940 . . . . . . . . . . . .DLB-215

Beresford, Anne 1929- . . . . . . . . . . . . . . . DLB-40

Beresford, John Davys
    1873-1947 . . . . . . . . . . . DLB-162, 178, 197

    "Experiment in the Novel" (1929)
    [excerpt] . . . . . . . . . . . . . . . . . . . . .DLB-36

Beresford-Howe, Constance 1922- . . . . . . DLB-88

R. G. Berford Company . . . . . . . . . . . . . . . .DLB-49

Berg, Elizabeth 1948- . . . . . . . . . . . . . . . .DLB-292

Berg, Stephen 1934- . . . . . . . . . . . . . . . . . . DLB-5

Bergengruen, Werner 1892-1964 . . . . . . . . .DLB-56

Berger, John 1926- . . . . . . . . . . . . . DLB-14, 207

Berger, Meyer 1898-1959 . . . . . . . . . . . . . . .DLB-29

Berger, Thomas 1924- . . . . . . . . . . . DLB-2; Y-80

    A Statement by Thomas Berger . . . . . . . . Y-80

Bergman, Hjalmar 1883-1931 . . . . . . . . . . .DLB-259

Bergman, Ingmar 1918- . . . . . . . . . . . . . .DLB-257

Berkeley, Anthony 1893-1971 . . . . . . . . . . . DLB-77

Berkeley, George 1685-1753 . . . . DLB-31, 101, 252

The Berkley Publishing Corporation. . . . . . DLB-46

Berlin, Irving 1888-1989 . . . . . . . . . . . . . . .DLB-265

Berlin, Lucia 1936- . . . . . . . . . . . . . . . . . .DLB-130

Berman, Marshall 1940- . . . . . . . . . . . . . .DLB-246

Bernal, Vicente J. 1888-1915 . . . . . . . . . . . . DLB-82

Bernanos, Georges 1888-1948. . . . . . . . . . . .DLB-72

Bernard, Catherine 1663?-1712 . . . . . . . . .DLB-268

Bernard, Harry 1898-1979. . . . . . . . . . . . . . DLB-92

Bernard, John 1756-1828 . . . . . . . . . . . . . . .DLB-37

Bernard of Chartres circa 1060-1124?. . . .DLB-115

Bernard of Clairvaux 1090-1153 . . . . . . . . .DLB-208

Bernard, Richard 1568-1641/1642. . . . . . .DLB-281

Bernard Silvestris
    flourished circa 1130-1160 . . . . . . . . .DLB-208

Bernari, Carlo 1909-1992 . . . . . . . . . . . . . .DLB-177

Bernhard, Thomas
    1931-1989 . . . . . . . . . DLB-85, 124; CDWLB-2

Berniéres, Louis de 1954- . . . . . . . . . . . . DLB-271

Bernstein, Charles 1950- . . . . . . . . . . . . . DLB-169

Berriault, Gina 1926-1999 . . . . . . . . . . . . .DLB-130

Berrigan, Daniel 1921- . . . . . . . . . . . . . . . . DLB-5

Berrigan, Ted 1934-1983. . . . . . . . . . .DLB-5, 169

Berry, Wendell 1934- . . . . . . DLB-5, 6, 234, 275

Berryman, John 1914-1972 . . . .DLB-48; CDALB-1

Bersianik, Louky 1930- . . . . . . . . . . . . . . .DLB-60

Thomas Berthelet [publishing house] . . . . DLB-170

Berto, Giuseppe 1914-1978 . . . . . . . . . . . . .DLB-177

Bertocci, Peter Anthony 1910-1989 . . . . . . .DLB-279

Bertolucci, Attilio 1911-2000 . . . . . . . . . . . .DLB-128

Berton, Pierre 1920- . . . . . . . . . . . . . . . . . DLB-68

Bertrand, Louis "Aloysius" 1807-1841 . . . .DLB-217

Besant, Sir Walter 1836-1901 . . . . . DLB-135, 190

Bessa-Luís, Agustina 1922- . . . . . . . . . . . .DLB-287

Bessette, Gerard 1920- . . . . . . . . . . . . . . . DLB-53

Bessie, Alvah 1904-1985 . . . . . . . . . . . . . . . DLB-26

Bester, Alfred 1913-1987 . . . . . . . . . . . . . . . .DLB-8

Besterman, Theodore 1904-1976. . . . . . . . .DLB-201

Beston, Henry (Henry Beston Sheahan)
    1888-1968 . . . . . . . . . . . . . . . . . . . . . . . DLB-275

Best-Seller Lists
    An Assessment . . . . . . . . . . . . . . . . . . . . Y-84

    What's Really Wrong With
    Bestseller Lists . . . . . . . . . . . . . . . . . . Y-84

Bestuzhev, Aleksandr Aleksandrovich
    (Marlinsky) 1797-1837 . . . . . . . . . . . . .DLB-198

Bestuzhev, Nikolai Aleksandrovich
    1791-1855 . . . . . . . . . . . . . . . . . . . . . . .DLB-198

Betham-Edwards, Matilda Barbara
    (see Edwards, Matilda Barbara Betham-)

Betjeman, John
    1906-1984 . . . . . . . . DLB-20; Y-84; CDBLB-7

Betocchi, Carlo 1899-1986. . . . . . . . . . . . . .DLB-128

Bettarini, Mariella 1942- . . . . . . . . . . . . .DLB-128

Betts, Doris 1932- . . . . . . . . . . . . . DLB-218; Y-82

Beveridge, Albert J. 1862-1927 . . . . . . . . . . DLB-17

Beverley, Robert circa 1673-1722. . . . . .DLB-24, 30

Bevilacqua, Alberto 1934- . . . . . . . . . . . .DLB-196

Bevington, Louisa Sarah 1845-1895 . . . . .DLB-199

Beyle, Marie-Henri (see Stendhal)

Białoszewski, Miron 1922-1983 . . . . . . . .DLB-232

# Cumulative Index

Bianco, Margery Williams 1881-1944 ... DLB-160
Bibaud, Adèle 1854-1941 ............. DLB-92
Bibaud, Michel 1782-1857............. DLB-99
Bibliography
   Bibliographical and Textual Scholarship
     Since World War II ............. Y-89
   Center for Bibliographical Studies and
     Research at the University of
     California, Riverside ............ Y-91
   The Great Bibliographers Series ....... Y-93
   Primary Bibliography: A Retrospective ... Y-95
Bichsel, Peter 1935- .................. DLB-75
Bickerstaff, Isaac John 1733-circa 1808... DLB-89
Drexel Biddle [publishing house] ....... DLB-49
Bidermann, Jacob
   1577 or 1578-1639 ............... DLB-164
Bidwell, Walter Hilliard 1798-1881 ...... DLB-79
Biehl, Charlotta Dorothea 1731-1788 .... DLB-300
Bienek, Horst 1930-1990 ............... DLB-75
Bierbaum, Otto Julius 1865-1910 ........ DLB-66
Bierce, Ambrose 1842-1914?
   ...... DLB-11, 12, 23, 71, 74, 186; CDALB-3
Bigelow, William F. 1879-1966 ......... DLB-91
Biggle, Lloyd, Jr. 1923- ................ DLB-8
Bigiaretti, Libero 1905-1993 ............DLB-177
Bigland, Eileen 1898-1970.............. DLB-195
Biglow, Hosea (see Lowell, James Russell)
Bigongiari, Piero 1914-1997 ........... DLB-128
Bilenchi, Romano 1909-1989 ........... DLB-264
Billinger, Richard 1890-1965 ........... DLB-124
Billings, Hammatt 1818-1874 .......... DLB-188
Billings, John Shaw 1898-1975 ......... DLB-137
Billings, Josh (see Shaw, Henry Wheeler)
Binding, Rudolf G. 1867-1938 ......... DLB-66
Bingay, Malcolm 1884-1953 ........... DLB-241
Bingham, Caleb 1757-1817 ............ DLB-42
Bingham, George Barry 1906-1988 ..... DLB-127
Bingham, Sallie 1937- ................. DLB-234
William Bingley [publishing house] .... DLB-154
Binyon, Laurence 1869-1943 ........... DLB-19
*Biographia Brittanica* ................... DLB-142
Biography
   Biographical Documents .......... Y-84, 85
   A Celebration of Literary Biography..... Y-98
   Conference on Modern Biography ...... Y-85
   The Cult of Biography
     Excerpts from the Second Folio Debate:
     "Biographies are generally a disease of
     English Literature" ................ Y-86
   New Approaches to Biography: Challenges
     from Critical Theory, USC Conference
     on Literary Studies, 1990 .......... Y-90
   "The New Biography," by Virginia Woolf,
     *New York Herald Tribune*,
     30 October 1927 ................. DLB-149
   "The Practice of Biography," in *The English
     Sense of Humour and Other Essays*, by
     Harold Nicolson ................. DLB-149
   "Principles of Biography," in *Elizabethan
     and Other Essays*, by Sidney Lee .. DLB-149

Remarks at the Opening of "The Biographical
   Part of Literature" Exhibition, by
   William R. Cagle................. Y-98
Survey of Literary Biographies ......... Y-00
A Transit of Poets and Others: American
   Biography in 1982................ Y-82
The Year in Literary
   Biography .................... Y-83–01
Biography, The Practice of:
   An Interview with B. L. Reid....... Y-83
   An Interview with David Herbert Donald .. Y-87
   An Interview with Humphrey Carpenter.... Y-84
   An Interview with Joan Mellen ...... Y-94
   An Interview with John Caldwell Guilds.... Y-92
   An Interview with William Manchester... Y-85
John Bioren [publishing house]......... DLB-49
Bioy Casares, Adolfo 1914-1999 ....... DLB-113
Bird, Isabella Lucy 1831-1904 ......... DLB-166
Bird, Robert Montgomery 1806-1854 ... DLB-202
Bird, William 1888-1963 .......... DLB-4; DS-15
   The Cost of the *Cantos:* William Bird
     to Ezra Pound .................. Y-01
Birken, Sigmund von 1626-1681 ....... DLB-164
Birney, Earle 1904-1995................ DLB-88
Birrell, Augustine 1850-1933 .......... DLB-98
Bisher, Furman 1918- .................DLB-171
Bishop, Elizabeth
   1911-1979......... DLB-5, 169; CDALB-6
   The Elizabeth Bishop Society........... Y-01
Bishop, John Peale 1892-1944 ...... DLB-4, 9, 45
Bismarck, Otto von 1815-1898......... DLB-129
Bisset, Robert 1759-1805 ............. DLB-142
Bissett, Bill 1939- ..................... DLB-53
Bitov, Andrei Georgievich 1937- ...... DLB-302
Bitzius, Albert (see Gotthelf, Jeremias)
Bjørnboe, Jens 1920-1976 ............. DLB-297
Bjørnvig, Thorkild 1918- .............. DLB-214
Black, David (D. M.) 1941- .......... DLB-40
Black, Gavin (Oswald Morris Wynd)
   1913-1998 ......................DLB-276
Black, Lionel (Dudley Barker)
   1910-1980 ......................DLB-276
Black, Winifred 1863-1936............. DLB-25
Walter J. Black [publishing house] ....... DLB-46
Blackamore, Arthur 1679-? ........ DLB-24, 39
Blackburn, Alexander L. 1929- ......... Y-85
Blackburn, John 1923-1993 .......... DLB-261
Blackburn, Paul 1926-1971.........DLB-16; Y-81
Blackburn, Thomas 1916-1977......... DLB-27
Blacker, Terence 1948- ...............DLB-271
Blackmore, R. D. 1825-1900 .......... DLB-18
Blackmore, Sir Richard 1654-1729 ..... DLB-131
Blackmur, R. P. 1904-1965............ DLB-63
Basil Blackwell, Publisher............ DLB-106
Blackwood, Algernon Henry
   1869-1951 ...........DLB-153, 156, 178
Blackwood, Caroline 1931-1996......DLB-14, 207

William Blackwood and Sons, Ltd...... DLB-154
*Blackwood's Edinburgh Magazine*
   1817-1980................... DLB-110
Blades, William 1824-1890............ DLB-184
Blaga, Lucian 1895-1961 ............. DLB-220
Blagden, Isabella 1817?-1873 ......... DLB-199
Blair, Eric Arthur (see Orwell, George)
Blair, Francis Preston 1791-1876......... DLB-43
Blair, Hugh
   *Lectures on Rhetoric and Belles Lettres* (1783),
     [excerpts] ................... DLB-31
Blair, James circa 1655-1743 ......... DLB-24
Blair, John Durburrow 1759-1823 ..... DLB-37
Blais, Marie-Claire 1939- ............. DLB-53
Blaise, Clark 1940- ................... DLB-53
Blake, George 1893-1961 ............. DLB-191
Blake, Lillie Devereux 1833-1913.... DLB-202, 221
Blake, Nicholas (C. Day Lewis)
   1904-1972 ..................... DLB-77
Blake, William
   1757-1827 ...... DLB-93, 154, 163; CDBLB-3
The Blakiston Company .............. DLB-49
Blanchard, Stephen 1950- ............ DLB-267
Blanchot, Maurice 1907-2003 ...... DLB-72, 296
Blanckenburg, Christian Friedrich von
   1744-1796...................... DLB-94
Blandiana, Ana 1942- ..... DLB-232; CDWLB-4
Blanshard, Brand 1892-1987 ...........DLB-279
Blaser, Robin 1925- .................. DLB-165
Blaumanis, Rūdolfs 1863-1908......... DLB-220
Bleasdale, Alan 1946- ................ DLB-245
Bledsoe, Albert Taylor
   1809-1877....................DLB-3, 79, 248
Bleecker, Ann Eliza 1752-1783 ....... DLB-200
Blelock and Company ............... DLB-49
Blennerhassett, Margaret Agnew
   1773-1842 ...................... DLB-99
Geoffrey Bles [publishing house] ....... DLB-112
Blessington, Marguerite, Countess of
   1789-1849...................... DLB-166
Blew, Mary Clearman 1939- ......... DLB-256
Blicher, Steen Steensen 1782-1848 ...... DLB-300
The Blickling Homilies circa 971 ...... DLB-146
Blind, Mathilde 1841-1896............ DLB-199
Blish, James 1921-1975 ................ DLB-8
E. Bliss and E. White
   [publishing house] ................ DLB-49
Bliven, Bruce 1889-1977 ..............DLB-137
Blixen, Karen 1885-1962 ............. DLB-214
Bloch, Ernst 1885-1977 .............. DLB-296
Bloch, Robert 1917-1994.............. DLB-44
   Tribute to John D. MacDonald ........ Y-86
Block, Lawrence 1938- ............... DLB-226
Block, Rudolph (see Lessing, Bruno)
Blok, Aleksandr Aleksandrovich
   1880-1921 ..................... DLB-295
Blondal, Patricia 1926-1959 ........... DLB-88
Bloom, Harold 1930- ................. DLB-67

| | | |
|---|---|---|
| Bloomer, Amelia 1818-1894 | DLB-79 | |
| Bloomfield, Robert 1766-1823 | DLB-93 | |
| Bloomsbury Group | DS-10 | |
| The *Dreadnought* Hoax | DS-10 | |
| Blotner, Joseph 1923- | DLB-111 | |
| Blount, Thomas 1618?-1679 | DLB-236 | |
| Bloy, Léon 1846-1917 | DLB-123 | |
| Blume, Judy 1938- | DLB-52 | |
| Tribute to Theodor Seuss Geisel | Y-91 | |
| Blunck, Hans Friedrich 1888-1961 | DLB-66 | |
| Blunden, Edmund 1896-1974 | DLB-20, 100, 155 | |
| Blundeville, Thomas 1522?-1606 | DLB-236 | |
| Blunt, Lady Anne Isabella Noel 1837-1917 | DLB-174 | |
| Blunt, Wilfrid Scawen 1840-1922 | DLB-19, 174 | |
| Bly, Nellie (see Cochrane, Elizabeth) | | |
| Bly, Robert 1926- | DLB-5 | |
| Blyton, Enid 1897-1968 | DLB-160 | |
| Boaden, James 1762-1839 | DLB-89 | |
| Boas, Frederick S. 1862-1957 | DLB-149 | |
| The Bobbs-Merrill Company | DLB-46, 291 | |
| The Bobbs-Merrill Archive at the Lilly Library, Indiana University | Y-90 | |
| Boborykin, Petr Dmitrievich 1836-1921 | DLB-238 | |
| Bobrov, Semen Sergeevich 1763?-1810 | DLB-150 | |
| Bobrowski, Johannes 1917-1965 | DLB-75 | |
| Bocage, Manuel Maria Barbosa du 1765-1805 | DLB-287 | |
| Bodenheim, Maxwell 1892-1954 | DLB-9, 45 | |
| Bodenstedt, Friedrich von 1819-1892 | DLB-129 | |
| Bodini, Vittorio 1914-1970 | DLB-128 | |
| Bodkin, M. McDonnell 1850-1933 | DLB-70 | |
| Bodley, Sir Thomas 1545-1613 | DLB-213 | |
| Bodley Head | DLB-112 | |
| Bodmer, Johann Jakob 1698-1783 | DLB-97 | |
| Bodmershof, Imma von 1895-1982 | DLB-85 | |
| Bodsworth, Fred 1918- | DLB-68 | |
| Böðvar Guðmundsson 1939- | DLB-293 | |
| Boehm, Sydney 1908- | DLB-44 | |
| Boer, Charles 1939- | DLB-5 | |
| Boethius circa 480-circa 524 | DLB-115 | |
| Boethius of Dacia circa 1240-? | DLB-115 | |
| Bogan, Louise 1897-1970 | DLB-45, 169 | |
| Bogarde, Dirk 1921-1999 | DLB-14 | |
| Bogdanov, Aleksandr Aleksandrovich 1873-1928 | DLB-295 | |
| Bogdanovich, Ippolit Fedorovich circa 1743-1803 | DLB-150 | |
| David Bogue [publishing house] | DLB-106 | |
| Bohjalian, Chris 1960- | DLB-292 | |
| Böhme, Jakob 1575-1624 | DLB-164 | |
| H. G. Bohn [publishing house] | DLB-106 | |
| Bohse, August 1661-1742 | DLB-168 | |
| Boie, Heinrich Christian 1744-1806 | DLB-94 | |
| Boileau-Despréaux, Nicolas 1636-1711 | DLB-268 | |
| Bok, Edward W. 1863-1930 | DLB-91; DS-16 | |
| Boland, Eavan 1944- | DLB-40 | |
| Boldrewood, Rolf (Thomas Alexander Browne) 1826?-1915 | DLB-230 | |
| Bolingbroke, Henry St. John, Viscount 1678-1751 | DLB-101 | |
| Böll, Heinrich 1917-1985 | DLB-69; Y-85; CDWLB-2 | |
| Bolling, Robert 1738-1775 | DLB-31 | |
| Bolotov, Andrei Timofeevich 1738-1833 | DLB-150 | |
| Bolt, Carol 1941- | DLB-60 | |
| Bolt, Robert 1924-1995 | DLB-13, 233 | |
| Bolton, Herbert E. 1870-1953 | DLB-17 | |
| Bonaventura | DLB-90 | |
| Bonaventure circa 1217-1274 | DLB-115 | |
| Bonaviri, Giuseppe 1924- | DLB-177 | |
| Bond, Edward 1934- | DLB-13 | |
| Bond, Michael 1926- | DLB-161 | |
| Bondarev, Iurii Vasil'evich 1924- | DLB-302 | |
| Albert and Charles Boni [publishing house] | DLB-46 | |
| Boni and Liveright | DLB-46 | |
| Bonnefoy, Yves 1923- | DLB-258 | |
| Bonner, Marita 1899-1971 | DLB-228 | |
| Bonner, Paul Hyde 1893-1968 | DS-17 | |
| Bonner, Sherwood (see McDowell, Katharine Sherwood Bonner) | | |
| Robert Bonner's Sons | DLB-49 | |
| Bonnin, Gertrude Simmons (see Zitkala-Ša) | | |
| Bonsanti, Alessandro 1904-1984 | DLB-177 | |
| Bontempelli, Massimo 1878-1960 | DLB-264 | |
| Bontemps, Arna 1902-1973 | DLB-48, 51 | |
| *The Book Buyer* 1867-1880, 1884-1918, 1935-1938 | DS-13 | |
| The Book League of America | DLB-46 | |
| Book Reviewing | | |
| The American Book Review: A Sketch | Y-92 | |
| Book Reviewing and the Literary Scene | Y-96, 97 | |
| Book Reviewing in America | Y-87–94 | |
| Book Reviewing in America and the Literary Scene | Y-95 | |
| Book Reviewing in Texas | Y-94 | |
| Book Reviews in Glossy Magazines | Y-95 | |
| Do They or Don't They? Writers Reading Book Reviews | Y-01 | |
| The Most Powerful Book Review in America [*New York Times Book Review*] | Y-82 | |
| Some Surprises and Universal Truths | Y-92 | |
| The Year in Book Reviewing and the Literary Situation | Y-98 | |
| Book Supply Company | DLB-49 | |
| The Book Trade History Group | Y-93 | |
| The Booker Prize | Y-96–98 | |
| Address by Anthony Thwaite, Chairman of the Booker Prize Judges | | |
| Comments from Former Booker Prize Winners | Y-86 | |
| Boorde, Andrew circa 1490-1549 | DLB-136 | |
| Boorstin, Daniel J. 1914- | DLB-17 | |
| Tribute to Archibald MacLeish | Y-82 | |
| Tribute to Charles Scribner Jr | Y-95 | |
| Booth, Franklin 1874-1948 | DLB-188 | |
| Booth, Mary L. 1831-1889 | DLB-79 | |
| Booth, Philip 1925- | Y-82 | |
| Booth, Wayne C. 1921- | DLB-67 | |
| Booth, William 1829-1912 | DLB-190 | |
| Bor, Josef 1906-1979 | DLB-299 | |
| Borchardt, Rudolf 1877-1945 | DLB-66 | |
| Borchert, Wolfgang 1921-1947 | DLB-69, 124 | |
| Bording, Anders 1619-1677 | DLB-300 | |
| Borel, Pétrus 1809-1859 | DLB-119 | |
| Borgen, Johan 1902-1979 | DLB-297 | |
| Borges, Jorge Luis 1899-1986 | DLB-113, 283; Y-86; CDWLB-3 | |
| The Poetry of Jorge Luis Borges | Y-86 | |
| A Personal Tribute | Y-86 | |
| Borgese, Giuseppe Antonio 1882-1952 | DLB-264 | |
| Börne, Ludwig 1786-1837 | DLB-90 | |
| Bornstein, Miriam 1950- | DLB-209 | |
| Borowski, Tadeusz 1922-1951 | DLB-215; CDWLB-4 | |
| Borrow, George 1803-1881 | DLB-21, 55, 166 | |
| Bosanquet, Bernard 1848-1923 | DLB-262 | |
| Bosch, Juan 1909-2001 | DLB-145 | |
| Bosco, Henri 1888-1976 | DLB-72 | |
| Bosco, Monique 1927- | DLB-53 | |
| Bosman, Herman Charles 1905-1951 | DLB-225 | |
| Bossuet, Jacques-Bénigne 1627-1704 | DLB-268 | |
| Bostic, Joe 1908-1988 | DLB-241 | |
| Boston, Lucy M. 1892-1990 | DLB-161 | |
| *Boston Quarterly Review* | DLB-1 | |
| Boston University | | |
| Editorial Institute at Boston University | Y-00 | |
| Special Collections at Boston University | Y-99 | |
| Boswell, James 1740-1795 | DLB-104, 142; CDBLB-2 | |
| Boswell, Robert 1953- | DLB-234 | |
| Bosworth, David | Y-82 | |
| Excerpt from "Excerpts from a Report of the Commission," in *The Death of Descartes* | Y-82 | |
| Bote, Hermann circa 1460-circa 1520 | DLB-179 | |
| Botev, Khristo 1847-1876 | DLB-147 | |
| Botkin, Vasilii Petrovich 1811-1869 | DLB-277 | |
| Botta, Anne C. Lynch 1815-1891 | DLB-3, 250 | |
| Botto, Ján (see Krasko, Ivan) | | |
| Bottome, Phyllis 1882-1963 | DLB-197 | |
| Bottomley, Gordon 1874-1948 | DLB-10 | |
| Bottoms, David 1949- | DLB-120; Y-83 | |
| Tribute to James Dickey | Y-97 | |
| Bottrall, Ronald 1906- | DLB-20 | |

## Cumulative Index

Bouchardy, Joseph 1810-1870.......... DLB-192
Boucher, Anthony 1911-1968............ DLB-8
Boucher, Jonathan 1738-1804........... DLB-31
Boucher de Boucherville, Georges
   1814-1894................... DLB-99
Boudreau, Daniel (see Coste, Donat)
Bouhours, Dominique 1628-1702....... DLB-268
Bourassa, Napoléon 1827-1916......... DLB-99
Bourget, Paul 1852-1935 ............. DLB-123
Bourinot, John George 1837-1902....... DLB-99
Bourjaily, Vance 1922- ........... DLB-2, 143
Bourne, Edward Gaylord 1860-1908..... DLB-47
Bourne, Randolph 1886-1918........... DLB-63
Bousoño, Carlos 1923- ............ DLB-108
Bousquet, Joë 1897-1950.............. DLB-72
Bova, Ben 1932- ....................... Y-81
Bovard, Oliver K. 1872-1945........... DLB-25
Bove, Emmanuel 1898-1945............. DLB-72
Bowen, Elizabeth
   1899-1973......... DLB-15, 162; CDBLB-7
Bowen, Francis 1811-1890 ....... DLB-1, 59, 235
Bowen, John 1924- ..................... DLB-13
Bowen, Marjorie 1886-1952 ........... DLB-153
Bowen-Merrill Company ............... DLB-49
Bowering, George 1935- ............... DLB-53
Bowers, Bathsheba 1671-1718.......... DLB-200
Bowers, Claude G. 1878-1958 .......... DLB-17
Bowers, Edgar 1924-2000............... DLB-5
Bowers, Fredson Thayer
   1905-1991 ............ DLB-140; Y-91
   The Editorial Style of Fredson Bowers ... Y-91
   Fredson Bowers and
     Studies in Bibliography ........... Y-91
   Fredson Bowers and the Cambridge
     Beaumont and Fletcher .......... Y-91
   Fredson Bowers as Critic of Renaissance
     Dramatic Literature.............. Y-91
   Fredson Bowers as Music Critic......... Y-91
   Fredson Bowers, Master Teacher ...... Y-91
   An Interview [on Nabokov] ........... Y-80
   Working with Fredson Bowers ........ Y-91
Bowles, Paul 1910-1999 ...... DLB-5, 6, 218; Y-99
Bowles, Samuel, III 1826-1878 .......... DLB-43
Bowles, William Lisle 1762-1850 ........ DLB-93
Bowman, Louise Morey 1882-1944 ...... DLB-68
Bowne, Borden Parker 1847-1919 ...... DLB-270
Boyd, James 1888-1944 .......... DLB-9; DS-16
Boyd, John 1919- ..................... DLB-8
Boyd, Martin 1893-1972 .............. DLB-260
Boyd, Thomas 1898-1935 ........ DLB-9; DS-16
Boyd, William 1952- ................. DLB-231
Boye, Karin 1900-1941............... DLB-259
Boyesen, Hjalmar Hjorth
   1848-1895 ............. DLB-12, 71; DS-13
Boylan, Clare 1948- ................. DLB-267
Boyle, Kay 1902-1992    DLB-4, 9, 48, 86; DS-15;
   .................................... Y-93

Boyle, Roger, Earl of Orrery 1621-1679... DLB-80
Boyle, T. Coraghessan
   1948- ............... DLB-218, 278; Y-86
Božić, Mirko 1919- ................. DLB-181
Brackenbury, Alison 1953- ........... DLB-40
Brackenridge, Hugh Henry
   1748-1816................... DLB-11, 37
   The Rising Glory of America........ DLB-37
Brackett, Charles 1892-1969........... DLB-26
Brackett, Leigh 1915-1978 ........... DLB-8, 26
John Bradburn [publishing house]...... DLB-49
Bradbury, Malcolm 1932-2000....... DLB-14, 207
Bradbury, Ray 1920- ..... DLB-2, 8; CDALB-6
Bradbury and Evans.................. DLB-106
Braddon, Mary Elizabeth
   1835-1915 ............. DLB-18, 70, 156
Bradford, Andrew 1686-1742 ...... DLB-43, 73
Bradford, Gamaliel 1863-1932 ......... DLB-17
Bradford, John 1749-1830............. DLB-43
Bradford, Roark 1896-1948 ........... DLB-86
Bradford, William 1590-1657...... DLB-24, 30
Bradford, William, III 1719-1791 .... DLB-43, 73
Bradlaugh, Charles 1833-1891.......... DLB-57
Bradley, David 1950- ................. DLB-33
Bradley, F. H. 1846-1924 ............. DLB-262
Bradley, Katherine Harris (see Field, Michael)
Bradley, Marion Zimmer 1930-1999 ..... DLB-8
Bradley, William Aspenwall 1878-1939 .... DLB-4
Ira Bradley and Company ............. DLB-49
J. W. Bradley and Company .......... DLB-49
Bradshaw, Henry 1831-1886 .......... DLB-184
Bradstreet, Anne
   1612 or 1613-1672 ....... DLB-24; CDALB-2
Bradūnas, Kazys 1917- ............. DLB-220
Bradwardine, Thomas circa 1295-1349 .. DLB-115
Brady, Frank 1924-1986............... DLB-111
Frederic A. Brady [publishing house] ..... DLB-49
Bragg, Melvyn 1939- ............ DLB-14, 271
Brahe, Tycho 1546-1601 ............. DLB-300
Charles H. Brainard [publishing house] ... DLB-49
Braine, John 1922-1986 . DLB-15; Y-86; CDBLB-7
Braithwait, Richard 1588-1673 ......... DLB-151
Braithwaite, William Stanley
   1878-1962................... DLB-50, 54
Bräker, Ulrich 1735-1798 ............. DLB-94
Bramah, Ernest 1868-1942............. DLB-70
Branagan, Thomas 1774-1843 ......... DLB-37
Brancati, Vitaliano 1907-1954......... DLB-264
Branch, William Blackwell 1927- ...... DLB-76
Brand, Christianna 1907-1988 .........DLB-276
Brand, Max (see Faust, Frederick Schiller)
Brandão, Raul 1867-1930 ............ DLB-287
Branden Press...................... DLB-46
Brandes, Georg 1842-1927............ DLB-300
Branner, H.C. 1903-1966............. DLB-214
Brant, Sebastian 1457-1521............DLB-179

Brassey, Lady Annie (Allnutt)
   1839-1887 .................. DLB-166
Brathwaite, Edward Kamau
   1930- ............ DLB-125; CDWLB-3
Brault, Jacques 1933- ............... DLB-53
Braun, Matt 1932- .................. DLB-212
Braun, Volker 1939- ............. DLB-75, 124
Brautigan, Richard
   1935-1984 ........ DLB-2, 5, 206; Y-80, 84
Braxton, Joanne M. 1950- ........... DLB-41
Bray, Anne Eliza 1790-1883 .......... DLB-116
Bray, Thomas 1656-1730 ............. DLB-24
Brazdžionis, Bernardas 1907- ........ DLB-220
George Braziller [publishing house] ..... DLB-46
The Bread Loaf Writers' Conference 1983 ... Y-84
Breasted, James Henry 1865-1935 ...... DLB-47
Brecht, Bertolt
   1898-1956 ........ DLB-56, 124; CDWLB-2
Bredel, Willi 1901-1964 ............. DLB-56
Bregendahl, Marie 1867-1940......... DLB-214
Breitinger, Johann Jakob 1701-1776 .... DLB-97
Brekke, Paal 1923-1993 .............. DLB-297
Bremser, Bonnie 1939- .............. DLB-16
Bremser, Ray 1934-1998 .............. DLB-16
Brennan, Christopher 1870-1932 ...... DLB-230
Brentano, Bernard von 1901-1964 ...... DLB-56
Brentano, Clemens 1778-1842 .......... DLB-90
Brentano, Franz 1838-1917............ DLB-296
Brentano's............................ DLB-49
Brenton, Howard 1942- .............. DLB-13
Breslin, Jimmy 1929-1996 ............ DLB-185
Breton, André 1896-1966............ DLB-65, 258
Breton, Nicholas circa 1555-circa 1626... DLB-136
The Breton Lays
   1300-early fifteenth century ........ DLB-146
Brett, Simon 1945- ................DLB-276
Brewer, Luther A. 1858-1933 .........DLB-187
Brewer, Warren and Putnam .......... DLB-46
Brewster, Elizabeth 1922- ........... DLB-60
Breytenbach, Breyten 1939- ......... DLB-225
Bridge, Ann (Lady Mary Dolling Sanders
   O'Malley) 1889-1974 ........... DLB-191
Bridge, Horatio 1806-1893 ........... DLB-183
Bridgers, Sue Ellen 1942- ........... DLB-52
Bridges, Robert
   1844-1930 ......... DLB-19, 98; CDBLB-5
The Bridgewater Library ............. DLB-213
Bridie, James 1888-1951.............. DLB-10
Brieux, Eugene 1858-1932 ........... DLB-192
Brigadere, Anna
   1861-1933 ........... DLB-220; CDWLB-4
Briggs, Charles Frederick
   1804-1877.................... DLB-3, 250
Brighouse, Harold 1882-1958.......... DLB-10
Bright, Mary Chavelita Dunne
   (see Egerton, George)
Brightman, Edgar Sheffield 1884-1953....DLB-270

B. J. Brimmer Company . . . . . . . . . . . . . .DLB-46
Brines, Francisco 1932- . . . . . . . . . . . . .DLB-134
Brink, André 1935- . . . . . . . . . . . . . . . .DLB-225
Brinley, George, Jr. 1817-1875 . . . . . . . . . .DLB-140
Brinnin, John Malcolm 1916-1998. . . . . . . . .DLB-48
Brisbane, Albert 1809-1890 . . . . . . . . . .DLB-3, 250
Brisbane, Arthur 1864-1936. . . . . . . . . . . . .DLB-25
British Academy. . . . . . . . . . . . . . . . . . .DLB-112
*The British Critic* 1793-1843 . . . . . . . . . . .DLB-110
British Library
    The American Trust for the
        British Library . . . . . . . . . . . . . . . . Y-96
    The British Library and the Regular
        Readers' Group . . . . . . . . . . . . . . . Y-91
    Building the New British Library
        at St Pancras . . . . . . . . . . . . . . . . . . Y-94
British Literary Prizes . . . . . . . . . .DLB-207; Y-98
British Literature
    The "Angry Young Men" . . . . . . . . . .DLB-15
    Author-Printers, 1476-1599 . . . . . . . .DLB-167
    The Comic Tradition Continued . . . . .DLB-15
    Documents on Sixteenth-Century
        Literature . . . . . . . . . . . . . DLB-167, 172
    *Eikon Basilike* 1649 . . . . . . . . . . . . . .DLB-151
    Letter from London . . . . . . . . . . . . . . . .Y-96
    *A Mirror for Magistrates* . . . . . . . . . . . .DLB-167
    "Modern English Prose" (1876),
        by George Saintsbury . . . . . . . . . . .DLB-57
    Sex, Class, Politics, and Religion [in the
        British Novel, 1930-1959] . . . . . . . .DLB-15
    Victorians on Rhetoric and Prose
        Style . . . . . . . . . . . . . . . . . . . . . . .DLB-57
    The Year in British Fiction . . . . . . . . .Y-99–01
    "You've Never Had It So Good," Gusted
        by "Winds of Change": British
        Fiction in the 1950s, 1960s,
        and After . . . . . . . . . . . . . . . . . . .DLB-14
British Literature, Old and Middle English
    Anglo-Norman Literature in the
        Development of Middle English
        Literature . . . . . . . . . . . . . . . . . .DLB-146
    The *Alliterative Morte Arthure and the*
        *Stanzaic Morte Arthur*
        circa 1350-1400. . . . . . . . . . . . . .DLB-146
    *Ancrene Riwle* circa 1200-1225 . . . . . . .DLB-146
    The *Anglo-Saxon Chronicle* circa
        890-1154 . . . . . . . . . . . . . . . . . .DLB-146
    *The Battle of Maldon* circa 1000 . . . . . .DLB-146
    *Beowulf* circa 900-1000 or
        790-825 . . . . . . . . . . DLB-146; CDBLB-1
    The Blickling Homilies circa 971. . . . .DLB-146
    The Breton Lays
        1300-early fifteenth century . . . . .DLB-146
    *The Castle of Perseverance*
        circa 1400-1425. . . . . . . . . . . . . .DLB-146
    The Celtic Background to Medieval
        English Literature . . . . . . . . . . . .DLB-146
    The Chester Plays circa 1505-1532;
        revisions until 1575 . . . . . . . . . . .DLB-146
    *Cursor Mundi* circa 1300 . . . . . . . . . .DLB-146
    The English Language: 410
        to 1500 . . . . . . . . . . . . . . . . . . .DLB-146

    The Germanic Epic and Old English
        Heroic Poetry: *Widsith, Waldere,*
        and *The Fight at Finnsburg* . . . . . .DLB-146
    *Judith* circa 930 . . . . . . . . . . . . . . . .DLB-146
    The Matter of England 1240-1400 . . .DLB-146
    The Matter of Rome early twelfth to
        late fifteenth centuries . . . . . . . . . .DLB-146
    Middle English Literature:
        An Introduction . . . . . . . . . . . . . .DLB-146
    The Middle English Lyric . . . . . . . . . .DLB-146
    Morality Plays: *Mankind* circa 1450-1500
        and *Everyman* circa 1500 . . . . . . .DLB-146
    N-Town Plays circa 1468 to early
        sixteenth century . . . . . . . . . . . . .DLB-146
    Old English Literature:
        An Introduction . . . . . . . . . . . . . .DLB-146
    Old English Riddles
        eighth to tenth centuries . . . . . . . .DLB-146
    *The Owl and the Nightingale*
        circa 1189-1199 . . . . . . . . . . . . . .DLB-146
    *The Paston Letters* 1422-1509 . . . . . . . .DLB-146
    *The Seafarer* circa 970 . . . . . . . . . . . .DLB-146
    The *South English Legendary* circa
        thirteenth to fifteenth centuries . . . .DLB-146
*The British Review and London Critical*
    *Journal* 1811-1825 . . . . . . . . . . . . . . .DLB-110
Brito, Aristeo 1942- . . . . . . . . . . . . . . . .DLB-122
Brittain, Vera 1893-1970 . . . . . . . . . . . .DLB-191
Briusov, Valerii Iakovlevich 1873-1924 . . .DLB-295
Brizeux, Auguste 1803-1858 . . . . . . . . . .DLB-217
Broadway Publishing Company . . . . . . . . .DLB-46
Broch, Hermann
    1886-1951 . . . . . . . . DLB-85, 124; CDWLB-2
Brochu, André 1942- . . . . . . . . . . . . . . .DLB-53
Brock, Edwin 1927-1997 . . . . . . . . . . . . .DLB-40
Brockes, Barthold Heinrich 1680-1747 . . .DLB-168
Brod, Max 1884-1968 . . . . . . . . . . . . . . .DLB-81
Brodber, Erna 1940- . . . . . . . . . . . . . . .DLB-157
Brodhead, John R. 1814-1873 . . . . . . . . . .DLB-30
Brodkey, Harold 1930-1996 . . . . . . . . . .DLB-130
Brodsky, Joseph (Iosif Aleksandrovich
    Brodsky) 1940-1996 . . . . . . . .DLB-285; Y-87
    Nobel Lecture 1987 . . . . . . . . . . . . . . .Y-87
Brodsky, Michael 1948- . . . . . . . . . . . . .DLB-244
Broeg, Bob 1918- . . . . . . . . . . . . . . . . .DLB-171
Brøgger, Suzanne 1944- . . . . . . . . . . . .DLB-214
Brome, Richard circa 1590-1652 . . . . . . . .DLB-58
Brome, Vincent 1910- . . . . . . . . . . . . . .DLB-155
Bromfield, Louis 1896-1956 . . . . . . . . .DLB-4, 9, 86
Bromige, David 1933- . . . . . . . . . . . . . .DLB-193
Broner, E. M. 1930- . . . . . . . . . . . . . . . .DLB-28
    Tribute to Bernard Malamud . . . . . . . . .Y-86
Bronk, William 1918-1999 . . . . . . . . . . .DLB-165
Bronnen, Arnolt 1895-1959 . . . . . . . . . . .DLB-124
Brontë, Anne 1820-1849 . . . . . . . . . .DLB-21, 199
Brontë, Charlotte
    1816-1855 . . . . . .DLB-21, 159, 199; CDBLB-4
Brontë, Emily
    1818-1848 . . . . . .DLB-21, 32, 199; CDBLB-4

The Brontë Society . . . . . . . . . . . . . . . . . .Y-98
Brook, Stephen 1947- . . . . . . . . . . . . . .DLB-204
Brook Farm 1841-1847 . . . . . . . .DLB-1; 223; DS-5
Brooke, Frances 1724-1789 . . . . . . . . . .DLB-39, 99
Brooke, Henry 1703?-1783 . . . . . . . . . . . .DLB-39
Brooke, L. Leslie 1862-1940 . . . . . . . . . .DLB-141
Brooke, Margaret, Ranee of Sarawak
    1849-1936 . . . . . . . . . . . . . . . . . . .DLB-174
Brooke, Rupert
    1887-1915 . . . . . . . . .DLB-19, 216; CDBLB-6
    The Friends of the Dymock Poets . . . . . .Y-00
Brooker, Bertram 1888-1955 . . . . . . . . . . .DLB-88
Brooke-Rose, Christine 1923- . . . . . . .DLB-14, 231
Brookner, Anita 1928- . . . . . . . . . .DLB-194; Y-87
Brooks, Charles Timothy 1813-1883 . . .DLB-1, 243
Brooks, Cleanth 1906-1994 . . . . . . . .DLB-63; Y-94
    Tribute to Katherine Anne Porter . . . . . .Y-80
    Tribute to Walker Percy . . . . . . . . . . . .Y-90
Brooks, Gwendolyn
    1917-2000 . . . . . . . .DLB-5, 76, 165; CDALB-1
    Tribute to Julian Mayfield. . . . . . . . . . . .Y-84
Brooks, Jeremy 1926- . . . . . . . . . . . . . . .DLB-14
Brooks, Mel 1926- . . . . . . . . . . . . . . . . .DLB-26
Brooks, Noah 1830-1903 . . . . . . . . .DLB-42; DS-13
Brooks, Richard 1912-1992 . . . . . . . . . . . .DLB-44
Brooks, Van Wyck 1886-1963 . . .DLB-45, 63, 103
Brophy, Brigid 1929-1995 . . . . . . .DLB-14, 70, 271
Brophy, John 1899-1965 . . . . . . . . . . . . .DLB-191
Brorson, Hans Adolph 1694-1764 . . . . . . .DLB-300
Brossard, Chandler 1922-1993 . . . . . . . . . .DLB-16
Brossard, Nicole 1943- . . . . . . . . . . . . . .DLB-53
Broster, Dorothy Kathleen 1877-1950 . . . .DLB-160
Brother Antoninus (see Everson, William)
Brotherton, Lord 1856-1930 . . . . . . . . . .DLB-184
Brougham, John 1810-1880 . . . . . . . . . . . .DLB-11
Brougham and Vaux, Henry Peter
    Brougham, Baron 1778-1868 . . . .DLB-110, 158
Broughton, James 1913-1999 . . . . . . . . . . .DLB-5
Broughton, Rhoda 1840-1920 . . . . . . . . . .DLB-18
Broun, Heywood 1888-1939 . . . . . . . .DLB-29, 171
Brown, Alice 1856-1948 . . . . . . . . . . . . . .DLB-78
Brown, Bob 1886-1959 . . . . . . . . .DLB-4, 45; DS-15
Brown, Cecil 1943- . . . . . . . . . . . . . . . . .DLB-33
Brown, Charles Brockden
    1771-1810 . . . . . . . .DLB-37, 59, 73; CDALB-2
Brown, Christy 1932-1981 . . . . . . . . . . . .DLB-14
Brown, Dee 1908-2002 . . . . . . . . . . . . . . . .Y-80
Brown, Frank London 1927-1962 . . . . . . . .DLB-76
Brown, Fredric 1906-1972 . . . . . . . . . . . . .DLB-8
Brown, George Mackay
    1921-1996 . . . . . . . . . . .DLB-14, 27, 139, 271
Brown, Harry 1917-1986 . . . . . . . . . . . . .DLB-26
Brown, Larry 1951- . . . . . . . . . . .DLB-234, 292
Brown, Lew 1893-1958 . . . . . . . . . . . . . .DLB-265
Brown, Marcia 1918- . . . . . . . . . . . . . . .DLB-61
Brown, Margaret Wise 1910-1952. . . . . . . .DLB-22

Brown, Morna Doris (see Ferrars, Elizabeth)

Brown, Oliver Madox 1855-1874 ........ DLB-21

Brown, Sterling 1901-1989 ....... DLB-48, 51, 63

Brown, T. E. 1830-1897 ................ DLB-35

Brown, Thomas Alexander (see Boldrewood, Rolf)

Brown, Warren 1894-1978 ............. DLB-241

Brown, William Hill 1765-1793 ......... DLB-37

Brown, William Wells
   1815-1884............. DLB-3, 50, 183, 248

Brown University
   The Festival of Vanguard Narrative ..... Y-93

Browne, Charles Farrar 1834-1867 ....... DLB-11

Browne, Frances 1816-1879 ............ DLB-199

Browne, Francis Fisher 1843-1913 ....... DLB-79

Browne, Howard 1908-1999 .......... DLB-226

Browne, J. Ross 1821-1875 ............. DLB-202

Browne, Michael Dennis 1940- ........ DLB-40

Browne, Sir Thomas 1605-1682 ........ DLB-151

Browne, William, of Tavistock
   1590-1645 ....................... DLB-121

Browne, Wynyard 1911-1964 ...... DLB-13, 233

Browne and Nolan .................. DLB-106

Brownell, W. C. 1851-1928 .............. DLB-71

Browning, Elizabeth Barrett
   1806-1861 ......... DLB-32, 199; CDBLB-4

Browning, Robert
   1812-1889 .......... DLB-32, 163; CDBLB-4

   Essay on Chatterton ............... DLB-32

   Introductory Essay: *Letters of Percy
   Bysshe Shelley* (1852) ............. DLB-32

   "The Novel in [Robert Browning's]
   'The Ring and the Book'" (1912),
   by Henry James................. DLB-32

Brownjohn, Allan 1931- ............. DLB-40

   Tribute to John Betjeman............. Y-84

Brownson, Orestes Augustus
   1803-1876......... DLB-1, 59, 73, 243; DS-5

Bruccoli, Matthew J. 1931- ........... DLB-103

   Joseph [Heller] and George [V. Higgins]... Y-99

   Response [to Busch on Fitzgerald] ....... Y-96

   Tribute to Albert Erskine.............. Y-93

   Tribute to Charles E. Feinberg.......... Y-88

   Working with Fredson Bowers ........ Y-91

Bruce, Charles 1906-1971.............. DLB-68

Bruce, John Edward 1856-1924

   Three Documents [African American
   poets]..................... DLB-50

Bruce, Leo 1903-1979.................. DLB-77

Bruce, Mary Grant 1878-1958 ......... DLB-230

Bruce, Philip Alexander 1856-1933 ....... DLB-47

Bruce-Novoa, Juan 1944- ............ DLB-82

Bruckman, Clyde 1894-1955 ........... DLB-26

Bruckner, Ferdinand 1891-1958 ........ DLB-118

Brundage, John Herbert (see Herbert, John)

Brunner, John 1934-1995 ............. DLB-261

   Tribute to Theodore Sturgeon.......... Y-85

Brutus, Dennis
   1924- ......... DLB-117, 225; CDWLB-3

Bryan, C. D. B. 1936- ............. DLB-185

Bryant, Arthur 1899-1985 ............ DLB-149

Bryant, William Cullen 1794-1878
   ......... DLB-3, 43, 59, 189, 250; CDALB-2

Bryce, James 1838-1922 ......... DLB-166, 190

Bryce Echenique, Alfredo
   1939- ............ DLB-145; CDWLB-3

Bryden, Bill 1942- ................. DLB-233

Brydges, Sir Samuel Egerton
   1762-1837................. DLB-107, 142

Bryskett, Lodowick 1546?-1612 ........ DLB-167

Buchan, John 1875-1940........ DLB-34, 70, 156

Buchanan, George 1506-1582 ......... DLB-132

Buchanan, Robert 1841-1901 ....... DLB-18, 35

   "The Fleshly School of Poetry and
   Other Phenomena of the Day"
   (1872)..................... DLB-35

   "The Fleshly School of Poetry:
   Mr. D. G. Rossetti" (1871),
   by Thomas Maitland........... DLB-35

Buchler, Justus 1914-1991 ............DLB-279

Buchman, Sidney 1902-1975........... DLB-26

Buchner, Augustus 1591-1661 ......... DLB-164

Büchner, Georg
   1813-1837............ DLB-133; CDWLB-2

Bucholtz, Andreas Heinrich 1607-1671..... DLB-168

Buck, Pearl S. 1892-1973 .. DLB-9, 102; CDALB-7

Bucke, Charles 1781-1846 ............ DLB-110

Bucke, Richard Maurice 1837-1902 ...... DLB-99

Buckingham, Edwin 1810-1833 ......... DLB-73

Buckingham, Joseph Tinker 1779-1861 ... DLB-73

Buckler, Ernest 1908-1984 ............. DLB-68

Buckley, Vincent 1925-1988............ DLB-289

Buckley, William F., Jr. 1925- ....DLB-137; Y-80

   Publisher's Statement From the
   Initial Issue of *National Review*
   (19 November 1955) .......... DLB-137

Buckminster, Joseph Stevens
   1784-1812....................... DLB-37

Buckner, Robert 1906- .............. DLB-26

Budd, Thomas ?-1698 ................ DLB-24

Budrys, A. J. 1931- ................. DLB-8

Buechner, Frederick 1926- ............ Y-80

Buell, John 1927- .................. DLB-53

Bufalino, Gesualdo 1920-1996 ........ DLB-196

Job Buffum [publishing house].......... DLB-49

Bugnet, Georges 1879-1981 ........... DLB-92

Buies, Arthur 1840-1901 .............. DLB-99

Bukiet, Melvin Jules 1953- ........... DLB-299

Bukowski, Charles 1920-1994 ... DLB-5, 130, 169

Bulatović, Miodrag
   1930-1991 ......... DLB-181; CDWLB-4

Bulgakov, Mikhail Afanas'evich
   1891-1940 .....................DLB-272

Bulgarin, Faddei Venediktovich
   1789-1859..................... DLB-198

Bulger, Bozeman 1877-1932 ...........DLB-171

Bull, Olaf 1883-1933................. DLB-297

Bullein, William
   between 1520 and 1530-1576....... DLB-167

Bullins, Ed 1935- .............DLB-7, 38, 249

Bulwer, John 1606-1656................ DLB-236

Bulwer-Lytton, Edward (also Edward
   Bulwer) 1803-1873................. DLB-21

   "On Art in Fiction "(1838).......... DLB-21

Bumpus, Jerry 1937- .................... Y-81

Bunce and Brother .................. DLB-49

Bunner, H. C. 1855-1896.............DLB-78, 79

Bunting, Basil 1900-1985 ............. DLB-20

Buntline, Ned (Edward Zane Carroll
   Judson) 1821-1886................ DLB-186

Bunyan, John 1628-1688 ..... DLB-39; CDBLB-2

   The Author's Apology for
   His Book.................. DLB-39

Burch, Robert 1925- ................ DLB-52

Burciaga, José Antonio 1940- ......... DLB-82

Burdekin, Katharine (Murray Constantine)
   1896-1963 .................... DLB-255

Bürger, Gottfried August 1747-1794 ...... DLB-94

Burgess, Anthony (John Anthony Burgess Wilson)
   1917-1993...... DLB-14, 194, 261; CDBLB-8

   The Anthony Burgess Archive at
   the Harry Ransom Humanities
   Research Center ............... Y-98

   Anthony Burgess's *99 Novels*:
   An Opinion Poll ................ Y-84

Burgess, Gelett 1866-1951 ............ DLB-11

Burgess, John W. 1844-1931 ........... DLB-47

Burgess, Thornton W. 1874-1965 ...... DLB-22

Burgess, Stringer and Company......... DLB-49

Burgos, Julia de 1914-1953 ........... DLB-290

Burick, Si 1909-1986 .................DLB-171

Burk, John Daly circa 1772-1808 ....... DLB-37

Burk, Ronnie 1955- ................ DLB-209

Burke, Edmund 1729?-1797 ....... DLB-104, 252

Burke, James Lee 1936- ............. DLB-226

Burke, Johnny 1908-1964............. DLB-265

Burke, Kenneth 1897-1993 ......... DLB-45, 63

Burke, Thomas 1886-1945 ............DLB-197

Burley, Dan 1907-1962............... DLB-241

Burley, W. J. 1914- .................DLB-276

Burlingame, Edward Livermore
   1848-1922 .................... DLB-79

Burman, Carina 1960- ............. DLB-257

Burnet, Gilbert 1643-1715 ............ DLB-101

Burnett, Frances Hodgson
   1849-1924 .........DLB-42, 141; DS-13, 14

Burnett, W. R. 1899-1982 .......... DLB-9, 226

Burnett, Whit 1899-1973 ..............DLB-137

Burney, Fanny 1752-1840.............. DLB-39

   Dedication, *The Wanderer* (1814) ..... DLB-39

   Preface to *Evelina* (1778) ............ DLB-39

Burns, Alan 1929- ............. DLB-14, 194

Burns, Joanne 1945- ................ DLB-289

Burns, John Horne 1916-1953 ........... Y-85

Burns, Robert 1759-1796 .... DLB-109; CDBLB-3

Burns and Oates ........................DLB-106

Burnshaw, Stanley 1906- ........DLB-48; Y-97

   James Dickey and Stanley Burnshaw Correspondence ..................Y-02

   Review of Stanley Burnshaw: The Collected Poems and Selected Prose........................Y-02

   Tribute to Robert Penn Warren ........Y-89

Burr, C. Chauncey 1815?-1883..........DLB-79

Burr, Esther Edwards 1732-1758........DLB-200

Burroughs, Edgar Rice 1875-1950......DLB-8

   The Burroughs Bibliophiles ............Y-98

Burroughs, John 1837-1921 .........DLB-64, 275

Burroughs, Margaret T. G. 1917- .......DLB-41

Burroughs, William S., Jr. 1947-1981......DLB-16

Burroughs, William Seward 1914-1997
.........DLB-2, 8, 16, 152, 237; Y-81, 97

Burroway, Janet 1936- .................DLB-6

Burt, Maxwell Struthers 1882-1954 ................DLB-86; DS-16

A. L. Burt and Company...............DLB-49

Burton, Hester 1913- ...............DLB-161

Burton, Isabel Arundell 1831-1896 ......DLB-166

Burton, Miles (see Rhode, John)

Burton, Richard Francis 1821-1890 ...............DLB-55, 166, 184

Burton, Robert 1577-1640 ...........DLB-151

Burton, Virginia Lee 1909-1968 ........DLB-22

Burton, William Evans 1804-1860........DLB-73

Burwell, Adam Hood 1790-1849 ........DLB-99

Bury, Lady Charlotte 1775-1861 .......DLB-116

Busch, Frederick 1941- ...........DLB-6, 218

   Excerpts from Frederick Busch's USC Remarks [on F. Scott Fitzgerald] ......Y-96

   Tribute to James Laughlin............Y-97

   Tribute to Raymond Carver..........Y-88

Busch, Niven 1903-1991 .................DLB-44

Bushnell, Horace 1802-1876 ............DS-13

Business & Literature
The Claims of Business and Literature: An Undergraduate Essay by Maxwell Perkins..................Y-01

Bussières, Arthur de 1877-1913 .........DLB-92

Butler, Charles circa 1560-1647........DLB-236

Butler, Guy 1918- ..................DLB-225

Butler, Joseph 1692-1752 ............DLB-252

Butler, Josephine Elizabeth 1828-1906 ..................DLB-190

Butler, Juan 1942-1981 ................DLB-53

Butler, Judith 1956- ................DLB-246

Butler, Octavia E. 1947- ..............DLB-33

Butler, Pierce 1884-1953 ..............DLB-187

Butler, Robert Olen 1945- ............DLB-173

Butler, Samuel 1613-1680 .........DLB-101, 126

Butler, Samuel 1835-1902 ........DLB-18, 57, 174; CDBLB-5

Butler, William Francis 1838-1910.......DLB-166

E. H. Butler and Company ...........DLB-49

Butor, Michel 1926- .................DLB-83

Nathaniel Butter [publishing house]......DLB-170

Butterworth, Hezekiah 1839-1905........DLB-42

Buttitta, Ignazio 1899-1997 ...........DLB-114

Butts, Mary 1890-1937 ...............DLB-240

Buzo, Alex 1944- ...................DLB-289

Buzzati, Dino 1906-1972 ..............DLB-177

Byars, Betsy 1928- ...................DLB-52

Byatt, A. S. 1936- ................DLB-14, 194

Byles, Mather 1707-1788...............DLB-24

Henry Bynneman [publishing house].....DLB-170

Bynner, Witter 1881-1968..............DLB-54

Byrd, William circa 1543-1623 ........DLB-172

Byrd, William, II 1674-1744..........DLB-24, 140

Byrne, John Keyes (see Leonard, Hugh)

Byron, George Gordon, Lord 1788-1824 .........DLB-96, 110; CDBLB-3

   The Byron Society of America ........Y-00

Byron, Robert 1905-1941 .............DLB-195

## C

Caballero Bonald, José Manuel 1926- ........................DLB-108

Cabañero, Eladio 1930- ..............DLB-134

Cabell, James Branch 1879-1958 .......DLB-9, 78

Cabeza de Baca, Manuel 1853-1915 .....DLB-122

Cabeza de Baca Gilbert, Fabiola 1898- .........................DLB-122

Cable, George Washington 1844-1925 ...............DLB-12, 74; DS-13

Cable, Mildred 1878-1952 .............DLB-195

Cabral, Manuel del 1907-1999..........DLB-283

Cabrera, Lydia 1900-1991...............DLB-145

Cabrera Infante, Guillermo 1929- ..............DLB-113; CDWLB-3

Cadell [publishing house]..............DLB-154

Cady, Edwin H. 1917- ...............DLB-103

Caedmon flourished 658-680 ..........DLB-146

Caedmon School circa 660-899 ........DLB-146

Caesar, Irving 1895-1996..............DLB-265

Cafés, Brasseries, and Bistros ..........DS-15

Cage, John 1912-1992 ................DLB-193

Cahan, Abraham 1860-1951 .......DLB-9, 25, 28

Cahn, Sammy 1913-1993 ..............DLB-265

Cain, George 1943- ...................DLB-33

Cain, James M. 1892-1977 ............DLB-226

Caird, Edward 1835-1908 .............DLB-262

Caird, Mona 1854-1932...............DLB-197

Čaks, Aleksandrs 1901-1950 ............DLB-220; CDWLB-4

Caldecott, Randolph 1846-1886 .......DLB-163

John Calder Limited [Publishing house]................DLB-112

Calderón de la Barca, Fanny 1804-1882 ....................DLB-183

Caldwell, Ben 1937- .................DLB-38

Caldwell, Erskine 1903-1987 .........DLB-9, 86

H. M. Caldwell Company.............DLB-49

Caldwell, Taylor 1900-1985 ............DS-17

Calhoun, John C. 1782-1850 .......DLB-3, 248

Călinescu, George 1899-1965 .........DLB-220

Calisher, Hortense 1911- .........DLB-2, 218

Calkins, Mary Whiton 1863-1930.......DLB-270

Callaghan, Mary Rose 1944- ..........DLB-207

Callaghan, Morley 1903-1990 .....DLB-68; DS-15

Callahan, S. Alice 1868-1894........DLB-175, 221

Callaloo [journal].........................Y-87

Callimachus circa 305 B.C.-240 B.C. .....DLB-176

Calmer, Edgar 1907- .................DLB-4

Calverley, C. S. 1831-1884 ..............DLB-35

Calvert, George Henry 1803-1889 .............DLB-1, 64, 248

Calvino, Italo 1923-1985.............DLB-196

Cambridge, Ada 1844-1926...........DLB-230

Cambridge Press ....................DLB-49

Cambridge Songs (Carmina Cantabrigensia) circa 1050 ..........................DLB-148

Cambridge University
   Cambridge and the Apostles............DS-5

Cambridge University Press ..........DLB-170

Camden, William 1551-1623..........DLB-172

Camden House: An Interview with James Hardin .......................Y-92

Cameron, Eleanor 1912-2000 ..........DLB-52

Cameron, George Frederick 1854-1885.........................DLB-99

Cameron, Lucy Lyttelton 1781-1858.....DLB-163

Cameron, Peter 1959- ................DLB-234

Cameron, William Bleasdell 1862-1951 ...DLB-99

Camm, John 1718-1778 ................DLB-31

Camões, Luís de 1524-1580 ...........DLB-287

Camon, Ferdinando 1935- ...........DLB-196

Camp, Walter 1859-1925 .............DLB-241

Campana, Dino 1885-1932 ...........DLB-114

Campbell, Bebe Moore 1950- .........DLB-227

Campbell, David 1915-1979 ..........DLB-260

Campbell, Gabrielle Margaret Vere (see Shearing, Joseph, and Bowen, Marjorie)

Campbell, James Dykes 1838-1895......DLB-144

Campbell, James Edwin 1867-1896 ......DLB-50

Campbell, John 1653-1728..............DLB-43

Campbell, John W., Jr. 1910-1971........DLB-8

Campbell, Ramsey 1946- ............DLB-261

Campbell, Roy 1901-1957 .........DLB-20, 225

Campbell, Thomas 1777-1844 ......DLB-93, 144

Campbell, William Edward (see March, William)

Campbell, William Wilfred 1858-1918 ....DLB-92

Campion, Edmund 1539-1581 ........DLB-167

Campion, Thomas 1567-1620 .........DLB-58, 172; CDBLB-1

Campo, Rafael 1964- ................DLB-282

Campton, David 1924- ..............DLB-245

Camus, Albert 1913-1960 .............DLB-72

Camus, Jean-Pierre 1584-1652 . . . . . . . . . . DLB-268

The Canadian Publishers' Records Database . . Y-96

Canby, Henry Seidel 1878-1961 . . . . . . . . DLB-91

Cancioneros . . . . . . . . . . . . . . . . . . . . . . . DLB-286

Candelaria, Cordelia 1943- . . . . . . . . . . . DLB-82

Candelaria, Nash 1928- . . . . . . . . . . . . . DLB-82

Canetti, Elias
   1905-1994 . . . . . . . . DLB-85, 124; CDWLB-2

Canham, Erwin Dain 1904-1982 . . . . . . . DLB-127

Canitz, Friedrich Rudolph Ludwig von
   1654-1699 . . . . . . . . . . . . . . . . . . . . DLB-168

Cankar, Ivan 1876-1918 . . . . . DLB-147; CDWLB-4

Cannan, Gilbert 1884-1955 . . . . . . . . . . DLB-10, 197

Cannan, Joanna 1896-1961 . . . . . . . . . . . DLB-191

Cannell, Kathleen 1891-1974 . . . . . . . . . . . DLB-4

Cannell, Skipwith 1887-1957 . . . . . . . . . . . DLB-45

Canning, George 1770-1827 . . . . . . . . . . . DLB-158

Cannon, Jimmy 1910-1973 . . . . . . . . . . . DLB-171

Cano, Daniel 1947- . . . . . . . . . . . . . . . . DLB-209

Old Dogs / New Tricks? New
   Technologies, the Canon, and the
   Structure of the Profession . . . . . . . . Y-02

Cantú, Norma Elia 1947- . . . . . . . . . . . . DLB-209

Cantwell, Robert 1908-1978 . . . . . . . . . . . . DLB-9

Jonathan Cape and Harrison Smith
   [publishing house] . . . . . . . . . . . . . . . DLB-46

Jonathan Cape Limited . . . . . . . . . . . . . . DLB-112

Čapek, Karel 1890-1938 . . . . DLB-215; CDWLB-4

Capen, Joseph 1658-1725 . . . . . . . . . . . . . DLB-24

Capes, Bernard 1854-1918 . . . . . . . . . . . . DLB-156

Capote, Truman 1924-1984
   . . . . . . . . DLB-2, 185, 227; Y-80, 84; CDALB-1

Capps, Benjamin 1922- . . . . . . . . . . . . . DLB-256

Caproni, Giorgio 1912-1990 . . . . . . . . . . . DLB-128

Caragiale, Mateiu Ioan 1885-1936 . . . . . . DLB-220

Cardarelli, Vincenzo 1887-1959 . . . . . . . . DLB-114

Cardenal, Ernesto 1925- . . . . . . . . . . . . DLB-290

Cárdenas, Reyes 1948- . . . . . . . . . . . . . DLB-122

Cardinal, Marie 1929-2001 . . . . . . . . . . . . DLB-83

Cardoza y Aragón, Luis 1901-1992 . . . . . DLB-290

Carew, Jan 1920- . . . . . . . . . . . . . . . . . DLB-157

Carew, Thomas 1594 or 1595-1640 . . . . DLB-126

Carey, Henry circa 1687-1689-1743 . . . . . . DLB-84

Carey, Mathew 1760-1839 . . . . . . . . . . DLB-37, 73

M. Carey and Company . . . . . . . . . . . . . . DLB-49

Carey, Peter 1943- . . . . . . . . . . . . . . . . DLB-289

Carey and Hart . . . . . . . . . . . . . . . . . . . . DLB-49

Carlell, Lodowick 1602-1675 . . . . . . . . . . . DLB-58

Carleton, William 1794-1869 . . . . . . . . . . DLB-159

G. W. Carleton [publishing house] . . . . . . DLB-49

Carlile, Richard 1790-1843 . . . . . . . DLB-110, 158

Carlson, Ron 1947- . . . . . . . . . . . . . . . . DLB-244

Carlyle, Jane Welsh 1801-1866 . . . . . . . . . DLB-55

Carlyle, Thomas
   1795-1881 . . . . . . . . DLB-55, 144; CDBLB-3

"The Hero as Man of Letters:
   Johnson, Rousseau, Burns"
   (1841) [excerpt] . . . . . . . . . . . . . . . DLB-57

The Hero as Poet. Dante; Shakspeare
   (1841) . . . . . . . . . . . . . . . . . . . . . . DLB-32

Carman, Bliss 1861-1929 . . . . . . . . . . . . . . DLB-92

Carmina Burana circa 1230 . . . . . . . . . . . DLB-138

Carnap, Rudolf 1891-1970 . . . . . . . . . . . . DLB-270

Carnero, Guillermo 1947- . . . . . . . . . . . DLB-108

Carossa, Hans 1878-1956 . . . . . . . . . . . . . DLB-66

Carpenter, Humphrey
   1946- . . . . . . . . . . . . . . . DLB-155; Y-84, 99

Carpenter, Stephen Cullen ?-1820? . . . . . . DLB-73

Carpentier, Alejo
   1904-1980 . . . . . . . . . . DLB-113; CDWLB-3

Carr, Emily (1871-1945) . . . . . . . . . . . . . . DLB-68

Carr, Marina 1964- . . . . . . . . . . . . . . . . DLB-245

Carr, Virginia Spencer 1929- . . . . . . DLB-111; Y-00

Carrera Andrade, Jorge 1903-1978 . . . . . . DLB-283

Carrier, Roch 1937- . . . . . . . . . . . . . . . . DLB-53

Carrillo, Adolfo 1855-1926 . . . . . . . . . . . DLB-122

Carroll, Gladys Hasty 1904- . . . . . . . . . . . DLB-9

Carroll, John 1735-1815 . . . . . . . . . . . . . . DLB-37

Carroll, John 1809-1884 . . . . . . . . . . . . . . DLB-99

Carroll, Lewis
   1832-1898 . . . . . . DLB-18, 163, 178; CDBLB-4

The Lewis Carroll Centenary . . . . . . . . . Y-98

The Lewis Carroll Society
   of North America . . . . . . . . . . . . . . Y-00

Carroll, Paul 1927- . . . . . . . . . . . . . . . . DLB-16

Carroll, Paul Vincent 1900-1968 . . . . . . . . DLB-10

Carroll and Graf Publishers . . . . . . . . . . . DLB-46

Carruth, Hayden 1921- . . . . . . . . . DLB-5, 165

   Tribute to James Dickey . . . . . . . . . . . . Y-97

   Tribute to Raymond Carver . . . . . . . . . Y-88

Carryl, Charles E. 1841-1920 . . . . . . . . . . DLB-42

Carson, Anne 1950- . . . . . . . . . . . . . . . DLB-193

Carson, Rachel 1907-1964 . . . . . . . . . . . . DLB-275

Carswell, Catherine 1879-1946 . . . . . . . . . DLB-36

Cartagena, Alfonso de ca. 1384-1456 . . . . DLB-286

Cartagena, Teresa de 1425?-? . . . . . . . . . . DLB-286

Cărtărescu, Mirea 1956- . . . . . . . . . . . . DLB-232

Carter, Angela 1940-1992 . . . . . . . DLB-14, 207, 261

Carter, Elizabeth 1717-1806 . . . . . . . . . . DLB-109

Carter, Henry (see Leslie, Frank)

Carter, Hodding, Jr. 1907-1972 . . . . . . . . DLB-127

Carter, Jared 1939- . . . . . . . . . . . . . . . . DLB-282

Carter, John 1905-1975 . . . . . . . . . . . . . . DLB-201

Carter, Landon 1710-1778 . . . . . . . . . . . . DLB-31

Carter, Lin 1930-1988 . . . . . . . . . . . . . . . . Y-81

Carter, Martin 1927-1997 . . . . DLB-117; CDWLB-3

Carter, Robert, and Brothers . . . . . . . . . . DLB-49

Carter and Hendee . . . . . . . . . . . . . . . . . DLB-49

Cartwright, Jim 1958- . . . . . . . . . . . . . . DLB-245

Cartwright, John 1740-1824 . . . . . . . . . . DLB-158

Cartwright, William circa 1611-1643 . . . . DLB-126

Caruthers, William Alexander
   1802-1846 . . . . . . . . . . . . . . . . . DLB-3, 248

Carver, Jonathan 1710-1780 . . . . . . . . . . . DLB-31

Carver, Raymond 1938-1988 . . . DLB-130; Y-83, 88

   First Strauss "Livings" Awarded to Cynthia
   Ozick and Raymond Carver
   An Interview with Raymond Carver . . . Y-83

Carvic, Heron 1917?-1980 . . . . . . . . . . . . DLB-276

Cary, Alice 1820-1871 . . . . . . . . . . . . . . DLB-202

Cary, Joyce 1888-1957 . . . DLB-15, 100; CDBLB-6

Cary, Patrick 1623?-1657 . . . . . . . . . . . . DLB-131

Casal, Julián del 1863-1893 . . . . . . . . . . . DLB-283

Case, John 1540-1600 . . . . . . . . . . . . . . . DLB-281

Casey, Gavin 1907-1964 . . . . . . . . . . . . . DLB-260

Casey, Juanita 1925- . . . . . . . . . . . . . . . DLB-14

Casey, Michael 1947- . . . . . . . . . . . . . . . DLB-5

Cassady, Carolyn 1923- . . . . . . . . . . . . . DLB-16

   "As I See It" . . . . . . . . . . . . . . . . . . . DLB-16

Cassady, Neal 1926-1968 . . . . . . . . . DLB-16, 237

Cassell and Company . . . . . . . . . . . . . . . DLB-106

Cassell Publishing Company . . . . . . . . . . DLB-49

Cassill, R. V. 1919- . . . . . . . . DLB-6, 218; Y-02

   Tribute to James Dickey . . . . . . . . . . . . Y-97

Cassity, Turner 1929- . . . . . . . . . DLB-105; Y-02

Cassius Dio circa 155/164-post 229 . . . . . DLB-176

Cassola, Carlo 1917-1987 . . . . . . . . . . . . DLB-177

Castellano, Olivia 1944- . . . . . . . . . . . . DLB-122

Castellanos, Rosario
   1925-1974 . . . . . . . . . DLB-113, 290; CDWLB-3

Castelo Branco, Camilo 1825-1890 . . . . . DLB-287

Castile, Protest Poetry in . . . . . . . . . . . . . DLB-286

Castile and Aragon, Vernacular Translations
   in Crowns of 1352-1515 . . . . . . . . . DLB-286

Castillo, Ana 1953- . . . . . . . . . . . DLB-122, 227

Castillo, Rafael C. 1950- . . . . . . . . . . . . DLB-209

The Castle of Perserverance
   circa 1400-1425 . . . . . . . . . . . . . . . . DLB-146

Castlemon, Harry (see Fosdick, Charles Austin)

Čašule, Kole 1921- . . . . . . . . . . . . . . . . DLB-181

Caswall, Edward 1814-1878 . . . . . . . . . . . DLB-32

Catacalos, Rosemary 1944- . . . . . . . . . . DLB-122

Cather, Willa 1873-1947
   . . . . . . . DLB-9, 54, 78, 256; DS-1; CDALB-3

   The Willa Cather Pioneer Memorial
   and Education Foundation . . . . . . . . Y-00

Catherine II (Ekaterina Alekseevna), "The Great,"
   Empress of Russia 1729-1796 . . . . . . DLB-150

Catherwood, Mary Hartwell 1847-1902 . . . DLB-78

Catledge, Turner 1901-1983 . . . . . . . . . . DLB-127

Catlin, George 1796-1872 . . . . . . . . DLB-186, 189

Cato the Elder 234 B.C.-149 B.C. . . . . . . DLB-211

Cattafi, Bartolo 1922-1979 . . . . . . . . . . . DLB-128

Catton, Bruce 1899-1978 . . . . . . . . . . . . . DLB-17

Catullus circa 84 B.C.-54 B.C.
   . . . . . . . . . . . . . . . . . . DLB-211; CDWLB-1

Causley, Charles 1917- . . . . . . . . . . . . . DLB-27

Caute, David 1936- . . . . . . . . . . . DLB-14, 231

Cavendish, Duchess of Newcastle,
 Margaret Lucas
 1623?-1673 . . . . . . . . . . . . .DLB-131, 252, 281

Cawein, Madison 1865-1914. . . . . . . . . . . .DLB-54

William Caxton [publishing house]. . . . . .DLB-170

The Caxton Printers, Limited . . . . . . . . . .DLB-46

Caylor, O. P. 1849-1897 . . . . . . . . . . . . . .DLB-241

Cayrol, Jean 1911- . . . . . . . . . . . . . . . . .DLB-83

Cecil, Lord David 1902-1986 . . . . . . . . .DLB-155

Cela, Camilo José 1916-2002. . . . . . . . . . . . .Y-89

 Nobel Lecture 1989. . . . . . . . . . . . . . . . .Y-89

Celan, Paul 1920-1970. . . . . . .DLB-69; CDWLB-2

Celati, Gianni 1937- . . . . . . . . . . . . . . .DLB-196

Celaya, Gabriel 1911-1991 . . . . . . . . . . . .DLB-108

Céline, Louis-Ferdinand 1894-1961. . . . . . .DLB-72

Celtis, Conrad 1459-1508 . . . . . . . . . . . . .DLB-179

Cendrars, Blaise 1887-1961 . . . . . . . . . . .DLB-258

The Steinbeck Centennial . . . . . . . . . . . . . . .Y-02

Censorship
 The Island Trees Case: A Symposium on
  School Library Censorship. . . . . . . . .Y-82

Center for Bibliographical Studies and
 Research at the University of
 California, Riverside . . . . . . . . . . . . . . . .Y-91

Center for Book Research . . . . . . . . . . . . . . .Y-84

The Center for the Book in the Library
 of Congress . . . . . . . . . . . . . . . . . . . . . . .Y-93

 A New Voice: The Center for the
  Book's First Five Years . . . . . . . . . . . .Y-83

Centlivre, Susanna 1669?-1723 . . . . . . . . . .DLB-84

The Centre for Writing, Publishing and
 Printing History at the University
 of Reading. . . . . . . . . . . . . . . . . . . . . . . .Y-00

The Century Company. . . . . . . . . . . . . . .DLB-49

A Century of Poetry, a Lifetime of Collecting:
 J. M. Edelstein's Collection of
 Twentieth-Century American Poetry . . . .Y-02

Cernuda, Luis 1902-1963 . . . . . . . . . . . . .DLB-134

Cerruto, Oscar 1912-1981 . . . . . . . . . . . . .DLB-283

Cervantes, Lorna Dee 1954- . . . . . . . . . . .DLB-82

de Céspedes, Alba 1911-1997 . . . . . . . . . .DLB-264

Ch., T. (see Marchenko, Anastasiia Iakovlevna)

Chaadaev, Petr Iakovlevich
 1794-1856 . . . . . . . . . . . . . . . . . . . . .DLB-198

Chabon, Michael 1963- . . . . . . . . . . . . .DLB-278

Chacel, Rosa 1898-1994 . . . . . . . . . . . . . .DLB-134

Chacón, Eusebio 1869-1948 . . . . . . . . . . . .DLB-82

Chacón, Felipe Maximiliano 1873-?. . . . . . .DLB-82

Chadwick, Henry 1824-1908. . . . . . . . . . .DLB-241

Chadwyck-Healey's Full-Text Literary Databases:
 Editing Commercial Databases of
 Primary Literary Texts . . . . . . . . . . . . . .Y-95

Challans, Eileen Mary (see Renault, Mary)

Chalmers, George 1742-1825. . . . . . . . . . .DLB-30

Chaloner, Sir Thomas 1520-1565 . . . . . . .DLB-167

Chamberlain, Samuel S. 1851-1916. . . . . . .DLB-25

Chamberland, Paul 1939- . . . . . . . . . . . .DLB-60

Chamberlin, William Henry 1897-1969. . . .DLB-29

Chambers, Charles Haddon 1860-1921 . . .DLB-10

Chambers, María Cristina (see Mena, María Cristina)

Chambers, Robert W. 1865-1933 . . . . . . .DLB-202

W. and R. Chambers
 [publishing house] . . . . . . . . . . . . . . .DLB-106

Chamisso, Adelbert von 1781-1838. . . . . . .DLB-90

Champfleury 1821-1889 . . . . . . . . . . . . . .DLB-119

Chandler, Harry 1864-1944 . . . . . . . . . . . .DLB-29

Chandler, Norman 1899-1973 . . . . . . . . .DLB-127

Chandler, Otis 1927- . . . . . . . . . . . . . .DLB-127

Chandler, Raymond
 1888-1959 . . . .DLB-226, 253; DS-6; CDALB-5

 Raymond Chandler Centenary. . . . . . . . .Y-88

Channing, Edward 1856-1931. . . . . . . . . . .DLB-17

Channing, Edward Tyrrell
 1790-1856 . . . . . . . . . . . . . . . .DLB-1, 59, 235

Channing, William Ellery
 1780-1842 . . . . . . . . . . . . . . . .DLB-1, 59, 235

Channing, William Ellery, II
 1817-1901 . . . . . . . . . . . . . . . . . . .DLB-1, 223

Channing, William Henry
 1810-1884 . . . . . . . . . . . . . . . .DLB-1, 59, 243

Chapelain, Jean 1595-1674. . . . . . . . . . . .DLB-268

Chaplin, Charlie 1889-1977. . . . . . . . . . . . .DLB-44

Chapman, George
 1559 or 1560-1634 . . . . . . . . . . .DLB-62, 121

Chapman, Olive Murray 1892-1977 . . . . .DLB-195

Chapman, R. W. 1881-1960 . . . . . . . . . . .DLB-201

Chapman, William 1850-1917. . . . . . . . . . .DLB-99

John Chapman [publishing house]. . . . . . .DLB-106

Chapman and Hall [publishing house] . . .DLB-106

Chappell, Fred 1936- . . . . . . . . . . .DLB-6, 105

 "A Detail in a Poem". . . . . . . . . . . . .DLB-105

 Tribute to Peter Taylor. . . . . . . . . . . . . . .Y-94

Chappell, William 1582-1649 . . . . . . . . . .DLB-236

Char, René 1907-1988 . . . . . . . . . . . . . . .DLB-258

Charbonneau, Jean 1875-1960. . . . . . . . . . .DLB-92

Charbonneau, Robert 1911-1967. . . . . . . . .DLB-68

Charles, Gerda 1914- . . . . . . . . . . . . . . .DLB-14

William Charles [publishing house]. . . . . . .DLB-49

Charles d'Orléans 1394-1465 . . . . . . . . . .DLB-208

Charley (see Mann, Charles)

Charskaia, Lidiia 1875-1937. . . . . . . . . . . .DLB-295

Charteris, Leslie 1907-1993 . . . . . . . . . . . .DLB-77

Chartier, Alain circa 1385-1430. . . . . . . . .DLB-208

Charyn, Jerome 1937- . . . . . . . . . . . . . . . .Y-83

Chase, Borden 1900-1971 . . . . . . . . . . . . . .DLB-26

Chase, Edna Woolman 1877-1957. . . . . . . .DLB-91

Chase, James Hadley (René Raymond)
 1906-1985 . . . . . . . . . . . . . . . . . . . . .DLB-276

Chase, Mary Coyle 1907-1981 . . . . . . . . .DLB-228

Chase-Riboud, Barbara 1936- . . . . . . . .DLB-33

Chateaubriand, François-René de
 1768-1848 . . . . . . . . . . . . . . . . . . . . .DLB-119

Chatterton, Thomas 1752-1770 . . . . . . . .DLB-109

 Essay on Chatterton (1842), by
  Robert Browning . . . . . . . . . . . . . .DLB-32

Chatto and Windus. . . . . . . . . . . . . . . . .DLB-106

Chatwin, Bruce 1940-1989 . . . . . . . .DLB-194, 204

Chaucer, Geoffrey
 1340?-1400 . . . . . . . . . . .DLB-146; CDBLB-1

 New Chaucer Society . . . . . . . . . . . . . . . .Y-00

Chaudhuri, Amit 1962- . . . . . . . . . . . .DLB-267

Chauncy, Charles 1705-1787 . . . . . . . . . . .DLB-24

Chauveau, Pierre-Joseph-Olivier
 1820-1890 . . . . . . . . . . . . . . . . . . . . . .DLB-99

Chávez, Denise 1948- . . . . . . . . . . . . .DLB-122

Chávez, Fray Angélico 1910-1996. . . . . . . .DLB-82

Chayefsky, Paddy 1923-1981 . . . . DLB-7, 44; Y-81

Cheesman, Evelyn 1881-1969 . . . . . . . . .DLB-195

Cheever, Ezekiel 1615-1708. . . . . . . . . . . . .DLB-24

Cheever, George Barrell 1807-1890. . . . . . .DLB-59

Cheever, John 1912-1982
 . . . . . . . DLB-2, 102, 227; Y-80, 82; CDALB-1

Cheever, Susan 1943- . . . . . . . . . . . . . . . .Y-82

Cheke, Sir John 1514-1557 . . . . . . . . . . . .DLB-132

Chekhov, Anton Pavlovich 1860-1904 . . .DLB-277

Chelsea House. . . . . . . . . . . . . . . . . . . . . .DLB-46

Chênedollé, Charles de 1769-1833 . . . . . .DLB-217

Cheney, Brainard
 Tribute to Caroline Gordon . . . . . . . . . .Y-81

Cheney, Ednah Dow 1824-1904 . . . . . .DLB-1, 223

Cheney, Harriet Vaughan 1796-1889 . . . . .DLB-99

Chénier, Marie-Joseph 1764-1811 . . . . . . .DLB-192

Chernyshevsky, Nikolai Gavrilovich
 1828-1889 . . . . . . . . . . . . . . . . . . . . .DLB-238

Cherry, Kelly 1940- . . . . . . . . . . . . . . . . .Y-83

Cherryh, C. J. 1942- . . . . . . . . . . . . . . . . .Y-80

Chesebro', Caroline 1825-1873 . . . . . . . .DLB-202

Chesney, Sir George Tomkyns
 1830-1895 . . . . . . . . . . . . . . . . . . . . .DLB-190

Chesnut, Mary Boykin 1823-1886 . . . . . .DLB-239

Chesnutt, Charles Waddell
 1858-1932 . . . . . . . . . . . . . . . DLB-12, 50, 78

Chesson, Mrs. Nora (see Hopper, Nora)

Chester, Alfred 1928-1971 . . . . . . . . . . . .DLB-130

Chester, George Randolph 1869-1924 . . . .DLB-78

The Chester Plays circa 1505-1532;
 revisions until 1575. . . . . . . . . . . . . .DLB-146

Chesterfield, Philip Dormer Stanhope,
 Fourth Earl of 1694-1773. . . . . . . . .DLB-104

Chesterton, G. K. 1874-1936
 . . DLB-10, 19, 34, 70, 98, 149, 178; CDBLB-6

 "The Ethics of Elfland" (1908) . . . . . .DLB-178

Chettle, Henry
 circa 1560-circa 1607. . . . . . . . . . . . .DLB-136

Cheuse, Alan 1940- . . . . . . . . . . . . . . .DLB-244

Chew, Ada Nield 1870-1945 . . . . . . . . . .DLB-135

Cheyney, Edward P. 1861-1947 . . . . . . . . .DLB-47

Chiara, Piero 1913-1986 . . . . . . . . . . . . .DLB-177

Chicanos
 Chicano History . . . . . . . . . . . . . . . . .DLB-82

 Chicano Language . . . . . . . . . . . . . . .DLB-82

 Chicano Literature: A Bibliography . .DLB-209

 A Contemporary Flourescence of Chicano
  Literature . . . . . . . . . . . . . . . . . . . . . .Y-84

461

# Cumulative Index  DLB 302

Literatura Chicanesca: The View From
   Without................. DLB-82
Child, Francis James 1825-1896... DLB-1, 64, 235
Child, Lydia Maria 1802-1880.... DLB-1, 74, 243
Child, Philip 1898-1978 ................. DLB-68
Childers, Erskine 1870-1922............. DLB-70
Children's Literature
   Afterword: Propaganda, Namby-Pamby,
      and Some Books of Distinction... DLB-52
   Children's Book Awards and Prizes... DLB-61
   Children's Book Illustration in the
      Twentieth Century ............ DLB-61
   Children's Illustrators, 1800-1880 ... DLB-163
   The Harry Potter Phenomenon......... Y-99
   Pony Stories, Omnibus
      Essay on .................... DLB-160
   The Reality of One Woman's Dream:
      The de Grummond Children's
      Literature Collection ............. Y-99
   School Stories, 1914-1960 ......... DLB-160
   The Year in Children's
      Books................. Y-92–96, 98–01
   The Year in Children's Literature ....... Y-97
Childress, Alice 1916-1994.........DLB-7, 38, 249
Childress, Mark 1957- ................ DLB-292
Childs, George W. 1829-1894 ........... DLB-23
Chilton Book Company ................. DLB-46
Chin, Frank 1940- ................... DLB-206
Chinweizu 1943- ..................... DLB-157
Chitham, Edward 1932- ............... DLB-155
Chittenden, Hiram Martin 1858-1917 .... DLB-47
Chivers, Thomas Holley 1809-1858... DLB-3, 248
Chkhartishvili, Grigorii Shalvovich
   (see Akunin, Boris)
Chocano, José Santos 1875-1934 ....... DLB-290
Cholmondeley, Mary 1859-1925 ........ DLB-197
Chomsky, Noam 1928- ................ DLB-246
Chopin, Kate 1850-1904... DLB-12, 78; CDALB-3
Chopin, René 1885-1953 ............... DLB-92
Choquette, Adrienne 1915-1973......... DLB-68
Choquette, Robert 1905-1991 .......... DLB-68
Choyce, Lesley 1951- ................. DLB-251
Chrétien de Troyes
   circa 1140-circa 1190 .............. DLB-208
Christensen, Inger 1935- ............. DLB-214
Christensen, Lars Saabye 1953- ........ DLB-297
*The Christian Examiner* ............... DLB-1
The Christian Publishing Company...... DLB-49
Christie, Agatha
   1890-1976........DLB-13, 77, 245; CDBLB-6
Christine de Pizan
   circa 1365-circa 1431 .............. DLB-208
Christopher, John (Sam Youd) 1922- .. DLB-255
*Christus und die Samariterin* circa 950..... DLB-148
Christy, Howard Chandler 1873-1952... DLB-188
Chukovskaia, Lidiia 1907-1996......... DLB-302
Chulkov, Mikhail Dmitrievich
   1743?-1792 .................... DLB-150

Church, Benjamin 1734-1778 .......... DLB-31
Church, Francis Pharcellus 1839-1906.... DLB-79
Church, Peggy Pond 1903-1986........ DLB-212
Church, Richard 1893-1972 ........... DLB-191
Church, William Conant 1836-1917 ..... DLB-79
Churchill, Caryl 1938- ................ DLB-13
Churchill, Charles 1731-1764 ......... DLB-109
Churchill, Winston 1871-1947 ......... DLB-202
Churchill, Sir Winston
   1874-1965....... DLB-100; DS-16; CDBLB-5
Churchyard, Thomas 1520?-1604 ...... DLB-132
E. Churton and Company ............ DLB-106
Chute, Marchette 1909-1994 .......... DLB-103
Ciardi, John 1916-1986.............DLB-5; Y-86
Cibber, Colley 1671-1757 .............. DLB-84
Cicero 106 B.C.-43 B.C.....DLB-211, CDWLB-1
Cima, Annalisa 1941- ................ DLB-128
Čingo, Živko 1935-1987............... DLB-181
Cioran, E. M. 1911-1995 .............. DLB-220
Čipkus, Alfonsas (see Nyka-Niliūnas, Alfonsas)
Cirese, Eugenio 1884-1955............ DLB-114
Cīrulis, Jānis (see Bels, Alberts)
Cisneros, Antonio 1942- .............. DLB-290
Cisneros, Sandra 1954- ........ DLB-122, 152
City Lights Books..................... DLB-46
Civil War (1861–1865)
   Battles and Leaders of the Civil War.. DLB-47
   Official Records of the Rebellion..... DLB-47
   Recording the Civil War ........... DLB-47
Cixous, Hélène 1937- ........... DLB-83, 242
Clampitt, Amy 1920-1994 ............ DLB-105
   Tribute to Alfred A. Knopf ........... Y-84
Clancy, Tom 1947- .................. DLB-227
Clapper, Raymond 1892-1944 .......... DLB-29
Clare, John 1793-1864 .............. DLB-55, 96
Clarendon, Edward Hyde, Earl of
   1609-1674..................... DLB-101
Clark, Alfred Alexander Gordon
   (see Hare, Cyril)
Clark, Ann Nolan 1896- .............. DLB-52
Clark, C. E. Frazer, Jr. 1925-2001 ..DLB-187; Y-01
   C. E. Frazer Clark Jr. and
      Hawthorne Bibliography....... DLB-269
   The Publications of C. E. Frazer
      Clark Jr.................... DLB-269
Clark, Catherine Anthony 1892-1977..... DLB-68
Clark, Charles Heber 1841-1915 ........ DLB-11
Clark, Davis Wasgatt 1812-1871 ........ DLB-79
Clark, Douglas 1919-1993 ............DLB-276
Clark, Eleanor 1913- ................. DLB-6
Clark, J. P. 1935- .........DLB-117; CDWLB-3
Clark, Lewis Gaylord
   1808-1873.............DLB-3, 64, 73, 250
Clark, Walter Van Tilburg
   1909-1971................. DLB-9, 206
Clark, William 1770-1838......... DLB-183, 186

Clark, William Andrews, Jr.
   1877-1934.....................DLB-187
C. M. Clark Publishing Company ....... DLB-46
Clarke, Sir Arthur C. 1917- ......... DLB-261
   Tribute to Theodore Sturgeon.......... Y-85
Clarke, Austin 1896-1974............ DLB-10, 20
Clarke, Austin C. 1934- ......... DLB-53, 125
Clarke, Gillian 1937- ................. DLB-40
Clarke, James Freeman
   1810-1888 ......... DLB-1, 59, 235; DS-5
Clarke, John circa 1596-1658......... DLB-281
Clarke, Lindsay 1939- ............... DLB-231
Clarke, Marcus 1846-1881 ........... DLB-230
Clarke, Pauline 1921- ............... DLB-161
Clarke, Rebecca Sophia 1833-1906 ..... DLB-42
Clarke, Samuel 1675-1729 ........... DLB-252
Robert Clarke and Company.......... DLB-49
Clarkson, Thomas 1760-1846.......... DLB-158
Claudel, Paul 1868-1955 ......... DLB-192, 258
Claudius, Matthias 1740-1815 ......... DLB-97
Clausen, Andy 1943- ................ DLB-16
Claussen, Sophus 1865-1931 ......... DLB-300
Clawson, John L. 1865-1933 ..........DLB-187
Claxton, Remsen and Haffelfinger....... DLB-49
Clay, Cassius Marcellus 1810-1903 ..... DLB-43
Clayton, Richard (seed Haggard, William)
Cleage, Pearl 1948- ................. DLB-228
Cleary, Beverly 1916- ................ DLB-52
Cleary, Kate McPhelim 1863-1905...... DLB-221
Cleaver, Vera 1919-1992 and
   Cleaver, Bill 1920-1981............ DLB-52
Cleeve, Brian 1921- .................DLB-276
Cleland, John 1710-1789.............. DLB-39
Clemens, Samuel Langhorne (Mark Twain)
   1835-1910 ......... DLB-11, 12, 23, 64, 74,
                                186, 189; CDALB-3
   Comments From Authors and Scholars on
      their First Reading of *Huck Finn*..... Y-85
   Huck at 100: How Old Is
      Huckleberry Finn? ............... Y-85
   Mark Twain on Perpetual Copyright ... Y-92
   A New Edition of *Huck Finn*............. Y-85
Clement, Hal 1922- ................... DLB-8
Clemo, Jack 1916- ................... DLB-27
Clephane, Elizabeth Cecilia 1830-1869 .. DLB-199
Cleveland, John 1613-1658 .......... DLB-126
Cliff, Michelle 1946- .......DLB-157; CDWLB-3
Clifford, Lady Anne 1590-1676 ....... DLB-151
Clifford, James L. 1901-1978 ......... DLB-103
Clifford, Lucy 1853?-1929.....DLB-135, 141, 197
Clift, Charmian 1923-1969............ DLB-260
Clifton, Lucille 1936- .............. DLB-5, 41
Clines, Francis X. 1938- ............. DLB-185
Clive, Caroline (V) 1801-1873 ........ DLB-199
Edward J. Clode [publishing house].... DLB-46
Clough, Arthur Hugh 1819-1861....... DLB-32

Cloutier, Cécile 1930- ................DLB-60

Clouts, Sidney 1926-1982 ............DLB-225

Clutton-Brock, Arthur 1868-1924 ......DLB-98

Coates, Robert M.
   1897-1973............DLB-4, 9, 102; DS-15

Coatsworth, Elizabeth 1893-1986 ......DLB-22

Cobb, Charles E., Jr. 1943- ...........DLB-41

Cobb, Frank I. 1869-1923 .............DLB-25

Cobb, Irvin S. 1876-1944........DLB-11, 25, 86

Cobbe, Frances Power 1822-1904 .......DLB-190

Cobbett, William 1763-1835 ....DLB-43, 107, 158

Cobbledick, Gordon 1898-1969 ........DLB-171

Cochran, Thomas C. 1902- ............DLB-17

Cochrane, Elizabeth 1867-1922 ......DLB-25, 189

Cockerell, Sir Sydney 1867-1962 ......DLB-201

Cockerill, John A. 1845-1896............DLB-23

Cocteau, Jean 1889-1963............DLB-65, 258

Coderre, Emile (see Jean Narrache)

Cody, Liza 1944- ....................DLB-276

Coe, Jonathan 1961- .................DLB-231

Coetzee, J. M. 1940- .................DLB-225

Coffee, Lenore J. 1900?-1984............DLB-44

Coffin, Robert P. Tristram 1892-1955.....DLB-45

Coghill, Mrs. Harry (see Walker, Anna Louisa)

Cogswell, Fred 1917- .................DLB-60

Cogswell, Mason Fitch 1761-1830 .......DLB-37

Cohan, George M. 1878-1942 ..........DLB-249

Cohen, Arthur A. 1928-1986............DLB-28

Cohen, Leonard 1934- ................DLB-53

Cohen, Matt 1942- ...................DLB-53

Cohen, Morris Raphael 1880-1947 ......DLB-270

Colbeck, Norman 1903-1987...........DLB-201

Colden, Cadwallader
   1688-1776 .............DLB-24, 30, 270

Colden, Jane 1724-1766 ..............DLB-200

Cole, Barry 1936- ...................DLB-14

Cole, George Watson 1850-1939.........DLB-140

Colegate, Isabel 1931- ............DLB-14, 231

Coleman, Emily Holmes 1899-1974 ......DLB-4

Coleman, Wanda 1946- ...............DLB-130

Coleridge, Hartley 1796-1849 ..........DLB-96

Coleridge, Mary 1861-1907 .........DLB-19, 98

Coleridge, Samuel Taylor
   1772-1834 .........DLB-93, 107; CDBLB-3

Coleridge, Sara 1802-1852 ............DLB-199

Colet, John 1467-1519 ................DLB-132

Colette 1873-1954 ....................DLB-65

Colette, Sidonie Gabrielle (see Colette)

Colinas, Antonio 1946- ..............DLB-134

Coll, Joseph Clement 1881-1921 ........DLB-188

A Century of Poetry, a Lifetime of Collecting:
   J. M. Edelstein's Collection of
   Twentieth-Century American Poetry ....Y-02

Collier, John 1901-1980............DLB-77, 255

Collier, John Payne 1789-1883 .........DLB-184

Collier, Mary 1690-1762 ..............DLB-95

Collier, Robert J. 1876-1918............DLB-91

P. F. Collier [publishing house] .........DLB-49

Collin and Small ......................DLB-49

Collingwood, R. G. 1889-1943 ..........DLB-262

Collingwood, W. G. 1854-1932..........DLB-149

Collins, An floruit circa 1653............DLB-131

Collins, Anthony 1676-1729............DLB-252

Collins, Merle 1950- .................DLB-157

Collins, Michael 1964- ................DLB-267
   Tribute to John D. MacDonald.........Y-86
   Tribute to Kenneth Millar.............Y-83
   Why I Write Mysteries: Night and Day ..Y-85

Collins, Mortimer 1827-1876 .........DLB-21, 35

Collins, Tom (see Furphy, Joseph)

Collins, Wilkie
   1824-1889........DLB-18, 70, 159; CDBLB-4
   "The Unknown Public" (1858)
   [excerpt] ....................DLB-57
   The Wilkie Collins Society ............Y-98

Collins, William 1721-1759 ............DLB-109

Isaac Collins [publishing house]..........DLB-49

William Collins, Sons and Company ....DLB-154

Collis, Maurice 1889-1973.............DLB-195

Collyer, Mary 1716?-1763? .............DLB-39

Colman, Benjamin 1673-1747 ..........DLB-24

Colman, George, the Elder 1732-1794.....DLB-89

Colman, George, the Younger
   1762-1836 .....................DLB-89

S. Colman [publishing house] ...........DLB-49

Colombo, John Robert 1936- ..........DLB-53

Colquhoun, Patrick 1745-1820 .........DLB-158

Colter, Cyrus 1910-2002 ..............DLB-33

Colum, Padraic 1881-1972.............DLB-19

*The Columbia History of the American Novel*
   A Symposium on....................Y-92

Columella fl. first century A.D..........DLB-211

Colvin, Sir Sidney 1845-1927 ..........DLB-149

Colwin, Laurie 1944-1992........DLB-218; Y-80

Comden, Betty 1915-  and
   Green, Adolph 1918- .........DLB-44, 265

Comi, Girolamo 1890-1968............DLB-114

Comisso, Giovanni 1895-1969 ..........DLB-264

Commager, Henry Steele 1902-1998......DLB-17

Commynes, Philippe de
   circa 1447-1511 ..................DLB-208

Compton, D. G. 1930- ...............DLB-261

Compton-Burnett, Ivy 1884?-1969 .......DLB-36

Conan, Laure (Félicité Angers)
   1845-1924 .....................DLB-99

Concord, Massachusetts
   Concord History and Life...........DLB-223
   Concord: Literary History
   of a Town....................DLB-223
   The Old Manse, by Hawthorne .....DLB-223
   The Thoreauvian Pilgrimage: The
   Structure of an American Cult ...DLB-223

Conde, Carmen 1901-1996 ............DLB-108

Congreve, William
   1670-1729 .........DLB-39, 84; CDBLB-2
   Preface to *Incognita* (1692) ..........DLB-39

W. B. Conkey Company................DLB-49

Conn, Stewart 1936- ................DLB-233

Connell, Evan S., Jr. 1924- .........DLB-2; Y-81

Connelly, Marc 1890-1980 .........DLB-7; Y-80

Connolly, Cyril 1903-1974 .............DLB-98

Connolly, James B. 1868-1957...........DLB-78

Connor, Ralph (Charles William Gordon)
   1860-1937 .....................DLB-92

Connor, Tony 1930- .................DLB-40

Conquest, Robert 1917- ..............DLB-27

Conrad, Joseph
   1857-1924 ....DLB-10, 34, 98, 156; CDBLB-5

John Conrad and Company ............DLB-49

Conroy, Jack 1899-1990 ...............Y-81
   A Tribute [to Nelson Algren] ..........Y-81

Conroy, Pat 1945- ...................DLB-6

Considine, Bob 1906-1975............DLB-241

Consolo, Vincenzo 1933- .............DLB-196

Constable, Henry 1562-1613............DLB-136

Archibald Constable and Company .....DLB-154

Constable and Company Limited .......DLB-112

Constant, Benjamin 1767-1830..........DLB-119

Constant de Rebecque, Henri-Benjamin de
   (see Constant, Benjamin)

Constantine, David 1944- .............DLB-40

Constantine, Murray (see Burdekin, Katharine)

Constantin-Weyer, Maurice 1881-1964....DLB-92

*Contempo* (magazine)
   Contempo Caravan:
   Kites in a Windstorm ............Y-85

The Continental Publishing Company ....DLB-49

A Conversation between William Riggan
   and Janette Turner Hospital ..........Y-02

Conversations with Editors ..............Y-95

Conway, Anne 1631-1679 .............DLB-252

Conway, Moncure Daniel
   1832-1907 ...................DLB-1, 223

Cook, Ebenezer circa 1667-circa 1732 .....DLB-24

Cook, Edward Tyas 1857-1919.........DLB-149

Cook, Eliza 1818-1889.................DLB-199

Cook, George Cram 1873-1924..........DLB-266

Cook, Michael 1933-1994 .............DLB-53

David C. Cook Publishing Company ....DLB-49

Cooke, George Willis 1848-1923 ........DLB-71

Cooke, John Esten 1830-1886........DLB-3, 248

Cooke, Philip Pendleton
   1816-1850 .................DLB-3, 59, 248

Cooke, Rose Terry 1827-1892........DLB-12, 74

Increase Cooke and Company ..........DLB-49

Cook-Lynn, Elizabeth 1930- ..........DLB-175

Coolbrith, Ina 1841-1928 .........DLB-54, 186

Cooley, Peter 1940- .................DLB-105
   "Into the Mirror" .................DLB-105

Coolidge, Clark 1939- ...............DLB-193

Coolidge, Susan
(see Woolsey, Sarah Chauncy)
George Coolidge [publishing house]......DLB-49
Cooper, Anna Julia 1858-1964........DLB-221
Cooper, Edith Emma 1862-1913.......DLB-240
Cooper, Giles 1918-1966..............DLB-13
Cooper, J. California 19??-..........DLB-212
Cooper, James Fenimore
1789-1851.......DLB-3, 183, 250; CDALB-2
 The Bicentennial of James Fenimore Cooper:
  An International Celebration........Y-89
 The James Fenimore Cooper Society.....Y-01
Cooper, Kent 1880-1965..............DLB-29
Cooper, Susan 1935-..........DLB-161, 261
Cooper, Susan Fenimore 1813-1894.....DLB-239
William Cooper [publishing house]......DLB-170
J. Coote [publishing house]............DLB-154
Coover, Robert 1932-........DLB-2, 227; Y-81
 Tribute to Donald Barthelme.........Y-89
 Tribute to Theodor Seuss Geisel......Y-91
Copeland and Day...................DLB-49
Ćopić, Branko 1915-1984..............DLB-181
Copland, Robert 1470?-1548..........DLB-136
Coppard, A. E. 1878-1957............DLB-162
Coppée, François 1842-1908..........DLB-217
Coppel, Alfred 1921-.................Y-83
 Tribute to Jessamyn West...........Y-84
Coppola, Francis Ford 1939-..........DLB-44
Copway, George (Kah-ge-ga-gah-bowh)
1818-1869...................DLB-175, 183
Copyright
 The Development of the Author's
  Copyright in Britain..........DLB-154
 The Digital Millennium Copyright Act:
  Expanding Copyright Protection in
  Cyberspace and Beyond...........Y-98
 Editorial: The Extension of Copyright...Y-02
 Mark Twain on Perpetual Copyright....Y-92
 Public Domain and the Violation
  of Texts....................Y-97
 The Question of American Copyright
  in the Nineteenth Century
  Preface, by George Haven Putnam
  The Evolution of Copyright, by
   Brander Matthews
  Summary of Copyright Legislation in
   the United States, by R. R. Bowker
  Analysis of the Provisions of the
   Copyright Law of 1891, by
   George Haven Putnam
  The Contest for International Copyright,
   by George Haven Putnam
  Cheap Books and Good Books,
   by Brander Matthews........DLB-49
 Writers and Their Copyright Holders:
  the WATCH Project.............Y-94
Corazzini, Sergio 1886-1907..........DLB-114
Corbett, Richard 1582-1635..........DLB-121
Corbière, Tristan 1845-1875..........DLB-217
Corcoran, Barbara 1911-............DLB-52
Cordelli, Franco 1943-...............DLB-196
Corelli, Marie 1855-1924.........DLB-34, 156

Corle, Edwin 1906-1956..............Y-85
Corman, Cid 1924-..............DLB-5, 193
Cormier, Robert 1925-2000...DLB-52; CDALB-6
 Tribute to Theodor Seuss Geisel......Y-91
Corn, Alfred 1943-.........DLB-120, 282; Y-80
Corneille, Pierre 1606-1684..........DLB-268
Cornford, Frances 1886-1960.........DLB-240
Cornish, Sam 1935-.................DLB-41
Cornish, William
circa 1465-circa 1524.............DLB-132
Cornwall, Barry (see Procter, Bryan Waller)
Cornwallis, Sir William, the Younger
circa 1579-1614.................DLB-151
Cornwell, David John Moore (see le Carré, John)
Coronel Urtecho, José 1906-1994......DLB-290
Corpi, Lucha 1945-.................DLB-82
Corrington, John William
1932-1988..................DLB-6, 244
Corriveau, Monique 1927-1976........DLB-251
Corrothers, James D. 1869-1917.......DLB-50
Corso, Gregory 1930-2001......DLB-5, 16, 237
Cortázar, Julio 1914-1984....DLB-113; CDWLB-3
Cortéz, Carlos 1923-................DLB-209
Cortez, Jayne 1936-.................DLB-41
Corvinus, Gottlieb Siegmund
1677-1746....................DLB-168
Corvo, Baron (see Rolfe, Frederick William)
Cory, Annie Sophie (see Cross, Victoria)
Cory, Desmond (Shaun Lloyd McCarthy)
1928-.......................DLB-276
Cory, William Johnson 1823-1892......DLB-35
Coryate, Thomas 1577?-1617.....DLB-151, 172
Ćosić, Dobrica 1921-......DLB-181; CDWLB-4
Cosin, John 1595-1672..........DLB-151, 213
Cosmopolitan Book Corporation........DLB-46
Costa, Maria Velho da (see The Three Marias:
A Landmark Case in Portuguese
Literary History)
Costain, Thomas B. 1885-1965.........DLB-9
Coste, Donat (Daniel Boudreau)
1912-1957.....................DLB-88
Costello, Louisa Stuart 1799-1870.....DLB-166
Cota-Cárdenas, Margarita 1941-.....DLB-122
Côté, Denis 1954-.................DLB-251
Cotten, Bruce 1873-1954............DLB-187
Cotter, Joseph Seamon, Jr. 1895-1919....DLB-50
Cotter, Joseph Seamon, Sr. 1861-1949...DLB-50
Joseph Cottle [publishing house].......DLB-154
Cotton, Charles 1630-1687...........DLB-131
Cotton, John 1584-1652.............DLB-24
Cotton, Sir Robert Bruce 1571-1631....DLB-213
Coulter, John 1888-1980.............DLB-68
Cournos, John 1881-1966............DLB-54
Courteline, Georges 1858-1929........DLB-192
Cousins, Margaret 1905-1996.........DLB-137
Cousins, Norman 1915-1990..........DLB-137
Couvreur, Jessie (see Tasma)

Coventry, Francis 1725-1754..........DLB-39
 Dedication, *The History of Pompey
  the Little* (1751)................DLB-39
Coverdale, Miles 1487 or 1488-1569....DLB-167
N. Coverly [publishing house].........DLB-49
Covici-Friede......................DLB-46
Cowan, Peter 1914-2002.............DLB-260
Coward, Noel
1899-1973.........DLB-10, 245; CDBLB-6
Coward, McCann and Geoghegan.......DLB-46
Cowles, Gardner 1861-1946..........DLB-29
Cowles, Gardner "Mike", Jr.
1903-1985................DLB-127, 137
Cowley, Abraham 1618-1667......DLB-131, 151
Cowley, Hannah 1743-1809...........DLB-89
Cowley, Malcolm
1898-1989.......DLB-4, 48; DS-15; Y-81, 89
Cowper, Richard (John Middleton Murry Jr.)
1926-2002....................DLB-261
Cowper, William 1731-1800.......DLB-104, 109
Cox, A. B. (see Berkeley, Anthony)
Cox, James McMahon 1903-1974......DLB-127
Cox, James Middleton 1870-1957......DLB-127
Cox, Leonard circa 1495-circa 1550.....DLB-281
Cox, Palmer 1840-1924..............DLB-42
Coxe, Louis 1918-1993...............DLB-5
Coxe, Tench 1755-1824..............DLB-37
Cozzens, Frederick S. 1818-1869......DLB-202
Cozzens, James Gould 1903-1978............
.........DLB-9, 294; Y-84; DS-2; CDALB-1
 Cozzens's *Michael Scarlett*............Y-97
 Ernest Hemingway's Reaction to
  James Gould Cozzens............Y-98
 James Gould Cozzens–A View
  from Afar....................Y-97
 James Gould Cozzens: How to
  Read Him....................Y-97
 James Gould Cozzens Symposium and
  Exhibition at the University of
  South Carolina, Columbia.........Y-00
 *Mens Rea* (or Something).............Y-97
 Novels for Grown-Ups...............Y-97
Crabbe, George 1754-1832............DLB-93
Crace, Jim 1946-..................DLB-231
Crackanthorpe, Hubert 1870-1896.....DLB-135
Craddock, Charles Egbert (see Murfree, Mary N.)
Cradock, Thomas 1718-1770..........DLB-31
Craig, Daniel H. 1811-1895...........DLB-43
Craik, Dinah Maria 1826-1887......DLB-35, 163
Cramer, Richard Ben 1950-..........DLB-185
Cranch, Christopher Pearse
1813-1892..........DLB-1, 42, 243; DS-5
Crane, Hart 1899-1932.....DLB-4, 48; CDALB-4
 Nathan Asch Remembers Ford Madox
  Ford, Sam Roth, and Hart Crane....Y-02
Crane, R. S. 1886-1967..............DLB-63
Crane, Stephen
1871-1900........DLB-12, 54, 78; CDALB-3

Stephen Crane: A Revaluation, Virginia
  Tech Conference, 1989 . . . . . . . . . . Y-89
The Stephen Crane Society. . . . . . . . Y-98, 01
Crane, Walter 1845-1915 . . . . . . . . . . . . . DLB-163
Cranmer, Thomas 1489-1556 . . . . . . DLB-132, 213
Crapsey, Adelaide 1878-1914. . . . . . . . . . . DLB-54
Crashaw, Richard 1612/1613-1649 . . . . . . DLB-126
Craven, Avery 1885-1980 . . . . . . . . . . . . . . DLB-17
Crawford, Charles 1752-circa 1815 . . . . . . . DLB-31
Crawford, F. Marion 1854-1909 . . . . . . . . DLB-71
Crawford, Isabel Valancy 1850-1887. . . . . . DLB-92
Crawley, Alan 1887-1975 . . . . . . . . . . . . . . DLB-68
Crayon, Geoffrey (see Irving, Washington)
Crayon, Porte (see Strother, David Hunter)
Creamer, Robert W. 1922- . . . . . . . . . DLB-171
Creasey, John 1908-1973 . . . . . . . . . . . . . . DLB-77
Creative Age Press. . . . . . . . . . . . . . . . . . . . DLB-46
Creative Nonfiction . . . . . . . . . . . . . . . . . . . . Y-02
William Creech [publishing house] . . . . . . DLB-154
Thomas Creede [publishing house] . . . . . . DLB-170
Creel, George 1876-1953 . . . . . . . . . . . . . . DLB-25
Creeley, Robert 1926-
  . . . . . . . . . . . . . . . . DLB-5, 16, 169; DS-17
Creelman, James
  1859-1915 . . . . . . . . . . . . . . . . . . . . . DLB-23
Cregan, David 1931- . . . . . . . . . . . . . . DLB-13
Creighton, Donald 1902-1979 . . . . . . . . . . DLB-88
Crémazie, Octave 1827-1879 . . . . . . . . . . . DLB-99
Crémer, Victoriano 1909?- . . . . . . . . . . . DLB-108
Crescas, Hasdai circa 1340-1412? . . . . . . . DLB-115
Crespo, Angel 1926-1995 . . . . . . . . . . . . . DLB-134
Cresset Press . . . . . . . . . . . . . . . . . . . . . . . DLB-112
Cresswell, Helen 1934- . . . . . . . . . . . . . DLB-161
Crèvecoeur, Michel Guillaume Jean de
  1735-1813 . . . . . . . . . . . . . . . . . . . . . DLB-37
Crewe, Candida 1964- . . . . . . . . . . . . . DLB-207
Crews, Harry 1935- . . . . . . . . DLB-6, 143, 185
Crichton, Michael (John Lange, Jeffrey Hudson,
  Michael Douglas) 1942- . . . . DLB-292; Y-81
Crispin, Edmund (Robert Bruce Montgomery)
  1921-1978 . . . . . . . . . . . . . . . . . . . . . DLB-87
Cristofer, Michael 1946- . . . . . . . . . . . . DLB-7
Criticism
  Afro-American Literary Critics:
    An Introduction . . . . . . . . . . . . . . DLB-33
  The Consolidation of Opinion: Critical
    Responses to the Modernists . . . . . DLB-36
  "Criticism in Relation to Novels"
    (1863), by G. H. Lewes . . . . . . . . DLB-21
  The Limits of Pluralism . . . . . . . . . . . DLB-67
  Modern Critical Terms, Schools, and
    Movements. . . . . . . . . . . . . . . . . . . DLB-67
  "Panic Among the Philistines":
    A Postscript, An Interview
    with Bryan Griffin . . . . . . . . . . . . . . Y-81
  The Recovery of Literature: Criticism
    in the 1990s: A Symposium . . . . . . . Y-91
  The Stealthy School of Criticism (1871),
    by Dante Gabriel Rossetti. . . . . . . DLB-35

Crnjanski, Miloš
  1893-1977 . . . . . . . . . DLB-147; CDWLB-4
Crocker, Hannah Mather 1752-1829. . . . . DLB-200
Crockett, David (Davy)
  1786-1836 . . . . . . . . . . . DLB-3, 11, 183, 248
Croft-Cooke, Rupert (see Bruce, Leo)
Crofts, Freeman Wills 1879-1957. . . . . . . . DLB-77
Croker, John Wilson 1780-1857 . . . . . . . . DLB-110
Croly, George 1780-1860. . . . . . . . . . . . . DLB-159
Croly, Herbert 1869-1930 . . . . . . . . . . . . . DLB-91
Croly, Jane Cunningham 1829-1901. . . . . . DLB-23
Crompton, Richmal 1890-1969 . . . . . . . . DLB-160
Cronin, A. J. 1896-1981. . . . . . . . . . . . . . DLB-191
Cros, Charles 1842-1888 . . . . . . . . . . . . . DLB-217
Crosby, Caresse 1892-1970 and
  Crosby, Harry 1898-1929 and . . DLB-4; DS-15
Crosby, Harry 1898-1929 . . . . . . . . . . . . . DLB-48
Crosland, Camilla Toulmin (Mrs. Newton
  Crosland) 1812-1895. . . . . . . . . . . . DLB-240
Cross, Gillian 1945- . . . . . . . . . . . . . DLB-161
Cross, Victoria 1868-1952 . . . . . . . . DLB-135, 197
Crossley-Holland, Kevin 1941- . . . . DLB-40, 161
Crothers, Rachel 1870-1958 . . . . . . . . DLB-7, 266
Thomas Y. Crowell Company . . . . . . . . . DLB-49
Crowley, John 1942- . . . . . . . . . . . . . . Y-82
Crowley, Mart 1935- . . . . . . . . DLB-7, 266
Crown Publishers . . . . . . . . . . . . . . . . . . . . DLB-46
Crowne, John 1641-1712 . . . . . . . . . . . . . DLB-80
Crowninshield, Edward Augustus
  1817-1859 . . . . . . . . . . . . . . . . . . . . DLB-140
Crowninshield, Frank 1872-1947 . . . . . . . DLB-91
Croy, Homer 1883-1965 . . . . . . . . . . . . . . . DLB-4
Crumley, James 1939- . . . . . . . DLB-226; Y-84
Cruse, Mary Anne 1825?-1910 . . . . . . . . DLB-239
Cruz, Migdalia 1958- . . . . . . . . . . . . . DLB-249
Cruz, Victor Hernández 1949- . . . . . . . DLB-41
Csokor, Franz Theodor 1885-1969 . . . . . . DLB-81
Csoóri, Sándor 1930- . . . . . DLB-232; CDWLB-4
Cuadra, Pablo Antonio 1912-2002 . . . . . . DLB-290
Cuala Press . . . . . . . . . . . . . . . . . . . . . . . . DLB-112
Cudworth, Ralph 1617-1688 . . . . . . . . . . DLB-252
Cugoano, Quobna Ottabah 1797-? . . . . . . . . Y-02
Cullen, Countee
  1903-1946 . . . . . . . . DLB-4, 48, 51; CDALB-4
Culler, Jonathan D. 1944- . . . . . . . DLB-67, 246
Cullinan, Elizabeth 1933- . . . . . . . . . . DLB-234
Culverwel, Nathaniel 1619?-1651? . . . . . . DLB-252
Cumberland, Richard 1732-1811. . . . . . . . DLB-89
Cummings, Constance Gordon
  1837-1924 . . . . . . . . . . . . . . . . . . . . DLB-174
Cummings, E. E.
  1894-1962 . . . . . . . . . . DLB-4, 48; CDALB-5
  The E. E. Cummings Society . . . . . . . . Y-01
Cummings, Ray 1887-1957 . . . . . . . . . . . . . DLB-8
Cummings and Hilliard . . . . . . . . . . . . . . . DLB-49
Cummins, Maria Susanna 1827-1866 . . . . . DLB-42
Cumpián, Carlos 1953- . . . . . . . . . . . . DLB-209

Cunard, Nancy 1896-1965 . . . . . . . . . . . DLB-240
Joseph Cundall [publishing house] . . . . . . DLB-106
Cuney, Waring 1906-1976 . . . . . . . . . . . . . DLB-51
Cuney-Hare, Maude 1874-1936 . . . . . . . . DLB-52
Cunningham, Allan 1784-1842 . . . . . DLB-116, 144
Cunningham, J. V. 1911-1985 . . . . . . . . . . DLB-5
Cunningham, Michael 1952- . . . . . . . DLB-292
Cunningham, Peter (Peter Lauder, Peter
  Benjamin) 1947- . . . . . . . . . . . . . . DLB-267
Peter F. Cunningham
  [publishing house] . . . . . . . . . . . . . . DLB-49
Cunquiero, Alvaro 1911-1981 . . . . . . . . . DLB-134
Cuomo, George 1929- . . . . . . . . . . . . . . Y-80
Cupples, Upham and Company . . . . . . . . DLB-49
Cupples and Leon . . . . . . . . . . . . . . . . . . . DLB-46
Cuppy, Will 1884-1949 . . . . . . . . . . . . . . . DLB-11
Curiel, Barbara Brinson 1956- . . . . . . . DLB-209
Edmund Curll [publishing house] . . . . . . DLB-154
Currie, James 1756-1805 . . . . . . . . . . . . . DLB-142
Currie, Mary Montgomerie Lamb Singleton,
  Lady Currie (see Fane, Violet)
Cursor Mundi circa 1300 . . . . . . . . . . . . . . DLB-146
Curti, Merle E. 1897-1996 . . . . . . . . . . . . DLB-17
Curtis, Anthony 1926- . . . . . . . . . . . . . DLB-155
Curtis, Cyrus H. K. 1850-1933 . . . . . . . . DLB-91
Curtis, George William
  1824-1892 . . . . . . . . . . . . . . . DLB-1, 43, 223
Curzon, Robert 1810-1873 . . . . . . . . . . . DLB-166
Curzon, Sarah Anne 1833-1898 . . . . . . . . DLB-99
Cusack, Dymphna 1902-1981 . . . . . . . . . DLB-260
Cushing, Eliza Lanesford 1794-1886 . . . . . DLB-99
Cushing, Harvey 1869-1939 . . . . . . . . . . DLB-187
Custance, Olive (Lady Alfred Douglas)
  1874-1944 . . . . . . . . . . . . . . . . . . . . DLB-240
Cynewulf circa 770-840 . . . . . . . . . . . . . . DLB-146
Cyrano de Bergerac, Savinien de
  1619-1655 . . . . . . . . . . . . . . . . . . . . DLB-268
Czepko, Daniel 1605-1660 . . . . . . . . . . . . DLB-164
Czerniawski, Adam 1934- . . . . . . . . . . DLB-232

# D

Dabit, Eugène 1898-1936 . . . . . . . . . . . . . DLB-65
Daborne, Robert circa 1580-1628 . . . . . . . DLB-58
Dąbrowska, Maria
  1889-1965 . . . . . . . . . DLB-215; CDWLB-4
Dacey, Philip 1939- . . . . . . . . . . . . . . DLB-105
  "Eyes Across Centuries:
    Contemporary Poetry and 'That
    Vision Thing,'" . . . . . . . . . . . . . DLB-105
Dach, Simon 1605-1659. . . . . . . . . . . . . . DLB-164
Dagerman, Stig 1923-1954. . . . . . . . . . . . DLB-259
Daggett, Rollin M. 1831-1901 . . . . . . . . . DLB-79
D'Aguiar, Fred 1960- . . . . . . . . . . . . . DLB-157
Dahl, Roald 1916-1990 . . . . . . . . . . DLB-139, 255
  Tribute to Alfred A. Knopf . . . . . . . . . . Y-84
Dahlberg, Edward 1900-1977 . . . . . . . . . . DLB-48
Dahn, Felix 1834-1912. . . . . . . . . . . . . . . DLB-129

# Cumulative Index

Dal', Vladimir Ivanovich (Kazak Vladimir Lugansky) 1801-1872............ DLB-198
Dale, Peter 1938- .................. DLB-40
Daley, Arthur 1904-1974 ............. DLB-171
Dall, Caroline Healey 1822-1912..... DLB-1, 235
Dallas, E. S. 1828-1879 ............ DLB-55
 *The Gay Science* [excerpt](1866)....... DLB-21
The Dallas Theater Center............. DLB-7
D'Alton, Louis 1900-1951 ............ DLB-10
Dalton, Roque 1935-1975............ DLB-283
Daly, Carroll John 1889-1958 ........ DLB-226
Daly, T. A. 1871-1948 ............... DLB-11
Damon, S. Foster 1893-1971....... DLB-45
William S. Damrell [publishing house].... DLB-49
Dana, Charles A. 1819-1897...... DLB-3, 23, 250
Dana, Richard Henry, Jr. 1815-1882.......... DLB-1, 183, 235
Dandridge, Ray Garfield ............ DLB-51
Dane, Clemence 1887-1965 ........DLB-10, 197
Danforth, John 1660-1730 ........... DLB-24
Danforth, Samuel, I 1626-1674......... DLB-24
Danforth, Samuel, II 1666-1727......... DLB-24
Daniel, John M. 1825-1865........... DLB-43
Daniel, Samuel 1562 or 1563-1619...... DLB-62
Daniel Press ..................... DLB-106
Daniel', Iulii (Nikolai Arzhak) 1925-1988 .................. DLB-302
Daniells, Roy 1902-1979............. DLB-68
Daniels, Jim 1956- ................. DLB-120
Daniels, Jonathan 1902-1981 ......... DLB-127
Daniels, Josephus 1862-1948 ........ DLB-29
Daniels, Sarah 1957- ............... DLB-245
Danilevsky, Grigorii Petrovich 1829-1890 .................. DLB-238
Dannay, Frederic 1905-1982 ......... DLB-137
Danner, Margaret Esse 1915- ........ DLB-41
John Danter [publishing house] ........DLB-170
Dantin, Louis (Eugene Seers) 1865-1945 .................. DLB-92
Danto, Arthur C. 1924- ..............DLB-279
Danzig, Allison 1898-1987 ...........DLB-171
D'Arcy, Ella circa 1857-1937......... DLB-135
Darío, Rubén 1867-1916.............. DLB-290
Dark, Eleanor 1901-1985 ............ DLB-260
Darke, Nick 1948- .................. DLB-233
Darley, Felix Octavious Carr 1822-1888 .................. DLB-188
Darley, George 1795-1846 ........... DLB-96
Darmesteter, Madame James (see Robinson, A. Mary F.)
Darwin, Charles 1809-1882 ........DLB-57, 166
Darwin, Erasmus 1731-1802........... DLB-93
Daryush, Elizabeth 1887-1977 ....... DLB-20
Dashkova, Ekaterina Romanovna (née Vorontsova) 1743-1810 ....... DLB-150
Dashwood, Edmée Elizabeth Monica de la Pasture (see Delafield, E. M.)

Daudet, Alphonse 1840-1897 ......... DLB-123
d'Aulaire, Edgar Parin 1898- and d'Aulaire, Ingri 1904- ........... DLB-22
Davenant, Sir William 1606-1668 ... DLB-58, 126
Davenport, Guy 1927- ............... DLB-130
 Tribute to John Gardner ............... Y-82
Davenport, Marcia 1903-1996 ............ DS-17
Davenport, Robert ?-? ............... DLB-58
Daves, Delmer 1904-1977............. DLB-26
Davey, Frank 1940- ................. DLB-53
Davidson, Avram 1923-1993 .......... DLB-8
Davidson, Donald 1893-1968........ DLB-45
Davidson, Donald 1917- ..............DLB-279
Davidson, John 1857-1909 ........... DLB-19
Davidson, Lionel 1922- ..............DLB-14, 276
Davidson, Robyn 1950- .............. DLB-204
Davidson, Sara 1943- ............... DLB-185
Davíð Stefánsson frá Fagraskógi 1895-1964 .................. DLB-293
Davie, Donald 1922- ................ DLB-27
Davie, Elspeth 1919-1995............ DLB-139
Davies, Sir John 1569-1626 ..........DLB-172
Davies, John, of Hereford 1565?-1618 ... DLB-121
Davies, Rhys 1901-1978 ............. DLB-139, 191
Davies, Robertson 1913-1995.......... DLB-68
Davies, Samuel 1723-1761 ........... DLB-31
Davies, Thomas 1712?-1785 ....... DLB-142, 154
Davies, W. H. 1871-1940 .............DLB-19, 174
Peter Davies Limited ................ DLB-112
Davin, Nicholas Flood 1840?-1901...... DLB-99
Daviot, Gordon 1896?-1952 ........... DLB-10
 (see also Tey, Josephine)
Davis, Arthur Hoey (see Rudd, Steele)
Davis, Charles A. (Major J. Downing) 1795-1867.......... DLB-11
Davis, Clyde Brion 1894-1962......... DLB-9
Davis, Dick 1945- .................. DLB-40, 282
Davis, Frank Marshall 1905-1987........ DLB-51
Davis, H. L. 1894-1960 ............. DLB-9, 206
Davis, John 1774-1854 .............. DLB-37
Davis, Lydia 1947- ................. DLB-130
Davis, Margaret Thomson 1926- ..... DLB-14
Davis, Ossie 1917- ................. DLB-7, 38, 249
Davis, Owen 1874-1956 .............. DLB-249
Davis, Paxton 1925-1994 ............. Y-89
Davis, Rebecca Harding 1831-1910 .................. DLB-74, 239
Davis, Richard Harding 1864-1916 .............DLB-12, 23, 78, 79, 189; DS-13
Davis, Samuel Cole 1764-1809 ....... DLB-37
Davis, Samuel Post 1850-1918 ....... DLB-202
Davison, Frank Dalby 1893-1970 ..... DLB-260
Davison, Peter 1928- ............... DLB-5
Davydov, Denis Vasil'evich 1784-1839 ... DLB-205
Davys, Mary 1674-1732 .............. DLB-39

Preface to *The Works of Mrs. Davy* (1725) .................. DLB-39
DAW Books....................... DLB-46
Dawe, Bruce 1930- ................. DLB-289
Dawson, Ernest 1882-1947........DLB-140; Y-02
Dawson, Fielding 1930- ............. DLB-130
Dawson, Sarah Morgan 1842-1909 ..... DLB-239
Dawson, William 1704-1752........... DLB-31
Day, Angel flourished 1583-1599....DLB-167, 236
Day, Benjamin Henry 1810-1889........ DLB-43
Day, Clarence 1874-1935 ............ DLB-11
Day, Dorothy 1897-1980 ............. DLB-29
Day, Frank Parker 1881-1950 ........ DLB-92
Day, John circa 1574-circa 1640 ........ DLB-62
Day, Thomas 1748-1789 .............. DLB-39
John Day [publishing house]..........DLB-170
The John Day Company ............. DLB-46
Mahlon Day [publishing house]......... DLB-49
Day Lewis, C. (see Blake, Nicholas)
Dazai Osamu 1909-1948 ............. DLB-182
Deacon, William Arthur 1890-1977 ...... DLB-68
Deal, Borden 1922-1985............... DLB-6
de Angeli, Marguerite 1889-1987 ....... DLB-22
De Angelis, Milo 1951- ............. DLB-128
Debord, Guy 1931-1994............... DLB-296
De Bow, J. D. B. 1820-1867 .......DLB-3, 79, 248
de Bruyn, Günter 1926- ............. DLB-75
de Camp, L. Sprague 1907-2000 ........ DLB-8
De Carlo, Andrea 1952- ............. DLB-196
De Casas, Celso A. 1944- ........... DLB-209
Dechert, Robert 1895-1975............DLB-187
Dedications, Inscriptions, and Annotations .................. Y-01–02
Dee, John 1527-1608 or 1609 ...... DLB-136, 213
Deeping, George Warwick 1877-1950 ... DLB-153
Defoe, Daniel 1660-1731....... DLB-39, 95, 101; CDBLB-2
 Preface to *Colonel Jack* (1722) ........ DLB-39
 Preface to *The Farther Adventures of Robinson Crusoe* (1719)........... DLB-39
 Preface to *Moll Flanders* (1722) ....... DLB-39
 Preface to *Robinson Crusoe* (1719)...... DLB-39
 Preface to *Roxana* (1724)........... DLB-39
de Fontaine, Felix Gregory 1834-1896 .... DLB-43
De Forest, John William 1826-1906 .. DLB-12, 189
DeFrees, Madeline 1919- ............ DLB-105
 "The Poet's Kaleidoscope: The Element of Surprise in the Making of the Poem" ......... DLB-105
DeGolyer, Everette Lee 1886-1956 ......DLB-187
de Graff, Robert 1895-1981 ............. Y-81
de Graft, Joe 1924-1978 .............DLB-117
*De Heinrico* circa 980? ................ DLB-148
Deighton, Len 1929- ....... DLB-87; CDBLB-8
DeJong, Meindert 1906-1991 ......... DLB-52

Dekker, Thomas
  circa 1572-1632 . . . . . . DLB-62, 172; CDBLB-1
Delacorte, George T., Jr. 1894-1991 . . . . . . DLB-91
Delafield, E. M. 1890-1943 . . . . . . . . . . . . . DLB-34
Delahaye, Guy (Guillaume Lahaise)
  1888-1969 . . . . . . . . . . . . . . . . . . . . . . DLB-92
de la Mare, Walter 1873-1956
  . . . . . . . . . DLB-19, 153, 162, 255; CDBLB-6
Deland, Margaret 1857-1945 . . . . . . . . . . . . DLB-78
Delaney, Shelagh 1939- . . . . DLB-13; CDBLB-8
Delano, Amasa 1763-1823 . . . . . . . . . . . . . DLB-183
Delany, Martin Robinson 1812-1885 . . . . . . DLB-50
Delany, Samuel R. 1942- . . . . . . . . . DLB-8, 33
de la Roche, Mazo 1879-1961 . . . . . . . . . . . DLB-68
Delavigne, Jean François Casimir
  1793-1843 . . . . . . . . . . . . . . . . . . . . . DLB-192
Delbanco, Nicholas 1942- . . . . . . . DLB-6, 234
Delblanc, Sven 1931-1992 . . . . . . . . . . . . . DLB-257
Del Castillo, Ramón 1949- . . . . . . . . . . . . DLB-209
Deledda, Grazia 1871-1936 . . . . . . . . . . . . DLB-264
De León, Nephtal 1945- . . . . . . . . . . . . . . DLB-82
Deleuze, Gilles 1925-1995 . . . . . . . . . . . . . DLB-296
Delfini, Antonio 1907-1963 . . . . . . . . . . . . DLB-264
Delgado, Abelardo Barrientos 1931- . . . . DLB-82
Del Giudice, Daniele 1949- . . . . . . . . . . . . DLB-196
De Libero, Libero 1906-1981 . . . . . . . . . . . DLB-114
DeLillo, Don 1936- . . . . . . . . . . . . DLB-6, 173
de Lint, Charles 1951- . . . . . . . . . . . . . . . DLB-251
de Lisser H. G. 1878-1944 . . . . . . . . . . . . . DLB-117
Dell, Floyd 1887-1969 . . . . . . . . . . . . . . . . DLB-9
Dell Publishing Company . . . . . . . . . . . . . DLB-46
delle Grazie, Marie Eugene 1864-1931 . . . . DLB-81
Deloney, Thomas died 1600 . . . . . . . . . . . DLB-167
Deloria, Ella C. 1889-1971 . . . . . . . . . . . . DLB-175
Deloria, Vine, Jr. 1933- . . . . . . . . . . . . . . DLB-175
del Rey, Lester 1915-1993 . . . . . . . . . . . . . . DLB-8
Del Vecchio, John M. 1947- . . . . . . . . . . . . . DS-9
Del'vig, Anton Antonovich 1798-1831 . . . . DLB-205
de Man, Paul 1919-1983 . . . . . . . . . . . . . . DLB-67
DeMarinis, Rick 1934- . . . . . . . . . . . . . . DLB-218
Demby, William 1922- . . . . . . . . . . . . . . . DLB-33
De Mille, James 1833-1880 . . . . . . . . DLB-99, 251
de Mille, William 1878-1955 . . . . . . . . . . . DLB-266
Deming, Philander 1829-1915 . . . . . . . . . . . DLB-74
Deml, Jakub 1878-1961 . . . . . . . . . . . . . . DLB-215
Demorest, William Jennings 1822-1895 . . . . DLB-79
De Morgan, William 1839-1917 . . . . . . . . DLB-153
Demosthenes 384 B.C.-322 B.C. . . . . . . . DLB-176
Henry Denham [publishing house] . . . . . . DLB-170
Denham, Sir John 1615-1669 . . . . . . . DLB-58, 126
Denison, Merrill 1893-1975 . . . . . . . . . . . . DLB-92
T. S. Denison and Company . . . . . . . . . . . DLB-49
Dennery, Adolphe Philippe 1811-1899 . . . DLB-192
Dennie, Joseph 1768-1812 . . . . . DLB-37, 43, 59, 73
Dennis, C. J. 1876-1938 . . . . . . . . . . . . . . DLB-260

Dennis, John 1658-1734 . . . . . . . . . . . . . . DLB-101
Dennis, Nigel 1912-1989 . . . . . . . DLB-13, 15, 233
Denslow, W. W. 1856-1915 . . . . . . . . . . . . DLB-188
Dent, J. M., and Sons . . . . . . . . . . . . . . . . DLB-112
Dent, Tom 1932-1998 . . . . . . . . . . . . . . . . DLB-38
Denton, Daniel circa 1626-1703 . . . . . . . . . DLB-24
DePaola, Tomie 1934- . . . . . . . . . . . . . . . DLB-61
De Quille, Dan 1829-1898 . . . . . . . . . . . . DLB-186
De Quincey, Thomas
  1785-1859 . . . . . . . DLB-110, 144; CDBLB-3
  "Rhetoric" (1828; revised, 1859)
    [excerpt] . . . . . . . . . . . . . . . . . . . . DLB-57
  "Style" (1840; revised, 1859)
    [excerpt] . . . . . . . . . . . . . . . . . . . . DLB-57
Derby, George Horatio 1823-1861 . . . . . . . DLB-11
J. C. Derby and Company . . . . . . . . . . . . . DLB-49
Derby and Miller . . . . . . . . . . . . . . . . . . . DLB-49
De Ricci, Seymour 1881-1942 . . . . . . . . . . DLB-201
Derleth, August 1909-1971 . . . . . . . DLB-9; DS-17
Derrida, Jacques 1930- . . . . . . . . . . . . . . DLB-242
The Derrydale Press . . . . . . . . . . . . . . . . . DLB-46
Derzhavin, Gavriil Romanovich
  1743-1816 . . . . . . . . . . . . . . . . . . . . . DLB-150
Desai, Anita 1937- . . . . . . . . . . . . . . . . . DLB-271
Desaulniers, Gonzalve 1863-1934 . . . . . . . . DLB-92
Desbordes-Valmore, Marceline
  1786-1859 . . . . . . . . . . . . . . . . . . . . . DLB-217
Descartes, René 1596-1650 . . . . . . . . . . . . DLB-268
Deschamps, Emile 1791-1871 . . . . . . . . . . DLB-217
Deschamps, Eustache 1340?-1404 . . . . . . . DLB-208
Desbiens, Jean-Paul 1927- . . . . . . . . . . . . . DLB-53
des Forêts, Louis-Rene 1918-2001 . . . . . . . . DLB-83
Desiato, Luca 1941- . . . . . . . . . . . . . . . . DLB-196
Desjardins, Marie-Catherine
  (see Villedieu, Madame de)
Desnica, Vladan 1905-1967 . . . . . . . . . . . . DLB-181
Desnos, Robert 1900-1945 . . . . . . . . . . . . DLB-258
DesRochers, Alfred 1901-1978 . . . . . . . . . . DLB-68
Desrosiers, Léo-Paul 1896-1967 . . . . . . . . . DLB-68
Dessaulles, Louis-Antoine 1819-1895 . . . . . DLB-99
Dessì, Giuseppe 1909-1977 . . . . . . . . . . . . DLB-177
Destouches, Louis-Ferdinand
  (see Céline, Louis-Ferdinand)
DeSylva, Buddy 1895-1950 . . . . . . . . . . . . DLB-265
De Tabley, Lord 1835-1895 . . . . . . . . . . . . DLB-35
Deutsch, Babette 1895-1982 . . . . . . . . . . . . DLB-45
Deutsch, Niklaus Manuel (see Manuel, Niklaus)
André Deutsch Limited . . . . . . . . . . . . . . DLB-112
Devanny, Jean 1894-1962 . . . . . . . . . . . . . DLB-260
Deveaux, Alexis 1948- . . . . . . . . . . . . . . . DLB-38
De Vere, Aubrey 1814-1902 . . . . . . . . . . . . DLB-35
Devereux, second Earl of Essex, Robert
  1565-1601 . . . . . . . . . . . . . . . . . . . . . DLB-136
The Devin-Adair Company . . . . . . . . . . . . DLB-46
De Vinne, Theodore Low
  1828-1914 . . . . . . . . . . . . . . . . . . . . . DLB-187
Devlin, Anne 1951- . . . . . . . . . . . . . . . . DLB-245

DeVoto, Bernard 1897-1955 . . . . . . . DLB-9, 256
De Vries, Peter 1910-1993 . . . . . . . . . DLB-6; Y-82
  Tribute to Albert Erskine . . . . . . . . . . . . Y-93
Dewart, Edward Hartley 1828-1903 . . . . . . DLB-99
Dewdney, Christopher 1951- . . . . . . . . . . DLB-60
Dewdney, Selwyn 1909-1979 . . . . . . . . . . . DLB-68
Dewey, John 1859-1952 . . . . . . . . . . DLB-246, 270
Dewey, Orville 1794-1882 . . . . . . . . . . . . DLB-243
Dewey, Thomas B. 1915-1981 . . . . . . . . . DLB-226
DeWitt, Robert M., Publisher . . . . . . . . . . DLB-49
DeWolfe, Fiske and Company . . . . . . . . . . DLB-49
Dexter, Colin 1930- . . . . . . . . . . . . . . . . . DLB-87
de Young, M. H. 1849-1925 . . . . . . . . . . . . DLB-25
Dhlomo, H. I. E. 1903-1956 . . . . . . . DLB-157, 225
Dhuoda circa 803-after 843 . . . . . . . . . . . DLB-148
*The Dial* 1840-1844 . . . . . . . . . . . . . . . . DLB-223
The Dial Press . . . . . . . . . . . . . . . . . . . . . DLB-46
Diamond, I. A. L. 1920-1988 . . . . . . . . . . . DLB-26
Dibble, L. Grace 1902-1998 . . . . . . . . . . . DLB-204
Dibdin, Thomas Frognall
  1776-1847 . . . . . . . . . . . . . . . . . . . . . DLB-184
Di Cicco, Pier Giorgio 1949- . . . . . . . . . . DLB-60
Dick, Philip K. 1928-1982 . . . . . . . . . . . . . . DLB-8
Dick and Fitzgerald . . . . . . . . . . . . . . . . . DLB-49
Dickens, Charles 1812-1870 . . . DLB-21, 55, 70, 159,
                            166; DS-5; CDBLB-4
Dickey, Eric Jerome 1961- . . . . . . . . . . . DLB-292
Dickey, James 1923-1997 . . . . . . . . . DLB-5, 193;
          Y-82, 93, 96, 97; DS-7, 19; CDALB-6
  James Dickey and Stanley Burnshaw
    Correspondence . . . . . . . . . . . . . . . . Y-02
  James Dickey at Seventy–A Tribute . . . . . Y-93
  James Dickey, American Poet . . . . . . . . . Y-96
  The James Dickey Society . . . . . . . . . . . Y-99
  The Life of James Dickey: A Lecture to
    the Friends of the Emory Libraries,
    by Henry Hart . . . . . . . . . . . . . . . . . Y-98
  Tribute to Archibald MacLeish . . . . . . . . Y-82
  Tribute to Malcolm Cowley . . . . . . . . . . Y-89
  Tribute to Truman Capote . . . . . . . . . . Y-84
  Tributes [to Dickey] . . . . . . . . . . . . . . . Y-97
Dickey, William 1928-1994 . . . . . . . . . . . . . DLB-5
Dickinson, Emily
  1830-1886 . . . . . . . . . DLB-1, 243; CDALB-3
Dickinson, John 1732-1808 . . . . . . . . . . . . DLB-31
Dickinson, Jonathan 1688-1747 . . . . . . . . . DLB-24
Dickinson, Patric 1914- . . . . . . . . . . . . . . DLB-27
Dickinson, Peter 1927- . . . . . . . DLB-87, 161, 276
John Dicks [publishing house] . . . . . . . . . DLB-106
Dickson, Gordon R. 1923-2001 . . . . . . . . . . DLB-8
*Dictionary of Literary Biography*
  Annual Awards for *Dictionary of
    Literary Biography* Editors and
    Contributors . . . . . . . . . . . . . . . . . Y-98–02
*Dictionary of Literary Biography*
  *Yearbook* Awards . . . . . . . . Y-92–93, 97–02
*The Dictionary of National Biography* . . . . . . . DLB-144

# Cumulative Index

Didion, Joan 1934-
......DLB-2, 173, 185; Y-81, 86; CDALB-6
Di Donato, Pietro 1911- .............DLB-9
Die Fürstliche Bibliothek Corvey ..........Y-96
Diego, Gerardo 1896-1987 ..........DLB-134
Dietz, Howard 1896-1983............DLB-265
Digby, Everard 1550?-1605 ..........DLB-281
Digges, Thomas circa 1546-1595 ....DLB-136
The Digital Millennium Copyright Act:
  Expanding Copyright Protection in
  Cyberspace and Beyond ............Y-98
Diktonius, Elmer 1896-1961..........DLB-259
Dillard, Annie 1945- ......DLB-275, 278; Y-80
Dillard, R. H. W. 1937- ...........DLB-5, 244
Charles T. Dillingham Company........DLB-49
G. W. Dillingham Company..........DLB-49
Edward and Charles Dilly
  [publishing house] ...............DLB-154
Dilthey, Wilhelm 1833-1911 ..........DLB-129
Dimitrova, Blaga 1922- ....DLB-181; CDWLB-4
Dimov, Dimitr 1909-1966 ...........DLB-181
Dimsdale, Thomas J. 1831?-1866.......DLB-186
Dinescu, Mircea 1950- ..............DLB-232
Dinesen, Isak (see Blixen, Karen)
Dingelstedt, Franz von 1814-1881 ......DLB-133
Dinis, Júlio (Joaquim Guilherme
  Gomes Coelho) 1839-1871.........DLB-287
Dintenfass, Mark 1941- ...............Y-84
Diogenes, Jr. (see Brougham, John)
Diogenes Laertius circa 200 ............DLB-176
DiPrima, Diane 1934- .............DLB-5, 16
Disch, Thomas M. 1940- .........DLB-8, 282
Diski, Jenny 1947- ..................DLB-271
Disney, Walt 1901-1966...............DLB-22
Disraeli, Benjamin 1804-1881.......DLB-21, 55
D'Israeli, Isaac 1766-1848 ............DLB-107
DLB Award for Distinguished
  Literary Criticism..................Y-02
Ditlevsen, Tove 1917-1976 ..........DLB-214
Ditzen, Rudolf (see Fallada, Hans)
Dix, Dorothea Lynde 1802-1887 .....DLB-1, 235
Dix, Dorothy (see Gilmer, Elizabeth Meriwether)
Dix, Edwards and Company ...........DLB-49
Dix, Gertrude circa 1874-? ...........DLB-197
Dixie, Florence Douglas 1857-1905.....DLB-174
Dixon, Ella Hepworth
  1855 or 1857-1932 ................DLB-197
Dixon, Paige (see Corcoran, Barbara)
Dixon, Richard Watson 1833-1900 ......DLB-19
Dixon, Stephen 1936- ...............DLB-130
DLB Award for Distinguished
  Literary Criticism..................Y-02
Dmitriev, Andrei Viktorovich 1956- ....DLB-285
Dmitriev, Ivan Ivanovich 1760-1837.....DLB-150
Dobell, Bertram 1842-1914............DLB-184
Dobell, Sydney 1824-1874 .............DLB-32
Dobie, J. Frank 1888-1964 ............DLB-212

Dobles Yzaguirre, Julieta 1943- .......DLB-283
Döblin, Alfred 1878-1957 ....DLB-66; CDWLB-2
Dobroliubov, Nikolai Aleksandrovich
  1836-1861 .....................DLB-277
Dobson, Austin 1840-1921.........DLB-35, 144
Dobson, Rosemary 1920- ............DLB-260
Doctorow, E. L.
  1931- .....DLB-2, 28, 173; Y-80; CDALB-6
Dodd, Susan M. 1946- ..............DLB-244
Dodd, William E. 1869-1940 ..........DLB-17
Anne Dodd [publishing house]........DLB-154
Dodd, Mead and Company ...........DLB-49
Doderer, Heimito von 1896-1966.......DLB-85
B. W. Dodge and Company...........DLB-46
Dodge, Mary Abigail 1833-1896 .......DLB-221
Dodge, Mary Mapes
  1831?-1905................DLB-42, 79; DS-13
Dodge Publishing Company ..........DLB-49
Dodgson, Charles Lutwidge (see Carroll, Lewis)
Dodsley, Robert 1703-1764............DLB-95
R. Dodsley [publishing house] ........DLB-154
Dodson, Owen 1914-1983 ............DLB-76
Dodwell, Christina 1951- ............DLB-204
Doesticks, Q. K. Philander, P. B.
  (see Thomson, Mortimer)
Doheny, Carrie Estelle 1875-1958 ......DLB-140
Doherty, John 1798?-1854 ............DLB-190
Doig, Ivan 1939- ...................DLB-206
Doinaș, Ștefan Augustin 1922- .......DLB-232
Domínguez, Sylvia Maida 1935- .......DLB-122
Donaghy, Michael 1954- .............DLB-282
Patrick Donahoe [publishing house]......DLB-49
Donald, David H. 1920- ........DLB-17; Y-87
Donaldson, Scott 1928- .............DLB-111
Doni, Rodolfo 1919- ................DLB-177
Donleavy, J. P. 1926- ............DLB-6, 173
Donnadieu, Marguerite (see Duras, Marguerite)
Donne, John
  1572-1631........DLB-121, 151; CDBLB-1
Donnelly, Ignatius 1831-1901 ..........DLB-12
R. R. Donnelley and Sons Company ....DLB-49
Donoghue, Emma 1969- ............DLB-267
Donohue and Henneberry ............DLB-49
Donoso, José 1924-1996.....DLB-113; CDWLB-3
M. Doolady [publishing house] ........DLB-49
Dooley, Ebon (see Ebon)
Doolittle, Hilda 1886-1961 .....DLB-4, 45; DS-15
Doplicher, Fabio 1938- ..............DLB-128
Dor, Milo 1923- ....................DLB-85
George H. Doran Company...........DLB-46
Dorgelès, Roland 1886-1973...........DLB-65
Dorn, Edward 1929-1999..............DLB-5
Dorr, Rheta Childe 1866-1948 .........DLB-25
Dorris, Michael 1945-1997 ...........DLB-175
Dorset and Middlesex, Charles Sackville,
  Lord Buckhurst, Earl of 1643-1706 ....DLB-131

Dorsey, Candas Jane 1952- ..........DLB-251
Dorst, Tankred 1925- .............DLB-75, 124
Dos Passos, John 1896-1970
  ...............DLB-4, 9; DS-1, 15; CDALB-5
  John Dos Passos: A Centennial
    Commemoration...................Y-96
  John Dos Passos: Artist ..............Y-99
  John Dos Passos Newsletter...........Y-00
  U.S.A. (Documentary) ............DLB-274
Dostoevsky, Fyodor 1821-1881 ........DLB-238
Doubleday and Company .............DLB-49
Doubrovsky, Serge 1928- ............DLB-299
Dougall, Lily 1858-1923...............DLB-92
Doughty, Charles M.
  1843-1926 ...............DLB-19, 57, 174
Douglas, Lady Alfred (see Custance, Olive)
Douglas, Ellen (Josephine Ayres Haxton)
  1921- .........................DLB-292
Douglas, Gavin 1476-1522 ...........DLB-132
Douglas, Keith 1920-1944 ............DLB-27
Douglas, Norman 1868-1952 .......DLB-34, 195
Douglass, Frederick 1817-1895
  .........DLB-1, 43, 50, 79, 243; CDALB-2
  Frederick Douglass Creative Arts Center  Y-01
Douglass, William circa 1691-1752......DLB-24
Dourado, Autran 1926- .............DLB-145
Dove, Arthur G. 1880-1946 ..........DLB-188
Dove, Rita 1952- .........DLB-120; CDALB-7
Dover Publications..................DLB-46
Doves Press ......................DLB-112
Dovlatov, Sergei Donatovich
  1941-1990 .....................DLB-285
Dowden, Edward 1843-1913 ......DLB-35, 149
Dowell, Coleman 1925-1985 .........DLB-130
Dowland, John 1563-1626 ...........DLB-172
Downes, Gwladys 1915- .............DLB-88
Downing, J., Major (see Davis, Charles A.)
Downing, Major Jack (see Smith, Seba)
Dowriche, Anne
  before 1560-after 1613 ............DLB-172
Dowson, Ernest 1867-1900 .......DLB-19, 135
William Doxey [publishing house].......DLB-49
Doyle, Sir Arthur Conan
  1859-1930 ...DLB-18, 70, 156, 178; CDBLB-5
  The Priory Scholars of New York .......Y-99
Doyle, Kirby 1932- .................DLB-16
Doyle, Roddy 1958- ................DLB-194
Drabble, Margaret
  1939- .......DLB-14, 155, 231; CDBLB-8
  Tribute to Graham Greene ............Y-91
Drach, Albert 1902-1995 .............DLB-85
Drachmann, Holger 1846-1908 .......DLB-300
Dragojević, Danijel 1934- ...........DLB-181
Drake, Samuel Gardner 1798-1875......DLB-187
Drama (See Theater)
The Dramatic Publishing Company......DLB-49
Dramatists Play Service ..............DLB-46

468

Drant, Thomas
 early 1540s?-1578 ................DLB-167
Draper, John W. 1811-1882..............DLB-30
Draper, Lyman C. 1815-1891 ...........DLB-30
Drayton, Michael 1563-1631...........DLB-121
Dreiser, Theodore 1871-1945
 ....... DLB-9, 12, 102, 137; DS-1; CDALB-3
 The International Theodore Dreiser
  Society ......................Y-01
 Notes from the Underground
  of *Sister Carrie* ................Y-01
Dresser, Davis 1904-1977 ............DLB-226
Drew, Elizabeth A.
 "A Note on Technique" [excerpt]
  (1926) .....................DLB-36
Drewitz, Ingeborg 1923-1986............DLB-75
Drieu La Rochelle, Pierre 1893-1945......DLB-72
Drinker, Elizabeth 1735-1807..........DLB-200
Drinkwater, John 1882-1937 .....DLB-10, 19, 149
 The Friends of the Dymock Poets.......Y-00
Droste-Hülshoff, Annette von
 1797-1848..............DLB-133; CDWLB-2
The Drue Heinz Literature Prize
 Excerpt from "Excerpts from a Report
 of the Commission," in David
 Bosworth's *The Death of Descartes*
 An Interview with David Bosworth .....Y-82
Drummond, William, of Hawthornden
 1585-1649 ...............DLB-121, 213
Drummond, William Henry 1854-1907 ...DLB-92
Druzhinin, Aleksandr Vasil'evich
 1824-1864 ...................DLB-238
Dryden, Charles 1860?-1931...........DLB-171
Dryden, John
 1631-1700 .....DLB-80, 101, 131; CDBLB-2
Držić, Marin
 circa 1508-1567 ........DLB-147; CDWLB-4
Duane, William 1760-1835 .............DLB-43
Dubé, Marcel 1930- ..................DLB-53
Dubé, Rodolphe (see Hertel, François)
Dubie, Norman 1945- ................DLB-120
Dubin, Al 1891-1945..................DLB-265
Dubois, Silvia 1788 or 1789?-1889........DLB-239
Du Bois, W. E. B.
 1868-1963 ....DLB-47, 50, 91, 246; CDALB-3
Du Bois, William Pène 1916-1993.........DLB-61
Dubrovina, Ekaterina Oskarovna
 1846-1913 ...................DLB-238
Dubus, Andre 1936-1999................DLB-130
 Tribute to Michael M. Rea ...........Y-97
Dubus, Andre, III 1959- .............DLB-292
Ducange, Victor 1783-1833 ...........DLB-192
Du Chaillu, Paul Belloni 1831?-1903.....DLB-189
Ducharme, Réjean 1941- .............DLB-60
Dučić, Jovan 1871-1943 .....DLB-147; CDWLB-4
Duck, Stephen 1705?-1756 .............DLB-95
Gerald Duckworth and Company
 Limited .....................DLB-112
Duclaux, Madame Mary (see Robinson, A. Mary F.)

Dudek, Louis 1918-2001 ...............DLB-88
Dudintsev, Vladimir Dmitrievich
 1918-1998 ....................DLB-302
Dudley-Smith, Trevor (see Hall, Adam)
Duell, Sloan and Pearce................DLB-46
Duerer, Albrecht 1471-1528............DLB-179
Duff Gordon, Lucie 1821-1869 .........DLB-166
Dufferin, Helen Lady, Countess of Gifford
 1807-1867 ....................DLB-199
Duffield and Green ...................DLB-46
Duffy, Maureen 1933- .................DLB-14
Dufief, Nicholas Gouin 1776-1834........DLB-187
Dufresne, John 1948- ................DLB-292
Dugan, Alan 1923- ....................DLB-5
Dugard, William 1606-1662 ......DLB-170, 281
 William Dugard [publishing house]......DLB-170
Dugas, Marcel 1883-1947 ..............DLB-92
 William Dugdale [publishing house].....DLB-106
Duhamel, Georges 1884-1966 ...........DLB-65
Dujardin, Edouard 1861-1949............DLB-123
Dukes, Ashley 1885-1959 ..............DLB-10
Dumas, Alexandre *fils* 1824-1895............DLB-192
Dumas, Alexandre *père* 1802-1870 .....DLB-119, 192
Dumas, Henry 1934-1968................DLB-41
du Maurier, Daphne 1907-1989.........DLB-191
Du Maurier, George 1834-1896 .... DLB-153, 178
Dummett, Michael 1925- ............DLB-262
Dunbar, Paul Laurence
 1872-1906 ........DLB-50, 54, 78; CDALB-3
 Introduction to *Lyrics of Lowly Life* (1896),
  by William Dean Howells .......DLB-50
Dunbar, William
 circa 1460-circa 1522..........DLB-132, 146
Duncan, Dave 1933- .................DLB-251
Duncan, David James 1952- .........DLB-256
Duncan, Norman 1871-1916 ............DLB-92
Duncan, Quince 1940- ...............DLB-145
Duncan, Robert 1919-1988 .......DLB-5, 16, 193
Duncan, Ronald 1914-1982.............DLB-13
Duncan, Sara Jeannette 1861-1922 .....DLB-92
Dunigan, Edward, and Brother .........DLB-49
Dunlap, John 1747-1812................DLB-43
Dunlap, William 1766-1839....... DLB-30, 37, 59
Dunlop, William "Tiger" 1792-1848 ......DLB-99
Dunmore, Helen 1952- ...............DLB-267
Dunn, Douglas 1942- .................DLB-40
Dunn, Harvey Thomas 1884-1952 .....DLB-188
Dunn, Stephen 1939- ................DLB-105
 "The Good, The Not So Good" .....DLB-105
Dunne, Finley Peter 1867-1936 .......DLB-11, 23
Dunne, John Gregory 1932- .............Y-80
Dunne, Philip 1908-1992...............DLB-26
Dunning, Ralph Cheever 1878-1930 ......DLB-4
Dunning, William A. 1857-1922 ........DLB-17
Duns Scotus, John circa 1266-1308 ......DLB-115

Dunsany, Lord (Edward John Moreton
 Drax Plunkett, Baron Dunsany)
 1878-1957 ....... DLB-10, 77, 153, 156, 255
Dunton, W. Herbert 1878-1936.........DLB-188
John Dunton [publishing house] .......DLB-170
Dupin, Amantine-Aurore-Lucile (see Sand, George)
Dupuy, Eliza Ann 1814-1880 ..........DLB-248
Durack, Mary 1913-1994 ..............DLB-260
Durand, Lucile (see Bersianik, Louky)
Duranti, Francesca 1935- ............DLB-196
Duranty, Walter 1884-1957.............DLB-29
Duras, Marguerite (Marguerite Donnadieu)
 1914-1996 ....................DLB-83
Durfey, Thomas 1653-1723.............DLB-80
Durova, Nadezhda Andreevna
 (Aleksandr Andreevich Aleksandrov)
 1783-1866 ...................DLB-198
Durrell, Lawrence 1912-1990
 ......... DLB-15, 27, 204; Y-90; CDBLB-7
William Durrell [publishing house] .......DLB-49
Dürrenmatt, Friedrich
 1921-1990 ........ DLB-69, 124; CDWLB-2
Duston, Hannah 1657-1737 ...........DLB-200
Dutt, Toru 1856-1877 ................DLB-240
E. P. Dutton and Company.............DLB-49
Duun, Olav 1876-1939 ...............DLB-297
Duvoisin, Roger 1904-1980.............DLB-61
Duyckinck, Evert Augustus
 1816-1878 ..............DLB-3, 64, 250
Duyckinck, George L.
 1823-1863 ................DLB-3, 250
Duyckinck and Company ..............DLB-49
Dwight, John Sullivan 1813-1893 .....DLB-1, 235
Dwight, Timothy 1752-1817 ............DLB-37
 America: or, A Poem on the Settlement
  of the British Colonies, by
  Timothy Dwight................DLB-37
Dybek, Stuart 1942- .................DLB-130
 Tribute to Michael M. Rea ............Y-97
Dyer, Charles 1928- ..................DLB-13
Dyer, Sir Edward 1543-1607 ...........DLB-136
Dyer, George 1755-1841 ...............DLB-93
Dyer, John 1699-1757 .................DLB-95
Dyk, Viktor 1877-1931 ...............DLB-215
Dylan, Bob 1941- ....................DLB-16

# E

Eager, Edward 1911-1964 ..............DLB-22
Eagleton, Terry 1943- ...............DLB-242
Eames, Wilberforce
 1855-1937 ....................DLB-140
Earle, Alice Morse
 1853-1911 ....................DLB-221
Earle, John 1600 or 1601-1665 ........DLB-151
James H. Earle and Company ..........DLB-49
East Europe
 Independence and Destruction,
  1918-1941...................DLB-220

| | | |
|---|---|---|
| Social Theory and Ethnography: Language and Ethnicity in Western versus Eastern Man ... DLB-220 | Edwards, Edward 1812-1886 ......... DLB-184 | Eliot, T. S. 1888-1965 ........ DLB-7, 10, 45, 63, 245; CDALB-5 |
| Eastlake, William 1917-1997 ........ DLB-6, 206 | Edwards, Jonathan 1703-1758 ....... DLB-24, 270 | T. S. Eliot Centennial: The Return of the Old Possum ................ Y-88 |
| Eastman, Carol ?- ................... DLB-44 | Edwards, Jonathan, Jr. 1745-1801 ...... DLB-37 | The T. S. Eliot Society: Celebration and Scholarship, 1980-1999 ......... Y-99 |
| Eastman, Charles A. (Ohiyesa) 1858-1939 ................... DLB-175 | Edwards, Junius 1929- .............. DLB-33 | Eliot's Court Press ................. DLB-170 |
| Eastman, Max 1883-1969 ............. DLB-91 | Edwards, Matilda Barbara Betham 1836-1919 ................... DLB-174 | Elizabeth I 1533-1603 ............... DLB-136 |
| Eaton, Daniel Isaac 1753-1814 ......... DLB-158 | Edwards, Richard 1524-1566 .......... DLB-62 | Elizabeth von Nassau-Saarbrücken after 1393-1456 ................ DLB-179 |
| Eaton, Edith Maude 1865-1914 ........ DLB-221 | Edwards, Sarah Pierpont 1710-1758 ..... DLB-200 | Elizondo, Salvador 1932- ............ DLB-145 |
| Eaton, Winnifred 1875-1954 .......... DLB-221 | James Edwards [publishing house] ...... DLB-154 | Elizondo, Sergio 1930- .............. DLB-82 |
| Eberhart, Richard 1904- .... DLB-48; CDALB-1 | Effinger, George Alec 1947- ........... DLB-8 | Elkin, Stanley 1930-1995 ........ DLB-2, 28, 218, 278; Y-80 |
| Tribute to Robert Penn Warren ....... Y-89 | Egerton, George 1859-1945 .......... DLB-135 | Elles, Dora Amy (see Wentworth, Patricia) |
| Ebner, Jeannie 1918- ................ DLB-85 | Eggleston, Edward 1837-1902 ......... DLB-12 | Ellet, Elizabeth F. 1818?-1877 ......... DLB-30 |
| Ebner-Eschenbach, Marie von 1830-1916 .................... DLB-81 | Eggleston, Wilfred 1901-1986 ......... DLB-92 | Elliot, Ebenezer 1781-1849 ....... DLB-96, 190 |
| Ebon 1942- ....................... DLB-41 | Eglītis, Anšlavs 1906-1993 ........... DLB-220 | Elliot, Frances Minto (Dickinson) 1820-1898 .................... DLB-166 |
| E-Books' Second Act in Libraries ......... Y-02 | Eguren, José María 1874-1942 ........ DLB-290 | Elliott, Charlotte 1789-1871 .......... DLB-199 |
| *Ecbasis Captivi* circa 1045 ............. DLB-148 | Ehrenreich, Barbara 1941- ........... DLB-246 | Elliott, George 1923- ................ DLB-68 |
| Ecco Press ........................ DLB-46 | Ehrenstein, Albert 1886-1950 .......... DLB-81 | Elliott, George P. 1918-1980 .......... DLB-244 |
| Eckhart, Meister circa 1260-circa 1328 ... DLB-115 | Ehrhart, W. D. 1948- ................ DS-9 | Elliott, Janice 1931-1995 ............. DLB-14 |
| *The Eclectic Review* 1805-1868 ......... DLB-110 | Ehrlich, Gretel 1946- ............ DLB-212, 275 | Elliott, Sarah Barnwell 1848-1928 ...... DLB-221 |
| Eco, Umberto 1932- ............ DLB-196, 242 | Eich, Günter 1907-1972 .......... DLB-69, 124 | Elliott, Sumner Locke 1917-1991 ....... DLB-289 |
| Eddison, E. R. 1882-1945 ............ DLB-255 | Eichendorff, Joseph Freiherr von 1788-1857 ................... DLB-90 | Elliott, Thomes and Talbot ........... DLB-49 |
| Edel, Leon 1907-1997 ............... DLB-103 | Eifukumon'in 1271-1342 ............ DLB-203 | Elliott, William, III 1788-1863 ...... DLB-3, 248 |
| Edelfeldt, Inger 1956- ............... DLB-257 | Eigner, Larry 1926-1996 .......... DLB-5, 193 | Ellis, Alice Thomas (Anna Margaret Haycraft) 1932- ....................... DLB-194 |
| A Century of Poetry, a Lifetime of Collecting: J. M. Edelstein's Collection of Twentieth-Century American Poetry ............ Y-02 | *Eikon Basilike* 1649 ................ DLB-151 | Ellis, Bret Easton 1964- ............. DLB-292 |
| Edes, Benjamin 1732-1803 ............ DLB-43 | Eilhart von Oberge circa 1140-circa 1195 ........... DLB-148 | Ellis, Edward S. 1840-1916 ........... DLB-42 |
| Edgar, David 1948- ............ DLB-13, 233 | Einar Benediktsson 1864-1940 ........ DLB-293 | Ellis, George E. "The New Controversy Concerning Miracles .................... DS-5 |
| Viewpoint: Politics and Performance ................. DLB-13 | Einar Kárason 1955- ............... DLB-293 | Ellis, Havelock 1859-1939 ........... DLB-190 |
| Edgerton, Clyde 1944- .............. DLB-278 | Einar Már Guðmundsson 1954- ...... DLB-293 | Frederick Staridge Ellis [publishing house] .............. DLB-106 |
| Edgeworth, Maria 1768-1849 ............. DLB-116, 159, 163 | Einhard circa 770-840 .............. DLB-148 | The George H. Ellis Company .......... DLB-49 |
| *The Edinburgh Review* 1802-1929 ....... DLB-110 | Eiseley, Loren 1907-1977 ....... DLB-275, DS-17 | Ellison, Harlan 1934- ................ DLB-8 |
| Edinburgh University Press ........... DLB-112 | Eisenberg, Deborah 1945- ........... DLB-244 | Tribute to Isaac Asimov ............. Y-92 |
| Editing Conversations with Editors ........... Y-95 | Eisenreich, Herbert 1925-1986 ......... DLB-85 | Ellison, Ralph 1914-1994 ... DLB-2, 76, 227; Y-94; CDALB-1 |
| Editorial Statements ............... DLB-137 | Eisner, Kurt 1867-1919 .............. DLB-66 | Ellmann, Richard 1918-1987 ...... DLB-103; Y-87 |
| The Editorial Style of Fredson Bowers ... Y-91 | Ekelöf, Gunnar 1907-1968 ........... DLB-259 | Ellroy, James 1948- ............. DLB-226; Y-91 |
| Editorial: The Extension of Copyright ... Y-02 | Eklund, Gordon 1945- .............. Y-83 | Tribute to John D. MacDonald ........ Y-86 |
| We See the Editor at Work .......... Y-97 | Ekman, Kerstin 1933- .............. DLB-257 | Tribute to Raymond Chandler ........ Y-88 |
| Whose *Ulysses*? The Function of Editing .. Y-97 | Ekwensi, Cyprian 1921- ..... DLB-117; CDWLB-3 | Eluard, Paul 1895-1952 .............. DLB-258 |
| The Editor Publishing Company ........ DLB-49 | Elaw, Zilpha circa 1790-? ............ DLB-239 | Elyot, Thomas 1490?-1546 ........... DLB-136 |
| Editorial Institute at Boston University ..... Y-00 | George Eld [publishing house] ......... DLB-170 | Emanuel, James Andrew 1921- ........ DLB-41 |
| Edmonds, Helen Woods Ferguson (see Kavan, Anna) | Elder, Lonne, III 1931- ......... DLB-7, 38, 44 | Emecheta, Buchi 1944- .... DLB-117; CDWLB-3 |
| Edmonds, Randolph 1900-1983 ........ DLB-51 | Paul Elder and Company ............ DLB-49 | Emerson, Ralph Waldo 1803-1882 ..... DLB-1, 59, 73, 183, 223, 270; DS-5; CDALB-2 |
| Edmonds, Walter D. 1903-1998 ......... DLB-9 | Eldershaw, Flora (M. Barnard Eldershaw) 1897-1956 ................... DLB-260 | Ralph Waldo Emerson in 1982 ........ Y-82 |
| Edric, Robert (see Armitage, G. E.) | Eldershaw, M. Barnard (see Barnard, Marjorie and Eldershaw, Flora) | The Ralph Waldo Emerson Society ..... Y-99 |
| Edschmid, Kasimir 1890-1966 ......... DLB-56 | The Electronic Text Center and the Electronic Archive of Early American Fiction at the University of Virginia Library ......... Y-98 | Emerson, William 1769-1811 .......... DLB-37 |
| Edson, Margaret 1961- .............. DLB-266 | | Emerson, William R. 1923-1997 ........ Y-97 |
| Edson, Russell 1935- ................ DLB-244 | Eliade, Mircea 1907-1986 ... DLB-220; CDWLB-4 | Emin, Fedor Aleksandrovich circa 1735-1770 ................ DLB-150 |
| Edwards, Amelia Anne Blandford 1831-1892 ................... DLB-174 | Elie, Robert 1915-1973 .............. DLB-88 | |
| Edwards, Dic 1953- ................ DLB-245 | Elin Pelin 1877-1949 ........ DLB-147; CDWLB-4 | |
| | Eliot, George 1819-1880 ....... DLB-21, 35, 55; CDBLB-4 | |
| | The George Eliot Fellowship .......... Y-99 | |
| | Eliot, John 1604-1690 ............... DLB-24 | |

| | | |
|---|---|---|
| Emmanuel, Pierre 1916-1984 . . . . . . . . . . DLB-258 | Esdaile, Arundell 1880-1956 . . . . . . . . . . DLB-201 | **F** |
| Empedocles fifth century B.C. . . . . . . DLB-176 | Esenin, Sergei Aleksandrovich 1895-1925 . . . . . . . . . . . . . . . . . . . . . DLB-295 | |
| Empson, William 1906-1984 . . . . . . . . . . DLB-20 | | Faber, Frederick William 1814-1863 . . . . . DLB-32 |
| Enchi Fumiko 1905-1986 . . . . . . . . . . DLB-182 | Eshleman, Clayton 1935- . . . . . . . . . . . . . . DLB-5 | Faber and Faber Limited . . . . . . . . . . . . . DLB-112 |
| Ende, Michael 1929-1995 . . . . . . . . . . . DLB-75 | Espaillat, Rhina P. 1932- . . . . . . . . . . DLB-282 | Faccio, Rena (see Aleramo, Sibilla) |
| Endō Shūsaku 1923-1996 . . . . . . . . . . DLB-182 | Espanca, Florbela 1894-1930 . . . . . . . . . . DLB-287 | Facsimiles |
| Engel, Marian 1933-1985 . . . . . . . . . . . . DLB-53 | Espriu, Salvador 1913-1985 . . . . . . . . . . DLB-134 | The Uses of Facsimile: A Symposium . . . . Y-90 |
| Engel'gardt, Sof'ia Vladimirovna 1828-1894 . . . . . . . . . . . . . . . . . . . . . DLB-277 | Ess Ess Publishing Company . . . . . . . . . . . DLB-49 | Fadeev, Aleksandr Aleksandrovich 1901-1956 . . . . . . . . . . . . . . . . . . . . . DLB-272 |
| | Essex House Press . . . . . . . . . . . . . . . . . . DLB-112 | Fagundo, Ana María 1938- . . . . . . . . DLB-134 |
| Engels, Friedrich 1820-1895 . . . . . . . . . . DLB-129 | Esson, Louis 1878-1943 . . . . . . . . . . . . . DLB-260 | Fainzil'berg, Il'ia Arnol'dovich |
| Engle, Paul 1908- . . . . . . . . . . . . . . . . . . DLB-48 | Essop, Ahmed 1931- . . . . . . . . . . . . . . . . DLB-225 | (see Il'f, Il'ia and Petrov, Evgenii) |
| Tribute to Robert Penn Warren . . . . . . . . Y-89 | Esterházy, Péter 1950- . . . . DLB-232; CDWLB-4 | Fair, Ronald L. 1932- . . . . . . . . . . . . . . . DLB-33 |
| English, Thomas Dunn 1819-1902 . . . . . DLB-202 | Estes, Eleanor 1906-1988 . . . . . . . . . . . . . DLB-22 | Fairfax, Beatrice (see Manning, Marie) |
| Ennius 239 B.C.-169 B.C. . . . . . . . . . . . . DLB-211 | Estes and Lauriat . . . . . . . . . . . . . . . . . . . DLB-49 | Fairlie, Gerard 1899-1983 . . . . . . . . . . . . . DLB-77 |
| Enquist, Per Olov 1934- . . . . . . . . . . . DLB-257 | Estleman, Loren D. 1952- . . . . . . . . . . DLB-226 | Faldbakken, Knut 1941- . . . . . . . . . . . . . DLB-297 |
| Enright, Anne 1962- . . . . . . . . . . . . . . DLB-267 | Eszterhas, Joe 1944- . . . . . . . . . . . . . . . . DLB-185 | Falkberget, Johan (Johan Petter Lillebakken) 1879-1967 . . . . . . . . . . . . . . . . . . . . . DLB-297 |
| Enright, D. J. 1920- . . . . . . . . . . . . . . . . DLB-27 | Etherege, George 1636-circa 1692 . . . . . . . DLB-80 | |
| Enright, Elizabeth 1909-1968 . . . . . . . . . . DLB-22 | Ethridge, Mark, Sr. 1896-1981 . . . . . . . . DLB-127 | Fallada, Hans 1893-1947 . . . . . . . . . . . . . DLB-56 |
| Epictetus circa 55-circa 125-130 . . . . . . DLB-176 | Ets, Marie Hall 1893-1984 . . . . . . . . . . . . DLB-22 | Fancher, Betsy 1928- . . . . . . . . . . . . . . . . . Y-83 |
| Epicurus 342/341 B.C.-271/270 B.C. . . . . . DLB-176 | Etter, David 1928- . . . . . . . . . . . . . . . . . DLB-105 | Fane, Violet 1843-1905 . . . . . . . . . . . . . . DLB-35 |
| Epps, Bernard 1936- . . . . . . . . . . . . . . . DLB-53 | Ettner, Johann Christoph 1654-1724 . . . . . . . . . . . . . . . . . . . . . DLB-168 | Fanfrolico Press . . . . . . . . . . . . . . . . . . . DLB-112 |
| Epshtein, Mikhail Naumovich 1950- . . . DLB-285 | | Fanning, Katherine 1927- . . . . . . . . . . . DLB-127 |
| Epstein, Julius 1909-2000 and Epstein, Philip 1909-1952 . . . . . . . . . DLB-26 | Eudora Welty Remembered in Two Exhibits . . . . . . . . . . . . . . . . . . . . . . Y-02 | Fanon, Frantz 1925-1961 . . . . . . . . . . . . DLB-296 |
| | | Fanshawe, Sir Richard 1608-1666 . . . . . . DLB-126 |
| Epstein, Leslie 1938- . . . . . . . . . . . . . . . DLB-299 | Eugene Gant's Projected Works . . . . . . . . . Y-01 | Fantasy Press Publishers . . . . . . . . . . . . . . DLB-46 |
| Editors, Conversations with . . . . . . . . . . . . . Y-95 | Eupolemius flourished circa 1095 . . . . . DLB-148 | Fante, John 1909-1983 . . . . . . . . . DLB-130; Y-83 |
| Equiano, Olaudah circa 1745-1797 . . . . . . DLB-37, 50; CDWLB-3 | Euripides circa 484 B.C.-407/406 B.C. . . . . . . . . . . . . . . . . DLB-176; CDWLB-1 | Al-Farabi circa 870-950 . . . . . . . . . . . . . . DLB-115 |
| | | Farabough, Laura 1949- . . . . . . . . . . . . DLB-228 |
| Olaudah Equiano and Unfinished Journeys: The Slave-Narrative Tradition and Twentieth-Century Continuities . . . . . . . . . . . . . . . . . . DLB-117 | Evans, Augusta Jane 1835-1909 . . . . . . . . DLB-239 | Farah, Nuruddin 1945- . . . DLB-125; CDWLB-3 |
| | Evans, Caradoc 1878-1945 . . . . . . . . . . . DLB-162 | Farber, Norma 1909-1984 . . . . . . . . . . . . DLB-61 |
| | Evans, Charles 1850-1935 . . . . . . . . . . . DLB-187 | Fargue, Léon-Paul 1876-1947 . . . . . . . . . DLB-258 |
| | Evans, Donald 1884-1921 . . . . . . . . . . . . DLB-54 | Farigoule, Louis (see Romains, Jules) |
| Eragny Press . . . . . . . . . . . . . . . . . . . . . . DLB-112 | Evans, George Henry 1805-1856 . . . . . . . DLB-43 | Farjeon, Eleanor 1881-1965 . . . . . . . . . . DLB-160 |
| Erasmus, Desiderius 1467-1536 . . . . . . . DLB-136 | Evans, Hubert 1892-1986 . . . . . . . . . . . . DLB-92 | Farley, Harriet 1812-1907 . . . . . . . . . . . DLB-239 |
| Erba, Luciano 1922- . . . . . . . . . . . . . . DLB-128 | Evans, Mari 1923- . . . . . . . . . . . . . . . . . DLB-41 | Farley, Walter 1920-1989 . . . . . . . . . . . . . DLB-22 |
| Erdman, Nikolai Robertovich 1900-1970 . . . . . . . . . . . . . . . . . . . . . DLB-272 | Evans, Mary Ann (see Eliot, George) | Farmborough, Florence 1887-1978 . . . . . DLB-204 |
| | Evans, Nathaniel 1742-1767 . . . . . . . . . . . DLB-31 | Farmer, Penelope 1939- . . . . . . . . . . . . DLB-161 |
| Erdrich, Louise 1954- . . . . . . . DLB-152, 175, 206; CDALB-7 | Evans, Sebastian 1830-1909 . . . . . . . . . . . DLB-35 | Farmer, Philip José 1918- . . . . . . . . . . . . . DLB-8 |
| | Evans, Ray 1915- . . . . . . . . . . . . . . . . . . DLB-265 | Farnaby, Thomas 1575?-1647 . . . . . . . . . DLB-236 |
| Erenburg, Il'ia Grigor'evich 1891-1967 . . . DLB-272 | M. Evans and Company . . . . . . . . . . . . . . DLB-46 | Farningham, Marianne (see Hearn, Mary Anne) |
| Erichsen-Brown, Gwethalyn Graham (see Graham, Gwethalyn) | Evaristi, Marcella 1953- . . . . . . . . . . . . DLB-233 | Farquhar, George circa 1677-1707 . . . . . . . DLB-84 |
| | Everett, Alexander Hill 1790-1847 . . . . . . DLB-59 | Farquharson, Martha (see Finley, Martha) |
| Eriugena, John Scottus circa 810-877 . . . . . DLB-115 | Everett, Edward 1794-1865 . . . . . DLB-1, 59, 235 | Farrar, Frederic William 1831-1903 . . . . . . DLB-163 |
| Ernst, Paul 1866-1933 . . . . . . . . . . . DLB-66, 118 | Everson, R. G. 1903- . . . . . . . . . . . . . . . DLB-88 | Farrar, Straus and Giroux . . . . . . . . . . . . . DLB-46 |
| Erofeev, Venedikt Vasil'evich 1938-1990 . . . . . . . . . . . . . . . . . . . . . DLB-285 | Everson, William 1912-1994 . . . . . DLB-5, 16, 212 | Farrar and Rinehart . . . . . . . . . . . . . . . . . DLB-46 |
| | Ewald, Johannes 1743-1781 . . . . . . . . . . DLB-300 | Farrell, J. G. 1935-1979 . . . . . . . . . . DLB-14, 271 |
| Erofeev, Viktor Vladimirovich 1947- . . . DLB-285 | Ewart, Gavin 1916-1995 . . . . . . . . . . . . . DLB-40 | Farrell, James T. 1904-1979 . . . . DLB-4, 9, 86; DS-2 |
| Ershov, Petr Pavlovich 1815-1869 . . . . . . DLB-205 | Ewing, Juliana Horatia 1841-1885 . . . . . . . . . . . . . . . . . . . . DLB-21, 163 | Fast, Howard 1914- . . . . . . . . . . . . . . . . . DLB-9 |
| Erskine, Albert 1911-1993 . . . . . . . . . . . . . Y-93 | | Faulkner, William 1897-1962 . . . DLB-9, 11, 44, 102; DS-2; Y-86; CDALB-5 |
| At Home with Albert Erskine . . . . . . . . . Y-00 | The Examiner 1808-1881 . . . . . . . . . . . . . DLB-110 | |
| Erskine, John 1879-1951 . . . . . . . . . . DLB-9, 102 | Exley, Frederick 1929-1992 . . . . . . DLB-143; Y-81 | Faulkner and Yoknapatawpha Conference, Oxford, Mississippi . . . . . Y-97 |
| Erskine, Mrs. Steuart ?-1948 . . . . . . . . . . DLB-195 | Editorial: The Extension of Copyright . . . . . Y-02 | |
| Ertel', Aleksandr Ivanovich 1855-1908 . . . . . . . . . . . . . . . . . . . . . DLB-238 | von Eyb, Albrecht 1420-1475 . . . . . . . . . DLB-179 | Faulkner Centennial Addresses . . . . . . . . . Y-97 |
| | Eyre and Spottiswoode . . . . . . . . . . . . . . DLB-106 | "Faulkner 100–Celebrating the Work," University of South Carolina, Columbia . . . . . . . . . . . . . . . . . . . . . . . Y-97 |
| Ervine, St. John Greer 1883-1971 . . . . . . . DLB-10 | Ezera, Regīna 1930- . . . . . . . . . . . . . . . DLB-232 | |
| Eschenburg, Johann Joachim 1743-1820 . . . . . . . . . . . . . . . . . . . . . . DLB-97 | Ezzo ?-after 1065 . . . . . . . . . . . . . . . . . . DLB-148 | |
| Escoto, Julio 1944- . . . . . . . . . . . . . . . . DLB-145 | | |

Impressions of William Faulkner ........ Y-97
    William Faulkner and the People-to-People
        Program. ....................... Y-86
    William Faulkner Centenary
        Celebrations ..................... Y-97
    The William Faulkner Society .......... Y-99
George Faulkner [publishing house] ..... DLB-154
Faulks, Sebastian 1953- ............ DLB-207
Fauset, Jessie Redmon 1882-1961 ........ DLB-51
Faust, Frederick Schiller (Max Brand)
    1892-1944 ..................... DLB-256
Faust, Irvin
    1924- ....... DLB-2, 28, 218, 278; Y-80, 00
    I Wake Up Screaming [Response to
        Ken Auletta] .................... Y-97
    Tribute to Bernard Malamud. ......... Y-86
    Tribute to Isaac Bashevis Singer ....... Y-91
    Tribute to Meyer Levin .............. Y-81
Fawcett, Edgar 1847-1904 ............ DLB-202
Fawcett, Millicent Garrett 1847-1929 .... DLB-190
Fawcett Books ...................... DLB-46
Fay, Theodore Sedgwick 1807-1898 ..... DLB-202
Fearing, Kenneth 1902-1961 ............ DLB-9
Federal Writers' Project ............. DLB-46
Federman, Raymond 1928- ............ Y-80
Fedin, Konstantin Aleksandrovich
    1892-1977 ..................... DLB-272
Fedorov, Innokentii Vasil'evich
    (see Omulevsky, Innokentii Vasil'evich)
Feiffer, Jules 1929- ............... DLB-7, 44
Feinberg, Charles E. 1899-1988 .... DLB-187; Y-88
Feind, Barthold 1678-1721 ............ DLB-168
Feinstein, Elaine 1930- ............ DLB-14, 40
Feirstein, Frederick 1940- ............ DLB-282
Feiss, Paul Louis 1875-1952 ............ DLB-187
Feldman, Irving 1928- ............... DLB-169
Felipe, Léon 1884-1968 .............. DLB-108
Fell, Frederick, Publishers .............. DLB-46
Fellowship of Southern Writers ............ Y-98
Felltham, Owen 1602?-1668 ...... DLB-126, 151
Felman, Shoshana 1942- ............ DLB-246
Fels, Ludwig 1946- .................. DLB-75
Felton, Cornelius Conway
    1807-1862 .................. DLB-1, 235
Mothe-Fénelon, François de Salignac de la
    1651-1715 ...................... DLB-268
Fenn, Harry 1837-1911 ............... DLB-188
Fennario, David 1947- ............... DLB-60
Fenner, Dudley 1558?-1587? ........... DLB-236
Fenno, Jenny 1765?-1803 ............. DLB-200
Fenno, John 1751-1798 ................ DLB-43
R. F. Fenno and Company ............. DLB-49
Fenoglio, Beppe 1922-1963 ............ DLB-177
Fenton, Geoffrey 1539?-1608 ........... DLB-136
Fenton, James 1949- ................. DLB-40
    The Hemingway/Fenton
        Correspondence .................. Y-02

Ferber, Edna 1885-1968 ...... DLB-9, 28, 86, 266
Ferdinand, Vallery, III (see Salaam, Kalamu ya)
Ferguson, Sir Samuel 1810-1886 ......... DLB-32
Ferguson, William Scott 1875-1954 ...... DLB-47
Fergusson, Robert 1750-1774 .......... DLB-109
Ferland, Albert 1872-1943 ............. DLB-92
Ferlinghetti, Lawrence
    1919- ............. DLB-5, 16; CDALB-1
    Tribute to Kenneth Rexroth ........... Y-82
Fermor, Patrick Leigh 1915- ......... DLB-204
Fern, Fanny (see Parton, Sara Payson Willis)
Ferrars, Elizabeth (Morna Doris Brown)
    1907-1995 ...................... DLB-87
Ferré, Rosario 1942- ................ DLB-145
Ferreira, Vergílio 1916-1996 .......... DLB-287
E. Ferret and Company ............... DLB-49
Ferrier, Susan 1782-1854 ............. DLB-116
Ferril, Thomas Hornsby 1896-1988 ..... DLB-206
Ferrini, Vincent 1913- ............... DLB-48
Ferron, Jacques 1921-1985 ............ DLB-60
Ferron, Madeleine 1922- ............. DLB-53
Ferrucci, Franco 1936- ............... DLB-196
Fet, Afanasii Afanas'evich
    1820?-1892 ..................... DLB-277
Fetridge and Company ............... DLB-49
Feuchtersleben, Ernst Freiherr von
    1806-1849 ..................... DLB-133
Feuchtwanger, Lion 1884-1958 ......... DLB-66
Feuerbach, Ludwig 1804-1872 ......... DLB-133
Feuillet, Octave 1821-1890 ............ DLB-192
Feydeau, Georges 1862-1921 .......... DLB-192
Fibiger, Mathilde 1830-1872 ........... DLB-300
Fichte, Johann Gottlieb 1762-1814 ...... DLB-90
Ficke, Arthur Davison 1883-1945 ....... DLB-54
Fiction
    American Fiction and the 1930s ....... DLB-9
    Fiction Best-Sellers, 1910-1945 ........ DLB-9
    Postmodern Holocaust Fiction ....... DLB-299
    The Year in Fiction ....... Y-84, 86, 89, 94–99
    The Year in Fiction: A Biased View ..... Y-83
    The Year in U.S. Fiction ........... Y-00, 01
    The Year's Work in Fiction: A Survey ... Y-82
Fiedler, Leslie A. 1917- ............ DLB-28, 67
    Tribute to Bernard Malamud .......... Y-86
    Tribute to James Dickey ............. Y-97
Field, Barron 1789-1846 .............. DLB-230
Field, Edward 1924- ................. DLB-105
Field, Eugene 1850-1895 . DLB-23, 42, 140; DS-13
Field, John 1545?-1588 ............... DLB-167
Field, Joseph M. 1810-1856 ........... DLB-248
Field, Marshall, III 1893-1956 ......... DLB-127
Field, Marshall, IV 1916-1965 ......... DLB-127
Field, Marshall, V 1941- ............. DLB-127
Field, Michael (Katherine Harris Bradley)
    1846-1914 ..................... DLB-240
    "The Poetry File" .................. DLB-105

Field, Nathan 1587-1619 or 1620 ........ DLB-58
Field, Rachel 1894-1942 ............. DLB-9, 22
Fielding, Helen 1958- ............... DLB-231
Fielding, Henry
    1707-1754 ....... DLB-39, 84, 101; CDBLB-2
    "Defense of *Amelia*" (1752) .......... DLB-39
    *The History of the Adventures of Joseph Andrews*
        [excerpt] (1742) ................ DLB-39
    Letter to [Samuel] Richardson on *Clarissa*
        (1748). ....................... DLB-39
    Preface to *Joseph Andrews* (1742) ...... DLB-39
    Preface to Sarah Fielding's *Familiar
        Letters* (1747) [excerpt] .......... DLB-39
    Preface to Sarah Fielding's *The
        Adventures of David Simple* (1744) ... DLB-39
    Review of *Clarissa* (1748) ........... DLB-39
    *Tom Jones* (1749) [excerpt] .......... DLB-39
Fielding, Sarah 1710-1768 ............. DLB-39
    Preface to *The Cry* (1754) ........... DLB-39
Fields, Annie Adams 1834-1915 ........ DLB-221
Fields, Dorothy 1905-1974 ............ DLB-265
Fields, James T. 1817-1881 .......... DLB-1, 235
Fields, Julia 1938- ................... DLB-41
Fields, Osgood and Company ........... DLB-49
Fields, W. C. 1880-1946 ............... DLB-44
Fierstein, Harvey 1954- .............. DLB-266
Figes, Eva 1932- .................. DLB-14, 271
Figuera, Angela 1902-1984 ............ DLB-108
Filmer, Sir Robert 1586-1653 .......... DLB-151
Filson, John circa 1753-1788 ........... DLB-37
Finch, Anne, Countess of Winchilsea
    1661-1720. ..................... DLB-95
Finch, Annie 1956- ................. DLB-282
Finch, Robert 1900- ................. DLB-88
Findley, Timothy 1930-2002 ........... DLB-53
Finlay, Ian Hamilton 1925- ........... DLB-40
Finley, Martha 1828-1909 ............. DLB-42
Finn, Elizabeth Anne (McCaul)
    1825-1921 ..................... DLB-166
Finnegan, Seamus 1949- ............. DLB-245
Finney, Jack 1911-1995 ................ DLB-8
Finney, Walter Braden (see Finney, Jack)
Firbank, Ronald 1886-1926 ............ DLB-36
Firmin, Giles 1615-1697 ............... DLB-24
First Edition Library/Collectors'
    Reprints, Inc. ..................... Y-91
Fischart, Johann
    1546 or 1547-1590 or 1591 ......... DLB-179
Fischer, Karoline Auguste Fernandine
    1764-1842 ...................... DLB-94
Fischer, Tibor 1959- ................ DLB-231
Fish, Stanley 1938- .................. DLB-67
Fishacre, Richard 1205-1248 .......... DLB-115
Fisher, Clay (see Allen, Henry W.)
Fisher, Dorothy Canfield 1879-1958 ... DLB-9, 102
Fisher, Leonard Everett 1924- ........ DLB-61
Fisher, Roy 1930- ................... DLB-40

| | | |
|---|---|---|
| Fisher, Rudolph 1897-1934 . . . . . . . . DLB-51, 102 | Fletcher, Phineas 1582-1650 . . . . . . . . . . DLB-121 | Ford, R. A. D. 1915- . . . . . . . . . . . . . . . . . DLB-88 |
| Fisher, Steve 1913-1980 . . . . . . . . . . . . . . DLB-226 | Flieg, Helmut (see Heym, Stefan) | Ford, Richard 1944- . . . . . . . . . . . . . . . . DLB-227 |
| Fisher, Sydney George 1856-1927 . . . . . . . DLB-47 | Flint, F. S. 1885-1960 . . . . . . . . . . . . . . . . . DLB-19 | Ford, Worthington C. 1858-1941 . . . . . . . DLB-47 |
| Fisher, Vardis 1895-1968 . . . . . . . . . . . DLB-9, 206 | Flint, Timothy 1780-1840 . . . . . . . . . DLB-73, 186 | Fords, Howard, and Hulbert . . . . . . . . . . DLB-49 |
| Fiske, John 1608-1677 . . . . . . . . . . . . . . . . DLB-24 | Fløgstad, Kjartan 1944- . . . . . . . . . . . . . DLB-297 | Foreman, Carl 1914-1984 . . . . . . . . . . . . DLB-26 |
| Fiske, John 1842-1901 . . . . . . . . . . . . . DLB-47, 64 | Florensky, Pavel Aleksandrovich 1882-1937 . . . . . . . . . . . . . . . . . . . . . . DLB-295 | Forester, C. S. 1899-1966 . . . . . . . . . . . . DLB-191 |
| Fitch, Thomas circa 1700-1774 . . . . . . . . . DLB-31 | | The C. S. Forester Society . . . . . . . . . . . Y-00 |
| Fitch, William Clyde 1865-1909 . . . . . . . . . DLB-7 | Flores, Juan de fl. 1470-1500 . . . . . . . . . DLB-286 | Forester, Frank (see Herbert, Henry William) |
| FitzGerald, Edward 1809-1883 . . . . . . . . . DLB-32 | Flores-Williams, Jason 1969- . . . . . . . . . DLB-209 | Anthologizing New Formalism . . . . . . . . DLB-282 |
| Fitzgerald, F. Scott 1896-1940 . . . . . . . . . . . . . . . . . DLB-4, 9, 86; Y-81, 92; DS-1, 15, 16; CDALB-4 | Florio, John 1553?-1625 . . . . . . . . . . . . . DLB-172 | The Little Magazines of the New Formalism . . . . . . . . . . . . . . . . . . DLB-282 |
| | Fludd, Robert 1574-1637 . . . . . . . . . . . . . DLB-281 | |
| | Fo, Dario 1926- . . . . . . . . . . . . . . . . . . . . . . Y-97 | The New Narrative Poetry . . . . . . . . . . DLB-282 |
| F. Scott Fitzgerald: A Descriptive Bibliography, Supplement (2001) . . . . Y-01 | Nobel Lecture 1997: Contra Jogulatores Obloquentes . . . . . . . . . . . . . . . . . . . . . Y-97 | Presses of the New Formalism and the New Narrative . . . . . . . . . . . . . . . . DLB-282 |
| F. Scott Fitzgerald Centenary Celebrations . . . . . . . . . . . . . . . . . . . . Y-96 | Foden, Giles 1967- . . . . . . . . . . . . . . . . . DLB-267 | The Prosody of the New Formalism . . . . . DLB-282 |
| F. Scott Fitzgerald Inducted into the American Poets' Corner at St. John the Divine; Ezra Pound Banned . . . . . Y-99 | Fofanov, Konstantin Mikhailovich 1862-1911 . . . . . . . . . . . . . . . . . . . . . . DLB-277 | Younger Women Poets of the New Formalism . . . . . . . . . . . . . . . . . . DLB-282 |
| | Foix, J. V. 1893-1987 . . . . . . . . . . . . . . . . DLB-134 | Forman, Harry Buxton 1842-1917 . . . . . . DLB-184 |
| "F. Scott Fitzgerald: St. Paul's Native Son and Distinguished American Writer": University of Minnesota Conference, 29-31 October 1982 . . . . . . . . . . . . . Y-82 | Foley, Martha 1897-1977 . . . . . . . . . . . . DLB-137 | Fornés, María Irene 1930- . . . . . . . . . . . . DLB-7 |
| | Folger, Henry Clay 1857-1930 . . . . . . . . . DLB-140 | Forrest, Leon 1937-1997 . . . . . . . . . . . . . DLB-33 |
| | Folio Society . . . . . . . . . . . . . . . . . . . . . . . DLB-112 | Forsh, Ol'ga Dmitrievna 1873-1961 . . . . . DLB-272 |
| | Follain, Jean 1903-1971 . . . . . . . . . . . . . DLB-258 | Forster, E. M. 1879-1970 . . . . . . . . DLB-34, 98, 162, 178, 195; DS-10; CDBLB-6 |
| First International F. Scott Fitzgerald Conference . . . . . . . . . . . . . . . . . . . . Y-92 | Follen, Charles 1796-1840 . . . . . . . . . . . DLB-235 | |
| *The Great Gatsby* (Documentary) . . . . . . DLB-219 | Follen, Eliza Lee (Cabot) 1787-1860 . . . . DLB-1, 235 | |
| *Tender Is the Night* (Documentary) . . . . DLB-273 | Follett, Ken 1949- . . . . . . . . . . . . . DLB-87; Y-81 | "Fantasy," from *Aspects of the Novel* (1927) . . . . . . . . . . . . . . . . . . . . . . . DLB-178 |
| Fitzgerald, Penelope 1916- . . . . . . . . DLB-14, 194 | Follett Publishing Company . . . . . . . . . . . DLB-46 | Forster, Georg 1754-1794 . . . . . . . . . . . . DLB-94 |
| Fitzgerald, Robert 1910-1985 . . . . . . . . . . . . Y-80 | John West Folsom [publishing house] . . . . DLB-49 | Forster, John 1812-1876 . . . . . . . . . . . . . DLB-144 |
| FitzGerald, Robert D. 1902-1987 . . . . . . . DLB-260 | Folz, Hans between 1435 and 1440-1513 . . . . . . DLB-179 | Forster, Margaret 1938- . . . . . . . . DLB-155, 271 |
| Fitzgerald, Thomas 1819-1891 . . . . . . . . . . DLB-23 | | Forsyth, Frederick 1938- . . . . . . . . . . . . . DLB-87 |
| Fitzgerald, Zelda Sayre 1900-1948 . . . . . . . . . Y-84 | Fonseca, Manuel da 1911-1993 . . . . . . . . DLB-287 | Forsyth, William "Literary Style" (1857) [excerpt] . . . . . . DLB-57 |
| Fitzhugh, Louise 1928-1974 . . . . . . . . . . . . DLB-52 | Fontane, Theodor 1819-1898 . . . . . . . . . . . DLB-129; CDWLB-2 | |
| Fitzhugh, William circa 1651-1701 . . . . . . . DLB-24 | | Forten, Charlotte L. 1837-1914 . . . . . . DLB-50, 239 |
| Flagg, James Montgomery 1877-1960 . . . . . DLB-188 | Fontenelle, Bernard Le Bovier de 1657-1757 . . . . . . . . . . . . . . . . . . . . . . DLB-268 | Pages from Her Diary . . . . . . . . . . . . DLB-50 |
| Flanagan, Thomas 1923-2002 . . . . . . . . . . . Y-80 | | Fortini, Franco 1917-1994 . . . . . . . . . . . DLB-128 |
| Flanner, Hildegarde 1899-1987 . . . . . . . . . DLB-48 | Fontes, Montserrat 1940- . . . . . . . . . . . DLB-209 | Fortune, Mary ca. 1833-ca. 1910 . . . . . . . DLB-230 |
| Flanner, Janet 1892-1978 . . . . . . . . . DLB-4; DS-15 | Fonvisin, Denis Ivanovich 1744 or 1745-1792 . . . . . . . . . . . . . . . DLB-150 | Fortune, T. Thomas 1856-1928 . . . . . . . . DLB-23 |
| Flannery, Peter 1951- . . . . . . . . . . . . . . DLB-233 | | Fosdick, Charles Austin 1842-1915 . . . . . . DLB-42 |
| Flaubert, Gustave 1821-1880 . . . . . . . DLB-119, 301 | Foote, Horton 1916- . . . . . . . . . . . DLB-26, 266 | Fosse, Jon 1959- . . . . . . . . . . . . . . . . . . DLB-297 |
| Flavin, Martin 1883-1967 . . . . . . . . . . . . . . . DLB-9 | Foote, Mary Hallock 1847-1938 . . . . . . . . DLB-186, 188, 202, 221 | Foster, David 1944- . . . . . . . . . . . . . . . . DLB-289 |
| Fleck, Konrad (flourished circa 1220) . . . . DLB-138 | | Foster, Genevieve 1893-1979 . . . . . . . . . . DLB-61 |
| Flecker, James Elroy 1884-1915 . . . . . . DLB-10, 19 | Foote, Samuel 1721-1777 . . . . . . . . . . . . . DLB-89 | Foster, Hannah Webster 1758-1840 . . . . . . . . . . . . . . . . . . DLB-37, 200 |
| Fleeson, Doris 1901-1970 . . . . . . . . . . . . . . DLB-29 | Foote, Shelby 1916- . . . . . . . . . . . . DLB-2, 17 | |
| Fleißer, Marieluise 1901-1974 . . . . . . . DLB-56, 124 | Forbes, Calvin 1945- . . . . . . . . . . . . . . . DLB-41 | Foster, John 1648-1681 . . . . . . . . . . . . . . DLB-24 |
| Fleischer, Nat 1887-1972 . . . . . . . . . . . . . . DLB-241 | Forbes, Ester 1891-1967 . . . . . . . . . . . . . DLB-22 | Foster, Michael 1904-1956 . . . . . . . . . . . . . DLB-9 |
| Fleming, Abraham 1552?-1607 . . . . . . . . . DLB-236 | Forbes, Rosita 1893?-1967 . . . . . . . . . . . DLB-195 | Foster, Myles Birket 1825-1899 . . . . . . . . DLB-184 |
| Fleming, Ian 1908-1964 . . . DLB-87, 201; CDBLB-7 | Forbes and Company . . . . . . . . . . . . . . . . DLB-49 | Foucault, Michel 1926-1984 . . . . . . . . . . DLB-242 |
| Fleming, Joan 1908-1980 . . . . . . . . . . . . . DLB-276 | Force, Peter 1790-1868 . . . . . . . . . . . . . . DLB-30 | Robert and Andrew Foulis [publishing house] . . . . . . . . . . . . . . . DLB-154 |
| Fleming, May Agnes 1840-1880 . . . . . . . . . DLB-99 | Forché, Carolyn 1950- . . . . . . . . . . . DLB-5, 193 | |
| Fleming, Paul 1609-1640 . . . . . . . . . . . . . DLB-164 | Ford, Charles Henri 1913-2002 . . . . . . . DLB-4, 48 | Fouqué, Caroline de la Motte 1774-1831 . . . DLB-90 |
| Fleming, Peter 1907-1971 . . . . . . . . . . . . . DLB-195 | Ford, Corey 1902-1969 . . . . . . . . . . . . . . DLB-11 | Fouqué, Friedrich de la Motte 1777-1843 . . . . . . . . . . . . . . . . . . . . . . . DLB-90 |
| Fletcher, Giles, the Elder 1546-1611 . . . . . DLB-136 | Ford, Ford Madox 1873-1939 . . . . . . . DLB-34, 98, 162; CDBLB-6 | |
| Fletcher, Giles, the Younger 1585 or 1586-1623 . . . . . . . . . . . . . . . DLB-121 | | Four Seas Company . . . . . . . . . . . . . . . . . DLB-46 |
| | Nathan Asch Remembers Ford Madox Ford, Sam Roth, and Hart Crane . . . . Y-02 | Four Winds Press . . . . . . . . . . . . . . . . . . DLB-46 |
| Fletcher, J. S. 1863-1935 . . . . . . . . . . . . . . DLB-70 | | Fournier, Henri Alban (see Alain-Fournier) |
| Fletcher, John 1579-1625 . . . . . . . . . . . . . DLB-58 | J. B. Ford and Company . . . . . . . . . . . . . DLB-49 | Fowler, Christopher 1953- . . . . . . . . . . . DLB-267 |
| Fletcher, John Gould 1886-1950 . . . . . . . DLB-4, 45 | Ford, Jesse Hill 1928-1996 . . . . . . . . . . . . . DLB-6 | Fowler, Connie May 1958- . . . . . . . . . . . DLB-292 |
| | Ford, John 1586-? . . . . . . . . . . . DLB-58; CDBLB-1 | |

# Cumulative Index

Fowler and Wells Company . . . . . . . . . . . DLB-49
Fowles, John 1926- . . . . . . . DLB-14, 139, 207; CDBLB-8
Fox, John 1939- . . . . . . . . . . . . . . . . . . DLB-245
Fox, John, Jr. 1862 or 1863-1919 . . . DLB-9; DS-13
Fox, Paula 1923- . . . . . . . . . . . . . . . . . . DLB-52
Fox, Richard Kyle 1846-1922 . . . . . . . . . DLB-79
Fox, William Price 1926- . . . . . . . DLB-2; Y-81
    Remembering Joe Heller . . . . . . . . . . . . . Y-99
Richard K. Fox [publishing house] . . . . . . . DLB-49
Foxe, John 1517-1587 . . . . . . . . . . . . . . . DLB-132
Fraenkel, Michael 1896-1957 . . . . . . . . . DLB-4
France, Anatole 1844-1924 . . . . . . . . . . . DLB-123
France, Richard 1938- . . . . . . . . . . . . . . DLB-7
Francis, Convers 1795-1863 . . . . . . . . . DLB-1, 235
Francis, Dick 1920- . . . . . . . DLB-87; CDBLB-8
Francis, Sir Frank 1901-1988 . . . . . . . . . DLB-201
Francis, Jeffrey, Lord 1773-1850 . . . . . . . DLB-107
C. S. Francis [publishing house] . . . . . . . . DLB-49
Franck, Sebastian 1499-1542 . . . . . . . . . DLB-179
Francke, Kuno 1855-1930 . . . . . . . . . . . DLB-71
Françoise (Robertine Barry) 1863-1910 . . . DLB-92
François, Louise von 1817-1893 . . . . . . . DLB-129
Frank, Bruno 1887-1945 . . . . . . . . . . . . . DLB-118
Frank, Leonhard 1882-1961 . . . . . DLB-56, 118
Frank, Melvin 1913-1988 . . . . . . . . . . . . DLB-26
Frank, Waldo 1889-1967 . . . . . . . . . . . . DLB-9, 63
Franken, Rose 1895?-1988 . . . . . . DLB-228, Y-84
Franklin, Benjamin 1706-1790 . . . . DLB-24, 43, 73, 183; CDALB-2
Franklin, James 1697-1735 . . . . . . . . . . . DLB-43
Franklin, John 1786-1847 . . . . . . . . . . . . DLB-99
Franklin, Miles 1879-1954 . . . . . . . . . . . DLB-230
Franklin Library . . . . . . . . . . . . . . . . . . DLB-46
Frantz, Ralph Jules 1902-1979 . . . . . . . . . DLB-4
Franzos, Karl Emil 1848-1904 . . . . . . . . . DLB-129
Fraser, Antonia 1932- . . . . . . . . . . . . . . DLB-276
Fraser, G. S. 1915-1980 . . . . . . . . . . . . . DLB-27
Fraser, Kathleen 1935- . . . . . . . . . . . . . . DLB-169
Frattini, Alberto 1922- . . . . . . . . . . . . . . DLB-128
Frau Ava ?-1127 . . . . . . . . . . . . . . . . . . DLB-148
Fraunce, Abraham 1558?-1592 or 1593 . . DLB-236
Frayn, Michael 1933- . . . . . DLB-13, 14, 194, 245
Frazier, Charles 1950- . . . . . . . . . . . . . . DLB-292
Fréchette, Louis-Honoré 1839-1908 . . . . . DLB-99
Frederic, Harold 1856-1898 . . . DLB-12, 23; DS-13
Freed, Arthur 1894-1973 . . . . . . . . . . . . DLB-265
Freeling, Nicolas 1927- . . . . . . . . . . . . . DLB-87
    Tribute to Georges Simenon . . . . . . . . . . Y-89
Freeman, Douglas Southall 1886-1953 . . . . . . . . . . . . . . DLB-17; DS-17
Freeman, Judith 1946- . . . . . . . . . . . . . . DLB-256
Freeman, Legh Richmond 1842-1915 . . . . DLB-23
Freeman, Mary E. Wilkins 1852-1930 . . . . . . . . . . . . . DLB-12, 78, 221

Freeman, R. Austin 1862-1943 . . . . . . . . DLB-70
Freidank circa 1170-circa 1233 . . . . . . . DLB-138
Freiligrath, Ferdinand 1810-1876 . . . . . . DLB-133
Fremlin, Celia 1914- . . . . . . . . . . . . . . . DLB-276
Frémont, Jessie Benton 1834-1902 . . . . . . DLB-183
Frémont, John Charles 1813-1890 . . . . . . . . . . . . . . . . . DLB-183, 186
French, Alice 1850-1934 . . . . . . . . DLB-74; DS-13
French, David 1939- . . . . . . . . . . . . . . . DLB-53
French, Evangeline 1869-1960 . . . . . . . . DLB-195
French, Francesca 1871-1960 . . . . . . . . . DLB-195
James French [publishing house] . . . . . . . DLB-49
Samuel French [publishing house] . . . . . . DLB-49
Samuel French, Limited . . . . . . . . . . . . DLB-106
French Literature
    Epic and Beast Epic . . . . . . . . . . . . . . DLB-208
    French Arthurian Literature . . . . . . . . DLB-208
    Lyric Poetry . . . . . . . . . . . . . . . . . . . DLB-268
    Other Poets . . . . . . . . . . . . . . . . . . . DLB-217
    Poetry in Nineteenth-Century France: Cultural Background and Critical Commentary . . . . . . . . . . . . . . . DLB-217
    *Roman de la Rose:* Guillaume de Lorris 1200 to 1205-circa 1230, Jean de Meun 1235/1240-circa 1305 . . . DLB-208
    Saints' Lives . . . . . . . . . . . . . . . . . . . DLB-208
    Troubadours, *Trobairitz,* and Trouvères . . . . . . . . . . . . . . . . . . DLB-208
French Theater
    Medieval French Drama . . . . . . . . . . DLB-208
    Parisian Theater, Fall 1984: Toward a New Baroque . . . . . . . . . . . . . . Y-85
Freneau, Philip 1752-1832 . . . . . . . . DLB-37, 43
    The Rising Glory of America . . . . . . . . DLB-37
Freni, Melo 1934- . . . . . . . . . . . . . . . . . DLB-128
Freshfield, Douglas W. 1845-1934 . . . . . . DLB-174
Freud, Sigmund 1856-1939 . . . . . . . . . . DLB-296
Freytag, Gustav 1816-1895 . . . . . . . . . . DLB-129
Fríða Á. Sigurðardóttir 1940- . . . . . . . . . DLB-293
Fridegård, Jan 1897-1968 . . . . . . . . . . . . DLB-259
Fried, Erich 1921-1988 . . . . . . . . . . . . . DLB-85
Friedan, Betty 1921- . . . . . . . . . . . . . . . DLB-246
Friedman, Bruce Jay 1930- . . . . DLB-2, 28, 244
Friedman, Carl 1952- . . . . . . . . . . . . . . DLB-299
Friedman, Kinky 1944- . . . . . . . . . . . . . DLB-292
Friedrich von Hausen circa 1171-1190 . . . DLB-138
Friel, Brian 1929- . . . . . . . . . . . . . . . . . DLB-13
Friend, Krebs 1895?-1967? . . . . . . . . . . . DLB-4
Fries, Fritz Rudolf 1935- . . . . . . . . . . . . DLB-75
Frisch, Max 1911-1991 . . . . . . . . DLB-69, 124; CDWLB-2
Frischlin, Nicodemus 1547-1590 . . . . . . . DLB-179
Frischmuth, Barbara 1941- . . . . . . . . . . DLB-85
Fritz, Jean 1915- . . . . . . . . . . . . . . . . . DLB-52
Froissart, Jean circa 1337-circa 1404 . . . . DLB-208
Fromm, Erich 1900-1980 . . . . . . . . . . . . DLB-296
Fromentin, Eugene 1820-1876 . . . . . . . . DLB-123

Frontinus circa A.D. 35-A.D. 103/104 . . . DLB-211
Frost, A. B. 1851-1928 . . . . . . . DLB-188; DS-13
Frost, Robert 1874-1963 . . . . . . . DLB-54; DS-7; CDALB-4
    The Friends of the Dymock Poets . . . . . . Y-00
Frostenson, Katarina 1953- . . . . . . . . . . DLB-257
Frothingham, Octavius Brooks 1822-1895 . . . . . . . . . . . . . . . . . DLB-1, 243
Froude, James Anthony 1818-1894 . . . . . . . . . . . . . . DLB-18, 57, 144
Fruitlands 1843-1844 . . . . . . . . DLB-1, 223; DS-5
Fry, Christopher 1907- . . . . . . . . . . . . . DLB-13
    Tribute to John Betjeman . . . . . . . . . . . . Y-84
Fry, Roger 1866-1934 . . . . . . . . . . . . . . . DS-10
Fry, Stephen 1957- . . . . . . . . . . . . . . . . DLB-207
Frye, Northrop 1912-1991 . . . . . DLB-67, 68, 246
Fuchs, Daniel 1909-1993 . . . . . DLB-9, 26, 28; Y-93
    Tribute to Isaac Bashevis Singer . . . . . . . Y-91
Fuentes, Carlos 1928- . . . . . DLB-113; CDWLB-3
Fuertes, Gloria 1918-1998 . . . . . . . . . . . DLB-108
Fugard, Athol 1932- . . . . . . . . . . . . . . . DLB-225
The Fugitives and the Agrarians: The First Exhibition . . . . . . . . . . . . . . Y-85
Fujiwara no Shunzei 1114-1204 . . . . . . . DLB-203
Fujiwara no Tameaki 1230s?-1290s? . . . . DLB-203
Fujiwara no Tameie 1198-1275 . . . . . . . . DLB-203
Fujiwara no Teika 1162-1241 . . . . . . . . . DLB-203
Fuks, Ladislav 1923-1994 . . . . . . . . . . . . DLB-299
Fulbecke, William 1560-1603? . . . . . . . . DLB-172
Fuller, Charles 1939- . . . . . . . . . . DLB-38, 266
Fuller, Henry Blake 1857-1929 . . . . . . . . DLB-12
Fuller, John 1937- . . . . . . . . . . . . . . . . . DLB-40
Fuller, Margaret (see Fuller, Sarah)
Fuller, Roy 1912-1991 . . . . . . . . . . . DLB-15, 20
    Tribute to Christopher Isherwood . . . . . . Y-86
Fuller, Samuel 1912-1997 . . . . . . . . . . . DLB-26
Fuller, Sarah 1810-1850 . . . . . . DLB-1, 59, 73, 183, 223, 239; DS-5; CDALB-2
Fuller, Thomas 1608-1661 . . . . . . . . . . . DLB-151
Fullerton, Hugh 1873-1945 . . . . . . . . . . DLB-171
Fullwood, William flourished 1568 . . . . . DLB-236
Fulton, Alice 1952- . . . . . . . . . . . . . . . . DLB-193
Fulton, Len 1934- . . . . . . . . . . . . . . . . . Y-86
Fulton, Robin 1937- . . . . . . . . . . . . . . . DLB-40
Furbank, P. N. 1920- . . . . . . . . . . . . . . . DLB-155
Furetière, Antoine 1619-1688 . . . . . . . . . DLB-268
Furman, Laura 1945- . . . . . . . . . . . . . . . Y-86
Furmanov, Dmitrii Andreevich 1891-1926 . . . . . . . . . . . . . . . . . . DLB-272
Furness, Horace Howard 1833-1912 . . . . DLB-64
Furness, William Henry 1802-1896 . . . . . . . . . . . . . . . . . . DLB-1, 235
Furnivall, Frederick James 1825-1910 . . . DLB-184
Furphy, Joseph (Tom Collins) 1843-1912 . . . . . . . . . . . . . . . . . . DLB-230
Furthman, Jules 1888-1966 . . . . . . . . . . DLB-26

Shakespeare and Montaigne: A Symposium by Jules Furthman......Y-02
Furui Yoshikichi 1937-......DLB-182
Fushimi, Emperor 1265-1317......DLB-203
Futabatei Shimei (Hasegawa Tatsunosuke) 1864-1909......DLB-180
Fyleman, Rose 1877-1957......DLB-160

# G

Gaarder, Jostein 1952-......DLB-297
Gadallah, Leslie 1939-......DLB-251
Gadamer, Hans-Georg 1900-2002......DLB-296
Gadda, Carlo Emilio 1893-1973......DLB-177
Gaddis, William 1922-1998......DLB-2, 278
William Gaddis: A Tribute......Y-99
Gág, Wanda 1893-1946......DLB-22
Gagarin, Ivan Sergeevich 1814-1882......DLB-198
Gagnon, Madeleine 1938-......DLB-60
Gaiman, Neil 1960-......DLB-261
Gaine, Hugh 1726-1807......DLB-43
Hugh Gaine [publishing house]......DLB-49
Gaines, Ernest J. 1933-......DLB-2, 33, 152; Y-80; CDALB-6
Gaiser, Gerd 1908-1976......DLB-69
Gaitskill, Mary 1954-......DLB-244
Galarza, Ernesto 1905-1984......DLB-122
Galaxy Science Fiction Novels......DLB-46
Galbraith, Robert (or Caubraith) circa 1483-1544......DLB-281
Gale, Zona 1874-1938......DLB-9, 228, 78
Galen of Pergamon 129-after 210......DLB-176
Gales, Winifred Marshall 1761-1839......DLB-200
Medieval Galician-Portuguese Poetry......DLB-287
Gall, Louise von 1815-1855......DLB-133
Gallagher, Tess 1943-......DLB-120, 212, 244
Gallagher, Wes 1911-......DLB-127
Gallagher, William Davis 1808-1894......DLB-73
Gallant, Mavis 1922-......DLB-53
Gallegos, María Magdalena 1935-......DLB-209
Gallico, Paul 1897-1976......DLB-9, 171
Gallop, Jane 1952-......DLB-246
Galloway, Grace Growden 1727-1782......DLB-200
Gallup, Donald 1913-2000......DLB-187
Galsworthy, John 1867-1933......DLB-10, 34, 98, 162; DS-16; CDBLB-5
Galt, John 1779-1839......DLB-99, 116, 159
Galton, Sir Francis 1822-1911......DLB-166
Galvin, Brendan 1938-......DLB-5
Gambit......DLB-46
Gamboa, Reymundo 1948-......DLB-122
*Gammer Gurton's Needle*......DLB-62
Gan, Elena Andreevna (Zeneida R-va) 1814-1842......DLB-198
Gandlevsky, Sergei Markovich 1952-......DLB-285
Gannett, Frank E. 1876-1957......DLB-29
Gao Xingjian 1940-......Y-00

Nobel Lecture 2000: "The Case for Literature"......Y-00
Gaos, Vicente 1919-1980......DLB-134
García, Andrew 1854?-1943......DLB-209
García, Cristina 1958-......DLB-292
García, Lionel G. 1935-......DLB-82
García, Richard 1941-......DLB-209
García Márquez, Gabriel 1928-......DLB-113; Y-82; CDWLB-3
The Magical World of Macondo......Y-82
Nobel Lecture 1982: The Solitude of Latin America......Y-82
A Tribute to Gabriel García Márquez......Y-82
García Marruz, Fina 1923-......DLB-283
García-Camarillo, Cecilio 1943-......DLB-209
Gardam, Jane 1928-......DLB-14, 161, 231
Gardell, Jonas 1963-......DLB-257
Garden, Alexander circa 1685-1756......DLB-31
Gardiner, John Rolfe 1936-......DLB-244
Gardiner, Margaret Power Farmer (see Blessington, Marguerite, Countess of)
Gardner, John 1933-1982......DLB-2; Y-82; CDALB-7
Garfield, Leon 1921-1996......DLB-161
Garis, Howard R. 1873-1962......DLB-22
Garland, Hamlin 1860-1940......DLB-12, 71, 78, 186
The Hamlin Garland Society......Y-01
Garneau, François-Xavier 1809-1866......DLB-99
Garneau, Hector de Saint-Denys 1912-1943......DLB-88
Garneau, Michel 1939-......DLB-53
Garner, Alan 1934-......DLB-161, 261
Garner, Hugh 1913-1979......DLB-68
Garnett, David 1892-1981......DLB-34
Garnett, Eve 1900-1991......DLB-160
Garnett, Richard 1835-1906......DLB-184
Garrard, Lewis H. 1829-1887......DLB-186
Garraty, John A. 1920-......DLB-17
Garrett, Almeida (João Baptista da Silva Leitão de Almeida Garrett) 1799-1854......DLB-287
Garrett, George 1929-......DLB-2, 5, 130, 152; Y-83
Literary Prizes......Y-00
My Summer Reading Orgy: Reading for Fun and Games: One Reader's Report on the Summer of 2001......Y-01
A Summing Up at Century's End......Y-99
Tribute to James Dickey......Y-97
Tribute to Michael M. Rea......Y-97
Tribute to Paxton Davis......Y-94
Tribute to Peter Taylor......Y-94
Tribute to William Goyen......Y-83
A Writer Talking: A Collage......Y-00
Garrett, John Work 1872-1942......DLB-187
Garrick, David 1717-1779......DLB-84, 213
Garrison, William Lloyd 1805-1879......DLB-1, 43, 235; CDALB-2

Garro, Elena 1920-1998......DLB-145
Garshin, Vsevolod Mikhailovich 1855-1888......DLB-277
Garth, Samuel 1661-1719......DLB-95
Garve, Andrew 1908-2001......DLB-87
Gary, Romain 1914-1980......DLB-83, 299
Gascoigne, George 1539?-1577......DLB-136
Gascoyne, David 1916-2001......DLB-20
Gash, Jonathan (John Grant) 1933-......DLB-276
Gaskell, Elizabeth Cleghorn 1810-1865......DLB-21, 144, 159; CDBLB-4
The Gaskell Society......Y-98
Gaskell, Jane 1941-......DLB-261
Gaspey, Thomas 1788-1871......DLB-116
Gass, William H. 1924-......DLB-2, 227
Gates, Doris 1901-1987......DLB-22
Gates, Henry Louis, Jr. 1950-......DLB-67
Gates, Lewis E. 1860-1924......DLB-71
Gatto, Alfonso 1909-1976......DLB-114
Gault, William Campbell 1910-1995......DLB-226
Tribute to Kenneth Millar......Y-83
Gaunt, Mary 1861-1942......DLB-174, 230
Gautier, Théophile 1811-1872......DLB-119
Gautreaux, Tim 1947-......DLB-292
Gauvreau, Claude 1925-1971......DLB-88
The *Gawain*-Poet flourished circa 1350-1400......DLB-146
Gawsworth, John (Terence Ian Fytton Armstrong) 1912-1970......DLB-255
Gay, Ebenezer 1696-1787......DLB-24
Gay, John 1685-1732......DLB-84, 95
Gayarré, Charles E. A. 1805-1895......DLB-30
Charles Gaylord [publishing house]......DLB-49
Gaylord, Edward King 1873-1974......DLB-127
Gaylord, Edward Lewis 1919-......DLB-127
Gébler, Carlo 1954-......DLB-271
Geda, Sigitas 1943-......DLB-232
Geddes, Gary 1940-......DLB-60
Geddes, Virgil 1897-......DLB-4
Gedeon (Georgii Andreevich Krinovsky) circa 1730-1763......DLB-150
Gee, Maggie 1948-......DLB-207
Gee, Shirley 1932-......DLB-245
Geibel, Emanuel 1815-1884......DLB-129
Geiogamah, Hanay 1945-......DLB-175
Geis, Bernard, Associates......DLB-46
Geisel, Theodor Seuss 1904-1991......DLB-61; Y-91
Gelb, Arthur 1924-......DLB-103
Gelb, Barbara 1926-......DLB-103
Gelber, Jack 1932-......DLB-7, 228
Gélinas, Gratien 1909-1999......DLB-88
Gellert, Christian Füerchtegott 1715-1769......DLB-97
Gellhorn, Martha 1908-1998......Y-82, 98
Gems, Pam 1925-......DLB-13
Genet, Jean 1910-1986......DLB-72; Y-86

# Cumulative Index

Genette, Gérard 1930- .............. DLB-242
Genevoix, Maurice 1890-1980 ......... DLB-65
Genis, Aleksandr Aleksandrovich
  1953- ...................... DLB-285
Genovese, Eugene D. 1930- ......... DLB-17
Gent, Peter 1942- ..................... Y-82
Geoffrey of Monmouth
  circa 1100-1155 ............... DLB-146
George, Henry 1839-1897 ............ DLB-23
George, Jean Craighead 1919- ....... DLB-52
George, W. L. 1882-1926 ............ DLB-197
George III, King of Great Britain
  and Ireland 1738-1820 ......... DLB-213
*Georgslied* 896? ..................... DLB-148
Gerber, Merrill Joan 1938- ......... DLB-218
Gerhardie, William 1895-1977 ....... DLB-36
Gerhardt, Paul 1607-1676 ........... DLB-164
Gérin, Winifred 1901-1981 .......... DLB-155
Gérin-Lajoie, Antoine 1824-1882 .... DLB-99
German Literature
  A Call to Letters and an Invitation
    to the Electric Chair ......... DLB-75
  The Conversion of an Unpolitical
    Man ......................... DLB-66
  The German Radio Play .......... DLB-124
  The German Transformation from the
    Baroque to the Enlightenment .... DLB-97
  Germanophilism ................. DLB-66
  A Letter from a New Germany ..... Y-90
  The Making of a People ......... DLB-66
  The Novel of Impressionism ..... DLB-66
  Pattern and Paradigm: History as
    Design ...................... DLB-75
  Premisses ..................... DLB-66
  The 'Twenties and Berlin ....... DLB-66
  Wolfram von Eschenbach's *Parzival*:
    Prologue and Book 3 ......... DLB-138
  Writers and Politics: 1871-1918 ..... DLB-66
German Literature, Middle Ages
  *Abrogans* circa 790-800 ........ DLB-148
  *Annolied* between 1077 and 1081 .... DLB-148
  The Arthurian Tradition and
    Its European Context ........ DLB-138
  *Cambridge Songs (Carmina Cantabrigensia)*
    circa 1050 .................. DLB-148
  *Christus und die Samariterin* circa 950 ... DLB-148
  *De Heinrico* circa 980? ........ DLB-148
  *Ecbasis Captivi* circa 1045 ..... DLB-148
  *Georgslied* 896? ............... DLB-148
  German Literature and Culture from
    Charlemagne to the Early Courtly
    Period ............. DLB-148; CDWLB-2
  The Germanic Epic and Old English
    Heroic Poetry: *Widsith, Waldere*,
    and *The Fight at Finnsburg* ... DLB-146
  *Graf Rudolf* between circa
    1170 and circa 1185 ......... DLB-148
  *Heliand* circa 850 ............. DLB-148
  *Das Hildesbrandslied*
    circa 820 .......... DLB-148; CDWLB-2

*Kaiserchronik* circa 1147 ........... DLB-148
The Legends of the Saints and a
  Medieval Christian
  Worldview .................... DLB-148
*Ludus de Antichristo* circa 1160 ..... DLB-148
*Ludwigslied* 881 or 882 ............ DLB-148
*Muspilli* circa 790-circa 850 ....... DLB-148
*Old German Genesis* and *Old German
  Exodus* circa 1050-circa 1130 ... DLB-148
Old High German Charms
  and Blessings ....... DLB-148; CDWLB-2
The *Old High German Isidor*
  circa 790-800 ................ DLB-148
*Petruslied* circa 854? ............. DLB-148
*Physiologus* circa 1070-circa 1150 ... DLB-148
*Ruodlieb* circa 1050-1075 .......... DLB-148
"Spielmannsepen" (circa 1152
  circa 1500) .................. DLB-148
The Strasbourg Oaths 842 ......... DLB-148
*Tatian* circa 830 .................. DLB-148
*Waltharius* circa 825 .............. DLB-148
*Wessobrunner Gebet* circa 787-815 ... DLB-148
German Theater
  German Drama 800-1280 ........ DLB-138
  German Drama from Naturalism
    to Fascism: 1889-1933 ....... DLB-118
Gernsback, Hugo 1884-1967 ....... DLB-8, 137
Gerould, Katharine Fullerton
  1879-1944 ..................... DLB-78
Samuel Gerrish [publishing house] ...... DLB-49
Gerrold, David 1944- ............... DLB-8
Gersão, Teolinda 1940- ............ DLB-287
Gershon, Karen 1923-1993 .......... DLB-299
Gershwin, Ira 1896-1983 ........... DLB-265
  The Ira Gershwin Centenary ........ Y-96
Gerson, Jean 1363-1429 ............ DLB-208
Gersonides 1288-1344 .............. DLB-115
Gerstäcker, Friedrich 1816-1872 ...... DLB-129
Gertsen, Aleksandr Ivanovich
  (see Herzen, Alexander)
Gerstenberg, Heinrich Wilhelm von
  1737-1823 ..................... DLB-97
Gervinus, Georg Gottfried
  1805-1871 .................... DLB-133
Gery, John 1953- .................. DLB-282
Geßner, Solomon 1730-1788 ......... DLB-97
Geston, Mark S. 1946- .............. DLB-8
Al-Ghazali 1058-1111 .............. DLB-115
Gibbings, Robert 1889-1958 ........ DLB-195
Gibbon, Edward 1737-1794 ......... DLB-104
Gibbon, John Murray 1875-1952 ..... DLB-92
Gibbon, Lewis Grassic (see Mitchell, James Leslie)
Gibbons, Floyd 1887-1939 .......... DLB-25
Gibbons, Kaye 1960- ............... DLB-292
Gibbons, Reginald 1947- ........... DLB-120
Gibbons, William ?-? ............... DLB-73
Gibson, Charles Dana
  1867-1944 ............. DLB-188; DS-13

Gibson, Graeme 1934- .............. DLB-53
Gibson, Margaret 1944- ............ DLB-120
Gibson, Margaret Dunlop 1843-1920 .... DLB-174
Gibson, Wilfrid 1878-1962 .......... DLB-19
  The Friends of the Dymock Poets ....... Y-00
Gibson, William 1914- .............. DLB-7
Gibson, William 1948- ............. DLB-251
Gide, André 1869-1951 ............. DLB-65
Giguère, Diane 1937- .............. DLB-53
Giguère, Roland 1929- ............. DLB-60
Gil de Biedma, Jaime 1929-1990 ...... DLB-108
Gil-Albert, Juan 1906-1994 ......... DLB-134
Gilbert, Anthony 1899-1973 ......... DLB-77
Gilbert, Elizabeth 1969- ........... DLB-292
Gilbert, Sir Humphrey 1537-1583 ...... DLB-136
Gilbert, Michael 1912- ............. DLB-87
Gilbert, Sandra M. 1936- ....... DLB-120, 246
Gilchrist, Alexander 1828-1861 ...... DLB-144
Gilchrist, Ellen 1935- ............. DLB-130
Gilder, Jeannette L. 1849-1916 ..... DLB-79
Gilder, Richard Watson 1844-1909 .... DLB-64, 79
Gildersleeve, Basil 1831-1924 ....... DLB-71
Giles, Henry 1809-1882 ............ DLB-64
Giles of Rome circa 1243-1316 ...... DLB-115
Gilfillan, George 1813-1878 ........ DLB-144
Gill, Eric 1882-1940 ............... DLB-98
Gill, Sarah Prince 1728-1771 ....... DLB-200
William F. Gill Company ........... DLB-49
Gillespie, A. Lincoln, Jr. 1895-1950 ..... DLB-4
Gillespie, Haven 1883-1975 ......... DLB-265
Gilliam, Florence ?-? ............... DLB-4
Gilliatt, Penelope 1932-1993 ....... DLB-14
Gillott, Jacky 1939-1980 ........... DLB-14
Gilman, Caroline H. 1794-1888 ...... DLB-3, 73
Gilman, Charlotte Perkins 1860-1935 ... DLB-221
  The Charlotte Perkins Gilman Society ..... Y-99
W. and J. Gilman [publishing house] ...... DLB-49
Gilmer, Elizabeth Meriwether
  1861-1951 ..................... DLB-29
Gilmer, Francis Walker 1790-1826 ..... DLB-37
Gilmore, Mary 1865-1962 ........... DLB-260
Gilroy, Frank D. 1925- ............. DLB-7
Gimferrer, Pere (Pedro) 1945- ...... DLB-134
Gingrich, Arnold 1903-1976 ......... DLB-137
  Prospectus From the Initial Issue of
    *Esquire* (Autumn 1933) ....... DLB-137
  "With the Editorial Ken," Prospectus
    From the Initial Issue of *Ken*
    (7 April 1938) ............... DLB-137
Ginsberg, Allen
  1926-1997 .... DLB-5, 16, 169, 237; CDALB-1
Ginzburg, Evgeniia
  1904-1977 .................... DLB-302
Ginzburg, Lidiia Iakovlevna
  1902-1990 .................... DLB-302
Ginzburg, Natalia 1916-1991 ........ DLB-177

| | | |
|---|---|---|
| Ginzkey, Franz Karl 1871-1963 . . . . . . . . . .DLB-81 | Godkin, E. L. 1831-1902 . . . . . . . . . . . . . . .DLB-79 | González, Angel 1925- . . . . . . . . . . . . . . .DLB-108 |
| Gioia, Dana 1950- . . . . . . . . . . . .DLB-120, 282 | Godolphin, Sidney 1610-1643 . . . . . . . . . .DLB-126 | Gonzalez, Genaro 1949- . . . . . . . . . . . .DLB-122 |
| Giono, Jean 1895-1970 . . . . . . . . . . . . . . . .DLB-72 | Godwin, Gail 1937- . . . . . . . . . . . . .DLB-6, 234 | González, Otto-Raúl 1921- . . . . . . . . . . .DLB-290 |
| Giotti, Virgilio 1885-1957 . . . . . . . . . . . . .DLB-114 | M. J. Godwin and Company . . . . . . . . . .DLB-154 | Gonzalez, Ray 1952- . . . . . . . . . . . . . . . .DLB-122 |
| Giovanni, Nikki 1943- . . . .DLB-5, 41; CDALB-7 | Godwin, Mary Jane Clairmont 1766-1841 . . . . . . . . . . . . . . . . . . . .DLB-163 | González de Mireles, Jovita 1899-1983 . . . . . . . . . . . . . . . . . . . .DLB-122 |
| Gipson, Lawrence Henry 1880-1971 . . . . . .DLB-17 | Godwin, Parke 1816-1904 . . . . . . . .DLB-3, 64, 250 | González Martínez, Enrique 1871-1952 . . .DLB-290 |
| Girard, Rodolphe 1879-1956 . . . . . . . . . . . .DLB-92 | Godwin, William 1756-1836 . . . . . . .DLB-39, 104, 142, 158, 163, 262; CDBLB-3 | González-T., César A. 1931- . . . . . . . . . .DLB-82 |
| Giraudoux, Jean 1882-1944 . . . . . . . . . . . . .DLB-65 | Preface to *St. Leon* (1799) . . . . . . . . . .DLB-39 | Goodis, David 1917-1967 . . . . . . . . . . . . .DLB-226 |
| Girondo, Oliverio 1891-1967 . . . . . . . . . . .DLB-283 | Goering, Reinhard 1887-1936 . . . . . . . . . .DLB-118 | Goodison, Lorna 1947- . . . . . . . . . . . . . .DLB-157 |
| Gissing, George 1857-1903 . . . . . .DLB-18, 135, 184 | Goes, Albrecht 1908- . . . . . . . . . . . . . . . .DLB-69 | Goodman, Allegra 1967- . . . . . . . . . . . . .DLB-244 |
| The Place of Realism in Fiction (1895) .DLB-18 | Goethe, Johann Wolfgang von 1749-1832 . . . . . . . . . . .DLB-94; CDWLB-2 | Goodman, Nelson 1906-1998 . . . . . . . . . .DLB-279 |
| Giudici, Giovanni 1924- . . . . . . . . . . . . . .DLB-128 | Goetz, Curt 1888-1960 . . . . . . . . . . . . . . .DLB-124 | Goodman, Paul 1911-1972 . . . . . . . .DLB-130, 246 |
| Giuliani, Alfredo 1924- . . . . . . . . . . . . . . .DLB-128 | Goffe, Thomas circa 1592-1629 . . . . . . . . .DLB-58 | The Goodman Theatre . . . . . . . . . . . . . . .DLB-7 |
| Gjellerup, Karl 1857-1919 . . . . . . . . . . . . .DLB-300 | Goffstein, M. B. 1940- . . . . . . . . . . . . . . . .DLB-61 | Goodrich, Frances 1891-1984 and Hackett, Albert 1900-1995 . . . . . . . . . .DLB-26 |
| Glackens, William J. 1870-1938 . . . . . . . . .DLB-188 | Gogarty, Oliver St. John 1878-1957 . . . .DLB-15, 19 | Goodrich, Samuel Griswold 1793-1860 . . . . . . . . . . . . . .DLB-1, 42, 73, 243 |
| Gladilin, Anatolii Tikhonovich 1935- . . . . . . . . . . . . . . . . . . . . . . . . . .DLB-302 | Gogol, Nikolai Vasil'evich 1809-1852 . . . . .DLB-198 | S. G. Goodrich [publishing house] . . . . . . . .DLB-49 |
| Gladkov, Fedor Vasil'evich 1883-1958 . . .DLB-272 | Goines, Donald 1937-1974 . . . . . . . . . . . . .DLB-33 | C. E. Goodspeed and Company . . . . . . . . .DLB-49 |
| Gladstone, William Ewart 1809-1898 . . . . . . . . . . . . . . . . . .DLB-57, 184 | Gold, Herbert 1924- . . . . . . . . . . . .DLB-2; Y-81 | Goodwin, Stephen 1943- . . . . . . . . . . . . . . .Y-82 |
| Glaeser, Ernst 1902-1963 . . . . . . . . . . . . . . .DLB-69 | Tribute to William Saroyan . . . . . . . . . .Y-81 | Googe, Barnabe 1540-1594 . . . . . . . . . . . .DLB-132 |
| Glancy, Diane 1941- . . . . . . . . . . . . . . . . .DLB-175 | Gold, Michael 1893-1967 . . . . . . . . . . . .DLB-9, 28 | Gookin, Daniel 1612-1687 . . . . . . . . . . . . .DLB-24 |
| Glanvill, Joseph 1636-1680 . . . . . . . . . . . .DLB-252 | Goldbarth, Albert 1948- . . . . . . . . . . . . . .DLB-120 | Goran, Lester 1928- . . . . . . . . . . . . . . . . .DLB-244 |
| Glanville, Brian 1931- . . . . . . . . . . .DLB-15, 139 | Goldberg, Dick 1947- . . . . . . . . . . . . . . . . . .DLB-7 | Gordimer, Nadine 1923- . . . . . . . .DLB-225; Y-91 |
| Glapthorne, Henry 1610-1643? . . . . . . . . . .DLB-58 | Golden Cockerel Press . . . . . . . . . . . . . .DLB-112 | Nobel Lecture 1991 . . . . . . . . . . . . . . . . .Y-91 |
| Glasgow, Ellen 1873-1945 . . . . . . . . . . .DLB-9, 12 | Golding, Arthur 1536-1606 . . . . . . . . . . . .DLB-136 | Gordon, Adam Lindsay 1833-1870 . . . . . .DLB-230 |
| The Ellen Glasgow Society . . . . . . . . . . . .Y-01 | Golding, Louis 1895-1958 . . . . . . . . . . . . .DLB-195 | Gordon, Caroline 1895-1981 . . . . . . .DLB-4, 9, 102; DS-17; Y-81 |
| Glasier, Katharine Bruce 1867-1950 . . . . . .DLB-190 | Golding, William 1911-1993 . . . . . . . .DLB-15, 100, 255; Y-83; CDBLB-7 | Gordon, Charles F. (see OyamO) |
| Glaspell, Susan 1876-1948 . . . . . .DLB-7, 9, 78, 228 | Nobel Lecture 1993 . . . . . . . . . . . . . . . . .Y-83 | Gordon, Charles William (see Connor, Ralph) |
| Glass, Montague 1877-1934 . . . . . . . . . . . . .DLB-11 | The Stature of William Golding . . . . . . . .Y-83 | Gordon, Giles 1940- . . . . . . . .DLB-14, 139, 207 |
| Glassco, John 1909-1981 . . . . . . . . . . . . . . .DLB-68 | Goldman, Emma 1869-1940 . . . . . . . . . . .DLB-221 | Gordon, Helen Cameron, Lady Russell 1867-1949 . . . . . . . . . . . . . . . . . . . .DLB-195 |
| Glauser, Friedrich 1896-1938 . . . . . . . . . . . .DLB-56 | Goldman, William 1931- . . . . . . . . . . . . . .DLB-44 | Gordon, Lyndall 1941- . . . . . . . . . . . . . .DLB-155 |
| F. Gleason's Publishing Hall . . . . . . . . . . . .DLB-49 | Goldring, Douglas 1887-1960 . . . . . . . . . .DLB-197 | Gordon, Mack 1904-1959 . . . . . . . . . . . . .DLB-265 |
| Gleim, Johann Wilhelm Ludwig 1719-1803 . . . . . . . . . . . . . . . . . . . . .DLB-97 | Goldschmidt, Meir Aron 1819-1887 . . . . .DLB-300 | Gordon, Mary 1949- . . . . . . . . . . . .DLB-6; Y-81 |
| Glendinning, Victoria 1937- . . . . . . . . . . .DLB-155 | Goldsmith, Oliver 1730?-1774 . . . . . . .DLB-39, 89, 104, 109, 142; CDBLB-2 | Gordone, Charles 1925-1995 . . . . . . . . . . . . .DLB-7 |
| Glidden, Frederick Dilley (Luke Short) 1908-1975 . . . . . . . . . . . . . . . . . . . . .DLB-256 | Goldsmith, Oliver 1794-1861 . . . . . . . . . . . .DLB-99 | Gore, Catherine 1800-1861 . . . . . . . . . . . .DLB-116 |
| Glinka, Fedor Nikolaevich 1786-1880 . . . .DLB-205 | Goldsmith Publishing Company . . . . . . . . .DLB-46 | Gore-Booth, Eva 1870-1926 . . . . . . . . . . .DLB-240 |
| Glover, Keith 1966- . . . . . . . . . . . . . . . . .DLB-249 | Goldstein, Richard 1944- . . . . . . . . . . . . . .DLB-185 | Gores, Joe 1931- . . . . . . . . . . . . . .DLB-226; Y-02 |
| Glover, Richard 1712-1785 . . . . . . . . . . . . .DLB-95 | Gollancz, Sir Israel 1864-1930 . . . . . . . . . .DLB-201 | Tribute to Kenneth Millar . . . . . . . . . . . . .Y-83 |
| Glück, Louise 1943- . . . . . . . . . . . . . . . . . . .DLB-5 | Victor Gollancz Limited . . . . . . . . . . . . .DLB-112 | Tribute to Raymond Chandler . . . . . . . . .Y-88 |
| Glyn, Elinor 1864-1943 . . . . . . . . . . . . . . .DLB-153 | Gomberville, Marin Le Roy, sieur de 1600?-1674 . . . . . . . . . . . . . . . . . . . .DLB-268 | Gorey, Edward 1925-2000 . . . . . . . . . . . . .DLB-61 |
| Gnedich, Nikolai Ivanovich 1784-1833 . . .DLB-205 | Gombrowicz, Witold 1904-1969 . . . . . . . . . . . . .DLB-215; CDWLB-4 | Gorgias of Leontini circa 485 B.C.-376 B.C. . . . . . . . . . . . .DLB-176 |
| Gobineau, Joseph-Arthur de 1816-1882 . . .DLB-123 | Gómez-Quiñones, Juan 1942- . . . . . . . .DLB-122 | Gor'ky, Maksim 1868-1936 . . . . . . . . . . . .DLB-295 |
| Godber, John 1956- . . . . . . . . . . . . . . . . .DLB-233 | Laurence James Gomme [publishing house] . . . . . . . . . . . . . . . .DLB-46 | Gorodetsky, Sergei Mitrofanovich 1884-1967 . . . . . . . . . . . . . . . . . . . .DLB-295 |
| Godbout, Jacques 1933- . . . . . . . . . . . . . . .DLB-53 | Goncharov, Ivan Aleksandrovich 1812-1891 . . . . . . . . . . . . . . . . . . . .DLB-238 | Gorostiza, José 1901-1979 . . . . . . . . . . . . .DLB-290 |
| Goddard, Morrill 1865-1937 . . . . . . . . . . . .DLB-25 | Goncourt, Edmond de 1822-1896 . . . . . . .DLB-123 | Görres, Joseph 1776-1848 . . . . . . . . . . . . .DLB-90 |
| Goddard, William 1740-1817 . . . . . . . . . . .DLB-43 | Goncourt, Jules de 1830-1870 . . . . . . . . . .DLB-123 | Gosse, Edmund 1849-1928 . . . . . .DLB-57, 144, 184 |
| Godden, Rumer 1907-1998 . . . . . . . . . . . .DLB-161 | Gonzales, Rodolfo "Corky" 1928- . . . . . .DLB-122 | Gosson, Stephen 1554-1624 . . . . . . . . . . . .DLB-172 |
| Godey, Louis A. 1804-1878 . . . . . . . . . . . . .DLB-73 | Gonzales-Berry, Erlinda 1942- . . . . . . . . .DLB-209 | *The Schoole of Abuse* (1579) . . . . . . . . . .DLB-172 |
| Godey and McMichael . . . . . . . . . . . . . . . .DLB-49 | "Chicano Language" . . . . . . . . . . . . . . .DLB-82 | Gotanda, Philip Kan 1951- . . . . . . . . . .DLB-266 |
| Godfrey, Dave 1938- . . . . . . . . . . . . . . . . .DLB-60 | | |
| Godfrey, Thomas 1736-1763 . . . . . . . . . . . .DLB-31 | | Gotlieb, Phyllis 1926- . . . . . . . . . . .DLB-88, 251 |
| Godine, David R., Publisher . . . . . . . . . . . .DLB-46 | | |

# Cumulative Index

Go-Toba 1180-1239 .................. DLB-203
Gottfried von Straßburg
    died before 1230 ...... DLB-138; CDWLB-2
Gotthelf, Jeremias 1797-1854........... DLB-133
Gottschalk circa 804/808-869 .......... DLB-148
Gottsched, Johann Christoph
    1700-1766...................... DLB-97
Götz, Johann Nikolaus 1721-1781........ DLB-97
Goudge, Elizabeth 1900-1984........... DLB-191
Gough, John B. 1817-1886 ............. DLB-243
Gould, Wallace 1882-1940.............. DLB-54
Govoni, Corrado 1884-1965 ............ DLB-114
Govrin, Michal 1950- ................. DLB-299
Gower, John circa 1330-1408 ........... DLB-146
Goyen, William 1915-1983......DLB-2, 218; Y-83
Goytisolo, José Augustín 1928- ........ DLB-134
Gozzano, Guido 1883-1916 ............ DLB-114
Grabbe, Christian Dietrich 1801-1836 ... DLB-133
Gracq, Julien (Louis Poirier) 1910- ..... DLB-83
Grady, Henry W. 1850-1889 ........... DLB-23
Graf, Oskar Maria 1894-1967........... DLB-56
*Graf Rudolf* between circa 1170 and
    circa 1185..................... DLB-148
Graff, Gerald 1937- .................. DLB-246
Richard Grafton [publishing house] .....DLB-170
Grafton, Sue 1940- ................... DLB-226
Graham, Frank 1893-1965 ............. DLB-241
Graham, George Rex 1813-1894 ........ DLB-73
Graham, Gwethalyn (Gwethalyn Graham
    Erichsen-Brown) 1913-1965......... DLB-88
Graham, Jorie 1951- ................. DLB-120
Graham, Katharine 1917-2001 ......... DLB-127
Graham, Lorenz 1902-1989 ........... DLB-76
Graham, Philip 1915-1963 ............ DLB-127
Graham, R. B. Cunninghame
    1852-1936 .............. DLB-98, 135, 174
Graham, Shirley 1896-1977 ........... DLB-76
Graham, Stephen 1884-1975........... DLB-195
Graham, W. S. 1918-1986 ............. DLB-20
William H. Graham [publishing house] ... DLB-49
Graham, Winston 1910- .............. DLB-77
Grahame, Kenneth 1859-1932 ...DLB-34, 141, 178
Grainger, Martin Allerdale 1874-1941 .... DLB-92
Gramatky, Hardie 1907-1979 .......... DLB-22
Gramcko, Ida 1924-1994 ............. DLB-290
Gramsci, Antonio 1891-1937 .......... DLB-296
Grand, Sarah 1854-1943............DLB-135, 197
Grandbois, Alain 1900-1975 ........... DLB-92
Grandson, Oton de circa 1345-1397.... DLB-208
Grange, John circa 1556-?............ DLB-136
Granger, Thomas 1578-1627 .......... DLB-281
Granich, Irwin (see Gold, Michael)
Granin, Daniil 1918- ................. DLB-302
Granovsky, Timofei Nikolaevich
    1813-1855..................... DLB-198

Grant, Anne MacVicar 1755-1838 ...... DLB-200
Grant, Duncan 1885-1978 .............. DS-10
Grant, George 1918-1988.............. DLB-88
Grant, George Monro 1835-1902 ....... DLB-99
Grant, Harry J. 1881-1963 ............. DLB-29
Grant, James Edward 1905-1966 ....... DLB-26
Grant, John (see Gash, Jonathan)
War of the Words (and Pictures): The Creation
    of a Graphic Novel................Y-02
Grass, Günter 1927- ...DLB-75, 124; CDWLB-2
    Nobel Lecture 1999:
        "To Be Continued . . ."........Y-99
    Tribute to Helen Wolff ............Y-94
Grasty, Charles H. 1863-1924 .......... DLB-25
Grau, Shirley Ann 1929- ............ DLB-2, 218
Graves, John 1920- ....................Y-83
Graves, Richard 1715-1804............. DLB-39
Graves, Robert 1895-1985
    ...DLB-20, 100, 191; DS-18; Y-85; CDBLB-6
    The St. John's College
        Robert Graves Trust..............Y-96
Gray, Alasdair 1934- ............ DLB-194, 261
Gray, Asa 1810-1888 ............. DLB-1, 235
Gray, David 1838-1861 ............... DLB-32
Gray, Simon 1936- .................. DLB-13
Gray, Thomas 1716-1771 .... DLB-109; CDBLB-2
Grayson, Richard 1951- ............. DLB-234
Grayson, William J. 1788-1863.... DLB-3, 64, 248
The Great Bibliographers Series...........Y-93
*The Great Gatsby* (Documentary) ........ DLB-219
"The Greatness of Southern Literature":
    League of the South Institute for the
    Study of Southern Culture and History
    .................................Y-02
Grech, Nikolai Ivanovich 1787-1867 ..... DLB-198
Greeley, Horace 1811-1872 .. DLB-3, 43, 189, 250
Green, Adolph 1915-2002 ......... DLB-44, 265
Green, Anna Katharine
    1846-1935 ................. DLB-202, 221
Green, Duff 1791-1875 ................ DLB-43
Green, Elizabeth Shippen 1871-1954 .... DLB-188
Green, Gerald 1922- .................. DLB-28
Green, Henry 1905-1973 .............. DLB-15
Green, Jonas 1712-1767............... DLB-31
Green, Joseph 1706-1780.............. DLB-31
Green, Julien 1900-1998 .......... DLB-4, 72
Green, Paul 1894-1981.......DLB-7, 9, 249; Y-81
Green, T. H. 1836-1882 .......... DLB-190, 262
Green, Terence M. 1947- ............. DLB-251
T. and S. Green
    [publishing house] ................ DLB-49
Green Tiger Press................... DLB-46
Timothy Green [publishing house]...... DLB-49
Greenaway, Kate 1846-1901 ........... DLB-141
Greenberg: Publisher ................. DLB-46
Greene, Asa 1789-1838................ DLB-11
Greene, Belle da Costa 1883-1950 ...... DLB-187

Greene, Graham 1904-1991
    ..........DLB-13, 15, 77, 100, 162, 201, 204;
                Y-85, 91; CDBLB-7
    Tribute to Christopher Isherwood....... Y-86
Greene, Robert 1558-1592......... .DLB-62, 167
Greene, Robert Bernard (Bob), Jr.
    1947- ....................... DLB-185
Benjamin H Greene [publishing house] ... DLB-49
Greenfield, George 1917-2000 .......... Y-91, 00
    Derek Robinson's Review of George
        Greenfield's *Rich Dust* ..........Y-02
Greenhow, Robert 1800-1854 ......... DLB-30
Greenlee, William B. 1872-1953.........DLB-187
Greenough, Horatio 1805-1852 ..... DLB-1, 235
Greenwell, Dora 1821-1882 ........ DLB-35, 199
Greenwillow Books ................. DLB-46
Greenwood, Grace (see Lippincott, Sara Jane Clarke)
Greenwood, Walter 1903-1974....... DLB-10, 191
Greer, Ben 1948- ..................... DLB-6
Greflinger, Georg 1620?-1677 ......... DLB-164
Greg, W. R. 1809-1881 ............... DLB-55
Greg, W. W. 1875-1959............... DLB-201
Gregg, Josiah 1806-1850......... DLB-183, 186
Gregg Press ........................ DLB-46
Gregory, Horace 1898-1982........... DLB-48
Gregory, Isabella Augusta Persse, Lady
    1852-1932 ..................... DLB-10
Gregory of Rimini circa 1300-1358 ..... DLB-115
Gregynog Press .................... DLB-112
Greiff, León de 1895-1976 ........... DLB-283
Greiffenberg, Catharina Regina von
    1633-1694 .................... DLB-168
Greig, Noël 1944- ................... DLB-245
Grekova, Irina (Elena Sergeevna Venttsel')
    1907-2002..................... DLB-302
Grenfell, Wilfred Thomason
    1865-1940......................DLB-92
Gress, Elsa 1919-1988 ............... DLB-214
Greve, Felix Paul (see Grove, Frederick Philip)
Greville, Fulke, First Lord Brooke
    1554-1628 ....................DLB-62, 172
Grey, Sir George, K.C.B. 1812-1898 .... DLB-184
Grey, Lady Jane 1537-1554 ........... DLB-132
Grey, Zane 1872-1939 ............ DLB-9, 212
    Zane Grey's West Society ............Y-00
Grey Owl (Archibald Stansfeld Belaney)
    1888-1938 .................DLB-92; DS-17
Grey Walls Press ................... DLB-112
Griboedov, Aleksandr Sergeevich
    1795?-1829..................... DLB-205
Grice, Paul 1913-1988 ...............DLB-279
Grier, Eldon 1917- .................. DLB-88
Grieve, C. M. (see MacDiarmid, Hugh)
Griffin, Bartholomew flourished 1596 ....DLB-172
Griffin, Bryan
    "Panic Among the Philistines":
        A Postscript, An Interview
        with Bryan Griffin................Y-81

| | | |
|---|---|---|
| Griffin, Gerald 1803-1840 . . . . . . . . . . . . .DLB-159 | Grymeston, Elizabeth before 1563-before 1604 . . . . . . . . . .DLB-136 | Guyot, Arnold 1807-1884 . . . . . . . . . . . . . . DS-13 |
| The Griffin Poetry Prize . . . . . . . . . . . . . . . . Y-00 | Grynberg, Henryk 1936- . . . . . . . . . . . . .DLB-299 | Gwynn, R. S. 1948- . . . . . . . . . . . . . . .DLB-282 |
| Griffith, Elizabeth 1727?-1793 . . . . . . . .DLB-39, 89 | Gryphius, Andreas 1616-1664 . . . . . . . . . . . DLB-164; CDWLB-2 | Gwynne, Erskine 1898-1948 . . . . . . . . . . .DLB-4 |
| Preface to *The Delicate Distress* (1769) . . .DLB-39 | Gryphius, Christian 1649-1706 . . . . . . . .DLB-168 | Gyles, John 1680-1755 . . . . . . . . . . . . . . .DLB-99 |
| Griffith, George 1857-1906 . . . . . . . . . . . . DLB-178 | Guare, John 1938- . . . . . . . . . . . . . . . DLB-7, 249 | Gyllembourg, Thomasine 1773-1856 . . . . .DLB-300 |
| Ralph Griffiths [publishing house] . . . . . . .DLB-154 | Guberman, Igor Mironovich 1936- . . . .DLB-285 | Gyllensten, Lars 1921- . . . . . . . . . . . . . .DLB-257 |
| Griffiths, Trevor 1935- . . . . . . . . . . .DLB-13, 245 | Guðbergur Bergsson 1932- . . . . . . . . . .DLB-293 | Gyrðir Elíasson 1961- . . . . . . . . . . . . . . .DLB-293 |
| S. C. Griggs and Company . . . . . . . . . . . . .DLB-49 | Guðmundur Böðvarsson 1904-1974 . . . . .DLB-293 | Gysin, Brion 1916-1986. . . . . . . . . . . . . . .DLB-16 |
| Griggs, Sutton Elbert 1872-1930 . . . . . . . . .DLB-50 | Guðmundur Gíslason Hagalín 1898-1985 . . . . . . . . . . . . . . . . . . . . .DLB-293 | # H |
| Grignon, Claude-Henri 1894-1976 . . . . . . .DLB-68 | Guðmundur Magnússon (see Jón Trausti) | H.D. (see Doolittle, Hilda) |
| Grigor'ev, Apollon Aleksandrovich 1822-1864 . . . . . . . . . . . . . . . . . . . . . DLB-277 | Guerra, Tonino 1920- . . . . . . . . . . . . . . .DLB-128 | Habermas, Jürgen 1929- . . . . . . . . . . .DLB-242 |
| Grigorovich, Dmitrii Vasil'evich 1822-1899 . . . . . . . . . . . . . . . . . . . . .DLB-238 | Guest, Barbara 1920- . . . . . . . . . . . .DLB-5, 193 | Habington, William 1605-1654 . . . . . . . .DLB-126 |
| Grigson, Geoffrey 1905-1985 . . . . . . . . . . .DLB-27 | Guèvremont, Germaine 1893-1968 . . . . . . .DLB-68 | Hacker, Marilyn 1942- . . . . . . . . . DLB-120, 282 |
| Grillparzer, Franz 1791-1872 . . . . . . . . . . . DLB-133; CDWLB-2 | Guglielminetti, Amalia 1881-1941 . . . . . . .DLB-264 | Hackett, Albert 1900-1995 . . . . . . . . . . . .DLB-26 |
| Grimald, Nicholas circa 1519-circa 1562 . . . . . . . . . . . . . .DLB-136 | Guidacci, Margherita 1921-1992 . . . . . . .DLB-128 | Hacks, Peter 1928- . . . . . . . . . . . . . . . .DLB-124 |
| Grimké, Angelina Weld 1880-1958 . . . .DLB-50, 54 | Guillén, Jorge 1893-1984 . . . . . . . . . . . . .DLB-108 | Hadas, Rachel 1948- . . . . . . . . . . DLB-120, 282 |
| Grimké, Sarah Moore 1792-1873 . . . . . . .DLB-239 | Guillén, Nicolás 1902-1989 . . . . . . . . . . .DLB-283 | Hadden, Briton 1898-1929 . . . . . . . . . . . .DLB-91 |
| Grimm, Hans 1875-1959 . . . . . . . . . . . . . .DLB-66 | Guilloux, Louis 1899-1980 . . . . . . . . . . . . DLB-72 | Hagedorn, Friedrich von 1708-1754 . . . . . .DLB-168 |
| Grimm, Jacob 1785-1863 . . . . . . . . . . . . . .DLB-90 | Guilpin, Everard circa 1572-after 1608? . . .DLB-136 | Hagelstange, Rudolf 1912-1984 . . . . . . . .DLB-69 |
| Grimm, Wilhelm 1786-1859 . . . . . . . . . . . DLB-90; CDWLB-2 | Guiney, Louise Imogen 1861-1920 . . . . . . .DLB-54 | Hagerup, Inger 1905-1985 . . . . . . . . . . .DLB-297 |
| Grimmelshausen, Johann Jacob Christoffel von 1621 or 1622-1676 . . . . . DLB-168; CDWLB-2 | Guiterman, Arthur 1871-1943 . . . . . . . . . .DLB-11 | Haggard, H. Rider 1856-1925 . . . . . . . . . . .DLB-70, 156, 174, 178 |
| Grimshaw, Beatrice Ethel 1871-1953 . . . . .DLB-174 | Gumilev, Nikolai Stepanovich 1886-1921 . . . . . . . . . . . . . . . . . . . . .DLB-295 | Haggard, William (Richard Clayton) 1907-1993 . . . . . . . . . . . . . . DLB-276; Y-93 |
| Grímur Thomsen 1820-1896 . . . . . . . . . .DLB-293 | Günderrode, Caroline von 1780-1806 . . . . . . . . . . . . . . . . . . . . . .DLB-90 | Hagy, Alyson 1960- . . . . . . . . . . . . . .DLB-244 |
| Grin, Aleksandr Stepanovich 1880-1932 . . . . . . . . . . . . . . . . . . . . .DLB-272 | Gundulić, Ivan 1589-1638 . . .DLB-147; CDWLB-4 | Hahn-Hahn, Ida Gräfin von 1805-1880 . . .DLB-133 |
| Grindal, Edmund 1519 or 1520-1583 . . . .DLB-132 | Gunesekera, Romesh 1954- . . . . . . . . . .DLB-267 | Haig-Brown, Roderick 1908-1976 . . . . . . .DLB-88 |
| Gripe, Maria (Kristina) 1923- . . . . . . . . .DLB-257 | Gunn, Bill 1934-1989 . . . . . . . . . . . . . . . .DLB-38 | Haight, Gordon S. 1901-1985 . . . . . . . . .DLB-103 |
| Griswold, Rufus Wilmot 1815-1857 . . . . . . . . . . . . . . . DLB-3, 59, 250 | Gunn, James E. 1923- . . . . . . . . . . . . . . . .DLB-8 | Hailey, Arthur 1920- . . . . . . . . . . DLB-88; Y-82 |
| Grosart, Alexander Balloch 1827-1899 . . . .DLB-184 | Gunn, Neil M. 1891-1973 . . . . . . . . . . . . .DLB-15 | Haines, John 1924- . . . . . . . . . . . . .DLB-5, 212 |
| Grosholz, Emily 1950- . . . . . . . . . . . . . .DLB-282 | Gunn, Thom 1929- . . . . . . . . DLB-27; CDBLB-8 | Hake, Edward flourished 1566-1604 . . . . .DLB-136 |
| Gross, Milt 1895-1953 . . . . . . . . . . . . . . . .DLB-11 | Gunnar Gunnarsson 1889-1975 . . . . . . . .DLB-293 | Hake, Thomas Gordon 1809-1895 . . . . . . .DLB-32 |
| Grosset and Dunlap . . . . . . . . . . . . . . . . . .DLB-49 | Gunnars, Kristjana 1948- . . . . . . . . . . . . .DLB-60 | Hakluyt, Richard 1552?-1616 . . . . . . . . . .DLB-136 |
| Grosseteste, Robert circa 1160-1253 . . . . .DLB-115 | Günther, Johann Christian 1695-1723 . . . .DLB-168 | Halas, František 1901-1949 . . . . . . . . . . .DLB-215 |
| Grossman, Allen 1932- . . . . . . . . . . . . . .DLB-193 | Gurik, Robert 1932- . . . . . . . . . . . . . . . . .DLB-60 | Halbe, Max 1865-1944 . . . . . . . . . . . . . .DLB-118 |
| Grossman, David 1954- . . . . . . . . . . . . . .DLB-299 | Gurney, A. R. 1930- . . . . . . . . . . . . . . . .DLB-266 | Halberstam, David 1934- . . . . . . . . . . . .DLB-241 |
| Grossman, Vasilii Semenovich 1905-1964 . . . . . . . . . . . . . . . . . . . . .DLB-272 | Gurney, Ivor 1890-1937 . . . . . . . . . . . . . . . . Y-02 | Haldane, Charlotte 1894-1969 . . . . . . . . .DLB-191 |
| Grossman Publishers . . . . . . . . . . . . . . . . .DLB-46 | The Ivor Gurney Society . . . . . . . . . . . Y-98 | Haldane, J. B. S. 1892-1964 . . . . . . . . . . .DLB-160 |
| Grosvenor, Gilbert H. 1875-1966 . . . . . . . .DLB-91 | Guro, Elena Genrikhovna 1877-1913 . . . . .DLB-295 | Haldeman, Joe 1943- . . . . . . . . . . . . . . . .DLB-8 |
| Groth, Klaus 1819-1899 . . . . . . . . . . . . . .DLB-129 | Gustafson, Ralph 1909-1995 . . . . . . . . . . .DLB-88 | Haldeman-Julius Company . . . . . . . . . . . .DLB-46 |
| Groulx, Lionel 1878-1967 . . . . . . . . . . . . .DLB-68 | Gustafsson, Lars 1936- . . . . . . . . . . . . . .DLB-257 | Hale, E. J., and Son . . . . . . . . . . . . . . . . .DLB-49 |
| Grove, Frederick Philip (Felix Paul Greve) 1879-1948 . . . . . . . . . . . . . . . . . . . . . .DLB-92 | Gütersloh, Albert Paris 1887-1973 . . . . . . .DLB-81 | Hale, Edward Everett 1822-1909 . . . . . . . . . . . . . . . DLB-1, 42, 74, 235 |
| Grove Press . . . . . . . . . . . . . . . . . . . . . . . .DLB-46 | Guterson, David 1956- . . . . . . . . . . . . . .DLB-292 | Hale, Janet Campbell 1946- . . . . . . . . . .DLB-175 |
| Groys, Boris Efimovich 1947- . . . . . . . .DLB-285 | Guthrie, A. B., Jr. 1901-1991 . . . . . . . .DLB-6, 212 | Hale, Kathleen 1898-2000 . . . . . . . . . . . .DLB-160 |
| Grubb, Davis 1919-1980 . . . . . . . . . . . . . . .DLB-6 | Guthrie, Ramon 1896-1973 . . . . . . . . . . . .DLB-4 | Hale, Leo Thomas (see Ebon) |
| Gruelle, Johnny 1880-1938 . . . . . . . . . . . .DLB-22 | Guthrie, Thomas Anstey (see Anstey, FC) | Hale, Lucretia Peabody 1820-1900 . . . . . . .DLB-42 |
| von Grumbach, Argula 1492-after 1563? . . . . . . . . . . . . . . . . .DLB-179 | The Guthrie Theater . . . . . . . . . . . . . . . . .DLB-7 | Hale, Nancy 1908-1988 . . . . . . . . DLB-86; DS-17; Y-80, 88 |
| Grundtvig, N. F. S. 1783-1872 . . . . . . . . .DLB-300 | Gutiérrez Nájera, Manuel 1859-1895 . . . . .DLB-290 | Hale, Sarah Josepha (Buell) 1788-1879 . . . . . . . . . . . . . DLB-1, 42, 73, 243 |
| | Guttormur J. Guttormsson 1878-1966 . . . .DLB-293 | Hale, Susan 1833-1910 . . . . . . . . . . . . . .DLB-221 |
| | Gutzkow, Karl 1811-1878 . . . . . . . . . . . .DLB-133 | Hales, John 1584-1656 . . . . . . . . . . . . . . .DLB-151 |
| | Guy, Ray 1939- . . . . . . . . . . . . . . . . . . . .DLB-60 | Halévy, Ludovic 1834-1908 . . . . . . . . . . .DLB-192 |
| | Guy, Rosa 1925- . . . . . . . . . . . . . . . . . . .DLB-33 | Haley, Alex 1921-1992 . . . . . . . . DLB-38; CDALB-7 |

# Cumulative Index

Haliburton, Thomas Chandler
1796-1865 .................. DLB-11, 99

Hall, Adam (Trevor Dudley-Smith)
1920-1995 ..................... DLB-276

Hall, Anna Maria 1800-1881 ......... DLB-159

Hall, Donald 1928- .................. DLB-5

Hall, Edward 1497-1547 ............. DLB-132

Hall, Halsey 1898-1977 .............. DLB-241

Hall, James 1793-1868 ............. DLB-73, 74

Hall, Joseph 1574-1656 ........ DLB-121, 151

Hall, Radclyffe 1880-1943 ........... DLB-191

Hall, Rodney 1935- .................. DLB-289

Hall, Sarah Ewing 1761-1830 .......... DLB-200

Hall, Stuart 1932- ................... DLB-242

Samuel Hall [publishing house] ........ DLB-49

Hallam, Arthur Henry 1811-1833 ....... DLB-32

On Some of the Characteristics of
Modern Poetry and On the
Lyrical Poems of Alfred
Tennyson (1831) ............... DLB-32

Halldór Laxness (Halldór Guðjónsson)
1902-1998 ................... DLB-293

Halleck, Fitz-Greene 1790-1867 ...... DLB-3, 250

Haller, Albrecht von 1708-1777 ......... DLB-168

Halliday, Brett (see Dresser, Davis)

Halliwell-Phillipps, James Orchard
1820-1889 .................... DLB-184

Hallmann, Johann Christian
1640-1704 or 1716? ............. DLB-168

Hallmark Editions ..................... DLB-46

Halper, Albert 1904-1984 .............. DLB-9

Halperin, John William 1941- ......... DLB-111

Halstead, Murat 1829-1908 ............ DLB-23

Hamann, Johann Georg 1730-1788 ....... DLB-97

Hamburger, Michael 1924- ............ DLB-27

Hamilton, Alexander 1712-1756 ........ DLB-31

Hamilton, Alexander 1755?-1804 ........ DLB-37

Hamilton, Cicely 1872-1952 ........ DLB-10, 197

Hamilton, Edmond 1904-1977 ........... DLB-8

Hamilton, Elizabeth 1758-1816 ..... DLB-116, 158

Hamilton, Gail (see Corcoran, Barbara)

Hamilton, Gail (see Dodge, Mary Abigail)

Hamish Hamilton Limited ............. DLB-112

Hamilton, Hugo 1953- ............... DLB-267

Hamilton, Ian 1938-2001 ........... DLB-40, 155

Hamilton, Janet 1795-1873 ........... DLB-199

Hamilton, Mary Agnes 1884-1962 ...... DLB-197

Hamilton, Patrick 1904-1962 ....... DLB-10, 191

Hamilton, Virginia 1936-2002 ... DLB-33, 52; Y-01

Hamilton, Sir William 1788-1856 ....... DLB-262

Hamilton-Paterson, James 1941- ....... DLB-267

Hammerstein, Oscar, 2nd 1895-1960 .... DLB-265

Hammett, Dashiell
1894-1961 ... DLB-226, 280; DS-6; CDALB-5

An Appeal in *TAC* ................. Y-91

*The Glass Key* and Other Dashiell
Hammett Mysteries ............... Y-96

Knopf to Hammett: The Editoral
Correspondence ................. Y-00

Hammon, Jupiter 1711-died between
1790 and 1806 ................ DLB-31, 50

Hammond, John ?-1663 ............... DLB-24

Hamner, Earl 1923- .................. DLB-6

Hampson, John 1901-1955 ............ DLB-191

Hampton, Christopher 1946- .......... DLB-13

Hamsun, Knut 1859-1952 ............. DLB-297

Handel-Mazzetti, Enrica von 1871-1955 ... DLB-81

Handke, Peter 1942- ............. DLB-85, 124

Handlin, Oscar 1915- ................ DLB-17

Hankin, St. John 1869-1909 ........... DLB-10

Hanley, Clifford 1922- ............... DLB-14

Hanley, James 1901-1985 ............. DLB-191

Hannah, Barry 1942- .............. DLB-6, 234

Hannay, James 1827-1873 ............. DLB-21

Hannes Hafstein 1861-1922 ........... DLB-293

Hano, Arnold 1922- .................. DLB-241

Hanrahan, Barbara 1939-1991 ......... DLB-289

Hansberry, Lorraine
1930-1965 ........... DLB-7, 38; CDALB-1

Hansen, Martin A. 1909-1955 ......... DLB-214

Hansen, Thorkild 1927-1989 .......... DLB-214

Hanson, Elizabeth 1684-1737 ......... DLB-200

Hapgood, Norman 1868-1937 ........... DLB-91

Happel, Eberhard Werner 1647-1690 .... DLB-168

Harbach, Otto 1873-1963 ............. DLB-265

*The Harbinger* 1845-1849 ........... DLB-1, 223

Harburg, E. Y. "Yip" 1896-1981 ....... DLB-265

Harcourt Brace Jovanovich ............ DLB-46

Hardenberg, Friedrich von (see Novalis)

Harding, Walter 1917- ............... DLB-111

Hardwick, Elizabeth 1916- ............. DLB-6

Hardy, Alexandre 1572?-1632 .......... DLB-268

Hardy, Frank 1917-1994 .............. DLB-260

Hardy, Thomas
1840-1928 ...... DLB-18, 19, 135; CDBLB-5

"Candour in English Fiction" (1890) .. DLB-18

Hare, Cyril 1900-1958 ............... DLB-77

Hare, David 1947- ................... DLB-13

Hare, R. M. 1919-2002 ............... DLB-262

Hargrove, Marion 1919- .............. DLB-11

Häring, Georg Wilhelm Heinrich
(see Alexis, Willibald)

Harington, Donald 1935- ............. DLB-152

Harington, Sir John 1560-1612 ........ DLB-136

Harjo, Joy 1951- ................ DLB-120, 175

Harkness, Margaret (John Law)
1854-1923 ..................... DLB-197

Harley, Edward, second Earl of Oxford
1689-1741 ..................... DLB-213

Harley, Robert, first Earl of Oxford
1661-1724 ..................... DLB-213

Harlow, Robert 1923- ................ DLB-60

Harman, Thomas flourished 1566-1573 .. DLB-136

Harness, Charles L. 1915- ............. DLB-8

Harnett, Cynthia 1893-1981 ........... DLB-161

Harnick, Sheldon 1924- .............. DLB-265

Tribute to Ira Gershwin .............. Y-96

Tribute to Lorenz Hart ............... Y-95

Harper, Edith Alice Mary (see Wickham, Anna)

Harper, Fletcher 1806-1877 ........... DLB-79

Harper, Frances Ellen Watkins
1825-1911 .................. DLB-50, 221

Harper, Michael S. 1938- ............. DLB-41

Harper and Brothers ................. DLB-49

Harpur, Charles 1813-1868 ........... DLB-230

Harraden, Beatrice 1864-1943 ........ DLB-153

George G. Harrap and Company
Limited ...................... DLB-112

Harriot, Thomas 1560-1621 ........... DLB-136

Harris, Alexander 1805-1874 ......... DLB-230

Harris, Benjamin ?-circa 1720 ...... DLB-42, 43

Harris, Christie 1907-2002 ............ DLB-88

Harris, Errol E. 1908- ............... DLB-279

Harris, Frank 1856-1931 ......... DLB-156, 197

Harris, George Washington
1814-1869 ................ DLB-3, 11, 248

Harris, Joanne 1964- ................ DLB-271

Harris, Joel Chandler
1848-1908 ......... DLB-11, 23, 42, 78, 91

The Joel Chandler Harris Association .... Y-99

Harris, Mark 1922- .............. DLB-2; Y-80

Tribute to Frederick A. Pottle ......... Y-87

Harris, William Torrey 1835-1909 ...... DLB-270

Harris, Wilson 1921- ...... DLB-117; CDWLB-3

Harrison, Mrs. Burton
(see Harrison, Constance Cary)

Harrison, Charles Yale 1898-1954 ....... DLB-68

Harrison, Constance Cary 1843-1920 ... DLB-221

Harrison, Frederic 1831-1923 ...... DLB-57, 190

"On Style in English Prose" (1898) ... DLB-57

Harrison, Harry 1925- ................ DLB-8

James P. Harrison Company ........... DLB-49

Harrison, Jim 1937- .................. Y-82

Harrison, M. John 1945- ............. DLB-261

Harrison, Mary St. Leger Kingsley
(see Malet, Lucas)

Harrison, Paul Carter 1936- ........... DLB-38

Harrison, Susan Frances 1859-1935 ...... DLB-99

Harrison, Tony 1937- ............. DLB-40, 245

Harrison, William 1535-1593 .......... DLB-136

Harrison, William 1933- ............. DLB-234

Harrisse, Henry 1829-1910 ............ DLB-47

The Harry Ransom Humanities Research Center
at the University of Texas at Austin ..... Y-00

Harryman, Carla 1952- ............... DLB-193

Harsdörffer, Georg Philipp 1607-1658 ... DLB-164

Harsent, David 1942- ................ DLB-40

Hart, Albert Bushnell 1854-1943 ....... DLB-17

Hart, Anne 1768-1834 ................ DLB-200

Hart, Elizabeth 1771-1833 ............ DLB-200

| | | |
|---|---|---|
| Hart, Julia Catherine 1796-1867 . . . . . . . . . .DLB-99 | Hawker, Robert Stephen 1803-1875 . . . . . .DLB-32 | Heath, Catherine 1924- . . . . . . . . . . . . .DLB-14 |
| Hart, Lorenz 1895-1943. . . . . . . . . . . . . .DLB-265 | Hawkes, John 1925-1998 . . . . . . . . .DLB-2, 7, 227; Y-80, Y-98 | Heath, James Ewell 1792-1862 . . . . . . . .DLB-248 |
| Larry Hart: Still an Influence . . . . . . . . . Y-95 | John Hawkes: A Tribute . . . . . . . . . . . . . . Y-98 | Heath, Roy A. K. 1926- . . . . . . . . . . . . .DLB-117 |
| Lorenz Hart: An American Lyricist . . . . . Y-95 | Tribute to Donald Barthelme . . . . . . . . . . Y-89 | Heath-Stubbs, John 1918- . . . . . . . . . . . .DLB-27 |
| The Lorenz Hart Centenary . . . . . . . . . . Y-95 | Hawkesworth, John 1720-1773. . . . . . . . . .DLB-142 | Heavysege, Charles 1816-1876 . . . . . . . . .DLB-99 |
| Hart, Moss 1904-1961 . . . . . . . . . . . . . . DLB-7, 266 | Hawkins, Sir Anthony Hope (see Hope, Anthony) | Hebbel, Friedrich 1813-1863 . . . . . . . . . . . DLB-129; CDWLB-2 |
| Hart, Oliver 1723-1795 . . . . . . . . . . . . . . .DLB-31 | Hawkins, Sir John 1719-1789 . . . . . . .DLB-104, 142 | Hebel, Johann Peter 1760-1826 . . . . . . . .DLB-90 |
| Rupert Hart-Davis Limited . . . . . . . . . . .DLB-112 | Hawkins, Walter Everette 1883-? . . . . . . . .DLB-50 | Heber, Richard 1774-1833 . . . . . . . . . . .DLB-184 |
| Harte, Bret 1836-1902 . . . . . . . . DLB-12, 64, 74, 79, 186; CDALB-3 | Hawthorne, Nathaniel 1804-1864 . . . DLB-1, 74, 183, 223, 269; DS-5; CDALB-2 | Hébert, Anne 1916-2000 . . . . . . . . . . . . .DLB-68 |
| Harte, Edward Holmead 1922- . . . . . .DLB-127 | The Nathaniel Hawthorne Society . . . . . . Y-00 | Hébert, Jacques 1923- . . . . . . . . . . . . . .DLB-53 |
| Harte, Houston Harriman 1927- . . . . . .DLB-127 | The Old Manse. . . . . . . . . . . . . . . . . .DLB-223 | Hecht, Anthony 1923- . . . . . . . . . . . DLB-5, 169 |
| Hartlaub, Felix 1913-1945 . . . . . . . . . . . . .DLB-56 | Hawthorne, Sophia Peabody 1809-1871 . . . . . . . . . . . . . . . . . .DLB-183, 239 | Hecht, Ben 1894-1964 . . . . DLB-7, 9, 25, 26, 28, 86 |
| Hartlebon, Otto Erich 1864-1905 . . . . . . . .DLB-118 | Hay, John 1835-1905 . . . . . . . . . . DLB-12, 47, 189 | Hecker, Isaac Thomas 1819-1888 . . . . .DLB-1, 243 |
| Hartley, David 1705-1757. . . . . . . . . . . . .DLB-252 | Hay, John 1915- . . . . . . . . . . . . . . . . .DLB-275 | Hedge, Frederic Henry 1805-1890 . . . . . . . . . . . DLB-1, 59, 243; DS-5 |
| Hartley, L. P. 1895-1972 . . . . . . . . . .DLB-15, 139 | Hayashi Fumiko 1903-1951. . . . . . . . . . . .DLB-180 | Hefner, Hugh M. 1926- . . . . . . . . . . . . .DLB-137 |
| Hartley, Marsden 1877-1943 . . . . . . . . . . .DLB-54 | Haycox, Ernest 1899-1950 . . . . . . . . . . . .DLB-206 | Hegel, Georg Wilhelm Friedrich 1770-1831 . . . . . . . . . . . . . . . . . . . . .DLB-90 |
| Hartling, Peter 1933- . . . . . . . . . . . . . . .DLB-75 | Haycraft, Anna Margaret (see Ellis, Alice Thomas) | Heiberg, Johan Ludvig 1791-1860 . . . . . . .DLB-300 |
| Hartman, Geoffrey H. 1929- . . . . . . . . .DLB-67 | Hayden, Robert 1913-1980 . . . . . . . . . . .DLB-5, 76; CDALB-1 | Heiberg, Johanne Luise 1812-1890 . . . . . .DLB-300 |
| Hartmann, Sadakichi 1867-1944 . . . . . . . .DLB-54 | Haydon, Benjamin Robert 1786-1846 . . . .DLB-110 | Heide, Robert 1939- . . . . . . . . . . . . . .DLB-249 |
| Hartmann von Aue circa 1160-circa 1205. . . .DLB-138; CDWLB-2 | Hayes, John Michael 1919- . . . . . . . . . .DLB-26 | Heidegger, Martin 1889-1976 . . . . . . . . .DLB-296 |
| Hartshorne, Charles 1897-2000 . . . . . . . . .DLB-270 | Hayley, William 1745-1820 . . . . . . . . .DLB-93, 142 | Heidish, Marcy 1947- . . . . . . . . . . . . . . . Y-82 |
| Haruf, Kent 1943- . . . . . . . . . . . . . . .DLB-292 | Haym, Rudolf 1821-1901 . . . . . . . . . . . .DLB-129 | Heißenbüttel, Helmut 1921-1996 . . . . . . .DLB-75 |
| Harvey, Gabriel 1550?-1631 . . . DLB-167, 213, 281 | Hayman, Robert 1575-1629. . . . . . . . . . . .DLB-99 | Heike monogatari . . . . . . . . . . . . . . . . .DLB-203 |
| Harvey, Jack (see Rankin, Ian) | Hayman, Ronald 1932- . . . . . . . . . . . . .DLB-155 | Hein, Christoph 1944- . . . . DLB-124; CDWLB-2 |
| Harvey, Jean-Charles 1891-1967 . . . . . . . .DLB-88 | Hayne, Paul Hamilton 1830-1886 . . . . . . . . . DLB-3, 64, 79, 248 | Hein, Piet 1905-1996 . . . . . . . . . . . . . .DLB-214 |
| Harvill Press Limited . . . . . . . . . . . . . .DLB-112 | Hays, Mary 1760-1843 . . . . . . . . .DLB-142, 158 | Heine, Heinrich 1797-1856. . . . DLB-90; CDWLB-2 |
| Harwood, Gwen 1920-1995. . . . . . . . . . .DLB-289 | Hayward, John 1905-1965. . . . . . . . . . . .DLB-201 | Heinemann, Larry 1944- . . . . . . . . . . . . . DS-9 |
| Harwood, Lee 1939- . . . . . . . . . . . . . . .DLB-40 | Haywood, Eliza 1693?-1756. . . . . . . . . . . .DLB-39 | William Heinemann Limited. . . . . . . . . .DLB-112 |
| Harwood, Ronald 1934- . . . . . . . . . . . . .DLB-13 | Dedication of *Lasselia* [excerpt] (1723) . . . . . . . . . . . . . . . . . . . . . . . .DLB-39 | Heinesen, William 1900-1991 . . . . . . . . .DLB-214 |
| Hašek, Jaroslav 1883-1923 . . .DLB-215; CDWLB-4 | Preface to *The Disguis'd Prince* [excerpt] (1723) . . . . . . . . . . . . . . .DLB-39 | Heinlein, Robert A. 1907-1988 . . . . . . . . .DLB-8 |
| Haskins, Charles Homer 1870-1937 . . . . . .DLB-47 | *The Tea-Table* [excerpt]. . . . . . . . . . . . . .DLB-39 | Heinrich, Willi 1920- . . . . . . . . . . . . . .DLB-75 |
| Haslam, Gerald 1937- . . . . . . . . . . . . . .DLB-212 | Willis P. Hazard [publishing house]. . . . . . .DLB-49 | Heinrich Julius of Brunswick 1564-1613 . .DLB-164 |
| Hass, Robert 1941- . . . . . . . . . .DLB-105, 206 | Hazlitt, William 1778-1830 . . . . . . .DLB-110, 158 | Heinrich von dem Türlîn flourished circa 1230. . . . . . . . . . . . . .DLB-138 |
| Hasselstrom, Linda M. 1943- . . . . . . . .DLB-256 | Hazzard, Shirley 1931- . . . . . . . .DLB-289; Y-82 | Heinrich von Melk flourished after 1160 . . . . . . . . . . . . . .DLB-148 |
| Hastings, Michael 1938- . . . . . . . . . . . . .DLB-233 | Head, Bessie 1937-1986 . . . . . . .DLB-117, 225; CDWLB-3 | Heinrich von Veldeke circa 1145-circa 1190. . . . . . . . . . . . . .DLB-138 |
| Hatar, Győző 1914- . . . . . . . . . . . . . . .DLB-215 | Headley, Joel T. 1813-1897 . . .DLB-30, 183; DS-13 | Heinse, Wilhelm 1746-1803. . . . . . . . . . .DLB-94 |
| The Hatch-Billops Collection. . . . . . . . . . .DLB-76 | Heaney, Seamus 1939- . . .DLB-40; Y-95; CDBLB-8 | Heinz, W. C. 1915- . . . . . . . . . . . . . . .DLB-171 |
| Hathaway, William 1944- . . . . . . . . . . . .DLB-120 | Nobel Lecture 1994: Crediting Poetry . . . Y-95 | Heiskell, John 1872-1972 . . . . . . . . . . . .DLB-127 |
| Hatherly, Ana 1929- . . . . . . . . . . . . . .DLB-287 | Heard, Nathan C. 1936- . . . . . . . . . . . .DLB-33 | Hejinian, Lyn 1941- . . . . . . . . . . . . . .DLB-165 |
| Hauch, Carsten 1790-1872 . . . . . . . . . . . .DLB-300 | Hearn, Lafcadio 1850-1904 . . . . . .DLB-12, 78, 189 | Helder, Herberto 1930- . . . . . . . . . . . .DLB-287 |
| Hauff, Wilhelm 1802-1827 . . . . . . . . . . . .DLB-90 | Hearn, Mary Anne (Marianne Farningham, Eva Hope) 1834-1909 . . . . . . . . . . .DLB-240 | *Heliand* circa 850 . . . . . . . . . . . . . . . . .DLB-148 |
| Hauge, Olav H. 1908-1994 . . . . . . . . . . .DLB-297 | Hearne, John 1926- . . . . . . . . . . . . . . .DLB-117 | Heller, Joseph 1923-1999 . . . . . . DLB-2, 28, 227; Y-80, 99, 02 |
| Haugen, Paal-Helge 1945- . . . . . . . . . . .DLB-297 | Hearne, Samuel 1745-1792. . . . . . . . . . . .DLB-99 | Excerpts from Joseph Heller's USC Address, "The Literature of Despair" . . . . . . . . . . . . . . . . . . . . Y-96 |
| Haugwitz, August Adolph von 1647-1706. . . . . . . . . . . . . . . . . . . . . . .DLB-168 | Hearne, Thomas 1678?-1735 . . . . . . . . . .DLB-213 | |
| Hauptmann, Carl 1858-1921 . . . . . . . .DLB-66, 118 | Hearst, William Randolph 1863-1951 . . . . .DLB-25 | Remembering Joe Heller, by William Price Fox. . . . . . . . . . . . . . . . . . . . . Y-99 |
| Hauptmann, Gerhart 1862-1946 . . . . . . . .DLB-66, 118; CDWLB-2 | Hearst, William Randolph, Jr. 1908-1993 . . . . . . . . . . . . . . . . . . . .DLB-127 | A Tribute to Joseph Heller . . . . . . . . . . . Y-99 |
| Hauser, Marianne 1910- . . . . . . . . . . . . Y-83 | Heartman, Charles Frederick 1883-1953 . .DLB-187 | Heller, Michael 1937- . . . . . . . . . . . . .DLB-165 |
| Havel, Václav 1936- . . . . . .DLB-232; CDWLB-4 | | |
| Haven, Alice B. Neal 1827-1863. . . . . . . . .DLB-250 | | |
| Havergal, Frances Ridley 1836-1879 . . . . .DLB-199 | | |
| Hawes, Stephen 1475?-before 1529 . . . . . .DLB-132 | | Hellman, Lillian 1906-1984 . . . . . DLB-7, 228; Y-84 |

Hellwig, Johann 1609-1674............ DLB-164
Helprin, Mark 1947- .........Y-85; CDALB-7
Helwig, David 1938- .............. DLB-60
Hemans, Felicia 1793-1835 ........... DLB-96
Hemenway, Abby Maria 1828-1890..... DLB-243
Hemingway, Ernest 1899-1961
........ DLB-4, 9, 102, 210; Y-81, 87, 99;
DS-1, 15, 16; CDALB-4
    A Centennial Celebration ............ Y-99
    Come to Papa .................... Y-99
    The Ernest Hemingway Collection at
        the John F. Kennedy Library........ Y-99
    Ernest Hemingway Declines to
        Introduce *War and Peace*........... Y-01
    Ernest Hemingway's Reaction to
        James Gould Cozzens ............. Y-98
    Ernest Hemingway's Toronto Journalism
        Revisited: With Three Previously
        Unrecorded Stories............... Y-92
    Falsifying Hemingway .............. Y-96
    Hemingway Centenary Celebration
        at the JFK Library............... Y-99
    The Hemingway/Fenton
        Correspondence ................ Y-02
    Hemingway in the JFK .............. Y-99
    The Hemingway Letters Project
        Finds an Editor ................ Y-02
    Hemingway Salesmen's Dummies....... Y-00
    Hemingway: Twenty-Five Years Later ... Y-85
    A Literary Archaeologist Digs On:
        A Brief Interview with Michael
        Reynolds ..................... Y-99
    Not Immediately Discernible ... but
        Eventually Quite Clear: The *First
        Light* and *Final Years* of
        Hemingway's Centenary........... Y-99
    Packaging Papa: *The Garden of Eden* ...... Y-86
    Second International Hemingway
        Colloquium: Cuba................ Y-98
Hémon, Louis 1880-1913 ............. DLB-92
Hempel, Amy 1951- ............... DLB-218
Hempel, Carl G. 1905-1997 ..........DLB-279
Hemphill, Paul 1936-  ................ Y-87
Hénault, Gilles 1920-1996 ............ DLB-88
Henchman, Daniel 1689-1761.......... DLB-24
Henderson, Alice Corbin 1881-1949 ..... DLB-54
Henderson, Archibald 1877-1963 ...... DLB-103
Henderson, David 1942- ............. DLB-41
Henderson, George Wylie 1904-1965 .... DLB-51
Henderson, Zenna 1917-1983........... DLB-8
Henighan, Tom 1934- ............. DLB-251
Henisch, Peter 1943- ............... DLB-85
Henley, Beth 1952- ................. Y-86
Henley, William Ernest 1849-1903 ...... DLB-19
Henniker, Florence 1855-1923 ........ DLB-135
Henning, Rachel 1826-1914 .......... DLB-230
Henningsen, Agnes 1868-1962 ........ DLB-214
Henry, Alexander 1739-1824 .......... DLB-99
Henry, Buck 1930- ................. DLB-26

Henry, Marguerite 1902-1997 ......... DLB-22
Henry, O. (see Porter, William Sydney)
Henry, Robert Selph 1889-1970 ........ DLB-17
Henry, Will (see Allen, Henry W.)
Henry VIII of England 1491-1547...... DLB-132
Henry of Ghent circa 1217-1229 - 1293 .. DLB-115
Henryson, Robert
    1420s or 1430s-circa 1505 ......... DLB-146
Henschke, Alfred (see Klabund)
Hensher, Philip 1965- .............. DLB-267
Hensley, Sophie Almon 1866-1946 ...... DLB-99
Henson, Lance 1944- ...............DLB-175
Henty, G. A. 1832-1902............ DLB-18, 141
    The Henty Society.................. Y-98
Hentz, Caroline Lee 1800-1856 ...... DLB-3, 248
Heraclitus
    flourished circa 500 B.C. ...........DLB-176
Herbert, Agnes circa 1880-1960.........DLB-174
Herbert, Alan Patrick 1890-1971 .... DLB-10, 191
Herbert, Edward, Lord, of Cherbury
    1582-1648 ............ DLB-121, 151, 252
Herbert, Frank 1920-1986 ..... DLB-8; CDALB-7
Herbert, George 1593-1633 .. DLB-126; CDBLB-1
Herbert, Henry William 1807-1858 .... DLB-3, 73
Herbert, John 1926- ................ DLB-53
Herbert, Mary Sidney, Countess of Pembroke
    (see Sidney, Mary)
Herbert, Xavier 1901-1984............ DLB-260
Herbert, Zbigniew
    1924-1998 ........... DLB-232; CDWLB-4
Herbst, Josephine 1892-1969 ........... DLB-9
Herburger, Gunter 1932- .........DLB-75, 124
Herculano, Alexandre 1810-1877 ...... DLB-287
Hercules, Frank E. M. 1917-1996........ DLB-33
Herder, Johann Gottfried 1744-1803 ..... DLB-97
B. Herder Book Company ............ DLB-49
Heredia, José-María de 1842-1905 ...... DLB-217
Herford, Charles Harold 1853-1931 .... DLB-149
Hergesheimer, Joseph 1880-1954 ..... DLB-9, 102
Heritage Press..................... DLB-46
Hermann the Lame 1013-1054 ........ DLB-148
Hermes, Johann Timotheu 1738-1821 .... DLB-97
Hermlin, Stephan 1915-1997 .......... DLB-69
Hernández, Alfonso C. 1938- ......... DLB-122
Hernández, Inés 1947- .............. DLB-122
Hernández, Miguel 1910-1942 ........ DLB-134
Hernton, Calvin C. 1932- ............ DLB-38
Herodotus circa 484 B.C.-circa 420 B.C.
    ....................DLB-176; CDWLB-1
Heron, Robert 1764-1807 ............ DLB-142
Herr, Michael 1940- ............... DLB-185
Herrera, Darío 1870-1914............ DLB-290
Herrera, Juan Felipe 1948- .......... DLB-122
E. R. Herrick and Company ........... DLB-49
Herrick, Robert 1591-1674 ........... DLB-126
Herrick, Robert 1868-1938.........DLB-9, 12, 78

Herrick, William 1915- ................Y-83
Herrmann, John 1900-1959 ............ DLB-4
Hersey, John
    1914-1993 ...DLB-6, 185, 278, 299; CDALB-7
Hertel, François 1905-1985............ DLB-68
Hervé-Bazin, Jean Pierre Marie (see Bazin, Hervé)
Hervey, John, Lord 1696-1743 ........ DLB-101
Herwig, Georg 1817-1875 ............ DLB-133
Herzen, Alexander (Aleksandr Ivanovich
    Gersten) 1812-1870 ..............DLB-277
Herzog, Emile Salomon Wilhelm
    (see Maurois, André)
Hesiod eighth century B.C...........DLB-176
Hesse, Hermann 1877-1962 .. DLB-66; CDWLB-2
Hessus, Eobanus 1488-1540...........DLB-179
Heureka! (see Kertész, Imre and Nobel Prize
    in Literature: 2002) .................Y-02
Hewat, Alexander circa 1743-circa 1824... DLB-30
Hewett, Dorothy 1923-2002 ......... DLB-289
Hewitt, John 1907-1987............... DLB-27
Hewlett, Maurice 1861-1923 ....... DLB-34, 156
Heyen, William 1940- ............... DLB-5
Heyer, Georgette 1902-1974..........DLB-77, 191
Heym, Stefan 1913-2001 .............. DLB-69
Heyse, Paul 1830-1914............... DLB-129
Heytesbury, William
    circa 1310-1372 or 1373 .......... DLB-115
Heyward, Dorothy 1890-1961 ........DLB-7, 249
Heyward, DuBose 1885-1940 ...DLB-7, 9, 45, 249
Heywood, John 1497?-1580? .......... DLB-136
Heywood, Thomas 1573 or 1574-1641 ... DLB-62
Hiaasen, Carl 1953- ............... DLB-292
Hibberd, Jack 1940- ............... DLB-289
Hibbs, Ben 1901-1975.................DLB-137
    "The Saturday Evening Post reaffirms
        a policy," Ben Hibb's Statement
        in *The Saturday Evening Post*
        (16 May 1942)..................DLB-137
Hichens, Robert S. 1864-1950 ........ DLB-153
Hickey, Emily 1845-1924 ............ DLB-199
Hickman, William Albert 1877-1957...... DLB-92
Hicks, Granville 1901-1982 .......... DLB-246
Hidalgo, José Luis 1919-1947 ........ DLB-108
Hiebert, Paul 1892-1987............... DLB-68
Hieng, Andrej 1925- ............... DLB-181
Hierro, José 1922-2002 ............. DLB-108
Higgins, Aidan 1927- ............... DLB-14
Higgins, Colin 1941-1988............. DLB-26
Higgins, George V.
    1939-1999 .............DLB-2; Y-81, 98–99
    Afterword [in response to Cozzen's
        *Mens Rea* (or Something)].......... Y-97
    *At End of Day:* The Last George V.
        Higgins Novel................... Y-99
    The Books of George V. Higgins:
        A Checklist of Editions
        and Printings.................. Y-00
    George V. Higgins in Class ........... Y-02

| | | |
|---|---|---|
| Tribute to Alfred A. Knopf . . . . . . . . . . . Y-84 | Hobsbawn, Eric (Francis Newton) 1917- . . . . . . . . . . . . . . . . . . . . . . . . . DLB-296 | Holden, Molly 1927-1981 . . . . . . . . . . . . . DLB-40 |
| Tributes to George V. Higgins . . . . . . . . Y-99 | Hobson, Laura Z. 1900- . . . . . . . . . . . . . . . DLB-28 | Hölderlin, Friedrich 1770-1843 . . . . . . . . . . . DLB-90; CDWLB-2 |
| "What You Lose on the Swings You Make Up on the Merry-Go-Round" . . . Y-99 | Hobson, Sarah 1947- . . . . . . . . . . . . . . . . DLB-204 | Holdstock, Robert 1948- . . . . . . . . . . DLB-261 |
| Higginson, Thomas Wentworth 1823-1911 . . . . . . . . . . . . . . . . . DLB-1, 64, 243 | Hoby, Thomas 1530-1566 . . . . . . . . . . . . DLB-132 | Holiday House . . . . . . . . . . . . . . . . . . . . . DLB-46 |
| Highwater, Jamake 1942?- . . . . . . . DLB-52; Y-85 | Hoccleve, Thomas circa 1368-circa 1437 . . . . . . . . . . . . . DLB-146 | Holinshed, Raphael died 1580 . . . . . . . . DLB-167 |
| Hijuelos, Oscar 1951- . . . . . . . . . . . . . . . DLB-145 | Hochhuth, Rolf 1931- . . . . . . . . . . . . . . . . DLB-124 | Holland, J. G. 1819-1881 . . . . . . . . . . . . . . . DS-13 |
| Hildegard von Bingen 1098-1179 . . . . . . . DLB-148 | Hochman, Sandra 1936- . . . . . . . . . . . . . . DLB-5 | Holland, Norman N. 1927- . . . . . . . . . . . DLB-67 |
| *Das Hildesbrandslied* circa 820 . . . . . . . . . . . DLB-148; CDWLB-2 | Hocken, Thomas Morland 1836-1910 . . . . DLB-184 | Hollander, John 1929- . . . . . . . . . . . . . . . . DLB-5 |
| Hildesheimer, Wolfgang 1916-1991 . . DLB-69, 124 | Hocking, William Ernest 1873-1966 . . . . . DLB-270 | Holley, Marietta 1836-1926 . . . . . . . . . . . . DLB-11 |
| Hildreth, Richard 1807-1865 . . . DLB-1, 30, 59, 235 | Hodder and Stoughton, Limited . . . . . . . . DLB-106 | Hollinghurst, Alan 1954- . . . . . . . . . . . . DLB-207 |
| Hill, Aaron 1685-1750 . . . . . . . . . . . . . . . . DLB-84 | Hodgins, Jack 1938- . . . . . . . . . . . . . . . . . DLB-60 | Hollingsworth, Margaret 1940- . . . . . . . . . DLB-60 |
| Hill, Geoffrey 1932- . . . . . . . DLB-40; CDBLB-8 | Hodgman, Helen 1945- . . . . . . . . . . . . . . . DLB-14 | Hollo, Anselm 1934- . . . . . . . . . . . . . . . . DLB-40 |
| George M. Hill Company . . . . . . . . . . . . . DLB-49 | Hodgskin, Thomas 1787-1869 . . . . . . . . . DLB-158 | Holloway, Emory 1885-1977 . . . . . . . . . . DLB-103 |
| Hill, "Sir" John 1714?-1775 . . . . . . . . . . . . DLB-39 | Hodgson, Ralph 1871-1962 . . . . . . . . . . . . DLB-19 | Holloway, John 1920- . . . . . . . . . . . . . . . DLB-27 |
| Lawrence Hill and Company, Publishers . . DLB-46 | Hodgson, William Hope 1877-1918 . . . . . . . . . . DLB-70, 153, 156, 178 | Holloway House Publishing Company . . . . DLB-46 |
| Hill, Leslie 1880-1960 . . . . . . . . . . . . . . . . DLB-51 | Hoe, Robert, III 1839-1909 . . . . . . . . . . . DLB-187 | Holme, Constance 1880-1955 . . . . . . . . . . DLB-34 |
| Hill, Reginald 1936- . . . . . . . . . . . . . . . . DLB-276 | Hoeg, Peter 1957- . . . . . . . . . . . . . . . . . . DLB-214 | Holmes, Abraham S. 1821?-1908 . . . . . . . . DLB-99 |
| Hill, Susan 1942- . . . . . . . . . . . . . . . DLB-14, 139 | Hoel, Sigurd 1890-1960 . . . . . . . . . . . . . . DLB-297 | Holmes, John Clellon 1926-1988 . . . . . DLB-16, 237 |
| Hill, Walter 1942- . . . . . . . . . . . . . . . . . . . DLB-44 | Hoem, Edvard 1949- . . . . . . . . . . . . . . . . DLB-297 | "Four Essays on the Beat Generation" . . . . . . . . . . . . . . . . . . . DLB-16 |
| Hill and Wang . . . . . . . . . . . . . . . . . . . . . . DLB-46 | Hoffenstein, Samuel 1890-1947 . . . . . . . . . DLB-11 | Holmes, Mary Jane 1825-1907 . . . . . DLB-202, 221 |
| Hillberry, Conrad 1928- . . . . . . . . . . . . . DLB-120 | Hoffman, Alice 1952- . . . . . . . . . . . . . . . . DLB-292 | Holmes, Oliver Wendell 1809-1894 . . . . . . . DLB-1, 189, 235; CDALB-2 |
| Hillerman, Tony 1925- . . . . . . . . . . . . . . DLB-206 | Hoffman, Charles Fenno 1806-1884 . . . DLB-3, 250 | Holmes, Richard 1945- . . . . . . . . . . . . . . DLB-155 |
| Hilliard, Gray and Company . . . . . . . . . . . DLB-49 | Hoffman, Daniel 1923- . . . . . . . . . . . . . . . . DLB-5 | Holmes, Thomas James 1874-1959 . . . . . . DLB-187 |
| Hills, Lee 1906-2000 . . . . . . . . . . . . . . . . DLB-127 | Tribute to Robert Graves . . . . . . . . . . . Y-85 | The Holocaust "Historical Novel" . . . . . . . DLB-299 |
| Hillyer, Robert 1895-1961 . . . . . . . . . . . . . DLB-54 | Hoffmann, E. T. A. 1776-1822 . . . . . . . . . . . DLB-90; CDWLB-2 | Holocaust Fiction, Postmodern . . . . . . . . . DLB-299 |
| Hilsenrath, Edgar 1926- . . . . . . . . . . . . . DLB-299 | Hoffman, Frank B. 1888-1958 . . . . . . . . . DLB-188 | Holocaust Novel, The "Second-Generation" . . . . . . . . . . . . . . . . . . . . . . . . . . . . . . . DLB-299 |
| Hilton, James 1900-1954 . . . . . . . . . . DLB-34, 77 | Hoffman, William 1925- . . . . . . . . . . . . . DLB-234 | Holroyd, Michael 1935- . . . . . . . DLB-155; Y-99 |
| Hilton, Walter died 1396 . . . . . . . . . . . . . DLB-146 | Tribute to Paxton Davis . . . . . . . . . . . Y-94 | Holst, Hermann E. von 1841-1904 . . . . . . DLB-47 |
| Hilton and Company . . . . . . . . . . . . . . . . DLB-49 | Hoffmanswaldau, Christian Hoffman von 1616-1679 . . . . . . . . . . . . . . . . . . . . . . DLB-168 | Holt, John 1721-1784 . . . . . . . . . . . . . . . . DLB-43 |
| Himes, Chester 1909-1984 . . . . DLB-2, 76, 143, 226 | Hofmann, Michael 1957- . . . . . . . . . . . . . . DLB-40 | Henry Holt and Company . . . . . . . . DLB-49, 284 |
| Joseph Hindmarsh [publishing house] . . . . DLB-170 | Hofmannsthal, Hugo von 1874-1929 . . . . . . . . DLB-81, 118; CDWLB-2 | Holt, Rinehart and Winston . . . . . . . . . . . DLB-46 |
| Hine, Daryl 1936- . . . . . . . . . . . . . . . . . . . DLB-60 | Hofmo, Gunvor 1921-1995 . . . . . . . . . . . DLB-297 | Holtby, Winifred 1898-1935 . . . . . . . . . . . DLB-191 |
| Hingley, Ronald 1920- . . . . . . . . . . . . . . . DLB-155 | Hofstadter, Richard 1916-1970 . . . . . DLB-17, 246 | Holthusen, Hans Egon 1913-1997 . . . . . . . DLB-69 |
| Hinojosa-Smith, Rolando 1929- . . . . . . . . DLB-82 | Hogan, Desmond 1950- . . . . . . . . . . . . . . DLB-14 | Hölty, Ludwig Christoph Heinrich 1748-1776 . . . . . . . . . . . . . . . . . . . . . . . DLB-94 |
| Hinton, S. E. 1948- . . . . . . . . . . . . . . . . CDALB-7 | Hogan, Linda 1947- . . . . . . . . . . . . . . . . DLB-175 | Holub, Miroslav 1923-1998 . . . . . . . . . . DLB-232; CDWLB-4 |
| Hippel, Theodor Gottlieb von 1741-1796 . . . . . . . . . . . . . . . . . . . . . . . . DLB-97 | Hogan and Thompson . . . . . . . . . . . . . . . . DLB-49 | Holz, Arno 1863-1929 . . . . . . . . . . . . . . . DLB-118 |
| Hippius, Zinaida Nikolaevna 1869-1945 . . . . . . . . . . . . . . . . . . . . . . DLB-295 | Hogarth Press . . . . . . . . . . . . . DLB-112; DS-10 | Home, Henry, Lord Kames (see Kames, Henry Home, Lord) |
| | Hogg, James 1770-1835 . . . . . . . DLB-93, 116, 159 | |
| Hippocrates of Cos flourished circa 425 B.C. . . . . . . . . . . DLB-176; CDWLB-1 | Hohberg, Wolfgang Helmhard Freiherr von 1612-1688 . . . . . . . . . . . . . . . . . . . . . . DLB-168 | Home, John 1722-1808 . . . . . . . . . . . . . . . DLB-84 |
| Hirabayashi Taiko 1905-1972 . . . . . . . . . DLB-180 | von Hohenheim, Philippus Aureolus Theophrastus Bombastus (see Paracelsus) | Home, William Douglas 1912- . . . . . . . . . DLB-13 |
| Hirsch, E. D., Jr. 1928- . . . . . . . . . . . . . . . DLB-67 | Hohl, Ludwig 1904-1980 . . . . . . . . . . . . . . DLB-56 | Home Publishing Company . . . . . . . . . . . . DLB-49 |
| Hirsch, Edward 1950- . . . . . . . . . . . . . . . DLB-120 | Højholt, Per 1928- . . . . . . . . . . . . . . . . . . DLB-214 | Homer circa eighth-seventh centuries B.C. . . . . . . . . . . . . . . . . . . DLB-176; CDWLB-1 |
| "Historical Novel," The Holocaust . . . . . . DLB-299 | Holan, Vladimir 1905-1980 . . . . . . . . . . . DLB-215 | Homer, Winslow 1836-1910 . . . . . . . . . . . DLB-188 |
| Hoagland, Edward 1932- . . . . . . . . . . . . . . DLB-6 | Holberg, Ludvig 1684-1754 . . . . . . . . . . . DLB-300 | Homes, Geoffrey (see Mainwaring, Daniel) |
| Hoagland, Everett H., III 1942- . . . . . . . . DLB-41 | Holbrook, David 1923- . . . . . . . . . . . DLB-14, 40 | Honan, Park 1928- . . . . . . . . . . . . . . . . . DLB-111 |
| Hoban, Russell 1925- . . . . . . . . . . DLB-52; Y-90 | Holcroft, Thomas 1745-1809 . . . . . DLB-39, 89, 158 | Hone, William 1780-1842 . . . . . . . . . DLB-110, 158 |
| Hobbes, Thomas 1588-1679 . . . DLB-151, 252, 281 | Preface to *Alwyn* (1780) . . . . . . . . . . . DLB-39 | Hongo, Garrett Kaoru 1951- . . . . . . . . . . DLB-120 |
| Hobby, Oveta 1905-1995 . . . . . . . . . . . . . DLB-127 | Holden, Jonathan 1941- . . . . . . . . . . . . . . DLB-105 | Honig, Edwin 1919- . . . . . . . . . . . . . . . . . . DLB-5 |
| Hobby, William 1878-1964 . . . . . . . . . . . DLB-127 | "Contemporary Verse Story-telling" . . . DLB-105 | Hood, Hugh 1928-2000 . . . . . . . . . . . . . . . DLB-53 |
| Hobsbaum, Philip 1932- . . . . . . . . . . . . . . DLB-40 | | Hood, Mary 1946- . . . . . . . . . . . . . . . . . DLB-234 |

483

| | | |
|---|---|---|
| Hood, Thomas 1799-1845 . . . . . . . . . . . . . DLB-96 | Hotchkiss and Company . . . . . . . . . . . . . . DLB-49 | Huddle, David 1942- . . . . . . . . . . . . . DLB-130 |
| Hook, Sidney 1902-1989 . . . . . . . . . . . . .DLB-279 | Hough, Emerson 1857-1923 . . . . . . . . . DLB-9, 212 | Hudgins, Andrew 1951- . . . . . . . . DLB-120, 282 |
| Hook, Theodore 1788-1841 . . . . . . . . . . . DLB-116 | Houghton, Stanley 1881-1913 . . . . . . . . . . DLB-10 | Hudson, Henry Norman 1814-1886 . . . . . DLB-64 |
| Hooker, Jeremy 1941- . . . . . . . . . . . . . . . DLB-40 | Houghton Mifflin Company . . . . . . . . . . . . DLB-49 | Hudson, Stephen 1868?-1944 . . . . . . . . . .DLB-197 |
| Hooker, Richard 1554-1600 . . . . . . . . . . . DLB-132 | *Hours at Home* . . . . . . . . . . . . . . . . . . . . . . .DS-13 | Hudson, W. H. 1841-1922 . . . . .DLB-98, 153, 174 |
| Hooker, Thomas 1586-1647 . . . . . . . . . . . . DLB-24 | Household, Geoffrey 1900-1988 . . . . . . . . . DLB-87 | Hudson and Goodwin . . . . . . . . . . . . . . . DLB-49 |
| hooks, bell 1952- . . . . . . . . . . . . . . . . . DLB-246 | Housman, A. E. 1859-1936 . . . DLB-19; CDBLB-5 | Huebsch, B. W., oral history . . . . . . . . . . . . .Y-99 |
| Hooper, Johnson Jones<br>1815-1862 . . . . . . . . . . . . . . . . . DLB-3, 11, 248 | Housman, Laurence 1865-1959 . . . . . . . . . DLB-10 | B. W. Huebsch [publishing house] . . . . . . . DLB-46 |
| Hope, A. D. 1907-2000 . . . . . . . . . . . . . . DLB-289 | Houston, Pam 1962- . . . . . . . . . . . . . . . DLB-244 | Hueffer, Oliver Madox 1876-1931 . . . . . . .DLB-197 |
| Hope, Anthony 1863-1933 . . . . . . . . DLB-153, 156 | Houwald, Ernst von 1778-1845 . . . . . . . . . DLB-90 | Huet, Pierre Daniel<br>Preface to *The History of Romances*<br>(1715) . . . . . . . . . . . . . . . . . . . . . . . DLB-39 |
| Hope, Christopher 1944- . . . . . . . . . . . . DLB-225 | Hovey, Richard 1864-1900 . . . . . . . . . . . . . DLB-54 | |
| Hope, Eva (see Hearn, Mary Anne) | Howard, Donald R. 1927-1987 . . . . . . . . . DLB-111 | |
| Hope, Laurence (Adela Florence<br>Cory Nicolson) 1865-1904 . . . . . . . . DLB-240 | Howard, Maureen 1930- . . . . . . . . . . . . . . .Y-83 | Hugh of St. Victor circa 1096-1141 . . . . . DLB-208 |
| | Howard, Richard 1929- . . . . . . . . . . . . . . . DLB-5 | Hughes, David 1930- . . . . . . . . . . . . . . . . DLB-14 |
| Hopkins, Ellice 1836-1904 . . . . . . . . . . . . DLB-190 | Howard, Roy W. 1883-1964 . . . . . . . . . . . DLB-29 | Hughes, Dusty 1947- . . . . . . . . . . . . . . . DLB-233 |
| Hopkins, Gerard Manley<br>1844-1889 . . . . . . . . . DLB-35, 57; CDBLB-5 | Howard, Sidney 1891-1939 . . . . . . .DLB-7, 26, 249 | Hughes, Hatcher 1881-1945 . . . . . . . . . . DLB-249 |
| Hopkins, John ?-1570 . . . . . . . . . . . . . . DLB-132 | Howard, Thomas, second Earl of Arundel<br>1585-1646 . . . . . . . . . . . . . . . . . . . DLB-213 | Hughes, John 1677-1720 . . . . . . . . . . . . . DLB-84 |
| Hopkins, John H., and Son . . . . . . . . . . . . DLB-46 | | Hughes, Langston 1902-1967 . . . . . . . DLB-4, 7, 48,<br>51, 86, 228; ; DS-15; CDALB-5 |
| Hopkins, Lemuel 1750-1801 . . . . . . . . . . . DLB-37 | Howe, E. W. 1853-1937 . . . . . . . . . . . DLB-12, 25 | |
| Hopkins, Pauline Elizabeth 1859-1930 . . . . DLB-50 | Howe, Henry 1816-1893 . . . . . . . . . . . . . . DLB-30 | Hughes, Richard 1900-1976 . . . . . . . . DLB-15, 161 |
| Hopkins, Samuel 1721-1803 . . . . . . . . . . . DLB-31 | Howe, Irving 1920-1993 . . . . . . . . . . . . . . DLB-67 | Hughes, Ted 1930-1998 . . . . . . . . . . . DLB-40, 161 |
| Hopkinson, Francis 1737-1791 . . . . . . . . . DLB-31 | Howe, Joseph 1804-1873 . . . . . . . . . . . . . . DLB-99 | Hughes, Thomas 1822-1896 . . . . . . . . DLB-18, 163 |
| Hopkinson, Nalo 1960- . . . . . . . . . . . . . DLB-251 | Howe, Julia Ward 1819-1910 . . . . DLB-1, 189, 235 | Hugo, Richard 1923-1982 . . . . . . . . . . DLB-5, 206 |
| Hopper, Nora (Mrs. Nora Chesson)<br>1871-1906 . . . . . . . . . . . . . . . . . . . DLB-240 | Howe, Percival Presland 1886-1944 . . . . . DLB-149 | Hugo, Victor 1802-1885 . . . . . . .DLB-119, 192, 217 |
| | Howe, Susan 1937- . . . . . . . . . . . . . . . . DLB-120 | Hugo Awards and Nebula Awards . . . . . . . . DLB-8 |
| Hoppin, Augustus 1828-1896 . . . . . . . . . . DLB-188 | Howell, Clark, Sr. 1863-1936 . . . . . . . . . . . DLB-25 | Huidobro, Vicente 1893-1948 . . . . . . . . . DLB-283 |
| Hora, Josef 1891-1945 . . . . . DLB-215; CDWLB-4 | Howell, Evan P. 1839-1905 . . . . . . . . . . . . DLB-23 | Hull, Richard 1896-1973 . . . . . . . . . . . . . DLB-77 |
| Horace 65 B.C.-8 B.C. . . . . . . DLB-211; CDWLB-1 | Howell, James 1594?-1666 . . . . . . . . . . . . DLB-151 | Hulda (Unnur Benediktsdóttir Bjarklind)<br>1881-1946 . . . . . . . . . . . . . . . . . . . DLB-293 |
| Horgan, Paul 1903-1995 . . . . . DLB-102, 212; Y-85 | Howell, Soskin and Company . . . . . . . . . . DLB-46 | |
| Tribute to Alfred A. Knopf . . . . . . . . . . .Y-84 | Howell, Warren Richardson<br>1912-1984 . . . . . . . . . . . . . . . . . . . DLB-140 | Hulme, T. E. 1883-1917 . . . . . . . . . . . . . . DLB-19 |
| Horizon Press . . . . . . . . . . . . . . . . . . . . . DLB-46 | | Hulton, Anne ?-1779? . . . . . . . . . . . . . . . DLB-200 |
| Horkheimer, Max 1895-1973 . . . . . . . . . . DLB-296 | Howells, William Dean 1837-1920<br>. . . . . . . . .DLB-12, 64, 74, 79, 189; CDALB-3 | Humboldt, Alexander von 1769-1859 . . . . DLB-90 |
| Hornby, C. H. St. John 1867-1946 . . . . . . DLB-201 | | Humboldt, Wilhelm von 1767-1835 . . . . . . DLB-90 |
| Hornby, Nick 1957- . . . . . . . . . . . . . . . DLB-207 | Introduction to Paul Laurence<br>Dunbar's *Lyrics of Lowly Life*<br>(1896) . . . . . . . . . . . . . . . . . . . . . . . DLB-50 | Hume, David 1711-1776 . . . . . . . . . DLB-104, 252 |
| Horne, Frank 1899-1974 . . . . . . . . . . . . . . DLB-51 | | Hume, Fergus 1859-1932 . . . . . . . . . . . . . DLB-70 |
| Horne, Richard Henry (Hengist)<br>1802 or 1803-1884 . . . . . . . . . . . . . . DLB-32 | | Hume, Sophia 1702-1774 . . . . . . . . . . . . DLB-200 |
| | The William Dean Howells Society . . . . . . .Y-01 | Hume-Rothery, Mary Catherine<br>1824-1885 . . . . . . . . . . . . . . . . . . . DLB-240 |
| Horne, Thomas 1608-1654 . . . . . . . . . . . DLB-281 | Howitt, Mary 1799-1888 . . . . . . . . . .DLB-110, 199 | |
| Horney, Karen 1885-1952 . . . . . . . . . . . . DLB-246 | Howitt, William 1792-1879 . . . . . . . . . . . DLB-110 | Humishuma<br>(see Mourning Dove) |
| Hornung, E. W. 1866-1921 . . . . . . . . . . . . DLB-70 | Hoyem, Andrew 1935- . . . . . . . . . . . . . . . DLB-5 | |
| Horovitz, Israel 1939- . . . . . . . . . . . . . . . . DLB-7 | Hoyers, Anna Ovena 1584-1655 . . . . . . . . DLB-164 | Hummer, T. R. 1950- . . . . . . . . . . . . . . DLB-120 |
| Horta, Maria Teresa (see The Three Marias:<br>A Landmark Case in Portuguese<br>Literary History) | Hoyle, Fred 1915-2001 . . . . . . . . . . . . . . DLB-261 | Humor<br>American Humor: A Historical<br>Survey . . . . . . . . . . . . . . . . . . . . . DLB-11 |
| | Hoyos, Angela de 1940- . . . . . . . . . . . . . . DLB-82 | |
| | Henry Hoyt [publishing house] . . . . . . . . . DLB-49 | American Humor Studies Association . . . .Y-99 |
| Horton, George Moses 1797?-1883? . . . . . . DLB-50 | Hoyt, Palmer 1897-1979 . . . . . . . . . . . . . DLB-127 | The Comic Tradition Continued<br>[in the British Novel] . . . . . . . . . . DLB-15 |
| George Moses Horton Society . . . . . . . . . .Y-99 | Hrabal, Bohumil 1914-1997 . . . . . . . . . . . DLB-232 | |
| Horváth, Ödön von 1901-1938 . . . . . DLB-85, 124 | Hrabanus Maurus 776?-856 . . . . . . . . . . . DLB-148 | Humorous Book Illustration . . . . . . . . . . DLB-11 |
| Horwood, Harold 1923- . . . . . . . . . . . . . . DLB-60 | Hronský, Josef Cíger 1896-1960 . . . . . . . . DLB-215 | International Society for Humor Studies . .Y-99 |
| E. and E. Hosford [publishing house] . . . . . DLB-49 | Hrotsvit of Gandersheim<br>circa 935-circa 1000 . . . . . . . . . . . . . DLB-148 | Newspaper Syndication of American<br>Humor . . . . . . . . . . . . . . . . . . . . . DLB-11 |
| Hoskens, Jane Fenn 1693-1770? . . . . . . . . DLB-200 | | |
| Hoskyns, John circa 1566-1638 . . . . DLB-121, 281 | Hubbard, Elbert 1856-1915 . . . . . . . . . . . . DLB-91 | Selected Humorous Magazines<br>(1820-1950) . . . . . . . . . . . . . . . . . DLB-11 |
| Hosokawa Yūsai 1535-1610 . . . . . . . . . . . DLB-203 | Hubbard, Kin 1868-1930 . . . . . . . . . . . . . . DLB-11 | |
| Hospers, John 1918- . . . . . . . . . . . . . . . .DLB-279 | Hubbard, William circa 1621-1704 . . . . . . . DLB-24 | Bruce Humphries [publishing house] . . . . DLB-46 |
| Hostovský, Egon 1908-1973 . . . . . . . . . . . DLB-215 | Huber, Therese 1764-1829 . . . . . . . . . . . . . DLB-90 | Humphrey, Duke of Gloucester<br>1391-1447 . . . . . . . . . . . . . . . . . . . DLB-213 |
| | Huch, Friedrich 1873-1913 . . . . . . . . . . . . DLB-66 | |
| | Huch, Ricarda 1864-1947 . . . . . . . . . . . . . DLB-66 | Humphrey, William<br>1924-1997 . . . . . . . . . . . . .DLB-6, 212, 234, 278 |

| | | |
|---|---|---|
| Humphreys, David 1752-1818 . . . . . . . . . . DLB-37 | Ibáñez, Sara de 1909-1971 . . . . . . . . . . . . DLB-290 | Internet (publishing and commerce) |
| Humphreys, Emyr 1919- . . . . . . . . . . . DLB-15 | Ibarbourou, Juana de 1892-1979 . . . . . . . . DLB-290 |    Author Websites . . . . . . . . . . . . . . . . . . . .Y-97 |
| Humphreys, Josephine 1945- . . . . . . . . DLB-292 | Ibn Bajja circa 1077-1138 . . . . . . . . . . . . . DLB-115 |    The Book Trade and the Internet . . . . . . . Y-00 |
| Huncke, Herbert 1915-1996 . . . . . . . . . . . . DLB-16 | Ibn Gabirol, Solomon |    E-Books Turn the Corner . . . . . . . . . . . . . Y-98 |
| Huneker, James Gibbons 1857-1921 . . . . . . DLB-71 |    circa 1021-circa 1058 . . . . . . . . . . . . DLB-115 |    The E-Researcher: Possibilities |
| Hunold, Christian Friedrich 1681-1721 . . . DLB-168 | Ibuse Masuji 1898-1993 . . . . . . . . . . . . . . . DLB-180 |       and Pitfalls . . . . . . . . . . . . . . . . . . . Y-00 |
| Hunt, Irene 1907- . . . . . . . . . . . . . . . . . . DLB-52 | Ichijō Kanera |    Interviews on E-publishing . . . . . . . . . . . Y-00 |
| Hunt, Leigh 1784-1859 . . . . . . . DLB-96, 110, 144 |    (see Ichijō Kaneyoshi) |    John Updike on the Internet . . . . . . . . . . .Y-97 |
| Hunt, Violet 1862-1942 . . . . . . . . . . . DLB-162, 197 | Ichijō Kaneyoshi (Ichijō Kanera) |    LitCheck Website . . . . . . . . . . . . . . . . . . Y-01 |
| Hunt, William Gibbes 1791-1833 . . . . . . . . DLB-73 |    1402-1481 . . . . . . . . . . . . . . . . . . . . . DLB-203 |    Virtual Books and Enemies of Books . . . . Y-00 |
| Hunter, Evan 1926- . . . . . . . . . . . . . . . . . Y-82 | Iffland, August Wilhelm | Interviews |
|    Tribute to John D. MacDonald . . . . . . . . Y-86 |    1759-1814 . . . . . . . . . . . . . . . . . . . . . DLB-94 |    Adoff, Arnold . . . . . . . . . . . . . . . . . . . . Y-01 |
| Hunter, Jim 1939- . . . . . . . . . . . . . . . . . DLB-14 | Iggulden, John 1917- . . . . . . . . . . . . . . . . DLB-289 |    Aldridge, John W. . . . . . . . . . . . . . . . . . Y-91 |
| Hunter, Kristin 1931- . . . . . . . . . . . . . . . DLB-33 | Ignatieff, Michael 1947- . . . . . . . . . . . . . JLB-267 |    Anastas, Benjamin. . . . . . . . . . . . . . . . . Y-98 |
|    Tribute to Julian Mayfield . . . . . . . . . . . . Y-84 | Ignatow, David 1914-1997 . . . . . . . . . . . . . . DLB-5 |    Baker, Nicholson. . . . . . . . . . . . . . . . . . Y-00 |
| Hunter, Mollie 1922- . . . . . . . . . . . . . . . DLB-161 | Ike, Chukwuemeka 1931- . . . . . . . . . . . . . DLB-157 |    Bank, Melissa . . . . . . . . . . . . . . . . . . . . Y-98 |
| Hunter, N. C. 1908-1971 . . . . . . . . . . . . . . DLB-10 | Ikkyū Sōjun 1394-1481 . . . . . . . . . . . . . . . DLB-203 |    Bass, T. J. . . . . . . . . . . . . . . . . . . . . . . . Y-80 |
| Hunter-Duvar, John 1821-1899 . . . . . . . . . DLB-99 | Iles, Francis (see Berkeley, Anthony) |    Bernstein, Harriet . . . . . . . . . . . . . . . . . Y-82 |
| Huntington, Henry E. 1850-1927 . . . . . . . DLB-140 | Il'f, Il'ia (Il'ia Arnol'dovich Fainzil'berg) |    Betts, Doris . . . . . . . . . . . . . . . . . . . . . . Y-82 |
|    The Henry E. Huntington Library . . . . . . Y-92 |    1897-1937 . . . . . . . . . . . . . . . . . . . . . DLB-272 |    Bosworth, David. . . . . . . . . . . . . . . . . . Y-82 |
| Huntington, Susan Mansfield 1791-1823 . . DLB-200 | Illich, Ivan 1926-2002 . . . . . . . . . . . . . . . . DLB-242 |    Bottoms, David . . . . . . . . . . . . . . . . . . . Y-83 |
| Hurd and Houghton . . . . . . . . . . . . . . . . . DLB-49 | Illustration |    Bowers, Fredson . . . . . . . . . . . . . . . . . . Y-80 |
| Hurst, Fannie 1889-1968 . . . . . . . . . . . . . . DLB-86 |    Children's Book Illustration in the |    Burnshaw, Stanley . . . . . . . . . . . . . . . . .Y-97 |
| Hurst and Blackett . . . . . . . . . . . . . . . . . . DLB-106 |       Twentieth Century . . . . . . . . . . . . . DLB-61 |    Carpenter, Humphrey . . . . . . . . . . Y-84, 99 |
| Hurst and Company . . . . . . . . . . . . . . . . . DLB-49 |    Children's Illustrators, 1800-1880 . . . . DLB-163 |    Carr, Virginia Spencer . . . . . . . . . . . . . Y-00 |
| Hurston, Zora Neale |    Early American Book Illustration . . . . . DLB-49 |    Carver, Raymond . . . . . . . . . . . . . . . . . Y-83 |
|    1901?-1960 . . . . . . . . . . DLB-51, 86; CDALB-7 |    The Iconography of Science-Fiction |    Cherry, Kelly . . . . . . . . . . . . . . . . . . . . Y-83 |
| Husserl, Edmund 1859-1938 . . . . . . . . . . . DLB-296 |       Art . . . . . . . . . . . . . . . . . . . . . . . . . . DLB-8 |    Conroy, Jack . . . . . . . . . . . . . . . . . . . . Y-81 |
| Husson, Jules-François-Félix (see Champfleury) |    The Illustration of Early German |    Coppel, Alfred . . . . . . . . . . . . . . . . . . . . Y-83 |
| Huston, John 1906-1987 . . . . . . . . . . . . . . DLB-26 |       Literary Manuscripts, circa |    Cowley, Malcolm . . . . . . . . . . . . . . . . . Y-81 |
| Hutcheson, Francis 1694-1746 . . . . . . . DLB-31, 252 |       1150-circa 1300 . . . . . . . . . . . . . . DLB-148 |    Davis, Paxton . . . . . . . . . . . . . . . . . . . . Y-89 |
| Hutchinson, Ron 1947- . . . . . . . . . . . . . . DLB-245 |    Minor Illustrators, 1880-1914 . . . . . . . DLB-141 |    Devito, Carlo . . . . . . . . . . . . . . . . . . . . Y-94 |
| Hutchinson, R. C. 1907-1975 . . . . . . . . . . . DLB-191 | Illyés, Gyula 1902-1983 . . . . . DLB-215; CDWLB-4 |    De Vries, Peter . . . . . . . . . . . . . . . . . . . Y-82 |
| Hutchinson, Thomas 1711-1780 . . . . . . DLB-30, 31 | Imbs, Bravig 1904-1946 . . . . . . . . . DLB-4; DS-15 |    Dickey, James . . . . . . . . . . . . . . . . . . . . Y-82 |
| Hutchinson and Company | Imbuga, Francis D. 1947- . . . . . . . . . . . . . DLB-157 |    Donald, David Herbert . . . . . . . . . . . . .Y-87 |
|    (Publishers) Limited . . . . . . . . . . . . . DLB-112 | Immermann, Karl 1796-1840 . . . . . . . . . . DLB-133 |    Editors, Conversations with . . . . . . . . . . Y-95 |
| Huth, Angela 1938- . . . . . . . . . . . . . . . . DLB-271 | Inchbald, Elizabeth 1753-1821 . . . . . . . DLB-39, 89 |    Ellroy, James . . . . . . . . . . . . . . . . . . . . Y-91 |
| Hutton, Richard Holt 1826-1897 . . . . . . . . DLB-57 | Indiana University Press . . . . . . . . . . . . . . . Y-02 |    Fancher, Betsy . . . . . . . . . . . . . . . . . . . Y-83 |
| von Hutten, Ulrich 1488-1523 . . . . . . . . . . DLB-179 | Ingamells, Rex 1913-1955 . . . . . . . . . . . . . DLB-260 |    Faust, Irvin . . . . . . . . . . . . . . . . . . . . . Y-00 |
| Huxley, Aldous 1894-1963 | Inge, William 1913-1973 . . . DLB-7, 249; CDALB-1 |    Fulton, Len . . . . . . . . . . . . . . . . . . . . . Y-86 |
|    . . . . . . DLB-36, 100, 162, 195, 255; CDBLB-6 | Ingelow, Jean 1820-1897 . . . . . . . . . . . DLB-35, 163 |    Furst, Alan. . . . . . . . . . . . . . . . . . . . . . Y-01 |
| Huxley, Elspeth Josceline | Ingemann, B. S. 1789-1862 . . . . . . . . . . . . DLB-300 |    Garrett, George . . . . . . . . . . . . . . . . . . Y-83 |
|    1907-1997 . . . . . . . . . . . . . . . . . DLB-77, 204 | Ingersoll, Ralph 1900-1985 . . . . . . . . . . . . DLB-127 |    Gelfman, Jane . . . . . . . . . . . . . . . . . . . Y-93 |
| Huxley, T. H. 1825-1895 . . . . . . . . . . . . . . . DLB-57 | The Ingersoll Prizes . . . . . . . . . . . . . . . . . . Y-84 |    Goldwater, Walter . . . . . . . . . . . . . . . . Y-93 |
| Huyghue, Douglas Smith 1816-1891 . . . . . . DLB-99 | Ingoldsby, Thomas (see Barham, Richard Harris) |    Gores, Joe . . . . . . . . . . . . . . . . . . . . . . Y-02 |
| Huysmans, Joris-Karl 1848-1907 . . . . . . . . DLB-123 | Ingraham, Joseph Holt 1809-1860 . . . . . DLB-3, 248 |    Greenfield, George . . . . . . . . . . . . . . . . Y-91 |
| Hwang, David Henry 1957- . . . . . DLB-212, 228 | Inman, John 1805-1850 . . . . . . . . . . . . . . . DLB-73 |    Griffin, Bryan . . . . . . . . . . . . . . . . . . . Y-81 |
| Hyde, Donald 1909-1966 . . . . . . . . . . . . . DLB-187 | Innerhofer, Franz 1944- . . . . . . . . . . . . . . DLB-85 |    Groom, Winston . . . . . . . . . . . . . . . . . . Y-01 |
| Hyde, Mary 1912- . . . . . . . . . . . . . . . . DLB-187 | Innes, Michael (J. I. M. Stewart) |    Guilds, John Caldwell . . . . . . . . . . . . . . Y-92 |
| Hyman, Trina Schart 1939- . . . . . . . . . . DLB-61 |    1906-1994 . . . . . . . . . . . . . . . . . . . . . DLB-276 |    Hamilton, Virginia . . . . . . . . . . . . . . . . Y-01 |
| | Innis, Harold Adams 1894-1952 . . . . . . . . . DLB-88 |    Hardin, James . . . . . . . . . . . . . . . . . . . Y-92 |
| **I** | Innis, Mary Quayle 1899-1972 . . . . . . . . . . DLB-88 |    Harris, Mark . . . . . . . . . . . . . . . . . . . . Y-80 |
| Iavorsky, Stefan 1658-1722 . . . . . . . . . . . . DLB-150 | Inō Sōgi 1421-1502 . . . . . . . . . . . . . . . . . DLB-203 |    Harrison, Jim. . . . . . . . . . . . . . . . . . . . Y-82 |
| Iazykov, Nikolai Mikhailovich | Inoue Yasushi 1907-1991 . . . . . . . . . . . . . DLB-182 |    Hazzard, Shirley . . . . . . . . . . . . . . . . . Y-82 |
|    1803-1846 . . . . . . . . . . . . . . . . . . . . . DLB-205 | "The Greatness of Southern Literature": |    Herrick, William . . . . . . . . . . . . . . . . . Y-01 |
| Ibáñez, Armando P. 1949- . . . . . . . . . DLB-209 |    League of the South Institute for the | |
| |    Study of Southern Culture and History | |
| |    . . . . . . . . . . . . . . . . . . . . . . . . . . . . . . Y-02 | |
| | International Publishers Company . . . . . . . DLB-46 | |

| | | |
|---|---|---|
| Higgins, George V. | Y-98 | |
| Hoban, Russell | Y-90 | |
| Holroyd, Michael | Y-99 | |
| Horowitz, Glen | Y-90 | |
| Iggulden, John | Y-01 | |
| Jakes, John | Y-83 | |
| Jenkinson, Edward B. | Y-82 | |
| Jenks, Tom | Y-86 | |
| Kaplan, Justin | Y-86 | |
| King, Florence | Y-85 | |
| Klopfer, Donald S. | Y-97 | |
| Krug, Judith | Y-82 | |
| Lamm, Donald | Y-95 | |
| Laughlin, James | Y-96 | |
| Lawrence, Starling | Y-95 | |
| Lindsay, Jack | Y-84 | |
| Mailer, Norman | Y-97 | |
| Manchester, William | Y-85 | |
| Max, D. T. | Y-94 | |
| McCormack, Thomas | Y-98 | |
| McNamara, Katherine | Y-97 | |
| Mellen, Joan | Y-94 | |
| Menaker, Daniel | Y-97 | |
| Mooneyham, Lamarr | Y-82 | |
| Murray, Les | Y-01 | |
| Nosworth, David | Y-82 | |
| O'Connor, Patrick | Y-84, 99 | |
| Ozick, Cynthia | Y-83 | |
| Penner, Jonathan | Y-83 | |
| Pennington, Lee | Y-82 | |
| Penzler, Otto | Y-96 | |
| Plimpton, George | Y-99 | |
| Potok, Chaim | Y-84 | |
| Powell, Padgett | Y-01 | |
| Prescott, Peter S. | Y-86 | |
| Rabe, David | Y-91 | |
| Rechy, John | Y-82 | |
| Reid, B. L. | Y-83 | |
| Reynolds, Michael | Y-95, 99 | |
| Robinson, Derek | Y-02 | |
| Rollyson, Carl | Y-97 | |
| Rosset, Barney | Y-02 | |
| Schlafly, Phyllis | Y-82 | |
| Schroeder, Patricia | Y-99 | |
| Schulberg, Budd | Y-81, 01 | |
| Scribner, Charles, III | Y-94 | |
| Sipper, Ralph | Y-94 | |
| Smith, Cork | Y-95 | |
| Staley, Thomas F. | Y-00 | |
| Styron, William | Y-80 | |
| Talese, Nan | Y-94 | |
| Thornton, John | Y-94 | |
| Toth, Susan Allen | Y-86 | |
| Tyler, Anne | Y-82 | |
| Vaughan, Samuel | Y-97 | |
| Von Ogtrop, Kristin | Y-92 | |
| Wallenstein, Barry | Y-92 | |
| Weintraub, Stanley | Y-82 | |
| Williams, J. Chamberlain | Y-84 | |

Into the Past: William Jovanovich's
Reflections in Publishing ............... Y-02

Ireland, David 1927- ............... DLB-289

The National Library of Ireland's
New James Joyce
Manuscripts ............... Y-02

Irigaray, Luce 1930- ............... DLB-296

Irving, John 1942- ............... DLB-6, 278; Y-82

Irving, Washington 1783-1859
............... DLB-3, 11, 30, 59, 73, 74,
183, 186, 250; CDALB-2

Irwin, Grace 1907- ............... DLB-68

Irwin, Will 1873-1948 ............... DLB-25

Isaksson, Ulla 1916-2000 ............... DLB-257

Iser, Wolfgang 1926- ............... DLB-242

Isherwood, Christopher
1904-1986 ............... DLB-15, 195; Y-86

The Christopher Isherwood Archive,
The Huntington Library ............ Y-99

Ishiguro, Kazuo 1954- ............... DLB-194

Ishikawa Jun 1899-1987 ............... DLB-182

Iskander, Fazil' Abdulevich 1929- ............ DLB-302

The Island Trees Case: A Symposium on
School Library Censorship
An Interview with Judith Krug
An Interview with Phyllis Schlafly
An Interview with Edward B. Jenkinson
An Interview with Lamarr Mooneyham
An Interview with Harriet Bernstein ..... Y-82

Islas, Arturo
1938-1991 ............... DLB-122

Issit, Debbie 1966- ............... DLB-233

Ivanišević, Drago 1907-1981 ............ DLB-181

Ivanov, Viacheslav Ivanovich
1866-1949 ............... DLB-295

Ivanov, Vsevolod Viacheslavovich
1895-1963 ............... DLB-272

Ivaska, Astrīde 1926- ............... DLB-232

M. J. Ivers and Company ............... DLB-49

Iwaniuk, Wacław 1915- ............... DLB-215

Iwano Hōmei 1873-1920 ............... DLB-180

Iwaszkiewicz, Jarosław 1894-1980 ............ DLB-215

Iyayi, Festus 1947- ............... DLB-157

Izumi Kyōka 1873-1939 ............... DLB-180

# J

Jackmon, Marvin E. (see Marvin X)

Jacks, L. P. 1860-1955 ............... DLB-135

Jackson, Angela 1951- ............... DLB-41

Jackson, Charles 1903-1968 ............... DLB-234

Jackson, Helen Hunt
1830-1885 ............... DLB-42, 47, 186, 189

Jackson, Holbrook 1874-1948 ............... DLB-98

Jackson, Laura Riding 1901-1991 ............ DLB-48

Jackson, Shirley
1916-1965 ............... DLB-6, 234; CDALB-1

Jacob, Max 1876-1944 ............... DLB-258

Jacob, Naomi 1884?-1964 ............... DLB-191

Jacob, Piers Anthony Dillingham
(see Anthony, Piers)

Jacob, Violet 1863-1946 ............... DLB-240

Jacobi, Friedrich Heinrich 1743-1819 ..... DLB-94

Jacobi, Johann Georg 1740-1841 ............ DLB-97

George W. Jacobs and Company ............... DLB-49

Jacobs, Harriet 1813-1897 ............... DLB-239

Jacobs, Joseph 1854-1916 ............... DLB-141

Jacobs, W. W. 1863-1943 ............... DLB-135

The W. W. Jacobs Appreciation Society .. Y-98

Jacobsen, J. P. 1847-1885 ............... DLB-300

Jacobsen, Jørgen-Frantz 1900-1938 ...... DLB-214

Jacobsen, Josephine 1908- ............ DLB-244

Jacobsen, Rolf 1907-1994 ............... DLB-297

Jacobson, Dan 1929- ............... DLB-14, 207, 225

Jacobson, Howard 1942- ............... DLB-207

Jacques de Vitry circa 1160/1170-1240 ... DLB-208

Jæger, Frank 1926-1977 ............... DLB-214

William Jaggard [publishing house] ...... DLB-170

Jahier, Piero 1884-1966 ............... DLB-114, 264

Jahnn, Hans Henny 1894-1959 ............ DLB-56, 124

Jaimes, Freyre, Ricardo 1866?-1933 ...... DLB-283

Jakes, John 1932- ............... DLB-278; Y-83

Tribute to John Gardner ............... Y-82

Tribute to John D. MacDonald ............ Y-86

Jakobína Johnson (Jakobína Sigurbjarnardóttir)
1883-1977 ............... DLB-293

Jakobson, Roman 1896-1982 ............... DLB-242

James, Alice 1848-1892 ............... DLB-221

James, C. L. R. 1901-1989 ............... DLB-125

James, George P. R. 1801-1860 ............ DLB-116

James, Henry 1843-1916
....... DLB-12, 71, 74, 189; DS-13; CDALB-3

"The Future of the Novel" (1899) .... DLB-18

"The Novel in [Robert Browning's]
'The Ring and the Book'"
(1912) ............... DLB-32

James, John circa 1633-1729 ............... DLB-24

James, M. R. 1862-1936 ............... DLB-156, 201

James, Naomi 1949- ............... DLB-204

James, P. D. (Phyllis Dorothy James White)
1920- ...... DLB-87, 276; DS-17; CDBLB-8

Tribute to Charles Scribner Jr. ............ Y-95

James, Thomas 1572?-1629 ............... DLB-213

U. P. James [publishing house] ............ DLB-49

James, Will 1892-1942 ............... DS-16

James, William 1842-1910 ............... DLB-270

James VI of Scotland, I of England
1566-1625 ............... DLB-151, 172

Ane Schort Treatise Conteining Some Revlis
and Cautelis to Be Obseruit and
Eschewit in Scottis Poesi (1584) ..... DLB-172

Jameson, Anna 1794-1860 ............... DLB-99, 166

| | | |
|---|---|---|
| Jameson, Fredric 1934- ..............DLB-67 | Jersild, Per Christian 1935- .........DLB-257 | Johnson, Nunnally 1897-1977 ..........DLB-26 |
| Jameson, J. Franklin 1859-1937 .........DLB-17 | Jesse, F. Tennyson 1888-1958 ..........DLB-77 | Johnson, Owen 1878-1952................Y-87 |
| Jameson, Storm 1891-1986 .............DLB-36 | Jewel, John 1522-1571 ................DLB-236 | Johnson, Pamela Hansford 1912-1981.....DLB-15 |
| Jančar, Drago 1948- ..................DLB-181 | John P. Jewett and Company............DLB-49 | Johnson, Pauline 1861-1913 .............DLB-92 |
| Janés, Clara 1940- ...................DLB-134 | Jewett, Sarah Orne 1849-1909.... DLB-12, 74, 221 | Johnson, Ronald 1935-1998.............DLB-169 |
| Janevski, Slavko 1920- ....DLB-181; CDWLB-4 | The Jewish Publication Society .........DLB-49 | Johnson, Samuel 1696-1772....DLB-24; CDBLB-2 |
| Janowitz, Tama 1957- ................DLB-292 | Studies in American Jewish Literature....... Y-02 | Johnson, Samuel 1709-1784 ........ DLB-39, 95, 104, 142, 213 |
| Jansson, Tove 1914-2001...............DLB-257 | Jewitt, John Rodgers 1783-1821..........DLB-99 | *Rambler,* no. 4 (1750) [excerpt].........DLB-39 |
| Janvier, Thomas 1849-1913.............DLB-202 | Jewsbury, Geraldine 1812-1880...........DLB-21 | The BBC Four Samuel Johnson Prize for Non-fiction..................... Y-02 |
| Japan | Jewsbury, Maria Jane 1800-1833.........DLB-199 | Johnson, Samuel 1822-1882...........DLB-1, 243 |
| "The Development of Meiji Japan"...DLB-180 | Jhabvala, Ruth Prawer 1927- .....DLB-139, 194 | Johnson, Susanna 1730-1810 ...........DLB-200 |
| "Encounter with the West".........DLB-180 | Jiménez, Juan Ramón 1881-1958.........DLB-134 | Johnson, Terry 1955- .................DLB-233 |
| Japanese Literature | Jin, Ha 1956- .................DLB-244, 292 | Johnson, Uwe 1934-1984..... DLB-75; CDWLB-2 |
| Letter from Japan ................ Y-94, 98 | Joans, Ted 1928- ................DLB-16, 41 | Benjamin Johnson [publishing house] .....DLB-49 |
| Medieval Travel Diaries ..........DLB-203 | Jōha 1525-1602 ........................DLB-203 | Benjamin, Jacob, and Robert Johnson [publishing house].................DLB-49 |
| Surveys: 1987-1995 ...............DLB-182 | Jóhann Sigurjónsson 1880-1919..........DLB-293 | Johnston, Annie Fellows 1863-1931.......DLB-42 |
| Jaramillo, Cleofas M. 1878-1956 ........DLB-122 | Jóhannes úr Kötlum 1899-1972 ..........DLB-293 | Johnston, Basil H. 1929- ...............DLB-60 |
| Jaramillo Levi, Enrique 1944- ........DLB-290 | Johannis de Garlandia (see John of Garland) | Johnston, David Claypole 1798?-1865....DLB-188 |
| Jarman, Mark 1952- ............DLB-120, 282 | John, Errol 1924-1988 .................DLB-233 | Johnston, Denis 1901-1984 ..............DLB-10 |
| Jarrell, Randall 1914-1965 ..........DLB-48, 52; CDALB-1 | John, Eugenie (see Marlitt, E.) | Johnston, Ellen 1835-1873 ............DLB-199 |
| Jarrold and Sons....................DLB-106 | John of Dumbleton circa 1310-circa 1349...............DLB-115 | Johnston, George 1912-1970 ...........DLB-260 |
| Jarry, Alfred 1873-1907 ...........DLB-192, 258 | John of Garland (Jean de Garlande, Johannis de Garlandia) circa 1195-circa 1272................DLB-208 | Johnston, George 1913- ................DLB-88 |
| Jarves, James Jackson 1818-1888 ........DLB-189 | | Johnston, Sir Harry 1858-1927 .........DLB-174 |
| Jasmin, Claude 1930- ..................DLB-60 | Johns, Captain W. E. 1893-1968..........DLB-160 | Johnston, Jennifer 1930- ...............DLB-14 |
| Jaunsudrabiņš, Jānis 1877-1962 ........DLB-220 | Johnson, Mrs. A. E. ca. 1858-1922 ......DLB-221 | Johnston, Mary 1870-1936.................DLB-9 |
| Jay, John 1745-1829...................DLB-31 | Johnson, Amelia (see Johnson, Mrs. A. E.) | Johnston, Richard Malcolm 1822-1898....DLB-74 |
| Jean de Garlande (see John of Garland) | Johnson, B. S. 1933-1973 .............DLB-14, 40 | Johnstone, Charles 1719?-1800?.........DLB-39 |
| Jefferies, Richard 1848-1887 ........DLB-98, 141 | Johnson, Charles 1679-1748..............DLB-84 | Johst, Hanns 1890-1978.................DLB-124 |
| The Richard Jefferies Society .......... Y-98 | Johnson, Charles 1948- ............DLB-33, 278 | Jökull Jakobsson 1933-1978 ............DLB-293 |
| Jeffers, Lance 1919-1985 ...............DLB-41 | Johnson, Charles S. 1893-1956 .......DLB-51, 91 | Jolas, Eugene 1894-1952 ............DLB-4, 45 |
| Jeffers, Robinson 1887-1962 .........DLB-45, 212; CDALB-4 | Johnson, Colin (Mudrooroo) 1938- ....DLB-289 | Jón Stefán Sveinsson or Svensson (see Nonni) |
| Jefferson, Thomas 1743-1826..........DLB-31, 183; CDALB-2 | Johnson, Denis 1949- .................DLB-120 | Jón Trausti (Guðmundur Magnússon) 1873-1918 ......................DLB-293 |
| Jégé 1866-1940.......................DLB-215 | Johnson, Diane 1934- ...................Y-80 | Jón úr Vör (Jón Jónsson) 1917-2000 .....DLB-293 |
| Jelinek, Elfriede 1946- .................DLB-85 | Johnson, Dorothy M. 1905–1984 ......DLB-206 | Jónas Hallgrímsson 1807-1845..........DLB-293 |
| Jellicoe, Ann 1927- ................DLB-13, 233 | Johnson, E. Pauline (Tekahionwake) 1861-1913 ......................DLB-175 | Jones, Alice C. 1853-1933 ...............DLB-92 |
| Jemison, Mary circa 1742-1833 .........DLB-239 | Johnson, Edgar 1901-1995..............DLB-103 | Jones, Charles C., Jr. 1831-1893...........DLB-30 |
| Jenkins, Dan 1929- ...................DLB-241 | Johnson, Edward 1598-1672 .............DLB-24 | Jones, D. G. 1929- ....................DLB-53 |
| Jenkins, Elizabeth 1905- ..............DLB-155 | Johnson, Eyvind 1900-1976 ............DLB-259 | Jones, David 1895-1974 .........DLB-20, 100; CDBLB-7 |
| Jenkins, Robin 1912- ...............DLB-14, 271 | Johnson, Fenton 1888-1958 .........DLB-45, 50 | Jones, Diana Wynne 1934- ............DLB-161 |
| Jenkins, William Fitzgerald (see Leinster, Murray) | Johnson, Georgia Douglas 1877?-1966 ...................DLB-51, 249 | Jones, Ebenezer 1820-1860 .............DLB-32 |
| Herbert Jenkins Limited..............DLB-112 | Johnson, Gerald W. 1890-1980..........DLB-29 | Jones, Ernest 1819-1868................DLB-32 |
| Jennings, Elizabeth 1926- ..............DLB-27 | Johnson, Greg 1953- ..................DLB-234 | Jones, Gayl 1949- ................DLB-33, 278 |
| Jens, Walter 1923- .....................DLB-69 | Johnson, Helene 1907-1995 .............DLB-51 | Jones, George 1800-1870 ..............DLB-183 |
| Jensen, Axel 1932-2003 ................DLB-297 | Jacob Johnson and Company ...........DLB-49 | Jones, Glyn 1905-1995 .................DLB-15 |
| Jensen, Johannes V. 1873-1950 .........DLB-214 | Johnson, James Weldon 1871-1938 ...............DLB-51; CDALB-4 | Jones, Gwyn 1907- ................DLB-15, 139 |
| Jensen, Merrill 1905-1980 ..............DLB-17 | Johnson, John H. 1918- ...............DLB-137 | Jones, Henry Arthur 1851-1929 .........DLB-10 |
| Jensen, Thit 1876-1957................DLB-214 | "Backstage," Statement From the Initial Issue of *Ebony* (November 1945................DLB-137 | Jones, Hugh circa 1692-1760 ...........DLB-24 |
| Jephson, Robert 1736-1803 .............DLB-89 | | Jones, James 1921-1977 .......DLB-2, 143; DS-17 |
| Jerome, Jerome K. 1859-1927 ....DLB-10, 34, 135 | Johnson, Joseph [publishing house] ......DLB-154 | James Jones Papers in the Handy Writers' Colony Collection at the University of Illinois at Springfield .................... Y-98 |
| The Jerome K. Jerome Society ......... Y-98 | Johnson, Linton Kwesi 1952- ..........DLB-157 | |
| Jerome, Judson 1927-1991 .............DLB-105 | Johnson, Lionel 1867-1902..............DLB-19 | |
| "Reflections: After a Tornado" .....DLB-105 | | |
| Jerrold, Douglas 1803-1857 .......DLB-158, 159 | | |

| | | |
|---|---|---|
| The James Jones Society. . . . . . . . . . . . . . Y-92 | The Quinn Draft of James Joyce's Circe Manuscript. . . . . . . . . . . . . . . . . Y-00 | Kant, Hermann 1926- . . . . . . . . . . . . . . . DLB-75 |
| Jones, Jenkin Lloyd 1911- . . . . . . . . . DLB-127 | Stephen Joyce's Letter to the Editor of *The Irish Times* . . . . . . . . . . . . . . . . . . . Y-97 | Kant, Immanuel 1724-1804 . . . . . . . . . DLB-94 |
| Jones, John Beauchamp 1810-1866. . . . . . DLB-202 | *Ulysses*, Reader's Edition: First Reactions . . Y-97 | Kantemir, Antiokh Dmitrievich 1708-1744 . . . . . . . . . . . . . . . . . . . . DLB-150 |
| Jones, Joseph, Major (see Thompson, William Tappan) | We See the Editor at Work . . . . . . . . . . . Y-97 | Kantor, MacKinlay 1904-1977 . . . . . . . DLB-9, 102 |
| Jones, LeRoi (see Baraka, Amiri) | Whose *Ulysses*? The Function of Editing . . Y-97 | Kanze Kōjirō Nobumitsu 1435-1516 . . . . DLB-203 |
| Jones, Lewis 1897-1939. . . . . . . . . . . . . DLB-15 | Jozsef, Attila 1905-1937. . . . . DLB-215; CDWLB-4 | Kanze Motokiyo (see Zeimi) |
| Jones, Madison 1925- . . . . . . . . . . . . . DLB-152 | Juarroz, Roberto 1925-1995 . . . . . . . . . DLB-283 | Kaplan, Fred 1937- . . . . . . . . . . . . . . DLB-111 |
| Jones, Marie 1951- . . . . . . . . . . . . . . . DLB-233 | Orange Judd Publishing Company. . . . . . . DLB-49 | Kaplan, Johanna 1942- . . . . . . . . . . . . DLB-28 |
| Jones, Preston 1936-1979 . . . . . . . . . . . DLB-7 | Judd, Sylvester 1813-1853 . . . . . . . . . DLB-1, 243 | Kaplan, Justin 1925- . . . . . . . . . . DLB-111; Y-86 |
| Jones, Rodney 1950- . . . . . . . . . . . . . DLB-120 | *Judith* circa 930. . . . . . . . . . . . . . . . . DLB-146 | Kaplinski, Jaan 1941- . . . . . . . . . . . . . DLB-232 |
| Jones, Thom 1945- . . . . . . . . . . . . . . . DLB-244 | Juel-Hansen, Erna 1845-1922 . . . . . . . . . DLB-300 | Kapnist, Vasilii Vasilevich 1758?-1823 . . . DLB-150 |
| Jones, Sir William 1746-1794 . . . . . . . . DLB-109 | Julian of Norwich 1342-circa 1420 . . . . DLB-1146 | Karadžić, Vuk Stefanović 1787-1864 . . . . . . . . . . . . . DLB-147; CDWLB-4 |
| Jones, William Alfred 1817-1900. . . . . . . DLB-59 | Julius Caesar 100 B.C.-44 B.C. . . . . . . DLB-211; CDWLB-1 | Karamzin, Nikolai Mikhailovich 1766-1826. . . . . . . . . . . . . . . . . . . . DLB-150 |
| Jones's Publishing House . . . . . . . . . . . . DLB-49 | June, Jennie (see Croly, Jane Cunningham) | Karinthy, Frigyes 1887-1938. . . . . . . . . DLB-215 |
| Jong, Erica 1942- . . . . . . . . . DLB-2, 5, 28, 152 | Jung, Carl Gustav 1875-1961 . . . . . . . . . DLB-296 | Karmel, Ilona 1925-2000 . . . . . . . . . . DLB-299 |
| Jonke, Gert F. 1946- . . . . . . . . . . . . . . DLB-85 | Jung, Franz 1888-1963 . . . . . . . . . . . . DLB-118 | Karsch, Anna Louisa 1722-1791 . . . . . . . DLB-97 |
| Jonson, Ben 1572?-1637 . . . . . . . . DLB-62, 121; CDBLB-1 | Jünger, Ernst 1895- . . . . . . DLB-56; CDWLB-2 | Kasack, Hermann 1896-1966 . . . . . . . . DLB-69 |
| Johsson, Tor 1916-1951 . . . . . . . . . . . DLB-297 | *Der jüngere Titurel* circa 1275 . . . . . . . . DLB-138 | Kasai Zenzō 1887-1927 . . . . . . . . . . . DLB-180 |
| Jordan, June 1936- . . . . . . . . . . . . . . . DLB-38 | Jung-Stilling, Johann Heinrich 1740-1817 . . . . . . . . . . . . . . . . . . . . DLB-94 | Kaschnitz, Marie Luise 1901-1974 . . . . . . DLB-69 |
| Jorgensen, Johannes 1866-1956 . . . . . . . DLB-300 | Junqueiro, Abílio Manuel Guerra 1850-1923 . . . . . . . . . . . . . . . . . . . . DLB-287 | Kassák, Lajos 1887-1967 . . . . . . . . . . . DLB-215 |
| Joseph, Jenny 1932- . . . . . . . . . . . . . . DLB-40 | Justice, Donald 1925- . . . . . . . . . . . . . . . Y-83 | Kaštelan, Jure 1919-1990 . . . . . . . . . . DLB-147 |
| Joseph and George . . . . . . . . . . . . . . . . Y-99 | Juvenal circa A.D. 60-circa A.D. 130 . . . . . . . . . . . . . . . . . DLB-211; CDWLB-1 | Kästner, Erich 1899-1974 . . . . . . . . . . . DLB-56 |
| Michael Joseph Limited . . . . . . . . . . . . DLB-112 | The Juvenile Library (see M. J. Godwin and Company) | Kataev, Evgenii Petrovich (see Il'f, Il'ia and Petrov, Evgenii) |
| Josephson, Matthew 1899-1978 . . . . . . . DLB-4 |  | Kataev, Valentin Petrovich 1897-1986 . . . . DLB-272 |
| Josephus, Flavius 37-100 . . . . . . . . . . DLB-176 | **K** | Katenin, Pavel Aleksandrovich 1792-1853. . . . . . . . . . . . . . . . . . . . DLB-205 |
| Josephy, Alvin M., Jr. Tribute to Alfred A. Knopf . . . . . . . . . . Y-84 | Kacew, Romain (see Gary, Romain) | Kattan, Naim 1928- . . . . . . . . . . . . . . DLB-53 |
| Josiah Allen's Wife (see Holley, Marietta) | Kafka, Franz 1883-1924 . . . . . DLB-81; CDWLB-2 | Katz, Steve 1935- . . . . . . . . . . . . . . . . Y-83 |
| Josipovici, Gabriel 1940- . . . . . . . . . . . DLB-14 | Kahn, Gus 1886-1941. . . . . . . . . . . . . DLB-265 | Ka-Tzetnik 135633 (Yehiel Dinur) 1909-2001 . . . . . . . . . . . . . . . . . . . DLB-299 |
| Josselyn, John ?-1675 . . . . . . . . . . . . . DLB-24 | Kahn, Roger 1927- . . . . . . . . . . . . . . DLB-171 | Kauffman, Janet 1945- . . . . . . . . . DLB-218; Y-86 |
| Joudry, Patricia 1921-2000 . . . . . . . . . . DLB-88 | Kaikō Takeshi 1939-1989. . . . . . . . . . . DLB-182 | Kauffmann, Samuel 1898-1971 . . . . . . . DLB-127 |
| Jouve, Pierre Jean 1887-1976. . . . . . . . . DLB-258 | Káinn (Kristján Níels Jónsson/Kristjan Niels Julius) 1860-1936 . . . . . . . . . . DLB-293 | Kaufman, Bob 1925-1986. . . . . . . . . . DLB-16, 41 |
| Jovanovich, William 1920-2001 . . . . . . . . Y-01 | Kaiser, Georg 1878-1945 . . . DLB-124; CDWLB-2 | Kaufman, George S. 1889-1961 . . . . . . . DLB-7 |
| Into the Past: William Jovanovich's Reflections on Publishing . . . . . . . . . Y-02 | *Kaiserchronik* circa 1147 . . . . . . . . . . . . DLB-148 | Kaufmann, Walter 1921-1980 . . . . . . . . DLB-279 |
| [Response to Ken Auletta] . . . . . . . . . . Y-97 | Kaleb, Vjekoslav 1905- . . . . . . . . . . . DLB-181 | Kavan, Anna (Helen Woods Ferguson Edmonds) 1901-1968. . . . . . . . . . . . DLB-255 |
| *The Temper of the West:* William Jovanovich . . . . . . . . . . . . . . . . . . Y-02 | Kalechofsky, Roberta 1931- . . . . . . . . . DLB-28 | Kavanagh, P. J. 1931- . . . . . . . . . . . . . DLB-40 |
| Tribute to Charles Scribner Jr. . . . . . . . . Y-95 | Kaler, James Otis 1848-1912. . . . . . . . DLB-12, 42 | Kavanagh, Patrick 1904-1967. . . . . . . . DLB-15, 20 |
| Jovine, Francesco 1902-1950 . . . . . . . . DLB-264 | Kalmar, Bert 1884-1947 . . . . . . . . . . . DLB-265 | Kaverin, Veniamin Aleksandrovich (Veniamin Aleksandrovich Zil'ber) 1902-1989 . . . . . . . . . . . . . . . . . . . DLB-272 |
| Jovine, Giuseppe 1922- . . . . . . . . . . . DLB-128 | Kamensky, Vasilii Vasil'evich 1884-1961 . . . . . . . . . . . . . . . . . . . . DLB-295 |  |
| Joyaux, Philippe (see Sollers, Philippe) | Kames, Henry Home, Lord 1696-1782. . . . . . . . . . . . . . . . . DLB-31, 104 | Kawabata Yasunari 1899-1972 . . . . . . . DLB-180 |
| Joyce, Adrien (see Eastman, Carol) | Kamo no Chōmei (Kamo no Nagaakira) 1153 or 1155-1216 . . . . . . . . . . . . . DLB-203 | Kay, Guy Gavriel 1954- . . . . . . . . . . . DLB-251 |
| Joyce, James 1882-1941 . . . . . . . DLB-10, 19, 36, 162, 247; CDBLB-6 | Kamo no Nagaakira (see Kamo no Chōmei) | Kaye-Smith, Sheila 1887-1956. . . . . . . . . DLB-36 |
| Danis Rose and the Rendering of *Ulysses* . . Y-97 | Kampmann, Christian 1939-1988. . . . . . . DLB-214 | Kazakov, Iurii Pavlovich 1927-1982 . . . . . DLB-302 |
| James Joyce Centenary: Dublin, 1982 . . . . Y-82 | Kandel, Lenore 1932- . . . . . . . . . . . . DLB-16 | Kazin, Alfred 1915-1998. . . . . . . . . . . . DLB-67 |
| James Joyce Conference. . . . . . . . . . . . Y-85 | Kanin, Garson 1912-1999. . . . . . . . . . . DLB-7 | Keane, John B. 1928- . . . . . . . . . . . . . DLB-13 |
| A Joyce (Con)Text: Danis Rose and the Remaking of *Ulysses* . . . . . . . . . . . . Y-97 | A Tribute (to Marc Connelly) . . . . . . . . Y-80 | Keary, Annie 1825-1879 . . . . . . . . . . . DLB-163 |
| The National Library of Ireland's New James Joyce Manuscripts. . . . . . Y-02 |  | Keary, Eliza 1827-1918 . . . . . . . . . . . . DLB-240 |
| The New *Ulysses*. . . . . . . . . . . . . . . . Y-84 |  | Keating, H. R. F. 1926- . . . . . . . . . . . . DLB-87 |
| Public Domain and the Violation of Texts . . . . . . . . . . . . . . . . . . . . . . Y-97 |  | Keatley, Charlotte 1960- . . . . . . . . . . . DLB-245 |
|  | Kaniuk, Yoram 1930- . . . . . . . . . . . . DLB-299 | Keats, Ezra Jack 1916-1983 . . . . . . . . . . DLB-61 |

| | | |
|---|---|---|
| Keats, John 1795-1821 . . . .DLB-96, 110; CDBLB-3 | Tribute to Cleanth Brooks . . . . . . . . . . . Y-80 | Khvostov, Dmitrii Ivanovich 1757-1835. . . . . . . . . . . . . . . . . . . . .DLB-150 |
| Keble, John 1792-1866. . . . . . . . . . . . . .DLB-32, 55 | Mitchell Kennerley [publishing house]. . . . .DLB-46 | Kibirov, Timur Iur'evich (Timur Iur'evich Zapoev) 1955- . . . . . . . .DLB-285 |
| Keckley, Elizabeth 1818?-1907. . . . . . . . .DLB-239 | Kenny, Maurice 1929- . . . . . . . . . . . . . . .DLB-175 | |
| Keeble, John 1944- . . . . . . . . . . . . . . . . . . Y-83 | Kent, Frank R. 1877-1958 . . . . . . . . . . . .DLB-29 | Kidd, Adam 1802?-1831 . . . . . . . . . . . . . .DLB-99 |
| Keeffe, Barrie 1945- . . . . . . . . . . . . .DLB-13, 245 | Kenyon, Jane 1947-1995 . . . . . . . . . . . . .DLB-120 | William Kidd [publishing house]. . . . . . .DLB-106 |
| Keeley, James 1867-1934 . . . . . . . . . . . . . .DLB-25 | Kenzheev, Bakhyt Shkurullaevich 1950- . . . . . . . . . . . . . . . . . . . . . . . .DLB-285 | Kidde, Harald 1878-1918. . . . . . . . . . . . .DLB-300 |
| W. B. Keen, Cooke and Company . . . . . . .DLB-49 | | Kidder, Tracy 1945- . . . . . . . . . . . . . . . .DLB-185 |
| The Mystery of Carolyn Keene. . . . . . . . . . . Y-02 | Keough, Hugh Edmund 1864-1912. . . . . .DLB-171 | Kiely, Benedict 1919- . . . . . . . . . . . . . . . .DLB-15 |
| Kefala, Antigone 1935- . . . . . . . . . . . . .DLB-289 | Keppler and Schwartzmann. . . . . . . . . . . .DLB-49 | Kieran, John 1892-1981. . . . . . . . . . . . . .DLB-171 |
| Keillor, Garrison 1942- . . . . . . . . . . . . . . . . Y-87 | Ker, John, third Duke of Roxburghe 1740-1804 . . . . . . . . . . . . . . . . . . . . .DLB-213 | Kierkegaard, Søren 1813-1855. . . . . . . . .DLB-300 |
| Keith, Marian (Mary Esther MacGregor) 1874?-1961 . . . . . . . . . . . . . . . . . . . .DLB-92 | | Kies, Marietta 1853-1899. . . . . . . . . . . . .DLB-270 |
| | Ker, N. R. 1908-1982. . . . . . . . . . . . . . . .DLB-201 | Kiggins and Kellogg. . . . . . . . . . . . . . . . . .DLB-49 |
| Keller, Gary D. 1943- . . . . . . . . . . . . . . .DLB-82 | Kerlan, Irvin 1912-1963. . . . . . . . . . . . . .DLB-187 | Kiley, Jed 1889-1962 . . . . . . . . . . . . . . . . .DLB-4 |
| Keller, Gottfried 1819-1890 . . . . . . . . . . . .DLB-129; CDWLB-2 | Kermode, Frank 1919- . . . . . . . . . . . . . .DLB-242 | Kilgore, Bernard 1908-1967. . . . . . . . . . .DLB-127 |
| | Kern, Jerome 1885-1945 . . . . . . . . . . . . .DLB-187 | Kilian, Crawford 1941- . . . . . . . . . . . . . .DLB-251 |
| Kelley, Edith Summers 1884-1956. . . . . . . .DLB-9 | Kernaghan, Eileen 1939- . . . . . . . . . . . . .DLB-251 | Killens, John Oliver 1916-1987 . . . . . . . . .DLB-33 |
| Kelley, Emma Dunham ?-? . . . . . . . . . . . .DLB-221 | Kerner, Justinus 1786-1862 . . . . . . . . . . . .DLB-90 | Tribute to Julian Mayfield. . . . . . . . . . . Y-84 |
| Kelley, William Melvin 1937- . . . . . . . . . .DLB-33 | Kerouac, Jack 1922-1969 . . .DLB-2, 16, 237; DS-3; CDALB-1 | Killigrew, Anne 1660-1685 . . . . . . . . . . .DLB-131 |
| Kellogg, Ansel Nash 1832-1886. . . . . . . . .DLB-23 | | Killigrew, Thomas 1612-1683 . . . . . . . . . .DLB-58 |
| Kellogg, Steven 1941- . . . . . . . . . . . . . . .DLB-61 | Auction of Jack Kerouac's On the Road Scroll . . . . . . . . . . . Y-01 | Kilmer, Joyce 1886-1918 . . . . . . . . . . . . . .DLB-45 |
| Kelly, George E. 1887-1974 . . . . . . . . .DLB-7, 249 | | Kilroy, Thomas 1934- . . . . . . . . . . . . . . .DLB-233 |
| Kelly, Hugh 1739-1777. . . . . . . . . . . . . . .DLB-89 | The Jack Kerouac Revival . . . . . . . . . . Y-95 | Kilwardby, Robert circa 1215-1279 . . . . .DLB-115 |
| Kelly, Piet and Company. . . . . . . . . . . . . .DLB-49 | "Re-meeting of Old Friends": The Jack Kerouac Conference . . . . . . Y-82 | Kilworth, Garry 1941- . . . . . . . . . . . . . .DLB-261 |
| Kelly, Robert 1935- . . . . . . . . .DLB-5, 130, 165 | | Kim, Anatolii Andreevich 1939- . . . . . .DLB-285 |
| Kelman, James 1946- . . . . . . . . . . . . . . .DLB-194 | Statement of Correction to "The Jack Kerouac Revival" . . . . . . . . . . . . . . . Y-96 | Kimball, Richard Burleigh 1816-1892 . . . .DLB-202 |
| Kelmscott Press . . . . . . . . . . . . . . . . . . . .DLB-112 | | Kincaid, Jamaica 1949- |
| Kelton, Elmer 1926- . . . . . . . . . . . . . . . .DLB-256 | Kerouac, Jan 1952-1996. . . . . . . . . . . . . .DLB-16 | . . . . . . . DLB-157, 227; CDALB-7; CDWLB-3 |
| Kemble, E. W. 1861-1933. . . . . . . . . . . . .DLB-188 | Charles H. Kerr and Company . . . . . . . . .DLB-49 | Kinck, Hans Ernst 1865-1926 . . . . . . . . .DLB-297 |
| Kemble, Fanny 1809-1893. . . . . . . . . . . . .DLB-32 | Kerr, Orpheus C. (see Newell, Robert Henry) | King, Charles 1844-1933 . . . . . . . . . . . . .DLB-186 |
| Kemelman, Harry 1908-1996 . . . . . . . . . .DLB-28 | Kersh, Gerald 1911-1968. . . . . . . . . . . . .DLB-255 | King, Clarence 1842-1901 . . . . . . . . . . . . .DLB-12 |
| Kempe, Margery circa 1373-1438 . . . . . . .DLB-146 | Kertész, Imre . . . . . . . . . . . . . . . .DLB-299; Y-02 | King, Florence 1936- . . . . . . . . . . . . . . . . . Y-85 |
| Kempner, Friederike 1836-1904 . . . . . . . .DLB-129 | Kesey, Ken 1935-2001 . . . . . . . .DLB-2, 16, 206; CDALB-6 | King, Francis 1923- . . . . . . . . . . . . .DLB-15, 139 |
| Kempowski, Walter 1929- . . . . . . . . . . . .DLB-75 | | King, Grace 1852-1932 . . . . . . . . . .DLB-12, 78 |
| Kenan, Randall 1963- . . . . . . . . . . . . . . .DLB-292 | Kessel, Joseph 1898-1979 . . . . . . . . . . . . .DLB-72 | King, Harriet Hamilton 1840-1920 . . . . . .DLB-199 |
| Claude Kendall [publishing company]. . . . .DLB-46 | Kessel, Martin 1901-1990 . . . . . . . . . . . . .DLB-56 | King, Henry 1592-1669 . . . . . . . . . . . . . .DLB-126 |
| Kendall, Henry 1839-1882. . . . . . . . . . . .DLB-230 | Kesten, Hermann 1900-1996 . . . . . . . . . . .DLB-56 | Solomon King [publishing house] . . . . . . .DLB-49 |
| Kendall, May 1861-1943 . . . . . . . . . . . . .DLB-240 | Keun, Irmgard 1905-1982 . . . . . . . . . . . . .DLB-69 | King, Stephen 1947- . . . . . . . . . . .DLB-143; Y-80 |
| Kendell, George 1809-1867 . . . . . . . . . . . .DLB-43 | Key, Ellen 1849-1926. . . . . . . . . . . . . . . .DLB-259 | |
| Keneally, Thomas 1935- . . . . . . . .DLB-289, 299 | Key and Biddle . . . . . . . . . . . . . . . . . . . . .DLB-49 | King, Susan Petigru 1824-1875 . . . . . . . .DLB-239 |
| Kenedy, P. J., and Sons . . . . . . . . . . . . . . .DLB-49 | Keynes, Sir Geoffrey 1887-1982. . . . . . . .DLB-201 | King, Thomas 1943- . . . . . . . . . . . . . . . .DLB-175 |
| Kenkō circa 1283-circa 1352 . . . . . . . . . .DLB-203 | Keynes, John Maynard 1883-1946 . . . . . . DS-10 | King, Woodie, Jr. 1937- . . . . . . . . . . . . . .DLB-38 |
| Kenna, Peter 1930-1987. . . . . . . . . . . . . .DLB-289 | Keyserling, Eduard von 1855-1918. . . . . . .DLB-66 | Kinglake, Alexander William 1809-1891 . . . . . . . . . . . . . . . .DLB-55, 166 |
| Kennan, George 1845-1924 . . . . . . . . . . .DLB-189 | Khan, Ismith 1925-2002 . . . . . . . . . . . . .DLB-125 | |
| Kennedy, A. L. 1965- . . . . . . . . . . . . . . .DLB-271 | Kharitonov, Evgenii Vladimirovich 1941-1981 . . . . . . . . . . . . . . . . . . . .DLB-285 | Kingo, Thomas 1634-1703. . . . . . . . . . . .DLB-300 |
| Kennedy, Adrienne 1931- . . . . . . . . . . . . .DLB-38 | | Kingsbury, Donald 1929- . . . . . . . . . . . .DLB-251 |
| Kennedy, John Pendleton 1795-1870 . . .DLB-3, 248 | Kharitonov, Mark Sergeevich 1937- . . . .DLB-285 | Kingsley, Charles 1819-1875 . . . . . . . DLB-21, 32, 163, 178, 190 |
| Kennedy, Leo 1907-2000 . . . . . . . . . . . . .DLB-88 | Khaytov, Nikolay 1919- . . . . . . . . . . . . .DLB-181 | |
| Kennedy, Margaret 1896-1967 . . . . . . . . .DLB-36 | Khemnitser, Ivan Ivanovich 1745-1784 . . . . . . . . . . . . . . . . . . . .DLB-150 | Kingsley, Henry 1830-1876 . . . . . . . .DLB-21, 230 |
| Kennedy, Patrick 1801-1873 . . . . . . . . . . .DLB-159 | | Kingsley, Mary Henrietta 1862-1900. . . . .DLB-174 |
| Kennedy, Richard S. 1920- . . . . .DLB-111; Y-02 | Kheraskov, Mikhail Matveevich 1733-1807 . . . . . . . . . . . . . . . . . . . .DLB-150 | Kingsley, Sidney 1906-1995. . . . . . . . . . . . .DLB-7 |
| Kennedy, William 1928- . . . . . . .DLB-143; Y-85 | | Kingsmill, Hugh 1889-1949. . . . . . . . . . .DLB-149 |
| Kennedy, X. J. 1929- . . . . . . . . . . . . . . . .DLB-5 | Khlebnikov, Velimir 1885-1922 . . . . . . . .DLB-295 | Kingsolver, Barbara 1955- . . . . . . . . . . . . .DLB-206; CDALB-7 |
| Tribute to John Ciardi . . . . . . . . . . . . Y-86 | Khomiakov, Aleksei Stepanovich 1804-1860 . . . . . . . . . . . . . . . . . . . .DLB-205 | |
| Kennelly, Brendan 1936- . . . . . . . . . . . . .DLB-40 | | Kingston, Maxine Hong 1940- . . . . . .DLB-173, 212; Y-80; CDALB-7 |
| Kenner, Hugh 1923- . . . . . . . . . . . . . . . .DLB-67 | Khristov, Boris 1945- . . . . . . . . . . . . . . .DLB-181 | |
| | Khvoshchinskaia, Nadezhda Dmitrievna 1824-1889 . . . . . . . . . . . . . . . . . . . .DLB-238 | Kingston, William Henry Giles 1814-1880 . . . . . . . . . . . . . . . . . . . .DLB-163 |

489

# Cumulative Index

Kinnan, Mary Lewis 1763-1848 . . . . . . . DLB-200
Kinnell, Galway 1927- . . . . . . . . . . . .DLB-5; Y-87
Kinsella, Thomas 1928- . . . . . . . . . . . . . DLB-27
Kipling, Rudyard 1865-1936
. . . . . . . . . . DLB-19, 34, 141, 156; CDBLB-5
Kipphardt, Heinar 1922-1982. . . . . . . . . DLB-124
Kirby, William 1817-1906. . . . . . . . . . . . DLB-99
Kircher, Athanasius 1602-1680. . . . . . . . DLB-164
Kireevsky, Ivan Vasil'evich 1806-1856. . . DLB-198
Kireevsky, Petr Vasil'evich 1808-1856. . . DLB-205
Kirk, Hans 1898-1962 . . . . . . . . . . . . . . DLB-214
Kirk, John Foster 1824-1904. . . . . . . . . . DLB-79
Kirkconnell, Watson 1895-1977 . . . . . . . . DLB-68
Kirkland, Caroline M.
1801-1864 . . . . . . . DLB-3, 73, 74, 250; DS-13
Kirkland, Joseph 1830-1893 . . . . . . . . . . DLB-12
Francis Kirkman [publishing house] . . . . . DLB-170
Kirkpatrick, Clayton 1915- . . . . . . . . . . DLB-127
Kirkup, James 1918- . . . . . . . . . . . . . . . DLB-27
Kirouac, Conrad (see Marie-Victorin, Frère)
Kirsch, Sarah 1935- . . . . . . . . . . . . . . . DLB-75
Kirst, Hans Hellmut 1914-1989 . . . . . . . . DLB-69
Kiš, Danilo 1935-1989 . . . . . DLB-181; CDWLB-4
Kita Morio 1927- . . . . . . . . . . . . . . . . DLB-182
Kitcat, Mabel Greenhow 1859-1922. . . . . DLB-135
Kitchin, C. H. B. 1895-1967 . . . . . . . . . . DLB-77
Kittredge, William 1932- . . . . . . DLB-212, 244
Kiukhel'beker, Vil'gel'm Karlovich
1797-1846 . . . . . . . . . . . . . . . . . . . DLB-205
Kizer, Carolyn 1925- . . . . . . . . . . DLB-5, 169
Kjaerstad, Jan 1953- . . . . . . . . . . . . . . DLB-297
Klabund 1890-1928 . . . . . . . . . . . . . . . DLB-66
Klaj, Johann 1616-1656 . . . . . . . . . . . . DLB-164
Klappert, Peter 1942- . . . . . . . . . . . . . . DLB-5
Klass, Philip (see Tenn, William)
Klein, A. M. 1909-1972. . . . . . . . . . . . . DLB-68
Kleist, Ewald von 1715-1759. . . . . . . . . . DLB-97
Kleist, Heinrich von
1777-1811. . . . . . . . . . . DLB-90; CDWLB-2
Klíma, Ivan 1931- . . . . . . . DLB-232; CDWLB-4
Klimentev, Andrei Platonovic
(see Platonov, Andrei Platonovich)
Klinger, Friedrich Maximilian
1752-1831. . . . . . . . . . . . . . . . . . . . DLB-94
Kliuev, Nikolai Alekseevich 1884-1937 . . DLB-295
Kliushnikov, Viktor Petrovich
1841-1892 . . . . . . . . . . . . . . . . . . . DLB-238
Klopfer, Donald S.
Impressions of William Faulkner . . . . . . . Y-97
Oral History Interview with Donald
S. Klopfer. . . . . . . . . . . . . . . . . . . . Y-97
Tribute to Alfred A. Knopf . . . . . . . . . . Y-84
Klopstock, Friedrich Gottlieb
1724-1803. . . . . . . . . . . . . . . . . . . . DLB-97
Klopstock, Meta 1728-1758. . . . . . . . . . . DLB-97
Kluge, Alexander 1932- . . . . . . . . . . . . DLB-75
Kluge, P. F. 1942- . . . . . . . . . . . . . . . . . Y-02

Knapp, Joseph Palmer 1864-1951. . . . . . . DLB-91
Knapp, Samuel Lorenzo 1783-1838 . . . . . DLB-59
J. J. and P. Knapton [publishing house] . . DLB-154
Kniazhnin, Iakov Borisovich 1740-1791 . . DLB-150
Knickerbocker, Diedrich (see Irving, Washington)
Knigge, Adolph Franz Friedrich Ludwig,
Freiherr von 1752-1796 . . . . . . . . . . . DLB-94
Charles Knight and Company . . . . . . . . DLB-106
Knight, Damon 1922-2002. . . . . . . . . . . . DLB-8
Knight, Etheridge 1931-1992 . . . . . . . . . DLB-41
Knight, John S. 1894-1981 . . . . . . . . . . . DLB-29
Knight, Sarah Kemble 1666-1727 . . . . DLB-24, 200
Knight-Bruce, G. W. H. 1852-1896 . . . . .DLB-174
Knister, Raymond 1899-1932. . . . . . . . . DLB-68
Knoblock, Edward 1874-1945 . . . . . . . . DLB-10
Knopf, Alfred A. 1892-1984 . . . . . . . . . . . Y-84
Knopf to Hammett: The Editoral
Correspondence . . . . . . . . . . . . . . . Y-00
Alfred A. Knopf [publishing house] . . . . DLB-46
Knorr von Rosenroth, Christian
1636-1689 . . . . . . . . . . . . . . . . . . . DLB-168
Knowles, John 1926- . . . . . . DLB-6; CDALB-6
Knox, Frank 1874-1944 . . . . . . . . . . . . . DLB-29
Knox, John circa 1514-1572 . . . . . . . . . DLB-132
Knox, John Armoy 1850-1906 . . . . . . . . DLB-23
Knox, Lucy 1845-1884. . . . . . . . . . . . . DLB-240
Knox, Ronald Arbuthnott 1888-1957. . . . . DLB-77
Knox, Thomas Wallace 1835-1896 . . . . . DLB-189
Knudsen, Jakob 1858-1917 . . . . . . . . . . DLB-300
Kobayashi Takiji 1903-1933. . . . . . . . . . DLB-180
Kober, Arthur 1900-1975 . . . . . . . . . . . DLB-11
Kobiakova, Aleksandra Petrovna
1823-1892 . . . . . . . . . . . . . . . . . . . DLB-238
Kocbek, Edvard 1904-1981 . .DLB-147; CDWLB-4
Koch, C. J. 1932- . . . . . . . . . . . . . . . . DLB-289
Koch, Howard 1902-1995 . . . . . . . . . . . DLB-26
Koch, Kenneth 1925-2002 . . . . . . . . . . . DLB-5
Kōda Rohan 1867-1947 . . . . . . . . . . . . DLB-180
Koehler, Ted 1894-1973. . . . . . . . . . . . DLB-265
Koenigsberg, Moses 1879-1945 . . . . . . . . DLB-25
Koeppen, Wolfgang 1906-1996 . . . . . . . . DLB-69
Koertge, Ronald 1940- . . . . . . . . . . . . DLB-105
Koestler, Arthur 1905-1983 . . . . . Y-83; CDBLB-7
Kohn, John S. Van E. 1906-1976 . . . . . . DLB-187
Kokhanovskaia
(see Sokhanskaia, Nadezhda Stepanova)
Kokoschka, Oskar 1886-1980 . . . . . . . . DLB-124
Kolb, Annette 1870-1967 . . . . . . . . . . . . DLB-66
Kolbenheyer, Erwin Guido
1878-1962. . . . . . . . . . . . . . . . DLB-66, 124
Kolleritsch, Alfred 1931- . . . . . . . . . . . DLB-85
Kolodny, Annette 1941- . . . . . . . . . . . . DLB-67
Kol'tsov, Aleksei Vasil'evich 1809-1842. . DLB-205
Komarov, Matvei circa 1730-1812 . . . . . DLB-150
Komroff, Manuel 1890-1974 . . . . . . . . . . DLB-4
Komunyakaa, Yusef 1947- . . . . . . . . . DLB-120

Kondoleon, Harry 1955-1994 . . . . . . . . DLB-266
Koneski, Blaže 1921-1993. . .DLB-181; CDWLB-4
Konigsburg, E. L. 1930- . . . . . . . . . . . . DLB-52
Konparu Zenchiku 1405-1468? . . . . . . . DLB-203
Konrád, György 1933- . . . . DLB-232; CDWLB-4
Konrad von Würzburg circa 1230-1287. . DLB-138
Konstantinov, Aleko 1863-1897 . . . . . . . .DLB-147
Konwicki, Tadeusz 1926- . . . . . . . . . . . DLB-232
Koontz, Dean 1945- . . . . . . . . . . . . . . DLB-292
Kooser, Ted 1939- . . . . . . . . . . . . . . . DLB-105
Kopit, Arthur 1937- . . . . . . . . . . . . . . . DLB-7
Kops, Bernard 1926?- . . . . . . . . . . . . . DLB-13
Kornbluth, C. M. 1923-1958 . . . . . . . . . . DLB-8
Körner, Theodor 1791-1813. . . . . . . . . . DLB-90
Kornfeld, Paul 1889-1942. . . . . . . . . . . DLB-118
Korolenko, Vladimir Galaktionovich
1853-1921 . . . . . . . . . . . . . . . . . . . .DLB-277
Kosinski, Jerzy 1933-1991 . . . . . .DLB-2, 299; Y-82
Kosmač, Ciril 1910-1980 . . . . . . . . . . . DLB-181
Kosovel, Srečko 1904-1926 . . . . . . . . . . .DLB-147
Kostrov, Ermil Ivanovich 1755-1796 . . . . DLB-150
Kotzebue, August von 1761-1819. . . . . . . DLB-94
Kotzwinkle, William 1938- . . . . . . . . . .DLB-173
Kovačić, Ante 1854-1889 . . . . . . . . . . . .DLB-147
Kovalevskaia, Sof'ia Vasil'evna
1850-1891 . . . . . . . . . . . . . . . . . . . .DLB-277
Kovič, Kajetan 1931- . . . . . . . . . . . . . DLB-181
Kozlov, Ivan Ivanovich 1779-1840 . . . . . DLB-205
Kracauer, Siegfried 1889-1966 . . . . . . . . DLB-296
Kraf, Elaine 1946- . . . . . . . . . . . . . . . . . Y-81
Kramer, Jane 1938- . . . . . . . . . . . . . . . DLB-185
Kramer, Larry 1935- . . . . . . . . . . . . . . DLB-249
Kramer, Mark 1944- . . . . . . . . . . . . . . DLB-185
Kranjčević, Silvije Strahimir 1865-1908 . . .DLB-147
Krasko, Ivan 1876-1958 . . . . . . . . . . . . DLB-215
Krasna, Norman 1909-1984 . . . . . . . . . . DLB-26
Kraus, Hans Peter 1907-1988 . . . . . . . . .DLB-187
Kraus, Karl 1874-1936 . . . . . . . . . . . . . DLB-118
Krause, Herbert 1905-1976. . . . . . . . . . DLB-256
Krauss, Ruth 1911-1993 . . . . . . . . . . . . DLB-52
Kreisel, Henry 1922-1991 . . . . . . . . . . . . DLB-88
Krestovsky V.
(see Khvoshchinskaia, Nadezhda Dmitrievna)
Krestovsky, Vsevolod Vladimirovich
1839-1895 . . . . . . . . . . . . . . . . . . . DLB-238
Kreuder, Ernst 1903-1972. . . . . . . . . . . DLB-69
Krėvė-Mickevičius, Vincas 1882-1954 . . . DLB-220
Kreymborg, Alfred 1883-1966 . . . . . . . DLB-4, 54
Krieger, Murray 1923- . . . . . . . . . . . . DLB-67
Krim, Seymour 1922-1989 . . . . . . . . . . . DLB-16
Kripke, Saul 1940- . . . . . . . . . . . . . . .DLB-279
Kristensen, Tom 1893-1974 . . . . . . . . . DLB-214
Kristeva, Julia 1941- . . . . . . . . . . . . . . DLB-242
Kristján Níels Jónsson/Kristjan Niels Julius
(see Káinn)
Kritzer, Hyman W. 1918-2002. . . . . . . . . . . . Y-02

Krivulin, Viktor Borisovich 1944-2001 . . .DLB-285

Krleža, Miroslav 1893-1981 . . . . . . . . . . . DLB-147; CDWLB-4

Krock, Arthur 1886-1974. . . . . . . . . . . . . . .DLB-29

Kroetsch, Robert 1927- . . . . . . . . . . . . . . . .DLB-53

Kropotkin, Petr Alekseevich 1842-1921 . . . . . . . . . . . . . . . . . . . . . .DLB-277

Kross, Jaan 1920- . . . . . . . . . . . . . . . . .DLB-232

Kruchenykh, Aleksei Eliseevich 1886-1968 . . . . . . . . . . . . . . . . . . . . . .DLB-295

Krúdy, Gyula 1878-1933 . . . . . . . . . . . .DLB-215

Krutch, Joseph Wood 1893-1970 . . . . . . . . . . . . . . .DLB-63, 206, 275

Krylov, Ivan Andreevich 1769-1844 . . . . .DLB-150

Krymov, Iurii Solomonovich (Iurii Solomonovich Beklemishev) 1908-1941 . . . . . . . . . . . . . . . . . . . . . .DLB-272

Kubin, Alfred 1877-1959 . . . . . . . . . . . . . .DLB-81

Kubrick, Stanley 1928-1999. . . . . . . . . . . . .DLB-26

*Kudrun* circa 1230-1240 . . . . . . . . . . . . . .DLB-138

Kuffstein, Hans Ludwig von 1582-1656 . .DLB-164

Kuhlmann, Quirinus 1651-1689 . . . . . . . .DLB-168

Kuhn, Thomas S. 1922-1996. . . . . . . . . . .DLB-279

Kuhnau, Johann 1660-1722 . . . . . . . . . . .DLB-168

Kukol'nik, Nestor Vasil'evich 1809-1868 . . . . . . . . . . . . . . . . . . . . . .DLB-205

Kukučín, Martin 1860-1928 . . . . . . . . . . . DLB-215; CDWLB-4

Kumin, Maxine 1925- . . . . . . . . . . . . . . . . .DLB-5

Kuncewicz, Maria 1895-1989. . . . . . . . . .DLB-215

Kundera, Milan 1929- . . . . . DLB-232; CDWLB-4

Kunene, Mazisi 1930- . . . . . . . . . . . . . . .DLB-117

Kunikida Doppo 1869-1908 . . . . . . . . . .DLB-180

Kunitz, Stanley 1905- . . . . . . . . . . . . . . . .DLB-48

Kunjufu, Johari M. (see Amini, Johari M.)

Kunnert, Gunter 1929- . . . . . . . . . . . . . . .DLB-75

Kunze, Reiner 1933- . . . . . . . . . . . . . . . . .DLB-75

Kupferberg, Tuli 1923- . . . . . . . . . . . . . . .DLB-16

Kuprin, Aleksandr Ivanovich 1870-1938 . . . . . . . . . . . . . . . . . . . . . .DLB-295

Kuraev, Mikhail Nikolaevich 1939- . . . .DLB-285

Kurahashi Yumiko 1935- . . . . . . . . . . . .DLB-182

Kureishi, Hanif 1954- . . . . . . . . . .DLB-194, 245

Kürnberger, Ferdinand 1821-1879 . . . . . .DLB-129

Kurz, Isolde 1853-1944 . . . . . . . . . . . . . . .DLB-66

Kusenberg, Kurt 1904-1983. . . . . . . . . . . .DLB-69

Kushchevsky, Ivan Afanas'evich 1847-1876. . . . . . . . . . . . . . . . . . . . . .DLB-238

Kushner, Tony 1956- . . . . . . . . . . . . . . . .DLB-228

Kuttner, Henry 1915-1958. . . . . . . . . . . . . .DLB-8

Kuzmin, Mikhail Alekseevich 1872-1936 . . . . . . . . . . . . . . . . . . . . . .DLB-295

Kuznetsov, Anatolii Vasil'evich (A. Anatoly) 1929-1979 . . . . . . . . . . . . . . . . .DLB-299, 302

Kyd, Thomas 1558-1594. . . . . . . . . . . . . . .DLB-62

Kyffin, Maurice circa 1560?-1598 . . . . . . .DLB-136

Kyger, Joanne 1934- . . . . . . . . . . . . . . . . .DLB-16

Kyne, Peter B. 1880-1957 . . . . . . . . . . . . . .DLB-78

Kyōgoku Tamekane 1254-1332 . . . . . . . .DLB-203

Kyrklund, Willy 1921- . . . . . . . . . . . . . . .DLB-257

# L

L. E. L. (see Landon, Letitia Elizabeth)

Laberge, Albert 1871-1960. . . . . . . . . . . . .DLB-68

Laberge, Marie 1950- . . . . . . . . . . . . . . . .DLB-60

Labiche, Eugène 1815-1888. . . . . . . . . . .DLB-192

Labrunie, Gerard (see Nerval, Gerard de)

La Bruyère, Jean de 1645-1696 . . . . . . . .DLB-268

La Calprenède 1609?-1663 . . . . . . . . . . .DLB-268

Lacan, Jacques 1901-1981 . . . . . . . . . . . .DLB-296

La Capria, Raffaele 1922- . . . . . . . . . . . .DLB-196

Lacombe, Patrice (see Trullier-Lacombe, Joseph Patrice)

Lacretelle, Jacques de 1888-1985 . . . . . . . .DLB-65

Lacy, Ed 1911-1968. . . . . . . . . . . . . . . . . .DLB-226

Lacy, Sam 1903- . . . . . . . . . . . . . . . . . . .DLB-171

Ladd, Joseph Brown 1764-1786 . . . . . . . . .DLB-37

La Farge, Oliver 1901-1963 . . . . . . . . . . . . .DLB-9

Lafayette, Marie-Madeleine, comtesse de 1634-1693 . . . . . . . . . . . . . . . . . . . . . .DLB-268

Laffan, Mrs. R. S. de Courcy (see Adams, Bertha Leith)

Lafferty, R. A. 1914-2002 . . . . . . . . . . . . . .DLB-8

La Flesche, Francis 1857-1932 . . . . . . . . .DLB-175

La Fontaine, Jean de 1621-1695. . . . . . . .DLB-268

Laforge, Jules 1860-1887 . . . . . . . . . . . . .DLB-217

Lagerkvist, Pär 1891-1974 . . . . . . . . . . . .DLB-259

Lagerlöf, Selma 1858-1940. . . . . . . . . . . . . . . . . . . . . .DLB-259

Lagorio, Gina 1922- . . . . . . . . . . . . . . . .DLB-196

La Guma, Alex 1925-1985 . . . . . . . DLB-117, 225; CDWLB-3

Lahaise, Guillaume (see Delahaye, Guy)

Lahontan, Louis-Armand de Lom d'Arce, Baron de 1666-1715?. . . . . . . . . . . . . . .DLB-99

Laing, Kojo 1946- . . . . . . . . . . . . . . . . .DLB-157

Laird, Caroberth 1895-1983 . . . . . . . . . . . . . Y-82

Laird and Lee . . . . . . . . . . . . . . . . . . . . . .DLB-49

Lake, Paul 1951- . . . . . . . . . . . . . . . . . .DLB-282

Lalić, Ivan V. 1931-1996 . . . . . . . . . . . . .DLB-181

Lalić, Mihailo 1914-1992 . . . . . . . . . . . . .DLB-181

Lalonde, Michèle 1937- . . . . . . . . . . . . . .DLB-60

Lamantia, Philip 1927- . . . . . . . . . . . . . . .DLB-16

Lamartine, Alphonse de 1790-1869. . . . . . . . . . . . . . . . . . . . . . .DLB-217

Lamb, Lady Caroline 1785-1828 . . . . . . . . . . . . . . . . . . . . . .DLB-116

Lamb, Charles 1775-1834 . . . . . . DLB-93, 107, 163; CDBLB-3

Lamb, Mary 1764-1874 . . . . . . . . . . . . . .DLB-163

Lambert, Angela 1940- . . . . . . . . . . . . . .DLB-271

Lambert, Betty 1933-1983 . . . . . . . . . . . . .DLB-60

Lamm, Donald Goodbye, Gutenberg? A Lecture at the New York Public Library, 18 April 1995 . . . . . . . . . . . . . . . . . . . Y-95

Lamming, George 1927- . . . . . . . . . . . . . DLB-125; CDWLB-3

La Mothe Le Vayer, François de 1588-1672 . . . . . . . . . . . . . . . . . . . . . .DLB-268

L'Amour, Louis 1908-1988 . . . . . . .DLB-206; Y-80

Lampman, Archibald 1861-1899. . . . . . . .DLB-92

Lamson, Wolffe and Company . . . . . . . . .DLB-49

Lancer Books. . . . . . . . . . . . . . . . . . . . . . .DLB-46

Lanchester, John 1962- . . . . . . . . . . . . . .DLB-267

Lander, Peter (see Cunningham, Peter)

Landesman, Jay 1919- and Landesman, Fran 1927- . . . . . . . . . . .DLB-16

Landolfi, Tommaso 1908-1979 . . . . . . . .DLB-177

Landon, Letitia Elizabeth 1802-1838 . . . . .DLB-96

Landor, Walter Savage 1775-1864. . . .DLB-93, 107

Landry, Napoléon-P. 1884-1956 . . . . . . . .DLB-92

Landvik, Lorna 1954- . . . . . . . . . . . . . . .DLB-292

Lane, Charles 1800-1870 . . . . . . .DLB-1, 223; DS-5

Lane, F. C. 1885-1984 . . . . . . . . . . . . . . .DLB-241

Lane, Laurence W. 1890-1967 . . . . . . . . . .DLB-91

Lane, M. Travis 1934- . . . . . . . . . . . . . . .DLB-60

Lane, Patrick 1939- . . . . . . . . . . . . . . . . .DLB-53

Lane, Pinkie Gordon 1923- . . . . . . . . . . .DLB-41

John Lane Company . . . . . . . . . . . . . . . . .DLB-49

Laney, Al 1896-1988 . . . . . . . . . . . . .DLB-4, 171

Lang, Andrew 1844-1912 . . . . . . DLB-98, 141, 184

Langer, Susanne K. 1895-1985 . . . . . . . .DLB-270

Langevin, André 1927- . . . . . . . . . . . . . .DLB-60

Langford, David 1953- . . . . . . . . . . . . . .DLB-261

Langgässer, Elisabeth 1899-1950. . . . . . . .DLB-69

Langhorne, John 1735-1779 . . . . . . . . . .DLB-109

Langland, William circa 1330-circa 1400. .DLB-146

Langton, Anna 1804-1893 . . . . . . . . . . . . .DLB-99

Lanham, Edwin 1904-1979 . . . . . . . . . . . . .DLB-4

Lanier, Sidney 1842-1881 . . . . . . . .DLB-64; DS-13

Lanyer, Aemilia 1569-1645 . . . . . . . . . . .DLB-121

Lapointe, Gatien 1931-1983 . . . . . . . . . . .DLB-88

Lapointe, Paul-Marie 1929- . . . . . . . . . . .DLB-88

Larcom, Lucy 1824-1893. . . . . . . . .DLB-221, 243

Lardner, John 1912-1960 . . . . . . . . . . . . .DLB-171

Lardner, Ring 1885-1933 . . . . . . DLB-11, 25, 86, 171; DS-16; CDALB-4

Lardner 100: Ring Lardner Centennial Symposium. . . . . . . . . . . . Y-85

Lardner, Ring, Jr. 1915-2000 . . . . . . DLB-26, Y-00

Larkin, Philip 1922-1985 . . . . . DLB-27; CDBLB-8

The Philip Larkin Society . . . . . . . . . . . . Y-99

La Roche, Sophie von 1730-1807. . . . . . . .DLB-94

La Rochefoucauld, François duc de 1613-1680 . . . . . . . . . . . . . . . . . . . . . .DLB-268

La Rocque, Gilbert 1943-1984. . . . . . . . . .DLB-60

Laroque de Roquebrune, Robert (see Roquebrune, Robert de)

Larrick, Nancy 1910- . . . . . . . . . . . . . . . .DLB-61

Lars, Claudia 1899-1974 . . . . . . . . . . . . .DLB-283

Larsen, Nella 1893-1964 . . . . . . . . . . . . . .DLB-51

| | | |
|---|---|---|
| Larsen, Thøger 1875-1928 . . . . . . . . . . . DLB-300 | Lawson, John ?-1711 . . . . . . . . . . . . . . . . . . DLB-24 | Lee, Sir Sidney 1859-1926 . . . . . . . . DLB-149, 184 |
| Larson, Clinton F. 1919-1994 . . . . . . . . . DLB-256 | Lawson, John Howard 1894-1977 . . . . DLB-228 | "Principles of Biography," in |
| La Sale, Antoine de | Lawson, Louisa Albury 1848-1920 . . . . . . DLB-230 | *Elizabethan and Other Essays* . . . . . . DLB-149 |
| circa 1386-1460/1467 . . . . . . . . . . . . . DLB-208 | Lawson, Robert 1892-1957 . . . . . . . . . . . . DLB-22 | Lee, Tanith 1947- . . . . . . . . . . . . . . . . . DLB-261 |
| Lasch, Christopher 1932-1994 . . . . . . . . DLB-246 | Lawson, Victor F. 1850-1925 . . . . . . . . . . . DLB-25 | Lee, Vernon |
| Lasker-Schüler, Else 1869-1945 . . . . . DLB-66, 124 | Layard, Austen Henry 1817-1894 . . . . . . DLB-166 | 1856-1935 . . . . . . . . DLB-57, 153, 156, 174, 178 |
| Lasnier, Rina 1915-1997 . . . . . . . . . . . . . . DLB-88 | Layton, Irving 1912- . . . . . . . . . . . . . . . . . DLB-88 | Lee and Shepard . . . . . . . . . . . . . . . . . . . . DLB-49 |
| Lassalle, Ferdinand 1825-1864 . . . . . . . . . DLB-129 | LaZamon flourished circa 1200 . . . . . . . DLB-146 | Le Fanu, Joseph Sheridan |
| Late-Medieval Castilian Theater . . . . . . DLB-286 | Lazarević, Laza K. 1851-1890 . . . . . . . . . DLB-147 | 1814-1873 . . . . . . . . . DLB-21, 70, 159, 178 |
| Latham, Robert 1912-1995 . . . . . . . . . . . DLB-201 | Lazarus, George 1904-1997 . . . . . . . . . . DLB-201 | Leffland, Ella 1931- . . . . . . . . . . . . . . . . . . Y-84 |
| Lathrop, Dorothy P. 1891-1980 . . . . . . . . DLB-22 | Lazhechnikov, Ivan Ivanovich | le Fort, Gertrud von 1876-1971 . . . . . . . . DLB-66 |
| Lathrop, George Parsons 1851-1898 . . . . DLB-71 | 1792-1869 . . . . . . . . . . . . . . . . . . . . . DLB-198 | Le Gallienne, Richard 1866-1947 . . . . . . . DLB-4 |
| Lathrop, John, Jr. 1772-1820 . . . . . . . . . . DLB-37 | Lea, Henry Charles 1825-1909 . . . . . . . . . DLB-47 | Legaré, Hugh Swinton |
| Latimer, Hugh 1492?-1555 . . . . . . . . . . . DLB-136 | Lea, Sydney 1942- . . . . . . . . . . . DLB-120, 282 | 1797-1843 . . . . . . . . . . . DLB-3, 59, 73, 248 |
| Latimore, Jewel Christine McLawler | Lea, Tom 1907-2001 . . . . . . . . . . . . . . . . . . DLB-6 | Legaré, James Mathewes 1823-1859 . . . DLB-3, 248 |
| (see Amini, Johari M.) | Leacock, John 1729-1802 . . . . . . . . . . . . . DLB-31 | Léger, Antoine-J. 1880-1950 . . . . . . . . . . . DLB-88 |
| Latin Literature, The Uniqueness of . . . . DLB-211 | Leacock, Stephen 1869-1944 . . . . . . . . . . DLB-92 | Leggett, William 1801-1839 . . . . . . . . . . DLB-250 |
| La Tour du Pin, Patrice de 1911-1975 . . . DLB-258 | Lead, Jane Ward 1623-1704 . . . . . . . . . . DLB-131 | Le Guin, Ursula K. |
| Latymer, William 1498-1583 . . . . . . . . . . DLB-132 | Leadenhall Press . . . . . . . . . . . . . . . . . . . DLB-106 | 1929- . . . . . . DLB-8, 52, 256, 275; CDALB-6 |
| Laube, Heinrich 1806-1884 . . . . . . . . . . . DLB-133 | "The Greatness of Southern Literature": | Lehman, Ernest 1920- . . . . . . . . . . . . . . . DLB-44 |
| Laud, William 1573-1645 . . . . . . . . . . . . DLB-213 | League of the South Institute for the | Lehmann, John 1907-1989 . . . . . . . . DLB-27, 100 |
| Laughlin, James 1914-1997 . . . . DLB-48; Y-96, 97 | Study of Southern Culture and History | John Lehmann Limited . . . . . . . . . . . . . . DLB-112 |
| A Tribute [to Henry Miller] . . . . . . . . . . . Y-80 | . . . . . . . . . . . . . . . . . . . . . . . . . . . . . . Y-02 | Lehmann, Rosamond 1901-1990 . . . . . . . DLB-15 |
| Tribute to Albert Erskine . . . . . . . . . . . . . Y-93 | Leakey, Caroline Woolmer 1827-1881 . . . DLB-230 | Lehmann, Wilhelm 1882-1968 . . . . . . . . . DLB-56 |
| Tribute to Kenneth Rexroth . . . . . . . . . . Y-82 | Leapor, Mary 1722-1746 . . . . . . . . . . . . . DLB-109 | Leiber, Fritz 1910-1992 . . . . . . . . . . . . . . . DLB-8 |
| Tribute to Malcolm Cowley . . . . . . . . . . . Y-89 | Lear, Edward 1812-1888 . . . . . . DLB-32, 163, 166 | Leibniz, Gottfried Wilhelm 1646-1716 . . . DLB-168 |
| Laumer, Keith 1925-1993 . . . . . . . . . . . . . . DLB-8 | Leary, Timothy 1920-1996 . . . . . . . . . . . . DLB-16 | Leicester University Press . . . . . . . . . . . . DLB-112 |
| Lauremberg, Johann 1590-1658 . . . . . . . DLB-164 | W. A. Leary and Company . . . . . . . . . . . DLB-49 | Leigh, Carolyn 1926-1983 . . . . . . . . . . . . DLB-265 |
| Laurence, Margaret 1926-1987 . . . . . . . . . DLB-53 | Léautaud, Paul 1872-1956 . . . . . . . . . . . . DLB-65 | Leigh, W. R. 1866-1955 . . . . . . . . . . . . . DLB-188 |
| Laurentius von Schnüffis 1633-1702 . . . . DLB-168 | Leavis, F. R. 1895-1978 . . . . . . . . . . . . . . DLB-242 | Leinster, Murray 1896-1975 . . . . . . . . . . . . DLB-8 |
| Laurents, Arthur 1918- . . . . . . . . . . . . . . . DLB-26 | Leavitt, David 1961- . . . . . . . . . . . . . . . . DLB-130 | Leiser, Bill 1898-1965 . . . . . . . . . . . . . . . DLB-241 |
| Laurie, Annie (see Black, Winifred) | Leavitt and Allen . . . . . . . . . . . . . . . . . . . DLB-49 | Leisewitz, Johann Anton 1752-1806 . . . . . DLB-94 |
| Laut, Agnes Christiana 1871-1936 . . . . . . DLB-92 | Le Blond, Mrs. Aubrey 1861-1934 . . . . . DLB-174 | Leitch, Maurice 1933- . . . . . . . . . . . . . . . DLB-14 |
| Lauterbach, Ann 1942- . . . . . . . . . . . . . . DLB-193 | le Carré, John (David John Moore Cornwell) | Leithauser, Brad 1943- . . . . . . . . DLB-120, 282 |
| Lautréamont, Isidore Lucien Ducasse, | 1931- . . . . . . . . . . . . . . . DLB-87; CDBLB-8 | Leland, Charles G. 1824-1903 . . . . . . . . . DLB-11 |
| Comte de 1846-1870 . . . . . . . . . . . DLB-217 | Tribute to Graham Greene . . . . . . . . . . . Y-91 | Leland, John 1503?-1552 . . . . . . . . . . . . DLB-136 |
| Lavater, Johann Kaspar 1741-1801 . . . . . . DLB-97 | Tribute to George Greenfield . . . . . . . . . Y-00 | Lemay, Pamphile 1837-1918 . . . . . . . . . . DLB-99 |
| Lavin, Mary 1912-1996 . . . . . . . . . . . . . . . DLB-15 | Lécavelé, Roland (see Dorgeles, Roland) | Lemelin, Roger 1919-1992 . . . . . . . . . . . . DLB-88 |
| Law, John (see Harkness, Margaret) | Lechlitner, Ruth 1901- . . . . . . . . . . . . . . . DLB-48 | Lemercier, Louis-Jean-Népomucène |
| Lawes, Henry 1596-1662 . . . . . . . . . . . . . DLB-126 | Leclerc, Félix 1914-1988 . . . . . . . . . . . . . . DLB-60 | 1771-1840 . . . . . . . . . . . . . . . . . . . . . DLB-192 |
| Lawler, Ray 1921- . . . . . . . . . . . . . . . . . . DLB-289 | Le Clézio, J. M. G. 1940- . . . . . . . . . . . . . DLB-83 | Le Moine, James MacPherson 1825-1912 . DLB-99 |
| Lawless, Anthony (see MacDonald, Philip) | Leder, Rudolf (see Hermlin, Stephan) | Lemon, Mark 1809-1870 . . . . . . . . . . . . . DLB-163 |
| Lawless, Emily (The Hon. Emily Lawless) | Lederer, Charles 1910-1976 . . . . . . . . . . . DLB-26 | Le Moyne, Jean 1913-1996 . . . . . . . . . . . . DLB-88 |
| 1845-1913 . . . . . . . . . . . . . . . . . . . . . DLB-240 | Ledwidge, Francis 1887-1917 . . . . . . . . . . DLB-20 | Lemperly, Paul 1858-1939 . . . . . . . . . . . DLB-187 |
| Lawrence, D. H. 1885-1930 | Lee, Dennis 1939- . . . . . . . . . . . . . . . . . . DLB-53 | L'Engle, Madeleine 1918- . . . . . . . . . . . . DLB-52 |
| . . . . . DLB-10, 19, 36, 98, 162, 195; CDBLB-6 | Lee, Don L. (see Madhubuti, Haki R.) | Lennart, Isobel 1915-1971 . . . . . . . . . . . . DLB-44 |
| The D. H. Lawrence Society of | Lee, George W. 1894-1976 . . . . . . . . . . . . DLB-51 | Lennox, Charlotte 1729 or 1730-1804 . . . . DLB-39 |
| North America . . . . . . . . . . . . . . . . . . . Y-00 | Lee, Harper 1926- . . . . . . . . . DLB-6; CDALB-1 | Lenox, James 1800-1880 . . . . . . . . . . . . . DLB-140 |
| Lawrence, David 1888-1973 . . . . . . . . . . . DLB-29 | Lee, Harriet 1757-1851 and | Lenski, Lois 1893-1974 . . . . . . . . . . . . . . . DLB-22 |
| Lawrence, Jerome 1915- . . . . . . . . . . . . DLB-228 | Lee, Sophia 1750-1824 . . . . . . . . . . . . DLB-39 | Lentricchia, Frank 1940- . . . . . . . . . . . . DLB-246 |
| Lawrence, Seymour 1926-1994 . . . . . . . . . . Y-94 | Lee, Laurie 1914-1997 . . . . . . . . . . . . . . . . DLB-27 | Lenz, Hermann 1913-1998 . . . . . . . . . . . . DLB-69 |
| Tribute to Richard Yates . . . . . . . . . . . . . Y-92 | Lee, Leslie 1935- . . . . . . . . . . . . . . . . . . DLB-266 | Lenz, J. M. R. 1751-1792 . . . . . . . . . . . . . DLB-94 |
| Lawrence, T. E. 1888-1935 . . . . . . . . . . . DLB-195 | Lee, Li-Young 1957- . . . . . . . . . . . . . . . . DLB-165 | Lenz, Siegfried 1926- . . . . . . . . . . . . . . . . DLB-75 |
| The T. E. Lawrence Society . . . . . . . . . . Y-98 | Lee, Manfred B. 1905-1971 . . . . . . . . . . . DLB-137 | Leonard, Elmore 1925- . . . . . . . . . DLB-173, 226 |
| Lawson, George 1598-1678 . . . . . . . . . . . DLB-213 | Lee, Nathaniel circa 1645-1692 . . . . . . . . . DLB-80 | Leonard, Hugh 1926- . . . . . . . . . . . . . . . DLB-13 |
| Lawson, Henry 1867-1922 . . . . . . . . . . . DLB-230 | Lee, Robert E. 1918-1994 . . . . . . . . . . . . DLB-228 | Leonard, William Ellery 1876-1944 . . . . . DLB-54 |

Leonov, Leonid Maksimovich 1899-1994...DLB-272
Leonowens, Anna 1834-1914...DLB-99, 166
Leont'ev, Konstantin Nikolaevich 1831-1891...DLB-277
Leopold, Aldo 1887-1948...DLB-275
LePan, Douglas 1914-1998...DLB-88
Lepik, Kalju 1920-1999...DLB-232
Leprohon, Rosanna Eleanor 1829-1879...DLB-99
Le Queux, William 1864-1927...DLB-70
Lermontov, Mikhail Iur'evich 1814-1841...DLB-205
Lerner, Alan Jay 1918-1986...DLB-265
Lerner, Max 1902-1992...DLB-29
Lernet-Holenia, Alexander 1897-1976...DLB-85
Le Rossignol, James 1866-1969...DLB-92
Lescarbot, Marc circa 1570-1642...DLB-99
LeSeur, William Dawson 1840-1917...DLB-92
LeSieg, Theo. (see Geisel, Theodor Seuss)
Leskov, Nikolai Semenovich 1831-1895...DLB-238
Leslie, Doris before 1902-1982...DLB-191
Leslie, Eliza 1787-1858...DLB-202
Leslie, Frank (Henry Carter) 1821-1880...DLB-43, 79
Frank Leslie [publishing house]...DLB-49
Leśmian, Bolesław 1878-1937...DLB-215
Lesperance, John 1835?-1891...DLB-99
Lessing, Bruno 1870-1940...DLB-28
Lessing, Doris 1919-...DLB-15, 139; Y-85; CDBLB-8
Lessing, Gotthold Ephraim 1729-1781...DLB-97; CDWLB-2
The Lessing Society...Y-00
Lettau, Reinhard 1929-1996...DLB-75
The Hemingway Letters Project Finds an Editor...Y-02
Lever, Charles 1806-1872...DLB-21
Lever, Ralph ca. 1527-1585...DLB-236
Leverson, Ada 1862-1933...DLB-153
Levertov, Denise 1923-1997...DLB-5, 165; CDALB-7
Levi, Peter 1931-2000...DLB-40
Levi, Primo 1919-1987...DLB-177, 299
Levien, Sonya 1888-1960...DLB-44
Levin, Meyer 1905-1981...DLB-9, 28; Y-81
Levin, Phillis 1954-...DLB-282
Lévinas, Emmanuel 1906-1995...DLB-296
Levine, Norman 1923-...DLB-88
Levine, Philip 1928-...DLB-5
Levis, Larry 1946-...DLB-120
Lévi-Strauss, Claude 1908-...DLB-242
Levitov, Aleksandr Ivanovich 1835?-1877...DLB-277
Levy, Amy 1861-1889...DLB-156, 240
Levy, Benn Wolfe 1900-1973...DLB-13; Y-81
Lewald, Fanny 1811-1889...DLB-129
Lewes, George Henry 1817-1878...DLB-55, 144

"Criticism in Relation to Novels" (1863)...DLB-21
*The Principles of Success in Literature* (1865) [excerpt]...DLB-57
Lewis, Agnes Smith 1843-1926...DLB-174
Lewis, Alfred H. 1857-1914...DLB-25, 186
Lewis, Alun 1915-1944...DLB-20, 162
Lewis, C. Day (see Day Lewis, C.)
Lewis, C. I. 1883-1964...DLB-270
Lewis, C. S. 1898-1963...DLB-15, 100, 160, 255; CDBLB-7
The New York C. S. Lewis Society...Y-99
Lewis, Charles B. 1842-1924...DLB-11
Lewis, David 1941-2001...DLB-279
Lewis, Henry Clay 1825-1850...DLB-3, 248
Lewis, Janet 1899-1999...Y-87
Tribute to Katherine Anne Porter...Y-80
Lewis, Matthew Gregory 1775-1818...DLB-39, 158, 178
Lewis, Meriwether 1774-1809...DLB-183, 186
Lewis, Norman 1908-...DLB-204
Lewis, R. W. B. 1917-...DLB-111
Lewis, Richard circa 1700-1734...DLB-24
Lewis, Sinclair 1885-1951...DLB-9, 102; DS-1; CDALB-4
Sinclair Lewis Centennial Conference...Y-85
The Sinclair Lewis Society...Y-99
Lewis, Wilmarth Sheldon 1895-1979...DLB-140
Lewis, Wyndham 1882-1957...DLB-15
*Time and Western Man* [excerpt] (1927)...DLB-36
Lewisohn, Ludwig 1882-1955...DLB-4, 9, 28, 102
Leyendecker, J. C. 1874-1951...DLB-188
Leyner, Mark 1956-...DLB-292
Lezama Lima, José 1910-1976...DLB-113, 283
L'Heureux, John 1934-...DLB-244
Libbey, Laura Jean 1862-1924...DLB-221
Libedinsky, Iurii Nikolaevich 1898-1959...DLB-272
Library History Group...Y-01
E-Books' Second Act in Libraries...Y-02
The Library of America...DLB-46
The Library of America: An Assessment After Two Decades...Y-02
Licensing Act of 1737...DLB-84
Leonard Lichfield I [publishing house]...DLB-170
Lichtenberg, Georg Christoph 1742-1799...DLB-94
The Liddle Collection...Y-97
Lidman, Sara 1923-...DLB-257
Lieb, Fred 1888-1980...DLB-171
Liebling, A. J. 1904-1963...DLB-4, 171
Lieutenant Murray (see Ballou, Maturin Murray)
Lighthall, William Douw 1857-1954...DLB-92
Lihn, Enrique 1929-1988...DLB-283
Lilar, Françoise (see Mallet-Joris, Françoise)
Lili'uokalani, Queen 1838-1917...DLB-221

Lillo, George 1691-1739...DLB-84
Lilly, J. K., Jr. 1893-1966...DLB-140
Lilly, Wait and Company...DLB-49
Lily, William circa 1468-1522...DLB-132
Limited Editions Club...DLB-46
Limón, Graciela 1938-...DLB-209
Lincoln and Edmands...DLB-49
Lind, Jakov 1927-...DLB-299
Linda Vilhjálmsdóttir 1958-...DLB-293
Lindesay, Ethel Forence (see Richardson, Henry Handel)
Lindgren, Astrid 1907-2002...DLB-257
Lindgren, Torgny 1938-...DLB-257
Lindsay, Alexander William, Twenty-fifth Earl of Crawford 1812-1880...DLB-184
Lindsay, Sir David circa 1485-1555...DLB-132
Lindsay, David 1878-1945...DLB-255
Lindsay, Jack 1900-1990...Y-84
Lindsay, Lady (Caroline Blanche Elizabeth Fitzroy Lindsay) 1844-1912...DLB-199
Lindsay, Norman 1879-1969...DLB-260
Lindsay, Vachel 1879-1931...DLB-54; CDALB-3
Linebarger, Paul Myron Anthony (see Smith, Cordwainer)
Link, Arthur S. 1920-1998...DLB-17
Linn, Ed 1922-2000...DLB-241
Linn, John Blair 1777-1804...DLB-37
Lins, Osman 1924-1978...DLB-145
Linton, Eliza Lynn 1822-1898...DLB-18
Linton, William James 1812-1897...DLB-32
Barnaby Bernard Lintot [publishing house]...DLB-170
Lion Books...DLB-46
Lionni, Leo 1910-1999...DLB-61
Lippard, George 1822-1854...DLB-202
Lippincott, Sara Jane Clarke 1823-1904...DLB-43
J. B. Lippincott Company...DLB-49
Lippmann, Walter 1889-1974...DLB-29
Lipton, Lawrence 1898-1975...DLB-16
Lisboa, Irene 1892-1958...DLB-287
Liscow, Christian Ludwig 1701-1760...DLB-97
Lish, Gordon 1934-...DLB-130
Tribute to Donald Barthelme...Y-89
Tribute to James Dickey...Y-97
Lisle, Charles-Marie-René Leconte de 1818-1894...DLB-217
Lispector, Clarice 1925-1977...DLB-113; CDWLB-3
LitCheck Website...Y-01
Literary Awards and Honors...Y-81–02
Booker Prize...Y-86, 96–98
The Drue Heinz Literature Prize...Y-82
The Elmer Holmes Bobst Awards in Arts and Letters...Y-87
The Griffin Poetry Prize...Y-00

Literary Prizes [British] ........ DLB-15, 207
National Book Critics Circle
  Awards................... Y-00–01
The National Jewish Book Awards ..... Y-85
Nobel Prize.................. Y-80–02
Winning an Edgar ................ Y-98
*The Literary Chronicle and Weekly Review*
  *1819-1828* ................. DLB-110
Literary Periodicals:
  *Callaloo* ...................... Y-87
  Expatriates in Paris .............. DS-15
  New Literary Periodicals:
    A Report for 1987 ............ Y-87
    A Report for 1988 ............ Y-88
    A Report for 1989 ............ Y-89
    A Report for 1990 ............ Y-90
    A Report for 1991 ............ Y-91
    A Report for 1992 ............ Y-92
    A Report for 1993 ............ Y-93
Literary Research Archives
  The Anthony Burgess Archive at
    the Harry Ransom Humanities
    Research Center ............ Y-98
  Archives of Charles Scribner's Sons..... DS-17
  Berg Collection of English and
    American Literature of the
    New York Public Library ........ Y-83
  The Bobbs-Merrill Archive at the
    Lilly Library, Indiana University ... Y-90
  Die Fürstliche Bibliothek Corvey....... Y-96
  Guide to the Archives of Publishers,
    Journals, and Literary Agents in
    North American Libraries ........ Y-93
  The Henry E. Huntington Library ..... Y-92
  The Humanities Research Center,
    University of Texas............. Y-82
  The John Carter Brown Library ........ Y-85
  Kent State Special Collections .......... Y-86
  The Lilly Library................... Y-84
  The Modern Literary Manuscripts
    Collection in the Special
    Collections of the Washington
    University Libraries............... Y-87
  A Publisher's Archives: G. P. Putnam .... Y-92
  Special Collections at Boston
    University ..................... Y-99
  The University of Virginia Libraries ..... Y-91
  The William Charvat American Fiction
    Collection at the Ohio State
    University Libraries............... Y-92
Literary Societies .............. Y-98–02
  The Margery Allingham Society ....... Y-98
  The American Studies Association
    of Norway .................... Y-00
  The Arnold Bennett Society.......... Y-98
  The Association for the Study of
    Literature and Environment
    (ASLE)....................... Y-99
  Belgian Luxembourg American Studies
    Association .................. Y-01
  The E. F. Benson Society............ Y-98
  The Elizabeth Bishop Society.......... Y-01

The [Edgar Rice] Burroughs
  Bibliophiles ................. Y-98
The Byron Society of America.......... Y-00
The Lewis Carroll Society
  of North America ............... Y-00
The Willa Cather Pioneer Memorial
  and Education Foundation ......... Y-00
New Chaucer Society................ Y-00
The Wilkie Collins Society .......... Y-98
The James Fenimore Cooper Society..... Y-01
The Stephen Crane Society ........ Y-98, 01
The E. E. Cummings Society.......... Y-01
The James Dickey Society ........... Y-99
John Dos Passos Newsletter........... Y-00
The Priory Scholars [Sir Arthur Conan
  Doyle] of New York ............. Y-99
The International Theodore Dreiser
  Society...................... Y-01
The Friends of the Dymock Poets ....... Y-00
The George Eliot Fellowship ......... Y-99
The T. S. Eliot Society: Celebration and
  Scholarship, 1980-1999 .......... Y-99
The Ralph Waldo Emerson Society ..... Y-99
The William Faulkner Society .......... Y-99
The C. S. Forester Society ........... Y-00
The Hamlin Garland Society........... Y-01
The [Elizabeth] Gaskell Society ......... Y-98
The Charlotte Perkins Gilman Society ... Y-99
The Ellen Glasgow Society .......... Y-01
Zane Grey's West Society ........... Y-00
The Ivor Gurney Society............. Y-98
The Joel Chandler Harris Association ... Y-99
The Nathaniel Hawthorne Society....... Y-00
The [George Alfred] Henty Society ..... Y-98
George Moses Horton Society......... Y-99
The William Dean Howells Society..... Y-01
WW2 HMSO Paperbacks Society....... Y-98
American Humor Studies Association ... Y-99
International Society for Humor Studies .. Y-99
The W. W. Jacobs Appreciation Society .. Y-98
The Richard Jefferies Society.......... Y-98
The Jerome K. Jerome Society ........ Y-98
The D. H. Lawrence Society of
  North America ................ Y-00
The T. E. Lawrence Society .......... Y-98
The [Gotthold] Lessing Society ....... Y-00
The New York C. S. Lewis Society ..... Y-99
The Sinclair Lewis Society........... Y-99
The Jack London Research Center ..... Y-00
The Jack London Society............ Y-99
The Cormac McCarthy Society ....... Y-99
The Melville Society ............... Y-01
The Arthur Miller Society ........... Y-01
The Milton Society of America ........ Y-00
International Marianne Moore Society ... Y-98
International Nabokov Society......... Y-99

The Vladimir Nabokov Society......... Y-01
The Flannery O'Connor Society ....... Y-99
The Wilfred Owen Association ........ Y-98
Penguin Collectors' Society .......... Y-98
The [E. A.] Poe Studies Association...... Y-99
The Katherine Anne Porter Society...... Y-01
The Beatrix Potter Society........... Y-98
The Ezra Pound Society ............ Y-01
The Powys Society.................. Y-98
Proust Society of America ........... Y-00
The Dorothy L. Sayers Society ........ Y-98
The Bernard Shaw Society........... Y-99
The Society for the Study of
  Southern Literature.............. Y-00
The Wallace Stevens Society.......... Y-99
The Harriet Beecher Stowe Center ..... Y-00
The R. S. Surtees Society ........... Y-98
The Thoreau Society................ Y-99
The Tilling [E. F. Benson] Society ..... Y-98
The Trollope Societies.............. Y-00
H. G. Wells Society ................ Y-98
The Western Literature Association ..... Y-99
The William Carlos Williams Society .... Y-99
The Henry Williamson Society ........ Y-98
The [Nero] Wolfe Pack ............. Y-99
The Thomas Wolfe Society........... Y-99
Worldwide Wodehouse Societies ...... Y-98
The W. B. Yeats Society of N.Y........ Y-99
The Charlotte M. Yonge Fellowship ..... Y-98
Literary Theory
  The Year in Literary Theory....... Y-92–Y-93
*Literature at Nurse, or Circulating Morals* (1885),
  by George Moore................ DLB-18
Litt, Toby 1968- ................ DLB-267
Littell, Eliakim 1797-1870 ........... DLB-79
Littell, Robert S. 1831-1896 .......... DLB-79
Little, Brown and Company.......... DLB-49
Little Magazines and Newspapers ........ DS-15
  Selected English-Language Little
    Magazines and Newspapers
    [France, 1920-1939]............ DLB-4
The Little Magazines of the
  New Formalism ............... DLB-282
*The Little Review* 1914-1929.............. DS-15
Littlewood, Joan 1914-2002 ........... DLB-13
Lively, Penelope 1933- ....... DLB-14, 161, 207
Liverpool University Press............ DLB-112
*The Lives of the Poets* (1753)............ DLB-142
Livesay, Dorothy 1909-1996 .......... DLB-68
Livesay, Florence Randal 1874-1953 ..... DLB-92
Livings, Henry 1929-1998 ........... DLB-13
Livingston, Anne Howe 1763-1841 ... DLB-37, 200
Livingston, Jay 1915-2001 ........... DLB-265
Livingston, Myra Cohn 1926-1996 ...... DLB-61
Livingston, William 1723-1790 ......... DLB-31
Livingstone, David 1813-1873 ........ DLB-166

Livingstone, Douglas 1932-1996 ........DLB-225

Livshits, Benedikt Konstantinovich
   1886-1938 or 1939 ...............DLB-295

Livy 59 B.C.-A.D. 17........DLB-211; CDWLB-1

Liyong, Taban lo (see Taban lo Liyong)

Lizárraga, Sylvia S. 1925- .............DLB-82

Llewellyn, Richard 1906-1983..........DLB-15

Lloréns Torres, Luis 1876-1944........DLB-290

Edward Lloyd [publishing house] .......DLB-106

Lobel, Arnold 1933- .................DLB-61

Lochridge, Betsy Hopkins (see Fancher, Betsy)

Locke, Alain 1886-1954................DLB-51

Locke, David Ross 1833-1888........DLB-11, 23

Locke, John 1632-1704.....DLB-31, 101, 213, 252

Locke, Richard Adams 1800-1871........DLB-43

Locker-Lampson, Frederick
   1821-1895 ...................DLB-35, 184

Lockhart, John Gibson
   1794-1854 .............. DLB-110, 116 144

Lockridge, Ross, Jr. 1914-1948 .... DLB-143; Y-80

*Locrine and Selimus*.....................DLB-62

Lodge, David 1935- .............DLB-14, 194

Lodge, George Cabot 1873-1909 ..........DLB-54

Lodge, Henry Cabot 1850-1924 .........DLB-47

Lodge, Thomas 1558-1625 ............DLB-172

   *Defence of Poetry* (1579) [excerpt] ......DLB-172

Loeb, Harold 1891-1974 .........DLB-4; DS-15

Loeb, William 1905-1981 ..............DLB-127

Loesser, Frank 1910-1969 ..............DLB-265

Lofting, Hugh 1886-1947...............DLB-160

Logan, Deborah Norris 1761-1839 .....DLB-200

Logan, James 1674-1751...........DLB-24, 140

Logan, John 1923-1987 ................DLB-5

Logan, Martha Daniell 1704?-1779 .....DLB-200

Logan, William 1950- ................DLB-120

Logau, Friedrich von 1605-1655........DLB-164

Logue, Christopher 1926- ............DLB-27

Lohenstein, Daniel Casper von
   1635-1683 ........................DLB-168

Lo-Johansson, Ivar 1901-1990 .........DLB-259

Lokert, George (or Lockhart)
   circa 1485-1547 ....................DLB-281

Lomonosov, Mikhail Vasil'evich
   1711-1765.........................DLB-150

London, Jack
   1876-1916 .....DLB-8, 12, 78, 212; CDALB-3

   The Jack London Research Center ...... Y-00

   The Jack London Society ............. Y-99

*The London Magazine* 1820-1829 .........DLB-110

Long, David 1948- ..................DLB-244

Long, H., and Brother.................DLB-49

Long, Haniel 1888-1956 ...............DLB-45

Long, Ray 1878-1935...................DLB-137

Longfellow, Henry Wadsworth
   1807-1882 .......DLB-1, 59, 235; CDALB-2

Longfellow, Samuel 1819-1892 ..........DLB-1

Longford, Elizabeth 1906-2002 ........DLB-155

   Tribute to Alfred A. Knopf............ Y-84

Longinus circa first century ...........DLB-176

Longley, Michael 1939- ..............DLB-40

T. Longman [publishing house]........DLB-154

Longmans, Green and Company ........DLB-49

Longmore, George 1793?-1867 ..........DLB-99

Longstreet, Augustus Baldwin
   1790-1870 ............. DLB-3, 11, 74, 248

D. Longworth [publishing house] .......DLB-49

Lønn, Øystein 1936- ................DLB-297

Lonsdale, Frederick 1881-1954 .........DLB-10

Loos, Anita 1893-1981..... DLB-11, 26, 228; Y-81

Lopate, Phillip 1943- ................. Y-80

Lopes, Fernão 1380/1390?-1460?.......DLB-287

Lopez, Barry 1945- ........ DLB-256, 275

López, Diana (see Isabella, Ríos)

López, Josefina 1969- .............DLB-209

López de Mendoza, Íñigo
   (see Santillana, Marqués de)

López Velarde, Ramón 1888-1921.......DLB-290

Loranger, Jean-Aubert 1896-1942 .......DLB-92

Lorca, Federico García 1898-1936.......DLB-108

Lord, John Keast 1818-1872 ............DLB-99

Lorde, Audre 1934-1992 ...............DLB-41

Lorimer, George Horace 1867-1937......DLB-91

A. K. Loring [publishing house]........DLB-49

Loring and Mussey ..................DLB-46

Lorris, Guillaume de (see *Roman de la Rose*)

Lossing, Benson J. 1813-1891 ..........DLB-30

Lothar, Ernst 1890-1974 ...............DLB-81

D. Lothrop and Company..............DLB-49

Lothrop, Harriet M. 1844-1924 .........DLB-42

Loti, Pierre 1850-1923 ................DLB-123

Lotichius Secundus, Petrus 1528-1560 ... DLB-179

Lott, Emmeline ?-?..................DLB-166

Louisiana State University Press ........ Y-97

Lounsbury, Thomas R. 1838-1915 .......DLB-71

Louÿs, Pierre 1870-1925 ..............DLB-123

Løveid, Cecile 1951- ...............DLB-297

Lovejoy, Arthur O. 1873-1962..........DLB-270

Lovelace, Earl 1935- ..... DLB-125; CDWLB-3

Lovelace, Richard 1618-1657..........DLB-131

John W. Lovell Company .............DLB-49

Lovell, Coryell and Company ..........DLB-49

Lover, Samuel 1797-1868........DLB-159, 190

Lovesey, Peter 1936- ................DLB-87

   Tribute to Georges Simenon.......... Y-89

Lovinescu, Eugen
   1881-1943 .......... DLB-220; CDWLB-4

Lovingood, Sut
   (see Harris, George Washington)

Low, Samuel 1765-? .................DLB-37

Lowell, Amy 1874-1925...........DLB-54, 140

Lowell, James Russell 1819-1891
   ...... DLB-1, 11, 64, 79, 189, 235; CDALB-2

Lowell, Robert
   1917-1977............DLB-5, 169; CDALB-7

Lowenfels, Walter 1897-1976.............DLB-4

Lowndes, Marie Belloc 1868-1947........DLB-70

Lowndes, William Thomas 1798-1843 ...DLB-184

Humphrey Lownes [publishing house] ... DLB-170

Lowry, Lois 1937-.....................DLB-52

Lowry, Malcolm 1909-1957....DLB-15; CDBLB-7

Lowther, Pat 1935-1975.................DLB-53

Loy, Mina 1882-1966 ..............DLB-4, 54

Loynaz, Dulce María 1902-1997 ........DLB-283

Lozeau, Albert 1878-1924 ..............DLB-92

Lubbock, Percy 1879-1965 .............DLB-149

Lucan A.D. 39-A.D. 65 ...............DLB-211

Lucas, E. V. 1868-1938 ........DLB-98, 149, 153

Fielding Lucas Jr. [publishing house]......DLB-49

Luce, Clare Booth 1903-1987 ..........DLB-228

Luce, Henry R. 1898-1967 .............DLB-91

John W. Luce and Company...........DLB-46

Lucena, Juan de ca. 1430-1501 .........DLB-286

Lucian circa 120-180 ................ DLB-176

Lucie-Smith, Edward 1933- ..........DLB-40

Lucilius circa 180 B.C.-102/101 B.C......DLB-211

Lucini, Gian Pietro 1867-1914 ........DLB-114

Lucretius circa 94 B.C.-circa 49 B.C.
   ................... DLB-211; CDWLB-1

Luder, Peter circa 1415-1472 ..........DLB-179

Ludlam, Charles 1943-1987............DLB-266

Ludlum, Robert 1927-2001 ............... Y-82

*Ludus de Antichristo* circa 1160 ..........DLB-148

Ludvigson, Susan 1942- ..............DLB-120

Ludwig, Jack 1922- .................DLB-60

Ludwig, Otto 1813-1865 ..............DLB-129

*Ludwigslied* 881 or 882 ..............DLB-148

Luera, Yolanda 1953- ...............DLB-122

Luft, Lya 1938- ...................DLB-145

Lugansky, Kazak Vladimir
   (see Dal', Vladimir Ivanovich)

Lugn, Kristina 1948- ...............DLB-257

Lugones, Leopoldo 1874-1938..........DLB-283

Lukács, Georg (see Lukács, György)

Lukács, György
   1885-1971 ........ DLB-215, 242; CDWLB-4

Luke, Peter 1919- ..................DLB-13

Lummis, Charles F. 1859-1928 .........DLB-186

Lundkvist, Artur 1906-1991 ...........DLB-259

Lunts, Lev Natanovich 1901-1924 ......DLB-272

F. M. Lupton Company................DLB-49

Lupus of Ferrières circa 805-circa 862 ....DLB-148

Lurie, Alison 1926- .................DLB-2

Lussu, Emilio 1890-1975 ..............DLB-264

Lustig, Arnošt 1926- ...........DLB-232, 299

Luther, Martin 1483-1546 ... DLB-179; CDWLB-2

Luzi, Mario 1914- ..................DLB-128

L'vov, Nikolai Aleksandrovich
   1751-1803........................DLB-150

| | | |
|---|---|---|
| Lyall, Gavin 1932- ................ DLB-87 | MacInnes, Colin 1914-1976 ........... DLB-14 | Madgett, Naomi Long 1923- ........ DLB-76 |
| Lydgate, John circa 1370-1450 ........ DLB-146 | MacInnes, Helen 1907-1985 ........... DLB-87 | Madhubuti, Haki R. 1942- .... DLB-5, 41; DS-8 |
| Lyly, John circa 1554-1606. ...... DLB-62, 167 | Mac Intyre, Tom 1931- .............. DLB-245 | Madison, James 1751-1836 ............ DLB-37 |
| Lynch, Patricia 1898-1972 ........... DLB-160 | Mačiulis, Jonas (see Maironis, Jonas) | Madsen, Svend Åge 1939- ......... DLB-214 |
| Lynch, Richard flourished 1596-1601 ... DLB-172 | Mack, Maynard 1909- .............. DLB-111 | Madrigal, Alfonso Fernández de (El Tostado) ca. 1405-1455 ..................... DLB-286 |
| Lynd, Robert 1879-1949 .............. DLB-98 | Mackall, Leonard L. 1879-1937 ........ DLB-140 | Maeterlinck, Maurice 1862-1949 ....... DLB-192 |
| Lyon, Matthew 1749-1822 ............. DLB-43 | MacKay, Isabel Ecclestone 1875-1928 .... DLB-92 | Mafūz, Najīb 1911- .................... Y-88 |
| Lyotard, Jean-François 1924-1998 ..... DLB-242 | MacKaye, Percy 1875-1956 ............ DLB-54 | Nobel Lecture 1988 ................ Y-88 |
| Lyricists Additional Lyricists: 1920-1960 ..... DLB-265 | Macken, Walter 1915-1967 ........... DLB-13 | The Little Magazines of the New Formalism .................. DLB-282 |
| Lysias circa 459 B.C.-circa 380 B.C. ....... DLB-176 | Mackenzie, Alexander 1763-1820 ....... DLB-99 | Magee, David 1905-1977 ............. DLB-187 |
| Lytle, Andrew 1902-1995 ...... DLB-6; Y-95 | Mackenzie, Alexander Slidell 1803-1848 ..................... DLB-183 | Maginn, William 1794-1842 ....... DLB-110, 159 |
| Tribute to Caroline Gordon .......... Y-81 | Mackenzie, Compton 1883-1972 .... DLB-34, 100 | Magoffin, Susan Shelby 1827-1855 ...... DLB-239 |
| Tribute to Katherine Anne Porter ...... Y-80 | Mackenzie, Henry 1745-1831 .......... DLB-39 | Mahan, Alfred Thayer 1840-1914 ....... DLB-47 |
| Lytton, Edward (see Bulwer-Lytton, Edward) | *The Lounger*, no. 20 (1785) .......... DLB-39 | Maheux-Forcier, Louise 1929- ........ DLB-60 |
| Lytton, Edward Robert Bulwer 1831-1891 ..................... DLB-32 | Mackenzie, Kenneth (Seaforth Mackenzie) 1913-1955 ................... DLB-260 | Mahin, John Lee 1902-1984 ........... DLB-44 |
| | Mackenzie, William 1758-1828 ......... DLB-187 | Mahon, Derek 1941- ................ DLB-40 |
| **M** | Mackey, Nathaniel 1947- ............ DLB-169 | Maiakovsky, Vladimir Vladimirovich 1893-1930 ..................... DLB-295 |
| | Mackey, Shena 1944- ............... DLB-231 | Maikov, Apollon Nikolaevich 1821-1897 ..................... DLB-277 |
| Maass, Joachim 1901-1972 ............ DLB-69 | Mackey, William Wellington 1937- ..... DLB-38 | |
| Mabie, Hamilton Wright 1845-1916 ..... DLB-71 | Mackintosh, Elizabeth (see Tey, Josephine) | Maikov, Vasilii Ivanovich 1728-1778 .... DLB-150 |
| Mac A'Ghobhainn, Iain (see Smith, Iain Crichton) | Mackintosh, Sir James 1765-1832 ...... DLB-158 | Mailer, Norman 1923- ........ DLB-2, 16, 28, 185, 278; Y-80, 83, 97; DS-3; CDALB-6 |
| MacArthur, Charles 1895-1956 ..... DLB-7, 25, 44 | Macklin, Charles 1699-1797 ........... DLB-89 | Tribute to Isaac Bashevis Singer ........ Y-91 |
| Macaulay, Catherine 1731-1791 ........ DLB-104 | Maclaren, Ian (see Watson, John) | Tribute to Meyer Levin ............. Y-81 |
| Macaulay, David 1945- .............. DLB-61 | MacLaverty, Bernard 1942- .......... DLB-267 | Maillart, Ella 1903-1997 ............. DLB-195 |
| Macaulay, Rose 1881-1958 ............ DLB-36 | MacLean, Alistair 1922-1987 .......... DLB-276 | Maillet, Adrienne 1885-1963 .......... DLB-68 |
| Macaulay, Thomas Babington 1800-1859 ......... DLB-32, 55; CDBLB-4 | MacLean, Katherine Anne 1925- ........ DLB-8 | Maillet, Antonine 1929- ............. DLB-60 |
| Macaulay Company ................. DLB-46 | Maclean, Norman 1902-1990 .......... DLB-206 | Maillu, David G. 1939- .............. DLB-157 |
| MacBeth, George 1932-1992 .......... DLB-40 | MacLeish, Archibald 1892-1982 ........ DLB-4, 7, 45; Y-82; DS-15; CDALB-7 | Maimonides, Moses 1138-1204 ....... DLB-115 |
| Macbeth, Madge 1880-1965 ........... DLB-92 | MacLennan, Hugh 1907-1990 ......... DLB-68 | Main Selections of the Book-of-the-Month Club, 1926-1945 ................. DLB-9 |
| MacCaig, Norman 1910-1996 ......... DLB-27 | MacLeod, Alistair 1936- ............. DLB-60 | Mainwaring, Daniel 1902-1977 ........ DLB-44 |
| MacDiarmid, Hugh 1892-1978 ............ DLB-20; CDBLB-7 | Macleod, Fiona (see Sharp, William) | Mair, Charles 1838-1927 ............. DLB-99 |
| MacDonald, Cynthia 1928- ......... DLB-105 | Macleod, Norman 1906-1985 .......... DLB-4 | Mair, John circa 1467-1550 ........... DLB-281 |
| MacDonald, George 1824-1905 ... DLB-18, 163, 178 | Mac Low, Jackson 1922- ............. DLB-193 | Maironis, Jonas 1862-1932 .. DLB-220; CDWLB-4 |
| MacDonald, John D. 1916-1986 ..... DLB-8; Y-86 | Macmillan and Company ............. DLB-106 | Mais, Roger 1905-1955 ..... DLB-125; CDWLB-3 |
| MacDonald, Philip 1899?-1980 ........ DLB-77 | The Macmillan Company ............ DLB-49 | Maitland, Sara 1950- ................ DLB-271 |
| Macdonald, Ross (see Millar, Kenneth) | Macmillan's English Men of Letters, First Series (1878-1892) ........... DLB-144 | Major, Andre 1942- ................ DLB-60 |
| Macdonald, Sharman 1951- ......... DLB-245 | MacNamara, Brinsley 1890-1963 ........ DLB-10 | Major, Charles 1856-1913 ............ DLB-202 |
| MacDonald, Wilson 1880-1967 ........ DLB-92 | MacNeice, Louis 1907-1963 ........ DLB-10, 20 | Major, Clarence 1936- .............. DLB-33 |
| Macdonald and Company (Publishers) .. DLB-112 | Macphail, Andrew 1864-1938 .......... DLB-92 | Major, Kevin 1949- ................. DLB-60 |
| MacEwen, Gwendolyn 1941-1987 ... DLB-53, 251 | Macpherson, James 1736-1796 ........ DLB-109 | Major Books ..................... DLB-46 |
| Macfadden, Bernarr 1868-1955 ...... DLB-25, 91 | Macpherson, Jay 1931- .............. DLB-53 | Makanin, Vladimir Semenovich 1937- .................. DLB-285 |
| MacGregor, John 1825-1892 .......... DLB-166 | Macpherson, Jeanie 1884-1946 ......... DLB-44 | Makarenko, Anton Semenovich 1888-1939 ..................... DLB-272 |
| MacGregor, Mary Esther (see Keith, Marian) | Macrae Smith Company .............. DLB-46 | Makemie, Francis circa 1658-1708 ...... DLB-24 |
| Macherey, Pierre 1938- ............. DLB-296 | MacRaye, Lucy Betty (see Webling, Lucy) | *The Making of Americans* Contract .......... Y-98 |
| Machado, Antonio 1875-1939 ........ DLB-108 | John Macrone [publishing house] ..... DLB-106 | Maksimov, Vladimir Emel'ianovich 1930-1995 ..................... DLB-302 |
| Machado, Manuel 1874-1947 ......... DLB-108 | MacShane, Frank 1927-1999 .......... DLB-111 | Maksimović, Desanka 1898-1993 ............ DLB-147; CDWLB-4 |
| Machar, Agnes Maule 1837-1927 ....... DLB-92 | Macy-Masius ..................... DLB-46 | Malamud, Bernard 1914-1986 ........ DLB-2, 28, 152; Y-80, 86; CDALB-1 |
| Machaut, Guillaume de circa 1300-1377 .................. DLB-208 | Madden, David 1933- ................ DLB-6 | |
| Machen, Arthur Llewelyn Jones 1863-1947 .............. DLB-36, 156, 178 | Madden, Sir Frederic 1801-1873 ....... DLB-184 | |
| MacIlmaine, Roland fl. 1574 .......... DLB-281 | Maddow, Ben 1909-1992 ............. DLB-44 | |
| | Maddux, Rachel 1912-1983 ....... DLB-234; Y-93 | |

| | | |
|---|---|---|
| Bernard Malamud Archive at the Harry Ransom Humanities Research Center . . . . . . . . . . . . . . . . Y-00 | Mann, Heinrich 1871-1950 . . . . . . . . DLB-66, 118 | Markham, Edwin 1852-1940 . . . . . . . DLB-54, 186 |
| Mălăncioiu, Ileana 1940- . . . . . . . . . . . DLB-232 | Mann, Horace 1796-1859 . . . . . . . . . . DLB-1, 235 | Markle, Fletcher 1921-1991 . . . . . . DLB-68; Y-91 |
| Malaparte, Curzio (Kurt Erich Suckert) 1898-1957 . . . . . DLB-264 | Mann, Klaus 1906-1949 . . . . . . . . . . . . . . . DLB-56 | Marlatt, Daphne 1942- . . . . . . . . . . . . . . DLB-60 |
| Malerba, Luigi 1927- . . . . . . . . . . . . . . DLB-196 | Mann, Mary Peabody 1806-1887 . . . . . . DLB-239 | Marlitt, E. 1825-1887 . . . . . . . . . . . . . . . DLB-129 |
| Malet, Lucas 1852-1931 . . . . . . . . . . . . . DLB-153 | Mann, Thomas 1875-1955 . . . . DLB-66; CDWLB-2 | Marlowe, Christopher 1564-1593 . . . . . . . . . . . . . DLB-62; CDBLB-1 |
| Mallarmé, Stéphane 1842-1898 . . . . . . . . DLB-217 | Mann, William D'Alton 1839-1920 . . . . . . DLB-137 | Marlyn, John 1912- . . . . . . . . . . . . . . . . . DLB-88 |
| Malleson, Lucy Beatrice (see Gilbert, Anthony) | Mannin, Ethel 1900-1984 . . . . . . . . DLB-191, 195 | Marmion, Shakerley 1603-1639 . . . . . . . . DLB-58 |
| Mallet-Joris, Françoise (Françoise Lilar) 1930- . . . . . . . . . . . . . . . . . . . . . . . . . DLB-83 | Manning, Emily (see Australie) | Der Marner before 1230-circa 1287 . . . . . . DLB-138 |
| Mallock, W. H. 1849-1923 . . . . . . . . . DLB-18, 57 | Manning, Frederic 1882-1935 . . . . . . . . DLB-260 | Marnham, Patrick 1943- . . . . . . . . . . . . DLB-204 |
| "Every Man His Own Poet; or, The Inspired Singer's Recipe Book" (1877) . . . . . . . . . . . . . . . . . DLB-35 | Manning, Laurence 1899-1972 . . . . . . . . DLB-251 | The *Marprelate Tracts* 1588-1589 . . . . . . . DLB-132 |
| | Manning, Marie 1873?-1945 . . . . . . . . . . DLB-29 | Marquand, John P. 1893-1960 . . . . . . . DLB-9, 102 |
| | Manning and Loring . . . . . . . . . . . . . . . . DLB-49 | Marques, Helena 1935- . . . . . . . . . . . . . DLB-287 |
| "Le Style c'est l'homme" (1892) . . . . . . DLB-57 | Mannyng, Robert flourished 1303-1338 . . DLB-146 | Marqués, René 1919-1979 . . . . . . . . . . . DLB-113 |
| *Memoirs of Life and Literature* (1920), [excerpt] . . . . . . . . . . . . . . . . . . DLB-57 | Mano, D. Keith 1942- . . . . . . . . . . . . . . . . DLB-6 | Marquis, Don 1878-1937 . . . . . . . . . . DLB-11, 25 |
| | Manor Books . . . . . . . . . . . . . . . . . . . . . . DLB-46 | Marriott, Anne 1913-1997 . . . . . . . . . . . . DLB-68 |
| Malone, Dumas 1892-1986 . . . . . . . . . . . . DLB-17 | Manrique, Gómez 1412?-1490 . . . . . . . . DLB-286 | Marryat, Frederick 1792-1848 . . . . . . . DLB-21, 163 |
| Malone, Edmond 1741-1812 . . . . . . . . . DLB-142 | Manrique, Jorge ca. 1440-1479 . . . . . . . . DLB-286 | Marsh, Capen, Lyon and Webb . . . . . . . . DLB-49 |
| Malory, Sir Thomas circa 1400-1410 - 1471 . . . DLB-146; CDBLB-1 | Mansfield, Katherine 1888-1923 . . . . . . . DLB-162 | Marsh, George Perkins 1801-1882 . . . . . . . . . . . . . . . . . DLB-1, 64, 243 |
| | Mantel, Hilary 1952- . . . . . . . . . . . . . . DLB-271 | |
| Malouf, David 1934- . . . . . . . . . . . . . . DLB-289 | Manuel, Niklaus circa 1484-1530 . . . . . . DLB-179 | Marsh, James 1794-1842 . . . . . . . . . . . . DLB-1, 59 |
| Malpede, Karen 1945- . . . . . . . . . . . . . DLB-249 | Manzini, Gianna 1896-1974 . . . . . . . . . . DLB-177 | Marsh, Narcissus 1638-1713 . . . . . . . . . . DLB-213 |
| Malraux, André 1901-1976 . . . . . . . . . . . DLB-72 | Mapanje, Jack 1944- . . . . . . . . . . . . . . . DLB-157 | Marsh, Ngaio 1899-1982 . . . . . . . . . . . . . DLB-77 |
| Malthus, Thomas Robert 1766-1834 . . . . . . . . . . . . . . DLB-107, 158 | Maraini, Dacia 1936- . . . . . . . . . . . . . . . DLB-196 | Marshall, Alan 1902-1984 . . . . . . . . . . . DLB-260 |
| | Maramzin, Vladimir Rafailovich 1934- . . . . . . . . . . . . . . . . . . . . . . . . . DLB-302 | Marshall, Edison 1894-1967 . . . . . . . . . . DLB-102 |
| Maltz, Albert 1908-1985 . . . . . . . . . . . . DLB-102 | | Marshall, Edward 1932- . . . . . . . . . . . . . DLB-16 |
| Malzberg, Barry N. 1939- . . . . . . . . . . . . . DLB-8 | March, William (William Edward Campbell) 1893-1954 . . . . . . . . . . . . . . . . . DLB-9, 86 | Marshall, Emma 1828-1899 . . . . . . . . . . DLB-163 |
| Mamet, David 1947- . . . . . . . . . . . . . . . . DLB-7 | Marchand, Leslie A. 1900-1999 . . . . . . . . DLB-103 | Marshall, James 1942-1992 . . . . . . . . . . . DLB-61 |
| Mamin, Dmitrii Narkisovich 1852-1912 . . DLB-238 | Marchant, Bessie 1862-1941 . . . . . . . . . . DLB-160 | Marshall, Joyce 1913- . . . . . . . . . . . . . . . DLB-88 |
| Manaka, Matsemela 1956- . . . . . . . . . . DLB-157 | Marchant, Tony 1959- . . . . . . . . . . . . . . DLB-245 | Marshall, Paule 1929- . . . DLB-33, 157, 227 |
| Manchester University Press . . . . . . . . . DLB-112 | Marchenko, Anastasiia Iakovlevna 1830-1880 . . . . . . . . . . . . . . . . . . . . . DLB-238 | Marshall, Tom 1938-1993 . . . . . . . . . . . . DLB-60 |
| Mandel, Eli 1922-1992 . . . . . . . . . . . . . . DLB-53 | | Marsilius of Padua circa 1275-circa 1342 . . . . . . . . . . . . . . DLB-115 |
| Mandel'shtam, Nadezhda Iakovlevna 1899-1980 . . . . . . . . . . . . . . . . . . . . . DLB-302 | Marchessault, Jovette 1938- . . . . . . . . . . DLB-60 | |
| | Marcinkevičius, Justinas 1930- . . . . . . . DLB-232 | Mars-Jones, Adam 1954- . . . . . . . . . . . . DLB-207 |
| Mandel'shtam, Osip Emil'evich 1891-1938 . . . . . . . . . . . . . . . . . . . . . DLB-295 | Marcus, Frank 1928- . . . . . . . . . . . . . . . . DLB-13 | Marson, Una 1905-1965 . . . . . . . . . . . . . DLB-157 |
| | Marcuse, Herbert 1898-1979 . . . . . . . . . DLB-242 | Marston, John 1576-1634 . . . . . . . . . . DLB-58, 172 |
| Mandeville, Bernard 1670-1733 . . . . . . . DLB-101 | Marden, Orison Swett 1850-1924 . . . . . . DLB-137 | Marston, Philip Bourke 1850-1887 . . . . . . DLB-35 |
| Mandeville, Sir John mid fourteenth century . . . . . . . . . . . . DLB-146 | Marechera, Dambudzo 1952-1987 . . . . . . DLB-157 | Martens, Kurt 1870-1945 . . . . . . . . . . . . . DLB-66 |
| | Marek, Richard, Books . . . . . . . . . . . . . . DLB-46 | Martí, José 1853-1895 . . . . . . . . . . . . . . DLB-290 |
| Mandiargues, André Pieyre de 1909-1991 . . . . . . . . . . . . . . . . . . . . . . DLB-83 | Mares, E. A. 1938- . . . . . . . . . . . . . . . . DLB-122 | Martial circa A.D. 40-circa A.D. 103 . . . . . . . . . . . . . . . . . . . DLB-211; CDWLB-1 |
| Manea, Norman 1936- . . . . . . . . . . . . . DLB-232 | Margulies, Donald 1954- . . . . . . . . . . . . DLB-228 | |
| Manfred, Frederick 1912-1994 . . . . DLB-6, 212, 227 | Mariani, Paul 1940- . . . . . . . . . . . . . . . . DLB-111 | William S. Martien [publishing house] . . . . DLB-49 |
| Manfredi, Gianfranco 1948- . . . . . . . . . DLB-196 | Marie de France flourished 1160-1178 . . . . DLB-208 | Martin, Abe (see Hubbard, Kin) |
| Mangan, Sherry 1904-1961 . . . . . . . . . . . . DLB-4 | Marie-Victorin, Frère (Conrad Kirouac) 1885-1944 . . . . . . . . . . . . . . . . . . . . . . DLB-92 | Martin, Catherine ca. 1847-1937 . . . . . . . DLB-230 |
| Manganelli, Giorgio 1922-1990 . . . . . . . DLB-196 | | Martin, Charles 1942- . . . . . . . . . . . DLB-120, 282 |
| Manilius fl. first century A.D. . . . . . . . . DLB-211 | Marin, Biagio 1891-1985 . . . . . . . . . . . . DLB-128 | Martin, Claire 1914- . . . . . . . . . . . . . . . . DLB-60 |
| Mankiewicz, Herman 1897-1953 . . . . . . . DLB-26 | Marinetti, Filippo Tommaso 1876-1944 . . . . . . . . . . . . . . . . . . DLB-114, 264 | Martin, David 1915-1997 . . . . . . . . . . . . DLB-260 |
| Mankiewicz, Joseph L. 1909-1993 . . . . . . DLB-44 | | Martin, Jay 1935- . . . . . . . . . . . . . . . . . DLB-111 |
| Mankowitz, Wolf 1924-1998 . . . . . . . . . . DLB-15 | Marinina, Aleksandra (Marina Anatol'evna Alekseeva) 1957- . . . . . . . . . . . . . . . DLB-285 | Martin, Johann (see Laurentius von Schnüffis) |
| Manley, Delarivière 1672?-1724 . . . . . . DLB-39, 80 | Marinkovič, Ranko 1913- . . . . . . . . . . . DLB-147; CDWLB-4 | Martin, Thomas 1696-1771 . . . . . . . . . . DLB-213 |
| Preface to *The Secret History, of Queen Zarah, and the Zarazians* (1705) . . . . . DLB-39 | | Martin, Violet Florence (see Ross, Martin) |
| | Marion, Frances 1886-1973 . . . . . . . . . . . DLB-44 | Martin du Gard, Roger 1881-1958 . . . . . . DLB-65 |
| Mann, Abby 1927- . . . . . . . . . . . . . . . . . DLB-44 | Marius, Richard C. 1933-1999 . . . . . . . . . . Y-85 | Martineau, Harriet 1802-1876 . . . . DLB-21, 55, 159, 163, 166, 190 |
| Mann, Charles 1929-1998 . . . . . . . . . . . . . Y-98 | Markevich, Boleslav Mikhailovich 1822-1884 . . . . . . . . . . . . . . . . . . . . . DLB-238 | |
| Mann, Emily 1952- . . . . . . . . . . . . . . . . DLB-266 | Markfield, Wallace 1926-2002 . . . . . . . . DLB-2, 28 | Martínez, Demetria 1960- . . . . . . . . . . . DLB-209 |

# Cumulative Index

Martínez de Toledo, Alfonso 1398?-1468................DLB-286
Martínez, Eliud 1935-............DLB-122
Martínez, Max 1943-..............DLB-82
Martínez, Rubén 1962-............DLB-209
Martinson, Harry 1904-1978.........DLB-259
Martinson, Moa 1890-1964..........DLB-259
Martone, Michael 1955-............DLB-218
Martyn, Edward 1859-1923..........DLB-10
Marvell, Andrew 1621-1678............DLB-131; CDBLB-2
Marvin X 1944-...................DLB-38
Marx, Karl 1818-1883..............DLB-129
Marzials, Theo 1850-1920...........DLB-35
Masefield, John 1878-1967...DLB-10, 19, 153, 160; CDBLB-5
Masham, Damaris Cudworth, Lady 1659-1708......................DLB-252
Masino, Paola 1908-1989...........DLB-264
Mason, A. E. W. 1865-1948..........DLB-70
Mason, Bobbie Ann 1940-..........DLB-173; Y-87; CDALB-7
Mason, William 1725-1797...........DLB-142
Mason Brothers....................DLB-49
*The Massachusetts Quarterly Review* 1847-1850......................DLB-1
Massey, Gerald 1828-1907...........DLB-32
Massey, Linton R. 1900-1974........DLB-187
Massie, Allan 1938-...............DLB-271
Massinger, Philip 1583-1640........DLB-58
Masson, David 1822-1907............DLB-144
Masters, Edgar Lee 1868-1950. DLB-54; CDALB-3
Masters, Hilary 1928-..............DLB-244
Mastronardi, Lucio 1930-1979.......DLB-177
Matevski, Mateja 1929-...DLB-181; CDWLB-4
Mather, Cotton 1663-1728........DLB-24, 30, 140; CDALB-2
Mather, Increase 1639-1723.........DLB-24
Mather, Richard 1596-1669..........DLB-24
Matheson, Annie 1853-1924..........DLB-240
Matheson, Richard 1926-............DLB-8, 44
Matheus, John F. 1887-.............DLB-51
Mathews, Cornelius 1817?-1889....DLB-3, 64, 250
Elkin Mathews [publishing house].....DLB-112
Mathews, John Joseph 1894-1979......DLB-175
Mathias, Roland 1915-..............DLB-27
Mathis, June 1892-1927.............DLB-44
Mathis, Sharon Bell 1937-..........DLB-33
Matković, Marijan 1915-1985........DLB-181
Matoš, Antun Gustav 1873-1914......DLB-147
Matos Paoli, Francisco 1915-2000....DLB-290
Matsumoto Seichō 1909-1992.........DLB-182
The Matter of England 1240-1400....DLB-146
The Matter of Rome early twelfth to late fifteenth century.................DLB-146
Matthew of Vendôme circa 1130-circa 1200.............DLB-208

Matthews, Brander 1852-1929..DLB-71, 78; DS-13
Matthews, Jack 1925-..............DLB-6
Matthews, Victoria Earle 1861-1907....DLB-221
Matthews, William 1942-1997........DLB-5
Matthías Jochumsson 1835-1920......DLB-293
Matthías Johannessen 1930-.........DLB-293
Matthiessen, F. O. 1902-1950........DLB-63
Matthiessen, Peter 1927-.......DLB-6, 173, 275
Maturin, Charles Robert 1780-1824....DLB-178
Maugham, W. Somerset 1874-1965 ......DLB-10, 36, 77, 100, 162, 195; CDBLB-6
Maupassant, Guy de 1850-1893........DLB-123
Maupin, Armistead 1944-............DLB-278
Mauriac, Claude 1914-1996..........DLB-83
Mauriac, François 1885-1970........DLB-65
Maurice, Frederick Denison 1805-1872...DLB-55
Maurois, André 1885-1967...........DLB-65
Maury, James 1718-1769.............DLB-31
Mavor, Elizabeth 1927-.............DLB-14
Mavor, Osborne Henry (see Bridie, James)
Maxwell, Gavin 1914-1969...........DLB-204
Maxwell, William 1908-2000.............DLB-218, 278; Y-80
Tribute to Nancy Hale..............Y-88
H. Maxwell [publishing house].......DLB-49
John Maxwell [publishing house].....DLB-106
May, Elaine 1932-..................DLB-44
May, Karl 1842-1912................DLB-129
May, Thomas 1595/1596-1650.........DLB-58
Mayer, Bernadette 1945-............DLB-165
Mayer, Mercer 1943-................DLB-61
Mayer, O. B. 1818-1891.............DLB-3, 248
Mayes, Herbert R. 1900-1987........DLB-137
Mayes, Wendell 1919-1992...........DLB-26
Mayfield, Julian 1928-1984.........DLB-33; Y-84
Mayhew, Henry 1812-1887............DLB-18, 55, 190
Mayhew, Jonathan 1720-1766.........DLB-31
Mayne, Ethel Colburn 1865-1941.....DLB-197
Mayne, Jasper 1604-1672............DLB-126
Mayne, Seymour 1944-...............DLB-60
Mayor, Flora Macdonald 1872-1932...DLB-36
Mayröcker, Friederike 1924-........DLB-85
Mazrui, Ali A. 1933-...............DLB-125
Mažuranić, Ivan 1814-1890..........DLB-147
Mazursky, Paul 1930-...............DLB-44
McAlmon, Robert 1896-1956...DLB-4, 45; DS-15
"A Night at Bricktop's"............Y-01
McArthur, Peter 1866-1924..........DLB-92
McAuley, James 1917-1976...........DLB-260
Robert M. McBride and Company......DLB-46
McCabe, Patrick 1955-..............DLB-194
McCaffrey, Anne 1926-..............DLB-8
McCann, Colum 1965-................DLB-267
McCarthy, Cormac 1933-..........DLB-6, 143, 256
The Cormac McCarthy Society........Y-99

McCarthy, Mary 1912-1989..........DLB-2; Y-81
McCarthy, Shaun Lloyd (see Cory, Desmond)
McCay, Winsor 1871-1934............DLB-22
McClane, Albert Jules 1922-1991....DLB-171
McClatchy, C. K. 1858-1936.........DLB-25
McClellan, George Marion 1860-1934....DLB-50
"The Negro as a Writer"............DLB-50
McCloskey, Robert 1914-............DLB-22
McClung, Nellie Letitia 1873-1951...DLB-92
McClure, James 1939-...............DLB-276
McClure, Joanna 1930-..............DLB-16
McClure, Michael 1932-.............DLB-16
McClure, Phillips and Company......DLB-46
McClure, S. S. 1857-1949...........DLB-91
A. C. McClurg and Company..........DLB-49
McCluskey, John A., Jr. 1944-......DLB-33
McCollum, Michael A. 1946-.........Y-87
McConnell, William C. 1917-........DLB-88
McCord, David 1897-1997............DLB-61
McCord, Louisa S. 1810-1879........DLB-248
McCorkle, Jill 1958-...............DLB-234; Y-87
McCorkle, Samuel Eusebius 1746-1811...DLB-37
McCormick, Anne O'Hare 1880-1954...DLB-29
McCormick, Kenneth Dale 1906-1997...Y-97
McCormick, Robert R. 1880-1955.....DLB-29
McCourt, Edward 1907-1972..........DLB-88
McCoy, Horace 1897-1955............DLB-9
McCrae, Hugh 1876-1958.............DLB-260
McCrae, John 1872-1918.............DLB-92
McCullagh, Joseph B. 1842-1896.....DLB-23
McCullers, Carson 1917-1967......DLB-2, 7, 173, 228; CDALB-1
McCulloch, Thomas 1776-1843........DLB-99
McDermott, Alice 1953-.............DLB-292
McDonald, Forrest 1927-............DLB-17
McDonald, Walter 1934-.............DLB-105, DS-9
"Getting Started: Accepting the Regions You Own—or Which Own You"........................DLB-105
Tribute to James Dickey............Y-97
McDougall, Colin 1917-1984.........DLB-68
McDowell, Katharine Sherwood Bonner 1849-1883......................DLB-202, 239
Obolensky McDowell [publishing house]................DLB-46
McEwan, Ian 1948-..................DLB-14, 194
McFadden, David 1940-..............DLB-60
McFall, Frances Elizabeth Clarke (see Grand, Sarah)
McFarland, Ron 1942-...............DLB-256
McFarlane, Leslie 1902-1977........DLB-88
McFee, William 1881-1966...........DLB-153
McGahern, John 1934-...............DLB-14, 231
McGee, Thomas D'Arcy 1825-1868....DLB-99
McGeehan, W. O. 1879-1933..........DLB-25, 171
McGill, Ralph 1898-1969............DLB-29

498

McGinley, Phyllis 1905-1978 . . . . . . . . DLB-11, 48

McGinniss, Joe 1942- . . . . . . . . . . . . . . . DLB-185

McGirt, James E. 1874-1930 . . . . . . . . . . . . DLB-50

McGlashan and Gill . . . . . . . . . . . . . . . . . DLB-106

McGough, Roger 1937- . . . . . . . . . . . . . . DLB-40

McGrath, John 1935- . . . . . . . . . . . . . . . DLB-233

McGrath, Patrick 1950- . . . . . . . . . . . . . . DLB-231

McGraw-Hill . . . . . . . . . . . . . . . . . . . . . . DLB-46

McGuane, Thomas 1939- . . . . DLB-2, 212; Y-80

    Tribute to Seymour Lawrence . . . . . . . . Y-94

McGuckian, Medbh 1950- . . . . . . . . . . . . DLB-40

McGuffey, William Holmes 1800-1873 . . . . DLB-42

McGuinness, Frank 1953- . . . . . . . . . . . DLB-245

McHenry, James 1785-1845 . . . . . . . . . . . DLB-202

McIlvanney, William 1936- . . . . . . DLB-14, 207

McIlwraith, Jean Newton 1859-1938 . . . . . . DLB-92

McInerney, Jay 1955- . . . . . . . . . . . . . . . DLB-292

McIntosh, Maria Jane 1803-1878 . . . . DLB-239, 248

McIntyre, James 1827-1906 . . . . . . . . . . . . DLB-99

McIntyre, O. O. 1884-1938 . . . . . . . . . . . . DLB-25

McKay, Claude 1889-1948 . . . . DLB-4, 45, 51, 117

The David McKay Company . . . . . . . . . . . DLB-49

McKean, William V. 1820-1903 . . . . . . . . . DLB-23

McKenna, Stephen 1888-1967 . . . . . . . . . DLB-197

The McKenzie Trust . . . . . . . . . . . . . . . . . . Y-96

McKerrow, R. B. 1872-1940 . . . . . . . . . . . DLB-201

McKinley, Robin 1952- . . . . . . . . . . . . . . DLB-52

McKnight, Reginald 1956- . . . . . . . . . . . DLB-234

McLachlan, Alexander 1818-1896 . . . . . . . . DLB-99

McLaren, Floris Clark 1904-1978 . . . . . . . . DLB-68

McLaverty, Michael 1907- . . . . . . . . . . . . DLB-15

McLean, Duncan 1964- . . . . . . . . . . . . . DLB-267

McLean, John R. 1848-1916 . . . . . . . . . . . . DLB-23

McLean, William L. 1852-1931 . . . . . . . . . . DLB-25

McLennan, William 1856-1904 . . . . . . . . . . DLB-92

McLoughlin Brothers . . . . . . . . . . . . . . . . DLB-49

McLuhan, Marshall 1911-1980 . . . . . . . . . . DLB-88

McMaster, John Bach 1852-1932 . . . . . . . . . DLB-47

McMillan, Terri 1951- . . . . . . . . . . . . . . DLB-292

McMurtry, Larry 1936-
    . . . . . . . DLB-2, 143, 256; Y-80, 87; CDALB-6

McNally, Terrence 1939- . . . . . . . . DLB-7, 249

McNeil, Florence 1937- . . . . . . . . . . . . . . DLB-60

McNeile, Herman Cyril 1888-1937 . . . . . . . DLB-77

McNickle, D'Arcy 1904-1977 . . . . . . DLB-175, 212

McPhee, John 1931- . . . . . . . . . . DLB-185, 275

McPherson, James Alan 1943- . . . . . DLB-38, 244

McPherson, Sandra 1943- . . . . . . . . . . . . . Y-86

McTaggart, J. M. E. 1866-1925 . . . . . . . . . DLB-262

McWhirter, George 1939- . . . . . . . . . . . . DLB-60

McWilliam, Candia 1955- . . . . . . . . . . . . DLB-267

McWilliams, Carey 1905-1980 . . . . . . . . . DLB-137

    "*The Nation's* Future," Carey
    McWilliams's Editorial Policy
    in *Nation* . . . . . . . . . . . . . . . . . DLB-137

Mda, Zakes 1948- . . . . . . . . . . . . . . . . DLB-225

Mead, George Herbert 1863-1931 . . . . . . . DLB-270

Mead, L. T. 1844-1914 . . . . . . . . . . . . . . DLB-141

Mead, Matthew 1924- . . . . . . . . . . . . . . . DLB-40

Mead, Taylor ?- . . . . . . . . . . . . . . . . . . . DLB-16

Meany, Tom 1903-1964 . . . . . . . . . . . . . DLB-171

Mechthild von Magdeburg
    circa 1207-circa 1282 . . . . . . . . . . . . DLB-138

Medieval Galician-Portuguese Poetry . . . . DLB-287

Medill, Joseph 1823-1899 . . . . . . . . . . . . . DLB-43

Medoff, Mark 1940- . . . . . . . . . . . . . . . . . DLB-7

Meek, Alexander Beaufort 1814-1865 . . DLB-3, 248

Meeke, Mary ?-1816? . . . . . . . . . . . . . . . DLB-116

Mei, Lev Aleksandrovich 1822-1862 . . . . . DLB-277

Meinke, Peter 1932- . . . . . . . . . . . . . . . . . DLB-5

Mejia Vallejo, Manuel 1923- . . . . . . . . . . DLB-113

Melanchthon, Philipp 1497-1560 . . . . . . . DLB-179

Melançon, Robert 1947- . . . . . . . . . . . . . DLB-60

Mell, Max 1882-1971 . . . . . . . . . . . . DLB-81, 124

Mellow, James R. 1926-1997 . . . . . . . . . . DLB-111

Mel'nikov, Pavel Ivanovich 1818-1883 . . . DLB-238

Meltzer, David 1937- . . . . . . . . . . . . . . . DLB-16

Meltzer, Milton 1915- . . . . . . . . . . . . . . . DLB-61

Melville, Elizabeth, Lady Culross
    circa 1585-1640 . . . . . . . . . . . . . . . DLB-172

Melville, Herman
    1819-1891 . . . . . . . . DLB-3, 74, 250; CDALB-2

    The Melville Society . . . . . . . . . . . . . . . Y-01

Melville, James
    (Roy Peter Martin) 1931- . . . . . . . DLB-276

Mena, Juan de 1411-1456 . . . . . . . . . . . . DLB-286

Mena, María Cristina 1893-1965 . . . . DLB-209, 221

Menander 342-341 B.C.-circa 292-291 B.C.
    . . . . . . . . . . . . . . . . . DLB-176; CDWLB-1

Menantes (see Hunold, Christian Friedrich)

Mencke, Johann Burckhard 1674-1732 . . . DLB-168

Mencken, H. L. 1880-1956
    . . . . . . . DLB-11, 29, 63, 137, 222; CDALB-4

    "Berlin, February, 1917" . . . . . . . . . . . . Y-00

    From the Initial Issue of *American Mercury*
    (January 1924) . . . . . . . . . . . . . . DLB-137

    Mencken and Nietzsche: An
    Unpublished Excerpt from H. L.
    Mencken's *My Life as Author and
    Editor* . . . . . . . . . . . . . . . . . . . . . . Y-93

Mendelssohn, Moses 1729-1786 . . . . . . . . . DLB-97

Mendes, Catulle 1841-1909 . . . . . . . . . . . DLB-217

Méndez M., Miguel 1930- . . . . . . . . . . . . DLB-82

The Mercantile Library of New York . . . . . . Y-96

Mercer, Cecil William (see Yates, Dornford)

Mercer, David 1928-1980 . . . . . . . . . . . . . DLB-13

Mercer, John 1704-1768 . . . . . . . . . . . . . . DLB-31

Mercer, Johnny 1909-1976 . . . . . . . . . . . DLB-265

Meredith, George
    1828-1909 . . . . DLB-18, 35, 57, 159; CDBLB-4

Meredith, Louisa Anne 1812-1895 . . DLB-166, 230

Meredith, Owen
    (see Lytton, Edward Robert Bulwer)

Meredith, William 1919- . . . . . . . . . . . . . DLB-5

Meres, Francis
    *Palladis Tamia, Wits Treasurie* (1598)
    [excerpt] . . . . . . . . . . . . . . . . DLB-172

Merezhkovsky, Dmitrii Sergeevich
    1865-1941 . . . . . . . . . . . . . . . . . . DLB-295

Mergerle, Johann Ulrich
    (see Abraham ä Sancta Clara)

Mérimée, Prosper 1803-1870 . . . . . . DLB-119, 192

Merivale, John Herman 1779-1844 . . . . . . . DLB-96

Meriwether, Louise 1923- . . . . . . . . . . . . DLB-33

Merleau-Ponty, Maurice 1908-1961 . . . . . DLB-296

Merlin Press . . . . . . . . . . . . . . . . . . . . . . DLB-112

Merriam, Eve 1916-1992 . . . . . . . . . . . . . . DLB-61

The Merriam Company . . . . . . . . . . . . . . . DLB-49

Merril, Judith 1923-1997 . . . . . . . . . . . . . DLB-251

    Tribute to Theodore Sturgeon. . . . . . . . . Y-85

Merrill, James 1926-1995 . . . . . . DLB-5, 165; Y-85

Merrill and Baker . . . . . . . . . . . . . . . . . . . DLB-49

The Mershon Company . . . . . . . . . . . . . . . DLB-49

Merton, Thomas 1915-1968 . . . . . . . DLB-48; Y-81

Merwin, W. S. 1927- . . . . . . . . . . . . DLB-5, 169

Julian Messner [publishing house] . . . . . . . . DLB-46

Mészöly, Miklós 1921- . . . . . . . . . . . . . . DLB-232

J. Metcalf [publishing house] . . . . . . . . . . . DLB-49

Metcalf, John 1938- . . . . . . . . . . . . . . . . DLB-60

The Methodist Book Concern . . . . . . . . . . . DLB-49

Methuen and Company . . . . . . . . . . . . . . DLB-112

Meun, Jean de (see *Roman de la Rose*)

Mew, Charlotte 1869-1928 . . . . . . . . DLB-19, 135

Mewshaw, Michael 1943- . . . . . . . . . . . . . Y-80

    Tribute to Albert Erskine . . . . . . . . . . . Y-93

Meyer, Conrad Ferdinand 1825-1898 . . . . DLB-129

Meyer, E. Y. 1946- . . . . . . . . . . . . . . . . . DLB-75

Meyer, Eugene 1875-1959 . . . . . . . . . . . . . DLB-29

Meyer, Michael 1921-2000 . . . . . . . . . . . DLB-155

Meyers, Jeffrey 1939- . . . . . . . . . . . . . . . DLB-111

Meynell, Alice 1847-1922 . . . . . . . . . DLB-19, 98

Meynell, Viola 1885-1956 . . . . . . . . . . . . DLB-153

Meyrink, Gustav 1868-1932 . . . . . . . . . . . . DLB-81

Mézières, Philipe de circa 1327-1405 . . . . . DLB-208

Michael, Ib 1945- . . . . . . . . . . . . . . . . . DLB-214

Michael, Livi 1960- . . . . . . . . . . . . . . . . DLB-267

Michaëlis, Karen 1872-1950 . . . . . . . . . . . DLB-214

Michaels, Anne 1958- . . . . . . . . . . . . . . DLB-299

Michaels, Leonard 1933- . . . . . . . . . . . . DLB-130

Michaux, Henri 1899-1984 . . . . . . . . . . . DLB-258

Micheaux, Oscar 1884-1951 . . . . . . . . . . . . DLB-50

Michel of Northgate, Dan
    circa 1265-circa 1340 . . . . . . . . . . . . DLB-146

Micheline, Jack 1929-1998 . . . . . . . . . . . . DLB-16

Michener, James A. 1907?-1997 . . . . . . . . . . DLB-6

Micklejohn, George circa 1717-1818 . . . . . . DLB-31

Middle Hill Press . . . . . . . . . . . . . . . . . . DLB-106

Middleton, Christopher 1926- . . . . . . . . DLB-40

Middleton, Richard 1882-1911 . . . . . . . . DLB-156

# Cumulative Index

Middleton, Stanley 1919- .............. DLB-14
Middleton, Thomas 1580-1627 ........ DLB-58
Miegel, Agnes 1879-1964 ............. DLB-56
Mieželaitis, Eduardas 1919-1997 ....... DLB-220
Miguéis, José Rodrigues 1901-1980 ..... DLB-287
Mihailović, Dragoslav 1930- .......... DLB-181
Mihalić, Slavko 1928- ............... DLB-181
Mikhailov, A.
  (see Sheller, Aleksandr Konstantinovich)
Mikhailov, Mikhail Larionovich
  1829-1865 ...................... DLB-238
Mikhailovsky, Nikolai Konstantinovich
  1842-1904 ..................... DLB-277
Miles, Josephine 1911-1985 ........... DLB-48
Miles, Susan (Ursula Wyllie Roberts)
  1888-1975 ...................... DLB-240
Miliković, Branko 1934-1961 .......... DLB-181
Milius, John 1944- .................. DLB-44
Mill, James 1773-1836 ......... DLB-107, 158, 262
Mill, John Stuart
  1806-1873 ...... DLB-55, 190, 262; CDBLB-4
  Thoughts on Poetry and Its Varieties
    (1833) ....................... DLB-32
Andrew Millar [publishing house] ...... DLB-154
Millar, Kenneth
  1915-1983 ........... DLB-2, 226; Y-83; DS-6
Millay, Edna St. Vincent
  1892-1950 .......... DLB-45, 249; CDALB-4
Millen, Sarah Gertrude 1888-1968 ...... DLB-225
Miller, Andrew 1960- ................ DLB-267
Miller, Arthur 1915- ...... DLB-7, 266; CDALB-1
  The Arthur Miller Society ........... Y-01
Miller, Caroline 1903-1992 ............ DLB-9
Miller, Eugene Ethelbert 1950- ........ DLB-41
  Tribute to Julian Mayfield ........... Y-84
Miller, Heather Ross 1939- ........... DLB-120
Miller, Henry
  1891-1980 ........ DLB-4, 9; Y-80; CDALB-5
Miller, Hugh 1802-1856 .............. DLB-190
Miller, J. Hillis 1928- ............... DLB-67
Miller, Jason 1939- .................. DLB-7
Miller, Joaquin 1839-1913 ............ DLB-186
Miller, May 1899-1995 ............... DLB-41
Miller, Paul 1906-1991 .............. DLB-127
Miller, Perry 1905-1963 ............. DLB-17, 63
Miller, Sue 1943- .................. DLB-143
Miller, Vassar 1924-1998 ............ DLB-105
Miller, Walter M., Jr. 1923-1996 ........ DLB-8
Miller, Webb 1892-1940 .............. DLB-29
James Miller [publishing house] ....... DLB-49
Millett, Kate 1934- ................ DLB-246
Millhauser, Steven 1943- ............. DLB-2
Millican, Arthenia J. Bates 1920- ....... DLB-38
Milligan, Alice 1866-1953 ............ DLB-240
Mills, Magnus 1954- ................ DLB-267
Mills and Boon .................... DLB-112
Milman, Henry Hart 1796-1868 ........ DLB-96

Milne, A. A. 1882-1956 ..... DLB-10, 77, 100, 160
Milner, Ron 1938- .................. DLB-38
William Milner [publishing house] ...... DLB-106
Milnes, Richard Monckton (Lord Houghton)
  1809-1885 ................... DLB-32, 184
Milton, John
  1608-1674 ..... DLB-131, 151, 281; CDBLB-2
  The Milton Society of America ........ Y-00
Miłosz, Czesław 1911- ... DLB-215; CDWLB-4
Minakami Tsutomu 1919- ............ DLB-182
Minamoto no Sanetomo 1192-1219 ..... DLB-203
Minco, Marga 1920- ................ DLB-299
The Minerva Press .................. DLB-154
*Minnesang* circa 1150-1280 ........... DLB-138
  The Music of *Minnesang* ........... DLB-138
Minns, Susan 1839-1938 .............. DLB-140
Minton, Balch and Company .......... DLB-46
Mirbeau, Octave 1848-1917 ....... DLB-123, 192
Mirk, John died after 1414? ........... DLB-146
Miró, Ricardo 1883-1940 ............. DLB-290
Miron, Gaston 1928-1996 ............. DLB-60
*A Mirror for Magistrates* .............. DLB-167
Mishima Yukio 1925-1970 ............ DLB-182
Mistral, Gabriela 1889-1957 .......... DLB-283
Mitchel, Jonathan 1624-1668 .......... DLB-24
Mitchell, Adrian 1932- ............... DLB-40
Mitchell, Donald Grant
  1822-1908 ............. DLB-1, 243; DS-13
Mitchell, Gladys 1901-1983 ........... DLB-77
Mitchell, James Leslie 1901-1935 ........ DLB-15
Mitchell, John (see Slater, Patrick)
Mitchell, John Ames 1845-1918 ........ DLB-79
Mitchell, Joseph 1908-1996 ....... DLB-185; Y-96
Mitchell, Julian 1935- ............... DLB-14
Mitchell, Ken 1940- ................. DLB-60
Mitchell, Langdon 1862-1935 ........... DLB-7
Mitchell, Loften 1919- ............... DLB-38
Mitchell, Margaret 1900-1949 .. DLB-9; CDALB-7
Mitchell, S. Weir 1829-1914 .......... DLB-202
Mitchell, W. J. T. 1942- ............. DLB-246
Mitchell, W. O. 1914-1998 ........... DLB-88
Mitchison, Naomi Margaret (Haldane)
  1897-1999 ............. DLB-160, 191, 255
Mitford, Mary Russell 1787-1855 .... DLB-110, 116
Mitford, Nancy 1904-1973 ........... DLB-191
Mittelholzer, Edgar
  1909-1965 .............. DLB-117; CDWLB-3
Mitterer, Erika 1906- ................ DLB-85
Mitterer, Felix 1948- ................ DLB-124
Mitternacht, Johann Sebastian
  1613-1679 ..................... DLB-168
Miyamoto Yuriko 1899-1951 .......... DLB-180
Mizener, Arthur 1907-1988 ........... DLB-103
Mo, Timothy 1950- ................. DLB-194
Moberg, Vilhelm 1898-1973 .......... DLB-259
Modern Age Books .................. DLB-46

Modern Language Association of America
  The Modern Language Association of
    America Celebrates Its Centennial ... Y-84
The Modern Library ................. DLB-46
Modiano, Patrick 1945- ......... DLB-83, 299
Moffat, Yard and Company ........... DLB-46
Moffet, Thomas 1553-1604 ........... DLB-136
Mofolo, Thomas 1876-1948 ........... DLB-225
Mohr, Nicholasa 1938- .............. DLB-145
Moix, Ana María 1947- .............. DLB-134
Molesworth, Louisa 1839-1921 ........ DLB-135
Molière (Jean-Baptiste Poquelin)
  1622-1673 ..................... DLB-268
Møller, Poul Martin 1794-1838 ........ DLB-300
Möllhausen, Balduin 1825-1905 ....... DLB-129
Molnár, Ferenc 1878-1952 ... DLB-215; CDWLB-4
Molnár, Miklós (see Mészöly, Miklós)
Momaday, N. Scott
  1934- ....... DLB-143, 175, 256; CDALB-7
Monkhouse, Allan 1858-1936 ......... DLB-10
Monro, Harold 1879-1932 ............ DLB-19
Monroe, Harriet 1860-1936 ......... DLB-54, 91
Monsarrat, Nicholas 1910-1979 ........ DLB-15
Montagu, Lady Mary Wortley
  1689-1762 .................. DLB-95, 101
Montague, C. E. 1867-1928 .......... DLB-197
Montague, John 1929- ............... DLB-40
Montale, Eugenio 1896-1981 ......... DLB-114
Montalvo, Garci Rodríguez de
  ca. 1450?-before 1505 ............ DLB-286
Montalvo, José 1946-1994 ............ DLB-209
Monterroso, Augusto 1921-2003 ....... DLB-145
Montesquiou, Robert de 1855-1921 ..... DLB-217
Montgomerie, Alexander
  circa 1550?-1598 ................ DLB-167
Montgomery, James 1771-1854 ..... DLB-93, 158
Montgomery, John 1919- ............. DLB-16
Montgomery, Lucy Maud
  1874-1942 ................ DLB-92; DS-14
Montgomery, Marion 1925- ............ DLB-6
Montgomery, Robert Bruce (see Crispin, Edmund)
Montherlant, Henry de 1896-1972 ...... DLB-72
*The Monthly Review* 1749-1844 ......... DLB-110
Montigny, Louvigny de 1876-1955 ..... DLB-92
Montoya, José 1932- ................ DLB-122
Moodie, John Wedderburn Dunbar
  1797-1869 ...................... DLB-99
Moodie, Susanna 1803-1885 .......... DLB-99
Moody, Joshua circa 1633-1697 ........ DLB-24
Moody, William Vaughn 1869-1910 ... DLB-7, 54
Moorcock, Michael 1939- ..... DLB-14, 231, 261
Moore, Alan 1953- ................. DLB-261
Moore, Brian 1921-1999 ............. DLB-251
Moore, Catherine L. 1911-1987 ......... DLB-8
Moore, Clement Clarke 1779-1863 ..... DLB-42
Moore, Dora Mavor 1888-1979 ........ DLB-92
Moore, G. E. 1873-1958 ............. DLB-262

500

Moore, George 1852-1933 .... DLB-10, 18, 57, 135
   *Literature at Nurse, or Circulating Morals* (1885) .................... DLB-18
Moore, Lorrie 1957- ................ DLB-234
Moore, Marianne 1887-1972 ......... DLB-45; DS-7; CDALB-5
   International Marianne Moore Society ... Y-98
Moore, Mavor 1919- ................ DLB-88
Moore, Richard 1927- ............... DLB-105
   "The No Self, the Little Self, and the Poets" .................... DLB-105
Moore, T. Sturge 1870-1944 ............ DLB-19
Moore, Thomas 1779-1852 ......... DLB-96, 144
Moore, Ward 1903-1978 ................ DLB-8
Moore, Wilstach, Keys and Company .... DLB-49
Moorehead, Alan 1901-1983 ........... DLB-204
Moorhouse, Frank 1938- ............. DLB-289
Moorhouse, Geoffrey 1931- ........... DLB-204
The Moorland-Spingarn Research Center .................... DLB-76
Moorman, Mary C. 1905-1994 ......... DLB-155
Mora, Pat 1942- ................... DLB-209
Moraga, Cherríe 1952- ........... DLB-82, 249
Morales, Alejandro 1944- ............. DLB-82
Morales, Mario Roberto 1947- ........ DLB-145
Morales, Rafael 1919- ................ DLB-108
Morality Plays: *Mankind* circa 1450-1500 and *Everyman* circa 1500 ........ DLB-146
Morand, Paul (1888-1976) ............ DLB-65
Morante, Elsa 1912-1985 ............. DLB-177
Morata, Olympia Fulvia 1526-1555 ..... DLB-179
Moravia, Alberto 1907-1990 .......... DLB-177
Mordaunt, Elinor 1872-1942 .......... DLB-174
Mordovtsev, Daniil Lukich 1830-1905 ... DLB-238
More, Hannah 1745-1833 .......... DLB-107, 109, 116, 158
More, Henry 1614-1687 .......... DLB-126, 252
More, Sir Thomas 1477/1478-1535 .......... DLB-136, 281
Morejón, Nancy 1944- ............... DLB-283
Morency, Pierre 1942- ............... DLB-60
Moreno, Dorinda 1939- .............. DLB-122
Moretti, Marino 1885-1979 ........ DLB-114, 264
Morgan, Berry 1919- .................. DLB-6
Morgan, Charles 1894-1958 ........ DLB-34, 100
Morgan, Edmund S. 1916- ............ DLB-17
Morgan, Edwin 1920- ................ DLB-27
Morgan, John Pierpont 1837-1913 ..... DLB-140
Morgan, John Pierpont, Jr. 1867-1943 ... DLB-140
Morgan, Robert 1944- ........... DLB-120, 292
Morgan, Sydney Owenson, Lady 1776?-1859 ................. DLB-116, 158
Morgner, Irmtraud 1933-1990 ......... DLB-75
Morhof, Daniel Georg 1639-1691 ...... DLB-164
Mori Ōgai 1862-1922 ................ DLB-180
Móricz, Zsigmond 1879-1942 .......... DLB-215

Morier, James Justinian 1782 or 1783?-1849 ............ DLB-116
Mörike, Eduard 1804-1875 ........... DLB-133
Morin, Paul 1889-1963 ............... DLB-92
Morison, Richard 1514?-1556 ......... DLB-136
Morison, Samuel Eliot 1887-1976 ...... DLB-17
Morison, Stanley 1889-1967 .......... DLB-201
Moritz, Karl Philipp 1756-1793 ........ DLB-94
*Moriz von Craûn* circa 1220-1230 ....... DLB-138
Morley, Christopher 1890-1957 ......... DLB-9
Morley, John 1838-1923 ....... DLB-57, 144, 190
Moro, César 1903-1956 .............. DLB-290
Morris, George Pope 1802-1864 ....... DLB-73
Morris, James Humphrey (see Morris, Jan)
Morris, Jan 1926- .................. DLB-204
Morris, Lewis 1833-1907 .............. DLB-35
Morris, Margaret 1737-1816 .......... DLB-200
Morris, Mary McGarry 1943- ......... DLB-292
Morris, Richard B. 1904-1989 ......... DLB-17
Morris, William 1834-1896 .... DLB-18, 35, 57, 156, 178, 184; CDBLB-4
Morris, Willie 1934-1999 .............. Y-80
   Tribute to Irwin Shaw ............... Y-84
   Tribute to James Dickey ............. Y-97
Morris, Wright 1910-1998 .......... DLB-2, 206, 218; Y-81
Morrison, Arthur 1863-1945 .... DLB-70, 135, 197
Morrison, Charles Clayton 1874-1966 .... DLB-91
Morrison, John 1904-1998 ........... DLB-260
Morrison, Toni 1931- .......... DLB-6, 33, 143; Y-81, 93; CDALB-6
   Nobel Lecture 1993 ................ Y-93
Morrissy, Mary 1957- ............... DLB-267
William Morrow and Company ........ DLB-46
Morse, James Herbert 1841-1923 ...... DLB-71
Morse, Jedidiah 1761-1826 ........... DLB-37
Morse, John T., Jr. 1840-1937 ......... DLB-47
Morselli, Guido 1912-1973 ........... DLB-177
*Morte Arthure,* the *Alliterative* and the *Stanzaic* circa 1350-1400 ........ DLB-146
Mortimer, Favell Lee 1802-1878 ....... DLB-163
Mortimer, John 1923- ......... DLB-13, 245, 271; CDBLB-8
Morton, Carlos 1942- ............... DLB-122
Morton, H. V. 1892-1979 ............. DLB-195
John P. Morton and Company ......... DLB-49
Morton, Nathaniel 1613-1685 .......... DLB-24
Morton, Sarah Wentworth 1759-1846 .... DLB-37
Morton, Thomas circa 1579-circa 1647 .... DLB-24
Moscherosch, Johann Michael 1601-1669 .................. DLB-164
Humphrey Moseley [publishing house] ................ DLB-170
Möser, Justus 1720-1794 ............. DLB-97
Mosley, Nicholas 1923- ......... DLB-14, 207
Moss, Arthur 1889-1969 ............... DLB-4
Moss, Howard 1922-1987 .............. DLB-5

Moss, Thylias 1954- ................ DLB-120
Motion, Andrew 1952- ............... DLB-40
Motley, John Lothrop 1814-1877 ............ DLB-1, 30, 59, 235
Motley, Willard 1909-1965 ........ DLB-76, 143
Mott, Lucretia 1793-1880 ............ DLB-239
Benjamin Motte Jr. [publishing house] ................ DLB-154
Motteux, Peter Anthony 1663-1718 ...... DLB-80
Mottram, R. H. 1883-1971 ............ DLB-36
Mount, Ferdinand 1939- ............. DLB-231
Mouré, Erin 1955- .................. DLB-60
Mourning Dove (Humishuma) between 1882 and 1888?-1936 ......... DLB-175, 221
Movies
   Fiction into Film, 1928-1975: A List of Movies Based on the Works of Authors in British Novelists, 1930-1959 .................. DLB-15
   Movies from Books, 1920-1974 ........ DLB-9
Mowat, Farley 1921- ................ DLB-68
A. R. Mowbray and Company, Limited .................... DLB-106
Mowrer, Edgar Ansel 1892-1977 ........ DLB-29
Mowrer, Paul Scott 1887-1971 ......... DLB-29
Edward Moxon [publishing house] ..... DLB-106
Joseph Moxon [publishing house] ...... DLB-170
Moyes, Patricia 1923-2000 ........... DLB-276
Mphahlele, Es'kia (Ezekiel) 1919- .......... DLB-125, 225; CDWLB-3
Mrożek, Sławomir 1930- ... DLB-232; CDWLB-4
Mtshali, Oswald Mbuyiseni 1940- ................. DLB-125, 225
*Mucedorus* .................... DLB-62
Mudford, William 1782-1848 ......... DLB-159
Mudrooroo (see Johnson, Colin)
Mueller, Lisel 1924- ................ DLB-105
Muhajir, El (see Marvin X)
Muhajir, Nazzam Al Fitnah (see Marvin X)
Mühlbach, Luise 1814-1873 ........... DLB-133
Muir, Edwin 1887-1959 ........ DLB-20, 100, 191
Muir, Helen 1937- .................. DLB-14
Muir, John 1838-1914 .......... DLB-186, 275
Muir, Percy 1894-1979 .............. DLB-201
Mujū Ichien 1226-1312 .............. DLB-203
Mukherjee, Bharati 1940- ......... DLB-60, 218
Mulcaster, Richard 1531 or 1532-1611 ... DLB-167
Muldoon, Paul 1951- ................ DLB-40
Mulisch, Harry 1927- ............... DLB-299
Müller, Friedrich (see Müller, Maler)
Müller, Heiner 1929-1995 ............ DLB-124
Müller, Maler 1749-1825 .............. DLB-94
Muller, Marcia 1944- ................ DLB-226
Müller, Wilhelm 1794-1827 ........... DLB-90
Mumford, Lewis 1895-1990 ............ DLB-63
Munby, A. N. L. 1913-1974 ........... DLB-201
Munby, Arthur Joseph 1828-1910 ....... DLB-35

# Cumulative Index  DLB 302

Munday, Anthony 1560-1633 . . . . . . . .DLB-62, 172
Mundt, Clara (see Mühlbach, Luise)
Mundt, Theodore 1808-1861 . . . . . . . . . . DLB-133
Munford, Robert circa 1737-1783 . . . . . . . DLB-31
Mungoshi, Charles 1947- . . . . . . . . . . . . . DLB-157
Munk, Kaj 1898-1944 . . . . . . . . . . . . . . . . DLB-214
Munonye, John 1929- . . . . . . . . . . . . . . . DLB-117
Munro, Alice 1931- . . . . . . . . . . . . . . . . . DLB-53
George Munro [publishing house] . . . . . . . DLB-49
Munro, H. H.
  1870-1916 . . . . . . . . . DLB-34, 162; CDBLB-5
Munro, Neil 1864-1930 . . . . . . . . . . . . . . DLB-156
Norman L. Munro [publishing house] . . . . DLB-49
Munroe, Kirk 1850-1930 . . . . . . . . . . . . . DLB-42
Munroe and Francis . . . . . . . . . . . . . . . . . DLB-49
James Munroe and Company . . . . . . . . . . DLB-49
Joel Munsell [publishing house] . . . . . . . . DLB-49
Munsey, Frank A. 1854-1925 . . . . . . . DLB-25, 91
Frank A. Munsey and Company . . . . . . . DLB-49
Murakami Haruki 1949- . . . . . . . . . . . . . DLB-182
Murav'ev, Mikhail Nikitich 1757-1807 . . . DLB-150
Murdoch, Iris 1919-1999
  . . . . . . . . . . . . . DLB-14, 194, 233; CDBLB-8
Murdock, James
  From Sketches of Modern Philosophy . . . . . . DS-5
Murdoch, Rupert 1931- . . . . . . . . . . . . . DLB-127
Murfree, Mary N. 1850-1922 . . . . . . . DLB-12, 74
Murger, Henry 1822-1861 . . . . . . . . . . . . DLB-119
Murger, Louis-Henri (see Murger, Henry)
Murnane, Gerald 1939- . . . . . . . . . . . . . DLB-289
Murner, Thomas 1475-1537 . . . . . . . . . . .DLB-179
Muro, Amado 1915-1971 . . . . . . . . . . . . DLB-82
Murphy, Arthur 1727-1805 . . . . . . . . DLB-89, 142
Murphy, Beatrice M. 1908-1992 . . . . . . . . DLB-76
Murphy, Dervla 1931- . . . . . . . . . . . . . . DLB-204
Murphy, Emily 1868-1933 . . . . . . . . . . . . DLB-99
Murphy, Jack 1923-1980 . . . . . . . . . . . . . DLB-241
Murphy, John H., III 1916- . . . . . . . . . . . DLB-127
Murphy, Richard 1927-1993 . . . . . . . . . . DLB-40
John Murphy and Company . . . . . . . . . . DLB-49
Murray, Albert L. 1916- . . . . . . . . . . . . . DLB-38
Murray, Gilbert 1866-1957 . . . . . . . . . . . DLB-10
Murray, Jim 1919-1998 . . . . . . . . . . . . . . DLB-241
John Murray [publishing house] . . . . . . . . DLB-154
Murray, Judith Sargent 1751-1820 . . . .DLB-37, 200
Murray, Les 1938- . . . . . . . . . . . . . . . . . DLB-289
Murray, Pauli 1910-1985 . . . . . . . . . . . . . DLB-41
Murry, John Middleton 1889-1957 . . . . . . DLB-149
  "The Break-Up of the Novel"
    (1922) . . . . . . . . . . . . . . . . . . . . . DLB-36
Murry, John Middleton, Jr. (see Cowper, Richard)
Musäus, Johann Karl August 1735-1787 . . . DLB-97
Muschg, Adolf 1934- . . . . . . . . . . . . . . . DLB-75
Musil, Robert
  1880-1942 . . . . . . . DLB-81, 124; CDWLB-2
Muspilli circa 790-circa 850 . . . . . . . . . . . DLB-148

Musset, Alfred de 1810-1857 . . . . . . .DLB-192, 217
Benjamin B. Mussey
  and Company . . . . . . . . . . . . . . . . . DLB-49
Mutafchieva, Vera 1929- . . . . . . . . . . . . DLB-181
Mutis, Alvaro 1923- . . . . . . . . . . . . . . . . DLB-283
Mwangi, Meja 1948- . . . . . . . . . . . . . . . DLB-125
Myers, Frederic W. H. 1843-1901 . . . . . . DLB-190
Myers, Gustavus 1872-1942 . . . . . . . . . . . DLB-47
Myers, L. H. 1881-1944 . . . . . . . . . . . . . DLB-15
Myers, Walter Dean 1937- . . . . . . . . . . . DLB-33
Myerson, Julie 1960- . . . . . . . . . . . . . . . DLB-267
Mykle, Agnar 1915-1994 . . . . . . . . . . . . . DLB-297
Mykolaitis-Putinas,
  Vincas 1893-1967 . . . . . . . . . . . . . . DLB-220
Myles, Eileen 1949- . . . . . . . . . . . . . . . . DLB-193
Myrdal, Jan 1927- . . . . . . . . . . . . . . . . . DLB-257
Mystery
  1985: The Year of the Mystery:
    A Symposium . . . . . . . . . . . . . . . . . Y-85
  Comments from Other Writers . . . . . . . . Y-85
  The Second Annual New York Festival
    of Mystery . . . . . . . . . . . . . . . . . . . Y-00
  Why I Read Mysteries . . . . . . . . . . . . . . Y-85
  Why I Write Mysteries: Night and Day,
    by Michael Collins . . . . . . . . . . . . . . Y-85

# N

Na Prous Boneta circa 1296-1328 . . . . . . DLB-208
Nabl, Franz 1883-1974 . . . . . . . . . . . . . . DLB-81
Nabokov, Véra 1902-1991 . . . . . . . . . . . . . Y-91
Nabokov, Vladimir 1899-1977 . . DLB-2, 244, 278;
                          Y-80, 91; DS-3; CDALB-1
  International Nabokov Society . . . . . . . . . Y-99
  An Interview [On Nabokov], by
    Fredson Bowers . . . . . . . . . . . . . . . . Y-80
  Nabokov Festival at Cornell . . . . . . . . . . Y-83
  The Vladimir Nabokov Archive in the
    Berg Collection of the New York
    Public Library: An Overview . . . . . . . Y-91
  The Vladimir Nabokov Society . . . . . . . . Y-01
Nádaši, Ladislav (see Jégé)
Naden, Constance 1858-1889 . . . . . . . . . DLB-199
Nadezhdin, Nikolai Ivanovich
  1804-1856 . . . . . . . . . . . . . . . . . . . DLB-198
Nadson, Semen Iakovlevich 1862-1887 . . .DLB-277
Naevius circa 265 B.C.-201 B.C. . . . . . . . DLB-211
Nafis and Cornish . . . . . . . . . . . . . . . . . DLB-49
Nagai Kafū 1879-1959 . . . . . . . . . . . . . . DLB-180
Nagel, Ernest 1901-1985 . . . . . . . . . . . . .DLB-279
Nagibin, Iurii Markovich 1920-1994 . . . . DLB-302
Nagrodskaia, Evdokiia Apollonovna
  1866-1930 . . . . . . . . . . . . . . . . . . . DLB-295
Naipaul, Shiva 1945-1985 . . . . . . . . .DLB-157; Y-85
Naipaul, V. S. 1932- . . . . . . . DLB-125, 204, 207;
                         Y-85, Y-01; CDBLB-8; CDWLB-3
  Nobel Lecture 2001: "Two Worlds" . . . . . Y-01
Nakagami Kenji 1946-1992 . . . . . . . . . . DLB-182
Nakano-in Masatada no Musume (see Nijō, Lady)

Nałkowska, Zofia 1884-1954 . . . . . . . . . DLB-215
Namora, Fernando 1919-1989 . . . . . . . . DLB-287
Joseph Nancrede [publishing house] . . . . . DLB-49
Naranjo, Carmen 1930- . . . . . . . . . . . . DLB-145
Narbikova, Valeriia Spartakovna
  1958- . . . . . . . . . . . . . . . . . . . . . . DLB-285
Narezhny, Vasilii Trofimovich
  1780-1825 . . . . . . . . . . . . . . . . . . . DLB-198
Narrache, Jean (Emile Coderre)
  1893-1970 . . . . . . . . . . . . . . . . . . . DLB-92
Nasby, Petroleum Vesuvius (see Locke, David Ross)
Eveleigh Nash [publishing house] . . . . . . . DLB-112
Nash, Ogden 1902-1971 . . . . . . . . . . . . . DLB-11
Nashe, Thomas 1567-1601? . . . . . . . . . . DLB-167
Nason, Jerry 1910-1986 . . . . . . . . . . . . . DLB-241
Nasr, Seyyed Hossein 1933- . . . . . . . . . .DLB-279
Nast, Condé 1873-1942 . . . . . . . . . . . . . DLB-91
Nast, Thomas 1840-1902 . . . . . . . . . . . . DLB-188
Nastasijević, Momčilo 1894-1938 . . . . . . .DLB-147
Nathan, George Jean 1882-1958 . . . . . . .DLB-137
Nathan, Robert 1894-1985 . . . . . . . . . . . DLB-9
National Book Critics Circle Awards . . . . . Y-00–01
The National Jewish Book Awards . . . . . . . . Y-85
Natsume Sōseki 1867-1916 . . . . . . . . . . . DLB-180
Naughton, Bill 1910-1992 . . . . . . . . . . . . DLB-13
Navarro, Joe 1953- . . . . . . . . . . . . . . . . DLB-209
Naylor, Gloria 1950- . . . . . . . . . . . . . . .DLB-173
Nazor, Vladimir 1876-1949 . . . . . . . . . . .DLB-147
Ndebele, Njabulo 1948- . . . . . . . . . .DLB-157, 225
Neagoe, Peter 1881-1960 . . . . . . . . . . . . DLB-4
Neal, John 1793-1876 . . . . . . . . . . DLB-1, 59, 243
Neal, Joseph C. 1807-1847 . . . . . . . . . . . DLB-11
Neal, Larry 1937-1981 . . . . . . . . . . . . . . DLB-38
The Neale Publishing Company . . . . . . . DLB-49
Nebel, Frederick 1903-1967 . . . . . . . . . . DLB-226
Nebrija, Antonio de 1442 or 1444-1522 . . DLB-286
Nedreaas, Torborg 1906-1987 . . . . . . . . . DLB-297
F. Tennyson Neely [publishing house] . . . . DLB-49
Negoițescu, Ion 1921-1993 . . . . . . . . . . . DLB-220
Negri, Ada 1870-1945 . . . . . . . . . . . . . . DLB-114
Neihardt, John G. 1881-1973 . . . . . DLB-9, 54, 256
Neidhart von Reuental
  circa 1185-circa 1240 . . . . . . . . . . . . . DLB-138
Neilson, John Shaw 1872-1942 . . . . . . . . DLB-230
Nekrasov, Nikolai Alekseevich
  1821-1877 . . . . . . . . . . . . . . . . . . . .DLB-277
Nekrasov, Viktor Platonovich
  1911-1987 . . . . . . . . . . . . . . . . . . . DLB-302
Neledinsky-Meletsky, Iurii Aleksandrovich
  1752-1828 . . . . . . . . . . . . . . . . . . . DLB-150
Nelligan, Emile 1879-1941 . . . . . . . . . . . DLB-92
Nelson, Alice Moore Dunbar 1875-1935 . . DLB-50
Nelson, Antonya 1961- . . . . . . . . . . . . . DLB-244
Nelson, Kent 1943- . . . . . . . . . . . . . . . . DLB-234
Nelson, Richard K. 1941- . . . . . . . . . . . .DLB-275
Nelson, Thomas, and Sons [U.K.] . . . . . . DLB-106

| | | |
|---|---|---|
| Nelson, Thomas, and Sons [U.S.] ........DLB-49 | The *Nibelungenlied* and the *Klage* circa 1200 ......................DLB-138 | Niven, Larry 1938- ..............DLB-8 |
| Nelson, William 1908-1978 ............DLB-103 | Nichol, B. P. 1944-1988................DLB-53 | Nixon, Howard M. 1909-1983 .........DLB-201 |
| Nelson, William Rockhill 1841-1915......DLB-23 | Nicholas of Cusa 1401-1464 ...........DLB-115 | Nizan, Paul 1905-1940................DLB-72 |
| Nemerov, Howard 1920-1991.....DLB-5, 6; Y-83 | Nichols, Ann 1891?-1966...............DLB-249 | Njegoš, Petar II Petrović 1813-1851 .........DLB-147; CDWLB-4 |
| Németh, László 1901-1975............DLB-215 | Nichols, Beverly 1898-1983............DLB-191 | Nkosi, Lewis 1936- ..........DLB-157, 225 |
| Nepos circa 100 B.C.-post 27 B.C........DLB-211 | Nichols, Dudley 1895-1960.............DLB-26 | Noah, Mordecai M. 1785-1851 .........DLB-250 |
| Nėris, Salomėja 1904-1945...DLB-220; CDWLB-4 | Nichols, Grace 1950- ................DLB-157 | Noailles, Anna de 1876-1933 ..........DLB-258 |
| Neruda, Pablo 1904-1973...............DLB-283 | Nichols, John 1940- .....................Y-82 | Nobel Peace Prize The Nobel Prize and Literary Politics.... Y-88 |
| Nerval, Gérard de 1808-1855 ...........DLB-217 | Nichols, Mary Sargeant (Neal) Gove 1810-1884 ...................DLB-1, 243 | Elie Wiesel .....................Y-86 |
| Nervo, Amado 1870-1919 ..............DLB-290 | Nichols, Peter 1927- .............DLB-13, 245 | Nobel Prize in Literature Joseph Brodsky..................Y-87 |
| Nesbit, E. 1858-1924 ........ DLB-141, 153, 178 | Nichols, Roy F. 1896-1973..............DLB-17 | Camilo José Cela.................Y-89 |
| Ness, Evaline 1911-1986 ................DLB-61 | Nichols, Ruth 1948-....................DLB-60 | Dario Fo ......................Y-97 |
| Nestroy, Johann 1801-1862 .............DLB-133 | Nicholson, Edward Williams Byron 1849-1912 ......................DLB-184 | Gabriel García Márquez ............Y-82 |
| Nettleship, R. L. 1846-1892.............DLB-262 | Nicholson, Geoff 1953-.................DLB-271 | William Golding..................Y-83 |
| Neugeboren, Jay 1938- .................DLB-28 | Nicholson, Norman 1914- ..............DLB-27 | Nadine Gordimer ................Y-91 |
| Neukirch, Benjamin 1655-1729 ........DLB-168 | Nicholson, William 1872-1949..........DLB-141 | Günter Grass....................Y-99 |
| Neumann, Alfred 1895-1952 ............DLB-56 | Ní Chuilleanáin, Eiléan 1942- ..........DLB-40 | Seamus Heaney..................Y-95 |
| Neumann, Ferenc (see Molnár, Ferenc) | Nicol, Eric 1919- .....................DLB-68 | Imre Kertész ...................Y-02 |
| Neumark, Georg 1621-1681 ............DLB-164 | Nicolai, Friedrich 1733-1811 ............DLB-97 | Najīb Mahfūz ...................Y-88 |
| Neumeister, Erdmann 1671-1756 ........DLB-168 | Nicolas de Clamanges circa 1363-1437 ...DLB-208 | Toni Morrison ..................Y-93 |
| Nevins, Allan 1890-1971 ........ DLB-17; DS-17 | Nicolay, John G. 1832-1901 and Hay, John 1838-1905 ..............DLB-47 | V. S. Naipaul....................Y-01 |
| Nevinson, Henry Woodd 1856-1941 ...DLB-135 | Nicole, Pierre 1625-1695 ..............DLB-268 | Kenzaburō Ōe...................Y-94 |
| The New American Library ............DLB-46 | Nicolson, Adela Florence Cory (see Hope, Laurence) | Octavio Paz.....................Y-90 |
| New Directions Publishing Corporation ...DLB-46 | Nicolson, Harold 1886-1968 ....... DLB-100, 149 | José Saramago...................Y-98 |
| *The New Monthly Magazine* 1814-1884.....DLB-110 | "The Practice of Biography," in *The English Sense of Humour and Other Essays* ..................DLB-149 | Jaroslav Seifert..................Y-84 |
| *New York Times Book Review* ............... Y-82 | | Claude Simon ...................Y-85 |
| John Newbery [publishing house] .......DLB-154 | Nicolson, Nigel 1917- .................DLB-155 | Wole Soyinka ...................Y-86 |
| Newbolt, Henry 1862-1938..............DLB-19 | Niebuhr, Reinhold 1892-1971 ..... DLB-17; DS-17 | Wisława Szymborska ..............Y-96 |
| Newbound, Bernard Slade (see Slade, Bernard) | Niedecker, Lorine 1903-1970...........DLB-48 | Derek Walcott...................Y-92 |
| Newby, Eric 1919- ....................DLB-204 | Nieman, Lucius W. 1857-1935..........DLB-25 | Gao Xingjian....................Y-00 |
| Newby, P. H. 1918- ...................DLB-15 | Nietzsche, Friedrich 1844-1900 ............DLB-129; CDWLB-2 | Nobre, António 1867-1900.............DLB-287 |
| Thomas Cautley Newby [publishing house]................DLB-106 | Mencken and Nietzsche: An Unpublished Excerpt from H. L. Mencken's *My Life as Author and Editor* ..............Y-93 | Nodier, Charles 1780-1844 ............DLB-119 |
| Newcomb, Charles King 1820-1894 ...DLB-1, 223 | | Noël, Marie (Marie Mélanie Rouget) 1883-1967 ......................DLB-258 |
| Newell, Peter 1862-1924 ................DLB-42 | Nievo, Stanislao 1928- ................DLB-196 | Noel, Roden 1834-1894................DLB-35 |
| Newell, Robert Henry 1836-1901 ........DLB-11 | Niggli, Josefina 1910-1983 ...............Y-80 | Nogami Yaeko 1885-1985.............DLB-180 |
| Newhouse, Samuel I. 1895-1979 .......DLB-127 | Nightingale, Florence 1820-1910 ......DLB-166 | Nogo, Rajko Petrov 1945- .............DLB-181 |
| Newman, Cecil Earl 1903-1976 ........DLB-127 | Nijō, Lady (Nakano-in Masatada no Musume) 1258-after 1306 ..................DLB-203 | Nolan, William F. 1928- ................DLB-8 |
| Newman, David 1937- .................DLB-44 | | Tribute to Raymond Chandler......... Y-88 |
| Newman, Frances 1883-1928.............Y-80 | Nijō Yoshimoto 1320-1388 ............DLB-203 | Noland, C. F. M. 1810?-1858 ..........DLB-11 |
| Newman, Francis William 1805-1897 ....DLB-190 | Nikitin, Ivan Savvich 1824-1861 .......DLB-277 | Noma Hiroshi 1915-1991 .............DLB-182 |
| Newman, John Henry 1801-1890 ..DLB-18, 32, 55 | Nikitin, Nikolai Nikolaevich 1895-1963 ..DLB-272 | Nonesuch Press ......................DLB-112 |
| Mark Newman [publishing house].......DLB-49 | Nikolev, Nikolai Petrovich 1758-1815....DLB-150 | Creative Nonfiction....................Y-02 |
| Newmarch, Rosa Harriet 1857-1940 ....DLB-240 | Niles, Hezekiah 1777-1839..............DLB-43 | Nonni (Jón Stefán Sveinsson or Svensson) 1857-1944 ......................DLB-293 |
| George Newnes Limited ...............DLB-112 | Nims, John Frederick 1913-1999 ..........DLB-5 | Noon, Jeff 1957-.......................DLB-267 |
| Newsome, Effie Lee 1885-1979 ..........DLB-76 | Tribute to Nancy Hale .................Y-88 | Noonan, Robert Phillipe (see Tressell, Robert) |
| Newton, A. Edward 1864-1940 .........DLB-140 | Nin, Anaïs 1903-1977............DLB-2, 4, 152 | Noonday Press........................DLB-46 |
| Newton, Sir Isaac 1642-1727 ...........DLB-252 | Nína Björk Árnadóttir 1941-2000 .......DLB-293 | Noone, John 1936- ...................DLB-14 |
| Nexø, Martin Andersen 1869-1954 ......DLB-214 | Niño, Raúl 1961- ....................DLB-209 | Nora, Eugenio de 1923- ...............DLB-134 |
| Nezval, Vítěslav 1900-1958 ...........DLB-215; CDWLB-4 | Nissenson, Hugh 1933- ................DLB-28 | Nordan, Lewis 1939-..................DLB-234 |
| Ngugi wa Thiong'o 1938- ...........DLB-125; CDWLB-3 | Niven, Frederick John 1878-1944........DLB-92 | Nordbrandt, Henrik 1945- ............DLB-214 |
| Niatum, Duane 1938- .................DLB-175 | | Nordhoff, Charles 1887-1947...........DLB-9 |

503

| | | |
|---|---|---|
| Norén, Lars 1944- ................. DLB-257 | "The Future of the Novel" (1899), by Henry James ................. DLB-18 | Oates, Joyce Carol 1938- ............ DLB-2, 5, 130; Y-81; CDALB-6 |
| Norfolk, Lawrence 1963- ........... DLB-267 | *The Gay Science* (1866), by E. S. Dallas [excerpt]..................... DLB-21 | Tribute to Michael M. Rea ........... Y-97 |
| Norman, Charles 1904-1996 ......... DLB-111 | A Haughty and Proud Generation (1922), by Ford Madox Hueffer .. DLB-36 | Ōba Minako 1930- .................. DLB-182 |
| Norman, Marsha 1947- ....... DLB-266; Y-84 | Literary Effects of World War II..... DLB-15 | Ober, Frederick Albion 1849-1913...... DLB-189 |
| Norris, Charles G. 1881-1945........... DLB-9 | "Modern Novelists –Great and Small" (1855), by Margaret Oliphant .... DLB-21 | Ober, William 1920-1993................ Y-93 |
| Norris, Frank 1870-1902....... DLB-12, 71, 186; CDALB-3 | The Modernists (1932), by Joseph Warren Beach........ DLB-36 | Oberholtzer, Ellis Paxson 1868-1936..... DLB-47 |
| Norris, Helen 1916- ................ DLB-292 | A Note on Technique (1926), by Elizabeth A. Drew [excerpts]..... DLB-36 | The Obituary as Literary Form ........... Y-02 |
| Norris, John 1657-1712 .............. DLB-252 | Novel-Reading: *The Works of Charles Dickens*; *The Works of W. Makepeace Thackeray* (1879), by Anthony Trollope .......... DLB-21 | Obradović, Dositej 1740?-1811.........DLB-147 |
| Norris, Leslie 1921- ...............DLB-27, 256 | | O'Brien, Charlotte Grace 1845-1909 .... DLB-240 |
| Norse, Harold 1916- ................. DLB-16 | | O'Brien, Edna 1932- ... DLB-14, 231; CDBLB-8 |
| Norte, Marisela 1955- ............... DLB-209 | | O'Brien, Fitz-James 1828-1862 ......... DLB-74 |
| North, Marianne 1830-1890...........DLB-174 | Novels with a Purpose (1864), by Justin M'Carthy ............. DLB-21 | O'Brien, Flann (see O'Nolan, Brian) |
| North Point Press .................... DLB-46 | | O'Brien, Kate 1897-1974................ DLB-15 |
| Nortje, Arthur 1942-1970 ........ DLB-125, 225 | "On Art in Fiction" (1838), by Edward Bulwer ............ DLB-21 | O'Brien, Tim 1946- .... DLB-152; Y-80; DS-9; CDALB-7 |
| Norton, Alice Mary (see Norton, Andre) | | |
| Norton, Andre 1912- ............... DLB-8, 52 | The Present State of the English Novel (1892), by George Saintsbury .... DLB-18 | O'Casey, Sean 1880-1964..... DLB-10; CDBLB-6 |
| Norton, Andrews 1786-1853.... DLB-1, 235; DS-5 | Representative Men and Women: A Historical Perspective on the British Novel, 1930-1960..... DLB-15 | Occom, Samson 1723-1792 ..........DLB-175 |
| Norton, Caroline 1808-1877 ... DLB-21, 159, 199 | | Occomy, Marita Bonner 1899-1971 ...... DLB-51 |
| Norton, Charles Eliot 1827-1908 .. DLB-1, 64, 235 | | Ochs, Adolph S. 1858-1935 ............ DLB-25 |
| Norton, John 1606-1663................ DLB-24 | "The Revolt" (1937), by Mary Colum [excerpts] ................... DLB-36 | Ochs-Oakes, George Washington 1861-1931 .....................DLB-137 |
| Norton, Mary 1903-1992 .............. DLB-160 | | |
| Norton, Thomas 1532-1584 ............ DLB-62 | "Sensation Novels" (1863), by H. L. Manse .................. DLB-21 | O'Connor, Flannery 1925-1964 ........DLB-2, 152; Y-80; DS-12; CDALB-1 |
| W. W. Norton and Company ......... DLB-46 | | |
| Norwood, Robert 1874-1932 .......... DLB-92 | Sex, Class, Politics, and Religion [in the British Novel, 1930-1959] .... DLB-15 | The Flannery O'Connor Society ........ Y-99 |
| Nosaka Akiyuki 1930- ............... DLB-182 | *Time and Western Man* (1927), by Wyndham Lewis [excerpts] .. DLB-36 | O'Connor, Frank 1903-1966 .......... DLB-162 |
| Nossack, Hans Erich 1901-1977 ......... DLB-69 | | O'Connor, Joseph 1963- .............. DLB-267 |
| Notker Balbulus circa 840-912 ......... DLB-148 | Noventa, Giacomo 1898-1960 ......... DLB-114 | Octopus Publishing Group............ DLB-112 |
| Notker III of Saint Gall circa 950-1022 .. DLB-148 | Novikov, Nikolai Ivanovich 1744-1818 .. DLB-150 | Oda Sakunosuke 1913-1947 ........... DLB-182 |
| Notker von Zweifalten ?-1095 ......... DLB-148 | Novomeský, Laco 1904-1976 .......... DLB-215 | Odell, Jonathan 1737-1818 ......... DLB-31, 99 |
| Nourse, Alan E. 1928- ................. DLB-8 | Nowlan, Alden 1933-1983 ............. DLB-53 | O'Dell, Scott 1903-1989 ............... DLB-52 |
| Novak, Slobodan 1924- ............... DLB-181 | Noyes, Alfred 1880-1958 .............. DLB-20 | Odets, Clifford 1906-1963 ...........DLB-7, 26 |
| Novak, Vjenceslav 1859-1905 .......... DLB-147 | Noyes, Crosby S. 1825-1908 ........... DLB-23 | Odhams Press Limited ............... DLB-112 |
| Novakovich, Josip 1956- .............. DLB-244 | Noyes, Nicholas 1647-1717 ............ DLB-24 | Odio, Eunice 1922-1974 .............. DLB-283 |
| Novalis 1772-1801.......... DLB-90; CDWLB-2 | Noyes, Theodore W. 1858-1946 ........ DLB-29 | Odoevsky, Aleksandr Ivanovich 1802-1839 ..................... DLB-205 |
| Novaro, Mario 1868-1944 ............. DLB-114 | Nozick, Robert 1938-2002 ............DLB-279 | |
| Novás Calvo, Lino 1903-1983 ......... DLB-145 | N-Town Plays circa 1468 to early sixteenth century................ DLB-146 | Odoevsky, Vladimir Fedorovich 1804 or 1803-1869 ............... DLB-198 |
| Novelists *Library Journal* Statements and Questionnaires from First Novelists.... Y-87 | | |
| | Nugent, Frank 1908-1965............. DLB-44 | O'Donnell, Peter 1920- ............... DLB-87 |
| Novels *The Columbia History of the American Novel* A Symposium on................. Y-92 | Nušić, Branislav 1864-1938 ..DLB-147; CDWLB-4 | O'Donovan, Michael (see O'Connor, Frank) |
| | David Nutt [publishing house] ........ DLB-106 | O'Dowd, Bernard 1866-1953.......... DLB-230 |
| The Great Modern Library Scam ....... Y-98 | Nwapa, Flora 1931-1993 ... DLB-125; CDWLB-3 | Ōe, Kenzaburō 1935- ...........DLB-182; Y-94 |
| Novels for Grown-Ups.................. Y-97 | Nye, Edgar Wilson (Bill) 1850-1896 ................ DLB-11, 23, 186 | Nobel Lecture 1994: Japan, the Ambiguous, and Myself .......... Y-94 |
| The Proletarian Novel ............... DLB-9 | | |
| Novel, The "Second-Generation" Holocaust ..................... DLB-299 | | Oehlenschläger, Adam 1779-1850....... DLB-300 |
| | Nye, Naomi Shihab 1952- .......... DLB-120 | O'Faolain, Julia 1932- ............ DLB-14, 231 |
| The Year in the Novel..... Y-87–88, Y-90–93 | Nye, Robert 1939- ...............DLB-14, 271 | O'Faolain, Sean 1900-1991 ......... DLB-15, 162 |
| Novels, British "The Break-Up of the Novel" (1922), by John Middleton Murry....... DLB-36 | Nyka-Niliūnas, Alfonsas 1919- ....... DLB-220 | Off-Loop Theatres .................... DLB-7 |
| | | Offord, Carl Ruthven 1910- ........... DLB-76 |
| | **O** | O'Flaherty, Liam 1896-1984 ...DLB-36, 162; Y-84 |
| The Consolidation of Opinion: Critical Responses to the Modernists..... DLB-36 | Oakes, Urian circa 1631-1681 .......... DLB-24 | Ogarev, Nikolai Platonovich 1813-1877 ...DLB-277 |
| | Oakes Smith, Elizabeth 1806-1893 ................ DLB-1, 239, 243 | J. S. Ogilvie and Company............ DLB-49 |
| "Criticism in Relation to Novels" (1863), by G. H. Lewes.......... DLB-21 | | Ogilvy, Eliza 1822-1912 .............. DLB-199 |
| | | Ogot, Grace 1930- .................. DLB-125 |
| "Experiment in the Novel" (1929) [excerpt], by John D. Beresford ... DLB-36 | Oakley, Violet 1874-1961 ............. DLB-188 | O'Grady, Desmond 1935- ............ DLB-40 |
| | | Ogunyemi, Wale 1939- .............DLB-157 |

O'Hagan, Howard 1902-1982 . . . . . . . . . . . DLB-68

O'Hara, Frank 1926-1966 . . . . . . . DLB-5, 16, 193

O'Hara, John
    1905-1970 . . . . . . . DLB-9, 86; DS-2; CDALB-5

    John O'Hara's Pottsville Journalism . . . . . Y-88

O'Hegarty, P. S. 1879-1955 . . . . . . . . . . . . DLB-201

Ohio State University
    The William Charvat American Fiction
        Collection at the Ohio State
        University Libraries . . . . . . . . . . . . . . Y-92

Okara, Gabriel 1921- . . . . . DLB-125; CDWLB-3

O'Keeffe, John 1747-1833 . . . . . . . . . . . . . . DLB-89

Nicholas Okes [publishing house] . . . . . . . DLB-170

Okigbo, Christopher
    1930-1967 . . . . . . . . . . . DLB-125; CDWLB-3

Okot p'Bitek 1931-1982 . . . . . DLB-125; CDWLB-3

Okpewho, Isidore 1941- . . . . . . . . . . . . . . DLB-157

Okri, Ben 1959- . . . . . . . . . . . . . . DLB-157, 231

Ólafur Jóhann Sigurðsson 1918-1988 . . . . DLB-293

Old Dogs / New Tricks? New Technologies,
    the Canon, and the Structure of
    the Profession . . . . . . . . . . . . . . . . . . . . Y-02

Old Franklin Publishing House . . . . . . . . . DLB-49

*Old German Genesis* and *Old German Exodus*
    circa 1050-circa 1130 . . . . . . . . . . . . . . DLB-148

The *Old High German Isidor*
    circa 790-800 . . . . . . . . . . . . . . . . . . . DLB-148

Older, Fremont 1856-1935 . . . . . . . . . . . . . . DLB-25

Oldham, John 1653-1683 . . . . . . . . . . . . . . DLB-131

Oldman, C. B. 1894-1969 . . . . . . . . . . . . . . DLB-201

Olds, Sharon 1942- . . . . . . . . . . . . . . . . . DLB-120

Olearius, Adam 1599-1671 . . . . . . . . . . . . . DLB-164

O'Leary, Ellen 1831-1889 . . . . . . . . . . . . . . DLB-240

O'Leary, Juan E. 1879-1969 . . . . . . . . . . . . DLB-290

Olesha, Iurii Karlovich 1899-1960 . . . . . . . DLB-272

Oliphant, Laurence 1829?-1888 . . . . . . DLB-18, 166

Oliphant, Margaret 1828-1897 . . . DLB-18, 159, 190

    "Modern Novelists–Great and Small"
        (1855) . . . . . . . . . . . . . . . . . . . . . . . DLB-21

Oliveira, Carlos de 1921-1981 . . . . . . . . . . DLB-287

Oliver, Chad 1928-1993 . . . . . . . . . . . . . . . . DLB-8

Oliver, Mary 1935- . . . . . . . . . . . . . . . DLB-5, 193

Ollier, Claude 1922- . . . . . . . . . . . . . . . . . DLB-83

Olsen, Tillie 1912/1913-
    . . . . . . . . . . . . . DLB-28, 206; Y-80; CDALB-7

Olson, Charles 1910-1970 . . . . . . . DLB-5, 16, 193

Olson, Elder 1909- . . . . . . . . . . . . . . DLB-48, 63

Olson, Sigurd F. 1899-1982 . . . . . . . . . . . . DLB-275

The Omega Workshops . . . . . . . . . . . . . . . DS-10

Omotoso, Kole 1943- . . . . . . . . . . . . . . . . DLB-125

Omulevsky, Innokentii Vasil'evich
    1836 [or 1837]-1883 . . . . . . . . . . . . . . DLB-238

Ondaatje, Michael 1943- . . . . . . . . . . . . . . DLB-60

O'Neill, Eugene 1888-1953 . . . . . DLB-7; CDALB-5

    Eugene O'Neill Memorial Theater
        Center . . . . . . . . . . . . . . . . . . . . . . . . DLB-7

    Eugene O'Neill's Letters: A Review . . . . . Y-88

Onetti, Juan Carlos
    1909-1994 . . . . . . . . . . . DLB-113; CDWLB-3

Onions, George Oliver 1872-1961 . . . . . . . DLB-153

Onofri, Arturo 1885-1928 . . . . . . . . . . . . . DLB-114

O'Nolan, Brian 1911-1966 . . . . . . . . . . . . . DLB-231

Oodgeroo of the Tribe Noonuccal
    (Kath Walker) 1920-1993 . . . . . . . . . . DLB-289

Opie, Amelia 1769-1853 . . . . . . . . . . DLB-116, 159

Opitz, Martin 1597-1639 . . . . . . . . . . . . . . DLB-164

Oppen, George 1908-1984 . . . . . . . . . . DLB-5, 165

Oppenheim, E. Phillips 1866-1946 . . . . . . . DLB-70

Oppenheim, James 1882-1932 . . . . . . . . . . DLB-28

Oppenheimer, Joel 1930-1988 . . . . . . . . DLB-5, 193

Optic, Oliver (see Adams, William Taylor)

Orczy, Emma, Baroness 1865-1947 . . . . . . . DLB-70

Oregon Shakespeare Festival . . . . . . . . . . . . Y-00

Origo, Iris 1902-1988 . . . . . . . . . . . . . . . . . DLB-155

O'Riordan, Kate 1960- . . . . . . . . . . . . . . . DLB-267

Orlovitz, Gil 1918-1973 . . . . . . . . . . . . . . DLB-2, 5

Orlovsky, Peter 1933- . . . . . . . . . . . . . . . . DLB-16

Ormond, John 1923- . . . . . . . . . . . . . . . . . DLB-27

Ornitz, Samuel 1890-1957 . . . . . . . . . . DLB-28, 44

O'Rourke, P. J. 1947- . . . . . . . . . . . . . . . . DLB-185

Orozco, Olga 1920-1999 . . . . . . . . . . . . . . DLB-283

Orten, Jiří 1919-1941 . . . . . . . . . . . . . . . . DLB-215

Ortese, Anna Maria 1914- . . . . . . . . . . . . DLB-177

Ortiz, Simon J. 1941- . . . . . . . DLB-120, 175, 256

*Ortnit* and *Wolfdietrich* circa 1225-1250 . . . . DLB-138

Orton, Joe 1933-1967 . . . . . . . . . DLB-13; CDBLB-8

Orwell, George (Eric Arthur Blair)
    1903-1950 . . . DLB-15, 98, 195, 255; CDBLB-7

    The Orwell Year . . . . . . . . . . . . . . . . . . . Y-84

    (Re-)Publishing Orwell . . . . . . . . . . . . . Y-86

Ory, Carlos Edmundo de 1923- . . . . . . . . DLB-134

Osbey, Brenda Marie 1957- . . . . . . . . . . . DLB-120

Osbon, B. S. 1827-1912 . . . . . . . . . . . . . . . DLB-43

Osborn, Sarah 1714-1796 . . . . . . . . . . . . . DLB-200

Osborne, John 1929-1994 . . . . . DLB-13; CDBLB-7

Osgood, Frances Sargent 1811-1850 . . . . . DLB-250

Osgood, Herbert L. 1855-1918 . . . . . . . . . . DLB-47

James R. Osgood and Company . . . . . . . . DLB-49

Osgood, McIlvaine and Company . . . . . . . DLB-112

O'Shaughnessy, Arthur 1844-1881 . . . . . . . DLB-35

Patrick O'Shea [publishing house] . . . . . . . DLB-49

Osipov, Nikolai Petrovich 1751-1799 . . . . . DLB-150

Oskison, John Milton 1879-1947 . . . . . . . . DLB-175

Osler, Sir William 1849-1919 . . . . . . . . . . . DLB-184

Osofisan, Femi 1946- . . . . . DLB-125; CDWLB-3

Ostenso, Martha 1900-1963 . . . . . . . . . . . . DLB-92

Ostrauskas, Kostas 1926- . . . . . . . . . . . . . DLB-232

Ostriker, Alicia 1937- . . . . . . . . . . . . . . . . DLB-120

Ostrovsky, Aleksandr Nikolaevich
    1823-1886 . . . . . . . . . . . . . . . . . . . . . DLB-277

Ostrovsky, Nikolai Alekseevich
    1904-1936 . . . . . . . . . . . . . . . . . . . . . DLB-272

Osundare, Niyi 1947- . . . . . DLB-157; CDWLB-3

Oswald, Eleazer 1755-1795 . . . . . . . . . . . . . DLB-43

Oswald von Wolkenstein
    1376 or 1377-1445 . . . . . . . . . . . . . . . DLB-179

Otero, Blas de 1916-1979 . . . . . . . . . . . . . DLB-134

Otero, Miguel Antonio 1859-1944 . . . . . . . DLB-82

Otero, Nina 1881-1965 . . . . . . . . . . . . . . . DLB-209

Otero Silva, Miguel 1908-1985 . . . . . . . . . DLB-145

Otfried von Weißenburg
    circa 800-circa 875? . . . . . . . . . . . . . . DLB-148

Otis, Broaders and Company . . . . . . . . . . . DLB-49

Otis, James (see Kaler, James Otis)

Otis, James, Jr. 1725-1783 . . . . . . . . . . . . . DLB-31

Ottaway, James 1911-2000 . . . . . . . . . . . . DLB-127

Ottendorfer, Oswald 1826-1900 . . . . . . . . . DLB-23

Ottieri, Ottiero 1924- . . . . . . . . . . . . . . . DLB-177

Otto-Peters, Louise 1819-1895 . . . . . . . . . DLB-129

Otway, Thomas 1652-1685 . . . . . . . . . . . . . DLB-80

Ouellette, Fernand 1930- . . . . . . . . . . . . . . DLB-60

Ouida 1839-1908 . . . . . . . . . . . . . . . . DLB-18, 156

Outing Publishing Company . . . . . . . . . . . DLB-46

Overbury, Sir Thomas
    circa 1581-1613 . . . . . . . . . . . . . . . . . DLB-151

The Overlook Press . . . . . . . . . . . . . . . . . . DLB-46

Ovid 43 B.C.-A.D. 17 . . . . . . DLB-211; CDWLB-1

Owen, Guy 1925- . . . . . . . . . . . . . . . . . . . DLB-5

Owen, John 1564-1622 . . . . . . . . . . . . . . . DLB-121

John Owen [publishing house] . . . . . . . . . . DLB-49

Peter Owen Limited . . . . . . . . . . . . . . . . . DLB-112

Owen, Robert 1771-1858 . . . . . . . . . DLB-107, 158

Owen, Wilfred
    1893-1918 . . . . . . . . DLB-20; DS-18; CDBLB-6

    A Centenary Celebration . . . . . . . . . . . . Y-93

    The Wilfred Owen Association . . . . . . . Y-98

*The Owl and the Nightingale*
    circa 1189-1199 . . . . . . . . . . . . . . . . . DLB-146

Owsley, Frank L. 1890-1956 . . . . . . . . . . . . DLB-17

Oxford, Seventeenth Earl of, Edward
    de Vere 1550-1604 . . . . . . . . . . . . . . . DLB-172

OyamO (Charles F. Gordon)
    1943- . . . . . . . . . . . . . . . . . . . . . . . . DLB-266

Ozerov, Vladislav Aleksandrovich
    1769-1816 . . . . . . . . . . . . . . . . . . . . . DLB-150

Ozick, Cynthia 1928- . . . DLB-28, 152, 299; Y-82

    First Strauss "Livings" Awarded
        to Cynthia Ozick and
        Raymond Carver
        An Interview with Cynthia Ozick . . . . Y-83

    Tribute to Michael M. Rea . . . . . . . . . . . Y-97

# P

Pace, Richard 1482?-1536 . . . . . . . . . . . . . DLB-167

Pacey, Desmond 1917-1975 . . . . . . . . . . . . DLB-88

Pacheco, José Emilio 1939- . . . . . . . . . . DLB-290

Pack, Robert 1929- . . . . . . . . . . . . . . . . . . DLB-5

Padell Publishing Company . . . . . . . . . . . . DLB-46

Padgett, Ron 1942- . . . . . . . . . . . . . . . . . . DLB-5

Padilla, Ernesto Chávez 1944- . . . . . . . . DLB-122

L. C. Page and Company . . . . . . . . . . . . . DLB-49

Page, Louise 1955- . . . . . . . . . . . . . . . . . DLB-233

# Cumulative Index

Page, P. K. 1916- .................. DLB-68
Page, Thomas Nelson
 1853-1922 ............. DLB-12, 78; DS-13
Page, Walter Hines 1855-1918 ....... DLB-71, 91
Paget, Francis Edward 1806-1882 ...... DLB-163
Paget, Violet (see Lee, Vernon)
Pagliarani, Elio 1927- ................ DLB-128
Pain, Barry 1864-1928 ............ DLB-135, 197
Pain, Philip ?-circa 1666 ............ DLB-24
Paine, Robert Treat, Jr. 1773-1811 ....... DLB-37
Paine, Thomas
 1737-1809 .... DLB-31, 43, 73, 158; CDALB-2
Painter, George D. 1914- ........... DLB-155
Painter, William 1540?-1594 .......... DLB-136
Palazzeschi, Aldo 1885-1974 ....... DLB-114, 264
Palei, Marina Anatol'evna 1955- ....... DLB-285
Palencia, Alfonso de 1424-1492 ........ DLB-286
Palés Matos, Luis 1898-1959 .......... DLB-290
Paley, Grace 1922- ............ DLB-28, 218
Paley, William 1743-1805 ............ DLB-252
Palfrey, John Gorham 1796-1881 .. DLB-1, 30, 235
Palgrave, Francis Turner 1824-1897 ...... DLB-35
Palmer, Joe H. 1904-1952 ........... DLB-171
Palmer, Michael 1943- ............. DLB-169
Palmer, Nettie 1885-1964 ........... DLB-260
Palmer, Vance 1885-1959 ........... DLB-260
Paltock, Robert 1697-1767 ............ DLB-39
Paludan, Jacob 1896-1975 ........... DLB-214
Paludin-Müller, Frederik 1809-1876 ..... DLB-300
Pan Books Limited ................ DLB-112
Panaev, Ivan Ivanovich 1812-1862 ...... DLB-198
Panaeva, Avdot'ia Iakovlevna
 1820-1893 ................... DLB-238
Panama, Norman 1914- and
 Frank, Melvin 1913-1988 .......... DLB-26
Pancake, Breece D'J 1952-1979 ........ DLB-130
Panduro, Leif 1923-1977 ............ DLB-214
Panero, Leopoldo 1909-1962 ......... DLB-108
Pangborn, Edgar 1909-1976 .......... DLB-8
Panizzi, Sir Anthony 1797-1879 ....... DLB-184
Panneton, Philippe (see Ringuet)
Panova, Vera Fedorovna 1905-1973 ..... DLB-302
Panshin, Alexei 1940- .............. DLB-8
Pansy (see Alden, Isabella)
Pantheon Books ................. DLB-46
Papadat-Bengescu, Hortensia
 1876-1955 ................... DLB-220
Papantonio, Michael 1907-1976 ....... DLB-187
Paperback Library ................ DLB-46
Paperback Science Fiction ........... DLB-8
Papini, Giovanni 1881-1956 .......... DLB-264
Paquet, Alfons 1881-1944 ........... DLB-66
Paracelsus 1493-1541 .............. DLB-179
Paradis, Suzanne 1936- ............ DLB-53
Páral, Vladimír, 1932- ............. DLB-232
Pardoe, Julia 1804-1862 ............ DLB-166

Paredes, Américo 1915-1999 ......... DLB-209
Pareja Diezcanseco, Alfredo 1908-1993 .. DLB-145
Parents' Magazine Press ............. DLB-46
Parfit, Derek 1942- ................ DLB-262
Parise, Goffredo 1929-1986 .......... DLB-177
Parish, Mitchell 1900-1993 .......... DLB-265
Parizeau, Alice 1930-1990 ........... DLB-60
Park, Ruth 1923?- ................ DLB-260
Parke, John 1754-1789 .............. DLB-31
Parker, Dan 1893-1967 ............. DLB-241
Parker, Dorothy 1893-1967 ..... DLB-11, 45, 86
Parker, Gilbert 1860-1932 ........... DLB-99
Parker, James 1714-1770 ............ DLB-43
Parker, John [publishing house] ....... DLB-106
Parker, Matthew 1504-1575 .......... DLB-213
Parker, Stewart 1941-1988 ........... DLB-245
Parker, Theodore 1810-1860 ... DLB-1, 235; DS-5
Parker, William Riley 1906-1968 ....... DLB-103
J. H. Parker [publishing house] ........ DLB-106
Parkes, Bessie Rayner (Madame Belloc)
 1829-1925 ................... DLB-240
Parkman, Francis
 1823-1893 ........ DLB-1, 30, 183, 186, 235
Parks, Gordon 1912- ............... DLB-33
Parks, Tim 1954- ................. DLB-231
Parks, William 1698-1750 ............ DLB-43
William Parks [publishing house] ...... DLB-49
Parley, Peter (see Goodrich, Samuel Griswold)
Parmenides late sixth-fifth century B.C. .. DLB-176
Parnell, Thomas 1679-1718 .......... DLB-95
Parnicki, Teodor 1908-1988 .......... DLB-215
Parnok, Sofiia Iakovlevna (Parnokh)
 1885-1933 ................... DLB-295
Parr, Catherine 1513?-1548 .......... DLB-136
Parra, Nicanor 1914- .............. DLB-283
Parrington, Vernon L. 1871-1929 ..... DLB-17, 63
Parrish, Maxfield 1870-1966 ......... DLB-188
Parronchi, Alessandro 1914- ......... DLB-128
Parshchikov, Aleksei Maksimovich
 (Raiderman) 1954- .............. DLB-285
Parton, James 1822-1891 ............ DLB-30
Parton, Sara Payson Willis
 1811-1872 .............. DLB-43, 74, 239
S. W. Partridge and Company ........ DLB-106
Parun, Vesna 1922- ...... DLB-181; CDWLB-4
Pascal, Blaise 1623-1662 ............ DLB-268
Pasinetti, Pier Maria 1913- .......... DLB-177
 Tribute to Albert Erskine ............ Y-93
Pasolini, Pier Paolo 1922-1975 ..... DLB-128, 177
Pastan, Linda 1932- ............... DLB-5
Pasternak, Boris
 1890-1960 ................... DLB-302
Paston, George (Emily Morse Symonds)
 1860-1936 ................ DLB-149, 197
The Paston Letters 1422-1509 ......... DLB-146
Pastorius, Francis Daniel
 1651-circa 1720 ................ DLB-24

Patchen, Kenneth 1911-1972 ....... DLB-16, 48
Pater, Walter 1839-1894 ... DLB-57, 156; CDBLB-4
 Aesthetic Poetry (1873) ............ DLB-35
 "Style" (1888) [excerpt] ............ DLB-57
Paterson, A. B. "Banjo" 1864-1941 ..... DLB-230
Paterson, Katherine 1932- .......... DLB-52
Patmore, Coventry 1823-1896 ....... DLB-35, 98
Paton, Alan 1903-1988 ......... DLB-225; DS-17
Paton, Joseph Noel 1821-1901 ........ DLB-35
Paton Walsh, Jill 1937- ............. DLB-161
Patrick, Edwin Hill ("Ted") 1901-1964 .. DLB-137
Patrick, John 1906-1995 ............ DLB-7
Pattee, Fred Lewis 1863-1950 ........ DLB-71
Patterson, Alicia 1906-1963 .......... DLB-127
Patterson, Eleanor Medill 1881-1948 .... DLB-29
Patterson, Eugene 1923- ........... DLB-127
Patterson, Joseph Medill 1879-1946 ..... DLB-29
Pattillo, Henry 1726-1801 ........... DLB-37
Paul, Elliot 1891-1958 ........... DLB-4; DS-15
Paul, Jean (see Richter, Johann Paul Friedrich)
Paul, Kegan, Trench, Trubner and
 Company Limited .............. DLB-106
Peter Paul Book Company ........... DLB-49
Stanley Paul and Company Limited .... DLB-112
Paulding, James Kirke
 1778-1860 ............. DLB-3, 59, 74, 250
Paulin, Tom 1949- ................ DLB-40
Pauper, Peter, Press ............... DLB-46
Paustovsky, Konstantin Georgievich
 1892-1968 ................... DLB-272
Pavese, Cesare 1908-1950 ........ DLB-128, 177
Pavić, Milorad 1929- ..... DLB-181; CDWLB-4
Pavlov, Konstantin 1933- ........... DLB-181
Pavlov, Nikolai Filippovich 1803-1864 ... DLB-198
Pavlova, Karolina Karlovna 1807-1893 ... DLB-205
Pavlović, Miodrag
 1928- ............... DLB-181; CDWLB-4
Paxton, John 1911-1985 ............ DLB-44
Payn, James 1830-1898 ............. DLB-18
Payne, John 1842-1916 ............. DLB-35
Payne, John Howard 1791-1852 ....... DLB-37
Payson and Clarke ................ DLB-46
Paz, Octavio 1914-1998 ...... DLB-290; Y-90, 98
 Nobel Lecture 1990 ................ Y-90
Pazzi, Roberto 1946- .............. DLB-196
Pea, Enrico 1881-1958 ............. DLB-264
Peabody, Elizabeth Palmer
 1804-1894 ................ DLB-1, 223
 Preface to Record of a School:
 Exemplifying the General Principles
 of Spiritual Culture ............... DS-5
Elizabeth Palmer Peabody
 [publishing house] .............. DLB-49
Peabody, Josephine Preston 1874-1922 .. DLB-249
Peabody, Oliver William Bourn
 1799-1848 .................... DLB-59
Peace, Roger 1899-1968 ............ DLB-127

Peacham, Henry 1578-1644?..........DLB-151
Peacham, Henry, the Elder
   1547-1634.................DLB-172, 236
Peachtree Publishers, Limited..........DLB-46
Peacock, Molly 1947-...............DLB-120
Peacock, Thomas Love 1785-1866...DLB-96, 116
Pead, Deuel ?-1727...................DLB-24
Peake, Mervyn 1911-1968......DLB-15, 160, 255
Peale, Rembrandt 1778-1860...........DLB-183
Pear Tree Press......................DLB-112
Pearce, Philippa 1920-...............DLB-161
H. B. Pearson [publishing house].........DLB-49
Pearson, Hesketh 1887-1964...........DLB-149
Peattie, Donald Culross 1898-1964......DLB-275
Pechersky, Andrei (see Mel'nikov, Pavel Ivanovich)
Peck, George W. 1840-1916........DLB-23, 42
H. C. Peck and Theo. Bliss
   [publishing house]................DLB-49
Peck, Harry Thurston 1856-1914.....DLB-71, 91
Peden, William 1913-1999...........DLB-234
   Tribute to William Goyen............Y-83
Peele, George 1556-1596.........DLB-62, 167
Pegler, Westbrook 1894-1969..........DLB-171
Péguy, Charles 1873-1914.............DLB-258
Peirce, Charles Sanders 1839-1914......DLB-270
Pekić, Borislav 1930-1992...DLB-181; CDWLB-4
Pelevin, Viktor Olegovich 1962-.......DLB-285
Pellegrini and Cudahy.................DLB-46
Pelletier, Aimé (see Vac, Bertrand)
Pelletier, Francine 1959-.............DLB-251
Pellicer, Carlos 1897?-1977...........DLB-290
Pemberton, Sir Max 1863-1950.........DLB-70
de la Peña, Terri 1947-...............DLB-209
Penfield, Edward 1866-1925...........DLB-188
Penguin Books [U.K.]................DLB-112
   Fifty Penguin Years.................Y-85
   Penguin Collectors' Society............Y-98
Penguin Books [U.S.].................DLB-46
Penn, William 1644-1718..............DLB-24
Penn Publishing Company.............DLB-49
Penna, Sandro 1906-1977.............DLB-114
Pennell, Joseph 1857-1926...........DLB-188
Penner, Jonathan 1940-................Y-83
Pennington, Lee 1939-.................Y-82
Penton, Brian 1904-1951..............DLB-260
Pepper, Stephen C. 1891-1972........DLB-270
Pepys, Samuel
   1633-1703.........DLB-101, 213; CDBLB-2
Percy, Thomas 1729-1811.............DLB-104
Percy, Walker 1916-1990.......DLB-2; Y-80, 90
   Tribute to Caroline Gordon...........Y-81
Percy, William 1575-1648.............DLB-172
Perec, Georges 1936-1982.........DLB-83, 299
Perelman, Bob 1947-..................DLB-193
Perelman, S. J. 1904-1979..........DLB-11, 44

Pérez de Guzmán, Fernán
   ca. 1377-ca. 1460.................DLB-286
Perez, Raymundo "Tigre" 1946-.......DLB-122
Peri Rossi, Cristina 1941-........DLB-145, 290
Perkins, Eugene 1932-................DLB-41
Perkins, Maxwell
   The Claims of Business and Literature:
   An Undergraduate Essay..........Y-01
Perkins, William 1558-1602...........DLB-281
Perkoff, Stuart Z. 1930-1974..........DLB-16
Perley, Moses Henry 1804-1862........DLB-99
Permabooks..........................DLB-46
Perovsky, Aleksei Alekseevich
   (Antonii Pogorel'sky) 1787-1836.....DLB-198
Perrault, Charles 1628-1703...........DLB-268
Perri, Henry 1561-1617..............DLB-236
Perrin, Alice 1867-1934..............DLB-156
Perry, Anne 1938-...................DLB-276
Perry, Bliss 1860-1954.................DLB-71
Perry, Eleanor 1915-1981...............DLB-44
Perry, Henry (see Perri, Henry)
Perry, Matthew 1794-1858.............DLB-183
Perry, Sampson 1747-1823............DLB-158
Perse, Saint-John 1887-1975...........DLB-258
Persius A.D. 34-A.D. 62..............DLB-211
Perutz, Leo 1882-1957.................DLB-81
Pesetsky, Bette 1932-................DLB-130
Pessanha, Camilo 1867-1926..........DLB-287
Pessoa, Fernando 1888-1935..........DLB-287
Pestalozzi, Johann Heinrich 1746-1827....DLB-94
Peter, Laurence J. 1919-1990..........DLB-53
Peter of Spain circa 1205-1277.........DLB-115
Peterkin, Julia 1880-1961..............DLB-9
Peters, Ellis (Edith Pargeter) 1913-1995...DLB-276
Peters, Lenrie 1932-.................DLB-117
Peters, Robert 1924-.................DLB-105
   "Foreword to *Ludwig of Baviria*".....DLB-105
Petersham, Maud 1889-1971 and
   Petersham, Miska 1888-1960.......DLB-22
Peterson, Charles Jacobs 1819-1887......DLB-79
Peterson, Len 1917-..................DLB-88
Peterson, Levi S. 1933-..............DLB-206
Peterson, Louis 1922-1998............DLB-76
Peterson, T. B., and Brothers..........DLB-49
Petitclair, Pierre 1813-1860............DLB-99
Petrescu, Camil 1894-1957............DLB-220
Petronius circa A.D. 20-A.D. 66
   ..........................DLB-211; CDWLB-1
Petrov, Aleksandar 1938-............DLB-181
Petrov, Evgenii (Evgenii Petrovich Kataev)
   1903-1942......................DLB-272
Petrov, Gavriil 1730-1801............DLB-150
Petrov, Valeri 1920-.................DLB-181
Petrov, Vasilii Petrovich 1736-1799......DLB-150
Petrović, Rastko
   1898-1949.............DLB-147; CDWLB-4

Petrushevskaia, Liudmila Stefanovna
   1938-..........................DLB-285
*Petruslied* circa 854?.................DLB-148
Petry, Ann 1908-1997.................DLB-76
Pettie, George circa 1548-1589........DLB-136
Pétur Gunnarsson 1947-..............DLB-293
Peyton, K. M. 1929-.................DLB-161
Pfaffe Konrad flourished circa 1172......DLB-148
Pfaffe Lamprecht flourished circa 1150...DLB-148
Pfeiffer, Emily 1827-1890.............DLB-199
Pforzheimer, Carl H. 1879-1957.......DLB-140
Phaedrus circa 18 B.C.-circa A.D. 50....DLB-211
Phaer, Thomas 1510?-1560............DLB-167
Phaidon Press Limited................DLB-112
Pharr, Robert Deane 1916-1992.........DLB-33
Phelps, Elizabeth Stuart 1815-1852.....DLB-202
Phelps, Elizabeth Stuart 1844-1911...DLB-74, 221
Philander von der Linde
   (see Mencke, Johann Burckhard)
Philby, H. St. John B. 1885-1960.......DLB-195
Philip, Marlene Nourbese 1947-.......DLB-157
Philippe, Charles-Louis 1874-1909......DLB-65
Philips, John 1676-1708...............DLB-95
Philips, Katherine 1632-1664...........DLB-131
Phillipps, Sir Thomas 1792-1872........DLB-184
Phillips, Caryl 1958-.................DLB-157
Phillips, David Graham 1867-1911.....DLB-9, 12
Phillips, Jayne Anne 1952-.......DLB-292; Y-80
   Tribute to Seymour Lawrence..........Y-94
Phillips, Robert 1938-................DLB-105
   "Finding, Losing, Reclaiming: A Note
   on My Poems"................DLB-105
   Tribute to William Goyen............Y-83
Phillips, Stephen 1864-1915...........DLB-10
Phillips, Ulrich B. 1877-1934..........DLB-17
Phillips, Wendell 1811-1884..........DLB-235
Phillips, Willard 1784-1873............DLB-59
Phillips, William 1907-2002...........DLB-137
Phillips, Sampson and Company........DLB-49
Phillpotts, Adelaide Eden (Adelaide Ross)
   1896-1993......................DLB-191
Phillpotts, Eden 1862-1960..DLB-10, 70, 135, 153
Philo circa 20-15 B.C.-circa A.D. 50.....DLB-176
Philosophical Library..................DLB-46
Philosophy
   Eighteenth-Century Philosophical
   Background....................DLB-31
   Philosophic Thought in Boston......DLB-235
   Translators of the Twelfth Century:
   Literary Issues Raised and
   Impact Created...............DLB-115
Elihu Phinney [publishing house]........DLB-49
Phoenix, John (see Derby, George Horatio)
PHYLON (Fourth Quarter, 1950),
   The Negro in Literature:
   The Current Scene...............DLB-76
*Physiologus* circa 1070-circa 1150.........DLB-148

# Cumulative Index

Piccolo, Lucio 1903-1969 . . . . . . . . . . . . . DLB-114
Pickard, Tom 1946- . . . . . . . . . . . . . . . . . DLB-40
William Pickering [publishing house] . . . . DLB-106
Pickthall, Marjorie 1883-1922 . . . . . . . . . . DLB-92
Picoult, Jodi 1966- . . . . . . . . . . . . . . . . . DLB-292
Pictorial Printing Company . . . . . . . . . . . DLB-49
Piel, Gerard 1915- . . . . . . . . . . . . . . . . . . DLB-137
 "An Announcement to Our Readers,"
  Gerard Piel's Statement in *Scientific
  American* (April 1948) . . . . . . . . . DLB-137
Pielmeier, John 1949- . . . . . . . . . . . . . . . DLB-266
Piercy, Marge 1936- . . . . . . . . . DLB-120, 227
Pierro, Albino 1916-1995 . . . . . . . . . . . . . DLB-128
Pignotti, Lamberto 1926- . . . . . . . . . . . . DLB-128
Pike, Albert 1809-1891 . . . . . . . . . . . . . . . DLB-74
Pike, Zebulon Montgomery 1779-1813 . . . DLB-183
Pillat, Ion 1891-1945 . . . . . . . . . . . . . . . . DLB-220
Pil'niak, Boris Andreevich (Boris Andreevich
 Vogau) 1894-1938 . . . . . . . . . . . . . DLB-272
Pilon, Jean-Guy 1930- . . . . . . . . . . . . . . DLB-60
Pinar, Florencia fl. ca. late
 fifteenth century . . . . . . . . . . . . . . . . DLB-286
Pinckney, Eliza Lucas 1722-1793 . . . . . . . DLB-200
Pinckney, Josephine 1895-1957 . . . . . . . . DLB-6
Pindar circa 518 B.C.-circa 438 B.C.
 . . . . . . . . . . . . . . . . . DLB-176; CDWLB-1
Pindar, Peter (see Wolcot, John)
Pineda, Cecile 1942- . . . . . . . . . . . . . . . . DLB-209
Pinero, Arthur Wing 1855-1934 . . . . . . . . DLB-10
Piñero, Miguel 1946-1988 . . . . . . . . . . . . DLB-266
Pinget, Robert 1919-1997 . . . . . . . . . . . . . DLB-83
Pinkney, Edward Coote 1802-1828 . . . . . DLB-248
Pinnacle Books . . . . . . . . . . . . . . . . . . . . . DLB-46
Piñon, Nélida 1935- . . . . . . . . . . . . . . . . DLB-145
Pinsky, Robert 1940- . . . . . . . . . . . . . . . . . Y-82
 Reappointed Poet Laureate . . . . . . . . . . Y-98
Pinter, Harold 1930- . . . . . . . DLB-13; CDBLB-8
 Writing for the Theatre . . . . . . . . . . . DLB-13
Pinto, Fernão Mendes 1509/1511?-1583 . . DLB-287
Piontek, Heinz 1925- . . . . . . . . . . . . . . . . DLB-75
Piozzi, Hester Lynch [Thrale]
 1741-1821 . . . . . . . . . . . . . . . . DLB-104, 142
Piper, H. Beam 1904-1964 . . . . . . . . . . . . DLB-8
Piper, Watty . . . . . . . . . . . . . . . . . . . . . . . DLB-22
Pirandello, Luigi 1867-1936 . . . . . . . . . . . DLB-264
Pirckheimer, Caritas 1467-1532 . . . . . . . . DLB-179
Pirckheimer, Willibald 1470-1530 . . . . . . . DLB-179
Pires, José Cardoso 1925-1998 . . . . . . . . . DLB-287
Pisar, Samuel 1929- . . . . . . . . . . . . . . . . . . Y-83
Pisarev, Dmitrii Ivanovich 1840-1868 . . . . DLB-277
Pisemsky, Aleksei Feofilaktovich
 1821-1881 . . . . . . . . . . . . . . . . . . . . DLB-238
Pitkin, Timothy 1766-1847 . . . . . . . . . . . . DLB-30
Pitter, Ruth 1897- . . . . . . . . . . . . . . . . . . DLB-20
Pix, Mary 1666-1709 . . . . . . . . . . . . . . . . DLB-80
Pixérécourt, René Charles Guilbert de
 1773-1844 . . . . . . . . . . . . . . . . . . . . DLB-192

Pizarnik, Alejandra 1936-1972 . . . . . . . . . DLB-283
Plá, Josefina 1909-1999 . . . . . . . . . . . . . . DLB-290
Plaatje, Sol T. 1876-1932 . . . . . . . . DLB-125, 225
Plante, David 1940- . . . . . . . . . . . . . . . . . . Y-83
Platen, August von 1796-1835 . . . . . . . . . DLB-90
Plantinga, Alvin 1932- . . . . . . . . . . . . . . DLB-279
Plath, Sylvia
 1932-1963 . . . . . . . . DLB-5, 6, 152; CDALB-1
Plato circa 428 B.C.-348-347 B.C.
 . . . . . . . . . . . . . . . . . DLB-176; CDWLB-1
Plato, Ann 1824?-? . . . . . . . . . . . . . . . . . DLB-239
Platon 1737-1812 . . . . . . . . . . . . . . . . . . . DLB-150
Platonov, Andrei Platonovich (Andrei
 Platonovich Klimentev) 1899-1951 . . DLB-272
Platt, Charles 1945- . . . . . . . . . . . . . . . . . DLB-261
Platt and Munk Company . . . . . . . . . . . . DLB-46
Plautus circa 254 B.C.-184 B.C.
 . . . . . . . . . . . . . . . . . DLB-211; CDWLB-1
Playboy Press . . . . . . . . . . . . . . . . . . . . . . DLB-46
John Playford [publishing house] . . . . . . . DLB-170
Der Pleier flourished circa 1250 . . . . . . . . DLB-138
Pleijel, Agneta 1940- . . . . . . . . . . . . . . . . DLB-257
Plenzdorf, Ulrich 1934- . . . . . . . . . . . . . . DLB-75
Pleshcheev, Aleksei Nikolaevich
 1825?-1893 . . . . . . . . . . . . . . . . . . . DLB-277
Plessen, Elizabeth 1944- . . . . . . . . . . . . . DLB-75
Pletnev, Petr Aleksandrovich
 1792-1865 . . . . . . . . . . . . . . . . . . . . DLB-205
Pliekšāne, Elza Rozenberga (see Aspazija)
Pliekšāns, Jānis (see Rainis, Jānis)
Plievier, Theodor 1892-1955 . . . . . . . . . . . DLB-69
Plimpton, George 1927-2003 . . DLB-185, 241; Y-99
Pliny the Elder A.D. 23/24-A.D. 79 . . . . . DLB-211
Pliny the Younger
 circa A.D. 61-A.D. 112 . . . . . . . . . . . DLB-211
Plomer, William
 1903-1973 . . . . . . . . . . DLB-20, 162, 191, 225
Plotinus 204-270 . . . . . . . . . . . DLB-176; CDWLB-1
Plowright, Teresa 1952- . . . . . . . . . . . . . DLB-251
Plume, Thomas 1630-1704 . . . . . . . . . . . . DLB-213
Plumly, Stanley 1939- . . . . . . . . . . . DLB-5, 193
Plumpp, Sterling D. 1940- . . . . . . . . . . . . DLB-41
Plunkett, James 1920- . . . . . . . . . . . . . . . DLB-14
Plutarch
 circa 46-circa 120 . . . . . . . DLB-176; CDWLB-1
Plymell, Charles 1935- . . . . . . . . . . . . . . . DLB-16
Pocket Books . . . . . . . . . . . . . . . . . . . . . . DLB-46
Poe, Edgar Allan 1809-1849
 . . . . . . . . . . DLB-3, 59, 73, 74, 248; CDALB-2
 The Poe Studies Association . . . . . . . . . . Y-99
Poe, James 1921-1980 . . . . . . . . . . . . . . . DLB-44
The Poet Laureate of the United States . . . . . Y-86
 Statements from Former Consultants
  in Poetry . . . . . . . . . . . . . . . . . . . . . . Y-86
Poetry
 Aesthetic Poetry (1873) . . . . . . . . . . . DLB-35
 A Century of Poetry, a Lifetime of
  Collecting: J. M. Edelstein's

  Collection of Twentieth-
   Century American Poetry . . . . . . . . . Y-02
 "Certain Gifts," by Betty Adcock . . . . DLB-105
 Contempo Caravan: Kites in a
  Windstorm . . . . . . . . . . . . . . . . . . . Y-85
 "Contemporary Verse Story-telling,"
  by Jonathan Holden . . . . . . . . . . DLB-105
 "A Detail in a Poem," by Fred
  Chappell . . . . . . . . . . . . . . . . . . DLB-105
 "The English Renaissance of Art"
  (1908), by Oscar Wilde . . . . . . . . DLB-35
 "Every Man His Own Poet; or,
  The Inspired Singer's Recipe
  Book" (1877), by
  H. W. Mallock . . . . . . . . . . . . . . DLB-35
 "Eyes Across Centuries: Contemporary
  Poetry and 'That Vision Thing,'"
  by Philip Dacey . . . . . . . . . . . . . DLB-105
 A Field Guide to Recent Schools
  of American Poetry . . . . . . . . . . . . . Y-86
 "Finding, Losing, Reclaiming:
  A Note on My Poems,
  by Robert Phillips" . . . . . . . . . . . DLB-105
 "The Fleshly School of Poetry and Other
  Phenomena of the Day" (1872) . . . DLB-35
 "The Fleshly School of Poetry:
  Mr. D. G. Rossetti" (1871) . . . . . . DLB-35
 The G. Ross Roy Scottish Poetry Collection
  at the University of South Carolina . . Y-89
 "Getting Started: Accepting the Regions
  You Own–or Which Own You,"
  by Walter McDonald . . . . . . . . . DLB-105
 "The Good, The Not So Good," by
  Stephen Dunn . . . . . . . . . . . . . . DLB-105
 The Griffin Poetry Prize . . . . . . . . . . . . Y-00
 The Hero as Poet. Dante; Shakspeare
  (1841), by Thomas Carlyle . . . . . . DLB-32
 "Images and 'Images,'" by Charles
  Simic . . . . . . . . . . . . . . . . . . . . . DLB-105
 "Into the Mirror," by Peter Cooley . . DLB-105
 "Knots into Webs: Some Autobiographical
  Sources," by Dabney Stuart . . . . DLB-105
 "L'Envoi" (1882), by Oscar Wilde . . . DLB-35
 "Living in Ruin," by Gerald Stern . . . DLB-105
 Looking for the Golden Mountain:
  Poetry Reviewing . . . . . . . . . . . . . . . Y-89
 Lyric Poetry (French) . . . . . . . . . . . . DLB-268
 Medieval Galician-Portuguese
  Poetry . . . . . . . . . . . . . . . . . . . . DLB-287
 "The No Self, the Little Self, and the
  Poets," by Richard Moore . . . . . . DLB-105
 On Some of the Characteristics of Modern
  Poetry and On the Lyrical Poems of
  Alfred Tennyson (1831) . . . . . . . . DLB-32
 The Pitt Poetry Series: Poetry Publishing
  Today . . . . . . . . . . . . . . . . . . . . . . . Y-85
 "The Poetry File," by Edward
  Field . . . . . . . . . . . . . . . . . . . . . DLB-105
 Poetry in Nineteenth-Century France:
  Cultural Background and Critical
  Commentary . . . . . . . . . . . . . . . DLB-217
 The Poetry of Jorge Luis Borges . . . . . . Y-86
 "The Poet's Kaleidoscope: The Element
  of Surprise in the Making of the
  Poem" by Madeline DeFrees . . . . DLB-105

| | | |
|---|---|---|
| The Pre-Raphaelite Controversy......DLB-35 | Pomialovsky, Nikolai Gerasimovich 1835-1863......................DLB-238 | Postans, Marianne circa 1810-1865......DLB-166 |
| Protest Poetry in Castile..........DLB-286 | Pomilio, Mario 1921-1990............DLB-177 | Postgate, Raymond 1896-1971..........DLB-276 |
| "Reflections: After a Tornado," by Judson Jerome.............DLB-105 | Ponce, Mary Helen 1938-............DLB-122 | Postl, Carl (see Sealsfield, Carl) |
| Statements from Former Consultants in Poetry......................Y-86 | Ponce-Montoya, Juanita 1949-........DLB-122 | Postmodern Holocaust Fiction..........DLB-299 |
| Statements on the Art of Poetry......DLB-54 | Ponet, John 1516?-1556.............DLB-132 | Poston, Ted 1906-1974................DLB-51 |
| The Study of Poetry (1880), by Matthew Arnold..............DLB-35 | Ponge, Francis 1899-1988........DLB-258; Y-02 | Potekhin, Aleksei Antipovich 1829-1908..DLB-238 |
| A Survey of Poetry Anthologies, 1879-1960....................DLB-54 | Poniatowska, Elena 1933-..............DLB-113; CDWLB-3 | Potok, Chaim 1929-2002.........DLB-28, 152 |
| Thoughts on Poetry and Its Varieties (1833), by John Stuart Mill......DLB-32 | Ponsard, François 1814-1867..........DLB-192 | A Conversation with Chaim Potok......Y-84 |
| Under the Microscope (1872), by A. C. Swinburne..............DLB-35 | William Ponsonby [publishing house]....DLB-170 | Tribute to Bernard Malamud..........Y-86 |
| The Unterberg Poetry Center of the 92nd Street Y..............Y-98 | Pontiggia, Giuseppe 1934-............DLB-196 | Potter, Beatrix 1866-1943.............DLB-141 |
| Victorian Poetry: Five Critical Views.....................DLBV-35 | Pontoppidan, Henrik 1857-1943........DLB-300 | The Beatrix Potter Society............Y-98 |
| Year in Poetry.............Y-83–92, 94–01 | Pony Stories, Omnibus Essay on........DLB-160 | Potter, David M. 1910-1971.............DLB-17 |
| Year's Work in American Poetry.......Y-82 | Poole, Ernest 1880-1950................DLB-9 | Potter, Dennis 1935-1994..............DLB-233 |
| Poets | Poole, Sophia 1804-1891..............DLB-166 | John E. Potter and Company..........DLB-49 |
| *The Lives of the Poets* (1753)..........DLB-142 | Poore, Benjamin Perley 1820-1887.......DLB-23 | Pottle, Frederick A. 1897-1987.....DLB-103; Y-87 |
| Minor Poets of the Earlier Seventeenth Century..........DLB-121 | Popa, Vasko 1922-1991.....DLB-181; CDWLB-4 | Poulin, Jacques 1937-.................DLB-60 |
| Other British Poets Who Fell in the Great War.............DLB-216 | Pope, Abbie Hanscom 1858-1894........DLB-140 | Pound, Ezra 1885-1972 ...........DLB-4, 45, 63; DS-15; CDALB-4 |
| Other Poets [French]..............DLB-217 | Pope, Alexander 1688-1744.......DLB-95, 101, 213; CDBLB-2 | The Cost of the *Cantos:* William Bird to Ezra Pound...................Y-01 |
| Second-Generation Minor Poets of the Seventeenth Century.......DLB-126 | Popov, Aleksandr Serafimovich (see Serafimovich, Aleksandr Serafimovich) | The Ezra Pound Society.............Y-01 |
| Third-Generation Minor Poets of the Seventeenth Century.......DLB-131 | Popov, Evgenii Anatol'evich 1946-....DLB-285 | Poverman, C. E. 1944-...............DLB-234 |
| Pogodin, Mikhail Petrovich 1800-1875...DLB-198 | Popov, Mikhail Ivanovich 1742-circa 1790..................DLB-150 | Povich, Shirley 1905-1998.............DLB-171 |
| Pogorel'sky, Antonii (see Perovsky, Aleksei Alekseevich) | Popović, Aleksandar 1929-1996..........DLB-181 | Powell, Anthony 1905-2000...DLB-15; CDBLB-7 |
| Pohl, Frederik 1919-...............DLB-8 | Popper, Karl 1902-1994.............DLB-262 | The Anthony Powell Society: Powell and the First Biennial Conference.......Y-01 |
| Tribute to Isaac Asimov.............Y-92 | Popular Culture Association/ American Culture Association........Y-99 | Powell, Dawn 1897-1965 Dawn Powell, Where Have You Been All Our Lives?...................Y-97 |
| Tribute to Theodore Sturgeon.........Y-85 | Popular Library....................DLB-46 | Powell, John Wesley 1834-1902.........DLB-186 |
| Poirier, Louis (see Gracq, Julien) | Poquelin, Jean-Baptiste (see Molière) | Powell, Padgett 1952-................DLB-234 |
| Poláček, Karel 1892-1945...DLB-215; CDWLB-4 | Porete, Marguerite ?-1310............DLB-208 | Powers, J. F. 1917-1999...............DLB-130 |
| Polanyi, Michael 1891-1976...........DLB-100 | Porlock, Martin (see MacDonald, Philip) | Powers, Jimmy 1903-1995.............DLB-241 |
| Pole, Reginald 1500-1558.............DLB-132 | Porpoise Press.....................DLB-112 | Pownall, David 1938-.................DLB-14 |
| Polevoi, Nikolai Alekseevich 1796-1846..DLB-198 | Porta, Antonio 1935-1989.............DLB-128 | Powys, John Cowper 1872-1963.....DLB-15, 255 |
| Polezhaev, Aleksandr Ivanovich 1804-1838....................DLB-205 | Porter, Anna Maria 1780-1832......DLB-116, 159 | Powys, Llewelyn 1884-1939.............DLB-98 |
| Poliakoff, Stephen 1952-.............DLB-13 | Porter, Cole 1891-1964..............DLB-265 | Powys, T. F. 1875-1953............DLB-36, 162 |
| Polidori, John William 1795-1821.......DLB-116 | Porter, David 1780-1843.............DLB-183 | The Powys Society..................Y-98 |
| Polite, Carlene Hatcher 1932-..........DLB-33 | Porter, Eleanor H. 1868-1920............DLB-9 | Poynter, Nelson 1903-1978............DLB-127 |
| Pollard, Alfred W. 1859-1944..........DLB-201 | Porter, Gene Stratton (see Stratton-Porter, Gene) | Prado, Pedro 1886-1952..............DLB-283 |
| Pollard, Edward A. 1832-1872..........DLB-30 | Porter, Hal 1911-1984................DLB-260 | Prados, Emilio 1899-1962.............DLB-134 |
| Pollard, Graham 1903-1976............DLB-201 | Porter, Henry ?-?...................DLB-62 | Praed, Mrs. Caroline (see Praed, Rosa) |
| Pollard, Percival 1869-1911............DLB-71 | Porter, Jane 1776-1850..........DLB-116, 159 | Praed, Rosa (Mrs. Caroline Praed) 1851-1935....................DLB-230 |
| Pollard and Moss...................DLB-49 | Porter, Katherine Anne 1890-1980 ......DLB-4, 9, 102; Y-80; DS-12; CDALB-7 | Praed, Winthrop Mackworth 1802-1839...DLB-96 |
| Pollock, Sharon 1936-................DLB-60 | The Katherine Anne Porter Society.....Y-01 | Praeger Publishers...................DLB-46 |
| Polonsky, Abraham 1910-1999..........DLB-26 | Porter, Peter 1929-.............DLB-40, 289 | Praetorius, Johannes 1630-1680.........DLB-168 |
| Polonsky, Iakov Petrovich 1819-1898....DLB-277 | Porter, William Sydney (O. Henry) 1862-1910........DLB-12, 78, 79; CDALB-3 | Pratolini, Vasco 1913-1991.............DLB-177 |
| Polotsky, Simeon 1629-1680...........DLB-150 | Porter, William T. 1809-1858.....DLB-3, 43, 250 | Pratt, E. J. 1882-1964.................DLB-92 |
| Polybius circa 200 B.C.-118 B.C........DLB-176 | Porter and Coates..................DLB-49 | Pratt, Samuel Jackson 1749-1814........DLB-39 |
| | Portillo Trambley, Estela 1927-1998....DLB-209 | Preciado Martin, Patricia 1939-.......DLB-209 |
| | Portis, Charles 1933-..................DLB-6 | Préfontaine, Yves 1937-...............DLB-53 |
| | Medieval Galician-Portuguese Poetry....DLB-287 | Prelutsky, Jack 1940-.................DLB-61 |
| | Posey, Alexander 1873-1908...........DLB-175 | Prentice, George D. 1802-1870..........DLB-43 |
| | | Prentice-Hall.......................DLB-46 |
| | | Prescott, Orville 1906-1996............Y-96 |

# Cumulative Index

Prescott, William Hickling
1796-1859............DLB-1, 30, 59, 235
Prešeren, Francè
1800-1849............DLB-147; CDWLB-4
Presses (*See also* Publishing)
   Small Presses in Great Britain and
     Ireland, 1960-1985............DLB-40
   Small Presses I: Jargon Society..........Y-84
   Small Presses II: The Spirit That Moves
     Us Press......................Y-85
   Small Presses III: Pushcart Press........Y-87
Preston, Margaret Junkin
1820-1897............DLB-239, 248
Preston, May Wilson 1873-1949.....DLB-188
Preston, Thomas 1537-1598..........DLB-62
Prévert, Jacques 1900-1977...........DLB-258
Price, Anthony 1928-................DLB-276
Price, Reynolds 1933-........DLB-2, 218, 278
Price, Richard 1723-1791............DLB-158
Price, Richard 1949-..................Y-81
Prichard, Katharine Susannah
1883-1969...................DLB-260
Prideaux, John 1578-1650............DLB-236
Priest, Christopher 1943-....DLB-14, 207, 261
Priestley, J. B. 1894-1984
....DLB-10, 34, 77, 100, 139; Y-84; CDBLB-6
Priestley, Joseph 1733-1804..........DLB-252
Prigov, Dmitrii Aleksandrovich 1940-.DLB-285
Prime, Benjamin Young
1733-1791....................DLB-31
Primrose, Diana floruit circa 1630.....DLB-126
Prince, F. T. 1912-..................DLB-20
Prince, Nancy Gardner 1799-?.......DLB-239
Prince, Thomas 1687-1758.......DLB-24, 140
Pringle, Thomas 1789-1834..........DLB-225
Printz, Wolfgang Casper 1641-1717..DLB-168
Prior, Matthew 1664-1721............DLB-95
Prisco, Michele 1920-................DLB-177
Prishvin, Mikhail Mikhailovich
1873-1954....................DLB-272
Pritchard, William H. 1932-.........DLB-111
Pritchett, V. S. 1900-1997........DLB-15, 139
Probyn, May 1856 or 1857-1909.....DLB-199
Procter, Adelaide Anne 1825-1864...DLB-32, 199
Procter, Bryan Waller 1787-1874....DLB-96, 144
Proctor, Robert 1868-1903............DLB-184
Prokopovich, Feofan 1681?-1736.....DLB-150
Prokosch, Frederic 1906-1989.........DLB-48
Pronzini, Bill 1943-..................DLB-226
Propertius circa 50 B.C.-post 16 B.C.
..................DLB-211; CDWLB-1
Propper, Dan 1937-..................DLB-16
Prose, Francine 1947-................DLB-234
Protagoras circa 490 B.C.-420 B.C.......DLB-176
Protest Poetry in Castile
ca. 1445-ca. 1506................DLB-286
Proud, Robert 1728-1813.............DLB-30
Proust, Marcel 1871-1922.............DLB-65

Marcel Proust at 129 and the Proust
  Society of America...............Y-00
Marcel Proust's *Remembrance of Things Past*:
  The Rediscovered Galley Proofs.....Y-00
Prutkov, Koz'ma Petrovich 1803-1863...DLB-277
Prynne, J. H. 1936-..................DLB-40
Przybyszewski, Stanislaw 1868-1927....DLB-66
Pseudo-Dionysius the Areopagite floruit
circa 500....................DLB-115
Public Lending Right in America
  PLR and the Meaning of Literary
    Property.....................Y-83
  Statement by Sen. Charles
    McC. Mathias, Jr. PLR...........Y-83
  Statements on PLR by American Writers..Y-83
Public Lending Right in the United Kingdom
  The First Year in the United Kingdom...Y-83
Publishers [listed by individual names]
  Publishers, Conversations with:
    An Interview with Charles Scribner III.Y-94
    An Interview with Donald Lamm.....Y-95
    An Interview with James Laughlin.....Y-96
    An Interview with Patrick O'Connor....Y-84
Publishing
  The Art and Mystery of Publishing:
    Interviews....................Y-97
  Book Publishing Accounting: Some Basic
    Concepts.....................Y-98
  1873 Publishers' Catalogues..........DLB-49
  The Literary Scene 2002: Publishing, Book
    Reviewing, and Literary Journalism..Y-02
  Main Trends in Twentieth-Century
    Book Clubs...................DLB-46
  Overview of U.S. Book Publishing,
    1910-1945....................DLB-9
  The Pitt Poetry Series: Poetry Publishing
    Today........................Y-85
  Publishing Fiction at LSU Press........Y-87
  The Publishing Industry in 1998:
    *Sturm-und-drang.com*...............Y-98
  The Publishing Industry in 1999........Y-99
  Publishers and Agents: The Columbia
    Connection...................Y-87
  Responses to Ken Auletta.............Y-97
  Southern Writers Between the Wars...DLB-9
  The State of Publishing...............Y-97
  Trends in Twentieth-Century
    Mass Market Publishing........DLB-46
  The Year in Book Publishing..........Y-86
Pückler-Muskau, Hermann von
1785-1871....................DLB-133
Pufendorf, Samuel von 1632-1694....DLB-168
Pugh, Edwin William 1874-1930....DLB-135
Pugin, A. Welby 1812-1852...........DLB-55
Puig, Manuel 1932-1990....DLB-113; CDWLB-3
Pulgar, Hernando del (Fernando del Pulgar)
ca. 1436-ca. 1492.............DLB-286
Pulitzer, Joseph 1847-1911............DLB-23
Pulitzer, Joseph, Jr. 1885-1955........DLB-29
Pulitzer Prizes for the Novel, 1917-1945...DLB-9
Pulliam, Eugene 1889-1975..........DLB-127

Purcell, Deirdre 1945-...............DLB-267
Purchas, Samuel 1577?-1626.........DLB-151
Purdy, Al 1918-2000.................DLB-88
Purdy, James 1923-...............DLB-2, 218
Purdy, Ken W. 1913-1972............DLB-137
Pusey, Edward Bouverie 1800-1882......DLB-55
Pushkin, Aleksandr Sergeevich
1799-1837....................DLB-205
Pushkin, Vasilii L'vovich
1766-1830....................DLB-205
Putnam, George Palmer
1814-1872............DLB-3, 79, 250, 254
G. P. Putnam [publishing house].......DLB-254
G. P. Putnam's Sons [U.K.]............DLB-106
G. P. Putnam's Sons [U.S.]............DLB-49
A Publisher's Archives: G. P. Putnam....Y-92
Putnam, Hilary 1926-................DLB-279
Putnam, Samuel 1892-1950.......DLB-4; DS-15
Puttenham, George 1529?-1590......DLB-281
Puzo, Mario 1920-1999................DLB-6
Pyle, Ernie 1900-1945................DLB-29
Pyle, Howard
1853-1911..........DLB-42, 188; DS-13
Pyle, Robert Michael 1947-..........DLB-275
Pym, Barbara 1913-1980.....DLB-14, 207; Y-87
Pynchon, Thomas 1937-..........DLB-2, 173
Pyramid Books.......................DLB-46
Pyrnelle, Louise-Clarke 1850-1907.....DLB-42
Pythagoras circa 570 B.C.-?...........DLB-176

# Q

Quad, M. (see Lewis, Charles B.)
Quaritch, Bernard 1819-1899.........DLB-184
Quarles, Francis 1592-1644...........DLB-126
*The Quarterly Review* 1809-1967......DLB-110
Quasimodo, Salvatore 1901-1968......DLB-114
Queen, Ellery (see Dannay, Frederic, and
  Manfred B. Lee)
Queen, Frank 1822-1882..............DLB-241
The Queen City Publishing House.....DLB-49
Queirós, Eça de 1845-1900............DLB-287
Queneau, Raymond 1903-1976....DLB-72, 258
Quennell, Peter 1905-1993........DLB-155, 195
Quental, Antero de 1842-1891........DLB-287
Quesada, José Luis 1948-.............DLB-290
Quesnel, Joseph 1746-1809............DLB-99
Quiller-Couch, Sir Arthur Thomas
1863-1944..........DLB-135, 153, 190
Quin, Ann 1936-1973...........DLB-14, 231
Quinault, Philippe 1635-1688.........DLB-268
Quincy, Samuel, of Georgia ?-?........DLB-31
Quincy, Samuel, of Massachusetts
1734-1789....................DLB-31
Quindlen, Anna 1952-...............DLB-292
Quine, W. V. 1908-2000..............DLB-279
Quinn, Anthony 1915-2001...........DLB-122

Quinn, John 1870-1924 . . . . . . . . . . . . . . .DLB-187
Quiñónez, Naomi 1951- . . . . . . . . . . . . .DLB-209
Quintana, Leroy V. 1944- . . . . . . . . . . . .DLB-82
Quintana, Miguel de 1671-1748
    A Forerunner of Chicano
        Literature . . . . . . . . . . . . . . . . . .DLB-122
Quintilian
    circa A.D. 40-circa A.D. 96 . . . . . . . .DLB-211
Quintus Curtius Rufus
    fl. A.D. 35 . . . . . . . . . . . . . . . . . . . . .DLB-211
Harlin Quist Books . . . . . . . . . . . . . . . . .DLB-46
Quoirez, Françoise (see Sagan, Françoise)

# R

Raabe, Wilhelm 1831-1910 . . . . . . . . . . . .DLB-129
Raban, Jonathan 1942- . . . . . . . . . . . . .DLB-204
Rabe, David 1940- . . . . . . . . DLB-7, 228; Y-91
Raboni, Giovanni 1932- . . . . . . . . . . . . .DLB-128
Rachilde 1860-1953 . . . . . . . . . . . . .DLB-123, 192
Racin, Kočo 1908-1943 . . . . . . . . . . . . .DLB-147
Racine, Jean 1639-1699 . . . . . . . . . . . . .DLB-268
Rackham, Arthur 1867-1939 . . . . . . . . . .DLB-141
Raczymow, Henri 1948- . . . . . . . . . . . .DLB-299
Radauskas, Henrikas
    1910-1970 . . . . . . . . . .DLB-220; CDWLB-4
Radcliffe, Ann 1764-1823 . . . . . . . . . .DLB-39, 178
Raddall, Thomas 1903-1994 . . . . . . . . . .DLB-68
Radford, Dollie 1858-1920 . . . . . . . . . . .DLB-240
Radichkov, Yordan 1929- . . . . . . . . . . .DLB-181
Radiguet, Raymond 1903-1923 . . . . . . . .DLB-65
Radishchev, Aleksandr Nikolaevich
    1749-1802 . . . . . . . . . . . . . . . . . . .DLB-150
Radnóti, Miklós
    1909-1944 . . . . . . . . . .DLB-215; CDWLB-4
Radványi, Netty Reiling (see Seghers, Anna)
Rahv, Philip 1908-1973 . . . . . . . . . . . . .DLB-137
Raich, Semen Egorovich 1792-1855 . . . . .DLB-205
Raičković, Stevan 1928- . . . . . . . . . . . .DLB-181
Raiderman (see Parshchikov, Aleksei Maksimovich)
Raimund, Ferdinand Jakob 1790-1836 . . . . .DLB-90
Raine, Craig 1944- . . . . . . . . . . . . . . . .DLB-40
Raine, Kathleen 1908- . . . . . . . . . . . . . .DLB-20
Rainis, Jānis 1865-1929 . . . . .DLB-220; CDWLB-4
Rainolde, Richard
    circa 1530-1606 . . . . . . . . . . . . .DLB-136, 236
Rainolds, John 1549-1607 . . . . . . . . . . . .DLB-281
Rakić, Milan 1876-1938 . . . . .DLB-147; CDWLB-4
Rakosi, Carl 1903- . . . . . . . . . . . . . . . . .DLB-193
Ralegh, Sir Walter
    1554?-1618 . . . . . . . . . . .DLB-172; CDBLB-1
Raleigh, Walter
    *Style* (1897) [excerpt] . . . . . . . . . . . . . .DLB-57
Ralin, Radoy 1923- . . . . . . . . . . . . . . . .DLB-181
Ralph, Julian 1853-1903 . . . . . . . . . . . . .DLB-23
Ramat, Silvio 1939- . . . . . . . . . . . . . . . .DLB-128
Ramée, Marie Louise de la (see Ouida)
Ramírez, Sergío 1942- . . . . . . . . . . . . . .DLB-145

Ramke, Bin 1947- . . . . . . . . . . . . . . . . .DLB-120
Ramler, Karl Wilhelm 1725-1798 . . . . . . . .DLB-97
Ramon Ribeyro, Julio 1929-1994 . . . . . . .DLB-145
Ramos, Manuel 1948- . . . . . . . . . . . . . .DLB-209
Ramos Sucre, José Antonio 1890-1930 . . .DLB-290
Ramous, Mario 1924- . . . . . . . . . . . . . .DLB-128
Rampersad, Arnold 1941- . . . . . . . . . . .DLB-111
Ramsay, Allan 1684 or 1685-1758 . . . . . . .DLB-95
Ramsay, David 1749-1815 . . . . . . . . . . . .DLB-30
Ramsay, Martha Laurens 1759-1811 . . . . .DLB-200
Ramsey, Frank P. 1903-1930 . . . . . . . . . .DLB-262
Ranch, Hieronimus Justesen
    1539-1607 . . . . . . . . . . . . . . . . . . .DLB-300
Ranck, Katherine Quintana 1942- . . . . . .DLB-122
Rand, Avery and Company . . . . . . . . . . .DLB-49
Rand, Ayn 1905-1982 . . . DLB-227, 279; CDALB-7
Rand McNally and Company . . . . . . . . . .DLB-49
Randall, David Anton 1905-1975 . . . . . . .DLB-140
Randall, Dudley 1914- . . . . . . . . . . . . . .DLB-41
Randall, Henry S. 1811-1876 . . . . . . . . . .DLB-30
Randall, James G. 1881-1953 . . . . . . . . . .DLB-17
    The Randall Jarrell Symposium: A Small
        Collection of Randall Jarrells . . . . . . . Y-86
    Excerpts From Papers Delivered at the
        Randall Jarrel Symposium . . . . . . . . . Y-86
Randall, John Herman, Jr. 1899-1980 . . . .DLB-279
Randolph, A. Philip 1889-1979 . . . . . . . .DLB-91
Anson D. F. Randolph
    [publishing house] . . . . . . . . . . . . . . . .DLB-49
Randolph, Thomas 1605-1635 . . . . . .DLB-58, 126
Random House . . . . . . . . . . . . . . . . . . .DLB-46
Rankin, Ian (Jack Harvey) 1960- . . . . . . .DLB-267
Henry Ranlet [publishing house] . . . . . . . .DLB-49
Ransom, Harry 1908-1976 . . . . . . . . . . . .DLB-187
Ransom, John Crowe
    1888-1974 . . . . . . . . . .DLB-45, 63; CDALB-7
Ransome, Arthur 1884-1967 . . . . . . . . . .DLB-160
Raphael, Frederic 1931- . . . . . . . . . . . . .DLB-14
Raphaelson, Samson 1896-1983 . . . . . . . .DLB-44
Rare Book Dealers
    Bertram Rota and His Bookshop . . . . . Y-91
    An Interview with Glenn Horowitz . . . . Y-90
    An Interview with Otto Penzler . . . . . . Y-96
    An Interview with Ralph Sipper . . . . . . Y-94
    New York City Bookshops in the
        1930s and 1940s: The Recollections
        of Walter Goldwater . . . . . . . . . . . . Y-93
Rare Books
    Research in the American Antiquarian
        Book Trade . . . . . . . . . . . . . . . . . Y-97
    Two Hundred Years of Rare Books and
        Literary Collections at the
        University of South Carolina . . . . . . Y-00
Rashi circa 1040-1105 . . . . . . . . . . . . . .DLB-208
Raskin, Ellen 1928-1984 . . . . . . . . . . . . .DLB-52
Rasputin, Valentin Grigor'evich
    1937- . . . . . . . . . . . . . . . . . . . . . .DLB-302
Rastell, John 1475?-1536 . . . . . .DLB-136, 170

Rattigan, Terence
    1911-1977 . . . . . . . . . . . . .DLB-13; CDBLB-7
Raven, Simon 1927-2001 . . . . . . . . . . . . .DLB-271
Ravnkilde, Adda 1862-1883 . . . . . . . . . .DLB-300
Rawicz, Piotr 1919-1982 . . . . . . . . . . . . .DLB-299
Rawlings, Marjorie Kinnan 1896-1953
    . . . . . . . . . . DLB-9, 22, 102; DS-17; CDALB-7
Rawlinson, Richard 1690-1755 . . . . . . . .DLB-213
Rawlinson, Thomas 1681-1725 . . . . . . . .DLB-213
Rawls, John 1921-2002 . . . . . . . . . . . . . .DLB-279
Raworth, Tom 1938- . . . . . . . . . . . . . . .DLB-40
Ray, David 1932- . . . . . . . . . . . . . . . . . .DLB-5
Ray, Gordon Norton 1915-1986 . . . .DLB-103, 140
Ray, Henrietta Cordelia 1849-1916 . . . . . .DLB-50
Raymond, Ernest 1888-1974 . . . . . . . . . .DLB-191
Raymond, Henry J. 1820-1869 . . . . . .DLB-43, 79
Raymond, René (see Chase, James Hadley)
Razaf, Andy 1895-1973 . . . . . . . . . . . . .DLB-265
Rea, Michael 1927-1996 . . . . . . . . . . . . . . .Y-97
    Michael M. Rea and the Rea Award for
        the Short Story . . . . . . . . . . . . . . . Y-97
Reach, Angus 1821-1856 . . . . . . . . . . . . .DLB-70
Read, Herbert 1893-1968 . . . . . . . . . .DLB-20, 149
Read, Martha Meredith . . . . . . . . . . . . .DLB-200
Read, Opie 1852-1939 . . . . . . . . . . . . . .DLB-23
Read, Piers Paul 1941- . . . . . . . . . . . . . .DLB-14
Reade, Charles 1814-1884 . . . . . . . . . . . .DLB-21
Reader's Digest Condensed Books . . . . . . .DLB-46
*Readers Ulysses* Symposium . . . . . . . . . . . .Y-97
Reading, Peter 1946- . . . . . . . . . . . . . . .DLB-40
Reading Series in New York City . . . . . . . Y-96
Reaney, James 1926- . . . . . . . . . . . . . . .DLB-68
Rebhun, Paul 1500?-1546 . . . . . . . . . . . .DLB-179
Rèbora, Clemente 1885-1957 . . . . . . . . . .DLB-114
Rebreanu, Liviu 1885-1944 . . . . . . . . . . .DLB-220
Rechy, John 1931- . . . . . . . . DLB-122, 278; Y-82
Redding, J. Saunders 1906-1988 . . . . . .DLB-63, 76
J. S. Redfield [publishing house] . . . . . . . .DLB-49
Redgrove, Peter 1932- . . . . . . . . . . . . . .DLB-40
Redmon, Anne 1943- . . . . . . . . . . . . . . . .Y-86
Redmond, Eugene B. 1937- . . . . . . . . . .DLB-41
Redol, Alves 1911-1969 . . . . . . . . . . . . .DLB-287
James Redpath [publishing house] . . . . . . .DLB-49
Reed, Henry 1808-1854 . . . . . . . . . . . . .DLB-59
Reed, Henry 1914-1986 . . . . . . . . . . . . . .DLB-27
Reed, Ishmael
    1938- . . . . .DLB-2, 5, 33, 169, 227; DS-8
Reed, Rex 1938- . . . . . . . . . . . . . . . . . .DLB-185
Reed, Sampson 1800-1880 . . . . . . . . .DLB-1, 235
Reed, Talbot Baines 1852-1893 . . . . . . . .DLB-141
Reedy, William Marion 1862-1920 . . . . . .DLB-91
Reese, Lizette Woodworth 1856-1935 . . . . .DLB-54
Reese, Thomas 1742-1796 . . . . . . . . . . . .DLB-37
Reeve, Clara 1729-1807 . . . . . . . . . . . . .DLB-39
    Preface to *The Old English Baron*
        (1778) . . . . . . . . . . . . . . . . . . . . .DLB-39

*The Progress of Romance* (1785)
[excerpt].....................DLB-39
Reeves, James 1909-1978 ............DLB-161
Reeves, John 1926- ..............DLB-88
Reeves-Stevens, Garfield 1953- .......DLB-251
Régio, José (José Maria dos Reis Pereira) 1901-1969 .....................DLB-287
Henry Regnery Company ............DLB-46
Rehberg, Hans 1901-1963 ............DLB-124
Rehfisch, Hans José 1891-1960.........DLB-124
Reich, Ebbe Kløvedal 1940- .......DLB-214
Reid, Alastair 1926- ..............DLB-27
Reid, B. L. 1918-1990.................DLB-111
Reid, Christopher 1949- ..........DLB-40
Reid, Forrest 1875-1947 ............DLB-153
Reid, Helen Rogers 1882-1970 .......DLB-29
Reid, James ?-? .....................DLB-31
Reid, Mayne 1818-1883 ...........DLB-21, 163
Reid, Thomas 1710-1796 ...........DLB-31, 252
Reid, V. S. (Vic) 1913-1987 ..........DLB-125
Reid, Whitelaw 1837-1912 ............DLB-23
Reilly and Lee Publishing Company .....DLB-46
Reimann, Brigitte 1933-1973 ............DLB-75
Reinmar der Alte circa 1165-circa 1205 ..DLB-138
Reinmar von Zweter circa 1200-circa 1250 .............DLB-138
Reisch, Walter 1903-1983 ............DLB-44
Reizei Family .....................DLB-203
Religion
    A Crisis of Culture: The Changing Role of Religion in the New Republic ................DLB-37
Remarque, Erich Maria 1898-1970............DLB-56; CDWLB-2
Remington, Frederic 1861-1909 .............DLB-12, 186, 188
Remizov, Aleksei Mikhailovich 1877-1957......................DLB-295
Renaud, Jacques 1943- ...........DLB-60
Renault, Mary 1905-1983...............Y-83
Rendell, Ruth (Barbara Vine) 1930-....................DLB-87, 276
Rensselaer, Maria van Cortlandt van 1645-1689 ................DLB-200
Repplier, Agnes 1855-1950............DLB-221
Reshetnikov, Fedor Mikhailovich 1841-1871......................DLB-238
Rettenbacher, Simon 1634-1706........DLB-168
Retz, Jean-François-Paul de Gondi, cardinal de 1613-1679 ..........DLB-268
Reuchlin, Johannes 1455-1522 .....DLB-179
Reuter, Christian 1665-after 1712........DLB-168
Fleming H. Revell Company ..........DLB-49
Reverdy, Pierre 1889-1960............DLB-258
Reuter, Fritz 1810-1874..............DLB-129
Reuter, Gabriele 1859-1941 ............DLB-66
Reventlow, Franziska Gräfin zu 1871-1918......................DLB-66
Review of Reviews Office............DLB-112

Rexroth, Kenneth 1905-1982
     .......DLB-16, 48, 165, 212; Y-82; CDALB-1
    The Commercialization of the Image of Revolt ...................DLB-16
Rey, H. A. 1898-1977................DLB-22
Reynal and Hitchcock ...............DLB-46
Reynolds, G. W. M. 1814-1879 .........DLB-21
Reynolds, John Hamilton 1794-1852 .....DLB-96
Reynolds, Sir Joshua 1723-1792 ........DLB-104
Reynolds, Mack 1917-1983.............DLB-8
Reznikoff, Charles 1894-1976........DLB-28, 45
Rhetoric
    Continental European Rhetoricians, 1400-1600, and Their Influence in Reaissance England ........DLB-236
    A Finding Guide to Key Works on Microfilm...............DLB-236
    Glossary of Terms and Definitions of Rhetoic and Logic ..........DLB-236
Rhett, Robert Barnwell 1800-1876 ......DLB-43
Rhode, John 1884-1964 ..............DLB-77
Rhodes, Eugene Manlove 1869-1934....DLB-256
Rhodes, James Ford 1848-1927..........DLB-47
Rhodes, Richard 1937- .............DLB-185
Rhys, Jean 1890-1979
    .....DLB-36, 117, 162; CDBLB-7; CDWLB-3
Ribeiro, Bernadim fl. ca. 1475/1482-1526/1544 ......DLB-287
Ricardo, David 1772-1823 .........DLB-107, 158
Ricardou, Jean 1932- ..............DLB-83
Rice, Anne (A. N. Roquelare, Anne Rampling) 1941- .....................DLB-292
Rice, Christopher 1978- ............DLB-292
Rice, Elmer 1892-1967 ..............DLB-4, 7
Rice, Grantland 1880-1954 .........DLB-29, 171
Rich, Adrienne 1929- ....DLB-5, 67; CDALB-7
Richard, Mark 1955- ..............DLB-234
Richard de Fournival 1201-1259 or 1260.............DLB-208
Richards, David Adams 1950- ........DLB-53
Richards, George circa 1760-1814 ......DLB-37
Richards, I. A. 1893-1979............DLB-27
Richards, Laura E. 1850-1943 ..........DLB-42
Richards, William Carey 1818-1892 .....DLB-73
Grant Richards [publishing house] .....DLB-112
Richardson, Charles F. 1851-1913 ......DLB-71
Richardson, Dorothy M. 1873-1957 ......DLB-36
    The Novels of Dorothy Richardson (1918), by May Sinclair.........DLB-36
Richardson, Henry Handel (Ethel Florence Lindesay Robertson) 1870-1946.................DLB-197, 230
Richardson, Jack 1935- ..............DLB-7
Richardson, John 1796-1852 ..........DLB-99
Richardson, Samuel 1689-1761...........DLB-39, 154; CDBLB-2
    Introductory Letters from the Second Edition of *Pamela* (1741)........DLB-39
    Postscript to [the Third Edition of] *Clarissa* (1751)............DLB-39

Preface to the First Edition of *Pamela* (1740) ...............DLB-39
Preface to the Third Edition of *Clarissa* (1751) [excerpt] .........DLB-39
Preface to Volume 1 of *Clarissa* (1747).....................DLB-39
Preface to Volume 3 of *Clarissa* (1748).....................DLB-39
Richardson, Willis 1889-1977...........DLB-51
Riche, Barnabe 1542-1617 ............DLB-136
Richepin, Jean 1849-1926.............DLB-192
Richler, Mordecai 1931-2001 ..........DLB-53
Richter, Conrad 1890-1968 .........DLB-9, 212
Richter, Hans Werner 1908-1993 .......DLB-69
Richter, Johann Paul Friedrich 1763-1825.............DLB-94; CDWLB-2
Joseph Rickerby [publishing house] .....DLB-106
Rickword, Edgell 1898-1982 ...........DLB-20
Riddell, Charlotte 1832-1906..........DLB-156
Riddell, John (see Ford, Corey)
Ridge, John Rollin 1827-1867..........DLB-175
Ridge, Lola 1873-1941 ..............DLB-54
Ridge, William Pett 1859-1930.........DLB-135
Riding, Laura (see Jackson, Laura Riding)
Ridler, Anne 1912- ..............DLB-27
Ridruego, Dionisio 1912-1975 .........DLB-108
Riel, Louis 1844-1885................DLB-99
Riemer, Johannes 1648-1714 .........DLB-168
Rifbjerg, Klaus 1931- ..............DLB-214
Riffaterre, Michael 1924- ..........DLB-67
A Conversation between William Riggan and Janette Turner Hospital.......Y-02
Riggs, Lynn 1899-1954 .............DLB-175
Riis, Jacob 1849-1914 ..............DLB-23
John C. Riker [publishing house] ........DLB-49
Riley, James 1777-1840 .............DLB-183
Riley, John 1938-1978................DLB-40
Rilke, Rainer Maria 1875-1926.............DLB-81; CDWLB-2
Rimanelli, Giose 1926- .............DLB-177
Rimbaud, Jean-Nicolas-Arthur 1854-1891 ....................DLB-217
Rinehart and Company ...............DLB-46
Ringuet 1895-1960 .................DLB-68
Ringwood, Gwen Pharis 1910-1984......DLB-88
Rinser, Luise 1911- ..............DLB-69
Ríos, Alberto 1952- .............DLB-122
Ríos, Isabella 1948- ............DLB-82
Ripley, Arthur 1895-1961.............DLB-44
Ripley, George 1802-1880 .....DLB-1, 64, 73, 235
The Rising Glory of America: Three Poems ..................DLB-37
The Rising Glory of America: Written in 1771 (1786), by Hugh Henry Brackenridge and Philip Freneau ..............DLB-37
Riskin, Robert 1897-1955.............DLB-26
Risse, Heinz 1898- .............DLB-69
Rist, Johann 1607-1667 .............DLB-164

| | | |
|---|---|---|
| Ristikivi, Karl 1912-1977 | DLB-220 |
| Ritchie, Anna Mowatt 1819-1870 | DLB-3, 250 |
| Ritchie, Anne Thackeray 1837-1919 | DLB-18 |
| Ritchie, Thomas 1778-1854 | DLB-43 |
| The Ritz Paris Hemingway Award | Y-85 |
| Mario Varga Llosa's Acceptance Speech | Y-85 |
| Rivard, Adjutor 1868-1945 | DLB-92 |
| Rive, Richard 1931-1989 | DLB-125, 225 |
| Rivera, José 1955- | DLB-249 |
| Rivera, Marina 1942- | DLB-122 |
| Rivera, Tomás 1935-1984 | DLB-82 |
| Rivers, Conrad Kent 1933-1968 | DLB-41 |
| Riverside Press | DLB-49 |
| Rivington, James circa 1724-1802 | DLB-43 |
| Charles Rivington [publishing house] | DLB-154 |
| Rivkin, Allen 1903-1990 | DLB-26 |
| Roa Bastos, Augusto 1917- | DLB-113 |
| Robbe-Grillet, Alain 1922- | DLB-83 |
| Robbins, Tom 1936- | Y-80 |
| Roberts, Charles G. D. 1860-1943 | DLB-92 |
| Roberts, Dorothy 1906-1993 | DLB-88 |
| Roberts, Elizabeth Madox 1881-1941 | DLB-9, 54, 102 |
| Roberts, John (see Swynnerton, Thomas) |
| Roberts, Keith 1935-2000 | DLB-261 |
| Roberts, Kenneth 1885-1957 | DLB-9 |
| Roberts, Michèle 1949- | DLB-231 |
| Roberts, Theodore Goodridge 1877-1953 | DLB-92 |
| Roberts, Ursula Wyllie (see Miles, Susan) |
| Roberts, William 1767-1849 | DLB-142 |
| James Roberts [publishing house] | DLB-154 |
| Roberts Brothers | DLB-49 |
| A. M. Robertson and Company | DLB-49 |
| Robertson, Ethel Florence Lindesay (see Richardson, Henry Handel) |
| Robertson, William 1721-1793 | DLB-104 |
| Robin, Leo 1895-1984 | DLB-265 |
| Robins, Elizabeth 1862-1952 | DLB-197 |
| Robinson, A. Mary F. (Madame James Darmesteter, Madame Mary Duclaux) 1857-1944 | DLB-240 |
| Robinson, Casey 1903-1979 | DLB-44 |
| Robinson, Derek | Y-02 |
| Robinson, Edwin Arlington 1869-1935 | DLB-54; CDALB-3 |
| Review by Derek Robinson of George Greenfield's *Rich Dust* | Y-02 |
| Robinson, Henry Crabb 1775-1867 | DLB-107 |
| Robinson, James Harvey 1863-1936 | DLB-47 |
| Robinson, Lennox 1886-1958 | DLB-10 |
| Robinson, Mabel Louise 1874-1962 | DLB-22 |
| Robinson, Marilynne 1943- | DLB-206 |
| Robinson, Mary 1758-1800 | DLB-158 |
| Robinson, Richard circa 1545-1607 | DLB-167 |
| Robinson, Therese 1797-1870 | DLB-59, 133 |
| Robison, Mary 1949- | DLB-130 |
| Roblès, Emmanuel 1914-1995 | DLB-83 |
| Roccatagliata Ceccardi, Ceccardo 1871-1919 | DLB-114 |
| Rocha, Adolfo Correira da (see Torga, Miguel) |
| Roche, Billy 1949- | DLB-233 |
| Rochester, John Wilmot, Earl of 1647-1680 | DLB-131 |
| Rochon, Esther 1948- | DLB-251 |
| Rock, Howard 1911-1976 | DLB-127 |
| Rockwell, Norman Perceval 1894-1978 | DLB-188 |
| Rodgers, Carolyn M. 1945- | DLB-41 |
| Rodgers, W. R. 1909-1969 | DLB-20 |
| Rodney, Lester 1911- | DLB-241 |
| Rodríguez, Claudio 1934-1999 | DLB-134 |
| Rodríguez, Joe D. 1943- | DLB-209 |
| Rodríguez, Luis J. 1954- | DLB-209 |
| Rodriguez, Richard 1944- | DLB-82, 256 |
| Rodríguez Julia, Edgardo 1946- | DLB-145 |
| Roe, E. P. 1838-1888 | DLB-202 |
| Roethke, Theodore 1908-1963 | DLB-5, 206; CDALB-1 |
| Rogers, Jane 1952- | DLB-194 |
| Rogers, Pattiann 1940- | DLB-105 |
| Rogers, Samuel 1763-1855 | DLB-93 |
| Rogers, Will 1879-1935 | DLB-11 |
| Rohmer, Sax 1883-1959 | DLB-70 |
| Roiphe, Anne 1935- | Y-80 |
| Rojas, Arnold R. 1896-1988 | DLB-82 |
| Rojas, Fernando de ca. 1475-1541 | DLB-286 |
| Rolfe, Frederick William 1860-1913 | DLB-34, 156 |
| Rolland, Romain 1866-1944 | DLB-65 |
| Rolle, Richard circa 1290-1300 - 1340 | DLB-146 |
| Rölvaag, O. E. 1876-1931 | DLB-9, 212 |
| Romains, Jules 1885-1972 | DLB-65 |
| A. Roman and Company | DLB-49 |
| *Roman de la Rose:* Guillaume de Lorris 1200/1205-circa 1230, Jean de Meun 1235-1240-circa 1305 | DLB-208 |
| Romano, Lalla 1906-2001 | DLB-177 |
| Romano, Octavio 1923- | DLB-122 |
| Rome, Harold 1908-1993 | DLB-265 |
| Romero, Leo 1950- | DLB-122 |
| Romero, Lin 1947- | DLB-122 |
| Romero, Orlando 1945- | DLB-82 |
| Rook, Clarence 1863-1915 | DLB-135 |
| Roosevelt, Theodore 1858-1919 | DLB-47, 186, 275 |
| Root, Waverley 1903-1982 | DLB-4 |
| Root, William Pitt 1941- | DLB-120 |
| Roquebrune, Robert de 1889-1978 | DLB-68 |
| Rorty, Richard 1931- | DLB-246, 279 |
| Rosa, João Guimarães 1908-1967 | DLB-113 |
| Rosales, Luis 1910-1992 | DLB-134 |
| Roscoe, William 1753-1831 | DLB-163 |
| Rose, Reginald 1920-2002 | DLB-26 |
| Rose, Wendy 1948- | DLB-175 |
| Rosegger, Peter 1843-1918 | DLB-129 |
| Rosei, Peter 1946- | DLB-85 |
| Rosen, Norma 1925- | DLB-28 |
| Rosenbach, A. S. W. 1876-1952 | DLB-140 |
| Rosenbaum, Ron 1946- | DLB-185 |
| Rosenbaum, Thane 1960- | DLB-299 |
| Rosenberg, Isaac 1890-1918 | DLB-20, 216 |
| Rosenfeld, Isaac 1918-1956 | DLB-28 |
| Rosenthal, Harold 1914-1999 | DLB-241 |
| Jimmy, Red, and Others: Harold Rosenthal Remembers the Stars of the Press Box | Y-01 |
| Rosenthal, M. L. 1917-1996 | DLB-5 |
| Rosenwald, Lessing J. 1891-1979 | DLB-187 |
| Ross, Alexander 1591-1654 | DLB-151 |
| Ross, Harold 1892-1951 | DLB-137 |
| Ross, Jerry 1926-1955 | DLB-265 |
| Ross, Leonard Q. (see Rosten, Leo) |
| Ross, Lillian 1927- | DLB-185 |
| Ross, Martin 1862-1915 | DLB-135 |
| Ross, Sinclair 1908-1996 | DLB-88 |
| Ross, W. W. E. 1894-1966 | DLB-88 |
| Rosselli, Amelia 1930-1996 | DLB-128 |
| Rossen, Robert 1908-1966 | DLB-26 |
| Rosset, Barney | Y-02 |
| Rossetti, Christina 1830-1894 | DLB-35, 163, 240 |
| Rossetti, Dante Gabriel 1828-1882 | DLB-35; CDBLB-4 |
| The Stealthy School of Criticism (1871) | DLB-35 |
| Rossner, Judith 1935- | DLB-6 |
| Rostand, Edmond 1868-1918 | DLB-192 |
| Rosten, Leo 1908-1997 | DLB-11 |
| Rostenberg, Leona 1908- | DLB-140 |
| Rostopchina, Evdokiia Petrovna 1811-1858 | DLB-205 |
| Rostovsky, Dimitrii 1651-1709 | DLB-150 |
| Rota, Bertram 1903-1966 | DLB-201 |
| Bertram Rota and His Bookshop | Y-91 |
| Roth, Gerhard 1942- | DLB-85, 124 |
| Roth, Henry 1906?-1995 | DLB-28 |
| Roth, Joseph 1894-1939 | DLB-85 |
| Roth, Philip 1933- | DLB-2, 28, 173; Y-82; CDALB-6 |
| Rothenberg, Jerome 1931- | DLB-5, 193 |
| Rothschild Family | DLB-184 |
| Rotimi, Ola 1938- | DLB-125 |
| Rotrou, Jean 1609-1650 | DLB-268 |
| Routhier, Adolphe-Basile 1839-1920 | DLB-99 |
| Routier, Simone 1901-1987 | DLB-88 |
| George Routledge and Sons | DLB-106 |
| Roversi, Roberto 1923- | DLB-128 |
| Rowe, Elizabeth Singer 1674-1737 | DLB-39, 95 |
| Rowe, Nicholas 1674-1718 | DLB-84 |

# Cumulative Index

Rowlands, Samuel circa 1570-1630......DLB-121
Rowlandson, Mary
   circa 1637-circa 1711..........DLB-24, 200
Rowley, William circa 1585-1626.......DLB-58
Rowling, J. K.
   The Harry Potter Phenomenon.........Y-99
Rowse, A. L. 1903-1997 .............DLB-155
Rowson, Susanna Haswell
   circa 1762-1824.................DLB-37, 200
Roy, Camille 1870-1943 ...............DLB-92
The G. Ross Roy Scottish Poetry Collection
   at the University of South Carolina......Y-89
Roy, Gabrielle 1909-1983..............DLB-68
Roy, Jules 1907-2000...................DLB-83
The Royal Court Theatre and the English
   Stage Company ..................DLB-13
The Royal Court Theatre and the New
   Drama .........................DLB-10
The Royal Shakespeare Company
   at the Swan......................Y-88
Royall, Anne Newport 1769-1854 ...DLB-43, 248
Royce, Josiah 1855-1916.............DLB-270
The Roycroft Printing Shop ............DLB-49
Royde-Smith, Naomi 1875-1964.......DLB-191
Royster, Vermont 1914-1996 .........DLB-127
Richard Royston [publishing house]......DLB-170
Rozanov, Vasilii Vasil'evich
   1856-1919......................DLB-295
Różewicz, Tadeusz 1921- ............DLB-232
Ruark, Gibbons 1941- ..............DLB-120
Ruban, Vasilii Grigorevich 1742-1795 ...DLB-150
Rubens, Bernice 1928- ..........DLB-14, 207
Rubina, Dina Il'inichna 1953- .......DLB-285
Rubinshtein, Lev Semenovich 1947- ...DLB-285
Rudd and Carleton....................DLB-49
Rudd, Steele (Arthur Hoey Davis) .....DLB-230
Rudkin, David 1936- ...............DLB-13
Rudnick, Paul 1957- ...............DLB-266
Rudnicki, Adolf 1909-1990...........DLB-299
Rudolf von Ems circa 1200-circa 1254 ...DLB-138
Ruffin, Josephine St. Pierre 1842-1924 ....DLB-79
Ruganda, John 1941- ..............DLB-157
Ruggles, Henry Joseph 1813-1906 .......DLB-64
Ruiz de Burton, María Amparo
   1832-1895 .................DLB-209, 221
Rukeyser, Muriel 1913-1980 ...........DLB-48
Rule, Jane 1931- ..................DLB-60
Rulfo, Juan 1918-1986 .....DLB-113; CDWLB-3
Rumaker, Michael 1932- ............DLB-16
Rumens, Carol 1944- ..............DLB-40
Rummo, Paul-Eerik 1942- ..........DLB-232
Runyon, Damon
   1880-1946 ...............DLB-11, 86, 171
*Ruodlieb* circa 1050-1075 ...........DLB-148
Rush, Benjamin 1746-1813............DLB-37
Rush, Rebecca 1779-?...............DLB-200
Rushdie, Salman 1947- ............DLB-194

Rusk, Ralph L. 1888-1962 ...........DLB-103
Ruskin, John
   1819-1900......DLB-55, 163, 190; CDBLB-4
Russ, Joanna 1937- .................DLB-8
Russell, Benjamin 1761-1845 ...........DLB-43
Russell, Bertrand 1872-1970 ......DLB-100, 262
Russell, Charles Edward 1860-1941......DLB-25
Russell, Charles M. 1864-1926........DLB-188
Russell, Eric Frank 1905-1978 ........DLB-255
Russell, Fred 1906-2003.............DLB-241
Russell, George William (see AE)
Russell, Countess Mary Annette Beauchamp
   (see Arnim, Elizabeth von)
Russell, Willy 1947- ..............DLB-233
B. B. Russell and Company ............DLB-49
R. H. Russell and Son ................DLB-49
Rutebeuf flourished 1249-1277.........DLB-208
Rutherford, Mark 1831-1913 ...........DLB-18
Ruxton, George Frederick
   1821-1848 .....................DLB-186
R-va, Zeneida (see Gan, Elena Andreevna)
Ryan, James 1952- ................DLB-267
Ryan, Michael 1946- ..................Y-82
Ryan, Oscar 1904- .................DLB-68
Rybakov, Anatolii Naumovich
   1911-1994......................DLB-302
Ryder, Jack 1871-1936 ..............DLB-241
Ryga, George 1932-1987 ..............DLB-60
Rylands, Enriqueta Augustina Tennant
   1843-1908 .....................DLB-184
Rylands, John 1801-1888 .............DLB-184
Ryle, Gilbert 1900-1976 .............DLB-262
Ryleev, Kondratii Fedorovich
   1795-1826......................DLB-205
Rymer, Thomas 1643?-1713...........DLB-101
Ryskind, Morrie 1895-1985 ............DLB-26
Rzhevsky, Aleksei Andreevich
   1737-1804 .....................DLB-150

# S

The Saalfield Publishing Company ......DLB-46
Saba, Umberto 1883-1957 ...........DLB-114
Sábato, Ernesto 1911- ....DLB-145; CDWLB-3
Saberhagen, Fred 1930- .............DLB-8
Sabin, Joseph 1821-1881.............DLB-187
Sacer, Gottfried Wilhelm 1635-1699 ....DLB-168
Sachs, Hans 1494-1576......DLB-179; CDWLB-2
Sá-Carneiro, Mário de 1890-1916 ......DLB-287
Sack, John 1930- .................DLB-185
Sackler, Howard 1929-1982 ............DLB-7
Sackville, Lady Margaret 1881-1963 ....DLB-240
Sackville, Thomas 1536-1608 and
   Norton, Thomas 1532-1584........DLB-62
Sackville, Thomas 1536-1608..........DLB-132
Sackville-West, Edward 1901-1965 .....DLB-191
Sackville-West, V. 1892-1962........DLB-34, 195

Sá de Miranda, Francisco de
   1481-1588?....................DLB-287
Sadlier, Mary Anne 1820-1903.........DLB-99
D. and J. Sadlier and Company ........DLB-49
Sadoff, Ira 1945- .................DLB-120
Sadoveanu, Mihail 1880-1961 ........DLB-220
Sadur, Nina Nikolaevna 1950- .......DLB-285
Sáenz, Benjamin Alire 1954- ........DLB-209
Saenz, Jaime 1921-1986 .......DLB-145, 283
Saffin, John circa 1626-1710 .........DLB-24
Sagan, Françoise 1935- .............DLB-83
Sage, Robert 1899-1962 ..............DLB-4
Sagel, Jim 1947- ..................DLB-82
Sagendorph, Robb Hansell 1900-1970 ....DLB-137
Sahagún, Carlos 1938- ............DLB-108
Sahkomaapii, Piitai (see Highwater, Jamake)
Sahl, Hans 1902-1993................DLB-69
Said, Edward W. 1935- .............DLB-67
Saigyō 1118-1190 ..................DLB-203
Saiko, George 1892-1962 .............DLB-85
Sainte-Beuve, Charles-Augustin
   1804-1869 .....................DLB-217
Saint-Exupéry, Antoine de 1900-1944 ....DLB-72
St. John, J. Allen 1872-1957 ..........DLB-188
St John, Madeleine 1942- ..........DLB-267
St. Johns, Adela Rogers 1894-1988......DLB-29
St. Omer, Garth 1931- .............DLB-117
Saint Pierre, Michel de 1916-1987 ......DLB-83
St. Dominic's Press ................DLB-112
The St. John's College Robert Graves Trust ..Y-96
St. Martin's Press ..................DLB-46
*St. Nicholas* 1873-1881 .................DS-13
Saintsbury, George 1845-1933 .......DLB-57, 149
   "Modern English Prose" (1876)......DLB-57
   The Present State of the English
     Novel (1892), ................DLB-18
Saiokuken Sōchō 1448-1532..........DLB-203
Saki (see Munro, H. H.)
Salaam, Kalamu ya 1947- ..........DLB-38
Šalamun, Tomaž 1941- ....DLB-181; CDWLB-4
Salas, Floyd 1931- .................DLB-82
Sálaz-Marquez, Rubén 1935- ........DLB-122
Salemson, Harold J. 1910-1988 .........DLB-4
Salesbury, William 1520?-1584? .......DLB-281
Salinas, Luis Omar 1937- ...........DLB-82
Salinas, Pedro 1891-1951 ............DLB-134
Salinger, J. D.
   1919- ........DLB-2, 102, 173; CDALB-1
Salkey, Andrew 1928- .............DLB-125
Sallust circa 86 B.C.-35 B.C.
   .....................DLB-211; CDWLB-1
Salt, Waldo 1914-1987 ...............DLB-44
Salter, James 1925- ...............DLB-130
Salter, Mary Jo 1954- .............DLB-120
Saltus, Edgar 1855-1921.............DLB-202

Saltykov, Mikhail Evgrafovich
   1826-1889 .......................DLB-238

Salustri, Carlo Alberto (see Trilussa)

Salverson, Laura Goodman 1890-1970 ....DLB-92

Samain, Albert 1858-1900 ...............DLB-217

Sampson, Richard Henry (see Hull, Richard)

Samuels, Ernest 1903-1996 ..............DLB-111

Sanborn, Franklin Benjamin
   1831-1917 ...................DLB-1, 223

Sánchez de Arévalo, Rodrigo
   1404-1470 .......................DLB-286

Sánchez, Luis Rafael 1936- ............DLB-145

Sánchez, Philomeno "Phil" 1917- ......DLB-122

Sánchez, Ricardo 1941-1995 ............DLB-82

Sánchez, Saúl 1943- ...................DLB-209

Sanchez, Sonia 1934- ..............DLB-41; DS-8

Sand, George 1804-1876 ..........DLB-119, 192

Sandburg, Carl
   1878-1967 ............DLB-17, 54; CDALB-3

Sandel, Cora (Sara Fabricius)
   1880-1974 .......................DLB-297

Sandemose, Aksel 1899-1965............DLB-297

Sanders, Edward 1939- ............DLB-16, 244

Sanderson, Robert 1587-1663 ...........DLB-281

Sandoz, Mari 1896-1966 ..............DLB-9, 212

Sandwell, B. K. 1876-1954 ..............DLB-92

Sandy, Stephen 1934- .................DLB-165

Sandys, George 1578-1644............DLB-24, 121

Sangster, Charles 1822-1893 ............DLB-99

Sanguineti, Edoardo 1930- .............DLB-128

Sanjōnishi Sanetaka 1455-1537 .........DLB-203

San Pedro, Diego de fl. ca. 1492 ........DLB-286

Sansay, Leonora ?-after 1823............DLB-200

Sansom, William 1912-1976.............DLB-139

Santayana, George
   1863-1952 ......DLB-54, 71, 246, 270; DS-13

Santiago, Danny 1911-1988.............DLB-122

Santillana, Marqués de (Íñigo López de Mendoza)
   1398-1458 .......................DLB-286

Santmyer, Helen Hooven 1895-1986........ Y-84

Sanvitale, Francesca 1928- ............DLB-196

Sapidus, Joannes 1490-1561............DLB-179

Sapir, Edward 1884-1939................DLB-92

Sapper (see McNeile, Herman Cyril)

Sappho circa 620 B.C.-circa 550 B.C.
   ...................... DLB-176; CDWLB-1

Saramago, José 1922- ..........DLB-287; Y-98

   Nobel Lecture 1998: How Characters
   Became the Masters and the Author
   Their Apprentice ................. Y-98

Sarban (John W. Wall) 1910-1989 ......DLB-255

Sardou, Victorien 1831-1908............DLB-192

Sarduy, Severo 1937-1993 ..............DLB-113

Sargent, Pamela 1948- ..................DLB-8

Saro-Wiwa, Ken 1941- ................DLB-157

Saroyan, Aram
   Rites of Passage [on William Saroyan] ... Y-83

Saroyan, William
   1908-1981 ..... DLB-7, 9, 86; Y-81; CDALB-7

Sarraute, Nathalie 1900-1999............DLB-83

Sarrazin, Albertine 1937-1967 ...........DLB-83

Sarris, Greg 1952- ....................DLB-175

Sarton, May 1912-1995 ...........DLB-48; Y-81

Sartre, Jean-Paul 1905-1980..........DLB-72, 296

Sassoon, Siegfried
   1886-1967 ............DLB-20, 191; DS-18

   A Centenary Essay .................. Y-86

   Tributes from Vivien F. Clarke and
   Michael Thorpe ................. Y-86

Sata Ineko 1904- ....................DLB-180

Saturday Review Press .................DLB-46

Saunders, James 1925- .................DLB-13

Saunders, John Monk 1897-1940 .........DLB-26

Saunders, Margaret Marshall
   1861-1947 ........................DLB-92

Saunders and Otley ...................DLB-106

Saussure, Ferdinand de 1857-1913 .......DLB-242

Savage, James 1784-1873 ...............DLB-30

Savage, Marmion W. 1803?-1872 ........DLB-21

Savage, Richard 1697?-1743.............DLB-95

Savard, Félix-Antoine 1896-1982.........DLB-68

Savery, Henry 1791-1842 ...............DLB-230

Saville, (Leonard) Malcolm 1901-1982 ...DLB-160

Savinio, Alberto 1891-1952 ............DLB-264

Sawyer, Robert J. 1960- ...............DLB-251

Sawyer, Ruth 1880-1970 ................DLB-22

Sayers, Dorothy L.
   1893-1957 .... DLB-10, 36, 77, 100; CDBLB-6

   The Dorothy L. Sayers Society ......... Y-98

Sayle, Charles Edward 1864-1924.......DLB-184

Sayles, John Thomas 1950- ............DLB-44

Sbarbaro, Camillo 1888-1967 ..........DLB-114

Scalapino, Leslie 1947- ...............DLB-193

Scannell, Vernon 1922- ................DLB-27

Scarry, Richard 1919-1994 ..............DLB-61

Schack, Hans Egede 1820-1859 ..........DLB-300

Schaefer, Jack 1907-1991 ...............DLB-212

Schaeffer, Albrecht 1885-1950...........DLB-66

Schaeffer, Susan Fromberg 1941- ...DLB-28, 299

Schaff, Philip 1819-1893 ................ DS-13

Schaper, Edzard 1908-1984 .............DLB-69

Scharf, J. Thomas 1843-1898............DLB-47

Schede, Paul Melissus 1539-1602 ........DLB-179

Scheffel, Joseph Viktor von 1826-1886 ...DLB-129

Scheffler, Johann 1624-1677.............DLB-164

Schelling, Friedrich Wilhelm Joseph von
   1775-1854 .......................DLB-90

Scherer, Wilhelm 1841-1886 ............DLB-129

Scherfig, Hans 1905-1979...............DLB-214

Schickele, René 1883-1940 ..............DLB-66

Schiff, Dorothy 1903-1989 ..............DLB-127

Schiller, Friedrich
   1759-1805 ..............DLB-94; CDWLB-2

Schirmer, David 1623-1687 .............DLB-164

Schlaf, Johannes 1862-1941 .............DLB-118

Schlegel, August Wilhelm 1767-1845 .....DLB-94

Schlegel, Dorothea 1763-1839 ...........DLB-90

Schlegel, Friedrich 1772-1829............DLB-90

Schleiermacher, Friedrich 1768-1834 .....DLB-90

Schlesinger, Arthur M., Jr. 1917- .......DLB-17

Schlumberger, Jean 1877-1968 ..........DLB-65

Schmid, Eduard Hermann Wilhelm
   (see Edschmid, Kasimir)

Schmidt, Arno 1914-1979 ...............DLB-69

Schmidt, Johann Kaspar (see Stirner, Max)

Schmidt, Michael 1947- ................DLB-40

Schmidtbonn, Wilhelm August
   1876-1952 ......................DLB-118

Schmitz, Aron Hector (see Svevo, Italo)

Schmitz, James H. 1911-1981 ............DLB-8

Schnabel, Johann Gottfried 1692-1760....DLB-168

Schnackenberg, Gjertrud 1953- ........DLB-120

Schnitzler, Arthur
   1862-1931 .........DLB-81, 118; CDWLB-2

Schnurre, Wolfdietrich 1920-1989........DLB-69

Schocken Books......................DLB-46

Scholartis Press .....................DLB-112

Scholderer, Victor 1880-1971...........DLB-201

The Schomburg Center for Research
   in Black Culture ..................DLB-76

Schönbeck, Virgilio (see Giotti, Virgilio)

Schönherr, Karl 1867-1943 .............DLB-118

Schoolcraft, Jane Johnston 1800-1841 ....DLB-175

School Stories, 1914-1960 ..............DLB-160

Schopenhauer, Arthur 1788-1860 ........DLB-90

Schopenhauer, Johanna 1766-1838 .......DLB-90

Schorer, Mark 1908-1977................DLB-103

Schottelius, Justus Georg 1612-1676 .....DLB-164

Schouler, James 1839-1920 .............DLB-47

Schoultz, Solveig von 1907-1996 ........DLB-259

Schrader, Paul 1946- ..................DLB-44

Schreiner, Olive
   1855-1920 ..........DLB-18, 156, 190, 225

Schroeder, Andreas 1946- .............DLB-53

Schubart, Christian Friedrich Daniel
   1739-1791 .......................DLB-97

Schubert, Gotthilf Heinrich 1780-1860 ....DLB-90

Schücking, Levin 1814-1883 ............DLB-133

Schulberg, Budd 1914- ..... DLB-6, 26, 28; Y-81

   Excerpts from USC Presentation
   [on F. Scott Fitzgerald] ............. Y-96

F. J. Schulte and Company .............DLB-49

Schulz, Bruno 1892-1942.... DLB-215; CDWLB-4

Schulze, Hans (see Praetorius, Johannes)

Schupp, Johann Balthasar 1610-1661.....DLB-164

Schurz, Carl 1829-1906 .................DLB-23

Schuyler, George S. 1895-1977 .......DLB-29, 51

Schuyler, James 1923-1991 ...........DLB-5, 169

Schwartz, Delmore 1913-1966 ........DLB-28, 48

# Cumulative Index  DLB 302

Schwartz, Jonathan 1938- .................Y-82
Schwartz, Lynne Sharon 1939- ........DLB-218
Schwarz, Sibylle 1621-1638 ............DLB-164
Schwarz-Bart, Andre 1928- ...........DLB-299
Schwerner, Armand 1927-1999........DLB-165
Schwob, Marcel 1867-1905............DLB-123
Sciascia, Leonardo 1921-1989.............DLB-177
Science Fiction and Fantasy
   Documents in British Fantasy and
     Science Fiction................DLB-178
   Hugo Awards and Nebula Awards.....DLB-8
   The Iconography of Science-Fiction
     Art....................DLB-8
   The New Wave...................DLB-8
   Paperback Science Fiction...........DLB-8
   Science Fantasy...................DLB-8
   Science-Fiction Fandom and
     Conventions................DLB-8
   Science-Fiction Fanzines: The Time
     Binders....................DLB-8
   Science-Fiction Films................DLB-8
   Science Fiction Writers of America
     and the Nebula Award............DLB-8
   Selected Science-Fiction Magazines and
     Anthologies..................DLB-8
   A World Chronology of Important Science
     Fiction Works (1818-1979).......DLB-8
   The Year in Science Fiction
     and Fantasy.................Y-00, 01
Scot, Reginald circa 1538-1599........DLB-136
Scotellaro, Rocco 1923-1953...........DLB-128
Scott, Alicia Anne (Lady John Scott)
   1810-1900......................DLB-240
Scott, Catharine Amy Dawson
   1865-1934......................DLB-240
Scott, Dennis 1939-1991...............DLB-125
Scott, Dixon 1881-1915..................DLB-98
Scott, Duncan Campbell 1862-1947......DLB-92
Scott, Evelyn 1893-1963............DLB-9, 48
Scott, F. R. 1899-1985...................DLB-88
Scott, Frederick George 1861-1944.......DLB-92
Scott, Geoffrey 1884-1929..............DLB-149
Scott, Harvey W. 1838-1910............DLB-23
Scott, Lady Jane (see Scott, Alicia Anne)
Scott, Paul 1920-1978...........DLB-14, 207
Scott, Sarah 1723-1795.................DLB-39
Scott, Tom 1918- ......................DLB-27
Scott, Sir Walter 1771-1832
   ......DLB-93, 107, 116, 144, 159; CDBLB-3
Scott, William Bell 1811-1890..........DLB-32
Walter Scott Publishing Company
   Limited......................DLB-112
William R. Scott [publishing house]......DLB-46
Scott-Heron, Gil 1949- ................DLB-41
Scribe, Eugene 1791-1861.............DLB-192
Scribner, Arthur Hawley 1859-1932.....DS-13, 16
Scribner, Charles 1854-1930..........DS-13, 16
Scribner, Charles, Jr. 1921-1995..........Y-95

   Reminiscences....................DS-17
Charles Scribner's Sons....DLB-49; DS-13, 16, 17
   Archives of Charles Scribner's Sons.....DS-17
*Scribner's Magazine*.....................DS-13
*Scribner's Monthly*.....................DS-13
Scripps, E. W. 1854-1926..............DLB-25
Scudder, Horace Elisha 1838-1902....DLB-42, 71
Scudder, Vida Dutton 1861-1954.......DLB-71
Scudéry, Madeleine de 1607-1701.......DLB-268
Scupham, Peter 1933- ................DLB-40
Seabrook, William 1886-1945...........DLB-4
Seabury, Samuel 1729-1796............DLB-31
Seacole, Mary Jane Grant 1805-1881....DLB-166
*The Seafarer* circa 970.................DLB-146
Sealsfield, Charles (Carl Postl)
   1793-1864................DLB-133, 186
Searle, John R. 1932- ..................DLB-279
Sears, Edward I. 1819?-1876............DLB-79
Sears Publishing Company............DLB-46
Seaton, George 1911-1979.............DLB-44
Seaton, William Winston 1785-1866.....DLB-43
Martin Secker [publishing house].......DLB-112
Martin Secker, and Warburg Limited...DLB-112
The "Second Generation" Holocaust
   Novel.........................DLB-299
Sedgwick, Arthur George 1844-1915.....DLB-64
Sedgwick, Catharine Maria
   1789-1867.........DLB-1, 74, 183, 239, 243
Sedgwick, Ellery 1872-1960............DLB-91
Sedgwick, Eve Kosofsky 1950- ........DLB-246
Sedley, Sir Charles 1639-1701.........DLB-131
Seeberg, Peter 1925-1999.............DLB-214
Seeger, Alan 1888-1916...............DLB-45
Seers, Eugene (see Dantin, Louis)
Segal, Erich 1937- ......................Y-86
Segal, Lore 1928- ....................DLB-299
Šegedin, Petar 1909- .................DLB-181
Seghers, Anna 1900-1983....DLB-69; CDWLB-2
Seid, Ruth (see Sinclair, Jo)
Seidel, Frederick Lewis 1936- ............Y-84
Seidel, Ina 1885-1974..................DLB-56
Seifert, Jaroslav
   1901-1986.......DLB-215; Y-84; CDWLB-4
   Jaroslav Seifert Through the Eyes of
     the English-Speaking Reader........Y-84
   Three Poems by Jaroslav Seifert.......Y-84
Seifullina, Lidiia Nikolaevna 1889-1954...DLB-272
Seigenthaler, John 1927- ..............DLB-127
Seizin Press...........................DLB-112
Séjour, Victor 1817-1874...............DLB-50
Séjour Marcou et Ferrand, Juan Victor
   (see Séjour, Victor)
Sekowski, Józef-Julian, Baron Brambeus
   (see Senkovsky, Osip Ivanovich)
Selby, Bettina 1934- .................DLB-204
Selby, Hubert, Jr. 1928- .........DLB-2, 227

Selden, George 1929-1989.............DLB-52
Selden, John 1584-1654...............DLB-213
Selenić, Slobodan 1933-1995..........DLB-181
Self, Edwin F. 1920- ..................DLB-137
Self, Will 1961- ......................DLB-207
Seligman, Edwin R. A. 1861-1939......DLB-47
Selimović, Meša
   1910-1982............DLB-181; CDWLB-4
Sellars, Wilfrid 1912-1989.............DLB-279
Sellings, Arthur (Arthur Gordon Ley)
   1911-1968....................DLB-261
Selous, Frederick Courteney 1851-1917...DLB-174
Seltzer, Chester E. (see Muro, Amado)
Thomas Seltzer [publishing house].......DLB-46
Selvon, Sam 1923-1994.....DLB-125; CDWLB-3
Semel, Nava 1954- ...................DLB-299
Semmes, Raphael 1809-1877..........DLB-189
Senancour, Etienne de 1770-1846.......DLB-119
Sena, Jorge de 1919-1978..............DLB-287
Sendak, Maurice 1928- ...............DLB-61
Seneca the Elder
   circa 54 B.C.-circa A.D. 40........DLB-211
Seneca the Younger
   circa 1 B.C.-A.D. 65.....DLB-211; CDWLB-1
Senécal, Eva 1905- ...................DLB-92
Sengstacke, John 1912-1997...........DLB-127
Senior, Olive 1941- ..................DLB-157
Senkovsky, Osip Ivanovich
   (Józef-Julian Sekowski, Baron Brambeus)
   1800-1858....................DLB-198
Šenoa, August 1838-1881....DLB-147; CDWLB-4
Sepamla, Sipho 1932- ............DLB-157, 225
Serafimovich, Aleksandr Serafimovich
   (Aleksandr Serafimovich Popov)
   1863-1949....................DLB-272
Serao, Matilde 1856-1927.............DLB-264
Seredy, Kate 1899-1975................DLB-22
Sereni, Vittorio 1913-1983............DLB-128
William Seres [publishing house].......DLB-170
Sergeev-Tsensky, Sergei Nikolaevich (Sergei
   Nikolaevich Sergeev) 1875-1958.....DLB-272
Serling, Rod 1924-1975................DLB-26
Sernine, Daniel 1955- ................DLB-251
Serote, Mongane Wally 1944- ....DLB-125, 225
Serraillier, Ian 1912-1994.............DLB-161
Serrano, Nina 1934- .................DLB-122
Service, Robert 1874-1958..............DLB-92
Sessler, Charles 1854-1935............DLB-187
Seth, Vikram 1952- ..............DLB-120, 271
Seton, Elizabeth Ann 1774-1821.......DLB-200
Seton, Ernest Thompson
   1860-1942................DLB-92; DS-13
Seton, John circa 1509-1567...........DLB-281
Setouchi Harumi 1922- ..............DLB-182
Settle, Mary Lee 1918- .................DLB-6
Seume, Johann Gottfried 1763-1810....DLB-94
Seuse, Heinrich 1295?-1366...........DLB-179

| | | |
|---|---|---|
| Seuss, Dr. (see Geisel, Theodor Seuss) | Shaw, Henry Wheeler 1818-1885........DLB-11 | Tribute to Graham Greene...........Y-91 |
| Severianin, Igor' 1887-1941............DLB-295 | Shaw, Irwin 1913-1984......DLB-6, 102; Y-84; CDALB-1 | Sherry, Richard 1506-1551 or 1555.....DLB-236 |
| Severin, Timothy 1940- ............DLB-204 | Shaw, Joseph T. 1874-1952..........DLB-137 | Sherwood, Mary Martha 1775-1851.....DLB-163 |
| Sévigné, Marie de Rabutin Chantal, Madame de 1626-1696...........DLB-268 | "As I Was Saying," Joseph T. Shaw's Editorial Rationale in *Black Mask* (January 1927)..............DLB-137 | Sherwood, Robert E. 1896-1955...DLB-7, 26, 249 |
| Sewall, Joseph 1688-1769..............DLB-24 | | Shevyrev, Stepan Petrovich 1806-1864...DLB-205 |
| Sewall, Richard B. 1908-   ..........DLB-111 | Shaw, Mary 1854-1929..............DLB-228 | Shiel, M. P. 1865-1947................DLB-153 |
| Sewall, Samuel 1652-1730..............DLB-24 | Shaw, Robert 1927-1978..........DLB-13, 14 | Shiels, George 1886-1949..............DLB-10 |
| Sewell, Anna 1820-1878...............DLB-163 | Shaw, Robert B. 1947-................DLB-120 | Shiga Naoya 1883-1971................DLB-180 |
| Sexton, Anne 1928-1974...DLB-5, 169; CDALB-1 | Shawn, Wallace 1943-.................DLB-266 | Shiina Rinzō 1911-1973................DLB-182 |
| Seymour-Smith, Martin 1928-1998......DLB-155 | Shawn, William 1907-1992............DLB-137 | Shikishi Naishinnō 1153?-1201.........DLB-203 |
| Sgorlon, Carlo 1930-..................DLB-196 | Frank Shay [publishing house]..........DLB-46 | Shillaber, Benjamin Penhallow 1814-1890.................DLB-1, 11, 235 |
| Shaara, Michael 1929-1988............Y-83 | Shchedrin, N. (see Saltykov, Mikhail Evgrafovich) | |
| Shabel'skaia, Aleksandra Stanislavovna 1845-1921.....................DLB-238 | Shcherbakova, Galina Nikolaevna 1932- ....................DLB-285 | Shimao Toshio 1917-1986.............DLB-182 |
| | | Shimazaki Tōson 1872-1943...........DLB-180 |
| Shadwell, Thomas 1641?-1692.........DLB-80 | Shcherbina, Nikolai Fedorovich 1821-1869.....................DLB-277 | Shimose, Pedro 1940-..................DLB-283 |
| Shaffer, Anthony 1926-  .............DLB-13 | | Shine, Ted 1931-   ..................DLB-38 |
| Shaffer, Peter 1926-  ....DLB-13, 233; CDBLB-8 | Shea, John Gilmary 1824-1892..........DLB-30 | Shinkei 1406-1475....................DLB-203 |
| Shaftesbury, Anthony Ashley Cooper, Third Earl of 1671-1713..........DLB-101 | Sheaffer, Louis 1912-1993.............DLB-103 | Ship, Reuben 1915-1975................DLB-88 |
| | Sheahan, Henry Beston (see Beston, Henry) | Shirer, William L. 1904-1993.............DLB-4 |
| Shaginian, Marietta Sergeevna 1888-1982.....................DLB-272 | Shearing, Joseph 1886-1952............DLB-70 | Shirinsky-Shikhmatov, Sergii Aleksandrovich 1783-1837.....................DLB-150 |
| | Shebbeare, John 1709-1788............DLB-39 | |
| Shairp, Mordaunt 1887-1939............DLB-10 | Sheckley, Robert 1928-    .............DLB-8 | Shirley, James 1596-1666...............DLB-58 |
| Shakespeare, Nicholas 1957-...........DLB-231 | Shedd, William G. T. 1820-1894........DLB-64 | Shishkov, Aleksandr Semenovich 1753-1841.....................DLB-150 |
| Shakespeare, William 1564-1616......DLB-62, 172, 263; CDBLB-1 | Sheed, Wilfrid 1930-....................DLB-6 | |
| | Sheed and Ward [U.S.]................DLB-46 | Shockley, Ann Allen 1927-   ..........DLB-33 |
| The New Variorum Shakespeare.......Y-85 | Sheed and Ward Limited [U.K.]........DLB-112 | Sholokhov, Mikhail Aleksandrovich 1905-1984.....................DLB-272 |
| Shakespeare and Montaigne: A Symposium by Jules Furthman...............Y-02 | Sheldon, Alice B. (see Tiptree, James, Jr.) | |
| | Sheldon, Edward 1886-1946............DLB-7 | Shōno Junzō 1921-...................DLB-182 |
| $6,166,000 for a *Book!* Observations on *The Shakespeare First Folio: The History of the Book*....................Y-01 | Sheldon and Company.................DLB-49 | Shore, Arabella 1820?-1901............DLB-199 |
| | Sheller, Aleksandr Konstantinovich 1838-1900.....................DLB-238 | Shore, Louisa 1824-1895...............DLB-199 |
| Taylor-Made Shakespeare? Or Is "Shall I Die?" the Long-Lost Text of Bottom's Dream?..............Y-85 | | Short, Luke (see Glidden, Frederick Dilley) |
| | Shelley, Mary Wollstonecraft 1797-1851 .....DLB-110, 116, 159, 178; CDBLB-3 | Peter Short [publishing house]..........DLB-170 |
| | | Shorter, Dora Sigerson 1866-1918......DLB-240 |
| The Shakespeare Globe Trust.............Y-93 | Preface to *Frankenstein; or, The Modern Prometheus* (1818)........DLB-178 | Shorthouse, Joseph Henry 1834-1903.....DLB-18 |
| Shakespeare Head Press..............DLB-112 | | Short Stories |
| Shakhova, Elisaveta Nikitichna 1822-1899.....................DLB-277 | Shelley, Percy Bysshe 1792-1822......DLB-96, 110, 158; CDBLB-3 | Michael M. Rea and the Rea Award for the Short Story..............Y-97 |
| Shakhovskoi, Aleksandr Aleksandrovich 1777-1846.....................DLB-150 | Shelnutt, Eve 1941-   ................DLB-130 | The Year in Short Stories............Y-87 |
| | Shenshin (see Fet, Afanasii Afanas'evich) | The Year in the Short Story......Y-88, 90–93 |
| Shalamov, Varlam Tikhonovich 1907-1982.....................DLB-302 | Shenstone, William 1714-1763..........DLB-95 | Shōtetsu 1381-1459..................DLB-203 |
| | Shepard, Clark and Brown.............DLB-49 | Showalter, Elaine 1941-   ............DLB-67 |
| Shange, Ntozake 1948-   ..........DLB-38, 249 | Shepard, Ernest Howard 1879-1976......DLB-160 | Shreve, Anita 1946-...................DLB-292 |
| Shapcott, Thomas W. 1935-    .......DLB-289 | Shepard, Sam 1943-   ............DLB-7, 212 | Shukshin, Vasilii Makarovich 1929-1974.....................DLB-302 |
| Shapir, Ol'ga Andreevna 1850-1916.....DLB-295 | Shepard, Thomas I, 1604 or 1605-1649...DLB-24 | |
| Shapiro, Karl 1913-2000................DLB-48 | Shepard, Thomas, II, 1635-1677........DLB-24 | Shulevitz, Uri 1935-...................DLB-61 |
| Sharon Publications..................DLB-46 | Shepherd, Luke flourished 1547-1554....DLB-136 | Shulman, Max 1919-1988..............DLB-11 |
| Sharov, Vladimir Aleksandrovich 1952-   ....................DLB-285 | Sherburne, Edward 1616-1702..........DLB-131 | Shute, Henry A. 1856-1943..............DLB-9 |
| | Sheridan, Frances 1724-1766........DLB-39, 84 | Shute, Nevil (Nevil Shute Norway) 1899-1960.....................DLB-255 |
| Sharp, Margery 1905-1991............DLB-161 | Sheridan, Richard Brinsley 1751-1816..............DLB-89; CDBLB-2 | |
| Sharp, William 1855-1905..............DLB-156 | | Shuttle, Penelope 1947-   ..........DLB-14, 40 |
| Sharpe, Tom 1928-   ............DLB-14, 231 | Sherman, Francis 1871-1926...........DLB-92 | Shvarts, Evgenii L'vovich 1896-1958....DLB-272 |
| Shaw, Albert 1857-1947................DLB-91 | Sherman, Martin 1938-   ............DLB-228 | Sibbes, Richard 1577-1635.............DLB-151 |
| Shaw, George Bernard 1856-1950......DLB-10, 57, 190, CDBLB-6 | Sherriff, R. C. 1896-1975........DLB-10, 191, 233 | Sibiriak, D. (see Mamin, Dmitrii Narkisovich) |
| | Sherrod, Blackie 1919-   ............DLB-241 | Siddal, Elizabeth Eleanor 1829-1862.....DLB-199 |
| The Bernard Shaw Society............Y-99 | Sherry, Norman 1935-................DLB-155 | Sidgwick, Ethel 1877-1970.............DLB-197 |
| "Stage Censorship: The Rejected Statement" (1911) [excerpts].....DLB-10 | | Sidgwick, Henry 1838-1900............DLB-262 |
| | | Sidgwick and Jackson Limited.........DLB-112 |

# Cumulative Index

Sidney, Margaret (see Lothrop, Harriet M.)
Sidney, Mary 1561-1621 ............. DLB-167
Sidney, Sir Philip 1554-1586.. DLB-167; CDBLB-1
    An Apologie for Poetrie (the Olney edition, 1595, of Defence of Poesie) ....... DLB-167
Sidney's Press ...................... DLB-49
Sierra, Rubén 1946- ................ DLB-122
Sierra Club Books................... DLB-49
Siger of Brabant circa 1240-circa 1284 ... DLB-115
Sigourney, Lydia Huntley
    1791-1865....... DLB-1, 42, 73, 183, 239, 243
Silkin, Jon 1930-1997 ................ DLB-27
Silko, Leslie Marmon
    1948- ............ DLB-143, 175, 256, 275
Silliman, Benjamin 1779-1864........... DLB-183
Silliman, Ron 1946- ................ DLB-169
Silliphant, Stirling 1918-1996 ......... DLB-26
Sillitoe, Alan 1928- .... DLB-14, 139; CDBLB-8
    Tribute to J. B. Priestly ............. Y-84
Silman, Roberta 1934- ............... DLB-28
Silone, Ignazio (Secondino Tranquilli)
    1900-1978................... DLB-264
Silva, Beverly 1930- ................ DLB-122
Silva, Clara 1905-1976 ............... DLB-290
Silva, José Asunció 1865-1896 .......... DLB-283
Silverberg, Robert 1935- .............. DLB-8
Silverman, Kaja 1947- ................ DLB-246
Silverman, Kenneth 1936- ............. DLB-111
Simak, Clifford D. 1904-1988........... DLB-8
Simcoe, Elizabeth 1762-1850............ DLB-99
Simcox, Edith Jemima 1844-1901........ DLB-190
Simcox, George Augustus 1841-1905..... DLB-35
Sime, Jessie Georgina 1868-1958 ........ DLB-92
Simenon, Georges 1903-1989........ DLB-72; Y-89
Simic, Charles 1938- ................. DLB-105
    "Images and 'Images'" ............. DLB-105
Simionescu, Mircea Horia 1928- ....... DLB-232
Simmel, Georg 1858-1918 .............. DLB-296
Simmel, Johannes Mario 1924- ......... DLB-69
Valentine Simmes [publishing house]..... DLB-170
Simmons, Ernest J. 1903-1972 .......... DLB-103
Simmons, Herbert Alfred 1930- ........ DLB-33
Simmons, James 1933- ............... DLB-40
Simms, William Gilmore
    1806-1870............DLB-3, 30, 59, 73, 248
Simms and M'Intyre.................. DLB-106
Simon, Claude 1913- ....... DLB-83; Y-85
    Nobel Lecture ................... Y-85
Simon, Neil 1927- ................. DLB-7, 266
Simon and Schuster .................. DLB-46
Simonov, Konstantin Mikhailovich
    1915-1979..................... DLB-302
Simons, Katherine Drayton Mayrant
    1890-1969...................... Y-83
Simović, Ljubomir 1935- ............. DLB-181
Simpkin and Marshall
    [publishing house] ............... DLB-154

Simpson, Helen 1897-1940 ............. DLB-77
Simpson, Louis 1923- ............... DLB-5
Simpson, N. F. 1919- ............... DLB-13
Sims, George 1923- ............. DLB-87; Y-99
Sims, George Robert 1847-1922 ... DLB-35, 70, 135
Sinán, Rogelio 1902-1994......... DLB-145, 290
Sinclair, Andrew 1935- .............. DLB-14
Sinclair, Bertrand William 1881-1972..... DLB-92
Sinclair, Catherine 1800-1864.......... DLB-163
Sinclair, Jo 1913-1995................ DLB-28
Sinclair, Lister 1921- ............... DLB-88
Sinclair, May 1863-1946.......... DLB-36, 135
    The Novels of Dorothy Richardson (1918) ....................... DLB-36
Sinclair, Upton 1878-1968 ...... DLB-9; CDALB-5
Upton Sinclair [publishing house]....... DLB-46
Singer, Isaac Bashevis 1904-1991
    ........DLB-6, 28, 52, 278; Y-91; CDALB-1
Singer, Mark 1950- ................. DLB-185
Singmaster, Elsie 1879-1958 ........... DLB-9
Siniavsky, Andrei Donatovich (Abram Tertz)
    1925-1997..................... DLB-302
Sinisgalli, Leonardo 1908-1981.......... DLB-114
Siodmak, Curt 1902-2000.............. DLB-44
Sîrbu, Ion D. 1919-1989............... DLB-232
Siringo, Charles A. 1855-1928 .......... DLB-186
Sissman, L. E. 1928-1976 .............. DLB-5
Sisson, C. H. 1914- .................. DLB-27
Sitwell, Edith 1887-1964 ...... DLB-20; CDBLB-7
Sitwell, Osbert 1892-1969..........DLB-100, 195
Skácel, Jan 1922-1989 ............... DLB-232
Skalbe, Kārlis 1879-1945............... DLB-220
Skármeta, Antonio
    1940- ............ DLB-145; CDWLB-3
Skavronsky, A. (see Danilevsky, Grigorii Petrovich)
Skeat, Walter W. 1835-1912 ........... DLB-184
William Skeffington [publishing house] .. DLB-106
Skelton, John 1463-1529............... DLB-136
Skelton, Robin 1925-1997..........DLB-27, 53
Škéma, Antanas 1910-1961............. DLB-220
Skinner, Constance Lindsay
    1877-1939..................... DLB-92
Skinner, John Stuart 1788-1851 ......... DLB-73
Skipsey, Joseph 1832-1903 ............. DLB-35
Skou-Hansen, Tage 1925- ............ DLB-214
Skrzynecki, Peter 1945- .............. DLB-289
Škvorecký, Josef 1924- .... DLB-232; CDWLB-4
Slade, Bernard 1930- ................. DLB-53
Slamnig, Ivan 1930- ................. DLB-181
Slančeková, Božena (see Timrava)
Slataper, Scipio 1888-1915 ............. DLB-264
Slater, Patrick 1880-1951 .............. DLB-68
Slaveykov, Pencho 1866-1912 .......... DLB-147
Slaviček, Milivoj 1929- ............... DLB-181
Slavitt, David 1935- ............... DLB-5, 6

Sleigh, Burrows Willcocks Arthur
    1821-1869 ..................... DLB-99
Sleptsov, Vasilii Alekseevich 1836-1878 ...DLB-277
Slesinger, Tess 1905-1945 ............. DLB-102
Slessor, Kenneth 1901-1971 ........... DLB-260
Slick, Sam (see Haliburton, Thomas Chandler)
Sloan, John 1871-1951 ................ DLB-188
Sloane, William, Associates ........... DLB-46
Slonimsky, Mikhail Leonidovich
    1897-1972.....................DLB-272
Sluchevsky, Konstantin Konstantinovich
    1837-1904.....................DLB-277
Small, Maynard and Company ........ DLB-49
Smart, Christopher 1722-1771 ......... DLB-109
Smart, David A. 1892-1957 ............DLB-137
Smart, Elizabeth 1913-1986 ........... DLB-88
Smart, J. J. C. 1920- ................ DLB-262
Smedley, Menella Bute 1820?-1877 ..... DLB-199
William Smellie [publishing house]...... DLB-154
Smiles, Samuel 1812-1904 ............. DLB-55
Smiley, Jane 1949- .............DLB-227, 234
Smith, A. J. M. 1902-1980 ............. DLB-88
Smith, Adam 1723-1790 ........ DLB-104, 252
Smith, Adam (George Jerome Waldo
    Goodman) 1930- ............... DLB-185
Smith, Alexander 1829-1867 ...... DLB-32, 55
    "On the Writing of Essays" (1862) ... DLB-57
Smith, Amanda 1837-1915 ............. DLB-221
Smith, Betty 1896-1972................ Y-82
Smith, Carol Sturm 1938- .............. Y-81
Smith, Charles Henry 1826-1903 ....... DLB-11
Smith, Charlotte 1749-1806 ........ DLB-39, 109
Smith, Chet 1899-1973 ................DLB-171
Smith, Cordwainer 1913-1966 .......... DLB-8
Smith, Dave 1942- .................. DLB-5
    Tribute to James Dickey ............. Y-97
    Tribute to John Gardner ............. Y-82
Smith, Dodie 1896- ................. DLB-10
Smith, Doris Buchanan 1934- ......... DLB-52
Smith, E. E. 1890-1965................. DLB-8
Smith, Elihu Hubbard 1771-1798 ....... DLB-37
Smith, Elizabeth Oakes (Prince)
    (see Oakes Smith, Elizabeth)
Smith, Eunice 1757-1823............... DLB-200
Smith, F. Hopkinson 1838-1915........... DS-13
Smith, George D. 1870-1920........... DLB-140
Smith, George O. 1911-1981 ............ DLB-8
Smith, Goldwin 1823-1910............. DLB-99
Smith, H. Allen 1907-1976 ......... DLB-11, 29
Smith, Harry B. 1860-1936 ............DLB-187
Smith, Hazel Brannon 1914-1994.......DLB-127
Smith, Henry circa 1560-circa 1591 ..... DLB-136
Smith, Horatio (Horace)
    1779-1849.................. DLB-96, 116
Smith, Iain Crichton 1928-1998 ..... DLB-40, 139
Smith, J. Allen 1860-1924 ............. DLB-47

| | | |
|---|---|---|
| Smith, James 1775-1839 . . . . . . . . . . . . . . . DLB-96 | The Society for Textual Scholarship and *TEXT* . . . . . . . . . . . . . . . . . . . . . . . Y-87 | Sotheby, William 1757-1833. . . . . . . . DLB-93, 213 |
| Smith, Jessie Willcox 1863-1935 . . . . . . . . DLB-188 | | Soto, Gary 1952- . . . . . . . . . . . . . . . . . . . DLB-82 |
| Smith, John 1580-1631. . . . . . . . . . . . . . DLB-24, 30 | The Society for the History of Authorship, Reading and Publishing . . . . . . . . . . . . Y-92 | Soueif, Ahdaf 1950- . . . . . . . . . . . . . . . . DLB-267 |
| Smith, John 1618-1652. . . . . . . . . . . . . . . . DLB-252 | Söderberg, Hjalmar 1869-1941 . . . . . . . . DLB-259 | Souster, Raymond 1921- . . . . . . . . . . . . . DLB-88 |
| Smith, Josiah 1704-1781 . . . . . . . . . . . . . . . DLB-24 | Södergran, Edith 1892-1923 . . . . . . . . . . DLB-259 | The *South English Legendary* circa thirteenth-fifteenth centuries . . . . . . . . DLB-146 |
| Smith, Ken 1938- . . . . . . . . . . . . . . . . . . . DLB-40 | Soffici, Ardengo 1879-1964 . . . . . . . DLB-114, 264 | |
| Smith, Lee 1944- . . . . . . . . . . . . . DLB-143; Y-83 | Sofola, 'Zulu 1938- . . . . . . . . . . . . . . . . DLB-157 | Southerland, Ellease 1943- . . . . . . . . . . . . DLB-33 |
| Smith, Logan Pearsall 1865-1946. . . . . . . . . DLB-98 | Sokhanskaia, Nadezhda Stepanovna (Kokhanovskaia) 1823?-1884 . . . . . . . DLB-277 | Southern, Terry 1924-1995 . . . . . . . . . . . . .DLB-2 |
| Smith, Margaret Bayard 1778-1844 . . . . . . DLB-248 | | Southern Illinois University Press . . . . . . . . . Y-95 |
| Smith, Mark 1935- . . . . . . . . . . . . . . . . . . . . Y-82 | Sokolov, Sasha (Aleksandr Vsevolodovich Sokolov) 1943- . . . . . . . . . . . . . . . . . DLB-285 | Southern Literature Fellowship of Southern Writers. . . . . . . . Y-98 |
| Smith, Michael 1698-circa 1771 . . . . . . . . . DLB-31 | Solano, Solita 1888-1975 . . . . . . . . . . . . . . DLB-4 | The Fugitives and the Agrarians: The First Exhibition . . . . . . . . . . . . Y-85 |
| Smith, Pauline 1882-1959 . . . . . . . . . . . . . DLB-225 | Soldati, Mario 1906-1999. . . . . . . . . . . . . DLB-177 | |
| Smith, Red 1905-1982 . . . . . . . . . . . . DLB-29, 171 | Soledad (see Zamudio, Adela) | "The Greatness of Southern Literature": League of the South Institute for the Study of Southern Culture and History . . . . . . . . . . . . . . . . . . . . . . Y-02 |
| Smith, Roswell 1829-1892 . . . . . . . . . . . . . DLB-79 | Šoljan, Antun 1932-1993 . . . . . . . . . . . . . DLB-181 | |
| Smith, Samuel Harrison 1772-1845 . . . . . . . DLB-43 | Sollers, Philippe (Philippe Joyaux) 1936- . . . . . . . . . . . . . . . . . . . . . . . . DLB-83 | |
| Smith, Samuel Stanhope 1751-1819 . . . . . . . DLB-37 | | The Society for the Study of Southern Literature . . . . . . . . . . . . . Y-00 |
| Smith, Sarah (see Stretton, Hesba) | Sollogub, Vladimir Aleksandrovich 1813-1882 . . . . . . . . . . . . . . . . . . . . . DLB-198 | |
| Smith, Sarah Pogson 1774-1870 . . . . . . . . DLB-200 | | Southern Writers Between the Wars . . . DLB-9 |
| Smith, Seba 1792-1868. . . . . . . . . . DLB-1, 11, 243 | Sollors, Werner 1943- . . . . . . . . . . . . . . . DBL-246 | Southerne, Thomas 1659-1746 . . . . . . . . . DLB-80 |
| Smith, Stevie 1902-1971 . . . . . . . . . . . . . . . DLB-20 | Solmi, Sergio 1899-1981 . . . . . . . . . . . . . DLB-114 | Southey, Caroline Anne Bowles 1786-1854 . . . . . . . . . . . . . . . . . . . . . DLB-116 |
| Smith, Sydney 1771-1845. . . . . . . . . . . . . DLB-107 | Sologub, Fedor 1863-1927 . . . . . . . . . . . . DLB-295 | |
| Smith, Sydney Goodsir 1915-1975 . . . . . . . DLB-27 | Solomon, Carl 1928- . . . . . . . . . . . . . . . . DLB-16 | Southey, Robert 1774-1843 . . . . . DLB-93, 107, 142 |
| Smith, Sir Thomas 1513-1577 . . . . . . . . . DLB-132 | Soloukhin, Vladimir Alekseevich 1924-1997 . . . . . . . . . . . . . . . . . . . . . DLB-302 | Southwell, Robert 1561?-1595. . . . . . . . . DLB-167 |
| Smith, Wendell 1914-1972. . . . . . . . . . . . . DLB-171 | | Southworth, E. D. E. N. 1819-1899. . . . . . DLB-239 |
| Smith, William flourished 1595-1597. . . . . DLB-136 | Solov'ev, Sergei Mikhailovich 1885-1942 . . . . . . . . . . . . . . . . . . . . . DLB-295 | Sowande, Bode 1948- . . . . . . . . . . . . . . . DLB-157 |
| Smith, William 1727-1803 . . . . . . . . . . . . . DLB-31 | | Tace Sowle [publishing house]. . . . . . . . . . DLB-170 |
| *A General Idea of the College of Mirania* (1753) [excerpts] . . . . . . . . . . . . . . . DLB-31 | Solov'ev, Vladimir Sergeevich 1853-1900 . . . . . . . . . . . . . . . . . . . . . DLB-295 | Soyfer, Jura 1912-1939 . . . . . . . . . . . . . . DLB-124 |
| | | Soyinka, Wole 1934- . . . . . DLB-125; Y-86, Y-87; CDWLB-3 |
| Smith, William 1728-1793 . . . . . . . . . . . . . DLB-30 | Solstad, Dag 1941- . . . . . . . . . . . . . . . . DLB-297 | |
| Smith, William Gardner 1927-1974 . . . . . . . DLB-76 | Solway, David 1941- . . . . . . . . . . . . . . . . DLB-53 | Nobel Lecture 1986: This Past Must Address Its Present. . . . . . . . . . . . . . Y-86 |
| Smith, William Henry 1808-1872 . . . . . . . DLB-159 | Solzhenitsyn, Aleksandr Isaevich 1918- . . . . . . . . . . . . . . . . . . . . . . . DLB-302 | |
| Smith, William Jay 1918- . . . . . . . . . . . . . . DLB-5 | Solzhenitsyn and America. . . . . . . . . . . Y-85 | Spacks, Barry 1931- . . . . . . . . . . . . . . . . DLB-105 |
| Smith, Elder and Company . . . . . . . . . . . . DLB-154 | | Spalding, Frances 1950- . . . . . . . . . . . . . DLB-155 |
| Harrison Smith and Robert Haas [publishing house] . . . . . . . . . . . . . . . . DLB-46 | Some Basic Notes on Three Modern Genres: Interview, Blurb, and Obituary. . . . . . . . Y-02 | Spanish Travel Writers of the Late Middle Ages . . . . . . . . . . . . . . . DLB-286 |
| | Somerville, Edith Œnone 1858-1949. . . . . DLB-135 | |
| J. Stilman Smith and Company . . . . . . . . . DLB-49 | Somov, Orest Mikhailovich 1793-1833 . . . DLB-198 | Spark, Muriel 1918- . . . . DLB-15, 139; CDBLB-7 |
| W. B. Smith and Company . . . . . . . . . . . DLB-49 | Sønderby, Knud 1909-1966. . . . . . . . . . . . DLB-214 | Michael Sparke [publishing house] . . . . . . DLB-170 |
| W. H. Smith and Son . . . . . . . . . . . . . . . DLB-106 | Song, Cathy 1955- . . . . . . . . . . . . . . . . . DLB-169 | Sparks, Jared 1789-1866. . . . . . . . . DLB-1, 30, 235 |
| Leonard Smithers [publishing house]. . . . . DLB-112 | Sonnevi, Göran 1939- . . . . . . . . . . . . . . . DLB-257 | Sparshott, Francis 1926- . . . . . . . . . . . . . . DLB-60 |
| Smollett, Tobias 1721-1771 . . . . . . . . . . . DLB-39, 104; CDBLB-2 | Sono Ayako 1931- . . . . . . . . . . . . . . . . . DLB-182 | Späth, Gerold 1939- . . . . . . . . . . . . . . . . . DLB-75 |
| | Sontag, Susan 1933- . . . . . . . . . . . . . . DLB-2, 67 | Spatola, Adriano 1941-1988. . . . . . . . . . . DLB-128 |
| Dedication to *Ferdinand Count Fathom* (1753) . . . . . . . . . . . . . . . . . . . . . . DLB-39 | Sophocles 497/496 B.C.-406/405 B.C. . . . . . . . . . . . . . . . . . DLB-176; CDWLB-1 | Spaziani, Maria Luisa 1924- . . . . . . . . . . DLB-128 |
| | | *Specimens of Foreign Standard Literature* 1838-1842 . . . . . . . . . . . . . . . . . . . . . . DLB-1 |
| Preface to *Ferdinand Count Fathom* (1753) . . . . . . . . . . . . . . . . . . . . . . DLB-39 | Šopov, Aco 1923-1982. . . . . . . . . . . . . . . DLB-181 | |
| | Sorel, Charles ca.1600-1674 . . . . . . . . . . . DLB-268 | *The Spectator* 1828- . . . . . . . . . . . . . . . . DLB-110 |
| Preface to *Roderick Random* (1748) . . . . . DLB-39 | Sørensen, Villy 1929- . . . . . . . . . . . . . . . DLB-214 | Spedding, James 1808-1881 . . . . . . . . . . . DLB-144 |
| Smythe, Francis Sydney 1900-1949 . . . . . . DLB-195 | Sorensen, Virginia 1912-1991 . . . . . . . . . . DLB-206 | Spee von Langenfeld, Friedrich 1591-1635 . . . . . . . . . . . . . . . . . . . . . DLB-164 |
| Snelling, William Joseph 1804-1848 . . . . . DLB-202 | Sorge, Reinhard Johannes 1892-1916 . . . . DLB-118 | |
| Snellings, Rolland (see Touré, Askia Muhammad) | Sorokin, Vladimir Georgievich 1955- . . . . . . . . . . . . . . . . . . . . . . . DLB-285 | Speght, Rachel 1597-after 1630 . . . . . . . . DLB-126 |
| Snodgrass, W. D. 1926- . . . . . . . . . . . . . . . DLB-5 | | Speke, John Hanning 1827-1864 . . . . . . . DLB-166 |
| Snorri Hjartarson 1906-1986 . . . . . . . . . . DLB-293 | Sorrentino, Gilbert 1929- . . . . . DLB-5, 173; Y-80 | Spellman, A. B. 1935- . . . . . . . . . . . . . . . DLB-41 |
| Snow, C. P. 1905-1980 . . . . . DLB-15, 77; DS-17; CDBLB-7 | Sosa, Roberto 1930- . . . . . . . . . . . . . . . . DLB-290 | Spence, Catherine Helen 1825-1910 . . . . . DLB-230 |
| | Sotheby, James 1682-1742 . . . . . . . . . . . . DLB-213 | Spence, Thomas 1750-1814 . . . . . . . . . . . DLB-158 |
| Snyder, Gary 1930- . . . . . . . DLB-5, 16, 165, 212, 237, 275 | Sotheby, John 1740-1807 . . . . . . . . . . . . . DLB-213 | Spencer, Anne 1882-1975. . . . . . . . . . . DLB-51, 54 |
| | Sotheby, Samuel 1771-1842 . . . . . . . . . . . DLB-213 | Spencer, Charles, third Earl of Sunderland 1674-1722 . . . . . . . . . . . . . . . . . . . . . DLB-213 |
| Sobiloff, Hy 1912-1970. . . . . . . . . . . . . . . DLB-48 | Sotheby, Samuel Leigh 1805-1861. . . . . . . DLB-213 | Spencer, Elizabeth 1921- . . . . . . . . . . DLB-6, 218 |

Spencer, George John, Second Earl Spencer 1758-1834 ................. DLB-184
Spencer, Herbert 1820-1903 ......... DLB-57, 262
   "The Philosophy of Style" (1852) .... DLB-57
Spencer, Scott 1945- ................ Y-86
Spender, J. A. 1862-1942 ............. DLB-98
Spender, Stephen 1909-1995 ... DLB-20; CDBLB-7
Spener, Philipp Jakob 1635-1705 ....... DLB-164
Spenser, Edmund circa 1552-1599 ....... DLB-167; CDBLB-1
   Envoy from *The Shepheardes Calender* . DLB-167
   "The Generall Argument of the Whole Booke," from *The Shepheardes Calender* ........ DLB-167
   "A Letter of the Authors Expounding His Whole Intention in the Course of this Worke: Which for that It Giueth Great Light to the Reader, for the Better Vnderstanding Is Hereunto Annexed," from *The Faerie Qveene* (1590) .... DLB-167
   "To His Booke," from *The Shepheardes Calender* (1579) ... DLB-167
   "To the Most Excellent and Learned Both Orator and Poete, Mayster Gabriell Haruey, His Verie Special and Singular Good Frend E. K. Commendeth the Good Lyking of This His Labour, and the Patronage of the New Poete," from *The Shepheardes Calender* ........ DLB-167
Sperr, Martin 1944- ................ DLB-124
Spewack, Bella Cowen 1899-1990 ...... DLB-266
Spewack, Samuel 1899-1971 .......... DLB-266
Spicer, Jack 1925-1965 .......... DLB-5, 16, 193
Spiegelman, Art 1948- ............... DLB-299
Spielberg, Peter 1929- ................ Y-81
Spielhagen, Friedrich 1829-1911 ........ DLB-129
"*Spielmannsepen*" (circa 1152-circa 1500) .. DLB-148
Spier, Peter 1927- ................... DLB-61
Spillane, Mickey 1918- .............. DLB-226
Spink, J. G. Taylor 1888-1962 ......... DLB-241
Spinrad, Norman 1940- .............. DLB-8
   Tribute to Isaac Asimov............. Y-92
Spires, Elizabeth 1952- .............. DLB-120
Spitteler, Carl 1845-1924 ............. DLB-129
Spivak, Lawrence E. 1900- ........... DLB-137
Spofford, Harriet Prescott 1835-1921 ................. DLB-74, 221
Sports
   Jimmy, Red, and Others: Harold Rosenthal Remembers the Stars of the Press Box................. Y-01
   The Literature of Boxing in England through Arthur Conan Doyle ...... Y-01
   Notable Twentieth-Century Books about Sports................. DLB-241
Sprigge, Timothy L. S. 1932- ........ DLB-262
Spring, Howard 1889-1965........... DLB-191
Squibob (see Derby, George Horatio)
Squier, E. G. 1821-1888 .............. DLB-189
Stableford, Brian 1948- .............. DLB-261

Stacpoole, H. de Vere 1863-1951 ....... DLB-153
Staël, Germaine de 1766-1817 ...... DLB-119, 192
Staël-Holstein, Anne-Louise Germaine de (see Staël, Germaine de)
Staffeldt, Schack 1769-1826............ DLB-300
Stafford, Jean 1915-1979 ............ DLB-2, 173
Stafford, William 1914-1993 ........ DLB-5, 206
Stallings, Laurence 1894-1968 ........ DLB-7, 44
Stallworthy, Jon 1935- ............... DLB-40
Stampp, Kenneth M. 1912- .......... DLB-17
Stănescu, Nichita 1933-1983........... DLB-232
Stanev, Emiliyan 1907-1979 .......... DLB-181
Stanford, Ann 1916- ................. DLB-5
Stangerup, Henrik 1937-1998 ........ DLB-214
Stanihurst, Richard 1547-1618 ........ DLB-281
Stanitsky, N. (see Panaeva, Avdot'ia Iakovlevna)
Stankevich, Nikolai Vladimirovich 1813-1840 ................ DLB-198
Stanković, Borisav ("Bora") 1876-1927............. DLB-147; CDWLB-4
Stanley, Henry M. 1841-1904 ... DLB-189; DS-13
Stanley, Thomas 1625-1678 .......... DLB-131
Stannard, Martin 1947- .............. DLB-155
William Stansby [publishing house] ...... DLB-170
Stanton, Elizabeth Cady 1815-1902 ...... DLB-79
Stanton, Frank L. 1857-1927........... DLB-25
Stanton, Maura 1946- ............... DLB-120
Stapledon, Olaf 1886-1950 ......... DLB-15, 255
Star Spangled Banner Office........... DLB-49
Stark, Freya 1893-1993............... DLB-195
Starkey, Thomas circa 1499-1538 ...... DLB-132
Starkie, Walter 1894-1976 ............ DLB-195
Starkweather, David 1935- ............ DLB-7
Starrett, Vincent 1886-1974 .......... DLB-187
Stationers' Company of London, The .... DLB-170
Statius circa A.D. 45-A.D. 96 ......... DLB-211
Stead, Christina 1902-1983............ DLB-260
Stead, Robert J. C. 1880-1959 ......... DLB-92
Steadman, Mark 1930- ............... DLB-6
Stearns, Harold E. 1891-1943....... DLB-4; DS-15
Stebnitsky, M. (see Leskov, Nikolai Semenovich)
Stedman, Edmund Clarence 1833-1908 ... DLB-64
Steegmuller, Francis 1906-1994 ........ DLB-111
Steel, Flora Annie 1847-1929 ....... DLB-153, 156
Steele, Max 1922- .................... Y-80
Steele, Richard 1672-1729 .......... DLB-84, 101; CDBLB-2
Steele, Timothy 1948- ............... DLB-120
Steele, Wilbur Daniel 1886-1970 ....... DLB-86
Wallace Markfield's "Steeplechase" ....... Y-02
Steere, Richard circa 1643-1721 ........ DLB-24
Stefán frá Hvítadal (Stefán Sigurðsson) 1887-1933................. DLB-293
Stefán Guðmundsson (see Stephan G. Stephansson)
Stefán Hörður Grímsson 1919 or 1920-2002.............. DLB-293

Stefanovski, Goran 1952- .......... DLB-181
Stegner, Wallace 1909-1993 .......... DLB-9, 206, 275; Y-93
Stehr, Hermann 1864-1940 .......... DLB-66
Steig, William 1907- ................. DLB-61
Stein, Gertrude 1874-1946 ........ DLB-4, 54, 86, 228; DS-15; CDALB-4
Stein, Leo 1872-1947................. DLB-4
Stein and Day Publishers ............. DLB-46
Steinbeck, John 1902-1968 ........ DLB-7, 9, 212, 275; DS-2; CDALB-5
   John Steinbeck Research Center, San Jose State University........... Y-85
   The Steinbeck Centennial ............ Y-02
Steinem, Gloria 1934- .............. DLB-246
Steiner, George 1929- ............. DLB-67, 299
Steinhoewel, Heinrich 1411/1412-1479.... DLB-179
Steinn Steinarr (Aðalsteinn Kristmundsson) 1908-1958 ................. DLB-293
Steinunn Sigurðardóttir 1950- ........ DLB-293
Steloff, Ida Frances 1887-1989 ......... DLB-187
Stendhal 1783-1842................. DLB-119
Stephan G. Stephansson (Stefán Guðmundsson) 1853-1927 ................. DLB-293
Stephen, Leslie 1832-1904 ...... DLB-57, 144, 190
Stephen Family (Bloomsbury Group)....... DS-10
Stephens, A. G. 1865-1933 .......... DLB-230
Stephens, Alexander H. 1812-1883 ...... DLB-47
Stephens, Alice Barber 1858-1932 ...... DLB-188
Stephens, Ann 1810-1886.......... DLB-3, 73, 250
Stephens, Charles Asbury 1844?-1931 .... DLB-42
Stephens, James 1882?-1950..... DLB-19, 153, 162
Stephens, John Lloyd 1805-1852 ... DLB-183, 250
Stephens, Michael 1946- ............ DLB-234
Stephensen, P. R. 1901-1965 .......... DLB-260
Sterling, George 1869-1926 ........... DLB-54
Sterling, James 1701-1763 ............ DLB-24
Sterling, John 1806-1844 ............. DLB-116
Stern, Gerald 1925- ................. DLB-105
   "Living in Ruin" ................. DLB-105
Stern, Gladys B. 1890-1973 .......... DLB-197
Stern, Madeleine B. 1912- ......... DLB-111, 140
Stern, Richard 1928- ............. DLB-218; Y-87
Stern, Stewart 1922- ................ DLB-26
Sterne, Laurence 1713-1768 ... DLB-39; CDBLB-2
Sternheim, Carl 1878-1942......... DLB-56, 118
Sternhold, Thomas ?-1549 .......... DLB-132
Steuart, David 1747-1824 ........... DLB-213
Stevens, Henry 1819-1886 .......... DLB-140
Stevens, Wallace 1879-1955 ... DLB-54; CDALB-5
   The Wallace Stevens Society .......... Y-99
Stevenson, Anne 1933- ............. DLB-40
Stevenson, D. E. 1892-1973 ......... DLB-191
Stevenson, Lionel 1902-1973 .......... DLB-155
Stevenson, Robert Louis 1850-1894 ........ DLB-18, 57, 141, 156, 174; DS-13; CDBLB-5

"On Style in Literature: Its Technical Elements" (1885)....DLB-57
Stewart, Donald Ogden 1894-1980............DLB-4, 11, 26; DS-15
Stewart, Douglas 1913-1985.........DLB-260
Stewart, Dugald 1753-1828............DLB-31
Stewart, George, Jr. 1848-1906..........DLB-99
Stewart, George R. 1895-1980...........DLB-8
Stewart, Harold 1916-1995..........DLB-260
Stewart, J. I. M. (see Innes, Michael)
Stewart, Maria W. 1803?-1879.........DLB-239
Stewart, Randall 1896-1964...........DLB-103
Stewart, Sean 1965-................DLB-251
Stewart and Kidd Company............DLB-46
Sthen, Hans Christensen 1544-1610.....DLB-300
Stickney, Trumbull 1874-1904..........DLB-54
Stieler, Caspar 1632-1707.............DLB-164
Stifter, Adalbert 1805-1868............DLB-133; CDWLB-2
Stiles, Ezra 1727-1795................DLB-31
Still, James 1906-2001............DLB-9; Y-01
Stirling, S. M. 1953-................DLB-251
Stirner, Max 1806-1856..............DLB-129
Stith, William 1707-1755..............DLB-31
Stivens, Dal 1911-1997...............DLB-260
Elliot Stock [publishing house].........DLB-106
Stockton, Annis Boudinot 1736-1801.....DLB-200
Stockton, Frank R. 1834-1902..DLB-42, 74; DS-13
Stockton, J. Roy 1892-1972............DLB-241
Ashbel Stoddard [publishing house].......DLB-49
Stoddard, Charles Warren 1843-1909....DLB-186
Stoddard, Elizabeth 1823-1902.........DLB-202
Stoddard, Richard Henry 1825-1903...........DLB-3, 64, 250; DS-13
Stoddard, Solomon 1643-1729..........DLB-24
Stoker, Bram 1847-1912.......DLB-36, 70, 178; CDBLB-5
  On Writing *Dracula,* from the Introduction to *Dracula* (1897)...DLB-178
Frederick A. Stokes Company...........DLB-49
Stokes, Thomas L. 1898-1958...........DLB-29
Stokesbury, Leon 1945-...............DLB-120
Stolberg, Christian Graf zu 1748-1821.....DLB-94
Stolberg, Friedrich Leopold Graf zu 1750-1819.....................DLB-94
Stone, Lucy 1818-1893............DLB-79, 239
Stone, Melville 1848-1929.............DLB-25
Stone, Robert 1937-.................DLB-152
Stone, Ruth 1915-...................DLB-105
Stone, Samuel 1602-1663..............DLB-24
Stone, William Leete 1792-1844........DLB-202
Herbert S. Stone and Company..........DLB-49
Stone and Kimball....................DLB-49
Stoppard, Tom 1937-.......DLB-13, 233; Y-85; CDBLB-8
  Playwrights and Professors..........DLB-13
Storey, Anthony 1928-................DLB-14

Storey, David 1933-........DLB-13, 14, 207, 245
Storm, Theodor 1817-1888............DLB-129; CDWLB-2
Storni, Alfonsina 1892-1938............DLB-283
Story, Thomas circa 1670-1742..........DLB-31
Story, William Wetmore 1819-1895...DLB-1, 235
Storytelling: A Contemporary Renaissance...Y-84
Stoughton, William 1631-1701...........DLB-24
Stow, John 1525-1605.................DLB-132
Stow, Randolph 1935-................DLB-260
Stowe, Harriet Beecher 1811-1896......DLB-1,12, 42, 74, 189, 239, 243; CDALB-3
  The Harriet Beecher Stowe Center.......Y-00
Stowe, Leland 1899-1994...............DLB-29
Stoyanov, Dimitr Ivanov (see Elin Pelin)
Strabo 64/63 B.C.-circa A.D. 25........DLB-176
Strachey, Lytton 1880-1932......DLB-149; DS-10
  Preface to *Eminent Victorians*.........DLB-149
William Strahan [publishing house]......DLB-154
Strahan and Company.................DLB-106
Strand, Mark 1934-....................DLB-5
The Strasbourg Oaths 842..............DLB-148
Stratemeyer, Edward 1862-1930.........DLB-42
Strati, Saverio 1924-..................DLB-177
Stratton and Barnard..................DLB-49
Stratton-Porter, Gene 1863-1924................DLB-221; DS-14
Straub, Peter 1943-.....................Y-84
Strauß, Botho 1944-..................DLB-124
Strauß, David Friedrich 1808-1874......DLB-133
The Strawberry Hill Press..............DLB-154
Strawson, P. F. 1919-.................DLB-262
Streatfeild, Noel 1895-1986............DLB-160
Street, Cecil John Charles (see Rhode, John)
Street, G. S. 1867-1936................DLB-135
Street and Smith.....................DLB-49
Streeter, Edward 1891-1976............DLB-11
Streeter, Thomas Winthrop 1883-1965...DLB-140
Stretton, Hesba 1832-1911.........DLB-163, 190
Stribling, T. S. 1881-1965..............DLB-9
Der Stricker circa 1190-circa 1250.......DLB-138
Strickland, Samuel 1804-1867...........DLB-99
Strindberg, August 1849-1912..........DLB-259
Stringer, Arthur 1874-1950.............DLB-92
Stringer and Townsend.................DLB-49
Strittmatter, Erwin 1912-1994...........DLB-69
Strniša, Gregor 1930-1987..............DLB-181
Strode, William 1630-1645.............DLB-126
Strong, L. A. G. 1896-1958.............DLB-191
Strother, David Hunter (Porte Crayon) 1816-1888..................DLB-3, 248
Strouse, Jean 1945-...................DLB-111
Strugatsky, Arkadii Natanovich 1925-1991...........................DLB-302
Strugatsky, Boris Natanovich 1933-....DLB-302
Stuart, Dabney 1937-.................DLB-105

"Knots into Webs: Some Autobiographical Sources"......DLB-105
Stuart, Jesse 1906-1984......DLB-9, 48, 102; Y-84
Lyle Stuart [publishing house]..........DLB-46
Stuart, Ruth McEnery 1849?-1917......DLB-202
Stub, Ambrosius 1705-1758............DLB-300
Stubbs, Harry Clement (see Clement, Hal)
Stubenberg, Johann Wilhelm von 1619-1663......................DLB-164
Stuckenberg, Viggo 1763-1905.........DLB-300
Studebaker, William V. 1947-..........DLB-256
Studies in American Jewish Literature......Y-02
Studio..............................DLB-112
Stump, Al 1916-1995.................DLB-241
Sturgeon, Theodore 1918-1985..............DLB-8; Y-85
Sturges, Preston 1898-1959............DLB-26
Styron, William 1925-......DLB-2, 143, 299; Y-80; CDALB-6
  Tribute to James Dickey...............Y-97
Suárez, Clementina 1902-1991.........DLB-290
Suárez, Mario 1925-..................DLB-82
Such, Peter 1939-....................DLB-60
Suckling, Sir John 1609-1641?......DLB-58, 126
Suckow, Ruth 1892-1960...........DLB-9, 102
Sudermann, Hermann 1857-1928.......DLB-118
Sue, Eugène 1804-1857...............DLB-119
Sue, Marie-Joseph (see Sue, Eugène)
Suetonius circa A.D. 69-post A.D. 122...DLB-211
Suggs, Simon (see Hooper, Johnson Jones)
Sui Sin Far (see Eaton, Edith Maude)
Suits, Gustav 1883-1956.....DLB-220; CDWLB-4
Sukenick, Ronald 1932-........DLB-173; Y-81
  An Author's Response................Y-82
Sukhovo-Kobylin, Aleksandr Vasil'evich 1817-1903........................DLB-277
Suknaski, Andrew 1942-..............DLB-53
Sullivan, Alan 1868-1947..............DLB-92
Sullivan, C. Gardner 1886-1965........DLB-26
Sullivan, Frank 1892-1976.............DLB-11
Sulte, Benjamin 1841-1923.............DLB-99
Sulzberger, Arthur Hays 1891-1968.....DLB-127
Sulzberger, Arthur Ochs 1926-........DLB-127
Sulzer, Johann Georg 1720-1779........DLB-97
Sumarokov, Aleksandr Petrovich 1717-1777.......................DLB-150
Summers, Hollis 1916-.................DLB-6
Sumner, Charles 1811-1874............DLB-235
Sumner, William Graham 1840-1910....DLB-270
Henry A. Sumner [publishing house]..................DLB-49
Sundman, Per Olof 1922-1992.........DLB-257
Supervielle, Jules 1884-1960...........DLB-258
Surtees, Robert Smith 1803-1864.......DLB-21
  The R. S. Surtees Society.............Y-98
Sutcliffe, Matthew 1550?-1629.........DLB-281

Sutcliffe, William 1971- .............DLB-271

Sutherland, Efua Theodora
   1924-1996 .................. DLB-117

Sutherland, John 1919-1956 ........... DLB-68

Sutro, Alfred 1863-1933 .............. DLB-10

Svava Jakobsdóttir 1930- ........... DLB-293

Svendsen, Hanne Marie 1933- ...... DLB-214

Svevo, Italo (Ettore Schmitz)
   1861-1928 .................. DLB-264

Swados, Harvey 1920-1972 ........... DLB-2

Swain, Charles 1801-1874............ DLB-32

Swallow Press...................... DLB-46

Swan Sonnenschein Limited.......... DLB-106

Swanberg, W. A. 1907-1992........... DLB-103

Swedish Literature
   The Literature of the Modern
    Breakthrough............... DLB-259

Swenson, May 1919-1989.............. DLB-5

Swerling, Jo 1897- ................. DLB-44

Swift, Graham 1949- ................ DLB-194

Swift, Jonathan
   1667-1745 ...... DLB-39, 95, 101; CDBLB-2

Swinburne, A. C.
   1837-1909........... DLB-35, 57; CDBLB-4

   Under the Microscope (1872)........ DLB-35

Swineshead, Richard floruit circa 1350... DLB-115

Swinnerton, Frank 1884-1982........... DLB-34

Swisshelm, Jane Grey 1815-1884 ....... DLB-43

Swope, Herbert Bayard 1882-1958..... DLB-25

Swords, James ?-1844 ................ DLB-73

Swords, Thomas 1763-1843 ............ DLB-73

T. and J. Swords and Company ........ DLB-49

Swynnerton, Thomas (John Roberts)
   circa 1500-1554 ............... DLB-281

Sykes, Ella C. ?-1939 ............... DLB-174

Sylvester, Josuah 1562 or 1563-1618 ... DLB-121

Symonds, Emily Morse (see Paston, George)

Symonds, John Addington
   1840-1893 .................DLB-57, 144

   "Personal Style" (1890) .......... DLB-57

Symons, A. J. A. 1900-1941 .......... DLB-149

Symons, Arthur 1865-1945....... DLB-19, 57, 149

Symons, Julian
   1912-1994................DLB-87, 155; Y-92

   Julian Symons at Eighty............... Y-92

Symons, Scott 1933- ................ DLB-53

Synge, John Millington
   1871-1909........... DLB-10, 19; CDBLB-5

   Synge Summer School: J. M. Synge
    and the Irish Theater, Rathdrum,
    County Wiclow, Ireland .......... Y-93

Syrett, Netta 1865-1943 ...........DLB-135, 197

Szabó, Lőrinc 1900-1957 ............ DLB-215

Szabó, Magda 1917- ................ DLB-215

Szymborska, Wisława
   1923- ............DLB-232, Y-96; CDWLB-4

   Nobel Lecture 1996:
    The Poet and the World .......... Y-96

# T

Taban lo Liyong 1939?- ............. DLB-125

Tablada, José Juan 1871-1945......... DLB-290

Tabori, George 1914- ............... DLB-245

Tabucchi, Antonio 1943- ............ DLB-196

Taché, Joseph-Charles 1820-1894 ....... DLB-99

Tachihara Masaaki 1926-1980 ........ DLB-182

Tacitus circa A.D. 55-circa A.D. 117
   .................. DLB-211; CDWLB-1

Tadijanović, Dragutin 1905- ......... DLB-181

Tafdrup, Pia 1952- ................. DLB-214

Tafolla, Carmen 1951- .............. DLB-82

Taggard, Genevieve 1894-1948 ......... DLB-45

Taggart, John 1942- ................ DLB-193

Tagger, Theodor (see Bruckner, Ferdinand)

Taiheiki late fourteenth century ........ DLB-203

Tait, J. Selwin, and Sons............. DLB-49

Tait's Edinburgh Magazine 1832-1861 ..... DLB-110

The Takarazaka Revue Company .......... Y-91

Talander (see Bohse, August)

Talese, Gay 1932- ................. DLB-185

   Tribute to Irwin Shaw ............. Y-84

Talev, Dimitr 1898-1966 ............ DLB-181

Taliaferro, H. E. 1811-1875 .......... DLB-202

Tallent, Elizabeth 1954- ............ DLB-130

TallMountain, Mary 1918-1994........ DLB-193

Talvj 1797-1870.................. DLB-59, 133

Tamási, Áron 1897-1966 ............ DLB-215

Tammsaare, A. H.
   1878-1940............ DLB-220; CDWLB-4

Tan, Amy 1952- ......... DLB-173; CDALB-7

Tandori, Dezső 1938- .............. DLB-232

Tanner, Thomas 1673/1674-1735....... DLB-213

Tanizaki Jun'ichirō 1886-1965 ........ DLB-180

Tapahonso, Luci 1953- .............DLB-175

The Mark Taper Forum.............. DLB-7

Taradash, Daniel 1913- ............. DLB-44

Tarasov-Rodionov, Aleksandr Ignat'evich
   1885-1938 ....................DLB-272

Tarbell, Ida M. 1857-1944 ........... DLB-47

Tardivel, Jules-Paul 1851-1905 ....... DLB-99

Targan, Barry 1932- ................ DLB-130

   Tribute to John Gardner ........... Y-82

Tarkington, Booth 1869-1946 ...... DLB-9, 102

Tashlin, Frank 1913-1972............ DLB-44

Tasma (Jessie Couvreur) 1848-1897 .... DLB-230

Tate, Allen 1899-1979.......DLB-4, 45, 63; DS-17

Tate, James 1943- ............... DLB-5, 169

Tate, Nahum circa 1652-1715........ DLB-80

Tatian circa 830.................... DLB-148

Taufer, Veno 1933- ................ DLB-181

Tauler, Johannes circa 1300-1361......DLB-179

Tavares, Salette 1922-1994........... DLB-287

Tavčar, Ivan 1851-1923 ............ DLB-147

Taverner, Richard ca. 1505-1575 ....... DLB-236

Taylor, Ann 1782-1866 ............. DLB-163

Taylor, Bayard 1825-1878 ...... DLB-3, 189, 250

Taylor, Bert Leston 1866-1921 ........ DLB-25

Taylor, Charles H. 1846-1921 .......... DLB-25

Taylor, Edward circa 1642-1729 ....... DLB-24

Taylor, Elizabeth 1912-1975........... DLB-139

Taylor, Sir Henry 1800-1886 ......... DLB-32

Taylor, Henry 1942- ................ DLB-5

   Who Owns American Literature ....... Y-94

Taylor, Jane 1783-1824............... DLB-163

Taylor, Jeremy circa 1613-1667 ....... DLB-151

Taylor, John 1577 or 1578 - 1653....... DLB-121

Taylor, Mildred D. 1943- ........... DLB-52

Taylor, Peter 1917-1994 ... DLB-218, 278; Y-81, 94

Taylor, Susie King 1848-1912 ........ DLB-221

Taylor, William Howland 1901-1966 ... DLB-241

William Taylor and Company.......... DLB-49

Teale, Edwin Way 1899-1980 .........DLB-275

Teasdale, Sara 1884-1933............. DLB-45

Teillier, Jorge 1935-1996 ........... DLB-283

Telles, Lygia Fagundes 1924- ........ DLB-113

The Temper of the West: William Jovanovich ... Y-02

Temple, Sir William 1555?-1627 ....... DLB-281

Temple, Sir William 1628-1699 ....... DLB-101

Temple, William F. 1914-1989......... DLB-255

Temrizov, A. (see Marchenko, Anastasia Iakovlevna)

Tench, Watkin ca. 1758-1833......... DLB-230

Tender Is the Night (Documentary) .......DLB-273

Tendriakov, Vladimir Fedorovich
   1923-1984 ..................... DLB-302

Tenn, William 1919- ............... DLB-8

Tennant, Emma 1937- .............. DLB-14

Tenney, Tabitha Gilman 1762-1837...DLB-37, 200

Tennyson, Alfred 1809-1892 .. DLB-32; CDBLB-4

   On Some of the Characteristics of
    Modern Poetry and On the Lyrical
    Poems of Alfred Tennyson
    (1831) .................. DLB-32

Tennyson, Frederick 1807-1898 ........ DLB-32

Tenorio, Arthur 1924- ............. DLB-209

Tepl, Johannes von
   circa 1350-1414/1415 ............DLB-179

Tepliakov, Viktor Grigor'evich
   1804-1842 ..................... DLB-205

Terence circa 184 B.C.-159 B.C. or after
   .................. DLB-211; CDWLB-1

Terhune, Albert Payson 1872-1942 ....... DLB-9

Terhune, Mary Virginia 1830-1922........DS-13

Terpigorev, Sergei Nikolaevich (S. Atava)
   1841-1895 .....................DLB-277

Terry, Megan 1932- ...............DLB-7, 249

Terson, Peter 1932- ................ DLB-13

Tesich, Steve 1943-1996 .............. Y-83

Tessa, Delio 1886-1939 ............. DLB-114

Testori, Giovanni
   1923-1993 ..................DLB-128, 177

Texas
    The Year in Texas Literature . . . . . . . . . . Y-98

Tey, Josephine 1896?-1952 . . . . . . . . . . . . . . DLB-77

Thacher, James 1754-1844 . . . . . . . . . . . . . . . DLB-37

Thacher, John Boyd 1847-1909 . . . . . . . . . . DLB-187

Thackeray, William Makepeace
1811-1863 . . . DLB-21, 55, 159, 163; CDBLB-4

Thames and Hudson Limited . . . . . . . . . . DLB-112

Thanet, Octave (see French, Alice)

Thaxter, Celia Laighton
1835-1894 . . . . . . . . . . . . . . . . . . . . . . . DLB-239

Thayer, Caroline Matilda Warren
1785-1844 . . . . . . . . . . . . . . . . . . . . . . . DLB-200

Thayer, Douglas H. 1929- . . . . . . . . . . DLB-256

Theater
    Black Theatre: A Forum [excerpts] . . . . DLB-38

    Community and Commentators:
        Black Theatre and Its Critics . . . . . DLB-38

    German Drama from Naturalism
        to Fascism: 1889-1933 . . . . . . . . . DLB-118

    A Look at the Contemporary Black
        Theatre Movement . . . . . . . . . . . . . DLB-38

    The Lord Chamberlain's Office and
        Stage Censorship in England . . . . . DLB-10

    New Forces at Work in the American
        Theatre: 1915-1925 . . . . . . . . . . . . . DLB-7

    Off Broadway and Off-Off Broadway . . DLB-7

    Oregon Shakespeare Festival . . . . . . . . . . . Y-00

    Plays, Playwrights, and Playgoers . . . . . DLB-84

    Playwrights on the Theater . . . . . . . . . . DLB-80

    Playwrights and Professors . . . . . . . . . . DLB-13

    Producing *Dear Bunny, Dear Volodya:*
        *The Friendship and the Feud* . . . . . . . . . Y-97

    Viewpoint: Politics and Performance,
        by David Edgar . . . . . . . . . . . . . . DLB-13

    Writing for the Theatre,
        by Harold Pinter . . . . . . . . . . . . . DLB-13

    The Year in Drama . . . . . . . . . Y-82–85, 87–98

    The Year in U.S. Drama . . . . . . . . . . . . . Y-00

Theater, English and Irish
    Anti-Theatrical Tracts . . . . . . . . . . . . . DLB-263

    The Chester Plays circa 1505-1532;
        revisions until 1575 . . . . . . . . . . . DLB-146

    Dangerous Years: London Theater,
        1939-1945 . . . . . . . . . . . . . . . . . . . DLB-10

    A Defense of Actors . . . . . . . . . . . . . . . DLB-263

    The Development of Lighting in the
        Staging of Drama, 1900-1945 . . . . DLB-10

    Education . . . . . . . . . . . . . . . . . . . . . . . DLB-263

    The End of English Stage Censorship,
        1945-1968 . . . . . . . . . . . . . . . . . . . DLB-13

    Epigrams and Satires . . . . . . . . . . . . . . DLB-263

    Eyewitnesses and Historians . . . . . . . . . DLB-263

    Fringe and Alternative Theater in
        Great Britain . . . . . . . . . . . . . . . . . DLB-13

    The Great War and the Theater,
        1914-1918 [Great Britain] . . . . . . . DLB-10

    Licensing Act of 1737 . . . . . . . . . . . . . . DLB-84

    Morality Plays: *Mankind* circa 1450-1500
        and *Everyman* circa 1500 . . . . . . . DLB-146

    The New Variorum Shakespeare . . . . . . . Y-85

    N-Town Plays circa 1468 to early
        sixteenth century . . . . . . . . . . . . . DLB-146

    Politics and the Theater . . . . . . . . . . . . DLB-263

    Practical Matters . . . . . . . . . . . . . . . . . DLB-263

    Prologues, Epilogues, Epistles to
        Readers, and Excerpts from
        Plays . . . . . . . . . . . . . . . . . . . . . . . DLB-263

    The Publication of English
        Renaissance Plays . . . . . . . . . . . . . DLB-62

    Regulations for the Theater . . . . . . . . DLB-263

    Sources for the Study of Tudor and
        Stuart Drama . . . . . . . . . . . . . . . . DLB-62

    Stage Censorship: "The Rejected
        Statement" (1911), by Bernard
        Shaw [excerpts] . . . . . . . . . . . . . . . DLB-10

    Synge Summer School: J. M. Synge and
        the Irish Theater, Rathdrum,
        County Wiclow, Ireland . . . . . . . . . . Y-93

    The Theater in Shakespeare's Time . . . DLB-62

    The Theatre Guild . . . . . . . . . . . . . . . . . . DLB-7

    The Townely Plays fifteenth and
        sixteenth centuries . . . . . . . . . . . . DLB-146

    The Year in British Drama . . . . . . . . . Y-99–01

    The Year in Drama: London . . . . . . . . . . Y-90

    The Year in London Theatre . . . . . . . . . . Y-92

    *A Yorkshire Tragedy* . . . . . . . . . . . . . . . . DLB-58

Theaters
    The Abbey Theatre and Irish Drama,
        1900-1945 . . . . . . . . . . . . . . . . . . . DLB-10

    Actors Theatre of Louisville . . . . . . . . . . . DLB-7

    American Conservatory Theatre . . . . . . . DLB-7

    Arena Stage . . . . . . . . . . . . . . . . . . . . . . . DLB-7

    Black Theaters and Theater
        Organizations in America,
        1961-1982: A Research List . . . . . DLB-38

    The Dallas Theater Center . . . . . . . . . . . DLB-7

    Eugene O'Neill Memorial Theater
        Center . . . . . . . . . . . . . . . . . . . . . . . DLB-7

    The Goodman Theatre . . . . . . . . . . . . . . DLB-7

    The Guthrie Theater . . . . . . . . . . . . . . . . DLB-7

    The Mark Taper Forum . . . . . . . . . . . . . DLB-7

    The National Theatre and the Royal
        Shakespeare Company: The
        National Companies . . . . . . . . . . . DLB-13

    Off-Loop Theatres . . . . . . . . . . . . . . . . . . DLB-7

    The Royal Court Theatre and the
        English Stage Company . . . . . . . . DLB-13

    The Royal Court Theatre and the
        New Drama . . . . . . . . . . . . . . . . . DLB-10

    The Takarazaka Revue Company . . . . . . Y-91

Thegan and the Astronomer
    flourished circa 850 . . . . . . . . . . . . . . . DLB-148

Thelwall, John 1764-1834 . . . . . . . . . . DLB-93, 158

Theocritus circa 300 B.C.-260 B.C. . . . . . . DLB-176

Theodorescu, Ion N. (see Arghezi, Tudor)

Theodulf circa 760-circa 821 . . . . . . . . . . . DLB-148

Theophrastus circa 371 B.C.-287 B.C. . . . . DLB-176

Thériault, Yves 1915-1983 . . . . . . . . . . . . . . DLB-88

Thério, Adrien 1925- . . . . . . . . . . . . . . . DLB-53

Theroux, Paul 1941- . . . . DLB-2, 218; CDALB-7

Thesiger, Wilfred 1910- . . . . . . . . . . . . . DLB-204

They All Came to Paris . . . . . . . . . . . . . . . . DS-15

Thibaudeau, Colleen 1925- . . . . . . . . . . DLB-88

Thiele, Colin 1920- . . . . . . . . . . . . . . . DLB-289

Thielen, Benedict 1903-1965 . . . . . . . . . . DLB-102

Thiong'o Ngugi wa (see Ngugi wa Thiong'o)

*This Quarter* 1925-1927, 1929-1932 . . . . . . . DS-15

Thoma, Ludwig 1867-1921 . . . . . . . . . . . . DLB-66

Thoma, Richard 1902- . . . . . . . . . . . . . . DLB-4

Thomas, Audrey 1935- . . . . . . . . . . . . . DLB-60

Thomas, D. M.
    1935- . . . DLB-40, 207, 299; Y-82; CDBLB-8

    The Plagiarism Controversy . . . . . . . . . . Y-82

Thomas, Dylan
    1914-1953 . . . . . . . DLB-13, 20, 139; CDBLB-7

    The Dylan Thomas Celebration . . . . . . . Y-99

Thomas, Edward
    1878-1917 . . . . . . . . . . DLB-19, 98, 156, 216

    The Friends of the Dymock Poets . . . . . . Y-00

Thomas, Frederick William 1806-1866 . . . DLB-202

Thomas, Gwyn 1913-1981 . . . . . . . . . DLB-15, 245

Thomas, Isaiah 1750-1831 . . . . . . DLB-43, 73, 187

Thomas, Johann 1624-1679 . . . . . . . . . . . DLB-168

Thomas, John 1900-1932 . . . . . . . . . . . . . . . DLB-4

Thomas, Joyce Carol 1938- . . . . . . . . . . DLB-33

Thomas, Lewis 1913-1993 . . . . . . . . . . . . DLB-275

Thomas, Lorenzo 1944- . . . . . . . . . . . . DLB-41

Thomas, R. S. 1915-2000 . . . . . DLB-27; CDBLB-8

Isaiah Thomas [publishing house] . . . . . . . . DLB-49

Thomasîn von Zerclære
    circa 1186-circa 1259 . . . . . . . . . . . . . . DLB-138

Thomason, George 1602?-1666 . . . . . . . . DLB-213

Thomasius, Christian 1655-1728 . . . . . . . . DLB-168

Thompson, Daniel Pierce 1795-1868 . . . . . DLB-202

Thompson, David 1770-1857 . . . . . . . . . . . DLB-99

Thompson, Dorothy 1893-1961 . . . . . . . . . DLB-29

Thompson, E. P. 1924-1993 . . . . . . . . . . . DLB-242

Thompson, Flora 1876-1947 . . . . . . . . . . . DLB-240

Thompson, Francis
    1859-1907 . . . . . . . . . . . . . DLB-19; CDBLB-5

Thompson, George Selden (see Selden, George)

Thompson, Henry Yates 1838-1928 . . . . . DLB-184

Thompson, Hunter S. 1939- . . . . . . . . DLB-185

Thompson, Jim 1906-1977 . . . . . . . . . . . . DLB-226

Thompson, John 1938-1976 . . . . . . . . . . . . DLB-60

Thompson, John R. 1823-1873 . . . DLB-3, 73, 248

Thompson, Lawrance 1906-1973 . . . . . . . DLB-103

Thompson, Maurice 1844-1901 . . . . . . DLB-71, 74

Thompson, Ruth Plumly 1891-1976 . . . . . . DLB-22

Thompson, Thomas Phillips 1843-1933 . . . DLB-99

Thompson, William 1775-1833 . . . . . . . . . DLB-158

Thompson, William Tappan
    1812-1882 . . . . . . . . . . . . . . . . DLB-3, 11, 248

Thomson, Cockburn
    "Modern Style" (1857) [excerpt] . . . . . DLB-57

Thomson, Edward William 1849-1924 . . . . DLB-92

Thomson, James 1700-1748 . . . . . . . . . . . . DLB-95

Thomson, James 1834-1882 .............. DLB-35
Thomson, Joseph 1858-1895 ............ DLB-174
Thomson, Mortimer 1831-1875 ......... DLB-11
Thomson, Rupert 1955- ................... DLB-267
Thon, Melanie Rae 1957- ................. DLB-244
Thor Vilhjálmsson 1925- .................. DLB-293
Þórarinn Eldjárn 1949- ..................... DLB-293
Þórbergur Þórðarson 1888-1974 ........ DLB-293
Thoreau, Henry David 1817-1862 .... DLB-1, 183, 223, 270, 298; DS-5; CDALB-2

    The Thoreau Society ................ Y-99

    The Thoreauvian Pilgrimage: The Structure of an American Cult .. DLB-223

Thorne, William 1568?-1630 ........... DLB-281

Thornton, John F.
    [Repsonse to Ken Auletta] ............. Y-97

Thorpe, Adam 1956- ....................... DLB-231

Thorpe, Thomas Bangs 1815-1878 ................ DLB-3, 11, 248

Thorup, Kirsten 1942- .................... DLB-214

Thotl, Birgitte 1610-1662 ................ DLB-300

Thrale, Hester Lynch
    (see Piozzi, Hester Lynch [Thrale])

The Three Marias: A Landmark Case in Portuguese Literary History
    (Maria Isabel Barreno, 1939-  ;
    Maria Teresa Horta, 1937-  ;
    Maria Velho da Costa, 1938-  ) .... DLB-287

Thubron, Colin 1939- .......... DLB-204, 231

Thucydides circa 455 B.C.-circa 395 B.C. ....... DLB-176

Thulstrup, Thure de 1848-1930 ........ DLB-188

Thümmel, Moritz August von 1738-1817 ................... DLB-97

Thurber, James 1894-1961 .... DLB-4, 11, 22, 102; CDALB-5

Thurman, Wallace 1902-1934 .......... DLB-51

    "Negro Poets and Their Poetry" ..... DLB-50

Thwaite, Anthony 1930- .................. DLB-40

    The Booker Prize, Address .............. Y-86

Thwaites, Reuben Gold 1853-1913 ...... DLB-47

Tibullus circa 54 B.C.-circa 19 B.C. ..... DLB-211

Ticknor, George 1791-1871 .. DLB-1, 59, 140, 235

Ticknor and Fields .................. DLB-49

Ticknor and Fields (revived) ............ DLB-46

Tieck, Ludwig 1773-1853 .... DLB-90; CDWLB-2

Tietjens, Eunice 1884-1944 .............. DLB-54

Tikkanen, Märta 1935- .................... DLB-257

Tilghman, Christopher circa 1948 ...... DLB-244

Tilney, Edmund circa 1536-1610 ....... DLB-136

Charles Tilt [publishing house] ......... DLB-106

J. E. Tilton and Company .............. DLB-49

Time-Life Books .................... DLB-46

Times Books ...................... DLB-46

Timothy, Peter circa 1725-1782 ......... DLB-43

Timrava 1867-1951 ................... DLB-215

Timrod, Henry 1828-1867 ........... DLB-3, 248

Tindal, Henrietta 1818?-1879 ........... DLB-199

Tinker, Chauncey Brewster 1876-1963 .. DLB-140

Tinsley Brothers .................... DLB-106

Tiptree, James, Jr. 1915-1987 ........... DLB-8

Tišma, Aleksandar 1924- ................ DLB-181

Titus, Edward William 1870-1952 ................. DLB-4; DS-15

Tiutchev, Fedor Ivanovich 1803-1873 ... DLB-205

Tlali, Miriam 1933- .............. DLB-157, 225

Todd, Barbara Euphan 1890-1976 ...... DLB-160

Todorov, Tzvetan 1939- ................. DLB-242

Tofte, Robert 1561 or 1562-1619 or 1620 ........ DLB-172

Tóibín, Colm 1955- ..................... DLB-271

Toklas, Alice B. 1877-1967 ........ DLB-4; DS-15

Tokuda Shūsei 1872-1943 ............... DLB-180

Toland, John 1670-1722 ................. DLB-252

Tolkien, J. R. R. 1892-1973 ...... DLB-15, 160, 255; CDBLB-6

Toller, Ernst 1893-1939 .................. DLB-124

Tollet, Elizabeth 1694-1754 ............. DLB-95

Tolson, Melvin B. 1898-1966 ....... DLB-48, 76

Tolstaya, Tatyana 1951- ................. DLB-285

Tolstoy, Aleksei Konstantinovich 1817-1875 ...................... DLB-238

Tolstoy, Aleksei Nikolaevich 1883-1945 .. DLB-272

Tolstoy, Leo 1828-1910 .................. DLB-238

Tomalin, Claire 1933- ................... DLB-155

Tómas Guðmundsson 1901-1983 ...... DLB-293

Tomasi di Lampedusa, Giuseppe 1896-1957 ....................... DLB-177

Tomlinson, Charles 1927- .............. DLB-40

Tomlinson, H. M. 1873-1958 .... DLB-36, 100, 195

Abel Tompkins [publishing house] ....... DLB-49

Tompson, Benjamin 1642-1714 ......... DLB-24

Tomson, Graham R.
    (see Watson, Rosamund Marriott)

Ton'a 1289-1372 ..................... DLB-203

Tondelli, Pier Vittorio 1955-1991 ....... DLB-196

Tonks, Rosemary 1932- ............ DLB-14, 207

Tonna, Charlotte Elizabeth 1790-1846 ... DLB-163

Jacob Tonson the Elder [publishing house] ................. DLB-170

Toole, John Kennedy 1937-1969 .......... Y-81

Toomer, Jean 1894-1967 .......... DLB-45, 51; CDALB-4

Topsoe, Vilhelm 1840-1881 ............ DLB-300

Tor Books ........................ DLB-46

Torberg, Friedrich 1908-1979 ........... DLB-85

Torga, Miguel (Adolfo Correira da Rocha) 1907-1995 ...................... DLB-287

Torrence, Ridgely 1874-1950 ....... DLB-54, 249

Torres-Metzger, Joseph V. 1933- ...... DLB-122

El Tostado (see Madrigal, Alfonso Fernández de)

Toth, Susan Allen 1940- ................. Y-86

Richard Tottell [publishing house] ....... DLB-170

    "The Printer to the Reader," (1557) ..................... DLB-167

Tough-Guy Literature ................. DLB-9

Touré, Askia Muhammad 1938- ...... DLB-41

Tourgée, Albion W. 1838-1905 ......... DLB-79

Tournemir, Elizaveta Sailhas de (see Tur, Evgeniia)

Tourneur, Cyril circa 1580-1626 ........ DLB-58

Tournier, Michel 1924- ................. DLB-83

Frank Tousey [publishing house] ....... DLB-49

Tower Publications ................... DLB-46

Towne, Benjamin circa 1740-1793 ...... DLB-43

Towne, Robert 1936- ................... DLB-44

The Townely Plays fifteenth and sixteenth centuries ...................... DLB-146

Townsend, Sue 1946- ................... DLB-271

Townshend, Aurelian by 1583-circa 1651 ............... DLB-121

Toy, Barbara 1908-2001 ................ DLB-204

Tozzi, Federigo 1883-1920 ............. DLB-264

Tracy, Honor 1913-1989 ............... DLB-15

Traherne, Thomas 1637?-1674 ......... DLB-131

Traill, Catharine Parr 1802-1899 ....... DLB-99

Train, Arthur 1875-1945 ........ DLB-86; DS-16

Tranquilli, Secondino (see Silone, Ignazio)

The Transatlantic Publishing Company .. DLB-49

*The Transatlantic Review* 1924-1925 ......... DS-15

The Transcendental Club 1836-1840 .............. DLB-1; DLB-223

Transcendentalism ....... DLB-1; DLB-223; DS-5

    "A Response from America," by John A. Heraud ................. DS-5

    Publications and Social Movements .... DLB-1

    The Rise of Transcendentalism, 1815-1860 ..................... DS-5

    Transcendentalists, American ......... DS-5

    "What Is Transcendentalism? By a Thinking Man," by James Kinnard Jr. .................... DS-5

*transition* 1927-1938 .................... DS-15

Translations (Vernacular) in the Crowns of Castile and Aragon 1352-1515 ...... DLB-286

Tranströmer, Tomas 1931- ............. DLB-257

Tranter, John 1943- .................... DLB-289

Travel Writing
    American Travel Writing, 1776-1864 (checklist) .................... DLB-183

    British Travel Writing, 1940-1997 (checklist) .................... DLB-204

    Travel Writers of the Late Middle Ages ................ DLB-286

    (1876-1909) ..................... DLB-174

    (1837-1875) ..................... DLB-166

    (1910-1939) ..................... DLB-195

Traven, B. 1882?/1890?-1969? ....... DLB-9, 56

Travers, Ben 1886-1980 .......... DLB-10, 233

Travers, P. L. (Pamela Lyndon) 1899-1996 ..................... DLB-160

Trediakovsky, Vasilii Kirillovich 1703-1769 ..................... DLB-150

Treece, Henry 1911-1966 .............. DLB-160

Treitel, Jonathan 1959- ................. DLB-267

Trejo, Ernesto 1950-1991 . . . . . . . . . . . . .DLB-122

Trelawny, Edward John
   1792-1881 . . . . . . . . . . . . . . DLB-110, 116, 144

Tremain, Rose 1943- . . . . . . . . . . . DLB-14, 271

Tremblay, Michel 1942- . . . . . . . . . . . . . . .DLB-60

Trent, William P. 1862-1939 . . . . . . . . DLB-47, 71

Trescot, William Henry 1822-1898 . . . . . . .DLB-30

Tressell, Robert (Robert Phillipe Noonan)
   1870-1911 . . . . . . . . . . . . . . . . . . . . . .DLB-197

Trevelyan, Sir George Otto
   1838-1928 . . . . . . . . . . . . . . . . . . . . . .DLB-144

Trevisa, John circa 1342-circa 1402 . . . . . .DLB-146

Trevor, William 1928- . . . . . . . . . . . DLB-14, 139

*Trierer Floyris* circa 1170-1180 . . . . . . . . .DLB-138

Trifonov, Iurii Valentinovich
   1925-1981 . . . . . . . . . . . . . . . . . . . . . .DLB-302

Trillin, Calvin 1935- . . . . . . . . . . . . . . . . .DLB-185

Trilling, Lionel 1905-1975 . . . . . . . . .DLB-28, 63

Trilussa 1871-1950 . . . . . . . . . . . . . . . . . .DLB-114

Trimmer, Sarah 1741-1810 . . . . . . . . . . . .DLB-158

Triolet, Elsa 1896-1970 . . . . . . . . . . . . . . .DLB-72

Tripp, John 1927- . . . . . . . . . . . . . . . . . .DLB-40

Trocchi, Alexander 1925-1984 . . . . . . . . . .DLB-15

Troisi, Dante 1920-1989 . . . . . . . . . . . . . .DLB-196

Trollope, Anthony
   1815-1882 . . . . . . .DLB-21, 57, 159; CDBLB-4

   Novel-Reading: *The Works of Charles
   Dickens; The Works of W. Makepeace
   Thackeray* (1879) . . . . . . . . . . . . . . .DLB-21

   The Trollope Societies . . . . . . . . . . . . . . Y-00

Trollope, Frances 1779-1863 . . . . . . . .DLB-21, 166

Trollope, Joanna 1943- . . . . . . . . . . . . . .DLB-207

Troop, Elizabeth 1931- . . . . . . . . . . . . . . .DLB-14

Trotter, Catharine 1679-1749 . . . . . . .DLB-84, 252

Trotti, Lamar 1898-1952 . . . . . . . . . . . . . .DLB-44

Trottier, Pierre 1925- . . . . . . . . . . . . . . . .DLB-60

Trotzig, Birgitta 1929- . . . . . . . . . . . . . . .DLB-257

Troupe, Quincy Thomas, Jr. 1943- . . . . . .DLB-41

John F. Trow and Company . . . . . . . . . . .DLB-49

Trowbridge, John Townsend 1827-1916 . .DLB-202

Trudel, Jean-Louis 1967- . . . . . . . . . . .DLB-251

Truillier-Lacombe, Joseph-Patrice
   1807-1863 . . . . . . . . . . . . . . . . . . . . . . .DLB-99

Trumbo, Dalton 1905-1976 . . . . . . . . . . . .DLB-26

Trumbull, Benjamin 1735-1820 . . . . . . . . .DLB-30

Trumbull, John 1750-1831 . . . . . . . . . . . . .DLB-31

Trumbull, John 1756-1843 . . . . . . . . . . . .DLB-183

Truth, Sojourner 1797?-1883 . . . . . . . . . .DLB-239

Tscherning, Andreas 1611-1659 . . . . . . . .DLB-164

Tsubouchi Shōyō 1859-1935 . . . . . . . . . . .DLB-180

Tsvetaeva, Marina Ivanovna 1892-1941 . . .DLB-295

Tuchman, Barbara W.
   Tribute to Alfred A. Knopf . . . . . . . . . . . Y-84

Tucholsky, Kurt 1890-1935 . . . . . . . . . . . .DLB-56

Tucker, Charlotte Maria
   1821-1893 . . . . . . . . . . . . . . . . . .DLB-163, 190

Tucker, George 1775-1861 . . . . . . . .DLB-3, 30, 248

Tucker, James 1808?-1866? . . . . . . . . . . . .DLB-230

Tucker, Nathaniel Beverley
   1784-1851 . . . . . . . . . . . . . . . . . . .DLB-3, 248

Tucker, St. George 1752-1827 . . . . . . . . . .DLB-37

Tuckerman, Frederick Goddard
   1821-1873 . . . . . . . . . . . . . . . . . . . . . . .DLB-243

Tuckerman, Henry Theodore 1813-1871 . .DLB-64

Tumas, Juozas (see Vaizgantas)

Tunis, John R. 1889-1975 . . . . . . . . .DLB-22, 171

Tunstall, Cuthbert 1474-1559 . . . . . . . . .DLB-132

Tunström, Göran 1937-2000 . . . . . . . . . .DLB-257

Tuohy, Frank 1925- . . . . . . . . . . . . .DLB-14, 139

Tupper, Martin F. 1810-1889 . . . . . . . . . . .DLB-32

Tur, Evgeniia 1815-1892 . . . . . . . . . . . . . .DLB-238

Turbyfill, Mark 1896-1991 . . . . . . . . . . . . .DLB-45

Turco, Lewis 1934- . . . . . . . . . . . . . . . . . . Y-84

   Tribute to John Ciardi . . . . . . . . . . . . . . Y-86

Turgenev, Aleksandr Ivanovich
   1784-1845 . . . . . . . . . . . . . . . . . . . . . . .DLB-198

Turgenev, Ivan Sergeevich 1818-1883 . . . .DLB-238

Turnbull, Alexander H. 1868-1918 . . . . . .DLB-184

Turnbull, Andrew 1921-1970 . . . . . . . . . .DLB-103

Turnbull, Gael 1928- . . . . . . . . . . . . . . . .DLB-40

Turner, Arlin 1909-1980 . . . . . . . . . . . . . .DLB-103

Turner, Charles (Tennyson) 1808-1879 . . . .DLB-32

Turner, Ethel 1872-1958 . . . . . . . . . . . . . .DLB-230

Turner, Frederick 1943- . . . . . . . . . . . . . .DLB-40

Turner, Frederick Jackson
   1861-1932 . . . . . . . . . . . . . . . . . .DLB-17, 186

A Conversation between William Riggan
   and Janette Turner Hospital . . . . . . . . . . Y-02

Turner, Joseph Addison 1826-1868 . . . . . .DLB-79

Turpin, Waters Edward 1910-1968 . . . . . . .DLB-51

Turrini, Peter 1944- . . . . . . . . . . . . . . . .DLB-124

Tutuola, Amos 1920-1997 . . . DLB-125; CDWLB-3

Twain, Mark (see Clemens, Samuel Langhorne)

Tweedie, Ethel Brilliana circa 1860-1940 . DLB-174

A Century of Poetry, a Lifetime of
   Collecting: J. M. Edelstein's
   Collection of Twentieth-
   Century American Poetry . . . . . . . . . . YB-02

Twombly, Wells 1935-1977 . . . . . . . . . . . .DLB-241

Twysden, Sir Roger 1597-1672 . . . . . . . .DLB-213

Tyler, Anne
   1941- . . . . . . . . DLB-6, 143; Y-82; CDALB-7

Tyler, Mary Palmer 1775-1866 . . . . . . . . .DLB-200

Tyler, Moses Coit 1835-1900 . . . . . . . DLB-47, 64

Tyler, Royall 1757-1826 . . . . . . . . . . . . . . .DLB-37

Tylor, Edward Burnett 1832-1917 . . . . . . .DLB-57

Tynan, Katharine 1861-1931 . . . . . . .DLB-153, 240

Tyndale, William circa 1494-1536 . . . . . . .DLB-132

Tyree, Omar 1969- . . . . . . . . . . . . . . . . .DLB-292

# U

Uchida, Yoshika 1921-1992 . . . . . . . . . . CDALB-7

Udall, Nicholas 1504-1556 . . . . . . . . . . . . .DLB-62

Ugrěsić, Dubravka 1949- . . . . . . . . . . . .DLB-181

Uhland, Ludwig 1787-1862 . . . . . . . . . . . .DLB-90

Uhse, Bodo 1904-1963 . . . . . . . . . . . . . . . .DLB-69

Ujević, Augustin "Tin"
   1891-1955 . . . . . . . . . . . . . . . . . . . . . . .DLB-147

Ulenhart, Niclas flourished circa 1600 . . . .DLB-164

Ulfeldt, Leonora Christina 1621-1698 . . . .DLB-300

Ulibarrí, Sabine R. 1919- . . . . . . . . . . . . .DLB-82

Ulica, Jorge 1870-1926 . . . . . . . . . . . . . . . .DLB-82

Ulitskaya, Liudmila Evgen'evna
   1943- . . . . . . . . . . . . . . . . . . . . . . . . . .DLB-285

Ulivi, Ferruccio 1912- . . . . . . . . . . . . . . .DLB-196

Ulizio, B. George 1889-1969 . . . . . . . . . . .DLB-140

Ulrich von Liechtenstein
   circa 1200-circa 1275 . . . . . . . . . . . . . . .DLB-138

Ulrich von Zatzikhoven
   before 1194-after 1214 . . . . . . . . . . . .DLB-138

Unaipon, David 1872-1967 . . . . . . . . . . . .DLB-230

Unamuno, Miguel de 1864-1936 . . . . . . . .DLB-108

Under, Marie 1883-1980 . . . DLB-220; CDWLB-4

Underhill, Evelyn 1875-1941 . . . . . . . . . . .DLB-240

Undset, Sigrid 1882-1949 . . . . . . . . . . . . .DLB-297

Ungaretti, Giuseppe 1888-1970 . . . . . . . . .DLB-114

Unger, Friederike Helene 1741-1813 . . . . . .DLB-94

United States Book Company . . . . . . . . . .DLB-49

Universal Publishing and Distributing
   Corporation . . . . . . . . . . . . . . . . . . . . .DLB-46

University of Colorado
   Special Collections at the University of
   Colorado at Boulder . . . . . . . . . . . . . . Y-98

Indiana University Press . . . . . . . . . . . . . . . Y-02

The University of Iowa
   Writers' Workshop Golden Jubilee . . . . . Y-86

University of Missouri Press . . . . . . . . . . . . . Y-01

University of South Carolina
   The G. Ross Roy Scottish
   Poetry Collection . . . . . . . . . . . . . . . . Y-89

   Two Hundred Years of Rare Books and
   Literary Collections at the
   University of South Carolina . . . . . . . Y-00

The University of South Carolina Press . . . . Y-94

University of Virginia
   The Book Arts Press at the University
   of Virginia . . . . . . . . . . . . . . . . . . . . . Y-96

   The Electronic Text Center and the
   Electronic Archive of Early American
   Fiction at the University of Virginia
   Library . . . . . . . . . . . . . . . . . . . . . . . . Y-98

   University of Virginia Libraries . . . . . . . Y-91

University of Wales Press . . . . . . . . . . . . .DLB-112

University Press of Florida . . . . . . . . . . . . . Y-00

University Press of Kansas . . . . . . . . . . . . . . Y-98

University Press of Mississippi . . . . . . . . . . . Y-99

Unnur Benediktsdóttir Bjarklind (see Hulda)

Uno Chiyo 1897-1996 . . . . . . . . . . . . . . . .DLB-180

Unruh, Fritz von 1885-1970 . . . . . . . .DLB-56, 118

Unsworth, Barry 1930- . . . . . . . . . . . . . .DLB-194

Unt, Mati 1944- . . . . . . . . . . . . . . . . . . . .DLB-232

The Unterberg Poetry Center of the
   92nd Street Y . . . . . . . . . . . . . . . . . . . . Y-98

T. Fisher Unwin [publishing house] . . . . .DLB-106

# Cumulative Index

Upchurch, Boyd B. (see Boyd, John)
Updike, John 1932- .... DLB-2, 5, 143, 218, 227; Y-80, 82; DS-3; CDALB-6
   John Updike on the Internet .......... Y-97
   Tribute to Alfred A. Knopf ........... Y-84
   Tribute to John Ciardi ............... Y-86
Upīts, Andrejs 1877-1970 ............. DLB-220
Uppdal, Kristofer 1878-1961........... DLB-297
Upton, Bertha 1849-1912.............. DLB-141
Upton, Charles 1948- ................. DLB-16
Upton, Florence K. 1873-1922 ......... DLB-141
Upward, Allen 1863-1926 .............. DLB-36
Urban, Milo 1904-1982 ................ DLB-215
Ureña de Henríquez, Salomé 1850-1897................ DLB-283
Urfé, Honoré d' 1567-1625 ............ DLB-268
Urista, Alberto Baltazar (see Alurista)
Urquhart, Fred 1912-1995 ............. DLB-139
Urrea, Luis Alberto 1955- ............. DLB-209
Urzidil, Johannes 1896-1970 ........... DLB-85
*U.S.A.* (Documentary) ................DLB-274
Usk, Thomas died 1388 ............... DLB-146
Uslar Pietri, Arturo 1906-2001......... DLB-113
Uspensky, Gleb Ivanovich 1843-1902 ...DLB-277
Ussher, James 1581-1656 .............. DLB-213
Ustinov, Peter 1921- ................... DLB-13
Uttley, Alison 1884-1976 .............. DLB-160
Uz, Johann Peter 1720-1796 ........... DLB-97

# V

Vadianus, Joachim 1484-1551 ..........DLB-179
Vac, Bertrand (Aimé Pelletier) 1914- ... DLB-88
Vācietis, Ojārs 1933-1983............. DLB-232
Vaculík, Ludvík 1926- ................ DLB-232
Vaičiulaitis, Antanas 1906-1992 ....... DLB-220
Vaičiūnaite, Judita 1937- .............. DLB-232
Vail, Laurence 1891-1968.............. DLB-4
Vail, Petr L'vovich 1949- .............. DLB-285
Vailland, Roger 1907-1965 ............ DLB-83
Vaižgantas 1869-1933................. DLB-220
Vajda, Ernest 1887-1954............... DLB-44
Valdés, Gina 1943- .................... DLB-122
Valdez, Luis Miguel 1940- ............ DLB-122
Valduga, Patrizia 1953- ............... DLB-128
Vale Press......................... DLB-112
Valente, José Angel 1929-2000 ........ DLB-108
Valenzuela, Luisa 1938- .. DLB-113; CDWLB-3
Valera, Diego de 1412-1488 ........... DLB-286
Valeri, Diego 1887-1976 .............. DLB-128
Valerius Flaccus fl. circa A.D. 92 ...... DLB-211
Valerius Maximus fl. circa A.D. 31 .... DLB-211
Valéry, Paul 1871-1945................ DLB-258
Valesio, Paolo 1939- .................. DLB-196
Valgardson, W. D. 1939- .............. DLB-60
Valle, Luz 1899-1971 ................. DLB-290

Valle, Víctor Manuel 1950- ......... DLB-122
Valle-Inclán, Ramón del 1866-1936 ..... DLB-134
Vallejo, Armando 1949- ............. DLB-122
Vallejo, César Abraham 1892-1938 ..... DLB-290
Vallès, Jules 1832-1885................ DLB-123
Vallette, Marguerite Eymery (see Rachilde)
Valverde, José María 1926-1996 ....... DLB-108
Vampilov, Aleksandr Valentinovich (A. Sanin) 1937-1972................ DLB-302
Van Allsburg, Chris 1949- ........... DLB-61
Van Anda, Carr 1864-1945 ........... DLB-25
Vanbrugh, Sir John 1664-1726 ......... DLB-80
Vance, Jack 1916?- ................... DLB-8
Vančura, Vladislav 1891-1942 .......... DLB-215; CDWLB-4
van der Post, Laurens 1906-1996 ...... DLB-204
Van Dine, S. S. (see Wright, Williard Huntington)
Van Doren, Mark 1894-1972 ......... DLB-45
van Druten, John 1901-1957........... DLB-10
Van Duyn, Mona 1921- ............. DLB-5
   Tribute to James Dickey ........... Y-97
Van Dyke, Henry 1852-1933..... DLB-71; DS-13
Van Dyke, Henry 1928- ............. DLB-33
Van Dyke, John C. 1856-1932......... DLB-186
Vane, Sutton 1888-1963............... DLB-10
Vanguard Press .................... DLB-46
van Gulik, Robert Hans 1910-1967 ........ DS-17
van Itallie, Jean-Claude 1936- .......... DLB-7
Van Loan, Charles E. 1876-1919 .......DLB-171
Vann, Robert L. 1879-1940 .......... DLB-29
Van Rensselaer, Mariana Griswold 1851-1934 .................... DLB-47
Van Rensselaer, Mrs. Schuyler (see Van Rensselaer, Mariana Griswold)
Van Vechten, Carl 1880-1964 ...... DLB-4, 9, 51
van Vogt, A. E. 1912-2000........... DLB-8, 251
Varela, Blanca 1926- ................ DLB-290
Vargas Llosa, Mario 1936- ............. DLB-145; CDWLB-3
   Acceptance Speech for the Ritz Paris Hemingway Award ............... Y-85
Varley, John 1947- .................... Y-81
Varnhagen von Ense, Karl August 1785-1858..................... DLB-90
Varnhagen von Ense, Rahel 1771-1833...................... DLB-90
Varro 116 B.C.-27 B.C. ............. DLB-211
Vasilenko, Svetlana Vladimirovna 1956- .................... DLB-285
Vasiliu, George (see Bacovia, George)
Vásquez, Richard 1928- ............ DLB-209
Vásquez Montalbán, Manuel 1939- ... DLB-134
Vassa, Gustavus (see Equiano, Olaudah)
Vassalli, Sebastiano 1941- ........ DLB-128, 196
Vaugelas, Claude Favre de 1585-1650 ... DLB-268
Vaughan, Henry 1621-1695 .......... DLB-131
Vaughan, Thomas 1621-1666 ........ DLB-131

Vaughn, Robert 1592?-1667........... DLB-213
Vaux, Thomas, Lord 1509-1556 ..... DLB-132
Vazov, Ivan 1850-1921......DLB-147; CDWLB-4
Véa, Alfredo, Jr. 1950- ............. DLB-209
Veblen, Thorstein 1857-1929 ........ DLB-246
Vedel, Anders Sørensen 1542-1616 ..... DLB-300
Vega, Janine Pommy 1942- .......... DLB-16
Veiller, Anthony 1903-1965........... DLB-44
Velásquez-Trevino, Gloria 1949- ..... DLB-122
Veley, Margaret 1843-1887 .......... DLB-199
Velleius Paterculus circa 20 B.C.-circa A.D. 30 ........ DLB-211
Veloz Maggiolo, Marcio 1936- ...... DLB-145
Vel'tman, Aleksandr Fomich 1800-1870...................... DLB-198
Venegas, Daniel ?-? ................. DLB-82
Venevitinov, Dmitrii Vladimirovich 1805-1827.................... DLB-205
Verbitskaia, Anastasiia Alekseevna 1861-1928 ................... DLB-295
Verde, Cesário 1855-1886............ DLB-287
Vergil, Polydore circa 1470-1555 ....... DLB-132
Veríssimo, Erico 1905-1975 .......... DLB-145
Verlaine, Paul 1844-1896..............DLB-217
Vernacular Translations in the Crowns of Castile and Aragon 1352-1515...... DLB-286
Verne, Jules 1828-1905................ DLB-123
Verplanck, Gulian C. 1786-1870........ DLB-59
Very, Jones 1813-1880 ....... DLB-1, 243; DS-5
Vesaas, Halldis Moren 1907-1995 ..... DLB-297
Vesaas, Tarjei 1897-1970 ............ DLB-297
Vian, Boris 1920-1959 ................ DLB-72
Viazemsky, Petr Andreevich 1792-1878..................... DLB-205
Vicars, Thomas 1591-1638 ........... DLB-236
Vicente, Gil 1465-1536/1540? ........ DLB-287
Vickers, Roy 1888?-1965 ............. DLB-77
Vickery, Sukey 1779-1821 ........... DLB-200
Victoria 1819-1901 ................. DLB-55
Victoria Press .................... DLB-106
Vidal, Gore 1925-    .... DLB-6, 152; CDALB-7
Vidal, Mary Theresa 1815-1873........ DLB-230
Vidmer, Richards 1898-1978 ......... DLB-241
Viebig, Clara 1860-1952.............. DLB-66
Viereck, George Sylvester 1884-1962..... DLB-54
Viereck, Peter 1916- ................. DLB-5
Vietnam War (ended 1975) Resources for the Study of Vietnam War Literature............... DLB-9
Viets, Roger 1738-1811 .............. DLB-99
Vigil-Piñon, Evangelina 1949- ....... DLB-122
Vigneault, Gilles 1928- .............. DLB-60
Vigny, Alfred de 1797-1863 ....DLB-119, 192, 217
Vigolo, Giorgio 1894-1983 ........... DLB-114
Vik, Bjorg 1935- .................... DLB-297
The Viking Press .................. DLB-46
Vilde, Eduard 1865-1933 ............ DLB-220

Vilinskaia, Mariia Aleksandrovna (see Vovchok, Marko)
Villanueva, Alma Luz 1944- .........DLB-122
Villanueva, Tino 1941- ............DLB-82
Villard, Henry 1835-1900 ...........DLB-23
Villard, Oswald Garrison 1872-1949...DLB-25, 91
Villarreal, Edit 1944- ..............DLB-209
Villarreal, José Antonio 1924- .......DLB-82
Villaseñor, Victor 1940- ............DLB-209
Villedieu, Madame de (Marie-Catherine Desjardins) 1640?-1683.............DLB-268
Villegas de Magnón, Leonor 1876-1955 ......................DLB-122
Villehardouin, Geoffroi de circa 1150-1215 .................DLB-208
Villemaire, Yolande 1949- ..........DLB-60
Villena, Enrique de ca. 1382/84-1432 ....DLB-286
Villena, Luis Antonio de 1951- .......DLB-134
Villiers, George, Second Duke of Buckingham 1628-1687..........DLB-80
Villiers de l'Isle-Adam, Jean-Marie Mathias Philippe-Auguste, Comte de 1838-1889.........DLB-123, 192
Villon, François 1431-circa 1463? .......DLB-208
Vine Press .......................DLB-112
Viorst, Judith ?- .................DLB-52
Vipont, Elfrida (Elfrida Vipont Foulds, Charles Vipont) 1902-1992.........DLB-160
Viramontes, Helena María 1954- .....DLB-122
Virgil 70 B.C.-19 B.C......DLB-211; CDWLB-1
Vischer, Friedrich Theodor 1807-1887....DLB-133
Vitier, Cintio 1921- ...............DLB-283
Vitruvius circa 85 B.C.-circa 15 B.C......DLB-211
Vitry, Philippe de 1291-1361........DLB-208
Vittorini, Elio 1908-1966 ...........DLB-264
Vivanco, Luis Felipe 1907-1975 ......DLB-108
Vivian, E. Charles (Charles Henry Cannell, Charles Henry Vivian, Jack Mann, Barry Lynd) 1882-1947..........DLB-255
Viviani, Cesare 1947- ..............DLB-128
Vivien, Renée 1877-1909 ...........DLB-217
Vizenor, Gerald 1934- .........DLB-175, 227
Vizetelly and Company.............DLB-106
Vladimov, Georgii Nikolaevich 1931-2003 ....................DLB-302
Voaden, Herman 1903-1991 ........DLB-88
Voß, Johann Heinrich 1751-1826 .......DLB-90
Vogau, Boris Andreevich (see Pil'niak, Boris Andreevich)
Voigt, Ellen Bryant 1943- ..........DLB-120
Voinovich, Vladimir Nikolaevich 1932- ........................DLB-302
Vojnović, Ivo 1857-1929 ....DLB-147; CDWLB-4
Vold, Jan Erik 1939- ...............DLB-297
Volkoff, Vladimir 1932- ............DLB-83
P. F. Volland Company.............DLB-46
Vollbehr, Otto H. F. 1872?-1945 or 1946..............DLB-187
Vologdin (see Zasodimsky, Pavel Vladimirovich)

Voloshin, Maksimilian Aleksandrovich 1877-1932 ....................DLB-295
Volponi, Paolo 1924-1994...........DLB-177
Vonarburg, Élisabeth 1947- .........DLB-251
von der Grün, Max 1926- ...........DLB-75
Vonnegut, Kurt 1922- ......DLB-2, 8, 152; Y-80; DS-3; CDALB-6
    Tribute to Isaac Asimov ............Y-92
    Tribute to Richard Brautigan .........Y-84
Voranc, Prežihov 1893-1950 .........DLB-147
Voronsky, Aleksandr Konstantinovich 1884-1937 ....................DLB-272
Vovchok, Marko 1833-1907 .........DLB-238
Voynich, E. L. 1864-1960 ...........DLB-197
Vroman, Mary Elizabeth circa 1924-1967..DLB-33

# W

Wace, Robert ("Maistre") circa 1100-circa 1175 ..............DLB-146
Wackenroder, Wilhelm Heinrich 1773-1798.....................DLB-90
Wackernagel, Wilhelm 1806-1869 ......DLB-133
Waddell, Helen 1889-1965 ..........DLB-240
Waddington, Miriam 1917- ..........DLB-68
Wade, Henry 1887-1969 ............DLB-77
Wagenknecht, Edward 1900- ........DLB-103
Wägner, Elin 1882-1949 ............DLB-259
Wagner, Heinrich Leopold 1747-1779 ....DLB-94
Wagner, Henry R. 1862-1957 ........DLB-140
Wagner, Richard 1813-1883 .........DLB-129
Wagoner, David 1926- ..........DLB-5, 256
Wah, Fred 1939- ..................DLB-60
Waiblinger, Wilhelm 1804-1830 ......DLB-90
Wain, John 1925-1994.........DLB-15, 27, 139, 155; CDBLB-8
    Tribute to J. B. Priestly ..............Y-84
Wainwright, Jeffrey 1944- ..........DLB-40
Waite, Peirce and Company .........DLB-49
Wakeman, Stephen H. 1859-1924......DLB-187
Wakoski, Diane 1937- ...............DLB-5
Walahfrid Strabo circa 808-849........DLB-148
Henry Z. Walck [publishing house].......DLB-46
Walcott, Derek 1930- ......DLB-117; Y-81, 92; CDWLB-3
    Nobel Lecture 1992: The Antilles: Fragments of Epic Memory ........Y-92
Robert Waldegrave [publishing house] ...DLB-170
Waldis, Burkhard circa 1490-1556? .....DLB-178
Waldman, Anne 1945- .............DLB-16
Waldrop, Rosmarie 1935- ..........DLB-169
Walker, Alice 1900-1982 ............DLB-201
Walker, Alice 1944- ..DLB-6, 33, 143; CDALB-6
Walker, Annie Louisa (Mrs. Harry Coghill) circa 1836-1907.................DLB-240
Walker, George F. 1947- ............DLB-60
Walker, John Brisben 1847-1931 ......DLB-79
Walker, Joseph A. 1935- ............DLB-38

Walker, Kath (see Oodgeroo of the Tribe Noonuccal)
Walker, Margaret 1915-1998........DLB-76, 152
Walker, Obadiah 1616-1699 ..........DLB-281
Walker, Ted 1934- .................DLB-40
Walker, Evans and Cogswell Company ...DLB-49
Wall, John F. (see Sarban)
Wallace, Alfred Russel 1823-1913 .....DLB-190
Wallace, Dewitt 1889-1981 ..........DLB-137
Wallace, Edgar 1875-1932 ...........DLB-70
Wallace, Lew 1827-1905 ............DLB-202
Wallace, Lila Acheson 1889-1984 .......DLB-137
    "A Word of Thanks," From the Initial Issue of *Reader's Digest* (February 1922) ..............DLB-137
Wallace, Naomi 1960- ..............DLB-249
Wallace Markfield's "Steeplechase".........Y-02
Wallace-Crabbe, Chris 1934- ........DLB-289
Wallant, Edward Lewis 1926-1962 ............DLB-2, 28, 143, 299
Waller, Edmund 1606-1687...........DLB-126
Walpole, Horace 1717-1797 .....DLB-39, 104, 213
    Preface to the First Edition of *The Castle of Otranto* (1764) ....DLB-39, 178
    Preface to the Second Edition of *The Castle of Otranto* (1765) ....DLB-39, 178
Walpole, Hugh 1884-1941 ...........DLB-34
Walrond, Eric 1898-1966 ............DLB-51
Walser, Martin 1927- .........DLB-75, 124
Walser, Robert 1878-1956 ...........DLB-66
Walsh, Ernest 1895-1926............DLB-4, 45
Walsh, Robert 1784-1859 ............DLB-59
Walters, Henry 1848-1931 ..........DLB-140
*Waltharius* circa 825 ................DLB-148
Walther von der Vogelweide circa 1170-circa 1230................DLB-138
Walton, Izaak 1593-1683 ........DLB-151, 213; CDBLB-1
Wambaugh, Joseph 1937- .........DLB-6; Y-83
Wand, Alfred Rudolph 1828-1891 .....DLB-188
Waniek, Marilyn Nelson 1946- ......DLB-120
Wanley, Humphrey 1672-1726 .......DLB-213
War of the Words (and Pictures): The Creation of a Graphic Novel........Y-02
Warburton, William 1698-1779........DLB-104
Ward, Aileen 1919- ................DLB-111
Ward, Artemus (see Browne, Charles Farrar)
Ward, Arthur Henry Sarsfield (see Rohmer, Sax)
Ward, Douglas Turner 1930- ......DLB-7, 38
Ward, Mrs. Humphry 1851-1920 ......DLB-18
Ward, James 1843-1925 ............DLB-262
Ward, Lynd 1905-1985 ..............DLB-22
Ward, Lock and Company ...........DLB-106
Ward, Nathaniel circa 1578-1652 .......DLB-24
Ward, Theodore 1902-1983 .........DLB-76
Wardle, Ralph 1909-1988 ...........DLB-103
Ware, Henry, Jr. 1794-1843..........DLB-235
Ware, William 1797-1852 ........DLB-1, 235

# Cumulative Index

Warfield, Catherine Ann 1816-1877 . . . . . . . DLB-248
Waring, Anna Letitia 1823-1910 . . . . . . . . . DLB-240
Frederick Warne and Company [U.K.] . . . . DLB-106
Frederick Warne and Company [U.S.] . . . . DLB-49
Warner, Anne 1869-1913 . . . . . . . . . . . . . . DLB-202
Warner, Charles Dudley 1829-1900 . . . . . . DLB-64
Warner, Marina 1946- . . . . . . . . . . . . . . . . DLB-194
Warner, Rex 1905-1986 . . . . . . . . . . . . . . . DLB-15
Warner, Susan 1819-1885 . . . DLB-3, 42, 239, 250
Warner, Sylvia Townsend
   1893-1978 . . . . . . . . . . . . . . . . . DLB-34, 139
Warner, William 1558-1609 . . . . . . . . . . . . DLB-172
Warner Books . . . . . . . . . . . . . . . . . . . . . . DLB-46
Warr, Bertram 1917-1943 . . . . . . . . . . . . . DLB-88
Warren, John Byrne Leicester (see De Tabley, Lord)
Warren, Lella 1899-1982 . . . . . . . . . . . . . . . . Y-83
Warren, Mercy Otis 1728-1814 . . . . . DLB-31, 200
Warren, Robert Penn 1905-1989 . . . . . DLB-2, 48,
   152; Y-80, 89; CDALB-6
   Tribute to Katherine Anne Porter . . . . . . . Y-80
Warren, Samuel 1807-1877 . . . . . . . . . . . . DLB-190
*Die Wartburgkrieg* circa 1230-circa 1280 . . . DLB-138
Warton, Joseph 1722-1800 . . . . . . . . DLB-104, 109
Warton, Thomas 1728-1790 . . . . . . . DLB-104, 109
Warung, Price (William Astley)
   1855-1911 . . . . . . . . . . . . . . . . . . . . DLB-230
Washington, George 1732-1799 . . . . . . . . . . DLB-31
Washington, Ned 1901-1976 . . . . . . . . . . . DLB-265
Wassermann, Jakob 1873-1934 . . . . . . . . . . . DLB-66
Wasserstein, Wendy 1950- . . . . . . . . . . . . DLB-228
Wassmo, Herbjorg 1942- . . . . . . . . . . . . . DLB-297
Wasson, David Atwood 1823-1887 . . . DLB-1, 223
Watanna, Onoto (see Eaton, Winnifred)
Waten, Judah 1911?-1985 . . . . . . . . . . . . . DLB-289
Waterhouse, Keith 1929- . . . . . . . . . . . DLB-13, 15
Waterman, Andrew 1940- . . . . . . . . . . . . . DLB-40
Waters, Frank 1902-1995 . . . . . . . . DLB-212; Y-86
Waters, Michael 1949- . . . . . . . . . . . . . . . DLB-120
Watkins, Tobias 1780-1855 . . . . . . . . . . . . . DLB-73
Watkins, Vernon 1906-1967 . . . . . . . . . . . . DLB-20
Watmough, David 1926- . . . . . . . . . . . . . . DLB-53
Watson, Colin 1920-1983 . . . . . . . . . . . . . DLB-276
Watson, Ian 1943- . . . . . . . . . . . . . . . . . . DLB-261
Watson, James Wreford (see Wreford, James)
Watson, John 1850-1907 . . . . . . . . . . . . . . DLB-156
Watson, Rosamund Marriott
   (Graham R. Tomson) 1860-1911 . . . . DLB-240
Watson, Sheila 1909-1998 . . . . . . . . . . . . . . DLB-60
Watson, Thomas 1545?-1592 . . . . . . . . . . . DLB-132
Watson, Wilfred 1911- . . . . . . . . . . . . . . . . DLB-60
W. J. Watt and Company . . . . . . . . . . . . . . DLB-46
Watten, Barrett 1948- . . . . . . . . . . . . . . . . DLB-193
Watterson, Henry 1840-1921 . . . . . . . . . . . DLB-25
Watts, Alan 1915-1973 . . . . . . . . . . . . . . . . DLB-16
Watts, Isaac 1674-1748 . . . . . . . . . . . . . . . . DLB-95

Franklin Watts [publishing house] . . . . . . . DLB-46
Waugh, Alec 1898-1981 . . . . . . . . . . . . . . . DLB-191
Waugh, Auberon 1939-2000 . . . DLB-14, 194; Y-00
Waugh, Evelyn 1903-1966 . . . . . DLB-15, 162, 195;
   CDBLB-6
Way and Williams . . . . . . . . . . . . . . . . . . . DLB-49
Wayman, Tom 1945- . . . . . . . . . . . . . . . . . DLB-53
Weatherly, Tom 1942- . . . . . . . . . . . . . . . . DLB-41
Weaver, Gordon 1937- . . . . . . . . . . . . . . . DLB-130
Weaver, Robert 1921- . . . . . . . . . . . . . . . . DLB-88
Webb, Beatrice 1858-1943 . . . . . . . . . . . . . DLB-190
Webb, Francis 1925-1973 . . . . . . . . . . . . . DLB-260
Webb, Frank J. ?-? . . . . . . . . . . . . . . . . . . DLB-50
Webb, James Watson 1802-1884 . . . . . . . . DLB-43
Webb, Mary 1881-1927 . . . . . . . . . . . . . . . DLB-34
Webb, Phyllis 1927- . . . . . . . . . . . . . . . . . DLB-53
Webb, Sidney 1859-1947 . . . . . . . . . . . . . DLB-190
Webb, Walter Prescott 1888-1963 . . . . . . . DLB-17
Webbe, William ?-1591 . . . . . . . . . . . . . . . DLB-132
Webber, Charles Wilkins 1819-1856? . . . DLB-202
Weber, Max 1864-1920 . . . . . . . . . . . . . . . DLB-296
Webling, Lucy (Lucy Betty MacRaye)
   1877-1952 . . . . . . . . . . . . . . . . . . . . DLB-240
Webling, Peggy (Arthur Weston)
   1871-1949 . . . . . . . . . . . . . . . . . . . . DLB-240
Webster, Augusta 1837-1894 . . . . . . DLB-35, 240
Webster, John
   1579 or 1580-1634? . . . . . . DLB-58; CDBLB-1
   The Melbourne Manuscript . . . . . . . . . . . . Y-86
Webster, Noah
   1758-1843 . . . . . . . . DLB-1, 37, 42, 43, 73, 243
Webster, Paul Francis 1907-1984 . . . . . . . DLB-265
Charles L. Webster and Company . . . . . . . DLB-49
Weckherlin, Georg Rodolf 1584-1653 . . . DLB-164
Wedekind, Frank
   1864-1918 . . . . . . . . . . . DLB-118; CDWLB-2
Weeks, Edward Augustus, Jr.
   1898-1989 . . . . . . . . . . . . . . . . . . . . DLB-137
Weeks, Stephen B. 1865-1918 . . . . . . . . . DLB-187
Weems, Mason Locke 1759-1825 . . . DLB-30, 37, 42
Weerth, Georg 1822-1856 . . . . . . . . . . . . . DLB-129
Weidenfeld and Nicolson . . . . . . . . . . . . . DLB-112
Weidman, Jerome 1913-1998 . . . . . . . . . . . DLB-28
Weigl, Bruce 1949- . . . . . . . . . . . . . . . . . . DLB-120
Weil, Jiří 1900-1959 . . . . . . . . . . . . . . . . . DLB-299
Weinbaum, Stanley Grauman 1902-1935 . . DLB-8
Weiner, Andrew 1949- . . . . . . . . . . . . . . . DLB-251
Weintraub, Stanley 1929- . . . . . . . . DLB-111; Y82
Weise, Christian 1642-1708 . . . . . . . . . . . DLB-168
Weisenborn, Gunther 1902-1969 . . . DLB-69, 124
Weiss, John 1818-1879 . . . . . . . . . . . . DLB-1, 243
Weiss, Paul 1901-2002 . . . . . . . . . . . . . . . DLB-279
Weiss, Peter 1916-1982 . . . . . . . . . . . DLB-69, 124
Weiss, Theodore 1916- . . . . . . . . . . . . . . . . DLB-5
Weiß, Ernst 1882-1940 . . . . . . . . . . . . . . . . DLB-81
Weiße, Christian Felix 1726-1804 . . . . . . . . DLB-97

Weitling, Wilhelm 1808-1871 . . . . . . . . . . DLB-129
Welch, James 1940- . . . . . . . . . . . . . . DLB-175, 256
Welch, Lew 1926-1971? . . . . . . . . . . . . . . . DLB-16
Weldon, Fay 1931- . . . . DLB-14, 194; CDBLB-8
Wellek, René 1903-1995 . . . . . . . . . . . . . . . DLB-63
Wells, Carolyn 1862-1942 . . . . . . . . . . . . . DLB-11
Wells, Charles Jeremiah
   circa 1800-1879 . . . . . . . . . . . . . . . . . DLB-32
Wells, Gabriel 1862-1946 . . . . . . . . . . . . . DLB-140
Wells, H. G. 1866-1946 . . . . DLB-34, 70, 156, 178;
   CDBLB-6
   H. G. Wells Society . . . . . . . . . . . . . . . . . Y-98
   Preface to *The Scientific Romances of
     H. G. Wells* (1933) . . . . . . . . . . . . . DLB-178
Wells, Helena 1758?-1824 . . . . . . . . . . . . . DLB-200
Wells, Rebecca 1952- . . . . . . . . . . . . . . . . DLB-292
Wells, Robert 1947- . . . . . . . . . . . . . . . . . . DLB-40
Wells-Barnett, Ida B. 1862-1931 . . . . . DLB-23, 221
Welsh, Irvine 1958- . . . . . . . . . . . . . . . . . DLB-271
Welty, Eudora 1909-2001 . . . . . . DLB-2, 102, 143;
   Y-87, 01; DS-12; CDALB-1
   Eudora Welty: Eye of the Storyteller . . . . . Y-87
   *Eudora Welty Newsletter* . . . . . . . . . . . . . . Y-99
   Eudora Welty's Funeral . . . . . . . . . . . . . . Y-01
   Eudora Welty's Ninetieth Birthday . . . . . . Y-99
   Eudora Welty Remembered in
     Two Exhibits . . . . . . . . . . . . . . . . . . Y-02
Wendell, Barrett 1855-1921 . . . . . . . . . . . . DLB-71
Wentworth, Patricia 1878-1961 . . . . . . . . . DLB-77
Wentworth, William Charles
   1790-1872 . . . . . . . . . . . . . . . . . . . . DLB-230
Werder, Diederich von dem 1584-1657 . . DLB-164
Werfel, Franz 1890-1945 . . . . . . . . . . . DLB-81, 124
Werner, Zacharias 1768-1823 . . . . . . . . . . . DLB-94
The Werner Company . . . . . . . . . . . . . . . . DLB-49
Wersba, Barbara 1932- . . . . . . . . . . . . . . . DLB-52
Wescott, Glenway
   1901-1987 . . . . . . . . . . . DLB-4, 9, 102; DS-15
Wesker, Arnold 1932- . . . . . DLB-13; CDBLB-8
Wesley, Charles 1707-1788 . . . . . . . . . . . . . DLB-95
Wesley, John 1703-1791 . . . . . . . . . . . . . . DLB-104
Wesley, Mary 1912-2002 . . . . . . . . . . . . . . DLB-231
Wesley, Richard 1945- . . . . . . . . . . . . . . . . DLB-38
Wessel, Johan Herman 1742-1785 . . . . . . DLB-300
A. Wessels and Company . . . . . . . . . . . . . . DLB-46
*Wessobrunner Gebet* circa 787-815 . . . . . . . DLB-148
West, Anthony 1914-1988 . . . . . . . . . . . . . DLB-15
   Tribute to Liam O'Flaherty . . . . . . . . . . . Y-84
West, Cheryl L. 1957- . . . . . . . . . . . . . . . DLB-266
West, Cornel 1953- . . . . . . . . . . . . . . . . . DLB-246
West, Dorothy 1907-1998 . . . . . . . . . . . . . . DLB-76
West, Jessamyn 1902-1984 . . . . . . . . . DLB-6; Y-84
West, Mae 1892-1980 . . . . . . . . . . . . . . . . . DLB-44
West, Michael Lee 1953- . . . . . . . . . . . . . DLB-292
West, Michelle Sagara 1963- . . . . . . . . . . DLB-251
West, Morris 1916-1999 . . . . . . . . . . . . . . DLB-289

West, Nathanael 1903-1940 .........DLB-4, 9, 28; CDALB-5
West, Paul 1930- .................DLB-14
West, Rebecca 1892-1983 .........DLB-36; Y-83
West, Richard 1941- ...............DLB-185
West and Johnson ..................DLB-49
Westcott, Edward Noyes 1846-1898 .....DLB-202
The Western Literature Association ........Y-99
*The Western Messenger* 1835-1841 ...............DLB-1; DLB-223
Western Publishing Company...........DLB-46
Western Writers of America ............Y-99
*The Westminster Review* 1824-1914 .......DLB-110
Weston, Arthur (see Webling, Peggy)
Weston, Elizabeth Jane circa 1582-1612 ..DLB-172
Wetherald, Agnes Ethelwyn 1857-1940....DLB-99
Wetherell, Elizabeth (see Warner, Susan)
Wetherell, W. D. 1948- ..............DLB-234
Wetzel, Friedrich Gottlob 1779-1819 ......DLB-90
Weyman, Stanley J. 1855-1928 .....DLB-141, 156
Wezel, Johann Karl 1747-1819..........DLB-94
Whalen, Philip 1923-2002.............DLB-16
Whalley, George 1915-1983 ............DLB-88
Wharton, Edith 1862-1937 ........ DLB-4, 9, 12, 78, 189; DS-13; CDALB-3
Wharton, William 1920s?- ............Y-80
Whately, Mary Louisa 1824-1889.......DLB-166
Whately, Richard 1787-1863 ..........DLB-190
*Elements of Rhetoric* (1828; revised, 1846) [excerpt]..........DLB-57
Wheatley, Dennis 1897-1977 ........ DLB-77, 255
Wheatley, Phillis circa 1754-1784 .......DLB-31, 50; CDALB-2
Wheeler, Anna Doyle 1785-1848?.......DLB-158
Wheeler, Charles Stearns 1816-1843...DLB-1, 223
Wheeler, Monroe 1900-1988.............DLB-4
Wheelock, John Hall 1886-1978 ........DLB-45
From John Hall Wheelock's Oral Memoir....................Y-01
Wheelwright, J. B. 1897-1940..........DLB-45
Wheelwright, John circa 1592-1679 .......DLB-24
Whetstone, George 1550-1587..........DLB-136
Whetstone, Colonel Pete (see Noland, C. F. M.)
Whewell, William 1794-1866............DLB-262
Whichcote, Benjamin 1609?-1683.......DLB-252
Whicher, Stephen E. 1915-1961 ........DLB-111
Whipple, Edwin Percy 1819-1886 .....DLB-1, 64
Whitaker, Alexander 1585-1617 .......DLB-24
Whitaker, Daniel K. 1801-1881.........DLB-73
Whitcher, Frances Miriam 1812-1852 ...............DLB-11, 202
White, Andrew 1579-1656..............DLB-24
White, Andrew Dickson 1832-1918 .....DLB-47
White, E. B. 1899-1985 ....DLB-11, 22; CDALB-7
White, Edgar B. 1947- .................DLB-38
White, Edmund 1940- ................DLB-227

White, Ethel Lina 1887-1944 ..........DLB-77
White, Hayden V. 1928- ..............DLB-246
White, Henry Kirke 1785-1806 .........DLB-96
White, Horace 1834-1916 ..............DLB-23
White, James 1928-1999 ..............DLB-261
White, Patrick 1912-1990 .............DLB-260
White, Phyllis Dorothy James (see James, P. D.)
White, Richard Grant 1821-1885 ........DLB-64
White, T. H. 1906-1964 ..........DLB-160, 255
White, Walter 1893-1955 ..............DLB-51
Wilcox, James 1949- .................DLB-292
William White and Company ...........DLB-49
White, William Allen 1868-1944 .....DLB-9, 25
White, William Anthony Parker (see Boucher, Anthony)
White, William Hale (see Rutherford, Mark)
Whitechurch, Victor L. 1868-1933 .......DLB-70
Whitehead, Alfred North 1861-1947 .................DLB-100, 262
Whitehead, James 1936- ...............Y-81
Whitehead, William 1715-1785 .....DLB-84, 109
Whitfield, James Monroe 1822-1871 .....DLB-50
Whitfield, Raoul 1898-1945...........DLB-226
Whitgift, John circa 1533-1604 .........DLB-132
Whiting, John 1917-1963 ..............DLB-13
Whiting, Samuel 1597-1679 ............DLB-24
Whitlock, Brand 1869-1934............DLB-12
Whitman, Albery Allson 1851-1901 .....DLB-50
Whitman, Alden 1913-1990 ............Y-91
Whitman, Sarah Helen (Power) 1803-1878 ..................DLB-1, 243
Whitman, Walt 1819-1892 ....DLB-3, 64, 224, 250; CDALB-2
Albert Whitman and Company..........DLB-46
Whitman Publishing Company..........DLB-46
Whitney, Geoffrey 1548 or 1552?-1601 ..DLB-136
Whitney, Isabella flourished 1566-1573...DLB-136
Whitney, John Hay 1904-1982 ........DLB-127
Whittemore, Reed 1919-1995 ...........DLB-5
Whittier, John Greenleaf 1807-1892 .........DLB-1, 243; CDALB-2
Whittlesey House ....................DLB-46
Wickham, Anna (Edith Alice Mary Harper) 1884-1947 .................DLB-240
Wickram, Georg circa 1505-circa 1561 ...DLB-179
Wicomb, Zoë 1948- ..................DLB-225
Wideman, John Edgar 1941- .......DLB-33, 143
Widener, Harry Elkins 1885-1912.......DLB-140
Wiebe, Rudy 1934- ...................DLB-60
Wiechert, Ernst 1887-1950.............DLB-56
Wied, Gustav 1858-1914...............DLB-300
Wied, Martina 1882-1957 ..............DLB-85
Wiehe, Evelyn May Clowes (see Mordaunt, Elinor)
Wieland, Christoph Martin 1733-1813 ....DLB-97
Wienbarg, Ludolf 1802-1872..........DLB-133

Wieners, John 1934- ..................DLB-16
Wier, Ester 1910- ....................DLB-52
Wiesel, Elie 1928- .....DLB-83, 299; Y-86, 87; CDALB-7
Nobel Lecture 1986: Hope, Despair and Memory .....................Y-86
Wiggin, Kate Douglas 1856-1923 ........DLB-42
Wigglesworth, Michael 1631-1705........DLB-24
Wilberforce, William 1759-1833 ........DLB-158
Wilbrandt, Adolf 1837-1911 ...........DLB-129
Wilbur, Richard 1921- ...DLB-5, 169; CDALB-7
Tribute to Robert Penn Warren ........Y-89
Wilcox, James 1949- .................DLB-292
Wild, Peter 1940- ....................DLB-5
Wilde, Lady Jane Francesca Elgee 1821?-1896 ....................DLB-199
Wilde, Oscar 1854-1900 ......DLB-10, 19, 34, 57, 141, 156, 190; CDBLB-5
"The Critic as Artist" (1891).........DLB-57
"The Decay of Lying" (1889) ........DLB-18
"The English Renaissance of Art" (1908)...................DLB-35
"L'Envoi" (1882)..................DLB-35
Oscar Wilde Conference at Hofstra University...................Y-00
Wilde, Richard Henry 1789-1847 .......DLB-3, 59
W. A. Wilde Company ................DLB-49
Wilder, Billy 1906- ..................DLB-26
Wilder, Laura Ingalls 1867-1957 .....DLB-22, 256
Wilder, Thornton 1897-1975........ DLB-4, 7, 9, 228; CDALB-7
Thornton Wilder Centenary at Yale......Y-97
Wildgans, Anton 1881-1932 ...........DLB-118
Wiley, Bell Irvin 1906-1980.............DLB-17
John Wiley and Sons..................DLB-49
Wilhelm, Kate 1928- ...................DLB-8
Wilkes, Charles 1798-1877.............DLB-183
Wilkes, George 1817-1885 .............DLB-79
Wilkins, John 1614-1672 ..............DLB-236
Wilkinson, Anne 1910-1961 ............DLB-88
Wilkinson, Eliza Yonge 1757-circa 1813 .................DLB-200
Wilkinson, Sylvia 1940- ................Y-86
Wilkinson, William Cleaver 1833-1920 ...DLB-71
Willard, Barbara 1909-1994 ...........DLB-161
Willard, Emma 1787-1870 .............DLB-239
Willard, Frances E. 1839-1898 .........DLB-221
Willard, Nancy 1936- ...............DLB-5, 52
Willard, Samuel 1640-1707 .............DLB-24
L. Willard [publishing house] ..........DLB-49
Willeford, Charles 1919-1988 ..........DLB-226
William of Auvergne 1190-1249 ........DLB-115
William of Conches circa 1090-circa 1154..............DLB-115
William of Ockham circa 1285-1347 .....DLB-115
William of Sherwood 1200/1205-1266/1271 .............DLB-115

# Cumulative Index

The William Charvat American Fiction
   Collection at the Ohio State
   University Libraries . . . . . . . . . . . . . . . . . . . Y-92
Williams, Ben Ames 1889-1953 . . . . . . . DLB-102
Williams, C. K. 1936- . . . . . . . . . . . . . . . . DLB-5
Williams, Chancellor 1905-1992 . . . . . . . DLB-76
Williams, Charles 1886-1945 . . . DLB-100, 153, 255
Williams, Denis 1923-1998 . . . . . . . . . . . DLB-117
Williams, Emlyn 1905-1987 . . . . . . . . . DLB-10, 77
Williams, Garth 1912-1996 . . . . . . . . . . . DLB-22
Williams, George Washington
   1849-1891 . . . . . . . . . . . . . . . . . . . . DLB-47
Williams, Heathcote 1941- . . . . . . . . . . . . DLB-13
Williams, Helen Maria 1761-1827 . . . . . . DLB-158
Williams, Hugo 1942- . . . . . . . . . . . . . . . DLB-40
Williams, Isaac 1802-1865 . . . . . . . . . . . . DLB-32
Williams, Joan 1928- . . . . . . . . . . . . . . . . DLB-6
Williams, Joe 1889-1972 . . . . . . . . . . . . . DLB-241
Williams, John A. 1925- . . . . . . . . . . . DLB-2, 33
Williams, John E. 1922-1994 . . . . . . . . . . DLB-6
Williams, Jonathan 1929- . . . . . . . . . . . . DLB-5
Williams, Miller 1930- . . . . . . . . . . . . . . DLB-105
Williams, Nigel 1948- . . . . . . . . . . . . . . . DLB-231
Williams, Raymond
   1921-1988 . . . . . . . . . . . . DLB-14, 231, 242
Williams, Roger circa 1603-1683 . . . . . . . DLB-24
Williams, Rowland 1817-1870 . . . . . . . . . DLB-184
Williams, Samm-Art 1946- . . . . . . . . . . . DLB-38
Williams, Sherley Anne 1944-1999 . . . . . . DLB-41
Williams, T. Harry 1909-1979 . . . . . . . . . DLB-17
Williams, Tennessee
   1911-1983 . . . . . DLB-7; Y-83; DS-4; CDALB-1
Williams, Terry Tempest 1955- . . . DLB-206, 275
Williams, Ursula Moray 1911- . . . . . . . DLB-160
Williams, Valentine 1883-1946 . . . . . . . . DLB-77
Williams, William Appleman 1921- . . . . DLB-17
Williams, William Carlos
   1883-1963 . . . . . DLB-4, 16, 54, 86; CDALB-4
   The William Carlos Williams Society . . . . Y-99
Williams, Wirt 1921- . . . . . . . . . . . . . . . . DLB-6
A. Williams and Company . . . . . . . . . . . . DLB-49
Williams Brothers . . . . . . . . . . . . . . . . . . . DLB-49
Wiliamson, David 1942- . . . . . . . . . . . . DLB-289
Williamson, Henry 1895-1977 . . . . . . . . DLB-191
   The Henry Williamson Society . . . . . . . . Y-98
Williamson, Jack 1908- . . . . . . . . . . . . . . DLB-8
Willingham, Calder Baynard, Jr.
   1922-1995 . . . . . . . . . . . . . . . . . DLB-2, 44
Williram of Ebersberg circa 1020-1085 . . DLB-148
Willis, John circa 1572-1625 . . . . . . . . . . DLB-281
Willis, Nathaniel Parker 1806-1867 . . . . DLB-3, 59,
                        73, 74, 183, 250; DS-13
Willkomm, Ernst 1810-1886 . . . . . . . . . DLB-133
Wills, Garry 1934- . . . . . . . . . . . . . . . . DLB-246
   Tribute to Kenneth Dale McCormick . . . . Y-97
Willson, Meredith 1902-1984 . . . . . . . . . DLB-265

Willumsen, Dorrit 1940- . . . . . . . . . . . . DLB-214
Wilmer, Clive 1945- . . . . . . . . . . . . . . . . DLB-40
Wilson, A. N. 1950- . . . . . . . . . DLB-14, 155, 194
Wilson, Angus 1913-1991 . . . . . DLB-15, 139, 155
Wilson, Arthur 1595-1652 . . . . . . . . . . . . DLB-58
Wilson, August 1945- . . . . . . . . . . . . . . DLB-228
Wilson, Augusta Jane Evans 1835-1909 . . . DLB-42
Wilson, Colin 1931- . . . . . . . . . . . . DLB-14, 194
   Tribute to J. B. Priestly . . . . . . . . . . . . . . Y-84
Wilson, Edmund 1895-1972 . . . . . . . . . . DLB-63
Wilson, Ethel 1888-1980 . . . . . . . . . . . . . DLB-68
Wilson, F. P. 1889-1963 . . . . . . . . . . . . . DLB-201
Wilson, Harriet E.
   1827/1828?-1863? . . . . . . . . DLB-50, 239, 243
Wilson, Harry Leon 1867-1939 . . . . . . . . DLB-9
Wilson, John 1588-1667 . . . . . . . . . . . . . DLB-24
Wilson, John 1785-1854 . . . . . . . . . . . . . DLB-110
Wilson, John Anthony Burgess
   (see Burgess, Anthony)
Wilson, John Dover 1881-1969 . . . . . . . DLB-201
Wilson, Lanford 1937- . . . . . . . . . . . . . . . DLB-7
Wilson, Margaret 1882-1973 . . . . . . . . . . DLB-9
Wilson, Michael 1914-1978 . . . . . . . . . . . DLB-44
Wilson, Mona 1872-1954 . . . . . . . . . . . . DLB-149
Wilson, Robert Charles 1953- . . . . . . . . DLB-251
Wilson, Robert McLiam 1964- . . . . . . . . DLB-267
Wilson, Robley 1930- . . . . . . . . . . . . . . DLB-218
Wilson, Romer 1891-1930 . . . . . . . . . . . DLB-191
Wilson, Thomas 1524-1581 . . . . . . . DLB-132, 236
Wilson, Woodrow 1856-1924 . . . . . . . . . DLB-47
Effingham Wilson [publishing house] . . . . DLB-154
Wimpfeling, Jakob 1450-1528 . . . . . . . . DLB-179
Wimsatt, William K., Jr. 1907-1975 . . . . . DLB-63
Winchell, Walter 1897-1972 . . . . . . . . . . DLB-29
J. Winchester [publishing house] . . . . . . . DLB-49
Winckelmann, Johann Joachim
   1717-1768 . . . . . . . . . . . . . . . . . . . . DLB-97
Winckler, Paul 1630-1686 . . . . . . . . . . . DLB-164
Wind, Herbert Warren 1916- . . . . . . . . DLB-171
John Windet [publishing house] . . . . . . . DLB-170
Windham, Donald 1920- . . . . . . . . . . . . . DLB-6
Wing, Donald Goddard 1904-1972 . . . . . DLB-187
Wing, John M. 1844-1917 . . . . . . . . . . . DLB-187
Allan Wingate [publishing house] . . . . . . DLB-112
Winnemucca, Sarah 1844-1921 . . . . . . . DLB-175
Winnifrith, Tom 1938- . . . . . . . . . . . . . DLB-155
Winsloe, Christa 1888-1944 . . . . . . . . . . DLB-124
Winslow, Anna Green 1759-1780 . . . . . . DLB-200
Winsor, Justin 1831-1897 . . . . . . . . . . . . DLB-47
John C. Winston Company . . . . . . . . . . . DLB-49
Winters, Yvor 1900-1968 . . . . . . . . . . . . DLB-48
Winterson, Jeanette 1959- . . . . . . . DLB-207, 261
Winther, Christian 1796-1876 . . . . . . . . DLB-300
Winthrop, John 1588-1649 . . . . . . . . DLB-24, 30
Winthrop, John, Jr. 1606-1676 . . . . . . . . DLB-24

Winthrop, Margaret Tyndal 1591-1647 . . DLB-200
Winthrop, Theodore 1828-1861 . . . . . . . DLB-202
Wirt, William 1772-1834 . . . . . . . . . . . . . DLB-37
Wise, John 1652-1725 . . . . . . . . . . . . . . . DLB-24
Wise, Thomas James 1859-1937 . . . . . . . DLB-184
Wiseman, Adele 1928-1992 . . . . . . . . . . . DLB-88
Wishart and Company . . . . . . . . . . . . . . DLB-112
Wisner, George 1812-1849 . . . . . . . . . . . DLB-43
Wister, Owen 1860-1938 . . . . . . . DLB-9, 78, 186
Wister, Sarah 1761-1804 . . . . . . . . . . . . . DLB-200
Wither, George 1588-1667 . . . . . . . . . . . DLB-121
Witherspoon, John 1723-1794 . . . . . . . . . DLB-31
   *The Works of the Rev. John Witherspoon*
   (1800-1801) [excerpts] . . . . . . . . . . . DLB-31
Withrow, William Henry 1839-1908 . . . . . DLB-99
Witkacy (see Witkiewicz, Stanisław Ignacy)
Witkiewicz, Stanisław Ignacy
   1885-1939 . . . . . . . . . . . DLB-215; CDWLB-4
Wittenwiler, Heinrich before 1387-
   circa 1414? . . . . . . . . . . . . . . . . . . . DLB-179
Wittgenstein, Ludwig 1889-1951 . . . . . . . DLB-262
Wittig, Monique 1935- . . . . . . . . . . . . . . DLB-83
Wodehouse, P. G.
   1881-1975 . . . . . . . . . DLB-34, 162; CDBLB-6
   Worldwide Wodehouse Societies . . . . . . . Y-98
Wohmann, Gabriele 1932- . . . . . . . . . . . DLB-75
Woiwode, Larry 1941- . . . . . . . . . . . . . . . DLB-6
   Tribute to John Gardner . . . . . . . . . . . . . Y-82
Wolcot, John 1738-1819 . . . . . . . . . . . . . DLB-109
Wolcott, Roger 1679-1767 . . . . . . . . . . . . DLB-24
Wolf, Christa 1929- . . . . . . . . DLB-75; CDWLB-2
Wolf, Friedrich 1888-1953 . . . . . . . . . . . DLB-124
Wolfe, Gene 1931- . . . . . . . . . . . . . . . . . . DLB-8
Wolfe, Thomas 1900-1938 . . . . . DLB-9, 102, 229;
                      Y-85; DS-2, DS-16; CDALB-5
   "All the Faults of Youth and Inexperience":
   A Reader's Report on
   Thomas Wolfe's *O Lost* . . . . . . . . . . . Y-01
   Emendations for *Look Homeward, Angel* . . . Y-00
   Eugene Gant's Projected Works . . . . . . . . Y-01
   Fire at the Old Kentucky Home
   [Thomas Wolfe Memorial] . . . . . . . . . Y-98
   Thomas Wolfe Centennial
   Celebration in Asheville . . . . . . . . . . . Y-00
   The Thomas Wolfe Collection at
   the University of North Carolina
   at Chapel Hill . . . . . . . . . . . . . . . . . . Y-97
   The Thomas Wolfe Society . . . . . . . . . Y-97, 99
Wolfe, Tom 1931- . . . . . . . . . . . . . . DLB-152, 185
John Wolfe [publishing house] . . . . . . . . DLB-170
Reyner (Reginald) Wolfe
   [publishing house] . . . . . . . . . . . . . . DLB-170
Wolfenstein, Martha 1869-1906 . . . . . . . DLB-221
Wolff, David (see Maddow, Ben)
Wolff, Helen 1906-1994 . . . . . . . . . . . . . . . Y-94
Wolff, Tobias 1945- . . . . . . . . . . . . . . . . DLB-130
   Tribute to Michael M. Rea . . . . . . . . . . . Y-97
   Tribute to Raymond Carver . . . . . . . . . . Y-88

Wolfram von Eschenbach
  circa 1170-after 1220 . . . . DLB-138; CDWLB-2
  Wolfram von Eschenbach's *Parzival*:
    Prologue and Book 3 . . . . . . . . . DLB-138
Wolker, Jiří 1900-1924 . . . . . . . . . . . . . DLB-215
Wollstonecraft, Mary 1759-1797 . . . . DLB-39, 104,
  158, 252; CDBLB-3
Women
  Women's Work, Women's Sphere:
    Selected Comments from Women
    Writers . . . . . . . . . . . . . . . . . . DLB-200
Wondratschek, Wolf 1943- . . . . . . . . . DLB-75
Wong, Elizabeth 1958- . . . . . . . . . . . DLB-266
Wood, Anthony à 1632-1695 . . . . . . . . DLB-213
Wood, Benjamin 1820-1900 . . . . . . . . DLB-23
Wood, Charles 1932-1980 . . . . . . . . . . DLB-13
  The Charles Wood Affair:
    A Playwright Revived . . . . . . . . . . Y-83
Wood, Mrs. Henry 1814-1887 . . . . . . . . DLB-18
Wood, Joanna E. 1867-1927 . . . . . . . . DLB-92
Wood, Sally Sayward Barrell Keating
  1759-1855 . . . . . . . . . . . . . . . . . DLB-200
Wood, William ?-? . . . . . . . . . . . . . . . DLB-24
Samuel Wood [publishing house] . . . . . . . DLB-49
Woodberry, George Edward
  1855-1930 . . . . . . . . . . . . . . DLB-71, 103
Woodbridge, Benjamin 1622-1684 . . . . . . DLB-24
Woodbridge, Frederick J. E. 1867-1940 . . . DLB-270
Woodcock, George 1912-1995 . . . . . . . . DLB-88
Woodhull, Victoria C. 1838-1927 . . . . . . DLB-79
Woodmason, Charles circa 1720-? . . . . . . DLB-31
Woodress, James Leslie, Jr. 1916- . . . . . . DLB-111
Woods, Margaret L. 1855-1945 . . . . . . . DLB-240
Woodson, Carter G. 1875-1950 . . . . . . . DLB-17
Woodward, C. Vann 1908-1999 . . . . . . . DLB-17
Woodward, Stanley 1895-1965 . . . . . . . DLB-171
Woodworth, Samuel 1785-1842 . . . . . . . DLB-250
Wooler, Thomas 1785 or 1786-1853 . . . . DLB-158
Woolf, David (see Maddow, Ben)
Woolf, Douglas 1922-1992 . . . . . . . . . . DLB-244
Woolf, Leonard 1880-1969 . . . . . DLB-100; DS-10
Woolf, Virginia 1882-1941 . . . DLB-36, 100, 162;
  DS-10; CDBLB-6
  "The New Biography," *New York Herald
    Tribune*, 30 October 1927 . . . . . . DLB-149
Woollcott, Alexander 1887-1943 . . . . . . DLB-29
Woolman, John 1720-1772 . . . . . . . . . DLB-31
Woolner, Thomas 1825-1892 . . . . . . . . DLB-35
Woolrich, Cornell 1903-1968 . . . . . . . . DLB-226
Woolsey, Sarah Chauncy 1835-1905 . . . . DLB-42
Woolson, Constance Fenimore
  1840-1894 . . . . . . . . . DLB-12, 74, 189, 221
Worcester, Joseph Emerson
  1784-1865 . . . . . . . . . . . . . . . . DLB-1, 235
Wynkyn de Worde [publishing house] . . . DLB-170
Wordsworth, Christopher 1807-1885 . . . . DLB-166
Wordsworth, Dorothy 1771-1855 . . . . . . DLB-107
Wordsworth, Elizabeth 1840-1932 . . . . . . DLB-98
Wordsworth, William
  1770-1850 . . . . . . . . DLB-93, 107; CDBLB-3

Workman, Fanny Bullock
  1859-1925 . . . . . . . . . . . . . . . . DLB-189
*World Literatue Today:* A Journal for the
  New Millennium . . . . . . . . . . . . . . Y-01
World Publishing Company . . . . . . . . . DLB-46
World War I (1914-1918) . . . . . . . . . . . DS-18
  The Great War Exhibit and Symposium
    at the University of South Carolina . . Y-97
  The Liddle Collection and First World
    War Research . . . . . . . . . . . . . . . Y-97
  Other British Poets Who Fell
    in the Great War . . . . . . . . . . . DLB-216
  The Seventy-Fifth Anniversary of
    the Armistice: The Wilfred Owen
    Centenary and the Great War Exhibit
    at the University of Virginia . . . . . . Y-93
World War II (1939-1945)
  Literary Effects of World War II . . . . . DLB-15
  World War II Writers Symposium
    at the University of South Carolina,
    12–14 April 1995 . . . . . . . . . . . . . Y-95
  WW2 HMSO Paperbacks Society . . . . . Y-98
R. Worthington and Company . . . . . . . DLB-49
Wotton, Sir Henry 1568-1639 . . . . . . . . DLB-121
Wouk, Herman 1915- . . . . . . . Y-82; CDALB-7
  Tribute to James Dickey . . . . . . . . . . Y-97
Wreford, James 1915- . . . . . . . . . . . . DLB-88
Wren, Sir Christopher 1632-1723 . . . . . . DLB-213
Wren, Percival Christopher 1885-1941 . . . DLB-153
Wrenn, John Henry 1841-1911 . . . . . . . DLB-140
Wright, C. D. 1949- . . . . . . . . . . . . . DLB-120
Wright, Charles 1935- . . . . . . . DLB-165; Y-82
Wright, Charles Stevenson 1932- . . . . . . DLB-33
Wright, Chauncey 1830-1875 . . . . . . . . DLB-270
Wright, Frances 1795-1852 . . . . . . . . . DLB-73
Wright, Harold Bell 1872-1944 . . . . . . . DLB-9
Wright, James 1927-1980
  . . . . . . . . . . . . . . . . DLB-5, 169; CDALB-7
Wright, Jay 1935- . . . . . . . . . . . . . . . DLB-41
Wright, Judith 1915-2000 . . . . . . . . . . DLB-260
Wright, Louis B. 1899-1984 . . . . . . . . . DLB-17
Wright, Richard 1908-1960 . . . . . . DLB-76, 102;
  DS-2; CDALB-5
Wright, Richard B. 1937- . . . . . . . . . . DLB-53
Wright, S. Fowler 1874-1965 . . . . . . . . DLB-255
Wright, Sarah Elizabeth 1928- . . . . . . . DLB-33
Wright, T. H. "Style" (1877) [excerpt] . . . DLB-57
Wright, Willard Huntington
  (S. S. Van Dine) 1888-1939 . . . . . . . DS-16
Wrightson, Patricia 1921- . . . . . . . . . DLB-289
Wrigley, Robert 1951- . . . . . . . . . . . DLB-256
*Writers' Forum* . . . . . . . . . . . . . . . . . Y-85
Writing
  A Writing Life . . . . . . . . . . . . . . . . Y-02
  On Learning to Write . . . . . . . . . . . . Y-88
  The Profession of Authorship:
    Scribblers for Bread . . . . . . . . . . . Y-89
  A Writer Talking: A Collage . . . . . . . . Y-00
Wroth, Lawrence C. 1884-1970 . . . . . . . DLB-187
Wroth, Lady Mary 1587-1653 . . . . . . . . DLB-121
Wurlitzer, Rudolph 1937- . . . . . . . . . . DLB-173

Wyatt, Sir Thomas circa 1503-1542 . . . . . DLB-132
Wycherley, William
  1641-1715 . . . . . . . . . . . DLB-80; CDBLB-2
Wyclif, John circa 1335-1384 . . . . . . . . DLB-146
Wyeth, N. C. 1882-1945 . . . . . . . DLB-188; DS-16
Wyle, Niklas von circa 1415-1479 . . . . . . DLB-179
Wylie, Elinor 1885-1928 . . . . . . . . . . DLB-9, 45
Wylie, Philip 1902-1971 . . . . . . . . . . . DLB-9
Wyllie, John Cook 1908-1968 . . . . . . . . DLB-140
Wyman, Lillie Buffum Chace
  1847-1929 . . . . . . . . . . . . . . . . DLB-202
Wymark, Olwen 1934- . . . . . . . . . . . DLB-233
Wynd, Oswald Morris (see Black, Gavin)
Wyndham, John (John Wyndham Parkes
  Lucas Beynon Harris) 1903-1969 . . . DLB-255
Wynne-Tyson, Esmé 1898-1972 . . . . . . . DLB-191

# X

Xenophon circa 430 B.C.-circa 356 B.C. . . . DLB-176

# Y

Yasuoka Shōtarō 1920- . . . . . . . . . . . DLB-182
Yates, Dornford 1885-1960 . . . . . . . DLB-77, 153
Yates, J. Michael 1938- . . . . . . . . . . . DLB-60
Yates, Richard 1926-1992 . . . DLB-2, 234; Y-81, 92
Yau, John 1950- . . . . . . . . . . . . . . . DLB-234
Yavorov, Peyo 1878-1914 . . . . . . . . . . DLB-147
Yearsley, Ann 1753-1806 . . . . . . . . . . DLB-109
Yeats, William Butler
  1865-1939 . . . . DLB-10, 19, 98, 156; CDBLB-5
  The W. B. Yeats Society of N.Y. . . . . . Y-99
Yellen, Jack 1892-1991 . . . . . . . . . . . DLB-265
Yep, Laurence 1948- . . . . . . . . . . . . DLB-52
Yerby, Frank 1916-1991 . . . . . . . . . . . DLB-76
Yezierska, Anzia 1880-1970 . . . . . . . DLB-28, 221
Yolen, Jane 1939- . . . . . . . . . . . . . . DLB-52
Yonge, Charlotte Mary 1823-1901 . . . DLB-18, 163
  The Charlotte M. Yonge Fellowship . . . Y-98
The York Cycle circa 1376-circa 1569 . . . . DLB-146
*A Yorkshire Tragedy* . . . . . . . . . . . . . DLB-58
Thomas Yoseloff [publishing house] . . . . . DLB-46
Youd, Sam (see Christopher, John)
Young, A. S. "Doc" 1919-1996 . . . . . . . DLB-241
Young, Al 1939- . . . . . . . . . . . . . . . DLB-33
Young, Arthur 1741-1820 . . . . . . . . . . DLB-158
Young, Dick 1917 or 1918-1987 . . . . . . . DLB-171
Young, Edward 1683-1765 . . . . . . . . . DLB-95
Young, Frank A. "Fay" 1884-1957 . . . . . . DLB-241
Young, Francis Brett 1884-1954 . . . . . . . DLB-191
Young, Gavin 1928- . . . . . . . . . . . . . DLB-204
Young, Stark 1881-1963 . . . . . DLB-9, 102; DS-16
Young, Waldeman 1880-1938 . . . . . . . . DLB-26
William Young [publishing house] . . . . . DLB-49
Young Bear, Ray A. 1950- . . . . . . . . . DLB-175
Yourcenar, Marguerite 1903-1987 . . . DLB-72; Y-88
Yovkov, Yordan 1880-1937 . . DLB-147; CDWLB-4

# Z

Zachariä, Friedrich Wilhelm 1726-1777 . . . . DLB-97
Zagajewski, Adam 1945- . . . . . . . . . . DLB-232

# Cumulative Index

Zagoskin, Mikhail Nikolaevich 1789-1852 ..................... DLB-198

Zajc, Dane 1929- .................. DLB-181

Zālīte, Māra 1952- ................. DLB-232

Zalygin, Sergei Pavlovich 1913-2000 ..................... DLB-302

Zamiatin, Evgenii Ivanovich 1884-1937 .. DLB-272

Zamora, Bernice 1938- ............. DLB-82

Zamudio, Adela (Soledad) 1854-1928 ... DLB-283

Zand, Herbert 1923-1970 ........... DLB-85

Zangwill, Israel 1864-1926 ...... DLB-10, 135, 197

Zanzotto, Andrea 1921- ............ DLB-128

Zapata Olivella, Manuel 1920- ....... DLB-113

Zapoev, Timur Iur'evich
(see Kibirov, Timur Iur'evich)

Zasodimsky, Pavel Vladimirovich 1843-1912 ...................... DLB-238

Zebra Books ...................... DLB-46

Zebrowski, George 1945- ............ DLB-8

Zech, Paul 1881-1946 ............... DLB-56

Zeidner, Lisa 1955- ................ DLB-120

Zeidonis, Imants 1933- ............. DLB-232

Zeimi (Kanze Motokiyo) 1363-1443 ..... DLB-203

Zelazny, Roger 1937-1995 ........... DLB-8

Zenger, John Peter 1697-1746 ....... DLB-24, 43

Zepheria ......................... DLB-172

Zesen, Philipp von 1619-1689 ........ DLB-164

Zhadovskaia, Iuliia Valerianovna 1824-1883 ..................... DLB-277

Zhukova, Mar'ia Semenovna 1805-1855 ..................... DLB-277

Zhukovsky, Vasilii Andreevich 1783-1852 ..................... DLB-205

Zhvanetsky, Mikhail Mikhailovich 1934- ......................... DLB-285

G. B. Zieber and Company ........... DLB-49

Ziedonis, Imants 1933- ............. CDWLB-4

Zieroth, Dale 1946- ................ DLB-60

Zigler und Kliphausen, Heinrich Anshelm von 1663-1697 .......... DLB-168

Zil'ber, Veniamin Aleksandrovich
(see Kaverin, Veniamin Aleksandrovich)

Zimmer, Paul 1934- ................. DLB-5

Zinberg, Len (see Lacy, Ed)

Zincgref, Julius Wilhelm 1591-1635 ..... DLB-164

Zindel, Paul 1936- ........ DLB-7, 52; CDALB-7

Zinnes, Harriet 1919- .............. DLB-193

Zinov'ev, Aleksandr Aleksandrovich 1922- ......................... DLB-302

Zinov'eva-Annibal, Lidiia Dmitrievna 1865 or 1866-1907 .............. DLB-295

Zinzendorf, Nikolaus Ludwig von 1700-1760 ..................... DLB-168

Zitkala-Ša 1876-1938 ............... DLB-175

Zīverts, Mārtiņš 1903-1990 .......... DLB-220

Zlatovratsky, Nikolai Nikolaevich 1845-1911 ..................... DLB-238

Zola, Emile 1840-1902 .............. DLB-123

Zolla, Elémire 1926- ............... DLB-196

Zolotow, Charlotte 1915- ........... DLB-52

Zoshchenko, Mikhail Mikhailovich 1895-1958 ..................... DLB-272

Zschokke, Heinrich 1771-1848 ....... DLB-94

Zubly, John Joachim 1724-1781 ...... DLB-31

Zu-Bolton, Ahmos, II 1936- ......... DLB-41

Zuckmayer, Carl 1896-1977 ......... DLB-56, 124

Zukofsky, Louis 1904-1978 ......... DLB-5, 165

Zupan, Vitomil 1914-1987 .......... DLB-181

Župančič, Oton 1878-1949 ... DLB-147; CDWLB-4

zur Mühlen, Hermynia 1883-1951 ...... DLB-56

Zweig, Arnold 1887-1968 ............ DLB-66

Zweig, Stefan 1881-1942 ........... DLB-81, 118

Zwinger, Ann 1925- ................ DLB-275

Zwingli, Huldrych 1484-1531 ........ DLB-179

# Ø

Øverland, Arnulf 1889-1968 ......... DLB-297

Wolfram von Eschenbach circa 1170-after 1220 .... DLB-138; CDWLB-2

Wolfram von Eschenbach's *Parzival*: Prologue and Book 3 .......... DLB-138

Wolker, Jiří 1900-1924 ............... DLB-215

Wollstonecraft, Mary 1759-1797 .... DLB-39, 104, 158, 252; CDBLB-3

Women
  Women's Work, Women's Sphere: Selected Comments from Women Writers ................. DLB-200

Wondratschek, Wolf 1943- .......... DLB-75

Wong, Elizabeth 1958- ............. DLB-266

Wood, Anthony à 1632-1695 ......... DLB-213

Wood, Benjamin 1820-1900 .......... DLB-23

Wood, Charles 1932-1980 ........... DLB-13

  The Charles Wood Affair: A Playwright Revived ............. Y-83

Wood, Mrs. Henry 1814-1887 ........ DLB-18

Wood, Joanna E. 1867-1927 ......... DLB-92

Wood, Sally Sayward Barrell Keating 1759-1855 .................... DLB-200

Wood, William ?-? ................. DLB-24

Samuel Wood [publishing house] ..... DLB-49

Woodberry, George Edward 1855-1930 .................. DLB-71, 103

Woodbridge, Benjamin 1622-1684 ..... DLB-24

Woodbridge, Frederick J. E. 1867-1940 .. DLB-270

Woodcock, George 1912-1995 ........ DLB-88

Woodhull, Victoria C. 1838-1927 ..... DLB-79

Woodmason, Charles circa 1720-? ... DLB-31

Woodress, James Leslie, Jr. 1916- ... DLB-111

Woods, Margaret L. 1855-1945 ...... DLB-240

Woodson, Carter G. 1875-1950 ...... DLB-17

Woodward, C. Vann 1908-1999 ...... DLB-17

Woodward, Stanley 1895-1965 ...... DLB-171

Woodworth, Samuel 1785-1842 ...... DLB-250

Wooler, Thomas 1785 or 1786-1853 .. DLB-158

Woolf, David (see Maddow, Ben)

Woolf, Douglas 1922-1992 .......... DLB-244

Woolf, Leonard 1880-1969 ..... DLB-100; DS-10

Woolf, Virginia 1882-1941 .... DLB-36, 100, 162; DS-10; CDBLB-6

"The New Biography," *New York Herald Tribune*, 30 October 1927 ...... DLB-149

Woollcott, Alexander 1887-1943 .... DLB-29

Woolman, John 1720-1772 .......... DLB-31

Woolner, Thomas 1825-1892 ........ DLB-35

Woolrich, Cornell 1903-1968 ....... DLB-226

Woolsey, Sarah Chauncy 1835-1905 ... DLB-42

Woolson, Constance Fenimore 1840-1894 ........... DLB-12, 74, 189, 221

Worcester, Joseph Emerson 1784-1865 .................. DLB-1, 235

Wynkyn de Worde [publishing house] .. DLB-170

Wordsworth, Christopher 1807-1885 ... DLB-166

Wordsworth, Dorothy 1771-1855 .... DLB-107

Wordsworth, Elizabeth 1840-1932 ... DLB-98

Wordsworth, William 1770-1850 .......... DLB-93, 107; CDBLB-3

Workman, Fanny Bullock 1859-1925 ................... DLB-189

*World Literature Today*: A Journal for the New Millennium .................. Y-01

World Publishing Company ........... DLB-46

World War I (1914-1918) ............... DS-18

  The Great War Exhibit and Symposium at the University of South Carolina .. Y-97

  The Liddle Collection and First World War Research .................. Y-97

  Other British Poets Who Fell in the Great War ........... DLB-216

  The Seventy-Fifth Anniversary of the Armistice: The Wilfred Owen Centenary and the Great War Exhibit at the University of Virginia ....... Y-93

World War II (1939-1945)
  Literary Effects of World War II ..... DLB-15

  World War II Writers Symposium at the University of South Carolina, 12-14 April 1995 ............... Y-95

  WW2 HMSO Paperbacks Society ...... Y-98

R. Worthington and Company ........ DLB-49

Wotton, Sir Henry 1568-1639 ........ DLB-121

Wouk, Herman 1915- ...... Y-82; CDALB-7

  Tribute to James Dickey ............ Y-97

Wreford, James 1915- .............. DLB-88

Wren, Sir Christopher 1632-1723 .... DLB-213

Wren, Percival Christopher 1885-1941 .. DLB-153

Wrenn, John Henry 1841-1911 ....... DLB-140

Wright, C. D. 1949- ............... DLB-120

Wright, Charles 1935- ......... DLB-165; Y-82

Wright, Charles Stevenson 1932- .... DLB-33

Wright, Chauncey 1830-1875 ....... DLB-270

Wright, Frances 1795-1852 ......... DLB-73

Wright, Harold Bell 1872-1944 ...... DLB-9

Wright, James 1927-1980 ............. DLB-5, 169; CDALB-7

Wright, Jay 1935- ................. DLB-41

Wright, Judith 1915-2000 .......... DLB-260

Wright, Louis B. 1899-1984 ........ DLB-17

Wright, Richard 1908-1960 ....... DLB-76, 102; DS-2; CDALB-5

Wright, Richard B. 1937- .......... DLB-53

Wright, S. Fowler 1874-1965 ....... DLB-255

Wright, Sarah Elizabeth 1928- ...... DLB-33

Wright, T. H. "Style" (1877) [excerpt] .. DLB-57

Wright, Willard Huntington (S. S. Van Dine) 1888-1939 ........ DS-16

Wrightson, Patricia 1921- ......... DLB-289

Wrigley, Robert 1951- ............. DLB-256

*Writers' Forum* .................... Y-85

Writing
  A Writing Life .................... Y-02
  On Learning to Write .............. Y-88
  The Profession of Authorship: Scribblers for Bread ............. Y-89
  A Writer Talking: A Collage ....... Y-00

Wroth, Lawrence C. 1884-1970 ...... DLB-187

Wroth, Lady Mary 1587-1653 ........ DLB-121

Wurlitzer, Rudolph 1937- .......... DLB-173

Wyatt, Sir Thomas circa 1503-1542 ..... DLB-132

Wycherley, William 1641-1715 .............. DLB-80; CDBLB-2

Wyclif, John circa 1335-1384 ........ DLB-146

Wyeth, N. C. 1882-1945 ........ DLB-188; DS-16

Wyle, Niklas von circa 1415-1479 .... DLB-179

Wylie, Elinor 1885-1928 ............ DLB-9, 45

Wylie, Philip 1902-1971 ............ DLB-9

Wyllie, John Cook 1908-1968 ....... DLB-140

Wyman, Lillie Buffum Chace 1847-1929 ................... DLB-202

Wymark, Olwen 1934- ............. DLB-233

Wynd, Oswald Morris (see Black, Gavin)

Wyndham, John (John Wyndham Parkes Lucas Beynon Harris) 1903-1969 ... DLB-255

Wynne-Tyson, Esmé 1898-1972 ...... DLB-191

# X

Xenophon circa 430 B.C.-circa 356 B.C. ... DLB-176

# Y

Yasuoka Shōtarō 1920- ............. DLB-182

Yates, Dornford 1885-1960 ....... DLB-77, 153

Yates, J. Michael 1938- ............ DLB-60

Yates, Richard 1926-1992 ... DLB-2, 234; Y-81, 92

Yau, John 1950- ................... DLB-234

Yavorov, Peyo 1878-1914 ............ DLB-147

Yearsley, Ann 1753-1806 ............ DLB-109

Yeats, William Butler 1865-1939 .... DLB-10, 19, 98, 156; CDBLB-5

  The W. B. Yeats Society of N.Y. ..... Y-99

Yellen, Jack 1892-1991 ............. DLB-265

Yep, Laurence 1948- ............... DLB-52

Yerby, Frank 1916-1991 ............ DLB-76

Yezierska, Anzia 1880-1970 ....... DLB-28, 221

Yolen, Jane 1939- ................. DLB-52

Yonge, Charlotte Mary 1823-1901 ... DLB-18, 163

  The Charlotte M. Yonge Fellowship ..... Y-98

The York Cycle circa 1376-circa 1569 .... DLB-146

*A Yorkshire Tragedy* ................. DLB-58

Thomas Yoseloff [publishing house] ..... DLB-46

Youd, Sam (see Christopher, John)

Young, A. S. "Doc" 1919-1996 ...... DLB-241

Young, Al 1939- ................... DLB-33

Young, Arthur 1741-1820 ........... DLB-158

Young, Dick 1917 or 1918-1987 ..... DLB-171

Young, Edward 1683-1765 .......... DLB-95

Young, Frank A. "Fay" 1884-1957 .... DLB-241

Young, Francis Brett 1884-1954 ..... DLB-191

Young, Gavin 1928- ............... DLB-204

Young, Stark 1881-1963 ....... DLB-9, 102; DS-16

Young, Waldeman 1880-1938 ........ DLB-26

William Young [publishing house] ...... DLB-49

Young Bear, Ray A. 1950- .......... DLB-175

Yourcenar, Marguerite 1903-1987 ... DLB-72; Y-88

Yovkov, Yordan 1880-1937 .. DLB-147; CDWLB-4

# Z

Zachariä, Friedrich Wilhelm 1726-1777 .... DLB-97

Zagajewski, Adam 1945- ............ DLB-232

Zagoskin, Mikhail Nikolaevich 1789-1852 .................... DLB-198

Zajc, Dane 1929- ................. DLB-181

Zālīte, Māra 1952- ................ DLB-232

Zalygin, Sergei Pavlovich 1913-2000 ...................... DLB-302

Zamiatin, Evgenii Ivanovich 1884-1937 .. DLB-272

Zamora, Bernice 1938- ............ DLB-82

Zamudio, Adela (Soledad) 1854-1928 ... DLB-283

Zand, Herbert 1923-1970 ............. DLB-85

Zangwill, Israel 1864-1926 ...... DLB-10, 135, 197

Zanzotto, Andrea 1921- ............. DLB-128

Zapata Olivella, Manuel 1920- ........ DLB-113

Zapoev, Timur Iur'evich (see Kibirov, Timur Iur'evich)

Zasodimsky, Pavel Vladimirovich 1843-1912 ..................... DLB-238

Zebra Books ...................... DLB-46

Zebrowski, George 1945- ............ DLB-8

Zech, Paul 1881-1946 ................ DLB-56

Zeidner, Lisa 1955- ................ DLB-120

Zeidonis, Imants 1933- ............. DLB-232

Zeimi (Kanze Motokiyo) 1363-1443 ..... DLB-203

Zelazny, Roger 1937-1995 ............ DLB-8

Zenger, John Peter 1697-1746 ........ DLB-24, 43

Zepheria ........................ DLB-172

Zesen, Philipp von 1619-1689 ........ DLB-164

Zhadovskaia, Iuliia Valerianovna 1824-1883 ..................... DLB-277

Zhukova, Mar'ia Semenovna 1805-1855 ..................... DLB-277

Zhukovsky, Vasilii Andreevich 1783-1852 ..................... DLB-205

Zhvanetsky, Mikhail Mikhailovich 1934- ........................ DLB-285

G. B. Zieber and Company ........... DLB-49

Ziedonis, Imants 1933- ........... CDWLB-4

Zieroth, Dale 1946- ............... DLB-60

Zigler und Kliphausen, Heinrich Anshelm von 1663-1697 ......... DLB-168

Zil'ber, Veniamin Aleksandrovich (see Kaverin, Veniamin Aleksandrovich)

Zimmer, Paul 1934- ............... DLB-5

Zinberg, Len (see Lacy, Ed)

Zincgref, Julius Wilhelm 1591-1635 ..... DLB-164

Zindel, Paul 1936- ....... DLB-7, 52; CDALB-7

Zinnes, Harriet 1919- .............. DLB-193

Zinov'ev, Aleksandr Aleksandrovich 1922- ........................ DLB-302

Zinov'eva-Annibal, Lidiia Dmitrievna 1865 or 1866-1907 .............. DLB-295

Zinzendorf, Nikolaus Ludwig von 1700-1760 ..................... DLB-168

Zitkala-Ša 1876-1938 ................ DLB-175

Zīverts, Mārtiņš 1903-1990 .......... DLB-220

Zlatovratsky, Nikolai Nikolaevich 1845-1911 ..................... DLB-238

Zola, Emile 1840-1902 ............... DLB-123

Zolla, Elémire 1926- ............... DLB-196

Zolotow, Charlotte 1915- ............ DLB-52

Zoshchenko, Mikhail Mikhailovich 1895-1958 ..................... DLB-272

Zschokke, Heinrich 1771-1848 ......... DLB-94

Zubly, John Joachim 1724-1781 ....... DLB-31

Zu-Bolton, Ahmos, II 1936- .......... DLB-41

Zuckmayer, Carl 1896-1977 ........ DLB-56, 124

Zukofsky, Louis 1904-1978 ......... DLB-5, 165

Zupan, Vitomil 1914-1987 ............ DLB-181

Župančič, Oton 1878-1949 ...DLB-147; CDWLB-4

zur Mühlen, Hermynia 1883-1951 ....... DLB-56

Zweig, Arnold 1887-1968 ............. DLB-66

Zweig, Stefan 1881-1942 ......... DLB-81, 118

Zwinger, Ann 1925- ................ DLB-275

Zwingli, Huldrych 1484-1531 ........ DLB-179

## Ø

Øverland, Arnulf 1889-1968 ......... DLB-297

ISBN 0-7876-6839-7

PG
3094
.R866

2005